808.899
DAU   128

Daughters of
an international
anthology of words
and writings by women
of African descent
from the ancient

W9-CCH-080

Hickory Flat Public Library
2740 East Cherokee Dr.
Canton, GA 30115

SEQUOYAH REGIONAL LIBRARY SYSTEM
3 8749 0012 8064 1

DAUGHTERS OF
AFRICA

DAUGHTERS OF AFRICA

An International Anthology of Words and Writings
by Women of African Descent: From
the Ancient Egyptian to the Present

EDITED AND WITH AN INTRODUCTION BY
MARGARET BUSBY

Pantheon Books, New York

THIS BOOK IS THE PROPERTY OF
SEQUOYAH REGIONAL LIBRARY
CANTON, GEORGIA

Compilation and Introduction copyright © 1992 by Margaret Busby

All rights reserved under International and Pan-American Copyright Conventions. Published in the United States by Pantheon Books, a division of Random House, Inc., New York. Originally published in Great Britain by Jonathan Cape Ltd., London.

Library of Congress Cataloging-in-Publication Data

Daughters of Africa: an international anthology of words and writings by women of African descent from the ancient Egyptian to the present / edited by Margaret Busby.
p. cm.
Includes bibliographical references and index.
ISBN 0-679-41634-X
1. Literature — Women authors.   2. Literature — Black authors — Translations into English.   3. English literature — Black authors — Translations from foreign languages.   I. Busby, Margaret.
PN6068.D38   1992   92-54116
808.8'99287 — dc20

Manufactured in the United States of America
4 6 8 9 7 5 3

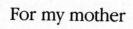

For my mother

Contents

Acknowledgements

Thanks

To all the contributors, authors, editors, publishers, translators and friends for offering advice, providing material and making suggestions, with special mention to: Pauline Melville, Jayne Cortez, Ayse Bircan, Pedro Perez Sarduy, Jean Stubbs, Astrid Roemer, Dorothy Kuya, Valerie Wilmer, Julio Finn, Kathleen Weaver, Anne Adams, Nancee Oku Bright, Ann Wallace, Ade Solanke, Burt Caesar, Sara Corrigall and the Casely-Hayford family.

To members of my family and extended family for their invaluable help, support and encouragement, particularly to George Busby, Eileen Busby, Moira Stuart, Vastiana Belfon and David Pallister.

To Candida Lacey of Jonathan Cape, who commissioned *Daughters of Africa* while part of the original and late-lamented Pandora team whose heroic behind-the-scenes efforts contributed so much to the making of this book – with special mention to Debbie Licorish and Sara Dunn.

Apologies

To all those excellent writers I have had to leave out – and for any inadvertent inaccuracies. . .

Introduction

To Black Women

Sisters,
where there is cold silence –
no hallelujahs, no hurrahs at all, no handshakes,
no neon red or blue, no smiling faces –
prevail.
Prevail across the editors of the world!
who are obsessed, self-honeying and self-crowned
in the seduced area,

   It has been a
hard trudge, with fainting, bandaging and death.
There have been startling confrontations.
There have been tramplings. Tramplings
of monarchs and of other men.

But there remain large countries in your eyes.
Shrewd sun.
The civil balance.
The listening secrets.

And you create and train your flowers still.

                 – Gwendolyn Brooks

"O, ye daughters of Africa, awake! awake! arise! no longer sleep nor slumber,
but distinguish yourselves,
Show forth to the world that ye are endowed with noble and exalted faculties."

          – Maria W. Stewart, *Productions of Mrs Maria W. Stewart* (1835)

Imagine a thirsty traveller trying to catch a flowing river in a calabash and you
may have some idea of the impossible task facing a compiler of an anthology
of this sort. The source may be known, the direction clear, but inevitably much
spills out, leaving only a taste of those precious waters. The thirst for literature
with personal relevance has inspired many Black women's creativity – Toni
Morrison has explained that what she writes are the kind of books she wants
to read, a sentiment endorsed by Alice Walker: "I write all the things *I should*

have been able to read,"[1] as well as by the young Zimbabwean novelist Tsitsi Dangarembga who has said: "I'd try to look for myself in the books that I read, but I didn't find me." Similarly, perhaps the first reason for the contents of this anthology is subjective: it is the sort of anthology I wish I had had access to years ago but which did not exist.

So it should be understood that in this way my selection is personal, and not meant to limit recognition of excellence to only those women included. In addition, my aim was to show the immense range, in terms of genre, country of origin and style, that a category such as "women writers of African descent" encompasses. Without doubt I, or anyone else, could compile a similar volume that would include a completely different selection and still leave out many women who deserve to be read and to be better known. It would be misleading to call this a definitive work, implying that everything excluded merits lesser consideration. I prefer to see it as a contribution to the cause of reclaiming for women of African descent a place in literary history. If its effect is to spur others on to do better, it will have achieved its purpose.

The description "women of African descent" is used in the title, in preference to "women of colour" or "Black women", to indicate the particular connectedness that the women in this anthology share – which is not to overlook our differences: the Russian upbringing of Yelena Khanga (see pages 955–9) has little in common with the Turkish upbringing of Ayse Bircan (pages 881–90), or the Kenyan upbringing of Charity Waciuma (pages 377–81), or the Mississippi upbringing of Ann Moody (pages 506–11), or the Brazilian upbringing of Pilar López Gonzales (pages 546–9). As Filomina Chioma Steady acknowledged, "the black woman, within a cross-cultural perspective, represents much diversity in terms of nationality, class affiliation, generational differences, and particular historical experiences".[2] On the most obvious level, we come in every possible skin shade, from deepest ebony to palest cream, and society and circumstance have in the past created, and sometimes still perpetuate, a hierarchy of tone that has exerted tyrannical sway over our lives – as is evident from many of the contributions in this anthology. The whole question of terminology is a complex one, fraught with pitfalls and ever-changing with the rise and fall of political and cultural ideologies. So whereas the complaint of crusading journalist Ida B. Wells in an 1878 editorial in the *Chicago Conservator*, "Spell It With a Capital", was: "We have noticed an error which all journalists seem to make. Whether from mistake or ill-intention, we are unable to say, but the profession universally begins Negro with a small letter.... The French, German, Irish, Dutch, Japanese, and other nationalities are honoured with a capital letter, but the poor sons of Ham must bear the burden of a small *n*" (pages 150–51), the campaigner Mary Church Terrell (see pages 151–3) by 1949 was writing to the editor of the *Washington Post*: "Please stop us using the word 'Negro'.... We are the only human beings

[1] Alice Walker, "Saving the Life That Is Your Own", *In Search of Our Mothers' Gardens: Womanist Prose*, New York: Harcourt Brace, 1983; London: Women's Press, 1984, p. 13.
[2] Filomina Chioma Steady (ed.), *The Black Woman Cross-Culturally*, Cambridge, Mass.: Schenkman, 1981, p. 7.

in the world with fifty-seven varieties of complexions who are classed together as a single racial unit. Therefore, we are really, truly colored people, and that is the only name in the English language which accurately describes us." Despite the continuing resistance of many journalists, the standard reference books (for example, *The Oxford Dictionary for Writers and Editors*) now accept the correctness of capitalizing the noun "Black" (or "White"), and in addition many Black writers as a matter of principle also capitalize the adjective. Maybe eventually we will, in the words of Gwendolyn Brooks, Poet Laureate of Illinois and the first Black writer awarded a Pulitzer Prize in 1950, "Prevail across the editors of the world!"

The arrangement of this anthology is chronological, by authors' date (or estimated date) of birth. (Where dates were not available from published sources or have not been personally confirmed, living authors are of course free to deny my guesses!) This attaches no spurious relevance to age but is simply a device to try to chart the development of a literary canon over the years, to restore links and show the continuity of expression that against all odds still exists in much of the material. Some selections were made because of their historical significance, others because of their representative nature, or indeed because they have mould-breaking importance. Clearly, African women have always played a central role as storytellers within their communities. However, as Lauretta Ngcobo has written:

> Oral tales are inclusive and in a variety of ways reach out to as many people as possible, so that ultimately they become the common property of the majority. Writing, on the other hand, is designed for a select class, those who can read. Essentially, therefore, it is exclusive, intended from the outset to reach only the eyes of those who have achieved literacy: the script itself automatically excludes those who do not have it.[3]

The fact that recent decades show a greater spread of printed material than previous centuries is linked to not just literacy problems but access to publishing. Many "slave narratives" by nineteenth-century African-American women saw the light of day either through private white patronage or the self-publishing efforts of the women themselves. (Harriet Wilson, the first African-American novelist, in 1859 published *Our Nig: Or Sketches from the Life of a Free Black* – see pages 58–66 – in a vain effort to raise money to save her dying son.) Hortense J. Spillers has written of the virtual suppression of Black women's realities until the Harlem Renaissance – also known as the New Negro movement, spanning approximately the years 1917 to 1935, a period of unprecedented creativity for Afro-Americans that saw the literary flowering of writers such as Georgia Douglas Johnson, Jessie Redmon Fauset (who from 1912 to 1926 was literary editor of the Black literary journal *The Crisis*), Nella Larsen and Zora Neale Hurston.

Essentially the black woman as artist, as intellectual spokesperson for

---

[3] Lauretta Ngcobo (ed.), *Let It Be Told: Black Women Writers in Britain*, London: Pluto Press, 1987, p. 2.

her own cultural apprenticeship, has not existed before, for anyone. At the source of her own symbol-making task, this community of writers confronts, therefore, a tradition of work that is quite recent, its continuities, broken and sporadic.[4]

It was initially Black men who were more readily taken up by the literary establishment, particularly as the US civil rights era stimulated demand for Black Studies courses in the late 1960s and early 1970s; and, coinciding with the growing militancy of the (white) women's liberation movement, more Black women too began to be published, such as Nikki Giovanni, Mari Evans and Carolyn Rodgers (pages 568–9, 299–301 and 544–6), who caught the defiant mood of the times in their poetry. Yet over a decade later, a Black women's studies anthology could still be aptly titled *All the Blacks Are Men, All the Women Are White, But Some of Us Are Brave*,[5] notwithstanding Faith Berry's observation: "More new Afro-American women writers were published between 1960 and 1975 than the total number published in two centuries of Afro-American literature."[6] Only comparatively recently have Black women begun to find receptive outlets and wider distribution for their work through mainstream publishing houses in the metropolitan West; nevertheless, it is commercial fashion that has usually dictated the agenda. Aside from the valiant efforts of academic publishers (notably Howard University Press, and Heinemann Educational Books, who published in 1966 the first work by Flora Nwapa, pioneer African woman novelist – see page 399), it has been left to autonomous Black companies (including, in the USA, Third World Press, Broadside Press, Harlem River Press and Africa World Press; in Britain, New Beacon Books, Jessica Huntley's Bogle-L'Ouverture Publications, Karnak House, Akira Press and Karia Press; in Canada, Anne Wallace's Williams–Wallace), and to small general presses (for example, Three Continents Press, Thunder's Mouth, Pluto, Zed Press or Allison & Busby) to demonstrate a consistent commitment to Black writing presented outside possibly ghettoizing series. The setting up since the mid 1970s of feminist imprints (in Britain: Virago, The Women's Press, Sheba Feminist Publishers, Pandora, Onlywomen; in the USA, Naiad, Shameless Hussy, Spinsters Ink) has enabled more Black women's voices to be heard. Rarest of all are thriving ventures run by/for Black women, such as Kitchen Table: Women of Color Press, or the British-based Black Womantalk and Urban Fox Press, all founded since the 1980s. Crucial to the proliferation of the writings of Black women, and their right to the critical attention they deserve, is the continuing existence of publishers such as these – and above all the encouragement of Black women to enter the publishing industry to build on the efforts of those

[4] Hortense J. Spillers, "A Hateful Passion, A Lost Love", *Feminist Studies* 9, no. 2 (Summer 1983), p. 297.

[5] Gloria T. Hull, Patricia Bell Scott and Barbara Smith (eds), *All the Blacks Are Men, All the Women Are White, But Some of Us Are Brave: Black Women's Studies*, Old Westbury, NY: Feminist Press, 1982.

[6] Faith Berry, "A Question of Publishers and a Question of Audience", *Black Scholar* 17:2 (March/April 1986), pp. 41–9.

brave women (among them New York literary agent Marie Dutton Brown, and Toni Morrison in her role as a senior editor for Random House) who have stood the storm.

Beginning *Daughters of Africa* with a selection of anonymous songs and poetry from Africa – often dealing with the universal theme of love relationships – underlines the oral tradition that runs throughout the diaspora and highlights the fact that African women's creativity has roots that extend beyond written records. In West African countries such as Senegal and The Gambia it was the duty of professional musicians known as *griots* to preserve and sing the history of a particular family or tribe going back several generations, as well as to improvise on current affairs – a facility echoed by calypsonians in the Caribbean. (That the oral tradition is closely linked with music makes it natural that the expression of Black female pain and joy are epitomized in the blues and songs of African-American artists such as Bessie Smith, Billie Holiday, Dinah Washington, Josephine Baker, Aretha Franklin, Nina Simone.) "Orature", the term coined by the late Ugandan literary critic Pio Zirimu, encompasses both the tradition of unwritten creativity and verbal transmission of that creativity. In the absence of literacy in many African communities, oral (and aural) communication is pre-eminent. In traditional African societies folktales and stories, many featuring "trickster" figures such as the spider (Ananse, in Ghana), the tortoise or the hare, functioned both as entertainment and instruction, passed down from generation to generation, resurfacing in the New World in the guise of the "Uncle Remus" stories in the USA or Anancy stories in the Caribbean (see Merle Hodge's *Crick Crack, Monkey*, pages 582–6).

The linguistic versatility demonstrated by people of Africa and the African diaspora is in itself a remarkable testament to survival of vicissitude in a history that has weathered subjugation and colonization by the powers of Europe. Those Africans transported to the New World in the course of the slave trade were forbidden to speak in their own native tongues, whether Yoruba or Asante Twi:

> What these languages had to do, however, was to submerge themselves, because officially the conquering people – the Spaniards, the English, the French and the Dutch – insisted that the language of public discourse and conversation, of obedience, command and conception, should be English, French, Spanish or Dutch.[7]

Thus, diaspora Africans draw both on an official "educated" language – in which, since the time the young slave Phillis Wheatley began to compose poetry in the eighteenth century, they have demonstrated literary skills beyond mere imitation – and on those submerged African retentions. Nor is it unusual in Africa itself for people to be multilingual – conversant with one or more of their own indigenous languages as well as with an imported European language, which may also have evolved a creolized or pidgin form (incorporated, for instance, in

---

[7] Edward Kamau Brathwaite, *History of the Voice: The Development of Nation Language in Anglophone Caribbean Poetry*, London: New Beacon Books, 1984, p. 7.

the work of Nigerian Adaora Lily Ulasi, see pages 422–31). The modern creative use of patois or dialect, or, lately, "dub poetry" in which reggae music forms a counterpoint to the words (see, for example, the poems of Jamaicans Louise Bennett, Valerie Bloom or Jean Binta Breeze, see pages 277–9. 900–902 amd 902–05), show an uninhibited departure from the received standard language in favour of what Edward Kamau Brathwaite calls *nation language*, the kind of English spoken by those brought to the Caribbean as slaves and labourers:

> I use the term in contrast to *dialect*. The word "dialect" has been bandied about for a long time, and it carried very pejorative overtones. Dialect is thought of as "bad English". Dialect is "inferior English". Dialect is the language used when you want to make fun of someone. Caricature speaks in dialect. Dialect has a long history coming from the plantation where people's dignity is distorted through their language and the descriptions which the dialect gave to them. Nation language, on the other hand, is the *submerged* area of that dialect which is much more closely allied to the African aspect of experience in the Caribbean. It may be in English: but often it is in an English which is like a howl, or a shout or a machine-gun or the wind or a wave. It is also like the blues. And sometimes it is English and African at the same time.[8]

Orthography and syntax may be used unconventionally to refreshing effect, as in the work of Ntozake Shange, who explains her style thus: "The spellings result from the way I talk or the way the character talks, or the way I heard something said. Basically the spellings reflect language as I hear it."[9] Informing her work is a refusal to conform to the norms of an imposed "educated" culture, in preference to "popular culture" or "vernacular culture":

> We do not have to refer continually to European art as the standard. That's absolutely absurd and racist, and I won't participate in that utter lie. My work is one of the few ways I can preserve the elements of our culture that need to be remembered and absolutely revered.[10]

Arguing for the legitimacy of Black English within the educational system, June Jordan wrote tellingly in a 1972 essay:

> both Black and white youngsters are compelled to attend school. Once inside this system, the white child is rewarded for mastery of his standard, white English: the language he learned at his mother's white and standard knee. But the Black child is punished for mastery of his non-standard, Black English: for the ruling elite of America have decided that *non*-standard is *sub*-standard, and even dangerous, and must be eradicated.[11]

[8] Ibid., p. 13.
[9] Claudia Tate (ed.), *Black Women Writers at Work*, New York: Continuum, 1983; Harpenden, Herts: Oldcastle, 1985, p. 163.
[10] Ibid., p. 164.
[11] June Jordan, "White English/Black English: The Politics of Translation", *Moving Towards Home: Political Essays*, London: Virago, 1988, p. 34.

She concluded: "If we lose our fluency in our language, we may irreversibly forsake elements of the spirit that have provided for our survival."[12]

Tradition and history are nurturing spirits for women of African descent. For without an understanding of where we have come from, we are less likely to be able to make sense of where we are going. But awareness of past trials and tribulations must not bow us, rather strengthen us for whatever the future holds. "Only history plants consciousness", asserts Lourdes Teodoro in her poem "The Generation of Fear" (pages 382–3). The legacy of the slave trade with Africa confronts us daily in the very existence of the diaspora. In the course of the commercial system that was the Atlantic slave trade, together with the slave trades of the trans-Sahara and East Africa, over a period of some four hundred years from the mid-1400s, 15 to 20 million Africans were against their will shipped to the Americas and Europe. Portugal, Britain, Denmark, France, Holland, Spain and other European countries, as well as America, were all implicated. To rehearse again the traumatic facts is not to wallow in victimhood but to ensure an understanding of what our foremothers had to survive.

During the Middle Passage, the journey from Africa to the Americas (Cuban Nancy Morejón's poem "Black Woman", on pages 854–5, imagines some of the emotions such a voyage may have engendered), female captives were subject to the seamen's advances. According to one former slave-ship captain:

> When the women and girls are taken on board a ship, naked, trembling, terrified, perhaps almost exhausted with cold, fatigue, and hunger, they are often exposed to the wanton rudeness of white savages. The poor creatures cannot understand the language they hear, but the looks and manner of the speakers are sufficiently intelligible. In imagination, the prey is divided, upon the spot, and only reserved till opportunity offers. Where resistance or refusal would be utterly in vain, even the solicitation of consent is seldom thought of.[13]

Brought naked from the ship's hold to the auction block, they were assessed for breeding potential, a scene recreated in "The Slave Auction" (page 82) by the popular poet Frances Ellen Watkins Harper (1825–1911), who wrote and spoke out forthrightly about the wrongs of slavery:

> The sale began – young girls were there,
>   Defenceless in their wretchedness,
> Whose stifled sobs of deep despair
>   Revealed their anguish and distress.
>
> And mothers stood with streaming eyes,
>   And saw their dearest children sold;

---

[12] Ibid., p. 40.
[13] John Newton, *The Journal of a Slave Trader 1750–1754*, ed. Bernard Martin and Mark Spurrell, London: Epworth Press, 1962, p. 104.

> Unheeded rose their bitter cries,
> While tyrants bartered them for gold. . . .

Brutalized and sexually exploited – and stereotyped – by white slaveholders, Black women bore mulatto offspring for their masters, or were forced to conceive babies for economic gain:

> She was to be had for the taking. Boys on and about the plantation inevitably learned to use her, and having acquired the habit, often continued it into manhood and after marriage. For she was natural and could give herself up to passion in a way impossible to wives inhibited by puritanical training.[14]

Then there was the pain of separation when children and mothers were sold to different masters; first-hand testimony of one such parting was given by Louisa Picquet, who recalls being sold away from her mother at the age of fourteen:

> "When I was going away I heard someone cryin' and prayin' the Lord to go with her only daughter, and protect me. I felt pretty bad then, but hadn't no time only to say goodbye. . . .it seems fresh in my memory when I think of it – no longer than yesterday. Mother was right on her knees, with her hands up, prayin' to the Lord for me. She didn't care who saw her: the people all lookin' at her. I often thought her prayers followed me, for I could never forget her. . . ."
> Q. – "Have you never seen her since?"
> A. – "No, never since that time. I went to New Orleans, and she went to Texas. So I understood."[15]

In the nineteenth century, abolition laws made slave trading illegal (although the emancipation of slaves was not immediate): Denmark led the way in 1802, Britain passed an Abolition Bill in 1807, followed by legislation in the USA in 1808, then Sweden in 1813, Holland in 1814, France in 1815, the British colonies in the Caribbean in 1833; Portugal and Spain continued to import slaves to work in Cuban and Brazilian plantations until the 1860s but by 1888 slavery and the slave trade were finally dead in Cuba and Brazil. Even for those American Blacks who were freed or born free there were continuing dangers, as Anthony G. Barthelemy notes:

> The notorious Fugitive Slave Act passed in Congress in 1850 threatened the safety of every *legally* free black person in the United States and forced hundreds of runaway slaves to run even farther to safety in Canada or Europe. Four years later, the Supreme Court, as if following the lead of

---

[14] W. J. Cash, *The Mind of the South*, New York, 1941, p. 87.
[15] H. Mattison, *Louisa Picquet, the Octoroon: or Inside Views of Southern Domestic Life*, 1861, p. 18; New York/Oxford: Oxford University Press, Schomburg Library of Nineteenth-Century Black Women Writers, 1988 (facsimile).

Congress, proclaimed in its Dred Scott Decision that blacks "had no rights which the white man was bound to respect".[16]

Some emancipated slaves, including Henrietta Fullor (see pages 79–80), were able to make the return journey back to Africa, to settlements in Liberia and Sierra Leone (unlike the speaker in Louise Bennett's "Back to Africa", pages 278–9). The earliest published African-American poet is Lucy Terry, born in about 1730 in Africa, from where she was kidnapped and brought to New England as a slave. Her historical position is guaranteed by only one poem, "Bars Fight" (page 17), written in about 1746. More substantial evidence of poetic skill is found in the work of Phillis Wheatley (pages 18–22), born in Senegal in about 1753, and taken as a seven-year-old slave to the USA. A child prodigy, she was reading and writing and learning Latin within sixteen months, and at the age of thirteen began writing poems of classical accomplishment, one of her earliest entitled "On being brought from Africa to America". Despite achieving celebrity, both in America and in Britain, where she travelled with her mistress, and being the first Black and only the second woman (after Anne Bradstreet) to publish a book of poetry in the USA, she died in poverty aged barely thirty.

The trauma of enslavement, the instinct to resist and escape, the striving for freedom, would have been material enough for many more volumes of testimony by nineteenth-century Black women than have in recent years been rediscovered and reprinted (notably in the 1988 Schomburg Library of Nineteenth-Century Black Women Writers series, under the general editorship of Henry Louis Gates, Jr). Sometimes these slave narratives were dictated to amanuenses sympathetic to the abolitionist cause; often they were published with the aim of raising funds for personal welfare or education:

A new variable constrained the telling of these stories, for these women had to sell their intimate memories and to sort out the property rights to their lives. The act of recording their lives, ironically, recorded their financial distress.[17]

From those accounts that survive, such as those by "Old Elizabeth", Mary Prince, Mattie Jackson, Annie Burton, Ann Drumgoold and Bethany Veney (see pages 22–6, 27–30, 109–15, 115–23, 145–8, 148–9), comes remarkable insight into these women's own efforts to rise above their unfortunate circumstances. Many of those African-American women who published work in the nineteenth century found sustenance in religion and undertook preaching tours, as was the case with Zilpha Elaw (see pages 31–6), who published her memoirs in 1840 at the end of a five-year mission to Britain. Occasionally they earned platforms as moving orators, speaking out against slavery and oppression by race and sex. Maria Stewart – whose exhortation to Black women to strive for

---

[16] Anthony G. Barthelemy (ed.), *Collected Black Women's Narratives*, Oxford/New York: Oxford University Press, Schomburg Library of Nineteenth-Century Black Women Writers, 1988, Introduction, p. xxix.
[17] Ibid., p. xxxiv.

education and political rights furnished the title for this anthology – became the first American-born woman to lecture in public in 1832 (see pages 47–52). The passion of Sojourner Truth's renowned address to the 1852 National Women's Suffrage Convention (page 38) echoes down the generations:

> Ain't I a woman?
>   Look at me
> Look at my arm!
>   I have plowed and planted
> and gathered into barns
>   and no man could head me. . . .
> And ain't I a woman?
>   I could work as much
> And eat as much as a man –
>   When I could get it –
> And bear the lash as well
>   and ain't I a woman?
> I have born thirteen children
>   and seen most all sold into slavery
> and when I cried out a mother's grief
>   none but Jesus heard me. . .
> and ain't I a woman?. . .
>   If the first woman God ever made
> was strong enough to turn the world
>   upside down, all alone
> together women ought to be able to turn it
>   rightside up again.

A Narrative of the Life and Travels of Mrs Nancy Prince (1853; see pages 40–46), recording the author's travels in Russia and the West Indies, is an example of the fact that nineteenth-century Black women's experiences and concerns extended far beyond the confines of enslavement. Mary Seacole, who was born in Jamaica twenty-five years before the abolition of slavery and died in London in 1881, was incontrovertible proof that in freedom Black women could undertake major roles in setting the wider world to rights. Her Wonderful Adventures of Mrs Seacole in Many Lands (see pages 53–7) – a success on its publication in 1857 but largely forgotten until it was reprinted in the 1980s – tells of her life of adventure and dedication that culminated in her becoming as notable a figure in the Crimean War as Florence Nightingale. Comparably revealing are Susie King Taylor's 1902 reminiscences of her life as laundress, teacher and nurse to the Union army during the US civil war (see pages 124–7).

The history of Black women in the United Kingdom since slavery days is inextricably linked with the economic needs of others, of Britain and British interests in the West Indies and Africa. The act of emancipation whereby slavery was "utterly and forever abolished and declared unlawful throughout the British Colonies" was passed in 1833, taking effect the next year. But under colonialism Black people in Africa and the Caribbean still had to endure domination by

Whites. In the West Indies the plantation system that lasted into the twentieth century, providing commodities such as sugar, cotton and cocoa for the British economy, depended on cheap labour, but with the growing reluctance of ex-slaves to continue to be exploited, indentured labourers were brought in from India, and even from China, to increase competition for work and so reduce wages. In the depression of the 1920s and 1930s, poverty and unemployment led some to emigrate to the American mainland where farm and factory work was available. (Coping with the societal differences involved with migration is a theme of works such as Joan Cambridge's *Clarise Cumberbatch Want to Go Home*, 604–8; and US-based writers such as Rosa Guy and Louise Meriwether have Caribbean origins, as does the generation that includes Dionne Brand and Marlene Nourbese Phillip, who settled in Canada.) During the Second World War, recruits from the British colonies contributed unstintingly to the war effort, coming to Britain to work as civilians or in the armed forces. After the war many West Indians were encouraged to emigrate to a Britain that needed assistance in rebuilding an economy that was short of labour. When on 22 June 1948 the *Empire Windrush* docked at Tilbury carrying 492 Jamaicans, some of whom were returning to "the Motherland" where they had seen war service, the headline of the London *Evening Standard* was "WELCOME HOME". Peter Fryer writes:

> In some industries the demand for labour was so great that members of the reserve army of black workers were actively recruited in their home countries. In April 1956 London Transport began recruiting staff in Barbados, and within 12 years a total of 3,787 Barbadians had been taken on. They were lent their fares to Britain, and the loans were repaid gradually from their wages. . . . And a Tory health minister by the name of Enoch Powell welcomed West Indian nurses to Britain.[18]

The jobs these Black immigrants came to fill, jobs in which they still predominate – driving tube trains, collecting bus fares, emptying hospital patients' bed-pans – were invariably the unglamorous ones at the lower end of the labour force:

> Black women are faced with no other prospect than to fill the jobs which the indigenous workforce were no longer willing to do, in the servicing, semi-skilled and unskilled sectors. Service work was little more than institutionalised housework, as night and daytime cleaners, canteen workers, laundry workers and chambermaids – an extension of the work we had done under colonialism in the Caribbean.[19]

Yet, the indigenous British workforce felt threatened; nor was their irrational worry a new one. The Black presence in London in 1764, when the capital's total

---

[18] Peter Fryer, *Staying Power: The History of Black People in Britain*, London: Pluto, 1984 p. 373.
[19] Beverley Bryan, Stella Dadzie, Suzanne Scafe, *Heart of the Race: Black Women's Lives in Britain*, London: Virago, 1985, p. 25.

population was 676,250, had prompted *The Gentleman's Magazine* to comment:

> The practice of importing Negroe servants into these kingdoms is said to be already a grievance that requires a remedy, and yet it is every day encouraged, insomuch that the number in this metropolis only, is supposed to be near 20,000; the main objections to their importation is, that they cease to consider themselves as slaves in this free country, nor will they put up with an inequality of treatment, nor more willingly perform the laborious offices of servitude than our own people, and if put to do it, are generally sullen, spiteful, treacherous, and revengeful. It is therefore highly impolitic to introduce them as servants here, where that rigour and severity is impracticable which is absolutely necessary to make them useful.[20]

The 1962 Commonwealth Immigration Act was introduced whose effect was to regulate the numbers of Black people entering Britain, institutionalizing the prejudice experienced as racist attacks and police brutality against Blacks. The inflammatory speech in April 1968 of Enoch Powell, a senior Conservative Member of Parliament, with its talk of rivers foaming with blood unless immigration was further curbed and "re-emigration" encouraged, was to bring race relations in Britain to a low ebb. Children left behind in the Caribbean were sent for, lest they be excluded for ever. (Iiola Ashundie's "Mother of Mine", pages 898–900, and Joan Riley's *The Unbelonging*, pages 909–14, give two aspects of the reactions of those offspring who came later.) The US civil rights movement, and high-profile participants such as Angela Davis, provided inspiration. In the early 1970s Black women in Britain began to organize within their own groups, most notably the Organization of Women of Asian and African Descent (OWAAD), which flourished between 1978 and 1983, holding annual conferences. A generation of young women since then – including Maud Sulter, Jackie Kay, Dinah Anuli Butler – have rallied to the challenge of exploring the British Black condition, with its particular ramifications according to race, class and gender.

Although women such as Maria Stewart, Sojourner Truth and Anna J. Cooper – who in her 1892 book *A Voice from the South by a Black Woman of the South* (pages 136–45) discussed from a feminist viewpoint the situation of Black women, seeing their progress as key to the advancement of the whole race, since "a stream cannot rise higher than its source" – were early speaking out against oppression by racism and sexism, it was only two decades ago that Frances Beale used the term "double jeopardy" to characterize the condition of being Black and female.[21] The poor social and economic conditions affecting a majority of Black women constitute a further oppression by class. The urgent need remains to surmount these oppressions. Far from complying with the passive, acquiescing stereotype, Black women through the centuries have been formidable leaders (like Queen Hatshepsut, whose magnificent obelisk at Luxor still stands as a monument to her defiant reign, and Makeda, Queen of Sheba),

[20] *The Gentleman's Magazine*, vol. 34, 1794, p. 483.
[21] "Double Jeopardy: To Be Black and Female", in Toni Cade Bambara (ed.), *The Black Woman: An Anthology*, New York: Signet/NAL, 1970, p. 92.

occupying central positions in the history of liberation struggles. Queen Nzinga in Angola in the 1630s and 1640s tried to coordinate resistance to Portuguese slave-traders; Nanny (celebrated in Lorna Goodison's poem, pages 723–4), leader of the Jamaican Maroons – runaway slaves – fought a guerrilla war against the British in 1733; Harriet Tubman became known as the Moses of her people for organizing in the 1850s an "Underground Railroad" that helped hundreds of slaves to escape; Ida Wells Barnett from the end of the nineteenth century waged a tireless crusade against lynchings and racial injustice; Rosa Parks's defiant refusal to move to a seat allocated for Blacks on a segregated bus in 1955 ignited the Civil Rights movement. Deborah K. King has written: "through the necessity of confronting and surviving racial oppression, black women have assumed responsibilities atypical of those assigned to white women under Western patriarchy".[22] King further argues that "a black feminist ideology presumes an image of black women as powerful, independent subjects. By concentrating on our multiple oppressions, scholarly descriptions have confounded our ability to discover and appreciate the ways in which black women are not victim".[23]

The concept of feminism is an uncomfortable one for many Black women who perceive the Western women's liberation movement as tainted by the racism evident in society as a whole. (Angela Davis, writing on the empowerment of Afro-American women – pages 570–71 – recalls that in 1895 Black women organized their own Club Movement, "having been repeatedly shunned by the racially homogeneous women's rights movement".) Many prefer instead to espouse Alice Walker's theory of *womanism*, as defined in the front of *In Search of Our Mothers' Gardens*: a womanist is "committed to the survival and wholeness of entire people, male *and* female.... Womanist is to feminist as purple to lavender."[24] Yet whatever the labels, it is an incontrovertible fact that for over a century Black women have been vocal in resisting sexism both within and without their own communities. Amy Jacques Garvey, writing in 1925 in an editorial in *The Negro World* (pages 209–11), served notice on Black men that any further vacillation on their part would force Black women to take over the sole lead in the struggle. Notwithstanding Christine Craig's tribute to her grandmothers and their mothers for keeping their silence "to compost up their strength" – "It must be known now how that silent legacy/nourished and infused such a line,/such a close linked chain/to hold us until we could speak/until we could speak out/loud enough to hear ourselves/and believe our own words" ("The Chain", pages 555–6) – Bell Hooks, a rare example of a Black woman whose writings have always embraced feminism, sees it not as a means to emerge from silence into speech, nor even to hold on to speech, "but to change the nature and direction of our speech, to make a speech that compels listeners, one that is heard" (pages 841–4).

---

[22] "Multiple jeopardy, multiple consciousness: the context of a black feminist ideology", in Micheline R. Malson, Elisabeth Mudimbe-Boyi, Jean F. O'Barr and Mary Wyer (eds), *Black Women in America: Social Science Perspectives*, Chicago/London: University of Chicago Press, 1990, p. 277.

[23] Ibid., p. 295.

[24] Walker, *In Search of Our Mothers' Gardens*, op. cit., pp. xi–xii.

Michele Wallace in her controversial book *Black Macho and the Myth of the Superwoman* (see pages 838–40) wrote in 1978 of the intricate web of mythology which surrounds the Black woman, according to which: "Less of a woman in that she is less 'feminine' and helpless, she is really *more* of a woman in that she is the embodiment of Mother Earth, the quintessential mother with infinite sexual, life-giving, and nurturing reserves." Indeed, the image of Black women as superhuman towers of strengrh and survivors of whatever misfortunes life has thrown at them is not always born out by the facts. The success and critical acclaim accorded to Pulitzer prizewinners Toni Morrison (for her superb *Beloved*, see pages 394–9) and Alice Walker, or the fortitude that enabled Buchi Emecheta to salvage a successful writing career from the jaws of adversity, are offset by the plight of other fine writers – among them Phillis Wheatley, Nella Larsen, Zora Neale Hurston, Bessie Head – who died in differing degrees of obscurity and penury, unfulfilled or in tragic circumstances.

When the toil and drudgery of slavery was done, Black women frequently could find work only as domestics in white households. Claudia Jones (1915–64), Trinidadian-born journalist and activist, wrote in 1930 (see pages 262–5): "Following the emancipation, and persisting to the present day, a large percentage of Negro women – married as well as single – were forced to work for a living. But despite the shift in employment of Negro women from rural to urban areas, Negro women are still generally confined to the lowest-paying jobs.... The low scale of earning of Negro women is directly related to her almost complete exclusion from virtually all fields of work except the most menial and underpaid, namely, domestic service." In 1978 Jeanne Noble could still observe: "While it is true that the numbers of black female domestics are diminishing...the image of the black domestic is still woven in the very fabric of America, especially in the South, where the role was perfected."[25] The image of the Black woman as domestic haunts works such as Ann Petry's *The Street* (the first novel by a Black woman to sell over a million copies; see pages 229–39) and Lorraine Hansberry's all-Black Broadway success *A Raisin in the Sun* (see pages 356–62). It is interesting to compare the way writers such as Alice Childress ("Like One of the Family", pages 280–81) and Barbara Makhalisa ("Different Values", pages 618–21), writing respectively about North American and South African contexts, use humour subversively.

Satire, polemic, fantasy – the moods and styles of expression vary and shift continuously. This anthology has aimed to give an idea of the wide range of genres explored by women of African descent: historical fiction (for example, Valerie Belgrave and Sherley Anne Williams, pages 681–4 and 671–6), science fiction (Octavia Butler, pages 705–13), literary novels, short stories, poetry, essays, journalism, oral history, memoirs, diaries, letters, essays, plays, folklore.... (The magical and supernatural as a part of ordinary life is a hallmark, as in Myriam Warner-Vieyra's *As the Sorcerer Said...* – see pages 621–30 – an acceptance of the inevitability of things: "The river does not wash away what is

[25] Jeanne Noble, *Beautiful, Also, Are the Souls of My Black Sisters: A History of the Black Woman in America*, Englewood Cliffs, NJ: Prentice-Hall, 1978, p. 76.

meant for you.") The significance of fiction for Black people was a belief held strongly by Pauline Hopkins (pages 127–35), who wrote in the preface to her novel *Contending Forces* (1900): "It is a record of growth and developement from generation to generation. No one will do this for us; we must develop the men and women who will faithfully protray the innermost thoughts and feelings of the Negro with all the fire and romance which lie dormant in our history." A predilection for autobiographical writing in one form or another is perhaps unsurprising, given the need to correct the misconceived images of the Black women that have proliferated through the ages in fact and fiction, generated by those who are not Black and female. As Mary Helen Washington has put it: "People other than the black woman herself try to define who she is, what she is supposed to look like, act like, and sound like. And most of these creations bear very little resemblance to real, live black women."[26] Washington further says: "If there is a single distinguishing feature of the literature of black women – and this accounts for their lack of recognition – it is this: their literature is about black women; it takes the trouble to record the thoughts, words, feelings, and deeds of black women".[27]

Through oral history and autobiography come memorable pictures of Black women's rites of passage and daily life: a young girl's arranged marriage, in *Nisa: The Life and Words of a !Kung Woman* (pages 282–6); the initiation of a Liberian girl in Alice Perry Johnson's "The Beginning of a Kpelle Woman" (pages 414–15); Jane Tapsubei Creider's glimpse of life among her Nandi people in *Two Lives: My Spirit and I* (pages 614–18); the vivid sights and smells of the Brazilian shantytown recorded in the diary of Carolina Maria de Jesús (pages 247–53), who despite the diurnal grind of foraging for herself and her children can still write at the end of the day, "The book is man's best invention yet." In creative writing too there are elements that seem precisely to capture the atmosphere of the societies that inspired them: Caribbean childhoods conjured up in Grace Nichols's *Whole of a Morning Sky* (pages 798–811), Zee Edgell's *Beka Lamb* (pages 520–25), Merle Collins's "The Walk" (pages 791–6), or Jamaica Kincaid's *Annie John* (pages 722–4); Elean Thomas's sensitive drawing of Josina, "everybody's woman and yet nobody's woman" (pages 733–6); Somali writer Saida Herzi's gruelling dramatization of the ordeal of female infibulation (page 777–82). Perspectives on Southern Africa include Joyce Sikakane's prison experiences (pages 557–64), Zoë Wicomb's honest depiction of the underside of romance across the colour bar (pages 752–62), Dulcie September's unvarnished look at urban life (pages 859–68), Bessie Head's perceptive vignettes of Botswana village life (pages 583–7) and Ellen Kuzwayo's unsentimental description of the realities of polygamy as they affect two ordinary women (pages 254–8).

The inescapable fact of polygamy in Africa is treated in a variety of illuminating ways – from Mabel Segun's cynical article "Polygamy – Ancient and Modern" (pages 373–6), to Buchi Emecheta's poignant chapter from her novel *The Joys of Motherhood*, "A Man Needs Many Wives" (pages 656–66), to the deft

[26] Introduction to Mary Helen Washington, *Black-Eyed Susans: Classic Stories by and about Black Women*, Garden City, NY: Anchor/Doubleday, 1975, p. ix.
[27] *Invented Lives: Narratives of Black Women 1860–1960*, Garden City, NY: Anchor/ Doubleday, 1987, Introduction, p. xxi.

touch of Mabel Dove-Danquah's short story "Anticipation" (pages 233–6). And unquestioning acceptance of custom and ritual – as indicated in Efua Sutherland's "New Life at Kyerefaso" (pages 314–18) – contrasts with the necessary adjustment that follows contact with Western education and society – typified by Noni Jabavu's account of her return to South Africa after many years abroad (see pages 287–97), Tsitsi Dangarembga's fictional treatment of the effects for a young girl in Zimbabwe of learning new values through missionary schooling (pages 924–31), or Mariama Bâ's epistolary picture of a Muslim woman liberated from "the bog of tradition, superstition and custom" (pages 340–45). The emergence of a younger generation of high-calibre women writers in Africa, including Tsitsi Dangarembga and Zeinab Alkali (who like Mariama Bâ comes from a Muslim background; see page 782), is an encouraging sign; so too is the comitment of African women, such as Abena Busia, 'Molara Ogundipe-Leslie and Ifi Amadiume, who are combining imaginative writing with literary criticism and other forms of non-fiction. But their number remains small and the prejudices and obstacles they face – for instance, being ignored by male critics – are great. Adeola James in her illuminating book of interviews, *In Their Own Voices: African Women Writers Talk*, draws attention to the particular situation of women writers in Africa today, who "in the twenty-five years since they started being published, have made a significant contribution, which until recently, has been only grudgingly acknowledged".[28]

The development of streetwise instincts to staunch the debilitating drain of poverty is a defence mechanism discovered by Rosa Guy's protagonist Dorrie in *A Measure of Time* (see pages 319–25). From another tributary flows the privileged angst of being born into genteel middle-class mores – clearly seen in Marita Bonner's essay "On Being Young – A Woman – and Colored" (pages 212–15), or Dorothy West's portrait of Boston's Black intelligentsia after the First World War (pages 240–46).

The "tragic mulatto" figure widespread in American literature finds echoes in the work of writers such as Jessie Fauset (see page 170) and Nella Larsen, who in her novels (see pages 200–8) explores the syndrome of light-skinned Blacks "passing" for white in order to achieve social advantage, a self-denial that Frances Harper's Iola Leroy (pages 85–9) eschews. As interracial relationships become more common throughout the diaspora, problems of cultural identity surface – for Jenneba Sie Jalloh in connection with her Irish heritage (pages 964–8), for Ayse Bircan, a Turkish Black woman married to a Kurdish man, in connection with her son's complexes (see pages 881–90), and for the Afro-German women Abena Adomako, Julia Berger, Angelika Eisenbrandt and May Opitz who contribute their frank personal stories (pages 960–62, 969–70, 870–72, 932–7). For yet others, something of a comedy of errors has evolved, with the problem – the "bequest of confusion" Dinah Anuli Butler writes about in her poem to her father (pages 923–4) – is external and in the eye of the beholder. The ultimate solution for Pauline Melville (author of the prizewinning short-story collection *Shape-shifter* that defies categorization) is to choose to take

---

[28] Adeola James (ed.), *In Their Own Voices: African Women Writers Talk*, London: James Currey/Portsmouth, NH: Heinemann, 1990, p. 2.

as her "tutelary spirits Legba, Exu and Hermes, the gods of boundaries" (see pages 939–43).

Occasionally the meeting of social and personal frustrations produces situations of unique poignancy, with characters for whom fulfilment seems impossible, as with the abandoned romantic heroine in Cuban Marta Rojas's *Rey Spencer's Swing* (pages 412–14); or Claire, the 39-year-old unmarried narrator of Haitian Marie Chauvet's novel (see pages 272–5), desperately in love with her brother-in-law, who describes the background that has shaped her:

> I was born in 1900. A time when prejudice was at its height in this little province. Three separate groups had formed and these three groups were as divided as enemies: the "aristocrats", to whom we belonged, the petits bourgeois and the common people. Torn apart by the ambiguity of a particularly delicate situation, I began to suffer from a very early age because of my dark skin, whose mahogany colour, inherited from some distant ancestor, stood out glaringly in the close circle of whites and light-skinned mulattos with whom my parents mixed. But all that is in the past, and for the moment at least, I don't feel inclined to turn towards what is over and done with.

Affirmation of self-image, or erosion of it, in the confrontation with white western concepts of beauty – usually in terms of skin shade and hair texture, often associated with their appeal to the opposite sex – feature as issues in many of the selections. The hairdressing salon (spotlighted by Marsha Prescod, pages 485–7) – which might be someone's front parlour – has always been a crucial meeting place for Black women, and talk of hair often figures large. Lucinda Roy, in her celebratory poem "If You Know Black Hair" (page 897), sees it is a prized symbol of indomitability; Gwendolyn Brooks's eponymous heroine in *Maud Martha* (see pages 269–71) is resigned to the knowledge that her father prefers her sister Helen's hair to her own because it "impressed him, not with its length and body, but simply with its apparent untamableness"; while Una Marson's "Kinky Hair Blues" (pages 221–2) epitomizes the paradox of our love/hate relationship with our unreconstructed appearance:

> ...I like me black face
> And me kinky hair,
> I like me black face
> And me kinky hair.
> But nobody loves dem,
> I jes don't tink it's fair.
>
> Now I's gwine press me hair
> And bleach me skin,
> I's gwine press me hair
> And bleach me skin.
> What won't a gal do
> Some kind of man to win.

Relationships between the sexes are another source of abundant subject matter, and though different generations have different mores, some ideas remain the same although they cannot always be taken at face value. Compare the advice on wifely duties given by Mwana Kupona Msham to her daughter in the nineteenth century (see pages 67–9) with the Bemba girls' initiation song ("The man is the peak of the house;/That is what we have understood./It is women who make the pinnacle/On top of the roof", page 1); or the attitude of Kristina Rungano's long-suffering wife in her subversively wry poem "The Woman" (pages 963–4), published in 1984 – whatever grievances she bears towards her man, however onerous and unreasonable his demands, she says:

Yet tomorrow I shall again wake up to you,
Milk the cow, plough the land and cook your food;
You shall again be my lord,
For isn't it right that woman should obey,
Love, serve and honour her man?
For are you not the fruit of the land?

Iyamidé Hazeley's poem "Political Union" (pages 907–9) takes a more modern view of male-female relationships within the context of social and political liberation. Yet the ultimate aim is, in Alda do Espírito Santo's words, "we may be all of us on the same side of the canoe" (see pages 326–8). Sometimes conflict results from interracial alliances, pointed up by Baby Palatine's disapproval of Joy's dating of a white boy in Marsha Hunt's novel (see pages 688–94), or as unfolds in Louise Meriwether's short story "A Happening in Barbados" (pages 302–8) or Maya Angelou's "The Reunion" (pages 332–5). Even more problematically received can be relationships between women.

"Yet women-identified women – those who sought their own destinies and attempted to execute them in the absence of male support – have been around in all of our communities for a long time, as Audre Lorde has pointed out."[29] Red Jordan Arobateau's perceived dilemma (see pages 593–603) of being a light-skinned Black woman is compounded by her sexual orientation: "My psychiatrist informs me; 'You are white.' (He also tells me it's wrong to be a lesbian. He is white. And not homosexual. This is brainwashing.)" Other attitudes emerge in Becky Birtha's story "Johnnieruth" (pages 744–8) and the extract "The Two" from Gloria Naylor's *The Women of Brewster Place* (pages 812–18). Other sisterly relationships are revealed, for example, in Ama Ata Aidoo's "Two Sisters" (pages 532–42), Sandi Russell's "Sister" (pages 694–8), Baba of Karo's recollection of special girlhood friendships (pages 166–8).

Woman-headed households are commonly depicted, in families where the man is absent possibly as a consequence of the realities of economic and social pressures. In line with the familiar phenomenon of "my mother who fathered me", portraits of strong mother-daughter, grandmother-granddaughter relationships abound both in creative writing and in memoirs (the inclusion

[29] Audre Lorde, "Scratching the Surface: Some Notes on Barriers to Women and Loving", *Sister Outsider: Essays and Speeches*, Freedom, CA: The Crossing Press, 1984,

of both Adelaide and Gladys Casely-Hayford provides a rare opportunity to observe generational differences in themes and concerns; see pages 153–60 and 217–20). Old women, in fact and in fiction, inspire some of the most tender writing. In Beryl Gilroy's *Frangipani House* (see pages 309–13), set in an old people's home, Mama King tries to come to terms with being deprived of "her faithful friends, work and hardship". Erna Brodber's Granny Tucker prays with her granddaughters Jane and Louisa (see pages 503–6). Jewelle Gomez remembers nostalgically a swimming lesson with her "Dahomean queen" grandmother (pages 763–5). Astrid Roemer tentatively unravels the psychology of a mother and grandmother (pages 725–32). Naomi Long Madgett compassionately senses the "heavy years" borne by a woman she observes, who "coaxes her fat in front of her like a loaded market basket with defective wheels" (page 298). An 84-year-old woman imparts the wisdom of her years in Sonia Sanchez's "Just Don't Never Give Up On Love" (pages 447–9). Paule Marshall pays an affectionate tribute to her grandmother in "To Da-Duh, In Memoriam" (pages 348–55). Yet there is also at times a feeling of regret for the loss of old values, the old ways – Mīcere Mūgo's poem (pages 551–3) asks "Where are those songs?" Similarly, Margaret Walker (pages 266–7), whose popular poem "For My People" speaks of "the gone years and the now years and the maybe years", wonders in "Lineage": "My grandmothers were strong...They were full of sturdiness and singing....Why am I not as they?"

If we should ever falter in our confidence of our power eventually to overcome, Hattie Gossett's poem "world view" (page 550) gives a timely reminder that:

> theres more poor than nonpoor
> theres more colored than noncolored
> theres more women than men

> All over the world the poor woman of color is the mainstay of
> the little daddy centred family which is the bottom line of big
> daddys industrial civilization.

Contemporary issues of global importance and scope are boldly and explicitly tackled in the work of writers such as Jayne Cortez (pages 466–8) and June Jordan (acknowledging, in "Declaration of an Independence I Would Just as Soon Not Have" – pages 471–5 – her own awareness that political change won't come about through lone activity, that only through connecting herself with liberation struggles in the Black Movement, in the Third World Movement and in the Women's Movement will she be free to be who she is, Black and female) and are in various ways implicit in that of many others.

Abena Busia's poem "Liberation" (pages 869–70) speaks uncompromisingly of that "fire within us":

of powerful women
whose spirits are so angry
we can laugh beauty into life
and still make you taste
the salt tears of our knowledge –
For we are not tortured
anymore;
we have seen beyond your lies and disguises,
and *we* have mastered the language of words,
we have mastered speech.
And know
we have also seen ourselves.
We have stripped ourselves raw
and naked piece by piece until our flesh lies flayed
with blood on our *own* hands.
What terrible thing can you do us
which we have not done to ourselves?. . .

Throughout these women's words runs the awareness of connectedness to a wider flow of history, to the precursors, our foremothers. Our collective strength, like that of a chain, derives from maintaining the links.

Geographical Listing and Bibliographies

E NSURING a wide geographical spread has meant cutting down particularly on contributions from US women, whose output alone could fill many volumes of comparable length, and the list of those I regret leaving out runs into scores. (Inevitably space considerations have meant that much material originally planned for inclusion has had to be left out. Also inevitably, financial constraints have played their awesome part, and it has proved impossible to accommodate the demands of some publishers' unyielding permissions departments.)

Nevertheless, the contributions finally chosen are from women born in or identifying with: Angola, Antigua, Aruba, Barbados, Belize, Benin, Bermuda, Botswana, Brazil, Canada, Costa Rica, Côte d'Ivoire, Cuba, Dominica, Egypt, England, Ethiopia, Germany, Ghana, Grenada, Guadeloupe, Guyana, Haiti, Ireland, Jamaica, Kenya, Lesotho, Liberia, Malawi, Mali, Mozambique, the Netherlands, Nigeria, Russia, Santo Domingo, St Kitts, Sao Tomé, Scotland, Senegal, Sierra Leone, Somalia, South Africa, Sudan, Surinam, Tigray, Trinidad and Tobago, Turkey, Uganda, Uruguay, the United States of America, Zaïre, Zambia and Zimbabwe. A rough listing by area is given at the end of the book.

Daughters of Africa extends a tradition begun by a few landmark works that placed Black women's experience centre-stage. Toni Cade Bambara's pioneering anthology *The Black Woman* (1970) grew partly "out of an impatience with the fact that in the whole bibliography of feminist literature, literature directly relevant to us [Afro-American women] wouldn't fill a page" (Preface, pp. 10–11). The twenty-one years since then have seen a coming of age for that literature, in so far as it is now possible to produce a bibliography of Further Reading featuring so many publications by and about women of African descent. A highlighting of some of those titles shows the proliferation of such material.

USA: Mary Helen Washington, (ed.), *Black-Eyed Susans: Classic Stories By and About Black Women* (1975), *Midnight Birds: Stories of Contemporary Black Women Writers* (1980) and *Invented Lives: Narratives of Black Women 1860–1960* (1987); Gerda Lerner (ed.), *Black Women in White America* (1972); Jeanne Noble, *Beautiful, Also, Are the Souls of my Black Sisters: A History of the Black Woman in America* (1978); Roseanne P. Bell, Bettye J. Parker and Beverly Guy-Sheftall (eds), *Sturdy Black Bridges: Visions of Black Women in Literature* (1979); La Frances Rodgers Rose, *The Black Woman* (1980); Erlene Stetson (ed.), *Black Sister: Poetry by Black American Women, 1746–1980* (1981); Cherrie Moraga and Gloria Anzaldúa (eds), *This Bridge Called My Back: Writings by Radical Women of Color* (1981); Pat Crutchfield Exum (ed.), *Keeping the Faith: Writings by Contemporary Black American Women* (1981); Gloria T. Hull, Patricia Bell Scott and Barbara Smith (eds), *All the Women Are White, All the Blacks Are Men, But Some of Us Are Brave: Black Women's Studies* (1982); Amina Baraka and Amiri Baraka (eds), *Confirmation: An Anthology of African-American Women* (1983); Claudia Tate (ed.), *Black Women Writers at Work* (1983); Barbara Christian, *Black Women Novelists* (1983) and *Black Feminist Criticism: Perspectives on Black Women Writers* (1985); Barbara Smith (ed.), *Home Girls: A Black Feminist Anthology* (1983); Mari Evans (ed.), *Black Women Writers* (1984); Paula Giddings, *When and Where I Enter: The Impact of Black Women on Race and Sex in America* (1984); Dorothy Sterling (ed.), *We Are Your Sisters: Black Women in the Nineteenth Century* (1984); Margaret B. Wilkerson (ed.), *Nine Plays by Black Women* (1986); Dorothy Hilton Chapman (comp.), *Index to Poetry by Black American Women* (1986); Hazel V. Carby, *Reconstructing Womanhood: The Emergence of the Afro-American Woman Novelist* (1987); Susan Willis, *Specifying: Black Women Writing the American Experience* (1987); Ann Allen Shockley, *Afro-American Women Writers 1746–1933* (1988); Michael Awkward, *Inspiriting Influences: Tradition, Revision, and Afro-American Women's Novels* (1989); Cheryl A. Wall (ed.), *Changing Our Own Words: Essays on Criticism, Theory, and Writing by Black Women* (1989); Maureen Honey (ed.), *Shadowed Dreams: Women's Poetry of the Harlem Renaissance* (1989); Gloria Anzaldúa (ed.), *Making Face, Making Soul – Haciendo Caras: Creative and Critical Perspectives by Women of Color* (1990); Sandi Russell, *Render Me My Song: African-American Women Writers from Slavery to the Present* (1990); Joanne M. Braxton and Andrée Nicola McLaughlin (eds), *Wild Women in the Whirlwind: Afra-American Culture and the Contemporary Literary Renaissance* (1990); Kathy A. Perkins (ed.), *Black Female Playwrights: An Anthology of Plays before 1950* (1990); Lorraine Elena Roses and Ruth Elizabeth Randolph, *Harlem Renaissance and Beyond: Literary Biographies of 100 Black Women Writers 1900–1945* (1990); Henry Louis Gates, Jr, *Reading Black/Reading Feminist* (1990); Melisa Walker, *Down from the Mountaintop: Black Women's Novels in the Wake of the Civil*

Rights Movement (1991). The Schomburg Library of Nineteenth-Century Black Women Writers, under the general editorship of Henry Louis Gates, Jr, and the Beacon Press Black Women Writers Series have made available since the late 1980s many out-of-print works by African-American women.

CANADA: Ann Wallace (ed.), *Daughters of the Sun, Women of the Moon: Anthology of Canadian Black Women Poets* (1991).

CROSS-CULTURAL PERSPECTIVES: Filomina Chioma-Steady (ed.), *The Black Woman Cross-Culturally* (1981); Mineke Schipper (ed.), *Unheard Words: Women and Literature in Africa, the Arab World, Asia, the Caribbean and Latin America* (1985); Rosalyn Terborg-Penn, Sharon Harley and Andrea Benton Rushing (eds), *Women in Africa and the African Diaspora* (1987); Carole Boyce Davies (ed.), *Black Women's Writing: Crossing the Boundaries* (1989); Susheila Nasta, *Motherlands: Black Women's Writing form the Caribbean, Africa and South Asia* (1991).

BRITAIN: Elyse Dodgson, *Motherland: West Indian Women in Britain in the 1960s* (1984); Beverley Bryan, Stella Dadzie and Suzanne Scafe (eds), *The Heart of the Race: Black Women's Lives in Britain* (1985); Rhonda Cobham and Merle Collins (eds), *Watchers and Seekers: Creative Writing by Black Women in Britain* (1987); Lauretta Ngcobo (ed.), *Let It Be Told: Black Women Writers in Britain* (1987); Da Choong, Olivette Cole Wilson, Gabriela Pearse, Bernardine Evaristo (eds), *Black Women Talk Poetry* (1987); Shabnam Grewal, Jackie Kay, Liliane Landor, Gail Lewis and Pratibha Parmar (eds), *Charting the Journey: Writings by Black and Third World Women* (1988); Zhana (ed.), *Sojourn* (1988); Audrey Osler, *Speaking Out: Black Girls in Britain* (1989); Maud Sulter (ed), *Passion: Discourses on Blackwomen's Creativity* (1990); Da Choong, Olivette Cole Wilson, Sylvia Parker and Gabriela Pearse (eds), *Don't Ask Me Why: An Anthology of Short Stories by Black Women* (1991).

THE CARIBBEAN: Pamela Mordecai and Mervyn Morris (eds), *Jamaica Woman* (1980); Sistren, *Lionheart Gal* (1986); Pamela Mordecai and Betty Wilson (eds), *Her True-True Name: An Anthology of Women's Writing from the Caribbean* (1989); Brenda F. Berrian, *Bibliography of Women Writers from the Caribbean* (1989); Carole Boyce Davies and Elaine Savory Fido (eds), *Out of the Kumbla: Caribbean Women and Literature* (1990); Ramabai Espinet (ed.), *Creation Fire: A CAFRA Anthology of Caribbean Women's Poetry* (1990); Selwyn R. Cudjoe (ed.), *Caribbean Women Writers* (1990); Margaret Watts (ed.), *Washerwoman Hangs her Poems in the Sun* (1991).

AFRICA: Charlotte Bruner (ed.), *Unwinding Threads: Writing by Women in Africa* (1983); Taiwo Oladele, *Female Novelists of Modern Africa* (1984); Brenda Berrian, *Bibliography of African Women Writers and Journalists* (1985); Carole Boyce Davies and Anne Adams Graves (eds), *Ngambika: Studies of Women in African Literature* (1986); Adeola James (ed.), *In Their Own Voices: African Women Writers Talk* (1990).

Many other general anthologies include various proportions of women contributors, and the bibliography of Further Reading attempts to give some idea of those included. The former "invisibility" of women writers of African descent makes it significant that many early anthologies of African writing or African-American, for example, seemed able to find only a few, if any, women they deemed worthy of inclusion. This under-representation is only in recent years being corrected.

The listing of Author Sources gives the main published works by those women whose contributions appear in *Daughters of Africa*, with details of selected individual works of biography or criticism.

Margaret Busby
London, December 1991.

DAUGHTERS OF
AFRICA

Traditional African Poems

The following poems and songs are mostly from sub-Saharan Africa. According to Leonard W. Doob, editor of Ants Will Not Eat Your Fingers: A Selection of Traditional African Poems *(New York, 1966), in which many of them appeared: "By and large the poems are traditional in three senses. They have been attributed to no known creators by their discoverers who have stated or implied that they are — or once were — part of the ritual of the society. Then, secondly, they have been relatively uninfluenced by European or Eastern poetic traditions. Finally. . .these poems are likely to be so embedded in an African ceremony or tradition that they affect almost every member of the group without being recognized as a separate genre; many are supposed to be sung or chanted; and most deal with the eternal themes of love, death, jealousy, anxiety."*

Initiation Song of Girls

The man is the peak of the house;
That is what we have understood.
It is women who make the pinnacle
On top of the roof.

Bemba [translated by Audrey I. Richards]

Love Song of a Girl

The far-off mountains hide you from me,
While the nearer ones overhang me.
Would that I had a heavy sledge
To crush the mountains near me.
Would that I had wings like a bird
To fly over those farther away.

Xhosa (South Africa) [translated by A. C. Jordan]

Girls' Secret Love Song

You shake the waist – we shake.
Let us shake the waist – we shake.
You shake the waist – we shake.
I am going to my lover – we shake.
Even if it is raining – we shake –
I am going to my lover – we shake.
He is at Chesumei – we shake.
Even when night comes – we shake –
I am going to my lover – we shake.
Even if he hits me – we shake –
I am going at night – we shake.
Even if there is a wild animal – we shake –
I am going to my lover – we shake.
A person not knowing a lover – we shake –
Knows nothing at all – we shake.

Kipsigi [translated by J. G. Peristiany]

Song for Dance of Young Girls

We mould a pot as our mothers did.
The pot, where is the pot?
The pot, it is here.
We mould the pot as our mothers did.

First, the base of the pot.
Strip by strip, and layer by layer.
Supple fingers moulding the clay,
Long fingers moulding the clay,
Layer by layer and strip by strip,
We build up the pot of our mother.

We build up the pot of our mother,
Strip by strip and layer by layer.
Its belly swells like the paunch of a hyena,
Of a hyena which has eaten a whole sheep.
Its belly swells like a mother of twins.
It is a beautiful pot, the pot of our mother,
It swells like a mother of twins.

Didinga (*Uganda*) [translated by J. H. Driberg]

A Woman Sings of Her Love

Oh, you are a kilt which a young dandy set out to choose,
Oh, you are like a costly ring for which thousands were paid,
Will I ever find your like – you who have been shown to me only once?
An umbrella comes apart; you are (as strong as) looped iron;
Oh, you (who are as) the gold of Nairobi, finely moulded,
You are the risen sun, and the early rays of dawn,
Will I ever find your like, you who have been shown to me only once?

(Somalia) [translated by B. W. Andrzejewski/I. M. Lewis]

"I Am Your Betrothed"

I heard it said that I was betrothed
And one afternoon when I was at home,
As I was sitting, I saw a fool coming,
He came dragging his coat on the ground
And his trousers were made of khaki.
I said to him, "Fool, where do you come from?"
He replied, "I am your betrothed."
I gave the dog a chair and his tail hung down.

Kgatla (Botswana) [translated by I. Schapera]

Taunts of Old Women to a Pregnant Wife

First you sought pleasure,
Now you will have pain instead;
You will no longer have your beauty,
For you are not a girl any more
But a child's mother.

While you ate, it was sweet,
But now it is sour:
Nasty, nasty, nasty.
Both day and night
It was your custom to sleep together:
Nasty, nasty, nasty.

Yao [translated by A. M. Hokororo]

A Mother to Her First-born

Speak to me, child of my heart.
Speak to me with your eyes, your round laughing eyes,
Wet and shining as Lupeyo's bull-calf.

Speak to me, little one,
Clutching my breast with your hand,
So strong and firm for all its littleness.
It will be the hand of a warrior, my son,
A hand that will gladden your father.
See how eagerly it fastens on me:
It thinks already of a spear:
It quivers as at the throwing a spear.
O son, you will have a warrior's name and be a leader of men.
And your sons, and your sons' sons, will remember you long after you
    have slipped into darkness.
But I, I shall always remember your hand clutching me so.
I shall recall how you lay in my arms,
And looked at me so, and so,
And how your tiny hands played with my bosom.
And when they name you great warrior, then will my eyes be wet with
    remembering.

And how shall we name you, little warrior?
See, let us play at naming.
It will not be a name of despisal, for you are my first-born.
Not as Nawal's son is named will you be named.
Our gods will be kinder to you than theirs.
Must we call you "Insolence" or "Worthless One"?
Shall you be named, like a child of fortune, after the dung of cattle?
Our gods need no cheating, my child:
They wish you no ill.
They have washed your body and clothed it with beauty.
The have set a fire in your eyes.
And the little, puckering ridges of your brow –
Are they not the seal of their fingerprints when they fashioned you?
They have given you beauty and strength, child of my heart,
And wisdom is already shining in your eyes,
And laughter.

So how shall we name you, little one?
Are you your father's father, or his brother, or yet another?
Whose spirit is it that is in you, little warrior?
Whose spear-hand tightens round my breast?
Who lives in you and quickens to life, like last year's melon seed?

Are you silent, then?
But your eyes are thinking, thinking, and glowing like the eyes of a leopard
    in a thicket.
Well, let be.
At the day of naming you will tell us.

O my child, now indeed I am happy.
Now indeed I am a wife –
No more a bride, but a Mother-of-one.
Be splendid and magnificent, child of desire.
Be proud, as I am proud.
Be happy, as I am happy.
Be loved, as now I am loved.
Child, child, child, love I have had from my man.
But now, only now, have I the fullness of love.
Now, only now, am I his wife and the mother of his first-born.
His soul is safe in your keeping, my child, and it was I, I, I, who made you.

Therefore am I loved.
Therefore am I happy.
Therefore am I a wife.
Therefore have I great honour.

You will tend his shrine when he is gone.
With sacrifice and oblation you will recall his name year by year.
He will live in your prayers, my child,
And there will be no more death for him, but everlasting life springing
    from your loins.
You are his shield and his spear, his hope and redemption from the
    dead.
Through you he will be reborn, as the saplings in Spring.
And I, I am the mother of his first-born.
Sleep, child of beauty and courage and fulfilment, sleep.
I am content.

(Sudan) [translated by J. H. Driberg]

Lullaby

Someone would like to have you for her child,
But you are my own.
Someone wished she had you to nurse on a good mat;
Someone wished you were hers, she would put you on a camel blanket;
But I have to rear you on a torn mat.
Someone wished she had you, but I have you.

Akan (Ghana)

A Mother Praises Her Baby

You son of a clear-eyed mother
You far-sighted one,
How you will see game one day,
You, who have strong arms and legs,
You strong-limbed one,
How surely you will shoot, plunder the Herreros,
And bring your mother their fat cattle to eat,
You child of a strong-thighed father,
How you will subdue strong oxen between your thighs one day,
You who have a mighty penis,
How many and what mighty children you will beget!

Khoikhoi (South Africa)

Mothers' Song

When a son leaves our womb,
We are joyously glad;
The gladness heals us.
When he leaves our larger womb,
The village, we lie torn, bleeding:
There is no healing, no healing
until a son returns to us,
There is no healing;
Only when he returns
Can there be healing.
Oh, oh, our sons,
Stay with us now
Until we come together
In the town of the Dead.

Loma [translated by Esther Warner]

Chorus Sung by Co-Wives to One Another

Woman, your soul is misshapen,
In haste was it made;
So fleshless a face speaks,
Saying your soul was formed without care.
The ancestral clay for your making
Was moulded in haste.
A thing of no beauty are you,
Your face unsuited for a face,
Your feet unsuited for feet.

(Dahomey/Benin) [translated by Frances Herskovits/Leonard Doob]

Love Song

He has two loves,
He has two loves,
I go to see him off.
I meet the other woman.
I cannot go on,
I cannot go back,
I burst into tears.

Akan (Ghana) [translated by J. H. Kwabena Nketia]

Lullaby of an Abandoned Mother

Hush, my forgotten one,
Hush, my child;
These labours of love
You have given me,
For the heart eats what is beloved
But rejects what is bestowed.

Kgatla [translated by I. Schapera]

Household Song

When I asked for him at Entoto, he was towards Akaki,
So they told me;
When I asked for him at Akaki, he was towards Jarer,
So they told me;
When I asked for him at Jarer, he was towards Mendar,
So they told me;
When I asked for him at Mendar, he was towards Awash,
So they told me;
When I asked for him at Awash, he was towards Chercher,
So they told me;
When I asked for him at Chercher, he was towards Harar,
So they told me;
When I asked for him at Harar, he was towards Djibouti,
So they told me;
When I asked for him at Djibouti, he had crossed the sea,
Or so they said:
I sent to find him a hundred times,
But I never found him.
I sit by the fire and weep:
What a fool he is
To hope he will ever find anyone to equal me.

Amhara (Ethiopia) [translated by Sylvia Pankhurst]

Trousers of Wind

[household song about a worthless lover, sung by the women as they work] .
(Ethiopia) [translated by Sylvia Pankhurst/Ato Menghestu Lemma]

Trousers of wind and buttons of hail;
A lump of Shoa earth, at Gondar nothing left;
A hyena bearing meat, led by a leather thong;
Some water in a glass left standing by the fire;
A measure of water thrown on the hearth;
A horse of mist and a swollen ford;
Useless for anything, useful to no one;
Why am I in love with such a man as he?

Two Pounding Songs

[sung as grain is pounded using pestle and mortar]

A shared husband I don't want!
I want my own
Who looks on proudly as I pound,
Not somebody else's
Who when I pound
Turns his back on me!
I want a beautiful child
Who sleeps on a mattress
In a house with a wooden door!

ChiChewa (Malawi)

Lazybones, let's go to the farm
 Sorry, I've got a headache
Lazybones, let's go pounding grain
 Sorry, my leg isn't right
Lazybones, let's go fetch firewood
 Sorry, my hands are hurting
Lazybones, come and have some food
 Hold on, let me wash my hands!

ChiTumbuka (Malawi)

Grinding Song

Hear me, my grains, my grains of wheat –
While I tell my tale.
When we brought you from the harvest fields
You filled the basket to the brim;
But after all that labour on the land,
When you come to the grindstone,
Instead of ten donkey-loads,
You are only a few handfuls.
The feudals have taken it all.

My hands, hear me as you grind,
Not to let fall the smallest grain
And waste it on the floor.
The Lady in the feudal's house
Sits idle, with her hands
Adorned with gold and henna.
But my hands are ground down
With work, and fighting
With this stone –
To ward off hunger.

Why am I born a woman?
For a priest, I make do with a hen;
My grindstone is my only friend.
I can open my heart to no one near,
Whether they are home or the house is empty,
No one speaks to me.
My priest is a hen and my friend a grindstone.

How do you feel, my husband,
As you labour for nothing on the land?
The fire burns bright in the feudal's home,
Where there is soup and meat and milk;
Coming home from the fields
To a house cold and dark
With no fire and no food –
How do you feel, my husband?

(Tigray)

Ancient Egyptian

There are four known manuscripts of love songs dating from the Egyptian New Kingdom, which spanned the eighteenth to twentieth dynasties, c. 1550–1080 BC. Miriam Lichtheim writes in Ancient Egyptian Literature: Volume II *(1976): "Though sophisticated in the context of their own times, the poems have the conceptual simplicity and terseness of language that are the hallmarks of ancient Egyptian literature." Papyrus Harris 500 (Papyrus British Museum 10060) contains three collections of such lyrics, and the following are from the second collection (II.b).*

Love Songs

Beginning of the delightful, beautiful songs of your beloved sister as she comes from the fields.

2

The voice of the wild goose shrills,
It is caught by its bait;
My love of you pervades me,
I cannot loosen it.
I shall retrieve my nets,
But what do I tell my mother,
To whom I go daily,
Laden with bird catch?
I have spread no snares today,
I am caught in my love of you!

3

The wild goose soars and swoops,
It alights on the net;
Many birds swarm about,
I have work to do.
I am held fast by my love,
Alone, my heart meets your heart,
From your beauty I'll not part!

6

The voice of the dove is calling,
It says: "It's day! Where are you?"
O bird, stop scolding me!
I found my brother in his bed,
My heart was overjoyed;
Each said: "I shall not leave you,
My hand is in your hand;
You and I shall wander
In all the places fair."
He makes me the foremost of women,
He does not aggrieve my heart.

7

My gaze is fixed on the garden gate,
My brother will come to me;
Eyes on the road, ears straining,
I wait for him who neglects me.
I made my brother's love my sole concern,
About him my heart is not silent;
It sends me a fleet-footed messenger
Who comes and goes to tell me:
"He deceives you, in other words,
He found another woman,
She is dazzling to his eyes."
Why vex another's heart to death?

8

My heart thought of my love of you,
When half of my hair was braided;
I came at a run to find you.
And neglected my hairdo.
Now if you let me braid my hair,
I shall be ready in a moment.

Queen Hatshepsut

1501–1447 BC

A formidable woman, she ruled Egypt in the eighteenth dynasty for twenty-one years (1490–1469 BC), portraying herself as man, wearing a false beard and the robes and royal insignia of a Pharaoh. Her father Thutmose I died in 1495 BC after a thirty-year rule, with no male heir from his principal wife, Hatshepsut's mother, though from another wife he had a son, Thutmose II, whose right to rule was ensured by marriage to Hatshepsut. Thutmose II had only a short reign (1495–1490 BC), and he too had no male heir from his principal wife (and half-sister), who bore him two daughters; he named as successor his son Thutmose III, born to a concubine. On the death of her husband and half-brother, Hatshepsut became regent for Thutmose III, then a minor. However, she usurped sole power, spreading the story that her real father was the god Amun Ra, that she had been chosen by the gods to rule Egypt. Her advisers included Senmut, her architect and lover, and she was responsible for the building of several fine monuments, including a huge sanctuary at the temple of Karnak and her great three-level temple in Deir el-Bahri, with wall paintings detailing her voyage in the ninth year of her reign to Punt (Somalia) to fetch incense trees and other agricultural products. She also erected four obelisks at the temple of Amun at Karnak. One of these, outside the eastern wall of the temple, still stands, after more than thirty-four centuries. The tallest surviving obelisk in Egypt, it is 29.5 metres in height, weighing 323 tons, made of a single monolith of red granite, and originally gilded at the top so that the upper half gleamed in the sun. On its side and base are hieroglyphic inscriptions, honouring Hatshepsut's divine father Amun and in memory of her earthly father Thutmose I, which are in part translated here.

Speech of the Queen

I have done this with a loving heart for my father Amun;
Initiated in his secret of the beginning,
Acquainted with his beneficent might,
I did not forget whatever he had ordained.

My majesty knows his divinity,
I acted under his command;
It was he who led me,
I did not plan a work without his doing.
It was he who gave directions,
I did not sleep because of his temple,
I did not stray from what he commanded.
My heart was Sia[1] before my father,
I entered into the plans of his heart.
I did not turn my back to the city of the All-Lord,
Rather did I turn my face to it.
I know that Ipet-sut is the lightland on earth,
The august hill of the beginning,
The Sacred Eye of the All-Lord,
His favoured place that bears his beauty,
That gathers in his followers.

It is the King himself who says:
I declare before the folk who shall be in the future,
Who shall deserve the monument I made for my father,
Who shall speak in discussion,
Who shall look to posterity –
It was when I sat in the palace,
And thought of my maker,
That my heart led me to make for him
Two obelisks of electrum,
Whose summits would reach the heavens,
In the august hall of columns,
Between the two great portals of the King,
The Strong Bull, King Aakheperkare, the Horus triumphant.[2]
Now my heart turns to and fro,
In thinking what will the people say,
They who shall see my monument in after years,
And shall speak of what I have done.

Beware of saying, "I know not, I know not:
Why has this been done?
To fashion a mountain of gold throughout,
Like something that just happened."
I swear, as I am loved of Re,
As Amun, my father, favours me,
As my nostrils are refreshed with life and dominion,

---

[1] The personification of the concept of understanding.
[2] Thutmose I had built the two pylons now numbered IV and V, and a hypostyle hall between them. Hatshepsut removed its wooden ceiling, thus turning the hall into a colonnaded court, and erected her two obelisks in it.

As I wear the white crown,
As I appear with the red crown,
As the Two Lords have joined their portions for me,
As I rule this land like the son of Isis,
As I am mighty like the son of Nut,
As Re rests in the evening bark,
As he prevails in the morning bark,
As he joins his two mothers in the god's ship,
As sky endures, as his creation lasts,
As I shall be eternal like an undying star,
As I shall rest in life like Atum –
So as regards these two great obelisks,
Wrought with electrum by my majesty for my father Amun,
In order that my name may endure in this temple,
For eternity and everlastingness,
They are each of one block of hard granite,
Without seam, with joining together!

My majesty began work on them in year 15, second month of winter, day 1, ending in year 16, fourth month of summer, last day totalling seven months of quarry work. I did it for him out of affection, as a king for a god. It was my wish to make them for him gilded with electrum. "Their foil lies on their body," is what I expect people to say. My mouth is effective in its speech; I do not go back on my word. Hear ye! I gave for them of the finest electrum. I measured it by the gallon like sacks of grain. My majesty summoned a quantity beyond what the Two Lands had yet seen. The ignorant and the wise know it.

Nor shall he who hears it say,
"It is a boast," what I have said;
Rather say, "How like her it is,
She is devoted to her father!"
Lo, the god knows me well,
Amun, Lord of Thrones-of-the-Two-Lands;
He made me rule Black Land and Red Land as reward,
No one rebels against me in all lands.
All foreign lands are my subjects,
He placed my border at the limits of heaven,
What Aten encircles labours for me.
He gave it to him who came from him,
Knowing I would rule it for him.
I am his daughter in very truth,
Who serves him, who knows what he ordains.
My reward from my father is life-stability-rule,
On the Horus throne of all the living, eternally like Re.

Makeda, Queen of Sheba

fl. 10th century BC

R uler of the kingdom of Saba', she is claimed by Ethiopians to be their Queen Makeda, from whom descended their monarchs. Hearing of the wisdom of Solomon, King of Israel, she travelled to Jersalem, as the Old Testament of the Bible records: "and she said to the king, It was a true report which I heard in mine own land of thine acts, and of thine wisdom: Howbeit I believed not their words, until I came, and mine own eyes had seen it: and, behold, the one half of the greatness of thy wisdom was not told me: for thou exceedest the fame that I hear. Happy are thy men, and happy are these thy servants, which stand continually before thee, and hear thy wisdom. Blessed be the Lord thy God, which delighted in thee to set thee on his throne, to be king for the Lord thy God: because thy God loved Israel, to establish thou for ever, therefore made he thee king over them, to do judgment and justice. And she gave the king an hundred and twenty talents of gold, and of spices great abundance, and precious stones: neither was there any such spice as the queen of Sheba gave king Solomon. . . . And king Solomon gave to the queen of Sheba all her desire, whatsoever she asked, beside that which she had brought unto the king. So she turned, and went away to her own land, she and her servants" (Chronicles II, 9). According to the Kebra Nagast (The Glory of the Kings), an ancient work venerated in Ethiopia for centuries, Makeda returned home carrying the child of her union with Solomon. Her words, translated by Sir E. A. Wallis Budge (from manuscript of Ishak's version in the British Museum) in The Queen of Sheba and her Only Son Menyelek (1922), illuminate her feelings before her journey to Solomon – "I love him merely on hearing concerning him and without seeing him, and the whole story of him that hath been told me is to me as the desire of my heart, and like water to the thirsty man" – and afterwards.

On the Wisdom of Solomon

I AM smitten with the love of wisdom, and I am constrained by the cords of understanding; for wisdom is far better than treasure of gold and silver, and wisdom is the best of everything that hath been created on the earth. . . . It is sweeter than honey, and it maketh one to rejoice more than wine, and it illumineth more than the sun, and it is to be loved more than precious stones. . . . Wisdom is an exalted thing and a rich thing; I will love her like a mother, and she will embrace me like her child. . . .

Through wisdom I have dived down into the great sea, and have seized in the place of her depths a pearl whereby I am rich. I went down like the great iron anchor whereby men anchor ships for the night on the high seas, and I received a lamp which lighteth me, and I came up by the ropes of the boat of understanding. I went to sleep in the depths of the sea, and not being overwhelmed with the water I dreamed a dream. And it seemed to me that there was a star in my womb, and I marvelled thereat, and I laid hold upon it and made it strong in the splendour of the sun. . . I went in through the doors of the treasury of wisdom and I drew for myself the waters of understanding. I went into the blaze of the flame of the sun, and it lighted me with the splendour thereof, and I made of it a shield for myself, and I saved myself by confidence therein, and not myself only but all those who travel in the footprints of wisdom, and not myself only but all the men of my country, the kingdom of Ethiopia, and not only those but those who travel in their ways, the nations that are round about.

Lucy Terry

c. 1730–1821

The earliest known published African-American poet, she is usu-ally considered more important for her place in history than the quality of her doggerel-like verse. Born in Africa, kidnapped and brought to New England as a slave, she was sold at the age of five to Ebenezer Wells of Deerfield, Massachusetts, where she experienced the raid described in "Bars Fight" – written in about 1746 and passed on orally for over a century until its appearance in print in 1855, in Josiah Gilbert Holland's History of Western Massachusetts. (Spellings are as in the original.) In 1756 she married Abijah Prince, a free Black twenty-four years her senior, a landowner and one of the charter founders of the town of Sunderland, Vermont. He bought her freedom and in 1760 they moved to Guildford, Vermont; they had six children. Apparently a

*forceful woman, she tried for three hours to convince the authorities
at Williams College to change their segregation policies and admit her
oldest son, and at another time successfully argued her own case in
court regarding a land dispute. She had a reputation as a raconteur,
and young people would come to her home to listen to her stories. After
her husband's death in 1794 she settled in Sunderland, where she ended
her life.*

Bars Fight

August 'twas, the twenty-fifth,
Seventeen hundred forty-six,
The Indians did in ambush lay,
Some very valient men to slay,
The names of whom I'll not leave out:
Samuel Allen like a hero fout,
And though he was so brave and bold,
His face no more shall we behold;
Eleazer Hawks was killed outright,
Before he had time to fight,
Before he did the Indians see,
Was shot and killed immediately;
Oliver Amsden, he was slain,
Which caused his friends much grief and pain;
Simeon Amsden they found dead,
Not many rods off from his head;
Adonijah Gillet, we do hear,
Did lose his life, which was so dear;
John Saddler fled across the water,
And so escaped the dreadful slaughter;
Eunice Allen see the Indians comeing,
And hoped to save herself by running,
And had not her petticoats stopt her,
The awful creatures had not cotched her,
And tommyhawked her on the head,
And left her on the ground for dead;
Young Samuel Allen, oh! lack-a-day,
Was taken and carried to Canada.

Phillis Wheatley
c. 1753–84

Born in Senegal, West Africa, she was taken as a seven-year-old slave to the USA and in 1761 was bought in a local slave-market by Boston tailor's wife Susannah Wheatley. Impressing her purchaser by her "humble and modest demeanor", "interesting features" and obvious brightness, she was taught to read and write, and revealed herself as something of a child prodigy, able to read the Bible fluently within sixteen months, and learning Latin. At about thirteen she began writing poems; one of her earliest is "On being brought from Africa to America". In 1773 she came to England with her former mistress (she become a freedwoman in 1772), achieving celebrity in high society, undoubtedly because of her youth, sex, age and position as much as for the accomplishment of her verse (which is much influenced by missionary attitudes and a neo-classical style). Her mistress died in 1774, and Phillis fended for herself as poet and seamstress, marrying in 1778 John Peters, a free Black man, and moving to Wilmington, Massachusetts. She had three children; two had died by 1783 and the third survived her only by a few hours. Her husband was jailed for debt and she died in poverty in 1784, barely thirty. She was the first Black (the second woman, after Anne Bradstreet) to publish a book of poetry in the USA, her Poems on Various Subjects, Religious and Moral (1773) going through eleven editions until 1816.

On Being Brought from Africa to America

'Twas mercy brought me from my *Pagan* land,
Taught my benighted soul to understand
That there's a God, that there's a *Saviour* too.
Once I redemption neither sought nor knew.
Some view our sable race with scornful eye;
"Their colour is a diabolic dye."
Remember, *Christians*, *Negroes*, black as *Cain*,
May be refined, and join th' angelic train.

To S. M. [Scipio Moorhead], A Young African Painter, On Seeing His Works

To show lab'ring bosom's deep intent,
And though in living characters to paint,
When first thy pencil did those beauties give,
And breathing figures learnt from thee to live,
How did those prospects give my soul delight,
A new creation rushing on my sight!
Still, wondrous youth! each noble path pursue;
On deathless glories fix thine ardent view:
Still may the painter's and the poet's fire,
To aid thy pencil and thy verse conspire!
And may the charms of each seraphic theme
Conduct thy footsteps to immortal fame!
High to the blissful wonders of the skies
Elate thy soul, and raise thy wishful eyes,
Thrice happy, when exalted to survey
That splendid city, crowned with endless day,
Whose twice six gates on radiant hinges ring:
Celestial Salem blooms in endless spring.
Calm and serene thy moments glide along,
And may the muse inspire each future song!
Still, with the sweets of contemplation blessed,
May peace with balmy wings your soul invest!
But when these shades of time are chased away,
And darkness ends in everlasting day,
On what seraphic pinions shall we move,
And view the landscapes in the realms above!
There shall thy tongue in heavenly murmurs flow,
And there my muse with heavenly transport glow;
No more to tell of Damon's tender sighs,
Or radiance of Aurora's eyes;
For nobler themes demand a nobler strain,
And purer language on the ethereal plain.
Cease, gentle Muse! the solemn gloom of night
Now seals the fair creation from my sight.

To the Right Honorable William, Earl of Dartmouth, His Majesty's Principal Secretary of State for North America

Hail, happy day! when, smiling like the morn,
Fair Freedom rose, New-England to adorn:

The northern clime beneath her genial ray,
Dartmouth! congratulates thy blissful sway;
Elate with hope, her race no longer mourns,
Each soul expands, each grateful bosom burns,
While in thine hand with pleasure we behold
The silken reins, and Freedom's charms unfold.
Long lost to realms beneath the northern skies,
She shines supreme, while hated faction dies:
Soon as appeared the Goddess long desired,
Sick at the view, she languished and expired;
Thus from the splendors of the morning light
The owl in sadness seeks the caves of night.

No more, America, in mournful strain,
Of wrongs, and grievance unredressed complain,
No longer shalt thou dread the iron chain,
Which wanton Tyranny with lawless hand
Had made, and with it meant t' enslave the land.

Should you, my lord, while you peruse my song,
Wonder from whence my love of Freedom sprung,
Whence flow these wishes for the common good,
By feeling hearts alone best understood,
I, young in life, by seeming cruel fate
Was snatch'd from Afric's fancied happy seat:
What pangs excruciating must molest,
What sorrows labour in my parent's breast?
Steeled was that soul, and by no misery moved
That from a father seized his babe beloved:
Such, such my case, And can I then but pray
Others may never feel tyrannic sway?

For favours past, great Sir, our thanks are due,
And thee we ask thy favours to renew,
Since in thy power, as in thy will before,
To soothe the griefs, which thou didst once deplore.
May heavenly grace the sacred sanction give
To all thy works, and thou forever live
Not only on the wings of fleeting Fame,
Though praise immortal crowns the patriot's name,
But to conduct to heaven's refulgent fane,
May fiery coursers sweep th' ethereal plain,
And bear thee upwards to that blest abode,
Where, like the prophet, thou shalt find thy God.

Liberty and Peace (1794)

Lo! Freedom comes, Th' prescient muse foretold,
All eyes th' accomplish'd prophecy behold:
Her port describ'd, "She moves divinely fair,
Olive and laurel bind her golden hair."
She, the bright progeny of Heaven, descends,
And every grace her sovereign step attends;
For now kind Heaven, indulgent to our prayer,
In smiling peace resolves the din of war.
Fix'd in Columbia her illustrious line,
And bids in thee her future council shine.
To every realm her portals open'd wide,
Receives from each the full commercial tide.
Each art and science now with rising charms,
Th' expanding heart with emulation warns.
E'en great Britannia sees with dread surprise,
And from the dazzling splendors turns her eyes.
Britain, whose navies swept th' Atlantic o'er,
And thunder sent to every distant shore;
E'en thou, in manners cruel as thou art,
The sword resign'd, resume the friendly part.
For Gallia's power espous'd Columbia's cause,
And new-born Rome shall give Britannia laws,
Nor unremember'd in the grateful strain,
Shall princely Louis' friendly deed remain;
The generous price th' impending vengeance eyes,
Sees the fierce wrong and to the rescue flies.
Perish that thirst of boundless power, that drew
On Albion's head the curse to tyrants due.
But thou appeas'd submit to heaven's decree,
That bids this realm of freedom rival thee.
Now sheath the sword that bade the brave atone
With guiltless blood for madness not their own.
Sent from th' enjoyment of their native shore,
Ill-fated – never to behold her more.
From every kingdom on Europa's coast
Throng'd various troops, their glory, strength, and boast.
With heart-felt pity fair Hibernia saw
Columbia menac'd by the Tyrant's law:
On hostile fields fraternal arms engage,
And mutual deaths, all dealt with mutual rage;
The muse's ear hears mother earth deplore
Her ample surface smoke with kindred gore:
The hostile field destroys the social ties,
And everlasting slumber seals their eyes.
Columbia mourns, the haughty foes deride,

Her treasures plunder'd and her towns destroy'd:
Witness how Charlestown's curling smokes arise,
In sable columns to the clouded skies.
The ample dome, high-wrought with curious toil,
In one sad hour the savage troops despoil.
Descending peace the power of war confounds;
From every tongue celestial peace resounds:
As from the east th' illustrious king of day,
With rising radiance drives the shades away,
So freedom comes array'd with charms divine,
And in her train commerce and plenty shine.
Britannia owns her independent reign,
Hibernia, Scotia, and the realms of Spain;
And great Germania's ample coast admires
The generous spirit that Columbia fires.
Auspicious Heaven shall fill with fav'ring gales,
Where'er Columbia spreads her swelling sails:
To every realm shall peace her charms display,
And heavenly freedom spread her golden ray.

Elizabeth ("Old Elizabeth")

· 1766–after 1863

*S*he spent her first thirty years in bondage in Maryland, and at the
age of forty-two undertook a preaching career. In the early nineteenth century she went to Virginia where (according to William L.
Andrews, editor of Six Women's Slave Narratives) "she inveighed against
both the slavery of sin and the sin of slavery". Unmarried and childless,
she wrote her Memoir of Old Elizabeth, a Coloured Woman (1863) at the
age of ninety-seven.

From

Memoir of Old Elizabeth

I WAS born in Maryland in the year 1766. My parents were slaves. Both my father and mother were religious people, and belonged to the Methodist Society. It was my father's practice to read in the Bible aloud to his children every sabbath morning. At these seasons, when I was but five years old, I often felt the overshadowing of the Lord's Spirit, without at all understanding what it meant; and these incomes and influences continued to attend me until I was eleven years old, particularly when I was alone, by which I was preserved from doing anything that I thought was wrong.

In the eleventh year of my age, my master sent me to another farm, several miles from my parents, brothers, and sisters, which was a great trouble to me. At last I grew so lonely and sad I thought I should die, if I did not see my mother. I asked the overseer if I might go, but being positively denied, I concluded to go without his knowledge. When I reached home my mother was away. I set off and walked twenty miles before I found her. I staid with her for several days, and we returned together. Next day I was sent back to my new place, which renewed my sorrow. At parting, my mother told me that I had "nobody in the wide world to look to but God." These words fell upon my heart with pondrous weight, and seemed to add to my grief. I went back repeating as I went, "none but God in the wide world." On reaching the farm, I found the overseer was displeased at me for going without his liberty. He tied me with a rope, and gave me some stripes of which I carried the marks for weeks.

After this time, finding as my mother said, I had none in the world to look to but God, I betook myself to prayer, and in every lonely place I found an altar. I mourned sore like a dove and chattered forth my sorrow, moaning in the corners of the field, and under the fences.

I continued in this state for about six months, feeling as though my head were waters, and I could do nothing but weep. I lost my appetite, and not being able to take enough food to sustain nature, I became so weak I had but little strength to work; still I was required to do all my duty. One evening, after the duties of the day were ended, I thought I could not live over the night, so threw myself on a bench, expecting to die, and without being prepared to meet my Maker; and my spirit cried within me, must I die in this state, and be banished from Thy presence forever? I own I am a sinner in Thy sight, and not fit to live where thou art. Still it was my fervent desire that the Lord would pardon me. Just at this season, I saw with my spiritual eye, an awful gulf of misery. As I thought I was about to plunge into it, I heard a voice saying, "rise up and pray," which strengthened me. I fell on my knees and prayed the best I could the Lord's prayer. Knowing no more to say, I halted, but continued on my knees. My spirit was then *taught* to pray, "Lord, have mercy on me – Christ save me." Immediately there appeared a director, clothed in white raiment. I thought he took me by the hand and said, "come with me." He led me down a long journey to a fiery gulf, and left me standing upon the brink of this awful pit. I began to scream for mercy, thinking I was about to be plunged to the belly of hell, and believed I should sink to endless ruin. Although I prayed and wrestled with all my might, it seemed in vain. Still, I felt all the while that I was sustained by some invisible power. At this solemn moment, I thought I saw a hand from which hung, as it were, a silver hair, and a voice told me that all the hope I had of being saved was no more than a hair; still, pray, and it will be sufficient. I then renewed my struggle, crying for mercy and salvation, until I found that every cry raised me higher and higher, and my head was quite above the fiery pillars. Then I thought I was permitted to look straight forward, and saw the Saviour standing with His hand stretched out to receive me. An indescribably glorious light was *in* Him, and He said, "peace, peace, come unto me." At this moment I felt that my sins were forgiven me, and the time of my deliverance was at hand. I sprang forward and fell at his feet, giving Him all the thanks and highest praises, crying, Thou hast redeemed me – Thou has redeemed me to thyself. I felt filled with light and love. At this moment I thought my former guide took me again by the hand and led me upward, till I came to the celestial world and to heaven's door, which I saw was open, and while I stood there, a power surrounded me which drew me in, and I saw millions of glorified spirits in white robes. After I had this view, I thought I heard a voice saying, "Art thou willing to be saved?" I said, Yes Lord. Again I was asked, "Art thou willing to be saved in my way?" I stood speechless until he asked me again, "Art thou willing to be saved in my way?" Then I heard a whispering voice say, "If thou art not saved in the Lord's way, thou canst not be saved at all;" at which I exclaimed, "Yes Lord, in thy own way." Immediately a light fell upon my head, and I was filled with light, and I was shown the world lying in wickedness, and was told I must go there, and call the people to repentance, for the day of the Lord was at hand; and this message was as a heavy yoke upon me, so that I wept bitterly at the thought of what I should have to pass through. While I wept, I heard a voice say, "weep not, some will laugh at thee, some will scoff at thee, and the dogs will bark at thee, but while thou doest my will, I will be with thee to the ends of the earth."

I was at this time not yet thirteen years old. The next day, when I had come to myself, I felt like a new creature in Christ, and all my desire was to see the Saviour.

I lived in a place where there was no preaching, and no religious instruction; but every day I went out amongst the hay-stacks, where the presence of the Lord overshadowed me, and I was filled with sweetness and joy, and was as a vessel filled with holy oil. In this way I continued for about a year; many times my hands were at my work, my spirit was carried away to spiritual things. One day as I was going to my old place behind the hay-stacks to pray, I was assailed with this language, "Are you going there to weep and pray? what a fool! there are older professors than you are, and they do not take that way to get to heaven; people whose sins are forgiven ought to be joyful and lively, and not be struggling and praying." With this I halted and concluded I would not go, but do as other professors did, and so went off to play; but at this moment the light that was in me became darkened, and the peace and joy that I once had, departed from me.

About this time I was moved back to the farm where my mother lived, and then sold to a stranger. Here I had deep sorrows and plungings, not having experienced a return of that sweet evidence and light with which I had been favoured formerly; but by watching unto prayer, and wrestling mightily with the Lord, my peace gradually returned, and with it a great exercise and weight upon my heart for the salvation of my fellow-creatures; and I was often carried to distant lands and shown places where I should have to travel and deliver the Lord's message. Years afterwards, I found myself visiting those towns and countries that I had seen in the light as I sat at home at my sewing, – places of which I had never heard.

Some years from this time I was sold to a Presbyterian for a term of years, as he did not think it right to hold slaves for life. Having served him faithfully my time out, he gave me my liberty, which was about the thirtieth year of my age.

As I now lived in a neighborhood where I could attend religious meetings, occasionally I felt moved to speak a few words therein; but I shrank from it – so great was the cross to my nature.

I did not speak much till I had reached my forty-second year, when it was revealed to me that the message which had been given to me I had not yet delivered, and the time had come. As I could read but little, I questioned within myself how it would be possible for me to deliver the message, when I did not understand the Scriptures. Whereupon I was moved to open a Bible that was near me, which I did, and my eyes fell upon this passage, "Gird up thy loins now like a man, and answer thou me. Obey God rather than man," &c. Here I fell into a great exercise of spirit, and was plunged very low. I went from one religious professor to another, enquiring of them what ailed me; but of all these I could find none who could throw any light upon such impressions. They all told me there was nothing in Scripture that would sanction such exercises. It was hard for men to travel, and what would women do? These things greatly discouraged me, and shut up my way, and caused me to resist the Spirit. After going to all that were accounted pious, and receiving no help, I returned to the Lord, feeling that I was nothing, and knew nothing, and wrestled and prayed to the Lord that He would fully reveal His will, and make the way plain. . . .

I felt very unworthy and small, notwithstanding the Lord had shown himself with great power, insomuch that conjecturers and critics were constrained to join in praise to his great name; for truly, we had times of refreshing from the presence of the Lord. At one of the meetings, a vast number of the white inhabitants of the place, and many coloured people, attended – many no doubt from curiosity to hear what the old coloured woman had to say. One, a great scripturian, fixed himself behind the door with pen and ink, in order to take down the discourse in short-hand; but the Almighty Being anointed me with such a portion of his Spirit, that he cast away his paper and pen, and heard the discourse with patience, and was much affected, for the Lord wrought powerfully on his heart. After meeting, he came forward and offered me his hand with solemnity on his countenance, and handed me something to pay for my conveyance home.

I returned, much strengthened by the Lord's power, to go on to the fulfilment of His work, although I was again pressed by the authorities of the church to which I belonged, for imprudency; and so much condemned, that I was sorely tempted by the enemy to turn aside into the wilderness. I was so embarrassed and encompassed, I wondered within myself whether all that were called to be mouth piece for the Lord, suffered such deep wadings as I experienced.

I now found I had to travel still more extensively in the work of the ministry, and I applied to the Lord for direction. I was often *invited* to go hither and thither, but felt that I must wait for the dictates of His Spirit.

At a meeting which I held in Maryland, I was led to speak from the passage, "Woe to the rebellious city," &c. After the meeting, the people came where I was, to take me before the squire; but the Lord delivered me from their hands.

I also held meetings in Virginia. The people there would not believe that a coloured woman could preach. And moreover, as she had no learning, they strove to imprison me because I spoke against slavery: and being brought up, they asked by what authority I spake? and if I had been ordained? I answered, not by the commission of men's hands: if the Lord had ordained me, I needed nothing better.

As I travelled along through the land, I was led at different times to converse with white men who were by profession ministers of the gospel. Many of them, up and down, confessed they did not believe in revelation, which gave me to see that men were sent forth as ministers without Christ's authority. In a conversation with one of these, he said, "You think you have these things by revelation, but there has been no such thing as revelation since Christ's ascension." I asked him where the apostle John got his revelation while he was in the Isle of Patmos. With this, he rose up and left me, and I said in my spirit, get thee behind me Satan.

I visited many remote places, where there were no meeting houses, and held many glorious meetings, for the Lord poured out his Spirit in sweet effusions. I also travelled in Canada, and visited several settlements of coloured people, and felt an open door amongst them.

I may here remark, that while journeying through the different states of the Union, I met with many of the Quaker Friends, and visited them in their families. I received much kindness and sympathy, and no opposition from them, in the prosecution of my labours. . .

From thence I went to Michigan, where I found a wide field of labour amongst my own colour. Here I remained four years. I established a school for coloured orphans, having always felt the great importance of the religious and moral *agri*culture of children, and the great need of it, especially amongst the coloured people. Having white teachers, I met with much encouragement.

My eighty-seventh year had now arrived, when suffering from disease, and feeling released from travelling further in my good Master's cause, I came on to Philadelphia, where I have remained until this time, which brings me to my ninety-seventh year. When I went forth, it was without purse or scrip – and I have come through great tribulation and temptation – not by any might of my own, for I feel that I am but as dust and ashes before my almighty Helper, who has, according to His promise, been with me and sustained me through all, and gives me now firm faith that he will be with me to the end, and, in his own good time, receive me into His everlasting rest.

Mary Prince

c. 1788–after 1833

Born in Bermuda, she became the first Black British woman to escape from slavery and publish a record of her experiences. In her autobiography and polemic against slavery, The History of Mary Prince, a West Indian Slave, Related by Herself *(published in London and Edinburgh in 1831 and into its third edition that year), she vividly recalls her life as a slave in Bermuda, Turks Island and Antigua, her rebellion against physical and psychological degradation, and her ultimate escape in London in 1828 from owners who refused to sell her, although she had traded for earnings to buy her own freedom.*

From

The History of Mary Prince

I WAS born at Brackish-Pond, in Bermuda, on a farm belonging to Mr Charles Myners. My mother was a household slave; and my father, whose name was Prince, was a sawyer belonging to Mr Trimmingham, a shipbuilder at Crow-Lane. When I was an infant, old Mr Myners died, and there was a division of the slaves and other property among the family. I was bought along with my mother by old Captain Darrel, and given to his grandchild, little Miss Betsey Williams. Captain Williams, Mr Darrel's son-in-law, was master of a vessel which traded to several places in America and the West Indies, and he was seldom at home long together.

Mrs Williams was a kind-hearted good woman, and she treated all her slaves well. She had only one daughter, Miss Betsey, for whom I was purchased, and who was about my own age. I was made quite a pet of by Miss Betsey, and loved her very much. She used to lead me about by the hand, and call me her little nigger. This was the happiest period of my life; for I was too young to under-stand rightly my condition as a slave, and too thoughtless and full of spirits to look forward to the days of toil and sorrow.

My mother was a household slave in the same family. I was under her own care, and my little brothers and sisters were my play-fellows and companions. My mother had several fine children after she came to Mrs Williams, – three girls and two boys. The tasks given out to us children were light, and we used to play together with Miss Betsey, with as much freedom almost as if she had been our sister.

My master, however, was a very harsh, selfish man; and we always dreaded his return from sea. His wife was herself much afraid of him; and, during his stay at home, seldom dared to shew her usual kindness to the slaves. He often left her, in the most distressed circumstances, to reside in other female society, at some place in the West Indies of which I have forgot the name. My poor mistress bore his ill-treatment with great patience, and all her slaves loved and pitied her. I was truly attached to her, and, next to my own mother, loved her better than any creature in the world. My obedience to her commands was cheerfully given: it sprung solely from the affection I felt for her, and not from fear of the power which the white people's law had given her over me.

I had scarcely reached my twelfth year when my mistress became too poor to keep so many of us at home; and she hired me out to Mrs Pruden, a lady who lived about five miles off, in the adjoining parish, in a large house near the sea. I cried bitterly at parting with my dear mistress and Miss Betsey, and when I kissed my mother and brothers and sisters, I thought my young heart would break, it pained me so. But there was no help; I was forced to go. Good Mrs Williams comforted me by saying that I should still be near the home I was about to quit, and might come over and see her and my kindred whenever I could obtain leave of absence from Mrs Pruden. A few hours after this I was taken to a strange house, and found myself among strange people. This separation seemed a sore trial to me then; but oh! 'twas light, light to the trials I have since endured! – 'twas nothing – nothing to be mentioned with them; but I was a child then, and it was according to my strength.

I knew that Mrs Williams could no longer maintain me; that she was fain to part with me for my food and clothing; and I tried to submit myself to the change. My new mistress was a passionate woman; but yet she did not treat me very unkindly. I do not remember her striking me but once, and that was for going to see Mrs Williams when I heard she was sick, and staying longer than she had given me leave to do. All my employment at this time was nursing a sweet baby, little Master Daniel; and I grew so fond of my nursling that it was my greatest delight to walk out with him by the sea-shore, accompanied by his brother and sister, Miss Fanny and Master James. – Dear Miss Fanny! She was a sweet, kind young lady, and so fond of me that she wished me to learn all that she knew herself; and her method of teaching me was as follows: – Directly she had said her lessons to her grandmamma, she used to come running to me, and make me repeat them one by one after her; and in a few months I was able not only to say my letters but to spell many small words. But this happy state was not to last long. Those days were too pleasant to last. My heart always softens when I think of them.

At this time Mrs Williams died. I was told suddenly of her death, and my grief was so great that, forgetting I had the baby in my arms, I ran away directly to my poor mistress's house; but reached it only in time to see the corpse carried out. Oh, that was a day of sorrow – a heavy day! All the slaves cried. My mother cried and lamented her sore; and I (foolish creature!) vainly entreated them to bring my dear mistress back to life. I knew nothing rightly about death then, and it seemed a hard thing to bear. When I thought about my mistress I felt as if the world was all gone wrong; and for many days and weeks I could think of nothing else. I returned to Mrs Pruden's; but my sorrow was too great to be comforted, for my own dear mistress was always in my mind. Whether in the house or abroad, my thoughts were always talking to me about her.

I staid at Mrs Pruden's about three months after this; I was then sent back to Mr Williams to be sold. Oh, that was a sad sad time! I recollect the day well. Mrs Pruden came to me and said, "Mary, you will have to go home directly; your master is going to be married, and he means to sell you and two of your sisters to raise money for the wedding." Hearing this I burst out a crying, – though I was then far from being sensible of the full weight of my misfortune, or of the misery that waited for me. Besides, I did not like to leave Mrs Pruden, and the dear baby, who had grown very fond of me. For some time I could scarcely believe that Mrs Pruden was in earnest, till I received orders for my immediate return. – Dear Miss Fanny! how she cried at parting with me, whilst I kissed and hugged the baby, thinking I should never see him again. I left Mrs Pruden's, and walked home with a heart full of sorrow. The idea of being sold away from my mother and Miss Betsey was so frightful, that I dared not trust myself to think about it. We had been bought of Mrs Myners, as I have mentioned, by Miss Betsey's grandfather, and given to her, so that we were by right *her* property, and I never thought we should be separated or sold away from her.

When I reached the house, I went in directly to Miss Betsey. I found her in great distress; and she cried out as soon as she saw me, "Oh, Mary! my father is going to sell you all to raise money to marry that wicked woman. You are *my* slaves, and he has no right to sell you; but it is all to please her." She then told me that my mother was living with her father's sister at a house close by, and I went there to see her. It was a sorrowful meeting; and we lamented with a great and sore crying our unfortunate situation. "Here comes one of my poor piccaninnies!" she said, the moment I came in, "one of the poor slave-brood who are to be sold to-morrow."

Oh, dear! I cannot bear to think of that day, – it is too much. – It recalls the great grief that filled my heart, and the woeful thoughts that passed to and fro through my mind, whilst listening to the pitiful words of my poor mother, weeping for the loss of her children. I wish I could find words to tell you all I then felt and suffered. The great God above alone knows the thoughts of the poor slave's heart, and the bitter pains which follow such separations as these. All that we love taken away from us – oh, it is sad, sad! and sore to be borne! – I got no sleep that night for thinking of the morrow; and dear Miss Betsey was scarcely less distressed. She could not bear to part with her old playmates and she cried sore and would not be pacified.

The black morning at length came; it came too soon for my poor mother and us. Whilst she was putting on us the new osnaburgs in which we were to be sold, she said, in a sorrowful voice, (I shall never forget it!) "See, I am *shrouding* my poor children; what a task for a mother!" – She then called Miss Betsey to take leave of us. "I am going to carry my little chickens to market," (these were her very words) "take your last look of them; may be you will see them no more." "Oh, my poor slaves! my own slaves!" said dear Miss Betsey, "you belong to me;

and it grieves my heart to part with you." – Miss Betsey kissed us all, and, when she left us, my mother called the rest of the slaves to bid us good bye. One of them, a woman named Moll, came with her infant in her arms. "Ay!" said my mother, seeing her turn away and look at her child with the tears in her eyes, "your turn will come next." The slaves could say nothing to comfort us; they could only weep and lament with us. When I left my dear little brothers and the house in which I had been brought up, I thought my heart would burst.

Our mother, weeping as she went, called me away with the children Hannah and Dinah, and we took the road that led to Hamble Town, which we reached about four o'clock in the afternoon. We followed my mother to the market-place, where she placed us in a row against a large house, with our backs to the wall and our arms folded across our breasts. I, as the eldest, stood first, Hannah next to me, then Dinah; and our mother stood beside, crying over us. My heart throbbed with grief and terror so violently, that I pressed my hands quite tightly across my breast, but I could not keep it still, and it continued to leap as though it would burst out of my body. But who cared for that? Did one of the many bystanders, who were looking at us so carelessly, think of the pain that wrung the hearts of the negro woman and her young ones? No, no! They were all not bad, I dare say, but slavery hardens white people's hearts towards the blacks; and many of them were not slow to make their remarks upon us aloud, without regard to our grief – though their light words fell like cayenne on the fresh wounds of our hearts. Oh those white people have small hearts who can only feel for themselves.

At length the vendue master, who was to offer us for sale like sheep or cattle, arrived, and asked my mother which was the eldest. She said nothing, but pointed to me. He took me by the hand, and led me out into the middle of the street, and, turning me slowly round, exposed me to the view of those who attended the vendue. I was soon surrounded by strange men, who examined and handled me in the same manner that a butcher would a calf or a lamb he was about to purchase, and who talked about my shape and size in like words – as if I could no more understand their meaning than the dumb beasts. I was then put up for sale. The bidding commenced at a few pounds, and gradually rose to fifty-seven,[1] when I was knocked down to the highest bidder; and the people who stood by said that I had fetched a great sum for so young a slave.

I then saw my sisters led forth, and sold to different owners; so that we had not the sad satisfaction of being partners in bondage. When the sale was over, my mother hugged and kissed us, and mourned over us, begging of us to keep up a good heart, and do our duty to our new masters. It was a sad parting; one went one way, one another, and our poor mammy went home with nothing.

[1] Bermuda currency; about £38 sterling.

Zilpha Elaw

c. 1790–after 1846

B orn to free parents, she was brought up near Philadelphia, Pennsylvania. She was twelve years old when her mother died in childbirth, after which her father put her into service with a Quaker family with whom she stayed until she was eighteen. Attracted to Methodism, she began to have religious visions in her mid-teens, was converted, and in 1808 joined a Methodist society. In 1810 she married Joseph Elaw, moving to Burlington, New Jersey, in 1811 and bearing him a daughter the next year. After her husband's death in 1823, she and her daughter worked in domestic service. Later she opened a school for Black children but closed it after two years and, placing her daughter in the care of a relative, began an evangelical career. She preached widely in the USA, and in July 1840 went to London; at the end of a five-year mission in Britain she published Memoirs of the Life, Religious Experience, Ministerial Travels and Labours of Mrs Zilpha Elaw, an American Female of Colour; Together with Some Account of the Great Religious Revivals in America [Written by Herself] (1846), extracts from which follow.

From

Memoirs of the Life ... of Mrs Zilpha Elaw

I REMAINED at home this time for the space of three years with the exception of an occasional short journey, and visit of a few weeks; and throughout this period, my mind was often burdened with the weight of a voyage to England. I often argued the matter before the Lord in prayer, pleading my ignorance, my sex, my colour and my inability to minister the gospel in a country so polished and enlightened, so furnished with Bibles, so blessed with ministers, so studded with temples; but the Lord said, "say not, I cannot speak; for thou shalt go to all to whom I send thee, and what I command thee, thou shalt speak" [Jer. 1:7].

In 1837, when on a visit to some religious friends, one morning, I saw a remarkable vision; I appeared to be in a strange place and conversing with a stranger, when three enormous balls of fire came perpendicularly over my head, and each of them exploded and burst at the same moment: I instantly appeared to fall to the ground; but was caught up by an unseen hand, and placed upon an animal, which darted with me through the regions of the air, with the velocity of lightning, and deposited me inside the window of an upper chamber. I there heard the voice of the Almighty, saying, "I have a message for her to go with upon the high seas, and she will go." This occurrence took place just three years prior to my departure from America.

In 1839, the Lord was pleased to send me again into the Southern states; and as I travelled from city to city, I felt the impression that the time was near when I must leave the land of my nativity for a foreign shore.(. . .)

The parting moment was painful in the extreme; for my daughter, and her two dear little boys, were entwined in the strongest affections of my heart; but I durst not disobey Him who had said unto me, as He had said unto Abraham, "Get thee out from thy country, and from thy kindred, and from thy father's house, unto a land that I will show thee" [Gen. 12:1]. On the 10th of June 1840, I rose from the bed on which I had laid for the last time; the recollection of that bitter morning even now suffuses my eyes with tears, and interrupts the delineations of my pen: the morning was calm, our minds resigned and peaceful, and we took, and held each other's hand, in silence; which was at length broken by my daughter, who said, "Mother, we part not, but I think we shall yet meet again; the will of the Lord be done, and God be with thee." At nine o'clock A.M., I bade farewell to those dear ties, and started for New York, where I tarried until the 1st July; and then I took the steam-boat to go to the ship Philadelphia, Captain Morgan, which vessel was lying in quarantine. Soon after our arrival on board, she got under weigh, and set sail for the port of London. My feelings on leaving the land of my nativity, and all that was dear to me on earth, were acutely indescribable; but God commanded, and I obeyed; bidding farewell to my country, and, committing my dear friends to the grace of God. The wind was fair, the passengers agreeable, and we were soon carried beyond the view of land. On the following morning, I awoke and presented my thanksgivings to my heavenly Father for His preserving care of me throughout the night. I then went upon deck, and surveyed the broad canopy above, and the rolling ocean beneath, gently moving wave after wave, as we glided over its tremulous surface. I observed the birds of the air flying over our heads, and wondered, at such a distance from land, that they were able to take such excursions without resting. I beheld the finny tribes pouring forth by thousands. I was now floating on the great and wide sea, wherein are things creeping innumerable, both small and great beasts. There go the ships! There is that great leviathan whom thou has made to play therein. These wait all upon thee, that thou mayest give them their meat in due season. Oh Lord, how manifold are thy works! in wisdom has thou made them all! the earth is full of thy riches [Psalm civ. 24, 27].

On the 23rd day of July, we were cheered with the sight of land; and on the 24th, we came to anchor off Falmouth, where most of the cabin passengers left us. On the evening of the 25th, we came safely into the London Docks: this was on a Saturday; and on the morning of the Lord's-day, I first set my foot on British ground. As I proceeded along Ratcliff Highway, I was much surprised to see the shops open, and many kinds of business in the course of transaction, women crying fruits for sale, and the people intent on traffic and marketing. I was indeed astonished, that in the metropolis of the most Christian country in the world, such a want of respect should be indicated towards the day which Jesus signalized by His resurrection, and His apostles practically set apart for the commemoration of His eucharistic sacrament, and the ordinances of His religion. Whether the literal and exact requirements of the fourth commandment be, in the case of Christians, transferred from the Jewish Sabbath to the "Lord's-day," is a point upon which all the disciples of Christ are not agreed; but if Christians are not bound to observe an absolute quietude and rest thereon, they certainly are bound to pay it that respect which is due to the day on which our redemption was assured by the Lord's resurrection – a day which was made sacred by the practice of His apostles, and by their inspired authority, called the "Lord's-day". Having taken apartments in Well-close-square, in the evening I attended at the Countess of Huntingdon's chapel, in Pell-street, and heard a discourse which afforded some encouragement to the heart of a female stranger in a foreign land. Some days elapsed ere I met with any of the Methodist family; but, going on the Wednesday evening again to Pell-street chapel, as I was passing a window, I caught sight of a lady, whose appearance powerfully arrested my attention; and it appeared that the feeling of surprise and interest was mutual. I turned back, and spoke to her, and inquired if she was acquainted with any section of the Methodist body? She said that her daughter should on the following evening conduct me to the Wesleyan chapel of St George, which she did accordingly; and I found that several class meetings were held on that evening; on that occasion, I met with Mr A— who introduced me to Mr C— one of the local preachers; and I was admitted into the class led by him, and enjoyed a very sweet time of refreshing from the presence of the Lord. I became acquainted also with Mrs T. – a true sister of the Lord, who has since fallen asleep in Jesus: and was introduced to a gentleman who interested himself greatly on my behalf, very considerably enlarged the circle of my acquaintance, and even ushered me before the committees of the peace and anti-slavery societies. I found my situation rather awkward in reference to the latter body. I was first received by a deputation of three gentlemen, and afterwards admitted before the board. It was really an august assembly; their dignity appeared so redundant, that they scarcely knew what to do with it all. Had I attended there on a matter of life and death, I think I could scarcely have been more closely interrogated or more rigidly examined; from the reception I met with, my impression was, that they imagined I wanted some pecuniary or other help from them; for they treated me as the proud do the needy. In this, however, they were mistaken. Among many other questions, they demanded to be informed, whether I had any new doctrine to advance, that the English Christians are not in possession of? To which I replied, no; but I was sent to preach Christ, and Him crucified: unto the Jews a stumbling-block, and unto the Greeks foolishness [1 Cor. 1:23]: they also wished to be informed, how it came about that God should send me? to which I replied, that I could not tell; but I knew that God required me to come hither, and that I came in obedience to His sovereign will; but that the Almighty's design therein was best known to Himself; but behold! said I, "I am here." Pride and arrogancy are among the master sins of rational beings; an high look, a stately bearing, and a proud heart, are abominations in the sight of God, and insure a woeful reverse in a future life. Infidels will indulge in pomposity and arrogance; but Christians are and must be humble and lowly. As a servant of Jesus, I am required to bear testimony in his name, who was meek and lowly, against the lofty looks of man, and the assumptions of such lordly authority and self-importance. Ere this work meets the eye of the public, I shall have sojourned in England five years: and I am justified in saying, that my God hath made my ministry a blessing to hundreds of persons; and many who were living in sin and darkness before they saw my coloured face, have risen up to praise the Lord, for having sent me to preach His Gospel on the shores of Britain; numbers who had been reared to maturity, and were resident in localities plentifully furnished with places of worship and ministers of the gospel, and had scarcely heard a sermon in their lives, were attracted to hear the coloured female preacher, were inclosed in the gospel net, and are now walking in the commandments and ordinances of the Lord. I have travelled in several parts of England, and I thank God He has given me some spiritual children in every place wherein I have laboured.

Soon after my arrival, I met with a gentleman, who advised my immediate return to my own country; adding that if he had been in America before my departure and had known my intention, he would have advised me better: I replied, that I had no will of my own in the matter; but my heavenly Father commanded, and I durst not confer with flesh and blood, but obeyed and came: but like other men destitute of faith in God, he did not comprehend this kind of argument; and persisted in his worldly reasonings, saying that people did not give away their gold here, and I had much better return. It is to be deplored that there are so many Christians of this person's cast: who are of the world; speak in accordance with its principles and sentiments, and walk according to its course. Instead of having little faith, they discover none at all: ignorant of the Scriptures and of the power of God, the love of the Father is not in them. Having parted with this Laodicean gentleman, I called upon Mrs H., in Princes-square: and my mind being somewhat damped, I sat a few minutes in silence, which Mrs H. broke by an affectionate inquiry into my circumstances; at the same time, presenting me with a handsome donation; telling me not to be discouraged, for the Lord would open my way and sustain me: my mind was cheered and my faith strengthened by this opportune proof of the power of God to furnish succours and raise up friends for His people even in a land of strangers.

In a few days after, Mrs T. introduced me to some of the Bible Christians, or Bryanites, as they are called; who are, I believe, a secession from the Wesleyan Methodists: our reception from them was very cool; but one of the brethren was about to preach in the street; and he invited me to preach in his stead. Accordingly at the time appointed, we repaired to the street and commenced the meeting; a very great crowd assembled, and I preached to them; but the meeting was broken up by two policemen, who came and tapped me on the shoulder, and desired me to desist; they demanded what authority I had for preaching? a gentleman present said, "she has her authority in her hand," that is, "the Word of God": we then departed.

On the following Lord's-day morning, I attended with Mrs T., at Salem chapel; and, in the afternoon, I preached in Stepney-fields, to a very numerous auditory. A very heavy shower fell during the service, yet very few persons retired in consequence of it. When the service was terminated, a gentleman and lady came, and inquired of me where I resided? and desired me to call and visit them; which, in the course of a few days, I did, and was very affectionately received: the lady, Mrs T., then invited me to spend a day with them, to which I consented, and enjoyed a heavenly day in their company. She then engaged me to spend a week with them; I did so, and a delightful week it was. The house was a little Bethel to us, and in the stated morning and evening worship of the family, the Lord manifested Himself in very rich displays of grace. Before my week expired, Mrs T. sent to my apartments for my truck, and bade me account her house my home during my sojourn in England. Their second daughter, who has since fallen asleep in Jesus, a most interesting and excellent young lady, was then greatly afflicted with a disease of the heart: our communion in the Spirit was exceedingly choice and precious; I richly enjoyed and highly prized her society.

I visited a number of small chapels in this vast metropolis, and endeavored to advance my heavenly Father's cause by attending many religious tea meetings; some of which I found very edifying and profitable to the soul. I also partook of a breakfast with a number of ministers and friends at Mr B. T—rs., by his special invitation; and after this, I was sent for to Ramsgate, and travelled through the county of Kent, preaching the word in many of the towns and villages as I passed through them. When in Canterbury, my mind was much struck with the mutations of time upon the works of man. I beheld there some stately edifices which were venerable with age; I ascended the eminence of the Dane John, from which I had a full view of the town; the spot where some of the martyrs of Jesus sealed the truth with their blood, was pointed out to me; and as I gazed upon the memorable place, I thought of those faithful servants of God with much sympathy and yearning of heart.

Having received an invitation from some of the Primitive Methodists in Yorkshire, to go down and labour among them, I went thither by railway, and reached Pontefract about eight o'clock on the evening of the 30th of December, 1840; the distance was great, being about 170 miles; and I was very much fatigued with the journey. The hireling will make the best bargain he can; but they who bear the commissions of Jesus will find no sinecures involved in them, but frequently hard labour and harder fare. On my arrival, I was very kindly received by Mrs Clift; and after a good night's repose, I was on the next morning much invigorated. On the following day, December 31, Mr Colson the superintendent minister, and Mr Crompton his assistant, called to see me, and explained the objects they had in view in sending for me. In the evening we attended a tea meeting of the Sunday School; on which occasion the children sang some beautiful anthems, and repeated some pieces with much correctness; the meeting was afterwards addressed by some of the brethren, and also by myself. At the conclusion of the meeting, we observed a watch night, as is customary with the Methodist societies, which was attended with much of the presence of God, the gracious manifestation of His Spirit, and with spiritual benefit to the souls of many. The weather was very inclement and rigorous; and

an abundance of labour was presented before me, which I entered into with
much delight and vigour, though with considerable weariness and distress to
the body.

> My shrinking flesh complains,
> And murmurs to contend so long;
> My mind superior is to pains:
> When I am weak, then am I strong.

On the 3rd of January, 1841, I went to Brotherton, and preached in the chapel
belonging to the brethren; it was completely crowded, and the Lord was in the
midst of us to bless His people with the manifestations of His grace and love.
After service, I returned the same evening to Pontefract, very much exhausted
with fatigue. On the following day Mr T— came to conduct me to Thorp, where
I preached in the evening, from "Enter ye at the strait gate," Matt. vii. 13, with
considerable energy of spirit; but, throughout my labours in England, I have
found a far less favourable soil for the seed of the kingdom in the British mind
than in the American. Human nature must be in every country radically the same;
God is the same; yet the word preached is generally attended in America with
far more powerful and converting results than in Britain. The population of the
United States have not been so extensively vitiated by the infidelity and sedition
of the press; and being more thinly spread over an immense territorial space,
there is less of contamination than in the more condensed masses of English
society; and they perhaps possess more honest simplicity of character, and less
of the self-sufficiency of a licentious intellectuality and worldly wisdom. It is
not for me, however, to account for the cause; the fact is but too apparent.
I had many seals to my ministry in Yorkshire, notwithstanding the general
barrenness of the mental soil; and found, in many of its towns, and especially
in Leeds, a very loving, lively and benevolent Christian people; not only in the
Methodist, but in other denominations also; and amongst the society of Friends.
I attended one of the meetings of the Friends there, and whilst sitting among
them, was moved by the Spirit to address them, and the dear friends received
the message which came through the medium of their coloured sister with
patience and delight.

Sojourner Truth

c. 1797–1883

The first African-American woman anti-slavery lecturer, abolitionist and crusader for women's rights, she was born on a Dutch landowner's estate in Ulster County, New York. Her father had been pirated from the Gold Coast; her mother nursed twelve children, all but two of whom were sold to other plantations. At the age of nine Isabella, as she was called, was taken from her parents and sold at auction. From 1810 to 1826 she worked on a farm in New York state, where she married a slave by whom she had at least five children. Though the state passed an emancipation law to take effect on 4 July 1827, her owner tried to enforce her services for a further year, but she escaped at dawn. When her five-year-old son was illegally seized and sold to a slaveholder in Alabama, she fought to regain him. In 1829 she took him to New York, becoming known for her power to move church groups with prayer and song; but, unhappy with a place where "the rich rob the poor, and the poor rob the poor", she moved to the country in 1843. She later said: "When I left the house of bondage, I left everything behind. I wasn't going to keep nothing of Egypt on me, and so I went to the Lord and asked him to give me a new name. And the Lord gave Sojourner, because I was to travel up and down the land, showing the people their sins, and being a sign unto them. Afterward I told the Lord I wanted another name, 'cause everybody else had two names; and the Lord gave me Truth, because I was to declare the truth to the people."

A well known activist, the only person speaking out for those doubly oppressed by race and sex, she made her renowned "Ain't I A Woman" address (here adapted to poetry by Erlene Stetson) at the second National Woman's Suffrage Convention in Akron, Ohio, in 1852; she also made a notable speech at the Fourth National Woman's Rights Convention in 1853. She dictated her autobiography, The Narrative of Sojourner Truth (1850), to a white friend and raised funds by selling copies at her lectures. Eventually settling in Battle Creek, Michigan, she worked for union causes, was received by President Abraham Lincoln in 1864, and worked for the Freedman's Relief Association.

Ain't I a Woman?

That man over there say
  a woman needs to be helped into carriages
and lifted over ditches
  and to have the best place everywhere.
Nobody ever helped me into carriages
  or over mud puddles
  or gives me a best place....

Ain't I a woman?
  Look at me
Look at my arm!
  I have plowed and planted
and gathered into barns
  and no man could head me....
And ain't I a woman?
  I could work as much
and eat as much as a man –
  when I could get to it –
and bear the lash as well
  and ain't I a woman?
I have born thirteen children
  and seen most all sold into slavery
and when I cried out a mother's grief
  none but Jesus heard me...
and ain't I a woman?
  That little man in black there say
a woman can't have as much rights as a man
  cause Christ wasn't a woman.
Where did your Christ come from?
  From God and a woman!
Man had nothing to do with him!
  If the first woman God ever made
was strong enough to turn the world
  upside down, all alone
together women ought to be able to turn it
  rightside up again.

Speech to the Convention of the American Equal Rights Association, New York City, 1867

M Y friends, I am rejoiced that you are glad, but I don't know how you will feel when I get through. I come from another field – the country of the slave. They have got their liberty – so much good luck to have slavery partly destroyed; not entirely. I want it root and branch destroyed. Then we will all be free indeed. I feel that if I have to answer for the deeds done in my body just as much as a man, I have a right to have just as much as a man. There is a great stir about colored men getting their rights, but not a word about the colored women; and if colored men get their rights, and not colored women theirs, you see the colored men will be masters over the women, and it will be just as bad as it was before. So I am for keeping the thing going while things are stirring; because if we wait till it is still, it will take a great while to get it going again. White women are a great deal smarter, and know more than colored women, while colored women do not know scarcely anything. They go out washing, which is about as high as a colored woman gets, and their men go about idle, strutting up and down; and when the women come home, they ask for their money and take it all, and then scold because there is no food. I want you to consider on that, chil'n. I call you chil'n; you are somebody's chil'n, and I am old enough to be mother of all that is here. I want women to have their rights. In the courts women have no rights, no voice; nobody speaks for them. I wish woman to have her voice there among the pettifoggers. If it is not a fit place for women, it is unfit for men to be there.

I am above eighty years old; it is about time for me to be going. I have been forty years a slave and forty years free, and would be here forty years more to have equal rights for all. I suppose I am kept here because something remains for me to do; I suppose I am yet to help to break the chain. I have done a great deal of work; as much as a man, but did not get so much pay. I used to work in the field and bind grain, keeping up with the cradler; but men doing no more, got twice as much pay. . . . We do as much, we eat as much, we want as much. I suppose I am about the only colored woman that goes about to speak for the rights of the colored women. I want to keep the thing stirring, now that the ice is cracked. What we want is a little money. You men know that you get as much again as women, when you write, or for what you do. When we get our rights, we shall not have to come to you for money, for then we shall have money enough in our own pockets; and maybe you will ask us for money. But help us now until we get it. It is a good consolation to know that when we have got this battle once fought we shall not be coming to you any more. . . .

I am glad to see that men are getting their rights, but I want women to get theirs, and while the water is stirring I will step into the pool. Now that there is a great stir about colored men's getting their rights is the time for women to step in and have theirs. I am sometimes told that "Women ain't fit to vote. Why, don't you know that a woman had seven devils in her: and do you suppose a woman is fit to rule the nation?" Seven devils ain't no account; a man had a legion in him. The devils didn't know where to go; and so they asked that they might go into the swine. They thought that was as good a place as they came out from. They didn't ask to go into the sheep – no, into the hog; that was the selfish beast; and man is so selfish that he has got women's rights and his own too, and yet he won't give women their rights. He keeps them all to himself. . . .

Nancy Gardner Prince
1799–?

B orn free in Newburyport, Massachusetts, of mixed African and Amerindian ancestry, she left her poverty-stricken home at the age of eight to become a domestic worker. After years of hard work, she decided at twenty-three to do something for herself. In 1823 she met Mr Prince, recently returned from a voyage to Russia (having gone there in the service of a sea captain and remained to become the servant of a princess in the tsar's court); they were married in February 1924 and by April set sail again for Russia. After nine and a half years the effect of cold weather on her health forced her to return to the USA; her husband was unable to leave immediately and died before he could follow her. In 1840 she went to newly emancipated Jamaica; her pamphlet about her trip was later incorporated in her book of memoirs, A Narrative of the Life and Travels of Mrs Nancy Prince written by Herself (1853), in which she writes of her exotic travels to Europe, Russia and Jamaica.

From

A Narrative of the Life and Travels of Mrs Nancy Prince

I WAS born in Newburyport, September the 15th 1799. My mother was born in Gloucester, Massachusetts – the daughter of Tobias Wornton, or Backus, so called. He was stolen from Africa, when a lad, and was a slave of Captain Winthrop Sargent; but, although a slave, he fought for liberty. He was in the Revolutionary army, and at the battle of Bunker Hill. He often used to tell us, when little children, the evils of Slavery, and how he was stolen from his native land. My grandmother was an Indian of this country; she became a captive to the English, or their descendants. She served as a domestic in the Parsons family. My father, Thomas Gardner, was born in Nantucket; his parents were of African descent. He died in Newburyport, when I was three months old. My mother was thus a second time left a widow, with her two children, and she returned to Gloucester to her father. My mother married her third husband, by whom she had six children. My step-father was stolen from Africa, and while the vessel was at anchor in one of our Eastern ports, he succeeded in making his escape from his captors, by swimming ashore. I have often heard him tell the tale. Having some knowledge of the English language, he found no trouble to pass. There were two of them, and they found, from observation, that they were in a free State. I have heard my father describe the beautiful moon-light night when they two launched their bodies into the deep, for liberty. When they got upon soundings, their feet were pricked with a sea-plant that grew under water, they had to retreat, and, at last they reached the shore. When day began to break, they laid down under a fence, as naked as they were born – soon they heard a rattling sound, and trembling, they looked to see what it meant. In a few minutes, a man with a broad-brimed hat on, looked over the fence and cried out, "Halloo boys! you are from that ship at anchor?" Trembling, we answered, yes. He kindly took us by the hand, and told us not to fear, for we were safe. "Jump, boys," said he, "into my cart," which we readily did. He turned about, and soon entered a large yard – we were taken to his house and carried to an apartment, where he brought us clothes and food, and cheered us with every kindness. No search was made for us; it was supposed we were drowned, as many had jumped over-board on the voyage, thinking they could get home to Africa again. I have often heard my step-father boast how brave they were, and say they stood like men and saw the ship set sail with less than half they stole from Africa. He was selling his bamboo baskets, when he was seized by white men, and put in a boat, and taken on board the ship that lay off; many such ships there were! He was called "Money Vose," and his name may be found on the Custom House books in Gloucester. His last voyage was with Captain Elias Davis, in the brig Romulus, belonging to Captain Fitz William Sargent, in whose employ he had been twelve years. During the war, the brig was taken by a British privateer, and he was pressed into their service. He was sick with the dropsy a long while, and died oppressed, in the English dominions. My mother was again left a widow, with an infant six weeks old, and seven other children. When she heard of her husband's death, she exclaimed, "I thought it; what shall I do with these children?" She was young, inexperienced, with no hope in God, and without the knowledge of her Saviour. Her grief, poverty, and responsibilities, were too much for her; she never again was the mother that she had been before. I was, at this time, in Captain F. W. Sargent's family. I shall never forget the feelings I experienced, on hearing of the decease of my father-in-law, although he was not kind to me or my sister; but, by industry a humble home was provided, for my mother and her younger children. Death had twice visited our family, in less than three months. My grandfather died before my father-in-law sailed. I thought I would go home a little while, and try and comfort my mother. The three oldest children were put into families.

My brother and myself stayed at home that Summer. We gathered berries and sold them in Gloucester; strawberries, raspberries, blackberries and whortle-berries, were in abundance, in the stony environs, growing spontaneously. With the sale of these fruits, my brother and myself nearly supported my mother and her children, that Summer. My brother George, young as he was, caught fish and sold them, and run of errands, and was always watching for something to do, that he might help his mother. At one time he was missing; we expected he was drowned; a search was made for him in the water; the neighbors were all on the alert. Poor mother returning from a hard day's work, supposing the boy was lost, was like a lunatic. The lad was supposed to have fallen from the wharf, where he was fishing. Our friends had all given up the search – it was then eleven o'clock at night. Mother and I locked up the children and went round to the harbor, to one Captain Warner, who traded to the Eastward. Mrs Warner informed us that my brother came there in the morning, with his bundle, and they supposed he was sent, as the Captain wished to take him with him. He went on board, and the vessel sailed that afternoon. In three weeks, he came home, to the comfort of his mother and all of us. He brought back, for his pay, four feet of wood and three dollars.

We stayed with our mother until every resource was exhausted; we then heard of a place eight miles out of town, where a boy and girl were wanted. We both went and were engaged. We often went home with our wages, and all the comforts we could get; but we could not approach our mother as we wished. God in mercy took one little boy of seven years, who had been in a consumption one year.

My oldest sister, Silvia, was seventy miles in the country, with the family that brought her up; so we were scattered all about. Soon as the war was over, I determined to get more for my labor. I left Essex and went to Salem, in the month of April, 1814, without a friend, without a guide. I first went to Gloucester, to bid my mother and the family adieu. George, my brother, I left with a promise to send for him when I should be settled. When I reached the Cove, about five miles from Gloucester, I stopped at a friend's who urged me not to go, holding up obstacles. It rained and snowed, but I travelled along, following the guide-posts, until I reached Beverly bridge. I crossed it when the clock struck four, in the afternoon. I now wished to find a friend in Becket Street, Salem, but was afraid of the people that I met near the Bridge, they were so covered with rags and dirt. I kept on until I reached the Common; I then asked a woman who was neatly dressed, for the the lady I wished to find. She did not know. I asked for another person, that I knew was not very good; she took me there, but I soon found my friend that I wished, and stopped there two weeks, and then went to live with a respectable colored family. My mother was not satisfied, and came after me. I would not go to Gloucester. She left me at a friend's, and this woman had a daughter, who came home from service, sick. I took her place, and thought myself fortunate to be with religious people, as I had enjoyed the happy privilege of religious instruction. My dear grandfather was a member of a Congregational Church, and a good man; he always attended meeting in the morning, and took his children with him. In the afternoon he took care of the smaller children, while my mother attended with her little group. He thought it was wrong for us to go to school where the teacher was not devoted to God. Thus I early knew the difference between right and wrong.

There were seven in the family, one sick with a fever, and another in a consumption; and of course, the work must have been very severe, especially the washings. Sabbath evening I had to prepare for the wash; soap the clothes and put them into the steamer, set the kettle of water to boiling, and then close in the steam, and let the pipe from the boiler into the steam box that held the clothes. At two o'clock, on the morning of Monday, the bell was rung for me to get up; but, that was not all, they said I was too slow, and the washing was not done well; I had to leave the tub to tend the door and wait on the family, and was not spoken kind to, at that.

Hard labor and unkindness was too much for me; in three months, my health and strength were gone. I often looked at my employers, and thought to myself, is this your religion? I did not wonder that the girl who had lived there previous to myself, went home to die. They had family prayers, morning and evening. Oh! yes, they were sanctimonious! I was a poor stranger, but fourteen years of age, imposed upon by these good people; but I must leave them. In the year 1814, they sent me to Gloucester in their chaise. I found my poor mother in bad health, and I was sick also; but, by the mercy of God, and the attention and skill of Dr Dale, and the kindness of friends, I was restored, so that in a few months, I was able again to go to work, although my side afflicted me, which I attributed to overworking myself.

In the Spring of 1815, I returned to Salem, accompanied by my eldest sister, and we obtained good places. She took it into her head to go to Boston, as a nursery girl, where she lived a few months and was then deluded away. February 7th, 1816, a friend came to Salem and informed me of it. To have heard of her death, would not have been so painful to me, as we loved each other very much, and more particularly, as our step-father was not very kind to us. When little girls, she used to cry about it, and we used to say, when we were large enough we would go away.

It was very cold; but notwithstanding, I was so distressed about my sister that I started the next morning for Boston, on foot. A friend was with me. At Lynn Hotel we refreshed ourselves, and all seemed much interested about me; two women took me aside, and inquired how it was that I was with that woman. I told my reason; she was well known all about; she lived as a cook in Boston, she came after her son, a little child whom she held in her arms. By the time we were seven miles from Salem, cold and fatigued, I could walk no farther, and we hired a horse and sleigh, and a man to drive us to Boston, where we arrived at seven o'clock in the evening. The house where we stopped was in Green street, the lady kindly invited me to stop; I refused; I was suspicious the house was not good; the woman I came with took me to Belknap street, where I found an old friend; I would not stop, they went with me to Bedford street, where I intended to put up. The inmates received me very kindly; my feet, hands and ears were all frostbitten. I needed all the hospitality that was extended to me. I was young and inexperienced, but God knew that my object was good. "In wisdom he chooses the weak things of the earth." Without his aid, how could I ever have rescued my lost sister? Mr Brown, when he learned my errand, kindly offered to assist me. He found where my sister resided, and taking with him a large cane, he accompanied me to the house, on Sabbath evening. My sister I found seated with a number of others round a fire, the mother of harlots at the head. My sister did not see me until I clasped her round the neck. The old woman flew at me, and bid me take my hands off of her; she opened a door that led down into a cellar kitchen, and told me to come down, she attempted to take my hands off of my sister. Mr Brown defended me with his cane; there were many men and girls there, and all was confusion. When my sister came to herself, she looked upon me and said: "Nancy, O Nancy, I am ruined!" I said, "Silvia, my dear sister, what are you here for? Will you not go with me?" She seemed thankful to get away; the enraged old woman cried out, "she owes me, she cannot go." Silvia replied, "I will go." The old woman seized her to drag her down into the kitchen; I held on to her, while Mr Brown at my side, used his great cane; he threatened her so that she was obliged to let my sister go, who, after collecting her things, accompanied Mr Brown and myself. . . .

Even now, I cannot refrain my feelings, although death has long separated us; but her soul is precious; she was very dear to me; she was five years older than myself, and often protected me from the blows of an unkind step-father. She often said she was not fit to live, nor fit to die.

The next day, after breakfast, one of Mrs Brown's daughters accompanied us to the stage office; we expected Mr Low, the driver of the Gloucester stage, who knew us as his towns-people, would let us take passage with him without any difficulty; but he refused unless we would ride upon the top. It was very cold; I had sent my mother my wages the week before, and what money I had, I had taken in advance, of my employers. We were greatly embarrassed, when a colored man, unknown to us, penetrated our difficulty, and asked us if we had two dollars; we told him we had; he very kindly took us to the stage office, and we bargained for a horse and sleigh to carry us to Salem, where we arrived safely in about two hours and a half; and we gave up our conveyance to the same owners, with ten thousand thanks to our colored friend, and to our Heavenly Father; had we attempted to walk, we must have frozen by the way. The horse and sleigh belonged to the stage-office, so we had no more care for that. The man who let it to us was very humane, although a stranger. The price was two dollars, of which he not only gave us back fifty cents to pay our toll, but went with us as far as to Charlestown bridge.

I often thought of the contrast between our townsman, Mr Low, and the stranger who was so kind to us. The lady I lived with, Mrs John Deland, received us very kindly, and permitted my sister to remain with me awhile; then she returned to Gloucester, to the family who brought her up, and I thought we had gained a great victory.

My brother George and myself were very desirous to make our mother comfortable: he went to sea for that purpose; the next April, I came to Boston to get a higher price for my labor; for we had agreed to support my mother, and hoped she would take home our little brother and take care of him, who was supported by the town. George came home, and sailed again in the same employ, leaving mother a draw bill for half his wages. My sister returned to Boston to find me, and wished to procure a place to work out. I had just changed my place for one more retired, and engaged my sister with me as a chamber maid; she tried me much. I thought it a needy time, for I had not yielded my heart to the will of God, though I had many impressions, and formed many resolutions; but the situations that I had been placed in, (having left my mother's house at the age of eight,) had not permitted me to do as I wished, although the kind counsels of my dear grandfather and pious teachers followed me wherever I went. Care after care oppressed me – my mother wandered about like a Jew – the young children who were in families were dissatisfied; all hope but in God was lost. I resolved, in my mind, to seek an interest in my Savior, and put my trust in Him; and never shall I forget the place or time when God spake to my troubled conscience. Justified by faith I found peace with God, the forgiveness of sin through Jesus Christ my Lord. After living sixteen years without hope, and without a guide, May 6th 1819, the Rev. Thomas Paul, baptized myself, and seven others, in obedience to the great command. . . .

My sister Silvia, was one of my greatest trials. Knowing she was in Boston, my mother, in one of her spells of insanity, got away from her home and travelled to Boston after her; she came where I lived, my employers were very kind to her, she tarried a few days, when I hired a horse and chaise and took them both back to Salem, and returned to my place in 1822, with a determination to do something for myself; I left my place after three months, and went to learn a trade; and after seven years of anxiety and toil, I made up my mind to leave my country. September 1st, 1823, Mr Prince arrived from Russia. February 15th, 1824, we were married. April 14th, we embarked on board the Romulus, captain Epes Sargent commander, bound for Russia. May 24th, arrived at Elsinore, left the same day for Copenhagen, where we remained twelve days. We visited the king's palace, and several other extensive and beautiful buildings. We attended a number of entertainments, among the Danes and English, who were religious; observed that their manners and customs were similar; they are attentive to strangers; the Sabbath is very strictly observed; the principal religion is Lutheran and Calvinistic, but all persuasions are tolerated. The languages are Dutch, French and English. The Danes are very modest and kind, but like all other nations, they know how to take the advantage. We left Copenhagen the 7th of June, and arrived at Cronstadt on the 19th; left there the 21st for St Petersburg, and in a few hours, were happy to find ourselves at our place of destination, through the blessing of God, in good health, and soon made welcome from all quarters. We took lodgings with a Mrs Robinson,

a native of our country, who was Patience Mott, of Providence, who left here
in the year 1813, in the family of Alexander Gabriel, the man who was taken
for Mr Prince. There I spent six weeks very pleasantly, visiting and receiving
friends, in the manner of the country. While there I attended two of their parties;
there were various amusements in which I did not partake, which caused them
much disappointment. I told them my religion did not allow of dancing or dice
playing, which formed part of the amusements. As they were very strict in their
religion, they indulged me in the same privilege. By the help of God I was ever
enabled to preserve my stand.

Mr Prince was born in Marlborough, and lived in families in this city. In 1810
he went to Gloucester, and sailed with captain Theodore Stanwood, for Russia.
He returned with him, and remained in his family, and at this time visited at my
mother's. He sailed with captain Stanwood in 1812, for the last time. The Captain
took with him his son Theodore, in order to place him in School in St Petersburg. When the Captain sailed for home, Mr Prince went to serve the Princess
Purtossof, one of the noble ladies of the Court. The palace where the imperial
family reside is called the court, or the seat of Government. This magnificent
building is adorned with all the ornaments that possibly can be explained;
there are hundreds of people that inhabit it, besides the soldiers that guard
it. There are several of these splendid edifices in the city and vicinity. The one
that I was presented in, was in a village, three miles from the city. After leaving
the carriage, we entered the first ward; where the usual salutation by the guards
was performed. As we passed through the beautiful hall, a door was opened by
two colored men in official dress. The Emperor Alexander, stood on his throne,
in his royal apparel. The throne is circular, elevated two steps from the floor,
and covered with scarlet velvet, tasseled with gold; as I entered, the Emperor
stepped forward with great politeness and condescension, and welcomed me,
and asked several questions; he then accompanied us to the Empress Elizabeth;
she stood in her dignity, and received me in the same manner the Emperor had.
They presented me with a watch, &c. It was customary in those days, when any
one married, belonging to the court, to present them with gifts, according to
their standard; there was no prejudice against color; there were there all casts,
and the people of all nations, each in their place.

The number of coloured men that filled this station was twenty; when
one dies, the number is immediately made up. Mr Prince filled the place of
one that had died. They serve in turns, four at a time, except on some great
occasions, when all are employed. Provision is made for the families within or
without the palace. Those without go to court at 8 o'clock in the morning; after
breakfasting, they take their station in the halls, for the purpose of opening the
doors, at signal given, when the Emperor and Empress pass.

Maria W. Stewart

1803–79

Born to free Black parents in Hartford, Connecticut, and orphaned at the age of five, she was bound out to a clergyman's family, with whom she stayed until she was fifteen. Her minimal education consisted mainly of Sunday schools until the age of twenty. In 1826 she married James W. Stewart, living in Boston, but after her husband's death in 1829 she was cheated out of her inheritance by lawyers and left impoverished. In her own words, she was "brought to the knowledge of the truth, as it is in Jesus, in 1830; in 1831 made a public profession of my faith in Christ". In 1832–3 she gave four public lectures in Boston, becoming the first American-born woman to lecture in public. The resulting notoriety led her to move to New York, where she attended school and then later became a teacher herself. Her first pamphlet, Productions of Mrs Maria W. Stewart (1835), collects together her devotional thoughts and essays on the condition of Black people; in it she addresses Black women, exhorting them to strive for education and political rights: "O, ye daughters of Africa, awake! awake! arise! no longer sleep nor slumber, but distinguish yourselves. Show forth to the world that ye are endowed with noble and exalted faculties." She tried organizing a school in Baltimore in 1852, and in 1863 moved to Washington, DC, where she successfully started her own school. Mediations from the Pen of Mrs Maria W. Stewart, an expanded volume of her writings, appeared in 1879. The following address was delivered at the African Masonic Hall in Boston, 27 February 1833.

On African Rights and Liberty

AFRICAN rights and liberty is a subject that ought to fire the breast of every free man of color in these United States, and excite in his bosom a lively, deep, decided and heart-felt interest. When I cast my eyes on the long list of illustrious names that are enrolled on the bright annals of fame among the whites, I turn my eyes within, and ask my thoughts, "Where are the names of our illustrious ones?" It must certainly have been for the want of energy on the part of the free people of color, that they have been long willing to bear the yoke of oppression. It must have been the want of ambition and force that has given the whites occasion to say that our natural abilities are not as good, and our capacities by nature inferior to theirs. They boldly assert that did we possess a natural independence of soul, and feel a love for liberty within our breasts, some one of our sable race, long before this, would have testified it, notwithstanding the disadvantages under which we labor. We have made ourselves appear altogether unqualified to speak in our own defence, and are therefore looked upon as objects of pity and commiseration. We have been imposed upon, insulted and derided on every side; and now, if we complain, it is considered as the height of impertinence. We have suffered ourselves to be considered as dastards, cowards, mean, faint-hearted wretches; and on this account (not because of our complexion) many despise us, and would gladly spurn us from their presence.

These things have fired my soul with a holy indignation, and compelled me thus to come forward, and endeavor to turn their attention to knowledge and improvement; for knowledge is power. I would ask, is it blindness of mind, or stupidity of soul, or the want of education that has caused our men who are 60 or 70 years of age, never to let their voices be heard, nor their hands be raised in behalf of their color? Or has it been for the fear of offending the whites? If it has, O ye fearful ones, throw off your fearfulness, and come forth in the name of the Lord, and in the strength of the God of Justice, and make yourselves useful and active members in society; for they admire a noble and patriotic spirit in others; and should they not admire it in us? If you are men, convince them that you possess the spirit of men; and as your day, so shall your strength be. Have the sons of Africa no souls? Feel they no ambitious desires? Shall the chains of ignorance forever confine them? Shall the insipid appellation of "clever negroes", or "good creatures", any longer content them? Where can we find among ourselves the man of science, or a philosopher, or an able statesman, or a counsellor at law? Show me our fearless and brave, our noble and gallant ones. Where are our lecturers in natural history, and our critics in useful knowledge? There may be a few such men among us, but they are rare. It is true our fathers bled and died in the revolutionary war, and others fought bravely under the command of Jackson, in defence of liberty. But where is the man that has distinguished himself in these modern days by acting wholly in the defence of African rights and liberty? There was one, although he sleeps, his memory lives.

I am sensible that there are many highly intelligent men of color in these United States, in the force of whose arguments, doubtless, I should discover my inferiority; but if they are blessed with wit and talent, friends and fortune, why have they not made themselves men of eminence, by striving to take all the reproach that is cast upon the people of color, and in endeavoring to alleviate the woes of their brethren in bondage? Talk, without effort, is nothing; you are abundantly capable, gentlemen, of making yourselves men of distinction; and this gross neglect, on your part, causes my blood to boil within me. Here is the grand cause which hinders the rise and progress of people of color. It is their want of laudable ambition and requisite courage.

Individuals have been distinguished according to their genius and talents, ever since the first formation of man, and will continue to be while the world stands. The different grades rise to honor and respectability as their merits may deserve. History informs us that we sprung from one of the most learned nations of the whole earth; from the seat, if not the parent, of science. Yes, poor despised Africa was once the resort of sages and legislators of other nations, was esteemed the school for learning, and the most illustrious men in Greece flocked thither for instruction. But it was our gross sins and abominations that provoked the Almighty to frown thus heavily upon us, and give our glory unto others. Sin and prodigality have caused the downfall of nations, kings and emperors; and were it not that God in wrath remembers mercy, we might indeed despair; but a promise is left us; "Ethiopia shall again stretch forth her hands unto God."

But it is of no use for us to boast that we sprung from this learned and enlightened nation, for this day a thick mist of moral gloom hangs over millions of our race. Our condition as a people has been low for hundreds of years, and it will continue to be so, unless by true piety and virtue, we strive to regain that which we have lost. White Americans, by their prudence, economy, and exertions, have sprung up and become one of the most flourishing nations in the world, distinguished for their knowledge of the arts and sciences, for their polite literature. While our minds are vacant and starve for want of knowledge, theirs are filled to overflowing. Most of our color have been taught to stand in fear of the white man from their earliest infancy, to work as soon as they could walk, and to call "master" before they could scare lisp the name of mother. Continual fear and laborious servitude have in some degree lessened in us that natural force and energy which belong to man; or else, in defiance of opposition, our men, before this, would have nobly and boldly contended for their rights. But give the man of color an equal opportunity with the white from the cradle to manhood, and from manhood to the grave, and you would discover the dignified statesman, the man of science, and the philosopher. But there is no such opportunity for the sons of Africa, and I fear that our powerful ones are fully determined that there never shall be. Forbid, ye Powers on high, that it should any longer be said that our men possess no force. O ye sons of Africa, when will your voices be heard in our legislative halls, in defiance of your enemies, contending for equal rights and liberty? How can you, when you reflect from what you have fallen, refrain from crying mightily unto God, to turn away from us the fierceness of his anger, and remember our transgressions against us no more forever? But a god of infinite purity will not regard the prayers of those who hold religion in one hand, and prejudice, sin and pollution in the other; he will not regard the prayers of self-righteousness and hypocrisy. Is it possible, I exclaim, that for the want of knowledge we have labored for hundreds of years to support others, and been content to receive what they chose to give us in return? Cast your eyes about, look as far as you can see; all, all is owned by the lordly white except here and there a lowly dwelling which the man of color, midst deprivations, fraud, and opposition has been scarce able to procure. Like King Solomon, who put neither nail or hammer to the temple, yet received the praise; so also have the white Americans gained themselves a name, like the names of the great men that are in the earth, while in reality we have been their principal foundation and support. We have pursued the shadow, they have obtained the substance; we have performed the labor, they have received the profits; we have planted the vines, they have eaten the fruits of them.

I would implore our men, and especially our rising youth, to flee from the gambling board and the dance-hall; for we are poor, and have no money to throw away. I do not consider dancing as criminal in itself, but it is astonishing to me that our fine young men are so blind to their own interest and the future welfare of their children as to spend their hard earnings for this frivolous amusement; for it has been carried on among us to such an unbecoming extent that it has become absolutely disgusting. "Faithful are the wounds of a friend, but the kisses of an enemy are deceitful" [Proverbs 27.6]. Had those men among us who had an opportunity, turned their attention as assiduously to mental and moral improvement as they have to gambling and dancing, I might have remained quietly at home and they stood contending in my place. These polite accomplishments will never enroll your names on the bright annals of fame who admire the belle void of intellectual knowledge, or applaud the dandy that talks largely on politics, without striving to assist his fellow in the revolution, when the nerves and muscles of every other man forced him into the field of action. You have a right to rejoice, and to let your hearts cheer you in the days of your youth; yet remember that for all these things God will bring you into judgment. Then, O ye sons of Africa, turn your mind from these perishable objects, and contend for the cause of God and the rights of man. Form yourselves into temperance societies. There are temperate men among you; then why will you any longer neglect to strive, by your example, to suppress vice in all its abhorrent forms? You have been told repeatedly of the glorious results arising from temperance, and can you bear to see the whites arising in honor and respectability without endeavoring to grasp after that honor and respectability also?

But I forbear. Let our money, instead of being thrown away as heretofore, be appropriated for schools and seminaries of learning for our children and youth. We ought to follow the example of the whites in this respect. Nothing would raise our respectability, add to our peace and happiness, and reflect so much honor upon us, as to be ourselves the promoters of temperance, and the supporters, as far as we are able, of useful and scientific knowledge. The rays of light and knowledge have been hid from our view; we have been taught to consider ourselves as scarce superior to the brute creation; and have performed the most laborious part of American drudgery. Had we as a people received one-half the early advantages the whites have received, I would defy the government of these United States to deprive us any longer of our rights.

I am informed that the agent of the Colonization Society has recently formed an association of young men for the purpose of influencing those of us to go to Liberia who may feel disposed. The colonizationists are blind to their own interest, for should the nations of the earth make war with America, they would find their forces much weakened by our absence; or should we remain here, can our "brave soldiers" and "fellow citizens", as they were termed in time of calamity, condescend to defend the rights of whites and be again deprived of their own, or sent to Liberia in return? Or, if the colonizationists are the real friends to Africa, let them expend the money which they collect in erecting a college to educate her injured sons in this land of gospel, light, and liberty; for it would be most thankfully received on our part, and convince us of the truth of their professions, and save time, expense, and anxiety. Let them place before us noble objects worthy of pursuit, and see if we prove ourselves to be those unambitious Negroes they term us. But, ah, methinks their hearts are so frozen toward us they had rather their money should be sunk in the ocean than to administer it to our relief: and I fear, if they dared, like Pharaoh, king of Egypt, they would order every male child among us to be drowned. But the most high God is still as able to subdue the lofty pride of these white Americans as He was the heart of that ancient rebel. They say, though we are looked upon as things, yet we sprang from a scientific people. Had our men the requisite force and energy they would soon convince them by their efforts, both in public and private, that they were men, or things in the shape of men. Well may the colonizationists laugh us to scorn for our negligence; well may they cry: "Shame to the sons of Africa." As the burden of the Israelites was too great for Moses to bear, so also is our burden too great for our noble advocate to bear. You must feel interested, my brethen, in what he undertakes, and hold up his hands by your good works, or in spite of himself his soul will become discouraged and his heart will die within him; for he has, as it were, the strong bulls of Bashan [Psalms 22:12] to contend with.

It is of no use for us to wait any longer for a generation of well-educated men to arise. We have slumbered and slept too long already; the day is far spent; the night of death approaches; and you have sound sense and good judgment sufficient to begin with, if you feel disposed to make a right use of it. Let every man of color throughout the United States, who possesses the spirit and principles of a man, sign a petition to Congress to abolish slavery in the District of Columbia, and grant you the rights and privileges of common free citizens; for if you had had faith as a grain of mustard seed [Matthew 13:31], long before this the mountain of prejudice might have been removed. We are all sensible that the Anti-Slavery Society has taken hold of the arm of our whole population, in order to raise them out of the mire. Now all we have to do is, by a spirit of virtuous ambition, to strive to raise ourselves; and I am happy to have it in my power thus publicly to say that the colored inhabitants of this city, in some respects, are beginning to improve. Had the free people of color in these United States nobly and freely contended for their rights, and showed a natural genius and talent, although not so brilliant as some; had they held up, encouraged and patronized each other, nothing could have hindered us from being a thriving and flourishing people. There has been a fault among us. The reason why our distinguished men have not made themselves more influential, is because they fear that the strong current of opposition through which they must pass would cause their downfall and prove their overthrow. And what gives rise to this opposition? Envy. And what has it amounted to? Nothing. And who are the cause of it? Our whited sepulchres [Matthew 23:27], who want to be great, and don't know how; who love to be called of men "Rabbi, Rabbi"; who put on false sanctity, and humble themselves to their brethren for the sake of acquiring the highest place in the synagogue and the uppermost seat at the feast. You, dearly beloved, who are the genuine followers of our

Lord Jesus Christ – the salt of the earth, and the light of the world – are not so culpable. As I told you in the very first of my writing, I will tell you again, I am but as a drop in the bucket – as one particle of the small dust of the earth [Isaiah 40:15]. God will surely raise up those among us who will plead the cause of virtue and the pure principles of morality more eloquently than I am able to do.

It appears to me that America has become like the great city of Babylon, for she has boasted in her heart: "I sit a queen and am no widow, and shall see no sorrow" [Revelation 18:7]! She is, indeed, a seller of slaves and the souls of men; she has made the Africans drunk with the wine of her fornication; she has put them completely beneath her feet, and she means to keep them there; her right hand supports the reins of government and her left hand the wheel of power, and she is determined not to let go her grasp. But many powerful sons and daughters of Africa will shortly arise, who will put down vice and immorality among us, and declare by Him that sitteth upon the throne that they will have their rights; and if refused, I am afraid they will spread horror and devastation around. I believe that the oppression of injured Africa has come up before the majesty of Heaven; and when our cries shall have reached the ears of the Most High, it will be a tremendous day for the people of this land; for strong is the hand of the Lord God Almighty.

Life has almost lost its charms for me; death has lost its sting, and the grave its terrors [I Corinthians 15:55]; and at times I have a strong desire to depart and dwell with Christ, which is far better. Let me entreat my white brethren to awake and save our sons from dissipation and our daughters from ruin. Lend the hand of assistance to feeble merit; plead the cause of virtue among our sable race; so shall our curses upon you be turned into blessings; and though you should endeavor to drive us from these shores, still we will cling to you the more firmly; nor will we attempt to rise above you; we will presume to be called your equals only.

The unfriendly whites first drove the native American from his much loved home. Then they stole our fathers from their peaceful and quiet dwellings, and brought them hither, and made bond-men and bond-women of them and their little ones. They have obliged our brethren to labor; kept them in utter ignorance; nourished them in vice, and raised them in degradation; and now that we have enriched their soil, and filled their coffers, they say that we are not capable of becoming like white men, and that we can never rise to respectability in this country. They would drive us to a strange land. But before I go, the bayonet shall pierce me through. African rights and liberty is a subject that ought to fire the breast of every free man of color in these United States, and excite in his bosom a lively, deep, decided, and heartfelt interest.

Mary Seacole
1805–81

B orn as Mary Jane Grant in Kingston, Jamaica, twenty-five years before the abolition of slavery, she was the daughter of a free Black woman and of a Scottish army officer. Before her brief marriage to Viscount Nelson's godson, Edwin Horatio Seacole (who died in 1836), she had travelled to England twice with relatives, and visited the Bahamas, Haiti and Cuba. Businesswoman, traveller, gold prospector, writer, "doctress", nurse, she led a varied and exciting life, depicted in her memoirs, and became a notable figure in the Crimean War, as deserving of attention as Florence Nightingale. Her autobiography, Wonderful Adventures of Mrs Seacole in Many Lands (1857), was an immediate success, reprinted in its publication year, and she later moved in royal circles that included Queen Victoria and the Princess of Wales. However, the autobiography had been largely forgotten until its reissue in London in 1984, edited by Ziggi Alexander and Audrey Dewjee.

From

Wonderful Adventures of Mrs Seacole in Many Lands

CHAPTER VIII

I LONG TO JOIN THE BRITISH ARMY BEFORE SEBASTOPOL

B EFORE I left Jamaica for Navy Bay, as narrated in the last chapter, war had been declared against Russia, and we were all anxiously expecting news of a descent upon the Crimea. Now, no sooner had I heard of war somewhere, than I longed to witness it; and when I was told that many of the regiments I had known so well in Jamaica had left England for the scene of action, the desire to join them became stronger than ever. I used to stand for hours in silent thought before an old map of the world, in a little corner of which some one had chalked a red cross, to enable me to distinguish where the Crimea was; and as I traced the route thither, all difficulties would vanish. But when I came to talk over the project with my friends, the best scheme I could devise seemed so wild and improbable, that I was fain to resign my hopes for a time, and so started for Navy Bay.

But all the way to England, from Navy Bay, I was turning my old wish over and over in my mind; and when I found myself in London, in the autumn of 1854, just after the battle of Alma had been fought, and my old friends were fairly before the walls of Sebastopol, how to join them there took up far more of my thoughts than that visionary gold-mining speculation on the river Palmilla which seemed so feasible to us in New Granada, but was considered so wild and unprofitable a speculation in London. And, as time wore on, the inclination to join my old friends of the 97th, 48th, and other regiments, battling with worse foes than yellow fever or cholera, took such exclusive possession of my mind, that I threw over the gold speculation altogether, and devoted all my energies to my new scheme.

Heaven knows it was visionary enough! I had no friends who could help me in such a project – nay, who would understand why I desired to go, and what I desired to do when I got there. My funds, although they might, carefully husbanded, carry me over the three thousand miles, and land me at Balaclava, would not support me there long; while to persuade the public that an unknown Creole woman would be useful to their army before Sebastopol was too improbable an achievement to be thought of for an instant. Circumstances, however, assisted me.

As the winter wore on, came hints from various quarters of mismanagement, want, and suffering in the Crimea; and after the battle of Balaclava and Inkermann, and the fearful storm of the 14th of November, the worst anticipations were realized. Then we knew that the hospitals were full to suffocation, that scarcity and exposure were the fate of all in the camp, and that the brave fellows for whom any of us at home would have split our last shilling, and shared our last meal, were dying thousands of miles away from the active sympathy of their fellow-countrymen. Fast and thick upon the news of Inkermann, fought by a handful of fasting and enfeebled men against eight times their number of picked Russians, brought fresh and animated to the contest, and while all England was reeling beneath the shock of that fearful victory, came the sad news that hundreds were dying whom the Russian shot and sword had spared, and that the hospitals of Scutari were utterly unable to shelter, or their inadequate staff to attend to, the ship-loads of sick and wounded which were sent to them across the stormy Black Sea.

But directly England knew the worst, she set about repairing her past neglect. In every household busy fingers were working for the poor soldiers – money flowed in golden streams wherever need was – and Christian ladies, mindful of the sublime example, "I was sick, and ye visited me," hastened to volunteer their services by those sick-beds which only women know how to soothe and bless.

Need I be ashamed to confess that I shared in the general enthusiasm, and longed more than ever to carry my busy (and the reader will not hesitate to add experienced) fingers where the sword or bullet had been busiest, and pestilence most rife. I had seen much of sorrow and death elsewhere, but they had never daunted me; and if I could feel happy binding up the wounds of quarrelsome Americans and treacherous Spaniards, what delight should I not experience if I could be useful to my own "sons", suffering for a cause it was so glorious to fight and bleed for! I never stayed to discuss probabilities, or enter into conjectures as to my chances of reaching the scene of action. I made up my mind that if the army wanted nurses, they would be glad of me, and with all the ardour of my nature, which ever carried me where inclination prompted, I decided that I *would* go to the Crimea; and go I did, as all the world knows.

Of course, had it not been for my old strong-mindedness (which has nothing to do with obstinacy, and is in no way related to it, the best term I can think of to express it being "judicious decisiveness"), I should have given up the scheme a score of times in as many days, so regularly did each successive day give birth to a fresh set of rebuffs and disappointments. I shall make no excuse to my readers for giving them a pretty full history of my struggles to become a Crimean *heroine!*

My first idea (and knowing that I was well fitted for the work, and would be the right woman in the right place, the reader can fancy my audacity) was to apply to the War Office for the post of hospital nurse. Among the diseases which I understood were most prevalent in the Crimea were cholera, diarrhoea, and dysentery, all of them more or less known in tropical climates; and with which, as the reader will remember, my Panama experience had made me tolerably familiar. Now, no one will accuse me of presumption, if I say that I thought (and so it afterwards proved) that my knowledge of these human ills would not only render my services as a nurse more valuable, but would enable me to be of use to the overworked doctors. That others thought so too, I took with me ample testimony. I cannot resist the temptation of giving my readers one of the testimonials I had, it seems so eminently practical and to the point:

I became acquainted with Mrs Seacole through the instrumentality of T. B. Cowan, Esq., H. B. M. Consul at Colon, on the Isthmus of Panama, and have had many opportunities of witnessing her professional zeal and ability in the treatment of aggravated forms of tropical diseases.

I am myself personally much indebted for her indefatigable kindness and skill at a time when I am apt to believe the advice of a practitioner qualified in the North would have little availed.

Her peculiar fitness, in a constitutional point of view, for the duties of medical attendant, needs no comment.

(Signed)

A.G.M.,
Late Medical Officer, West Granada
Gold-mining Company.

So I made long and unwearied application at the War Office, in blissful ignorance of the labour and time I was throwing away. I have reason to believe that I considerably interfered with the repose of sundry messengers, and disturbed, to an alarming degree, the official gravity of some nice gentlemanly

young fellows, who were working out their salaries in an easy, off-hand way.
But my ridiculous endeavours to gain an interview with the Secretary-at-War
of course failed, and glad at last to oblige a distracted messenger, I transferred
my attentions to the Quartermaster-General's department. Here I saw another
gentleman, who listened to me with a great deal of polite enjoyment, and – his
amusement ended – hinted, had I not better apply to the Medical Department;
and accordingly I attached myself to their quarters with the same unwearying
ardour. But, of course, I grew tired at last, and then I changed my plans.

Now, I am not for a single instant going to blame the authorities who would
not listen to the offer of a motherly yellow woman to go to the Crimea and
nurse her "sons" there, suffering from cholera, diarrhoea, and a host of lesser
ills. In my country, where people know our use, it would have been different;
but here it was natural enough – although I had references, and other voices
spoke for me – that they should laugh, goodnaturedly enough, at my offer. War,
I know, is a serious game, but sometimes very humble actors are of great use
in it, and if the reader, when he comes in time to peruse the evidence of those
who had to do with the Sebastopol drama, of my share in it, will turn back to
this chapter, he will confess perhaps that, after all, the impulse which led me to
the War Department was not unnatural.

My new scheme was, I candidly confess, worse devised than the one which
had failed. Miss Nightingale had left England for the Crimea, but other nurses
were still to follow, and my new plan was simply to offer myself to Mrs H—[1] as
a recruit. Feeling that I was one of the very women they most wanted, experienced and fond of the work, I jumped at once to the conclusion that they would
gladly enrol me in their number. To go to Cox's, the army agents, who were
most obliging to me, and obtain the Secretary-at-War's private address, did not
take long; and that done, I laid the same pertinacious siege to his great house
in —Square,[2] as I had previously done to his place of business.

Many a long hour did I wait in his great hall, while scores passed in and
out; many of them looking curiously at me. The flunkeys, noble creatures!
marvelled exceedingly at the yellow woman whom no excuses could get rid
of, nor impertinence dismay, and showed me very clearly that they resented my
persisting in remaining there in mute appeal from their sovereign will. At last I
gave that up, after a message from Mrs H. that the full complement of nurses had
been secured, and that my offer could not be entertained. Once again I tried, and
had an interview this time with one of Miss Nightingale's companions. She gave
me the same reply, and I read in her face the fact, that had there been a vacancy,
I should not have been chosen to fill it.

As a last resort, I applied to the managers of the Crimean Fund to know
whether they would give me a passage to the camp – once there I would trust
to something turning up. But this failed also, and one cold evening I stood in
the twilight, which was fast deepening into wintry night, and looked back upon
the ruins of my last castle in the air. The disappointment seemed a cruel one. I

---

[1] Elizabeth Herbert, wife of Sidney Herbert, Secretary at War, who co-ordinated
the recruitment of nurses.
[2] Belgrave Square.

was so conscious of the unselfishness of the motives which induced me to leave England – so certain of the service I could render among the sick soldiery, and yet I found it so difficult to convince others of these facts. Doubts and suspicions arose in my heart for the first and last time, thank Heaven. Was it possible that American prejudices against colour had some root here? Did these ladies shrink from accepting my aid because my blood flowed beneath a somewhat duskier skin than theirs? Tears streamed down my foolish cheeks, as I stood in the fast thinning streets; tears of grief that any should doubt my motives – that Heaven should deny me the opportunity that I sought. Then I stood still, and looking upward through and through the dark clouds that shadowed London, prayed aloud for help. I dare say that I was a strange sight to the few passers-by, who hastened homeward through the gloom and mist of that wintry night. I dare say those who read these pages will wonder at me as much as they who saw me did; but you must remember that I am one of an impulsive people, and find it hard to put that restraint upon my feelings, which to you is so easy and natural.

The morrow, however, brought fresh hope. A good night's rest had served to strengthen my determination. Let what might happen, to the Crimea I would go. If in no other way, then would I upon my own responsibility and at my own cost. There were those there who had known me in Jamaica, who had been under my care; doctors who would vouch for my skill and willingness to aid them, and a general who had more than once helped me, and would do so still. Why not trust to their welcome and kindness, and start at once? If the authorities had allowed me, I would willingly have given them my services as a nurse; but as they declined them, should I not open an hotel for invalids in the Crimea in my own way? I had no more idea of what the Crimea was than the home authorities themselves perhaps, but having once made up my mind, it was not long before cards were printed and speeding across the Mediterranean to my friends before Sebastopol. Here is one of them:

BRITISH HOTEL

Mrs Mary Seacole
(Late of Kingston, Jamaica),

Respectfully announces to her former kind friends, and to the
Officers of the Army and Navy generally,

That she has taken her passage in the screw-steamer "Hollander", to start from London on the 25th of January, intending on her arrival at Balaclava to establish a mess-table and comfortable quarters for sick and convalescent officers.

Harriet E. Adams Wilson

? c. 1808–c. 1870

*S*he was born possibly in Fredericksburg, Virginia (her birth date is
also open to question, some placing it as late as 1828), and lived
in Philadelphia before moving to New England. In about 1851 she
married a sailor, who left her but by whom she had a son in 1852.
Publishing in 1859 Our Nig; or, Sketches from the Life of a Free Black,
the fictional autobiography of a mulatto girl – rediscovered in 1983 by
Henry Louis Gates, Jr – she became the earliest African-American novelist.
(Another Black woman, Maria F. dos Reis, also in 1859 published a
novel, Ursula, in Brazil.) Her preface states "In offering to the public
the following pages, the writer confesses her inability to minister to the
refined and cultivated, the pleasure supplied by abler pens. It is not for
such these crude narrations appear. Deserted by kindred, disabled by
failing health, I am forced to some experiment which shall aid me in
maintaining myself and child without extinguishing this feeble life." Five
months later her son died, aged seven. She herself was frail in health since
her teens, and probably died in Boston.

From

Our Nig; or, Sketches from the Life of a Free Black

CHAPTER II

MY FATHER'S DEATH

Misery! we have known each other,
Like a sister and a brother,
Living in the same lone home
Many years – we must live some
Hours or ages yet to come.
                                        SHELLEY

J IM, proud of his treasure – a white wife, – tried hard to fulfil his promises;
and furnished her with a more comfortable dwelling, diet, and apparel. It was
comparatively a comfortable winter she passed after her marriage. When Jim
could work, all went on well. Industrious, and fond of Mag, he was determined
she should not regret her union to him. Time levied an additional charge upon
him, in the form of two pretty mulattos, whose infantile pranks amply repaid the
additional toil. A few years, and a severe cough and pain in his side compelled

him to be an idler for weeks together, and Mag had thus a reminder of by-gones. She cared for him only as a means to subserve her own comfort; yet she nursed him faithfully and true to marriage vows till death released her. He became the victim of consumption. He loved Mag to the last. So long as life continued, he stifled his sensibility to pain, and toiled for her sustenance long after he was able to do so.

A few expressive wishes for her welfare; a hope of better days for her; an anxiety lest they should not all go to the "good place"; brief advice about their children; a hope expressed that Mag would not be neglected as she used to be; the manifestation of Christian patience; these were *all* the legacy of miserable Mag. A feeling of cold desolation came over her, as she turned from the grave of one who had been truly faithful to her.

She was now expelled from companionship with white people; this last step – her union with a black – was the climax of repulsion.

Seth Shipley, a partner in Jim's business, wished her to remain in her present home; but she declined, and returned to her hovel again, with obstacles threefold more insurmountable than before. Seth accompanied her, giving her a weekly allowance which furnished most of the food necessary for the four inmates. After a time, work failed; their means were reduced.

How Mag toiled and suffered, yielding to fits of desperation, bursts of anger, and uttering curses too fearful to repeat. When both were supplied with work, they prospered; if idle, they were hungry together. In this way their interests became united; they planned for the future together. Mag had lived an outcast for years. She had ceased to feel the gushings of penitence; she had crushed the sharp agonies of an awakened conscience. She had no longings for a purer heart, a better life. Far easier to descend lower. She entered the darkness of perpetual infamy. She asked not the rite of civilization or Christianity. Her will made her the wife of Seth. Soon followed scenes familiar and trying.

"It's no use," said Seth one day; "we must give the children away, and try to get work in some other place."

"Who'll take the black devils?" snarled Mag.

"They're none of mine," said Seth; "what you growling about?"

"Nobody will want any thing of mine, or yours either," she replied.

"We'll make 'em, p'r'aps," he said. "There's Frado's six years old, and pretty, if she is yours, and white folks 'll say so. She'd be a prize somewhere," he continued, tipping his chair back against the wall, and placing his feet upon the rounds, as if he had much more to say when in the right position.

Frado, as they called one of Mag's children, was a beautiful mulatto, with long, curly black hair, and handsome, roguish eyes, sparkling with an exuberance of spirit almost beyond restraint.

Hearing her name mentioned, she looked up from her play, to see what Seth had to say of her.

"Wouldn't the Bellmonts take her?" asked Seth.

"Bellmonts?" shouted Mag. "His wife is a right she-devil! and if – "

"Hadn't they better be all together?" interrupted Seth, reminding her of a like epithet used in reference to her little ones.

Without seeming to notice him, she continued, "She can't keep a girl in the house over a week; and Mr Bellmont wants to hire a boy to work for him, but he can't find one that will live in the house with her; she's so ugly, they can't."

"Well, we've got to make a move soon," answered Seth; "if you go with me, we shall go right off. Had you rather spare the other one?" asked Seth, after a short pause.

"One's as bad as t'other," replied Mag. "Frado is such a wild, frolicky thing, and means to do jest as she's a mind to; she won't go if she don't want to. I don't want to tell her she is to be given away."

"I will," said Seth. "Come here, Frado?"

The child seemed to have some dim foreshadowing of evil, and declined.

"Come here," he continued; "I want to tell you something."

She came reluctantly. He took her hand and said: "We're going to move, by-'m-bye; will you go?"

"No!" screamed she; and giving a sudden jerk which destroyed Seth's equilibrium, left him sprawling on the floor, while she escaped through the open door.

"She's a hard one," said Seth, brushing his patched coat sleeve. "I'd risk her at Bellmont's."

They discussed the expediency of a speedy departure. Seth would first seek employment, and then return for Mag. They would take with them what they could carry, and leave the rest with Pete Greene, and come for them when they were wanted. They were long in arranging affairs satisfactorily, and were not a little startled at the close of their conference to find Frado missing. They thought approaching night would bring her. Twilight passed into darkness, and she did not come. They thought she had understood their plans, and had, perhaps, permanently withdrawn. They could not rest without making some effort to ascertain her retreat. Seth went in pursuit, and returned without her. They rallied others when they discovered that another little colored girl was missing, a favorite playmate of Frado's. All effort proved unavailing. Mag felt sure her fears were realized, and that she might never see her again. Before her anxieties became realities, both were safely returned, and from them and their attendant they learned that they went to walk, and not minding the direction soon found themselves lost. They had climbed fences and walls, passed through thickets and marshes, and when night approached selected a thick cluster of shrubbery as a covert for the night. They were discovered by the person who now restored them, chatting of their prospects, Frado attempting to banish the childish fears of her companion. As they were some miles from home, they were kindly cared for until morning. Mag was relieved to know her child was not driven to desperation by their intentions to relieve themselves of her, and she was inclined to think severe restraint would be healthful.

The removal was all arranged; the few days necessary for such migrations passed quickly, and one bright summer morning they bade farewell to their Singleton hovel, and with budgets and bundles commenced their weary march. As they neared the village, they heard the merry shouts of children gathered around the schoolroom, awaiting the coming of their teacher.

"Halloo!" screamed one, "Black, white and yeller!" "Black, white and yeller," echoed a dozen voices.

It did not grate so harshly on poor Mag as once it would. She did not even turn her head to look at them. She had passed into an insensibility no childish taunt could penetrate, else she would have reproached herself as she passed familiar scenes, for extending the separation once so easily annihilated by steadfast integrity. Two miles beyond lived the Bellmonts, in a large, old-fashioned, two-story white house, environed by fruitful acres, and embellished by shrubbery and shade trees. Years ago a youthful couple consecrated it as home; and after many little feet had worn paths to favorite fruit trees, and over its green hills, and mingled at last with brother man in the race which belongs neither to the swift or strong, the sire became grey-haired and decrepid, and went to his last repose. His aged consort soon followed him. The old homestead thus passed into the hands of a son, to whose wife Mag had applied the epithet "she-devil", as may be remembered. John, the son, had not in his family arrangements departed from the example of the father. The pastimes of his boyhood were ever freshly revived by witnessing the games of his own sons as they rallied about the same goal his youthful feet had often won; as well as by the amusements of his daughters in their imitations of maternal duties.

At the time we introduce them, however, John is wearing the badge of age. Most of his children were from home; some seeking employment; some were already settled in homes of their own. A maiden sister shared with him the estate on which he resided, and occupied a portion of the house.

Within sight of the house, Seth seated himself with his bundles and the child he had been leading, while Mag walked onward to the house leading Frado. A knock at the door brought Mrs Bellmont, and Mag asked if she would be willing to let that child stop there while she went to the Reed's house to wash, and when she came back she would call and get her. It seemed a novel request, but she consented. Why the impetuous child entered the house, we cannot tell; the door closed, and Mag hastily departed. Frado waited for the close of day, which was to bring back her mother. Alas! it never came. It was the last time she ever saw or heard of her mother.

CHAPTER III

A NEW HOME FOR ME

Oh! did we but know of the shadows so nigh,
    The world would indeed be a prison of gloom;
All light would be quenched in youth's eloquent eye,
    And the prayer-lisping infant would ask for the tomb.

For if Hope be a star that may lead us astray,
    And "deceiveth the heart," as the aged ones preach;
Yet 'twas Mercy that gave it, to beacon our way,
    Though its halo illumes where it never can reach.

ELIZA COOK

A S the day closed and Mag did not appear, surmises were expressed by the family that she never intended to return. Mr Bellmont was a kind, humane man, who would not grudge ospitality to the poorest wanderer, nor fail to sympathize with any sufferer, however humble. The child's desertion by her mother appealed to his sympathy, and he felt inclined to succor her. To do this in opposition to Mrs Bellmont's wishes, would be like encountering a whirlwind charged with fire, daggers and spikes. She was not as susceptible of fine emotions as her spouse. Mag's opinion of her was not without foundation. She was self-willed, haughty, undisciplined, arbitrary and severe. In common parlance, she was a *scold*, a thorough one. Mr B. remained silent during the consultation which follows, engaged in by mother, Mary and John, or Jack, as he was familiarly called.

"Send her to the County House," said Mary, in reply to the query what should be done with her, in a tone which indicated self-importance in the speaker. She was indeed the idol of her mother, and more nearly resembled her in disposition and manners than the others.

Jane, an invalid daughter, the eldest of those at home, was reclining on a sofa apparently uninterested.

"Keep her," said Jack. "She's real handsome and bright, and not very black, either."

"Yes," rejoined Mary; "that's just like you, Jack. She'll be of no use at all these three years, right under foot all the time."

"Poh! Miss Mary; if she should stay, it wouldn't be two days before you would be telling the girls about *our* nig, *our* nig!" retorted Jack.

"I don't want a nigger 'round *me*, do you, mother?" asked Mary.

"I don't mind the nigger in the child. I should like a dozen better than one," replied her mother. "If I could make her do my work in a few years, I would keep her. I have so much trouble with girls I hire, I am almost persuaded if I have one to train up in my way from a child, I shall be able to keep them awhile. I am tired of changing every few months."

"Where could she sleep?" asked Mary. "I don't want her near me."

"In the L chamber," answered the mother.

"How'll she get there?" asked Jack. "She'll be afraid to go through that dark passage, and she can't climb the ladder safely."

"She'll have to go there; it's good enough for a nigger," was the reply.

Jack was sent on horseback to ascertain if Mag was at her home. He returned with the testimony of Pete Greene that they were fairly departed, and that the child was intentionally thrust upon their family.

The imposition was not at all relished by Mrs B., or the pert, haughty Mary, who had just glided into her teens.

"Show the child to bed, Jack," said his mother. "You seem most pleased with the little nigger, so you may introduce her to her room."

He went to the kitchen, and, taking Frado gently by the hand, told her he would put her in bed now; perhaps her mother would come the next night after her.

It was not yet quite dark, so they ascended the stairs without any light, passing through nicely furnished rooms, which were a source of great amazement to the child. He opened the door which connected with her room by a dark, unfinished passage-way. "Don't bump your head," said Jack, and stepped before to open the door leading into her apartment, – an unfinished chamber over the kitchen, the roof slanting nearly to the floor, so that the bed could stand only in the middle of the room. A small half window furnished light and air. Jack returned to the sitting room with the remark that the child would soon outgrow those quarters.

"When she *does*, she'll outgrow the house," remarked the mother.

"What can she do to help you?" asked Mary. "She came just in the right time, didn't she? Just the very day after Bridget left," continued she.

"I'll see what she can do in the morning," was the answer.

While this conversation was passing below, Frado lay, revolving in her little mind whether she would remain or not until her mother's return. She was of wilful determined nature, a stranger to fear, and would not hesitate to wander away should she decide to. She remembered the conversation of her mother with Seth, the words "given away" which she heard used in reference to herself; and though she did not know their full import, she thought she should, by remaining, be in some relation to white people she was never favored with before. So she resolved to tarry, with the hope that mother would come and get her some time. The hot sun had penetrated her room, and it was long before a cooling breeze reduced the temperature so that she could sleep.

Frado was called early in the morning by her new mistress. Her first work was to feed the hens. She was shown how it was *always* to be done, and in no other way; any departure from this rule to be punished by a whipping. She was then accompanied by Jack to drive the cows to pasture, so she might learn the way. Upon her return she was allowed to eat her breakfast, consisting of a bowl of skimmed milk, with brown bread crusts, which she was told to eat, standing, by the kitchen table, and must not be over ten minutes about it. Meanwhile the family were taking their morning meal in the dining-room. This over, she was placed on a cricket to wash the common dishes; she was to be in waiting always to bring wood and chips, to run hither and thither from room to room.

A large amount of dish-washing for small hands followed dinner. Then the same after tea and going after the cows finished her first day's work. It was a new discipline to the child. She found some attractions about the place, and she retired to rest at night more willing to remain. The same routine followed day after day, with slight variation; adding a little more work, and spicing the toil with "words that burn", and frequent blows on her head. These were great annoyances to Frado, and had she known where her mother was, she would have gone at once to her. She was often greatly wearied, and silently wept over her sad fate. At first she wept aloud, which Mrs Bellmont noticed by applying a rawhide, always at hand in the kitchen. It was a symptom of discontent and complaining which must be "nipped in the bud", she said.

Thus passed a year. No intelligence of Mag. It was now certain Frado was to become a permanent member of the family. Her labors were multiplied; she was quite indispensable, although but seven years old. She had never learned to read, never heard of a school until her residence in the family.

Mrs Bellmont was in doubt about the utility of attempting to educate people of color, who were incapable of elevation. This subject occasioned a lengthy

discussion in the family. Mr Bellmont, Jane and Jack arguing for Frado's education; Mary and her mother objecting. At last Mr Bellmont declared decisively
that she *should* go to school. He was a man who seldom decided controversies
at home. The word once spoken admitted of no appeal; so, notwithstanding
Mary's objection that she would have to attend the same school she did, the
word became law.

It was to be a new scene to Frado, and Jack had many queries and conjectures
to answer. He was himself too far advanced to attend the summer school, which
Frado regretted, having had too many opportunities of witnessing Miss Mary's
temper to feel safe in her company alone.

The opening day of school came. Frado sauntered on far in the rear of Mary,
who was ashamed to be seen "walking with a nigger". As soon as she appeared,
with scanty clothing and bared feet, the children assembled, noisily published
her approach: "See that nigger," shouted one. "Look! Look!" cried another. "I
won't play with her," said one little girl. "Nor I neither," replied another.

Mary evidently relished these sharp attacks, and saw a fair prospect of lowering
Nig where, according to her views, she belonged. Poor Frado, chagrined and
grieved, felt that her anticipations of pleasure at such a place were far from
being realized. She was just deciding to return home, and never come there
again, when the teacher appeared, and observing the downcast looks of the
child, took her by the hand, and led her into the school-room. All followed, and,
after the bustle of securing seats was over, Miss Marsh inquired if the children
knew "any cause for the sorrow of that little girl?" pointing to Frado. It was soon
all told. She then reminded them of their duties to the poor and friendless; their
cowardice in attacking a young innocent child; referred them to one who looks
not on outward appearances, but on the heart. "She looks like a good girl; I think
I shall love her, so lay aside all prejudice, and vie with each other in shewing
kindness and good-will to one who seems different from you," were the closing
remarks of the kind lady. Those kind words! The most agreeable sound which
ever meets the ear of sorrowing, grieving childhood.

Example rendered her words efficacious. Day by day there was a manifest
change of deportment towards "Nig". Her speeches often drew merriment
from the children; no one could do more to enliven their favorite pastimes
than Frado. Mary could not endure to see her thus noticed, yet knew not how
to prevent it. She could not influence her schoolmates as she wished. She had
not gained their affections by winning ways and yielding points of controversy.
On the contrary, she was self-willed, domineering; every day reported "mad"
by some of her companions. She availed herself of the only alternative, abuse
and taunts, as they returned from school. This was not satisfactory; she wanted
to use physical force "to subdue her", to "keep her down".

There was, on their way home, a field intersected by a stream over which
a single plank was placed for a crossing. It occurred to Mary that it would be
a punishment to Nig to compel her to cross over; so she dragged her to the
edge, and told her authoritatively to go over. Nig hesitated, resisted. Mary placed
herself behind the child, and, in the struggle to force her over, lost her footing
and plunged into the stream. Some of the larger scholars being in sight, ran,
and thus prevented Mary from drowning and Frado from falling. Nig scampered

home fast as possible, and Mary went to the nearest house, dripping, to procure a change of garments. She came loitering home, half crying, exclaiming, "Nig pushed me into the stream!" She then related the particulars. Nig was called from the kitchen. Mary stood with anger flashing in her eyes. Mr Bellmont sat quietly reading his paper. He had witnessed too many of Miss Mary's outbreaks to be startled. Mrs Bellmony interrogated Nig.

"I didn't do it! I didn't do it!" answered Nig, passionately, and then related the occurrence truthfully.

The discrepancy greatly enraged Mrs Bellmont. With loud accusations and angry gestures she approached the child. Turning to her husband, she asked,

"Will you sit still, there, and hear that black nigger call Mary a liar?"

"How do we know but she has told the truth? I shall not punish her," he replied, and left the house, as he usually did when a tempest threatened to envelop him. No sooner was he out of sight than Mrs B. and Mary commenced beating her inhumanly; then propping her mouth open with a piece of wood, shut her up in a dark room, without any supper. For employment, while the tempest raged within, Mr Bellmont went for the cows, a task belonging to Frado, and thus unintentionally prolonged her pain. At dark Jack came in, and seeing Mary, accosted her with, "So you thought you'd vent your spite on Nig, did you? Why can't you let her alone? It was good enough for you to get a ducking, only you did not stay in half long enough."

"Stop!" said his mother. "You shall never talk so before me. You would have that little nigger trample on Mary, would you? She came home with a lie; it made Mary's story false."

"What was Mary's story?" asked Jack.

It was related.

"Now," said Jack, sallying into a chair, "the school-children happened to see it all, and they tell the same story Nig does. Which is most likely to be true, what a dozen agree they saw, or the contrary?"

"It is very strange you will believe what others say against your sister," retorted his mother, with flashing eye. "I think it is time your father subdued you."

"Father is a sensible man," argued Jack. "He would not wrong a dog. Where *is* Frado?" he continued.

"Mother gave her a good whipping and shut her up," replied Mary.

Just then Mr Bellmont entered, and asked if Frado was "shut up yet".

The knowledge of her innocence, the perfidy of his sister, worked fearfully on Jack. He bounded from his chair, searched every room till he found the child; her mouth wedged apart, her face swollen, and full of pain.

How Jack pitied her! He relieved her jaws, brought her some supper, took her to her room, comforted her as well as he knew how, sat by her till she fell asleep, and then left for the sitting room. As he passed his mother, he remarked, "If that was the way Frado was to be treated, he hoped she would never wake again!" He then imparted her situation to his father, who seemed untouched, till a glance at Jack exposed a tearful eye. Jack went early to her next morning. She awoke sad, but refreshed. After breakfast Jack took her with him to the field, and kept her through the day. But it could not be so generally. She must return to school,

to her household duties. He resolved to do what he could to protect her from
Mary and his mother. He bought her a dog, which became a great favorite with
both. The invalid, Jane, would gladly befriend her; but she had not the strength
to brave the iron will of her mother. Kind words and affectionate glances were
the only expressions of sympathy she could safely indulge in. The men employed
on the farm were always glad to hear her prattle; she was a great favorite with
them. Mrs Bellmont allowed them the privilege of talking with her in the kitchen.
She did not fear but she should have ample opportunity of subduing her when
they were away. Three months of schooling, summer and winter, she enjoyed
for three years. Her winter over-dress was a cast-off overcoat, once worn by
Jack, and a sun-bonnet. It was a source of great merriment to the scholars, but
Nig's retorts were so mirthful, and their satisfaction so evident in attributing the
selection to "Old Granny Bellmont," that it was not painful to Nig or pleasurable
to Mary. Her jollity was not to be quenched by whipping or scolding. In Mrs
Bellmont's presence she was under restraint; but in the kitchen, and among
her schoolmates, the pent up fires burst forth. She was ever at some sly prank
when unseen by her teacher, in school hours; not unfrequently some outburst
of merriment, of which she was the original, was charged upon some innocent
mate, and punishment inflicted which she merited. They enjoyed her antics so
fully that any of them would suffer wrongfully to keep open the avenues of mirth.
She would venture far beyond propriety, thus shielded and countenanced.

The teacher's desk was supplied with drawers, in which were stored his
books and other *et ceteras* of the profession. The children observed Nig very
busy there one morning before school, as they flitted in occasionally from their
play outside. The master came; called the children to order; opened a drawer
to take the book the occasion required; when out poured a volume of smoke.
"Fire! Fire!" screamed he, at the top of his voice. By this time he had become
sufficiently acquainted with the peculiar odor, to know he was imposed upon.
The scholars shouted with laughter to see the terror of the dupe, who, feeling
abashed at the needless fright, made no very strict investigation, and Nig once
more escaped punishment. She had provided herself with cigars, and puffing,
puffing away at the crack of the drawer, had filled it with smoke, and then
closed it tightly to deceive the teacher, and amuse the scholars. The interim
of terms was filled up with a variety of duties new and peculiar. At home,
no matter how powerful the heat when sent to rake hay or guard the grazing
herd, she was never permitted to shield her skin from the sun. She was not
many shades darker than Mary now; what a calamity it would be ever to hear
the contrast spoken of. Mrs Bellmont was determined the sun should have full
power to darken the shade which nature had first bestowed upon her as best
befitting.

Mwana Kupona binti Msham

1810–60

S he was the wife of Bwana Mataka, sheikh of the Siu region in the Lamu archipelago of Kenya, who for two decades conducted a guerrilla battle against Zanzibar Island's Sultan Saiyid Said. This is an extract (translated by Alice Werner) from "Utendi wa Mwana Kupona" – a utendi is an epic verse form in the Swahili poetic tradition, generally steeped in Islamic doctrine – composed about two years before her death, in which she advises her daughter about correct behaviour in matters religious, social and domestic – above all in showing complete obedience and deference towards her husband.

From

Poem of Mwana Kupona

Let your husband be content, all the days that you live together – do not worry him with requests, let it be he who recognizes you.

And as you go on, still seek to please him; and that is how you will find the way.

And in the day of resurrection, the decision is his; he will ask what he wants, and what he wishes will be done.

If he wishes you to go to Paradise, you will forthwith be brought there: if he says you are to go to the fire, there is no escape, you will be placed there.

Live with him befittingly, do not provoke him to anger: if he does speak out, do not answer him, endeavour to be silent.

Keep faith with him always; what he wishes do not withhold; let not you and him quarrel: the quarreller gets hurt.

If he goes out first, take leave of him; when he returns, salute him; then prepare a place for him beside you.

If he lies down, do not disturb him; come near him that you may massage him, and as to fresh air, let him not want someone to fan him.

If he sleeps, do not awaken him: neither speak in a loud voice; sit there and do not rise, that he may not have to look for you when he wakes.

When he awakes, delay not in preparing his meal, and look after his body, rubbing him and bathing him.

Shave him, backwards and forwards, and trim his beard for him; pour water over him and fumigate him morning and evening.

Look after him just like a child who knows not how to speak – look well
   after everything that goes out and comes in!
Make him comfortable that he may be at ease, do not refuse his commands;
   if he treats you badly God will rebuke him for it.
My child, do not be slovenly, do as you know best; but sweeping and washing
   out the bathroom, do not neglect it even once;
Nor washing and scenting yourself, and plaiting your hair, nor stringing jasmine
   blossoms and placing them on the coverlet.
And adorn yourself with garments like a bride – put anklets on your legs
   and bracelets on your arms.
Take not from your neck the necklace and clasp, nor cease perfuming your
   body with rosewater and dalia.
Take not the rings off your fingers nor cease dyeing your nails with henna; do
   not remove the antimony from your eyes nor refrain from putting it on your
   eyebrows.
Let your house be clean; honour your husband – when people meet together
   you will bring him praise.
Know what he likes and follow that; a matter that he hates, do not enter into it.
When you wish to go out, you must ask leave; if you see that he is annoyed
   return and stay.
Follow his directions and you will be truly at peace; do not stay on the
   road till the fourth hour has come.
And do not talk by the way, neither open your eyes to evil: look down
   on the ground with a modest countenance.
Return home quickly and sit with your master, and prepare the bedding
   that he may lie down at his ease.
Take every opportunity to exalt your lord, spread his praises, and do not
   require of him more than he can to perform.
What he gives you, receive and let your heart rejoice; what he does not
   do of his own accord, you have no need to tell him.
When you see him, uncover your teeth in a smile; what he says, attend
   to it, unless it be something impious.
My child, do not sharpen your tongue; be like your mother: I was married
   ten years and we did not quarrel once.
I married your father with joy and laughter; there was no want of mutual
   respect all the days that we lived together.
Not one day did we quarrel; he met no ill from me, neither did I from
   him, till the day of his election.
When death comes, if he tells me he is content with me, I shall praise God
   and follow His commands; [but at that time] my heart was astounded. . . .

I wish to warn her – see that you pay attention and follow God; return
   together with the women:
Read this, all you women, so you may understand, and bear no blame before
   the blessed Lord.
Read [these words like] wheat springing up: obey your husbands, that you
   may meet with no loss in this world and the next.

She who obeys her husband, power and prosperity are hers; wherever she
goes to she becomes known, and it is spread abroad.
She who wrote this poem is lonely and acquainted with grief: and if she
was ever uplifted in spirit the Lord will pardon it.
Let me give you the number [of verses]; it is a hundred and one; and two
in addition: they are what I have added.

Completed by the help of God.

Harriet Jacobs ("Linda Brent")

c. 1815–97

*S*he was born near Edenton, North Carolina, according to Jean
Fagan Yellin: "Her parents died while she was a child, and ... at
the death of her beloved mistress (who had taught her to read and
spell) she was sent to a licentious master. He subjected her to unrelenting
sexual harassment. In her teens she bore two children to another white
man. When her jealous master threatened her with concubinage, Jacobs
ran away. Aided by sympathetic black and white neighbors, she was sheltered by her family and for years remained hidden in the home of her
grandmother, a freed slave. During this time the father of her children,
who had bought them from her master, allowed them to live with her
grandmother. Although later he took their little girl to a free state, he
failed to keep his promise to emancipate the children. About 1842, Harriet
Jacobs finally escaped North, contacted her daughter, was joined by her
son, and found work in New York City."

In 1840 she moved to Rochester, New York, and with her brother,
a fugitive slave active in the abolitionist movement, ran an anti-
slavery reading room. In the American Civil War she went to Washington,
DC, to nurse Black troops, later returning to the South to help the freedmen. Her book Linda, or Incidents in the Life of a Slave Girl (1861) was
published under the name "Linda Brent" (edited by Lydia Maria Child),
and by circulating it she attempted to encourage support for emancipation. The following edited extract appeared in Child's The Freedmen's
Book (1865).

From

Incidents in the Life of a Slave Girl

THE GOOD GRANDMOTHER

I HAD a great treasure in my maternal grandmother, who was a remarkable woman in many respects. She was the daughter of a planter in South Carolina, who, at his death, left her and her mother free, with money to go to St Augustine, where they had relatives. It was during the Revolutionary War, and they were captured on their passage, carried back, and sold to different purchasers. Such was the story my grandmother used to tell me. She was sold to the keeper of a large hotel, and I have often heard her tell how hard she fared during childhood. But as she grew older she evinced so much intelligence, and was so faithful, that her master and mistress could not help seeing it was for their interest to take care of such a valuable piece of property. She became an indispensable person in the household, officiating in all capacities, from cook and wet-nurse to seamstress. She was much praised for her cooking; and her nice crackers became so famous in the neighborhood that many people were desirous of obtaining them. In consequence of numerous requests of this kind, she asked permission of her mistress to bake crackers at night, after all the household work was done; and she obtained leave to do it, provided she would clothe herself and the children from the profits. Upon these terms, after working hard all day for her mistress, she began her midnight bakings, assisted by her two oldest children. The business proved profitable; and each year she laid by a little, to create a fund for the purchase of her children. Her master died, and his property was divided among the heirs. My grandmother remained in the service of his widow, as a slave. Her children were divided among her master's children; but as she had five, Benjamin, the youngest, was sold, in order that the heirs might have an equal portion of dollars and cents. There was so little difference in our ages, that he always seemed to me more like a brother than an uncle. He was a bright, handsome lad, nearly white; for he inherited the complexion my grandmother had derived from Anglo-Saxon ancestors. His sale was a terrible blow to his mother; but she was naturally hopeful, and she went to work with redoubled energy, trusting in time to be able to purchase her children. One day, her mistress begged the loan of three hundred dollars from the little fund she had laid up from the proceeds of her baking. She promised to pay her soon; but as no promise or writing given to a slave is legally binding, she was obliged to trust solely to her honor.

In my master's house very little attention was paid to the slaves' meals. If they could catch a bit of food while it was going, well and good. But I gave myself no trouble on that score; for on my various errands I passed my grandmother's house, and she always had surrounded herself with the necessaries of life. She would have been happy, if her family could have shared them with her. There remained to her but three children and two grandchildren; and they were all slaves. Most earnestly did she strive to make us feel that it was the will of God;

that He had seen fit to place us under such circumstances, and though it seemed hard, we ought to pray for contentment. It was a beautiful faith, coming from a mother who could not call her children her own. But I and Benjamin, her youngest boy, condemned it. It appeared to us that it was much more according to the will of God that we should be free, and able to make a home for ourselves, as she had done. There we always found balsam for our troubles. She was so loving, so sympathizing! She always met us with a smile, and listened with patience to all our sorrows. She spoke so hopefully, that unconsciously the clouds gave place to sunshine. There was a grand big oven there, too, that baked bread and nice things for the town; and we knew there was always a choice bit in store for us. But even the charms of that old oven failed to reconcile us to our hard lot. Benjamin was now a tall, handsome lad, strongly and gracefully made, and with a spirit too bold and daring for a slave.

One day his master attempted to flog him for not obeying his summons quickly enough. Benjamin resisted, and in the struggle threw his master down. To raise his hand against a white man was a great crime, according to the laws of the state; and to avoid a cruel, public whipping, Benjamin hid himself and made his escape. My grandmother was absent, visiting an old friend in the country, when this happened. When she returned, and found her youngest child had fled, great was her sorrow. But, with characteristic piety, she said, "God's will be done." Every morning she inquired whether any news had been heard from her boy. Alas! news did come, – sad news. The master received a letter, and was rejoicing over the capture of his human chattel.

That day seems to me but as yesterday, so well do I remember it. I saw him led through the streets in chains to jail. His face was ghastly pale, but full of determination. He had sent some one to his mother's house to ask her not to come to meet him. He said the sight of her distress would take from him all self-control. Her heart yearned to see him, and she went; but she screened herself in the crowd, that it might be as her child had said.

We were not allowed to visit him. But we had known the jailer for years, and he was a kind-hearted man. At midnight he opened the door for my grandmother and myself to enter, in disguise. When we entered the cell, not a sound broke the stillness. "Benjamin," whispered my grandmother. No answer. "Benjamin!" said she, again, in faltering tone. There was a jingling of chains. The moon had just risen, and cast an uncertain light through the bars. We knelt down and took Benjamin's cold hands in ours. Sobs alone were heard, while she wept upon his neck. At last Benjamin's lips were unsealed. Mother and son talked together. He asked her pardon for the suffering he had caused her. She told him she had nothing to forgive; that she could not blame him for wanting to be free. He told her that he broke away from his captors, and was about to throw himself into the river, but thoughts of her came over him and arrested the movement. She asked him if he did not also think of God. He replied: "No, mother, I did not. When a man is hunted like a wild beast, he forgets that there *is* a God."

The pious mother shuddered, as she said: "Don't talk so, Benjamin. Try to be humble, and put your trust in God."

"I wish I had some of your goodness," he replied. "You bear everything patiently, just as though you thought it was all right. I wish I could."

She told him it had not always been so with her; that once she was like him; but when sore troubles came upon her, and she had no arm to lean upon, she learned to call on God, and he lightened her burdens. She besought him to do so likewise.

The jailer came to tell us we had overstayed our time, and we were obliged to hurry away. Grandmother went to the master and tried to intercede for her son. But he was inexorable. He said Benjamin should be made an example of. That he should be kept in jail till he was sold. For three months he remained within the walls of the prison, during which time grandmother secretly conveyed him changes of clothes, and as often as possible carried him something warm for supper, accompanied with some little luxury for her friend the jailer. He was finally sold to a slave-trader from New Orleans. When they fastened irons upon his wrists to drive him off with the coffle, it was heart-rending to hear the groans of that poor mother, as she clung to the Benjamin of her family, – her youngest, her pet. He was pale and thin now, from hardships and long confinement; but still his good looks were so observable that the slave-trader remarked he would give any price for the handsome lad, if he were a girl. We, who knew so well what Slavery was, were thankful that he was not.

Grandmother stifled her grief, and with strong arms and unwavering faith set to work to purchase freedom for Benjamin. She knew the slave-trader would charge three times as much as he gave for him; but she was not discouraged. She employed a lawyer to write to New Orleans, and try to negotiate the business for her. But word came that Benjamin was missing; he had run away again.

Philip, my grandmother's only remaining son, inherited his mother's intelligence. His mistress sometimes trusted him to go with a cargo to New York. One of these occasions occurred not long after Benjamin's second escape. Through God's good providence the brothers met in the streets of New York. It was a happy meeting, though Benjamin was very pale and thin; for on his way from bondage he had been taken violently ill, and brought nigh unto death. Eagerly he embraced his brother, exclaiming: "O Phil! here I am at last. I came nigh dying when I was almost in sight of freedom; and O how I prayed that I might live just to get one breath of free air! And here I am. In the old jail, I used to wish I was dead. But life is worth something now, and it would be hard to die." He begged his brother not to go back to the South, but to stay and work with him till they earned enough to buy their relatives.

Philip replied: "It would kill mother if I deserted her. She has pledged her house, and is working harder than ever to buy you. Will you be bought?"

"Never!" replied Benjamin, in his resolute tone. "When I have got so far out of their clutches, do you suppose, Phil, that I would ever let them be paid one red cent? Do you think I would consent to have mother turned out of her hard-earned home in her old age? And she never to see me after she had bought me? For you know, Phil, she would never leave the South while any of her children or grandchildren remained in Slavery. What a good mother! Tell her to buy *you*, Phil. You have always been a comfort to her; and I have always been making her trouble."

Philip furnished his brother with some clothes, and gave him what money he had. Benjamin pressed his hand, and said, with moistened eyes, "I part from all my kindred." And so it proved. We never heard from him afterwards.

When Uncle Philip came home, the first words he said, on entering the house, were: "O mother, Ben is free! I have seen him in New York." For a moment she seemed bewildered. He laid his hand gently on her shoulder and repeated what he had said. She raised her hands devoutly, and exclaimed, "God be praised! Let us thank Him." She dropped on her knees and poured forth her heart in prayer. When she grew calmer, she begged Philip to sit down and repeat every word her son had said. He told her all, except that Benjamin had nearly died on the way and was looking very pale and thin.

Still the brave old women toiled on to accomplish the rescue of her remaining children. After a while she succeeded in buying Philip, for whom she paid eight hundred dollars, and came home with the precious document that secured his freedom. The happy mother and son sat by her hearthstone that night, telling how proud they were of each other, and how they would prove to the world that they could take care of themselves, as they had long taken care of others. We all concluded by saying, "He that is *willing* to be a slave, let him be a slave."

My grandmother had still one daughter remaining in Slavery. She belonged to the same master that I did; and a hard time she had of it. She was a good soul, this old Aunt Nancy. She did all she could to supply the place of my lost mother to us orphans. She was the *factotum* in our master's household. She was housekeeper, waiting-maid, and everything else: nothing went on well without her, by day or by night. She wore herself out in their service. Grandmother toiled on, hoping to purchase release for her. But one evening word was brought that she had been suddenly attacked with paralysis, and grandmother hastened to her bedside. Mother and daughter had always been devotedly attached to each other; and now they looked lovingly and earnestly into each other's eyes, longing to speak of secrets that weighed on the hearts of both. She lived but two days, and on the last day she was speechless. It was sad to witness the grief of her bereaved mother. She had always been strong to bear, and religious faith still supported her; but her dark life had become still darker, and age and trouble were leaving deep traces on her withered face. The poor old back was fitted to its burden. It bent under it, but did not break.

Uncle Philip asked permission to bury his sister at his own expense; and slaveholders are always ready to grant *such* favors to slaves and their relatives. The arrangements were very plain, but perfectly respectable. It was talked of by the slaves as a mighty grand funeral. If Northern travellers had been passing through the place, perhaps they would have described it as a beautiful tribute to the humble dead, a touching proof of the attachment between slaveholders and their slaves; and very likely the mistress would have confirmed this impression, with her handkerchief at her eyes. *We* could have told them how the poor old mother had toiled, year after year, to buy her son Philip's right to his own earnings; and how that same Philip had paid the expenses of the funeral which they regarded as doing so much credit to the master.

There were some redeeming features in our hard destiny. Very pleasant are my recollections of the good old lady who paid fifty dollars for the purpose of making my grandmother free, when she stood on the auction-block. She loved this old lady, whom we all called Miss Fanny. She often took tea at grandmother's house. On such occasions, the table was spread with a snow-white cloth, and the china cups and silver spoons were taken from the old-fashioned buffet. There were hot muffins, tea-rusks, and delicious sweetmeats. My grandmother always had a supply of such articles, because she furnished the ladies of the town with such things for their parties. She kept two cows for that purpose, and the fresh cream was Miss Fanny's delight. She invariably repeated that it was the very best in town. The old ladies had cosey times together. They would work and chat, and sometimes, while talking over old times, their spectacles would get dim with tears, and would have to be taken off and wiped. When Miss Fanny bade us "Good by", her bag was always filled with grandmother's best cakes, and she was urged to come again soon.

[Here follows a long account of persecutions endured by the granddaughter, who tells this story. She finally made her escape, after encountering great dangers and hardships. The faithful old grandmother concealed her for a long time at great risk to them both, during which time she tried in vain to buy free papers for her. At last there came a chance to escape in a vessel Northward bound. She goes on to say:]

"All arrangements were made for me to go on board at dusk. Grandmother came to me with a small bag of money, which she wanted me to take. I begged her to keep at least part of it; but she insisted, while her tears fell fast, that I should take the whole. 'You may be sick among strangers,' said she; 'and they would send you to the poor-house to die.' Ah, that good grandmother! Though I had the blessed prospect of freedom before me, I felt dreadfully sad at leaving forever that old homestead, that had received and sheltered me in so many sorrows. Grandmother took me by the hand and said, 'My child, let us pray.' We knelt down together, with my arm clasped round the faithful, loving old friend I was about to leave forever. On no other occasion has it been my lot to listen to so fervent a supplication for mercy and protection. It thrilled through my heart and inspired me with trust in God. I staggered into the street, faint in body, though strong of purpose. I did not look back upon the dear old place, though I felt that I should never see it again."

[The granddaughter found friends at the North, and, being uncommonly quick in her perceptions, she soon did much to supply the deficiencies of early education. While leading a worthy, industrious life in New York, she twice very narrowly escaped becoming a victim to the infamous Fugitive Slave Law. A noble-hearted lady purchased her freedom, and thereby rescued her from further danger. She thus closes the story of her venerable ancestor: –]

"My grandmother lived to rejoice in the knowledge of my freedom; but not long afterward a letter came to me with a black seal. It was from a friend at the South, who informed me that she had gone 'where the wicked cease from troubling, and where the weary are at rest.' Among the gloomy recollections of my life in bondage come tender memories of that good grandmother, like a few fleecy clouds floating over a dark and troubled sea.

Ann Plato
c. 1820–?

Born in Hartford, Connecticut, she was a teacher in the (Black) Zion Methodist Church School there. Her Essays; Including Biographies and Miscellaneous Pieces in Prose and Poetry (1841), somewhat moralistic in tone, is thought to be the only essay collection by a Black writer issued between 1840 and 1865. Little is known about her, but the book's introduction by Rev. W. C. Pennington, pastor of the Colored Congregational Church of Hartford, suggests that she was aged about twenty, although some of the poetry may have been written in her early teens. "To the First of August" deals with a theme rare in her work, slavery and its abolition by the British in the West Indies in 1838.

To The First of August

Britannia's isles proclaim
  That freedom is their theme;
And we do view those honored lands
  with soul-delighting mien.

And unto those they held in gloom,
  Gave ev'ry one their right;
They did disdain fell slavery's shade,
  And trust in freedom's light.

Then unto ev'ry British blood,
  Their noble worth revere,
And think them ever noble men,
  And like them hence appear.

And when on Britain's isles remote
  We're then in freedom's bounds,
And while we stand on British ground,
  "You're free – you're free!" resounds.

Lift ye that country's banner high,
   And may it nobly wave,
Until beneath the azure sky,
   Man shall be no more a slave.

And, oh, when youth's ecstatic hour,
   When winds and torrents foam,
And passion's glowing noon are past
   To bless that free-born home;

Then let us celebrate the day
   And lay the thought to heart,
And teach the rising race the way
   That they may not depart.

Harriet Tubman

?c. 1821–1913

Born to slave parents in Dorchester County, Maryland, she suffered a brutal childhood, at the age of thirteen being injured by a rock thrown by her master, as a result of which she had occasional blackouts throughout her life. She married a freedman in 1844 or 1845, but they soon separated. In 1849 she escaped to the North and for the next decade devoted her energies and ingenuity to rescuing over 300 slaves in nineteen trips to the South and Canada, as a conductor of what was known as the Underground Railroad, becoming a legendary figure with a $40,000 reward on her head. She was known as the Moses of her people, for delivering them to "the promised land" of freedom. She said: "I had seen their tears and sighs, and I had heard their groans, and I would give every drop of blood in my veins

*to free them." Later she had three years of outstanding war service
as spy, scout, guerrilla leader and nurse for the Union army. Her
most spectacular scouting exploit was when she piloted Colonel James
Montgomery and his Black troops up the Combahee River, rescuing 756
slaves. She attended women's suffrage conventions and participated in
organizing the National Federation of Afro-American Women. Her letter
below refers to her efforts to raise funds through selling reprints of
her biography. She was belatedly granted a government pension, which
helped her support a home for aged freedmen in Auburn, New York,
where she lived until her death in relative poverty.*

Dictated letter to Mary Wright

Syracuse, N.Y.
May 29, 1896

M RS Mary Wright,
   I received the trunk and package which you sent me and I am very
thankful to you for them. I have been appointed by the pastors of the first M.E.
and the A.M.E. [African Methodist Episcopal] Churches of Auburn, to collect
clothes for the destitute colored children and the things which you sent are
very acceptable. . . .
   I would like for you to see Miss Edna Cheny [*sic*] for me. I would like to
get out another edition of books. The editor says he can publish five hundred
books for $100 before he destroyed the plates. I would like to have another set
of books published to take to the Methodists Centennial at New York this fall. I
can raise fifty dollars and if Miss Cheny can see Mr Sanburn [*sic*] and some of
those anti-slavery friends and have them raise fifty dollars more that will enable
me to get the books out before the editor destroys the plate. If they will help me
raise the money they can hold the books until I can sell enough to pay them back.
I would like to come and see you but my brother is sick and I cannot very well
leave him at this time. I am not doing anything now as I am not able.
   Miss Cheny has done very well by me and I do not wish to ask for money
by [but] if through her influence I can get the friends to help me I shall be very
thankful. My home is incorperated [*sic*] for an asylum for aged colored people
that will hold the mortage and I wont be troubled now. Remember me in your
prayers as your father did before you. If I never see you again I hope to see you
in the kingdom. Good by, God bless you all, from your friend who loves you all,

Harriet Tubman

Harriet Tubman's Petition, 1898

I AM about 75 years of age. I was born and reared in Dorchester County, Md. My maiden name was Araminta Ross. [S]ometime prior to the late War of the rebellion I married John Tubman who died in the State of Maryland on the 30th day of September, 1867. I married Nelson Davis, a soldier of the late war, on the 18th day of March, 1869, at Auburn, N.Y.

I furnished the original papers in my claim to one Charles P. Wood, then of Auburn, N.Y., who died several years ago. Said Wood made copies of said original papers which are hereunto annexed. I was informed by said Wood that he sent said original papers to one James Barrett, an attorney on 4½ Street, Washington, D.C., and I was told by the wife of said Barrett that she handed the original papers to the Hon. C. D. MacDougall, then a member of the House of Representatives.

My claim against the U.S. is for three years' service as nurse and cook in hospitals, and as commander of Several men (eight or nine) as scouts during the late war of the Rebellion, under directions and orders of Edwin M. Stanton, Secretary of War, and of several Generals.

I claim for my services above named the sum of Eighteen hundred dollars. The annexed copies have recently been read over to me and are true to the best of my knowledge information and belief.

I further declare that I have interest in said case and am concerned in it's prosecution and allowance.

her

Harriet   ×   Davis

mark

late Harriet Tubman

Henrietta Fullor

fl. 1849

I n 1822, the first Black emigrants from America were settled on a stretch of coastal land in West Africa near Mesurado River. The colony was called Liberia and its capital, Monrovia, was named after US President James Monroe, a slave-owner. As Liberian writer Zinnah Tamia Porte has observed (Guardian, 24 September 1990): "The country was created less out of American philanthropy than a fear of emancipated Blacks subversively leading slaves into revolt." The American Colonization Society (ACS), a white organization established in 1817 to devise schemes to rid America of troublesome Blacks by deportation, had by 1867 transported to Africa 5,000 freeborn Black Americans and 7,000 ex-slaves, many emancipated by their masters on condition that they go to Africa (there they joined 7,000 other Blacks from Barbados, Ghana and Sierra Leone, and several thousand Congolese rescued by anti-slavers from ships bound for the USA or Britain). An active participant in the ACS after 1830 was John McDonogh of Louisiana, owner of some 200 slaves, whom he claimed to treat well. On 11 June 1842 more than 80 of them sailed for Liberia. In a letter to the New Orleans Commercial Bulletin a month later, he exposed the real motives behind his colonization plans: "My own opinion is that without separation of the races, extermination of one or other must inevitably take place. The two races can never inhabit together in a state of equality in the same country. They may for a short time live together in the capacity of Master and slave, but as equals and Brethren never. . . ." Once in Africa, many of his ex-slaves corresponded with him. Some addressed him as "Father", "Parent", "Beloved Benefactor", signed themselves "Faithful servant" and "affectionate son", even retained his surname – responding perhaps sincerely to his paternalism, perhaps in a cynical exercise to elicit material assistance. Henrietta Fullor's dignified letter (in the John McDonogh Papers at Tulane University) – written two years after Liberia became an independent republic under a freeborn president from Oberlin College in the USA – is reproduced here.

Letter to a Slaveholder

St Pauls River New Orleans, Liberia
October 24th 1849.

Mr John McDonough [*sic*],

D EAR Sir,
    Having an opportunity of forwarding letters to the United States by the Liberia Packet which will sail in a few days I embrace this good opportunity of writing you by her.

This Sir I am happy to say leave in the enjoyment of good health also my family and wishing these times may find you and yours enjoying the same blessing. Since we have heard from you we have had some deaths out of our member. They are Mr James Fullor, Alexander Jackson, Manuel Fullor and Catherine Travis, the rest of our number are all well and doing well. We are doing pretty well in the Agricultural line growing coffee, rice, sugar and we have no right to complain of our situation it is true when we first landed after the expiration of the six months maintainance for the Society then we found it a little difficult to do as well as we could wish yet we have partially surmounted the difficulties and we are perfectly satisfied. We now are in the strictest sense of the word Free. We have a church in our village where we worship God and a school house where our children are sent daily to receive instructions.

The individuals whose death I have mentioned died in the triumps of faith and requested us to meet them in heaven they left abright testimony behind them of being heirs to the Kingdom above.

You will please rember us to all acquaintances and especially to our colored friends and say to them that Liberia is the home of our race and as good a country as they can find. Industry and perserverance is only required to make a man happy and wealthy in this our Adopted Country, its soil yeilds abundant harvest to the husbandmon, its climate is healthy its laws are founded upon justice and equity here, we sit under our own vine and Palm Tree, we all enjoy the same rights and priviledges that our white brethren does in America it is our only home.

It has been some time since I received a letter from you I would be happy to hear from you at all times, with these few lines I close wishing God in his alwise providence to continue and bless you and all the friends in America and also to continue to extend his hands of care over us and at last bring us to live with him where parting no more shall be.

Respectfully yours &c.
Henrietta Fullor

Frances Ellen Watkins Harper

1825–1911

Born in Baltimore, Maryland, only child of free parents, she was orphaned when she was three and was raised by an aunt and uncle. Self-supporting by age thirteen and largely self-educated, she published in 1845 a book of poetry and prose – Forest Leaves (alternatively called Autumn Leaves), of which no copies survive – going on to publish a dozen books between 1851 and her death. Iola LeRoy; or Shadows Uplifted (extracted here) was one of the first novels by a Black woman, written when she was sixty-seven and published in 1892. Writing in a mostly traditional style, she was the most popular woman poet of her day; Moses (1854) went through twenty editions by 1871 and her Poems on Miscellaneous Subjects (1857) sold 10,000 copies in its first five years. She was active in the movements for abolition, temperance and women's rights, and raised the question of whether Black authors should dwell on racial problems or address wider issues. She lectured widely and after the Civil War travelled in southern USA, holding meetings for Black women. Her story "The Two Offers" was the first known to have been published by a Black woman, in 1859, the same year Harriet E. Wilson became the first recorded African-American novelist._

She's Free!

How say that by law we may torture and chase
A woman whose crime is the hue of her face? –
With her step on the ice, and her arm on her child,
The danger was fearful, the pathway was wild. . . .
But she's free! yes, free from the land where the slave,
From the hand of oppression, must rest in the grave;
Where bondage and blood, where scourges and chains,
Have placed on our banner indelible stains. . . .
The bloodhounds have miss'd the scent of her way,
The hunter is rifled and foiled of his prey,
The cursing of men and clanking of chains
Make sounds of strange discord on Liberty's plains. . . .
Oh! poverty, danger and death she can brave,
For the child of her love is no longer a slave.

The Slave Auction

The sale began – young girls were there,
  Defenceless in their wretchedness,
Whose stifled sobs of deep despair
  Revealed their anguish and distress.

And mothers stood with streaming eyes,
  And saw their dearest children sold;
Unheeded rose their bitter cries,
  While tyrants bartered them for gold.

And woman, with her love and truth –
  For these in sable forms may dwell –
Gaz'd on the husband of her youth,
  With anguish none may paint or tell.

And men, whose sole crime was their hue,
  The impress of their Maker's hand,
And frail and shrinking children, too,
  Were gathered in that mournful band.

Ye who have laid your love to rest,
  And wept above their lifeless clay,
Know not the anguish of that breast,
  Whose lov'd are rudely torn away.

Ye may not know how desolate
  Are bosoms rudely forced to part,
And how a dull and heavy weight
  Will press the life-drops from the heart.

Bury Me in a Free Land

Make me a grave where'er you will,
In a lowly plain or a lofty hill;
Make it among earth's humblest graves,
But not in a land where men are slaves.

I could not rest, if around my grave
I heard the steps of a trembling slave;
His shadow above my silent tomb
Would make it a place of fearful gloom.

I could not sleep, if I heard the tread
Of a coffle-gang to the shambles led,
And the mother's shriek of wild despair
Rise, like a curse, on the trembling air.

I could not rest, if I saw the lash
Drinking her blood at each fearful gash;
And I saw her babes torn from her breast,
Like trembling doves from their parent nest.

I'd shudder and start, if I heard the bay
Of a bloodhound seizing his human prey;
And I heard the captive plead in vain,
As they bound, afresh, his galling chain.

If I saw young girls from their mother's arms
Bartered and sold for their youthful charms,
My eye would flash with a mournful flame,
My death-pale cheek grow red with shame.

I would sleep, dear friends, where bloated Might
Can rob no man of his dearest right;
My rest shall be calm in any grave
Where none can call his brother a slave.

I ask no monument, proud and high,
To arrest the gaze of the passers by;
All that my yearning spirit craves
Is – *Bury me not in a land of slaves!*

A Double Standard

Do you blame me that I loved him?
    If when standing all alone
I cried for bread, a careless world
    Pressed to my lips a stone?

Do you blame me that I loved him,
    That my heart beat glad and free,
When he told me in the sweetest tones
    He loved but only me?

Can you blame me that I did not see,
    Beneath his burning kiss,
The serpent's wiles, nor even less hear
    The deadly adder hiss?

Can you blame me that my heart grew cold,
   That the tempted, tempter turned –
When he was feted and caressed
   And I was coldly spurned?

Would you blame him, when you drew from me
   Your dainty robes aside,
If he with gilded baits should claim
   Your fairest as his bride?

Would you blame the world if it should press
   On him a civic crown;
And see me struggling in the depth,
   Then harshly press me down?

Crime has no sex and yet today
   I wear the brand of shame;
Whilst he amid the gay and proud
   Still bears an honored name.

Can you blame me if I've learned to think
   Your hate of vice a sham,
When you so coldly crushed me down,
   And then excused the man?

Would you blame me if tomorrow
   The coroner should say,
A wretched girl, outcast, forlorn,
   Has thrown her life away?

Yes, blame me for my downward course,
   But oh! remember well,
Within your homes you press the hand
   That led me down to hell.

I'm glad God's ways are not our ways,
   He does not see as man;
Within His love I know there's room
   For those whom others ban.

I think before His great white throne,
   His throne of spotless light,
That whited sepulchres shall wear
   The hue of endless night.

That I who fell, and he who sinned,
　　Shall reap as we have sown;
That each the burden of his loss
　　Must bear and bear alone.

No golden weights can turn the scale
　　Of justice in His sight;
And what is wrong in woman's life
　　In man's cannot be right.

Miss Watkins and the Constitution

(from letter published in *National Anti-Slavery Standard*, 9 April 1859)

I NEVER saw so clearly the nature and intent of the Constitution before. Oh, was it not strangely inconsistent that men, fresh, so fresh, from the baptism of the Revolution should make such concessions to the foul spirit of Despotism! that, when fresh from gaining their own liberty, they could permit the African slave trade – could let their national flag hang a sign of death on Guinea's coast and Congo's shore! Twenty-one years the slave-ships of the new Republic could gorge the sea monsters with their prey; twenty-one years of mourning and desolation for the children of the tropics, to gratify the avarice and cupidity of men styling themselves free! And then the dark intent of the fugitive clause veiled under words so specious that a stranger unacquainted with our nefarious government would not know that such a thing was meant by it. Alas for these fatal concessions. They remind me of the fabulous teeth sown by Cadmus – they rise, armed men, to smite. Is it a great mystery to you why these things are permitted? Wait, my brother, awhile; the end is not yet. The Psalmist was rather puzzled when he saw the wicked in power and spreading like a Bay tree; but how soon their end! Rest assured that, as nations and individuals, God will do right by us, and we should not ask of either God or man to do less than that. In the freedom of man's will I read the philosophy of his crimes, and the impossibility of his actions having a responsible moral character without it; and hence the continuance of slavery does not strike me as being so very mysterious.

From

Iola Leroy; or Shadows Uplifted

NORTHERN EXPERIENCE

"UNCLE Robert," said Iola, after she had been North several weeks, "I have a theory that every woman ought to know how to earn her own living. I believe that a great amount of sin and misery springs from the weakness and inefficiency of women."

"Perhaps that's so, but what are you going to do about it?"

"I am going to join the great rank of bread-winners. Mr Waterman has advertised for a number of saleswomen, and I intend to make application."

"When he advertises for help he means white women," said Robert.

"He said nothing about color," responded Iola.

"I don't suppose he did. He doesn't expect any colored girl to apply."

"Well, I think I could fill the place. At least I should like to try. And I do not think when I apply that I am in duty bound to tell him my great-grandmother was a negro."

"Well, child, there is no necessity for you to go out to work. You are perfectly welcome here, and I hope that you feel so."

"Oh, I certainly do. But still I would rather earn my own living."

That morning Iola applied for the situation, and, being prepossessing in her appearance, she obtained it.

For a while everything went as pleasantly as a marriage bell. But one day a young colored lady, well-dressed and well-bred in her manner, entered the store. It was an acquaintance which Iola had formed in the colored church which she attended. Iola gave her a few words of cordial greeting, and spent a few moments chatting with her. The attention of the girls who sold at the same counter was attracted, and their suspicion awakened. Iola was a stranger in that city. Who was she, and who were her people? At last it was decided that one of the girls should act as a spy, and bring what information she could concerning Iola.

The spy was successful. She found out that Iola was living in a good neighborhood, but that none of the neighbors knew her. The man of the house was very fair, but there was an old woman whom Iola called "Grandma," and she was unmistakably colored. The story was sufficient. If that were true, Iola must be colored, and she should be treated accordingly.

Without knowing the cause, Iola noticed a chill in the social atmosphere of the store, which communicated itself to the cash-boys, and they treated her so insolently that her situation became very uncomfortable. She saw the proprietor, resigned her position, and asked for and obtained a letter of recommendation to another merchant who had advertised for a saleswoman.

In applying for the place, she took the precaution to inform her employer that she was colored. It made no difference to him; but he said:–

"Don't say anything about it to the girls. They might not be willing to work with you."

Iola smiled, did not promise, and accepted the situation. She entered upon her duties, and proved quite acceptable as a saleswoman.

One day, during an interval in business, the girls began to talk of their respective churches, and the question was put to Iola:–

"Where do you go to church?"

"I go," she replied, "to Rev. River's church, corner of Eighth and L Streets."

"Oh, no; you must be mistaken. There is no church there except a colored one."

"That is where I go."

"Why do you go there?"

"Because I liked it when I came here, and joined it."

"A member of a colored church? What under heaven possessed you to do such a thing?"

"Because I wished to be with my own people."

Here the interrogator stopped, and looked surprised and pained, and almost instinctively moved a little farther from her. After the store was closed, the girls had an animated discussion, which resulted in the information being sent to Mr Cohen that Iola was a colored girl, and that they protested against her being continued in his employ. Mr Cohen yielded to the pressure, and informed Iola that her services were no longer needed.

When Robert came home in the evening, he found that Iola had lost her situation, and was looking somewhat discouraged.

"Well, uncle," she said, "I feel out of heart. It seems as if the prejudice pursues us through every avenue of life, and assigns us the lowest places."

"That is so," replied Robert, thoughtfully.

"And yet I am determined," said Iola, "to win for myself a place in the fields of labor. I have heard of a place in New England, and I mean to try for it, even if I only stay a few months."

"Well, if you *will* go, say nothing about your color."

"Uncle Robert, I see no necessity for proclaiming that fact on the housetop. Yet I am resolved that nothing shall tempt me to deny it. The best blood in my veins is African blood, and I am not ashamed of it."

"Hurrah for you!" exclaimed Robert, laughing heartily.

As Iola wished to try the world for herself, and so be prepared for any emergency, her uncle and grandmother were content to have her go to New England. The town to which she journeyed was only a few hours' ride from the city of P—, and Robert, knowing that there is no teacher like experience, was willing that Iola should have the benefit of her teaching.

Iola, on arriving in H—, sought the firm, and was informed that her services were needed. She found it a pleasant and lucrative position. There was only one drawback – her boarding place was too far from her work. There was an institution conducted by professed Christian women, which was for the special use of respectable young working girls. This was in such a desirable location that she called at the house to engage board.

The matron conducted her over the house, and grew so friendly in the interview that she put her arm around her, and seemed to look upon Iola as a desirable accession to the home. But, just as Iola was leaving, she said to the matron: "I must be honest with you; I am a colored woman."

Swift as light a change passed over the face of the matron. She withdrew her arm from Iola, and said: "I must see the board of managers about it."

When the board met, Iola's case was put before them, but they decided not to receive her. And these women, professors of a religion which taught, "If ye have respect to persons ye commit sin," virtually shut the door in her face because of the outcast blood in her veins.

Considerable feeling was aroused by the action of these women, who, to say the least, had not put their religion in the most favorable light.

Iola continued to work for the firm until she received letters from her mother and uncle, which informed her that her mother, having arranged her affairs in the South, was ready to come North. She then resolved to return to the city of P—, to be ready to welcome her mother on her arrival.

Iola arrived in time to see that everything was in order for her mother's reception. Her room was furnished neatly, but with those touches of beauty that womanly hands are such adepts in giving. A few charming pictures adorned the walls, and an easy chair stood waiting to receive the travel-worn mother. Robert and Iola met her at the depot; and grandma was on her feet at the first sound of the bell, opened the door, clasped Marie to her heart, and nearly fainted for joy.

"Can it be possible dat dis is my little Marie?" she exclaimed.

It did seem almost almost impossible to realize that this faded woman, with pale cheeks and prematurely whitened hair, was the rosy-cheeked child from whom she had been parted more than thirty years.

"Well," said Robert, after the first joyous greeting was over, "love is a very good thing, but Marie has had a long journey and needs something that will stick by the ribs. How about dinner, mother?"

"It's all ready," said Mrs Johnson.

After Marie had gone to her room and changed her dress, she came down and partook of the delicious repast which her mother and Iola had prepared for her.

In a few days Marie was settled in the home, and was well pleased with the change. The only drawback to her happiness was the absence of her son, and she expected him to come North after the closing of his school.

"Uncle Robert," said Iola, after her mother had been with them several weeks, "I am tired of being idle."

"What's the matter now?" asked Robert. "You are surely not going East again, and leave your mother?"

"Oh, I hope not," said Marie, anxiously. "I have been so long without you."

"No, mamma, I am not going East. I can get suitable employment here in the city of P—."

"But, Iola," said Robert, "you have tried, and been defeated. Why subject yourself to the same experience again?"

"Uncle Robert, I think that every woman should have some skill or art which would insure her at least a comfortable support. I believe there would be less unhappy marriages if labor were more honored among women."

"Well, Iola," said her mother, "what is your skill?"

"Nursing. I was very young when I went into the hospital, but I succeeded so well that the doctor said I must have been a born nurse. Now, I see by the papers, that a gentleman who has an invalid daughter wants some one who can be a nurse and companion for her, and I mean to apply for the situation. I do not think, if I do my part well in that position, that the blood in my veins will be any bar to my success."

A troubled look stole over Marie's face. She sighed faintly, but made no remonstrance. And so it was decided that Iola should apply for the situation.

Iola made application, and was readily accepted. Her patient was a frail girl of fifteen summers, who was ill with a low fever. Iola nursed her carefully, and soon had the satisfaction of seeing her restored to health. During her stay, Mr Cloten, the father of the invalid, had learned some of the particulars of Iola's Northern experience as a bread-winner, and he resolved to give her employment in his store when her services were no longer needed in the house. As soon as a vacancy occurred he gave Iola a place in his store.

The morning she entered on her work he called his employés together, and told them that Miss Iola had colored blood in her veins, but that he was going to employ her and give her a desk. If any one objected to working with her, he or she could step to the cashier's desk and receive what was due. Not a man remonstrated, not a woman demurred; and Iola at last found a place in the great army of bread-winners, which the traditions of her blood could not affect.

"How did you succeed?" asked Mrs Cloten of her husband, when he returned to dinner.

"Admirably! 'Everything is lovely and the goose hangs high,' I gave my employés understand that they could leave if they did not wish to work with Miss Leroy. Not one of them left, or showed any disposition to rebel."

"I am very glad," said Mrs Cloten. "I am ashamed of the way she has been treated in our city, when seeking to do her share in the world's work. I am glad that you were brave enough to face this cruel prejudice, and give her a situation."

"Well, my dear, do not make me a hero for a single act. I am grateful for the care Miss Leroy gave our Daisy. Money can buy services, but it cannot purchase tender, loving sympathy. I was also determined to let my employés know that I, not they, commanded my business. So, do not crown me a hero until I have won a niche in the temple of fame. In dealing with Southern prejudice against the negro, we Northerners could do it with better grace if we divested ourselves of our own. We irritate the South by our criticisms, and, while I confess that there is much that is reprehensible in their treatment of colored people, yet if our Northern civilization is higher than theirs we should 'criticize by creation.' We should stamp ourselves on the South, and not let the South stamp itself on us. When we have learned to treat men according to the complexion of their souls, and not the color of their skins, we will have given our best contribution towards the solution of the negro problem."

"I feel, my dear," said Mrs Cloten, "that what you have done is a right step in the right direction, and I hope that other merchants will do the same. We have numbers of business men, rich enough to afford themselves the luxury of a good conscience."

Lucy Delaney
?1820s–?

Her narrative From the Darkness Cometh the Light or Struggles for Freedom *(c. 1891) brings the reader "face to face with but only a few of the painful facts engendered by slavery", telling the story of how her mother Polly was kidnapped as a child in Illinois, taken to St Louis and sold into slavery, but pursued a lawsuit to win freedom in 1844 for herself and her daughter, who had been held in a prison cell for seventeen months. Lucy married Zachariah Delaney in 1849, and they had been together forty-two years at the time she wrote the book, outliving their four children: "yet one consolation was always mine! Our children were born free and died free!"*

From

From the Darkness Cometh the Light, or Struggles for Freedom

CHAPTER I

Soon is the echo and the shadow o'er,
Soon, soon we lie with lid-encumbered eyes
And the great fabrics that we reared before
Crumble to make a dust to hide who dies.

In the year 18—, Mr and Mrs John Woods and Mr and Mrs Andrew Posey lived as one family in the State of Illinois. Living with Mrs Posey was a little negro girl, named Polly Crocket, who had made it her home there, in peace and happiness, for five years. On a dismal night in the month of September, Polly, with four other colored persons, were kidnapped, and, after being securely bound and gagged, were put into a skiff and carried across the Mississippi River to the city of St Louis. Shortly after, these unfortunate negroes were taken up the Missouri River and sold into slavery. Polly was purchased by a farmer, Thomas Botts, with whom she resided for a year, when, overtaken by business reverses, he was obliged to sell all he possessed, including his negroes.

Among those present on the day set apart for the sale was Major Taylor Berry, a wealthy gentleman who had travelled a long distance for the purpose of purchasing a servant girl for his wife. As was the custom, all the negroes were brought out and placed in a line, so that the buyers could examine their good points at leisure. Major Berry was immediately attracted by the bright and alert appearance of Polly, and at once negotiated with the trader, paid the price agreed upon, and started for home to present his wife with this flesh and blood commodity, which money could so easily procure in our vaunted land of freedom.

Mrs Fanny Berry was highly pleased with Polly's manner and appearance, and concluded to make a seamstress of her. Major Berry had a mulatto servant, who was as handsome as an Apollo, and when he and Polly met each other, day after day, the natural result followed, and in a short time, with the full consent of Major Berry and his wife, were married. Two children were the fruit of this marriage, my sister Nancy and myself, Lucy A. Delaney.

While living in Franklin county, Major Berry became involved in a quarrel with some gentleman, and a duel was resorted to, to settle difficulty and avenge some fancied insult. The major arranged his affairs and made his will, leaving his negroes to his wife during her life-time and at her death they were to be free; this was his expressed wish.

My father accompanied Major Berry to New Madrid, where the fatal duel was fought, and stayed by him until the end came, received his last sigh, his last words, and closed his dying eyes, and afterwards conveyed the remains of his best friend to the bereaved family with a sad heart. Though sympathizing deeply with them in their affliction, my father was much disturbed as to what disposition would be made of him, and after Major Berry was consigned with loving hands to his last resting place, these haunting thoughts obtruded, even in his sleeping hours.

A few years after, Major Berry's widow married Robert Wash, an eminent lawyer, who afterwards became Judge of the Supreme Court. One child was born to them, who, when she grew to womanhood, became Mrs Francis W. Goode, whom I shall always hold in grateful remembrance as long as life lasts, and God bless her in her old age, is my fervent prayer for her kindness to me, a poor little slave girl!

We lived in the old "Wash" mansion some time after the marriage of the Judge, until their daughter Frances was born. How well I remember those happy days! Slavery had no horror then for me, as I played about the place, with the same joyful freedom as the little white children. With mother, father and sister, a pleasant home and surroundings, what happier child than I!

As I carelessly played away the hours, mother's smiles would fade away, and her brow contract into a heavy frown. I wondered much thereat, but the time came – ah! only too soon, when I learned the secret of her ever-changing face!

CHAPTER II

M RS Wash lost her health, and, on the advice of a physician, went to Pensacola, Florida, accompanied by my mother. There she died, and her body was brought back to St Louis and there interred. After Mrs Wash's death, the troubles of my parents and their children may be said to have really commenced.

Though in direct opposition to the will of Major Berry, my father's quondam master and friend, Judge Wash tore my father from his wife and children and sold him "way down South!"

Slavery! cursed slavery! what crimes has it invoked! and, oh! what retribution has a righteous God visited upon these traders in human flesh! The rivers of tears shed by us helpless ones, in captivity were turned to lakes of blood! How often have we cried in our anguish, "Oh! Lord, how long, how long?" But the handwriting was on the wall, and tardy justice came at last and avenged the woes of an oppressed race! Chickamauga, Shiloh, Atlanta and Gettyburgh, spoke in thunder tones! John Brown's body had indeed marched on, and we, the ransomed ones, glorify God and dedicate ourselves to His service, and acknowledge His greatness and goodness in rescuing us from such bondage as parts husband from wife, the mother from her children, aye, even the babe from her breast!

Major Berry's daughter Mary, shortly after, married H. S. Cox, of Philadelphia, and they went to that city to pass their honeymoon, taking my sister Nancy with them as waiting-maid. When my father was sold South, my mother registered a solemn vow that her children should not continue in slavery all their lives, and she never spared an opportunity to impress it upon us, that we must get our freedom whenever the chance offered. So here was an unlooked-for avenue of escape which presented much that was favorable in carrying out her desire to see Nancy a free woman.

Having been brought up in a free State, mother had learned much to her advantage, which would have been impossible in a slave State, and which she now proposed to turn to account for the benefit of her daughter. So mother instructed my sister not to return with Mr and Mrs Cox, but to run away, as soon as chance offered, to Canada, where a friend of our mother's lived who was also a runaway slave, living in freedom and happiness in Toronto.

As the happy couple wandered from city to city, in search of pleasure, my sister was constantly turning over in her mind various plans of escape. Fortune finally favored Nancy, for on their homeward trip they stopped at Niagara Falls for a few days. In her own words I will describe her escape:

"In the morning, Mr and Mrs Cox went for a drive, telling me that I could have the day to do as I pleased. The shores of Canada had been tantalizing my longing gaze for some days, and I was bound to reach there long before my mistress returned. So I locked up Mrs Cox's trunk and put the key under the pillow, where I was sure she would find it, and I made a strike for freedom! A servant in the hotel gave me all necessary information and even assisted me in getting away. Some kind of a festival was going on, and a large crowd was marching from the rink to the river, headed by a band of music. In such a motley throng I was unnoticed, but was trembling with fear of being detected. It seemed an age before the ferry boat arrived, which at last appeared, enveloped in a gigantic wreath of black smoke. Hastily I embarked, and as the boat stole away into the misty twilight and among crushing fields of ice, though the air was chill and gloomy, I felt the warmth of freedom as I neared the Canada shore. I landed, without question, and found my mother's friend with but little difficulty, who assisted me to get work and support myself. Not long afterwards, I married a prosperous farmer, who provided me with a happy home, where I brought my children into the world without the sin of slavery to strive against."

On the return of Mrs Cox to St Louis she sent for my mother and told her that Nancy had run away. Mother was very thankful, and in her heart arose a prayer of thanksgiving, but outwardly she pretended to be vexed and angry. Oh! the impenetrable mask of these poor black creatures! how much of joy, of sorrow, of misery and anguish have they hidden from their tormentors!

I was a small girl at that time, but remember how wildly mother showed her joy at Nancy's escape when we were alone together. She would dance, clap her hands, and, waving them above her head, would indulge in one of those weird negro melodies, which so charm and fascinate the listener.

Mrs Cox commenced housekeeping on a grand and extended scale, having a large acquaintance, she entertained lavishly. My mother cared for the laundry, and I, who was living with a Mrs Underhill, from New York, and was having rather good times, was compelled to go live with Mrs Cox to mind the baby. My pathway was thorny enough, and though there may be no roses without thorns, I had thorns in plenty with no roses.

I was beginning to plan for freedom, and was forever on the alert for a chance to escape and join my sister. I was then twelve years old, and often talked the matter over with mother and canvassed the probabilities of both of us getting away. No schemes were too wild for us to consider! Mother was especially restless, because she was a free woman up to the time of her being kidnapped, so the injustice and weight of slavery bore more heavily upon her than upon me. She did not dare to talk it over with anyone for fear that they would sell her further down the river, so I was her only confidant. Mother was always planning and getting ready to go, and while the fire was burning brightly, it but needed a little more provocation to add to the flames.

CHAPTER III

M RS Cox was always very severe and exacting with my mother, and one occasion, when something did not suit her, she turned on mother like a fury, and declared, "I am just tired out with the 'white airs' you put on, and if you don't behave differently, I will make Mr Cox sell you down the river at once."

Although mother turned grey with fear, she presented a bold front and retorted that "she didn't care, she was tired of that place, and didn't like to live there, nohow." This so infuriated Mr Cox that he cried, "How dare a negro say what she liked or what she did not like; and he would show her what he should do."

So, on the day following, he took my mother to an auction-room on Main Street and sold her to the highest bidder, for five hundred and fifty dollars. Oh! God! the pity of it! "In the home of the brave and the land of the free," in the sight of the stars and stripes – that symbol of freedom – sold away from her child, to satisfy the anger of a peevish mistress!

My mother returned to the house to get her few belongings, and straining me to her breast, begged me to be a good girl, that she was going to run away, and would buy me as soon as she could. With all the inborn faith of a child, I believed it most fondly, and when I heard that she had actually made her escape, three weeks after, my heart gave an exultant throb and cried, "God is good!"

A large reward was offered, the bloodhounds (curse them and curse their masters) were set loose on her trail. In the day time she hid in caves and the surrounding woods, and in the night time, guided by the wondrous North Star, that blessed lodestone of a slave people, my mother finally reached Chicago, where she was arrested by the negro-catchers. At this time the Fugitive Slave Law was in full operation, and it was against the law of the whole country to aid and protect an escaped slave; not even a drink of water, for the love of the Master, might be given, and those who dared to do it (and there were many such brave hearts, thank God!) placed their lives in danger.

The presence of bloodhounds and "nigger-catchers" in their midst, created great excitement and scandalized the community. Feeling ran high and hundreds of people gathered together and declared that mother should not be returned to slavery; but fearing that Mr Cox would wreak his vengeance upon me, my mother finally gave herself up to her captors, and returned to St Louis. And so the mothers of Israel have been ever slain through their deepest affections!

After my mother's return, she decided to sue for her freedom, and for that purpose employed a good lawyer. She had ample testimony to prove that she was kidnapped, and it was so fully verified that the jury decided that she was a free woman, and papers were made out accordingly.

In the meanwhile, Miss Martha Berry had married Mr Mitchell and taken me to live with her. I had never been taught to work, as playing with the babies had been my sole occupation; therefore, when Mrs Mitchell commanded me to do the weekly washing and ironing, I had no more idea how it was to be done than Mrs Mitchell herself. But I made the effort to do what she required, and my failure would have been amusing had it not been so appalling. In those days filtering was unknown and the many ways of clearing water were to me an unsolved riddle. I never had to do it, so it never concerned me how the clothes were ever washed clean.

As the Mississippi water was even muddier than now, the results of my washing can be better imagined than described. After soaking and boiling the clothes in its earthy depths, for a couple of days, in vain attempt to get them clean, and rinsing through several waters, I found the clothes were getting darker and darker, until they nearly approximated my own color. In my despair, I frantically rushed to my mother and sobbed out my troubles on her kindly breast. So in the morning, before the white people had arisen, a friend of my mother came to the house and washed out the clothes. During all this time, Mrs Mitchell was scolding vigorously, saying over and over again, "Lucy, you do not want to work, you are a lazy, good-for-nothing nigger!" I was angry at being called a nigger, and replied, "You don't know nothing, yourself, about it, and you expect a poor ignorant girl to know more than you do yourself; if you have any feeling you would get somebody to teach me, and then I'd do well enough."

She then gave me a wrapper to do up, and told me if I ruined that as I did the other clothes, she would whip me severely. I answered, "You have no business to whip me. I don't belong to you."

My mother had so often told me that she was a free woman and that I should not die a slave, I always had a feeling of independence, which would invariably crop out in these encounters with my mistress; and when I thus spoke, saucily, I must confess, she opened her eyes in angry amazement and cried:

"You *do* belong to me, for my papa left you to me in his will, when you were a baby, and you ought to be ashamed of yourself to talk so to one that you have been raised with; now, you take that wrapper, and if you don't do it up properly, I will bring you up with a round turn."

Without further comment, I took the wrapper, which was too handsome to trust to an inexperienced hand, like Mrs Mitchell very well knew I was, and washed it, with the same direful results as chronicled before. But I could not help it, as heaven is my witness. I was entirely and hopelessly ignorant! But of course my mistress would not believe it, and declared over and over again, that I did it on purpose to provoke her and show my defiance of her wishes. In vain did I disclaim any such intentions. She was bound to carry out her threat of whipping me.

I rebelled against such government, and would not permit her to strike me; she used shovel, tongs and broomstick in vain, as I disarmed her as fast as she picked up each weapon. Infuriated at her failure, my opposition and determination not to be whipped, Mrs Mitchell declared she would report me to Mr Mitchell and have him punish me.

When her husband returned home, she immediately entered a list of complaints against me as long as the moral law, including my failure to wash her clothes properly, and her inability to break my head for it; the last indictment seemed to be the heaviest she could bring against me. I was in the shadow of the doorway as the woman raved, while Mr Mitchell listened patiently until the end of his wife's grievances reached an appeal to him to whip me with the strength that a man alone could possess.

Then he declared. "Martha, this thing of cutting up and slashing servants is something I know nothing about, and positively will not do. I don't believe in slavery, anyhow; it is a curse on this land, and I wish we were well rid of it."

"Mr Mitchell, I will not have that saucy baggage around this house, for if she finds you won't whip her, there will be no living with her, so you shall just sell her, and I insist upon it."

"Well, Martha," he answered, "I found the girl with you when we were married, and as you claim her as yours, I shall not interpose any objections to the disposal of what you choose to call your property, in any manner you see fit, and I will make arrangements for selling her at once."

I distinctly overheard all that was said, and was just as determined not to be sold as I was not to be whipped. My mother's lawyer had told her to caution me never to go out of the city, if, at any time, the white people wanted me to go, so I was quite settled as to my course, in case Mr Mitchell undertook to sell me.

Several days after this conversation took place, Mrs Mitchell, with her baby and nurse, Lucy Wash, made a visit to her grandmother's, leaving orders that I should be sold before her return; so I was not surprised to be ordered by Mr Mitchell to pack up my clothes and get ready to go down the river, for I was to be sold that morning, and leave, on the steamboat Alex Scott, at 3 o'clock in the afternoon.

"Can't I go see my mother, first?" I asked.

"No," he replied, not very gently, "there is no time for that, you can see her when you come back. So hurry up and get ready, and let us have no more words about it!"

How I did hate him! To hear him talk as if I were going to take a pleasure trip, when he knew that if he sold me South, as he intended, I would never see my dear mother again.

However, I hastily ran up stairs and packed my trunk, but my mother's injunction "never to go out of the city" was ever present in my mind.

Mr Mitchell was Superintendent of Indian Affairs, his office being in the dwelling house, and I could hear him giving orders to his clerk, as I ran lightly down the stairs, out of the front door to the street, and with fleet foot, I skimmed the road which led to my mother's door, and, reaching it, stood trembling in every limb with terror and fatigue.

I could not gain admittance, as my mother was away to work and the door was locked. A white woman, living next door, and who was always friendly to mother, told me that she would not return until night. I clasped my hands in despair and cried, "Oh! the white people have sold me, and I had to run away to keep from being sent down the river."

This white lady, whose name I am sorry I cannot remember, sympathized with me, as she knew my mother's story and had written many letters for her, so she offered me the key of her house, which, fortunately, fitted my mother's door, and I was soon inside, cowering with fear in the darkness, magnifying every noise and every passing wind, until my imagination had almost converted the little cottage into a boat, and I was streaming down South, away from my mother, as fast as I could go.

Late at night mother returned, and was told all that had happened, and after getting supper, she took me to a friend's house for concealment, until the next day.

As soon as Mr Mitchell had discovered my unlooked-for departure, he was furious, for he did not think I had sense enough to run away; he accused the coachman of helping me off, and, despite the poor man's denials, hurried him away to the calaboose and put him under the lash, in order to force a confession. Finding this course unavailing, he offered a reward to the negro catchers, on the same evening, but their efforts were equally fruitless.

Charlotte Forten (Grimké)

1837–1914

B orn in Philadelphia, Pennsylvania, to free Black abolitionists, she moved to Salem, Massachusetts, at the age of sixteen, to complete her education, and on 24 May 1854 she began a journal which she intermittently continued until 1864. In 1855 she graduated with distinction from Higginson Grammar School and after a year's course at Salem Normal School, taught in the all-white Epes Grammar School, the first Black teacher in the Salem public school system. She was active in the anti-slavery movement and when the American Civil War broke out, she applied as a teacher to the Philadelphia Port Royal Relief Association, and in 1862 taught in St Helena, in the sea islands off the coast of South Carolina, the first Black teacher to participate in the experiment of educating ex-slaves. Drawing on her journals, she wrote sketches about her experiences in the sea islands, which were published in 1864 in Atlantic Monthly. She later worked in the Freedman's Society and published poems and essays in Christian Register, Boston Commonwealth, Liberator and New England Magazine. She married Francis J. Grimké (brother of Angelina Weld Grimké) in 1878, moving to Washington, DC, where she lived for the rest of her life.

From

The Journal of Charlotte Forten

WEDNESDAY, Sept. 12 [1855]. To-day school commenced – Most happy am I to return to the companionship of my studies, – ever my most valued friends. It is pleasant to meet the scholars again; most of them greeted me cordially, and were it not for the thought that *will* intrude, of the want of *entire sympathy* even of those I know and like best, I should greatly enjoy their society. There is one young girl and only one – Miss [Sarah] B[rown] who I believe thoroughly and heartily appreciates anti-slavery, – *racial* anti-slavery, and has no prejudice against color. I wonder that every colored person is not a misanthrope. Surely we have everything to make us hate mankind. I have met girls in the schoolroom [–] they have been thoroughly kind and cordial to me, – perhaps the next day met them in the street – they feared to recognize me; these I can but regard now with scorn and contempt, – once I liked them, believing them incapable of such meanness. Others give the most distant recognition possible, – I, of course, acknowledge no such recognitions, and they soon cease entirely. These are but trifles, certainly, to the great, public wrongs which we as a people are obliged to endure. But to those who experience them, these apparent trifles are most wearing and discouraging; even to the child's mind they reveal volumes of deceit and heartlessness, and early teach a lesson of suspicion and distrust. Oh! it is hard to go through life meeting contempt with contempt, hatred with hatred, fearing, with too good reason, to love and trust hardly any one whose skin is white – however lovable, attractive and congenial in seeming. In the bitter, passionate feelings of my soul again and again there rises the questions "When oh! when shall this cease?" "Is there no help?" "How long oh! how long must we continue to suffer – to endure?" Conscience answers it is wrong, it is ignoble to despair; let us labor earnestly and faithfully to acquire knowledge, to break down the barriers of prejudice and oppression. Let us take courage; never ceasing to work – hoping and believing that if not for us, for another generation there is a better, brighter day in store – when slavery and prejudice shall vanish before the glorious light of Liberty and Truth; when the rights of every colored man shall everywhere be acknowledged and respected, and he shall be treated as a *man* and a *brother!*

Wednesday, Nov. 5 [1862]. Had my first regular teaching experience, and to you and you only friend beloved, will I acknowledge that it was *not* a very pleasant one. Part of my scholars are very tiny, – babies, I call them – and it is hard to keep them quiet and interested while I am hearing the larger ones. They are too young even for the alphabet, it seems to me. I think I must write home and ask somebody to send me picture-books and toys to amuse them with. I fancied Miss T[owne] looked annoyed when, at one time the little ones were unusually restless. Perhaps it was only my fancy. Dear Miss M[urray] was kind and considerate as usual. She is very lovable. Well, I *must* not be discouraged. Perhaps things will go on better to-morrow. . . .

We've established our household on – as we hope – a firm basis. We have *Rose* for our little maid-of-all-work, *Amaretta* for cook, washer, and ironer, and *Cupid*, yes Cupid himself, for clerk, oysterman and future coachman. I must also inform you dear A., that we have made ourselves a bed, whereon we hope to rest to-night, for rest *I* certainly did not last night, despite innumerable blankets designed to conceal and render inactive the bones of the bed. But said bones did so protrude that sleep was almost an impossibility to our poor little body.

Thursday, Nov. 13 . . . Talked to the children a little while to-day about the noble Toussaint [L'Ouverture]. They listened very attentively. It is well that they sh'ld know what one of their own color c'ld do for his race. I long to inspire them with courage and ambition (of a noble sort), and high purpose. . . .

This eve, Harry, one of the men on the place, came in for a lesson. He is most eager to learn, and is really a scholar to be proud of. He learns rapidly. I gave him his first lesson in writing to-night, and his progress was wonderful.

He held the pen almost perfectly right the first time. He will very soon learn to write, I think. I must inquire if there are not more of the grown people who w'ld like to take lessons at night. Whenever I am well enough it will be a real happiness to me to teach them. . . .

Monday, Nov. 17. Had a dreadfully wearying day in school, of which the less said the better. Afterward drove with the ladies to "The Corner", a colection [*sic*] of negro houses, whither Miss T[owne] went on a doctoring expedition. The people there are very pleasant. Saw a little baby, just borne [*sic*] today – and another – old Venus' great-grandchild for whom I made the little pink frock. These people are very gratiful [*sic*]. The least kindness that you do them they insist on repaying in some way. We have had a quantity of eggs and potatoes brought us despite our remonstrances. Today one of the women gave me some Tanias. Tania is a queer looking root. After it is boiled it looks like a potato, but is much larger. I don't like the taste.
Tuesday, Nov. 18. After school went to The Corner again. Stopped at old Susy's house to see some sick children. Old Susy is a character. Miss T[owne] asked her if she wanted her old master to come back again. Most emphatically she answered. "No *indeed*, missus, no indeed dey treat we too bad. Dey tuk ebery one of my chilen away from me. When we sick and c'ldnt work dey tuk away all our food from us; gib us nutten to eat. Dey's orful hard Missis." When Miss T[owne] told her that some of the people said they wanted their old masters to come back, a look of supreme contempt came to old Susy's withered face. "Dat's 'cause dey's got no sense, den missus."

Sunday, Nov. 23. This eve. our boys and girls with others from across the creek came in and sang a long time for us. Of course we had the old favorites "Down in the Lonesome Valley", and "Roll, Jordan, Roll", and "No man can hender me", and beside those several shouting tunes that we had not heard before; they are very wild and strange. It was impossible for me to understand many of the words although I asked them to repeat them for me. I only know that one had something about "De Nell Am Ringing". I think that was the refrain; and of another, some of the words were "Christ build the church widout no hammer nor nail". "Jehovah Halleluhiah", which is a grand thing, and "Hold the light", an especial favorite of mine – they sang with great spirit. The leader of the singing was Prince, a large black boy, from Mr R[uggles]'s place. He was full of the shouting spirit, and c'ld not possibly keep still. It was amusing to see his gymnastic performances. They were quite in the Ethiopian Methodists' style. He has really a very fine bass voice. I enjoyed their singing so much, and sh'ld have enjoyed it so much more if some dear ones who are far away c'ld have listened it to [*sic*] with me. How delighted they would have been. . . .

Jan. 31 [1863]. . . . In B[eaufort] we spent nearly all our time at Harriet Tubman's – otherwise "Moses". She is a wonderful woman – a real heroine. Has helped off a large number of slaves, after taking her own freedom. She told us that she used to hide them in the woods during the day and go around to get provisions for them. Once she had with her a man named Joe, for whom a reward of

$1500 was offered. Frequently, in different places she found handbills exactly describing him, but at last they reached in safety the Suspension Bridge over the Falls and found themselves in Canada. Until then, she said, Joe had been very silent. In vain had she called his attention to the glory of the Falls. He sat perfectly still – moody, it seemed, and w'ld not even glance at them. But when she said. "Now we are in Can[ada]" he sprang to his feet with a great shout, and sang and clapped his hand [*sic*] in a perfect delirium of joy. So when they got out, and he first touched *free* soil, he shouted and hurrahed "as if he were crazy" – she said.

How exciting it was to hear her tell the story. And to hear her sing the very scraps of jubilant hymns that he sang. She said the ladies crowded around them, and some laughed and some cried. My own eyes were full as I listened to her – the heroic woman! A reward of $10,000 was offered for her by the Southerners, and her friends deemed it best that she sh'ld, for a time find refuge in Can[ada]. And she did so, but only for a short time. She came back and was soon at the good brave work again. She is living in B[eaufort] now; keeping an eating house. But she wants to go North, and will probably do so ere long. I am glad I saw her – *very* glad . . .

Life on the Sea Islands

IT was on the late afternoon of a warm, murky day late in October that our steamer, the United States, touched the landing at Hilton Head. A motley assemblage had collected on the wharf, – officers, soldiers, and "contraband" of every size and hue: black was, however, the prevailing color. The first view of Hilton Head is desolate enough, – a long, low, sandy point, stretching out into the sea, with no visible dwellings upon it, except the rows of small white-roofed houses which have lately been built for the freed people.

After signing a paper wherein we declared ourselves loyal to the Government, and wherein, also, were set forth fearful penalties, should we ever be found guilty of treason, we were allowed to land, and immediately took General Saxton's boat, the Flora, for Beaufort. The General was on board, and we were presented to him. He is handsome, courteous, and affable, and looks – as he is – the gentleman and the soldier.

From Hilton Head to Beaufort the same long, low line of sandy coast, bordered by trees; formidable gunboats in the distance, and the gray ruins of an old fort, said to have been built by the Huguenots more than two hundred years ago. Arrived at Beaufort, we found that we had not yet reached our journey's end. While waiting for the boat which was to take us to our island of St Helena, we had a little time to observe the ancient town. The houses in the main street, which fronts the "Bay", are large and handsome, built of wood, in the usual Southern style, with spacious piazzas, and surrounded by fine trees. We noticed in one yard a magnolia, as high as some of our largest shade-maples, with rich, dark, shining foliage. A large building which was once the Public Library is now a shelter for freed people from Fernandina. Did the Rebels know it, they would doubtless upturn their aristocratic noses, and exclaim in disgust, "To what base uses," etc. We confess that it was highly satisfactory to us to see how the tables had turned, now that "the whirligig of time has brought about its revenges." We saw the market-place, in which slaves were sometimes sold; but we were told that the buying and selling at auction were usually done in Charleston. The arsenal, a large stone structure, was guarded by cannon and sentinels. The houses in the smaller streets had mostly a dismantled, desolate look. We saw no one in the streets but soldiers and freed people. There were indications that already Northern improvements had reached this Southern town. Among them was a wharf, a convenience that one wonders how the Southerners could so long have existed without. The more we know of their mode of life, the more are we inclined to marvel at its utter shiftlessness.

Little colored children of every hue were playing about the streets, looking as merry and happy as children ought to look, – now that the evil shadow of Slavery no longer hangs over them. Some of the officers we met did not impress us favorably. They talked flippantly, and sneeringly of the negroes, whom they found we had come down to teach, using an epithet more offensive than gentlemanly. They assured us that there was great danger of Rebel attacks, that the yellow fever prevailed to an alarming extent, and that, indeed, the manufacture of coffins was the only business that was at all flourishing at present. Although by no means daunted by these alarming stories, we were glad when the announcement of our boat relieved us from their edifying conversation.

We rowed across to Ladies Island, which adjoins St Helena, through the splendors of a grand Southern sunset. The gorgeous clouds of crimson and gold were reflected as in a mirror in the smooth, clear waters below. As we glided along, the rich tones of the negro boatmen broke upon the evening stillness, – sweet strange, and solemn:–

> Jesus make de blind to see,
> Jesus make de cripple walk,
> Jesus make de deaf to hear.
> Walk in, kind Jesus!
> No man can hender me.

It was nearly dark when we reached the island, and then had a three-miles' drive through the lonely roads to the house of the superintendent. We thought how easy it would be for a band of guerrillas, had they chanced that way, to seize and hang us; but we were in that excited, jubilant state of mind which makes fear impossible, and sang "John Brown" with a will, as we drove through the pines and palmettos. Oh, it was good to sing that song in the very heart of Rebeldom! Harry, our driver, amused us much. He was surprised to find that we had not heard of him before. "Why, I thought eberybody at de Nort had heard o' me!" he said, very innocently. We learned afterward that Mrs F., who made the tour of the islands last summer, had publicly mentioned Harry. Some one had told him of it, and he of course imagined that he had become quite famous. Notwithstanding this little touch of vanity, Harry is one of the best and smartest men on the island.

Gates occurred, it seemed to us, at every few yards' distance, made in the

oldest fashion, – opening in the middle, like folding doors, for the accom-
modation of horsemen. The little boy who accompanied us as gate-opener
answered to the name of Cupid. Arrived at the headquarters of the general
superintendent, Mr S., we were kindly received by him and the ladies, and
shown into a large parlor, where a cheerful wood-fire glowed in the grate. It
had a home-like look; but still there was a sense of unreality about everything,
and I felt that nothing less than a vigorous "shaking-up", such as Grandfather
Smallweed daily experienced, would arouse me thoroughly to the fact that I was
in South Carolina.

The next morning L. and I were awakened by the cheerful voices of men
and women, children and chickens, in the yard below. We ran to the window,
and looked out. Women in bright-colored handkerchiefs, some carrying pails
on their heads, were crossing the yard, busy with their morning work; children
were playing and tumbling around them. On every face there was a look of
serenity and cheerfulness. My heart gave a great throb of happiness as I looked
at them, and thought, "They are free! so long down-trodden, so long crushed
to the earth, but now in their old homes, forever free!" And I thanked God that
I had lived to see this day.

After breakfast Miss T. drove us to Oaklands, our future home. The road
leading to the house was nearly choked with weeds. The house itself was in
a dilapidated condition, and the yard and garden had a sadly neglected look.
But there were roses in bloom; we plucked handfuls of feathery, fragrant acacia-
blossoms; ivy crept along the ground and under the house. The freed people
on the place seemed glad to see us. After talking with them, and giving some
directions for cleaning the house, we drove to the school, in which I was to teach.
It is kept in the Baptist Church, – a brick building, beautifully situated in a grove
of live-oaks. These trees are the first objects that attract one's attention here: not
that they are finer than our Northern oaks, but because of the singular gray moss
with which every branch is heavily draped. This hanging moss grows on nearly
all the trees, but on none so luxuriantly as on the live-oak. The pendants are
often four or five feet long, very graceful and beautiful, but giving the trees a
solemn, almost funereal look. The school was opened in September. Many of the
children had, however, received instruction during the summer. It was evident
that they had made very rapid improvement, and we noticed with pleasure how
bright and eager to learn many of them seemed. They sang in rich, sweet tones,
and with a peculiar swaying motion of the body, which made their singing the
more effective. They sang "Marching Along", with great spirit, and then one of
their own hymns, the air of which is beautiful and touching:

> My sister, you want to git religion,
>   Go down in de Lonesome Valley;
> My brudder, you want to git religion,
>   Go down in de Lonesome Valley.

Chorus

Go down in de Lonesome Valley,
Go down in de Lonesome Valley, my Lord,
Go down in de Lonesome Valley,
 To meet my Jesus dere!

Oh, feed on milk and honey,
Oh, feed on milk and honey, my Lord,
Oh, feed on milk and honey,
 Meet my Jesus dere!

Oh, John he brought a letter,
Oh, John he brought a letter, my Lord,
Oh, Mary and Marta read 'em,
 Meet my Jesus dere!

Chorus

Go down in de Lonesome Valley, etc.

They repeat their hymns several times, and while singing keep perfect time with their hands and feet.

On our way homeward we noticed that a few of the trees were beginning to turn, but we looked in vain for the glowing autumnal hues of our Northern forests. Some brilliant scarlet berries – the cassena – were growing along the road-side, and on every hand we saw the live-oak with its moss-drapery. The palmettos disappointed me; stiff and ungraceful, they have a bristling, defiant look, suggestive of Rebels starting up and defying everybody. The land is low and level – not the slightest approach to a hill, not a rock, nor even a stone to be seen. It would have a desolate look, were it not for the trees, and the hanging moss and numberless vines which festoon them. These vines overrun the hedges, form graceful arches between the trees, encircle their trunks, and sometimes cling to the topmost branches. In February they begin to bloom, and then throughout the spring and summer we have a succession of beautiful flowers. First comes the yellow jessamine, with its perfect, gold-colored, and deliciously fragrant blossoms. It lights up the hedges, and completely canopies some of the trees. Of all the wild-flowers this seems to me the most beautiful and fragrant. Then we have the snow-white, but scentless Cherokee rose, with its lovely, shining leaves. Later in the season come the brilliant trumpet-flower, the passion flower, and innumerable others.

The Sunday after our arrival we attended service at the Baptist Church. The people came in slowly; for they have no way of knowing the hour, except by the sun. By eleven they had all assembled, and the church was well filled. They were neatly dressed in their Sunday attire, the women mostly wearing clean, dark frocks, with white aprons and bright-colored head-handkerchiefs. Some had attained to the dignity of straw hats with gay feathers, but these were not nearly as becoming nor as picturesque as the handkerchiefs. The day was warm, and the windows were thrown open as if it were summer, although it was the second day of November. It was very pleasant to listen to the beautiful hymns, and look from the crowd of dark, earnest faces within, upon the grove of noble oaks without. The people sang, "Roll, Jordan, Roll", the grandest of all their hymns. There is a great, rolling wave of sound through it all.

> Mr Fuller settin' on de Tree ob Life,
> Fur to hear de Jordan roll.
> Oh, roll, Jordan! roll, Jordan! roll, Jordan, roll!

> Chorus

> Oh, roll, Jordan, roll! oh, roll, Jordan, roll!
> My soul arise in heab'n, Lord,
> Fur to hear de Jordan roll!

> Little chil'en, learn to fear de Lord,
> And let your days be long.
> Oh, roll, Jordan! roll, Jordan, roll!

> Chorus

> Oh, march, de angel, march! oh, march, de angel, march!
> My soul arise in heab'n, Lord,
> Fur to hear de Jordan roll!

The "Mr Fuller" referred to was their former minister, to whom they seem to have been much attached. He is a Southerner, but loyal, and is now, I believe, living in Baltimore. After the sermon the minister called upon one of the elders, a gray-headed old man, to pray. His manner was very fervent and impressive, but his language was so broken that to our unaccustomed ears it was quite intelligible. After the services the people gathered in groups outside, talking among themselves, and exchanging kindly greetings with the superintendents and teachers. In their bright handkerchiefs and white aprons they made a striking picture under the gray-mossed trees. We drove afterward a mile farther, to the Episcopal Church, in which the aristocracy of the island used to worship. It is a small white building, situated in a fine grove of live-oaks, at the junction of several roads. On one of the tombstones in the yard is the touching inscription in memory of two children, – "Blessed little lambs, and *art thou* gathered into the fold of the only true shepherd? Sweet *lillies* of the valley, and *art thou* removed to a more congenial soil?" The floor of the church is of stone, the pews of polished oak. It has an organ, which is not so entirely out of tune as are the pianos on the island. One of the ladies played, while the gentlemen sang, – old-fashioned New-England church-music, which it was pleasant to hear, but it did not thrill us as the singing of the people had done.

During the week we moved to Oaklands, our future home. The house was of one story, with a low-roofed piazza running the whole length. The interior had been thoroughly scrubbed and whitewashed; the exterior was guiltless of whitewash or paint. There were five rooms, all quite small, and several dark little entries, in one of which we found shelves lined with old medicine-bottles. These were a part of the possessions of the former owner, a Rebel physician, Dr Sams by name. Some of them were still filled with his nostrums. Our furniture consisted of a bedstead, two bureaus, three small pine tables, and two chairs, one of which had a broken back. These were lent to us by the people. The masters, in their hasty flight from the islands, left nearly all their furniture; but much of it was destroyed or taken by the soldiers who came first, and what they left was removed by the people to their own houses. Certainly, they have the best rights to it. We had made up our minds to dispense with all luxuries and even many conveniences; but it was rather distressing to have no fire, and nothing to eat. Mr H. had already appropriated a room for the store which he was going to open for the benefit of the freed people, and was superintending the removal of his goods. So L. and I were left to our own resources. But Cupid the elder came to the rescue, – Cupid, who, we were told, was to be our right-hand man, and who very graciously informed us that he would take care of us; which he at once proceeded to do by bringing in some wood, and busying himself in making a fire in the open fire-place. While he is thus engaged, I will try to describe him. A small, wiry figure, stockingless, shoeless, out at the knees and elbows, and wearing the remnant of an old straw hat, which looked as if it might have done good service in scaring the crows from a cornfield. The face nearly black, very ugly, but with the shrewdest expression I ever saw, and the brightest, most humorous twinkle in the eyes. One glance at Cupid's face showed that he was not a person to be imposed upon, and that he was abundantly able to take care of himself, as well as of us. The chimney obstinately refused to draw; in spite of the original and very uncomplimentary epithets which Cupid heaped upon it, – while we stood by, listening to him in amusement, although nearly suffocated by the smoke. At last perseverance conquered, and the fire began to burn cheerily. Then Amaretta, our cook, – a neat-looking black woman, adorned with the gayest of head-handkerchiefs, – made her appearance with some eggs and hominy, after partaking of which we proceeded to arrange our scanty furniture, which was soon done. In a few days we began to look civilized, having made a table-cover of some red and yellow handkerchiefs which we found among the store-goods, – a carpet of red and black woolen plaid, originally intended for frocks and shirts, – a cushion, stuffed with corn-husks and covered with calico, for a lounge, which Ben, the carpenter, had made for us of pine boards, – and lastly some corn-husk beds, which were an unspeakable luxury, after having endured agonies for several nights, sleeping on the slats of a bedstead. It is true, the said slats were covered with blankets, but these might as well have been sheets of paper for all the good they did us. What a resting-place it was: compared to it, the gridiron of St Lawrence – fire excepted – was a bed of roses.

The first day at school was rather trying. Most of my children were very small, and consequently restless. Some were too young to learn the alphabet. These little ones were brought to school because the older children – in whose care their parents leave them while at work – could not come without them.

We were therefore willing to have them come, although they seemed to have discovered the secret of perpetual motion, and tried one's patience sadly. But after some days of positive, though not severe treatment, order was brought out of chaos, and I found but little difficulty in managing and quieting the tiniest and most restless spirits. I never before saw children so eager to learn, although I had had several years' experience in New-England schools. Coming to school is a constant delight and recreation to them. They come here as other children go to play. The older ones, during the summer, work in the fields from early morning until eleven or twelve o'clock, and then come into school, after their hard toil in the hot sun, as bright and as anxious to learn as ever.

Of course there are some stupid ones, but these are the minority. The majority learn with wonderful rapidity. Many of the grown people are desirous of learning to read. It is wonderful how a people who have been so long crushed to the earth, so imbruted as these have been – and they are said to be among the most degraded negroes of the South – can have so great a desire for knowledge, and such a capability for attaining it. One cannot believe that the haughty Anglo-Saxon race, after centuries of such an experience as these people have had, would be very much superior to them. And one's indignation increases against those who, North as well as South, taunt the colored race with inferiority while they themselves use every means in their power to crush and degrade them, denying them every right and privilege, closing against them every avenue of elevation and improvement. Were they, under such circumstances, intellectual and refined, they would certainly be vastly superior to any other race that ever existed.

After the lessons, we used to talk freely to the children, often giving them slight sketches of some of the great and good men. Before teaching them the "John Brown" song, which they learned to sing with great spirit, Miss T. told them the story of the brave old man who had died for them. I told them about Toussaint, thinking it well they should know what one of their own color had done for his race. They listened attentively, and seemed to understand. We found it rather hard to keep their attention in school. It is not strange, as they have been so entirely unused to intellectual concentration. It is necessary to interest them every moment, in order to keep their thoughts from wandering. Teaching here is consequently far more fatiguing than at the North. In the church, we had of course but one room in which to hear all the children; and to make one's self heard, when there were often as many as a hundred and forty reciting at once, it was necessary to tax the lungs very severely.

My walk to school, of about a mile, was part of the way through a road lined with trees, – on one side stately pines, on the other noble live-oaks, hung with moss and canopied with vines. The ground was carpeted with brown, fragrant pine-leaves; and as I passed through in the morning, the woods were enlivened by the delicious songs of mocking-birds, which abound here, making one realize the truthful felicity of the description in "Evangeline",–

> The mocking-bird, wildest of singers,
> Shook from his little throat such floods of delirious music
> That the whole air and the woods and the waves seemed to listen.

The hedges were all aglow with the brilliant scarlet berries of the cassena, and on some of the oaks we observed the mistletoe, laden with its pure white, pearl-like berries. Out of the woods the roads are generally bad, and we found it hard work plodding through the deep sand.

In the evenings, the children frequently came in to sing and shout for us. These "shouts" are very strange, – in truth, almost indescribable. It is necessary to hear and see in order to have any clear idea of them. The children form a ring, and move around in a kind of shuffling dance, singing all the time. Four or five stand apart, and sing very energetically, clapping their hands, stamping their feet, and rocking their bodies to and fro. These are the musicians, to whose performance the shouters keep perfect time. The grown people on this plantation did not shout, but they do on some of the other plantations. It is very comical to see little children, not more than three or four years old, entering into the performance with all their might. But the shouting of the grown people is rather solemn and impressive than otherwise. We cannot determine whether it has a religious character or not. Some of the people tell us that it has, others that it has not. But as the shouts of the grown people are always in connection with their religious meetings, it is probable that they are the barbarous expression of religion, handed down to them from their African ancestors, and destined to pass away under the influence of Christian teachings. The people of this island have no songs. They sing only hymns, and most of these are sad. Prince, a large black boy from a neighboring plantation, was the principal shouter among the children. It seemed impossible for him to keep still for a moment. His performances were most amusing specimens of Ethiopian gymnastics. Amaretta the younger, a cunning, kittenish little creature of only six years old, had a remarkably sweet voice. Her favorite hymn, which we used to hear her singing to herself as she walked through the yard, is one of the oddest we have heard:–

What makes ole Satan follow me so?
Satan got nuttin' 't all fur to do wid me.

Chorus

Tiddy Rosa, hold your light!
Brudder Tony; hold your light!
All de member, hold bright light
On Canaan's shore!

This is one of the most spirited shouting tunes. "Tiddy" is their word for sister.

A very queer-looking old man came into the store one day. He was dressed in a complete suit of brilliant Brussels carpeting. Probably it had been taken from his master's house after the "gun-shoot"; but he looked so very dignified that we did not like to question him about it. The people called him Doctor Crofts, – which was, I believe, his master's name, his own being Scipio. He was very jubilant over the new state of things, and said to Mr H., – "Don't hab me feelins hurt now. Used to hab me feelins hurt all de time. But don't hab 'em hurt now no more." Poor old soul! We rejoiced with him that he and his brethren no longer have their "feelins" hurt, as in the old time.

On the Sunday before Thanksgiving, General Saxton's noble Proclamation was read at church. We could not listen to it without emotion. The people listened with the deepest attention, and seemed to understand and appreciate it. Whittier has said of it and its writer, – "It is the most beautiful and touching official document I ever read. God bless him! 'The bravest are the tenderest.'"

General Saxton is truly worthy of the gratitude and admiration with which the people regard him. His unfailing kindness and consideration for them – so different from the treatment they have sometimes received at the hands of other officers – have caused them to have unbounded confidence in General *"Saxby"*, as they call him.

After the service, there were six couples married. Some of the dresses were unique. One was particularly fine, – doubtless a cast-off dress of the bride's former mistress. The silk and lace, ribbons, feathers and flowers, were in a rather faded condition. But, comical as the costumes were, we were not disposed to laugh at them. We were too glad to see the poor creatures trying to lead right and virtuous lives. The legal ceremony, which was formerly scarcely known among them, is now everywhere consecrated. The constant and earnest advice of the minister and teachers has not been given in vain; nearly every Sunday there are several couples married in church. Some of them are people who have grown old together.

Thanksgiving-Day was observed as a general holiday. According to General Saxton's orders, an ox had been killed on each plantation, that the people might that day have fresh meat, which was a great luxury to them, and, indeed, to all of us. In the morning, a large number – superintendents, teachers, and freed people – assembled in the Baptist Church. It was a sight not soon to be forgotten, – that crowd of eager, happy black faces, from which the shadow of Slavery had forever passed. "Forever free! forever free!" those magical words of the Proclamation were constantly singing themselves in my soul. After an appropriate prayer and sermon by Mr P., and singing by the people, General Saxton made a short, but spirited speech, urging the young men to enlist in the regiment then forming under Colonel Higginson. Mrs Gage told the people how the slaves in Santa Cruz had secured their liberty. It was something entirely new and strange to them to hear a woman speak in public; but they listened with great attention, and seemed much interested. Before dispersing, they sang "Marching Alone", which is an especial favorite with them. It was a very happy Thanksgiving-Day for all of us. The weather was delightful; oranges and figs were hanging on the trees; roses, oleanders, and japonicas were blooming out-of-doors; the sun was warm and bright; and over all shone gloriously the blessed light of Freedom, – Freedom forevermore!

A Parting Hymn

When Winter's royal robes of white
From hill and vale are gone
And the glad voices of the spring
Upon the air are borne,
Friends who have met with us before,
Within these walls shall meet no more.

Forth to a noble work they go:
O, may their hearts keep pure,
And hopeful zeal and strength be theirs
To labor and endure,
That they an earnest faith may prove
By words of truth and deeds of love.

May those, whose holy task it is,
To guide impulsive youth,
Fail not to cherish in their souls
A reverence for truth;
For teachings which the lips impart
Must have their source within the heart.

May all who suffer share their love –
The poor and the oppressed;
So shall the blessing of our God
Upon their labors rest.
And may we meet again where all
Are blest and freed from every thrall.

Bethany Veney

fl. 1889

Born into slavery in Virginia, she was emancipated in 1858 by a man who took her North, where she was his employee for a few years. The Narrative of Bethany Veney, A Slave Woman was *published in 1889, probably written down by an amanuensis. In this poignant extract she describes her marriage to and parting from her first husband Jerry, also a slave, who was eventually sold away.*

From

The Narrative of Bethany Veney

AUNT BETTY'S STORY

CHAPTER I

CHILDHOOD – FIRST LESSONS IN MORALITY – FIRST LESSON IN
THE ART OF ENTERTAINING

I HAVE but little recollection of my very early life. My mother and her five children were owned by one James Fletcher, Pass Run, town of Luray, Page County, Virginia. Of my father I know nothing.

The first thing I remember with any distinctness was when, about seven years old, I was, with other children, knocking apples from a tree, when we were surprised by my young mistress, Miss Nasenath Fletcher, calling to us, in a loud and threatening tone, demanding what we were doing. Without waiting for reply, she told us to follow her; and, as she led the way down to a blackberry pasture not far off, she endeavored, in a very solemn manner, to impress us with the importance of always telling the truth. "If asked a question," she said, "we must answer directly, yes or no." I asked her "what we must say if asked something which we did not know." She answered, "Why, you must say you don't know, of course." I said, "I shall say, 'Maybe 'tis, and maybe 'tain't.'" I remember well how the children laughed at this; and then Miss Nasenath went on to tell us that *some time* all this world that we saw would be burned up, – that the moon would be turned into blood, the stars would fall out of the sky, and everything would melt away with a great heat, and that everybody, *every little child* that had told a lie, would be cast into a lake of fire and brimstone, and would burn there for ever and ever, and, what was more, though they should burn for ever and ever, they would never be burned up.

I was dreadfully frightened; and, as soon as I could get away, I ran to my mammy, and, repeating what mistress had said, begged to know if it could be true. To my great sorrow, she confirmed it all, but added what Miss Nasenath had failed to do; namely, that those who told the truth and were good would always have everything they should want. It seemed to me then there was nothing so good as molasses and sugar; and I eagerly asked, "Shall I have all the molasses and sugar I want, if I tell the truth?" "Yes," she replied, "*if you are good*; but remember, if you tell lies, you will be burned in the lake that burns for ever and ever."

This made a very strong impression upon me. I can never forget my mammy's manner at the time. I believed every word she said, and from that day to this I have never doubted its truth.

Though my conception of what constituted the truth was very dim, my fear of what should befall me, if I were to tell a lie, was very great. Still, I was only a young child, and could not, long at a time, be very unhappy.

My old master, who at times was inclined to be jolly, had a way of entertaining his friends by my singing and dancing. Supper over, he would call me into his room, and, giving me to understand what he wanted of me, I would, with all manner of grotesque grimaces, gestures, and positions, dance and sing:

> "Where are you going, Jim?
> Where are you going, Sam?
> To get a proper larning,
> To Jump Jim Crow,"

> or

> "David the king was grievit and worrit,
> He went to his chamber –
> His chamber and weppit;
> And, as he went, he weppit and said,
> 'O my son, O my son!
> Would to God I had died
> For thee, O Absalom,
> My son, my son,'"

and many other similar songs, of the meaning of which I had of course no idea, and I have since thought neither he nor his friends could have had any more than I.

CHAPTER IV

COURTSHIP AND MARRIAGE – A SLAVEHOLDER'S IDEA OF ITS REQUIREMENTS – SEPARATION

YEAR after year rolled on. Master Jonas Mannyfield lived seven miles from us, on the other side of the Blue Ridge; and he owned a likely young fellow called Jerry. We had always known each other, and now he wanted to marry me. Our masters were both willing; and there was nothing to hinder, except that there was no minister about there to marry us. "No matter for that," Kibbler said to Jerry. "If you want Bett, and she wants you, that's the whole of it." But I didn't think so. I said, "No: never till somebody comes along who can marry us." So it happened, one day, there was a colored man – a pedler, with his cart – on the road, and Jerry brought him in, and said he was ready to be minister for us. He asked us a few questions, which we answered in a satisfactory manner, and then he declared us husband and wife. I did not want him to make us promise that we would always be true to each other forsaking all others, as the white people do in their marriage service, because I knew that at any time our masters could compel us to break such a promise; and I had never forgotten the lesson learned, so many years before, in the blackberry pasture.

So Jerry and I were happy as, under all the circumstances we could well be. When he asked his master's consent to our marriage, he told him he had had thoughts of removing to Missouri, in which case he should take him with him, and we would have to be separated; but, if he chose to run the risk, he had nothing to say. Jerry did not think there was any danger, and we were not dissuaded; for hearts that love are much the same in bond or free, in white or black.

Eight or ten months passed on, when one night my brother Stephen, who lived on the Blue Ridge, near Master Mannyfield, came to see me, and, as we talked of many things, he spoke of Jerry in a way that instantly roused my suspicion. I said: "Tell me what is the matter? I know there is something. Is Jerry dead? Is he sold? Tell me what it is." I saw he dreaded to speak, and that frightened me the more.

At last, he said: "'Tis no use, Betty. You have got to know it. Old Look-a-here's people are all in jail for debt." "Old Look-a-here" was the nickname by which Mannyfield was known by the colored people far and near, because he had a way of saying, when he was about to whip one of his slaves, "Now look-a-here, you black rascal," or "you black wench."

The next day was Saturday, and I hurried to complete my task in the corn-field, and then asked my master if I could go to see Jerry. He objected at first, but at last gave me a pass to see my brother, and be gone until Monday morning.

The sun might have been two hours high when I started; but, before I was half over the mountain, night had closed round me its deepest gloom. The vivid flashes of lightning made the carriage path plain at times, and then I could not see a step before me; and the rolling thunder added to my fear and dread. I was dripping wet when, about nine o'clock, I reached the house. It had been my plan to get Stephen to go on with me to Jerry's mother's, and stay the night there; but his mistress, who was sister to my Miss Lucy, declared we must not go on in the storm, and, giving me supper, brought bedding, that I might lie on the kitchen floor and rest me there. In the morning, after a good breakfast, she started us off, with a bag of biscuits to eat by the way. Jerry's mother was glad to go with us; and we hurried along to Jerry, in jail at Little Washington, where he with his fellow-slaves was confined, like sheep or oxen, shut up in stalls, to be sold to pay their owner's debts.

Jerry saw us, as we came along the road, through the prison bars; and the jailer allowed us to talk together there, not, however, without a witness to all we might say. We had committed no offence against God or man. Jerry had not; and yet, like base criminals, we were denied even the consolation of privacy. This was a necessary part of the system of American slavery. Neither wife nor mother could intervene to soften its rigors one jot.

Several months passed, and Mannyfield was still unable to redeem his property; and they were at last put up at auction, and sold to the highest bidder. Frank White, a slave-trader, bought the entire lot, and proceeded at once to make up a gang for the Southern market.

Arrangements were made to start Friday morning; and on Thursday afternoon, chained together, the gang were taken across the stream, and encamped on its banks. White then went to Jerry, and, taking the handcuffs from his wrists, told him to go and stay the night with his wife, and see if he could persuade her to go with him. If he could, he would buy her, and so they need not be separated. He would pass that way in the morning, and see. Of course, Jerry was only too glad to come; and, at first, I thought I would go with him. Then came the consciousness that this inducement was only a sham, and that, once exposed for sale in a Southern market, the bidder with the largest sum of money would be our purchaser singly quite as surely as together; and, if separated, what would I do in a strange land? No: I would not go. It was far better for me to stay where, for miles and miles, I knew every one, and every one knew me. Then came the wish to secrete ourselves together in the mountains, or elsewhere, till White should be gone; but, to do this, detection was sure. Then we remembered that White had trusted us, in letting him come to me, and we felt ashamed, for a moment, as if we had tried to cheat; but what *right* had White to carry him away, or even to own him at all? Our poor, ignorant reasoning found it hard to understand his rights or our own; and we at last decided that, as soon as it was light, Jerry should take to the mountains, and, when White was surely gone, either I would join him there, and we would make for the North together, or he would come back, go to White's mother, who lived a few miles distant, and tell her he would work for her and obey her, but he would never go South to be worked to death in the rice-swamps or cotton-fields.

We talked late into the night; and at last, in the silence and dread, worn out with sorrow and fear, my head on his shoulder, we both dropped asleep.

Daylight was upon us when we waked. The sad consciousness of our condition, and our utter helplessness, overpowered us. I opened the door, and there was my mistress, with pail in hand, going to the spring for water. "Oh, what shall I do? Where shall I go?" cried Jerry, as he saw her. "Have no fear," I said. "Go right along. I know mistress will never betray you." And, with a bound, he was over the fence, into the fields, and off to the mountains.

In a very short time, White and his poor, doomed company came along, and called for Jerry. I had taken my pail to milk the cows; and, seeing me, he sung out, "Woman, where is Jerry, I say?" "I don't know where Jerry is," I answered. Then, turning to Kibbler, who, hearing the outcry, now came out, he said, "You told me that woman wouldn't lie; and you know well enough she is lying now, when she says she don't know where that — rascal is." Kibbler answered very slowly and thoughtfully, "I never knowed her to lie; but may be this time, – may be this time." White then turned to me, and said, "I took off his handcuffs, and let him go to you, and you had no business to serve me so."

It was true I did not know where Jerry was at that time. We had agreed that we would meet that night near the blacksmith's old shop, on the other side of the run; and that was all I knew of his whereabouts, though he had not been gone long enough to be far away. It was true he had trusted us, and I felt very badly; but what else *could* we have done? Kind reader, *what* think you?

I then told him that Jerry had said he was willing to work, and would go to his mother's and serve her, but *never* if he could help it, would he be carried South.

Then White tried to bargain with Kibbler for my purchase, saying he would give any price he should name for me, because he knew I would then find Jerry. But it was no use. Kibbler had a kind spot in his heart, and would not consent to let me go. So the slave-trader moved on with his human cattle.

Five miles on the road lived David McCoy, another slave-trader. When White reached his house, it was agreed by them that, if McCoy could find Jerry within two days, he should bring him on, and they would meet at Stanton, Va.

CHAPTER V

MEETING – A LAST INTERVIEW – SEPARATION

THE place where I was to meet Jerry was, as I have said, across the run, in a corn-field, near the blacksmith's shop, the time Friday night.

It had rained hard all day, and the stream was swollen, and pouring and rushing at a fearful rate. I waited till everybody was in bed and asleep, when I lighted my pine knot, and started for the Pass. It was still raining, and the night was very dark. Only by my torch could I see a step before me; and, when I attempted to wade in, as I did in many different places, I found it was no use. I should surely be drowned if I persisted. So, disappointed and grieved, I gave up and went home. The next morning I was able to get over on horseback to milk the cows, but I neither heard nor saw anything of Jerry.

Saturday night came. I knew well that, if not caught by White, Jerry would be round. At last, every one was in bed, and all was still. I waited and listened. I listened and waited. Then I heard his step at the door. I hurriedly opened it, and he came in. His clothes were still damp and stiff from the rain of yesterday. He was frightened and uneasy. He had been hiding around in different places, constantly fearing detection. He had seen me from behind the old blacksmith's shop when I had tried the night before, with my pine knot, to ford the stream; and he was glad, he said, when he saw me go back, for he knew I should be carried down by the current and be drowned, if I had persisted. I went to my mistress's bedroom, and asked her if I might go to the cellar. She knew at once what I meant, and whispered softly, "Betty, has Jerry come?" then, without waiting for reply, added, "get him some milk and light bread and butter." I was not long in doing so; and the poor fellow ate like one famishing. Then he wanted to know all that had happened, and what White had said when he found he was gone. We talked a long time, and tried to devise some plans for our mutual safety and possible escape from slavery altogether; but, every way we looked, the path was beset with danger and exposure. We were both utterly disheartened. But sleep came at last and, for the time being, relieved us of our fears.

In the morning, which was Sunday, we had our breakfast together, and, as the hours passed, began to feel a little comforted. After dinner, we walked out to the field and strolled about for some time; and, when ready to go back to the house, we each took an armful of fodder along for the horses. As we laid it down and turned to go into the house, David McCoy rode up on horseback. He saw Jerry at once, and called him to come to the fence. The excitement of the last days – the fasting and the fear – had completely cowed and broken whatever of manhood, or even of brute courage, a slave might by any possibility be presumed at any time to be possessed of, and the last remains of these qualities in poor Jerry were gone. He mutely obeyed; and when, with an oath, McCoy commanded him to mount the horse behind him, he mutely seated himself there. McCoy then called to me to go to the house and bring Jerry's clothes. "Never," – I screamed back to him, – "never, not to save your miserable life." But Jerry said: "O Betty, 'tis no use. We can't help it." I knew this was so. I stifled my anger and my grief, brought his little bundle, into which I tucked a testament and catechism some one had given me, and shook hands "good-by" with him. So we *parted forever*, in this world.

Mattie J. Jackson
1846–?

From St Louis, she was twenty when she dictated her autobiography to Dr L. S. Thompson, herself a Black woman. In her preface to The Story of Mattie J. Jackson *(subtitled "Her Parentage – Experience of Eighteen Years of Slavery – Incidents During the War – Her Escape from Slavery. A True Story", published in 1866), Mattie says: "I feel it a duty to improve the mind, and have ever had a thirst for education to fill that vacuum for which the soul has ever yearned since my earliest remembrance. Thus I ask you to buy my little book to aid me in obtaining an education, that I may be enabled to do some good in behalf of the elevation on my emancipated brothers and sisters." William*

L. Andrews, introducing his 1988 edition, writes: "Mattie Jackson's story illustrates an important fact about the female slave narrative tradition. It calls for justice, not mere sympathy or pity, as the great aim and need of black women in America."

From

The Story of Mattie J. Jackson

M Y ancestors were transported from Africa to America at the time the slave trade flourished in the Eastern States. I cannot give dates, as my progenitors, being slaves, had no means of keeping them. By all accounts my great grandfather was captured and brought from Africa. His original name I never learned. His master's name was Jackson, and he resided in the State of New York. My grandfather was born in the same State, and also remained a slave for some length of time, when he was emancipated, his master presenting him with quite an amount of property. He was true, honest and responsible, and this present was given him as a reward. He was much encouraged by the cheering prospect of better days. A better condition of things now presented itself. As he possessed a large share of confidence, he came to the conclusion, as he was free, that he was capable of selecting his own residence and manage his own affairs with prudence and economy. But, alas, his hopes were soon blighted. More heart rending sorrow and degradation awaited him. He was earnestly invited by a white decoyer to relinquish his former design and accompany him to Missouri and join him in speculation and become wealthy. As partners, they embarked on board a schooner for St Charles, Mo. On the passage, my grandfather was seized with a fever, and for a while was totally unconscious. When he regained his reason he found himself, near his journey's end, divested of his free papers and all others. On his arrival at St Charles he was seized by a huge, surly looking slaveholder who claimed him as his property. The contract had previously been concluded by his Judas-like friend, who had received the bounty. Oh, what a sad disappointment. After serving for thirty years to be thrust again into bondage where a deeper degradation and sorrow and hopeless toil were to be his portion for the remaining years of his existence. In deep despair and overwhelmed with grief, he made his escape to the woods, determined to put an end to his sorrows, by perishing with cold and hunger. His master immediately pursued him, and in twenty-four hours found him with hands and feet frost-bitten, in consequence of which he lost the use of his fingers and toes, and was thenceforth of little use to his new master. He remained with him, however, and married a woman in the same station in life. They lived as happily as their circumstances would permit. As Providence allotted, they only had one son, which was my father, Westly Jackson. He had a deep affection for his family, which the slave ever cherishes for his dear ones. He had no other link to fasten him to the human family but his fervent love for those who were bound to him by love and sympathy in their wrongs and sufferings. My grandfather remained in the same family until his death. My father, Westly Jackson, married, at the age of twenty-two, a girl owned by James Harris, named Ellen Turner. Nothing of importance occurred until three years after their marriage, when her master, Harris failed through the extravagance and mismanagement of his wife, who was a great spendthrift and a dreaded terror to the poor slaves and all others with whom she associated in common circumstances, consequently the entire stock was sold by the sheriff to a trader residing in Virginia. On account of the good reputation my mother sustained as a worthy servant and excellent cook, a tyrannical and much dreaded slaveholder watched for an opportunity to purchase her, but fortunately arrived a few moments too late, and she was bid off in too poor a condition of health to remain long a subject of banter and speculation. Her husband was allowed to carefully lift her down from the block and accompany her to her new master's, Charles Canory, who treated her very kindly while she remained in his family. Mr Canory resided in St Charles County for five years after he purchased my mother. During that time my father and mother were in the same neighborhood, but a short distance from each other. But another trial awaited them. Her master removed twenty miles away to a village called Bremen, near St Louis, Mo. My father, thereafter, visited my mother once a week, walking the distance every Saturday evening and returning on Sunday evening. But through all her trials and deprivations her trust and confidence was in Him who rescued his faithful followers from the fiery furnace and the lion's den, and led Moses through the Red Sea. Her trust and confidence was in Jesus. She relied on His precious promises, and ever found Him a present help in every time of need. Two years after this separation my father was sold and separated from us, but previous to his delivery to his new master he made his escape to a free State. My mother was then left with two children. She had three during the time they were permitted to remain together, and buried one. There names were Sarah Ann, Mattie Jane and Esther J. When my father left I was about three years of age, yet I can well remember the little kindnesses my father used to bestow upon us, and the deep affection and fondness he manifested for us. I shall never forget the bitter anguish of my parents' hearts, the sighs they uttered or the profusion of tears which coursed down their sable cheeks. O, what a horrid scene, but he was not her's, for cruel hands had separated them.

> The strongest tie of earthly joy that bound the aching heart –
> His love was e'er a joyous light that o er the pathway shone –
> A fountain gushing ever new amid life's desert wild –
> His slightest word was a sweet tone of music round her heart –
> Their lives a streamlet blent in one. O, Father, must they part?
> They tore him from her circling arms, her last and fond embrace –
> O never again can her sad eyes gaze upon his mournful face.
> It is not strange these bitter sighs are constant bursting forth.
> Amid mirth and glee and revelry she never took a part,
> She was a mother left alone with sorrow in her heart.

But my mother was conscious some time previous of the change that was to take place with my father, and if he was sold in the immediate vicinity he would be likely to be sold again at their will, and she concluded to assist him to make his escape from bondage. Though the parting was painful, it afforded her solace in the contemplation of her husband becoming a free man, and cherishing a hope that her little family, through the aid of some angel of mercy, might be enabled to make their escape also, and meet to part no more on earth. My father came to spend the night with us, according to his usual custom. It was the last time, and sadness brooded upon his brow. It was the only opportunity he had to make his escape without suspicion and detection, as he was immediately to fall into the hands of a new master. He had never been sold from the place of his birth before, and was determined never to be sold again if God would verify his promise. My father was not educated, but was a preacher, and administered the Word of God according to the dictation and revelation of the spirit. His former master had allowed him the privilege of holding meetings in the village within the limits of his pass on the Sundays when he visited my mother. But on this Saturday evening he arrived and gave us all his farewell kiss, and hurried away. My mother's people were aware of my father's intention, but rather than spare my mother, and for fear she might be detected, they secreted his escape. His master called a number of times and enquired for him and strongly pressed my mother to give him an account of my father, but she never gave it. We waited patiently, hoping to learn if he succeeded in gaining his freedom. Many anxious weeks and months passed before we could get any tidings from him, until at length my mother heard that he was in Chicago, a free man and preaching the Gospel. He made every effort to get his family, but all in vain. The spirit of slavery so strongly existed that letters could not reach her; they were all destroyed. My parents had never learned the rescuing scheme of the underground railroad which had borne so many thousands to the standard of freedom and victories. They knew no other resource than to depend upon their own chance in running away and secreting themselves. If caught they were in a worse condition than before.

THEIR ATTEMPT TO MAKE THEIR ESCAPE

Two years after my father's departure, my mother, with her two children, my sister and myself, attempted to make her escape. After traveling two days we reached Illinois. We slept in the woods at night. I believe my mother had food to supply us but fasted herself. But the advertisement had reached there before us, and loafers were already in search of us, and as soon as we were discovered on the brink of the river one of the spies made enquiries respecting her suspicious appearance. She was aware that she was arrested, consequently she gave a true account of herself – that she was in search of her husband. We were then destitute of any articles of clothing excepting our wearing apparel. Mother had become so weary that she was compelled to leave our package of clothing on the way. We were taken back to St Louis and committed to prison and remained there one week, after which they put us in Linch's trader's yard, where we remained about four weeks. We were then sold to William Lewis. Mr Lewis was a very severe master, and inflicted such punishment upon us as he thought proper. However, I only remember one severe contest Mr Lewis had with my mother. For some slight offence Mrs Lewis became offended and was tartly and loudly reprimanding her, when Mr L. came in and rashly felled her to the floor with his fist. But his wife was constantly pulling our ears, snapping us with her thimble, rapping us on the head and sides of it. It appeared impossible to please her. When we first went to Mr L.'s they had a cowhide which she used to inflict on a little slave girl she previously owned, nearly every night. This was done to learn the little girl to wake early to wait on her children. But my mother was a cook, as I before stated, and was in the habit of roasting meats and toasting bread. As they stinted us for food my mother roasted the cowhide. It was rather poor picking, but it was the last cowhide my mother ever had an opportunity to cook while we remained in his family. Mr L. soon moved about six miles from the city, and entered in partnership with his brother-in-law. The servants were then divided and distributed in both families. It unfortunately fell to my lot to live with Mrs Larry, my mistress' sister, which rendered my condition worse than the first. My master even disapproved of my ill treatment and took me to another place; the place my mother resided before my father's escape. After a short time Mr Lewis again returned to the city. My mother still remained as cook in his family. After six years' absence of my father my mother married again a man by the name of George Brown, and lived with her second husband about four years, and had two children, when he was sold for requesting a different kind and enough food. His master considered it a great insult, and declared he would sell him. But previous to this insult, as he called it, my step-father was foreman in Mr L.'s tobacco factory. He was trusty and of good moral habits, and was calculated to bring the highest price in the human market; therefore the excuse to sell him for the above offence was only a plot. The morning this offence occurred, Mr L. bid my father to remain in the kitchen till he had taken his breakfast. After pulling his ears and slapping his face bade him come to the factory; but instead of going to the factory he went to Canada. Thus my poor mother was again left alone with two more children added to her misery and sorrow to toil on her weary pilgrimage.

> Racked with agony and pain she was left alone again,
> With a purpose nought could move
> And the zeal of woman's love,
> Down she knelt in agony
> To ask the Lord to clear the way.

> True she said O gracious Lord,
> True and faithful is thy word;
> But the humblest, poorest, may
> Eat the crumbs they cast away.

> Though nine long years had passed
> Without one glimmering light of day
> She never did forget to pray
> And has not yet though whips and chains are cast away.

> For thus said the blessed Lord,
> I will verify my word;
> By the faith that has not failed,
> Thou has asked and shall prevail.

We remained but a short time at the same residence when Mr Lewis moved again to the country. Soon after, my little brother was taken sick in consequence of being confined in a box in which my mother was obliged to keep him. If permitted to creep around the floor her mistress thought it would take too much time to attend to him. He was two years old and never walked. His limbs were perfectly paralyzed for want of exercise. We now saw him gradually failing, but was not allowed to render him due attention. Even the morning he died she was compelled to attend to her usual work. She watched over him for three months by night and attended to her domestic affairs by day. The night previous to his death we were aware he could not survive through the approaching day, but it made no impression on my mistress until she came into the kitchen and saw his life fast ebbing away, then she put on a sad countenance for fear of being exposed, and told my mother to take the child to her room, where he only lived one hour. When she found he was dead she ordered grave clothes to be brought and gave my mother time to bury him. O that morning, that solemn morning. It appears to me that when that little spirit departed as though all heaven rejoiced and angels veiled their faces.

> My mother too in concert joined,–
> Her mingled praise with them combined.
> Her little saint had gone to God
> Who saved him with his precious blood.

Who said, "Suffer little children to come unto me and forbid them not."

MATTIE IN INDIANAPOLIS – THE GLORY OF FREEDOM – PRESIDENT LINCOLN'S REMAINS EXHIBITED

MY first business, after my arrival at Indianapolis was to find a boarding place in which I at once succeeded, and in a few hours thereafter was at a place of service of my own choice. I had always been under the yoke of oppression, compelled to submit to its laws, and not allowed to advance a rod from the house, or even out of call, without a severe punishment. Now this constant fear and restless yearning was over. It appeared as though I had emerged into a new world, or had never lived in the old one before. The people I lived with were Unionists, and became immediately interested in teaching and encouraging me in my literary advancement and all other important improvements, which precisely met the natural desires for which my soul had ever yearned since my earliest recollection. I could read a little, but was not allowed to learn in slavery. I was obliged to pay twenty-five cents for every letter written for me. I now began to feel that as I was free I could learn to write, as well as others; consequently Mrs Harris, the lady with whom I lived, volunteered to assist me. I was soon enabled to write quite a legible hand, which I find a great convenience. I would advise all, young, middle aged or old, in a free country to learn to read and write. If this little book should fall into the hands of one deficient of the important knowledge of writing, I hope they will remember the old maxim:– "Never too old to learn." Manage your own secrets, and divulge them by the silent language of your own pen. Had our blessed President considered it too humiliating to learn in advanced years, our race would yet have remained under the galling yoke of oppression. After I had been with Mrs Harris seven months, the joyful news came of the surrender of Lee's army and the capture of Richmond.

> Whilst the country's hearts were throbbing,
>   Filled with joy for victories won;
> Whilst the stars and stripes were waving
>   O'er each cottage, ship and dome,
> Came upon like winged lightning
>   Words that turned each joy to dread,
> Froze with horror as we listened:
>   Our beloved chieftain, Lincoln's dead.
>
> War's dark clouds has long held o'er us,
>   They have rolled their gloomy fold's away,
> And all the world is anxious, waiting
>   For that promised peaceful day.
> But that fearful blow inflicted,
>   Fell on his devoted head,
> And from every town and hamlet
>   Came the cry our Chieftain's dead.
>
> Weep, weep, O bleeding nation
>   For the patriot spirit fled,
> All untold our country's future –
>   Buried with the silent dead.

God of battles, God of nations to our country send relief
Turn each lamentation into joy whilst we mourn our murdered chief.

On the Saturday after the assassination of the President there was a meeting held on the Common, and a vote taken to have the President's body brought through Indianapolis, for the people to see his dear dead face. The vote was taken by raising the hands, and when the question was put in favor of it a thousand black hands were extended in the air, seemingly higher and more visible than all the rest. Nor were their hands alone raised, for in their deep sorrow and gloom they raised their hearts to God, for well they knew that He, through martyred blood, had made them free. It was some time before the remains reached Indianapolis, as it was near the last of the route. The body was placed in the centre of the hall of the State House, and we marched in by fours, and divided into two on each side of the casket, and passed directly through the hall. It was very rainy, – nothing but umbrellas were to be seen in any direction. The multitude were passing in and out from eight o'clock in the morning till four o'clock in the afternoon. His body remained until twelve o'clock in the evening, many distinguished persons visiting it, when amid the booming of cannon, it moved on its way to Springfield, its final resting-place. The death of the President was like an electric shock to my soul. I could not feel convinced of his death until I gazed upon his remains, and heard the last roll of the muffled drum and the farewell boom of the cannon. I was then convinced that though we were left to the tender mercies of God, we were without a leader.

> Gone, gone is our chieftain,
> The tried and the true;
> The grief of our nation the world never knew.
> We mourn as a nation has never yet mourned;
> The foe to our freedom more deeply has scorned.
>
> In the height of his glory in manhood's full prime,
> Our country's preserver through darkest of time;
> A merciful being, whose kindness all shared
> Shown mercy to others. Why was he not spared?
>
> The lover of Justice, the friend of the slave,
> He struck at oppression and made it a grave;
> He spoke for our bond-men, and chains from them fell,
> By making them soldiers they served our land well.
>
> Because he had spoken from sea unto sea
> Glad tidings go heavenward, our country is free,
> And angels I'm thinking looked down from above,
> With sweet smiles approving his great works of love.
>
> His name with the honor forever will live,
> And time to his laurels new lustre will give;
> He lived so unselfish, so loyal and true,
> That his deeds will shine brighter at every view.
>
> Then honor and cherish the name of the brave,
> The champion of freedom, the friend to the slave,
> The far-sighted statesman who saw a fair end,
> When north land and south land one flag shall defend.
>
> Rest, rest, fallen chieftain, thy labors are o'er,
> For thee mourns a nation as never before;
> Farewell honored chieftain whom millions adore,
> Farewell gentle spirit, whom heaven has won.

SISTER LOST – MOTHER'S ESCAPE

IN two or three weeks after the body of the President was carried through, my sister made her escape, but by some means we entirely lost trace of her. We heard she was in a free State. In three months my mother also escaped. She rose quite early in the morning, took my little brother, and arrived at my place of service in the afternoon. I was much surprised, and asked my mother how she came there. She could scarcely tell me for weeping, but I soon found out the mystery. After so many long years and so many attempts, for this was her seventh, she at last succeeded, and we were now all free. My mother had been a slave for more than forty-three years, and liberty was very sweet to her. The sound of freedom was music in our ears; the air was pure and fragrant; the genial rays of the glorious sun burst forth with a new lustre upon us, and all creation resounded in responses of praise to the author and creator of him who proclaimed life and freedom to the slave. I was overjoyed with my personal freedom, but the joy at my mother's escape was greater than anything I had ever known. It was a joy that reaches beyond the tide and anchors in the harbor of eternal rest. While in oppression, this eternal life-preserver had continually wafted her toward the land of freedom, which she was confident of gaining, whatever might betide. Our joy that we were permitted to mingle together our earthly bliss in glorious strains of freedom was indescribable. My mother responded with the children of Israel, – "The Lord is my strength and my song. The Lord is a man of war, and the Lord is his name." We left Indianapolis the day after my mother arrived, and took the cars at eleven o'clock the following evening for St Louis, my native State. We were then free, and instead of being hurried along, bare headed and half naked, through cars and boats, by a brutal master with a bill of sale in his pocket, we were our own, comfortably clothed, and having the true emblems of freedom.

Susie King Taylor
1848–1912

orn a slave near Savannah, Georgia, her parents' eldest child, she acquired some learning surreptitiously and gained her freedom by escaping behind Union lines with her family in 1862. During the US civil war she served as laundress, teacher and nurse to the Union army but received no compensation for her services. Her first husband, Sergeant King, died in 1866, shortly before the birth of their son, and she supported the child and herself by teaching. She later opened a night school for adults in Liberty County, Georgia, but this paid so little that she had to go into domestic service. She married Russell L. Taylor in 1879 and moved to Boston, where she helped organize the Women's Auxiliary Corps of the Grand Army of Republic, and in 1879 she compiled a roster of surviving Union veterans in Massachusetts. Her memoir, Reminiscences of My life in Camp with the 33rd United States Colored Troops Late 1st SC Volunteers *(1902), vividly describes life in a Black army camp.*

From

Reminiscences of My Life in Camp

XIII

THOUGHTS ON PRESENT CONDITIONS

LIVING here in Boston where the black man is given equal justice, I must say a word on the general treatment of my race, both in the North and South, in this twentieth century. I wonder if our white fellow men realize the true sense or meaning of brotherhood? For two hundred years we had toiled for them; the war of 1861 came and was ended, and we thought our race was forever freed from bondage, and that the two races could live in unity with each other, but when we read almost every day of what is being done to my race by some whites in the South, I sometimes ask, "Was the war in vain? Has it brought freedom, in the full sense of the word, or has it not made our condition more hopeless?"

In this "land of the free" we are burned, tortured, and denied a fair trial, murdered for any imaginary wrong conceived in the brain of the negro-hating white man. There is no redress for us from a government which promised to protect all under its flag. It seems a mystery to me. They say, "One flag, one nation, one country indivisible." Is this true? Can we say this truthfully, when one race is allowed to burn, hang, and inflict the most horrible torture weekly, monthly, on another? No, we cannot sing, "My country, 't is of thee, Sweet land of Liberty"! It is hollow mockery. The Southland laws are all on the side of the white, and they do just as they like to the negro, whether in the right or not.

I do not uphold my race when they do wrong. They ought to be punished, but the innocent are made to suffer as well as the guilty, and I hope the time will hasten when it will be stopped forever. Let us remember God says, "He that sheds blood, his blood shall be required again." I may not live to see it, but the time is approaching when the South will again have cause to repent for the blood it has shed of innocent black men, for their blood cries out for vengeance. For the South still cherishes a hatred toward the blacks, although there are some true Southern gentlemen left who abhor the stigma brought upon them, and feel it very keenly, and I hope the day is not far distant when the two races will reside in peace in the Southland, and we will sing with sincere and truthful hearts, "My country, 't is thee, Sweet land of Liberty, of thee I sing."

I have been in many States and cities, and in each I have looked for liberty and justice, equal for the black as for the white; but it was not until I was within the borders of New England, and reached old Massachusetts, that I found it. Here is found liberty in the full sense of the word, liberty for the stranger within her gates, irrespective of race or creed, liberty and justice for all.

We have before us still another problem to solve. With the close of the Spanish war, and on the entrance of the Americans into Cuba, the same conditions confront us as the war of 1861 left. The Cubans are free, but it is a limited freedom, for prejudice, deep-rooted, has been brought to them and a separation made between the white and black Cubans, a thing that had never existed between them before; but to-day there is the same intense hatred toward the negro in Cuba that there is in some parts of this country.

I helped to furnish and pack boxes to be sent to the soldiers and hospitals during the first part of the Spanish war; there were black soldiers there too. At the battle of San Juan Hill, they were in the front, just as brave, loyal, and true as those other black men who fought for freedom and the right; and yet their bravery and faithfulness were reluctantly acknowledged, and praise grudgingly given. All we ask for is equal justice," the same that is accorded to all other races who come to this country, of their free will (not forced to, as we were), and are allowed to enjoy every privilege, unrestricted, while we are denied what is rightfully our own in a country which the labor of our forefathers helpd to make what it is.

One thing I have noticed among my people in the South: they have accumulated a large amount of real estate, far surpassing the colored owners in the North, who seem to let their opportunity slip by them. Nearly all of Brownsville (a suburb of Savannah) is owned by colored people, and so it is in a great many other places throughout the State, and all that is needed is the protection of the law as citizens.

In 1867, soon after the death of my father, who had served on a gunboard during the war, my mother opened a grocery store, where she kept general merchandise always on hand. These she traded for cash or would exchange for crops of cotton, corn, or rice, which she would ship once a month, to F. Lloyd & Co., or Johnson & Jackson, in Savannah. These were colored merchants, doing business on Bay Street in that city. Mother bought her first property, which contained ten acres. She next purchased fifty acres of land. Then she had a chance to get a place with seven hundred acres of land, and she bought this.

In 1870, Colonel Hamilton and Major Devendorft, of Oswego, N.Y., came to the town and bought up a tract of land at a place called Doctortown, and started a mill. Mrs Devendorft heard of my mother and went to see her, and persuaded her to come to live with her, assuring her she would be as one of the family. Mother went with her, but after a few months she went to Doctortown, where she has been since, and now owns the largest settlement there. All trains going to Florida pass her place, just across the Altamaha River. She is well known by both white and black; the people are fond of her, and will not allow any one to harm her.

Mr Devendorft sold out his place in 1880 and went back to New York, where later he died.

I read an article, which said the ex-Confederate Daughters had sent a petition to the managers of the local theatres in Tennessee to prohibit the performance of "Uncle Tom's Cabin," claiming it was exaggerated (that is, the treatment of the slaves), and would have a very bad effect on the children who might see the drama. I paused and thought back a few years of the heart-rending scenes I have witnessed; I have seen many times, when I was a mere girl, thirty or forty men, handcuffed, and as many women and children, come every first Tuesday of each month from Mr Wiley's trade office to the auction blocks, one of them being situated on Drayton Street and Court Lane, the other on Bryant Street, near the Pulaski House. The route was down our principal street, Bull Street, to the court-house, which was only a block from where I resided.

All people in those days got all their water from the city pumps, which stood about a block apart throughout the city. The one we used to get water from was opposite the court-house, on Bull Street. I remember, as if it were yesterday, seeing droves of negroes going to be sold, and I often went to look at them, and I could hear the auctioneer very plainly from my house, auctioning these poor people off.

Do these Confederate Daughters ever send petitions to prohibit the atrocious lynchings and wholesale murdering and torture of the negro? Do you ever hear of them fearing this would have a bad effect on the children? Which of these two, the drama or the present state of affairs, makes a degrading impression upon the minds of our young generation? In my opinion it is not "Uncle Tom's Cabin," but it should be the one that has caused the world to cry "Shame!" It does not seem as if our land is yet civilized. It is like times long past, when rulers and high officers had to flee for their lives, and the negro has been dealt with in the same way since the war by those he lived with and toiled for two hundred years or more. I do not condemn all the Caucasian race because the negro is badly treated by a few of the race. No! for had it not been for the true whites, assisted by God and the prayers of our forefathers, I should not be here to-day.

There are still good friends to the negro. Why, there are still thousands that have not bowed to Baal. So it is with us. Man thinks two hundred years is a long time, and it is, too; but it is only as a week to God, and in his own time – I know I shall not live to see the day, but it will come – the South will be like the North, and when it comes it will be prized higher than we prize the North to-day. God is just; when he created man he made him in his image, and never intended one should misuse the other. All men are born free and equal in his sight.

Pauline Elizabeth Hopkins
("Sarah A. Allen")
1859–1930

Born *in Portland, Maine, she was taken to Boston while young and graduated from Boston Girls High School. A versatile writer, editor and singer, she had her first writing success at fifteen, winning a prize for best essay on "Evils of Intemperance and Their Remedy" in a contest among Black youth in local schools. She became a playwright in 1879, when the Hopkins Colored Troubadours (including her and her family) performed her musical drama* Escape from Slavery *(later renamed* Peculiar Sam; or, the Underground Railroad*). In her forties she began to achieve recognition as a fiction writer through her association with the* Colored American Magazine *(1902–04), a pioneering forum for Black literary talent. Her novels appeared serially (March 1901–November 1903) and when the magazine changed hands in May 1903 she was appointed literary editor; under her editorship its circulation rose to 15,000. Among writers the journal published were Frances E. W. Harper and Angelina Weld Grimké. She believed fiction has great significance for Black people, writing in the preface to her novel* Contending Forces *(1900): "It is a record of growth and development from generation to generation. No one will do this for us: we must ourselves develop the men and women who will faithfully portray the innermost thoughts and*

*feelings of the Negro with all the fire and romance which lie dormant
in our history." She travelled and lectured throughout the USA seeking
support for the* Colored American *and she was a founder of the Colored
American League, which tried to gain subscriptions and business for the
magazine. Eventually the magazine was sold and moved to New York;
Hopkins was initially assistant editor but resigned some months later. She
continued to write and edited the short-lived* New Era. *She made a living
working as a stenographer for the Massachusetts Institute of Technology.
She died of burns received in an accidental fire.*

From

Contending Forces

CHAPTER I

A RETROSPECT OF THE PAST

We wait beneath the furnace-blast
    The pangs of transformation;
Not painlessly doth God recast
    And mould anew the nation.
    Hot burns the fire
    Where wrongs expire;
    Nor spares the hand
    That from the land
    Uproots the ancient evil.

J. G. WHITTIER

I N the early part of the year 1800 the agitation of the inhabitants of Great
Britain over the increasing horrors of the slave trade carried on in the West
Indian possessions of the Empire was about reaching a climax. Every day the
terrible things done to slaves were becoming public talk, until the best English
humanitarians, searching for light upon the subject, became sick at heart over
the discoveries that they made and were led to declare the principle: "The air
of England is too pure for any slave to breathe."

To go back a little way in the romantic history of the emancipation of the
slaves in the islands will not take much time, and will, I hope, be as instructive
as interesting. Tales of the abuses of the slaves, with all the sickening details, had
reached the Quaker community as early as 1783, and that tender-hearted people

looked about themselves to see what steps they could take to ameliorate the condition of the Negroes in the West Indies, and to discourage the continuation of the trade along the African coast.

Thomas Clarkson, a student at Cambridge, was drawn into writing a prize essay on the subject, and became so interested that he allied himself with the Quakers and investigated the subject for himself, thereby confirming his own belief, "that Providence had never made that to be wise that was immoral; and that the slave trade was as impolitic as it was unjust."

After strenuous efforts by Mr Pitt and Mr Fox, Parliament became interested and instituted an inquiry into the abuses of the slave trade. Finally, Mr Wilberforce was drawn into the controversy, and for sixteen years waged an incessant warfare against the planters, meeting with defeat in his plans for ten consecutive years; but finally, in 1807, he was successful, and the slave trade was abolished.

These assailants of the slave trade had promised not to try to abolish slavery; but in a short time they learned that the trade was still carried on in ships sailing under the protection of false flags. Tales of the cruelties practiced upon the helpless chattels were continually reaching the ears of the British public, some of them such as to sicken the most cold-hearted and indifferent. For instance: causing a child to whip his mother until the blood ran; if a slave looked his master in the face, his limbs were broken; women in the first stages of their accouchement, upon refusing to work, were placed in the treadmill, where terrible things happened, too dreadful to relate.

Through the efforts of Granville Sharpe, the chairman of the London committee, Lord Stanley, minister of the colonies, introduced into the House of Commons his bill for emancipation.

Lord Stanley's bill proposed *gradual* emancipation, and was the best thing those men of wisdom could devise. Earnestly devoted to their task, they sought to wipe from the fair escutcheon of the Empire the awful blot which was upon it. By the adoption of the bill Great Britain not only liberated a people from the cruelties of their masters, but at the same time took an important step forward in the onward march of progress, which the most enlightened nations are unconsciously forced to make by the great law of advancement; "for the civility of no race can be perfect whilst another race is degraded."

In this bill of gradual emancipation certain conditions were proposed. All slaves were entitled to be known as apprenticed laborers, and to acquire thereby all the rights and privileges of freemen. "These conditions were that prædials should owe three-fourths of the profits of their labors to their masters for six years, and the non-prædials for four years. The other fourth of the apprentice's time was to be his own, which he might sell to his master or to other persons; and at the end of the term of years fixed, he should be free."

In the winter of 1790, when these important changes in the life of the Negro in the West Indies were pending, many planters were following the course of events with great anxiety. Many feared that in the end their slaves would be taken from them without recompense, and thereby render them and their families destitute. Among these planters was the family of Charles Montfort, of the island of Bermuda.

Bermuda's fifteen square miles of area lays six hundred miles from the nearest American coast. Delightful is this land, formed from coral reefs, flat and fertile, which to the eye appears as but a pin point upon the ocean's broad bosom, one of "a thousand islands in a tropic sea."

Once Bermuda was second only to Virginia in its importance as a British colony; once it held the carrying trade of the New World; once was known as the "Gibraltar of the Atlantic," although its history has been that of a simple and peaceful people. Its importance to the mother country as a military and naval station has drawn the paternal bonds of interest closer as the years have flown by. Indeed, Great Britain has been kind to the colonists of this favored island from its infancy, sheltering and shielding them so carefully that the iron hand of the master has never shown beneath the velvet glove. So Bermuda has always been intensely British, – intensely loyal. Today, at the beginning of the new century, Bermuda presents itself, outside of its importance as a military station for a great power, as a vast sanatorium for the benefit of invalids. A temperate climate, limpid rivers, the balmy fragrance and freshness of the air, no winter, – nature changing only in the tints of its foliage, – have contributed to its renown as a health-giving region; and thus Shakespeare's magic island of Prospero and Miranda has become, indeed, to the traveler

> The spot of earth uncurst,
> To show how all things were created first.

Mr Montfort was the owner of about seven hundred slaves. He was well known as an exporter of tobacco, sugar, coffee, onions and other products so easily grown in that salubrious climate, from which he received large returns. He was neither a cruel man, nor an avaricious one; but like all men in commercial life, or traders doing business in their own productions, he lost sight of the individual right or wrong of the matter, or we might say with more truth, that he perverted right to be what was conducive to this own interests, and felt that by owning slaves he did no man a wrong, since it was the common practice of those all about him, and he had been accustomed to this peculiar institution all his life.

Indeed, slavery never reached its lowest depths in this beautiful island; but a desire for England's honor and greatness had become a passion with the inhabitants, and restrained the planters from committing the ferocious acts of brutality so commonly practiced by the Spaniards. In many cases African blood had become diluted from amalgamation with the higher race, and many of these "colored" people became rich planters or business men (themselves owning slaves) through the favors heaped upon them by their white parents. This being the case, there might even have been a strain of African blood polluting the fair stream of Montfort's vitality, or even his wife's, which fact would not have caused him one instant's uneasiness. Moreover, he was a good master, and felt that while he housed his slaves well, fed them with the best of food suited to their occupations and the climate, and did not cruelly beat them, they fared better with him than they would have with another, perhaps, or even if they held property themselves.

The speeches of Mr Pitt, Mr Burke and others, together with the general trend of public sentiment as expressed through the medium of the British press, had now begun to make an impression upon some of the more humane of the planters on this island, and among them was Mr Montfort. Uneasiness now took the place of his former security; thought would obtrude itself upon him, and in the quiet hours of the night this man fought out the battle which conscience waged within him, and right prevailed to the extent of his deciding that he would free his slaves, but in his own way. He determined to leave Bermuda, and after settling in some other land, he would gradually free his slaves without impoverishing himself; bestow on each one a piece of land, and finally, with easy conscience, he would retire to England, and there lead the happy life of an English gentleman of fortune.

With this end in view, being a man of affairs and well acquainted with the whole of the American continent, he naturally turned his eyes towards the United States, where the institution flourished, and the people had not yet actually awakened to the folly and wickedness exemplified in the enslavement of their fellow-beings. For reasons which were never known, he finally made choice of Newbern, N. C., for a home. . . .

CHAPTER II

THE DAYS "BEFORE THE WAR."

O FREEDOM! thou art not as poets dream,
A fair young girl with light and delicate limbs,
. . . .
Thy birthright was not given by human hands:
Thou wert twinborn with man.

THE shores of Pamlico Sound presented a motley crowd of slaves, overseers, owners of vessels, and a phantasmagoric landscape very charming to eyes unaccustomed to such scenes. It was near the noon siesta. In the harbor lay three or four vessels ready to be loaded with their freight of rice, tobacco or cotton. The sun poured its level rays straight down upon the heads of all. A band of slaves sang in a musical monotone, and kept time to the music of their song as they unloaded a barge that had just arrived:

Turn dat han' spike roun' an' roun',
  Hol' hard, honey; hol' hard, honey.
Brack man tote de buckra's load,
  Hol' hard, honey; hol' hard, honey.

Neber 'fo' seed a nigger like you,
  Hol' hard, honey; hol' hard, honey.
Allers tinkin' 'bout yer ol' brack Sue,
  Hol' hard, honey; hol' hard, honey.

Ef I was an alligater what'd I do?
    Hol' hard, honey; hol' hard, honey.
Run 'way wid ol' brack Sue,
    Hol' hard, honey; hol' hard, honey.

Massa ketch yer, what'd he do?
    Hi, hi, honey; hi, hi, honey.
Cut yer back an' ol' brack Sue's,
    He, he, honey; he, he, honey.

I cuss massa 'hin' de fence,
    Hol' hard, honey; hol' hard, honey.
Massa don' hyar make no differyence,
    Hol' hard, honey; hol' hard, honey.

Turn dat han' spike roun' an' roun',
    Hol' hard, honey; hol' hard, honey.
Brack man tote de buckra's load,
    Hol' hard, honey; hol' hard, honey.

As the refrain died away the bell for the noon rest sounded faintly in the distance, gradually drawing nearer, and again their rich and plaintive voices blended together in sweet cadences as they finished placing the heavy load to the satisfaction of their drivers:

Hark, dat merry, purty bell go
    Jing-a-lingle, jing-a-lingle, jingle bell,
Jing-a-lingle, jing-a-lingle, jing-a-lingle bell,
    Jingle bell, jingle bell.

Even so sang the children of Israel in their captivity, as they sat by the rivers of Babylon awaiting deliverance.

Just now a ship, which had some time since appeared as a dark spot on the horizon, turned her majestic prow and steered for the entrance to the sound. Immediately the pilot boat in the harbor put out to her. Everyone on the shore became eagerly intent upon the strange ship, and they watched the pilot climb aboard with all the interest which usually attends the slightest cause for excitement in a small community.

The ship came on very slowly, for there was little wind, under topsail, jib and foresail, the British flag at the peak and the American flag at the fore. The people on shore could see the captain standing by the pilot, the anchor ready to be dropped, and the bowsprit shrouds loose. But now their interest was divided with a new arrival. A man on horseback rode down to the shaky wooden platform which served as a landing place for passengers; behind him, at a respectful distance, rode a white-haired Mulatto. The man leaped from his horse and threw his reins to the slave, signaled a couple of Negroes in a boat, jumped into it as they, obedient to his sign, pulled alongside the wharf, and was rowed swiftly out to the advancing ship, which was now making considerable headway toward the shore.

Among the idlers on the wharf was one whom everyone addressed as Bill. He was large, or rather burly, carried a rawhide in his hand, and from his air of authority toward them, was evidently the overseer of the gang of slaves who were loading the tobacco barge. From out the crowd a man who had been sitting idly on a bale of cotton moved toward him.

"Holloa, Bill," he said, addressing the owner of the rawhide.

"Howdy, Hank," returned Bill, surveying the other curiously, "whar in time did you drap from?"

Hank did not reply directly. He shifted the tobacco quid in his mouth from one cheek to the other, then with a nod of the head toward the approaching vessel, asked: "Whar's she from?"

"Hain't been in town lately, I reckon, or you'd know all about the 'Island Queen' from Bermudy. Planter named Montfort on her. He's movin' his niggers here to Caroliny; gittin' too hot fer him back thar," replied Bill, with a backward jerk of his thumb in the supposed direction of Bermuda. "How's things up yer way?"

"Fair, fair to middlin', Bill; thar's been some talk 'bout a risin' among the niggers, and so we jes tuk a few o' them an' strun' 'em up fer a eggsample to the res'. I tell you, Bill, we jes don't spec' to hav' no foolin' 'bout this yer question of who's on top as regards a gentleman's owning his niggers, an' whomsoeveder goes ter foolin' with that ar pertickler pint o' discusshun is gwine ter be made a eggsample of, even ef it's a white man. Didn' hyar nuthin' 'bout a circus up our way, did yer?"

Bill scratched his chin and shook his head in the negative.

"Wall, 'twas this here way: Jed Powers, you 'member Dan Powers' Jed, don' yer? Dan thet was tarred an' feathered fer selling good likely whiskey ter niggers?" Bill nodded in the affirmative. "Jed Powers wuz seed walkin' with Jimison's wench Violy. Be blowed ef he wasn't gittin' ready ter cut an' run ter Canidy with her!"

"Don' b'lieve yer, durned ef I do," said Bill.

"Fact! Be durned ef it ain't jes so."

"Wall! of all the onnat'rall cusses!"

"But his wurst offense, in gineral, wuz thet he wuz meanin' fer to marry her!" Hank paused in his narrative to allow a full appreciation of his statement to be impressed upon Bill's mind.

"Wus an' wus!" groaned the latter. "What is we comin' to, by thunder! I allays took Jed to be a decen' sort o' cuss, too. What's the committee doin' 'bout it?"

"Wall, we sot out to stop thet fun, anyhow. We got him after a hot chase, an' we put him in jail; an' las' week we guv him his trial. Jedge sentenced him to fifty lashes an' hangin' by the neck untell he wuz dead. But somehow or nuther folks is gittin' squeamish. Jedge don' durst to hang him; he'll jes guv him the fifty lashes an' a talking' to on the immoralty o' his acts an' ways. Jedge tol' him he wuz young an' had a chance to 'pent from the desolate ways o' his youth, of which his wurst failin' wuz a-wantin' to marry niggers, leastwise he'd end in hell, shure. Jedge tol' him everythin' 'cording ter law an' jestice. We wuz calkerlatin' ter have a celebrashun to which all the leading citizens o' this county would 'a' been bid, but, o' course, not havin' the hangin' sort o' took the ginger out o' the whole business."

"I hain't a doubt o' yer horsepertality in case o' the event, Hank; we's allays got along mighty comf'table tergether," replied Bill, nodding an emphatic approval of all that Hank had said. The whole speech had been liberally punctuated with copious floods of tobacco juice, which formed a small river between the two men.

"Best thing I know of down our way," said Bill, after they had taken another good look at the ship, "the best thing I know of was a raffle over ter Jellison's auction-rooms. A raffle's a great thing fer pickin up bargains in niggers an' horses. This pertickler one was fer a bay horse, a new light buggy an' harness, an' a Mulatto gal Sal. The whole thing wuz wurth fifteen hundred dollars, an' we had fifteen hundred chances at a dollar a head. Highest throw took first choice; lowest, the remainder. Winners to pay twenty dollars each fer refreshments."

"Leetle bit selfish o' you, Bill, ter keep all thet to yerself," said Hank, giving Bill a reproachful glance.

"Mabby so, mabby so. But you won't lose nuthin', Hank, ef I can help yer in the footur. 'Pears like some one wuz a-tellin' me," he continued reflectively, "thet yer wuz a-wurkin' fer the county 'bout thet time fer board an' clo's."

"Be durned ef I wuzn't," replied Hank with great candor. "Shot at a free nigger an' killed Brady's dog Pete. Ef it'd been the nigger I'd happened ter kill, hit would 'a' been all right; but bein' 'twas a bluded hound thet had tred hundreds o' runaways, it wuz anuther question; an' not havin' the muney ter pay a fine, an' Brady bein' purty mad, why in I went fer a munth."

"Wall, as I was a-sayin', ter perceed, by a lucky chance it wuz my fust choice, an' I choose the gal. I knowed she wuz a fust-class breeder an' my muney wuz shure fer a hundred per cent on her."

"I swear ter gosh, but yer right, Bill; mate her with the right sort an' you's got yer own muney."

Both men now turned their attention to the advancing ship.

"I see ol' Pollock's got 'em in tow," remarked Hank reflectively, after a moment's silence. "Ans Pollock's as crafty as can be. No 'fense meant, yer know; seems he's yer boss still; mean cuss ef he's rich's a jedge;" he continued, "s'pose they've got a heap o' money, too."

"Can't say as to thet," replied Bill, "but they bought Pollock's ol' place, an' it looks as though money might be plenty the way everything has been fixed up fer the missis."

The noon hours were now over, and a great deal of confusion reigned, caused by the arrival of a ship in port with so rich a man as Mr Montfort aboard. The two friends became separated in the ensuing bustle which attended the landing of the party. During the preceding conversation a carriage and teams for transporting the baggage and slaves had drawn up alongside the shore; and as Mr Montfort stepped on the rickety wharf and assisted his wife to do the same, a murmur of involuntary admiration ran through the motley crowd of rough white men and ignorant slaves.

Grace Montfort was a dream of beauty even among beautiful women. Tall and slender; her form was willowy, although perfectly molded. Her complexion was creamy in its whiteness, of the tint of the camellia; her hair, a rich golden brown, fell in rippling masses far below the waist line; brown eyes, large and soft as those seen in the fawn; heavy black eyebrows marking a high white forehead, and features as clearly cut as a cameo, completed a most lovely type of Southern beauty.

The two children followed their mother closely. They were sturdy boys, who resembled her in the beauty of their features; and in Jess, the baby, a still greater resemblance could be traced, because the hair had been allowed to remain in long, soft curls. So they came ashore to their new home, obsequiously waited upon by Mr Pollock, and lovingly attended by their numerous slaves. In an instant the family was seated in the waiting vehicle; and before the spectators could fully realize the beauty and elegance of the newcomers, they were whirled away, and the carriage was lost in a cloud of dust.

Hank Davis and Bill Sampson met once more before they left the wharf. "Ef they hain't got an overseer, I'm goin' to 'ply fer the job," said Hank, "never seed sich a booty in my life."

Bill Sampson scratched his head meditatively: "Strikes me, Hank, thet thet ar female's got a black streak in her somewhar."

Hank stared at Bill a moment, as though he thought he had suddenly lost his senses; then he burst into a loud guffaw.

"You git out, Bill Sampson."

"Wall, maybe," said Bill, "maybe so. Thar's too much cream color in the face and too little blud seen under the skin fer a genooine white 'ooman. You can't tell nothin' 'bout these Britishers; they're allers squeamish 'bout thar nigger brats; yas, sah, very squeamish. I've hern tell that they think nuthin of ejcatin' thar black brats, and freein' 'em, an' makin' 'em rich."

"You go to the devil," returned Hank, as he moved away, "you're wus nan ol' nigger, allers seein' a possum up a tree; an' 'taint no possum 'tall, – nuthin' but er skunk."

Apologists tell us as an excuse for the barbarous practice of slavery, that it was a godlike institution for the spread of the gospel of the meek and lowly carpenter's son, and that the African savage brought to these shores in chains was a most favored being.

Such may be the thoughts of the careless and superficial mind; but when we survey the flotsam and jetsam left from the wreck of the Civil War, we can deceive ourselves no longer; we must confess that the natural laws which govern individuals and communities never relax in their operation. The fruit of slavery was poisonous and bitter; let us rejoice that it no longer exists.

Anna J. Cooper
1859–1964

Born in Wake County, North Carolina, daughter of a slave mother
and a white father, she graduated from St Augustine Normal and
Collegiate Institute, Raleigh (1869), becoming a pupil-teacher at the
age of nine. She married Rev. George Cooper in June 1877; widowed
two years later, she completed her education at Oberlin College, obtaining a BA in 1884 (one of the first three Black women graduates in the
USA) and an MA in 1887. Scholar, writer, educator, civil rights activist,
she took a particular interest in the social status of Black women. She
was women's editor of Southland magazine in 1890, writing on race
and gender, and lecturing (with writers such as Frances E. W. Harper
and Alice Dunbar-Nelson). She was a delegate at the first Pan-African
Conference in London in 1900. In 1901 she became principal at M
Street High School, Washington, DC, where she began teaching in 1887,
but, despite being successful in raising academic standards, was dropped
from the staff in 1906. Determined to improve her own education, she
began doctoral studies at Columbia University in 1914, transferring to
university in France; in 1925, at the age of sixty-seven, she earned a
PhD from the Sorbonne. That same year her autobiographical work The
Third Step was published. She continued to write after retiring from
teaching, and she also edited the diaries of her friend Charlotte [Forten]
Grimké. This extract is from her book of essays and reflections, A Voice
from the South by a Black Woman of the South (1892), one of the earliest
publications to discuss the position and problems of Black women from
a feminist point of view.

From

A Voice from the South by a Black Woman of the South

WE are the heirs of a past which was not our fathers' moulding. "Every man
the arbiter of his own destiny" was not true for the American Negro of the

past: and it is no fault of his that he finds himself to-day the inheritor of a manhood and womanhood impoverished and debased by two centuries and more of compression and degradation.

But weaknesses and malformations, which to-day are attributable to a vicious schoolmaster and a pernicious system, will a century hence be rightly regarded as proofs of innate corruptness and radical incurability.

Now the fundamental agency under God in the regeneration, the re-training of the race, as well as the ground work and starting point of its progress upward, must be the *black woman*.

With all the wrongs and neglects of her past, with all the weakness, the debasement, the moral thralldom of her present, the black woman of to-day stands mute and wondering at the Herculean task devolving upon her. But the cycles wait for her. No other hand can move the lever. She must be loosed from her bands and set to work.

Our meager and superficial results from past efforts prove their futility; and every attempt to elevate the Negro, whether undertaken by himself or through the philanthropy of others, cannot but prove abortive unless so directed as to utilize the indispensable agency of an elevated and trained womanhood.

A race cannot be purified from without. Preachers and teachers are helps, and stimulants and conditions as necessary as the gracious rain and sunshine are to plant growth. But what are rain and dew and sunshine and cloud if there be no life in the plant germ? We must go to the root and see that that is sound and healthy and vigorous; and not deceive ourselves with waxen flowers and painted leaves of mock chlorophyll.

We too often mistake individuals' honor for race development and so are ready to substitute pretty accomplishments for sound sense and earnest purpose.

A stream cannot rise higher than its source. The atmosphere of homes is no rarer and purer and sweeter than are the mothers in those homes. A race is but a total of families. The nation is the aggregate of its homes. As the whole is sum of all its parts, so the character of the parts will determine the characteristics of the whole. These are all axioms and so evident that it seems gratuitous to remark it; and yet, unless I am greatly mistaken, most of the unsatisfaction from our past results arises from just such a radical and palpable error, as much almost on our own part as on that of our benevolent white friends.

The Negro is constitutionally hopeful and proverbially irrepressible; and naturally stands in danger of being dazzled by the shimmer and tinsel of superficials. We often mistake foliage for fruit and overestimate or wrongly estimate brilliant results.

The late Martin R. Delany, who was an unadulterated black man, used to say when honors of state fell upon him, that when he entered the council of kings the black race entered with him; meaning, I suppose, that there was no discounting his race identity and attributing his achievements to some admixture of Saxon blood. But our present record of eminent men, when placed beside the actual status of the race in America to-day, proves that no man can represent the race. Whatever the attainments of the individual may be, unless his home has moved on *pari passu*, he can never be regarded as identical with or representative of the whole.

Not by pointing to sun-bathed mountain tops do we prove that Phoebus warms the valleys. We must point to homes, average homes, homes of the rank and file of horny handed toiling men and women of the South (where the masses are) lighted and cheered by the good, the beautiful, and the true, – then and not till then will the whole plateau be lifted into the sunlight.

Only the BLACK WOMAN can say "when and where I enter, in the quiet, undisputed dignity of my womanhood, without violence and without suing or special patronage, then and there the whole *Negro race enters with me.*" Is it not evident then that as individual workers for this race we must address ourselves with no half-hearted zeal to this feature of our mission. The need is felt and must be recognized by all. There is a call for workers, for missionaries, for men and women with the double consecration of a fundamental love of humanity and a desire for its melioration through the Gospel; but superadded to this we demand an intelligent and sympathetic comprehension of the interests and special needs of the Negro.

I see not why there should not be an organized effort for the protection and elevation of our girls such as the White Cross League in England. English women are strengthened and protected by more than twelve centuries of Christian influences, freedom and civilization; English girls are dispirited and crushed down by no such all-levelling prejudice as that supercilious caste spirit in America which cynically assumes "A Negro woman cannot be a lady". English womanhood is beset by no such snares and traps as betray the unprotected, untrained colored girl of the South, whose only crime and dire destruction often is her unconscious and marvelous beauty. Surely then if English indignation is aroused and English manhood thrilled under the leadership of a Bishop of the English church to build up bulwarks around their wronged sisters, Negro sentiment cannot remain callous and Negro effort nerveless in view of the imminent peril of the mothers of the next generation. "*I am my Sister's keeper!*" should be the hearty response of every man and woman of the race, and this conviction should purify and exalt the narrow, selfish and petty personal aims of life into a noble and sacred purpose.

We need men who can let their interest and gallantry extend outside the circle of their æsthetic appreciation; men who can be a father, a brother, a friend to every weak, struggling unshielded girl. We need women who are so sure of their own social footing that they need not fear leaning to lend a hand to a fallen or falling sister. We need men and women who do not exhaust their genius splitting hairs on aristocratic distinctions and thanking God they are not as others; but earnest, unselfish souls, who can go into the highways and byways, lifting up and leading, advising and encouraging with the truly catholic benevolence of the Gospel of Christ. . . .

There is, then, a real and special influence of woman. An influence subtle and often involuntary, an influence so intimately interwoven in, so intricately interpenetrated by the masculine influence of the time that it is often difficult to extricate the delicate meshes and analyze and identify the closely clinging fibers. And yet, without this influence – so long as woman sat with bandaged eyes and manacled hands, fast bound in the clamps of ignorance and inaction, the world of thought moved in its orbit like the revolutions of the moon; with one face (the man's face) always out, so that the spectator could not distinguish whether it was disc or sphere.

Now I claim that it is the prevalence of the Higher Education among women, the making it a common everyday affair for women to reason and think and express their thought, the training and stimulus which enable and encourage women to administer to the world the bread it needs as well as the sugar it cries for; in short it is the transmitting the potential forces of her soul into dynamic factors that has given symmetry and completeness to the world's agencies. So only could it be consummated that Mercy, the lesson she teaches, and Truth, the task man has set himself, should meet together: that righteousness, or *rightness*, man's ideal, – and *peace*, its necessary "other half", should kiss each other.

We must thank the general enlightenment and independence of woman (which we may now regard as a *fait accompli*) that both these forces are now at work in the world, and it is fair to demand from them for the twentieth century a higher type of civilization than any attained in the nineteenth. Religion, science, art, economics, have all needed the feminine flavor; and literature, the expression of what is permanent and best in all of these, may be gauged at any time to measure the strength of the feminine ingredient. You will not find theology consigning infants to lakes of unquenchable fire long after women have had a chance to grasp, master, and wield its dogmas. You will not find science annihilating personality from the government of the Universe and making of God an ungovernable, unintelligible, blind, often destructive physical force; you will not find jurisprudence formulating as an axiom the absurdity that man and wife are one, and that one the man – that the married woman may not hold or bequeath her own property save as subject to her husband's direction; you will not find political economists declaring that the only possible adjustment between laborers and capitalists is that of selfishness and rapacity – that each must get all he can and keep all that he gets, while the world cries *laissez faire* and the lawyers explain, "it is the beautiful working of the law of supply and demand"; in fine, you will not find the law of love shut out from the affairs of men after the feminine half of the world's truth is completed.

Nay, put your ear now close to the pulse of the time. What is the key-note of the literature of these days? What is the banner cry of all the activities of the last half decade? What is the dominant seventh which is to add richness and tone to the final cadences of this century and lead by a grand modulation into the triumphant harmonies of the next? Is it not compassion for the poor and unfortunate, and, as Bellamy has expressed it, "indignant outcry against the failure of the social machinery as it is, to ameliorate the miseries of men!" Even Christianity is being brought to the bar of humanity and tried by the standard of its ability to alleviate the world's suffering and lighten and brighten its woe. What else can be the meaning of Matthew Arnold's saddening protest, "We cannot do without Christianity," cried he, "and we cannot endure it as it is."

When went there by an age, when so much time and thought, so much money and labor were given to God's poor and God's invalids, the lowly and unlovely, the sinning as well as the suffering – homes for inebriates and homes for lunatics, shelter for the aged and shelter for babes, hospitals for the sick, props and braces for the falling, reformatory prisons and prison reformatories, all show that a "mothering" influence from some source is leavening the nation.

Now please understand me. I do not ask you to admit that these benefactions and virtues are the exclusive possession of women, or even that women are their chief and only advocates. It may be a man who formulates and makes them vocal. It may be, and often is, a man who weeps over the wrongs and struggles for the amelioration: but that man has imbibed those impulses from a mother rather than from a father and is simply materializing and giving back to the world in tangible form the ideal love and tenderness, devotion and care that have cherished and nourished the helpless period of his own existence.

All I claim is that there is a feminine as well as a masculine side to truth; that these are related not as inferior and superior, not as better and worse, not as weaker and stronger, but as complements – complements in one necessary and symmetric whole. That as the man is more noble in reason, so the woman is more quick in sympathy. That as he is indefatigable in pursuit of abstract truth, so is she in caring for the interests by the way – striving tenderly and lovingly that not one of the least of these "little ones" should perish. That while we not unfrequently see women who reason, we say, with the coolness and precision of a man, and men as considerate of helplessness as a woman, still there is a general consensus of mankind that the one trait is essentially masculine and the other is peculiarly feminine. That both are needed to be worked into the training of children, in order that our boys may supplement their virility by tenderness and sensibility, and our girls may round out their gentleness by strength and self-reliance. That, as both are alike necessary in giving symmetry to the individual, so a nation or a race will degenerate into mere emotionalism on the one hand, or bullyism on the other, if dominated by either exclusively; lastly, and most emphatically, that the feminine factor can have its proper effect only through woman's development and education so that she may fitly and intelligently stamp her force on the forces of her day, and add her modicum to the riches of the world's thought.

> For woman's cause is man's: they rise or sink
> Together, dwarfed or godlike, bond or free:
> For she that out of Lethe scales with man
> The shining steps of nature, shares with man
> His nights, his days, moves with him to one goal.
> If she be small, slight-natured, miserable,
> How shall men grow?
> ... Let her make herself her own
> To give or keep, to live and learn and be
> All that not harms distinctive womanhood.
> For woman is not undeveloped man
> But diverse: could we make her as the man
> Sweet love were slain; his dearest bond is this,
> Not like to like, but like in difference.
> Yet in the long years liker must they grow;
> The man be more of woman, she of man;

He gain in sweetness and in moral height,
Nor lose the wrestling thews that throw the world;
She mental breadth, nor fail in childward care,
Nor lose the childlike in the larger mind;
Till at the last she set herself to man,
Like perfect music unto noble words.

Now you will argue, perhaps, and rightly, that higher education for women is not a modern idea, and that, if that is the means of setting free and invigorating the long desired feminine force in the world, it has already had a trial and should, in the past, have produced some of these glowing effects. Sappho, the bright, sweet singer of Lesbos, "the violet-crowned, pure, sweetly smiling Sappho" as Alcaeus calls her, chanted her lyrics and poured forth her soul nearly six centuries before Christ, in notes as full and free, as passionate and eloquent as did ever Archilochus or Anacreon.

Aspasia, that earliest queen of the drawing-room, a century later ministered to the intellectual entertainment of Socrates and the leading wits and philosophers of her time. Indeed, to her is attributed, by the best critics, the authorship of one of the most noted speeches ever delivered by Pericles.

Later on, during the Renaissance period, women were professors in mathematics, physics, metaphysics, and the classic languages in Bologna, Pavia, Padua, and Brescia. Olympia Fulvia Morata, of Ferrara, a most interesting character, whose magnificent library was destroyed in 1553 in the invasion of Schweinfurt by Albert of Brandenburg, had acquired a most extensive education. It is said that this wonderful girl gave lectures on classical subjects in her sixteenth year, and had even before that written several very remarkable Greek and Latin poems, and what is also to the point, she married a professor at Heidelberg, and became a *help-meet for him*.

It is true then that the higher education for women – in fact, the highest that the world has ever witnessed – belongs to the past; but we must remember that it was possible, down to the middle of our own century, only to a select few; and that the fashions and traditions of the times were before that all against it. . . .

The colored woman of to-day occupies, one may say, a unique position in this country. In a period of itself transitional and unsettled, her status seems one of the least ascertainable and definitive of all the forces which make for our civilization. She is confronted by both a woman question and a race problem, and is as yet an unknown or an unacknowledged factor in both. While the women of the white race can with calm assurance enter upon the work they feel by nature appointed to do, while their men give loyal support and appreciative countenance to their efforts, recognizing in most avenues of usefulness the propriety and the need of woman's distinctive co-operation, the colored woman too often finds herself hampered and shamed by a less liberal sentiment and a more conservative attitude on the part of those for whose opinion she cares most. That this is not universally true I am glad to admit. There are to be found both intensely conservative white men and exceedingly liberal colored men. But as far as my experience goes the average man of our race is less frequently ready to admit the actual need among the sturdier forces of the world for woman's help or influence. That great social and economic questions await her interference, that she could throw any light on problems of national import, that her intermeddling could improve the management of school systems, or elevate the tone of public institutions, or humanize and sanctify the far reaching influence of prisons and reformatories and improve the treatment of lunatics and imbeciles, – that she has a word worth hearing on mooted questions in political economy, that she could contribute a suggestion on the relations of labor and capital, or offer a thought on honest money and honorable trade, I fear the majority of "Americans of the colored variety" are not yet prepared to concede. It may be that they do not yet see these questions in their right perspective, being absorbed in the immediate needs of their own political complications. A good deal depends on where we put the emphasis in this world; and our men are not perhaps to blame if they see everything colored by the light of those agitations in the midst of which they live and move and have their being. The part they have had to play in American history during the last twenty-five or thirty years has tended rather to exaggerate the importance of mere political advantage, as well as to set a fictitious valuation on those able to secure such advantage. It is the astute politician, the manager who can gain preferment for himself and his favorites, the demagogue known to stand in with the powers at the White House and consulted on the bestowal of government plums, whom we set in high places and denominate great. It is they who receive the hosannas of the multitude and are regarded as leaders of the people. The thinker and the doer, the man who solves the problem by enriching his country with an invention worth thousands or by a thought inestimable and precious is given neither bread nor a stone. He is too often left to die in obscurity and neglect even if spared in his life the bitterness of fanatical jealousies and detraction.

And yet politics, and surely American politics, is hardly a school for great minds. Sharpening rather than deepening, it develops the faculty of taking advantage of present emergencies rather than the insight to distinguish between the true and the false, the lasting and the ephemeral advantage. Highly cultivated selfishness rather than consecrated benevolence is its passport to success. Its votaries are never seers. At best they are but manipulators – often only jugglers. It is conducive neither to profound statesmanship nor to the higher type of manhood. Altruism is its *mauvais succès* and naturally enough it is indifferent to any factor which cannot be worked into its own immediate aims and purposes. As woman's influence as a political element is as yet nil in most of the commonwealths of our republic, it is not surprising that with those who place the emphasis on mere political capital she may yet seem almost a nonentity so far as it concerns the solution of great national or even racial perplexities.

There are those, however, who value the calm elevation of the thoughtful spectator who stands aloof from the heated scramble; and, above the turmoil and din of corruption and selfishness, can listen to the teachings of eternal truth and righteousness. There are even those who feel that the black man's unjust and unlawful exclusion temporarily from participation in the elective franchise in certain states is after all but a lesson "in the desert" fitted to develop in him insight and discrimination against the day of his own appointed time. One needs occasionally to stand aside from the hum and rush of human interests and passions to hear the voices of God. And it not unfrequently happens that the All-loving gives a great push to certain souls to thrust them out, as it were, from the distracting current for awhile to promote their discipline and growth, or to enrich them by communion and reflection. And similarly it may be woman's privilege from her peculiar coigne of vantage as a quiet observer, to whisper just the needed suggestion or the almost forgotten truth. The colored woman, then, should not be ignored because her bark is resting in the silent waters of the sheltered cove. She is watching the movements of the contestants none the less and is all the better qualified, perhaps, to weigh and judge and advise because not herself in the excitement of the race. Her voice, too, has always been heard in clear, unfaltering tones, ringing the changes on those deeper interests which make for permanent good. She is always sound and orthodox on questions affecting the well-being of her race. You do not find the colored woman selling her birthright for a mess of pottage. Nay, even after reason has retired from the contest, she has been known to cling blindly with the instinct of a turtle dove to those principles and policies which to her mind promise hope and safety for children yet unborn. . . .

Not unfelt, then, if unproclaimed has been the work and influence of the colored women of America. Our list of chieftains in the service, though not long, is not inferior in strength and excellence, I dare believe, to any similar list which this country can produce.

Among the pioneers, Frances Watkins Harper could sing with prophetic exaltation in the darkest days, when as yet there was not a rift in the clouds overhanging her people:

> Yes, Ethiopia shall stretch
> Her bleeding hands abroad;
> Her cry of agony shall reach the burning throne of God.
> Redeemed from dust and freed from chains
> Her sons shall lift their eyes,
> From cloud-capt hills and verdant plains
> Shall shouts of triumph rise.

Among preachers of righteousness, an unanswerable silencer of cavilers and objectors, was Sojourner Truth, that unique and rugged genius who seemed carved out without hand or chisel from the solid mountain mass; and in pleasing contrast, Amanda Smith, sweetest of natural singers and pleaders in dulcet tones for the things of God and of His Christ.

Sarah Woodson Early and Martha Briggs, planting and watering in the school room, and giving off from their matchless and irresistible personality an impetus and inspiration which can never die so long as there lives and breathes a remote descendant of their disciples and friends.

Charlotte Fortin Grimké, the gentle spirit whose verses and life link her so beautifully with America's great Quaker poet and loving reformer.

Hallie Quinn Brown, charming reader, earnest, effective lecturer and devoted worker of unflagging zeal and unquestioned power.

Fannie Jackson Coppin, the teacher and organizer, pre-eminent among women of whatever country or race in constructive and executive force.

These women represent all shades of belief and as many departments of activity; but they have one thing in common – their sympathy with the oppressed race in America and the consecration of their several talents in whatever line to the work of its deliverance and development.

Fifty years ago woman's activity according to orthodox definitions was on a pretty clearly cut "sphere", including primarily the kitchen and the nursery, and rescued from the barrenness of prison bars by the womanly mania for adorning every discoverable bit of china or canvass with forlorn looking cranes balanced idiotically on one foot. The woman of to-day finds herself in the presence of responsibilities which ramify through the profoundest and most varied interests of her country and race. Not one of the issues of this plodding, toiling, sinning, repenting, falling, aspiring humanity can afford to shut her out, or can deny the reality of her influence. No plan for renovating society, no scheme for purifying politics, no reform in church or in state, no moral, social, or economic question, no movement upward or downward in the human plane is lost on her. A man once said when told his house was afire: "Go tell my wife; I never meddle with household affairs." But no woman can possibly put herself or her sex outside any of the interests that affect humanity. All departments in the new era are to be hers, in the sense that her interests are in all and through all; and it is incumbent on her to keep intelligently and sympathetically *en rapport* with all the great movements of her time, that she may know on which side to throw the weight of her influence. She stands now at the gateway of this new era of American civilization. In her hands must be moulded the strength, the wit, the statesmanship, the morality, all the psychic force, the social and economic intercourse of that era. To be alive at such an epoch is a privilege, to be a woman then is sublime.

In this last decade of our century, changes of such moment are in progress, such new and alluring vistas are opening out before us, such original and radical suggestions for the adjustment of labor and capital, of government and the governed, of the family, the church and the state, that to be a possible factor though an infinitesimal in such a movement is pregnant with hope and weighty with responsibility. To be a woman in such an age carries with it a privilege and an opportunity never implied before. But to be a woman of the Negro race in America, and to be able to grasp the deep significance of the possibilities of the crisis, is to have a heritage, it seems to me, unique in the ages. In the first place, the race is young and full of the elasticity and hopefulness of youth. All its achievements are before it. It does not look on the masterly triumphs of nineteenth century civilization with that *blasé* world-weary look which characterizes the old washed out and worn out races which have already, so to speak, seen their best days.

Said a European writer recently: "Except the Sclavonic, the Negro is the only original and distinctive genius which has yet to come to growth – and the feeling is to cherish and develop it."

Everything to this race is new and strange and inspiring. There is a quickening of its pulses and a glowing of its self-consciousness. Aha, I can rival that! I can aspire to that! I can honor my name and vindicate my race! Something like this, it strikes me, is the enthusiasm which stirs the genius of young Africa in America; and the memory of past oppression and the fact of present attempted repression only serve to gather momentum for its irrepressible powers. Then again, a race in such a stage of growth is peculiarly sensitive to impressions. Not the photographer's sensitized plate is more delicately impressionable to outer influences than is this high strung people here on the threshold of a career.

What a responsibility then to have the sole management of the primal lights and shadows! Such is the colored woman's office. She must stamp weal or woe on the coming history of this people. May she see her opportunity and vindicate her high prerogative.

Annie L. Burton

c. 1860–?

B orn into slavery – her father was a white man from Liverpool, England – she was liberated in childhood by the Union army. Moving North in 1879, she was among the earliest Black emigrants there from the US South during the post-Civil War era. First as a laundress and later as a cook, she successfully supported herself in Boston and New York. She took on the responsibility of raising her sister's son, moved to Georgia, and eventually became a restaurateur in Jacksonville, Florida, and subsequently in Boston, seeing her nephew through college. She married Samuel Burton in 1888. Memories of Childhood's Slavery Days was published in 1909.

From

Memories of Childhood's Slavery Days

RECOLLECTIONS OF A HAPPY LIFE

T HE memory of my happy, care-free childhood days on the plantation, with my little white and black companions, is often with me. Neither master nor mistress nor neighbors had time to bestow a thought upon us, for the great Civil War was raging. That great event in American history was a matter wholly outside the realm of our childish interests. Of course we heard our elders discuss the various events of the great struggle, but it meant nothing to us.

On the plantation there were ten white children and fourteen colored children. Our days were spent roaming about from plantation to plantation, not knowing or caring what things were going on in the great world outside our little realm. Planting time and harvest time were happy days for us. How often at the harvest time the planters discovered cornstalks missing from the ends of the rows, and blamed the crows! We were called the "little fairy devils". To the sweet potatoes and peanuts and sugar cane we also helped ourselves.

Those slaves that were not married served the food from the great house, and about half-past eleven they would send the older children with food to the workers in the fields. Of course, I followed, and before we got to the fields, we had eaten the food nearly all up. When the workers returned home they complained, and we were whipped.

The slaves got their allowance every Monday night of molasses, meat, corn meal, and a kind of flour called "dredgings" or "shorts". Perhaps this allowance would be gone before the next Monday night, in which case the slaves would steal hogs and chickens. Then would come the whipping-post. Master himself never whipped his slaves; this was left to the overseer.

We children had no supper, and only a little piece of bread or something of the kind in the morning. Our dishes consisted of one wooden bowl, and oyster shells were our spoons. This bowl served for about fifteen children, and often the dogs and the ducks and the peafowl had a dip in it. Sometimes we had buttermilk and bread in our bowl, sometimes greens or bones.

Our clothes were little homespun cotton slips, with short sleeves. I never knew what shoes were until I got big enough to earn them myself.

If a slave man and woman wished to marry, a party would be arranged some Saturday night among the slaves. The marriage ceremony consisted of the pair jumping over a stick. If no children were born within a year or so, the wife was sold.

At New Year's, if there was any debt or mortgage on the plantation, the extra slaves were taken to Clayton and sold at the court house. In this way families were separated.

When they were getting recruits for the war, we were allowed to go to Clayton to see the soldiers.

I remember, at the beginning of the war, two colored men were hung in Clayton; one, Cæsar King, for killing a blood hound and biting off an overseer's ear; the other, Dabney Madison, for the murder of his master. Dabney Madison's master was really shot by a man named Houston, who was infatuated with Madison's mistress, and who had hired Madison to make the bullets for him. Houston escaped after the deed, and the blame fell on Dabney Madison, as he was the only slave of his master and mistress. The clothes of the two victims were hung on two pine trees, and no colored person would touch them. Since I have grown up, I have seen the skeleton of one of these men in the office of a doctor in Clayton.

After the men were hung, the bones were put in an old deserted house. Somebody that cared for the bones used to put them in the sun in the bright weather, and back in the house when it rained. Finally the bones disappeared, although the boxes that had contained them still remained.

At one time, when they were building barns on the plantation, one of the big boys got a little brandy and gave us children all a drink, enough to make us drunk. Four doctors were sent for, but nobody could tell what was the matter with us, except they thought we had eaten something poisonous. They wanted to give us some castor oil, but we refused to take it, because we thought that the oil was made from the bones of the dead men we had seen. Finally, we told about the big white boy giving us the brandy, and the mystery was cleared up.

Young as I was then, I remember this conversation between master and mistress, on master's return from the gate one day, when he had received the latest news: "William, what is the news from the seat of war?" "A great battle was fought at Bull Run, and the Confederates won," he replied. "Oh, good, good," said mistress, "and what did Jeff Davis say?" "Look out for the blockade. I do not know what the end may be soon," he answered. "What does Jeff Davis mean by that?" she asked. "Sarah Anne, I don't know, unless he means that the niggers will be free." "O, my God, what shall we do?" "I presume," he said, "we shall have to put our boys to work and hire help." "But," she said, "what will the niggers do if they are free? Why, they will starve if we don't keep them." "Oh, well," he said, "let them wander, if they will not stay with their owners. I don't doubt that many owners have been good to their slaves, and they would rather remain with their owners than wander about without home or country."

My mistress often told me that my father was a planter who owned a plantation about two miles from ours. He was a white man, born in Liverpool, England. He died in Lewisville, Alabama, in the year 1875.

I will venture to say that I only saw my father a dozen times, when I was about four years old; and those times I saw him only from a distance, as he was driving by the great house of our plantation. Whenever my mistress saw him going by, she would take me by the hand and run out upon the piazza, and exclaim, "Stop there, I say! Don't you want to see and speak to and caress your darling child? She often speaks of you and wants to embrace her dear father. See what a bright and beautiful daughter she is, a perfect picture of yourself. Well, I declare, you are an affectionate father." I well remember that whenever my mistress would speak thus and upbraid him, he would whip up his horse and get out of sight and hearing as quickly as possible. My mistress's action was, of course, intended to humble and shame my father. I never spoke to him, and cannot remember that he ever noticed me, or in any way acknowledged me to be his child.

My mother and my mistress were children together, and grew up to be mothers together. My mother was the cook in my mistress's household. One morning when master had gone to Eufaula, my mother and my mistress got into an argument, the consequence of which was that my mother was whipped, for the first time in her life. Whereupon, my mother refused to do any more work, and ran away from the plantation. For three years we did not see her again.

Our plantation was one of several thousand acres, comprising large level fields, upland, and considerable forests of Southern pine. Cotton, corn, sweet potatoes, sugar cane, wheat, and rye were the principal crops raised on the plantation. It was situated near the P— River, and about twenty-three miles from Clayton, Ala.

One day my master heard that the Yankees were coming our way, and he immediately made preparations to get his goods and valuables out of their reach. The big six-mule team was brought to the smoke-house door, and loaded with hams and provisions. After being loaded, the team was put in the care of two of the most trustworthy and valuable slaves that my master owned, and driven away. It was master's intention to have these things taken to a swamp, and there concealed in a pit that had recently been made for the purpose. But just before the team left the main road for the by-road that led to the swamp, the two slaves were surprised by the Yankees, who at once took possession of the provisions, and started the team toward Clayton, where the Yankees had headquarters. The road to Clayton ran past our plantation. One of the slave children happened to look up the road, and saw the Yankees coming, and gave warning. Whereupon my master left unceremoniously for the woods, and remained concealed there for five days. The niggers had run away whenever they got a chance, but now it was master's and the other white folks' turn to run.

Kate Drumgoold
?1860s–?

S he and Annie Burton were among the earliest Black emigrants from the Southern United States to the North after the American Civil War. In 1865 she went with her mother to Brooklyn, New York, where she was converted to Christianity. She worked as a domestic servant and dedicated herself to obtaining an education so that she could become a

*teacher. Despite sickness and poverty, she saved enough of her earnings
to attend boarding schools and by the age of twenty had received almost
four years of formal training at Wayland Seminary, Washington, DC; in
this brief extract from* A Slave Girl's Story: Being an Autobiography of Kate
Drumgoold *(1898) she touchingly comments on the manners of her male
fellow students there. After further schooling at Harper's Ferry, she began
her teaching career, which she continued for eleven years until forced by
poor health to stop.*

From

A Slave Girl's Story

ETIQUETTE OF YOUNG MEN

I WAS wondering a few days since if the men of the present day had lost
the respect that men used to have for the women. I was carried back to
the year 1884 while in school with so many of the young men of my own
race, when I saw so much of the respect that they showed to us girls and that
was what caused me to write this to their honor. I think that true etiquette is
one of the greatest blessings that young men can have for the women, for it is
to them that we look to for the protection and love, and if we fail to find it in
them where shall we look? This is one of the greatest fortunes that one can
have, and it is that which makes a young man what he ought to be. We, as the
women, need so many of such ones and the world needs them fully as much,
and the God who made them looks for more and when he does not find it in
the dear creatures that He has made it makes Him feel sad.

I found a number of young men that used to attend the Wayland Seminary
that had the greatest regard for the girls, and I could not but notice them in this
respect and their kind acts while there, although I was not in the same classes
with them, but I never saw them make any difference while I was in school. I
always found good friends among them and I never saw a young man meet
one of the young ladies but they lifted their hats, and that made the people
of Washington, D. C., always speak of it in the kindest terms. One never loses
anything in this way, and their virtues are greater than gold.

When the weather was very bad one day and I was coming from school and a
young man saw me fall down, he came to help me home and I felt very grateful
and I feel that wherever that young man shall go he will have favor in the eyes
of all, and God will be his leader for he has made a good beginning.

Ida B. Wells (Barnett)

1862–1931

A crusading journalist, she was active in the civil rights movement and anti-lynching campaigns. Born to slaves in Holly Springs, Mississippi, she was educated at the local freedmen's school and, when orphaned at fourteen, became a teacher in order to support her brothers and sisters. In 1883 she moved to Memphis, where she continued to teach and began to write for a local Black weekly, while attending Fisk University and Lemoyne Institute. In 1891 she lost her teaching job after complaining about facilities for Blacks, and she devoted herself to exposing their conditions in her newspaper Free Speech and Headlight. Later she was a reporter for the New York Age. She moved to Chicago after her marriage to Ferdinand L. Barnett and was active in politics there. She undertook anti-lynching speaking tours in the USA and abroad, travelling to Britain in 1893 and 1894 and addressing audiences of thousands. She founded, in 1914, the first Black women's suffrage organization, the Alpha Suffrage Club, and co-founded the National Association of Colored Women, the National Afro-American Council and the National Association for the Advancement of Colored People. Working as a probation officer, she organized legal aid for people such as the victims of the 1918 Race Riots. She began her posthumously published autobiography, Crusade for Justice (1970), in 1928. The earliest printed appeal for capitalizing the word "Negro" was in this editorial by her in 1878 in the Chicago Conservator, which she owned and edited.

Spell It With a Capital

WE have noticed an error which all journalists seem to make. Whether from mistake or ill-intention, we are unable to say, but the profession universally begins Negro with a small letter. It is certainly improper, and as no one has ever given a good reason for this breach of orthography, we will offer one. White men began printing long before Colored men dared read their works; had power to establish any rule they saw fit. As a mark of disrespect, as a stigma, as a badge of inferiority, they tacitly agreed to spell his name without a capital. The French, German, Irish, Dutch, Japanese, and other nationalities are honored with a capital letter, but the poor sons of Ham must bear the burden of a small *n*.

To our Colored journalistic brothers we present this as a matter of self-interest. Spell it with a capital. To the Democratic journals we present this as a matter of good grammar. To the Republicans we present it as a matter of right. Spell it with a capital. To all persons who would take from our wearied shoulders a hair's weight of the burden of prejudice and ill will we bear, we present this as a matter of human charity and beg you SPELL IT WITH A CAPITAL.

Mary Church Terrell

1863–1954

A lifelong leader in anti-discrimination fights, she was born in Memphis, Tennessee, to newly emancipated parents. She enjoyed a good education, and in 1884 graduated head of her class from Oberlin College. She taught at Wilberforce University and at the High School for Colored Youth, Washington, DC, studied for two years (1888–90) in Europe, and in 1891 married teacher and lawyer Robert H. Terrell. In 1895 she was the first Black woman appointed to the DC Board of Education, serving for eleven years. She was first president of the National Association of Colored Women (1896–1901) and a founder of the National Association for the Advancement of Colored People. In the 1890s she became a public speaker, campaigning against lynching and discriminatory laws. She represented Black women at international congresses in Berlin, Zurich and London, spoke on "The Progress of Coloured Women" at the 1898 convention of the National American Woman Suffrage Association, and at the 1904 International Council of Women in Germany. Politically active till the end of her life, she was, at the age of eighty-nine, a plaintiff in a civil rights test case which resulted in the outlawing of racial discrimination in eating places in Washington in 1949. Her book A Colored Woman in a White World, introduced by H. G. Wells, was published in 1940.

Letter to the Editor of the Washington Post
(14 May, 1949)

DEAR Sir:
Please stop using the word "Negro". Several days ago "BAN ON WORD ASKED" was the *Post*'s title of an appeal made by a leper who stood before a congressional committee urging that the Federal Government ban the use of the word "leper". He said the word "leper" should be removed from the dictionary because of its unjust and shameful stigma which hurts its victims and efforts to control and wipe the disease out. He wants the affliction to be called "Hanson's Disease", because lepers are treated unfairly owing to "public misunderstanding".

For a reason similar to the one given by the leper I am urging the *Post* and others willing to advance our interests and deal justly with our group to stop using the word "Negro". The word is a misnomer from every point of view. It does not represent a country or anything else except one single, solitary color. And no one color can describe the various and varied complexions in our group. In complexion we range from deep black to the fairest white with all the colors of the rainbow thrown in for good measure. When twenty or thirty of us are meeting together it would be as hard to find three or four of us with the same complexion as it would be to catch greased lightning in a bottle. We are the only human beings in the world with fifty seven variety of complexions who are classed together as a single racial unit. Therefore, we are really, truly colored people, and that is the only name in the English language which accurately describes us.

To be sure the complexion of the Chinese and Japanese is yellow. But nobody refers to an individual in either group as a colored man ... They say he is Chinese.... When I studied abroad and was introduced as an "American", (generally speaking, everybody from the United States used to be called an "American" in Europe) occasionally somebody would say, "You are rather dark to be an American, aren't you?" "Yes," I would reply, "I am dark, because some of my ancestors were Africans." I was proud of having the continent of Africa part of my ancestral background. "I am an African-American," I would explain. I am not ashamed of my African descent. Africa had great universities before there were any in England and the African was the first man industrious and skillful enough to work in iron. If our group must have a special name setting it apart, the sensible way to settle it would be to refer to our ancestors, the Africans, from whom our swarthy complexions come.

There are at least two strong reasons why I object to designating our group as Negroes. If a man is a Negro, it follows as the night the day that a woman is a Negress. "Negress" is an ugly, repulsive word – virtually a term of degradation and reproach which colored women of this country can not live down in a thousand years. I have questioned scores of men who call themselves "Negroes", and each and every one of them strenuously objected to having his wife, or daughter or mother or any woman in his family called a "Negress".

In the second place, I object to ... Negro because our meanest detractors and most cruel persecutors insist that we shall be called by that name, so that they can humiliate us by referring contemptuously to us as "niggers", or "Negras" as Bilbo used to do. Some of our group say they will continue to classify us as Negroes, until an individual referred to as such will be proud of that name. But that is a case of wishful thinking and nothing else. For the moment one hears the word Negro in this country, instantly, automatically, in his mind's eye he sees a human being who is ignorant, segregated, discriminated against, considered inferior and objectionable on general principles from every point of view. God alone knows how long it will take our minority group under prevailing conditions in this country to reach such heights that a representative of it will be proud to be called a Negro. That would be a double, back action, super-duper miracle indeed! ...

It is a great pity the word "Negro" was not outlawed in the Emancipation Proclamation as it certainly should have been. After people have been freed, it is a cruel injustice to call them by the same name they bore as slaves. It is painful and shocking indeed that those in our group who have enjoyed educational opportunities; that officials in the National Association for the Advancement of Colored People, founded forty years ago, which repudiated the word "Negro", should continue to use the slave term and thereby increase the difficulties of their group in their effort to reach the worthy goal toward which they strive.

The founders of the NAACP which has been and still is waging such a holy warfare against disfranchisement, segregation and discrimination of all kinds certainly deserves our gratitude for not naming that wonderful, powerful instrument for good "The National Association for the Advancement of Negroes".

Adelaide Casely-Hayford

1868–1959

Born in Sierra Leone of Fanti and English ancestry (her grandfather was a Yorkshireman who worked for the Royal African Company and married the daughter of a Fanti chief), she and her family migrated in 1872 to England, where she spent her schooldays, later study-

ing music in Germany for three years from 1885. Returning to Freetown in 1897, after her father's death, she began to search for her identity, feeling herself "a black white woman". At the age of thirty-five, she married the Gold Coast lawyer, writer and political activist J. E. Casely-Hayford and their daughter Gladys was born in 1904. Adelaide and her husband separated after some years and with her sister she established the Girls Vocational School in Freetown; in 1926 she and her niece undertook a US lecture tour to raise money for her project, the first West African women to lecture there.

Her writings, published late in her life – or posthumously, as in the case of "Mista Courifer", which in 1961 was included in Langston Hughes's An African Treasury *– show her deep awareness of being first and foremost an African. She began her memoirs, in the form of a series of long essays, some time after her retirement in 1940, adding to them in the years up to the 1950s. "My Life and Times", edited by her grand-daughter-in-law Lucilda Hunter, appears in* Memoirs and Poems *(1983), alongside a selection of poetry by her daughter, and ends with the words: "If I have any advice worth giving to the rising generation of Africa, it is this: NEVER be ashamed of your colour. Be representative of the best of African life. I found from experience that this is the only way to happiness, the only way to retain one's self-respect, the only way to win the respect of other races, and the only way in which we can ever give a real contribution to the world."*

Mista Courifer

NOT a sound was heard in the coffin-maker's workshop, that is to say no human sound. Mista Courifer, a solid citizen of Sierra Leone, was not given to much speech. His apprentices, knowing this, never dared address him unless he spoke first. Then they only carried on their conversation in whispers. Not that Mista Courifer did not know how to use his tongue. It was incessantly wagging to and fro in his mouth at every blow of the hammer. But his shop in the heart of Freetown was a part of his house. And, as he had once confided to a friend, he was a silent member of his own household from necessity. His wife, given to much speaking, could outtalk him.

"It's no use for argue wid woman," he said cautiously. "Just like 'e no use for teach woman carpentering; she nebba sabi for hit de nail on de head. If 'e argue, she'll hit eberyting but de nail; and so wid de carpentering."

So, around his wife, with the exception of his tongue's continual wagging like a pendulum, his mouth was kept more or less shut. But whatever self-control he exercised in this respect at home was completely sent to the wind in his official capacity as the local preacher at chapel, for Mista Courifer was one of the pillars of the church, being equally at home in conducting a prayer meeting, superintending the Sunday school or occupying the pulpit.

His voice was remarkable for its wonderful graduations of pitch. He would insist on starting most of his tunes himself: consequently they nearly always ended in a solo. If he happened to pitch in the bass, he descended into such a *de profundis* that his congregations were left to flounder in a higher key; if he started in the treble, he soared so high that the children stared at him openmouthed and their elders were lost in wonder and amazement. As for his prayers, he roared and volleyed and thundered to such an extent that poor little mites were quickly reduced to a state of collapse and started to whisper from sheer fright.

But he was most at home in the pulpit. It is true, his labours were altogether confined to the outlying village districts of Regent, Gloucester and Leicester, an arrangement with which he was by no means satisfied. Still, a village congregation is better than none at all.

His favourite themes were Jonah and Noah and he was forever pointing out the great similarity between the two, generally finishing his discourse after this manner: "You see, my beloved Brebren, den two man berry much alike. All two lived in a sinful and adulturous generation. One get inside an ark; de odder one get inside a whale. Day bof seek a refuge fom de swelling waves.

"And so it is today, my beloved Brebren. No matter if we get inside a whale or get inside an ark, as long as we get inside some place of safety – as long as we can find some refuge, some hiding place from de wiles ob de debil."

But his congregation was by no means convinced.

Mr Courifer always wore black. He was one of the Sierra Leone gentlemen who consider everything European to be not only the right thing, but the *only* thing for the African, and having read somewhere that English undertakers generally appeared in sombre attire, he immediately followed suit.

He even went so far as to build a European house. During his short stay in England, he had noticed how the houses were built and furnished and had forthwith erected himself one after the approved pattern – a house with stuffy little passages, narrow little staircases and poky rooms, all crammed with saddlebags and carpeted with Axminsters. No wonder his wife had to talk. It was so hopelessly uncomfortable, stuffy and unsanitary.

So Mr Courifer wore black. It never struck him for a single moment that red would have been more appropriate, far more becoming, far less expensive and far more national. No! It must be black. He would have liked blue black, but he wore rusty black for economy.

There was one subject upon which Mr Courifer could talk even at home, so no one ever mentioned it: his son, Tomas. Mista Courifer had great expectations for his son; indeed in the back of his mind he had hopes of seeing him reach the high-water mark of red-tape officialism, for Tomas was in the government service. Not very high up, it is true, but still he was in it. It was an honour that impressed his father deeply, but Tomas unfortunately did not seem to think quite so much of it. The youth in question, however, was altogether neutral in his opinions in his father's presence. Although somewhat feminine as to attire, he was distinctly masculine in his speech. His neutrality was not a matter of choice, since no one was allowed to choose anything in the Courifer family but the paterfamilias himself.

From start to finish, Tomas's career had been cut out, and in spite of the fact that nature had endowed him with a black skin and an African temperament, Tomas was to be an Englishman. He was even to be an Englishman in appearance.

Consequently, once a year mysterious bundles arrived by parcel post. When opened, they revealed marvellous checks and plaids in vivid greens and blues after the fashion of a Liverpool counterjumper, waistcoats decorative in the extreme with their bold designs and rows of brass buttons, socks vying with the rainbow in glory and pumps very patent in appearance and very fragile as to texture.

Now, Tomas was no longer a minor and he keenly resented having his clothes chosen for him like a boy going to school for the first time. Indeed on one occasion, had it not been for his sister's timely interference, he would have chucked the whole collection in the fire.

Dear little Keren-happuch, eight years his junior and not at all attractive, with a very diminutive body and a very large heart. Such a mistake! People's hearts ought always to be in proportion to their size, otherwise it upsets the dimensions of the whole structure and often ends in its total collapse.

Keren was that type of little individual whom nobody worshipped, consequently she understood the art of worshipping others to the full. Tomas was the object of her adoration. Upon him she lavished the whole store of her boundless wealth and whatever hurt Tomas became positive torture as far as Keren-happuch was concerned.

"Tomas!" she said clinging to him with the tenacity of a bear, as she saw the faggots piled up high, ready for the conflagration. "Do yah! No burn am oh! Ole man go flog you oh! Den clos berry fine! I like am myself too much. I wish" – she added wistfully – "me na boy; I wish I could use am."

This was quite a new feature which had never struck Tomas before. Keren-happuch had never received a bundle of English clothes in her life, hence her great appreciation of them.

At first Tomas only laughed – the superior daredevil don't-care-a-damn-about-consequences laugh of the brave before the deed. But after hearing that wistful little sentence, he forgot his own annoyance and awoke to his responsibilities as an elder brother.

A few Sundays later, Tomas Courifer, Jr., marched up the aisle of the little Wesleyan chapel in all his Liverpool magnificence accompanied by a very elated little Keren-happuch whose natural unattractiveness had been further accentuated by a vivid cerise costume – a heterogeneous mass of frill and furbelows. But the glory of her array by no means outshone the brightness of her smile. Indeed that smile seemed to illuminate the whole church and to dispel the usual melancholy preceding the recital of Jonah and his woes.

Unfortunately, Tomas had a very poor opinion of the government service and in a burst of confidence he had told Keren that he meant to chuck it at the very first opportunity. In vain his sister expostulated and pointed out the advantages connected with it – the honour, the pension – and the awful nemesis upon the head of anyone incurring the head-of-the-family's ire.

"Why you want leave am, Tomas?" she asked desperately.

"Because I never got a proper holiday. I have been in the office four and a half years and have never had a whole week off yet. And," he went on vehemently, "these white chaps come and go, and a fresh one upsets what the old one has done and a newcomer upsets what he does and they all only stay for a year and a half and go away for four months, drawing big fat pay all the time, not to speak of passages, whereas a poor African like me has to work year in and year out with never a chance of a decent break. But you needn't be afraid, Keren dear," he added consolingly. "I shan't resign, I shall just behave so badly that they'll chuck me and then my ole man can't say very much."

Accordingly when Tomas, puffing a cigarette, sauntered into the office at 9 a.m. instead of 8 a.m. for the fourth time that week, Mr Buckmaster, who had hitherto maintained a discreet silence and kept his eyes shut, opened them wide and administered a sharp rebuke. Tomas's conscience was profoundly stirred. Mr Buckmaster was one of the few white men for whom he had a deep respect, aye, in the depth of his heart, he really had a sneaking regard. It was for fear of offending him that he had remained so long at his post.

But he had only lately heard that his chief was due for leave so he decided there and then to say a long good-bye to a service which had treated him so shabbily. He was a vociferous reader of halfpenny newspapers and he knew that the humblest shop assistant in England was entitled to a fortnight's holiday every year. Therefore it was ridiculous to argue that because he was an African working in Africa there was no need for a holiday. All his applications for leave were quietly pigeonholed for a more convenient season.

"Courifer!" Mr Buckmaster said sternly. "Walk into my private office please." And Courifer knew that this was the beginning of the end.

"I suppose you know that the office hours are from 8 a.m. till 4 p.m. daily," commenced Mr Buckmaster, in a freezing tone.

"Yes, er – Sir!" stammered Courifer with his heart in his mouth and his mouth twisted up into a hard sailor's knot.

"And I suppose you also know that smoking is strictly forbidden in the office?"

"Yes, er – er – Sir!" stammered the youth.

"Now hitherto," the even tones went on, "I have always looked upon you as an exemplary clerk, strictly obliging, punctual, accurate and honest, but for the last two or three weeks I have had nothing but complaints about you. And from what I myself have seen, I am afraid they are not altogether unmerited."

Mr Buckmaster rose as he spoke, took a bunch of keys out of his pocket and, unlocking his roll-top desk, drew out a sheaf of papers. "This is your work, is it not?" he said to the youth.

"Yes, er – er – Sir!" he stuttered, looking shamefacedly at the dirty, ink-stained, blotched sheets of closely typewritten matter.

"Then what in Heaven's name is the matter with you to produce such work?"

Tomas remained silent for a moment or two. He summoned up courage to look boldly at the stern countenance of his chief. And as he looked, the sternness seemed to melt away and he could see genuine concern there.

"Please, er – Sir!" he stammered. "May – I – er – just tell you everything?"

Half an hour later, a very quiet, subdued, penitent Tomas Courifer walked out of the office by a side door. Mr Buckmaster followed later, taking with him an increased respect for the powers of endurance exercised by the growing West African youth.

Six weeks later, Mista Courifer was busily occupied wagging his tongue when he looked up from his work to see a European man standing in his doorway.

The undertaker found speech and a chair simultaneously. "Good afternoon, Sah!" he said, dusting the chair before offering it to his visitor. "I hope you don't want a coffin, Sah!" which was a deep-sea lie for nothing pleased him more than the opportunity of making a coffin for a European. He was always so sure of the money. Such handsome money – paid it is true with a few ejaculations, but paid on the nail and without any deductions whatsoever. Now with his own people things were different. They demurred, they haggled, they bartered, they gave him detailed accounts of all their other expenses and then, after keeping him waiting for weeks, they would end by sending him half the amount with a stern exhortation to be thankful for that.

Mr Buckmaster took the proffered chair and answered pleasantly: "No, thank you, I don't intend dying just yet. I happened to be passing so I thought I should just like a word with you about your son."

Mr Courifer bristled all over with exultation and expectation. Perhaps they were going to make his son a kind of undersecretary of state. What an unexpected honour for the Courifer family. What a rise in their social status; what a rise out of their neighbours. How good God was!

"Of course you know he is in my office?"

"Oh, yes, Sah. He often speaks about you."

"Well, I am going home very soon and as I may not be returning to Sierra Leone, I just wanted to tell you how pleased I should be at any time to give him a decent testimonial."

Mr Courifer's countenance fell. What a comedown!

"Yes, Sah," he answered somewhat dubiously.

"I can recommend him highly as being steady, persevering, reliable and trustworthy. And you can always apply to me if ever such a thing be necessary."

Was that all! What a disappointment! Still it was something worth having. Mr Buckmaster was an Englishman and a testimonial from him would certainly be a very valuable possession. He rubbed his hands together as he said: "Well, I am berry much obliged to you, Sah, berry much obliged. And as time is short and we nebba know what a day may bring forth, would you mind writing one down now, Sah?"

"Certainly. If you will give me a sheet of paper, I shall do so at once."

Before Tomas returned home from his evening work, the testimonial was already framed and hanging up amidst the moth-eaten velvet of the drawing-room.

On the following Monday morning, Courifer Jr. bounced into his father's workshop, upsetting the equilibrium of the carpenter's bench and also of the voiceless apprentice hard at work.

"Well, Sah?" ejaculated his father, surveying him in disgust. "You berry late. Why you no go office dis morning?"

"Because I've got a whole two months' holiday, Sir! Just think of it – two whole months – with nothing to do but just enjoy myself!"

"Tomas," his father said solemnly, peering at him over his glasses, "you must larn for make coffin. You get fine chance now."

Sotto voce: "I'll be damned if I will!" Aloud: "No, thank you, Sir. I am going to learn how to make love, after which I am going to learn how to build myself a nice mud hut."

"And who dis gal you want married?" thundered his father, ignoring the latter part of the sentence altogether.

A broad smile illuminated Tomas's countenance. "She is a very nice girl, Sir, a very nice girl. Very quiet and gentle and sweet, and she doesn't talk too much."

"I see. Is dat all?"

"Oh, no. She can sew and clean and make a nice little home. And she has plenty sense; she will made a good mother."

"Yes, notting pass dat!"

"She has been to school for a long time. She reads nice books and she writes, oh, such a nice letter," said Tomas, patting his breast-pocket affectionately.

"I see. I suppose she sabi cook fashion?"

"I don't know, I don't think so, and it doesn't matter very much."

"What!" roared the old man. "You mean tell me you want married woman who no sabi cook?"

"I want to marry her because I love her, Sir!"

"Dat's all right, but for we country, de heart and de stomach always go togedder. For we country, black man no want married woman who no sabi cook! Dat de berry first requistional. You own mudder sabi cook."

That's the reason why she has been nothing but your miserable drudge all these years, thought the young man. His face was very grave as he rejoined: "The style in our country is not at all nice, Sir. I don't like to see a wife slaving away in the kitchen all times to make good chop for her husband who sits down alone and eats the best of everything himself, and she and the children only get the leavings. No thank you! And besides, Sir, you are always telling me that you want me to be an Englishman. That is why I always try to talk good English to you."

"Yes, dat's all right. Dat's berry good. But I want make you *look* like Englishman. I don't say you must copy all der different way!"

"Well, Sir, if I try till I die, I shall never look like an Englishman, and I don't know that I want to. But there are some English customs that I like very much indeed. I like the way white men treat their wives; I like their home life; I life to see mother and father and the little family all sitting down eating their meals together."

"I see," retorted his father sarcastically. "And who go cook den meal? You tink say wid your four pound a month, you go able hire a perfessional cook?"

"Oh, I don't say so, Sir. And I am sure if Accastasia does not know how to cook now, she will before we are married. But what I want you to understand is just this, that whether she is able to cook or not, I shall marry her just the same."

"Berry well," shouted his father, wrath delineated in every feature, "but instead of building one mud hut you better go one time build one madhouse."

"Sir, thank you. But I know what I am about and a mud hut will suit as perfectly for the present."

"A mud hut!" ejaculated his father in horror. "You done use fine England house wid staircase and balustrade and tick carpet and handsome furnitures. You want to go live in mud hut? You ungrateful boy, you shame me, oh!"

"Dear me, no, Sir. I won't shame you. It's going to be a nice clean spacious mud hut. And what is more, it is going to be a sweet little home, just big enough for two. I am going to distemper the walls pale green, like at the principal's rooms at Keren's school."

"How you sabi den woman's rooms?"

"Because you have sent me two or three times to pay her school fees, so I have looked at those walls and I like them too much."

"I see. And what else you go do?" asked his father ironically.

"I am going to order some nice wicker chairs from the Islands and a few good pieces of linoleum for the floors and then – "

"And den what?"

"I shall bring home my bride."

Mr Courifer's objection grew deeper with each moment. A mud hut! This son of his – the hope of his life! A government officer! A would-be Englishman! To live in a mud hut! His disgust knew no bounds. "You ungrateful wretch!" he bellowed. "You go disgrace me. You go lower your pore father. You go lower your position for de office."

"I am sorry, Sir," retorted the young man. "I don't wish to offend you. I'm grateful for all you have done for me. But I have had a raise in salary and I want a home of my own which, after all, is only natural, and" – he went on steadily, staring his father straight in the face – "I may as well tell you at once, you need not order any more Liverpool suits for me."

"Why not?" thundered his irate parent, removing his specs lest any harm should befall them.

"Well, I am sorry to grieve you, Sir, but I have been trying to live up to your European standards all this time. Now I am going to chuck it once and for all. I am going back to the native costume of my mother's people, and the next time I appear in chapel it will be as a Wolof."

The very next Sunday the awful shock of seeing his son walk up the aisle of the church in pantaloons and the bright loose overjacket of a Wolof from Gambia, escorting a pretty young bride the colour of chocolate, also in native dress, so unnerved Mista Courifer that his mind suddenly became a complete blank. He could not even remember Jonah and the whale, nor could his tongue possess one word to let fly, not one. The service had to be turned into a prayer meeting.

Mister Courifer is the local preacher no longer. Now he only makes coffins.

Alice Dunbar-Nelson
1875–1935

B orn in New Orleans to middle-class parents, she went to public schools and Dillard University. Graduating in 1892, she taught in New Orleans and Brooklyn, did further studies at the University of Pennsylvania, Cornell University and the School of Industrial Art, and began to submit poetry to Monthly Review. She came to the attention of poet Paul Lawrence Dunbar, and they married three years later, in 1898. She achieved national prominence as a poet in her own right and her work appeared in the major publications of the Harlem Renaissance; she also wrote drama and short stories, and her publications include Violets, and Other Tales (1895) – in which "The Woman" appeared – and The Goodness of St Rocque, and Other Stories (1899). After she and Dunbar separated in 1902, she returned to teaching for eighteen years. She became associate editor of the Wilmington Advocate, a weekly paper published by her second husband Robert John Nelson (whom she married in 1916), dedicated to the achievement of equal rights for Black people. She was associate editor of the African Methodist Episcopal Church Review, columnist for the Pittsburgh Courier and the Washington Eagle and contributor to the Crisis, Opportunity, Collier's and Messenger. She also compiled two substantial collections, Masterpieces of Negro Eloquence: The Best Speeches by the Negro from the Days of Slavery to the Present Time (1914) and The Dunbar Speaker and Entertainer, containing the best prose and poetic selections by and about the Negro race (1920); "I Sit and Sew" was included in the latter. Three years after moving to Philadelphia, she died of a heart attack, leaving two unfinished novels.

The Woman

T HE literary manager of the club arose, cleared his throat, adjusted his cravat, fixed his eyes sternly upon the young man, and in a sonorous voice, a little marred by his habitual lisp, asked: "Mr —, will you please tell us your opinion upon the question, whether woman's chances for matrimony are increased or decreased when she becomes man's equal as a wage earner?"

The secretary adjusted her eye-glass, and held her pencil alertly poised above her book, ready to note which side Mr — took. Mr — fidgeted, pulled himself together with a violent jerk, and finally spoke his mind. Someone else did likewise, also someone else, then the women interposed, and jumped on the men, the men retaliated, a wordy war ensued, and the whole matter ended by nothing being decided, pro or con – generally the case in wordy discussions. *Moi?* Well, I sawed wood and said nothing, but all the while there was forming in my mind, no, I won't say forming, it was there already. It was this, *Why should well-salaried women marry?* Take the average working-woman of to-day. She works from five to ten hours a day, doing extra night work, sometimes, of course. Her work over, she goes home or to her boarding-house, as the case may be. Her meals are prepared for her, she has no household cares upon her shoulders, no troublesome dinners to prepare for a fault-finding husband, no fretful children to try her patience, no petty bread and meat economies to adjust. She has her cares, her money-troubles, her debts, and her scrimpings, it is true, but they only make her independent, instead of reducing her to a dead level of despair. Her day's work ends at the office, school, factory or store; the rest of the time is hers, undisturbed by the restless going to and fro of housewifely cares, and she can employ it in mental or social diversions. She does not incessantly rely upon the whims of a cross man to take her to such amusements as she desires. In this nineteenth century she is free to go where she pleases – provided it be in a moral atmosphere – without comment. Theatres, concerts, lectures, and the lighter amusements of social affairs among her associates, are open to her, and there she can go, see, and be seen, admire and be admired, enjoy and be enjoyed, without a single harrowing thought of the baby's milk or the husband's coffee.

Her earnings are her own, indisputably, unreservedly, undividedly. She knows to a certainty just how much she can spend, how well she can dress, how far her earnings will go. If there is a dress, a book, a bit of music, a bunch of flowers, or a bit of furniture that she wants, she can get it, and there is no need of asking anyone's advice, or gently hinting to John that Mrs So and So has a lovely new hat, and there is one ever so much prettier and cheaper down at Thus & Co's. To an independent spirit there is a certain sense of humiliation and wounded pride in asking for money, be it five cents or five hundred dollars. The working woman knows no such pang; she has but to question her account and all is over. In the summer she takes her savings of the winter, packs her trunk and takes a trip more or less extensive, and there is none to say her nay, – nothing to bother her save the accumulation of her own baggage. There is an independent, happy, free-and-easy swing about the motion of her life. Her mind is constantly being broadened by contact with the world in its working clothes; in her leisure moments by the better thought of dead and living men which she meets in her applications to books and periodicals; in her vacations, by her studies of nature, or it may be other communities than her own. The freedom which she enjoys she does not trespass upon, for if she did not learn at school she has acquired since habits of strong self-reliance, self-support, earnest thinking, deep discriminations, and firmly believes that the most perfect liberty is that state in which humanity conforms itself to and obeys strictly, without deviation, those laws which are best fitted for their mutual self-advancement.

And so your independent working woman of to-day comes as near being ideal in her equable self poise as can be imagined. So why should she hasten to give this liberty up in exchange for a serfdom, sweet sometimes, it is true, but which too often becomes galling and unendurable.

It is not marriage that I decry, for I don't think any really sane person would do this, but it is this wholesale marrying of girls in their teens, this rushing into an unknown plane of life to avoid work. Avoid work! What housewife dares call a moment her own?

Marriages might be made in Heaven, but too often they are consummated right here on earth, based on a desire to possess the physical attractions of the woman by the man, pretty much as a child desires a toy, and an innate love of man, a wild desire not to be ridiculed by the foolish as an "old maid," and a certain delicate shrinking from the work of the world – laziness is a good name for it – by the woman. The attraction of mind to mind, the ability of one to compliment the lights and shadows in the other, the capacity of either to fulfil the duties of wife or husband – these do not enter into the contract. That is why we have divorce courts.

And so our independent woman in every year of her full, rich, well-rounded life, gaining fresh knowledge and experience, learning humanity, and particularly that portion of it which is the other gender, so well as to avoid clay-footed idols, and finally when she does consent to bear the yoke upon her shoulders, does so with perhaps less romance and glamor than her younger scoffing sisters, but with an assurance of solid and more lasting happiness. Why should she have hastened this; was aught lost by the delay?

"They say" that men don't admire this type of woman, that they prefer the soft, dainty, winning, mindless creature who cuddles into men's arms, agrees to everything they say, and looks upon them as a race of gods turned loose upon this earth for the edification of womankind. Well, may be so, but there is one thing positive, they certainly respect the independent one, and admire her, too, even if it is at a distance, and that in itself is something. As to the other part, no matter how sensible a woman is on other questions, when she falls in love she is fool enough to believe her adored one a veritable Solomon. Cuddling? Well, she may preside over conventions, brandish her umbrella at board meetings, tramp the streets soliciting subscriptions, wield the blue pencil in an editorial sanctum, hammer a type-writer, smear her nose with ink from a galley full of pied type, lead infant ideas through the tortuous mazes of c-a-t and r-a-t, plead at the bar, or wield the scalpel in a dissecting room, yet when the right moment comes, she will sink as gracefully into his manly embrace, throw her arms as lovingly around his neck, and cuddle as warmly and sweetly to his bosom as her little sister who has done nothing else but think, dream, and practice for that hour. It comes natural, you see.

From a Woman's Point of View
(column in *Pittsburgh Courier*, 9 January 1926)

WE have come a long way in the appreciation of our own, and the realization of our own possibilities. The writer can remember one day in a well known school when, in company with the other students, she helped stage a student musical strike because some visitors from the North asked the students to "sing some of the songs of your own people." It was considered degrading even to refer to the old songs of slavery, much less sing them. And this attitude was by no means uncommon. Colored people felt uncomfortable and self-conscious and humiliated when the old songs were sung, and few were there who saw any beauty in them. And now this book season brings three well edited, authentic, beautifully arranged editions of the "sorrow songs" out in one month, and the Negro public is falling over itself to buy and own them.

So with our standard of beauty. Nordic, vs. Hawaiian. Two little girls sat playing dolls on the porch of a summer hotel where a goodly group of women of the race tilted their rocking chairs to and fro. The little golden skinned child played with a brown skin doll, with shorty curly black hair, wine dark tints in its bisque cheeks, and brown eyes that opened and closed most realistically. The little dusky maiden played with a big blonde doll, all golden curls and pink lace. And she was frankly amused at her little friend's brown hued doll.

"I wouldn't play with a funny looking doll like that," she giggled, "Why it's DARK. Who ever saw a dark doll?"

Mother No. 2 registered fury. What mother could brook an insult to her own child?

"And look at her hair!" continued Mother No. 1, as she smoothed the golden curls of her own child. "Why it's funny stuff, I wouldn't have a doll with hair like that."

Mother No. 2 gathered her insulted brown baby to her outraged bosom and rose in dignified wrath.

"It's not funny," she sobbed. "And if it is, it's hair's heaps better'n yours!" and fled with all the honors of war.

This was less than fifteen years ago. Yet what Negro mother now would buy her child a Nordic doll in preference to one of the color of its own race? And every little colored girl treasures her little brown doll as the most cherished of her family. It shows progress in racial ideals more strikingly than any one thing that we can notice.

And have you noticed how the prevalence of the brown doll has tinged the characteristics of the dolls made for little white girls? The so-called "character doll," with the tinted complexion? The Negro pigmentizes all American life, literature, music, art, dancing, dolls, dress, oratory, law and love. Is it a subtle overtone of brown, or a deep-rooted foundation of the great mother-heart of Africa, reaching out and embracing America?

I Sit and Sew

I sit and sew – a useless task it seems,
My hands grown tired, my head weighed down with dreams –
The panoply of war, the martial tread of men,
Grim faced, stern eyed, gazing beyond the ken
Of lesser souls, whose eyes have not seen Death,
Nor learned to hold their lives but as a breath –
But – I must sit and sew.

I sit and sew – my heart aches with desire –
That pageant terrible, that fiercely pouring fire
On wasted fields, and writhing grotesque things
Once men. My soul in pity flings
Appealing cries, yearning only to go
There in that holocaust of hell, those fields of woe –
But – I must sit and sew

The little useless seam, the idle patch;
Why dream I here beneath my homely thatch,
When there they lie in sodden mud and rain,
Pitifully calling me, the quick ones and the slain?
You need me, Christ. It is no roseate dream
That beckons me – this pretty futile seam
It stifles me – God, *must* I sit and sew?

Baba

c. 1877–1951

F rom Northern Nigeria, she told her life story in a series of interviews conducted by Mary F. Smith between 1949 and 1950. A
gifted storyteller with a remarkable memory, Baba related her
experiences from about 1890, before the coming of the British, until after
the Second World War. Her oral history was published in Baba of Karo:
A Woman of the Muslim Hausa (1954). This extract refers to the lifelong
bond-friendships between women of her community, whose obligations
include the exchange of gifts on ceremonial occasions. There could be
jealousy between kawaye (female bond-friends) of the same woman, just
as between co-wives.

From

Baba of Karo: A Woman of the Muslim Hausa

CHAPTER III

A GIRL'S FRIENDS

I HAD four *kawaye* at Zarewa; a *kawa* is your special girl-friend. There was
Kande, a Maguzawa girl, Zaila a daughter of butchers, Matan Sarki who was
my "sister";' Matan Sarki's mother was married and Matan Sarki was born in
that house, then her mother broke up that marriage and came to our ward and
married one of our "fathers"; she brought Matan Sarki with her. She was nine
years old and I was nine at the time, too. When we put on our best clothes and
went to market, our mothers looked at us and saw that we were both handsome,
so they said it would be nice to make us *kawaye*. Since I was already living here
in the town, I bought ten kolanuts and some perfume and henna and I called my
younger sister and gave them to her to take to Matan Sarki's mother who had
married our "father". They gave her the gift-bearer's dues, a small share of the
gift she had brought them. The following Friday Matan Sarki sent her younger
sister to bring gifts to me. There we were, then when the Great Festival came
round one friend would get out her money and buy oil and perfume and henna
and kolanuts and take them to the other, so that she could dress her hair for
the Feast. Matan Sarki would send her younger sister, who would come to our
mother's hut. Mother would give her threepence or sixpence, her dues, and say
to me, "Here are your things." She was pleased.

This sort of friendship between women who are *kawaye* has nothing to do with men – men have their own sorts of friends. In the morning we would go off to market together, the five of us, and when we came back we would take each other home and all eat food together. At night we used to go dancing. When one *kawa* got married, the others escorted her to her husband's home.

There was Zaila – they used to drum to her a lot, I remember her song:

> *Zaila from a distant town,*
> *Zaila from a distant town,*
> *Whoever sees Zaila gives a thousand (cowries),*
> *Even if it breaks a poor man,*
> *Or he gives her five hundred.*

This was my drum-rhythm:

> *Baba with many Gwari,*[1]
> *Baba with many Gwari,*
> *Everyone sees Baba with many Gwari.*
> *In your house they don't say* 'yar kwaliya
>   *They say* dan kwaliya,
> *In your house they don't say* dan koko,
>   *They say* dan koko.
> *Baba with many Gwari.*

Zaila was a daughter of the Zarewa butchers, she lived in their ward. We met in the market and we exchanged gifts. She died four years ago over at Jos. I liked Zaila, she was handsome. Matan Sarki, in our own kin, was dark like me but she had a longer nose. Among us all there wasn't one ugly one. Kande lived near the market, when we went to market we used to see her, the daughter of the sellers of salt. One day she said, "Do you like me?" I said, "Yes, I like you." I said, "*Kawa?*" she said, "*Kawa.*" There was no more discussion, we liked one another. It had nothing to do with our parents, Kande and I became *kawaye* on our own. I had been seeing her for a long time, then the day that desire came we became *kawaye*.

The girls of our family did not go to a Koran school, we were a farmer's family. At that time our male relatives did not farm, the slaves did that. The boys of the family went to Koran school.

In the evenings we used to play and dance and sing songs; there was one I remember about Maikano the *jakada*'s grandson, he was a young man who used to steal and give the stolen goods to the drummers and singers; when he gave them things they made songs about him.

There was a splendid drummer, and there was a song about him:

---

[1] *Gwari* – i.e. pagans, slaves. "*Yar kwaliya, dan kwaliya*, etc. – wrong genders, mistakes with implosive "d", in general a play on the incorrect Hausa spoken by pagan slaves.
[2] *Jakada* – the fiefholder's agent.

There was a splendid drummer, and there was a song about him:

> *The drum drums health,*
> *The drum drums wealth,*
> *He takes his wife six hundred thousand cowries.*
> *The drum drums health,*
> *The drum drums wealth,*
> *He takes his son six hundred thousand cowries,*
> *The drum drums health,*
> *The drum drums wealth . . .*

Then we danced. Another of Mai Zaria the drummer's songs went like this:

> *If I were like Mai Zaria*
> *I would not farm, I would not hoe,*
> *I would not even go to market,*
> *If I were like Mai Zaria!*

His drumming was so good that everyone gave him money, they gave him gowns, and he felt good. Then the praise-singers would sing:

> *Son of the house, take out your money,*
> *Take it out and give me some,*
> *Take out your money and give it to me,*
> *Indeed friends are made with laughter,*
> *Cheeriness is what takes a man.*
> *You aren't like the orphan*
> *On whom Allah turned his back,*
> *Because you have your parents*
> *You have gifts in your house,*
> *You have inherited happiness.*
> *For your mother looks at her son,*
> *Your father looks at his son,*
> *Indeed you've inherited gifts in your house.*
> *Because your mother sees her son —*
> *Because your father sees his son —*
> *Take out your money and give it to the singers,*
> *Because you inherited such gifts in your house.*

The praise-singers are cunning – they undoubtedly are. I don't remember all the words of their songs, those are what I remember.

Angelina Weld Grimké
1880–1958

B orn in Boston, Massachusetts, she was the only child of a prominent Black lawyer and his white wife, who left him when their daughter was young. Living with her father after 1887, she was educated at various schools where she was invariably the only Black, graduating in 1902. She taught English from 1903 and continued writing poems, having first been published in 1893. After her father's death in 1930, she gave up teaching and moved to New York to write, maintaining contact with Georgia Douglas Johnson, her longtime friend in Washington, DC. Using a romantic and lyrical style, she was one of the first Black poets to receive general recognition. She wrote a pioneering protest play Rachel (the programme notes claimed: "This is the first attempt to use the stage for race propaganda in order to enlighten the American people relative to the lamentable condition of ten millions of colored citizens in this free republic"), as well as other dramas and short stories. Her writing reflects something of the confusion of her life – born of mixed race into a privileged background, over-protected by an ambitious father whose death devastated her, and ambivalent about her sexuality. Her poems have appeared in many anthologies through the decades.

The Black Finger

I have just seen a beautiful thing
   Slim and still,
Against a gold, gold sky
  A straight cypress,
  Sensitive,
  Exquisite,
A black finger
Pointing upwards.
Why, beautiful, still finger are you black?
And why are you pointing upwards?

At April

Toss your gay heads,
  Brown girl trees;
Toss your gay lovely heads;
Shake your downy russet curls
All about your brown faces;
Stretch your brown slim bodies;
Stretch your brown slim arms'
Stretch your brown slim toes.
Who knows better than we
With the dark, dark bodies,
What it means
When April comes a-laughing and a-weeping
Once again
At our hearts?

Jessie Redmon Fauset

1882–1961

*S*he was born in Camden County, New Jersey, and educated in
public schools in Philadelphia (the only Black student in her high
school classes) and at Cornell (gaining a BA in 1905, one of its first
Black women graduates), the University of Pennsylvania (MA, 1919) and
the Sorbonne. She was literary editor of Crisis (1912–26), publishing
many writers who achieved prominence in the Harlem Renaissance, as
well as her own poems, stories and essays. In 1921 she attended the Pan-
African Congress abroad and subsequently returned to the Sorbonne to
study French. She taught French in New York and for a time in 1949
was visiting professor of English at Hampton Institute, Virginia. In

1929 she married and in the early 1950s moved to New Jersey, where she remained until her husband's death in 1958, when she moved to Philadelphia. The most accomplished of her novels is Plum Bun *(extracted below), which has as its theme a mulatto woman passing for white. Introducing the 1985 edition, Gloria McDowell writes: "Like black women before her – Sojourner Truth, Anna J. Cooper, Frances W. Harper, Mary Church Terrell, among them – Fauset saw both blackness and femaleness as essential parts of her identity. Her writings demonstrate that the 'race' question and the 'woman' question are necessarily and unavoidably interconnected. Each of her four novels –* There Is Confusion *(1924),* Plum Bun *(1929),* The Chinaberry Tree *(1931), and* Comedy, American Style *(1933) – deals with some aspect of this connection, but none as effectively as* Plum Bun.*

Oriflamme

"I can remember when I was a little, young girl, how my old mammy would sit out of doors in the evenings and look up at the stars and groan, and I would say, 'Mammy, what makes you groan so?' And she would say, 'I am groaning to think of my poor children; they do not know where I be and I don't know where they be. I look up at the stars and they look up at the stars!'"

– *Sojourner Truth*

I think I see her sitting bowed and black,
    Stricken and seared with slavery's mortal scars,
Reft of her children, lonely, anguished yet
    Still looking at the stars.

Symbolic mother, we thy myriad sons,
    Pounding our stubborn hearts on Freedom's bars,
Clutching our birthright, fight with faces set,
    Still visioning the stars!

Dead Fires

If this is peace, this dead and leaden thing,
    Then better far the hateful fret, the sting.
Better the wound forever seeking balm
    Than this gray calm!

Is this pain's surcease? Better far the ache,
   The long-drawn dreary day, the night's white wake,
Better the choking sigh, the sobbing breath
   Than passion's death!

From

Plum Bun

CHAPTER IV

T HE third-storey front was Angela's bedroom. She was glad of its loneliness
and security tonight, – even if her mother had not suggested her going to
bed early she would have sought its shelter immediately after supper. Study for
its own sake held no attractions for her; she did not care for any of her subjects
really except Drawing and French. And when she was drawing she did not consider that she was studying, it was too naturally a means of self-expression. As for
French, she did have to study that with great care, for languages did not come to
her with any great readiness, but there was an element of fine ladyism about the
beautiful, logical tongue that made her in accordance with some secret subconscious ambition resolve to make it her own.

The other subjects, History, English, and Physical Geography, were not
drudgery, for she had a fair enough mind; but then they were not attractive
either, and she was lacking in Virginia's dogged resignation to unwelcome
duties. Even when Jinny was a little girl she had been known to say manfully in
the face of an uncongenial task: "Well, I dotta det it done." Angela was not like
that. But tonight she was concentrating with all her power on her work. During
the day she had been badly hurt; she had received a wound whose depth and
violence she would not reveal even to her parents, – because, and this only
increased the pain, young as she was she knew that there was nothing they
could do about it. There was nothing to be done but to get over it. Only she
was not developed enough to state this stoicism to herself. She was like a little
pet cat that had once formed part of their household; its leg had been badly torn
by a passing dog and the poor thing had dragged itself into the house and lain
on its cushion patiently, waiting stolidly for this unfamiliar agony to subside. So
Angela waited for the hurt in her mind to cease.

But across the history dates on the printed page and through the stately lines
of Lycidas she kept seeing Mary Hastings' accusing face, hearing Mary Hastings'
accusing voice:

"Coloured! Angela, you never told me that you were coloured!"

And then her own voice in tragic but proud bewilderment. "Tell you that
I was coloured! Why of course I never told you that I was coloured. Why
should I?"

She had been so proud of Mary Hastings' friendship. In the dark and tortured
spaces of her difficult life it had been a lovely, hidden refuge. It had been an

experience so rarely sweet that she had hardly spoken of it even to Virginia. The other girls in her classes had meant nothing to her. At least she had schooled herself to have them mean nothing. Some of them she had known since early childhood; they had lived in her neighbourhood and had gone to the graded schools with her. They had known that she was coloured, for they had seen her with Virginia, and sometimes her tall, black father had come to fetch her home on a rainy day. There had been pleasant enough contacts and intimacies; in the quiet of Jefferson Street they had played "The Farmer in the Dell" and "Here come three jolly, jolly sailor-boys", dark retreats of the old market had afforded endless satisfaction for "Hide and Go Seek". She and those other children had gone shopping arm in arm for school supplies, threading their way in and out of the bustle and confusion that were Columbia Avenue.

As she grew older many of these intimacies lessened, in some cases ceased altogether. But she was never conscious of being left completely alone; there was always some one with whom to eat lunch or who was going her way after school. It was not until she reached the high school that she began to realize how solitary her life was becoming. There were no other coloured girls in her class but there had been only two or three during her school-life, and if there had been any she would not necessarily have confined herself to them; that this might be a good thing to do in sheer self-defence would hardly have occurred to her. But this problem did not confront her; what did confront her was that the very girls with whom she had grown up were evading her; when she went to the Assembly none of them sat next to her unless no other seat were vacant; little groups toward which she drifted during lunch, inexplicably dissolved to re-form in another portion of the room. Sometimes a girl in this new group threw her a backward glance charged either with a mean amusement or with annoyance.

Angela was proud; she did not need such a hint more than once, but she was bewildered and hurt. She took stories to school to read at recess, or wandered into the drawing laboratory and touched up her designs. Miss Barrington thought her an unusually industrious student.

And then in the middle of the term Mary Hastings had come, a slender, well-bred girl of fifteen. She was rather stupid in her work, in fact she shone in nothing but French and good manners. Undeniably she had an air, and her accent was remarkable. The other pupils, giggling, produced certain uncouth and unheard of sounds, but Mary said in French: "No, I have lent my knife to the brother-in-law of the gardener but here is my cane," quite as though the idiotic phrase were part of an imaginary conversation which she was conducting and appreciating. "She really knows what she's talking about," little Esther Bayliss commented, and added that Mary's family had lost some money and they had had to send her to public school. But it was some time before this knowledge, dispensed by Esther with mysterious yet absolute authenticity, became generally known. Meanwhile Mary was left to her own devices while the class with complete but tacit unanimity "tried her out". Mary, unaware of this, looked with her near-sighted, slightly supercilious gaze about the room at recess and seeing only one girl, and that girl Angela, who approached in dress, manner and deportment her own rather set ideas, had taken her lunch over to the other pupil's desk and said: "Come on, let's eat together while you tell me who everybody is."

Angela took the invitation as simply as the other had offered. "That little girl in the purplish dress is Esther Bayliss and the tall one in the thick glasses –"

Mary, sitting with her back to the feeding groups, never troubled to look around. "I don't mean the girls. I expect I'll know them soon enough when I get around to it. I mean the teachers. Do you have to dig for them?" She liked Angela and she showed it plainly and directly. Her home was in some remote fastness of West Philadelphia which she could reach with comparative swiftness by taking the car at Spring Garden Street. Instead she walked half-way home with her new friend, up Seventeenth Street as far as Girard Avenue where, after a final exchange of school matters and farewells, she took the car, leaving Angela to her happy, satisfied thoughts. And presently she began to know more than happiness and satisfaction, she was knowing the extreme gratification of being the chosen companion of a popular and important girl, for Mary, although not quick at her studies, was a power in everything else. She dressed well, she had plenty of pocket money, she could play the latest marches in the gymnasium, she received a certain indefinable but flattering attention from the teachers, and she could make things "go". The school paper was moribund and Mary knew how to resuscitate it; she brought in advertisements from her father's business; she made her married sisters obtain subscriptions. Without being obtrusive or over-bearing, without condescension and without toadying she was the leader of her class. And with it all she stuck to Angela. She accepted popularity because it was thrust upon her, but she was friendly with Angela because the latter suited her.

Angela was happy. She had a friend and the friendship brought her unexpected advantages. She was no longer left out of groups because there could be no class plans without Mary and Mary would remain nowhere for any length of time without Angela. So to save time and arguments, and also to avoid offending the regent, Angela was always included. Not that she cared much about this, but she did like Mary; as is the way of a "fidus Achates", she gave her friendship wholeheartedly. And it was gratifying to be in the midst of things.

In April the school magazine announced a new departure. Henceforth the editorial staff was to be composed of two representatives from each class; of these one was to be the chief representative chosen by vote of the class, the other was to be assistant, selected by the chief. The chief representative, said the announcement pompously, would sit in at executive meetings and have a voice in the policy of the paper. The assistant would solicit and collect subscriptions, collect fees, receive and report complaints and in brief, said Esther Bayliss, "do all the dirty work". But she coveted the position and title for all that.

Angela's class held a brief meeting after school and elected Mary Hastings as representative without a dissenting vote. "No," said Angela holding up a last rather grimy bit of paper. "Here is one for Esther Bayliss." Two or three of the girls giggled; everyone knew that she must have voted for herself; indeed it had been she who had insisted on taking a ballot rather than a vote by acclaim. Mary was already on her feet. She had been sure of the result of the election, would have been astonished indeed had it turned out any other way. "Well, girls," she began in her rather high, refined voice, "I wish to thank you for the – er – confidence you have bestowed, that is, placed in me and I'm sure you all know I'll do my best to keep the old paper going. And while I'm about it I might just as well announce that I'm choosing Angela Murray for my assistant."

There was a moment's silence. The girls who had thought about it at all had known that if Mary were elected, as assuredly she would be, this meant also the election of Angela. And those who had taken no thought saw no reason to object to her appointment. And anyway there was nothing to be done. But Esther Bayliss pushed forward: "I don't know how it is with the rest of you, but I should have to think twice before I'd trust my subscription money to a coloured girl."

Mary said in utter astonishment: "Coloured, why what are you talking about? Who's coloured?"

"Angela, Angela Murray, that's who's coloured. At least she used to be when we all went to school at Eighteenth and Oxford."

Mary said again: "Coloured!" And then, "Angela, you never told me you were coloured!"

Angela's voice was as amazed as her own: "Tell you that I was coloured! Why of course I never told you that I was coloured! Why should I?"

"There," said Esther, "see she never told Mary that she was coloured. What wouldn't she have done with our money!"

Angela had picked up her books and strolled out the door. But she flew down the north staircase and out the Brandywine Street entrance and so to Sixteenth Street where she would meet no one she knew, especially at this belated hour. At home there would be work to do, her lessons to get and the long, long hours of the night must pass before she would have to face again the hurt and humiliation of the classroom; before she would have to steel her heart and her nerves to drop Mary Hastings before Mary Hastings could drop her. No one, no one, Mary least of all, should guess how completely she had been wounded. Mary and her shrinking bewilderment! Mary and her exclamation: "Coloured!" This was a curious business, this colour. It was the one god apparently to whom you could sacrifice everything. On account of it her mother had neglected to greet her own husband on the street. Mary Hastings could let it come between her and her friend.

In the morning she was at school early; the girls should all see her there and their individual attitude should be her attitude. She would remember each one's greetings, would store it away for future guidance. Some of the girls were especially careful to speak to her, one or two gave her a meaning smile, or so she took it, and turned away. Some did not speak at all. When Mary Hastings came in Angela rose and sauntered unseeing and unheeding deliberately past her through the doorway, across the hall to Miss Barrington's laboratory. As she returned she passed Mary's desk, and the girl lifted troubled but not unfriendly eyes to meet her own; Angela met the glance fully but without recognition. She thought to herself: "Coloured! If they said to me Mary Hastings is a voodoo, I'd have answered, 'What of it? She's my friend.'"

Before June Mary Hastings came up to her and asked her to wait after school.

Angela who had been neither avoiding nor seeking her gave a cool nod. They walked out of the French classroom together. When they reached the corner Mary spoke:

"Oh, Angela, let's be friends again. It doesn't really make any difference. See, I don't care any more."

"But that's what I don't understand. Why should it have made any difference in the first place? I'm just the same as I was before you knew I was coloured and just the same afterwards. Why should it ever have made any difference at all?"

"I don't know, I'm sure. I was just surprised. It was all so unexpected."

"What was unexpected?"

"Oh, I don't know. I can't explain it. But let's be friends."

"Well," said Angela slowly, "I'm willing, but I don't think it will ever be the same again."

It wasn't. Some element, spontaneity, trustfulness was lacking. Mary, who had never thought of speaking of colour, was suddenly conscious that here was a subject which she must not discuss. She was less frank, at times even restrained. Angela, too young to define her thoughts, yet felt vaguely: "She failed me once, – I was her friend, – yet she failed me for something with which I had nothing to do. She's just as likely to do it again. It's in her."

Definitely she said to herself, "Mary withdrew herself not because I was coloured but because she didn't know I was coloured. Therefore if she had never known I was coloured she would always have been my friend. We would have kept on having our good times together." And she began to wonder which was the more important, a patent insistence on the fact of colour or an acceptance of the good things of life which could come to you in America if either you were not coloured or the fact of your racial connections was not made known.

During the summer Mary Hastings' family, it appeared, recovered their fallen fortunes. At any rate she did not return to school in the fall and Angela never saw her again.

Anne Spencer
1882–1975

*A*n *only child born on a plantation in Henry Country, Virginia,
she was sent in 1893 to the Virginia Seminary, Lynchburg,
graduating in 1899. In 1901 she married Edward A. Spencer
and their house became a centre visited by literary figures such as Georgia
Douglas Jackson, W. E. B. Du Bois, Langston Hughes, Paul Robeson and
Claude McKay. Her poetry, which appeared in the major anthologies of the
Harlem Renaissance, is lyrical in form, rarely on Black subjects, although
she observed: "We are the PROBLEM – the great national game of TABOO."*

Letter to My Sister

It is dangerous for a woman to defy the gods;
To taunt them with the tongue's thin tip,
Or strut in the weakness of mere humanity,
Or draw a line daring them to cross;
The gods own the searing lightning,
The drowning waters, tormenting fears
And anger of red sins.

Oh, but worse still if you mince timidly –
Dodge this way or that, or kneel or pray,
Be kind, or sweat agony drops
Or lay your quick body over your feeble young;
If you have beauty or none, if celibate
Or vowed – the gods are Juggernaut,
Passing over. . .over. . .
This you may do:
Lock your heart, then, quietly,
And lest they peer within,
Light no lamp when dark comes down
Raise no shade for sun;
Breathless must your breath come through
If you die and dare deny
The gods their god-like fun.

White Things

Most things are colorful things – the sky, earth, and sea,
   Black men are most men; but the white are free!
White things are rare things; so rare, so rare
They stole from out a silvered world – somewhere.
Finding earth-plains fair plains, save greenly grassed,
They strewed white feathers of cowardice, as they passed;
   The golden stars with lances fine,
   The hills all red and darkened pine,
They blanched with their wand of power;
And turned the blood in a ruby rose
To a poor white poppy-flower.
They pyred a race of black, black men,
And burned them to ashes white; then,
Laughing, a young one claimed a skull,
For the skull of a black is white, not dull,
   But a glistening awful thing;
   Made, it seems, for this ghoul to swing
In the face of God with all his might,
And swear by the hell that sired him:
   "Man-maker, make white!"

Lady, Lady

Lady, Lady, I saw your face,
Dark as night withholding a star...
The chisel fell, or it might have been
You had borne so long the yoke of men.

Lady, Lady, I saw your hands,
Twisted, awry, like crumpled roots,
Bleached poor white in a sudsy tub,
Wrinkled and drawn from your rub-a-dub.

Lady, Lady, I saw your heart,
And altared there in its darksome place
Were the tongues of flame the ancients knew,
Where the good God sits to spangle through.

Elise Johnson McDougald
1885–1971

*T*he *daughter of a founder of the National Urban League, she graduated from Columbia University and taught in the New York elementary school system (1905–11), resigning to marry and raise a family. She was head of the women's department of the US employment Bureau and a social investigator and vocational guidance expert for the New York City Board of Education. She also worked for a time with the Manhattan Trade School and the New York branch of the Department of Labor. She later became the first Black principal in the New York City public school system, until her retirement in 1954. Her writings were published in the journals* Crisis *and* Opportunity *and with Jessie Clark she co-authored* New Day for the Colored Woman in Industry in NY City *(1919). "The Double Task: The Struggle of Negro Women for Sex and Race Emancipation" was first published in* Survey Graphic *(March 1925).*

From

The Double Task: The Struggle of Negro Women for Sex and Race Emancipation

THROUGHOUT the long years of history, woman has been the weather-vane, the indicator, showing in which direction the wind of destiny blows. Her status and development have augured now calm and stability, now swift currents of progress. What then is to be said of the Negro woman today?

In Harlem, more than anywhere else, the Negro woman is free from the cruder handicaps of primitive household hardships and the grosser forms of sex and race subjugation. Here she has considerable opportunity to measure her powers in the intellectual and industrial fields of the great city. Here the questions naturally arise: "What are her problems?" and "How is she solving them?"

To answer these questions, one must have in mind not any one Negro woman, but rather a colorful pageant of individuals, each differently endowed.

Like the red and yellow of the tiger-lily, the skin of one is brilliant against the star-lit darkness of a racial sister. From grace to strength, they vary in infinite degree, with traces of the race's history left in physical and mental outline on each. With a discerning mind, one catches the multiform charm, beauty and character of Negro women; and grasps the fact that their problem cannot be thought of in mass.

Because only a few caught this vision, the attitude of mind of most New Yorkers causes the Negro woman serious difficulty. She is conscious that what is left of chivalry is not directed toward her. She realizes that the ideals of beauty, built up in the fine arts, exclude her almost entirely. Instead, the grotesque Aunt Jemimas of the street-car advertisements proclaim only an ability to serve, without grace or loveliness. Nor does the drama catch her finest spirit. She is most often used to provoke the mirthless laugh of ridicule; or to portray feminine viciousness or vulgarity not peculiar to Negroes. This is the shadow over her. To a race naturally sunny comes the twilight of self-doubt and a sense of personal inferiority. It cannot be denied that these are potent and detrimental influences, though not generally recognized because they are in the realm of the mental and spiritual. More apparent are the economic handicaps which follow her recent entrance into industry. It is conceded that she has special difficulties because of the poor working conditions and low wages of her men. It is not surprising that only the determined women forge ahead to results other than mere survival. The few who do prove their mettle stimulate one to a closer study of how this achievement is won in Harlem.

Better to visualize the Negro woman at her job, our vision of a host of individuals must once more resolve itself into groups on the basis of activity. First, come a very small leisure group – the wives and daughters of men who are in business, in the professions and in a few well-paid personal service occupations. Second, a most active and progressive group, the women in business and the professions. Third, the many women in the trades and industry. Fourth, a group weighty in numbers struggling on in domestic service, with an even less fortunate fringe of casual workers, fluctuating with the economic temper of the times.

The first is a pleasing group to see. It is picked for outward beauty by Negro men with much the same feeling as other Americans of the same economic class. Keeping their women free to preside over the family, these women are affected by the problems of every wife and mother, but touched only faintly by their race's hardships. They do share acutely in the prevailing difficulty of finding competent household help. Negro wives find Negro maids unwilling generally to work in their own neighborhoods, for various reasons. They do not wish to work where there is a possibility of acquaintances coming into contact with them while they serve and they still harbor the misconception that Negroes of any station are unable to pay as much as persons of the other race. It is in these homes of comparative ease that we find the polite activities of social exclusiveness. The luxuries of well-appointed homes, modest motors, tennis, golf and country clubs, trips to Europe and California, make for social standing. The problem confronting the refined Negro family is to know others of the same achievement. The search for kindred spirits gradually grows less difficult; in the past it led to the custom of visiting all the large cities in order to know similar groups of cultured Negro people.

A spirit of stress and struggle characterizes the second two groups. These women of business, profession and trade are the hub of the wheel of progress. Their burden is twofold. Many are wives and mothers whose husbands are insufficiently paid, or who have succumbed to social maladjustment and have abandoned their families. An appalling number are widows. They face the great problem of leaving home each day and at the same time trying to rear children in their spare time – this too in neighborhoods where rents are large, standards of dress and recreation high and costly, and social danger on the increase.

The great commercial life of New York City is only slightly touched by the Negro woman of our second group. Negro business men offer her most of their work, but their number is limited. Outside of this field, custom is once more against her and competition is keen for all. However, Negro girls are training and some are holding exceptional jobs. One of the professors in a New York college has had a young colored woman as secretary for the past three years. Another holds the head clerical position in an organization where reliable handling of detail and a sense of business ethics are essential. For four years she has steadily advanced. Quietly these women prove their worth, so that when a vacancy exists and there is a call, it is difficult to find even one competent colored secretary who is not employed. As a result of opportunity in clerical work in the educational system of New York City a number have qualified for such positions, one being appointed within the year to the office work of a high school. In other departments the civil service in New York City is no longer free from discrimination. The casual personal interview, that tenacious and retrogressive practice introduced in the Federal administration during the World War, has spread and often nullifies the Negro woman's success in written tests. The successful young woman just cited above was three times "turned down" as undesirable on the basis of the personal interview. In the great mercantile houses, the many young Negro girls who might be well suited to salesmanship are barred from all but the menial positions. Even so, one Negro woman, beginning as a uniformed maid, has pulled herself up to the position of "head of stock".

Again, the telephone and insurance companies which receive considerable patronage from Negroes deny them proportionate employment. Fortunately, this is an era of changing customs. There is hope that a less selfish racial attitude will prevail. It is a heartening fact that there is an increasing number of Americans who will lend a hand in the game fight of the worthy.

In the less crowded professional vocations, the outlook is more cheerful. In these fields, the Negro woman is dependent largely upon herself and her own race for work. In the legal, dental, medical and nursing professions, successful women practitioners have usually worked their way through college and are "managing" on the small fees that can be received from an underpaid public. Social conditions in America are hardest upon the Negro because he is lowest in the economic scale. This gives rise to a demand for trained college women in the profession of social work. It has met with a response from young college women, anxious to devote their education and lives to the needs of the submerged classes. In New York City, some fifty-odd women are engaged in social work, other than nursing. In the latter profession there are over two hundred and fifty. Much of the social work has been pioneer in nature: the pay has been small with little possibility of advancement. For even in work among Negroes, the better paying positions are reserved for whites. The Negro college woman is doing her bit in this field at a sacrifice, along such lines as these: in the correctional departments of the city, as probation officers, investigators, and police women; as Big Sisters attached to the Childrens' Court; as field workers and visitors for relief organizations and missions; as secretaries for travelers-aid and mission societies; as visiting teachers and vocational guides for the schools of the city; and, in the many branches of public health nursing, in schools, organizations devoted to preventive and educational medicine, in hospitals and in private nursing.

In New York City, nearly three hundred Negro women share the good conditions in the teaching profession. They measure up to the high pedagogical requirements of the city and state law and are, increasingly, leaders in the community. Here too the Negro woman finds evidence of the white workers' fear of competition. The need for teachers is still so strong that little friction exists. When it does seem to be imminent, it is smoothed away, as it recently was at a meeting of school principals. From the floor, a discussion began with: "What are we going to do about this problem of the increasing number of Negro teachers coming into our schools?" It ended promptly through the suggestion of another principal: "Send all you get and don't want over to my school. I have two now and I'll match their work to any two of your best whom you name." One might go on to such interesting and more unusual professions as journalism, chiropody, bacteriology, pharmacy, etc., and find that, though the number in any one may be small, the Negro woman is creditably represented in practically every one. According to individual ability she is meeting with success.

Closing the door on the home anxieties, the woman engaged in trades and in industry faces equally serious difficulty in competition in the open working field. Custom is against her in all but a few trade and industrial occupations. She has, however been established long in the dressmaking trade among the helpers and finishers, and more recently among the drapers and fitters in some of the best establishments. Several Negro women are themselves proprietors of shops in the country's greatest fashion district. Each of them has, against great odds, convinced skeptical employers of her business value; and, at the same time, has educated fellow workers of other races, doing much to show the oneness of interest of all workers. In millinery, power sewing-machine operating on cloth, straw and leather, there are few Negro women. The laissez-faire attitude of practically all trade unions makes the Negro woman an unwilling menace to the cause of labor.

In trade cookery, the Negro woman's talent and past experience is recognized. Her problem here is to find employers who will let her work her way to managerial positions, in tea-rooms, candy shops and institutions. One such employer became convinced that the managing cook, a young colored graduate of Pratt Institute, would continue to build up a business that had been failing. She offered her a partnership. As in the cases of a number of such women, her barrier was lack of capital. No matter how highly trained, nor how much speed and business acumen has been acquired, the Negro's credit is held in doubt. An exception in this matter of capital will serve to prove the rule. Thirty years ago, a young Negro girl began learning all branches of the fur trade. She is now in business for herself, employing three women of her race and one Jewish man. She has made fur experts of still another half-dozen colored girls. Such instances as these justify the prediction that the foothold gained in the trade world will, year by year, become more secure.

Because of the limited fields for workers in this group, many of the unsuccessful drift into the fourth social grade, the domestic and casual workers. These drifters increase the difficulties of the Negro woman suited to housework. New standards of household management are forming and the problem of the Negro woman is to meet these new business-like ideals. The constant influx of workers unfamiliar with household conditions in New York keeps the situation one of turmoil. The Negro woman, moreover, is revolting against residential domestic service. It is a last stand in her fight to maintain a semblance of family life. For this reason, principally, the number of day or casual workers is on the increase. Happiness is almost impossible under the strain of these conditions. Health and morale suffer, but how else can her children, loose all afternoon, be gathered together at night-fall? Through it all she manages to give satisfactory service and the Negro woman is sought after for this unpopular work largely because her honesty, loyalty and cleanliness have stood the test of time. Through her drudgery, the women of other groups find leisure time for progress. This is one of her conditions to America.

It is apparent from what has been said, that even in New York City, Negro women are of a race which is free neither economically, socially nor spiritually. Like women in general, but more particularly like those of other oppressed minorities, the Negro woman has been forced to submit to over-powering conditions. Pressure has been exerted upon her, both from without and within her group. Her emotional and sex life is a reflex of her economic station. The women of the working class will react, emotionally and sexually, similarly to the working-class women of other races. The Negro woman does not maintain any moral standard which may be assigned chiefly to qualities of race, any more than a white woman does. Yet she has been singled out and advertised as having lower sex standards. Superficial critics who have had contact only with the lower grades of Negro women, claim that they are more immoral than other groups of women. This I deny. This is the sort of criticism which predicates of one race, to its detriment, that which is common to all races. Sex irregularities are not a matter of race, but of socio-economic conditions. Research shows that most of the African tribes from which the Negro sprang have strict codes for sex relations. There is no proof of inherent weakness in the ethnic group.

Gradually overcoming the habitual limits imposed upon her by slave masters, she increasingly seeks legal sanction for the consummation and dissolution of sex contracts. Contrary to popular belief, illegitimacy among Negroes is cause for shame and grief. When economic, social and biological forces combined bring about unwed motherhood, the reaction is much the same as in families of other racial groups. Secrecy is maintained if possible. Generally the married aunt, or even the mother, claims that the illegitimate child is her own. The foundling asylum is seldom sought. Schooled in this kind of suffering in the days of slavery, Negro women often temper scorn with sympathy for weakness. Stigma does fall upon the unmarried mother, but perhaps in this matter the Negroes' attitude is nearer the modern enlightened ideal for the social treatment of the unfortunate. May this not be considered another contribution to America?

With all these forces at work, true sex equality has not been approximated. The ratio of opportunity in the sex, social, economic and political spheres is about that which exists between white men and women. In the large, I would say that the Negro woman is the cultural equal of her man because she is generally kept in school longer. Negro boys, like white boys, are usually put to work to subsidize the family income. The growing economic independence of the Negro working woman is causing her to rebel against the domineering family attitude of the cruder working-class Negro man. The masses of Negro men are engaged in menial occupations throughout the working day. Their baffled and suppressed desires to determine their economic life are manifested in over-bearing domination at home. Working mothers are unable to instill different ideals in their sons. Conditions change slowly. Nevertheless, education and opportunity are modifying the spirit of the younger Negro men. Trained in modern schools of thought, they begin to show a wholesome attitude of fellowship and freedom for their women. The challenge to young Negro womanhood is to see clearly this trend and grasp the proferred comradeship with sincerity. In this matter of sex equality, Negro women have contributed few outstanding militants. Their feminist efforts are directed chiefly toward the realization of the equality of the races, the sex struggle assuming a subordinate place. . . .

We find the Negro woman, figuratively, struck in the face daily by contempt from the world about her. Within her soul, she knows little of peace and happiness. Through it all, she is courageously standing erect, developing within herself the moral strength to rise above and conquer false attitudes. She is maintaining her natural beauty and charm and improving her mind and opportunity. She is measuring up to the needs and demands of her family, community and race, and radiating from Harlem a hope that is cherished by her sisters in less propitious circumstances throughout the land. The wind of the race's destiny stirs more briskly because of her striving.

Georgia Douglas Johnson
1886–1966

Born in Atlanta of racially mixed ancestry (English, Indian and African-American), she attended Atlanta University and Oberlin College Conservatory of Music, Ohio. She taught in Alabama until her husband (whom she married in 1903) took up a political appointment in Washington, DC, where she moved with him and their two sons. She held some government posts, worked in women's organizations and wrote poetry, plays and columns for numerous Black newspapers. Her home became a centre for Black literary life for over forty years. She was the first Black woman after Frances E. W. Harper to win national recognition as a poet. Her books include The Heart of a Woman (1918), on themes to do with womanhood, Bronze (1922) – a collection she referred to as "entirely racial", with poems such as "Cosmopolite" reflecting her concern about her different heritages – and An Autumn Love Cycle (1928), in which "I Want to Die While You Love Me" appeared.

I Want to Die While You Love Me

I want to die while you love me,
   While yet you hold me fair,
While laughter lies upon my lips
   And lights are in my hair.

I want to die while you love me,
   And bear to that still bed,
Your kisses turbulent, unspent,
   To warm me when I'm dead.

I want to die while you love me,
   Oh, who would care to live
Till love has nothing more to ask
   And nothing more to give!

I want to die while you love me
   And never, never see
The glory of this perfect day
   Grow dim or cease to be.

The Heart of a Woman

The heart of a woman goes forth with the dawn,
As a lone bird, soft winging, so restlessly on,
Afar o'er life's turrets and vales does it roam
In the wake of those echoes the heart calls home.

The heart of a woman falls back with the night,
And enters some alien cage in its plight,
And tries to forget it has dreamed of the stars,
While it breaks, breaks, breaks on the sheltering bars.

Black Woman

Don't knock at my door, little child,
    I cannot let you in,
You know not what a world this is
    Of cruelty and sin.
Wait in the still eternity
    Until I come to you,
The world is cruel, cruel, child,
    I cannot let you in!

Don't knock at my door, little one,
    I cannot bear the pain
Of turning deaf-ear to your call
    Time and time again!

Cosmopolite

Not wholly this or that,
But wrought
Of alien bloods am I,
A product of the interplay
Of traveled hearts.
Estranged, yet not estranged, I stand
All comprehending;
From my estate
I view earth's frail dilemma;
Scion of fused strengths am I,
All understanding,
Nor this nor that
Contains me.

Celibacy

Where is the love that might have been
Flung to the four far ends of earth?
In my body, stamping round,
In my body, like a hound leashed and restless
Biding time!

Zora Neale Hurston
1891–1960

Born in the all-Black town of Eatonville, Florida, she was essentially left on her own on her mother's death in 1904, lived with various relatives, drifted from job to job and travelled north as a maid with the Gilbert & Sullivan Company. She attended Morgan Academy, Baltimore, and Howard University, and became involved in the Harlem Renaissance of the 1920s. She moved to New York in 1925, became secretary, then chauffeur, to white novelist Fannie Hurst, and was awarded a scholarship to Barnard College, where she studied folklore under anthropologist Franz Boas. Graduating with a BA in 1928, she spent four years researching the folk customs of Black Americans in the South, on which she drew in works such as Mules and Men (1935), a collection of tales, sermons and rural practices. She received a Guggenheim Fellowship to study folklore in the Caribbean, after which she wrote Tell My Horse (1938; also published as Voodoo Gods). She was one of the first African-American women writers to assimilate folk tradition into modern literature. Her other publications include an autobiography, Dust Tracks on a Road (1942), novels – Jonah's Gourd Vine (1934), Their Eyes Were Watching God (1937), Seraph on the Suwanee (1948) – and short stories. Despite being among the most prolific and talented writers of her era, she fell into obscurity and died in Florida twelve years after

*disappearing from New York. Her grave in Fort Pierce was unmarked
until Alice Walker, who has edited a Zora Neale Hurston reader,* I Love
Myself When I am Laughing. . .And Then Again When I'm Looking Mean
and Impressive *(1979), placed a tombstone on it.*

From

Their Eyes Were Watching God

CHAPTER II

J ANE saw her life like a great tree in leaf with the things suffered, things
enjoyed, things done and undone. Dawn and doom was in the branches.
"Ah know exactly what Ah got to tell yuh, but it's hard to know where
to start at."

"Ah ain't never seen mah papa. And Ah didn't know 'im if Ah did. Mah mama
neither. She was gone from round dere long before Ah wuz big enough tuh
know. Mah grandma raised me. Mah grandma and de white folks she worked
wid. She had a house out in de back-yard and dat's where Ah wuz born. They
was quality white folks up dere in West Florida. Named Washburn. She had four
gran'chillun on de place and all of us played together and dat's how come Ah
never called mah Grandma nothin' but Nanny, 'cause dat's what everybody on
de place called her. Nanny used to ketch us in our devilment and lick every
youngun on de place and Mis' Washburn did de same. Ah reckon dey never hit
us ah lick amiss 'cause dem three boys and us two girls wuz pretty aggravatin',
Ah speck.

"Ah was wid dem white chillun so much till Ah didn't know Ah wuzn't
white till Ah was round six years old. Wouldn't have found it out then, but
a man come long takin' pictures and without askin' anybody, Shelby, dat was
de oldest boy, he told him to take us. Round a week later de man brought de
picture for Mis' Washburn to see and pay him which she did, then give us all a
good lickin.'

"So when we looked at de picture and everybody got pointed out there wasn't
nobody left except a real dark little girl with long hair standing by Eleanor. Dat's
where Ah wuz s'posed to be, but Ah couldn't recognize dat dark chile as me. So
Ah ast, 'where is me? Ah don'e see me.'

"Everybody laughed, even Mr Washburn. Miss Nellie, de Mama of de chillun
who come back home after her husband dead, she pointed to de dark one and
said, 'Dat's you, Alphabet, don't you know yo' ownself?'

"Dey all useter call me Alphabet 'cause so many people had done named me
different names. Ah looked at de picture a long time and seen it was mah dress
and mah hair so Ah said:

"'Aw, aw! Ah'm colored!'

"Den dey all laughed real hard. But before Ah see de picture Ah thought
Ah wuz just like de rest.

"Us lived dere havin' fun till de chillun at school got to teasin' me 'bout livin' in de white folks backyard. Dere wuz uh knotty head gal name Mayrella dat useter git mad every time she look at me. Mis' Washburn useter dress me up in all de clothes her gran'chillun didn't need no mo' which still wuz better'n whut de rest uh de colored chillun had. And then she useter put hair ribbon on mah head fuh me tuh wear. Dat useter rile Mayrella uh lot. So she would pick at me all de time and put some others up tuh do de same. They'd push me 'way from de ring plays and make out they couldn't play wid nobody dat lived on premises. Den they'd tell me not to be takin' on over mah looks 'cause they mama told 'em 'bout de hound dawgs huntin' mah papa all night long. 'Bout Mr Washburn and de sheriff puttin' de bloodhounds on de trail tuh ketch mah papa for whut he done tuh mah mama. Dey didn't tell about how he wuz seen tryin' tuh git in touch wid mah mama later on so he could marry her. Naw, dey didn't talk dat part of it atall. Dey made it sound real bad so as tuh crumple mah feathers. None of 'em didn't even remember whut his name wuz, but dey all knowed de bloodhound part by heart. Nanny didn't love tuh see me wid mah head hung down, so she figgered it would be mo' better fuh me if us had uh house. She got de land and everything and then Mis' Washburn helped out uh whole heap wid things."

Pheoby's hungry listening helped Janie to tell her story. So she went on thinking back to her young years and explaining them to her friend in soft, easy phrases while all around the house, the night time put on flesh and blackness.

She thought awhile and decided that her conscious life had commenced at Nanny's gate. On a late afternoon Nanny had called her to come inside the house because she had spied Janie letting Johnny Taylor kiss her over the gatepost.

It was a spring afternoon in West Florida. Janie had spent most of the day under a blossoming pear tree in the back-yard. She had been spending every minute that she could steal from her chores under that tree for the last three days. That was to say, ever since the first tiny bloom had opened. It had called her to come and gaze on a mystery. From barren brown stems to glistening leaf-buds; from the leaf-buds to snowy virginity of bloom. It stirred her tremendously. How? Why? It was like a flute song forgotten in another existence and remembered again. What? How? Why? This singing she heard that had nothing to do with her ears. The rose of the world was breathing out smell. It followed her through all her waking moments and caressed her in her sleep. It connected itself with other vaguely felt matters that had struck her outside observation and buried themselves in her flesh. Now they emerged and quested about her consciousness.

She was stretched on her back beneath the pear tree soaking in the alto chant of the visiting bees, the gold of the sun and the panting breath of the breeze when the inaudible voice of it all came to her. She saw a dust-bearing bee sink into the sanctum of a bloom; the thousand sister-calyxes arch to meet the love embrace and the ecstatic shiver of the tree from root to tiniest branch creaming in every blossom and frothing with delight. So this was a marriage! She had been summoned to behold a revelation. Then Janie felt a pain remorseless sweet that left her limp and languid.

After a while she got up from where she was and went over the little garden field entire. She was seeking confirmation of the voice and vision, and everywhere she found and acknowledged answers. A personal answer for all other creations except herself. She felt an answer seeking her, but where? When? How? She found herself at the kitchen door and stumbled inside. In the air of the room were flies tumbling and singing, marrying and giving in marriage. When she reached the narrow hallway she was reminded that her grandmother was home with a sick headache. She was lying across the bed asleep so Janie tipped on out of the front door. Oh to be a pear tree – *any* tree in bloom! With kissing bees singing of the beginning of the world! She was sixteen. She had glossy leaves and bursting buds and she wanted to struggle with life but it seemed to elude her. Where were the singing bees for her? Nothing on the place nor in her grandma's house answered her. She searched as much of the world as she could from the top of the front steps and then went on down to the front gate and leaned over to gaze up and down the road. Looking, waiting, breathing short with impatience. Waiting for the world to be made.

Through pollinated air she saw a glorious being coming up the road. In her former blindness she had known him as shiftless Johnny Taylor, tall and lean. That was before the golden dust of pollen had beglamored his rags and her eyes.

In the last stages of Nanny's sleep, she dreamed of voices. Voices far-off but persistent, and gradually coming nearer. Janie's voice. Janie talking in whispery snatches with a male voice she couldn't quite place. That brought her wide awake. She bolted upright and peered out of the window and saw Johnny Taylor lacerating her Janie with a kiss.

"Janie!"

The old woman's voice was so lacking in command and reproof, so full of crumbling dissolution, – that Janie half believed that Nanny had not seen her. So she extended herself outside of her dream and went inside of the house. That was the end of her childhood.

Nanny's head and face looked like the standing roots of some old tree that had been torn away by storm. Foundation of ancient power that no longer mattered. The cooling palma christi leaves that Janie had bound about her grandma's head with a white rag had wilted down and become part and parcel of the woman. Her eyes didn't bore and pierce. They diffused and melted Jane, the room and the world into one comprehension.

"Janie, youse uh 'oman, now, so – "

"Naw, Nanny, naw Ah ain't no real 'oman yet."

The thought was too new and heavy for Janie. She fought it away.

Nanny closed her eyes and nodded a slow, weary affirmation many times before she gave it voice.

"Yeah, Janie, youse got yo' womanhood on yuh. So Ah mout ez well tell yuh whut Ah been savin' up for uh spell. Ah wants to see you married right away."

"Me, married? Naw, Nanny, no ma'am! Whut Ah know 'bout uh husband?"

"Whut Ah seen just now is plenty for me, honey, Ah don't want no trashy nigger, no breath-and-britches, lak Johnny Taylor usin' yo' to wipe his foots on."

Nanny's words made Janie's kiss across the gatepost seem like a manure pile after a rain.

"Look at me, Janie. Don't set dere wid yo' head hung down. Look at yo' ole grandma!" Her voice began snagging on the prongs of her feelings. "Ah don't want to be talkin' to you lak dis. Fact is Ah done been on mah knees to mah Maker many's de time askin' *please* – for Him not to make de burden too heavy for me to bear."

"Nanny, Ah just – Ah didn't mean nothin' bad."

"Dat's what makes me skeered. You don't mean no harm. You don't even know where harm is at. Ah'm ole now. Ah can't be always guidin' yo' feet from harm and danger. Ah wants to see you married right away."

"Who Ah'm goin' tuh marry off-hand lak dat? Ah don't know nobody."

"De Lawd will provide. He know Ah done bore de burden in de heat uh de day. Somebody done spoke to me 'bout you long time ago. Ah ain't said nothin' 'cause dat wasn't de way Ah placed you. Ah wanted yuh to school out and pick from a higher bush and a sweeter berry. But dat ain't yo' idea, Ah see."

"Nanny, who – who dat been askin' you for me?"

"Brother Logan Killicks. He's a good man, too."

"Naw, Nanny, no ma'am! Is dat whut he been hangin' round here for? He look like some ole skullhead in de grave yard."

The older woman sat bolt upright and put her feet to the floor, and thrust back the leaves from her face.

"So you don't want to marry off decent like, do yuh? You just wants to hug and kiss and feel around with first one man and then another, huh? You wants to make me suck de same sorrow yo' mama did, eh? Mah ole head ain't gray enough. Mah back ain't bowed enough to suit yuh!"

The vision of Logan Killicks was desecrating the pear tree, but Janie didn't know how to tell Nanny that. She merely hunched over and pouted at the floor.

"Janie."

"Yes, ma'am."

"You answer me when Ah speak. Don't you set dere poutin' wid me after all Ah done went through for you!"

She slapped the girl's face violently, and forced her head back so that their eyes met in struggle. With her hand uplifted for the second blow she saw the huge tear that welled up from Janie's heart and stood in each eye. She saw the terrible agony and the lips tightened down to hold back the cry and desisted. Instead she brushed back the heavy hair from Janie's face and stood there suffering and loving and weeping internally for both of them.

"Come to yo' Grandma, honey. Set in her lap lak yo' use tuh. Yo' Nanny wouldn't harm a hair uh yo' head. She don't want nobody else to do it neither if she kin help it. Honey, de white man is de ruler of everything as fur as Ah been able tuh find out. Maybe it's some place way off in de ocean where de black man is in power, but we don't know nothin' but what we see. So de white man throw down de load and tell de nigger man tuh pick it up. He pick it up because he have to, but he don't tote it. He hand it to his womenfolks. De nigger woman is de mule uh de world so fur as Ah can see. Ah been prayin' fuh it tuh be different wid you. Lawd, Lawd, Lawd!"

For a long time she sat rocking with the girl held tightly to her sunken breast. Janie's long legs dangled over one arm of the chair and the long braids of her hair swung low on the other side. Nanny half sung, half sobbed a running chant-prayer over the head of the weeping girl.

"Lawd have mercy! It was a long time on de way but Ah reckon it had to come. Oh Jesus! Do, Jesus! Ah done de best Ah could."

Finally, they both grew calm.

"Janie, how long you been 'lowin' Johnny Taylor to kiss you?"

"Only dis one time, Nanny. Ah don't love him at all. Whut made me do it is – oh, Ah don't know."

"Thank yuh, Massa Jesus."

"Ah ain't gointuh do it no mo', Nanny. Please don't make me marry Mr Killicks."

"'Tain't Logan Killicks Ah wants you to have, baby, it's protection. Ah ain't gittin' ole, honey. Ah'm *done* ole. One mornin' soon, now, de angel wid de sword is gointuh stop by here. De day and de hour is hid from me, but it won't be long. Ah ast de Lawd when you was uh infant in mah arms to let me stay here till you got grown. He done spared me to see de day. Mah daily prayer now is tuh let dese golden moments rolls on a few days longer till Ah see you safe in life."

"Lemme wait, Nanny, please, jus' a lil bit mo'."

"Don't think Ah don't feel wid you, Janie, 'cause Ah do. Ah couldn't love yuh no more if Ah had uh felt yo' birth pains mahself. Fact uh de matter, Ah loves yuh a whole heap more'n Ah do yo' mama, de one Ah did birth. But you got to take in consideration you ain't no everyday chile like most of 'em. You ain't got no papa, you might jus' as well say no mama, for de good she do yuh. You ain't got nobody but me. And mah head is ole and tilted towards de grave. Neither can you stand alone by yo'self. De thought uh you bein' kicked around from pillar tuh post is uh hurtin' thing. Every tear you drop squeezes a cup uh blood outa mah heart. Ah got tuh try and do for you befo' mah head is cold."

A sobbing sigh burst out of Janie. The old woman answered her with little soothing pats of the hand.

"You know, honey, us colored folks is branches without roots and that makes things come round in queer ways. You in particular. Ah was born back due in slavery so it wasn't for me to fulfill my dreams of whut a woman oughta be and to do. Dat's one of de hold-backs of slavery. But nothing can't stop you from wishin'. You can't beat nobody down so low till you can rob 'em of they will. Ah didn't want to be used for a work-ox and a brood-sow and Ah didn't want mah daughter used dat way neither. It sho wasn't mah will for things to happen lak they did. Ah even hated de way you was born. But, all de same Ah said thank God, Ah got another chance. Ah wanted to preach a great sermon about colored women sittin' on high, but they wasn't no pulpit for me. Freedom found me wid a baby daughter in mah arms, so Ah said Ah'd take a broom and a cook-pot and throw up a highway through de wilderness for her. She would expound what Ah felt. But somehow she got lost offa de highway and next thing Ah knowed here you was in de world. So whilst Ah was tendin' you of nights Ah said Ah'd save de text for you. Ah been waitin' a long time, Janie, but nothin' Ah been through ain't too much if you just take a stand on high ground lak Ah dreamed."

Old Nanny sat there rocking Janie like an infant and thinking back and back. Mind-pictures brought feelings, and feelings dragged out dramas from the hollows of her heart.

"Dat mornin' on de big planation close to Savannah, a rider come in a gallop tellin' 'bout Sherman takin' Atlanta. Marse Robert's son had done been kilt at Chickamauga. So he grabbed his gun and straddled his best horse and went off wid de rest of de gray-headed men and young boys to drive de Yankees back into Tennessee.

"They was all cheerin' and cryin' and shoutin' for de men dat was ridin' off. Ah couldn't see nothin' cause yo' mama wasn't but a week old, and Ah was flat uh mah back. But pretty soon he let on he forgot somethin' and run into mah cabin and made me let down mah hair for de last time. He sorta wropped his hand in it, pulled mah big toe, lak he always done, and was gone after de rest lak lightnin'. Ah heard 'em give one last whoop for him. Then de big house and de quarters got sober and silent.

"It was de cool of de evenin' when Mistis come walkin' in mah door. She throwed de door wide open and stood dere lookin' at me outa her eyes and her face. Look lak she been livin' through uh hundred years in January without one day of spring. She come stood over me in de bed.

"'Nanny, Ah come to see that baby uh yourn.'

"Ah tried not to feel de breeze off her face, but it got so cold in dere dat Ah was freezin' to death under the kivvers. So Ah couldn't move right away lak Ah aimed to. But Ah knowed Ah had to make haste and do it.

"'You better git dat kivver offa dat youngun and dat quick!' she clashed at me. 'Look lak you don't know who is Mistis on dis plantation, Madam. But Ah aims to show you.'

"By dat time I had done managed tuh unkivver mah baby enough for her to see de head and face.

"'Nigger, whut's yo' baby doin' wid gray eyes and yaller hair?' She begin tuh slap mah jaws ever which a'way. Ah never felt the fust ones 'cause Ah wuz too busy gittin' de kivver back over mah chile. But dem last lick burnt me lak fire. Ah had too many feelin's tuh tell which one tuh follow so Ah didn't cry and Ah didn't do nothin' else. But then she kept on astin me how come mah baby look white. She asted me dat maybe twenty-five or thirty times, lak she got tuh sayin' dat and couldn't help herself. So Ah told her, 'Ah don't know nothin' but what Ah'm told tuh do, 'cause Ah ain't nothin' but uh nigger and uh slave.'

"Instead of pacifyin' her lak Ah thought, look lak she got madder. But Ah reckon she was tired and wore out 'cause she didn't hit me no more. She went to de foot of de bed and wiped her hands on her handksher. 'Ah wouldn't dirty mah hands on yuh. But first thing in de mornin' de overseer will take you to de whippin' post and tie you down on yo' knees and cut de hide offa yo' yaller back. One hundred lashes wid a raw-hide on yo' bare back. Ah'll have you whipped till de blood run down to yo' heels! Ah mean to count de licks mahself. And if it kills you Ah'll stand de loss. Anyhow, as soon as dat brat is a month old Ah'm going to sell if offa dis place.'

"She flounced on off and left her wintertime wid me. Ah knowed mah body wasn't healed, but Ah couldn't consider dat. In de black dark Ah wrapped mah baby de best Ah knowed how and made it to de swamp by de river. Ah knowed de place was full uh moccasins and other bitin' snakes, but Ah was more skeered uh whut was behind me. Ah hide in dere day and night and suckled de baby every time she start to cry, for fear somebody might hear her and Ah'd git found. Ah ain't sayin' uh friend or two didn't feel mah care. And den de Good Lawd seen to it dat Ah wasn't taken. Ah don't see how come mah milk didn't kill mah chile, wid me so skeered and worried all de time. De noise uh de owls skeered me; de limbs of dem cypress trees took to crawlin' and movin' round after dark, and two three times Ah heered panthers prowlin' round. But nothin' never hurt me 'cause de Lawd knowed how it was.

"Den, one night Ah heard de big guns boomin' lak thunder. It kept up all night long. And de next mornin' Ah could see uh big ship at a distance and a great stirrin' round. So Ah wrapped Leafy up in moss and fixed her good in a tree and picked mah way on down to de landin'. The men was all in blue, and Ah heard people say Sherman was comin' to meet de boats in Savannah, and all of us slaves was free. So Ah run got mah baby and got in quotation wid people and found a place Ah could stay.

"But it was a long time after dat befo' de Big Surrender at Richmond. Den de big bell in Atlanta and all de men in gray uniforms had to go to Moultrie, and bury their swords in de ground to show they was never to fight about slavery no mo'. So den we knowed we was free.

"Ah wouldn't marry nobody, though Ah could have uh heap uh times, cause Ah didn't want nobody mistreating mah baby. So Ah got with some good white people and come down here in West Florida to work and make de sun shine on both sides of de street for Leafy.

"Mah Madam help me wid her just lak she been doin' wid you. Ah put her in school when it got so it was a school to put her in. Ah was 'spectin' to make a school teacher outa her.

"But one day she didn't come home at de usual time and Ah waited and waited, but she never come all dat night. Ah took a lantern and went round askin' everybody but nobody ain't seen her. De next mornin' she come crawlin' in on her hands and knees. A sight to see. Dat school teacher had done hid her in de woods all night long, and he had done raped mah baby and run on off just before day.

"She was only seventeen, and somethin' lak dat to happen! Lawd a'mussy! Look lak Ah kin see it all over agin. It was a long time before she was well, and by dat time we knowed you was on de way. And after you were born she took to drinkin' likker and stayin' out nights. Couldn't git her to stay here and nowhere else. Lawd knows where she is right now. She ain't dead, 'cause Ah'd know it by mah feelings, but sometimes Ah wish she was at rest.

"And, Janie, maybe it wasn't much, but Ah done de best Ah kin by you. Ah raked and scraped and bought dis lil piece uh land so you wouldn't have to stay in de white folks' yard and tuck yo' head befo' other chillun at school. Dat was all right when you was little. But when you got big enough to understand things, Ah wanted you to look upon yo'self. Ah don't want yo' feathers always crumpled by folks throwin' up things in yo' face. And Ah can't die easy thinkin' maybe de menfolks white or black is makin' a spit cup outa you: Have some sympathy fuh me. Put me down easy, Janie, Ah'm a cracked plate."

From

Mules and Men

I

WINTER passed and caterpillars began to cross the road again. I had spent a year in gathering and culling over folk-tales. I loved it, but I had to bear in mind that there was a limit to the money to be spent on the project, and as yet, I had done nothing about hoodoo.

So I slept a night, and the next morning I headed my toe-nails toward Louisiana and New Orleans in particular.

New Orleans is now and has ever been the hoodoo capital of America. Great names in rites that vie with those of Hayti in deeds that keep alive the powers of Africa.

Hoodoo, or Voodoo, as pronounced by the whites, is burning with a flame in America, with all the intensity of a suppressed religion. It has its thousands of secret adherents. It adapts itself like Christianity to its locale, reclaiming some of its borrowed characteristics to itself. Such as fire-worship as signified in the Christian church by the altar and the candles. And the belief in the power of water to sanctify as in baptism.

Belief in magic is older than writing. So nobody knows how it started.

The way we tell it, hoodoo started way back there before everything. Six days of magic spells and mighty words and the world with its elements above and below was made. And now, God is leaning back taking a seventh day rest. When the eighth day comes around, He'll start to making new again.

Man wasn't made until around half-past five on the sixth day, so he can't know how anything was done. Kingdoms crushed and crumbled whilst man went gazing up into the sky and down into the hollows of the earth trying to catch God working with His hands so he could find out His secrets and learn how to accomplish and do. But no man yet has seen God's hand, nor yet His finger-nails. All they could know was that God made everything to pass and perish except stones. God made stones for memory. He builds a mountain Himself when He wants things not forgot. Then His voice is heard in rumbling judgment.

Moses was the first man who ever learned God's power-compelling words and it took him forty years to learn ten words. So he made ten plagues and ten commandments. But God gave him His rod for a present, and showed him the back part of His glory. Then too, Moses could walk out of the sight of man. But Moses never would have stood before the Burning Bush, if he had not married Jethro's daughter. Jethro was a great hoodoo man. Jethro could tell Moses could carry power as soon as he saw him. In fact he felt him coming. Therefore, he

took Moses and crowned him and taught him. So Moses passed on beyond
Jethro with his rod. He lifted it up and tore a nation out of Pharaoh's side,
and Pharaoh couldn't help himself. Moses talked with the snake that lives in a
hole right under God's foot-rest. Moses had fire in his head and a cloud in his
mouth. The snake had told him God's making words. The words of doing and
the words of obedience. Many a man thinks he is making something when he's
only changing things around. But God let Moses make. And then Moses had so
much power he made the eight winged angels split open a mountain to bury
him in, and shut up the hole behind them.

And ever since the days of Moses, kings have been toting rods for a sign
of power. But it's mostly sham-polish because no king has ever had the power
of even one of Moses' ten words. Because Moses made a nation and a book, a
thousand million leaves of ordinary men's writing couldn't tell what Moses said.

Then when the moon had dragged a thousand tides behind her, Solomon
was a man. So Sheba, from her country where she was, felt him carrying power
and therefore she came to talk with Solomon and hear him.

The Queen of Sheba was an Ethiopian just like Jethro, with power unequal
to man. She didn't have to deny herself to give gold to Solomon. She had
gold-making words. But she was thirsty, and the country where she lived was
dry to her mouth. So she listened to her talking ring and went to see Solomon,
and the fountain in his garden quenched her thirst.

So she made Solomon wise and gave him her talking ring. And Solomon built
a room with a secret door and everyday he shut himself inside and listened to
his ring. So he wrote down the ring-talk in books.

That's what the old ones said in ancient times and we talk it again.

It was way back there – the old folks told it – that Raw-Head-And-Bloody-Bones
had reached down and laid hold of the taproot that points to the center of the
world. And they talked about High Walker too. But they talked in people's language and nobody knew them but the old folks.

Nobody knows for sure how many thousands in America are warmed by the
fire of hoodoo, because the worship is bound in secrecy. It is not the accepted
theology of the Nation and so believers conceal their faith. Brother from sister,
husband from wife. Nobody can say where it begins or ends. Mouths don't empty
themselves unless the ears are sympathetic and knowing.

That is why these voodoo ritualistic orgies of Broadway and popular fiction are
so laughable. The profound silence of the initiated remains what it is. Hoodoo
is not drum beating and dancing. There are no moon-worshippers among the
Negroes in America.

I was once talking to Mrs Rachel Silas of Sanford, Florida, so I asked
her where I could find a good hoodoo doctor.

"Do you believe in dat ole fogeyism, chile? Ah don't see how nobody
could do none of dat work, do you?" She laughed unnecessarily. "Ah been
hearin' 'bout dat mess ever since Ah been big enough tuh know mahself, but
shucks! Ah don't believe nobody kin do me no harm lessen they git somethin'
in mah mouth."

"Don't fool yourself," I answered with assurance. "People can do things
to you. I done seen things happen."

"Sho nuff? Well, well, well! Maybe things *kin* be don tuh harm yuh, cause Ah done heard *good* folks – folks dat ought to know – say dat it sho is a fact. Anyhow Ah figger it pays tuh be keerful."

"Oh, yeah, Mrs Rachel, Ah've seen a woman full of scorpions."

"Oh, it kin be done, honey, no effs and ands 'bout de thing. There's things that kin be done. Ah seen uh 'oman wid uh gopher in her belly. You could see 'm movin' round in her. And once every day he'd turn hisself clear over and then you could hear her hollerin' for a more'n a mile. Dat hard shell would be cuttin' her insides. Way after 'while she took down ill sick from it and died. Ah knowed de man dat done dat trick. Dat wuz done in uh dish of hoppin-johns"[1].

Mrs Viney White, a neighbor, was sitting there so she spoke. "Ah knowed into dat mahself. It wuz done over her breaking de leg of one of his hens dat wuz scratchin' up her garden. When she took down sick Ah went to see her and Ah told her folks right then dat somebody had done throwed at her, but they didn't b'lieve in nothin'. Went and got a Medical doctor, and they can't do them kind of cases no good at all. Fact is it makes it worser." She stopped short and nodded her head apprehensively towards the window. Rachel nodded her head knowingly. "She out dere now, tryin' tuh eavesdrop."

"Who you talkin' 'bout?" I asked.

"De one dat does all de underhand work 'round here. She even throwed at *me* once, but she can't do nothin'. Ah totes mah Big John de Conquerer wid me. And Ah sprinkles mustard seed 'round my door every night before Ah goes tuh bed."

"Yeah, and another thing," Mrs Rachel said, "Ah keeps her offa me too. She tries tuh come in dis yard so she kin put something down for me too, but air Lawd, Ah got something buried at dat gate dat she can't cross. She done been dere several times, but she can't cross."

"Ah'd git her tuh go if Ah wuz you, Rachel," Mrs Viney said.

"Wisht Ah knowed how. Ah'd sho do it."

"You throw salt behind her, everytime she go out of her gate. Do dat nine times and Ah bet she'll move so fast she won't even know where she's going. Somebody salted a woman over in Georgetown and she done moved so much she done wore out her furniture on de movin' wagon. But looka here, Zora, whut you want wid a two-headed doctor? Is somebody done throwed a old shoe at *you*?"

"Not exactly neither one, Mrs Viney. Just want to learn how to do things myself."

"Oh, honey, Ah wouldn't mess with it if Ah wuz you. Dat's a thing dat's got to be handled just so, do it'll kill you. Me and Rachel both knows somebody that could teach you if they will. Dis woman ain't lak some of these hoodoo doctors. She don't do nothin' but good. You couldn't pay her to be rottin' people's teeths out, and fillin' folks wid snakes and lizards and spiders and things like dat."

So I went to study with Eulalia, who specialized in Man-and-woman cases. Everyday somebody came to get Eulalia to tie them up with some man or woman

[1]Peas and rice cooked together.

[2]A root, extensively used in conjure.

or to loose them from love.

Eulalia was average sized with dark skin and bushy eyebrows. Her house was squatting among the palmettoes and the mossy scrub oaks. Nothing pretty in the house nor outside. No paint and no flowers. So one day a woman came to get tied to a man.

"Who is dis man?" Eulalia wanted to know.

"Jerry Moore," the woman told her. "He want me and Ah know it, but dat 'oman he got she got roots buried and he can't git shet of her – do we would of done been married."

Eulalia sat still and thought awhile. Then she said: "Course Ah'm uh Christian woman and don't believe in partin' no husband and wife but since she done worked roots on him, to hold him where he don't want to be, it tain't no sin for me to loose him. Where they live at?"

"Down Young's Quarters. De third house from dis end."

"Do she ever go off from home and stays a good while durin' de time he ain't there neither?"

"Yas Ma'am! She all de time way from dat house – off fanfootin' whilst he workin' lak a dog! It's a shame!"

"Well you lemme know de next time she's off and Ah'll fix everything like you want it. Put that money back in yo' purse, Ah don't want a thing till de work is done."

Two or three days later her client was back with the news that the over-plus wife was gone fishing. Eulalia sent her away and put on her shoes.

"Git dat salt-bowl and a lemon," she said to me. "Now write Jerry's name and his wife's nine times on a piece of paper and cut a little hole in the stem end of that lemon and pour some of that gun-powder in de hole and roll that paper tight and shove it inside the lemon. Wrap de lemon and de bowl of salt up and less go."

In Jerry Moore's yard, Eulalia looked all around and looked up at the sun a great deal, then pointed out a spot.

"Dig a little hole right here and bury dat lemon. It's got to be buried with the bloom-end down and it's got to be where de settin' sun will shine on it."

So I buried the lemon and Eulalia walked around to the kitchen door. By the time I had the lemon buried the door was open and we went inside. She looked all about and found some red pepper.

"Lift dat stove-lid for me," she ordered, and I did. She threw some of the pepper into the stove and we went on into the other room which was the bedroom and living-room all in one. Then Eulalia took the bowl and went from corner to corner "salting" the room. She'd toss a sprinkling into a corner and say, "Just fuss and fuss till you part and go away." Under the bed was sprinkled also. It was all over in a minute or two. Then we went out and shut the kitchen door and hurried away. And Saturday night Eulalia got her pay and the next day she set the ceremony to bring about the marriage.

FORMULAE OF HOODOO DOCTORS

TO MAKE PEOPLE LOVE YOU

T AKE nine lumps of starch, nine of sugar, nine teaspoons of steel dust. Wet it all with Jockey Club cologne. Take nine pieces of ribbon, blue, red or yellow. Take a dessertspoonful and put it on a piece of ribbon and tie it in a bag. As each fold is gathered together call his name. As you wrap it with yellow thread call his name till you finish. Make nine bags and place them under a rug, behind an armoire, under a step or over a door. They will love you and give you everything they can get. Distance makes no difference. Your mind is talking to his mind and nothing beats that.

TO BREAK UP A LOVE AFFAIR

T AKE nine needles, break each needle in three pieces. Write each person's name three times on paper. Write one name backwards and one forwards and lay the broken needles on the paper. Take five black candles, four red and three green.

Tie a string across the door from it, suspend a large candle upside down. It will hang low on the door; burn one each day for one hour. If you burn your first in the daytime, keep on in the day; if at night, continue at night. A tin plate with paper and needles in it must be placed to catch wax in.

When the ninth day is finished, go out into the street and get some white or black dog dung. A dog only drops his dung in the street when he is running and barking, and whoever you curse will run and bark likewise. Put it in a bag with the paper and carry it to running water, and one of the parties will leave town.

Nella Larsen
1893–1964

*S*he was born in Chicago to a Danish mother and a Black father
*from the Danish Virgin Islands; her father died when she was a
child and her mother remarried a white man who did not get on
with his stepdaughter. She briefly studied science at Fisk University and,
after an unsatisfactory marriage to a professor there, Dr Elmer Samuel
Imes, went to Denmark and attended the University of Copenhagen
for three years. On her return she trained as a nurse in New York,
graduating in 1915 and remaining in nursing for the next six years.
She then studied library science and was children's librarian at the New
York Public Library. After resigning in 1926 because of ill health, she took
up writing seriously, working on her acclaimed first novel,* Quicksand.
*Published in 1928, the story of Helga Crane, a mixed-race woman try-
ing to balance sexual fulfilment with middle-class respectability, it won
second prize in literature from the Harmon Foundation. The following
year her novel* Passing *was published, about Blacks who "pass" for white
but also about sexual desire between women. In 1930 she became the first
Black woman writer to win a Guggenheim Award, to do research abroad
on a third (unpublished) novel. After her divorce and in the wake of a
controversy over one of her stories resembling another writer's, she left
the literary scene and returned to nursing. Her novels deal with identity
and marginality, significant themes in her own life. She has been seen by
critics as something of a trailblazer among African-American women
writers, in that her novels are pioneer works in dealing with issues of
Black female sexuality.*

From

Quicksand

CHAPTER VIII

A YEAR thick with various adventures had sped by since that spring day on
which Helga Crane had set out away from Chicago's indifferent unkindness
for New York in the company of Mrs Hayes-Rore. New York she had found not

so unkind, not so unfriendly, not so indifferent. There she had been happy, and secured work, had made acquaintances and another friend. Again she had had that strange transforming experience, this time not so fleetingly, that magic sense of having come home. Harlem, teeming black Harlem, had welcomed her and lulled her into something that was, she was certain, peace and contentment.

The request and recommendation of Mrs Hayes-Rore had been sufficient for her to obtain work with the insurance company in which that energetic woman was interested. And through Anne it had been possible for her to meet and to know people with tastes and ideas similar to her own. Their sophisticated cynical talk, their elaborate parties, the unobtrusive correctness of their clothes and homes, all appealed to her craving for smartness, for enjoyment. Soon she was able to reflect with a flicker of amusement on that constant feeling of humiliation and inferiority which had encompassed her in Naxos. Her New York friends looked with contempt and scorn on Naxos and all its works. This gave Helga a pleasant sense of avengement. Any shreds of self-consciousness or apprehension which at first she may have felt vanished quickly, escaped in the keenness of her joy at seeming at last to belong somewhere. For she considered that she had, as she put it "found herself".

Between Anne Grey and Helga Crane there had sprung one of those immediate and peculiarly sympathetic friendships. Uneasy at first, Helga had been relieved that Anne had never returned to the uncomfortable subject of her mother's death so intentionally mentioned on their first meeting by Mrs Hayes-Rore, beyond a tremulous brief: "You won't talk to me about it, will you? I can't bear the thought of death. Nobody ever talks to me about it. My husband, you know." This Helga discovered to be true. Later, when she knew Anne better, she suspected that it was a bit of a pose assumed for the purpose of doing away with the necessity of speaking regretfully of a husband who had been perhaps not too greatly loved.

After the first pleasant weeks, feeling that her obligation to Anne was already too great, Helga began to look about for a permanent place to live. It was, she found, difficult. She eschewed the "Y" as too bare, impersonal, and restrictive. Nor did furnished rooms or the idea of a solitary or a shared apartment appeal to her. So she rejoiced when one day Anne, looking up from her book, said lightly: "Helga, since you're going to be in New York, why don't you stay here with me? I don't usually take people. It's too disrupting. Still, it *is* sort of pleasant having somebody in the house and I don't seem to mind you. You don't bore me, or bother me. If you'd like to stay – Think it over."

Helga didn't, of course, require to think it over, because lodgment in Anne's home was in complete accord with what she designated as her "æsthetic sense". Even Helga Crane approved of Anne's house and the furnishings which so admirably graced the big cream-colored rooms. Beds with long, tapering posts to which tremendous age lent dignity and interest, bonneted old highboys, tables that might be by Duncan Phyfe, rare spindle-legged chairs, and others whose ladder backs gracefully climbed the delicate wall panels. These historic things mingled harmoniously and comfortably with brass-bound Chinese tea-chests, luxurious deep chairs and davenports, tiny tables of gay color, a lacquered jade-green settee with gleaming black satin cushions, lustrous Eastern rugs,

ancient copper, Japanese prints, some fine etchings, a profusion of precious
bric-a-brac, and endless shelves filled with books.

Anne Grey herself was, as Helga expressed it, "almost too good to be
true." Thirty, maybe, brownly beautiful, she had the face of a golden Madonna,
grave and calm and sweet, with shining black hair and eyes. She carried herself
as queens are reputed to bear themselves, and probably do not. Her manners
were as agreeably gentle as her own soft name. She possessed an impeccably
fastidious taste in clothes, knowing what suited her and wearing it with an air of
unconscious assurance. The unusual thing, a native New Yorker, she was also a
person of distinction, financially independent, well connected and much sought
after. And she was interesting, an odd confusion of wit and intense earnestness;
a vivid and remarkable person. Yes, undoubtedly, Anne was almost too good to
be true. She was almost perfect.

Thus established, secure, comfortable, Helga soon became thoroughly absorbed in the distracting interests of life in New York. Her secretarial work
with the Negro insurance company filled her day. Books, the theater, parties,
used up the nights. Gradually in the charm of this new and delightful pattern
of her life she lost that tantalizing oppression of loneliness and isolation which
always, it seemed, had been a part of her existence.

But, while the continuously gorgeous panorama of Harlem fascinated her,
thrilled her, the sober mad rush of white New York failed entirely to stir her.
Like thousands of other Harlem dwellers, she patronized its shops, its theaters,
its art galleries, and its restaurants, and read its papers, without considering
herself a part of the monster. And she was satisfied, unenvious. For her this
Harlem was enough. Of that white world, so distant, so near, she asked only
indifference. No, not at all did she crave, from those pale and powerful people,
awareness. Sinister folk, she considered them, who had stolen her birthright.
Their past contribution to her life, which had been but shame and grief, she
had hidden away from brown folk in a locked closet, "never," she told herself,
"to be reopened."

Some day she intended to marry one of those alluring brown or yellow
men who danced attendance on her. Already financially successful, any one of
them could give to her the things which she had now come to desire, a home
like Anne's, cars of expensive makes such as lined the avenue, clothes and furs
from Bendel's and Revillon Frères', servants, and leisure.

Always her forehead wrinkled in distaste whenever, involuntarily, which was
somehow frequently, her mind turned on the speculative gray eyes and visionary
uplifting plans of Dr Anderson. That other, James Vayle, had slipped absolutely
from her consciousness. Of him she never thought. Helga Crane meant, now, to
have a home and perhaps laughing, appealing dark-eyed children in Harlem.
Her existence was bounded by Central Park, Fifth Avenue, St Nicholas Park, and
One Hundred and Forty-fifth street. Not at all a narrow life, as Negroes live it,
as Helga Crane knew it. Everything was there, vice and goodness, sadness and
gayety, ignorance and wisdom, ugliness and beauty, poverty and richness. And
it seemed to her that somehow of goodness, gayety, wisdom, and beauty always
there was a little more than of vice, sadness, ignorance, and ugliness. It was only
riches that did not quite transcend poverty.

"But," said Helga Crane, "what of that? Money isn't everything. It isn't even the half of everything. And here we have so much else – and by ourselves. It's only outside of Harlem among those others that money really counts for everything."

In the actuality of the pleasant present and the delightful vision of an agreeable future she was contented, and happy. She did not analyze this contentment, this happiness, but vaguely, without putting it into words or even so tangible a thing as a thought, she knew it sprang from a sense of freedom, a release from the feeling of smallness which had hedged her in, first during her sorry, unchildlike childhood among hostile white folk in Chicago, and later during her uncomfortable sojourn among snobbish black folk in Naxos.

From

Passing

CHAPTER II

I RENE wondered if it was tears that made Clare's eyes so luminous.
"And now, 'Rene, I want to hear all about you and everybody and everything. You're married, I s'pose?"

Irene nodded.

"Yes," Clare said knowingly, "you would be. Tell me about it."

And so for an hour or more they had sat there smoking and drinking tea and filling in the gap of twelve years with talk. That is, Irene did. She told Clare about her marriage and removal to New York, about her husband, and about her two sons, who were having their first experience of being separated from their parents at a summer camp, about her mother's death, about the marriages of her two brothers. She told of the marriages, births and deaths in other families that Clare had known, opening up, for her, new vistas on the lives of old friends and acquaintances.

Clare drank it all in, these things which for so long she had wanted to know and hadn't been able to learn. She sat motionless, her bright lips slightly parted, her whole face lit by the radiance of her happy eyes. Now and then she put a question, but for the most part she was silent.

Somewhere outside, a clock struck. Brought back to the present, Irene looked down at her watch and exclaimed: "Oh, I must go, Clare!"

A moment passed during which she was the prey of uneasiness. It had suddenly occurred to her that she hadn't asked Clare anything about her own life and that she had a very definite unwillingness to do so. And she was quite well aware of the reason for that reluctance. But, she asked herself, wouldn't it, all things considered, be the kindest thing not to ask? If things with Clare were as she – as they all – had suspected, wouldn't it be more tactful to seem to forget to inquire how she had spent those twelve years?

If? It was that "if" which bothered her. It might be, it might just be, in spite of all gossip and even appearances to the contrary, that there was nothing, had been nothing, that couldn't be simply and innocently explained. Appearances, she knew now, had a way sometimes of not fitting facts, and if Clare hadn't – Well, if they had all been wrong, then certainly she ought to express some interest in what had happened to her. It would seem queer and rude if she didn't. But how was she to know? There was, she at last decided, no way; so she merely said again, "I must go, Clare."

"Please, not so soon, 'Rene," Clare begged, not moving.

Irene thought: "She's really almost too good-looking. It's hardly any wonder that she – "

"And now, 'Rene dear, that I've found you, I mean to see lots and lots of you. We're here for a month at least. Jack, that's my husband, is here on business. Poor dear! in this heat. Isn't it beastly? Come to dinner with us tonight, won't you?" And she gave Irene a curious little sidelong glance and a sly, ironical smile peeped out on her full red lips, as if she had been in the secret of the other's thoughts and was mocking her.

Irene was conscious of a sharp intake of breath, but whether it was relief or chagrin that she felt, she herself could not have told. She said hastily: "I'm afraid I can't, Clare. I'm filled up. Dinner and bridge. I'm so sorry."

"Come tomorrow instead, to tea," Clare insisted. "Then you'll see Margery – she's just ten – and Jack too, maybe, if he hasn't got an appointment or something."

From Irene came an uneasy little laugh. She had an engagement for tomorrow also and she was afraid that Clare would not believe it. Suddenly, now, that possibility disturbed her. Therefore it was with a half-vexed feeling at the sense of undeserved guilt that had come upon her that she explained that it wouldn't be possible because she wouldn't be free for tea, or for luncheon or dinner either. "And the next day's Friday when I'll be going away for the week-end, Idlewild, you know. It's quite the thing now." And then she had an inspiration.

"Clare!" she exclaimed, "why don't you come up with me? Our place is probably full up – Jim's wife has a way of collecting mobs of the most impossible people – but we can always manage to find room for one more. And you'll see absolutely everybody."

In the very moment of giving the invitation she regretted it. What a foolish, what an idiotic impulse to have given way to! She groaned inwardly as she thought of the endless explanations in which it would involve her, of the curiosity, and the talk, and the lifted eye-brows. It wasn't she assured herself, that she was a snob, that she cared greatly for the petty restrictions and distinctions with which what called itself Negro society chose to hedge itself about; but that she had a natural and deeply rooted aversion to the kind of front-page notoriety that Clare Kendry's presence in Idlewild, as her guest, would expose her to. And here she was, perversely and against all reason, inviting her.

But Clare shook her head. "Really, I'd love to, 'Rene," she said, a little mournfully. "There's nothing I'd like better. But I couldn't. I mustn't, you see. It wouldn't do at all. I'm sure you understand. I'm simply crazy to go, but I can't." The dark eyes glistened and there was a suspicion of a quaver in the husky voice. "And believe me, 'Rene, I do thank you for asking me. Don't think I've entirely forgotten just what it would mean for you if I went. That is, if you still care about such things."

All indication of tears had gone from her eyes and voice, and Irene Redfield, searching her face, had an offended feeling that behind what was now only an ivory mask lurked a scornful amusement. She looked away, at the wall far beyond Clare. Well, she deserved it, for, as she acknowledged to herself, she *was* relieved. And for the very reason at which Clare had hinted. The fact that Clare had guessed her perturbation did not, however, in any degree lessen that relief. She was annoyed at having been detected in what might seem to be an insincerity; but that was all.

The waiter came with Clare's change. Irene reminded herself that she ought immediately to go. But she didn't move.

The truth was, she was curious. There were things that she wanted to ask Clare Kendry. She wished to find out about this hazardous business of "passing," this breaking away from all that was familiar and friendly to take one's chances in another environment, not entirely strange, perhaps, but certainly not entirely friendly. What, for example, one did about background, how one accounted for oneself. And how one felt when one came into contact with other Negroes. But she couldn't. She was unable to think of a single question that in its context or its phrasing was not too frankly curious, if not actually impertinent.

As if aware of her desire and her hesitation, Clare remarked, thoughtfully: "You know, 'Rene, I've often wondered why more coloured girls, girls like you and Margaret Hammer and Esther Dawson and – oh, lots of others – never 'passed' over. It's such a frightfully easy thing to do. If one's the type, all that's needed is a little nerve."

"What about background? Family, I mean. Surely you can't just drop down on people from nowhere and expect them to receive you with open arms, can you?"

"Almost," Clare asserted. "You'd be surprised. 'Rene, how much easier that is with white people than with us. Maybe because there are so many more of them, or maybe because they are secure and so don't have to bother. I've never quite decided."

Irene was inclined to be incredulous. "You mean that you didn't have to explain where you came from? It seems impossible."

Clare cast a glance of repressed amusement across the table at her. "As a matter of fact, I didn't. Though I suppose under any other circumstances I might have had to provide some plausible tale to account for myself. I've a good imagination, so I'm sure I could have done it quite creditably, and credibly. But it wasn't necessary. There were my aunts, you see, respectable and authentic enough for anything or anybody."

"I see. They were 'passing' too."

"No. They weren't. They were white."

"Oh!" And in the next instant it came back to Irene that she had heard this mentioned before; by her father, or, more likely, her mother. They were Bob Kendry's aunts. He had been a son of their brother's, on the left hand. A wild oat.

"They were nice old ladies," Clare explained, "very religious and as poor as church mice. That adored brother of theirs, my grandfather, got through every penny they had after he'd finished his own little bit."

Clare paused in her narrative to light another cigarette. Her smile, her expression, Irene noticed, was faintly resentful.

"Being good Christians," she continued, "when dad came to his tipsy end, they did their duty and gave me a home of sorts. I was, it was true, expected to earn my keep by doing all the housework, and most of the washing. But do you realize, 'Rene, that if it hadn't been for them, I shouldn't have had a home in the world?"

Irene's nod and little murmur were comprehensive, understanding.

Clare made a small mischievous grimace and proceeded. "Besides, to their notion, hard labour was good for me. I had Negro blood and they belonged to the generation that had written and read long articles headed: 'Will the Blacks Work?' Too, they weren't quite sure that the good God hadn't intended the sons and daughters of Ham to sweat because he had poked fun at old man Noah once when he had taken a drop too much. I remember the aunts telling me that that old drunkard had cursed Ham and his sons for all time."

Irene laughed. But Clare remained quite serious.

"It was more than a joke, I assure you, 'Rene. It was a hard life for a girl of sixteen. Still, I had a roof over my head, and food, and clothes – such as they were. And there were the Scriptures, and talks on morals and thrift and industry and the loving-kindness of the good Lord."

"Have you ever stopped to think, Clare," Irene demanded, "how much unhappiness and downright cruelty are laid to the loving-kindness of the Lord? And always by His most ardent followers, it seems."

"Have I?" Clare exclaimed. "It, they, made me what I am today. For, of course, I was determined to get away, to be a person and not a charity or a problem, or even a daughter of the indiscreet Ham. Then, too, I wanted things. I knew I wasn't bad-looking and that I could 'pass'. You can't know, 'Rene, how, when I used to go over to the south side, I used almost to hate all of you. You had all the things I wanted and never had had. It made me all the more determined to get them, and others. Do you, can you understand what I felt?"

She looked up with a pointed and appealing effect, and, evidently finding the sympathetic expression on Irene's face sufficient answer, went on. "The aunts were queer. For all their Bibles and praying and ranting about honesty, they didn't want anyone to know that their darling brother had seduced – ruined, they called it – a Negro girl. They could excuse the ruin, but they couldn't forgive the tar-brush. They forbade me to mention Negroes to the neighbours, or even to mention the south side. You may be sure that I didn't. I'll bet they were good and sorry afterwards."

She laughed and the ringing bells in her laugh had a hard metallic sound.

"When the chance to get away came, that omission was of great value to me. When Jack, a schoolboy acquaintance of some people in the neighbourhood, turned up from South America with untold gold, there was no one to tell him that I was coloured, and many to tell him about the severity and the religiousness of Aunt Grace and Aunt Edna. You can guess the rest. After he came, I stopped slipping off to the south side and slipped off to meet him instead. I couldn't manage both. In the end I had no great difficulty in convincing him that it was useless to talk marriage to the aunts. So on the day that I was eighteen, we went off and were married. So that's that. Nothing could have been easier."

"Yes, I do see that for you it was easy enough. By the way! I wonder why they didn't tell father that you were married. He went over to find out about you when you stopped coming over to see us. I'm sure they didn't tell him. Not that you were married."

Clare Kendry's eyes were bright with tears that didn't fall. "Oh, how lovely! To have cared enough about me to do that. The dear sweet man! Well, they couldn't tell him because they didn't know it. I took care of that, for I couldn't be sure that those consciences of theirs wouldn't begin to work on them afterwards and make them let the cat out of the bag. The old things probably thought I was living in sin, wherever I was. And it would be about what they expected."

An amused smile lit the lovely face for the smallest fraction of a second. After a little silence she said soberly: "But I'm sorry if they told your father so. That was something I hadn't counted on."

"I'm not sure that they did," Irene told her. "He didn't say so, anyway."

"He wouldn't, 'Rene dear. Not your father."

"Thanks, I'm sure he wouldn't."

"But you've never answered my question. Tell me, honestly, haven't you ever thought of 'passing'?"

Irene answered promptly: "No. Why should I?" And so disdainful was her voice and manner that Clare's face flushed and her eyes glinted. Irene hastened to add: "You see, Clare, I've everything I want. Except, perhaps, a little more money."

At that Clare laughed, her spark of anger vanished as quickly as it had appeared. "Of course," she declared, "that's what everybody wants, just a little more money, even the people who have it. And I must say I don't blame them. Money's awfully nice to have. In fact, all things considered, I think, 'Rene, that it's even worth the price."

Irene could only shrug her shoulders. Her reason partly agreed, her instinct wholly rebelled. And she could not say why. And though conscious that if she didn't hurry away, she was going to be late to dinner, she still lingered. It was as if the woman sitting on the other side of the table, a girl that she had known, who had done this rather dangerous and, to Irene Redfield, abhorrent thing successfully and had announced herself well satisfied, had for her a fascination, strange and compelling.

Clare Kendry was still leaning back in the tall chair, her sloping shoulders against the carved top. She sat with an air of indifferent assurance, as if arranged for, desired. About her clung that dim suggestion of polite insolence with which a few women are born and which some acquire with the coming of riches or importance.

Clare, it gave Irene a little prick of satisfaction to recall, hadn't got that by passing herself off as white. She herself had always had it.

Just as she'd always had that pale gold hair, which, unsheared still, was drawn loosely back from a broad brow, partly hidden by the small close hat. Her lips, painted a brilliant geranium-red, were sweet and sensitive and a little obstinate. A tempting mouth. The face across the forehead and cheeks was a trifle too wide, but the ivory skin had a peculiar soft lustre. And the eyes were magnificent! dark, sometimes absolutely black, always luminous, and set in long, black lashes. Arresting eyes, slow and mesmeric, and with, for all their warmth, something withdrawn and secret about them.

Ah! Surely! They were Negro eyes! mysterious and concealing. And set in that ivory face under that bright hair, there was about them something exotic.

Yes, Clare Kendry's loveliness was absolute, beyond challenge, thanks to those eyes which her grandmother and later her mother and father had given her.

Into those eyes there came a smile and over Irene the sense of being petted and caressed. She smiled back.

"Maybe," Clare suggested, "you can come Monday, if you're back. Or, if you're not, then Tuesday."

With a small regretful sigh, Irene informed Clare that she was afraid she wouldn't be back by Monday and that she was sure she had dozens of things for Tuesday, and that she was leaving Wednesday. It might be, however, that she could get out of something Tuesday.

"Oh, do try. Do put somebody else off. The others can see you any time, while I – Why, I may never see you again! Think of that, 'Rene! You'll have to come. You'll simply have to! I'll never forgive you if you don't."

At that moment it seemed a dreadful thing to think of never seeing Clare Kendry again. Standing there under the appeal, the caress, of her eyes, Irene had the desire, the hope, that this parting wouldn't be the last.

"I'll try, Clare," she promised gently. "I'll call you – or will you call me?"

"I think, perhaps, I'd better call you. Your father's in the book, I know, and the address is the same. Sixty-four eighteen. Some memory, what? Now remember, I'm going to expect you. You've got to be able to come."

Again that peculiar mellowing smile.

"I'll do my best, Clare."

Irene gathered up her gloves and bag. They stood up. She put out her hand. Clare took it and held it.

"It has been nice seeing you again, Clare. How pleased and glad father'll be to hear about you!"

"Until Tuesday, then," Clare Kendry replied. "I'll spend every minute of the time from now on looking forward to seeing you again. Goodbye, 'Rene dear. My love to your father, and this kiss for him."

Amy Jacques Garvey
1896–1973

B orn in Jamaica, she moved to the USA in 1917 and in 1922 became the second wife (after Amy Ashwood) of Jamaican pan-Africanist Marcus Garvey, founder in 1911 of the United Negro Improvement Association (UNIA) that advocated the "Back to Africa" movement. His secretary and co-worker, and in her own right a race activist, she was associate editor (1924–7) of the UNIA paper, Negro World. Introducing a page called "Our Women and What They Think", she expressed strongly feminist views, saying: "If the US Senate and Congress can open their doors to White women, we serve notice on our men that Negro women will demand equal opportunity to fill any position in the Universal Negro Improvement Association or anywhere else without discrimination because of sex. We are sorry if it hurts your old-fashioned tyrannical feelings, and we not only make the demand but we intend to enforce it." While her husband was in prison on trumped-up charges related to his shipping line that was to take Blacks to Africa, she published the first two volumes of Philosophy and Opinions of Marcus Garvey (1923). When he was deported from the USA in 1927, she toured England, France and Germany with him, writing articles for Negro World. Their sons were born in 1930 and 1933, and she remained in Jamaica when Garvey went to England in 1934. After his death in 1940 she continued working for Black nationalism, becoming contributing editor to the African, a journal published in Harlem in the 1940s, and founding the African Study Circle of the World in Jamaica in the late 1940s. She wrote the biography Garvey and Garveyism (1963) and published a book of articles in 1966. "Women as Leaders" was her editorial in Negro World on 24 October 1925.

Women as Leaders

T HE exigencies of this present age require that women take their places beside their men. White women are rallying all their forces and uniting regardless of national boundaries to save their race from destruction, and preserve its ideals for posterity.... White men have begun to realize that as women are the backbone of the home, so can they, by their economic experience and their aptitude for details, participate effectively in guiding the destiny of nation and race.

No line of endeavor remains closed for long to the modern woman. She agitates for equal opportunities and gets them; she makes good on the job and gains the respect of men who heretofore opposed her. She prefers to be a bread-winner than a half-starved wife at home. She is not afraid of hard work, and by being independent she gets more out of the present-day husband than her grandmother did in the good old days.

The women of the East, both yellow and black, are slowly but surely imitating the women of the Western world, and as the white women are bolstering up a decaying white civilization, even so women of the darker races are sallying forth to help their men establish a civilization according to their own standards, and to strive for world leadership.

Women of all climes and races have as great a part to play in the development of their particular group as the men. Some readers may not agree with us on this issue, but do they not mould the minds of their children, the future men and women? Even before birth a mother can so direct her thoughts and conduct as to bring into the world either a genius or an idiot. Imagine the early years of contact between mother and child, when she directs his form of speech, and is responsible for his conduct and deportment. Many a man has risen from the depths of poverty and obscurity and made his mark in life because of the advices and councils of a good mother whose influence guided his footsteps throughout his life.

Women therefore are extending this holy influence outside the realms of the home, softening the ills of the world by their gracious and kindly contact.

Some men may argue that the home will be broken up and women will become coarse and lose their gentle appeal. We do not think so, because everything can be done with moderation.... The doll-baby type of woman is a thing of the past, and the wide-awake woman is forging ahead prepared for all emergencies, and ready to answer any call, even if it be to face the cannons on the battlefield.

New York has a woman Secretary of State. Two States have women Governors, and we would not be surprised if within the next ten years a woman graces the White House in Washington D.C. Women are also filling diplomatic positions, and from time immemorial women have been used as spies to get information for their country.

White women have greater opportunities to display their ability because of the standing of both races, and due to the fact that black men are less appreciative of their women than white men. The former will more readily sing the praises of white women than their own; yet who is more deserving of admiration than the black woman, she who has borne the rigors of slavery, the deprivations consequent on a pauperized race, and the indignities heaped upon a weak and defenseless people? Yet she has suffered all with fortitude, and stands ever ready to help in the onward march to freedom and power.

Be not discouraged, black women of the world, but push forward, regardless of the lack of appreciation shown you. A race must be saved, a country must be redeemed, and unless you strengthen the leadership of vacillating Negro men, we will remain marking time until the Yellow race gains leadership of the world, and we be forced to subserviency under them, or extermination.

We are tired of hearing Negro men say, "There is a better day coming," while they do nothing to usher in the day. We are becoming so impatient that we are getting in the front ranks, and serve notice on the world that we will brush aside the halting, cowardly Negro men, and with prayer on our lips and arms prepared for any fray, we will press on and on until victory is ours.

Africa must be for Africans, and Negroes everywhere must be independent, God being our guide. Mr Black man, watch your step! Ethiopia's queens will reign again, and her Amazons protect her shores and people. Strengthen your shaking knees, and move forward, or we will displace you and lead on to victory and to glory.

Marita Bonner

1899–1971

B orn in Massachusetts, she studied English and comparative literature at Radcliffe College, graduating in 1922 and becoming a teacher in Virginia, Washington, DC, and subsequently Chicago. A frequent contributor between 1925 and 1940 to Crisis (published by the National Association for the Advancement of Colored People) and Opportunity (official publication of the National Urban League), she wrote plays, essays and short stories, many of which appear in Frye Street and Environs: The Collected Works of Marita Bonner, co-edited by her daughter Joyce Occomy Sticklin and Joyce Flynn. "On Being Young – a Woman – and Colored", which as its title implies, deals with the alienation she felt as a young, middle-class Black woman, won the 1925 essay contest sponsored by Crisis. She died after a fire in her Chicago apartment.

On Being Young – a Woman – and Colored

YOU start out after you have gone from kindergarten to sheepskin covered with sundry Latin phrases.

At least you know what you want life to give you. A career as fixed and as calmly brilliant as the North Star. The one real thing that money buys. Time. Time to do things. A house that can be as delectably out of order and as easily put in order as the doll-house of "playing-house" days. And of course, a husband you can look up to without looking down on yourself.

Somehow you feel like a kitten in a sunny catnip field that sees sleek, plump brown field mice and yellow baby chicks sitting coyly, side by side, under each leaf. A desire to dash three or four ways seizes you.

That's Youth.

But you know that things learned need testing – acid testing – to see if they are really after all, an interwoven part of you. All your life you have heard of the debt you owe "Your People" because you have managed to have the things they have not largely had.

So you find a spot where there are hordes of them – of course below the Line – to be your catnip field while you close your eyes to mice and chickens alike.

If you have never lived among your own, you feel prodigal. Some warm untouched current flows through them – through you – and drags you out into the deep waters of a new sea of human foibles and mannerisms; of a peculiar psychology and prejudices. And one day you find yourself entangled – enmeshed – pinioned in the seaweed of a Black Ghetto.

Not a Ghetto, placid like the Strasse that flows, outwardly unperturbed and calm in a stream of religious belief, but a peculiar group. Cut off, flung together, shoved aside in a bundle because of color and with no more in common.

Unless color is, after all, the real bond.

Milling around like live fish in a basket. Those at the bottom crushed into a sort of stupid apathy by the weight of those on top. Those on top leaping, leaping; leaping to scale the sides; to get out.

There are two "colored" movies, innumerable parties – and cards. Cards played so intensely that it fascinates and repulses at once.

Movies.

Movies worthy and worthless – but not even a low-caste spoken stage.

Parties, plentiful. Music and dancing and much that is wit and color and gaiety. But they are like the richest chocolate; stuffed costly chocolates that make the taste go stale if you have too many of them. That make plain whole bread taste like ashes.

There are all the earmarks of a group within a group. Cut off all around from ingress from or egress to other groups. A sameness of type. The smug self-satisfaction of an inner measurement; a measurement by standards known within a limited group and not those of an unlimited, seeing world.... Like the blind, blind mice. Mice whose eyes have been blinded.

Strange longing seizes hold of you. You wish yourself back where you can lay your bottom dollar down and sit in a dollar seat to hear voices, strings, reeds that have lifted the World out, up, beyond things that have bodies and walls. Where you can marvel at new marbles and bronzes and flat colors that will make men forget that things exist in a flesh more often than in spirit. Where you can sink your body in a cushioned seat and sink your soul at the same time into a section of life set before you on the boards for a few hours.

You hear that up at New York this is to be seen; that, to be heard.

You decide the next train will take you there.

You decide the next second that that train will not take you, nor the next – nor the next for some time to come.

For you know that – being a woman – you cannot twice a month or twice a year, for that matter, break away to see or hear anything in a city that is supposed to see and hear too much.

That's being a woman. A woman of any color.

You decide that something is wrong with a world that stifles and chokes; that cuts off and stunts; hedging in, pressing down on eyes, ears and throat. Somehow all wrong.

You wonder how it happens there that – say five hundred miles from the Bay State – Anglo Saxon intelligence is so warped and stunted.

How judgment and discernment are bred out of the race. And what has become of discrimination? Discrimination of the right sort. Discrimination that the best minds have told you weighs shadows and nuances and spiritual differences before it catalogues. The kind they have taught you all of your life was best: that looks clearly past generalization and past appearance to dissect, to dig down to the real heart of matters. That casts aside rapid summary conclusions, drawn from primary inference, as Daniel did the spiced meats.

Why can't they then perceive that there is a difference in the glance from a pair of eyes that look, mildly docile, at "white ladies" and those that, impersonally and perceptively – aware of distinctions – see only women who happen to be white?

Why do they see a colored woman only as a gross collection of desires, all uncontrolled, reaching out for their Apollos and the Quasimodos with avid indiscrimination?

Why, unless you talk in staccato squawks – brittle as sea-shells – unless you "champ" gum – unless you cover two yards square when you laugh – unless your taste runs to violent colors – impossible perfumes and more impossible clothes – are you a feminine Caliban craving to pass for Ariel?

An empty imitation of an empty invitation. A mime; a sham; a copy-cat. A hollow re-echo. A froth, a foam. A fleck of the ashes of superficiality?

Everything you touch or taste now is like the flesh of an unripe persimmon.
. . . Do you need to be told what that is being . . . ?

Old ideas, old fundamentals seem worm-eaten, out-grown, worthless, bitter; fit for the scrap-heap of Wisdom.

What you had thought tangible and practical has turned out to be a collection of "blue-flower" theories.

If they have not discovered how to use their accumulation of facts, they are useless to you in Their world.

Every part of you becomes bitter.

But – "In Heaven's name, do not grow bitter. Be bigger than they are" –
exhort white friends who have never had to draw breath in a Jim-Crow train.
Who have never had petty putrid insult dragged over them – drawing blood
– like pebbled sand on your body where the skin is tenderest. On your body
where the skin is thinnest and tenderest.

You long to explode and hurt everything white; friendly; unfriendly. But
you know that you cannot live with a chip on your shoulder even if you can
manage a smile around your eyes – without getting steely and brittle and losing
the softness that makes you a woman.

For chips make you bend your body to balance them. And once you bend,
you lose your poise, your balance, and the chip gets into you. The real you. You
get hard.

... And many things in you can ossify. ...

And you know, being a woman, you have to go about it gently and quietly,
to find out and to discover just what is wrong. Just what can be done.

You see clearly that they have acquired things.

Money; money. Money to build with, money to destroy. Money to swim
in. Money to drown in. Money.

An ascendancy of wisdom. An incalculable hoard of wisdom in all fields,
in all things collected from all quarters of humanity.

A stupendous mass of things.

Things.

So, too, the Greeks. ... Things.

And the Romans. ...

And you wonder and wonder why they have not discovered how to handle
deftly and skillfully, Wisdom, stored up for them – like the honey for the Gods
on Olympus – since time unknown.

You wonder and you wonder until you wander out into Infinity, where
– if it is to be found anywhere – Truth really exists.

The Greeks had possessions, culture. They were lost because they did
not understand.

The Romans owned more than anyone else. Trampled under the heel
of Vandals and Civilization, because they would not understand.

Greeks. Did not understand.

Romans. Would not understand.

"They." Will not understand.

So you find they have shut Wisdom up and have forgotten to find the key
that will let her out. They have trapped, trammeled, lashed her to themselves
with thews and thongs and theories. They have ransacked sea and earth and air
to bring every treasure to her. But she sulks and will not work for a world with
a whitish hue because it has snubbed her twin sister, Understanding.

You see clearly – off there is Infinity – Understanding. Standing alone,
waiting for someone to really want her.

But she is so far out there is no way to snatch at her and really drag her in.

So – being a woman – you can wait.

You must sit quietly without a chip. Not sodden – and weighted as if
your feet were cast in the iron of your soul. Not wasting strength in enervating

gestures as if two hundred years of bonds and whips had really tricked you into nervous uncertainty.

But quiet; quiet. Like Buddha – who brown like I am – sat entirely at ease, entirely sure of himself; motionless and knowing, a thousand years before the white man knew there was so very much difference between feet and hands.

Motionless on the outside. But on the inside?

Silent.

Still. . . . "Perhaps Buddha is a woman."

So you too. Still; quiet; with a smile, ever so slight, at the eyes so that Life will flow into and not by you. And you can gather, as it passes, the essences, the overtones, the tints, the shadows; draw understanding to yourself.

And then you can, when Time is ripe, swoop to your feet – at your full height – at a single gesture.

Ready to go where?

Why. . . . Wherever God motions.

Gwendolyn B. Bennett

1902–81

B orn in Giddings, Texas, she was educated in Washington, DC, and Brooklyn, where she was the first Black to be elected to the Literary and Dramatic Societies at Girls High School. She studied fine arts for two years at Teachers College, Columbia University, and later at the Pratt Institute, Brooklyn, and received a scholarship to study art in France in 1925. On her return to New York in 1926 she became assistant editor of Opportunity magazine. She taught design, watercolour and crafts at Howard University (she was forced to resign in 1927 because of disapproval of her planned marriage to a medical student there) and was director of the Harlem Community Art Center (1937–40). She contributed poems and stories to many publications, including American Mercury, Opportunity, Crisis, Messenger and Fire!! during the 1920s. Her drawings also appeared in Crisis and Messenger, and she and Aaron Douglas were the first Black artists to receive a Barnes Foundation Fellowship in 1927, and she and Aaron Douglas were the first Black artists to receive a Barnes Foundation Fellowship, in 1927.

To a Dark Girl

I love you for your brownness
And the rounded darkness of your breast.
I love you for the breaking sadness in your voice
And shadows where your wayward eye-lids rest.

Something of old forgotten queens
Lurks in the lithe abandon of your walk,
And something of the shackled slave
Sobs in the rhythm of your talk.

Oh, little brown girl, born for sorrow's mate,
Keep all you have of queenliness,
Forgetting that you once were slave,
And let your full lips laugh at Fate!

Hatred

I shall hate you
Like a dart of singing steel
Shot through still air
At even-tide.
Or solemnly
As pines are sober
When they stand etched
Against the sky.
Hating you shall be a game
Played with cool hands
And slim fingers.
Your heart will yearn
For the lonely splendor
Of the pine tree;
While rekindled fires
In my eyes
Shall wound you like swift arrows.
Memory will lay its hands
Upon your breast
And you will understand
My hatred.

Advice

You were a sophist,
Pale and quite remote,
As you bade me
Write poems –
Brown poems
Of dark words
And prehistoric rhythms . . .
Your pallor stifled my poesy
But I remembered a tapestry
That I would some day weave
Of dim purples and fine reds
And blues
Like night and death –
The keen precision of your words
Wove a silver thread
Through the dusk softness
Of my dream-stuff. . . .

Gladys May Casely-Hayford ("Aquah Laluah")

1904–50

B orn in Axim, Gold Coast (Ghana), only child of Adelaide Casely-Hayford (who in a reminiscence of her daughter wrote: "We had quite a lot in common, my darling one gial pickin and I. We were both premature, utterly negligible, puny infants causing our parents a lot of anxiety and trouble. We were both Wednesday's children – full of woe"). She had a lonely childhood, first attending local schools then in 1919, at the age of fifteen, she went to Britain and began to write poems while a pupil at Penrhos College, Colwyn Bay, Wales. Returning to Africa after some years, she taught in the Girls' Vocational School

*founded in Sierra Leone by her mother. The passage of her life was never
smooth but, as her mother recalled, her "outstanding capacity for love
and kindness swallowed up her many eccentricities". She suffered chronic
financial hardship, particularly after her marriage and the birth of her
son Kobina. Although in the 1930s her writing began to appear (under
the pseudonym Aquah Laluah) in US publications such as* Opportunity,
Atlantic Monthly *and the* Philadelphia Tribune, *she never followed up
opportunities afforded by her literary talent. Also an accomplished
musician, she made an impact on the Freetown cultural scene in the
1930s and 1940s. She eventually died of blackwater fever in Freetown,
relatively young and unfulfilled. She was one of the first Sierra
Leoneans to write poems in Krio, her collection* Take 'um So *appearing
in 1948. She left many unpublished poems and in 1983 "Palm Fronds",
a selection of her work, which ranges widely in style and theme –
encompassing poems of love and patriotism as well as poems for children
– was published alongside her mother's reminiscences in* Memoirs and
Poems, *edited by her daughter-in-law Lucilda Hunter.*

The Serving Girl

The calabash wherein she served my food
Was smooth and polished as sandalwood.
Fish, as white as the foam of the sea,
Peppered and golden-fried for me.
She brought palm wine that carelessly slips
From the sleeping palm tree's honeyed lips.
But who can guess, or even surmise
The countless things she served with her eyes?

Junior Geography Lesson

Here are the British Isles, girls, beyond the Atlantic Sea.
(Jes now somebody er go cry, if e no listen me.)
England is in Britain, where most white people stay.
(Tete, if you no careful, some good whip go pass you way.)
Now London is in England, where King George sits on his throne.
(No bring no crossness, Jane, to me, 'cos meself get me own.)
Now you and I and all of us are King George's subjects too,
For Sierra Leone belongs to him. (Ayo, if I hol' you. . .)
We help to form the Empire of Britain o'er the seas.
(You know say you dey laugh, don' you pretend you dey sneeze.)

What is the song about the Crown I taught you girls to sing?
Now everybody answer: "God Save Our Gracious King".
(Mercy! Dis here na wallah. Tank God, de bell done ring,
Dem dry-eye pickin whey dey now, no sabe anyting.)

To My Mother

Mother, I need you. Though a woman grown,
Mine own self's arbitrator, mine own law,
My need of you is deeper than I've known,
And far more urgent than it was before.
Into her tender arms I'd love to creep,
Pour out my woes, and cry myself to sleep.

But even were you here, this could not be,
Convention kills the sobbing child in me,
Since soft white luster crowned your smooth fair brow,
'Tis I, the child, turns Mother to you now.
Then whilst my firm hand smooths your long white hair,
And my young lips press from your eyes the tears,
Whilst my strong arms are round you, resting there in my embrace
I loose the weight of years.
And when you smile, confiding tilt your head,
To gaze into my eyes, I'm comforted.

The Ideal

I do not glorify the great ideal, the Ethiopian woman that I see,
I glorify that simple jet-skinned soul, the Mother of the coloured race to be,
Because she fought through danger and cried shame unto those
Who trample in the sod humanity; she should be glorified.
Because she raised her soul through stone to God; because she uncomplaining
   bore the weight
Of cradling men, and suffering whilst they lived, the strain of their encounters
   with swift fate,
Because she dried their eyes, and staunched their blood;
Because her breasts were warm on which to rest, hid in her bosom from
   the avenging flood,
As respite from the character's great test.
Because she is still simple, will remain so simple that men fail to recognize
She is the Mother of a wisdom tried, and taught in vain attempt to reach the skies.

Distance

Distance has robbed me of so many things
That make humdrum existence very dear.
The sun no shadow on the pathway flings
As certainty that you are somewhere near.
No longer may I raise the curtain frill
And gaze expectant at the crowd below
With a delicious sweet ecstatic thrill
To watch unseen, beloved, where you go.
No longer may I startled wake from sleep
Your name from my lips dropping like sweet dew
To curb my hungry longing, let it keep,
Knowing the morrow's dawning will bring you.
No longer may I lift my warm face up
For your soft kiss, pressed down upon my lips.
This is the yearning which we women feel,
Prone wanderers who sail the seas in ships.
And yet with all this anguish, had you wings,
Soul whom I love, I would not have you here.
Distance has robbed me of so many things
That made life's dull monotony so dear.

The Might Have Been

I cannot blame you for what is past,
Fate took a hand in it, joy did not last,
Misunderstanding held us both in thrall,
Better for each had we ne'er met at all.

When I think of the joy that might have been,
Had the dream of our love come true,
When I think of the grey in the skies above,
That should have been glorious blue.

When I think of the waste of the best life holds,
And the empty receipt of the years,
When I think of the golden might have been,
It fills my eyes with tears.

Una Marson

1905–65

J amaican feminist, journalist, playwright and one of the first Caribbean women to win recognition as a poet, she was an early
innovator of vernacular poetry; her blues poems were the first to
adapt musical rhythms to verse in the Caribbean. Born in St Elizabeth,
she was educated locally and had published two volumes of poetry –
Tropic Reveries (1930) and Heights and Depths (1931) – by 1932, when
she left for England. She was secretary of the League of Coloured Peoples
in London, and edited their journal, and was later private secretary to
Emperor Haile Selassie of Ethiopia while he was in exile in Britain.
She was active with the Women's International League for Peace and
Freedom, and the International Alliance of Women. Returning home
in 1936, she undertook social work, was involved with establishing
the weekly progressive paper Public Opinion and the journal Jamaica
Standard and produced several of her own plays. During a second
stay in England, from 1938, she was a radio broadcaster with the BBC
World Service, starting the Caribbean Voices programme. She went back
to Jamaica after the war, remaining active as a publisher, journalist
and social worker until her death.

Kinky Hair Blues

Gwine find a beauty shop
Cause I ain't a belle.
Gwine find a beauty shop
Cause I ain't a lovely belle.
The boys pass me by,
They say I's not so swell.

See oder young gals
So slick and smart.
See dose oder young gals
So slick and smart.
I jes gwine die on de shelf
If I don't mek a start.

I hate dat ironed hair
And dat bleaching skin.

Hate dat ironed hair
And dat bleaching skin.
But I'll be all alone
If I don't fall in.

Lord, 'tis you did gie me
All dis kinky hair.
'Tis you did gie me
All dis kinky hair,
And I don't envy gals
What got dose locks so fair.

I like me black face
And me kinky hair.
I like me black face
And me kinky hair.
But nobody loves dem,
I jes don't tink it's fair.

Now I's gwine press me hair
And bleach me skin,
I's gwine press me hair
And bleach me skin.
What won't a gal do
Some kind of man to win.

Brown Baby Blues

I got a brown baby
Sweet as she can be.
I got a brown baby
Sweet as she can be.
But she ain't got no papa,
Cause he's gone to sea.

I love me baby
But she don't got no name.
I love me baby
She don't got no name.
Well wha' fe do,
Dat is not her shame.

Maybe she'll ask me
Why I is so black,
Maybe she'll ask me
Why I is so black,

An' she's so brown;
Lord, send her papa back.

My sweet brown baby
Don't you cry.
My sweet brown baby
Don't you cry,
Your mama does love you
And you colour is high.

Mabel Dove-Danquah
1910–

Born in the Gold Coast (now Ghana), she married the scholar, playwright and diplomat J. B. Danquah and travelled with him in Europe and the USA. Before Ghana's independence, she served in parliament in 1952, the first woman to be elected a member of any African legislative assembly. She was editor of the Accra Evening News and, as "Marjorie Mensah", contributed a column a column to the West African Times. She was co-author of The Torn Veil and other stories (with Phebean Itayemi-Ogundipe, 1978). Her concern with the traditional role of women in Ghana is evident in her writing._

Anticipation

NANA Adaku II, Omanhene[1] Akwasin, was celebrating the twentieth anniversary of his accession to the stool[2] of Akwasin. The capital, Nkwabi, was thronged with people from the outlying towns and villages.

[1] *Omanhene:* the male ruler of the Akan state.
[2] *stool:* among the Akan peoples, the stool is the material symbol of the state.

It was in the height of the cocoa season, money was circulating freely and farmers were spending to their hearts' content. Friends who had not seen one another for a long time were renewing their friendship. They called with gifts of gin, champagne or whisky, recalled old days with gusto and before departing imbibed most of the drinks they brought as gifts. No one cared, everyone was happy. Few could be seen in European attire; nearly all were in Gold Coast costume. The men had tokota sandals on their feet, and rich multi-coloured velvet and gorgeous, hand-woven kente cloths nicely wrapped round their bodies. The women, with golden ear-rings dangling, with golden chains and bracelets, looked dignified in their colourful native attire.

The state drums were beating paeans of joy.

It was four o'clock in the afternoon and people were walking to the state park where the Odwira[3] was to be staged. Enclosures of palm leaves decorated the grounds.

The Omanhene arrived in a palanquin under a brightly-patterned state umbrella, a golden crown on his head, his kente studded with tiny golden beads, rows upon rows of golden necklaces piled high on his chest. He wore bracelets of gold from the wrists right up to the elbows. He held in his right hand a decorated elephant tail which he waved to his enthusiastic, cheering people. In front of him sat his "soul",[4] a young boy of twelve, holding the sword of office.

After the Omanhene came the Adontehene,[5] the next in importance. He was resplendent in rich green and red velvet cloth; his head band was studded with golden bars. Other chiefs came one after the other under their brightly-coloured state umbrellas. The procession was long. The crowd raised cheers as each palanquin was lowered, and the drums went on beating resounding joys of jubilation. The Omanhene took his seat on the dais with the Elders. The District Commissioner, Captain Hobbs, was near him. Sasa, the jester, looked ludicrous in his motley pair of trousers and his cap of monkey skin. He made faces at the Omanhene, he leered, did acrobatic stunts; the Omanhene could not laugh; it was against custom for the great Chief to be moved to laughter in public.

The state park presented a scene of barbaric splendour. Chiefs and their retinue sat on native stools under state umbrellas of diverse colours. The golden linguist staves of office gleamed in the sunlight. The women, like tropical butterflies, looked charming in their multi-coloured brocaded silk, kente and velvet, and the Oduku headdress, black and shiny, studded with long golden pins and slides. Young men paraded the grounds, their flowing cloths trailing behind them, their silken plaited headbands glittering in the sun.

The drums beat on.

---

[3] *Odwira*: "cleansing" or "purification," a festival occurring at the end of the Akan year and celebrating, usually, the yam harvest.

[4] *"soul"*: This refers to the Omanhene's *okrafo*, "soul-bearer," so called because the Omanhene had projected his actual soul (*kra*) to a person he loved dearly.

[5] *Adontehene*: the commander of the main body of the army in the Ashante state.

The women are going to perform the celebrated Adowa dance. The decorated calabashes make rhythm. The women run a few steps, move slowly sideways and sway their shoulders. One dancer looks particularly enchanting in her green, blue and red square kente, moving with the simple, charming grace of a wild woodland creature; the Chief is stirred, and throws a handful of loose cash into the crowd of dancers. She smiles as the coins fall on her and tinkle to the ground. There is a rush. She makes no sign but keeps on dancing.

The Omanhene turns to his trusted linguist:

"Who is that beautiful dancer?"

"I am sorry, I do not know her."

"I must have her as a wife."

Nana Adaku II was fifty-five and he had already forty wives, but a new beauty gave him the same new thrill as it did the man who is blessed – or cursed – with only one better half. Desire again burned fiercely in his veins; he was bored with his forty wives. He usually got so mixed up among them that lately he kept calling them by the wrong names. His new wife cried bitterly when he called her Oda, the name of an old, ugly wife.

"This dancer is totally different," thought the Chief; "she will be a joy to the palace." He turned round to the linguist:

"I will pay one hundred pounds for her."

"She might already be married, Nana."

"I shall pay the husband any moneys he demands."

The linguist knew his Omanhene: when he desired a woman he usually had his way.

"Get fifty pounds from the chief treasurer, find the relatives, give them the money and when she is in my palace tonight I shall give her the balance of fifty pounds. Give the linguist staff to Kojo and begin your investigations now."

Nana Adaku II was a fast worker. He was like men all over the world when they are stirred by feminine charm: a shapely leg, the flash of an eye, the quiver of a nostril, the timbre of a voice, and the male species becomes frenzy personified. Many men go through this sort of mania until they reach their dotage. The cynics among them treat women with a little flattery, bland tolerance, and take fine care not to become seriously entangled for life. Women, on the other hand, use quite a lot of common sense: they are not particularly thrilled by the physical charms of a man; if his pockets are heavy and his income sure, he is a good matrimonial risk. But there is evolving a new type of hardheaded modern woman who insists on the perfect lover as well as an income and other necessaries, or stays forever from the unbliss of marriage.

By 6 p.m. Nana Adaku II was getting bored with the whole assembly and was very glad to get into his palanquin. The state umbrellas danced, the chiefs sat again in their palanquins, the crowd cheered wildly, the drums beat. Soon the shadows of evening fell and the enclosures of palm leaves in the state park stood empty and deserted.

The Omanhene had taken his bath after dusk and changed into a gold and green brocaded cloth. Two male servants stood on either side and fanned him with large ostrich feathers as he reclined on a velvet-cushioned settee in his private sitting-room. An envelope containing fifty golden sovereigns was near him.

He knew his linguist as a man of tact and diplomacy and he was sure that night would bring him a wife to help him celebrate the anniversary of his accession to the Akwasin Stool.

He must have dozed. When he woke up the young woman was kneeling by his feet. He raised her on to the settee.

"Were you pleased to come?"

"I was pleased to do Nana's bidding."

"Good girl. What is your name?"

"Effua, my lord and master."

"It is beautiful name, and you are a beautiful woman, too. Here are fifty gold sovereigns, the balance of the marriage dowry. We will marry privately tonight and do the necessary custom afterward." Nana Adaku II is not the first man to use this technique. Civilized, semi-civilized, and primitive men all over the world have said the very same thing in nearly the same words.

"I shall give the money to my mother," said the sensible girl. "She is in the corridor. May I?" The Chief nodded assent.

Effua returned.

"Nana, my mother and other relatives want to thank you for the hundred pounds."

"There is no need, my beauty," and he played with the ivory beads lying so snugly on her bosom.

"They think you must have noticed some extraordinary charm in me for you to have spent so much money," she smiled shyly at the Omanhene.

"But, my dear, you are charming. Haven't they eyes?"

"But, Nana, I cannot understand it myself."

"You cannot, you modest woman? Look at yourself in that long mirror over there."

The girl smiled mischievously, went to the mirror, looked at herself. She came back and sat on the settee and leaned her head on his bosom.

"You are a lovely girl, Effua." He caressed her shiny black hair, so artistically plaited.

"But, my master, I have always been like this, haven't I?"

"I suppose so, beautiful, but I only saw you today."

"You only saw me today?"

"Today."

"Have you forgotten?"

"Forgotten what, my love?"

"You paid fifty pounds ... and married me two years ago."

Pauli Murray
1910–

Born in Baltimore, she was orphaned at the age of three and raised by her aunt, a teacher in a small Black school. Her maternal grandmother was a slave, her maternal grandfather fought with the Union armies in the American Civil War and later helped establish the first school system for the free Blacks of Virginia and North Carolina. She studied at Hunter College (BA, 1933), Howard University Law School (LLB cum laude, 1944) and at the universities of California and Yale, receiving a doctorate in 1965. Active in the civil rights and women's movements, she was arrested and convicted in Virginia in 1940, for refusing to move to a segregated seat on an interstate bus, and later was one of the Howard University student leaders of the sit-ins in restaurants in Washington, DC. In 1946 she became the first Black woman Deputy Attorney-General in California and she has lectured at the Ghana School of Law and at Boston and Brandeis universities. Taking up theological studies in 1973, she was the first Black female priest ordained by the Episcopal Church in 1977. Among her publications are Proud Shoes: The Story of an American Family (1956) and Dark Testament and Other Poems (1970).

Ruth

Brown girl chanting Te Deums on Sunday
Rust-coloured peasant with strength of granite,
Bronze girl wielding ship hulls on Monday,
Let nothing smirch you, let no one crush you.

Queen of ghetto, sturdy hill-climber,
Walk with the lilt of a ballet dancer,
Walk like a strong down-East wind blowing,
Walk with the majesty of the First Woman.

Gallant challenger, millioned-hop bearer,
The stars are your beacons, earth your inheritance,
Meet blaze and cannon with your own heart's passion,
Surrender to none the fire of your soul.

Virginia Brindis de Salas

?1910s–

*S*he was born in Uruguay and her published works of poetry include
Pregón de marimorena *(1946) and* Cien Cárceles de Amor *[One
Hundred Prisons of Love] (1949). The following poem was translated by Julio Finn and appears in his* Voices of Négritude *(1988).*

Song for a South American Black Boy

Boy with the pride of the Bantu
who sings:

Hey ho. . .
hey. . ., hey. . .,
hey. . ., hey. . .,
tango!

Little grandfather
of the grasslands –
he never forgets you
tell this American boy
that he's a Bantu.

He
came in the black slave ships,
shackled in its bowels
without so much as a "goodbye" to his tribe
or to the jungle.

Little grandfather
of the grasslands,
tell him, you tell
this American boy
how it is that he's Bantu.

Hey ho. . .
hey. . ., hey. . .,
hey. . ., hey. . .,
tango!

Ann Petry
1911–

Born to a poor family in Old Saybrook, Connecticut, she studied pharmacy at the University of Connecticut, receiving her degree in 1931, then working in the family drugstore. Marrying in 1928, she moved to New York and earned her living as a reporter for Harlem newspapers and for several social agencies concerned with urban slum conditions, out of which experience came her first novel, The Street (1946), written on a Houghton Mifflin Literary Fellowship. A member of the American Negro Theater, she also wrote children's plays. She studied creative writing at Columbia University, publishing her first stories in Crisis and Phylon. The Street was the first novel by a Black woman to sell over a million copies. Her later books are Country Place (1947) and The Narrows (1954). She has lectured at Berkeley, Miami University and Suffolk University and was visiting professor of English at the University of Hawaii.

From

The Street

CHAPTER VI

THERE was always a crowd in front of the Junto Bar and Grill on 116th Street. For in winter the street was cold. The wind blew the snow into great drifts that stayed along the kerb for weeks, gradually blackening with soot until it was no longer recognizable as snow, but appeared to be some dark eruption from the street itself.

As one cold day followed swiftly on the heels of another, the surface of the frozen piles became encrusted with bags of garbage, old shoes, newspapers, corset lacings. The frozen debris and the icy wind made the street a desolate place in winter and the people found a certain measure of escape from it by standing in front of the Junto where the light streaming from the windows and the music from its gramophone created an oasis of warmth.

In summer the street was hot and dusty, for no trees shaded it, and the sun beat straight down on the concrete pavement and the brick buildings. The inside of the houses fairly steamed; the dark passages were like ovens. Even the railings on the high steep stairways were warm to the touch.

As the thermometer crawled higher and higher, the people who lived on the street moved outdoors because the inside of the buildings was unbearable. The grown-ups lounging in chairs in front of the houses, the half-naked children playing along the kerb, transformed the street into an outdoor living-room. And because the people took to sleeping on roof-tops and fire escapes and park benches, the street also became a great outdoor bedroom.

The same people who found warmth by standing in front of the Junto in winter continued to stand there in summer. In fact, the number of people in front of the Junto increased in summer, for the whirr of its electric fans and the sound of ice clinking in tall glasses reached out to the street and created an illusion of coolness.

Thus, in winter and in summer people stood in front of the Junto from the time its doors opened early in the morning until they were firmly shut behind the last drunk the following morning.

The men who didn't work at all – the ones who never had and never would – stood in front of it in the morning. As the day slid toward afternoon, they were joined by tipsters, men who worked at night in factories and warehouses. And at night the pavement spilled over with the men who ran elevators and cleaned buildings and swept out subways.

All of them – the idle ones and the ones tired from their day's labour – found surcease and refreshment either inside or outside the Junto's doors. It served as social club and meeting place. By standing outside it a man could pick up all the day's news: the baseball scores, the number that came out, the latest neighbourhood gossip. Those who were interested in women could get an accurate evaluation of the girls who switched past in short tight skirts. A drinking man who was dead broke knew that if he stood there long enough a friend with funds would stroll by and offer to buy him a drink. And a man who was lonely and not interested in drinking or in women could absorb some of the warmth and laughter that seeped out to the street from the long bar.

The inside of the Junto was always crowded, too, because the white bartenders in their immaculate coats greeted the customers graciously. Their courteous friendliness was a heart-warming thing that helped rebuild egos battered and bruised during the course of the day's work.

The Junto represented something entirely different to the women on the street and what it meant to them depended in large measure on their age. Old women plodding past scowled ferociously and jerked the heavy shopping bags they carried until the stalks of celery and the mustard greens within seemed to tremble with rage at the sight of the Junto's doors. Some of the old women paused to mutter their hatred of it, to shake their fists in a sudden access of passion against it, and the men standing on the pavement moved closer to each other, forming a protective island with their shoulders, talking louder, laughing harder so as to shut out the sound and the sight of the old women.

Young women coming home from work – dirty, tired, depressed – looked forward to the moment when they could change their clothes and head towards the gracious spaciousness of the Junto. They dressed hurriedly in their small dark bedrooms, so impatient for the soft lights and the music and the fun that awaited them that they fumbled in their haste.

For the young women had an urgent hunger for companionship and the Junto offered men of all sizes and descriptions: sleek, well-dressed men who earned their living as tipsters; even better-dressed and better-looking men who earned a fatter living supplying women to an eager market; huge, grimy longshoremen who were given to sudden bursts of generosity; Pullman porters in on overnight runs from Washington, Chicago, Boston; and around the first of the month the sailors and soldiers flush with crisp pay-day money.

On the other hand, some of the young women went to the Junto only because they were hungry for the sight and sound of other young people and because the creeping silence that could be heard under the blaring radios, under the drunken quarrels in the bedrooms, was no longer bearable.

Lutie Johnson was one of these. For she wasn't going to the Junto to pick up a man or to quench a consuming, constant thirst. She was going there so that she could for a moment capture the illusion of having some of the things that she lacked.

As he hurried toward the Junto, she acknowledged the fact that she couldn't afford a glass of beer there. It would be cheaper to buy a bottle at the delicatessen and take it home and drink it if beer was what she wanted. The beer was incidental and unimportant. It was the other things that the Junto offered that she sought: the sound of laughter, the hum of talk, the sight of people and brilliant lights, the sparkle of the big mirror, the rhythmic music from the gramophone.

Once inside, she hesitated, trying to decide whether she should stand at the crowded bar or sit alone at one of the small tables in the centre of the room or in one of the booths at the side. She turned abruptly to the long bar, thinking that she needed people around her tonight, even all these people who were jammed against each other at the bar.

They were here for the same reason that she was – because they couldn't bear to spend an evening alone in some small dark room; because they couldn't bear to look what they could see of the future smack in the face while listening to radios or trying to read an evening paper.

"Beer, please," she said to the bartender.

There were rows of bottles on the shelves on each side of the big mirror behind the bar. They were reflected in the mirror, and looking at the reflection Lutie saw that they were magnified in size, shining so that they had the appearance of being filled with liquid, molten gold.

She examined herself and the people standing at the bar to see what changes the mirror wrought in them. There was a pleasant gaiety and charm about all of them. She found that she herself looked young, very young and happy in the mirror.

Her eyes wandered over the whole room. It sparkled in the mirror. The people had a kind of buoyancy about them. All except Old Man Junto, who was sitting alone at the table near the back.

She looked at him again and again, for his reflection in the mirror fascinated her. Somehow even at this distance his squat figure managed to dominate the whole room. It was, she decided, due to the bulk of his shoulders which were completely out of proportion to the rest of him.

Whenever she had been in here, he had been sitting at that same table, his hand cupped behind his ear as though he were listening to the sound of the cash register; sitting there alone watching everything – the customers, the bartenders, the waiters. For the barest fraction of a second, his eyes met hers in the mirror and then he looked away.

Then she forgot about him, for the gramophone in the far corner of the room started playing "Swing It, Sister". She hummed as she listened to it, not really aware that she was humming or why, knowing only that she felt free here where there was so much space.

The big mirror in front of her made the Junto an enormous room. It pushed the walls back and back into space. It reflected the lights from the ceiling and the concealed lighting that glowed in the corners of the room. It added a rosy radiance to the men and women standing at the bar; it pushed the world of other people's kitchen sinks back where it belonged and destroyed the existence of dirty streets and small shadowed rooms.

She finished the beer in one long gulp. Its pleasant bitter taste was still in her mouth when the bartender handed her a bill for the drink.

"I'll have another one," she said softly.

No matter what it cost them, people had to come to places like the Junto, she thought. They had to replace the haunting silences of rented rooms and little flats with the murmur of voices, the sound of laughter; they had to empty two or three small glasses of liquid gold so they could believe in themselves again.

She frowned. Two beers and the films for Bub and the budget she had planned so carefully was ruined. If she did this very often, there wouldn't be much point in having a budget – for she couldn't budget what she didn't have.

For a brief moment she tried to look into the future. She still couldn't see anything – couldn't see anything at all but 116th Street and a job that paid barely enough for food and rent and a handful of clothes. Year after year like that. She tried to recapture the feeling of self-confidence she had had earlier in the evening, but it refused to return, for she rebelled at the thought of day after day of work and night after night caged in that flat that no amount of scrubbing would ever get really clean.

She moved the beer glass on the bar. It left a wet ring and she moved it again in an effort to superimpose the rings on each other. It was warm in the Junto, the lights were soft, and the music coming from the gramophone was sweet. She listened intently to the record. It was "Darlin'", and when the voice on the record stopped she started singing: "There's no sun, Darlin'. There's no fun, Darlin'."

The men and women crowded at the bar stopped drinking to look at her. Her voice had a thin thread of sadness running through it that made the song important, that made it tell a story that wasn't in the words – a story of despair, of loneliness, of frustration. It was a story that all of them knew by heart and had always known because they had learned it soon after they were born and would go on adding to it until the day they died.

Just before the record ended, her voice stopped on a note so low and so long sustained that it was impossible to tell where it left off. There was a moment's silence around the bar, and then glasses were raised, the bartenders started counting change, and opening long-necked bottles, conversations were resumed.

The bartender handed her another bill. She picked it up mechanically and then placed it on top of the first one, held both of them loosely in her hand. That made two glasses and she'd better go before she weakened and bought another one. She put her gloves on slowly, transferring the bills from one hand to the other, wanting to linger here in this big high-ceilinged room where there were no shadowed silences, no dark corners; thinking that she should have made the beer last a long time by careful sipping instead of the greedy gulping that had made it disappear so quickly.

A man's hand closed over hers, gently extracted the two slips. "Let me take 'em," said a voice in her ear.

She looked down at the hand. The nails were clean, filed short. There was a thin coating of colourless polish on them. The skin was smooth. It was the hand of a man who earned his living in some way that didn't call for any wear and tear on his hands. She looked in the mirror and saw that the man who had reached for the bills was directly behind her.

He was wearing a brown overcoat. It was unfastened so that she caught a glimpse of a brown suit, of a tan-coloured shirt. His eyes met hers in the mirror and he said, "Do you sing for a living?"

She was aware that Old Man Junto was studying her in the mirror and she shifted her gaze back to the man standing behind her. He was waiting to find out whether she was going to ignore him or whether she was going to answer him. It would be so simple and so easy if she could say point-blank that all she wanted was a little companionship, someone to laugh with, someone to talk to, someone who would take her to places like the Junto and to the films without her having to think about how much it cost – just that and no more; and then to explain all at once and quickly that she couldn't get married because she didn't have a divorce, that there wasn't any inducement he could offer that would make her sleep with him.

It was out of the question to say any of those things. There wasn't any point even in talking to him, for when he found out, which he would eventually, that she wasn't going to sleep with him, he would disappear. It might take a week or a month, but that was how it would end.

No. There wasn't any point in answering him. What she should do was to take the bills out of his hand without replying and go on home. Go home to wash out a pair of stockings for herself, a pair of socks and a shirt for Bub. There had been night after night like that, and as far as she knew the same thing lay ahead in the future. There would be the three rooms with the silence and the walls pressing in –

"No, I don't," she said, and turned around and faced him. "I've never thought of trying." And knew as she said it that the walls had beaten her or she had beaten the walls. Whichever way she cared to look at it.

"You could, you know," he said. "How about another drink?"

"Make it beer, please." She hesitated, and then said, "Do you mean that you think I could earn my living singing?"

"Sure. You got the kind of voice that would go over big." He elbowed space for himself beside her at the bar. "Beer for the lady," he said to the bartender. "The usual for me." He leaned nearer to Lutie. "I know what I'm talkin' about. My band plays at the Casino."

"Oh," she said. "You're –"

"Boots Smith." He said it before she could finish her sentence. And his eyes on her face were so knowing, so hard, that she thought instantly of the robins she had seen on the Chandlers' lawn in Lyme, and the cat, lean, stretched out full length, drawing itself along on its belly, intent on its prey. The image flashed across her mind and was gone, for he said, "You want to try out with the band tomorrow night?"

"You mean sing at a dance? Without rehearsing?"

"Come up around ten o'clock and we'll run over some stuff. See how it goes."

She was holding the beer glass so tightly that she could feel the impression of the glass on her fingers and she let go of it for fear it would snap in two. She couldn't seem to stop the excitement that bubbled up in her; couldn't stop the flow of planning that ran through her mind. A singing job would mean she and Bub could leave 116th Street. She could get a flat where there were trees and the streets were clean and the rooms would be full of sunlight. There wouldn't be any more worry about rent and gas bills and she could be home when Bub came from school.

He was standing so close to her, watching her so intently, that again she thought of a cat slinking through grass, waiting, going slowly, barely making the grass move, but always getting nearer and nearer.

The only difference in the technique was that he had placed a piece of bait in front of her – succulent, tantalizing bait. He was waiting, watching to see whether she would nibble at it or whether he would have to use a different bait.

She tried to think about it dispassionately. Her voice wasn't any better or any worse than that of the women who sang with the dance bands over the radio. It was just an average good voice and with some coaching it might well be better than average. He had probably tossed out this sudden offer with the hope that she just might nibble at it.

Only she wasn't going to nibble. She was going to swallow it whole and come back for more until she ended up as vocalist with his band. She turned to look at him, to estimate him, to add up her chances.

His face was tough, hard-boiled, unscrupulous. There was a long, thin scar on his left cheek. It was a dark line that stood out sharply against the dark brown of his skin. And she thought that at some time someone had found his lack of scruple unbearable and had in desperation tried to do something about it. His body was lean, broad-shouldered, and as he lounged there, his arm on the bar, his muscles relaxed, she thought again of a cat slinking quietly after its prey.

There was no expression in his eyes, no softness, nothing to indicate that he would ever bother to lift a finger to help anyone but himself. It wouldn't be easy to use him. But what she wanted she wanted so badly that she decided to gamble to get it.

"Come on. Let's get out of here," he suggested. He shoved a crisp ten-dollar bill toward the barman and smiled at her while he waited for his change, quite obviously satisfied with whatever he had read in her face. She noticed that, though his mouth curved upward when he smiled, his eyes stayed expressionless, and she thought that he had completely lost the knack of really smiling.

He guided her toward the street, his hand under her elbow. "Want to go for a ride?" he asked. "I've got about three hours to kill before I go to work."

"I'd love to," she said.

Eighth Avenue was lined with small shops. And as they walked toward 117th Street, Lutie looked at each shop, closely reacting to it as violently as though she had never seen it before. All of them provided a sudden shocking contrast to the big softly lit interior of the Junto.

The windows of the butchers' shops were piled high with pigs' feet, hog maw, neck bones, chitterlings, ox tails, tripe – all the parts that didn't cost much because they didn't have much solid meat on them, she thought. The drapers' shops were a jumble of dark red stockings, imitation leather purses, gaudy rayon underwear edged with coarse yellow lace, flimsy blouses – most of it good for one wearing and no more, for the underwear would fade and ravel after the first washing and the purses would begin to disintegrate after they had been opened and closed a few times.

Withered oranges and sweet potatoes, wilting kale and okra, were stacked up on the vegetable stalls – the culls, the windfalls, all the bruised rotten fruit and vegetables were here. She stole a side glance at Boots striding along cat-footed, silent beside her.

It was a good thing that she had walked past these mean little shops with Boots Smith because the sight of them stiffened her determination to leave streets like this behind her – dark streets filled with shadowy figures that carried with them the horror of the places they lived in, places like her own flat. Otherwise she might have been afraid of him.

She thought about the shops again. All of them – the butchers' shops, the drapers', the vegetable stalls – all of them sold the leavings, the sweepings, the impossible unsaleable merchandise, the dregs and dross that were reserved especially for Harlem.

Yet the people went on living and reproducing in spite of the bad food. Most of the children had straight bones, strong white teeth. But it couldn't go on like that. Even the strongest heritage would one day run out. Bub was healthy, sturdy, strong, but he couldn't remain that way living here.

"I ain't seen you in Junto's before, baby," said Boots Smith.

"I don't go there very often," she said. There was something faintly contemptuous about the way he said "baby". He made it sound like "bebe", and it slipped casually, easily, out of his mouth as though it were his own handy, one-word index of women.

Then, because she was still thinking about the shops and their contents, she said, "When you look at the meat in these windows it's a wonder people in Harlem go on living."

"They don't have to eat it," he said indifferently.

"What are they going to do – stop eating?"

"If they make enough money they don't have to buy that stuff."

"But that's just it. Most of them don't make enough to buy anything else."

"There's plenty of money to be made in Harlem if you know how."

"Sure," she said. "It's on the trees and bushes. All you have to do is shake 'em."

"Look, baby," he said. "I ain't interested in how they eat or what they eat. Only thing I'm interested in right now is you."

They were silent after that. So there's plenty of money to be made in Harlem. She supposed there was if people were willing to earn it by doing something that kept them just two jumps ahead of the law. Otherwise they eked out a miserable existence.

They turned down 117th Street, and she wondered whether a ride with him meant a taxi or a car of his own. If there was plenty of money floating through the town, then she assumed he must have a car of his own. So when he opened the door of car drawn in close to the kerb, she wasn't over surprised at its length, its shiny, expensive look. It was about what she had expected from the red leather upholstery to the white-walled tyres and the top that could be thrown back when the weather was warm.

She got in, thinking, This is the kind of car you see in the films, the kind that swings insolently past you on Park Avenue, the kind that pulls up in front of the snooty stores on Fifth Avenue where a doorman all braid and brass buttons opens the door for you. The girls that got out of cars like this had mink coats swung carelessly from their shoulders, wore sable scarves tossed over slim wool suits.

This world was one of great contrasts, she thought, and if the richest part of it was to be fenced off so that people like herself could only look at it with no expectation of ever being able to get inside it, then it would be better to have been born blind so you couldn't see it, born deaf so you couldn't hear it, born with no sense of touch so you couldn't feel it. Better still, born with no brain so that you would be completely unaware of anything, so that you would never know there were places that were filled with sunlight and good food and where children were safe.

Boots started the car and for a moment he leaned so close to her that she could smell the lotion that he used and the faint, fruity smell of the bourbon he had been drinking. She didn't draw away from him; she simply stared at him with a cold kind of surprise that made him start fumbling with the clutch. Then the car drew away from the kerb.

He headed it uptown. "We got time to get up Hudson way. Okay?"

"Swell. It's been years since I've been up that way."

"Lived in New York long, baby?"

"I was born here." And next he would ask if she was married. She didn't know what her answer would be.

Because this time she wanted something and it made a difference. Ordinarily she knew exactly how it would go – like a pattern repeated over and over or the beginning of a meal. The table set with knife, fork, and spoons, napkin to the left of the fork and a glass filled with water at the tip end of the knife. Only sometimes the glass was a thin, delicate one and the napkin, instead of being paper, was thick linen still shining because a hot iron had been used on it when it was wet;

and the knife and fork, instead of being red-handled steel, were silver.

He had said there was plenty of money in Harlem, so evidently this was one of the thin glass, thick napkin, thin china, polished silver affairs. But the pattern was just the same. The soup plate would be removed and the main course brought on. She always ducked before the main course was served, but this time she had to dawdle with the main course, appear to welcome it, and yet not actually partake of it, and continue trifling and toying with it until she was successfully launched as a singer.

They had left Harlem before she noticed that there was a full moon – pale and remote despite its size. As they went steadily uptown, through the commercial business streets, and then swiftly out of Manhattan, she thought that the streets had a cold, deserted look. The buildings they passed were without lights. Whenever she caught a glimpse of the sky, it was over the tops of the buildings, so that it, too, had a far-away look. The buildings loomed darkly against it.

Then they were on a four-way concrete road that wound ahead grey-white in the moonlight. They were going faster and faster. And she got the feeling that Boots Smith's relationship to this swiftly moving car was no ordinary one. He wasn't just a black man driving a car at a pell-mell pace. He had lost all sense of time and space as the car plunged forward into the cold, white night.

The act of driving the car made him feel he was a powerful being who could conquer the world. Up over hills, fast down on the other side. It was like playing god and commanding everything within hearing to awaken and listen to him. The people sleeping in the white farmhouses were at the mercy of the sound of his engine roaring past in the night. It brought them half-awake – disturbed, uneasy. The cattle in the barns moved in protest, the chickens stirred on their roosts and before any of them could analyse the sound that had alarmed them, he was gone – on and on into the night.

And she knew, too, that this was the reason white people turned scornfully to look at Negroes who swooped past them on the highways. "Crazy niggers with cars" in the way they looked. Because they sensed that the black men had to roar past them, had for a brief moment to feel equal, feel superior; had to take reckless chances going round curves, passing on hills, so that they would be better able to face a world that took pains to make them feel that they didn't belong, that they were inferior.

Because in that one moment of passing a white man in a car they could feel good and the good feeling would last long enough so that they could hold their heads up the next day and the day after that. And the white people in the cars hated it because – and her mind stumbled over the thought and then went on – because possibly they too, needed to go on feeling superior. Because if they didn't, it upset the delicate balance of the world they moved in when they could see for themselves that a black man in a ratclap car could overtake and pass them on a hill. Because if there was nothing left for them but that business of feeling superior to black people, and that was taken away even for the split second of one car going ahead of another, it left them with nothing.

She stopped staring at the road ahead to look at Boots. He was leaning over the steering wheel, his hands cupped close on the sides of it. Yes, she thought, at this moment he has forgotten he's black. At this moment and in the act of sending this car hurtling through the night, he is making up for a lot of the things that have happened to him to make him what he is. He is proving all kinds of things to himself.

"Are you married, baby?" he asked. His voice was loud above the sound of the engine. He didn't look at her. His eyes were on the road. After he asked the question, he sent the car forward at a faster pace.

"I'm separated from my husband," she said. It was strange when he asked the question, the answer was on the tip of her tongue. It was true and it was the right answer. It put up no barriers to the next step – the removal of the soup plates and the bringing-on of the main course. Neither did it hurry the process.

"I thought you musta been married," he said. "Never saw a goodlooking chick yet who didn't belong to somebody."

She saw no point in telling him that she didn't belong to anybody; that she and Jim were as sharply separated as though they had been divorced, and that the separation wasn't the result of some sudden quarrel but a clean-cut break of years' standing. She had deliberately omitted all mention of Bub because Boots Smith obviously wasn't the kind of man who would maintain even a passing interest in a woman who was the mother of an eight-year-old child. She felt as though she had pushed Bub out of her life, disowned him, by not telling Boots about him.

He slowed the car down when they went through Poughkeepsie, stopping just long enough to pay the toll at the entrance of the Mid-Hudson Bridge. Once across the river, she became aware of the closeness of the hills, for the moon etched them clearly against the sky. They seemed to go up and up over her head.

"I don't like mountains," she said.

"Why?"

"I get the feeling they're closing in on me. Just a crazy notion," she added hastily, because she was reluctant to have him get the slightest inkling of the trapped feeling she got when there wasn't a lot of unfilled space around her.

"Probably why you sing so well," he said. "You feel things stronger than other folks." And then, "What songs do you know?"

"All the usual ones. Night and Day. Darlin'. Hurry Up, Sammy, and Let's Go Home."

"Have any trouble learnin' 'em?"

"No. I've never really tried to learn them. Just picked them up from hearing them on the radio."

"You'll have to learn some new ones" – he steered the car to the side of the road and parked it where there was an unobstructed view of the river.

The river was very wide at this point and she moved closer to him to get a better look at it. It made no sound, though she could see the direction of its flow between the great hills on either side. It had been flowing quietly along like this for years, she thought. It would go on for ever – silent, strong, knowing where it was going and not stopping for storms or bridges or factories. That was what had been wrong with her these last few weeks – she hadn't known where she was going. As a matter of fact, she had probably never known. But if she could sing – work hard at it, study, really get somewhere, it would give direction to her life – she would know where she was going.

"I don't know your name, baby," Boots said softly.

"Lutie Johnson," she said.

"Mrs Lutie Johnson," he said slowly. "Very nice. Very, very nice."

The soft, satisfied way he said the words made her sharply aware that there wasn't a house in sight, there wasn't a car passing along the road and hadn't been since they parked. She hadn't walked into this situation. She had run headlong into it, snatching greedily at the bait he had dangled in front of her. Because she had reached such a state of despair that she would have clutched at a straw if it appeared to offer the means by which she could get Bub and herself out of that street.

As his tough, unscrupulous face came closer and closer to hers, she reminded herself that all she knew about him was that he had a dance band, that he drove a high-priced car, and that he believed there was plenty of money in Harlem. And she had gone leaping and running into his car, emitting little cries of joy as she went. It hadn't occurred to her until this moment that from his viewpoint she was a pick-up girl.

When he turned her face toward his, she could feel the hardness of his hands under the suede gloves he wore. He looked at her for a long moment. "Very, very nice," he repeated, and bent forward and kissed her.

Her mind sought some plausible way of frustrating him without offending him. She couldn't think of anything. He was holding her so tightly and his mouth was so insistent, so brutal, that she twisted out of his arms, not caring what he thought, intent only on escaping from his ruthless hands and mouth.

The dashboard clock said nine-thirty. She wanted to pat it in gratitude.

"You're going to be late," she said, pointing at the clock.

"Damn!" he muttered, and reached for the ignition switch.

Dorothy West
1912–

Born in Boston, where she was educated at public school and
Boston University, she was the only child of well-to-do parents
and decided at the age of seven that she wanted to be a writer.
She joined the Saturday Evening Quill Club, organized by young Black
would-be writers, and when she was seventeen a story of hers won a
national competition sponsored by Opportunity magazine. Moving to
New York in the early 1930s she became involved with the Harlem Renaissance movement of writers. She studied at Columbia University's School
of Journalism and in 1934 founded the magazine Challenge, publishing many young Black writers. She was the first Black writer published by the New York Daily News, for which she wrote stories for the
next twenty years. Eventually she returned to Boston and since 1948 has
lived on Martha's Vineyard. Her only published novel is The Living Is
Easy (1948), from which this excerpt is taken. Drawing on her own background, it was the first book to focus on Boston's Black upper class
in the years before the First World War, with its hierarchy of businessmen,
intellectuals and socialites, and the increasingly familiar "tragic mulatto" as central female character, all informed with a subtle humour; she
writes of the untimely end of a Black businessman: "Everybody was just
a little bit proud of Mr Hartnett. . .who blew his brains out just like a white
man."

From

The Living Is Easy

CHAPTER X

CLEO read the guiding sign above a tippler's head and turned down the street
she sought. Here were no amiable loafers. Here were the sullen and shifty-

eyed, the denizens of the dark. These were the dregs, the men without women, the women without men. These were the haters who thought they were beaten because they were black. There were no children here. Sometimes a wizened, rat-faced gnome in the shape of a child hugged the shadows of a stoop, from which he would never emerge to walk in the sun. Here were the hunted, the thieves and killers, the nameless, the faceless. These were the blood brothers of all men everywhere who are born without race pride.

The men and women looked at Cleo with hate. They did not want her to walk with her head erect. For a black is a black, their thoughts ran, and as no-account as the next.

They stood silent. They stood motionless, and the sick smoldering went on inside them because here was one of their own who would disown them. The minds of the men shouted whore as she passed, because they knew she was not. The women's thoughts hurled Miss White Lady at her because they could not bear to admit she could walk with dignity and still be colored.

Cleo knew she had better not ask anybody anything. The thing to do was to keep on going down this ruined street of rotting frame houses until she found one with some distinguishing mark, a clean curtain or a swept walk, that would set it apart from the others.

In the middle of the block she saw it. A two-storied, flat-roofed, snow-white house, with open green shutters and sparkling windows. She pulled at the doorbell and heard its muted tinkle. In a moment or so the door opened. A round-faced, gray-haired colored maid stared at her without expression.

Cleo felt a quick resentment that this sporting woman could flaunt a maid. Like enough the maid had had to teach the mistress manners.

She said coldly, "Will you tell your madam that a lady" – the word was underlined – "wishes to see her? It's a very urgent matter."

The woman hesitated, then stepped aside to let her enter. "Will you wait here, please?" She left Cleo in the long reception hall and started up the stairs.

Again Cleo had a moment of wonder that this West End Duchess had found a colored woman willing to work for her. Cleo's friends who could afford maids had never been able to get colored help. The experienced domestics from the South could not be induced to work for people of color, feeling a natural embarrassment at the scorn to be found in their own stratum that they would use the back doors of a social group who could not use the front doors of their former employers.

In the employ of this upper colored class were the "green girls", the young, untutored immigrant girls who held their jobs until their more sophisticated countrymen explained the insurmountable distinction between a man who looked white and a man who was white.

There were only twenty-odd colored families who counted themselves the élite. Since most of that number could not afford maids, there was not really a servant problem.

While she waited impatiently, Cleo became aware of the graceful Chippendale pieces in the hall and the darkly glowing mahogany in the long parlor and dining room beyond. A magnificent grand piano engulfed a corner of the parlor. Cleo yearned to own it. She had been working on Bart a year to buy Judy an upright.

All nice children started piano lessons at five. She sighed. For a moment she pictured this beautiful furniture in the high-ceilinged rooms of her new house. She knew that their cost was far beyond anything Bart would consider paying for tables and chairs to eat at and sit in, which depreciated in value the more you ate and sat.

The maid returned. "Will you follow me, please."

They reached the upper hall. The maid murmured, "The lady." Cleo crossed the threshold of a charming morning room.

A woman rose from behind a tea-table set with exquisitely patterned china and surveyed Cleo quietly, with a still, unrevealing smile. She was ash-blond. Her imperial eyes were blue. Cleo was thoroughly disconcerted, for she was unprepared for the dignity of the West End Duchess. She had come for a fishwives' brawl, and the woman before her was patrician. There was breeding in every fragile bone.

"Won't you sit down?" the Duchess said.

Cleo sat down dumbly, though she had meant to stand, as befitting her position as a man's wife when faced with a sporting woman. But despite herself, she was impressed by this woman's superior status.

The Duchess appraised her. "I don't think we've ever met."

Cleo braced herself for the next observation, the common knowledge of Negroes forewarning her that the Duchess would make some casual mention of her servants, with the subtle intention of reminding Cleo that all colored people were in the same category.

Cleo said lightly, "You are not entirely a stranger to me. My cook has mentioned you often, but, of course, she may know you only by reputation."

The imperial eyes were veiled. The delicate chin lifted a little. "I cannot believe that you have come to exchange backstairs gossip. May I ask you who you are and why you are here?"

Cleo could feel herself getting mad. Did this outcast from her own kind consider herself too good to waste her expensive time on a colored woman? Still she could not unleash the hot words that would reduce her to a level beneath the dignity of this Duchess.

"I'm Mrs Bart Judson. I've come on behalf of Miss Althea Binney. Her father is dying."

The Duchess said quietly, almost reprovingly, "You cannot mean that. I am seeing him tonight."

"Not after the stroke he had this morning. He'll never live to see daybreak. You might as well make up your mind you've seen him for the last time."

The Duchess said witheringly: "Since Althea could not face me with such a grisly fabrication, I am sure she must admire the boldness which enables you to do so. You may tell Carter Binney that I would have more respect for him if he had chosen a less unscrupulous way to send word that he is dead to me."

"It was God's way," said Cleo furiously. "God's way of punishing that old fool for getting mixed up with your kind of trash. I never told a lie in my life, and I wouldn't perjure myself for you. When they put Carter Binney in the ground, you go tell the police he was buried alive, and see how long it takes them to cart you off to the booby hatch."

There was a pause, and Cleo's angry breathing filled it. Her green eyes blazed. After a little the Duchess said painfully, "I believe you now. It is God's way of punishing me for wanting Carter Binney."

Cleo lost complete control of her temper. She jumped to her feet and flung herself into that bitter, unending, secret war between white and colored women.

"Don't fool yourself!" she shouted. "God's forgotten you're on earth. It's the Devil who's licking his lips over you. And you've been a good disciple. I know why you hated Carter Binney. You couldn't stay out of bed with him, and you hated him instead of yourself. Well, you've got him lying at death's door, with not a penny to bury him, and not a penny to leave behind. There's no more damage you can do. Get out of my race and stay out."

The Duchess said, out of her suffering, "It is my race, too."

Cleo's mouth fell open. She said, in a soft, incredulous voice, "God have mercy, you're not all white?"

"My mother was colored."

Cleo sank back on her chair, and wished for her fan. "It wasn't your skin and hair that fooled me. We come every color under the sun. But the way you carry yourself, I thought you were born on Beacon Hill."

The Duchess said, without expression, "My father was."

Cleo thought of Thea, who had come to her for help, Thea with the tear stains on her pretty face. And Thea's image paled a little. Nothing tremendous had ever happened to Thea except her father's taking a fit because a born lady wanted to marry him. All of Cleo's zest for life, her insatiable love of conspiracy were roused to search behind the imperial eyes.

"If I had known you were colored, I wouldn't have hit you from so many sides. If I had known you were such a lady, I wouldn't have come for a fight at all. I never heard of you until an hour ago, and all I heard was one side of the story. There has to be another side. And you have a right to tell me yours."

Her eyes were gray again, and very gentle. Her voice was tender and persuasive. The Duchess felt her warm sympathy, and was drawn to it. And Cleo's sympathy was real. In this moment she wanted nothing more than to know about this lovely woman. Her whole intensity was directed to that end. The power of her personality was like a tongue of fire that ignored locked doors and penetrated whatever reticences might stand in the way of her passion to probe the lives of other women and tell them how to live them.

"May I give you tea?" the Duchess asked.

Cleo smiled radiantly. "I'd love a cup of tea while we talk."

The Duchess poured. This was her first tea party. She found a thin amusement in the fact that she was pouring for Mrs Bart Judson. She knew of Bart Judson and his wholesale business. She had never invited him to her gaming tables because he had nothing she wanted. She did not want money. The men who lost at her roulette wheel were the husbands of the women she wanted around her tea-table.

They were the women whose impregnable positions had been established by Boston birth and genteel breeding. They acknowledgeed no more than a hundred best families in Boston, New York, Philadelphia, and Washington.

Their lives were narrowly confined to a daily desperate effort to ignore their racial heritage. They did not consider themselves a minority group. The Irish were a minority group, the Jews, the Italians, the Greeks, who were barred from belonging by old country memories, accents, and mores. These gentlewomen felt that they had nothing in common except a facial resemblance. Though they scorned the Jew, they were secretly pleased when they could pass for one. Though they were contemptuous of the Latins, they were proud when they looked European. They were not too dismayed by a darkish skin if it was counterbalanced by a straight nose and straight hair that established an Indian origin. There was nothing that disturbed them more than knowing that no one would take them for anything but colored.

It was a bitter truth, to be discussed only in special groups, that a sporting woman in the West End was, by these standards, the most beautiful colored woman in Boston.

The Duchess passed Cleo a cup of tea. Cleo sipped it with her little finger crooked carefully. She wondered what Mr Judson would say if he could see her sipping tea with the Duchess. It wouldn't make a bit of difference to him that she carried herself like a lady. She had passed money across a green table. She had entertained married men. Mr Judson believed there were good women and bad women and no in-between. That was what made it so easy to pull the wool over his eyes.

Cleo put her cup down and assumed an attentive expression. It was getting on to four. In an hour Mr Judson would be starting home for supper. Men were nothing but stomach and the other thing. It would be a happy day for women if both could be cut out.

"Tell me about yourself," said Cleo richly.

The imperial eyes widened and darkened. The Spode cups cooled. The Duchess gave a little sigh and began her story.

"Althea Binney's mother and mine were foster sisters. My grandfather married her grandmother. Their marriage gave back their children the parents they had lost. Grandfather was butler for a Beacon Hill bachelor, who had never married because the only women to whom he would have given his name bored him in every way.

"Grandfather died in his employ. And this man, Thad Tewksbury, came to the funeral and saw my mother for the first time. To him she looked exotic. Her mother had been Irish."

Cleo remembered a tintype that she had seen in Thea's album, a regal brown man, an austere-faced woman stiffly corseted, and two little girls with their arms entwined, one as lovely as dawn. That lovely child had had a white mother, an Irish maid who had married a colored butler. And she, this immigrant Irisher, had obligingly died at her daughter's birth, thus removing herself from the circle of the colored élite, in which her peasant background would have been embarrassing. No one Cleo knew in the North admitted to having a white relation of the lower classes. When such a bride was chosen, it was considered very poor taste to discuss her humble origins. Her marriage had elevated her to her husband's higher station. White antecedence was only exploited when the daughter of bluebloods eloped with her coachman.

The Duchess said: "Thad made my mother his mistress. He defiled her the day he sent his carriage to fetch her to his house. The coachman said it was some matter concerning her continuing in Normal School. With her father dead, her stepmother could not support her while she finished her teacher's training. Her stepmother helped her dress in her best to go to see Thad Tewksbury. They thought it was important that she impress him with her neat appearance.

"My mother never reached the house on Beacon Hill. She was driven here. Thad was waiting. He showed her this house, and said he had bought it with the intention of giving it to her father, whom he had planned to retire because of his failing health. My mother was too ignorant of the world to know that no one would furnish a house in such style for a servant. She supposed that Thad knew no better than to buy the best. He gave my mother the deed to this house. He gave her a bank book. And she wept with gratitude. For one hour of her life she loved him: the hour they sat and talked during dinner. For a caterer came, and they celebrated his investment in her teaching career. My mother had never touched wine in her life, but she did not want to offend Thad by refusing the champagne he had ordered especially for her. And after the first glass, she never knew how many times it was refilled.

"When she waked, it was morning. The clothes she had worn were nowhere. She opened a closet door and found a dozen expensive costumes. But she knew she could not go home in them. She could not go home at all. Her stepmother would never believe that she had been innocent of Thad's intentions. She was a fallen woman. She looked at herself in the mirror, and saw her sin in her face, and did not know it was mostly the after-effect of champagne. She was too ashamed to walk out of this house, and sat and waited in a fine gown for Thad to come and tell her what to do."

Through the first years of Thad's fantastic indulgence, and forever after, Corinne never stopped regretting her acquiescence, or feeling self-pity. To the listening child in the fine French frocks her mother's nostalgic stories of the stern simplicity of her prim upbringing became the pattern of all her thinking.

At six the silver-haired child began to pray God to turn her a color that would make her unmistakably a member of her mother's race. The servants were her only contact with her kind. They were resentful that she and Corinne, without lifting a finger, lived in a luxury they could never hope to attain, no matter how long they labored in God's vineyard. They showed their resentment in their manner, which was just a shade under scorn, and were deliberately indifferent to the child, never stopping to listen to her prattle, never permitting her to play around them, speaking sharply whenever she strayed across the threshold of their privacy.

Her nurse was a pious old Frenchwoman, who loved her because she was a small innocent, and had forgotten that a child of sin should be treated as if that child had committed it. It was a natural thing for the child to love her in return. Seeing this, Corinne, her pride in her past increasing as the years made her return to it more remote than the moon, taught her daughter to dismiss the servants' churlishness as envy of her class superiority. The child dreamed of her mother's world of remembering as a paradise which some day she might enter.

Corinne's New England conscience deplored the life that she had grown too indolent to leave. She did not want her daughter to grow up with the belief that a wealthy white protector was worth a colored woman's loss of caste. For there was no city to which a notorious woman of color could escape where her reputation would not follow her. The special Negro groups were too small and too interlocked by marriage and old friendships for an aspirant to seek to disclaim her past.

As the years advanced, and passion slaked in Thad, the habit of Corinne's hearth grew stronger in him. He wanted to be with her, for she was his wife, in the way that woman's complete dependency makes a man cherish her in spite of himself. She was not amusing. She sat too quietly with her interminable tatting, and her little sad smile, and her velvet eyes with their veiled reproach. He could not stay away. Yet the dull evenings were unendurable, with Corinne occasionally consenting to a game of checkers, which she played with an exasperating lack of skill.

So it was that Thad got in the way of bringing in a friend or two to while away the night with cards. Other friends pressed him for invitations. To them it seemed an enormous adventure to see the inside of a colored concubine's house, and watch her walk among them with her sadness and disdain and her little gold box, in which she deposited her share of this new sin with imperceptible cleansing of the fingertips.

Carolina Maria de Jesús

1913–

*B*orn in Sacramento, Minas Gerais state, Brazil, she ended up living in a shantytown shack near São Paulo, surviving and feeding her three children by foraging in garbage and selling scrap paper. Educated to second-grade level, she wrote to distract herself from her troubles: "for when I was writing I was in a golden palace, with crystal windows and silver chandeliers. My dress was finest satin and diamonds *sat shining in my black hair. Then I put away my book and the smells came in through the rotting walls and rats ran over my feet. My satin turned to rags and the only things shining in my hair were lice." Her life of poverty changed when her graphic three-year diary of slum life in a favela –* Beyond All Pity *– was published in 1960 with the help of a young reporter, Audalio Dantas, and became a literary sensation in Brazil, selling out its first edition of 10,000 copies in three days. In less than six months 90,000 copies were sold, and two years later it was still on the bestseller list, having sold more than any other Brazilian book in history.*

From

Beyond All Pity

DIARY: 1955

J ULY 15, 1955 The birthday of my daughter Vera Eunice. I wanted to buy a pair of shoes for her, but the price of food keeps us from realizing our desires. Actually we are slaves to the cost of living. I found a pair of shoes in the garbage, washed them, and patched them for her to wear.

I didn't have one cent to buy bread. so I washed three bottles and traded them to Arnaldo. He kept the bottles and gave me bread. Then I went to sell my paper. I received 65 cruzeiros. I spent 20 cruzeiros for meat. I got one kilo of ham and one kilo of sugar and spent six cruzeiros on cheese. And the money was gone.

I was ill all day. I thought I had a cold. At night my chest pained me. I started to cough. I decided not to go out at night to look for paper. I searched for my son João. He was at Felisberto de Carvalho Street near the market. A bus had knocked a boy into the sidewalk and a crowd gathered. João was in the middle of it all. I poked him a couple of times and within five minutes he was home.

I washed the children, put them to bed, then washed myself and went to bed. I waited until 11:00 for a certain someone. He didn't come. I took an aspirin and laid down again. When I awoke the sun was sliding in space. My daughter Vera Eunice said: "Go get some water, Mother!"

July 16 I got up and obeyed Vera Eunice. I went to get the water. I made coffee. I told the children that I didn't have any bread, that they would have to drink their coffee plain and eat meat with *farinha*.[1] I was feeling ill and decided to cure myself. I stuck my finger down my throat twice, vomited and knew I was under the evil eye. The upset feeling left and I went to Senhor Manuel, carrying some cans to sell. Everything that I find in the garbage I sell. He gave me 13 cruzeiros. I kept thinking that I had to buy bread, soap, and milk for Vera Eunice. The 13

---

[1] *Farinha*: a coarse wheat flour.

cruzeiros wouldn't make it. I returned home, or rather to my shack, nervous and exhausted. I thought of the worrisome life that I led. Carrying paper, washing clothes for the children, staying in the street all day long. Yet I'm always lacking things, Vera doesn't have shoes and she doesn't like to go barefoot. For at least two years I've wanted to buy a meat mincer. And a sewing machine.

I came home and made lunch for the two boys. Rice, beans, and meat, and I'm going out to look for paper. I left the children, told them to play in the yard and not go into the street, because the terrible neighbours I have won't leave my children alone. I was feeling ill and wished I could lie down. But the poor don't rest nor are they permitted the pleasure of relaxation. I was nervous inside, cursing my luck. I collected two sacks full of paper. Afterward I went back and gathered up some scrap metal, some cans, and some kindling wood. As I walked I thought – when I return to the *favela* there is going to be something new. Maybe Dona Rosa or the insolent Angel Mary fought with my children. I found Vera Eunice sleeping and the boys playing in the street. I thought: it's 2:00. Maybe I'm going to get through this day without anything happening. João told me that the truck that gives out money was here to give out food. I took a sack and hurried out. It was the leader of the Spiritist Centre at 103 Vergueiro Street. I got two kilos of rice, two of beans, and two kilos of macaroni. I was happy. The truck went away. The nervousness that I had inside left me. I took advantage of my calmness to read. I picked up a magazine and sat on the grass, letting the rays of the sun warm me as I read a story. I wrote a note and gave it to my boy João to take to Senhor Arnaldo to buy soap, two aspirins, and some bread. Then I put water on the stove to make coffee. João came back saying he had lost the aspirins. I went back with him to look. We didn't find them.

When I came home there was a crowd at my door. Children and women claiming José Carlos had thrown stones at their houses. They wanted me to punish him.

July 17, Sunday A marvellous day. The sky was blue without one cloud. The sun was warm. I got out of bed at 6:30 and went to get water. I only had one piece of bread and three cruzeiros. I gave a small piece to each child and put the beans, that I got yesterday from the Spiritist Centre, on the fire. Then I went to wash clothes. When I returned from the river the beans were cooked. The children asked for bread. I gave the three cruzeiros to João to go and buy some. Today it was Nair Mathias who started an argument with my children. Silvia and her husband have begun an open-air spectacle. He is hitting her and I'm disgusted because the children are present. They heard words of the lowest kind. Oh, if I could move from here to a more decent neighbourhood!

I went to Dona Florela to ask for a piece of garlic. I went to Dona Analia and got exactly what I expected:

"I don't have any!"

I went to collect my clothes. Dona Aparecida asked me:

"Are you pregnant?"

"No, Senhora," I replied gently.

I cursed her under my breath. If I am pregnant it's not your business. I can't stand these *favela* women, they want to know everything. Their tongues are like chicken feet. Scratching at everything. The rumour is circulating that I am pregnant! If I am, I don't know about it!

I went out at night to look for paper. When I was passing the São Paulo football stadium many people were coming out. All of them were white and only one black. And the black started to insult me:

"Are you looking for paper, auntie? Watch your step, auntie dear!"

I was ill and wanted to lie down, but I went on. I met several friends and stopped to talk to them. When I was going up Tiradentes Avenue I met some women. One of them asked me:

"Are your legs healed?"

After I was operated on, I got better, thanks to God. I could even dance at Carnival in my feather costume. . . .

July 19 My children talking woke me up at 7 a.m. I got out of bed and went to look for water. The women were already at the tap. Their cans in a row. . . .

My turn came and I put my can under the tap to fill. . . . The water in the tap began to diminish. They blamed Rosa. Because she had been carrying water since 4 a.m. and washed all her clothes at home. She must pay 20 cruzeiros a month. My can filled, I went away.

I've been thinking of the problems I've had these days. I can take the ups and downs of life. If I can't store up courage to live, I've resolved to store up patience.

I've never hurt anybody. I'm smarter than that. I don't want any lawsuits. My identification card number is 845.936.

I went to the junk dealer to sell the paper. 55 cruzeiros. I hurried back, bought milk and bread. I made a chocolate drink for the children, made the beds, put beans on the stove, and swept the shack. I called Senhor Ireno Venancio da Silva to make a see-saw for the boys. To see if they would stay in the yard so the neighbours won't fight with them. I paid him 16 cruzeiros. While he was making the see-saw I went to soap the clothes. When I returned Senhor Ireno was finishing it, and a few more touches and he was done. The children liked the board when it was ready. Everybody wanted to ride at the same time.

I locked the door and went to sell some tin cans. I took the children with me. The day is hot and I like them to get the rays of the sun. What an ordeal! I carried Vera and put the sack on my head. I sold the cans and the scrap. I got 31 cruzeiros. I was happy. I asked:

"Senhor Manuel, didn't you make a mistake?"

"No, why?"

"Because the sack didn't weigh as much as 31 cruzeiros' worth. This amount is just what I need to pay the light bill."

I said good-bye and returned home. I made lunch. While the pots boiled, I wrote a little. I gave the children their lunch and went to Klabin paper mill to look for paper. I left the children playing in the yard. I got a lot of paper. I worked fast, thinking that those human beasts are capable of invading my shack and mistreating my children. I worked on, nervous and upset. My head began to ache. They wait for me to leave so they can come to my shack and hurt my children. Always when I'm not at home. When the children are alone they can't defend themselves.

In the *favelas* children of 15 stay out as late as they want. They mess around with prostitutes and listen to their adventures. There are those who work and those who just drift. The older people work. It's the younger ones who refuse to work. They have their mothers who pick up fruits and vegetables that fall from the street markets. They have the churches who give them bread. They have San Francisco church that once a month gives away necessities like coffee and soap.

They go to the fish market, pick up fish heads, anything they can find. They eat anything. They must have stomachs of reinforced concrete. Sometimes I turn on the radio and dance with the children; we pretend we're boxing. Today I bought sweets for them. I gave each one a piece and felt them looking at me a bit differently. My João said:

"What a good mother!"

When those female witches invade my shack, my children throw stones at them. The women scream:

"What uneducated brats!"

I reply:

"My children are defending me. You are ignorant and can't understand that. I'm going to write a book about the *favela*, and I'm going to tell everything that happened here. And everything that you do to me. I want to write a book, and you with these disgusting scenes are furnishing me with material."

Silvia asked me to take her name out of my book. She said:

"You are a tramp too. You slept in the flophouse. When you end up, you'll be crazy!"

I replied:

"That's true. Those who sleep in the flophouse are the poor. They have nowhere else to turn to, and one place is as good as another. But you, who say you never sleep in the flophouse, what are you doing here in a shack? You were born to live in a fine house. How come your life turned out like mine?"

She said:

"The only thing you know how to do is pick up paper."

I said:

"I pick up paper. I'm proving that I'm alive, at least."

I am living in a *favela*. But if God helps me, I'll get out of here. I hope the politicians tear down the *favelas*. There are people who take advantage of the way they live to bully those weaker than themselves. There is a house here that has five children and an old women who walks the entire day begging. There are wives that when their husbands are ill go out and support the family. The husbands, when they see their wives taking care of the home, never get well again.

Today I didn't go out looking for paper. I'm going to lie down. I'm not tired or sleepy. Yesterday I drank a beer and today I want another. But I'm not going to drink. I don't want that curse. I have responsibilities. My children! And the money that I spend on beer takes away from the essentials we need. What I can't stand in the *favelas* are the fathers who send their children out to buy *pinga*[2] and then give some to the children to drink.

They laugh:

"He's got worms. He's gotta drink it. Doctor's orders!"

My children can't stand alcohol. My son João said:

"Mama, when I grow up I'm not going to drink. A man who drinks doesn't buy clothes, doesn't have a radio, and doesn't build himself a brick house."

Today was a blessed day for me. The troublemakers of the *favela* see that I'm writing and know that it's about them. They decided to leave me in peace. In the *favelas* the men are more tolerant, more understanding. The rowdies are the women. Their intrigues are like Carlos Lacerda's and grate against the nerves. My nerves can't stand it. But I'm strong. I don't let anything bother me deeply. I don't get discouraged.

July 20 I got out of bed 4 a.m. to write. I opened the door and gazed at the starry sky. When the sun started to climb I went for water. I was lucky! The women weren't at the tap. I filled my cans and hurried off. I went to Arnaldo to get bread and milk. When I was returning I met Ismael with a knife at least a foot long. He told me he was waiting for Binidito and Miguel to kill them, for they had beaten him up while he was drunk.

I advised him not to fight, because crime doesn't work to anyone's advantage and only disrupts life. Then I smelled the alcohol and stopped. I know that drunks don't pay attention. Ismael, when he's not boozed up, shows his intelligence. He used to be a telegraph operator and a member of the Esoteric Circle Church. He can quote from the Bible and likes to give advice. But now he's not worth anything. He lets alcohol control him, but even so at times his advice is good for those who want to lead a decent life.

I prepared breakfast. Every child wants something different. Vera: oatmeal. João: black coffee. José Carlos: milk. And I: cream of wheat.

At this moment I can't give my children a decent house to live in, so I try to give them decent food.

They finished breakfast and I washed the dishes. Then I went to wash clothes. I don't have a man at home. There is just me and my children, so I can't relax. My dream is to be very clean, to wear expensive clothes and live in a comfortable house, but it's not possible. I am not unhappy with the work I do. I am used to being dirty. I've carried paper for eight years. What disgusts me is that I must live in a *favela*.

During the day the youths of 15 to 18 sit on the ground and talk of robbery. They just tried to hold up Senhor Raymundo Guello's store. One of them was wounded by a bullet and scattered the loot as he fell. The robbery took place at 4 a.m. When the dawn came children looked for the money in the street and a vacant lot. There was a child who found 20 cruzeiros. He showed the money around the *favela* and smiled. But the judge was severe, punishing without pity.

I went to the river to wash clothes and met Dona Mariana. She is a pleasant and decent woman with nine children and a nice home. She and her husband have given them an education. She tells them to live in peace and to raise children.

---

[2] *Pinga*: a white fiery liquor made from sugar cane. Powerful and potent, it is the favourite drink of Brazil's poor, who can get drunk on it for less than ten cents a bottle.

She was also going to wash clothes. She told me that Dona Geralda's Binidito was locked up all day. The radio patrol is tired of coming to look for him. They found him some work to do at the police station. I thought that was very funny and I laughed. Meanwhile I spread the clothes on the grass and went to look for paper. What an ordeal it is to search for paper. I have to carry my daughter Vera Eunice. She is only two years old and doesn't like to stay at home. I put the sack on my head and carried her in my arms. I bore the weight of the sack on my head and the weight of Vera Eunice in my arms. Sometimes it makes me angry. Then I get a hold of myself. She's not guilty because she's in the world.

I reflected: I've got to be tolerant with my children. They don't have anyone in the world but me. How sad is the condition of a woman alone without a man at home.

Here all the women pick on me. They say that I talk too well and that I know how to attract men. When I'm nervous I don't like to argue. I prefer to write. Every day I write. I sit in the yard and write.

I can't go looking for paper. Vera Eunice doesn't want to sleep and neither does José Carlos. Silvia and her husband are quarrelling. They've got nine children but don't respect them. Every day they fight.

I sold the paper and got 140 cruzeiros. I worked too hard and felt ill. I took some Dr Ross's "Pills of Life" for my liver and lay down. When I was sleeping I was awakened by the voice of Antonio Andrade arguing with his wife.

July 21 I woke with the voice of Dona Maria asking me if I wanted to buy any bananas or lettuce. I glanced at the children. They were still sleeping. I didn't answer. When they see fruit I have to buy it. I sent my boy João to Arnaldo's to buy sugar and bread. Then I went to wash clothes. While the clothes were bleaching I sat on the sidewalk and wrote. A man passed by and asked me:

"What are you writing?"

"All the cheating that the *favela* dwellers practise. Those human wrecks."

He said:

"Write it and give it to an editor so he can make revisions."

He looked at the children around me and asked:

"These kids are yours?"

I looked at the children. Of mine, there were only two. But as they were all the same colour, I told him yes.

"Where does your husband work?"

"I don't have a husband and I don't want one!"

A white woman who was listening hurried away. I thought: maybe she didn't appreciate my answer.

"That's a lot of children to take care of."

He opened his wallet. I thought: now he's going to give money to one of those kids thinking that all of them are mine. That was a stupid lie!

But Vera Eunice grabbed his arm and said:

"Give. Me. Shoes."

I said:

"She's saying that she wants the money to buy shoes."

He said:

"Give this to your mother."

I raised my eyes and looked at him. Two little girls with him called him "Daddy". I've seen him. Once I talked with him in a drugstore when I took Vera to get a flue shot. He walked on. I looked at the money he gave Vera. A hundred cruzeiros!

In a few minutes the story spread that Vera had got a hundred cruzeiros. I thought of the efficiency of the human tongue to transmit news. The children crowded around. I got up and went to sit near Dona Mariana's house. I asked her for a little coffee. I'm used to drinking coffee in Senhor Lino's house. Everything I ask them to loan me, they loan me. When I go to pay them, they never take it.

Afterward I went to wring out the clothes and returned to make lunch. Today I'm singing. I'm happy and I've asked the neighbours not to bother me. All of us have one happy day – today is mine!

A girl by the name of Amalia said that a spirit had possessed her mother. She was running around and trying to throw herself into the river. Many women tried to stop her. I spent the rest of the afternoon writing. At 4:30 Senhor Heitor turned on the lights. I gave the children a bath and got ready to go out. I went out to pick up paper but felt ill. I hurried because it was cold. When I got home it was 10:30. I turned on the radio, took a bath, and heated some food. I read a little. I don't know how to sleep without reading. I like to leaf through a book. The book is man's best invention so far.

Ellen Kuzwayo

1914–

Growing up in the South African countryside but having lived most of her life in the city, she has been a teacher and social worker, and in her sixties went to study at the University of Witwatersrand for a higher qualification in social work. She was for twelve years General Secretary of the YWCA and a member of the Soweto Committee

*of Ten, a body of moderate Black leaders, and with other members of
the committee was detained without trial for five months in 1977. She is
active in community life of Soweto, is president of the Black Consumer
Union of South Africa (since 1984) and of the Maggie Magaba Trust,
which promotes the women's self-help movement. She also serves on the
Urban Foundation Commitee. She has helped in the making of two films,*
Awake From Mourning *and* Tsiamelo: A Place of Goodness. *Her
autobiography* Call Me Woman *was published in 1985 and she is also the
author of the collection* Sit Down and Listen: Stories from South Africa
(1990), in which the following story appears.

The Reward of Waiting

A T the turn of the century, polygamy was the accepted norm in some tribal
communities in South Africa. It was a common occurrence to find wives of
one man very friendly with each other, to the point of wearing similar garments in
colour and style. To an outsider, such relationships often seemed unreal and full
of pretence; but they were real enough, and were the source of much satisfaction
and joy, to the man and women themselves.

Of course, some households were happier than others. A great deal depended
on the ability of the husband to maintain peace and order within his family.
There was always the danger of petty jealousies and subtle envy spreading
among the wives and children.

Khotso was one husband who tried to create the conditions for a harmonious
household. He was in his late forties and had one wife. They had two lovely
daughters, aged fourteen and ten. For some time, the couple had tried in vain to
conceive another child, hoping for a son. Their failure to do so weighed heavily
on them both, but especially so on Khotso, who felt his chances of ever having
a son were slipping away. In those years, failure to have a son was regarded as a
serious setback, since tradition laid it down that sons were the legitimate heirs
to the estate of their parents. His wife, Mosidi, also longed for another child but
she would have been equally delighted with a girl or a boy.

After much thought and deliberation, Khotso approached his wife and asked
her to think seriously about what they should do in order to have a son in the
family. The thought of her husband finding a second wife, young enough to
bear children, immediately crossed Mosidi's mind. She wondered if that was
what her husband meant, and went on to weigh up the implications of such an
event. Without making any positive suggestion, Khotso put the problem to his
wife several times. His persistence in the matter confirmed her feeling that her
husband was indeed entertaining the idea of a second wife. She decided that if
he referred to the matter again, she would have a direct reply for him.

It did not take Khotso long to return to the subject; it had clearly become a burning issue for him. Calmly, Mosidi turned to her husband and said, "Have you ever thought of finding a younger wife who could give birth to your son?" Taken aback by this blunt question, Khotso stumbled over his response. Meanwhile, Mosidi looked straight into his eyes and awaited his reply. It came eventually: "You – *you* mean I should find another wife? How will you manage in that situation?" Still very cool and calm, Mosidi replied, "If you do not find another wife, how else do you hope to get a son, seeing that I am no longer able to conceive?" Still bewildered by his wife's forthright manner, Khotso hung down his head, as if in shame, and said, "Mosidi, please give me time to consider your suggestion. I will return to you with my reply." Mosidi responded, "When you do, please also let me know what alternative you had in mind." In a daze, Khotso left the house and, in a pensive mood, sat under a tree.

That night, as they sat chatting after the evening meal, Khotso returned to the subject – much sooner than his wife had anticipated. "*Mma Lerato* [Lerato's mother]," he said, "I have given our talk very serious thought. To be honest, I never had any alternative thought. I entertained the same idea of finding a second wife. My problem is finding someone to take into the family who will bring blessings and peace, because I never contemplated having any wife other than you."

This statement came to Mosidi as a revelation. She suddenly felt very guilty, realizing that she had suspected that her husband had always wanted a second wife. She had also suspected that he already had someone in mind. She could not look Khotso directly in the eye; instead she looked down, trying to find an answer to her husband's unexpected words. She finally managed these words: "Thank you for sharing your thoughts so openly, Khotso. I hope you will find guidance in your search for the right woman." Khotso replied, "You must be aware, Mosidi, that this is not a task I can undertake without your support and co-operation. The best junior wives are those selected by their senior counterparts. If ever I take a second wife, Mosidi, she will be your choice."

Khotso was expressing what was common practice in traditional communities in those days. Husbands did indeed rely on their senior wives to recommend someone they felt would be suitable for their husbands and families.

Mosidi felt the weight of the responsibility descend on her. It was a problem she had never dreamt that she would have to address. But she knew that it was imperative for their family to have a son: the peace and harmony of the household depended on it. Recently, she had seen Khotso drifting into a tense, solemn mood; and she found it increasingly difficult to cheer him up, a task which previously she had always carried out easily and with joy. She decided that she would have to consider her husband's wish with seriousness and urgency.

Mosidi's relaxed nature and respect for people had earned her many friends among the community's women, young and old. She knew several homes in which there lived respectable young women – one of whom might make a suitable junior wife for Khotso. Any decision of this type, Mosidi knew, was a risky one; and she gave herself ample time to look for the right woman. Meanwhile, Khotso kept his thoughts, fears and expectations to himself and asked no questions about this sensitive and important subject.

After a month or two – a period which to Khotso seemed like a decade – Mosidi reopened the difficult subject. She chose a time late at night when they had already gone to bed. "Khotso," she began, "you know I have never rested since you expressed your fervent desire to have a son. Because I have accepted the Christian faith, I have found it very difficult to accept that we should introduce polygamy into our home. All the same, having said that, I want you to know that I have been very vigilant in looking for a mature young woman who would fit into our home, whom you would love and cherish at all times, and who, I would hope, would have love and respect for our family." Mosidi's voice became shaky and soft as she uttered her final sentence: "She comes from a good home, if that should mean anything."

The only words that managed to leave Khotso's lips were, "Thank you, Mosidi. You will tell me the rest tomorrow." Khotso was a Christian worshipper in name only; but he understood the importance of the Church to his wife. Mosidi was pleased and surprised that her husband asked no more at this point. The candle light was put out and they soon fell asleep.

After about two days of tense silence, Khotso resumed the talk, saying, "Mosidi, I am now ready to hear your full report of the woman you have found to be your helper in this home." Khotso was overwhelmed by what Mosidi had to tell him. She had selected Fumane, daughter of the right-hand man of the Chief of Bafokeng village. She was a good-looking woman in her middle twenties, well-groomed and from a good background and home. She was known in the community as an industrious, diligent woman – qualities highly prized in wives-to-be.

Khotso and Mosidi were not wealthy. They worked hard for what they owned; and they were respected in their community. It was counted an honour, then, for Fumane's family to be brought together with Khotso's family in this way. In a short time, all the negotiations were completed and Fumane proudly joined Khotso's family as his second wife. Because of her youth, Fumane was very confident that she would soon be mother to Khotso's only son.

At the beginning, everything seemed to go according to plan. There appeared to be a healthy relationship between Mosidi and Fumane. Fumane was indeed an asset to the family in terms of her contribution to the household chores. She was also a warm, pleasant young woman who soon took to Khotso's children. In their turn, they responded to her with love. Before too long, Khotso's family became the envy of the village because of the easy harmony prevailing there.

From month to month, Fumane's family anxiously monitored her appearance, trying to judge whether she was yet expectant. But months passed by without any sign of such a condition. And then, to everybody's shock, some six months after Fumane's arrival in the family, it came to light that Mosidi herself was expectant. Her youngest girl at that time was ten years of age. This discovery started a series of conflicts within the family.

Within two months of the confirmation of Mosidi's pregnancy, Fumane began to show signs of depression and withdrawal. She took less and less part in household work – an area in which she had previously excelled. She spoke less, too, keeping to herself most of the time. Khotso and Mosidi guessed that she was overcome by self-pity on account of her failure to conceive before

Mosidi, who was by far her senior in years. But all their efforts to make her feel better failed. These developments clearly embarrassed her family. Gradually, the atmosphere in the home, which had earlier been the envy of the village, turned sour.

Mosidi tried to support Fumane by looking to her for help in all ways when her pregnancy advanced and became a burden to her. She hoped in this way to win Fumane round, to bring them closer together and to reduce Fumane's tension, anxiety and insecurity. But Fumane closed up, sharing her problems and concerns with nobody in her new home – not even with Khotso. She ended up by distancing herself from all members of the family.

In those early years, when black people lived from the land, custom demanded that after confinement the new mother remained in the house for a period of three months. During that time, she had people around her who were assigned the special duties of nursing her, cooking for her, carrying out all the normal household tasks, and helping her with the baby. Under normal circumstances Fumane, as Khotso's second wife, would have been responsible for allocating duties to those who came to assist in the house at the time when Mosidi was due for confinement. But her sudden change of attitude made it difficult for people in the home to communicate and plan with her.

Fumane's state of mind also affected her relationship with her husband. Khotso began to show signs of embarrassment and guilt; also perhaps of regret over his decision to take a second wife, since Mosidi's baby might well be a boy. All in all, his life was not a comfortable one at this time, though he awaited the birth of his baby with great excitement. Fumane's difficult manner had brought Khotso and Mosidi closer together. Meanwhile, much against Khotso's will, Fumane became a constant visitor to her parents' home.

The arrival of the new baby – a son – was the greatest day in the life of Khotso's family. But it seemed to spell doom for Fumane. The baby, who resembled his father and was Khotso's great pride and joy, seemed to cement the parents' relationship still further. But Fumane appeared to be even more strained and tense and took to going to her parents even more frequently. Sometimes she spent the night at their home. Khotso's family tried to understand her problem and to accommodate her to the best of their ability. They took it that she was suffering from the pain of failing to conceive while Mosidi, a much older woman, had given birth to the first son in the family. They did their best to show her that they felt for her; but Fumane did not respond to their support.

The baby was about two months old when Fumane left for her parents' home without telling her husband that she was leaving. When she had stayed away for the unusually long period of three or four days, Khotso discussed the matter with Mosidi and then went after Fumane to find out what had happened to her. Before leaving, he checked the room which he shared with Fumane – and found that she had removed all that belonged to her. This came as a shock to Khotso; and he refrained from sharing the discovery with Mosidi through fear of unsettling her.

At Fumane's parents' house, Khotso was dismayed to learn that their daughter had reported that she had suffered emotional torture and humiliation in her new home. And because of that, she had pleaded with them not to intervene in any way. Finally, she had left her parents' home to go to the city to find a job and, she hoped, to forget the traumatic experience she had gone through. It has to be remembered that, in those years, failure to conceive was seen as a general indictment of a woman's behaviour and character.

Fumane's abrupt and unhappy departure made a deep impression on Khotso. He was convinced that the events of the previous months held a message for him. He began to see his wife in a fresh light, putting a new value on her calm nature, her confidence in herself and in others, and her respect for other people. In his mind, he relived the time when Fumane was part of their family; and he thought of the difficulties created by Fumane's attitude. Once again, he was filled with admiration and respect for the way in which Mosidi had responded to Fumane's whims and moods.

Their baby was about a year old when Khotso unfolded himself to his wife. "*Mma Lerato*," he started, "all through our married life of sixteen years, I have never doubted your integrity, dependability, good judgment, unselfishness at all times, and your honesty and sincerity when making decisions. I have always been fully aware of these rare qualities and attributes of yours. Today I am openly acknowledging them to you. I thank you for who you are. I thank my God and my ancestors for giving me a wife with such rare gifts of understanding and accepting, sometimes at your own expense, other people's shortcomings and abilities, failures and successes, likes and dislikes. This acknowledgement of who you are has increased my faith in my Creator and persuaded me that I alone do not have the power to direct my destiny. I thank you for all that. I thank all the powers which gave us this son." Here, Khotso cuddled the baby, Mpho ["Gift"]. "He is fully the brother of Lerato ["Love"] and Basetsana ["Girl"]. For this I am grateful."

Mosidi had been listening with concentration to what her husband said. Once Khotso had finished his long, cathartic speech, she took some time to respond to him. Then, in her usual calm manner, she turned to him, saying, "Thank you, *Rra Lerato* [Lerato's father], for all the kind things you have said to me about me. For me, the greatest message that has come out of this experience has been the affirmation of the love, support and guidance of our Creator. My faith is anchored in these realities. Time and again, I have shared with you my commitment to worship and my dedication to my faith. Somehow I was convinced that our prayers and pleas for a son would be rewarded. At the time, however, I found it very difficult to communicate that to you. My trust has not been in vain. My hopes have been fulfilled."

In complete surrender, Khotso handed over everything, saying, "From today, your faith will be my faith, your God my God, your hopes my hopes, your trust my trust. You have been the pillar, strength, support and guide of this family. Let it always be so."

Within six months, Khotso was dead. Those words of his remained a mainstay in Mosidi's life. In her grief, she was much comforted by the fact that her husband died a convert and a devoted worshipper.

Billie Holiday
1915–59

B orn Eleanora Fagan in Baltimore, she was as a child shunted
from relative to relative and suffered an attempted rape when
she was ten, after which she was sent to a home for wayward girls.
*In 1928, aged sixteen, she moved with her mother to Harlem and stayed
in a boardinghouse-cum-brothel, becoming a prostitute for a time. Her
singing career began in 1931 in a Harlem nightclub, where she was an
instant success. In the 1930s she worked with musicians such as Benny
Goodman, Artie Shaw and saxophonist Lester Young (who named her
"Lady Day"), but though she received musical acclaim – among her
classic songs are "Strange Fruit", "My Man" and "God Bless the Child" –
her personal life was unhappy. As she succumbed to drugs and drink, her
health declined as did her work opportunities. She made her last public
appearance in May 1959 before being admitted to hospital; while there,
she was once more arrested for possessing narcotics. By July she was
dead. A film based on her life,* Lady Sings the Blues, *was released in
1973, starring Diana Ross. The following extract is from the beginning
of her autobiography of the same name.*

From

Lady Sings the Blues

SOME OTHER SPRING

M OM and Pop were just a couple of kids when they got married. He
was eighteen, she was sixteen, and I was three.

Mom was working as a maid with a white family. When they found out she
was going to have a baby they just threw her out. Pop's family just about had
a fit, too, when they heard about it. They were real society folks and they never
heard of things like that going on in their part of East Baltimore.

But both kids were poor. And when you're poor, you grow up fast.

It's a wonder my mother didn't end up in the workhouse and me as a
foundling. But Sadie Fagan loved me from the time I was just a swift kick in
the ribs while she scrubbed the floors. She went to the hospital and made a
deal with the head woman there. She told them she'd scrub floors and wait

on the other bitches laying up there to have their kids so she could pay her way and mine. And she did. Mom was thirteen that Wednesday, April 7, 1915, in Baltimore when I was born. . . .

I was a woman when I was six. I was big for my age, with big breasts, big bones, a big fat healthy broad, that's all. So I started working out then, before school and after, minding babies, running errands, and scrubbing those damn white steps all over Baltimore.

White families in the neighbourhood used to pay me a nickel for scrubbing them down. I decided I had to have more money so I figured out a way. I bought me a brush of my own, a bucket, some rags, some Octagon soap, and a big white bar of that stuff I can't ever forget – Bon Ami.

The first time I stood on a white doorstep and asked this woman for fifteen cents for the job, she like to had a fit. But I explained to her the higher price came from me bringing my own supplies. She thought I had a damn nerve, I guess, but while she was thinking it over I said I'd scrub the kitchen or bathroom floor for the same price. That did it. I had the job. . . .

When I went into the scrubbing business it was the end of roller skating, bike riding, and boxing too. I used to like boxing. In school they used to teach us girls to box. But I didn't keep it up. Once a girl hit me on the nose and it just about finished me. I took my gloves off and beat the pants off her. The gym teacher got so sore, I never went near the school gym again.

But whether I was riding a bike or scrubbing somebody's dirty bathroom floor, I used to love to sing all the time. I liked music. If there was a place where I could go and hear it, I went.

Alice Dean used to keep a whorehouse on the corner nearest our place, and I used to run errands for her and the girls. I was very commercial in those days. I'd never go to the store for anybody for less than a nickel or a dime. But I'd run all over for Alice and the girls, and I'd wash basins, put out the Lifebuoy soap and towels. When it came time to pay me, I used to tell her she could keep the money if she'd let me come up in her front parlour and listen to Louis Armstrong and Bessie Smith on her victrola. . . . I spent many a wonderful hour there listening to Pops and Bessie. I remember Pops' recording of "West End Blues" and how it used to gas me. . . . Sometimes the record would make me so sad I'd cry up a storm. Other times the same damn record would make me so happy I'd forget about how much hard-earned money the session in the parlour was costing me.

But Mom didn't favour her daughter hanging around the house on the corner. And especially she couldn't understand why I wasn't bringing home any loot. "I know Eleanora," she used to complain, Eleanora being the name I'd been baptized under, "and she don't work for nobody for nothing." When Mom found out I was using my hard-earned money paying rent on Alice's parlour to listen to jazz on the victrola, she nearly had a fit too.

. . .There were other things I missed when I went into the scrubbing business full time. I used to love to go to the five-and-dime store in Baltimore and buy hot dogs. They never used to wait on Negroes there. But they'd sell me a hot dog because I was a kid and I guess they could use the business if nobody was looking. But if they caught me eating that hot dog before I got outside on the street, they'd give me hell for cluttering up the place.

I used to love white silk socks, too, and of course black patent-leather shoes. I could never afford them. But I used to sneak in the five-and-dime and grab the white socks off the counter and run like hell. Why not? They wouldn't let me buy them even if I did have the money.

I learned to crawl in the back way at the movies to save the dime it cost going in the front way. I don't think I missed a single picture Billie Dove ever made. I was crazy for her. I tried to do my hair like her and eventually I borrowed her name.

My name, Eleanora, was too damn long for anyone to say. Besides, I never liked it. Especially not after my grandma shortened it and used to scream "Nora!" at me from the back porch. My father had started calling me Bill because I was such a young tomboy. I didn't mind that, but I wanted to be pretty, too, and have a pretty name. So I decided Billie was it and I made it stick.

Claudia Jones
1915–64

B orn in Port of Spain, Trinidad, she emigrated with her family
in 1924 at the age of eight to the USA, where she experienced the
poverty and racism that led her to dedicate her life to the liberation
struggle. In 1948, in the McCarthy era, she was arrested, charged with
seeking "the overthrow of the government by force and violence", tried
and imprisoned. When illness forced her to give up legal appeals against
deportation, she left the USA and in 1956 took up residence in Britain.
She was the co-ordinator of the first Caribbean Carnival in London,
out of which developed what is now Europe's largest street festival, the
Notting Hill Carnival. In 1958 she founded and edited The West Indian
Gazette (and Afro-Asian-Caribbean News), the first campaigning Black
newspaper in Britain, was involved in many campaigns and visited the

USSR, Japan and China to contribute to the struggle for world peace. She died in London and is buried in a grave next to that of Karl Marx in Highgate Cemetery.

An End to The Neglect
of the Problems of Negro Women!

A N outstanding feature of the present stage of the Negro liberation movement is the growth in the militant participation of Negro women in all aspects of the struggle for peace, civil rights, and economic security. Symptomatic of this new militancy is the fact that Negro women have become symbols of many present-day struggles of the Negro people. This growth of militancy among Negro women has profound meaning, both for the Negro liberation movement and for the emerging anti-fascist, anti-imperialist coalition.

To understand this militancy correctly, to deepen and extend the role of Negro women in the struggle for peace and for all interests of the working class and the Negro people, means primarily to overcome the gross neglect of the special problems of Negro women. This neglect has too long permeated the ranks of the labour movement generally, of Left-progressives and also of the Communist Party. The most serious assessment of these shortcomings by progressives, especially by Marxist-Leninists, is vitally necessary if we are to help accelerate this development and integrate Negro women in the progressive and labour movement in our own Party.

The bourgeoisie is fearful of the militancy of the Negro woman, and for good reason. The capitalists know, far better than many progressives seem to know, that once Negro women undertake action, the militancy of the whole Negro people, and thus of the anti-imperialist coalition, is greatly enhanced.

Historically, the Negro woman has been the guardian, the protector, of the Negro family. From the days of the slave-traders down to the present, the Negro woman has had the responsibility of caring for the needs of the family, of shielding it from the blows of Jim Crow insults, of rearing children in an atmosphere of lynch terror, segregation and police brutality, and of fighting for an education for the children. The intensified oppression of the Negro people, which has been the hallmark of the post-war reactionary offensive, cannot therefore but lead to an acceleration of the militancy of the Negro woman. As mother, as Negro, and as worker, the Negro woman fights against the wiping out of the Negro family, against the Jim Crow ghetto existence which destroys the health, morale and the very life of millions of her sisters, brothers and children.

Viewed in this light, it is not accidental that the American bourgeoisie has intensified its oppression, not only of the Negro people in general but of Negro women in particular. Nothing so exposes the drive to fascism in the nation as the callous attitude which the bourgeoisie displays and cultivates toward Negro women. The vaunted boast of the ideologists of Big Business – that American women possess "the greatest equality" in the world – is exposed in all its hypocrisy; in the Soviet Union, the New Democracies and the formerly oppressed land of China, women are attaining new heights of equality. But above all else, Wall Street's boast stops at the water's edge where Negro and working-class women are concerned. Not equality, but degradation and super-exploitation: this is the actual lot of Negro women! . . .

Very much to the contrary, Negro women – as workers, as Negroes, and as women – are the most oppressed stratum of the whole population.

In 1940, two out of every five Negro women, in contrast to two out of every eight white women, worked for a living. By virtue of their majority status among the Negro people, Negro women not only constitute the largest percentage of women heads of families but are the main breadwinners of the Negro family. The large proportion of Negro women in the labour market is primarily a result of the low-scale earnings of Negro men. This disproportion also has its roots in the treatment and position of Negro women over the centuries.

Following the emancipation, and persisting to the present day, a large percentage of Negro women – married as well as single – were forced to work for a living. But despite the shift in employment of Negro women from rural to urban areas, Negro women are still generally confined to the lowest-paying jobs. . . . The super-exploitation of the Negro woman worker is thus revealed not only in that she receives, as a woman, less than equal pay for equal work with men, but in that the majority of Negro women get less than half the pay of white women. Little wonder, then, that in Negro communities the conditions of ghetto-living – low salaries, high rents, high prices, etc. – virtually become an iron curtain hemming in the lives of Negro children and undermining their health and spirit! Little wonder that the maternity death rate for Negro women is triple that of white women! Little wonder that one out of every ten Negro children born in the United States does not grow to manhood or womanhood!

The low scale of earnings of the Negro woman is directly related to her almost complete exclusion from virtually all fields of work except the most menial and underpaid, namely, domestic service. Revealing are the following data given in the report of 1945, *Negro Women War Workers* (Women's Bureau, US Department of Labor, Bulletin 205): Of a total 7 ½ million Negro women, over a million are in domestic and personal service. The overwhelming bulk – about 918,000 – of these women workers are employed in private families, and some 98,000 are employed as cooks, waitresses, and in like services in other than private homes. The remaining 60,000 workers in service trades are in miscellaneous personal service occupations (beauticians, boarding-house and lodging-house keepers, charwomen, janitors, practical nurses, housekeepers, hostesses, and elevator operators).

The next largest number of Negro women workers are engaged in agricultural work. In 1940, about 245,000 were agricultural workers. Of them, some 128,000 were unpaid family workers.

Industrial and other workers numbered more than 96,000 of the Negro women reported. Thirty-six thousand of these women were in manufacturing, the chief groups being 11,300 in apparel and other fabricated textile products, 1,000 in tobacco manufacturers, and 5,600 in food and related products.

The rest of the Negro women who work for a living were distributed along the following lines: teachers, 50,000; nurses and student nurses, 6,700; social and welfare workers, 1,700; dentists, pharmacists and veterinarians, 120; physicians and surgeons, 129; actresses, 200; authors, editors and reporters, 100; lawyers and judges, 39; librarians, 400; and other categories likewise illustrating the large-scale exclusion of Negro women from the professions. . . .

Inherently connected with the question of job opportunities where the Negro woman is concerned is the special oppression she faces as Negro, as woman and as worker. She is the victim of the white chauvinist stereotype as to where her place should be. In the film, radio and press, the Negro woman is not pictured in her real role as breadwinner, mother and protector of the family, but as a traditional "mammy" who puts the care of children and families of others above her own. This traditional stereotype of the Negro slave mother, which to this day appears in commercial advertisements, must be combated and rejected as a device of the imperialists to perpetuate the white chauvinist ideology that Negro women are "backward", "inferior" and the "natural slaves" of others.

Actually, the history of the Negro woman shows that the Negro mother under slavery held a key position and played a dominant role in her own family grouping. This was due primarily to two factors: the conditions of slavery, under which marriage, as such, was non-existent and the Negro's social status was derived from the mother and not the father; and the fact that most of the Negro people brought to these shores by the slave-traders came from West Africa where the position of women, based on active participation in property control, was relatively higher in the family than that of European women.

Early historians of the slave trade recall the testimony of travellers indicating that the love of the African mother for her child was unsurpassed in any part of the world. There are numerous stories attesting to the self-sacrificial way in which East African mothers offered themselves to the slave-traders in order to save their sons, and Hottentot women refused food during famines until after their children were fed.

It is impossible within the confines of this article to relate the terrible sufferings and degradations undergone by Negro mothers and Negro women generally under slavery. Subject to legalized rape by the slave-owners, confined to slave pens, forced to march for eight to fourteen hours with loads on their backs and to perform back-breaking work even during pregnancy, Negro women bore a burning hatred for slavery, and undertook a large share of the responsibility for defending and nurturing the Negro family.

The Negro mother was mistress in the slave cabin, and despite the interference of master or overseer, her wishes in regard to mating and in family matters were paramount. During and after slavery, Negro women had to support themselves and the children, necessarily playing an important role in the economic and social life of her people. . . .

The continued relegation of Negro women to domestic work has helped to perpetuate and intensify chauvinism directed against all Negro women. Despite the fact that Negro women may be grandmothers or mothers, the use of the chauvinist term "girl" for adult Negro women is a common expression. The very economic relationship of Negro women to white women, which perpetuates "madam-maid" relationships, feeds chauvinist attitudes and makes it incumbent on white women progressives, and particularly Communists, to fight consciously against all manifestations of white chauvinism, open and subtle.

Chauvinism on the part of progressive white women is often expressed in their failure to have close ties of friendship with Negro women and to realize that this fight for equality of Negro women is in their own self-interest, in as much as the super-exploitation and oppression of Negro women tends to depress the standard of all women. . . .

Some of the crassest expressions of chauvinism are to be found at social affairs, where, all too often, white men and women and Negro men participate in dancing, but Negro women are neglected, the acceptance of white ruling-class standards of "desirability" for women (such as light skin). The failure to extend courtesy to Negro women and to integrate Negro women into organizational leadership are other forms of chauvinism. . . .

The bourgeois ideologists have not failed, of course, to develop a special ideological offensive aimed at degrading Negro women, as part and parcel of the general reactionary ideological offensive against women of "kitchen, church and children". They cannot, however, with equanimity or credibility speak of the Negro woman's "place" as in the home; for Negro women are in other people's kitchens. Hence their task has been to intensify their theories of male "superiority" as regards the Negro woman by developing introspective attitudes which coincide with the "new school" of "psychological inferiority" of women. The whole intent of a host of articles, books, etc., has been to obscure the main responsibility for the oppression of Negro women by spreading the rotten bourgeois notion about a "battle of the sexes" and "ignoring" the fight of both Negro men and women – the whole Negro people – against their common oppressors, the white ruling class.

Chauvinist expressions also include paternalistic surprise when it is learned that Negroes are professional people. Negro professional women workers are often confronted with such remarks as "Isn't your family proud of you?" Then, there is the reverse practice of inquiring whether "someone in the family" would like to take a job as a domestic worker.

The responsibility for overcoming these special forms of white chauvinism rests not with the "subjectivity" of Negro women, as it is often put, but squarely on the shoulders of white men and white women. Negro men have a special responsibility particularly in relation to rooting out attitudes of male superiority as regards women in general. There is need to root out all "humanitarian" and patronizing attitudes towards Negro women.

Margaret Walker (Alexander)

1915–

orn in Birmingham, Alabama, she began writing poetry at the
age of twelve. She graduated from Gilbert Academy in 1930, has a
BA from Northwestern University and from the University of Iowa
an MA and PhD. She worked on the federal government's Writers Project
in Chicago and also as a typist, reporter and newspaper and magazine
editor. Her poems and articles have been widely published since the
1940s. She was the first Black poet to be given the Yale Younger Poets
Award, in 1942, for her first collection For My People, which celebrates
the African-American heritage, and in 1944 she received a Rosenwald
Fellowship. Her later poetry books include Prophet for a New day (1970)
and October Journey (1973). She taught for many years, notably at
Jackson State College, Mississippi, where she established a Black studies
programme. Her best known work of fiction is the historical novel Jubilee
(1966), which was based on the life of her great-grandmother, and the
creation of which she describes in her book How I Wrote Jubilee and
Other Essays on Life and Literature (1990).

For My People

For my people everywhere singing their slave songs repeatedly: their dirges
and their ditties and their blues and jubilees, praying their prayers nightly
to an unknown god, bending their knees humbly to an unseen power;
For my people lending their strength to the years: to the gone years and the
now years and the maybe years, washing ironing cooking scrubbing sewing
mending hoeing plowing digging planting pruning patching dragging along
never gaining never reaping never knowing and never understanding;
For my playmates in the clay and dust and sand of Alabama backyards playing
baptizing and preaching, and doctor and jail and soldier and school and mama
and cooking and playhouse and concert and store and Miss Choomby and hair
and company;
For the cramped bewildered years we went to school to learn to know the
reasons why and the answers to and the people who and the places where
and the days when, in memory of the bitter hours when we discovered we
were black and poor and small and different and nobody cared and nobody
wondered and nobody understood;

For the boys and girls who grew in spite of these to be Man and Woman,
    to laugh and dance and sing and play and drink their wine and religion
    and success, to marry their playmates and bear children and then die of
    consumption and anemia and lynching;

For my people thronging 47th Street in Chicago, and Lenox Avenue in New
    York and Rampart Street in New Orleans, lost disinherited dispossessed and
    HAPPY people filling the cabarets and taverns and other people's pockets
    needing bread and shoes and milk and land and money and Something –
    something all our own;

For my people walking blindly, spreading joy, losing time being lazy, sleeping
    when hungry, shouting when burdened, drinking when hopeless, tied and
    shackled and tangled among ourselves by the unseen creatures who tower
    over us omnisciently and laugh;

For my people blundering and groping and floundering in the dark of
    churches and schools and clubs and societies, associations and councils
    and committees and conventions, distressed and disturbed and deceived
    and devoured by money-hungry glory-craving leeches, preyed on by facile
    force of state and fad and novelty, by false prophet and holy believer;

For my people standing staring trying to fashion a better way from confusion,
    from hypocrisy and misunderstanding, trying to fashion a world that will
    hold all the people, all the faces, all the adams and eves and their countless
    generations;

Let a new earth rise. Let another world be born. Let a bloody peace be
    written in the sky. Let a second generation full of courage issue forth; let
    a people loving freedom come to growth, let a beauty full of healing and
    a strength of final clenching be the pulsing in our spirits and our bloods.
    Let the martial songs be written, let the dirges disappear. Let a race of men
    now rise and take control!

Lineage

My grandmothers were strong.
They followed plows and bent to toil.
They moved through fields sowing seed.
They touched earth and grain grew.
They were full of sturdiness and singing.
My grandmothers were strong.

My grandmothers are full of memories
Smelling of soap and onions and wet clay
With veins rolling roughly over quick hands
They have many clean words to say.
My grandmothers were strong.
Why am I not as they?

Gwendolyn Brooks

1917–

T he first Black writer to win a Pulitzer Prize, for her 1950 book of poems Annie Allen, she was born in Kansas and has lived mostly in Chicago. She graduated from Wilson Junior College in 1936, married in 1939 and had two children. She was Publicity Director of the NAACP Youth Council and taught on the faculties of various universities. Her many honours include the American Academy of Arts & Letters Award, Guggenheim Fellowships and honorary doctoral degrees. She has been Consultant in Poetry to the Library of Congress, editor/publisher of the journal Black Position, was named Poet Laureate of Illinois in 11968 (succeeding Carl Sandberg), and founded a publishing house in Chicago, the David Company. She is the author of a novel, Maud Martha (1953), children's books, several notable poetry collections, including A Street in Bronzeville (1946) and The Bean Eaters (1956), and an autobiography, Report from Part One (1972).

To Black Women

Sisters,
where there is cold silence –
no hallelujahs, no hurrahs at all, no handshakes,
no neon red or blue, no smiling faces –
prevail.
Prevail across the editors of the world!
who are obsessed, self-honeying and self-crowned
in the seduced area.

It has been a
hard trudge, with fainting, bandaging and death.
There have been startling confrontations.
There have been tramplings. Tramplings
of monarchs and of other men.

But there remain large countries in your eyes.
Shrewd sun.
The civil balance.
The listening secrets.

And you create and train your flowers still.

From

Maud Martha

HELEN

WHAT she remembered was Emmanuel; laughing, glinting in the sun; kneeing his wagon toward them, as they walked tardily home from school. Six years ago.

"How about a ride?" Emmanuel had hailed.

She had, daringly – it was not her way, not her native way – made a quip. A "sophisticated" quip. "Hi, handsome!" Instantly he had scowled, his dark face darkening.

"I don't mean you, you old black gal," little Emmanuel had exclaimed. "I mean Helen."

He had meant Helen, and Helen on the reissue of the invitation had climbed, without a word, into the wagon and was off and away.

Even now, at seventeen – high-school graduate, mistress of her fate, and a ten-dollar-a-week file clerk in the very Forty-seventh Street lawyer's office where Helen was a fifteen-dollar-a-week typist – as she sat on Helen's bed and watched Helen primp for a party, the memory hurt. There was no consolation in the thought that not now and not then would she have *had* Emmanuel "off a Christmas tree". For the basic situation had never changed. Helen was still the one they wanted in the wagon, still "the pretty one", "the dainty one". The lovely one.

She did not know what it was. She had tried to find the something that must be there to imitate, that she might imitate it. But she did not know what it was. I wash as much as Helen does, she thought. My hair is longer and thicker, she thought. I'm much smarter. I read books and newspapers and old folks like to talk with me, she thought.

But the kernel of the matter was that, in spite of these things, she was poor, and Helen was still the ranking queen, not only with the Emmanuels of the world, but even with their father – their mother – their brother. She did not blame the family. It was not their fault. She understood. They could not help it. They were enslaved, were fascinated, and they were not at all to blame.

Her noble understanding of their blamelessness did not make any easier to bear such a circumstance as Harry's springing to open a door so that Helen's soft little hands might not have to cope with the sullyings of a doorknob, or running her errands, to save the sweet and fine little feet, or shouldering Helen's part against Maud Martha. Especially could these items burn when Maud Martha recalled her comradely rompings with Harry, watched by the gentle Helen from the clean and gentle harbor of the porch: take the day, for example, when Harry had been chased by those five big boys from Forty-first and Wabash, cursing, smelling, beastlike boys! with bats and rocks, and little stones that were more worrying than rocks; on that occasion out Maud Martha had dashed, when she saw from the front-room window Harry, panting and torn, racing for home; out she had dashed and down into the street with one of the smaller porch chairs held high over her head, and while Harry gained first the porch and next the safety side of the front door she had swung left, swung right, clouting a head here, a head there, and screaming at the top of her lungs, "Y' leave my brother alone! Y' leave my brother alone!" And who had washed those bloody wounds, and afterward vaselined them down? Really – in spite of everything she could not understand why Harry had to hold open doors for Helen, and calmly let them slam in her, Maud Martha's his friend's, face.

It did not please her either, at the breakfast table, to watch her father drink his coffee and contentedly think (oh, she knew it!), as Helen started on her grapefruit, how daintily she ate, how gracefully she sat in her chair, how pure was her robe and unwrinkled, how neatly she had arranged her hair. Their father preferred Helen's hair to Maud Martha's (Maud Martha knew), which impressed him, not with its length and body, but simply with its apparent untamableness; for he would never get over that zeal of his for order in all things, in character, in housekeeping, in his own labor, in grooming, in human relationships. Always he had worried about Helen's homework, Helen's health. And now that boys were taking her out, he believed not one of them worthy of her, not one of them good enough to receive a note of her sweet voice: he insisted that she be returned before midnight. Yet who was it who sympathized with him in his decision to remain, for the rest of his days, the simple janitor! when everyone else was urging him to get out, get prestige, make more money? Who was it who sympathized with him in his almost desperate love for this old house? Who followed him about, emotionally speaking, loving this, doting on that? The kitchen, for instance, that was not beautiful in any way! The walls and ceilings, that were cracked. The chairs, which cried when people sat in them. The tables, that grieved audibly if anyone rested more than two fingers upon them. The huge cabinets, old and tired (when you shut their doors or drawers there was a sick, bickering little sound). The radiators, high and hideous. And underneath the low sink coiled unlovely pipes, that Helen said made her think of a careless woman's underwear, peeping out. In fact, often had Helen given her opinion, unasked, of the whole house, of the whole "hulk of rotten wood". Often had her cool and gentle eyes sneered, gently and coolly, at her father's determination to hold his poor estate. But take that kitchen, for instance! Maud Martha, taking it, saw herself there, up and down her seventeen years, eating apples after school; making sweet potato tarts; drawing, on the pathetic table, the horse that won her the sixth-grade prize; getting her hair curled for her first party, at that stove; washing dishes by summer twilight, with the back door wide open; making cheese and peanut-butter sandwiches for a picnic. And even crying, crying in that pantry, when no one knew. The old sorrows brought there! – now dried, flattened out, breaking into interesting dust at the merest look. . . .

"You'll never get a boy friend," said Helen, fluffing on her Golden Peacock powder, "if you don't stop reading those books."

Marie Chauvet

1917–75

*S*he was born in Port-au-Prince, Haiti, and was educated there at the Normal School for girls. Twice married (the name Chauvet is from her second marriage), she was a teacher for many years and died in New York. Her published fiction includes* Fille d'Haiti *(1954),* La danse sur le volcan *(1957; translated by Salvator Attanasio as* Dance on the Volcano, *1959),* Fonds-des-Nègres *(1961) and* Amour, colère et folie *(1968), from which this extract (translated by Betty Wilson) is taken. She also wrote a play,* La Légende des fleurs *(1949).*

From

Love

I WATCH the drama unfolding, scene by scene, unobtrusive as a shadow.
I, the only lucid one, the only dangerous one, and yet nobody around me
suspects a thing. The old maid! The one who has never had a husband, who
doesn't know what love is, who has never really lived in the true sense of the
word. They are wrong. I am savouring my vengeance in silence. It is my silence,
my vengeance. I know just whose arms Annette is going to throw herself into
and I have no intention whatsoever of opening my sister Felicia's eyes. She is
too blissfully happy and is too proudly carrying the three-month-old foetus in
her womb. If she was clever enough to catch a husband I hope she will be smart
enough to keep him. She is much too trusting. Her serenity exasperates me. She
smiles contentedly as she embroiders her son's chemises; for of course it will
be a son! And Annette will be his godmother, I can bet on that....

I am leaning on my window-sill watching them: Annette is offering Jean
Luze her fresh, young 22-year-old body, standing upright, in full daylight. They
turn away from Felicia and possess each other without touching. Desire burns
in their eyes, Jean Luze struggles with himself but the outcome is inevitable.

I am thirty-nine and still a virgin. A fate not to be envied in the eyes
of most women from the Haitian provinces. Is it like that everywhere? Are
there other little towns in the world like this one, half buried in ancient
customs, where people spy on each other? My town! my country! As they
proudly call this dreary *morne* where you hardly see any men apart from the
doctor, the druggist, the priest, the district commandant, the local magistrate,
the *préfet*, all new appointees and so typically "people from the coast" that it
is disheartening. The candidates for these posts represent the rare bird, whose
parents' greatest ambition had always been to send their son to Port-au-Prince
or abroad to make a scholar out of him. One of them has come back to us in
the person of Dr Audier who studied in France and whom I examine in vain for
signs of the superman....

I was born in 1900. A time when prejudice was at its height in this little
province. Three separate groups had formed and these three groups were as
divided as enemies: the "aristocrats", to whom we belonged, the petits bourgeois and the common people. Torn apart by the ambiguity of a particularly
delicate situation, I began to suffer from a very early age because of my dark
skin, whose mahogany colour, inherited from some distant ancestor, stood out
glaringly in the close circle of whites and light-skinned mulattos with whom my
parents mixed. But all that is in the past, and for the moment at least, I don't feel
inclined to turn towards what is over and done with....

The leaves fall from the trees, dance and whirl in the air before they fall
to the ground. Insomnia has made the living breath of night familiar. I can
distinguish the cry of every insect, of every lizard, the movement of every star,
each quiver of the earth. I am naked, on my bed, damp with sweat, palpitating
with desire. A man's arm's encircle my body. I am possessed. How can it be that

a moment afterwards, it is all over? Not even a crumb of memory? Ah! How lonely suffering is! I dress and softly approach the door of Annette's room. She is sobbing in the darkness. I knock. A voice hoarse from weeping asks who is there. I answer; she opens. My presence does not embarrass her, I am the silly idiot, the one on whom life has left no marks. She sobs again and then she asks me: "What do you want?"

I look at her silently and she clings to me.

"If only you knew, Claire ..."

"Shhh! Don't wear yourself out talking," I say to her silently: "I know what you are feeling and I share your feelings. The soul is a millstone, an albatross. It meddles in everything. It creates ties to torture us. Memories mark us, they go deep into our psyches. You are like a flower blown about by the wind. I wish you could be snatched from your ordinary everyday joys and carried away in a huge whirlwind, in danger of your life ..."

"I want to die! I want to die!" she cries out suddenly, so passionately that it leaves her bewildered. It was not she who spoke, but I. How tired she looks! How draining this love affair is for her! How morally weak she is! Jean Luze is not for her. The feeling he arouses in her is so strong that it is destroying her. Will it kill her? Too bad! I need her to serve as my intermediary. I am old. It is as if I am slowly going sour with my starved virginity locked tight between my thighs.

"Cry with me. It won't be for long, you'll see. Have confidence in your charms. You have all that it takes to seduce him. His armour is only a show. You have already seen that. You must not give up. You are experienced. At fifteen, in full control of your feelings, you are already frolicking in search of a male. I was the first to reap what I had sown. I am going to torture you, torture you both until you cry out for mercy ..."

"Next month is your birthday, I am going to have a little party for you. Invite whoever you want ..."

"You are treating me like a child," she protested.

My offer seems childish, but I want Annette to regain her composure, to dance and laugh as Jean Luze watches. I am going to bring her to the limit of her endurance. Suffering does not excite one, it either arouses pity or annoyance. I, who am so tight-fisted, am determined to sacrifice a lot of money on this reception.

The couple is with us, morning, noon and night, closer than ever. Felicia becomes more and more alive as her stomach swells. She is as tranquil as a statue. Jean Luze is eating heartily. He no longer smokes at the table, he claims the smell of tobacco bothers his wife.

"Pregnancy suits you," he tells her, putting his arm around her.

Every time I see him being affectionate to her in my presence, I hate her for being so easily contented with this lukewarm, bourgeois feeling she inspires in him.

I swear to shake him out of his tepid contentment. I will load him like a powder keg. He loses nothing by waiting. I will melt his ice. Let him continue to gaze fondly at us, let him smile. I love to see the dimple appear in his chin, his lips curl over his teeth.

Time passes. The wretchedness of the people grows. To each his lot. Our selfishness becomes the rule. We sink deeper and deeper into cowardice and become resigned. I am more in love with my sister's husband than ever and I don't want to think of anything beside this love. It becomes my refuge, my consolation. Once again Felicia is so sure of herself and of her man that she kissed Annette this morning and wished her happy birthday. They gave her perfume and talcum powder.

"Powder and perfume yourself all you want. I am not afraid of anything any more," Jean Luze's smile seemed to say. We'll see.

For the past few days, I have watched Annette trying in vain to waylay him, on the landing, in the drawing-room, at his room door! He foiled all her attempts without even seeming to feel superior about it. She does not know what to do now to entrap him. Yesterday she came out of her room in a bathing-suit she had made herself and pretending that she couldn't fasten the bra, she asked Jean Luze to help her. A friendly tap on the shoulder sent her off with these words: "There you are."

I hated him for a moment. I feel as if my pains are to no avail. He is more untouched then ever. His attitude, which has become too correct, is all the more offensive for that fact. He wants to make Annette know that: "You had me where you wanted for a while but you are not going to catch me again."

And he is not toying with her either. He has completely wiped out everything from his memory overnight. But what is desire if, once appeased, it does not find the strength to renew itself? How could I bear to see myself repulsed? Could it be that life wanted to spare me up till now by keeping me away from certain disappointing realities? Am I tempting fate by becoming hopelessly involved in an affair which leads nowhere? What I feel for this man has become so central to my existence that I can no longer do without it. Nothing seems to move him. It will drive me mad. Annette allowed Bob to kiss her right in front of him and he did not flinch. He gazed at them with a gentle and disinterested look, a pure angelic look, which was like a slap in the face.

... It rained last night. A torrential rain which lasted for four hours. And the weather has not improved since. Heavy, dirty-grey clouds hang in the sky like pieces of rags. We wade about through mud-puddles like pigs. The roads, full of cracks, have been transformed into ponds. The boat, indifferent, carries away its cargo of wood piled up on the wharf. Business is booming in this area. Mr Long, as red as a rooster, is directing operations himself. The peasants look like whipped dogs. They stretch out their hands to be paid, resentfully staring into the distance at the devastated mountain slopes. Huge white blotches spread over the mountains like leprosy. Immense rocks protrude from their flanks like tombs. The peasants are there, dressed in work clothes, barefooted, their halfort around their necks, their faces taut with discontent.

"Our land is ruined," one of them said. "We have cut down too many trees."

"I had said no, I had said no," cried another. "We should have stuck together, and refused every proposition. But blacks from the hills never stick together for long. They are weak before the whites and the bourgeois. And now the rains are coming and our lands are ruined. The American is getting rich, and he's not the only one. They are all against us."

The magistrate and the *préfet* go with Mr Long to the office, a small building with a sign "Long & Co., Export Corp". That's where Jean Luze spends his days, hunched over papers. He knows all their secrets. An expert accountant, it's his job and he draws up the figures, his handsome face bent over his ledgers.

Nobody is suspicious of him. He is white. And a white man can only be on Mr Long's side. He listens to them talking. And he learns a lot from them. I am waiting for Jean Luze under the shutters of my windows. It is four o'clock, time for him to come home from work. I am holding the book and the paper-cutter that he gave me yesterday with the words:

"You spoil me, I am spoiling you too. No, it's true, you are a great girl. Look, it's from Mexico. It's a dagger. One of the best. Keep it as a souvenir of me."

"Are you going away?"

"One never knows!"

He is not happy. What can I think of to keep him here? If he goes away, what becomes of me? How can the things around us be changed? For the first time in my life I want to redouble my efforts for a common goal. I would transform this place and make it into a little bit of the paradise which he longs for.

Caroline Ntseliseng Khaketla
1918–

A teacher and the first published woman writer of Lesotho, where she was born and received her education, she played an important role in the movement to create a written literature in tribal languages. Her book of poems, Mantsopa, appeared in 1963 and she is also a published dramatist, writing in the Sotho language.

The White and the Black

While I am gone, white mother, kill the fattened oxen
And feed your dear ones well, prime meat and curds
Overspilling so the dogs too lap the juice,
And still enough is left to throw a surplus
To your close kin across the seas.

And you, black mother, hold on firm –
There is a mystery in things to come
And a fierce look lights behind your eyes.
As the world-ball turns around and round
The fleeing partridge finds the forbidden grain.

Aída Cartagena Portalatín
1918-

Born in Moca, Dominican Republic, she took her degree at the Universidad Autónoma de Santo Domingo and studied music and theory at the School of Plastic Arts in Paris. She collaborated on and later edited La Poesía sorprendida, the literary journal closed down in 1947 by Trujillo's régime. She was also director of the Museo de Antropologia in Santo Domingo. Since the 1940s she has had several books of poetry published, including Mi mundo el mar (1953), Tierra Yania (1981) and En la casa del tiempo (1984); she has also written fiction and criticism and edited the volume Narradores dominicanos (Venzuela: Monte Editores, 1969). In December 1961 she founded the press Brigadas Dominicanas. The following poem appeared in Antología panorámica de la poesía dominicana, ed. Rueda (Santiago: UCMM, 1972), translated by Daisy C. DeFilippis in her article "Indias y Trigueñas No Longer: Contemporary Dominican Women Poets Speak", in Cimarrón: Caribbean Women (Vol. 1, No. 3, Spring 1988).

Black Autumn

elegy
"Echoing drums, echoing on. . ."

I know it was already autumn,
without leaves and a lark's song
I, who cry for the trees, for fish and for doves,
reject the white men of the South,
Those whites with their hatred aimed at black men.

I'd never question their motives
because they would answer
that in Alabama both races can blossom.
But, after the summer of Medgar W. Evers,
came the fall of four black girls.

Louise Bennett

1919–

Born in Kingston, Jamaica, she began to write as a teenager, and has performed her work professionally since 1938. She broadcast on radio and wrote a Sunday column in the Jamaican Gleaner newspaper, collected folklore material all over Jamaica and in 1945 won a British Council scholarship to the Royal Academy of Dramatic Art in London. She produced a Caribbean radio programme for the BBC, worked in repertory theatre in England and performed and broadcast in the USA. Returning to Jamaica in 1955, she was drama specialist in the Jamaica Social Welfare Commission and continued her distinguished *career as "Miss Lou", the persona of her poems. She has toured and lectured internationally and her honours include the MBE, Order of Jamaica and a DLitt (UWI). She has featured in many films, has been much anthologized and has made numerous recordings of her work, which includes* Jamaica Labrish *(1966), in which the following poem appears.*

Back to Africa

Back to Africa, Miss Mattie?
Yuh no know what yuh dah seh?
Yuh haffi come from somewhere fus
Before yuh go back deh!

Me know seh dat yuh great great great
Granma was African,
But, Mattie, doan yuh great great great
Granpa was Englishman?

Den yuh great granmodder fader
By yuh fader side was Jew?
An yuh grampa by yuh modder side
Was Frenchie parlez-vous!

But de balance a yuh family,
Yuh whole generation
Oonoo all bawn dung a Bung Grung[1] –
Oonoo all is Jamaican!

Den is weh yuh gwine, Miss Mattie?
Oh, yuh view de countenance,
An between yuh an de Africans
Is great resemblance!

Ascorden to dat, all dem blue-yeye
Wite American
Who-for great grampa was Englishman
Mus go back a Englan!

Wat a debil of a bump-an-bore,
Rig-jig an palam-pam
Ef de whole worl start fi go back
Whe dem great grampa come from!

---

[1] Burnt Ground – a village in Jamaica, i.e. local soil.

Ef a hard time yuh dah run from
Teck yuh chance! But Mattie, do
Sure a whe yuh come from so yuh got
Somewhe fi come back to!

Go a foreign, seek yuh fortune,
But no tell nobody seh
Yuh dah go fi seek yuh homelan,
For a right deh so yuh deh!

Alice Childress

1920–

B orn in Charleston, South Carolina, she was brought up in Harlem,
New York, where she studied drama and writing while working at
various jobs, including machinist, photo-negative retoucher, gov-
erness, sales woman and insurance agent. She became director of the
American Negro Theater School (1914–52) and was nominated for a
Tony award for her acting role in Anna Lucasta on Broadway in 1944.
A prolific playwright since the 1940s – among her plays are Florence
(1950), Wedding Band (1961) and Wine in the Wilderness (1969) – she
has also written fiction, including A Hero Ain't Nothing But a Sandwich
(1973) and A Short Walk (1979). These extracts are from her book Like
One of the Family: Conversations from a Domestic's Life (1956), in which
Mildred, a Black maid, makes humorous observations to he friend Marge
about the prejudiced ways of her well-heeled employers. Childress has
said, "My writing attempts to interpret the 'ordinary' because they are
not ordinary. Each human is uniquely different. Like snowflakes, the
human pattern is never cast twice. We are uncommonly and marvel-
lously intricate in thought and action, our problems are most complex
and, too often, silently borne."

From

Like One of the Family

LIKE ONE OF THE FAMILY

HI, Marge! I have had me one hectic day.... Well, I had to take out my crystal ball and give Mrs C— a thorough reading. She's the woman that I took over from Naomi after Naomi got married.... Well, she's a pretty nice woman as they go and I have never had too much trouble with her, but from time to time she really gripes me with her ways.

When she has company, for example, she'll holler out to me from the living-room to the kitchen: "Mildred dear! Be sure and eat *both* of those lamb chops for your lunch!" Now you know she wasn't doing a thing but tryin' to prove to the company how "good" and "kind" she was to the servant, because she had told me *already* to eat those chops.

Today she had a girl-friend of hers over to lunch and I was real busy afterwards clearing the things away and she called me over and introduced me to the woman.... Oh, no, Marge! I didn't object to that at all. I greeted the lady and then went back to me work.... And then it started! I could hear her talkin' just as loud . . . and she says to her friend, "We *just* love her! She's *like* one of the family and she *just adores* our little Carol! We don't know *what* we'd do without her! We don't think of her as a servant!" And on and on she went . . . and every time I came in to move a plate off the table both of them would grin at me like chessy cats.

After I couldn't stand it any more, I went in and took the platter off the table and gave 'em both a look that would have frizzled a egg.... Well, you might have heard a pin drop and then they started talkin' about something else.

When the guest leaves, I go in the living-room and says, "Mrs C—, I want to have a talk with you."

"By all means," she says.

I drew up a chair and read her thusly: "Mrs C—, you are a pretty nice person to work for, but I wish you would please stop talkin' about me like I was a *cocker spaniel* or a *poll parrot* or a *kitten.* . . . Now you just sit there and hear me out.

"In the first place, you do not *love* me; you may be fond of me, but that is all.... In the second place, I am *not* just like one of the family at all! The family eats in the dining-room and I eat in the kitchen. Your mama borrows your lace table-cloth for her company and your son entertains his friends in your parlor, your daughter takes her afternoon nap on the living-room couch and the puppy sleeps on your satin spread . . . and whenever your husband gets tired of something you are talkin' about he says, 'Oh, for Pete's sake, forget it. . . .' So you can see I am not *just* like one of the family.

"Now for another thing, I do not *just* adore your little Carol. I think she is a likable child, but she is also fresh and sassy. I know you call it 'uninhibited' and that is the way you want your child to be, but *luckily* my mother taught me some inhibitions or else I would smack little Carol once in a while when she's talkin' to you like you're a dog, but as it is I just laugh it off the way you do because she is *your* child and I am *not* like one of the family.

"Now when you say, 'We don't know *what* we'd do without her' this is a polite lie . . . because I know that if I dropped dead or had a stroke, you would get somebody to replace me.

"You think it is a compliment when you say, 'We don't think of her as a servant. . .' but after I have worked myself into a sweat cleaning the bathroom and the kitchen . . . making the beds . . . cooking the lunch . . . washing the dishes and ironing Carol's pinafores . . . I do not feel like no weekend house guest. I feel like a servant, and in the face of that I have been meaning to ask you for a slight raise which will make me feel much better toward everyone here and make me know my work is appreciated.

"Now I hope you will stop talkin' about me in my presence and that we will get along like a good employer and employee should."

Marge! She was almost speechless but she *apologized* and said she'd talk to her husband about the raise. . . . I knew things were progressing because this evening Carol came in the kitchen and she did not say, "I want some bread and jam!" but she did say, "*Please*, Mildred, will you fix me a slice of bread and jam."

I'm going upstairs, Marge. Just look . . . you done messed up that buttonhole!

THE POCKETBOOK GAME

M ARGE . . . day's work is an education! Well, I mean workin' in different homes you learn much more than if you was steady in one place. . . . I tell you, it really keeps your mind sharp tryin' to watch for what folks will put over on you.

What? . . . No, Marge, I do not want to help shell no beans, but I'd be more than glad to stay and have supper with you, and I'll wash the dishes after. Is that all right?

Who put anything over on who? . . . Oh, yes! It's like this. . . . I been working for Mrs E— one day a week for several months and I notice that she has some peculiar ways. Well, there was only one thing that really bothered me and that was her pocketbook habit. . . . No, not those little novels. . . . I mean her purse – her handbag.

Marge, she's got a big old pocketbook with two long straps on it . . . and whenever I'd go there, she'd be propped up in her chair with her handbag double wrapped tight around her wrist, and from room to room she'd roam with that purse hugged to her bosom. . . . Yes, girl! This happens every time! No, there's nobody there but me and her. . . . Marge, I couldn't say nothin' to her! It's her purse, ain't it? She can hold on to it if she wants to!

I held my peace for months, tryin' to figure out how I'd make my point. . . . Well, bless Bess! *Today was the day!* . . . Please, Marge, keep shellin' the beans so we can eat! I know you're listenin', but you listen with your ears, not your hands. . . . Well, anyway, I was almost ready to go home when she steps in the room hangin' on to her bag as usual and says, "Mildred, will you ask the super to come up and fix the kitchen faucet?" "Yes, Mrs E—," I says, "as soon as I leave." "Oh, no," she says, "he may be gone by then. Please go now." "All right," I says, and out the door I went, still wearin' my Hoover apron.

I just went down the hall and stood there a few minutes . . . and then I rushed back to the door and knocked on it as hard and frantic as I could. She flung the door open sayin', "What's the matter? Did you see the super?" . . . "No," I says, gaspin' hard for breath, "I was almost downstairs when I remembered . . . *I left my pocketbook!*"

With that I dashed in, grabbed my purse and then went down to get the super! Later, when I was leavin' she says real timid-like, "Mildred, I hope that you don't think I distrust you because – " I cut her off real quick. "That's all right, Mrs E—, I understand. 'Cause if I paid anybody as little as you pay me, I'd hold my pocketbook, too!"

Marge, you fool . . . lookout! . . . You gonna drop the beans on the floor!

Nisa

c. 1921–

M arried at twelve, then separated, divorced and widowed, the mother of four children none of whom survived, she lived in a remote corner of Botswana on the northern edge of the Kalahari desert at the time she was interviewed by anthropologist Marjorie Shostak in 1971. Nisa's story is told in Shostak's Nisa: The Life and Words of a !Kung Woman *(1981) and is particularly revealing about relationships between the sexes among the !Kung San people, who are traditionally hunters and gatherers.*

From

Nisa: The Life and Words of a !Kung Woman

L ONG ago, my parents traveled far, to a distant water hole. There we met Old Kantla and his son Tashay, who had also come to live near the well.

One day soon after we had arrived, I went with my friend Nukha to get at the well. That's when Tashay saw me. He thought, "That woman . . . that's the young woman I'm going to marry." He called Nukha over to him and asked, "Nukha, that young woman, that beautiful young woman . . . what is her name?" Nukha told him, "Her name is Nisa." He said, "Mmm . . . that young woman . . . I'm going to tell my mother and father about her. I'm going to ask them if I can marry her."

Nukha came back and we finished filling the water containers. We left and walked the long way back to our village. When Nukha saw my mother, she said, "Nisa and I were getting water and while we were there, some other people came to the well and began filling their water containers. That's when a young man saw Nisa and said he would ask his parents to ask for her in marriage."

I didn't say anything. Because when you are a child and someone wants to marry you, you don't talk. But when they first talked about it, my heart didn't agree. Later, I did agree, just a little; he was, after all, very handsome.

The next night there was a dance at our village. We were already singing and dancing when Tashay and his family came. They joined us and we danced and sang into the night. I was sitting with Nukha when Tashay came over to me. He touched my hand. I said, "What? What is the matter with this person? What is he doing? This person . . . how come I was just sitting here and he came and took hold of me?" Nukha said, "That's your husband . . . your husband has taken hold of you. Is that not so?" I said, "Won't he take you? You're older. Let him marry you." But she said, "He's my uncle. I won't marry my uncle. Anyway, he, himself, wants to marry you."

Later his mother and father went to my mother and father. His father said, "We came here and joined the dance, but now that the dancing is finished, I've come to speak to you, to Gau and Chuko. Give me your child, the one you both gave birth to. Give her to me and I will give her to my son. Yesterday, while he was at the well, he saw your child. When he returned, he told me that in the name of what he felt, I should today ask for her. Then I can give her to him. He said he wants to marry her."

My mother said, "Eh, but I didn't give birth to a woman, I gave birth to a child. She doesn't think about marriage, she just doesn't think about the inside of a marriage hut." Then my father said, "Eh, it's true. The child I gave birth to is still a child. She doesn't think about her marriage hut. When she marries a man, she just drops him. Then she get up, marries another, and drops him, too. She's already refused two men."

My father continued, "There is even another man, Dem, his hut stands over there. He is also asking to marry her. Dem's first wife wants Nisa to sit beside her as a co-wife. She goes out and collects food for Nisa. When she comes back, she gives Nisa food to cook so Nisa can give it to her husband. But when the woman unties the ends of her kaross and leaves it full of food beside Nisa, Nisa throws the food down, ruins it in the sand and kicks the kaross away. When I see that, I say that perhaps Nisa is not yet a woman."

Tashay's father answered, "I have listened to what you have said. That, of course, is the way of a child; it is a child's custom to do that. When she first marries, she stays with her husband for a while, then she refuses him. Then she goes to another. But one day, she stays with one man. That is also a child's way."

They talked about marriage and agreed to it. I was in my aunt's hut and couldn't see them, but I could hear their voices. Later, I went and joined them in my father's hut. When I got there, Tashay was looking at me. I sat down and he just kept looking at me.

When Tashay's mother saw me, she said, "Ohhh! How beautiful this person is! You are certainly a young woman already. Why do they say that you don't want to get married?" Tashay said, "Yes, there she is. I want you to give me the one who just arrived."

The day of the wedding, everyone was there. All of Tashay's friends were sitting around, laughing and laughing. His younger brother said, "Tashay, you're too old. Get out of the way so I can marry her. Give her to me." And his nephew said, "Uncle, you're already old. Now, let *me* marry her." They were all sitting around, talking like that. They all wanted me.

I went to my mother's hut and sat there. I was wearing lots of beads and my hair was completely covered and full with ornaments.

That night there was another dance. We danced, and some people fell asleep and others kept dancing. In the early morning, Tashay and his relatives went back to their camp; we went into our huts to sleep. When morning was late in the sky, they came back. They stayed around and then his parents said, "Because we are only staying a short while – tomorrow, let's start building the marriage hut."

The next day they started. There were lots of people there – Tashay's mother, my mother, and my aunt worked on the hut; everyone else sat around, talking. Late in the day, the young men went and brought Tashay to the finished hut. They set him down beside it and stayed there with him, sitting around the fire.

I was still at my mother's hut. I heard them tell two of my friends to go and bring me to the hut. I thought, "Oohh ... I'll run away." When they came for me, they couldn't find me. They said, "Where did Nisa go? Did she run away? It's getting dark. Doesn't she know that things may bite and kill her?" My father said, "Go tell Nisa that if this is what she's going to do, I'll hit her and she won't run away again. What made her want to run away, anyway?"

I was already far off in the bush. They came looking for me. I heard them calling, "Nisa ... Nisa ..." I sat down at the base of a tree. Then I heard Nukha, "Nisa ... Nisao ... my friend ... a hyena's out there ... things will bite and kill you ... come back ... Nisa ... Nisao ..."

When Nukha finally saw me, I started to run. She ran after me, chasing me and finally caught me. She called out to the others, "Hey! Nisa's here! Everyone, come! Help me! Take Nisa, she's here!"

They came and brought me back. Then they laid me down inside the hut. I cried and cried. People told me, "A man is not something that kills you; he is someone who marries you, who becomes like your father or your older brother. He kills animals and gives you things to eat. Even tomorrow, while you are crying, Tashay may kill an animal. But when he returns, he won't give you any meat; only he will eat. Beads, too. He will get beads but he won't give them to you. Why are you so afraid of your husband and what are you crying about?"

I listened and was quiet. Later, we went to sleep. Tashay lay down beside the opening of the hut, near the fire, and I lay down inside; he thought I might try and run away again. He covered himself with a blanket and slept.

While it was dark, I woke up. I sat up. I thought, "How am I going to jump over him? How can I get out and go to mother's hut to sleep beside her?" I looked at him sleeping. Then came other thoughts, other thoughts in the middle of the night, "Eh . . . this person has just married me . . ." and I lay down again. But I kept thinking, "Why did people give me this man in marriage? The older people say he is a good person, yet . . ."

I lay there and didn't move. The rain came beating down. It fell steadily and kept falling. Finally, I slept. Much later dawn broke.

In the morning, Tashay got up and sat by the fire. I was so frightened I just lay there, waiting for him to leave. When he went to urinate, I went and sat down inside my mother's hut.

That day, all his relatives came to our new hut – his mother, his father, his brothers . . . everyone! They all came. They said, "Go tell Nisa she should come and her in-laws will put the marriage oil on her. Can you see her sitting over there? Why isn't she coming so we can put the oil on her in her new hut?"

I refused to go. They kept calling for me until finally, my older brother said, "Uhn uhn. Nisa, if you act like this, I'll hit you. Now, get up and go over there. Sit over there so they can put the oil on you."

I still refused and just sat there. My older brother grabbed a switch from a nearby tree and started coming toward me. I got up. I was afraid. I followed him to where the others were sitting. Tashay's mother rubbed the oil on me and my aunt rubbed it on Tashay.

Then they left and it was just Tashay and me.

We began to live together, but I ran away, again and again. A part of my heart kept thinking, "How come I'm a child and have taken another husband?"

One night, I ran away and slept in the bush, the far away bush. We had been lying together inside the hut, sleeping. But I woke up and quietly tiptoed around his feet and then, very quickly, ran off. I went far, very far, past the mongongo groves near where we were living. It was very dark and I had no fire. I lay down beside the base of a tree and slept.

Dawn broke. People started to look for me and then saw my tracks. They followed them past the mongongo groves and came to where I had slept that night. But I had already left and was digging sha roots in the shade of some trees far away. They came closer. Nukha rushed ahead and, following my tracks, found me. She said that she had come alone looking for me and that the others were elsewhere. She said that we should stay together and dig roots together. I thanked her and told her she was a good friend.

We dug sha roots, and after a while she said, "Let's sit in the shade of that tree. After we rest awhile, we'll dig more roots. I'll stay with you the rest of the day, but when the sun is late in the sky, I'll leave you to return to the village. You can stay alone in the bush again. Tomorrow, I'll roast some of the roots and come back and give them to you to eat." I praised her, "My friend! You are very kind. But when you return to the village, don't tell them you saw me."

We sat in the shade together, resting. Then I looked around and saw the others approaching. I said, "Nukha, people are coming! You lied to me. You said they were in the village, but they're already here. I can't leave now. I'll just have to sit here with you."

The others found us sitting in the shade, full with the sha roots we had dug. They sat down with us. They were many – my older brother, my father, and Tashay. My father said, "What's the matter with you, leaving in the middle of the night like that, running away and sleeping among things of the night? If a lion had seen you, it would have killed you. Or a hyena. Or wild dogs. Any one of these would have killed you. What's the matter with you? Who is responsible for this? You are. You're the one trying to kill yourself."

I said, "Yes, if I want to sleep among the things of the night, what am I taking with me that belongs to any of you? I didn't take anything. I just left and slept by myself. Even if my heart desired it right now, I'd go as far as I wanted. Because that *is* what I want to do, to go far away. If I go back and stay with you, you'll just find me another husband. But everything that I am at this moment refuses one."

My older brother said, "Why should a husband be refused? Isn't a husband like a father? He helps you live and he gives you food. If you refuse to marry, where do you think you'll find foot to eat?" I cried, "As I am now, if you take me and bring me back to the village, I will take a poison arrow and kill myself. I don't want to be married!"

My older brother answered, "If you say you are going to stick yourself with a poison arrow, then I'll beat you until you understand what a poison arrow is and what you think you are going to do with it. You're insulting your very self. You are a person, a woman, and you aren't alive to talk like that; you are alive to play and to be happy."

He continued, "Look at your friends, all of them are married. Even Nukha, who is sitting with you, has taken herself in marriage. Why don't you think about how you and Nukha will be married and have homes? Why should your friend have a home and not you?"

I said, "This friend of mine may have taken a husband, but she is certainly older than I am. She is already a grown woman. But me, I'm a child and don't know what I would do with a husband."

He said, "Mm ... put the roots in your kaross and let's go, because the person who sits here *is* your husband and he isn't anyone else's. He is the man we gave you. You will grow up with him, lie down with him, and give birth to children with him."

We all got up and returned to the village. I didn't go to my hut but went to my mother's hut, put down the sha roots, and stayed there. Tashay went and sat by our hut. After a while he called to me, "Nisa ... Nisa ..." I thought, "What does he want?" and went over to him. He gave me some roots he had dug. I took a few and gave them to my mother; I took the others and went back to our hut and stayed there. In the late afternoon, when dusk was falling and the red sky began to stand, I started roasting food by the fire outside our hut. I took the food out of the coals and set it aside. Then I took some and gave it to Tashay. When they had cooled, we ate them – together.

Noni (Nontando) Jabavu

c. 1921–

S*he was born in Cape Province, South Africa, into a Xhosa family of intellectuals. At the age of fourteen she went to England in the care of English friends and continued her education there until 1939, studying at London's Royal Academy of Music. She has written two illuminating autobiographical novels, and she said in an author's note in the first (*Drawn in Colour: African Contrasts, *1960): "I belong to two worlds with two loyalties; South Africa where I was born and England where I was educated." When the Second World War broke out, she gave up studies as a film technician and trained to become a semi-skilled engineer and oxyacetylene welder, working on bomber engine parts. After the war she stayed in London, becoming a feature writer and television personality, but paying long visits to South Africa until her marriage to the English film director Michael Cadbury Crosfield broke the South African miscegenation laws. Thereafter she also travelled and lived in Mozambique, Uganda and Zimbabwe.* The Ochre People: Scenes from a South African Life *(1963) is in three sections, each dealing with her observations of a different geographical region; this extract is from the third part, "Johannesburg".*

From

The Ochre People

CHAPTER XVI

A JOURNEY not unlike other South African train journeys that I have described elsewhere, and at last we were on the final lap to the big city, gathering speed across the High Veld – vast, enormous bareness. The sight of these particular plains did not reassure. They were not like those of the Transkei when my long-distance bus had crossed into them over the Kei River. These seemed of a foreign country, huge stretches inhabited by total strangers; no locality – as through stretches in Ciskei and Transkei – where I could think: "Such and such a family, friends, live here." It seemed harsh, hostile, and made you feel ill at ease. The emptiness began to give way to the occasional Boer small town, *dorp*: bungalows with verandas crouched on straggly streets, squat Dutch Reformed Church. The *dorps* in turn began to run into one another and to spread into suburbs. Looking out of the window as we raced past I thought them dreary, featureless. But then a willow tree would stand out against the skyline, strikingly tall here in the Transvaal, far bigger than the ones I was accustomed to in the Eastern Cape. I was filled by a mounting nostalgia for "the Cape Colony" as people even in the Transkei called my part of the country, despite their region having for so long been incorporated into the Cape Province. Northerners here too called it that.

The Border was of course in the front of my mind, the buffer state with its olden fortifications – Forts: Wellington, Beresford, Murray, White, to say nothing of Fort Hare or Fort Cox, Fort Beaufort, our localized stamping-grounds. Their very names took me back to those conflicts the uncles had talked about in the car, when black and white "Cattle-keeping tribes" had wrestled over pastures and living room; of the equivocal role that "the second white tribe" had played when dominant; and of its policies of expediency. These had doubled back on the British. Now they were themselves dominated by Transvaal Boers. Even their splendid English language was demoted to a secondary status. How any of my relations could bear to live here was a mystery. The more I looked at their adoptive territory the more I missed the kind of veld I was used to – undulating, contoured, not dead flat like the land I was now crossing. I missed my kind of mountains, their folds, the *kloofs* covered with dark green forests, their crowns of majestic granite crags. But I reproached myself for being parochial, for in fact I loved South Africa's variety and vastness.

As the suburbs grew denser, my uneasiness deepened. I had seldom been to Johannesburg and this was the third visit in my whole life. The first had been when I was about nine years old. My mother had brought me and my tiny sister – my brother not quite born – on a prolonged visit to a suburb called West Rand, where she organized some Women's Clubs, and was also visiting her youngest sister, my aunt Linda, whose husband had been drowned when fording a river on horseback and overtaken midway by one of those outbreaks of sudden storm and flood during a drought – the sort my Uncle Rosebery had been so wary of. She had a baby girl. We stayed for what seemed years but may have been perhaps three months, with a family into which Aunt Linda afterwards married. Possibly that was the purpose of my mother's trip, I never knew, only that I had never remembered the visit with pleasure but with deep disquiet. For our hosts lived in a house that was on the edge of a native location and I was forbidden to leave their yard and go into the location as I longed to do and play with the children. I could see them swarming in its streets all day, never apparently going to school while I had to submit to morning lessons from my mother. My baby sister's nurse who came with us from the Cape and watched that I should not escape, told me of unnamable terrors that went on inside Jo'burg locations; of dirt, disease, robbers and gangsters, squalor, and of "*the language*" that I would pick up. The grown-ups confirmed her proscription, probably initiated it; it seemed everybody was frightened of the very word "location, *elokishini*", and I trembled, dreading it yet wanting to go – for I had no playmates. Occasionally the younger children of my eldest aunt (to whom I was now travelling) were brought from Klipspruit near Nancefield where they lived before moving to their present home at Pimville. They came miles in the train, and had to be shepherded home again before dark "because of the terrors of the location". When I saw my mother begin to pack and was told we were going home, my relief was immense. The thought of returning home to "the Colony" was heaven, idyllic – back to grass, veld, mountains. No more dirt, disease, fear of robbers. No more barred windows or locked doors. And I would be allowed to wander about freely again with my friends.

My second trip to Johannesburg had been last year to my Big Mother. I had been unaccompanied, and petrified – this time with cause: those Jo'burg gangsters, of whom everyone had gone in dread, had finally moved into *my* family's life far off in the Cape when they murdered my only brother up here studying at the University. I had had to come to my aunt because she was unable to travel south on that occasion because of her age and health.

The reason I was making this third visit was again because of her – would I *ever* come to this place otherwise? I sat tight in my seat realizing, and admitting, that this time, too, I was scared. My trip had been preceded, like last year's, by an avalanche of letters from my aunt, she and my uncle at Tsolo writing back and forth arranging which train I was to catch, times of connections at junctions, so that I should be met at Park Station by one or other of her daughters and shepherded from the heart of the city to where they lived eighteen miles out. All my cousins worked and were not able to take time off too easily. The arrangements therefore were intricate, everyone wanting to be sure that none of them should miscarry and leave me high and dry, alone and unprotected. In the end letters were followed by telegrams, in turn followed by others confirming and acknowledging. The whole thing was beset with anxieties and they welled up in me now that I was nearly there. Suppose something went wrong at the last moment and nobody came to Park Station, I asked myself gazing at the Rand, the string of towns that made up greater Johannesburg. I looked at the dumps beside the gold mines – those huge hills of white dust dredged up from six thousand feet below and more. I saw cranes and derricks with wheels in the air, gaunt mining machinery, cables, rusty fences plastered with bill boards – all of it a jumble amid a conglomeration of factories cheek by jowl with bungalows and double-storeyed houses that gave on to tarred roads, street lamps, blue-gum trees, motor cars, lorries, bicycles, people of different races hurrying. Where in this hideous mess would I go if my cousins did not turn up?

Fellow passengers began to stir and walk up and down the corridor and sort out baggage.

Of course I had the addresses of many families on the Rand; but I would have to hire a car, not knowing the local trains and being an absolute fool about arranging any detail in my own travels. But the thought of a cab was terrifying. We all knew down in the Cape that for a green-horn to hail an unknown taxi in Johannesburg was suicide; you would be robbed, probably knifed, your body abandoned on the veld or in some location back-yard. I turned the problem over in my mind. How had my young brother adapted himself and managed to live, let alone study in such surroundings? He had had difficulty I knew, and could understand, looking at the metropolitan spread. Towards the end of his course he had been afflicted by bouts of what was diagnosed as narcolepsy, a condition of the nerves of which we had never heard until then. It made him drop off to sleep anywhere, often during lecturers or at sports, even at times when driving his motor car. In my case just to sit and look at Johannesburg was making me wish I could fall asleep, and wake up to see Middledrift again or Tsolo.

Voices around began to rise, swell into a hubbub: Sesutho, Xhosa, Sechuana, Zulu, and mostly Afrikaans. The people were becoming excited, the journey almost over. They pointed out landmarks to one another with animation. I felt out of it, not interested. The train drew into Park Station. My heart began to pound. I went into the corridor and leaned out of a window to scan the faces of the crowd on the platforms, saw scores, black, white, brown, lifted up, preoccupied, they in turn scanning ours as the train passed. I noticed that even Africans were unsmiling with dour expressions. They were not passing the time of day by joking with those standing next to them as people did at country stations. This was the cold anonymity of the Golden City, *eGoli, eRautini*; I had arrived. The train slowed right down. I became absolutely filled with terror. Then I saw a woman wave to me. She was in a thick belted tweed coat, wore a sports felt hat and under its level brim I saw a preoccupied light brown face break into a rapturous smile when our eyes met and she shouted out my name – it was my cousin *Sis'* Tandiswa and I thanked God.

She stepped forward and walked alongside, her arm lifted to my window to try and hold my hand as I reached down. But she fell behind, having to dodge carrier carts and mounds of luggage. At last the train ground to a standstill. Passengers flung corridor doors open, leapt out shouting, joyful, laughing, and joined their friends. I too grabbed my case and was on the platform embracing my cousin, overwhelmed by the feeling of having been rescued from danger. I flung my arms around her and clung until after a while she held me off and looked down at my face, her brows knitted quizzically. Then she hugged me again and finally said, smiling and pretending to scold, "*Now*, child, are you *reassured?*"

She was the second oldest of my known cousins on both sides, the eldest of my aunt's four daughters, the second born, the *mazibulo* being an older brother. She had been named after my mother. I called her "*Sisi*" rather than "*Sis'* Tandiswa" because to pronounce that name made me feel somewhat uncomfortable. But I did sometimes called her "*Sis'* Tandi". The diminutive did not embarrass. I only realized later that this was because it had never been used for my mother. She was so much my senior that I did not know her exact age, and taller than me, buxom, and unmarried like all this particular family except for one. *Sis'* Tandi taught in a primary school, loved teaching. I knew that it was out of devotion to "the blood", that she had freed herself to come, instructed of course by "our" mother who in her old age now stayed in her home, never leaving it; a queen-bee in her hive, arranging, planning. The last time Big Mother had travelled was when my mother died and she was driven down to the Colony by my brother in his little English car. He brought a friend, a fellow medical student, Caleb Mokhesi, who was no relation but whom the big people at home at once treated as one, "the only way to thank him sufficiently for the service he had rendered us". He had interrupted his work to act as my brother's co-driver over the huge distance which had to be covered practically non-stop, my mother's death had been so unexpected. And I would never forget the picture Big Mother made when the trio arrived.

Our house was thronged with relations, friends, mourners, and we all stood and watched the small round bundle of elderly womanhood, black satin turban wound tightly like a toque round her head, wearing spectacles, a shawl over her coat, dressed entirely in black; and absolutely covered with dust, even to the crow's feet at her eyes. Nor would I forget my impression of the two young men as they skipped out from the front of the car to help her out before any of us could move. She was stiff after the journey, and blinked in the sunlight. My father, already tense, became excited and shouted with joy, relief "because the sons of the house had safely delivered their precious cargo"; while her brothers Cecil and Tennyson murmured "*Wafika uSis'* Daisy". Her presence comforted the household. She was so much my elders' senior that even *their* generation felt as if a protectress had come. Neither would I forget how she had afterwards sat, as if on a throne in our sitting-room or under the wintry leafless vine on the veranda and taken charge, delegating the duties that had to be performed. The reunion with *Sis'* Tandi in Johannesburg provoked such thoughts all over again and they affected me; her mother stood for much that had gone, was going, for ever. And my cousin was now teasing me, by way of dispelling some of the tensions. We both knew that the old lady was going to speak with me about these matters, about the people we had shared and loved, and of the diminishing number who were still here – some of whom (it had to be faced because of the unique situation of my living so far away) it was probable that I would not meet again.

"*Kulungile* Jili, let us go," she said, and added on glancing down at our feet, "Where is your luggage?" I pointed at the suitcase and small hold-all for books and overnight things.

"Is this all? Good gracious! And I ordered the big taxi from our man at Pimville, imagining you would have so much since you have travelled so far and for so long."

We looked at each other and smiled. She had forgotten about the aeroplane weight limits. We were not very well acquainted because of the gap in age. My intimates were her two youngest sisters. They had often stayed with us in the Cape when I was a child: Ntombizodwa ("Daughters Only") she was slightly older than me, and Constance Nontutuzelo ("Comforter"). She was younger and had been born soon after their father died; the reason for her second name. 'Zodwa was a trained nurse and worked in a hospital at Benoni, one of the towns along the Rand. *Sis'* Nora, the married one, lived with her husband and children at Pimville not far from home. Their brother was a mine clerk and lived at his work in bachelor quarters. At the house at Pimville my aunt had her eldest and youngest with her, and 'Zodwa when off duty.

The distance between the eldest and myself was modified by my aunt's industry as a letter writer – Victorian journalist background perhaps transmuting itself in old age, and because she was Big Mother to many scattered nephews and nieces. When each of us had lost one or both parents over the years, she filled their places in our lives at however long range, wrote regular letters to us individually; none of those futile round robin family letters that some overseas dynasties engage in that turn out to have been meaningless when the writers met in the flesh. Her especial "affection" was my cousin Boniswa, her mother (Aunt Linda whom we had visited at West Rand) having died soon after her second marriage. *Mam'omKhulu* was the anchor of all those linked through the Makiwane navel. She seemed to be with us as my cousin grasped my suitcase and led me through the "Non-European" Exit from the station and out to the "Non-European Taxi Rank".

Sis' Tandi kept looking round over her shoulder to tease me. "How are the palpitations, Ntando? Still bad? I could feel your heart – my, was it pumping. *Lunjan' uvalo!* You're really scared of Jo'burg, eh? You people from *eKoloni* are all the same, your faces like an open book; you act as though you are at the entrance of a lions' den when you arrive at this poor old city of ours!"

We climbed into the cab, a very elderly American saloon, its driver welcoming her back. He drove us through the city. I had eyes for very little. *Sis'* Tandi pointed out landmarks, historical monuments, read out the names of famous streets. None of them made an impression, they glanced off my closed mind. To this day it is as a clean slate about Johannesburg, as if I have never been there. The atmosphere hampered my reactions; and my fear of the violence up there blots out memory almost of anything I glimpsed on arriving or leaving. I never wanted to go up to town when my cousins went shopping and offered to take me sightseeing. Only when the cab had driven into their location called Pimville *Township*, and approached her house did my nervousness begin to subside. This was a house I knew, where I had people.

It was in Timana Street. They had lived in it for over twenty years and were themselves something of a landmark; everybody seemed to know them. I saw people on the road or in haggard doorways greet my cousin as we drove by in bottom gear because of the usual un-made up condition of township roads. Voices hailed her and the driver; he too was a local landmark. I began to feel I was among friends.

Yet the sight of the friends did not yet reassure altogether. Their houses looked dreadful from the outside – to me they could be gangsters' and lions' dens, thieves' kitchens. As for the road we were grinding and bumping along on! Potholes, refuse, dirt, disease, squalor – and sure enough, the "*language*" too, for I heard harsh-sounding words above the greetings directed at my companions, and my nurse's warnings of long ago crowded back into my mind. Probably I was only mishearing unfamiliar accents. Later, on going into some of these houses I found I had to amend my first impressions. But for the moment I was wrestling with fears of the unknown. *Sis'* Tandi noticed signs of this and said, while acknowledging greetings, "Believe me, you would get used to things if you lived here, Nontando." I shivered with a sudden wave of relief that this visit was to be short and cried, "Never!" but immediately felt stricken by my disloyalty and could not speak.

"Oh, yes, you would," she said hurriedly leaning forward to look out of the window, adding in a whisper, "One must be careful not to cut people. They know why I am home today and not at school. Greet them, Ntando, they are looking out for you." She was in the act of raising her hand to a woman on the wayside (where there should have been a pavement but I saw only an open drain), so I did the same. The woman smiled, renewed her waving and shouted, "*Teacheress! Uzenaye uMa Jili*, you have brought your relation? She is welcome – yet such a *girl*, where is the grown woman and mother you spoke of? Wonder of wonders" (this with a burst of laughter, her head now at the window for the driver had slowed right down for her). "Salute MaGambu for us please, Teacheress, on the lovely day of the coming of her late one's children, '*nonwabe torwana*, be happy together!'"

Again I was thankful for the conversation that forbids you to attempt an answer. It seemed incredible that in the midst of such squalor, conditions so purgatorial, antipathetic to life, people could be fine. At least at Middledrift and at Tsolo everything was on their side – the peace, the grandeurs of the scene, the environment to which they could feel they belonged. Did not those settings enable people to share their life's sacraments and pleasures? And what in heaven's name, in these other surroundings could prompt the spirit? As the woman's voice rang out, her face alive and glad, I began to look at the location with shifting emotion. "Began" only; for I was still repelled as last year on arrival; and filled with a disgust of which I was ashamed because I knew well enough that the surroundings were not of my relations' choosing, nor of friends and neighbours such as this woman.

Sis' Tandi went on prompting me as the taxi started up again, "I tell you, Ntando, you would get used to it. There are *people* living here among thieves and gangsters, *people* like back home in your beloved Colony. Why, before your brother was shot, he once told my mother of something that happened when he was coming down in the train from town one afternoon to visit her. It was what decided her to write and advise your parents, you know, to buy him a car, to use while he was a student up here." I hadn't known.

"That train was suddenly boarded by robbers, *otsotsi*, as so often of course; one of the facts of life. They held up each passenger with a revolver, made them hand over their wages, wallets. But one of them stopped his mate who was just starting on your brother and shouted in Afrikaans, '*Loes hom! Loes hom, man. Hy es Professor Jabavu's se sien* [Leave him – Professor Jabavu's son].' You see? Even some of the robber savages are people; twisted but not to be dismissed; perhaps even to be forgiven for 'They know not what they do' – Do not be afraid."

I admired her serenity but was not yet able to envy it.

So was my aunt serene, watching us arrive and dismount from the taxi when it stopped beyond her fence. She was at the front door, standing on the raised entrance which I noticed with surprise was smeared with cattle dung. She looked smaller than I had remembered from last year; and rounder, compact in warm clothes, knitted jersey, cardigan. And about her head, the tight widow's toque that she always wore. This time she leaned on a man's walking-stick, a new feature and to see it gave me a pang, realizing that the passage of a year at her age was not what it was at mine and my cousin's. I came level with her and she put out both arms, the walking-stick in one hand and now lifted in the air above my shoulder. Her eyes, behind the tortoise-shell rims of her spectacles glistened. The sight unnerved me although I expected it.

She let go in order to fumble and pull out a white handkerchief from an old-fashioned style of pocket at her waist. It had been a tense moment and I looked away and around me. Beyond the fence in the street, my cousin was paying off the driver. He had climbed out of his cab and now lifted his battered hat to my aunt, burly figure framed by a square building whose plaster was peeling away in patches – a Native Separatist Church of some sort, with the poverty-stricken houses and shacks huddled close to it confronting your eyes on all sides. "God keep you, Gambu," the man said and wished us a happy reunion. My aunt finished using her handkerchief and acknowledged his words with the grace one was accustomed to hear from old people, and he stepped into the car and started up his engine ready to go on down the street. This too was like the others, unmade up, pot-holed, and bounded by the same appalling squalor; yet men and women were in it, about their business in apparent unconcern; and ragged children were at play, darting out from the low doorways; teeming life – some quite young little girls had tinier tots slung on hips or tied to backs but managed to play hopscotch. To look at my aunt's carefully tended pocket of front garden forced me to more adjustments. A staggering spectacle in such a scene; the contrast with its surroundings seemed more striking than when I had come before. Presumably I had been numbed because of the reason for that year's visit. When the taxi finally pulled away, I cried out, "*Man'omkhulu*, how do you *sinda* this entrance, where is the kraal? Who does it for you?" I stopped, surprised to hear my aunt break into a gentle laugh. She said, to herself more than to me, "*Kwek!* this child!" then raised her voice, "Do you hear, Tandiswa? This person is truly fresh from her father. It is he who greets people, talks to them all the time not missing an item about their condition." Her face was radiant now as if the pain of the first sight of me was giving way to the pleasures of thinking about those of whom I reminded her.

"'Where's the kraal'? *Kaloku* Ntando, even here *e*Goli, people try to maintain an animal or two to milk for their young children. What I do is to beg them for the dung. This smearing is the work of a girl whose parents send her round from time to time 'to beautify their former teacher's home' – mine. Does she not do it exactly like a country girl? Of course we ought not to keep cattle in the location, Verwoerd forbids it. It has always been forbidden; even under sly Smuts. But since the location is uncared for, the municipality surrounding it with the open sewage farms that serve the European suburbs and are disgorged here, since our roads are never made up, what difference in hygiene does the presence of a cow or two make? And people's children must eat. Besides, it is good for these town-bred youngsters to know that milk does not come out of tins only, condensed. And since some of them never *go* to the country, *emaXhoseni*, or Basutoland, Portuguese East or wherever their people came from, would they ever *know* cattle except from hearsay if they did not see them in the location? We are lawbreakers, sinners, and you are looking at your mother who 'is an accessory after the fact', I suppose."

We laughed and moved indoors already launched on talk about the facts of life in urban areas. All the same the house was reminiscent of both my home at Middledrift and my uncle's for intangible reasons, one of them because it felt lived in; the family had been long established. It was well built, as "our" others were; indeed seemed more so, after the sight of the others around it. My aunt lived in the same style as we in the country. She liked stained and polished floors, liked covering them with rugs that had been used over the years, liked the same kind of furniture, sofas, rocking-chairs, roll-top desks, things that seemed to have been always with us while other families changed and renewed their possessions every time a catalogue arrived from the stores in the nearest big towns. I was glad now that my elders were the conservative type, although I had not been as a child on seeing other people's houses gleaming with smart new things and chromium fittings. Here at my aunt's too, another link with home and not so good – there was no electricity or running water. Although they were in town, such amenities were lacking for a reason which, as usual, we recapitulated as we ambled through the house – the one about "Natives" being under the perpetual threat of being "moved on" as "white" suburbs spread themselves. With these plans in the air, broadcast, published daily, would it not be "folly" as the authorities put it, for municipalities to spend money on services to locations that were only temporarily where they were? Government policy being what it was, first to discourage and now to forbid permanent life in towns for the blacks who have to work in them, continued the survival of migratory shacks that people put up, desperate for somewhere to live. It cast a blight on municipalities like Johannesburg, which often wanted to act.

"Jo'burg had a good record, as municipalities go," I heard my aunt say – and gasped, incredulous after what I had seen outside. But she insisted on being fair, in her elderly way, and on reminding me of the city's industrialists, businessmen, chambers of commerce: that these did not all share the Boer Government's dedication to the idea of migrant labour. Some of them spoke about the *benefit* to the whole country of the existence of a settled working class with roots and belongings in the cities.

We were automatically talking about these things because the noises from the over-crowded location wafted into the house and would not let you forget. Or at any rate, would not so soon let me, I should say. We walked along the passage, my cousin and I regulating our speed to my aunt's steps, her walking-stick punctuating our remarks and interrupting the glances I was casting into the rooms on either side. They, I saw, had not changed since my last visit, and looked orderly, secure, as always, amid the surrounding insecurity. Our conversation was a kind of small talk about familiar things that acted as a tranquillizer, for we were excited; moved by the ritual of being together again, by the different levels on which we were being reunited, to say nothing of the personal reason for my being here.

So we talked about the unrest that had gripped "the country", meaning our people, the tensions risen higher in the last two years because here in Johannesburg, Sophiatown, the location closest to the city, White "Western Area" and serviced with water, drainage, electricity, was being demolished and its inhabitants "moved from the European Ethnic Group Area". We talked about those belonging to us or close, who were in the front line of this phase of our country's social strife. My brother's digs had been at Sophiatown – after a prolonged effort on his part to get as near to the University in town (at Milner Park) as possible. Sophiatown provided that proximity. I had been taken last year to see where he had lived, in Toby Street, which afterwards made history because its houses were the first to be destroyed. It was on the edge of the "Buffer Zone", a strip of unoccupied grass thirty yards wide maintained in order to separate whites in their suburb called Westdene from the blacks in theirs called Sophiatown.

Newspapers where I happened to be at the time in Italy showed pictures of the destruction, of the inhabitants watching the bulldozers work while soldiers and Saracen tanks imported from Britain stood by. Armed white policemen scanned the evicted Africans whose belongings were in sad bundles on the ground waiting to be transported by military lorries. In one of his last letters my brother (not a prolific correspondent) had described what he had seen:

"*Sisi*, you should have been here. The Boers' (policemen's) pale blue eyes were glinting steelier than ever that day. Their fingers tickled the triggers of revolvers and the hands clenched and unclenched the handles of those *sjambok* (leather) whips until the knuckles were white."

And my aunt now murmured of him, "At the end of that scene our young son was translated, in God's wisdom, to spare his sensitive soul. He did not see the acts that were to follow in this play." But we had friends who had been settled citizens of "Sophia" for decades – Dr Xuma and his American wife; Mrs Motsieloa; many others, with homes better appointed, more elegant than any of ours. They were among those awaiting their turn in the great "removal of Natives". They had become property owners before racial demarcations, and had lived in pleasant spaces; but over the years became crowded by later arrivals who had nowhere to live and therefore put up the shacks, creating slums. Our friends' houses were to be destroyed too, which seemed to us extraordinary. And their titles to freeholds were to be ended – a decree that alarmed the country; for black freehold owners were a tiny number, less than one per cent in all South Africa. You have to use a magnifying-glass to see the statistic on a graph. It was the evolution of these "property-owning natives" whose existence had provoked the Group Areas Act. Under Verwoerd the Government looked on their enterprise as a threat to white people; and at the new "Native" Areas on the Rand to which they were being removed, Africans would be offered a thirty-year lease on Government property, on certain conditions. The property consisted of rows of structures recently built, miles from the city. They were small houses, uniform in type, described as "simple and rectangular, self-contained, asbestos roofed, with brick walls, divided inside with rough-plastered partitions; fitted with a front and a back door and windows, a hole in the roof to take a coal-stove chimney; no other fittings; running water outside next to the lavatory; also a drain under the tap." So ran the official Press hand-out, evidently sincerely calculated to make it sound delightful. It also announced that the Native Areas would be commanded by white superintendents. We all knew that it was no mere slum clearance.

Thoughts about it were therefore constantly in our minds. *Sis'* Tandi showed me the bedroom I was to share with my age-mate, cousin Nontutuzelo. I was impatient for her to come home from her job. She taught in a school too, in the location. I unpacked, washed and changed, hung my things in the wardrobe where she had made room for me. I sorted out the presents and mementoes that I had brought for everyone and for the house. *Sis'* Tandi reappeared, took me to the little sitting-room at the front where my aunt was waiting. I was still feeling unnerved because of the unfamiliar location sounds beyond the house. As we walked in to my aunt, she looked up at me keenly, and then told my cousin to close the front door.

"This person-of-yours is still half-ears outside," and they both smiled – which I knew concealed their concern. And to me she said, pointing her stick at an armchair next to hers, "It is early, but we will sit here in the *voorhuis*." She did not notice my smile at her Transvaal use of the Afrikaans; in the Cape none of us called the sitting-room that: for some extraordinary reason, when we did borrow a word for it, we young ones said *eroomini* and I could never fathom why it was not *esitting-roomini*. And more puzzling still, why did we refer to "borrow" a *Xhosa* word (for this particular room) which was simply the locative for "house"? And why never *eroomini* for example for *bed*room but ekamer*ini* from the Afrikaans? I worked out the puzzles later. My aunt was speaking. "We will sit here in the *voorhuis* while your cousin prepares: for you must give me the news of your Uncle Cecil, of MaDholomo there at home, and of your father."

We were to sit for many hours talking together in that little *voorhuis* with Makiwane and Majombozi portraits gazing down from its walls; and to the accompaniment of the noises in the street between us and the rickety Separatist Church.

Naomi Long Madgett
1923–

Born in Virginia, she spent part of her childhood in New Jersey, attended high school in St Louis and studied at Virginia State College. She went to New York University in 1946 and has an MA from Wayne State University. In 1965 she was the first recipient of the $10,000 Mott Fellowship in English at Oakland University. A mother

*of three, she has been a journalist and teacher and is professor of English
at Eastern Michigan University. Since 1974 she has been publisher and
associate editor at Lotus Press in Detroit. Her poetry collections include*
Pink Ladies in the Afternoon *(1972) and* Exits and Entrances *(1978).*

New Day

*"Keep a-inchin' along, keep a-inchin' along,
Jesus'll come bye an' bye.
Keep a-inchin' along like a po' inchworm,
Jesus'll come bye an' bye."*
                              (Negro Spiritual)

She coaxes her fat in front of her
like a loaded market basket with defective wheels.
Then she pursues it, slowly catches up, and
the cycle begins again.
Every step is a hardship and a triumph.

As she inches her way along in my direction
I sense the stretching and drawings of
her heavy years. I feel the thunderous
effort of her movement reverberating through
a wilderness of multiple betrayals.
As gently as I can, I say, "Good morning, Sister,"
as we come face to face, and wonder
if she can understand what I am saying.

Black Woman

My hair is springy like the forest grasses
that cushion the feet of squirrels –
crinkled and blown in a south breeze
like the small leaves of native bushes.

My black eyes are coals burning
like a low, full jungle moon
through the darkness of my being.
In a clear pool I see my face,
know my knowing.

My hands move pianissimo
over the music of the night:
gentle birds fluttering through leaves and grasses
they have not always loved,
nesting, finding home.

Where are my lovers?
Where are my tall, my lovely princes
dancing in slow grace
toward knowledge of my beauty?
Where
are my beautiful
black men?

Mari E. Evans

1923–

*B*orn *in Ohio, she studied at the University of Toledo. She has been a university professor, producer-director-writer of a television series, a civil servant, musician, choir director, church organist and director of adult programme promotion at an Indianapolis YMCA. She is a much anthologized poet, and has written theatre pieces and children's literature; her poetry collections include* Where Is All the Music *(1968),* I Am a Black Woman *(1970) and* Nightstar 1973–1978 *(1981). In addition she is editor of an invaluable critical work,* Black Women Writers *(1984). She says of her own work: "If there are those outside the Black experience who hear the music and can catch the beat, that is serendipity; I have no objections. But when I write, I write according to the title of poet Margaret Walker's classic: 'for my people'."*

I Am a Black Woman

I am a black woman
the music of my song
some sweet arpeggio of tears
is written in a minor key
and I
can be heard humming in the night
Can be heard
                    humming
in the night

I saw my mate leap screaming to the sea
and I/with these hands/cupped the lifebreath
from my issue in the canebrake
I lost Nat's swinging body in a rain of tears
and heard my son scream all the way from Anzio
for Peace he never knew. . . . I
learned Da Nang and Pork Chop Hill
in anguish
Now my nostrils know the gas
and these trigger tire/d fingers
seek the softness in my warrior's beard

I
am a black woman
tall as a cypress
strong
beyond all definition still
defying place
and time
and circumstance
   assailed
      impervious
         indestructible
Look
   on me and be
renewed

Where Have you Gone

Where have you gone

with your confident
walk with
your crooked smile

why did you leave
me
when you took your
laughter
and departed

are you aware that
with you
went the sun
all light
and what few stars
there were?

where have you gone
with your confident
walk your
crooked smile the
rent money
in one pocket and
my heart
in another. . .

Louise Meriwether
1923–

The only girl in a family of five children, she was raised in
Harlem, New York, where her parents had migrated from South
Carolina. After graduating from high school, she worked as a secre-
tary, studying at night school for a degree in English from New York
University, and later a master's degree in journalism from the University
of California. She was active in the civil rights movement, with the
Congress on Racial Equality in Los Angeles, and lived on the West Coast
for eighteen years before returning to the Bronx, New York. In addition
to short stories, she has written an acclaimed novel, Daddy Was a
Number Runner (1970) and several biographical books for children.

A Happening in Barbados

THE best way to pick up a Barbadian man, I hoped, was to walk alone down the beach with my tall, brown frame squeezed into a skintight bathing suit. Since my hotel was near the beach, and Dorothy and Alison, my two traveling companions, had gone shopping, I managed this quite well. I had not taken more than a few steps on the glittering, white sand before two black men were on either side of me vying for attention.

I chose the tall, slim-hipped one over the squat, muscle-bound man who was also grinning at me. But apparently they were friends, because Edwin had no sooner settled me under his umbrella than the squat one showed up with a beach chair and two other boys in tow.

Edwin made the introductions. His temporary rival was Gregory, and the other two were Alphonse and Dimitri.

Gregory was ugly. He had thick, rubbery lips, a scarcity of teeth, and a broad nose splattered like a pyramid across his face. He was all massive shoulders and bulging biceps. No doubt he had a certain animal magnetism, but personally I preferred a lean man like Edwin, who was well built but slender, his whole body fitting together like a symphony. Alphonse and Dimitri were clean-cut and pleasant looking.

They were all too young – twenty to twenty-five at the most – and Gregory seemed the oldest. I inwardly mourned their youth and settled down to make the most of my catch.

The crystal-blue sky rivaled the royal blue of the Caribbean for beauty, and our black bodies on the white sand added to the munificence of colors. We ran into the sea like squealing children when the sudden raindrops came, then shivered on the sand under a makeshift tent of umbrellas and damp towels waiting for the sun to reappear while nourishing ourselves with straight Barbados rum.

As with most of the West Indians I had already met on my whirlwind tour of Trinidad and Jamaica, who welcomed American Negroes with open arms, my new friends loved their island home, but work was scarce and they yearned to go to America. They were hungry for news of how Negroes were faring in the States.

Edwin's arm rested casually on my knee in a proprietary manner, and I smiled at him. His thin, serious face was smooth, too young for a razor, and when he smiled back, he looked even younger. He told me he was a waiter at the Hilton, saving his money to make it to the States. I had already learned not to be snobbish with the island's help. Yesterday's waiter may be tomorrow's waiter may be tomorrow's prime minister.

Dimitri, very black with an infectious grin, was also a waiter, and lanky Alphonse was a tile setter.

Gregory's occupation was apparently women, for that's all he talked about. He was able to launch this subject when a bony white woman – more peeling red than white, really looking like a gaunt cadaver in a loose-fitting bathing suit – came out of the sea and walked up to us. She smiled archly at Gregory.

"Are you going to take me to the Pigeon Club tonight, sugar?"

"No, mon," he said pleasantly, with a toothless grin. "I'm taking a younger pigeon."

The woman turned a deeper red, if that was possible, and, mumbling something incoherent, walked away.

"That one is always after me to take her some place," Gregory said. "She's rich, and she pays the bills but, mon, I don't want an old hag nobody else wants. I like to take my women away from white men and watch them squirm."

"Come down, mon," Dimitri said, grinning. "She look like she's starving for what you got to spare."

We all laughed. The boys exchanged stories about their experiences with predatory white women who came to the islands looking for some black action. But, one and all, they declared they liked dark-skinned meat the best, and I felt like a black queen of the Nile when Gregory winked at me and said, "The blacker the berry, mon, the sweeter the juice."

They had all been pursued and had chased some white tail, too, no doubt, but while the others took it all in good humor, it soon became apparent that Gregory's exploits were exercises in vengeance.

Gregory was saying: "I told that bastard, 'You in my country now, mon, and I'll kick your ass all the way back to Texas. The girl agreed to dance with me, and she don't need your permission.' That white man's face turned purple, but he sat back down, and I dance with his girl. Mon, they hate to see me rubbing bellies with their women because they know once she rub bellies with me she wanna rub something else, too." He laughed, and we all joined in. Serves the white men right, I thought. Let's see how they liked licking *that* end of the stick for a change.

"Mon, you gonna get killed yet," Edwin said, moving closer to me on the towel we shared. "You're crazy. You don't care whose woman you mess with. But it's not gonna be a white man who kill you but some bad Bajan."

Gregory led in the laughter, then held us spellbound for the next hour with intimate details of his affair with Glenda, a young white girl spending the summer with her father on their yacht. Whatever he had, Glenda wanted it desperately, or so Gregory told it.

Yeah, I thought to myself, like LSD, a black lover is the thing this year. I had seen the white girls in the Village and at off-Broadway theaters clutching their black men tightly while I, manless, looked on with bitterness. I often vowed I would find me an ofay in self-defense, but I could never bring myself to condone the wholesale rape of my slave ancestors by letting a white man touch me.

We finished the rum, and the three boys stood up to leave, making arrangements to get together later with us and my two girl friends and go clubbing.

Edwin and I were left alone. He stretched out his muscled leg and touched my toes with his. I smiled at him and let our thighs come together. Why did he have to be so damned young? Then our lips met, his warm and demanding, and I thought, what the hell, maybe I will. I was thirty-nine – good-bye, sweet bird of youth – an ungay divorcee, uptight and drinking too much, trying to disown the years which had brought only loneliness and pain. I had clawed my way up from the slums of Harlem via night school and was now a law clerk on Wall Street. But the fight upward had taken its toll. My husband, who couldn't claw as well as I, got lost somewhere in that concrete jungle. The last I saw of him, he was peering under every skirt around, searching for his lost manhood.

I had always felt contempt for women who found their kicks by robbing the cradle. Now here I was on a Barbados beach with an amorous child young enough to be my son. Two sayings flitted unbidden across my mind. "Judge not, that ye be not judged" and "The thing which I feared is come upon me." I thought, ain't it the goddamned truth?

Edwin kissed me again, pressing the length of his body against mine.

"I've got to go," I gasped. "My friends have probably returned and are looking for me. About ten tonight?"

He nodded; I smiled at him and ran all the way to my hotel.

At exactly ten o'clock, the telephone in our room announced we had company downstairs.

"Hot damn," Alison said, putting on her eyebrows in front of the mirror. "We're not going to be stood up."

"Island men," I said loftily, "are dependable, not like the bums you're used to in America."

Alison, freckled and willowy, had been married three times and was looking for her fourth. Her motto was, if at first you don't succeed, find another mother. She was a real-estate broker in Los Angeles, and we had been childhood friends in Harlem.

"What I can't stand," Dorothy said from the bathroom, "are those creeps who come to your apartment, drink up your liquor, then dirty up your sheets. You don't even get a dinner out of the deal."

She came out of the bathroom in her slip. Petite and delicate with a pixie grin, at thirty-five Dorothy looked more like one of the high school girls she taught than their teacher. She had never been married. Years before, while she was holding onto her virginity with a miser's grip, her fiancé messed up and knocked up one of her friends.

Since then, all of Dorothy's affairs had been with married men, displaying perhaps a subconscious vendetta against all wives.

By ten-twenty we were downstairs and I was introducing the girls to our four escorts, who eyed us with unconcealed admiration. We were looking good in our Saks Fifth Avenue finery. They were looking good, too, in soft shirts and loose slacks, all except Gregory, whose bulging muscles confined in clothing made him seem more gargantuan.

We took a cab and a few minutes later were squeezing behind a table in a small, smoky room called the Pigeon Club. A Trinidad steel band was blasting out the walls, and the tiny dance area was jammed with wiggling bottoms and shuffling feet. The white tourists trying to do the hip-shaking calypso were having a ball and looking awkward.

I got up to dance with Edwin. He had a natural grace and was easy to follow. Our bodies found the rhythm and became one with it while our eyes locked in silent ancient combat, his pleading, mine teasing.

We returned to our seats and to tall glasses of rum and cola tonic. The party had begun.

I danced every dance with Edwin, his clasp becoming gradually tighter until my face was smothered in his shoulder, my arms locked around his neck. He was adorable. Very good for my ego. The other boys took turns dancing with my friends, but soon preferences were set – Alison with Alphonse and Dorothy with Dimitri. With good humor, Gregory ordered another round and didn't seem to mind being odd man out, but he wasn't alone for long.

During the floor show, featuring the inevitable limbo dancers, a pretty white girl, about twenty-two, with straight, red hair hanging down to her shoulders, appeared at Gregory's elbow. From his wink at me and self-satisfied grin, I knew this was Glenda from the yacht.

"Hello," she said to Gregory. "Can I join you, or do you have a date?"

Well, I thought, that's the direct approach.

"What are you doing here?" Gregory asked.

"Looking for you."

Gregory slid over on the bench, next to the wall, and Glenda sat down as he introduced her to the rest of us. Somehow, her presence spoiled my mood. We had been happy being black, and I resented this intrusion from the white world. But Glenda was happy. She had found the man she'd set out to find and a swinging party to boot. She beamed a dazzling smile around the table.

Alphonse led Alison onto the dance floor, and Edwin and I followed. The steel band was playing a wild calypso, and I could feel my hair rising with the heat as I joined in the wildness.

When we returned to the table, Glenda applauded us, then turned to Gregory. "Why don't you teach me to dance like that?"

He answered with his toothless grin and a leer, implying he had better things to teach her.

White women were always snatching our men, I thought, and now they want to dance like us.

I turned my attention back to Edwin and met his full stare.

I teased him with a smile, refusing to commit myself. He had a lusty, healthy appetite, which was natural, I supposed, for a twenty-one-year-old lad. Lord, but why did he have to be that young? I stood up to go to the ladies' room.

"Wait for me," Glenda cried, trailing behind me.

The single toilet stall was occupied, and Glenda leaned against the wall waiting for it while I flipped open my compact and powdered my grimy face.

"You married?" she asked.

"Divorced."

"When I get married, I want to stay hooked forever."

"That's the way I planned it, too," I said dryly.

"What I mean," she rushed on, "is that I've gotta find a cat who wants to groove only with me."

Oh Lord, I thought, don't try to sound like us, too. Use your own, sterile language.

"I really dug this guy I was engaged to," Glenda continued, "but he couldn't function without a harem. I could have stood that, maybe, but when he didn't mind if I made it with some other guy, too, I knew I didn't want that kind of life."

I looked at her in the mirror as I applied my lipstick. She had been hurt, and badly. She shook right down to her naked soul. So she was dropping down a social notch, according to her scale of values, and trying to repair her damaged ego with a black brother.

"You gonna make it with Edwin?" she asked, as if we were college chums comparing dates.

"I'm not a one-night stand." My tone was frigid. That's another thing I can't stand about white people. Too familiar, because we're colored.

"I dig Gregory," she said, pushing her hair out of her eyes. "He's kind of rough, but who wouldn't be, the kind of life he's led."

"And what kind of life is that?" I asked.

"Didn't you know? His mother was a whore in an exclusive brothel for white men only. That was before, when the British owned the island."

"I take it you like rough men?" I asked.

"There's usually something gentle and lost underneath," she replied.

A white woman came out of the toilet and Glenda went in. Jesus, I thought, Gregory gentle? The woman walked to the basin, flung some water in the general direction of her hands, and left.

"Poor Daddy is having a fit," Glenda volunteered from the john, "but there's not much he can do about it. He's afraid I'll leave him again, and he gets lonely without me, so he just tags along and tries to keep me out of trouble."

"And he pays the bills?"

She answered with a laugh. "Why not? He's loaded."

Why not, I thought with bitterness. You white women have always managed to have your cake and eat it, too. The toilet flushed with a roar like Niagara Falls. I opened the door and went back to our table. Let Glenda find her way back alone.

Edwin pulled my chair out and brushed his lips across the nape of my neck as I sat down. He still had not danced with anyone else, and his apparent desire was flattering. For a moment, I considered it. That's what I really needed, wasn't it? To walk down the moonlit beach wrapped in his arms, making it to some pad to be made? It would be a delightful story to tell at bridge sessions. But I shook my head at him, and this time my smile was more sad than teasing.

Glenda came back and crawled over Gregory's legs to the seat beside him. The bastard. He made no pretense of being a gentleman. Suddenly, I didn't know which of them I disliked the most. Gregory winked at me. I don't know where he got the impression I was his conspirator, but I got up to dance with him.

"That Glenda," he grinned, "she's the one I was on the boat with last night. I banged her plenty, in the room right next to her father. We could hear him coughing to let us know he was awake, but he didn't come in."

He laughed like a naughty schoolboy, and I joined in. He was a nerveless bastard all right, and it served Glenda right that we were laughing at her. Who asked her to crash our party, anyway? That's when I got the idea to take Gregory away from her.

"You gonna bang her again tonight?" I asked, a new, teasing quality in my voice. "Or are you gonna find something better to do?" To help him get the message I rubbed bellies with him.

He couldn't believe this sudden turn of events. I could almost see him thinking. With one stroke he could slap Glenda down a peg and repay Edwin for beating his time with me on the beach that morning.

"You wanna come with me?" he asked, making sure of his quarry.

"What you got to offer?" I peered at him through half-closed lids.

"Big Bamboo," he sang, the title of a popular calypso. We both laughed.

I felt a heady excitement of impending danger as Gregory pulled me back to the table. The men paid the bill, and suddenly we were standing outside the club in the bright moonlight. Gregory deliberately uncurled Glenda's arm from his and took a step toward me. Looking at Edwin and nodding in my direction, he said, "She's coming with me. Any objections?"

Edwin inhaled a mouthful of smoke. His face was inscrutable. "You want to go with him?" he asked me quietly.

I avoided his eyes and nodded. "Yes."

He flipped the cigarette with contempt at my feet and lit another one. "Help yourself to the garbage," he said, and leaned back against the building, one leg braced behind him. The others suddenly stilled their chatter, sensing trouble.

I was holding Gregory's arm now, and I felt his muscles tense. "No," I said as he moved toward Edwin. "You've got what you want. Forget it."

Glenda was ungracious in defeat. "What about me?" she screamed. She stared from one black face to another, her glance lingering on Edwin. But he wasn't about to come to her aid and take Gregory's leavings.

"You can go home in a cab," Gregory said, pushing her ahead of him and pulling me behind him to a taxi waiting at the curb.

Glenda broke from his grasp. "You bastard. Who in the hell do you think you are, King Solomon? You can't dump me like this." She raised her hands as if to strike Gregory on the chest, but he caught them before they landed.

"Careful, white girl," he said. His voice was low but ominous. She froze.

"But why," she whimpered, all hurt child now. "You liked me last night. I know you did. Why are you treating me like this?"

"I didn't bring you here" – his voice was pleasant again – "so don't be trailing me all over town. When I want you, I'll come to that damn boat and get you. Now get in that cab before I throw you in. I'll see you tomorrow night. Maybe."

"You go to hell." She eluded him and turned on me, asking with incredible innocence, "What did I ever do to you?" Then she was running past toward the beach, her sobs drifting back to haunt me like a forlorn melody.

What had she ever done to me? And what had I just done? In order to degrade her for the crime of being white, I had sunk to the gutter. Suddenly Glenda was just another woman, vulnerable and lonely, like me.

We were sick, sick, sick. All fucked up. I had thought only Gregory was hung up in his love-hate, black-white syndrome, decades of suppressed hatred having sickened his soul. But I was tainted, too. I had forgotten my own misery long enough to inflict it on another woman who was only trying to ease her loneliness by making it with a soul brother. Was I jealous because she was able to function as a woman where I couldn't, because she realized that a man is a man, color be damned, while I was crucified on my own, anti-white-man cross?

What if she were going black trying to repent for some ancient Nordic sin? How else could she atone except with the gift of herself? And if some black brother wanted to help a chick off her lily-white pedestal, he was entitled to that freedom, and it was none of my damned business anyway.

"Let's go, baby," Gregory said, tucking my arm under his.

The black bastard. I didn't even like the ugly ape. I backed away from him. "Leave me alone," I screamed. "Goddamit, just leave me alone!"

For a moment, we were all frozen into an absurd fresco – Alison, Dorothy, and the two boys looking at me in shocked disbelief, Edwin hiding behind a nonchalant smokescreen, Gregory off balance and confused, reaching out toward me.

I moved first, toward Edwin, but I had slammed the door behind me. He laughed, a mirthless sound in the stillness. He knew. I had forsaken him, but at least not for Gregory.

Then I was running down the beach looking for Glenda, hot tears of shame burning my face. How could I have been such a bitch? But the white beach, shimmering in the moonlight, was empty. And once again, I was alone.

Beryl Gilroy

1924–

Born in Berbice, Guyana, she was among the 150,000 people who left the Caribbean for Britain in the 1950s, and she worked as a clerk in a shop and as a maid before she could find a teaching job. A teacher for over forty years, she was the first Black headmistress in her North London borough; she relates her experiences in her autobiography Black Teacher (1976). After completing a PhD in counselling psychology in the 1980s, she became a child psychotherapist

and multi-cultural researcher at London University's Institute of Educa-
tion. She has written several books for young people and novels which
include Frangipani House *(1986), extracted below. Set in the twilight*
world of a Guyanese woman sent to an old people's home, it won the
GLC Black Literature Prize; it was followed in 1989 by Boy-Sandwich.

From

Frangipani House

CHAPTER IV

Miss Mason stealthily dressed herself in all her nighties,, her head scarves and
her hats. The nighties gave her frail body a comically layered look and the
hats were incongruously piled one on top of the other, making her already
shrunken features more wizened then ever. Then as if someone had quietly
actuated an old gramophone and an ancient record, she started to sing and
dance in a stilted, rudimentary manner.

"I like a nice cup of tea in the morning. I like a nice cup of tea with my
tea." The nurses' laughter rang around the room. Miss Mason was encouraged
by it and lifting up all her nighties to show a dark-brown flabby bottom, she
turned to the four points of the compass and wiggled in brief, timid bursts.

"That's what I did when my mother was not looking," she yelled. "Like a
ball of twine, I trolled my botty round, and round. Hip! Hip! Hooray! There's
a black girl in the ring. Tra la – Tra la la."

"That's enough, Miss Mason," said Nurse Tubbs. "We not your mother.
So lie down and you can sing and wiggle in bed. You want a heart attack?"

The old woman climbed into bed, still wearing all her nightclothes, scarves
and hats. The nurses waited patiently for the time when sleep overwhelmed
her before they would undress her.

"We must make sure she don't do that again," said Nurse Douglas. "She
fake-happy that one. Paper happy! When we undress her, we have to hide
them things so she don't find them."

"But her antics make the day go quick, you know. I like her," replied
Nurse Tibbs appreciatively. "I really like her. The other day she offer to teach
me to play bridge. But we play Thirty-One – three cents a game and she beat
me too! All the while we playing, Miss Tilley keep on muttering, 'Gamblin is
an abomination unto the Lord.' Miss Mason does make me laugh. She say, 'The
Lord is everybody God-father. He like a little Abomination in his rum.'"

"Nurse Tibbs!" shouted Mama King, "I wan' go outside. The day look
clean. All its sins wash away. And look at dem trees. They look so nice!"

The frangipani trees were laden with sweet-scented orange-coloured flowers,
but the most wanton of their petals took short rides astride the wind and slowly

swirled to the ground. They had the appearance of snippets of ribbon strewn across a green baize carpet by wilful hands.

The more keenly Mama King watched the petals dancing and gliding on the wind the more memories escaped from her, causing her mind to scurry and scamper after them. Were those memories about her girls or about Miss Tilley's house that smelt of rotting oranges? She shook her head as if trying to jerk memory from some secluded corner of her brain – out of the crevice in which time had buried it but the memory stayed in its grave. Nurse Tibbs watched her and wondered what was going on. She continued her circular walk around an area heaped with petals, and picked some up and then, like a child caught doing some forbidden thing, she shyly dropped them again. She walked towards the low shed and scraped off those petals that adorned its bald, corrugated pate. Once more she thought of Danny. The house in which they first lived had such a roof, and when the sun heated it to boiling point, large, black spiders came out, seeking shade. But she walked with Danny when work was done and sat on the clean sand, and listened to the river chortling as it flowed, and watched the mangrove trees motionless in the dull, leaden darkness.

She hardly noticed when the memory she had been seeking came out of hiding. But she greeted it with a welcome smile. Of course, the colour reminded her of her daughters, both dressed in orange-coloured costumes for the school play. She stared out into the distance, allowing spools of recollections to unwind.

"They did want Token for Snow White. But she too tall. She make a good dwarf, though. She say everything she had to say. Everybody clap. I feel so proud. I take in plenty washing to rig them out for the play and when it happen I forget the rheumatism in me hand from the hot an' cold water. The teacher so please wid Token. I notice how she grown – fullin' out and then all of a sudden, Token sick. She wouldn't eat a thing – only drink, an even that. She get fine – fine – fine! I say, 'God if you wan' she, take she,' and I watch she turnin' to skeleton before me eyes. Then somebody tell me 'bout Maraj – a old, coolie man who know 'bout sickness.

"Where he live no bus does go. So Token an' me, we go by Donkey Cart for five hours and we reach there. He look at Token – she got nara. She guts twist. It easy for children guts to twist. He 'noint Token belly – she holler for mercy, but he 'noint her two more time. She eat dat same night. I kneel down in front of Maraj. I say, 'I ain' got money – only dis brooch. It solid gold. Take it.'

"'Keep your brooch. We all is poor people,' he tell me. 'Feed ten beggar one for every year you chile livin'. I don' wan' money. Tonight I go to sleep. Tomorrow I can wake up somewhere else. Thank God for everything.'

"People always good to me. The teacher never charge me a cent. She teach Token for nothing. Then she teach Cyclette. When I ask her about money – how much I got to pay – she say, 'Who talkin' 'bout payin! They will remember me when I get old. Cast your bread on the water. Dat's what the Bible say.' It look like yesterday when Token pass for nurse and Cyclette for secretary. Because they had a little complexion, they get work easy. Token was a good nurse. The patient dem like her and Cyclette could make a typewriter sing, laugh – run *and jump. Only yesterday they was little. Danny would proud of them. Poor Danny – I wonder where he stay now. Dead and gone. I believe so. Nobody see him or meet him. Even people who been to Aruba. I wonder where Danny gone?"*

"Mama King," Matron shouted from the door. "Your staring like you mad! People who stare like that have empty, idle mind. Why don't you think positive, instead of standing around and staring at nothing?"

"Since I come here I look, but all I see is what past and gone. You have now. All I have is long ago. Go and count you money. It got old people blood on it!"

In a mocking, over-deferential manner she curtsied to the Matron, then twisting her body through the small space that the Matron's bulk had left unoccupied, she went back into her room to rock her feelings to rest. She walked round and round the bed and then once again, unable to resist its beckoning, lay down and closed her eyes.

"Matron think I doing nothing," she said quietly to herself, "but thinking is hard work."

"I sit down and my whole life pass before – like a film at a picture show. I get so tired but yet I can't stop. And everybody think my mind empty, my head empty and my heart empty. I see people, dead and gone, walking and talking and young. And out of my old worn out body, a young woman walk out and life is like roll of new cloth waiting to roll out."

She fell asleep.

She woke around dusk but she did not get up, and when Nurse Douglas entered her room she faked sleep.

"Come on, Mama King. I know you wake up. You want cocoa-tea or coffee?"

"I want cocoa-tea."

While she sipped the cocoa, a flight of blue Sakis hurrying home in the dying light caught her eyes. The sun, plump and comfortable behind wisps of gossamer-mauve clouds, sank slowly out of sight. It was the end of another day.

"I wonder how long I been here. How long they keeping me here! How long I going to live Lord? I wonder how long?"

"Nurse," she called, "I want to go home. I miss everything."

"Mama King, you lucky. Life is a treadmill. You been on it for years and years. You daughters push you off. Don't grumble. Don't complain. Count your blessings."

Mama King sucked her teeth. "You don' teach you grandmother to suck egg. I wan' go home, I wan' pen and paper to write me daughters. They must come and take me out of this terble place."

"Well, tell you what, when you mind clear you can write. Wait till tomorrow. I will get you pen and paper and I will post the letter for you."

"I wan' the paper now," Mama King insisted. "And the pen, and the ink." Lucid, aggressive and determined, she kept on demanding writing materials until the nurse complied. She wrote a message to Token like a child given lines for punishment.

"Token, I want go home. I better. I hate this place.

Token, I want go home. I better. I hate this place."

She wrote until all the lines on the paper were covered. She had written it thirty times. Then she addressed the envelope and sealed in the letter allowing the nurse to take it from her and put it in her pocket.

"I will post it for you," Nurse Douglas promised. "I going home just now."

Mama King had doubts about the letters she asked the nurses to post. She never received any replies and every complaint she made was either swept aside like rotten wood in a rough wind, or ignored as if she complained in a foreign language. The women were expected to think themselves privileged and lucky to be under Matron's care.

The timid knock on her door went unanswered until she gathered her limbs, her wits, her feelings about her as if she was picking up shells out of loose sand.

Miss Mason stood there wearing a slipper on one foot, and a shoe on the other and on her head a battered cloche hat that could have come out of a hobo's pocket.

"Hello," Miss Mason twittered. "How are you today? I came to see you."

"You sure? I see you got a bag. You come to thief again? You thief me orange, me guava, me biscuit and whatever else you could lay your hands on."

Miss Mason frowned. "I only took your banana. I'm keeping everything just in case Matron drops dead and there's no food for us. Then you'll all have to come and beg food of me."

"I see," Mama King replied tentatively.

"I came to tell you about your husband. You always worry about him. Well he's all right. He's across water and there is gold too. Don't get married again and you'll be ship-shape to get to the end of time. He loves you just as much as ever."

"Don' talk about love. Is something you think about when you young and then you live it through your children when you old," snapped Mama King.

"Just as you wish. I thought I'll give you the message." Miss Mason's eyes revolved around the room. There was nothing edible for her to pilfer but the clatter of dishes drew her to the dining-room.

Mama King resumed her seat by the window, and on the grass outside, a patchwork of events from her life lay sprawled before her in a kind of half-light.

"*Since Danny gone my feelings for men shrivel like grass in dry weather. Ben Le Cage did come roun' once or twice but he is like mucka-mucka.[1] He make you scratch yourself morning, noon and night with worry. He live wid woman after woman – get chile after chile and as fas' as he get them, he forget 'bout them. I can' believe he get them normal. He mus' get fed up doin' the same thing so much time with so much women. He never think 'bout God dat man! I didn't take notice of him. I say I is a married woman – I aint one*"

---

[1] A plant, the juice causes itching when in contact with skin.

of you hole an' corner. He didn't like that. 'You got two girl children,' he say. Who will take you wid two girl? Boy more useful. Girl is trouble. Before they twenty they go and get belly.' I chase him out when he say that. He want to bring bad luck on my two girl."

The cadences of her voice seemed to lull her into a deep sleep. Only the muffled sounds of moans and sighs that seemed to be fragments of anguish rising from the graveyard inside her synchronized with her breathing. "She never dreamt," she said. She had never been able to recall a single dream but that evening one stuck in her mind and frightened her.

She was a child again walking demurely beside her mother along a road stretching far into the distance. There was no one else in sight but she could hear voices singing familiar tunes. The road suddenly became liquid and there she was swimming in the cool, chattering water. But her mother had disappeared and there was Matron scowling and scolding and shouting at her. Everything happened in an instant. She had grown old and Danny, as young as when she last saw him, had appeared on the scene. She rushed up to him but he eyed her with suspicion and cutting resentment.

"I don' want you," he said. *"You old! You ugly! I want this nice clean-skin woman."*

He embraced Matron and then pushed his wife out of their way. She felt a searing pain on her shoulder where he had touched her and she screamed. The nurses rushed in. Her face, covered with sweat emphasized the astonishment and pain in her eyes. "I dream," she whispered, "I dream...."

"It's only a nightmare, Mama King," comforted Nurse Carey. "It's gone now. Only me and you here now."

Mama King still sobbed. Her heart was so full of hatred, although she did not know for whom, that at the slightest touch she would split open like a ripe calabash dropped on stone.

"Ginchi," she called, "Ginchi!" But her friend had long since gone home. She rushed to the window. There was nothing to see – just a slither of moon and whipped egg-white clouds scurrying away to the other side of the globe.

More than anything else she wanted work. She always had a special relationship with work. Her body needed it as it needed food and clothes. And now, time and life, her daughters and the matron had all conspired to deprive her of her faithful friends, work and hardship. She felt as though they had punched and kicked her and given her many terrible blows.

She began once more to prowl round and round the room like a caged animal. Even the window had clouded over. She ran her fingers along the sill and so found comfort and peace. Why had work deserted her for no reason to speak of? True, she had been sick, and even getting older but since when work turn its back on poor, old people?

"If work come now and stan' up before me, I give her a big-big cuffing. Lord, how wonderful are thy works! All works belong to God."

Efua Sutherland
1924–

*S*he *was born and grew up in Cape Coast, Ghana, and attend-
ed school and teacher training college in Ghana. She went to
Homerton College, Cambridge University (earning a BA), and the
School of Oriental and African Studies, London University. Returning
to Ghana she taught at a secondary school and at St Monica's Teacher
Training College, Mampong, and was a lecturer at the University of
Ghana. In 1958 she founded her Experimental Theatre Group, drawing
on local folklore, lyrics and dances, performing both in Twi and English.
She founded the Ghana Drama Studio in Accra and in 1960 built a
courtyard theatre using the concept of traditional performance areas.
The earliest Ghanaian playwright-director and a popular broadcaster,
she writes for children and adults, in Fanti and in English. Her works
include* Foriwa *(1967),* Edufa *(1969) and* The Marriage of Anansewa
(1977).

New Life at Kyerefaso

S HALL we say
Shall we put it this way
Shall we say that the maid of Kyerefaso, Foruwa, daughter of the Queen
Mother, was as a young deer, graceful in limb? Such was she, with head
held high, eyes soft and wide with wonder. And she was light of foot, light in
all her moving.

Stepping springily along the water path like a deer that had strayed from
the thicket, springily stepping along the water path, she was a picture to give
the eye a feast. And nobody passed her by but turned to look at her again.

Those of her village said that her voice in speech was like the murmur
of a river quietly flowing beneath shadows of bamboo leaves. They said her
smile would sometimes blossom like a lily on her lips and sometimes rise like
sunrise.

The butterflies do not fly away from the flowers, they draw near. Foruwa
was the flower of her village.

So shall we say,

Shall we put it this way, that all the village butterflies, the men, tried to
draw near her at every turn, crossed and crossed her path? Men said of her,

"She shall be my wife, mine, and mine and mine."

But suns rose and set, moons silvered and died and as the days passed Foruwa grew more lovesome, yet she became no one's wife. She smiled at the butterflies and waved her hand lightly to greet them as she went swiftly about her daily work:

"Morning, Kweku
Morning, Kwesi
Morning, Kodwo"
but that was all.

And so they said, even while their hearts thumped for her:
"Proud!
Foruwa is proud . . . and very strange."

And so the men when they gathered would say:
"There goes a strange girl. She is not just the stiff-in-the-neck proud, not just breasts-stuck-out I-am-the-only-girl-in-the-village proud. What kind of pride is hers?"

The end of the year came round again, bringing the season of festivals. For the gathering in of corn, yams and cocoa there were harvest celebrations. There were bride-meetings too. And it came to the time when the Asafo companies should hold their festival. The village was full of manly sounds, loud musketry and swelling choruses.

The pathfinding, path-clearing ceremony came to an end. The Asafo marched on toward the Queen Mother's house, the women fussing round them, prancing round them, spreading their cloths in their way.

"Osee!" rang the cry. "Osee!" to the manly men of old. They crouched like leopards upon the branches.

Before the drums beat
Before the danger drums beat, beware!
Before the horns moaned
Before the wailing horns moaned, beware!

They were upright, they sprang. They sprang. They sprang upon the enemy. But now, blood no more! No more thundershot on thundershot.

But still we are the leopards on the branches. We are those who roar and cannot be answered back. Beware, we are they who cannot be answered back.

There was excitement outside the Queen Mother's courtyard gate.

"Gently, gently," warned the Asafo leader. "Here comes the Queen Mother.
Spread skins of the gentle sheep in her way.
Lightly, lightly walks our Mother Queen.
Shower her with silver,
Shower her with silver for she is peace."

And the Queen Mother stood there, tall, beautiful, before the men and there was silence.

"What news, what news do you bring?" she quietly asked.

"We come with dusty brows from our pathfinding, Mother. We come with tired, thorn-pricked feet. We come to bathe in the coolness of your peaceful stream. We come to offer our manliness to new life."

The Queen Mother stood there, tall and beautiful and quiet. Her fanbearers stood by her and all the women clustered near. One by one the men laid their guns at her feet and then she said:

"It is well. The gun is laid aside. The gun's rage is silenced in the stream. Let your weapons from now on be your minds and your hands' toil.

"Come, maidens, women all, join the men in dance for they offer themselves to new life."

There was one girl who did not dance.

"What, Foruwa!" urged the Queen Mother, "Will you not dance? The men are tired of parading in the ashes of their grandfathers' glorious deeds. That should make you smile. They are tired of the empty croak: 'We are men, we are men.'

"They are tired of sitting like vultures upon the rubbish heaps they have piled upon the half-built walls of their grandfathers. Smile, then, Foruwa, smile.

"Their brows shall now indeed be dusty, their feet thorn-picked, and 'I love my land' shall cease to be the empty croaking of a vulture upon the rubbish heap. Dance, Foruwa, dance!"

Foruwa opened her lips and this was all she said: "Mother, I do not find him here."

"Who? Who do you not find here?"

"He with whom this new life shall be built. He is not here, Mother. These men's faces are empty; there is nothing in them, nothing at all."

"Alas, Foruwa, alas, alas! What will become of you, my daughter?"

"The day I find him, Mother, the day I find the man, I shall come running to you, and your worries will come to an end."

"But, Foruwa, Foruwa," argued the Queen Mother, although in her heart she understood her daughter, "five years ago your rites were fulfilled. Where is the child of your womb? Your friend Maanan married. Your friend Esi married. Both had their rites with you."

"Yes, Mother, they married and see how their steps once lively now drag in the dust. The sparkle has died out of their eyes. Their husbands drink palm wine the day long under the mango trees, drink palm wine and push counters across the draughtboards all the day, and are they not already looking for other wives? Mother, the man I say is not here."

This conversation had been overheard by one of the men and soon others heard what Foruwa had said. That evening there was heard a new song in the village.

> There was a woman long ago,
> Tell that maid, tell that maid,
> There was a woman long ago,
> She would not marry Kwesi,
> She would not marry Kwaw,
> She would not, would not, would not.
> One day she came home with hurrying feet,
> I've found the man, the man, the man,
> Tell that maid, tell that maid,

Her man looked like a chief,
Tell that maid, tell that maid,
Her man looked like a chief,
Most splendid to see,
But he turned into a python,
He turned into a python
And swallowed her up.

From that time onward there were some in the village who turned their backs on Foruwa when she passed.

Shall we say

Shall we put it this way

Shall we say that a day came when Foruwa with hurrying feet came running to her mother? She burst through the courtyard gate; and there she stood in the courtyard, joy all over. And a stranger walked in after her and stood in the courtyard beside her, stood tall and strong as a pillar. Foruwa said to the astonished Queen Mother:

"Here he is, Mother, here is the man."

The Queen Mother took a slow look at the stranger standing there strong as a forest tree, and she said:

"You carry the light of wisdom on your face, my son. Greetings, you are welcome. But who are you, my son?"

"Greetings, Mother," replied the stranger quietly, "I am a worker. My hands are all I have to offer your daughter, for they are all my riches, I have travelled to see how men work in other lands. I have that knowledge and my strength. That is all my story."

Shall we say,

Shall we put it this way,

strange as the story is, that Foruwa was given in marriage to the stranger.

There was a rage in the village and many openly mocked saying, "Now the proud ones eat the dust."

Shall we say,

Shall we put it this way

that soon, quite soon, the people of Kyerefaso began to take notice of the stranger in quite a different way.

"Who," some said, "is this who has come among us? He who mingles sweat and song, he for whom toil is joy and life is full and abundant?"

"See," said others, "what a harvest the land yields under his ceaseless care."

"He has taken the earth and moulded it into bricks. See what a home he has built, how it graces the village where it stands."

"Look at the craft of his fingers, baskets or kente, stool or mat, the man makes them all."

"And our children swarm about him, gazing at him with wonder and delight."

Then it did not satisfy them any more to sit all day at their draughtboards under the mango trees.

"See what Foruwa's husband has done," they declared; "shall the sons of the land not do the same?"

And soon they began to seek out the stranger to talk with him. Soon they too were toiling, their fields began to yield as never before, and the women laboured joyfully to bring in the harvest. A new spirit stirred the village. As the carelessly built houses disappeared one by one, and new homes built after the fashion of the stranger's grew up, it seemed as if the village of Kyerefaso had been born afresh.

The people themselves became more alive and a new pride possessed them. They were no longer just grabbing from the land what they desired for their stomachs' present hunger and for their present comfort. They were looking at the land with new eyes, feeling it in their blood, and thoughtfully building a permanent and beautiful place for themselves and their children.

"Osee!" It was festival-time again. "Osee!" Blood no more. Our fathers found for us the paths. We are the roadmakers. They bought for us the land with their blood. We shall build it with our strength. We shall create it with our minds.

Following the men were the women and children. On their heads they carried every kind of produce that the land had yielded and crafts that their fingers had created. Green plantains and yellow bananas were carried by the bunch in large white wooden trays. Garden eggs, tomatoes, red oil-palm nuts warmed by the sun were piled high in black earthen vessels. Oranges, yams, maize filled shining brass trays and golden calabashes. Here and there were children proudly carrying colourful mats, baskets and toys which they themselves had made.

The Queen Mother watched the procession gathering on the new village playground now richly green from recent rains. She watched the people palpitating in a massive dance toward her where she stood with her fanbearers outside the royal house. She caught sight of Foruwa. Her load of charcoal in a large brass tray which she had adorned with red hibiscus danced with her body. Happiness filled the Queen Mother when she saw her daughter thus.

Then she caught sight of Foruwa's husband. He was carrying a white lamb in his arms, and he was singing happily with the men. She looked on him with pride. The procession had approached the royal house.

"See!" rang the cry of the Asafo leader. "See how the best in all the land stands. See how she stands waiting, our Queen Mother. Waiting to wash the dust from our brow in the coolness of her peaceful stream. Spread skins of the gentle sheep in her way, gently. Spread the yield of the land before her. Spread the craft of your hands before her, gently, gently.

"Lightly, lightly walks our Queen Mother, for she is peace."

Rosa Guy
1925–

T *rinidadian-born, she migrated to Harlem, New York, at the age of*
seven and was orphaned by the time she was fourteen, when she left
school to start work. She took factory employment and, realizing
that she got the worst jobs because she was Black, became involved with
the unions at her workplace, and later in the larger struggle for Black
freedom. She became involved with the American Negro Theatre, and
after the war divided her time between going to night school, studying
drama and making her living as a piece worker, before turning to writ-
ing. In the 1950s she and other established artists founded the Harlem
Writers' Guild to help Black writers develop their craft, and she became
its President. She had a play performed off Broadway in 1954 but it
was only much later that her stories and novels began to receive critical
attention, particularly her fiction for young adults, which includes The
Friends *(1973),* Edith Jackson *(1978) and* Ruby *(1981). Her first novel*
was Bird at My Window *(1966), and* A Measure of Time *(extracted here)*
– the story of streetwise Dorine Davis who leaves behind the racism of
Alabama and tries to make her way on the fast-track in Harlem – was
published in 1983.

From

A Measure of Time

CHAPTER II

T HE feeling that things had changed between us kept slipping and sliding
beneath our laughing. We laughed a lot. But sensing the change kept me
from telling him how much I hated living in that one goddamn room. Then,
too, Sonny kept taking me out, showing me *his* town.

He took me to Starlight Park. We rode on the merry-go-round, on the Ferris
wheel, playing at a childhood we never had. We walked around sightseeing,
eating ice-cream cones.

At Coney Island, we rode the merry-go-round, and the roller coaster, then
we walked on the boardwalk eating hot dogs and ice-cream cones.

At Rockaway, we rode the merry-go-round, and the roller coaster, then we walked on the boardwalk eating hot dogs and ice-cream cones.

At Far Rockaway, we rode the merry-go-round, and the Ferris wheel, and stood on the beach while the breakers rolled over our naked feet. The water pulled the sand from beneath our feet, stealing our support. And we ate ice-cream cones and hot dogs and laughed more than we had ever laughed together, even while our eyes kept gliding past each other's.

Sonny parked his car to take me for a subway ride (something he never again did). "The scuffler's pullman," Sonny called it. We rode down to City Hall, took a street car, working our way to midtown, then took the double-decker bus back up to Harlem. Driving up Fifth Avenue, looking down at shoppers going in and out of stores, Sonny said, "Here's where the rich white folks do their buying, baby."

His voice, so proud, made me bite down on my tongue to keep from asking which one he thought he was: rich? white? both?

Going out to the Statue of Liberty, standing on the ferry, salt water spraying my face, and hearing folks, foreign folks, around me talking: "Ay, but is goot, goot. Yass. It's symbol. We see her in a liddle, liddle while." It seemed fitting when seeing the lady, her arm pushed in the sky, to say:

"There she is, there she is." Shouting to the boatload of foreigners oohing and aahing and crying. My throat got right tight. "She sure is grand, Sonny, just like you said she'd be."

"What else? We Americans," Sonny said, "builds the best."

"But who thought of building her?"

"Dunno, baby."

"Who thought of putting her way out here?"

"Dunno, baby."

"Why they put her so far?" I asked.

"Search me," he said. "All I know is that our lady's out here welcoming them foreigners when they comes in."

"Should put one like her in the Penn Station to welcome folks coming up from the South," I said.

"You crazy, woman? We ain't no damn foreigners." That twisted my heart. More than the words, the feeling that even our thinking about things together had changed.

And the sick feeling played around my heart, when standing on the roof of our seven-story building, we looked out to see the orange-red ball of the late sun, sinking fast behind the low buildings where clotheslines – sheets, dresses, shorts, drawers – strung out against a sky bright enough to blind a feller with tomorrow's promises reduced everything to shadows – the Power and the Glory – the Lord making of man's necessities shadows flapping in the wind. And then darkness. The sun going out. Electric taking over, stretching darkness for miles. Such excitement! Knowing that beneath the darkness, promises were being kept. Folks were dancing, or about to; going to shows, or getting dressed to; girls, guys getting set to take on the whole town. What a joy! If water had brought Jonah to the belly of the whale and darkness, electric had brought folks to the center of the world and life. And what about me in this new life?

"New York," I sighed.

"Yeah, one hell of a city," Sonny said, not understanding my deep-down, sick feeling.

When we went downstairs and Sonny got to dressing, it didn't surprise me. He had been feeding me knowledge right along. He had been doing the "right thing" by me, but sight-seeing time was over.

Back in the little room sitting by the window, I got to filing my nails, pretending not to see the way he matched the stripes of his pinstriped suit, untied and retied his tie so that it looked the same, brushed his heavy eyebrows trying to look like the devil himself, wiggled his pinky to catch the light on his diamond, splashed toilet water over his face – overdoing, sure I'd try to stop him, try to keep him home. But if he thought that, he had another thought coming.

I kept on filing my nails. From the corner of my eye I saw him turn to give himself a last look, and the admiration stinking out of him for the life of me made the words slip out:

"If a whore didn't have more confidence," I said, "she'd best give up the trade and go to hog calling."

"What's that?" Sonny had always been deaf to all but compliments. I looked through the curtains, out into the air shaft. "I ain't heard," he said.

"I ain't said a word."

I examined my fingernails. One more shave and I've have to grow a new set. My hands dropped to my lap. To keep my eyes away from the slime of having the right answers on his face, I examined the curtains separating me from the brick of the next building. Trapped. I had to start marking the days until I freed myself from that room. Upstairs on the roof, looking over the city, at the sunset, the wide-open space about me, I had for a second been free – even happy. . . .

Six months! Six months ought not to have made that kind of difference. We had been too close. Had I changed? Babies do more to women than make mothers of them. That thought brought me to the mirror where, standing beside Sonny, I let my robe fall to my waist. I examined my titties. Still firm. Plump. I threw my kimono up to look at my backside. I prodded it, searched for telltale stretch marks. Smooth as peaches, round.

"Whatcha doin', baby?" Conceit blinded Sonny to my kind of reasoning. He smiled, put his arms around me, pinched my nipples. "Ain't got time," he said.

I hunched up my shoulders – I didn't care. Then I heard myself say: "Where you going?" – and wanted to stick my fingers in my ears to shut out his lies.

"Got to meet a man."

"How come you ain't taking me?"

"Business, baby." He smiled a soft, sorry-I-must smile, blinking all the while. "Business. I'm already over an hour late on account of looking at them stars." So – even if he wanted to, he didn't have time to wait.

I sat on the edge of the bed listening to his footsteps up the hall. The door slammed. I put my head in my hands. Lord, it had happened. Was happening. I couldn't take it. I needed to get to bed and cry and cry and cry – get it all out.

Ten minutes later, my high heels clicking down the hallway, I went into the living room where Big Red knelt, trying to fix a Victrola that hadn't worked since a slickster had palmed if off on him. (I kept puzzling on how this big-time sport kept getting "took" by every small-time hustler. But then Tom Rumley thought he was still down home, the way he liked to "do things myself".) "If Sonny gets back, tell him I stepped out, will you?"

Freckle-face looked up. "If Sonny gets back, I reckon he'll see for hisself." A fourteen-carat wisecrack. "Tell me, pretty lady, where you off to?"

"That's for me to know and for you to find out."

Giving short answers happened to be my specialty, but it had to be a sin how that golden smile turned them out of me. A decent word from me would have sent him to the nuthouse.

On the avenue, my feet knew better than my head where they were heading. Sonny had been keeping me clear of the West Indians, so of course that's where my feet led me. And they led me to the right corner. The crowd stood looking up at the same tall, handsome black man with his shaking mustache that I had seen on my first day. His sweaty face shone in the glow of the streetlight as he shouted: "I tell you the white mahn wicked. . . ."

"Yes, he wicked, wicked," folks standing near to me agreed.

"The white mahn is criminal. . . ." The hot flannel suit he wore had to add to his discomfort. He took off his hat, wiped the leather band inside, wiped his head, then his face. For a moment his face looked clean, calm – then the sweat commenced again, the mustache commenced to shaking. "You say he ain't criminal?" he asked those folks who had done nothing but agree. "Then let me ask you – how come this mahn thief we ships? How come, I ask you? How come he stick we leader – the honorable Marcus Garvey – in jail on a bogus charge!"

"True, true" from the crowd. "The charge bogus – bogus as hell. . . . Bogus, I tell you!" He said every word to its last letter. "And I will tell you why. Is because he think that by jailing we leader, he can stop we from leaving this country! He think that by so doing, he can force we to remain here – to live like pigs and to work like slaves! But he lie!"

"Ohgod, he lie. He lie." The woman standing in front of me spoke in an angry voice that went up at the end surprised-like. She looked around, her wide face with its high cheekbones expressionless, as though set in stone. Tall, narrow hips and broad shoulders, she stood as solid as a pillar. His pillar. She looked at me from small beady eyes, and I tried to ease away from her. But the crowd had thickened around me. I couldn't move. That scared me – being alone in Harlem surrounded by a bunch of foreigners! The woman looked down at me. She nodded.

"We ain't come here to live like nobody pig," she said. "We ain't nobody slave."

I half smiled, keeping my eyes on the speaker. I didn't want to get entangled with that bird-eyed, nonmoving force of a woman.

"Life is one big struggle," the speaker said. "Never forget that! So if the white mahn want struggle, we'll give it."

"You bet your life," an American voice said from behind me.

"We gon' gi' he in he teeth," Stone-face said.

"We. Shall. Endure! Struggle! We. Shall. And we shall endure!" Something about that shining, sweaty face, the shaking mustache, his feeling, entered me and grew. The crowd heaved. Excited. "Yes. We shall endure in this struggle. We shall free our leader – the honorable, the glorious Marcus Garvey!"

"Hear! Hear! Hear!" the crowd shouted. Sweat pushed out on my brow. "Hear, hear," I echoed them.

The preacher raised his arms, hushing the crowd. "The white mahn strong," he whispered. "Don't forget that!" Then raising his voice again: "But we blacks are strong. . . ."

"Hear! Hear! Hear!" we shouted.

"We must not forget that! And so we must be – all for one." He raised a fist over his head. Hundreds of fists went up in the air. "All for one!" the crowd echoed.

"And one for all!"

"And one for all!"

"And one for all!" I joined in.

"We. Shall. Be. Free!"

"We shall be free!"

"Or die!"

"Or die!" Lord, I had never been together with so many folks.

"What good if we ain't stick together?" Stone-face said in her singsong, surprised voice.

"You said it, sister." A broad smile spread out my face. "You just about said it."

"We shall be free." Our handsome leader promised. "Our honorable Marcus Garvey shall be free. . . ."

"Free! Free! Free!" the crowd chanted.

"We shall make good our vow. And we shall sail from these shores, back to the motherland. Africa! Africa for we Africans!"

"Africa for we Africans!" the crowd cheered. But they had lost me.

Africa? What damn Africa? Here I had just got to New York and loved it, and these folks talking about leaving? I looked around at the hot faces, the thrown-back heads, the mouths tight and determined. I had come to find West Indians, and instead found a bunch of Africans.

I eased my shoulders, trying to get through the crowd. But folks stood still – an unmoving wall. Stone-face turned, her face friendly. But I was ready to go. "I-I-I come out here to-to look for West Indians . . ." I said.

"How you mean?" she asked, her face still unmoving.

"I-I-I mean – I don't know nothing 'bout no Africans. . . ."

"What you talking?" she asked.

"I come looking for West . . ."

"And what you think we is?"

"The man up there says you all is Africans."

"And what you think you is?" She looked so far down to me, I swore I had shrunk to the size of a maggot.

"I-I-I'm American," I whispered.

"How you mean?" Her smooth-as-stone brow cracked into wrinkles.

"I-I-I-don't know nothing 'bout no Africans. . . ."

The wrinkles faded, settling her mouth into folds at the sides. She hunched her shoulders and turned from me, digging herself deeper into her footsteps.

"We must work together like one mighty fist!" my lost leader kept on as I fought to get through. The man behind me smiled kindly. And knowing he had heard me, I said, "You see – I come out looking for West Indians."

"Most are West Indians out here," he said. And recognizing him as the American who had spoken before, I whispered to him: "That man up there says they's Africans."

"Like you, like me, sister."

"Mister, I come from Alabama."

Stone-face spun around. "And where you think your ancestors from?" she asked.

"Alabama, ma'am. All my folks come from Alabama. I can prove it."

Her mouth dropped. "But the woman a fool?" she said in a loud voice, then resettled herself in her footsteps, adding: "But then, what you expect from the children of slaves?"

"Ma'am," I shot back, "I'll have you all know that I was born in the Cradle of the Federation." (I swear we used to brag about that.)

Hot out of my mind, I pushed my way through the crowd and made it back home, still steaming. Marching down the hallway into the living room, I found Tom still kneeling over is Victrola.

"What ails you?" he asked after one look at my face.

"Them damn West Indians – or Africans – or whatever in the hell they is – they can go to hell – "

"Whoa," Tom said, sitting back on his heels. "Who done gone and got my brown gal all lit up?"

"Tom, I declare, I ain't even met this woman, and she come telling me about my folks."

"How's that?" he asked.

"Got a damn nerve, saying my folks come from Africa."

"Oh, you been out there with them Garvey folks," Tom said.

"I declare that woman looked at me like I was dirt."

"Pay them monkey chasers no mind," Tom said. "They always blowing hard. Never did figger why they come here in the first place if Africa was where they wanted to be."

"I ain't never seen her before. And there she go. . . ."

Tom went on with his tinkering. "Was a time I hung out there listening – near every night," he said. "Not lately – not since they put Marcus Garvey in jail. I got tired of hearing the same thing night after night. Way I see it, Marcus Garvey ain't Jesus Christ. He can't walk them waters to get back to Africa – and they ain't gonna sell no black man decent boats. . . ."

"Tom Rumley, it ain't Jesus Christ what walked them waters. It was Moses."

"Moses? That right?" He looked up, thoughtful for one second. "You sure? Seems Jesus Christ's the one done all them things."

"Goes to show you ain't no good Baptist."

"I ain't no good nothing 'cept a hustling man." He had dropped a screw and went looking for it on all fours. "Anyhow, the way I see it, so what if we comes from Africa? We here to stay now. I ain't thinking of ever leaving New York –

except one way. . . ."

"Tom Rumley! Don't tell me you believe that shit?"

"Shit? What shit?" He kept searching for the screw.

"'Bout us coming from Africa."

"Makes sense," he said. He found the screw and sat back on his heels to look at me. "We had to come from someplace."

"Ain't you from Baltimore?"

"Sure thing. But where was we when this whole shebang belonged to them Indians? We had to belong to someplace."

"What shebang?"

"This country, Dorine lady. This country."

"This whole country!"

"Sure."

"Belonged to them West Indians?"

"Naw. American Indians."

"American Indians!"

"American Indians!"

Education comes in drips and drops to a feller who never went to school. Sure, I knew about us being slaves. Mama had been born to a slave (but only years later did I hear black folks bragging of their Indian blood, trying to prove they weren't out-and-out niggers or bloodline to slaves and white masters). Up to that time, I and lots of black folks took it for granted that but two kinds of folks lived on these shores: white folks and black folks.

"All I know is them West Indians is a simple bunch," I said. "Trying to make out a feller's dirt on account of he's from the South. Tom, you ain't heard nothing till you heard that woman say to me that I was the child of slaves. If it weren't for all those folks being around, I declare I'd have gone upside her head. . . ."

"Why you wants to get all riled up over that?" Tom said. "They was slaves, too."

"They was. . . ?"

"Sure they was."

"Tom, you putting me on? How you know?"

"Well, now . . ." He stopped his finagling and looked at the mess of magazines and newspapers all around the room. "Sure is enough wrote about it. And they know it. I heard Marcus Garvey hisself talk about it. We all was slaves, Dorine. We got brought to these here parts on ships. Only some got dropped off on them islands. Others got brung over here. Sure – we all was slaves."

"You swear to that, Tom Rumley?"

"A hell of a lot quicker than I'd swear to Moses. . . ."

I hit the streets running, all the way to that corner. But the speaker had gone, the crowd had thinned. Stone-face had disappeared. I searched the streets. . . .

Alda do Espírito Santo
1926–

Born on the island of São Tomé e Principe, the former Portuguese colony off the coast of West Africa, she worked as a teacher and was active in nationalist circles and at one point her identification with the African liberation movement led to her arrest and imprisonment for some months by the Portuguese authorities. Her published work includes O Jorgal das Ilhas (1976) and O Nosso o Solo Sagrado de Terra (1978).

The Same Side of the Canoe

The words of our day
are simple words
clear as brook waters
spurting from rust-red slopes
in the clear morning of each day.

So it is I speak to you,
my brother contracted to the coffee plantation
my brother leaving your blood on the bridge
or sailing the sea, a part of yourself lost
    battling the shark
My sister, laundering, laundering
for bread to feed your sons,
my sister selling pits of fruit
to the nearest shop
for the mourning of your dead,
my adjusted sister
selling yourself for a life of greater ease,
in the end only suffering more. . . .

It is for you, my brothers, companions of the road
my cry of hope
with you I feel I am dancing
on idle nights
on some plantation where people gather

together, brothers, in the harvest of cacao
together again on market day
where roasted breadfruit and chicken will bring money.
Together, impelling the canoe along the shore,
joining myself with you,
around the brimming bowl,
joining in the feast
flying through
the ten toasts.

Yet our age-old hands part
on the immense sands
of the São João beach,
because I know, my brother, blackened like you by life,
you think, brother of the canoe,
that we two, flesh of one flesh,
battered by hurricane tempests,
are not on the same side of the canoe.

It is suddenly dark.
There on the far side of the beach
on the Point of São Marcal
there are lights, many lights
in the dark palm-thatched sheds. . .
the sweet whistle thrills –
strange beckonings –
invitation to this ritual night. . . .

Here, only the initiated
in the frenetic rhythm of the dance of propitiation
here, the brothers of the *Santu*
madly wrenching their hips
releasing wild cries,
words, gestures
in the madness of the age-old rite.
In this side of the canoe I also am, my brother,
in your agonizing voice uttering prayers, oaths and maledictions.
Yes, I am here, my brother,
in the endless wakes for the dead
where the people play
with the life of their sons,
I am here, yes, my brother,
in the same side of the canoe.

But we want something still more beautiful.
We want to join our millenary hands,
hands of the cranes on the docks,

hands of the plantations and beaches,
in a great league encompassing
the earth from pole to pole
for our children's dreams
so we may be all of us on the same side of the canoe.

Afternoon descends. . .
The canoe slips away, serene,
on course to the marvellous beach
where our arms join
and we sit side by side
together in the canoe of our beaches.

Noémia De Sousa

1927–

Born in Lourenço Marquez (now Maputo), Mozambique, she attended secondary school in Brazil. She was a politically active journalist in Mozambique under Portuguese colonialism during the 1950s, when she produced some of her best poetry. For some years she lived with her Portuguese husband in Lisbon, Portugal, continually writing and protesting against Salazar's repressive government there, until in 1964 she was forced to seek refuge in France, writing under the pseudonym Vera Micaia. Her work is strongly influenced by African-American and Caribbean writing. It appears in many anthologies, including When Bullets Begin to Flower (1972), edited by Margaret Dickinson, who translated the following poem.

If You Want to Know Me

If you want to know me
examine with careful eyes
this bit of black wood
which some unknown Makonde brother
cut and carved
with his inspired hands
in the distant lands of the North.

This is what I am
empty sockets despairing of possessing life
a mouth torn open in an anguished wound
huge hands outspread
and raised in imprecation and in threat
a body tattooed with wounds seen and unseen
from the harsh whipstrokes of slavery
tortured and magnificent
proud and mysterious
Africa from head to foot
This is what I am.

If you want to understand me
come, bend over this soul of Africa
in the black dockworker's groans
the Chope's frenzied dances
the Changanas'[1] rebellion
in the strange sadness which flows
from an African song, through the night.[1]

And ask no more
to know me
for I am nothing but a shell of flesh
where Africa's revolt congealed
its cry pregnant with hope.

[1] Changanas – people of the Limpopo river basin.

Annette M'Baye
1927–

orn in Sokhone, Senegal, and locally educated, she began her working life as a teacher and in 1947 she went to France to study journalism. She has been active in Radio Senegal since 1963, rising to Director of Programmes, and she is also a journalist specializing in women's issues. In 1963 she launched Awa magazine, the first publication in French for African women. She has published books for children, fiction and poetry collections, including Poèmes Africains (1965).

Silhouette
(for Henri Bathily)

Behind, sun, before, shadow!
A waterground on a stately head,
A breast, a strip of loincloth fluttering,
Two feet that erase the pattern on the sand.

Maya Angelou
1928–

ctivist, poet, playwright, director, autobiographer and former dancer and nightclub singer, she was born Marguerite Johnson in St Louis, spent her early years with her grandmother and

*brother in the deep South, in Stamps and Arkansas, and went to live
with her mother in California aged five. She studied dance with Martha
Graham and drama with Frank Silvera, and joined the Harlem Writers'
Guild in New York. She published her first autobiographical book,* I Know
Why the Caged Bird Sings, *in 1970, followed by* Gather Together in My
Name *(1974),* Singin' and Swingin' and Gettin' Merry Like Christmas
(1976), The Heart of a Woman *(1981) and* All God's Children Need
Traveling Shoes *(1989). Her poetry books include* Just Give Me a Cool
Drink of Water 'fore I Diiie *(1988). She has produced, directed and acted
in film and television, and has written screenplays. Active in the civil
rights movement, she became Northern Co-ordinator for the Southern
Christian Leadership Conference in the 1960s, at the request of Dr Martin
Luther King, Jr. She lived in Africa for some years, in Egypt and in Ghana,
and now lives and works in North Carolina.*

A Good Woman Feeling Bad

The blues may be the life you've led
Or midnight hours in
An empty bed. But persecuting
Blues I've known
Could stalk
Like tigers, break like bone,

Pend like rope in
A gallows tree,
Make me curse
My pedigree,

Bitterness thick on
A rankling tongue,
A psalm to love that's
Left unsung.

Rivers heading north
But ending South,
Funeral music
In a going-home mouth.

All riddles are blues,
And all blues are sad,
And I'm only mentioning
Some blues I've had.

The Reunion

NOBODY could have told me that she'd be out with a black man; out, like going out. But there she was, in 1958, sitting up in the Blue Palm Cafe, when I played the Sunday matinee with Cal Callen's band.

Here's how it was. After we got on the stage, the place was packed, first Cal led us into "D. B. Blues". Of course I know just like everybody else that Cal's got a thing for Lester Young. Maybe because Cal plays the tenor sax, or maybe because he's about as red as Lester Young, or maybe just cause Lester is the Prez. Anybody that's played with Cal knows that the kickoff tune is gotta be "D. B. Blues". So I was ready. We romped.

I'd played with some of those guys, but never all together, but we took off on that tune like we were headed for Birdland in New York City. The audience liked it. Applauded as much as black audiences ever applaud. Black folks act like they are sure that with a little bit of study they could do whatever you're doing on the stage as well as you do it. If not better. So they clap for your luck. Lucky for you that they're not up there to show you where it's really at.

Anyway, after the applause, Cal started to introduce the band. That's his style. Everybody knows that too. After he's through introducing everybody, he's not going to say anything else till the next set, it doesn't matter how many times we play. So he's got a little comedy worked into the introduction patter. He started with Olly, the trumpet man. . . . "And here we have a real Chicagoan . . . by way of Atlanta, Georgia . . . bringing soul to Soulville . . . Mr Olly Martin."

He went on. Looked out into the audience. People sitting, not listening, or better, listening with one side of their ears and talking with both sides of their mouths. Some couples were making a little love . . . and some whites were there trying hard to act natural . . . like they come to the South Side of Chicago every day or maybe like they live there . . . then I saw her. Saw Miss Beth Ann Baker, sitting up with her blond self with a big black man . . . pretty black man. What? White girls, when they look alike, can look so much alike, I thought maybe it wasn't Beth. I looked again. It was her. I remember too well the turn of her cheek. The sliding way her jaw goes up to her hair. That was her. I might have missed a few notes, I might have in fact missed the whole interlude music.

What was she doing in Chicago? On the South Side. And with a black man? Beth Ann Baker of the Baker Cotton Gin. Miss Cotton Queen Baker of Georgia . . .

Then I heard Cal get round to me. He saved me for the last. Mainly cause I'm female and he can get a little rise out of the audience if he says, as he did say, "And our piano man is a lady. And what a lady. A cooker and a looker. Ladies and Gentlemen, I'd like to introduce to you Miss Philomena Jenkins. Folks call her Meanie." I noticed some applause, but mainly I was watching Beth. She heard my name and she looked right into my eyes. Her blue ones got as big as my black ones. She recognized me, in fact in a second we tipped eyelids at each other. Not winking. Just squinting, to see better. There was something that I couldn't recognize. Something I'd never seen in all those years in Baker, Georgia. Not panic, and it wasn't fear. Whatever was in that face seemed familiar, but before I could really read it, Cal announced our next number. "Round 'bout Midnight".

That used to be my song, for so many reasons. In Baker, the only time I could practice jazz, in the church, was round 'bout midnight. When the best chord changes came to me it was generally round 'bout midnight. When my first lover held me in his arms, it was round 'bout midnight. Usually when it's time to play that tune I dig right in it. But this time, I was too busy thinking about Beth and her family . . . and what she was doing in Chicago, on the South Side, escorted by the grooviest looking cat I'd seen in a long time. I was really trying to figure it out, then Cal's saxophone pushed its way into my figurings. Forced me to remember "Round 'bout Midnight". Reminded me of the years of loneliness, the doing-without days, the C.M.E. church, and the old ladies with hands like men and the round 'bout midnight dreams of crossing over Jordan. Then I took thirty-two bars. My fingers found the places between the keys where the blues and the truth lay hiding. I dug out the story of a woman without a man, and a man without hope. I tried to wedge myself in and lay down in the groove between B-flat and B-natural. I must of gotten close to it, because the audience brought me out with their clapping. Even Cal said, "Yeah baby, that's it." I nodded to him then to the audience and looked around for Beth.

How did she like them apples? What did she think of little Philomena that used to shake the farts out of her sheets, wash her dirty drawers, pick up after her slovenly mama? What did she think now? Did she know that I was still aching from the hurt Georgia put on me? But Beth was gone. So was her boyfriend.

I had lived with my parents until I was thirteen, in the servants' quarters. A house behind the Baker main house. Daddy was the butler, my mother was the cook, and I went to a segregated school on the other side of town where the other kids called me the Baker Nigger. Momma's nimble fingers were never able to sew away the truth of Beth's hand-me-down and thrown away clothing. I had a lot to say to Beth, and she was gone.

That was a bring-down. I guess what I wanted was to rub her face in "See now, you thought all I would ever be was you and your mama's flunky." And "See now, how folks, even you, pay to listen to me," and "See now, I'm saying something nobody else can say. Not the way I say it, anyway." But her table was empty.

We did the rest of the set. Some of my favorite tunes, "Sophisticated Lady", "Misty" and "Cool Blues". I admit that I never got back into the groove until we did "When Your Lover Has Gone".

After the closing tune, "Lester Leaps In", which Cal set at a tempo like he was trying to catch the last train to Mobile, was over, the audience gave us their usual thank-you, and we were off for a twenty-minute intermission.

Some of the guys went out to turn on and a couple went to tables where they had ladies waiting for them. But I went to the back of the dark smoky bar where even the occasional sunlight from the front door made no difference. My blood was still fluttering in my fingertips, throbbing. If she was listed in the phone directory I would call her. Hello Miss Beth . . . this is Philomena . . . who was your maid, whose whole family worked for you. Or could I say, Hello Beth.

Is this Beth? Well, this is Miss Jenkins. I saw you yesterday at the Blue Palm Cafe.
I used to know your parents. In fact your mother said my mother was a gem, and
my father was a treasure. I used to laugh 'cause your mother drank so much
whiskey, but my Momma said, "Judge not, that ye be not judged." Then I found
out that your father had three children down in our part of town and they all
looked just like you, only prettier. Oh Beth, now . . . now . . . shouldn't have a
chip . . . mustn't be bitter. . . . She of course would hang up.

Just imagining what I would have said to her cheered me up. I ordered a
drink from the bartender and settled back into my reverie. . . . Hello Beth . . .
this is a friend from Baker. What were you doing with that black man
Sunday? . . .

"Philomena? Remember me?" She stood before me absorbing the light. The
drawl was still there. The soft accent rich white girls practice in Georgia to show
that they had breeding. I couldn't think of anything to say. Did I remember her?
There was no way I could answer the question.

"I asked Willard to wait for me in the car. I wanted to talk to you."

I sipped my drink and looked in the mirror over the bar and wondered
what she really wanted. Her reflection wasn't threatening at all.

"I told him that we grew up . . . in the same town."

I was relieved that she hadn't said we grew up together. By the time I
was ten, I knew growing up meant going to work. She smiled and I held my
drink.

"I'm engaged to Willard and very happy."

I'm proud of my face. I didn't jump up and walk the bar.

She gave a practiced nod to the bartender and ordered a drink. "He teaches
high school here on the South Side." Her drink came and she lifted the glass
and our eyes met in the mirror. "I met him two years ago in Canada. We are
very happy."

Why the hell was she telling me her fairy story? We weren't kin. So she
had a black man. Did she think like most whites in mixed marriages that she
had done the whole race a favor?

"My parents . . ." her voice, became small, whispery. "My parents don't
understand. They think I'm with Willard just to spite them. They . . . When's
the last time you went home, Mena?" She didn't wait for my answer.

"They hate him. So much, they say they will disown me." Disbelief made her
voice strong again. "They said I could never set foot in Baker again." She tried
to catch my eyes in the mirror but I looked down at my drink. "I know there's
a lot wrong with Baker, but it's my home." The drawl was turning into a whine.
"Mother said, now mind you, she has never laid eyes on Willard, she said, if
she had dreamed when I was a baby that I would grow up to marry a nig . . .
a black man, she'd have choked me to death on her breast. That's a cruel thing
for a mother to say. I told her so."

She bent forward and I shifted to see her expression, but her profile was
hidden by the blonde hair. "He doesn't understand, and me either. He didn't
grow up in the South." I thought, no matter where he grew up, he wasn't white
and rich and spoiled. "I just wanted to talk to somebody who knew me. Knew
Baker. You know, a person can get lonely. . . . I don't see any of my friends, any

more. Do you understand, Mena? My parents gave me everything."

Well, they owned everything.

"Willard is the first thing I ever got for myself. And I'm not going to give him up."

We faced each other for the first time. She sounded like her mother and looked like a ten-year-old just before a tantrum.

"He's mine. He belongs to me."

The musicians were tuning up on the bandstand. I drained my glass and stood.

"Mena, I really enjoyed seeing you again, and talking about old times. I live in New York, but I come to Chicago every other weekend. Say, will you come to our wedding? We haven't set the date yet. Please come. It's going to be here . . . in a black church . . . somewhere."

"Good-bye, Beth. Tell your parents I said go to hell and take you with them, just for company."

I sat down at the piano. She still had everything. Her mother would understand the stubbornness and send her off to Paris or the Moon. Her father couldn't deny that black skin was beautiful. She had money and a wonderful-looking man to play with. If she stopped wanting him she could always walk away. She'd still be white.

The band was halfway into the "D. B. Blues" release before I thought, she had the money, but I had the music. She and her parents had had the power to hurt me when I was young, but look, the stuff in me lifted me up high above them. No matter how bad times became, I would always be the song struggling to be heard.

The piano keys were slippery with tears. I know, I sure as hell wasn't crying for myself.

Sylvia Wynter

1928–

Born to Jamaican parents in Holguin Oriente Province, Cuba, she returned to Jamaica at the age of two. In 1946 she was awarded a Jamaican scholarship which took her to England to

*read for a BA Honours degree in Modern Languages (Spanish) at King's
College, London University, after which she worked as a writer for radio
and television. A Spanish government scholarship enabled her to spend
a year studying philology in Spain and she earned an MA for her thesis
on seventeenth-century Spanish drama. Drama has always been a major
interest of hers, particularly in the context of Caribbean folk culture, and
she has written a number of plays, many of which have been produced in
Jamaica. In 1962 she published her novel* The Hills of Hebron *(extracted
here), which deals perceptively with religious revivalism in a rural Jamaican community. She began her academic career in 1963 as a lecturer
at the University of the West Indies, has held posts at the Universities of
Michigan and California (San Diego) and in 1977 became Professor
of African and Afro-American Studies and Comparative Literature at
Stanford University. A prolific literary critic and committed feminist, she
has written widely on culture, politics and history, and is a frequent
participant in academic conferences and forums on women's studies.*

From

The Hills of Hebron

THE DROUGHT

THE hills of Hebron were bare and parched under the sun. In places where
the thickly-wooded slopes had been cleared, the naked earth looked like
sores. The houses were stranded, dilapidated arks. Seated on their doorsteps
the New Believers looked out over the dead world of Hebron and felt a strange
lassitude in their limbs. They could not tame the sun. It was a distant and mer-
ciless enemy moving across a cloudless blue sky, day after day. It was the Will of
God. In their plots of ground there were stunted growths of cassava and corn.
The young banana shoots and the arrowing blossoms of the sugar-cane bowed
their crests to the ground.

In the yards around their houses, withered pumpkin vines, flame-coloured
"ackee" pods, black in the heat, and the shrivelled blossoms of the breadfruit
tree, littered the earth. Only the Jerusalem candlesticks that fenced in one barren
acre from the other, the cactus that grew wild all over the hills, the croton plants
that lingered in a few front gardens, their shiny leaves ribbed with bright yellow,
were unaffected by the drought – they sent their roots down to the secret places
of the earth's heart where moisture was hidden. Up on the further reaches of
the hills, the great trees allowed their branches to be raped, and hoarded life
in their roots, their trunks. Beneath them the exposed coffee plants, the cocoa
trees that had once drooped golden pods like rich gifts, perished. The New

Believers looked out on a skeletal world, etched in muted browns and beaten down, subdued, under the conqueror sun.

In the square the shadows under the trees were long and stark. It was nearing ten o'clock and silence held sway. The spring was dry. In the sediment of mud that remained at the bottom, a few tadpoles darted about. On the slope above the spring a dead frog lay on its back, its mottled belly like cured leather. Beside him a banana tree trailed its leaves like defeated banners; and the gashes in the leaves striped the shadow cast by the trunk with slivers of light that gleamed like pools of water.

Sister Eufemia stood near the spring, leaning against a cotton-tree stump. She held an empty petrol can (a kerosene tin, as the Hebronites called it) under her arm. She was of average height, pleasantly rounded, with a coffee-coloured skin and pale hazel eyes, the result of recessive genes left by some anonymous white ancestor. She could relax so completely it was as though the sun had dissolved her bones. She was waiting for Sister Gee. That morning the distance between her house and the spring had seemed to multiply itself and she felt tired. She wiped the sweat from her face and her apron, and shifted her position. Years of malnutrition made her movements indolent, like a sluggish river. As she raised her left foot to prop it behind her, she gave a startled jerk. Her foot had caught in a hollow concealed under the tangle of vines that covered the stump. She eased it out, stuck her finger in her mouth. Then she settled back to wait. She had been in the shade long enough to forget how hot the sun was, and she began to sing:

"June and July is a dry, dry hard time,
But drought in November, Lord, Massa,
A-sweat out me substance . . ."

Gee rounded the bend. She was balancing the empty tin on her head, swaying as she walked. She had a small face with a pointed chin, a long neck set well back on her shoulders, and high young breasts. But her hips were wide, her legs thick and sturdy. She had not really come for water. She knew there was none. But meeting Eufemia at the spring, talking with her, was a habit. Besides, there was nothing else to do. She lowered her water tin, took up a bamboo pole and stuck it into the spring, stirring up mud and tadpoles.

"Not a drop, eh?" Eufemia called out to her.

"Not a drop!"

Gee flung away the pole, up-ended her tin and sat, resting her elbows on her knees and propping her face in her hands. Eufemia came across to her.

"I dipped the pole down too, but it was the same as yesterday, the same as the day before!"

"Same like the day before that and the day before that, eh?"

"Same way so!" Eufemia affirmed. She seated herself in the same position as her friend.

A gust of wind sent the dry leaves spinning in a vortex. It spent itself and the leaves subsided once more. A trail of fat red ants disappeared into the undergrowth beside the tree-stump, a living caravan taking over an abandoned world; and the two women could have been petrified beings, relics of a people who had carved into face, attitude, posture, their long history of waiting for death, a waiting people, striving for nothing, accepting all.

Sister Gee glanced at the spring and her face was suddenly sombre.

"You know," she said, "it seems strange not to find Aunt Kate waiting by the spring, watching whilst we dip up the water, warning us to be careful not to wake up Maverlyn!"

"Yes, it seem strange not to see her!"

Eufemia looked over her shoulder at the spot where Aunt Kate used to sit. The old woman's absence emphasized for them the sharp change that had come upon Hebron. The two girls were the new generation, born and brought up in Hebron and without memories of the town from which their parents had made a triumphant exodus. On occasions they had visited Cockpit Centre with their elders, but had seen only evil lurking at every hand, the evil that they had been told about, and that they, born in the promised land, had been spared. But they had been reared under the shadow of Prophet Moses's sacrifice, his crucifixion. And they were still young enough to reject unconsciously, the constant worship of a wooden Cross and of death.

Aunt Kate's fantasy that her child was still alive, that she was only sleeping, touched a responsive chord in them. Her mad hope had become theirs. Some mornings, standing around her as she sat and cradled her arms, they had almost been persuaded that they could see, glancing on the surface of the water, her child Maverlyn, like some spirit celebrating the eternal life that their youth expected and demanded. And now the spring had dried up. They, as well as Aunt Kate, had been forced into accepting that Maverlyn was drowned and a long time buried, that Maverlyn was dead.

"I went up to see her last night," Eufemia said. "But Sister Ann wouldn't let me in. You know how fussy she is. But from the doorway I could hear poor Aunt Kate talking and laughing to herself and burning up with the fever!"

"Till my dying day," Gee said, "I am not going to forget Aunt Kate's face that day when the sun dry up the last sheet of water from the bottom of the spring and she was looking and looking and in no part of it she could find Maverlyn. Till my dying day I am not going to forget Aunt Kate's face that day!"

"Me neither," Eufemia agreed. Then she yawned, hugged herself and said:

"I hope the meeting today is not another prayer-for-rain one. I can't see what purpose they are serving!"

"This is not prayer-for-rain meeting, I can tell you that!"

"Then what sort of meeting it is then?"

"Hugh say that I am not tell anybody. Only the Senior Brothers and Sisters are to know about it."

"Well, I will soon know, anyway!"

"Wait until you know, then!"

"Cho, you don't know any more than I know myself," Eufemia taunted.

Gee bent close to her and whispered:

"Hugh arranged with the others to ask Miss Gatha to take over as Elder."

"But what about . . . Elder Obadiah?"

"What about him?" Gee's voice was hard.

"Well . . ." Eufemia explained hesitantly, "Brother Hugh . . . going to throw over his long-time friend like that?"

"What you mean throw over? Don't Hugh have the all of us to consider?"

"Yes, I know, but . . ."

"But what?"

"Nothing, nothing!"

Eufemia's disclaimer had been too hasty, and Gee frowned. Eufemia tried to apologize:

"Gee, I wasn't saying anything against Brother Hugh, you know . . ."

"I didn't say you were saying anything against him!" Gee snapped at her.

With Eufemia, Gee was always very touchy on the subject of Hugh. She never forgot the incredulity with which her friend received her disclosure that Brother Hugh, Chief Recorder of the Church of the New Believers of Hebron, had asked her to marry him on the same day that the Elder Obadiah was to marry Rose.

"But Gee, Brother Hugh . . . is . . . old!" Eufemia had protested.

"Then what about Obadiah and Rose?" she herself had argued.

"That is different!"

"And why it should be different? Rose is only a little bit older than me! Why it should be different?"

"I don't know, but . . ."

And Eufemia had left it at that, with the "but" remaining like a wasp's sting in Gee's memory. At the wedding, too, Eufemia, who was only her bridesmaid, had enjoyed the ceremony more than she, the bride; had laughed and talked with Brother Ananias whom she had not even dared to look at before when Gee was around. Even when, after the months had passed, the two made up their differences and once again met at the spring to gossip, or wandered over Hebron, their bare arms linked and nuzzling against each other as they told their "secrets", even then Gee had felt cheated. Eufemia had so much more to tell about what took place between herself and Ananias. Instead, she had to embroider details to elaborate the brief ritual which, every Friday, Hugh performed with her in bed, without ever seeming to pause in his endless talk about his plans for the greater glory of himself, of Obadiah, and of Hebron; and leaving her wondering if this was all that there was to it. . . .

Gee got up abruptly and left her water-tin by the tree-stump. Eufemia hesitated, then followed suit. They walked up to the church in silence.

Mariama Bâ
1929–81

S he was born to Muslim parents in Dakar, Senegal. Her mother
died when she was very young, and she was brought up by
her maternal grandparents in a well-to-do family. As she said,
"Normally I should have grown up in the midst of this family without
ever having gone to school, my only education being a traditional one
including initiation rites." However, her civil servant father's insistence
that she had a French education led to her attending the École Normal
for girls to Rufisque, where two essays she wrote were published. Becom-
int involved in Senegalese women's associations, she began to write and
speak on issues such as polygamy and clitoridectomy. She married a
Senegalese politician and had nine children before separating from
him, and she also worked as a secretary and primary school teacher.
Her own experience of marriage and motherhood contributed much to
her epistolary first novel, So Long a Letter (Une Si longue lettre, 1970),
which won the first Noma Award for Publishing in Africa. She wrote one
other novel, Scarlet Song (Le Chant écarlate) but before its publication in
1981 she died in Dakar after a long illness.

From

So Long A Letter

CHAPTER VII

A ISSATOU, I will never forget the white woman who was the first to desire
for us an "uncommon" destiny. Together, let us recall our school, green,
pink, blue, yellow, a veritable rainbow: green, blue and yellow, the colours of
the flowers everywhere in the compound; pink the colour of the dormitories,
with the beds impeccably made. Let us hear the walls of our school come to life
with the intensity of our study. Let us relive its intoxicating atmosphere at night,
while the evening song, our joint prayer, rang out, full of hope. The admission
policy, which was based on an entrance examination for the whole of former
French West Africa, now broken up into autonomous republics, made possible
a fruitful blend of different intellects, characters, manners and customs. Nothing
differentiated us, apart from specific racial features, the Fon girl from Dahomey

and the Malinke one from Guinea. Friendships were made that have endured the test of time and distance. We were true sisters, destined for the same mission of emancipation.

To lift us out of the bog of tradition, superstition and custom, to make us appreciate a multitude of civilizations without renouncing our own, to raise our vision of the world, cultivate our personalities, strengthen our qualities, to make up for our inadequacies, to develop universal moral values in us: these were the aims of our admirable headmistress. The word "love" had a particular resonance in her. She loved us without patronizing us, with our plaits either standing on end or bent down, with our loose blouses, our wrappers. She knew how to discover and appreciate our qualities.

How I think of her! If the memory of her has triumphed over the ingratitude of time, now that flowers no longer smell as sweetly or as strongly as before, now that age and mature reflection have stripped our dreams of their poetic virtue, it is because the path chosen for our training and our blossoming has not been at all fortuitous. It has accorded with the profound choices made by New Africa for the promotion of the black woman.

Thus, free from frustrating taboos and capable now of discernment, why should I follow my mother's finger pointing at Daouda Dieng, still a bachelor but too mature for my eighteen years. Working as an African doctor at the Polyclinique, he was well-to-do and knew how to use his position to advantage. His villa, perched on a rock on the Corniche facing the sea, was the meeting place for the young élite. Nothing was missing, from the refrigerator, containing its pleasant drinks, to the record player, which exuded sometimes languorous, sometimes frenzied music.

Daouda Dieng also knew how to win hearts. Useful presents for my mother, ranging from a sack of rice, appreciated in that period of war penury, to the frivolous gift for me, daintily wrapped in paper and tied with ribbons. But I preferred the man in the eternal khaki suit. Our marriage was celebrated without dowry, without pomp, under the disapproving looks of my father, before the painful indignation of my frustrated mother, under the sarcasm of my surprised sisters, in our town struck dumb with astonishment.

CHAPTER VIII

THEN came your marriage with Mawdo Bâ, recently graduated from the African School of Medicine and Pharmacy. A controversial marriage. I can stil hear the angry rumours in town:

"What, a Toucouleur marrying a goldsmith's daughter? He will never 'make money'."

"Mawdo's mother is a Dioufene, a *Guelewar*[1] from the Sine. What an insult to her, before her former co-wives." (Mawdo's father was dead.)

[1] Princess.

"In the desire to marry a 'short skirt' come what may, this is what one gets."

"School turns our girls into devils who lure our men away from the right path."

And I haven't recounted all. But Mawdo remained firm. "Marriage is a personal thing," he retorted to anyone who cared to hear.

He emphasized his total commitment to his choice of life partner by visiting your father, not at home but at his place of work. He would return from his outings illuminated, happy to have "moved in the right direction", he would say triumphantly. He would speak of your father as a "creative artist". He admired the man, weakened as he was by the daily dose of carbon dioxide he inhaled working in the acrid atmosphere of the dusty fumes. Gold is his medium, which he melts, pours, twists, flattens, refines, chases. "You should see him," Mawdo would add. "You should see him breathe over the flame." His cheeks would swell with the life from his lungs. This life would animate the flame, sometimes red, sometimes blue, which would rise or curve, wax or wane at his command, depending on what the work demanded. And the gold specks in the showers of red sparks, and the uncouth songs of the apprentices punctuating the strokes of the hammer here, and the pressure of hands on the bellows there would make passers-by turn round.

Aissatou, your father knew all the rites that protect the working of gold, the metal of the djinns. Each profession has its code, known only to the initiated and transmitted from father to son. As soon as your elder brothers left the huts of the circumcised, they moved into this particular world, the whole compound's source of nourishment.

But what about your younger brothers? Their steps were directed towards the white man's school. Hard is the climb up the steep hill of knowledge to the white man's school: kindergarten remains a luxury that only those who are financially sound can offer their young ones. Yet it is necessary, for this is what sharpens and channels the young ones' attention and sensibilities.

Even though the primary schools are rapidly increasing, access to them has not become any easier. They leave out in the streets an impressive number of children because of the lack of places.

Entrance into secondary school is no panacea for the child at an age fraught with the problems of consolidating his personality, with the explosion of puberty, with the discovery of the various pitfalls: drugs, vagrancy, sensuality.

The university has its own large number of despairing rejects.

What will the unsuccessful do? Apprenticeship to traditional crafts seems degrading to whoever has the slightest book-learning. The dream is to become a clerk. The trowel is spurned.

The horde of the jobless swells the flood of delinquency.

Should we have been happy at the desertion of the forges, the workshops, the shoemaker's shops? Should we have rejoiced so wholeheartedly? Were we not beginning to witness the disappearance of an elite of traditional manual workers?

Eternal questions of our eternal debates. We all agreed that much dismantling was needed to introduce modernity within our traditions. Torn between the past and the present, we deplored the "hard sweat" that would be inevitable. We counted the possible losses. But we knew that nothing would be as before. We were full of nostalgia but were resolutely progressive.

CHAPTER IX

MAWDO raised you to his own level, he the son of a princess and you a child from the forges. His mother's rejection did not frighten him.

Our lives developed in parallel. We experienced the tiffs and reconciliations of married life. In our different ways, we suffered the social constraints and heavy burden of custom. I loved Modou. I compromised with his people. I tolerated his sisters, who too often would desert their own homes to encumber my own. They allowed themselves to be fed and petted. They would look on, without reacting, as their children romped around on my chairs. I tolerated their spitting, the phlegm expertly secreted under my carpets.

His mother would stop by again and again while on her outings, always flanked by different friends, just to show off her son's social success but particularly so that they might see, at close quarters, her supremacy in this beautiful house in which she did not live. I would receive her with all the respect due to a queen, and she would leave satisfied, especially if her hand closed over the banknote I had carefully placed there. But hardly would she be out than she would think of the new band of friends she would soon be dazzling.

Modou's father was more understanding. More often than not, he would visit us without sitting down. He would accept a glass of cold water and would leave, after repeating his prayers for the protection of the house.

I knew how to smile at them all, and consented to wasting useful time in futile chatter. My sisters-in-law believed me to be spared the drudgery of housework.

"With your two housemaids!" they would say with emphasis.

Try explaining to them that a working woman is no less responsible for her home. Try explaining to them that nothing is done if you do not step in, that you have to see to everything, do everything all over again: cleaning up, cooking, ironing. There are the children to be washed, the husband to be looked after. The working woman has a dual task, of which both halves, equally arduous, must be reconciled. How does one go about this? Therein lies the skill that makes all the difference to a home.

Some of my sisters-in-law did not envy my way of living at all. They saw me dashing around the house after a hard day at school. They appreciated their comfort, their peace of mind, their moments of leisure and allowed themselves to be looked after by their husbands, who were crushed under their duties.

Others, limited in their way of thinking, envied my comfort and purchasing power. They would go into raptures over the many "gadgets" in my house: gas cooker, vegetable grater, sugar tongs. They forgot the source of this easy life; first up in the morning, last to go to bed, always working.

You, Aissatou, you forsook your family-in-law, tightly shut in with their hurt dignity. You would lament to me: "Your family-in-law respects you. You must treat them well. As for me, they look down on me from the height of their lost nobility. What can I do?"

While Mawdo's mother planned her revenge, we lived: Christmas Eve parties organized by several couples, with the costs shared equally, and held in turns in the different homes. Without self-consciousness, we would revive the dances of yester-year: the lively beguine, frenzied rumbas, languid tangos. We re-discovered the old beatings of the heart that strengthened our feelings.

We would also leave the stifling city to breathe in the healthy air of seaside suburbs.

We would walk along the Dakar Corniche, one of the most beautiful in West Africa, a sheer work of art wrought by nature. Rounded or pointed rocks, black or ochre-coloured, overlooking the ocean Greenery, sometimes a veritable hanging garden spread out under the clear sky. We would go on to the road to Ouakam, which also leads to Ngor and further on to Yoff airport. We would recognize on the way the narrow road leading farther on to Almadies beach.

Our favourite spot was Ngor beach, situated near the village of the same name, where old bearded fishermen repaired their nets under the silk-cotton trees. Naked and snotty children played in complete freedom when they were not frolicking about in the sea.

On the fine sand, washed by the waves and swollen with water, naively painted canoes awaited their turn to be launched into the waters. In their hollows small pools of blue water would glisten, full of light from the sky and sun.

What a crowd on public holidays! Numerous families would stroll about, thirsty for space and fresh air. People would undress, without embarrassment, tempted by the benevolent care of the iodized breeze and the warmth from the sun's rays. The idle would sleep under spread parasols. A few children, spade and bucket in hand, would build and demolish the castles of their imagination.

In the evening the fishermen would return from their laborious outings. Once more, they had escaped the moving snare of the sea. At first simple points on the horizon, the boats would become more distinct from one another as they drew nearer. They would dance in the hollows of the waves, then would lazily let themselves be dragged along. Fishermen would gaily furl their sails and draw in their tackle. While some of them would gather together the wriggling catch, others would wring out their soaked clothes and mop their faces.

Under the wondering gaze of the kids, the live fish would flip up as the long sea snakes would curve themselves inwards. There is nothing more beautiful than a fish just out of water, its eye clear and fresh, with golden or silvery scales and beautiful blueish glints!

Hands would sort out, group, divide. We would buy a good selection at bargain prices for the house.

The sea air would put us in good humour. The pleasure we indulged in and in which all our senses rejoiced would intoxicate both rich and poor with health. Our communion with deep, bottomless and unlimited nature refreshed our souls. Depression and sadness would disappear, suddenly to be replaced by feelings of plenitude and expansiveness.

Reinvigorated, we would set out for home. How jealously we guarded the secret of simple pleasures, health-giving remedy for the daily tensions of life.

Do you remember the picnics we organized at Sangalkam, in the farm Mawdo Bâ inherited from his father? Sangalkam remains the refuge of people from Dakar, those who want a break from the frenzy of the city. The younger set, in particular, has bought land there and built country residences: these green, open spaces are conducive to rest, meditation and the letting off of steam by children. This oasis lies on the road to Rufisque.

Mawdo's mother had looked after the farm before her son's marriage. The memory of her husband had made her attached to this plot of land, where their joint and patient hands had disciplined the vegetation that filled our eyes with admiration.

Yourself, you added the small building at the far end: three small, simple bedrooms, a bathroom, a kitchen. You grew many flowers in a few corners. You had a hen run built, then a closed pen for sheep.

Coconut trees, with their interlacing leaves, gave protection from the sun. Suculent sapodilla stood next to sweet-smelling pomegranates. Heavy mangoes weighed down the branches. Pawpaws resembling breasts of different shapes hung tempting and inaccessible from the tops of elongated trunks.

Green leaves and browned leaves, new grass and withered grass were strewn all over the ground. Under our feet the ants untiringly built and rebuilt their homes.

How warm the shades over the camp beds! Teams for games were formed one after the other amid cries of victory or lamentations of defeat.

And we stuffed ourselves with fruits within easy reach. And we drank the milk from coconuts. And we told "juicy stories"! And we danced about, roused by the strident notes of a gramophone. And the lamb, seasoned with white pepper, garlic, butter, hot pepper, would be roasting over the wood fire.

And we lived. When we stood in front of our over-crowded classes, we represented a force in the enormous effort to be accomplished in order to overcome ignorance.

Each profession, intellectual or manual, deserves consideration, whether it requires painful physical effort or manual dexterity, wide knowledge or the patience of an ant. Ours, like that of the doctor, does not allow for any mistake. You don't joke with life, and life is both body and mind. To warp a soul is as much a sacrilege as murder. Teachers – at kindergarten level, as at university level – form a noble army accomplishing daily feats, never praised, never decorated. An army forever on the move, forever vigilant. An army without drums, without gleaming uniforms. This army, thwarting traps and snares, everywhere plants the flag of knowledge and morality.

How we loved this priesthood, humble teachers in humble local schools. How faithfully we served our profession, and how we spent ourselves in order to do it honour. Like all apprentices, we had learned how to practise it well at the demonstration school, a few steps away from our own, where experienced teachers taught the novices that we were how to apply, in the lessons we gave, our knowledge of psychology and method. . . . In those children we set in motion waves that, breaking, carried away in their furl a bit of ourselves.

Citèkù Ndaaya
?1929–

Born into the Luba tribe in Zaïre, she was a professional poet. Her kàsàlà – *a very ancient song form that probably originated in songs of lamentation for important members of the tribe – was sung on* 16 September 1965 at Katende-Kabooke village, Eastern Kasai; she was about thirty-six at time of its recital. It was translated from combined French-Luba texts by Judith Gleason.

From

Ndaaya's Kàsàlà

Ndaaya, I, am so poor
   you can hear my pestle pounding after sundown.
Already I stand at the crossing of the roads,
   why then have I come to these lamentations. . . ?
This death of yours is men's affair, O Ntumba,
   were it women's affair I'd brandish my pestle.
Why I am what I am remains impenetrable:
   born a man – they would have handed me a sword –
   would I not have become a hero?
Am I not as things are vagabond with a strong gullet?
Could I not then fight as they fight. . .
Dear brothers,
   death came to me like a thief in the night,
   as I went to bed with a divided heart.
The drums of a famous musician, the intrepid one,
   today they are sounding my rhythm.
Ah, daughter of the Ngandu,
   were voice strong as drum
   it would already have reached my mother. . .
But tears will never awaken the dead,
   sooner vase will fill up. . .
War has ravaged me today, sister of Cibangu,
   but who remains to protect Ndaaya?

I must call my comrades, but who will respond?
  who dares summon the strong?
At the crossroads
  I have trapped bitter crickets
  I have grubbed for ashen cicadas
And I go to bed with a divided heart
  restless, I have counted beams
  vagabond, have counted roofs
Daughter of those who bathe till their bodies gleam as with oil,
  ah, my brothers, misfortunes weigh me down:
  one part orphan
  one part sterile
But what can I say that men might give me credence?
Ah, sister of Cibangu, human things alter:
  a young woman becomes old
  she-goat turns billy-goat
  another, having given birth,
  look – suddenly she's sterile,
  like Ndaaya.
Did I not give birth to a child with gums strong as cut-teeth?
O daughter, quickened in me by ritual,
  since you left, I've been inconsolable
  at the crossroads
Child planted in me by ritual
  see how women of my age prosper:
  third wives moved up to first place
  others demoted
At dangerous crossroads I call
  daughter, returned to my womb by ritual
  Mbombo
  Silence

Paule Marshall

1929–

Born in Brooklyn to Barbadian parents who emigrated to New York shortly after the First World War, she has a BA from Brooklyn College (1953), did postgraduate studies at Hunter College (1955) and has been a librarian, journalist and lecturer in Black literature at universities in the USA and Europe, including Columbia, Oxford and Paris. A member of the Harlem Writers' Guild and associated with American Youth for Democracy and with Artists for Freedom, she has received a Guggenheim Fellowship (1960), Rosenthal Fellowship (1961) and Ford Foundation grant. Describing her work as "both West Indian and American", she is the author of several books of fiction: Brown Girl, Brownstones (1959), Praisesong for the Widow (1983) and Reena and Other Stories (1983). Of "To Da-Duh, In Memoriam" she says: "This is the most autobiographical of the stories, a reminiscence largely of a visit I paid to my grandmother (whose nickname was Da-duh) on the island of Barbados when I was nine. Ours was a complex relationship – close, affectionate yet rivalrous. During the year I spent with her a subtle kind of power struggle went on between us. It was as if we both knew, at a level beyond words, that I had come into the world not only to love her and to continue her line but to take her very life in order that I might live.... Apart from this story, Da-duh also appears in one form or another in my other work as well.... She's an ancestor figure, symbolic for me of the long line of black women and men – African and New World – who made my being possible, and whose spirit I believe continues to animate my life and work. I wish to acknowledge and celebrate them. I am, in a word, an unabashed ancestor worshipper."

To Da-Duh, In Memoriam

"... Oh Nana! all of you is not involved in this evil business Death,
Nor all of us in life."
                            – From "At My Grandmother's Grave" by Lebert Bethune

I DID not see her at first I remember. For not only was it dark inside
the crowded disembarkation shed in spite of the daylight flooding in from
outside, but standing there waiting for her with my mother and sister I was still
somewhat blinded from the sheen of tropical sunlight on the water of the bay
which we had just crossed in the landing boat, leaving behind us the ship that
had brought us from New York lying in the offing. Besides, being only nine years
of age at the time and knowing nothing of islands I was busy attending to the
alien sights and sounds of Barbados, the unfamiliar smells.

I did not see her, but I was alerted to her approach by my mother's hand which
suddenly tightened around mine, and looking up I traced her gaze through the
gloom in the shed until I finally made out the small, purposeful, painfully erect
figure of the old woman headed our way.

Her face was drowned in the shadow of an ugly rolled-brim brown felt
hat, but the details of her slight body and of the struggle taking place within it
were clear enough – an intense, unrelenting struggle between her back which
was beginning to bend ever so slightly under the weight of her eighty-odd years
and the rest of her which sought to deny those years and hold that back straight,
keep it in line. Moving swiftly toward us (so swiftly it seemed she did not intend
stopping when she reached us but would sweep past us out the doorway which
opened onto the sea and like Christ walk upon the water!), she was caught
between the sunlight at her end of the building and the darkness inside – and
for a moment she appeared to contain them both: the light in the long severe
old-fashioned white dress she wore which brought the sense of a past that was
still alive into our bustling present and in the snatch of white at her eye; the
darkness in her black high-top shoes and in her face which was visible now
that she was closer.

It was as stark and fleshless as a death mask, that face. The maggots might have
already done their work, leaving only the framework of bone beneath the ruined
skin and deep wells at the temple and jaw. But her eyes were alive, unnervingly
so for one so old, with a sharp light that flicked out of the dim clouded depths
like a lizard's tongue to snap up all in her view. Those eyes betrayed a child's
curiosity about the world, and I wondered vaguely seeing them, and seeing the
way the bodice of her ancient dress had collapsed in on her flat chest (what had
happened to her breasts?), whether she might not be some kind of child at the
same time that she was a woman, with fourteen children, my mother included,
to prove it. Perhaps she was both, both child and woman, darkness and light,
past and present, life and death – all the opposites contained and reconciled in
her.

"My Da-duh," my mother said formally and stepped forward. The name
sounded like thunder fading softly in the distance.

"Child," Da-duh said, and her tone, her quick scrutiny of my mother,
the brief embrace in which they appeared to shy from each other rather than
touch, wiped out the fifteen years my mother had been away and restored the
old relationship. My mother, who was such a formidable figure in my eyes, had
suddenly with a word been reduced to my status.

"Yes, God is good," Da-duh said with a nod that was like a tic. "He
has spared me to see my child again."

We were led forward then, apologetically because not only did Da-duh prefer boys but she also liked her grandchildren to be "white", that is, fair-skinned; and we had, I was to discover, a number of cousins, the outside children of white estate managers and the like, who qualified. We, though, were as black as she.

My sister being the oldest was presented first. "This one takes after the father," my mother said and waited to be reproved.

Frowning, Da-duh tilted my sister's face toward the light. But her frown soon gave way to a grudging smile, for my sister with her large mild eyes and little broad winged nose, with our father's high-cheeked Barbadian cast to her face, was pretty.

"She's goin' be lucky," Da-duh said and patted her once on the cheek. "Any girl child that takes after the father does be lucky."

She turned then to me. But oddly enough she did not touch me. Instead leaning close, she peered hard at me, and then quickly drew back. I thought I saw her hand start up as though to shield her eyes. It was almost as if she saw not only me, a thin truculent child who it was said took after no one but myself, but something in me which for some reason she found disturbing, even threatening. We looked silently at each other for a long time there in the noisy shed, our gaze locked. She was the first to look away.

"But, Adry," she said to my mother and her laugh was cracked, thin, apprehensive. "Where did you get this one here with this fierce look?"

"We don't know where she came out of, my Da-duh," my mother said, laughing also. Even I smiled to myself. After all I had won the encounter. Da-duh had recognized my small strength – and this was all I ever asked of the adults in my life then.

"Come, soul," Da-duh said and took my hand. "You must be one of those New York terrors you hear so much about."

She led us, me at her side and my sister and mother behind, out of the shed into the sunlight that was like a bright driving summer rain and over to a group of people clustered beside a decrepit lorry. They were our relatives, most of them from St Andrews although Da-duh herself lived in St Thomas, the women wearing bright print dresses, the colors vivid against their darkness, the men rusty black suits that encased them like straitjackets. Da-duh, holding fast to my hand, became my anchor as they circled round us like a nervous sea, exclaiming, touching us with their calloused hands, embracing us shyly. They laughed in awed bursts: "But look Adry got big-big children!"/ "And see the nice things they wearing, wrist watch and all!"/ "I tell you, Adry has done all right for sheself in New York. . . ."

Da-duh, ashamed at their wonder, embarrassed for them, admonished them the while. "But, oh Christ," she said, "why you all got to get on like you never saw people from 'Away' before? You would think New York is the only place in the world to hear wunna. That's why I don't like to go anyplace with you St Andrews people, you know. You all ain't been colonized."

We were in the back of the lorry finally, packed in among the barrels of ham, flour, cornmeal and rice and the trucks of clothes that my mother had brought as gifts. We made our way slowly through Bridgetown's clogged streets, part of a funeral procession of cars and open-sided buses, bicycles and donkey carts. The dim little limestone shops and offices along the way marched with us, at the same mournful pace, towards the same grave ceremony – as did the people, the women balancing huge baskets on top their heads as if they were no more than hats they wore to shade them from the sun. Looking over the edge of the lorry I watched as their feet slurred the dust. I listened, and their voices, raw and loud and dissonant in the heat, seemed to be grappling with each other high overhead.

Da-duh sat on a trunk in our midst, a monarch amid her court. She still held my hand, but it was different now. I had suddenly become her anchor, for I felt her fear of the lorry with its asthmatic motor (a fear and distrust, I later learned, she had of all machines) beating like a pulse in her rough palm.

As soon as we left Bridgetown behind though, she relaxed, and while the others around us talked she gazed at the canes standing tall on either side of the winding marl road. "C'dear," she said softly to herself after a time. "The canes this side are pretty enough."

They were too much for me. I thought of them as giant weeds that had overrun the island, leaving scarcely any room for the small tottering houses of sunbleached pine we passed or the people, dark streaks as our lorry hurtled by. I suddenly feared that we were journeying, unaware that we were, toward some dangerous place where the canes, grown as high and thick as a forest, would close in on us and run us through with their stiletto blades. I longed then for the familiar: for the street in Brooklyn where I lived, for my father who had refused to accompany us ("Blowing out good money on foolishness," he had said of the trip), for a game of tag with my friends under the chestnut tree outside our aging brownstone house.

"Yes, but wait till you see St Thomas canes," Da-duh was saying to me. "They's canes father, bo," she gave a proud arrogant nod. "Tomorrow, God willing, I goin' take you out in the ground and show them to you."

True to her word Da-duh took me with her the following day out into the ground. It was a fairly large plot adjoining her weathered board and shingle house and consisting of a small orchard, a good-sized canepiece and behind the canes, where the land sloped abruptly down, a gully. She had purchased it with Panama money sent her by her eldest son, my uncle Joseph, who had died working on the canal. We entered the ground along a trail no wider than her body and as devious and complex as her reasons for showing me her land. Da-duh strode briskly ahead, her slight form filled out this morning by the layers of sacking petticoats she wore under her working dress to protect her against the damp. A fresh white cloth, elaborately arranged around her head, added to her height, and lent her a vain, almost roguish air.

Her pace slowed once we reached the orchard, and glancing back at me occasionally over her shoulder, she pointed out the various trees.

"This here is a breadfruit," she said. "That one yonder is a papaw. Here's a guava. This is a mango. I know you don't have anything like these in New York. Here's a sugar apple." (The fruit looked more like artichokes than apples to me.) "This one bears limes. . . ." She went on for some time, intoning the names of the trees as though they were those of her gods. Finally, turning to

me, she said, "I know you don't have anything this nice where you come from."
Then, as I hesitated: "I said I know you don't have anything this nice where you
come from. . . ."

"No," I said and my world did seem suddenly lacking.

Da-duh nodded and passed on. The orchard ended and we were on the
narrow cart road that led through the canepiece, the canes clashing like swords
above my cowering head. Again she turned and her thin muscular arms spread
wide, her dim gaze embracing the small field of canes, she said – and her voice
almost broke under the weight of her pride, "Tell me, have you got anything like
these in that place where you were born?"

"No."

"I din' think so. I bet you don't even know that these canes here and the
sugar you eat is one and the same thing. That they does throw the canes into
some damn machine at the factory and squeeze out all the little life in them to
make sugar for you all so in New York to eat. I bet you don't know that."

"I've got two cavities and I'm not allowed to eat a lot of sugar."

But Da-duh didn't hear me. She had turned with an inexplicably angry
motion and was making her way rapidly out of the canes and down the
slope at the edge of the field which led to the gully below. Following her
apprehensively down the incline amid a stand of banana plants whose leaves
flapped like elephants ears in the wind, I found myself in the middle of a small
tropical wood – a place dense and damp and gloomy and tremulous with the
fitful play of light and shadow as the leaves high above moved against the sun that
was almost hidden from view. It was a violent place, the tangled foliage fighting
each other for a chance at the sunlight, the branches of the trees locked in what
seemed an immemorial struggle, one both necessary and inevitable. But despite
the violence, it was pleasant, almost peaceful in the gully, and beneath the
thick undergrowth the earth smelled like spring.

This time Da-duh didn't even bother to ask her usual question, but simply
turned and waited for me to speak.

"No," I said, my head bowed. "We don't have anything like this in New York."

"Ah," she cried, her triumph complete. "I din' think so. Why, I've heard
that's a place where you can walk till you near drop and never see a tree."

"We've got a chestnut tree in front of our house," I said.

"Does it bear?" She waited. "I ask you, does it bear?"

"Not any more," I muttered. "It used to, but not anymore."

She gave the nod that was like a nervous twitch. "You see," she said. "Nothing
can bear there." Then, secure behind her scorn, she added, "But tell me, what's
this snow like that you hear so much about?"

Looking up, I studied her closely, sensing my chance, and then I told
her, describing at length and with as much drama as I could summon not
only what snow in the city was like, but what it would be like here, in her
perennial summer kingdom.

". . . And you see all these trees you got here," I said. "Well, they'd be
bare. No leaves, no fruit, nothing. They'd be covered in snow. You see your
canes. They'd be buried under tons of snow. The snow would be higher than
your head, higher than your house, and you wouldn't be able to come down

into this here gully because it would be snowed under. . . ."

She searched my face for the lie, still scornful but intrigued. "What a thing, huh?" she said finally, whispering it softly to herself.

"And when it snows you couldn't dress like you are now," I said. "Oh, no, you'd freeze to death. You'd have to wear a hat and gloves and galoshes and ear muffs so your ears wouldn't freeze and drop off, and a heavy coat. I've got a Shirley Temple coat with fur on the collar. I can dance. You wanna see?"

Before she could answer I began, with a dance called the Truck which was popular back then in the 1930s. My right forefinger waving, I trucked around the nearby trees and around Da-duh's awed and rigid form. After the Trunk I did the Suzy-Q, my lean hips swishing, my sneakers sidling zigzag over the ground. "I can sing," I said and did so, starting with "I'm Gonna Sit Right Down and Write Myself a Letter", then without pausing, "Tea For Two", and ending with "I Found a Million Dollar Baby in a Five and Ten Cent Store".

For long moments afterwards Da-duh stared at me as if I were a creature from Mars, an emissary from some world she did not know but which intrigued her and whose power she both felt and feared. Yet something about my performance must have pleased her, because bending down she slowly lifted her long skirt and then, one by one, the layers of petticoats until she came to a drawstring purse dangling at the end of a long strip of cloth tied round her waist. Opening the purse she handed me a penny. "Here," she said half-smiling against her will. "Take this to buy yourself a sweet at the shop up the road. There's nothing to be done with you, soul."

From then on, whenever 1 wasn't taken to visit relatives, I accompanied Da-duh out into the ground, and alone with her amid the canes or down in the gully I told her about New York. It always began with some slighting remark on her part: "I know they don't have anything this nice where you come from," or "Tell me, I hear those foolish people in New York does do such and such. . . ." But as I answered, recreating my towering world of steel and concrete and machines for her, building the city out of words, I would feel her give way. I came to know the signs of her surrender: the total stillness that would come over her little hard dry form, the probing gaze that like a surgeon's knife sought to cut through my skull to get at the images there, to see if I were lying; above all, her fear, a fear nameless and profound, the same one I had felt beating in the palm of her hand that day in the lorry.

Over the weeks I told her about refrigerators, radios, gas stoves, elevators, trolley cars, wringer washing machines, movies, airplanes, the cyclone at Coney Island, subways, toasters, electric lights: "At night, see, all you have to do is flip this little switch on the wall and all the lights in the house go on. Just like that. Like magic. It's like turning on the sun at night."

"But tell me," she said to me once with a faint mocking smile, "do the white people have all these things too or it's only the people looking like us?"

I laughed. "What d'ya mean," I said. "The white people have even better." Then: "I beat up a white girl in my class last term."

"Beating up white people!" Her tone was incredulous.

"How you mean!" I said, using an expression of hers. "She called me a name."

For some reason Da-duh could not quite get over this and repeated in the same hushed, shocked voice, "Beating up white people now! Oh, the lord, the world's changing up so I can scarce recognize it anymore."

One morning toward the end of our stay, Da-duh led me into a part of the gully that we had never visited before, an area darker and more thickly overgrown than the rest, almost impenetrable. There in a small clearing amid the dense bush, she stopped before an incredibly tall royal palm which rose cleanly out of the ground, and, drawing the eye up with it, soared high above the trees around it into the sky. It appeared to be touching the blue dome of sky, to be flaunting its dark crown of fronds right in the blinding white face of the late morning sun.

Da-duh watched me a long time before she spoke, and then she said, very quietly, "All right, now, tell me if you've got anything this tall in that place you're from."

I almost wished, seeing her face, that I could have said no. "Yes," I said. "We've got buildings hundreds of times this tall in New York. There's one called the Empire State building that's the tallest in the world. My class visited it last year and I went all the way to the top. It's got over a hundred floors. I can't describe how tall it is. Wait a minute. What's the name of that hill I went to visit the other day, where they have the police station?"

"You mean Bissex?"

"Yes, Bissex. Well, the Empire State Building is way taller than that."

"You're lying now!" she shouted, trembling with rage. Her hand lifted to strike me.

"No, I'm not," I said. "It really is, if you don't believe me I'll send you a picture postcard of it soon as I get back home so you can see for yourself. But it's way taller than Bissex."

All the fight went out of her at that. The hand poised to strike me fell limp to her side, and as she stared at me, seeing not me but the building that was taller than the highest hill she knew, the small stubborn light in her eyes (it was the same amber as the flame in the kerosene lamp she lit at dusk) began to fail. Finally, with a vague gesture that even in the midst of her defeat still tried to dismiss me and my world, she turned and started back through the gully, walking slowly, her steps groping and uncertain, as if she were suddenly no longer sure of the way, while I followed triumphant yet strangely saddened behind.

The next morning I found her dressed for our morning walk but stretched out on the Berbice chair in the tiny drawing room where she sometimes napped during the afternoon heat, her face turned to the window beside her. She appeared thinner and suddenly indescribably old.

"My Da-duh," I said.

"Yes, nuh," she said. Her voice was listless and the face she slowly turned my way was, now that I think back on it, like a Benin mask, the features drawn and almost distorted by an ancient abstract sorrow.

"Don't you feel well?" I asked.

"Girl, I don't know."

"My Da-duh, I goin' boil you some bush tea," my aunt, Da-duh's youngest child, who lived with her, called from the shed roof kitchen.

"Who tell you I need bush tea?" she cried, her voice assuming for a moment its old authority. "You can't even rest nowadays without some malicious person looking for you to be dead. Come, girl," she motioned me to a place beside her on the old-fashioned lounge chair, "give us a tune."

I sang for her until breakfast at eleven, all my brash irreverent Tin Pan Alley songs, and then just before noon we went out into the ground. But it was a short, dispirited walk. Da-duh didn't even notice that the mangoes were beginning to ripen and would have to be picked before the village boys got to them. And when she paused occasionally and looked out across the canes or up at her trees it wasn't as if she were seeing them but something else. Some huge, monolithic shape had imposed itself, it seemed, between her and the land, obstructing her vision. Returning to the house she slept the entire afternoon on the Berbice chair.

She remained like this until we left, languishing away the mornings on the chair at the window gazing out at the land as if it were already doomed; then, at noon, taking the brief stroll with me through the ground during which she seldom spoke, and afterwards returning home to sleep till almost dusk sometimes.

On the day of our departure she put on the austere, ankle-length white dress, the black shoes and brown felt hat (her town clothes she called them), but she did not go with us to town. She saw us off on the road outside her house and in the midst of my mother's tearful protracted farewell, she leaned down and whispered in my ear, "Girl, you're not to forget now to send me the picture of that building, you hear."

By the time I mailed her the large colored picture postcard of the Empire State building she was dead. She died during the famous '37 strike which began shortly after we left. On the day of her death England sent planes flying low over the island in a show of force – so low, according to my aunt's letter, that the downdraft from them shook the ripened mangoes from the trees in Da-duh's orchard. Frightened, everyone in the village fled into the canes. Except Da-duh. She remained in the house at the window so my aunt said, watching as the planes came swooping and screaming like monstrous birds down over the village, over her house, rattling her trees and flattening the young canes in her field. It must have seemed to her lying there that they did not intend pulling out of their dive, but like the hard-back beetles which hurled themselves with suicidal force against the walls of the house at night, those menacing silver shapes would hurl themselves in an ecstasy of self-immolation onto the land, destroying it utterly.

When the planes finally left and the villagers returned they found her dead on the Berbice chair at the window.

She died and I lived, but always, to this day even, within the shadow of her death. For a brief period after I was grown I went to live alone, like one doing penance, in a loft above a noisy factory in downtown New York and there painted seas of sugar-cane and huge swirling Van Gogh suns and palm trees striding like brightly-plumed Tutsi warriors across a tropical landscape, while the thunderous tread of the machines downstairs jarred the floor beneath my easel, mocking my efforts.

Lorraine Hansberry
1930–65

B orn to well-to-do parents in Chicago, she became interested in the
theatre while attending high school, and at the University of Wisconsin studied stage design and drama for two years, from 1948.
*She studied painting at the Art Institute of Chicago, Roosevelt College,
and in Guadalajara, Mexico. She then worked as a journalist (1951–3)
and married theatrical director Robert Nemiroff in 1953. Her first play,*
A Raisin in the Sun *(its title from a Langston Hughes poem), took
Broadway by storm, winning the New York Drama Critics' Circle Award
for best play of 1959; at twenty-nine she was the youngest American,
fifth woman and first Black playwright to win this accolade. (In 1973
the play was revived as a musical,* Raisin, *winning a Tony Award.)
Extracted here, it draws on the experience of her family who, when
she was eight, bought a house in a "white neighbourhood" and were
harassed and evicted, then had their complaint upheld in the Supreme
Court. Her next dramatic work,* The Sign in Sidney Brustein's Window
*(1965), dealing with prejudice in the context of anti-semitism and local
politics, had a brief run in New York (produced by her husband, from
whom she was divorced in 1964), closing on the day of her death from
cancer at the age of thirty-four.* To Be Young, Gifted and Black: Lorraine
Hansberry in Her Own Words, *compiled by Nemiroff, was dramatized in
1968 (published in 1969), the longest running play of the off-Broadway
season. Other works are collected in* Last Plays *(1972).*

From

A Raisin in the Sun

MAMA: Well – this all the packing got done since I left out of here this
morning? I testify before God that my children got all the energy of
the *dead*. What time the moving men due?

BENEATHA: Four o'clock. You had a caller, Mama.

She is smiling teasingly.

MAMA: Sure enough – who?

BENEATHA (*her arms folded saucily*): The Welcoming Committee.

WALTER *and* RUTH *giggle.*

MAMA (*innocently*): Who?

BENEATHA: The Welcoming Committee. They said they're sure going to be glad to see you when you get there.

WALTER (*devilishly*): Yeah, they said they can't hardly wait to see your face.

Laughter.

MAMA (*sensing their facetiousness*): What's the matter with you all?

WALTER: Ain't nothing the matter with us. We just telling you 'bout the gentleman who came to see you this afternoon. From the Clybourne Park Improvement Association.

MAMA: What he want?

RUTH (*in the same mood as* BENEATHA *and* WALTER): To welcome you, honey.

WALTER: He said they can't hardly wait. He said the one thing they don't have, that they just *dying* to have out there is a fine family of coloured people! (*To* RUTH *and* BENEATHA:) Ain't that right!

RUTH *and* BENEATHA (*mockingly*): Yeah! He left his card in case –

They indicate the card, and MAMA *picks it up and throws it on the floor – understanding and looking off as she draws her chair up to the table on which she has put her plant and some sticks and some cord.*

MAMA: Father, give us strength. (*Knowingly – and without fun:*) Did he threaten us?

BENEATHA: Oh – Mama – they don't do it like that anymore. He talked Brotherhood. He said everybody ought to learn how to sit down and hate each other with good Christian fellowship.

She and WALTER *shake hands to ridicule the remark.*

MAMA (*sadly*): Lord, protect us . . .

RUTH: You should hear the money those folks raised to buy the house from us. All we paid and then some.

BENEATHA: What they think we going to do – eat 'em?

RUTH: No, honey, marry 'em.

MAMA (*shaking her head*): Lord, Lord, Lord . . .

RUTH: Well – that's way the crackers crumble. Joke.

BENEATHA (*laughingly noticing what her mother is doing*): Mama, what are you doing?

MAMA: Fixing my plant so it won't get hurt none on the way . . .

BENEATHA: Mama, you going to take *that* to the new house?

MAMA: Un-huh –

BENEATHA: That raggedy-looked old thing?

MAMA (*stopping and looking at her, enunciating, grandly*): It expresses ME.

RUTH (*with delight, to* BENEATHA): So there, Miss Thing!

WALTER *comes to* MAMA *suddenly and bends down behind her and squeezes her in his arms with all his strength. She is overwhelmed by the suddenness of it and, though delighted, her manner is like that of* RUTH *with* TRAVIS.

MAMA: Look out now, boy! You make me mess up my thing here!

WALTER (*his face lit, he slips down on his knees beside her, his arms still about her*): Mama . . . you know what it means to climb up in the chariot?

MAMA (*gruffly, very happy*): Get on away from me now . . .

RUTH (*near the gift-wrapped package, trying to catch* WALTER's *eye*): Psst –

WALTER: What the old song say, Mama –

RUTH: Walter – Now?

She is pointing at the package.

WALTER (*speaking the lines, sweetly, playfully, in his mother's face*):

I got wings . . . you got wings . . .
All God's children got wings . . .

MAMA: Boy – get out of my face and do some work . . .

WALTER:

When I get to heaven gonna put on my wings,
Gonna fly all over God's heaven . . .

BENEATHA (*teasingly, from across the room*): Everybody talking 'bout heaven ain't going there!

WALTER (*to* RUTH, *who is carrying the box across the them*): I don't know, you think we ought to give her that . . . Seems to me she ain't been very appreciative around here.

MAMA (*eyeing the box, which is obviously a gift*): What is that?

WALTER (*taking it from* RUTH *and putting it on the table in front of* MAMA): Well – what you all think? Should we give it to her?

RUTH: Oh – she was pretty good today.

MAMA: I'll good you –

She turns her eyes to the box again.

BENEATHA: Open it, Mama.

She stands up, looks at it, turns and looks at all of them, and then presses her hands together and does not open her package.

WALTER (*sweetly*): Open it, Mama. It's for you. (MAMA *looks in his eyes. It is the first present in her life without its being Christmas. Slowly she opens her package and lifts out, one by one, a brand new sparkling set of gardening tools.* WALTER *continues, prodding:*) Ruth made up the note – read it . . .

MAMA (*picking up the card and adjusting her glasses*): "To our own Mrs Miniver – Love from Brother, Ruth and Beneatha." Ain't that lovely . . .

TRAVIS (*tugging at his father's sleeve*): Daddy, can I give her mine now?

WALTER: All right, son (TRAVIS *flies to get his gift*). Travis didn't want to go in with the rest of us, Mama. He got his own. (*Somewhat amused:*) We don't know what it is . . .

TRAVIS (*racing back in the room with a large hatbox and putting it in front of his grandmother*): Here!

MAMA: Lord have mercy, baby. You done gone and bought your grandmother a hat?

TRAVIS (*very proud*): Open it.

She does and lifts out an elaborate, but very elaborate, wide gardening hat, and all the adults break up at the sight of it.

RUTH: Travis, honey, what is that?

TRAVIS (*who thinks it is beautiful and appropriate*): It's a gardening hat! Like the ladies always have on in the magazines when they work in their gardens.

BENEATHA (*giggling fiercely*): Travis – we were trying to make Mama Mrs Miniver – not Scarlett O'Hara!

MAMA (*indignantly*): What's the matter with you all! This here is a beautiful hat! (*Absurdly:*) I always wanted me one just like it!

She pops it on her head to prove it to her grandson, and the hat is ludicrous and considerably oversized.

RUTH: Hot dog! Go, Mama!

WALTER (*doubled over with laughter*): I'm sorry, Mama – but you look like you ready to go out and chop you some cotton sure enough!

They all laugh except MAMA, *out of deference to* TRAVIS's *feelings.*

MAMA (*gathering the boy up to her*): Bless your heart – this is the prettiest hat I ever owned – (WALTER, RUTH *and* BENEATHA *chime in – noisily, festively and insincerely congratulating* TRAVIS *on his gift.*) What are we all standing around here for? We ain't finished packin' yet. Bennie, you ain't packed one book.

The bell rings.

BENEATHA: That couldn't be the movers . . . it's not hardly two good yet –

BENEATHA *goes into her room.* MAMA *starts for the door.*

WALTER (*turning, stiffening*): Wait – wait – I'll get it.

He stands and looks at the door.

MAMA: You expecting company, son?

WALTER (*just looking at the door*): Yeah – Yeah . . .

MAMA *looks at* RUTH, *and they exchange innocent and unfrightened glances.*

MAMA (*not understanding*): Well, let them in, son.

BENEATHA (*from her room*): We need some more string.

MAMA: Travis – you run to the hardware and get me some string cord.

> MAMA *goes out and* WALTER *turns and looks at* RUTH. TRAVIS *goes to a dish for money.*

RUTH: Why don't you answer the door, man?

WALTER (*suddenly bounding across the floor to her*): 'Cause sometimes it hard to let the future begin!

> *Stooping down in her face:*

> I got wings! You got wings!
> All God's children got wings!

> *He crosses to the door and throws it open. Standing there is a very slight little man in a not too prosperous business suit and with haunted frightened eyes and a hat pulled down tightly, brim up, around his forehead.* TRAVIS *passes between the men and exits.* WALTER *leans deep in the man's face, still in his jubilance.*

> When I get to heaven gonna put on my wings,
> Gonna fly all over God's heaven . . .

> *The little man just stares at him.*

> Heaven –

> *Suddenly he stops and looks past the little man into the empty hallway:*

> Where's Willy, man?

BOBO: He ain't with me.

WALTER (*not disturbed*): Oh – come on in. You know my wife.

BOBO (*dumbly, taking off his hat*): Yes – h'you, Miss Ruth.

RUTH (*quietly, a mood apart from her husband already, seeing* BOBO): Hello, Bobo.

WALTER: You right on time today . . . Right on time. That's the way! (*He slaps* BOBO *on his back.*) Sit down . . . lemme hear.

> RUTH *stands stiffly and quietly in back of them, as though somehow she senses death, her eyes fixed on her husband.*

BOBO (*his frightened eyes on the floor, his hat in his hand*): Could I please get a drink of water, before I tell you about it. Walter Lee?

> WALTER *does not take his eyes off the man.* RUTH *goes blindly to the tap and gets a glass of water and brings it to* BOBO.

WALTER: There ain't nothing wrong, is there?

BOBO: Lemme tell you –

WALTER: Man – didn't nothing go wrong?

BOBO: Lemme tell you – Walter Lee. (*Looking at* RUTH *and talking to her more than to* WALTER:) You know how it was. I got to tell you how it was. I mean first I got to tell you how it was all the way ... I mean about the money I put in, Walter Lee ...

WALTER (*with taut agitation now*): What about the money you put in?

BOBO: Well – it wasn't much as we told you – me and Willy – (*He stops.*) I'm sorry, Walter. I got a bad feeling about it. I got a real bad feeling about it ...

WALTER: Man, what you telling me about all this for? ... Tell me what happened in Springfield ...

BOBO: Springfield.

RUTH (*like a dead woman*): What was supposed to happen in Springfield?

BOBO (*to her*): This deal that me and Walter went into with Willy – Me and Willy are going to go down to Springfield and spread some money 'round so's we wouldn't have to wait so long for the liquor licence ... That's what we are going to do. Everybody said that was the way you had to do, you understand, Miss Ruth?

WALTER: Man – what happened down there?

BOBO (*a pitiful man, near tears*): I'm trying to tell you, Walter.

WALTER (*screaming at him suddenly*): THEN TELL ME, GODDAMMIT.... WHAT'S THE MATTER WITH YOU?

BOBO: Man... I didn't go to no Springfield, yesterday.

WALTER (*halted, life hanging in the moment:*) Why not?

BOBO (*the long way, the hard way to tell*): 'Cause I didn't have no reasons to ...

WALTER: Man, what are you talking about!

BOBO: I'm talking about the fact that when I got to the train station yesterday morning – eight o'clock like we planned ... Man – *Willy didn't never show up*.

WALTER: Why ... where was he ... where is he?

BOBO: That's what I'm trying to tell you ... I don't know ... I waited six hours ... I called his house ... and I waited ... six hours ... I waited in that train station six hours ... (*Breaking into tears:*) That was all the extra money I had in the world ...

Looking up at WALTER *with the tears running down his face.*

Man, *Willy is gone.*

WALTER: Gone, what you mean Willy is gone? Gone where? You mean he went by himself. You mean he went off to Springfield by himself – to take care of getting the licence – (*Turns and looks anxiously at* RUTH.) You mean maybe he didn't want too many people in on the business down there? (*Looks to* RUTH *again, as before.*) You know Willy got his own ways. (*Looks back to* BOBO.) Maybe you was late yesterday and he just went on down there without you. Maybe – maybe – he's been callin' you at home tryin' to tell you what happened or something. Maybe – maybe – he just got sick. He's somewhere – he's got to be somewhere. We just got to find him – me and you got to find him.

He grabs BOBO *senselessly by the collar and starts to shake him.*

We got to!

BOBO (*in sudden angry, frightened agony*): What's the matter with you, Walter! *When a cat take off with your money he don't leave you no maps!*

WALTER (*turning madly, as though he is looking for* WILLY *in the very room*): Willy! . . . Willy . . . don't do it . . . Please don't do it . . . Man, not with that money . . . Man, please, not with that money . . . Oh, God . . . Don't let it be true . . . (*He is wandering around, crying out for* WILLY *and looking for him or perhaps for help from God.*) Man . . . I trusted you . . . Man, I put my life in your hands . . . (*He starts to crumple down on the floor as* RUTH *just covers her face in horror.* MAMA *opens the door and comes into the room, with* BENEATHA *behind her.*) Man . . . (*He starts to pound the floor with his fists, sobbing wildly.*) *That money is made out of my father's flesh* . . .

BOBO (*standing over him helplessly*): I'm sorry, Walter . . . (*Only* WALTER'S *sobs reply.* BOBO *puts on his hat.*) I had my life staked on this deal, too . . .

He exits.

MAMA (*to* WALTER): Son – (*She goes to him, bends down to him, talks to his bent head.*) Son . . . Is it gone? Son, I gave you sixty-five hundred dollars. Is it gone? All of it? Beneatha's money too?

WALTER (*lifting his head slowly*): Mama . . . I never . . . went to the bank at all . . .

MAMA (*not wanting to believe him*): You mean . . . your sister's school money . . . you used that too . . . Walter? . . .

WALTER: Yessss! . . . All of it . . . It's all gone . . .

There is total silence. RUTH *stands with her face covered with her hands;* BENEATHA *leans forlornly against a wall fingering a piece of red ribbon from the mother's gift.* MAMA *stops and looks at her son without recognition and then, quite without thinking about it, starts to beat him senselessly in the face.* BENEATHA *goes to them and stops it.*

BENEATHA: Mama!

MAMA *stops and looks at both of her children and rises slowly and wanders vaguely, aimlessly away from them.*

MAMA: I seen . . . him . . . night after night . . . come in . . . and look at that rug . . . and then look at me . . . the red showing in his eyes . . . the veins moving in his head . . . I seen him grow thin and old before he was forty . . . working and working and working like somebody's old horse . . . killing himself . . . and you – you give it all away in a day . . .

BENEATHA: Mama –

MAMA: Oh, God … (*She looks up to Him:*) Look down here – and show
    me the strength.

BENEATHA: Mama –

MAMA (*folding over*): Strength …

BENEATHA (*plaintively*): Mama …

MAMA: Strength!

    Curtain.

Alda Lara
1930–62

Born in Bengeula, Angola, she studied medicine in Portugal, dur-*
ing which time she began an involvement with literature, publish-
ing her poems in the Angolan journal Mensagem *and in various
anthologies. Her collection* Poemas *was posthumously published in
1966 and her stories,* Tempo de Chuva *in 1973. After her death the
municipal government of Sá de Bandeira instituted the Alda Lara Prize
for poetry.*

Testament

To the youngest prostitute
In the oldest and darkest barrio
I leave my earrings
Cut in crystal, limpid and pure. . . .

And to that forgotten virgin
Girl without tenderness
Dreaming somewhere of a happy story
I leave my white dress
My wedding dress
Trimmed with lace. . . .

I offer my old rosary
To that old friend of mine
Who does not believe in God. . . .

And my books, my rosary beads
Of a different suffering
Are for humble folk
Who never learned to read.

As for my crazy poems
Those that echo sincerely
The confusion and sadness in my heart
Those that sing of hope
Where none can be found
Those I give to you, my love. . . .

So that in a moment of peace
When my soul comes from afar
To kiss your eyes

You will go into the night
Accompanied by the moon
To read them to children
That you meet along each street. . . .

Grace Ogot

1930–

O ne of Africa's best known writers of short stories, she was
born in Kenya's Central Nyanza district and studied nursing
and midwifery in Uganda and England. She has been a radio

broadcaster, community development officer, nursing sister, midwifery tutor, public relations officer, newspaper columnist and politician. She was founding chair of the Writers' Association of Kenya, a delegate to the UN and UNESCO, and in 1985 became an MP. In 1959 she married the historian Dr Bethwell Ogot. Explaining how she began to write, she has said: "When I was in England in 1956, I had known the man I later on married. And I wrote him a letter. After several letters he one day wrote back and said, 'Do you know, Grace, you can write poetry. Because your letters are so romantic.' Of course I thought, well, maybe the man is in love and that was all. I wrote back and said, 'Listen, brother, I can't understand poems, I don't read them so I'll never write one.' He was so persistent about it that eventually he said, 'If you can't write poetry why not try short stories?' And I tried one and it worked. . . ." Her novel The Promised Land *(1966) was the first imaginative book in English by a Luo writer, and she has subsequently published collections of short stories* – Land Without Thunder *(1968), in which "The Rain Came" appears,* The Other Woman and Other Stories *(1976) and* The Island of Tears *(1980) – and another novel,* The Graduate *(1980).*

The Rain Came

THE chief was still far from the gate when his daughter Oganda saw him. She ran to meet him. Breathlessly she asked her father, "What is the news, great Chief? Everyone in the village is anxiously waiting to hear when it will rain." Labong'o held out his hands for his daughter but he did not say a word. Puzzled by her father's cold attitude Oganda ran back to the village to warn the others that the chief was back.

The atmosphere in the village was tense and confused. Everyone moved aimlessly and fussed in the yard without actually doing any work. A young woman whispered to her co-wife, "If they have not solved this rain business today, the chief will crack." They had watched him getting thinner and thinner as the people kept on pestering him. "Our cattle lie dying in the fields," they reported. "Soon it will be our children and then ourselves. Tell us what to do to save our lives, oh great Chief." So the chief had daily prayed with the Almighty through the ancestors to deliver them from their distress.

Instead of calling the family together and giving them the news immediately, Labong'o went to his own hut, a sign that he was not to be disturbed. Having replaced the shutter, he sat in the dimly-lit hut to contemplate.

It was no longer a question of being the chief of hunger-stricken people that weighed Labong'o's heart. It was the life of his only daughter that was at stake. At the time when Oganda came to meet him, he saw the glittering chain shining around her waist. The prophecy was complete. "It is Oganda, Oganda, my only daughter, who must die so young." Labong'o burst into tears before finishing the sentence. The chief must not weep. Society had declared him the bravest of men. But Labong'o did not care any more. He assumed the position of a simple father and wept bitterly. He loved his people, the Luo, but what were the Luo for him without Oganda? Her life had brought a new life in Labong'o's world and he ruled better than he could remember. How would the spirit of the village survive his beautiful daughter? "There are so many homes and so many parents who have daughters. Why choose this one? She is all I have." Labong'o spoke as if the ancestors were there in the hut and he could see them face to face. Perhaps they were there, warning him to remember his promise on the day he was enthroned when he said aloud, before the elders, "I will lay down life, if necessary, and the life of my household, to save this tribe from the hands of the enemy." "Deny! Deny!" he could hear the voice of his forefathers mocking him.

When Labong'o was consecrated chief he was only a young man. Unlike his father, he ruled for many years with only one wife. But people rebuked him because his only wife did not bear him a daughter. He married a second, a third, and a fourth wife. but they all gave birth to male children. When Labong'o married a fifth wife she bore him a daughter. They called her Oganda, meaning "beans", because her skin was very fair. Out of Labong'o's twenty children, Oganda was the only girl. Though she was the chief's favourite, her mother's co-wives swallowed their jealous feelings and showered her with love. After all, they said, Oganda was a female child whose days in the royal family were numbered. She would soon marry at a tender age and leave the enviable position to someone else.

Never in his life had he been faced with such an impossible decision. Refusing to yield to the rainmaker's request would mean sacrificing the whole tribe, putting the interests of the individual above those of the society. More than that. It would mean disobeying the ancestors, and most probably wiping the Luo people from the surface of the earth. On the other hand, to let Oganda die as a ransom for the people would permanently cripple Labong'o spiritually. He knew he would never be the same chief again.

The words of Ndithi, the medicine man, still echoed in his ears. "Podho, the ancestor of the Luo, appeared to me in a dream last night, and he asked me to speak to the chief and the people," Ndithi had said to the gathering of tribesmen. "A young woman who has not known a man must die so that the country may have rain. While Podho was still talking to me, I saw a young woman standing at the lakeside, her hands raised, above her head. Her skin was as fair as the skin of young deer in the wilderness. Her tall slender figure stood like a lonely reed at the river bank. Her sleepy eyes wore a sad look like that of a bereaved mother. She wore a gold ring on her left ear, and a glittering brass chain around her waist. As I still marvelled at the beauty of this young woman, Podho told me, 'Out of all the women in this land, we have chosen this one. Let her offer herself as a sacrifice to the lake monster! And on that day, the rain will come down in torrents. Let everyone stay at home on that day, lest he be carried away by the floods.'"

Outside there was a strange stillness, except for the thirsty birds that sang lazily on the dying trees. The blinding mid-day heat had forced the people to retire to their huts. Not far away from the chief's hut, two guards were snoring away quietly. Labong'o removed his crown and the large eagle-head that hung loosely on his shoulders. He left the hut, and instead of asking Nyabog'o the messenger to beat the drum, he went straight and beat it himself. In no time the whole household had assembled under the siala tree where he usually addressed them. He told Oganda to wait a while in her grandmother's hut.

When Labong'o stood to address his household, his voice was hoarse and the tears choked him. He started to speak, but words refused to leave his lips. His wives and sons knew there was great danger. Perhaps their enemies had declared war on them. Labong'o eyes were red, and they could see he had been weeping. At last he told them. "One whom we love and treasure must be taken away from us. Oganda is to die." Labong'o's voice was so faint, that he could not hear it himself. But he continued, "The ancestors have chosen her to be offered as a sacrifice to the lake monster in order that we may have rain."

They were completely stunned. As a confused murmur broke out, Oganda's mother fainted and was carried off to her own hut. But the other people rejoiced. They danced around singing and chanting, "Oganda is the lucky one to die for the people. If it is to save the people, let Oganda go."

In her grandmother's hut Oganda wondered what the whole family were discussing about her that she could not hear. Her grandmother's hut was well away from the chief's court and, much as she strained her ears, she could not hear what was said. "It must be marriage," she concluded. It was an accepted custom for the family to discuss their daughter's future marriage behind her back. A faint smile played on Oganda's lips as she thought of the several young men who swallowed saliva at the mere mention of her name.

There was Kech, the son of a neighbouring clan elder. Kech was very handsome. He had sweet, meek eyes and a roaring laughter. He would make a wonderful father, Oganda thought. But they would not be a good match. Kech was a bit too short to be her husband. It would humiliate her to have to look down at Kech each time she spoke to him. Then she thought of Dimo, the tall young man who had already distinguished himself as a brave warrior and an outstanding wrestler. Dimo adored Oganda, but Oganda thought he would make a cruel husband, always quarrelling and ready to fight. No, she did not like him. Oganda fingered the glittering chain on her waist as she thought of Osinda. A long time ago when she was quite young Osinda had given her that chain, and instead of wearing it around her neck several times, she wore it round her waist where it could stay permanently. She heard her heart pounding so loudly as she thought of him. She whispered, "Let it be you they are discussing, Osinda, the lovely one. Come now and take me away . . ."

The lean figure in the doorway startled Oganda, who was rapt in thought about the man she loved. "You have frightened me, Grandma," said Oganda laughing. "Tell me, is it my marriage you are discussing? You can take it from me that I won't marry any of them." A smile played on her lips again. She was coaxing the old lady to tell her quickly, to tell her they were pleased with Osinda.

In the open space outside the excited relatives were dancing and singing. They were coming to the hut now, each carrying a gift to put at Oganda's feet. As their singing got nearer Oganda was able to hear what they were saying: "If it is to save the people, if it is to give us rain, let Oganda go. Let Oganda die for her people, and for her ancestors." Was she mad to think that they were singing about her?

How could she die? She found the lean figure of her grandmother barring the door. She could not get out. The look on her grandmother's face warned her that there was danger around the corner. "Mother, it is not marriage then?" Oganda asked urgently. She suddenly felt panicky like a mouse cornered by a hungry cat. Forgetting that there was only one door in the hut Oganda fought desperately to find another exit. She must fight for her life. But there was none.

She closed her eyes, leapt like a wild tiger through the door, knocking her grandmother flat to the ground. There outside in mourning garments Labong'o stood motionless, his hands folded at the back. He held his daughter's hand and led her away from the excited crowd to the little red-painted hut where her mother was resting. Here he broke the news officially to his daughter.

For a long time the three souls who loved one another dearly sat in darkness. It was no good speaking. And even if they tried, the words could not have come out. In the past they had been like three cooking stones, sharing their burdens. Taking Oganda away from them would leave two useless stones which would not hold a cooking-pot.

News that the beautiful daughter of the chief was to be sacrificed to give the people rain spread across the country like wind. At sunset the chief's village was full of relatives and friends who had come to congratulate Oganda. Many more were on their way coming, carrying their gifts. They would dance till morning to keep her company. And in the morning they would prepare her a big farewell feast. All these relatives thought it a great honour to be selected by the spirits to die, in order that the society may live. "Oganda's name will always remain a living name among us," they boasted.

But was it maternal love that prevented Minya from rejoicing with the other women? Was it the memory of the agony and pain of child-birth that made her feel so sorrowful? Or was it the deep warmth and understanding that passes between a suckling babe and her mother that made Oganda part of her life, her flesh? Of course it was an honour, a great honour, for her daughter to be chosen to die for the country. But what could she gain once her daughter was blown away by the wind? There were so many other women in the land, why choose her daughter, her only child! Had human life any meaning at all – other women had houses full of children while she, Minya, had to lose her only child!

In the cloudless sky the moon shone brightly, and the numerous stars glittered with a bewitching beauty. The dancers of all age-groups assembled to dance before Oganda, who sat close to her mother, sobbing quietly. All these years she had been with her people she thought she understood them. But now she discovered that she was a stranger among them. If they loved her as they had always professed why were they not making any attempt to save her? Did her people really understand what it felt like to die young? Unable to restrain her emotions any longer, she sobbed loudly as her age-group got up to dance. They were young and beautiful and very soon they would marry and have their own children. They would have husbands to love and little huts for themselves. They would have reached maturity. Oganda touched the chain around her waist as she thought of Osinda. She wished Osinda was there too, among her friends. "Perhaps he is ill," she thought gravely. The chain comforted Oganda – she would die with it around her waist and wear it in the underground world.

In the morning a big feast was prepared for Oganda. The women prepared many different tasty dishes so that she could pick and choose. "People don't eat after death," they said. Delicious though the food looked, Oganda touched none of it. Let the happy people eat. She contented herself with sips of water from a little calabash.

The time for her departure was drawing near, and each minute was precious. It was a day's journey to the lake. She was to walk all night, passing through the great forest. But nothing could touch her, not even the denizens of the forest. She was already anointed with sacred oil. From the time Oganda received the sad news she had expected Osinda to appear any moment. But he was not there. A relative told her that Osinda was away on a private visit. Oganda realized that she would never see her beloved again.

In the afternoon the whole village stood at the gate to say good-bye and to see her for the last time. Her mother wept on her neck for a long time. The great chief in a mourning skin came to the gate bare-footed, and mingled with the people – a simple father in grief. He took off his wrist bracelet and put it on his daughter's wrist saying, "You will always live among us. The spirit of our forefathers is with you."

Tongue-tied and unbelieving Oganda stood there before the people. She had nothing to say. She looked at her home once more. She could hear her heart beating so painfully within her. All her childhood plans were coming to an end. She felt like a flower nipped in the bud never to enjoy the morning dew again. She looked at her weeping mother, and whispered, "Whenever you want to see me, always look at the sunset. I will be there."

Oganda turned southwards to start her trek to the lake. Her parents, relatives, friends and admirers stood at the gate and watcher her go.

Her beautiful slender figure grew smaller and smaller till she mingled with the thin dry trees in the forest. As Oganda walked the lonely path that wound its way in the wilderness, she sang a song, and her own voice kept her company.

> The ancestors have said Oganda must die
> The daughter of the chief must be sacrificed,
> When the lake monster feeds on my flesh.
> The people will have rain.
> Yes, the rain will come down in torrents.
> And the floods will wash away the sandy beaches
> When the daughter of the chief dies in the lake.
> My age-group has consented
> My parents have consented
> So have my friends and relatives.
> Let Oganda die to give us rain.
> My age-group are young and ripe,
> Ripe for womanhood and motherhood
> But Oganda must die young,
> Oganda must sleep with the ancestors.
> Yes, rain will come down in torrents.

The red rays of the setting sun embraced Oganda, and she looked like a burning candle in the wilderness.

The people who came to hear her sad song were touched by her beauty. But they all said the same thing: "If it is to save the people, if it is to give us rain, then be not afraid. Your name will forever live among us."

At midnight Oganda was tired and weary. She could walk no more. She sat under a big tree, and having sipped water from her calabash, she rested her head on the tree trunk and slept.

When Oganda woke up in the morning the sun was high in the sky. After walking for many hours, she reached the *tong'*, a strip of land that separated the inhabited part of the country from the sacred place (*kar lamo*). No layman could enter this place and come out alive – only those who had direct contact with the spirits and the Almighty were allowed to enter this holy of holies. But Oganda had to pass through this sacred land on her way to the lake, which she had to reach at sunset.

A large crowd gathered to see her for the last time. Her voice was now hoarse and painful, but there was no need to worry any more. Soon she would not have to sing. The crowd looked at Oganda sympathetically, mumbling words she could not hear. But none of them pleaded for life. As Oganda opened the gate, a child, a young child, broke loose from the crowd, and ran towards her. The child took a small earring from her sweaty hands and gave it to Oganda saying, "When you reach the world of the dead, give this earring to my sister. She died last week. She forgot this ring." Oganda, taken aback by the strange request, took the little ring, and handed her precious water and food to the child. She did not need them now. Oganda did not know whether to laugh or cry. She had heard mourners sending their love to their sweethearts, long dead, but this idea of sending gifts was new to her.

Oganda held her breath as she crossed the barrier to enter the sacred land. She looked appealingly at the crowd, but there was no response. Their minds were too preoccupied with their own survival. Rain was the precious medicine they were longing for, and the sooner Oganda could get to her destination the better.

A strange feeling possessed Oganda as she picked her way in the sacred land. There were strange noises that often startled her, and her first reaction was to take to her heels. But she remembered that she had to fulfil the wish of her people. She was exhausted, but the path was still winding. Then suddenly the path ended on sandy land. The water had retreated miles away from the shore leaving a wide stretch of sand. Beyond this was the vast expanse of water.

Oganda felt afraid. She wanted to picture the size and shape of the monster, but fear would not let her. The society did not talk about it, nor did the crying children who were silenced by the mention of its name. The sun was still up, but it was no longer hot. For a long time Oganda walked ankle-deep in the sand. She was exhausted and longed desperately for her calabash of water. As she moved on, she had a strange feeling that something was following her. Was it the monster? Her hair stood erect, and a cold paralysing feeling ran along her spine. She looked behind, sideways and in front, but there was nothing, except a cloud of dust.

Oganda pulled up and hurried but the feeling did not leave her, and her whole body became saturated with perspiration.

The sun was going down fast and the lake shore seemed to move along with it.

Oganda started to run. She must be at the lake before sunset. As she ran she heard a noise from behind. She looked back sharply, and something resembling a moving bush was frantically running after her. It was about to catch up with her.

Oganda ran with all her strength. She was now determined to throw herself into the water even before sunset. She did not look back, but the creature was upon her. She made an effort to cry out, as in a nightmare, but she could not hear her own voice. The creature caught up with Oganda. In the utter confusion, as Oganda came face to face with the unidentified creature, a strong hand grabbed her. But she fell flat on the sand and fainted.

When the lake breeze brought her back to consciousness, a man was bending over her. ". . . . . !" Oganda opened her mouth to speak, but she had lost her voice. She swallowed a mouthful of water poured into her mouth by the stranger.

"Osinda, Osinda! Please let me die. Let me run, the sun is going down. Let me die, let them have rain." Osinda fondled the glittering chain around Oganda's waist and wiped the tears from her face.

"We must escape quickly to the unknown land," Osinda said urgently. "We must run away from the wrath of the ancestors and the retaliation of the monster."

"But the curse is upon me, Osinda, I am no good to you any more. And moreover the eyes of the ancestors will follow us everywhere and bad luck will befall us. Nor can we escape from the monster."

Oganda broke loose, afraid to escape, but Osinda grabbed her hands again.

"Listen to me, Oganda! Listen! Here are two coats!" He then covered the whole of Oganda's body, except her eyes, with a leafy attire made from the twigs of *Bwombwe*. "These will protect us from the eyes of the ancestors and the wrath of the monster. Now let us run out of here." He held Oganda's hand and they ran from the sacred land, avoiding the path that Oganda had followed.

The bush was thick, and the long grass entangled their feet as they ran. Halfway through the sacred land they stopped and looked back. The sun was almost touching the surface of the water. They were frightened. They continued to run, now faster, to avoid the sinking sun.

"Have faith, Oganda – that thing will not reach us."

When they reached the barrier and looked behind them trembling, only a tip of the sun could be seen above the water's surface.

"It is gone! It is gone!" Oganda wept, hiding her face in her hands.

"Weep not, daughter of the chief. Let us run, let us escape."

There was a bright lightning. They looked up, frightened. Above them black furious clouds started to gather. They began to run. Then the thunder roared, and the rain came down in torrents.

Mabel Segun
1930-

B orn in Bendel State, Nigeria, she attended school in Lagos, then
University College, Ibadan, graduating in 1953 with a BA in English, Latin and History. She taught these subjects in Nigerian schools
and later became Head of the Department of English and Social Studies
and Vice-Principal at the National Technical Teachers' College, Yaba. She
is a broadcaster (winning the Nigerian Broadcasting Corporation 1977
Artiste of the Year award), a keen sportswoman, singer and pianist, has
been an advertising copywriter and editor. She writes non-fiction, poetry
– including Conflict and Other Poems (1987) – and books for young
people, such as My Father's Daughter (1965). "Polygamy – Ancient and
Modern" is from Friends, Nigerians, Countrymen (1965; published as
Sorry, No Vacancy, 1985), a lighthearted look at the ways and attitudes
of Nigerians, compiled from her radio broadcasts, 1961–74.

The Pigeon-Hole

How I wish I could pigeon-hole myself
and neatly fix a label on!
But self-knowledge comes too late
and by the time I've known myself
I am no longer what I was.

I knew a woman once
who had a delinquent child.
she never had a moment's peace of mind
waiting in constant fear,
listening for the dreaded knock
and the cold tones of policeman:
"Madam, you're wanted at the station."
I don't know if the knock ever came
but she feared on right till
we moved away from the street.
She used to say,

"It's the uncertainty that worries me –
if only I knew for certain. . . ."

If only I knew for certain
what my delinquent self would do. . .
But I never know
until the deed is done
and I live on fearing,
wondering which part of me will be supreme –
the old and tested one, the present
or the future unknown.
Sometimes all three have equal power
and then
how I long for a pigeon-hole.

Polygamy – Ancient and Modern

POLYGAMY has been a subject of debate for as long as I can remember. In the days when I was a schoolgirl, everybody understood what was meant by polygamy. It did not have to be defined. It simply meant having more than one wife. But nowadays when you talk about polygamy people ask, "Which kind?" For it seems there are now three kinds of polygamy. One is the traditional form practised by our forefathers and a number of unprogressive contemporaries. Under this system a man has two or more wives all of whom are officially recognized under customary law. This form is considered by educated people as "bush" and out-of-date.

The more enlightened form of polygamy and one that benefits the educated man of the twentieth century is the one in which ostensibly monogamous husbands have what some people refer to as "external affairs". The third form of polygamy is the "one-by-one" type popularized by Hollywood. The advantage in this is that you are not stuck with an ageing spouse.

There have been many spokesmen on behalf of polygamy. However, its case has never been so well put as in a poem in pidgin English by a young Nigerian poet, Frank Aig-Imoukhuede. In it he denounces the "one man one wife" doctrine and looks back with nostalgia to the days when "his fader before his fader get him wife borku".

He says:

I done try go to church, I done go for court
Dem all dey talk about di new culture,
Dem talk about "equality", dem mention "divorce"
Dem holler am so-tay my ear nearly cut;
    One wife be for one man.

My fader before my fader get him wife borku.
E no' get equality palaver; he live well

For he be oga for 'im own house.
Bot dat time done pass before white man come
Wit'im
    One wife for one man.

Tell me how una woman no go make yanga
Wen 'e know say na 'im only dey.
Suppose say – make God no gree – 'e no born at all.
A tell you dat man bin dey craze wey start
    One wife for one man.

Jus tell me how one wife fit do one man;
How man go fit stay all time for him house
For time when belleh done kommot.
How many pickin, self, one woman fit born
    Wen one wife be for one man?

Suppose, self, say na so-so woman your wife dey born
Suppose your wife sabe book, no sabe make chop;
Den, how you go tell man make 'e no go out
Sake of dis divorce? Bo, dis culture na waya O!
    Wen one wife be for one man.

That poem was obviously written from the point of view of a man. That is why he makes the polygamous life sound such an ideal state of existence. But is it ideal? I refuse to agree. A man may be *Oga* in his own house, true enough. Women may kneel down while handing him a drink, they may rival one another in trying to minister unto him. Yes, he will enjoy all these favours – but at what a price! The day he marries a second wife is the day he says goodbye to peace, for you cannot have two women in the same house without expecting some quarrelling, and when these women are wives of the same man, well, you may expect bedlam. What causes these quarrels? Sometimes there are grave causes such as wife No. 2, who has three children, parading her blessings before wife No. 1, who has none. This being a fundamental issue, the quarrelling is recurrent. Most times, however, the causes are trivial, such as wife No. 2 sweeping the room while wife No. 3 is having a meal, or wife No. 3 giving wife No. 4 contemptuous looks, or singing uncomplimentary proverbs.

Did I say these were trivial causes? Not really. They all stem from an untrivial cause – jealousy. And because jealousy has many faces, no husband can ever hope to stamp it out entirely. And this is why the quarrelling continues.

I once lived in a polygamous household where there were three wives. I don't know how the poor husband ever got any work done in the hospital where he worked, for neighbours were always sending for him. He would be in the middle of giving a patient an injection and someone would rush up and shout, "They are fighting again." He did not have to ask, "Who?" He knew without being told and he would hastily finish giving the injection and rush to his quarters near the hospital. These days I don't suppose hospital authorities would tolerate such goings on, but those were real polygamous days and everybody understood and sympathized.

So the big drawback to polygamy is the quarrelling among wives. How can husbands try to reduce it to a minimum – for this is about all they can do? Some husbands get angry and beat their wives, but this method is not always successful – some wives enjoy being beaten; it seems to tone up their muscles and give them a new zest for living. Besides, some wives regard beating as a mark of affection – I once heard a woman lamenting that her husband must have stopped loving her since he no longer beat her.

Well, then, if beating it out, what else can an exasperated husband do? He could take a cue from a former neighbour of mine. He had a very successful system based on the motto "Prevention is better than cure". Under this system, none of his wives ever met each other face to face. He had only one wife with him at any one time while the other two lived with their parents. Then he rotated them. As wife No. 1 was boarding a lorry in Ijebu-Ode where the husband lived, wife No. 2 would be boarding another in Ibadan. Wife No. 2 arrived in Ijebu-Ode to find a wifeless house, and took over. Since housework is a universal function, she required no handing-over notes.

This was a very effective system and had the added advantage of ensuring that two wives were not pregnant at the same time – an unfortunate predicament in which less organized polygamous husbands sometimes find themselves.

A third method of combating quarrelling among wives is rustication. Rustication is a term commonly used in universities. It means to send down a student temporarily from the university as a punishment. Well, I knew a husband who adopted this system. Whenever his wives were caught quarrelling, he would send them to his home town for a couple of months – until they sobered up. This was an effective form of punishment, for each time the wives went home they missed television. It did not stop them from quarrelling, however, but it did stop them from quarrelling in the presence of their husband. One minute they would be at it, yelling at each other at the tops of their voices, the next moment they would shut up suddenly as their husband's car drove round the corner. I've no doubt the husband thought his wives had learnt their lessons and stopped quarrelling. He certainly got the peace that is denied to most polygamous men, but I cannot say the same for his neighbours whose siestas were ruined by the noisy quarrels. Rustication has its limitations, however. It can only be used by the city dweller. For he that is down need fear no fall and she that is already in the bush need fear no rustication.

During noisy quarrels between wives one sometimes hears expressions such as this: "After all, it was my money that was used to pay your bride price. If I'd known you would become a thorn in my flesh I would not have given our husband money."

From this it can be seen that it is not only men who desire polygamy. Polygamy is actively encouraged by some women, which is surprising, considering the amount of unhappiness they derive from it. Why do they do it?

There are a number of reasons. First, women are by nature good strategists. Knowing that most husbands possess a roving eye, they persuade theirs to bring his new sweetheart into the home where they can keep a vigilant eye on the goings on. Besides, as everyone knows, the woman outside the home tends to get a larger share of the family cake. A wife can keep an eye on the sharing of the family cake when the sharers are all together under one roof. For example, it would be impossible for a second wife to hide a new gold trinket or a new buba and iro outfit, evidence of her husband's partiality.

Another reason is that these wives want "an helpmeet" – to use a Biblical expression. Housework done with traditional tools is pretty exacting. Cooking delicious stew to earn the praise of a gourmet husband may be a pleasure, but preparing the ingredients certainly isn't. Few women enjoy grinding pepper on a grindstone; even after grinding machines were introduced into the country, carrying the ingredients to market to be ground was still an effort. So, wife No. 1 looked for a drudge to relieve her of this chore. A husband who was not too well off might refuse to pay for the services of a housemaid, but could hardly resist a plea to take another wife. Wife No. 2 could therefore be regarded as a glorified unpaid servant whose doubtful compensation was a share in the man's affections.

A third reason is wife No. 1's desire for a gossip mate. It can be pretty frustrating to sit in front of your house and watch another woman strutting by and have no one to gossip with about her ugly face, the shabby funeral she gave her mother a month ago and the fact that she is a very lazy woman who cannot cook a decent meal for her husband.

One can then understand why wife No. 1 would want a mate. Buy why on earth would a woman agree to become a drudge to another woman when she could become wife No. 1 in another man's home? The reason is that a woman prefers to have one-third of a good husband – and the word "good" may also mean "rich" – than to have a hundred per cent of a nonentity. Quality is preferred to quantity.

Polygamy is still commonly practised in a number of places, but as I said before, highly educated people are rejecting the traditional form of polygamy and substituting it with the modern form. I think this is a pity for under the old system a man usually kept all his wives under one roof and managing them called for a lot of ingenuity. Any man who succeeded deserved to be highly commended. Considering all the tact, diplomacy, strength and patience such a man must possess he would surely be well equipped to rule a nation. And he'd get my vote every time!

Charity Waciuma

?1930s–

er memories of a Kenyan adolescence during the Mau Mau emergency period are movingly described in her autobiographical book Daughter of Mumbi *(1969), from which this extract is taken. She is also a children's writer, drawing on Kikuyu legends and storytelling traditions, author of books such as* The Golden Feather *(1966),* Mweru, the Ostrich Girl *(1966) and* Who's Calling? *(1973).*

From

Daughter of Mumbi

ITEGA AND IRUA

ONE year, as the last heavy rains were falling, my mother went to the Local Council Hospital. Before she left she called us children together and said, "You will have to look after yourselves for a few days because Mummy is going to have a baby and Papa will be busy working."

We asked how long she was to be away and she said for one week. This seemed an eternity for me, at the age of nine or ten, because I depended upon her so much. Although my grandmother came and spoiled me, I still longed for my mother to be back. I hated to think of the baby she would bring back from the hospital which would, I thought, take my place in her affections, though I was not even then the youngest.

As I stood waving to my parents in the bus on their way to the hospital, the rain became lighter and lighter as it fell in bright, slanting showers. Sometimes the sun shone through the rain and a warmer breeze blew. A rainbow formed in the sky and in my excitement I forgot about my parents' departure. I ran to my grandmother who was cooking in our grass-thatched kitchen and breathlessly asked her, "What is a rainbow?"

"It is a long, bright snake that dwells in the water. When the rain falls heavily and the river becomes clouded with mud the snake gets so angry that it rises from the river into the sky to stop the rain. Sometimes two snakes climb upwards and then they always succeed."

My grandmother, my aunts and my mother's women friends came and planted our shamba. It is our tribal custom that if a woman becomes sick, her women friends tend her crops and look after her house and children until she is better.

The days passed quickly and the joyful time soon arrived for my father to go to fetch my mother home. Although I tried very hard to dislike the new baby, which was the centre of my mother's attention, I could not for she was so small and beautiful. I grew to love and cherish her, to care for her and want to protect her. It was the busiest week I had ever known in my home. Every day women brought my mother maize and millet gruel in large gourds while others came with firewood for cooking. This also is a Gikuyu custom. To regain her strength and make up for the blood she has lost, the new mother must eat this tasty dish and since she cannot prepare it herself, her friends must do it.

The new baby was named Muthoni after my mother's eldest sister so, according to tradition, her husband brought a big fat ram to be slaughtered for my mother, for giving birth to "his bride". Jokingly the child would always be his bride. If at any time as a grown-up girl she ran away to his house, he would have the right to come and ask the parents the cause and if he thought the girl was in the right he could decide that she should stay with him and his wife.

After a fortnight my mother was able to look after the house by herself but still she could not go to the shamba. As we needed extra milk, an old man who lived a mile from our home brought a pint every morning and each evening we went to his place for another pint. It was a great joy to walk across the smooth, green meadows every evening and I wished that my mother could always be having babies so that the freedom of the evening stroll with my brother or a friend would go on and on. I looked forward to the errand so much. Each time I looked through the ancient Gikuyu trees to the restful plump hills, saffron-yellow in the soft African twilight, across the river which divided my location from Location One. Coming back with the milk at sunset I used to gather the wild white lilies which sprang up only during the rainy season. Everything I saw reminded me of the greatness and the freedom of our land in the days of my grandfather's stories, when a man could travel about the country without being stopped by the White Man's messengers to produce his tax certificates or by rogues to rob him.

I longed for that time to come again but I knew with sadness that it never would. I could see to the north of us the White Man smoking a pipe, riding his horse across the acres of his coffee estate. His wife wore trousers like a man and her face was as hard and bleached as a stone in the river bed. I did not see how they could ever be dislodged from their fine, feudal life.

The sky turned a pale blue or violet just before the sunset and great smoky clouds drifted across the countryside, turning the emerald green of the coffee estate to a deep, hazy blue.

After the long rains we used to go early for milk in order to have time for swimming in the water which had gathered in a pond on our pathway.

Some moonlit nights we danced under an enormous old fig tree which stood in the centre of my grandfather's village. Then we were allowed to sit and listen to the old men's stories because of my grandfather's position in the clan, and because he was the leading storyteller. Afterwards we stayed at the house of one of my uncles instead of going home. At the end of every evening we stood round the fire, facing Mount Kirinyaga, and thanked Mwenenyaga, the God of our father Gikuyu, for the wonderful land he had given us, for the past and for the future. No one prayed for the present.

We joined in the prayers asking him to help us get rid of the white man who had taken the plains and the forests from us so that the members of the clan, who were the rightful owners, were deprived of it and wandered about as beggars. These prayers made a great impression upon me during my formative years. I was filled with a desire to study and become educated in the White Man's ways and in his knowledge so that I could help in turning him out of my country. By this time there were only five or six Africans in the whole country who had been abroad to study in Britain, in America or in India. The thirst for education and the desire to be free forced the spectacular growth of Kikuyu Independent Schools from mud structures to magnificent stone buildings. Everyone contributed in whatever way he or she could to ensure that the young boys and girls became educated. The pupils flooded to school in thousands.

Towards the end of the afternoon in the dry season my sisters and I used to go to fetch water from the river. Any little rain that fell at that time was collected in a tank for drinking. Although we got tired on the steep climb back from the valley with a "debe" of water on our backs secured by a head strap we still enjoyed the journeys: it was an opportunity to meet our girl friends, down there away from our parents. As we met we would give the traditional greeting of one girl to another, by raising the right hand level with the mouth, the palm towards the other person. With short jerky movements the hands went out to meet theirs, my head turning sideways as I said, "Wakia, Wakia," my age-grade greeting. There were proper words of greeting laid down for people of various ages and sexes and proper things to do when one met a person of another age group or sex.

It was very common to give one's closest friends a nickname and always to use it among ourselves. We would talk about everything under the sun. Especially boys. If we found married women by the river we talked among ourselves in riddles and by twisting the language in a special way. They did not know what we were saying and we could laugh and joke and tell stories about them without their understanding us. Even before the formal initiation ceremonies to bind them a very close communion grew up among the girls of an age set.

Near the river there lived an old witchdoctor whom we feared very much, to whom we gave the funny meaningless nickname of "Gathege". He had a large cockerel which had once bitten a headman so badly that the doctor had to pay compensation. His hut had a very small door and, happy-go-lucky young girls that we were, we found even this a source of amusement. He had a short wife, even shorter than he was, and we used to giggle and say that the door was so small because to have a large one would only have been a waste. His home was surrounded by tall banana trees and we used to watch as we sat by the river. As the fruit ripened we counted the weeks and days before it was ready. When the bananas were about to be picked by the old man we went on our way back from the river late in the evening and took them.

Gleefully we raced up the hill, our faces lit with the exhilaration of our achievement. We had stolen his bananas. He would never guess that young girls would dare to do such a thing to one who had such powerful magic.

In those far-off days school-age girls had little work to do after attending the classes, except fetching water from the river. On the route by which we went for water, there lived a young man who had recently returned from college to be a teacher at the local secondary school. Somehow, when we passed his house, we would lose my eldest sister and find her empty "debe" with one of us. We would take it and fill it and return to find her talking to that young man. Then she would return with us carrying her load. It was surprising to see how keen she was to go and fetch water and, sometimes, she would go two or three times in the same afternoon.

About this time, we lost many of our good friends when they went through the circumcision ceremony. Because we Christian girls had not "been to the river" we were unclean. We were not decent respectable people and mothers would not have the shame of letting their daughters be seen in our company. It was believed that a girl who was uncircumcised would cause the death of a circumcised husband. Moreover, an uncircumcised woman would be barren. When the other boys and girls – and their parents – came to realize that we really never would be circumcised it was something of a scandal. We became a laughing-stock, the butt of their jokes. They would whisper about us and shout riddles to us. They made up a song, which they used to chant at us, that if a young man was passing and it began to rain he should not ask our mother for shelter. For, if he came in and joked with us, we, being uncircumcised and therefore immature, would answer like children, and say childish things to him. Another song emphasized the belief that no woman could begin to grow up until she was circumcised; it asked how many castor trees our father was planting for us to climb and play in like children.

In the face of these taunts we held our heads high and walked all the more proudly to the river. We were healthy and full of energy and, according to the place and time, were very smartly dressed. Certainly we thought so, at any rate. We made new friends with uncircumised girls from across the river. They envied us because we were not ashamed of being uncircumcised and they copied our proud demeanour and some also tried to follow the new fashions we wore.

What did hurt us was the way my grandfather acted. Being a man of some position in the traditional set up, he was greatly embarrassed by our family's having abandoned the tribal custom. Not only was he personally affronted but he was put under considerable pressure from the other elders. He told my parents that they had brought shame and derision to the proud name of our family and our clan. It would be better if none of us ever went to see him again. This was a terrible prohibition. The grandfather was such a key figure in our society. We all loved him so dearly and he cherished all of us. The ban was relaxed in respect to my brothers. Being boys, they went to the hospital to be circumcised. Although this was not so significant as passing through the ceremonial operation, it was better than nothing. They were just about acceptable in proper Kikuyu society. Nevertheless, they stood solidly with us, their sisters, and refused to visit the old man. It was the old man who broke the prohibition in the end. He arrived one day with a big fat ram which was to be slaughtered and eaten to cleanse the bad words he had used against us. Although this restored our relationship with him, other people continued to insult us and there were frequent fights between my brothers and some of the young men who taunted us.

Although many of the people were Christians and did not observe all the traditional rites, this was one which they were most loath to give up. Those who had not observed all the earlier practices were not entitled to participate in all the ceremonies, but many nevertheless underwent the physical operation. All those who wanted to be full initiates had to have been through the rite of "Gaciaruo ringi" – rebirth. The day after a child was born a ram was killed and some of its fat cooked in a pot. The mother and the child each drank of the fat. When the child was from three to six years old the ceremony was completed, signifying the separation of the mother and child. The father killed another ram and this time he cut two narrow strips of its skin. If the child were a girl the skin was tied to the top of her right arm and round her calf. If a boy, to the left arm and leg. Before the tying on of the skin the child had to lie alongside its mother and cry like a baby. Once the skin was tied on and stayed there for three days, the boy or girl was supposed to put away such childish behaviour.

After the circumcision ceremony, the women who were Christians took offerings of the produce of their shambas to the harvest festival in the Church. In addition to the basket of maize which I took, I put a shilling, which I had raised by selling mangoes, in the collection. The Sunday service was so long that we children became bored and went outside to play in the field. We saw those women who were not Christians taking their harvest offerings to the traditional sacred place. I went nearer and saw how beautifully they had coloured themselves for the occasion with lime and clay from the river. They went to and fro carrying baskets of maize, beans and millet on their backs. As I watched from my hiding place, I saw the elders take a lamb and kill it a short distance away from the holy fig tree. Its skin was torn into strips and a band was placed round the waist of each woman. The women then went off in a party singing thanksgiving hymns to Mwenenyaga while the old men stayed behind and ate the meat. Although I said nothing at home about the beautiful ceremony, I treasured all that I had seen in my heart. I spent many days wishing that my mother gave her offering to Mwenenyaga instead of taking it to church.

Lourdes Teodoro
?1930s-

B orn in Brazil, she is a professor in the Institute of Architecture
at the University of Brasilia, and is the author of several books of
poetry, including Agua-Marinha Ou Tempo Sem Palavra. (1978).
The following poem was translated from the Portuguese by Iain Bruce.

The Generation of Fear

Beyond the belt of the horizon
our wrists are squeezed
and without a word the clouds disperse
further and further
squeezing our wrists.

our heads emptied
into the generation we brought into the world,
all anointed with prison lime.
our fruits grow without flavour or smell
and we accuse them of betraying the seed
but they, innocent, know nothing of betrayal.

they are children of the generation of fear
wand from the moment they saw the sun, it was already dark during the daytime.
but from some order they got the courage
to walk in the streets with empty hands.

our children are fruits that do not reflect
beyond the table where dinner happens
when they're not just the looks of a frightened lizard
hearing footsteps and hiding in the bushes on the look-out
for their share of rubbish.

They are children of the generation of fear
whose smothered scream blocked the artery,
and pressure was brought down

through the emptying out of thought.
they want flowers and hymns in my blood
but in my blood there is only blood
and fear of speaking out and fear of remaining silent

because our children

are our children
and we need them to be the children of their times
these times we have built
with silence and death.

without horizons, this time is cold
without horizons, this time is ugly
for our children.

It's necessary to plant and plough the land now
when all has been forgotten so it can last.
like the ancient oaks
just providing shadow.

the generation of fear files past and wants to think
ants to say, tell, recall.
only history plants consciousness
in the opaque moment.
desperate embroiderer, the generation of fear
hunts for scraps, dyes bits and pieces
and tries to build,
shows its face and hands out the old outburst.

how difficult it's become to be
but it was always difficult to be in vain.

Toni Cade Bambara
1931–

B orn and brought up in Harlem, New York (the setting for many
of her stories), she adopted the name "Bambara" after finding
it written on her grandmother's notebook in an old trunk. She
has a BA from Queens College, an MA from City University of New
York and attended the University of Florence. She has been a welfare
investigator, a community centre programme director and a teacher,
and has been writer-in-residence at various universities. Active in Black
community politics in Atlanta, where she moved in 1974, she runs writing
workshops. She has said: "As black and woman in a society systematically
orchestrated to oppress each and both, we have a very particular vantage
point and, therefore, have a special contribution to make to the collective
intelligence, to the literatures of this historical moment." Her books
include collections of short stories – Gorilla, My Love (in which
the following story appears), published in 1972, and The Sea Birds Are
Still Alive (1977) – and a novel, The Salt Eaters (1980), which won
the American Book Award. She was also editor of The Black Woman
(1970), a pioneering anthology of writings by African-American
women.

Maggie of the Green Bottles

M AGGIE had not intended to get sucked in on this thing, sleeping straight
through the christening, steering clear of the punch bowl, and refusing to
dress for company. But when she glanced over my grandfather's shoulder and
saw "Aspire, Enspire, Perspire" scrawled across the first page in that hard-core
Protestant hand, and a grease stain from the fried chicken too, something
snapped in her head. She snatched up the book and retired rapidly to her
room, locked my mother out, and explained through the door that my mother
was a fool to encourage a lot of misspelled nonsense from Mr Tyler's kin, and
an even bigger fool for having married the monster in the first place.

I imagine that Maggie sat at her great oak desk, rolled the lace cuffs gently
back, and dipped her quill into the lavender ink pot with all the ceremony
due the Emancipation Proclamation, which was, after all, exactly what she was
drafting. Writing to me, she explained, was serious business, for she felt called
upon to liberate me from all historical and genealogical connections except the

most divine. In short, the family was a disgrace, degrading Maggie's and my capacity for wings, as they say. I can only say that Maggie was truly inspired. And she probably ruined my life from the get-go.

There is a photo of the two of us on the second page. There's Maggie in Minnie Mouse shoes and a long polka-dot affair with her stockings rolled up at the shins, looking like muffins. There's me with nothing much at all on, in her arms, and looking almost like a normal, mortal, everyday-type baby – raw, wrinkled, ugly. Except that it must be clearly understood straightaway that I sprang into the world full wise and invulnerable and gorgeous like a goddess. Behind us is the player piano with the spooky keys. And behind that, the window outlining Maggie's crosshatched face and looking out over the yard, overgrown even then, where later I lay lost in the high grass, never hoping to be found till Maggie picked me up into her hair and told me all about the earth's moons.

Once just a raggedy thing holding telegrams from well-wishers, the book was pleasant reading on those rainy days when I didn't risk rusting my skates, or maybe just wasn't up to trailing up and down the city streets with the kids, preferring to study Maggie's drawings and try to grab hold of the fearsome machinery which turned the planets and coursed the stars and told me in no uncertain terms that as an Aries babe I was obligated to carry on the work of other Aries greats from Alexander right on down to anyone you care to mention. I could go on to relate all the wise-alecky responses I gave to Maggie's document as an older child rummaging in the trunks among the canceled checks and old sheet music, looking for some suspicioned love letters or some small proof that my mother had once had romance in her life, and finding instead the raggedy little book I thought was just a raggedy little book. But it is much too easy to smile at one's ignorant youth just to flatter one's present wisdom, but I digress.

Because, on my birthday, Saturn was sitting on its ass and Mars was taken unawares, getting bumped by Jupiter's flunkies, I would not be into my own till well past twenty. But according to the cards, and my palm line bore it out, the hangman would spare me till well into my hundredth year. So all in all, the tea leaves having had their say and the coffee-ground patterns being what they were, I was destined for greatness. She assured me. And I was certain of my success, as I was certain that my parents were not my parents, that I was descended, anointed and ready to gobble up the world, from urgent, noble Olympiads.

I am told by those who knew her, whose memories consist of something more substantial than a frantic gray lady who poured coffee into her saucer, that Margaret Cooper Williams wanted something she could not have. And it was the sorrow of her life that all her children and theirs and theirs were uncooperative – worse, squeamish. Too busy taking in laundry, buckling at the knees, putting their faith in Jesus, mute and sullen in their sorrow, too squeamish to band together and take the world by storm, make history, or even to appreciate the calling of Maggie the Ram, or the Aries that came after. Other things they told me, things I put aside to learn later though I always knew, perhaps, but never quite wanted to, the way you hold your breath and steady yourself to the knowledge secretly, but never let yourself understand. They called her crazy.

It is to Maggie's guts that I bow forehead to the floor and kiss her hand, because she'd tackle the lot of them right there in the yard, blood kin or by marriage, and neighbors or no. And anybody who'd stand up to my father, gross Neanderthal that he was, simply had to be some kind of weird combination of David, Aries, and lunatic. It began with the cooking usually, especially the pots of things Maggie concocted. Witchcraft, he called it. Home cooking, she'd counter. Then he'd come over to the stove, lift a lid with an incredible face, and comment about cesspools and fertilizers. But she'd remind him of his favorite dish, chitlins, addressing the bread box, though. He'd turn up the radio and make some remark about good church music and her crazy voodoo records. Then she'd tell the curtains that some men, who put magic down with nothing to replace it and nothing much to recommend them in the first place but their magic wand, lived a runabout life, practicing black magic on other men's wives. Then he'd say something about freeloading relatives and dancing to the piper's tune. And she'd whisper to the kettles that there wasn't no sense in begging from a beggar. Depending on how large an audience they drew, this could go on for hours until my father would cock his head to the side, listening, and then try to make his getaway.

"Ain't nobody calling you, Mr Tyler, cause don't nobody want you." And I'd feel kind of bad about my father like I do about the wolf man and the phantom of the opera. Monsters, you know, more than anybody else, need your pity cause they need beauty and love so bad.

One day, right about the time Maggie would say something painful that made him bring up freeloaders and piper's tunes, he began to sputter so bad it made me want to cry. But Maggie put the big wooden spoon down and whistled for Mister T – at least that's what Maggie and my grandmother, before she died, insisted on calling him. The dog, always hungry, came bounding through the screen door, stopped on a dime by the sink, and slinked over to Maggie's legs the way beat-up dogs can do, their tails all confused as to just what to do, their eyes unblinkingly watchful. Maggie offered him something from the pot. And when Mister T had finished, he licked Maggie's hand. She began to cackle. And then, before I could even put my milk down, up went Maggie's palm, and *bam*, Mister T went skidding across the linoleum and banged all the seltzer bottles down.

"Damn-fool mutt," said Maggie to her wooden spoon, "too dumb to even know you're supposed to bite the hand that feeds you."

My father threw his hand back and yelled for my mother to drop whatever she was doing, which was standing in the doorway shaking her head, and pack up the old lady's things posthaste. Maggie went right on laughing and talking to the spoon. And Mister T slinked over to the table so Baby Jason could pet him. And then it was name-calling time. And again I must genuflect and kiss her ring, because my father was no slouch when it came to names. He could malign your mother and work your father's lineage over in one short breath, describing in absolute detail all the incredible alliances made between your ancestors and all sorts of weird creatures. But Maggie had him beat there too, old lady in lace talking to spoons or no.

My mother came in weary and worn and gave me a nod. I slid my peanut-butter sandwich off the icebox, grabbed Baby Jason by his harness, and dragged him into our room, where I was supposed to read to him real loud. But I listened, I always listened to my mother's footfalls on the porch to the gravel path and down the hard mud road to the woodshed. Then I could give my attention to the kitchen, for "Goldilocks", keep in mind, never was enough to keep the brain alive. Then, right in the middle of some fierce curse or other, my father did this unbelievable thing. He stomped right into Maggie's room – that sanctuary of heaven charts and incense pots and dream books and magic stuffs. Only Jason, hiding from an August storm, had ever been allowed in there, and that was on his knees crawling. But in he stomped all big and bad like some terrible giant, this man whom Grandma Williams used to say was just the sort of size man put on this earth for the "'spress purpose of clubbing us all to death." And he came out with these green bottles, one in each hand, snorting and laughing at the same time. And I figured, peeping into the kitchen, that these bottles were enchanted, for they had a strange effect on Maggie, she shut right up. They had a strange effect on me too, gleaming there up in the air, nearly touching the ceiling, glinting off the shots of sunshine, grasped in the giant's fist. I was awed.

Whenever I saw them piled in the garbage out back I was tempted to touch them and make a wish, knowing all the while that the charm was all used up and that that was why they were in the garbage in the first place. But there was no doubt that they were special. And whenever Baby Jason managed to drag one out from under the bed, there was much whispering and shuffling on my mother's part. And when Sweet Basil, the grocer's boy, delivered these green bottles to Maggie, it was all hush-hush and backdoor and in the corner dealings, slipping it in and out of innumerable paper bags, holding it up to the light, then off she'd run to her room and be gone for hours, days sometimes, and when she did appear, looking mysterious and in a trance, her face all full of shadows. And she'd sit at the sideboard with that famous cup from the World's Fair, pouring coffee into the saucer and blowing on it very carefully, nodding and humming and swirling the grinds. She called me over once to look at the grinds.

"What does this look like, Peaches?"

"Looks like a star with a piece out of it."

"Hmm," she mumbled, and swirled again. "And now?"

Me peering into the cup and lost for words. "Looks like a face that lost its eyes."

"Hmm," again, as she thrust the cup right under my nose, and me wishing it was a box of falling glass I could look at where I knew what was what instead of looking into the bottom of a fat yellow cup at what looked like nothing but coffee grinds.

"Looks like a mouth losing its breath, Great Granny."

"Let's not get too outrageous, Peaches. This is serious business."

"Yes, ma'am." Peering again and trying to be worthy of Alexander and the Ram and all my other forebears. "What it really seems to be" – stalling for time and praying for inspiration – "is an upside-down bird, dead on its back with his heart chopped out and the hole bleeding."

She flicked my hand away when I tried to point the picture out which by now I was beginning to believe. "Go play somewhere, girl," she said. She was mad. "And quit calling me Granny."

"What happened here today?" my mother kept asking all evening, thumping out the fragrant dough and wringing the dishtowel, which was supposed to help the dough rise, wringing it to pieces. I couldn't remember anything particular, following her gaze to Maggie's door. "Was Sweet Basil here this afternoon?" Couldn't remember that either, but tried to show I was her daughter by staring hard at the closed door too. "Was Great Granny up and around at all today?" My memory failed me there too. "You ain't got much memory to speak of at all, do you?" said my father. I hung onto my mother's apron and helped her wring the dishtowel to pieces.

They told me she was very sick, so I had to drag Baby Jason out to the high grass and play with him. It was a hot day and the smell of the kerosene soaking the weeds that were stubborn about dying made my eyes tear. I was face down in the grass just listening, waiting for the afternoon siren which last year I thought was Judgment Day because it blew so long to say that the war was over and that we didn't have to eat Spam any more and that there was a circus coming and a parade and Uncle Bubba too, but with only one leg to show for it all. Maggie came into the yard with her basket of vegetables. She sat down at the edge of the gravel path and began stringing the peppers, red and green, red and green. And, like always, she was humming one of those weird songs of hers which always made her seem holier and blacker than she could've been. I tied Baby Jason to a tree so he wouldn't crawl into her lap, which always annoyed her. Maggie didn't like baby boys, or any kind of boys I'm thinking, but especially baby boys born in Cancer and Pisces or anything but in Aries.

"Look here, Peaches," she called, working the twine through the peppers and dropping her voice real low. "I want you to do this thing for your Great Granny."

"What must I do?" I waited a long time till I almost thought she'd fallen asleep, her head rolling around on her chest and her hands fumbling with slippery peppers, ripping them.

"I want you to go to my room and pull out the big pink box from under the bed." She looked around and woke up a bit. "This is a secret you-and-me thing now, Peaches." I nodded and waited some more. "Open the box and you'll see a green bottle. Wrap this apron around it and tuck it under your arm like so. Then grab up the mushrooms I left on the sideboard like that's what you came for in the first place. But get yourself back here right quick." I repeated the instructions, flopped a necklace of peppers around me, and dashed into the hot and dusty house. When I got back she dumped the mushrooms into her lap, tucked the bottle under her skirt, and smiled at the poor little peppers her nervous hands had strung. They hung wet and ruined off the twine like broken-necked little animals.

I was down in the bottom playing with the state-farm kids when Uncle Bubba came sliding down the sand pile on his one good leg. Jason was already in the station wagon hanging onto my old doll. We stayed at Aunt Min's till my father came to get us in the pickup. Everybody was in the kitchen dividing up Maggie's things. The linen chest went to Aunt Thelma. And the souvenirs from Maggie's honeymoons went to the freckle-faced cousins from town. The clothes were packed for the church. And Reverend Elson was directing the pianist's carrying from the kitchen window. The scattered sopranos, who never ever seemed to get together on their high notes or on their visits like this, were making my mother drink tea and kept nodding at me, saying she was sitting in the mourner's seat, which was just like all the other chairs in the set; same as the amen corner was no better or any less duty than the rest of the church and not even a corner. Then Reverend Elson turned to say that no matter how crazy she'd been, no matter how hateful she'd acted toward the church in general and him in particular, no matter how spiteful she'd behaved towards her neighbors and even her blood kin, and even though everyone was better off without her, seeing how she died as proof of her heathen character, and right there in the front yard too, with a bottle under her skirts, the sopranos joined in scattered as ever, despite all that, the Reverend Elson continued, God rest her soul, if He saw fit, that is.

The china darning egg went into Jason's overalls. And the desk went into my room. Bubba said he wanted the books for his children. And they all gave him such a look. My mother just sat in the kitchen chair called the mourner's seat and said nothing at all except that they were selling the house and moving to the city.

"Well, Peaches," my father said. "You were her special, what you want?"

"I'll take the bottles," I said.

"Let us pray," said the Reverend.

That night I sat at the desk and read the baby book for the first time. It sounded like Maggie for the world, holding me in her lap and spreading the charts on the kitchen table. I looked my new bottle collection over. There were purple bottles with glass stoppers and labels. There were squat blue bottles with squeeze tops but nothing in them. There were flat red bottles that could hold only one flower at a time. I had meant the green bottles. I was going to tell them and then I didn't. I was too small for so much enchantment anyway. I went to bed feeling much too small. And it seemed a shame that the hope of the Aries line should have to sleep with a light on still, and blame it on Jason and cry with balled fists in the eyes just like an ordinary, mortal, everyday-type baby.

Kristin Hunter

1931–

B orn in Philadelphia, Pennsylvania, she began her writing career
at the age of fourteen with a weekly column in the Pittsburgh
Courier. She studied Education at the University of Pennsylvania (BS,
1951) and made a living through writing and teaching, accepting an appointment as Senior Lecturer in English at the University of Pittsburgh in 1972. Her
first novel, God Bless the Child (1964), is the story of Rosie Fleming, who
grows up in a roach-infested tenement with a grandmother imbued by
genteel pretensions from years of domestic service to a rich white family,
and with a downpressed hairdresser mother ("In this world, it ain't an
easy job, making black women think they're beautiful"). She sets out to
get "her own" – like the child in the Billie Holiday song from which
the title is borrowed – but succumbs to a self-destructive pursuit of the
materialistic white American dream. In this extract, Rosie's underworld
friends try to assume behaviour appropriate to a social visit with Granny
and her companions. The book won the Philadelphia Athenaeum Literary
Award and was followed by other prizewinning works of fiction, both for
adults and for younger readers, including The Landlord (1966, later
filmed), The Soul Brothers and Sister Lou (1968; Council for Interracial
Books for Children Award), Guests in the Promised Land (1973; National
Book Award nomination) and The Lakestown Rebellion (1978).

From

God Bless the Child

CHAPTER XXIV

R OSIE'S cream cheese sandwiches were magnificent and inedible. They
were tinted pastel pink and green and arranged on a three-tiered crystal
tray in patterns that were obviously not meant to be disturbed. After they had
been passed and refused, the bar that silently churned its rainbows into the room
was used for the serving of pale pink lemonade and bright green Kool-Aid.

As each couple arrived, Rosie led them to Granny's chair for elaborate
introductions, then separated them into the seating arrangement she had
designed. Soon an uncomfortable row of girls sat facing an uneasy row of
men.

Rosie darted restlessly from background to foreground, harvesting invisible bits of litter from the floor, feeding the hi-fi a steady diet of Nelson Eddy and Jeanette Mac Donald, and urging liquids and sandwiches on her underworld friends, who all strove heroically to balance cut-glass cups and plates and lacy napkins on their knees with grace. The only topics permitted for general discussion were the state of your health and the weather. Men were also allowed to exchange low comments about sports with their neighbors, and women might engage, if they wished, in whispered discussions of clothes. Both sexes were supposed to cough discreetly, at regular intervals, into elegant handkerchiefs.

The three old ladies who surrounded Granny, sipping daintily and sighing and rustling their fans, were the only ones who seemed to be enjoying themselves. Everyone else seemed afflicted by a terrible itch. They looked about desperately, but no opportunities for scratching were in sight. As the minutes creaked along, the old ladies' fans flew more and more furiously, whipping up the air like egg white until it was stiff with discomfort. The little smile on Granny's face grew broader and broader. Twenty people crossed and uncrossed their legs thirty times.

Of all the young people, only Dolly seemed comfortable within the constraints Rosie had imposed. She sat with the calm propriety of a nun, hands resting quietly in her lap. On her right Ginger and Amber tugged nervously at identical tight satin dresses which kept doing exactly what they had been designed to do, ride high above the knee. On her left Bettina, the shapely stripper from The Cotton Club, suddenly ashamed of the endowment that earned her salary, seemed to be trying to wriggle down lower into her low-cut dress.

"Aw, don't hide it, honey," rumbled Pockets Robinson from across the room. "It looks good."

While everyone else looked shocked, the old ladies calmly took command and healed the breach of deportment.

"I went to see Miss Jenny Hankins laid out today," said Mrs Olive Fussell, the oldest of the three. "Sad."

"Mmm, yes," agreed Miss Bessie Harris, "but wasn't she a lovely co'pse?"

"Mmm, yes," Miss Olive replied. "She looked so sweet. Like she was just lyin' there dreamin' and would wake up by and by."

"Sad," said Miss Mary Scott. "Did you stay for the wedding?"

"No," Miss Olive replied with regret.

"Oh, that's too bad," Miss Mary said. "It was Lucia Luby's child. She made a lovely bride."

"I was there," Miss Bessie said. "Mmm yes, I was there. I was glad they had the viewing first. I always like to get there early and see everything. It sho' was a lovely ceremony."

"Mmm yes," said Mrs Lourinda Huggs, who had lately taken up church and embroidery to fill the gaps left in her life by her white folks, "that it was."

Except for a cough from Miltie Newton in the corner, the rest of the room was painfully silent. Bettina, wriggling and tugging miserably, pulled out a cigarette and asked Dolly if she had a match. Dolly shook her head, and the unhappy dancer, after a quick look around, stowed the contraband cylinder down her splendid bosom. She was not unobserved.

"Mm-hmm *yes*," Miss Mary emphasized with a decisive downward flourish of her fan.

Silence. Deadly oppressive silence, like a vacuum; all the air seemed to have been sucked out of the room.

Suffocating, poolroom owner Bud Lewis fished a sphere from his cup and said, with nervous humor, "First cherry I had all year."

There was scattered laughter until Rosie's baleful glance searched the room and found it out. Another hush fell.

Pockets Robinson leaned forward with a courteous cough and said to Granny, "I think he meant they ain't been in season, ma'am."

This only drew forth a more widespread ripple of laughter. Rosie, seeing that the thin bubble of her party's propriety was ready to burst, gave an imperious signal to Larnie.

Gravely, with only a slight held-in dance in his walk to betray his drunken amusement, he got up and went over to the piano in one corner. The group quickened slightly. Any distraction was preferable to what had gone before.

But Larnie chose to give them the most well-tempered, orderly Bach he could think of, unsullied by ornaments of dynamics. On and on it went, in monotonous machinelike progressions, while faces looked at each other in dull, baffled anger, and feet that had been poised for tapping drooped limply. At the end there was applause, but only from the old ladies.

Larnie did not wait until their genteel clapping was over. He plunged immediately, with drunken assurance, into the "Chromatic Fantasy and Fugue," and this time he held even the most sluggish attentions. The first runs seemed to fling open the ceiling to the sky. Notes flew overhead like swallows over city roofs, flock after flock, only to be scattered into gray clouds homing toward the south by rapid changes of key. Then the miracle happened.

The theme twisted, turned inside out, shed its solemn skin and was transformed into something quite different. A nimble arrangement of notes like bursting pinwheels above, and underneath a rhythm which was compellingly familiar, like blues, like gospel, like an amplification of the human heart. As it pulled in and out, back and forth, hands began to clap softly, and feet began to shuffle. Even Queenie, who had planned to stay aloof from the proceedings, found this music irresistible. She perched on the top step, eyes closed, swaying dreamily.

Larnie went on chasing star-trails until they were breathless from keeping up with him. Finally he took pity and, with chords hewn of solid stone, brought the thing to its ponderous climax. It still swung majestically in the after-echoes, like a rock balancing on the edge of a chasm.

Dolly forgot herself and cried, "Wonderful!" in the ensuing cave of silence.

Larnie stood up, smiling, glassy-eyed, pleased, acknowledging waves of applause and cries of "More, man! More!"

"Now, lemme give you the lowdown on this cat Bach," he said with a confidential wink at his audience. They sank into expectant silence as he sat down and launched into a skipping Gigue from one of the *English Suites*.

"Now Mister Bach was church folks and all that, you understand, but he had his lighter moments too. Wasn't nothin' he liked better than jammin' awhile." Larnie sneaked a subtle syncopation into the rhythm, then let it disappear. There were appreciative chuckles.

"'Course, now, when the Deacon or the Archbishop was in church, Bach played it real dignified." Larnie put his nose in the air and curled his fingers with dandified precision. "But when they cut out, man, that church started jumpin'."

The Gigue became a boogie, fast and driving, with a tickling antiphonal movement high in the treble. "Now one day Bach was jivin' around like this, compin' with his left hand and soloin' with his right, when the Bishop sneaked in the back way. But Bach dug him soon's the door opened. He got right back on that righteous kick."

The music was solemn again. "The Bishop digs it, and he nods real pious, and says, 'Fine, fine, Brother Johann, just what I like to hear.' And he goes out of church again, so naturally Bach gets back in the groove right away . . . till he hears some of the congregation filin' in."

Larnie closed the jazz improvisation with the traditional figure and chord. Still in his role, he half rose from the piano bench, smiled, and bowed. "The congregation applauded. And Bach stood up and took a bow, just as proper as you please." Intoxicated with his own acting, Larnie dragged a finger down the keyboard. "Bach just knew he was slick, see. He just knew he had 'em all fooled."

He paused significantly.

" – and then, somebody in the congregation yelled out, 'Crazy!'"

A great roar of laughter went up from every throat, and a cannonade of applause followed. B. J., the gambler, got up to clap Larnie on the shoulder.

"Man," he said, "I'd sure like to get you a drink, if this wasn't such a lame, dry party."

Only one small tinkling note of condemnation sounded in the swell of praise. But Granny's "Disgraceful!" was sweeping enough to include both B. J.'s remark and Larnie's performance.

She suddenly rose, and her three companions rose with her.

It was eleven o'clock, they explained sweetly: their bedtime. They conveyed the guilty impression that it was the bedtime of all decent Christians, but there was also, in their worn voices, a sighing admission that young people will be young. Rosie tried to stop their swift exodus and her mother's, but other urgencies were demanding her attention. Long before the cellar door had closed behind the last pair of sensible heels, her guests were clamoring around the bar.

She produced fifteen bottles, four of bourbon, four rye, and seven of White Horse Scotch. "Everybody get on the Horse!" she shouted. "Let's ride!"

Toni Morrison
1931–

Born in the steelmill town of Lorain, Ohio, she attended Howard
University (BA, 1953) and Cornell University (MA, 1955). She
taught English and creative writing at Texas South University
(1955–7) and Howard University (1957–64), during which time she
began to write; her first novel grew out of a story written after joining a
writers group. She also taught at Columbia, Yale and the State University
of New York amongst others. She was a senior editor with publishers Random House, where she worked from 1965 to 1983, notably publishing
writers such as Toni Cade Bambara, Alice Walker, Angela Davis and
Gayl Jones, until she left to concentrate on her won writing. Drawing
inspiration from the lives and ancestral experiences of the Black community, she has said: "I have always tried to establish a voice in the
work of a narrator which worked like a chorus, like what I think is
going on in the black church, or in jazz, where people respond, where
the reader is participating. So the problem is always how do you get that
feeling, which I call Black writing, which is not dropping 'g's, it's much
more subtle than that – the way people do it in churches, the way you
do it in jazz concerts, the way you say, 'yes', 'amen', get up and move,
so whoever is up there is not working alone." A novelist of undisputed
international stature, author of The Bluest Eye (1970), Sula (1974),
Song of Solomon (1977) and Tar Baby (1981), she received the 1988
Pulitzer Prize for fiction for Beloved (1987), a story which illuminates
a Black past haunted by violence and tenderness, centring on a mother
desperate to save her children from slavery.

From

Beloved

SHE led him to the top of the stairs, where light came straight from the
sky because the second-story windows of that house had been placed in
the pitched ceiling and not the walls. There were two rooms and she took him
into one of them, hoping he wouldn't mind the fact that she was not prepared;
that though she could remember desire, she had forgotten how it worked; the
clutch and helplessness that resided in the hands; how blindness was altered so

that what leapt to the eye were places to lie down, and all else – door knobs, straps, hooks, the sadness that crouched in corners, and the passing of time – was interference.

It was over before they could get their clothes off. Half-dressed and short of breath, they lay side by side resentful of one another and the skylight above them. His dreaming of her had been too long and too long ago. Her deprivation had been not having any dreams of her own at all. Now they were sorry and too shy to make talk. . .

Paul D looked through the window above his feet and folded his hands behind his head. An elbow grazed Sethe's shoulder. The touch of cloth on her skin startled her. She had forgotten he had not taken off his shirt. Dog, she thought, and then remembered that she had not allowed him the time for taking it off. Nor herself time to take off her petticoat, and considering she had begun undressing before she saw him on the porch, that her shoes and stockings were already in her hand and she had never put them back on; that he had looked at her wet bare feet and asked to join her; that when she rose to cook he had undressed her further; considering how quickly they had started getting naked, you'd think by now they would be. But maybe a man was nothing but a man, which is what Baby Suggs always said. They encouraged you to put some of your weight in their hands and soon as you felt how light and lovely that was, they studied your scars and tribulations, after which they did what he had done: ran her children out and tore up the house.

She needed to get up from there, go downstairs and piece it all back together. This house he told her to leave as though a house was a little thing – a shirtwaist or a sewing basket you could walk off from or give away any old time. She who had never had one but this one; she who left a dirt floor to come to this one; she who had to bring a fistful of salsify into Mrs Garner's kitchen every day just to be able to work in it, feel like some part of it was hers, because she wanted to love the work she did, to take the ugly out of it, and the only way she could feel at home on Sweet Home was if she picked some pretty growing thing and took it with her. The day she forgot was the day butter wouldn't come or the brine in the barrel blistered her arms.

At least it seemed so. A few yellow flowers on the table, some myrtle tied around the handle of the flatiron holding the door open for a breeze calmed her, and when Mrs Garner and she sat down to sort bristle, or make ink, she felt fine. Not scared of the men beyond. The five who slept in quarters near her, but never came in the night. Just touched their raggedy hats when they saw her and stared. And if she brought food to them in the fields, bacon and bread wrapped in a piece of clean sheeting, they never took it from her hands. They stood back and waited for her to put it on the ground (at the foot of a tree) and leave. Either they did not want to take anything from her, or did not want her to see them eat. Twice or three times she lingered. Hidden behind honeysuckle she watched them. How different they were without her, how they laughed and played and urinated and sang. All but Sixo, who laughed once – at the very end. Halle, of course, was the nicest. Baby Suggs' eighth and last child, who rented himself out all over the county to buy her away from there. But he too, as it turned out, was nothing but a man.

"A man ain't nothing but a man," said Baby Suggs. "But a son? Well now, that's *somebody*."

It made sense for a lot of reasons because in all of Baby's life, as well as Sethe's own, men and women were moved around like checkers. Anybody Baby Suggs knew, let alone loved, who hadn't run off or been hanged, got rented out, loaned out, bought up, brought back, stored up, mortgaged, won, stolen or seized. So Baby's eight children had six fathers. What she called the nastiness of life was the shock she received upon learning that nobody stopped playing checkers just because the pieces included her children. Halle she was able to keep the longest. Twenty years. A lifetime. Given to her, no doubt, to make up for *hearing* that her two girls, neither of whom had their adult teeth, were sold and gone and she had not been able to wave goodbye. To make up for coupling with a straw boss for four months in exchange for keeping her third child, a boy, with her – only to have him traded for lumber in the spring of the next year and to find herself pregnant by the man who promised not to and did. That child she could not love and the rest she would not. "God take what He would," she said. And He did, and He did, and He did and then gave her Halle who gave her freedom when it didn't mean a thing.

Sethe had the amazing luck of six whole years of marriage to that "somebody" son who had fathered every one of her children. A blessing she was reckless enough to take for granted, lean on, as though Sweet Home really was one. As though a handful of myrtle stuck in the handle of a pressing iron propped against the door in a whitewoman's kitchen could make it hers. As though mint sprig in the mouth changed the breath as well as its odor. A bigger fool never lived.

Sethe started to turn over on her stomach but changed her mind. She did not want to call Paul D's attention back to her, so she settled for crossing her ankles.

But Paul D noticed the movement as well as the change in her breathing. He felt obliged to try again, slower this time, but the appetite was gone. Actually it was a good feeling – not wanting her. Twenty-five years and blip! The kind of thing Sixo would do – like the time he arranged a meeting with Patsy the Thirty-Mile Woman. It took three months and two thirty-four-mile round trips to do it. To persuade her to walk one-third of the way toward him, to a place he knew. A deserted stone structure that Redmen used way back when they thought the land was theirs. Sixo discovered it on one of his night creeps, and asked its permission to enter. Inside, having felt what it felt like, he asked the Redmen's Presence if he could bring his woman there. It said yes and Sixo painstakingly instructed her how to get there, exactly when to start out, how his welcoming or warning whistles would sound. Since neither could go anywhere on business of their own, and since the Thirty-Mile Woman was already fourteen and scheduled for somebody's arms, the danger was real. When he arrived, she had not. He whistled and got no answer. He went into the Redmen's deserted lodge. She was not there. He returned to the meeting spot. She was not there. He waited longer. She still did not come. He grew frightened for her and walked down the road in the direction she should be coming from. Three or four miles, and he stopped. It was hopeless to go on that way, so he stood in the wind and asked for help.

Listening close for some sign, he heard a whimper. He turned toward it, waited and heard it again. Uncautious now, he hollered her name. She answered in a voice that sounded like life to him – not death. "Not move!" he shouted. "Breathe hard I can find you." He did. She believed she was already at the meeting place and was crying because she thought he had not kept his promise. Now it was too late for the rendezvous to happen at the Redmen's house, so they dropped where they were. Later he punctured her calf to simulate snakebite so she could use it in some way as an excuse for not being on time to shake worms from tobacco leaves. He gave her detailed directions about following the stream as a shortcut back, and saw her off. When he got to the road it was very light and he had his clothes in his hands. Suddenly from around a bend a wagon trundled toward him. Its driver, wide-eyed, raised a whip while the woman seated beside him covered her face. But Sixo had already melted into the woods before the lash could unfurl itself on his indigo behind.

He told the story to Paul F, Halle, Paul A and Paul D in the peculiar way that made them cry-laugh. Sixo went among trees at night. For dancing, he said, to keep his bloodlines open, he said. Privately, alone, he did it. None of the rest of them had seen him at it, but they could imagine it, and the picture they pictured made them eager to laugh at him – in daylight, that is, when it was safe.

But that was before he stopped speaking English because there was no future in it. Because of the Thirty-Mile Woman Sixo was the only one not paralyzed by yearning for Sethe. Nothing could be as good as the sex with her Paul D had been imagining off and on for twenty-five years. His foolishness made him smile and think fondly of himself as he turned over on his side, facing her. Sethe's eyes were closed, her hair a mess. Looked at this way, minus the polished eyes, her face was not so attractive. So it must have been her eyes that kept him both guarded and stirred up. Without them her face was manageable – a face he could handle. Maybe if she would keep them closed like that . . . But no, there was her mouth. Nice. Halle never knew what he had.

Although her eyes were closed, Sethe knew his gaze was on her face, and a paper picture of just how bad she must look raised itself up before her mind's eye. Still, there was no mockery coming from his gaze. Soft. It felt soft in a waiting kind of way. He was not judging her – or rather he was judging but not comparing her. Not since Halle had a man looked at her that way: not loving or passionate, but interested, as though he were examining an ear of corn for quality. Halle was more like a brother than a husband. His care suggested a family relationship rather than a man's laying claim. For years they saw each other in full daylight only on Sundays. The rest of the time they spoke or touched or ate in darkness. Predawn darkness and the afterlight of sunset. So looking at each other intently was a Sunday-morning pleasure and Halle examined her as though storing up what he saw in sunlight for the shadow he saw the rest of the week. And he had so little time. After his Sweet Home work and on Sunday afternoons was the debt work he owed for his mother. When he asked her to be his wife, Sethe happily agreed and then was stuck not knowing the next step. There should be a ceremony, shouldn't there? A preacher, some dancing, a party, a something. She and Mrs Garner were the only women there, so she decided to ask her.

"Halle and me want to be married, Mrs Garner."

"So I heard." She smiled. "He talked to Mr Garner about it. Are you already expecting?"

"No, ma'am."

"Well, you will be. You know that, don't you?"

"Yes, ma'am."

"Halle's nice, Sethe. He'll be good to you."

"But I mean we want to get married."

"You just said so. And I said all right."

"Is there a wedding?"

Mrs Garner put down her cooking spoon. Laughing a little, she touched Sethe on the head, saying, "You are one sweet child." And then no more.

Sethe made a dress on the sly and Halle hung his hitching rope from a nail on the wall of her cabin. And there on top of a mattress on top of the dirt floor of the cabin they coupled for the third time, the first two having been in the tiny cornfield Mr Garner kept because it was a crop animals could use as well as humans. Both Halle and Sethe were under the impression that they were hidden. Scrunched down among the stalks they couldn't see anything, including the corn tops waving over their heads and visible to everyone else.

Sethe smiled at her and Halle's stupidity. Even the crows knew and came to look. Uncrossing her ankles, she managed not to laugh aloud.

The jump, thought Paul D, from a calf to a girl wasn't all that mighty. Not the leap Halle believed it would be. And taking her in the corn rather than her quarters, a yard away from the cabins of the others who had lost out, was a gesture of tenderness. Halle wanted privacy for her and got public display. Who could miss a ripple in a cornfield on a quiet cloudless day? He, Sixo and both of the Pauls sat under Brother pouring water from a gourd over their heads, and through eyes streaming with well water, they watched the confusion of tassels in the field below. It had been hard, hard, hard sitting there erect as dogs, watching corn stalks dance at noon. The water running over their heads made it worse.

Paul D sighed and turned over. Sethe took the opportunity afforded by his movement to shift as well. Looking at Paul D's back, she remembered that some of the corn stalks broke, folded down over Halle's back, and among the things her fingers clutched were husk and cornsilk hair.

How loose the silk. How jailed down the juice.

The jealous admiration of the watching men melted with the feast of new corn they allowed themselves that night. Plucked from the broken stalks that Mr Garner could not doubt was the fault of the raccoon. Paul F wanted his roasted; Paul A wanted his boiled and now Paul D couldn't remember how finally they'd cooked those ears too young to eat. What he did remember was parting the hair to get to the tip, the edge of his fingernail just under, so as not to graze a single kernel.

The pulling down of the tight sheath, the ripping sound always convinced her it hurt.

As soon as one strip of husk was down, the rest obeyed and the ear yielded up to him its shy rows, exposed at last. How loose the silk. How quick the jailed-up flavor ran free.

No matter what all your teeth and wet fingers anticipated, there was no accounting for the way that simple joy could shake you.
How loose the silk. How fine and loose and free.

Flora Nwapa
1931–

B orn in Oguta, eastern Nigeria, she attended school in Port Har-court and Lagos, received a BA from University College, Ibadan, and a Diploma in Education from Edinburgh University. She has worked as a teacher and in public service, after the Nigerian civil war accepting a cabinet post in the Ministry of Health and Social Welfare in East-Central State (1970–5). She was the first African woman novelist to be published in Britain and achieve international recognition. Her many books include the novels Efuru (1966), Idu (1967), Never Again (1975), One Is Enough (1981) and Women Are Different (1986), a volume of poems entitled Cassava Song and Rice Song (1986), collec-tions of short stories – This Is Lagos and Other Stories (1971) and Wives at War and Other Stories – and several children's works. In the 1970s she founded Tana Press and the Flora Nwapa Company, publishing adult and juvenile literature of her own as well as by others. She gives as one of her objectives: "to inform and educate women all over the world, especially Feminists (both with capital F and small 'f') about the role of women in Nigeria, their economic independence, their relationship with their husbands and children, their traditional beliefs and their status in the community as a whole".

This Is Lagos

"THEY say Lagos men do not just chase women, they snatch them," Soha's mother told her on the eve of her departure to Lagos. "So, my daughter, be careful. My sister will take care of you. You should help her with her housework and her children, just as you have been doing here."

Soha was fond of her aunt. She called her Mama Eze. Eze was her aunt's first son. And Mama Eze called Soha "my sister's daughter". She too was fond of Soha whom she looked after when she was a little girl.

Soha was a sweet girl. She was just twenty when she came to Lagos. She was not beautiful in the real sense of the word. But she was very pretty and charming. She was full of life. She pretended that she knew her mind, and showed a confidence rare in a girl who had all her education in a village.

Her aunt and her family lived in Shomolu in the outskirts of Lagos. There was a primary school nearby, and it was in the school that her uncle by marriage got her a teaching job. Soha did not like teaching, but there was no other job, and so, like so many teachers, the job was just a stepping stone.

In the morning before she went to school, Soha saw that her aunt's children, five in all, were well prepared for school. She would see that they had their baths, wore their uniforms, and looked neat and tidy. Then she prepared their breakfast, and before seven each morning, the children were ready to go to school.

Everybody in the "yard" thought how dutiful Soha was. Her aunt's husband who was a quiet man praised Soha, and told his wife that she was a good girl. Her aunt was proud of her. Since she came to stay with them, her aunt had had time for relaxation. She did less housework, and paid more attention to her trade, which was selling bread.

For some time, everything went well with them. But Mama Eza did not like the way Soha refused to go on holiday when the school closed at the end of the first term. She was surprised when Soha told her that she did not want to go home to see her mother, despite the fact that her mother had been ill, and was recovering.

"Why don't you want to go home, my sister's daughter?"

"Who will look after the children if I go home?" she asked.

Mama Eze did not like the tone of Soha's voice. "Who had been looking after the children before you came, my sister's daughter? Your mother wants you to come home. You know how fond she is of you. I don't want her to think that I prevented you from coming home."

"She won't think so. I shall go during the Christmas holiday. This is a short holiday, only three weeks. And the roads. Remember what Lagos – Onitsha road is like." But she did not go home during the Christmas holiday either.

It was that argument that sort of did the trick. Mama Eze remembered the accident she witnessed not long ago. She was returning from the market, a huge load on her head, when, just in a flash it happened. It was a huge tipper-lorry and a Volkswagen car. She saw blood, and bodies, and the wreck of the Volkswagen. She covered her face with her hands. When she opened them, she looked the other way, and what did she see, a human tongue on the ground.

When she returned home, she told her husband. She swore that from thenceforth she would travel home by train.

She did not suggest going home by train to her niece. Soha had long rejected that idea. She did not see the sanity of it all. Why should a man in Lagos, wishing to go to Port Harcourt, decide to go up to Kaduna in the North first, then down south to Port Harcourt, and to take three days and three nights doing the journey he would do in a few hours if he were travelling by road?

One Saturday, during the holiday a brand new car stopped in front of the big "yard". The children in the "yard" including Mama Eze's children trooped out to have a closer look. A young man stepped out of the car and asked one of the children whether Soha lived there. "Yes, sister Soha lives here. Let me go and call her for you," Eze said, and ran into the house.

Soha was powdering her face when Eze pushed open the door and announced, "Sister Soha, a man is asking for you. He came in a car, a brand new car. I have not seen that car before. Come and see him. He wants you." Eze held her hand and began dragging her to the sitting-room.

"No, Eze, ask him to sit down in the sitting room and wait for me," Soha said quietly to Eze.

Eze dropped her hand and ran outside again. "She is coming. She says I should ask you to sit down in the sitting-room and wait for her," he said to the man. The man followed him to the sitting-room.

The children stood admiring the car. "It is a Volkswagen," one said.

"How can that be a Volkswagen? It is a Peugeot," another said.

"Can't you people see? It is a Record," yet another child said. They were coming close now. Some were touching the body of the car and leaving their dirty fingerprints on it when Eze came out again and drove them out.

"Let me see who says he is strong, dare come near this car." He planted himself in front of the car, looking bigger than he really was.

"Does the car belong to Eze's father?" a child asked.

"No. It belongs to sister Soha's friend," one of Eze's brothers replied without hesitation.

"I thought it belonged to your father," the same child said again.

"Keep quiet. Can't my father buy a car?" Eze shouted, standing menacingly in front of the child.

Soha was still in front of the mirror admiring herself. She was not in a hurry at all. Her mother had told her that she should never show a man that she was anxious about him. She should rather keep him waiting as long as she wished. She was wearing one of the dresses she sewed for herself when she was at home. She suddenly thought of changing it. But she changed her mind, and instead came out. She was looking very shy as she took the outstretched hand of the man who had come to visit her.

"Are you ready?"

"For . . ."

"We are going to Kingsway Stores."

"Kingsway Stores?"

"Of course. But we discussed it last night, and you asked me to come at nine thirty," the man said looking at his watch.

"I am sorry. But I can't go again."

"You can't go?"

"No."

"Why?"

"Can't I change my mind?"

"Of course you can," the man said quietly, a little surprised.

"I am going then."

"Already?"

"Yes."

"Don't you work on Saturdays?"

"No."

"Go well then," Soha said.

"When am I seeing you again?"

"I don't know. I have no car."

"Let's go to the cinema tonight."

"No, my mother will kill me."

"Your aunt."

"Yes. She is my mother. You said you will buy something for me today."

"Let's go to the Kingsway Stores then. I don't know how to buy things for women."

"Don't you buy things for your wife?"

"I told you, I have no wife." Soha laughed long and loud. The man watched her.

"Who are you deceiving? Please go to your wife and don't bother me. Lagos men, I know Lagos men."

"How many of them do you know?"

She did not answer. She rather rolled her eyes and shifted in the chair in which she sat.

"I am going," he said, standing up.

"Don't go now," she said. They heard the horn of a car.

"That's my car," he said.

"So?"

"The children are playing with the horn."

"So?"

"You are exasperating! I like you all the same. Let's go to this shopping, Soha. What is wrong with you? You are so stubborn."

"No, I won't go. I shall go next Saturday. I did not tell Mama Eze."

"You said you would."

"So I said."

He got up. It did not seem to him that there would be an end to this conversation.

"You are going?"

"I am going."

"Wait, I'll come with you." He breathed in and breathed out again.

"Go and change then."

"Change. Don't you like my dress?"

"I like it, but change into a better dress."

"I have no other dress. I might as well stay. You are ashamed of me."

"You have started again."

"I won't go again. How dare you say that my dress is not respectable. Well, maybe you will buy dresses for me before I go out with you." He put his hand in his back pocket and brought out his wallet. He pressed a five-pound note into her hand. She smiled and they went out.

"Eze, you have been watching his car?" Soha said.

Eze nodded. He dipped into his pocket and gave Eze a shilling. Eze jumped with joy.

"We watched with him," the other children chorused.

"Yes. They watched with him," Soha said. He brought out another shilling and gave to them. Then he drove away.

Mama Eze did not know about the young man who visited Soha. Soha warned the children not to tell their parents. But it was obvious to her that Soha had secrets. It was easy for a mother of five children who had watched so many girls growing up in the "yard" to know when they were involved in men. At first, she thought of asking Soha, but she thought better of it until one day when Soha told her she was going to the shops and did not come back until late in the evening. She called her in.

"Where did you go, my sister's daughter?"

"I told you I went to the shops."

"Many people went to the shops from this 'yard', but they returned long before you."

"Well, we did not go to the same shops," Soha said.

Mama Eze did not like the way Soha talked to her. She smiled. "Soha," she called her. That was the first time Mama Eze called her by her name. "Soha," she called again. "This is Lagos. Lagos is different from home. Lagos is big. You must be careful here. You are a mere child. Lagos men are too deep for you. Don't think you are clever. You are not. You can never be cleverer than a Lagos man. I am older than you are, so take my advice."

Soha said nothing. She did not give a thought to what her aunt told her. But that night, Mama Eze did not sleep well. She told her husband.

"You worry yourself unnecessarily. Didn't she tell you before she went to the shops?"

"She did."

"Well, then?"

"Well, then," Mama Eze echoed mockingly. "Well, then. Go on speaking English, 'well, then'. When something happens to Soha now, you will stay there. This is the time you should do something."

"Why are you talking like that, Mama Eze? What has the girl done? She is such a nice girl. She doesn't go out. She has been helping you with your housework. You yourself say so."

Mama Eze said nothing to him any more. One evening when Soha returned from school, she asked her aunt if she would allow her to go to the cinema. Her aunt clapped her hands in excitement, and rushed out of the room. "Mama Bisi, come out and hear what Soha is saying."

Mama Bisi, who was her neighbour, came out. "What did she say?" she asked clasping her chest. She was afraid.

"Soha, my sister's daughter, wants to go to the cinema."

Mama Bisi hissed. "Is that all? You are excited because she has told you today. What about the other nights she has been going?"

"Other nights? Other nights?"

"Go and sit down, *Ojari*. You don't know what you are saying. Soha, your sister's daughter, has been going out with different men for a long time now. You don't even see the dresses she wears, and the shoes. Do they look like the dresses a girl like her would wear?"

Mama Eze said nothing. Soha said nothing. "When Papa Eze returns, ask him whether you can go to the cinema," Mama Eze finally said after looking at her niece for a long time.

It wasn't long after this that Soha came to her aunt and told her that she wanted to move to a hostel.

"To a hostel, my sister's daughter. Who will pay for you?"

"I receive a salary."

"I see. I know you receive a salary. Those of us who have never received salaries in our lives know about salaries. But why now? Why do you want to leave us now? Don't you like my home any more? Is it too small for you? Or too humble? Are you ashamed of entertaining your friends here?"

"I want to start reading again. That's why I want to move to a hostel. It will be more convenient for me there."

"That is true. When you sing well, the dancer dances well. I understand my sister's daughter. I have to tell my husband and my sister. Your mother said you should stay with me. It is only reasonable that I tell her that you are leaving me to go to a hostel. What hostel is that by the way?"

"The one at Ajagba Street."

"I see."

When Soha went to school, Mama Eze went over to Mama Bisi and told her what Soha said. "I have told you," Mama Bisi said. "Soha is not a better girl. Do you know the kind of girls who live in that hostel at Ajagba street? Rotten girls who will never marry. No man will bring them into his home and call them wives. You know that my sister who is at Abeokuta whom I went to see last week."

"Yes, I know her, Iyabo."

"That's right. Iyabo. One of her friends who stayed in that hostel, nearly took Iyabo there. I stopped it. As soon as I heard it, I went to her mother at Abeokuta and told her. She came down, and both of us went to her. After talking to her, she changed her mind. So that's the place Soha wants to go and live. I no tell you, they say to go Lagos no hard, na return. Soha will be lost if she goes there."

Mama Eze returned home one evening from the market and was told that Soha had not been home from school. She put down her basket of unsold bread and sat down. "Didn't she tell you where she went?" she asked Eze. Eze shook his head. "And where is your father?" Mama Eze asked Eze.

"He has gone out."

"Where has be gone?"

"I don't know."

"You don't know. Every question, you don't know. Do you think you are still a child? Let me have some water quickly." Eze brought the water. Then Eze's father returned.

"They say Soha has not returned home," Mama Eze said to her husband.

"So Eze told me."

"And you went out, because Soha is not your sister. If Soha were your sister you would have been hysterical."

Then Mama Bisi came in, and sat down. She had heard of course.

"Eze, why not tell them the truth?" Mama Bisi said. Eze said nothing.

"Eze, so you know where Soha went?" Mama Eze asked.

"I don't know," Eze protested vehemently.

"You helped Soha with her box. I saw you," Mama Bisi accused.

She did not see Eze do this, but what she said was true. Mama Eze and her husband were confused.

"Mama Bisi, please, tell me what you know."

"Ask your son there. He knows everything. He knows where Soha went."

"I don't know. You are lying, Mama Bisi." Mama Eze got up and slapped Eze's face. "How dare you, how dare you say that Mama Bisi is lying, you, you good-for-nothing child."

"*Ewo*, Mama Eze, that will do. If you slap the boy again you'll have it hot."

"*Jo*, don't quarrel," Mama Bisi begged. She went over to Papa Eze. "Please don't. But, Eze, you are a bad child. Why are you hiding evil? A child like you behaving in this way."

Eze knew a lot. He helped Soha pack her things, and it was the gentleman with the car who took Soha away. Soha told him not to breathe a word to anybody. She also told him that she and her husband would come in the night to see his parents.

As they were wondering what to do, Eze slipped out. He was the only one who heard the sound of the car. He had grown to like Soha's friend since the day he watched his car for him. And he had also had many rides in his car as well, for anywhere Soha's friend saw Eze, he stopped to give him a lift, and he had enjoyed this very much.

Soha and the gentleman stepped out of the car, Soha leading the way. Mama Eze, Mama Bisi and Papa Eze stared at them. Soha and her friend stood. They stared at them.

"Can we sit down?" Soha asked as she sat down. The gentleman stood.

"Sit down," Papa Eze said. He sat down.

None found words. Soha's gentleman was completely lost.

"Is Soha living with you?" Papa Eze asked after a long time.

"Yes," he said.

"In fact we were married a month ago," Soha said.

"No!" Mama Eze shouted. "You, you married to my sister's daughter. Impossible. You are going to be 'un-married'. Do you hear? Mama Bisi, is that what they do here?"

"This is Lagos. Anything can happen here," Mama Bisi said. Then she turned to the gentleman and spoke in Yoruba to him. It was only Papa Eze who did not understand.

"It is true, Papa Eze. They are married. What is this country turning into? Soha, you, you who left home only yesterday to come to Lagos, you are married, married to a Lagos man, without telling anybody. It is a slight and nothing else. What do I know? I didn't go to school. If I had gone to school, you wouldn't have treated me in this way."

"So you pregnated her," Mama Bisi said to Soha's husband in Yoruba. He did not immediately reply.

Soha's heart missed a beat. "So it is showing already," she said to herself.

Mama Bisi smiled bitterly. "You children. You think you can deceive us. I have seven children."

"What is your name?" Mama Bisi asked Soha's husband in Yoruba.

"Ibikunle," he replied.

"Ibikunle, we don't marry like this in the place where we come from. . ." Mama Eze did not finish.

"Even in the place where he comes from *kpa kpa*," Mama Bisi interrupted. "It is Lagos. When they come to Lagos they forget their home background. Imagine coming here to say they are married. Where in the world do they do this sort of thing?"

"You hear, Mr Ibikunle, we don't marry like that in my home," Mama Eze said. "Home people will not regard you as married. This is unheard of. And you tell me this is what the white people do. So when white people wish to marry, they don't seek the consent of their parents, they don't even inform them. My sister's daughter," she turned to Soha, "you have not done well. You have rewarded me with evil. Why did you not take me into confidence? Am I not married? Is marriage a sin? Will I prevent you from marrying? Isn't it the prayer of every woman?"

"It is enough, Mama Eze," Mama Bisi said. "And besides. . . ."

"You women talk too much. Mr Ibikunle has acted like a gentleman. What if he had run away after pregnating Soha? What would you do?"

"Hear what my husband is saying. I don't blame you. What am I saying? Aren't you a man? Aren't all men the same? Mr Ibikunle, take your wife to your house, and get ready to go home to see your father and mother-in-law. I'll help you with the preparations."

Husband and wife went home. Mama Eze went home and told Soha's parents what had happened. A whole year passed. Mr Ibikunle did not have the courage, or was it the money to travel to Soha's home to present himself to Soha's parents as their son-in-law.

Lauretta Ngcobo

1931–

orn in Ixopo, Natal, the first girl of her parents' four children,
she was influenced by the family tradition of storytelling as well
as her grandmother's poetry. She received a BA in Education from
Fort Hare University. After the 1960s political upheavals in South Africa,
she went into exile with her husband and three of her children, living in
Swaziland, Tanzania and Zambia before settling in Britain in the early
1970s, where she worked as a teacher. She has said that literature to
her has a "curative quality", enabling writer and reader to stand apart
from issues and conflicts both internal and external and thereby find
solutions instead of being submerged by them. She has lectured on Black
women in literature, edited Let It Be Told: Essays by Black Women
Writers in Britain *(1987) and is the author of two novels,* Cross of
Gold *(1981) and* And They Didn't Die *(1990), from which this extract*
is taken. Set in South Africa of the 1950s and 1960s, it tells the story
of Jezile, a spirited young woman who works as a domestic to a white
family, is raped by the man of the household and after bearing his child
faces ostracism by her own community.

From

And They Didn't Die

CHAPTER XIII

ASIBIYA was out in the fields weeding when she received a message
that Jezile had arrived with a baby in her arms. She threw her implement
aside and strode home with the little messenger at her heels. When they were
some distance away and out of earshot she turned to the child, and lowering her
voice she asked, "What baby are you talking about? You don't mean Ndondo, do
you?"

"No, not Ndondo, Ndondo is big, I know her."

"It's a small baby, is it?"

"Yes, it's very, very small."

"We Nkulumkulu wami, my God, what's going on?"

MaSibiya almost ran the rest of the way, leaving the child lagging behind.

MaSibiya collapsed on her knees right beside Jezile where she sat in the shade of the house.

"Jezile, Jezile, my child, what's that you've got in your arms? Where did you get it from? What shall I say to the Majolas? What shall I say? Have you come from there or straight from Bloemfontein?" Jezile shook her head, but said nothing.

"You mean MaBiyela does not know about this baby? Have you told them? It's yours, Jezile, is it? Bring it here."

She took one look at the child and she screamed. "Jezile, what child is this? This can't be your child. And it's so small, how old is it?" She began to show concern for Jezile. She looked her up and down.

"Jezile, my child, my child. What's been happening to you? Who's the father of this child?" She asked repeatedly with tears streaming down her face. "But it's white, Jezile, it's white!"

Jezile began to sob uncontrollably. With the child forgotten on the mat, mother and daughter clung to each other. By then a group of young children stood watching, confounded. Jezile wept on and on as though she would never stop and MaSibiya rocked her daughter as though she was the infant instead of the little bundle on the mat. Slowly Jezile's sobs became quieter, but more convulsive. MaSibiya put her head down gently on the mat and rushed to make some tea for her. When Jezile had recovered, MaSibiya concentrated on the baby and asked no further questions of Jezile. When friends and relations and neighbours came to see her they were all subdued. None of them rushed to see the baby. Others pretended there was no baby to speak about, while some talked discreetly about the inescapable temptations that face all young women without husbands, with God being the only protection. It did not escape some that MaSibiya sat with the baby carefully covered and facing the wall throughout the time of their visit. It was one thing to tell the people of Luve that Jezile had a baby, and it was quite another to tell them that it was a white man's child, which was not only a transgression of their own customs but a crime as well.

It was three days before MaSibiya summoned up enough courage to tackle the subject with Jezile again. She dreaded another scene, but she had to know; she simply had to know for the Majolas' sake, if for no one else's. She had a responsibility to let them know that their daughter-in-law was here, or better still to take her there herself, before the local gossips carried the news. To MaSibiya's surprise, Jezile seemed drained of all feeling and ready to talk. She sat her mother down quietly and in an even voice she told the story about how she first went to work for the men on the road, how MaBiyela had advised her to go to Bloemfontein, and about her unspeakable life there. When she had finished MaSibiya summoned all the relations that were within reach and asked Jezile to tell them the whole story over again. Calmly, Jezile did, and the whole place was thrown into utter confusion. Many believed her, but it was clear that there were those who doubted the details of the story. Nobody dared to ask too many questions. The matter stopped being MaSibiya's problem – it affected all the Mapangas. This child would be called a Mapanga, one of them; a white child among them; a child born in this unorthodox way, if Jezile was to be believed. Others said the child could not be a Mapanga – it was a Majola child; Jezile was no longer a Mapanga herself – if she was unmarried, yes, it would be a Mapanga. But now, according to custom, the white child was a Majola. The older women treated Jezile with such tenderness as though she had only been raped the day before. MaSibiya, who was overwrought, told the gathering that she needed a few women to accompany her and Jezile to the Majolas within the next day or two for she daren't keep a Majola wife and child for too long without reporting her presence. But the general opinion was that Jezile should stay until she had fully recovered – after all, it was only a few days since she had had the baby, followed by the long journey from Bloemfontein. So, the next day, two men were sent to report to MaBiyela and all the Majolas that Jezile was with the Mapangas.

Two weeks later, when Jezile was a little stronger, she and MaSibiya accompanied by a group of six women travelled to Sigageni to the Majolas. Jezile dreaded facing her mother-in-law. But to her surprise MaBiyela looked a shadow of her former self. She sat them all down and in a quiet voice she sent the children to call the other Majola relations. The visitors were served tea in silence. When everyone had arrived, the two families sat facing each other. Jezile's eldest aunt on her father's side began to tell the whole story from the start while the others listened. Not a cough interrupted, and when she had finished the stunned silence was followed by a restless shuffle in the room. In an even voice MaBiyela asked to see the baby. When she opened the bundle and looked at its little face, she gave one deep groan. After some moments she asked one question of Jezile, a question directed more at destiny than her.

"Why didn't you just leave this child with the white man? The child does not belong here; it does not belong anywhere. This child will bring the white law on us. Who will face them when they come? This is not a Majola nor is it a Mapanga."

It was no longer Jezile's misfortune that lay in front of them, it was a communal catastrophe. There was a long silence; then, the oldest man in the room told the Mapangas that the matter could not be discussed further because Siyalo was away in jail. It would have to wait until he came back. It would have to wait for seven long years. No one spoke after the old man. The Mapangas were served with a light meal and they left after that. Then the Majolas left one by one mumbling their goodbyes softly with their heads bent low.

It was hard for Jezile to relate to the community as before. They received her back as they would any of their many unavoidable natural disasters. Her two friends, Gaba and Nomawa, came to see her, but even they had little to say and less to laugh about. But at least they were openly sympathetic. They carried the baby, admiring it and expressing the usual "oohs" and "ahs". Until that point everyone had treated him like a curse, a thing to be discarded, and she herself had not explored her true feelings towards the child. She had ministered to its needs mechanically, but now she knew that she cared. She wanted him to be loved, to belong. For the first time she told herself she loved him and so it did not matter that he had no second name. From that moment a new determination grew in her: she would face that community, she would live in it. She would give the child every chance to live normally. From that day she raised her head and talked normally to the people that she met along the pathways.

The baby was about two months old when the minister came to Sigageni to administer his quarterly Communion to his parishioners. As usual, the Deacon had to report to the minister about the state of the community. And Jezile was on his list. She and MaBiyela did not go to Church that Sunday to avoid the embarrassment of being discussed in the presence of the entire congregation. Later that afternoon, when the minister had left, the Deacon went to see MaBiyela. Within a few minutes of his entering MaBiyela's house Jezile heard the sound of weeping. She was curious but she thought it better to wait. When the Deacon had gone, Jezile went down to see MaBiyela. She was on her knees, sobbing and whimpering in a most pitiful way.

"What is it, Mother, what is it?"

"Oh, MaMapanga, this is truly a curse . . . The minister has censured me for keeping you here. He has banned me from attending Service. He said I have condoned everything you have done; that I should have sent you back to your people. Oh, MaMapanga, I've been excommunicated. I wasn't there; I could not have stopped what happened to you . . . and I cannot do anything now, without Siyalo . . . He is hard, MaMapanga, God's ways are hard."

Jezile was "excommunicated" as well. She had broken a strict moral code. But at that point she was more deeply concerned about MaBiyela, and less about herself. She looked on compassionately, but she was stunned. She had never once thought that she stood condemned by the Church and by God. Surely God who saw everything knew that she had not sinned; she had been sinned against. Now he was punishing not only her but MaBiyela as well; it simply made no sense. She wanted to say something to the crumpled shape on the floor, but the words would not come. The life of the Church was a lifeline for everyone in this community. When life was hard to bear, that is where they all went. Other aspects of life in the community were channelled through the Church. That was why this judgment was like a death sentence.

Some members of the community were sympathetic and others cynical. Jezile could not bear to see MaBiyela suffering. They were both cast out and it was unbearable. By the end of the week, Jezile could bear it no longer. She picked up the baby and went with her other two children down to MaBiyela's house.

"Mother, I've decided, I'll have to go. I'll go back to my people until Siyalo comes back. I cannot bear to see you suffer for something you have so little to do with. God's ways are not easy to understand and cannot be argued with. If you let me, I'll go away tomorrow."

"It's not for me to let you go. This is a matter for the Majolas. I hear you. I'll have to call them all back again to discuss this. If they let you go, then you will go. Tomorrow I'll call them. But for tonight go and sleep with the children."

MaBiyela looked grey and thinner than when there was no food around. Jezile had not expected her to crumble in this way. Once she had seemed so strong and powerful. But all that power was gone now and seemed never to have been hers in the first place. Even Siyalo behind his prison walls had more power than MaBiyela.

At the meeting with the Majolas the following day it was agreed that Jezile should go back to her people to release MaBiyela from her remote responsibility. They allowed her to take the Majola children with her as well. But they were not unanimous on this point. Some argued that Jezile's children could not be taken away from the Majolas. But others said they were too young to be separated from their mother. MaBiyela cried bitterly to see them go. She had become attached to them in the year that Jezile was away. Besides, they were her grandchildren, Siyalo's own children, the only real link with him in his long absence and she loved them dearly.

By the beginning of the following week Jezile left Sigageni, her mind in torment and her loyalties deeply divided. The burden of shame was growing heavier with every decision and every decision was completely out of her control. She had always known she was weak; she had fought hard against this helplessness. Yet it seemed that all her efforts were in vain; she felt as if she was suspended in space, at the mercy of all nameless authorities. However, after a few days with her mother, she began to feel safe. In her house she learned to laugh again.

Marta Rojas (Rodriguez)
1931–

*C*uban-born *writer and journalist, she was the only journalist present in court when Fidel Castro was tried after the 1953 attack on the Moncada army barracks in Santiago, Cuba's second-largest military installation; her first book,* El Juicio del Moncada *(1964), is therefore an invaluable historical testimony. Her subsequent books include:* Viet Nam del Sur *(1966) and* Scenas de Viet Nam *(1959), drawing on her experiences as a war correspondent;* Tania, la guerrillera inolvidable *(1974) and* El que debe vivir *(Casa de las Américas*

*Prize, 1978). El aula verde (1981) and El médico de la familia (1986)
are chronicles based on her journalistic work. Her first work of fiction
was La Cueva del Muerto (1988). The following extract (translated from
Spanish by Jean Stubbs and Pedro Perez Sarduy) is from an as yet
unpublished novel,* El Columpio de Rey Spencer, *a love story set in
eastern Cuba. Its many subtexts are firmly located in racial, social and
psychological tensions, as the narrative travels back and forth through
time from the early twentieth-century sugar boom, with its accompanying wave of Caribbean migrant labour, to the present day.*

From

Rey Spencer's Swing

ONE of the letters from when Juliana and Andrés the highbrown amused
themselves playing post, kept by her, explained why Arturo Cassamajour
broke off with Clarita Spencer, and Antonio's role in it. It was a moving and
sincere love letter. Written in the shaky child writing of Andrés, who had copied
it, the letter went:

Clarita dear,
    Never doubt my love; it's precisely because I love you, because of how
much you mean to me and how much I respect you, because of the quality
of our union, that I have decided to free you from the beautiful relationship
we have had. I have submitted you to biting comments, unwonted humiliation and scorn, which tears my soul and damns my conscience.
    I should never have taken you to the masked ball and I don't want to
blame my cousin Antonio and his perhaps undue insistence; he is different
from others you met, who lifted your "hooded cloak" under the pretext
of being drunk, to vex and humiliate you the moment I left your side. I
had confessed our love, all the details of how we met, to Antonio, and he
wanted you to enjoy the ball with us. As soon as I spoke to him about you,
he asked me to take you to meet him, and when he met you was so taken
by your nature, your personality, your charm, your beauty, that anything
seemed little to please you.
    Do you know something? I was jealous of him when you talked in
English at Carol's home the night we invited you to the society ball, and
he, as always, went that much further: he said he would have you enter
the Catalan club on his arm, unmasked, which he did, and his friends were
your beaux. I know perhaps they were amused by Pinera's daring, but the
fact is that nobody humiliated you; on the contrary, even the women were
courteous and kind to you.
    You are right to reproach me for not having thought through the
consequences, realizing that I must know how stupid and imbecilic these
self-styled sophisticated browns of my society are, though there are in all
parts exceptions. Since neither my cousin Antonio nor I think like they do,
we did not weigh up the consequences. I know you won't hate me from

now on because there could never be those feelings in you towards me, otherwise I wouldn't have faith in our love, which exists, and which is for me the only clear, true thing in life. If anything, you will be embarrassed for me or by me, a man of no character who gives in to a social group that places itself above those of its very origin, corrupted by prevailing social and racial prejudice, wanting to "better the race" at all costs to have a place. You would have reason to think I already have that place and yet, to hold on to it, cast aside your and my happiness.

When I learned that Tito Ojeda, the Puerto Rican, was marrying Carol I understood how wretched I am; he is white and she is black, and I am just a little more laundered than you; but society takes a high toll of me because of my position as a doctor, it sets a limit, and unfortunately you are that limit; the same isn't demanded of me as of Tito Ojeda, perhaps even because Tito is white and has a right to choose, whereas I don't.

Those would be my pusillanimous reflections; were you to think that way, there would be reason enough, and I do not blame you. But that's not how it is. Clarita, you're the one I want to protect from the vermin on the loose out there.

I did think of proposing as an alternative going off to France together and getting married there; but I can't ask that of you because it would mean a new uprooting for you, separation from Mrs Christie Spencer, your mother, and your loved ones, and it wouldn't seem right to me, unless you were to ask me to.

My love, what can I do for you not to suffer as I do? Antonio loathes me, my cousin urges in good faith for us to defy the world or be secret lovers until people grow accustomed. But I cannot accept either, I will never again expose you to shame, though rhetorically speaking they are the ones who should be ashamed of what they did to us. Neither will I disown you.

Do you remember how happy we were that first day of carnival, lost in the avalanche of Martí Promenade, kissing on the street, holding hands, eating goatmeat at the stand by the fountain? Ah, neither you nor I even tried to unmask. Carol did. You could tell intuitively, you were concerned about me, and I about you, afraid of what finally came to pass at our society ball because you're black and Jamaican, "an undesirable immigrant". I'm cruel to repeat it but I say it to myself. I'm no good for you, Clarita, I don't deserve you; you must find your happiness and peace elsewhere, not from me. Mine is gone. It will not be easy but you will achieve this with your pride, talent and dignity; they are your lance and shield. Of one thing I rest assured, that I did not take advantage of you. We were meant for each other always, we were passionate though perhaps unthinking in our love; we felt so much for one another, we respected each other, we enjoyed each other and now we are both suffering.

I hope for a letter from you, if you wish to write to me. I do not demand it of you.

I close this letter offering my services to you, your family and your friends. Please do not punish me by concealing any need that I might remedy, no matter what; it may be I shall know and be with you, claim my place to help you or them. Without bothering you, I shall follow your steps. For now, I kiss and take comfort from your shadow that is left me. Though you may not know it, you will live within me wherever I go; I shall hear your voice, that voice of yours, everywhere.

I shall keep up paying the rent of 'the outhouse to Carol: it shall be ours, or yours if you prefer; if not, I shall come here whenever I can as one seeking shelter in a temple to meditate or cry. I shall always come alone; I repeat, my thoughts will be of you. This I swear to you, sister, in the grief that binds us.

Allow me a joke, which I wish at this moment were a reality, not an illusion, a dream like the many we had in so short a time. It will be my last "poor" joke; I would like to have you, Clarita, by my side like Zizi Cassamajour populating a whole locality with my children – I, Prudencio.

Save yourself, my dear.

Yours, with all my heart,

Arturo Cassamajour.

Alice Perry Johnson
1932–

A resident of Liberia since her marriage to physician Archibald Johnson in 1956, she was born in Newark, New Jersey, and is the mother of three children. She is the author of two books of verse and prose, Step Ahead (1972), in which this poem of initiation into womanhood appears, and Africa Is a Woman (1976). She is also a painter.

The Beginning of a Kpelle Woman

Tomorrow the drums will beat and I will
dance my last dance as a child.

The beating drums will sound here and
the echoes will reach Nimba –
My footsteps will echo on the hollow
ground and keep time with the drums.
My body will be washed and the white chalk
will run down and sink into the ground
with my footsteps –
And the drums will beat, and we all will dance.
Being a child are over – and I must start the
dance of womanhood – while the drums beat out my life.
Gourds shaking, drums beating and the sound of
dancing feet together with the clicking of beads
on soft bodies.
Beautiful bodies gleaming with the oil of youth.
Bells on the slim ankles and white chalk in fine
designs on brown and black bodies –
The grigri bush has ended and the young girls
come forth eagerly – they stand and watch –
then, slowly, with a small shrug of a shoulder,
then the other – the small sway of a hip – then the other
The foot stamping the ground, impatiently. . .
waiting for the other as the whole body begins its
dance in celebrating the final days of a child!

Rebeka Njau

1932–

S*he was born in Kanyariri, Kenya, attended Alliance School for*
Girls and later received a diploma in education from Makerere
University College. She subsequently taught at Alliance Girls' School
(1958–9) and Makerere College School (1960–62), and became head-

mistress of Nairobi Girls' Secondary School in 1964. She was also Kenyan representative to the University College Council (1965–6). Her early ambitions were in the field of theatre, as evidenced by her plays In a Round Chain *(performed in 1964) and the prizewinning one-act drama* The Scar *(1965). She was awarded the East African Writing Committee Prize for her first novel, then called* Alone with the Fig Tree *and later developed into* Ripples in the Pool *(1975), from which this is an extract. Her collection of stories,* The Hypocrite, *was published in 1980.*

From

Ripples in the Pool

CHAPTER I

No one could explain why Gikere married Selina even in the face of the strong protests of his own mother. Nor could they understand why Selina herself chose to live with a man of Gikere's kind. The whole thing seemed somehow wrong and men talked about it everywhere in town. For Selina was no ordinary girl: she was arrogant, self-centred, highly expensive and feared no man. Once every year she visited the village of her birth like a tourist who goes sight-seeing in underdeveloped lands. As she walked along the narrow village paths, she felt a kind of power lifting her up and making her walk with a swing in her high heels. Now and again she took out her mirror and smiled at the reflection of her face. She was pleased that the cream she had used for several months had burnt out what she called the "primitive darkness" she had been born with. Children followed behind calling her "muthungu" (*European*) and she smiled to herself and felt the term "light" she had several times used to describe her skin colouring was quite appropriate. She held her head high, her chest out, and almost popped out her eyes to make them look bigger and brighter than they were.

But she was well built. She was five foot five and her body was compact and full in the right places. Her face was smooth, not a pimple on it. Her colour was rich and creamy and the tight-fitting gowns she wore flattered the shape of her body and made photographers who worked for local dailies and magazines pursue her for cover-girl pictures. She framed the one that showed her dressed in pants and bra with legs astride two branches of a wattle tree, and hung it above her bedstead in the Nurses Hostel where she lived.

"It is a woman's duty to make herself attractive," she often said to Sophia who usually modelled with her. "I know how to use make-up. That's why men are always after me. They think I have charm but that is because I know how to treat them. Although I'm free with them, they cannot cheat me. I know what I want from them. Have you ever met executives who behave like animals when they fall in love? They are pathetic. I call them bush creatures. They're ticks. They suck your blood, if you are a fool, and leave you dry. Always demanding more and more, in fact more than one can give. But they cannot treat *me* like that. Do you know what I do, Sophia? I make them bow seven times before I will speak to them. I treat them roughly and get away with it! You can do anything in the city, you know."

Selina continued talking in that same tone as she sat on the edge of an armchair in the waiting-room of a prosperous advertising agency. Sophia stared at her as she talked, admiring the way her lips moved. She seemed so full of life, so free. Self-sufficient. And she had money. Every man knew that. She could afford to buy the most expensive dresses and jewellery in town but she never spent a single cent of her own money to do so. There was always a man somewhere to foot her bills. No wonder so many girls envied her.

"I love beautiful things," she went on. "I like to possess them, to make them my own. It's a disease with me. But I make men pay for them. If they want me, they must spend their money."

She paused, stood up and looked out of the window.

"I want to settle down now, though," she continued. "I know you'll think I'm crazy to hear me say this, but I want a home and a man to care for me. A decent man, not the type that just wants a good time. I want a man who will take me for what I am. What do you think, Sophia?"

Sophia did not answer immediately. She nodded her head slightly and continued staring at Selina. Selina also studied Sophia's face. She noticed that her lips were dry and there were two dark rings under her eyelids. She seemed in bad shape for modelling that morning. But she had to work. She needed money. She had just given birth to a baby girl and the man who had conceived her, a Permanent Secretary in a Government office, had denied he was responsible and had deserted her. As she continued staring at Sophia, Selina swore she would never let such a thing happen to her.

"I've got more guts than you, Sophia," she continued. "That's why I can't find the kind of man I want."

Sophia kept quiet but, after a while, a little smile, a kind of sarcastic smile, played on her cracked lips and she said:

"But your game will not last long, Selina!"

"I'm not like you, Sophia. You are too submissive. That's why men treat you like dirt! I shall never allow any man to treat me the way they have treated you!"

"What kind of man do you really want, Selina?"

"I know you've been disillusioned, Sophia. It's not your fault. You didn't know better. You thought that by becoming an adaptable woman, men would love you and want to live with you. But you were wrong. Men do not know what kind of woman they want. If you are a 'yes' woman, they soon get tired of you; if you are intelligent and have your own mind, they don't have enough guts to deal with that! So whatever you do, Sophia, just be yourself. Let men take you as you are. I want a real companion myself, a real friend who will not desert me when I'm old and full of wrinkles on my face!"

"Get a white man, then," Sophia said. "They're not difficult to find these days. I'm tired of our men. It's true that they don't know how to deal with an intelligent woman. Look at the way Jim has treated me. Look at Mary. Look at

Ciku! They were all decent girls, but where are they now? What has happened to their jobs? Look at the number of girls in the streets! Think of their parents who had high hopes for them! If you don't want trouble, my friend, don't think of getting married to one of our men. Marry a European. There are many of them looking for sophisticated black girls!"

"Sophia, I know the white men and I know what they are after. I've seen them hunting for girls in the night clubs and I've sworn I shall never waste my life on tired old men."

"But they will never beat you up. They will never be cruel to you. If you don't want to be a cabbage for an African man, you should marry a white man. An African will beat you up like a dog, he will persecute you until you are nothing and have no will of your own!"

"No, Sophia, I shall never marry a white man. I know them too well."

It was true Selina had gone through many of them. By now she no longer cared for them. They had given her money and bought her clothes. One of them had even bought her a car which she had sold afterwards for a lot of money. But now she did not want their kind of world. Instead she went to the Star every Saturday evening where she found African men to accompany her to the more fashionable night clubs frequented by top government officials, MPs, executives and bosses of big companies. She had no constant boyfriend. She felt she did not need one. She knew she was the most desired woman in town. Men waved at her from their cars. She was sophisticated, attractive and, what is more, she knew how to charm men. She had a cover-girl look about her and men liked to have her company at big dinner parties hosted by rich company executives. At such parties, she glided along confidently talking to this man and that and played her game with them all. There was never a moment Selina was not in control. She was always the same girl, the girl who loved no one but herself, the girl who got what she desired without giving an inch of her real self.

But now she was beginning to tire of the game. She was getting weary of floating in darkness without a clear path to follow. She was going to be thirty-three next year and she needed a steady man. She needed him urgently. She needed a man she could handle with ease, a man who would idolize her and make her feel indispensable. But a man like that was not easy to find. She knew that too well. However, she was determined to try. So when Gikere appeared at the Star that evening, she did not hesitate to approach him. She had been restless and hungry for attention all evening. Her eyes had been wandering from one man to another. She had seen Gikere many times around the Nurses Hostel, but had never felt any wish to talk to him. He did not look masculine enough and it was rumoured that he had no interest in women. He had been very religious and narrow-minded and considered it sinful to have a girlfriend. But he was good at his job. At Mbagathi Hospital, everyone talked of his devotion to his work and, though recently he had started to frequent the Star, he was not interested in chasing girls. He was still naive in matters connected with love-making but strangely enough this was the man Selina was determined to possess, a man no other woman had ever touched, a man six years younger than she was.

"Come, dance with me, Gikere," she said, taking hold of his arm. Gikere got up, followed her and started to dance. He liked the way she moved. She hugged him. She seemed determined to possess him that night. He felt a strange kind of warmth when he rubbed against her bosom.

"You dance well," he said shyly.

"I want to be your partner tonight," she said, smiling seductively.

"I am not a good dancer, Selina."

"I'll teach you."

"All right."

They danced for a while. Then Gikere said, "Let's sit down. I want to talk to you."

They sat down.

"Would you like a drink?" Gikere asked.

"Lemonade," she answered.

"Is that what you drink these days?"

"I hate alcohol. It makes my head go round."

"So you are a teetotaller?"

"More or less."

"What do you mean?"

"Sometimes I take one or two sips of brandy but that's all."

"You're a lucky woman."

"I don't know. I've lost a lot of friends that way. These days you have to drink to keep your friends."

"I never used to drink at all but when you keep company with people who like to drink, then you fall into their trap. I wish I could be strong-minded like you, Selina."

"Let's go and dance again," Selina said, smiling in her usual way.

"I'm not a dancer, Selina."

"Then let's go somewhere else."

"You know the night clubs."

"Let's go to the Casino."

"Don't you want to finish your lemonade?"

"I've had enough," she said, pressing his hand warmly.

"But you know I'm not an executive. Selina."

"Don't worry, I've got some money."

"And I've got a car."

They left and went to the Casino. There they found several men who knew Selina. They got free drinks all evening. But when Selina noticed that Gikere was feeling uneasy there, she whispered in his ear and said, "I like you, Gikere."

"I like you too," he answered emotionally.

"I feel so near you, tonight. I want to be just with you."

"Let's go to my house. I don't like this place."

"All right."

They left the Casino and went directly to Gikere's house near the hospital. When they got out of the car, Gikere held her hand and led her into the sitting room. The room was simply furnished. It was clean and neat, but the walls were almost bare. The only decorations were enlarged photographs of Gikere with his mother, a big framed picture of the hospital staff at Mbagathi taken in 1953, and a few pictures of cover girls cut out from magazines.

"I want one of you," he said when he noticed her looking keenly at the photos of the cover girls.

"You will have one, or two, or three, or as many as you like. I have a whole album full of photographs. You know, I do modelling in my spare time. I've made a lot of money from it but now I'm tired of being used cheaply. I'm not a doll to play with. I've been living a superficial type of life. You are a serious man, Gikere. I want you to share your life with me." She paused and looked at Gikere's face. He was smiling. She smiled back in a most seductive manner.

"I like you, Gikere, and I like this room."

Gikere was pleased. He had never imagined that a girl like Selina would be attracted to him. The girls he had met before did not interest him. He thought they were too narrow-minded. He needed a girl who would make him important, a girl who was ambitious and adventurous, a girl who would work side by side with him and help him to set up a private clinic somewhere. This clinic was his greatest ambition. He dreamt about it often. He saw himself visiting the sick and the poor village folk and giving them food and clothes. He saw himself as a saviour for the have-nots in the villages, the deserted poor whom no one bothered about. He dreamt of bringing life to these people. His colleagues knew that one day he would set up his own clinic somewhere in a village. He was a very hardworking man and they were certain he would succeed.

Selina was a nurse. He was attracted by her personality, her lack of fear, her confidence and her good looks. He thought she was the kind of woman who could help him fulfil his dreams. And she seemed to like him. What more than that did he need?

"I shall make this house more comfortable," he said.

"This is a wonderful place. I like it, Gikere."

"It is yours when you want it. Feel at home here," he said, his mouth feeling the first sensations of desire.

She glued her lips to his when she heard that. A wave of desire passed through his veins. He pulled her down onto the settee where they remained, their arms round each other, kissing and caressing till dawn.

In the next few weeks, the whole town was to know of the friendship between Gikere and Selina. They did not hide the fact that they were in love, madly in love. They walked hand in hand everywhere. After three months, Selina discovered she was pregnant. So, one evening she moved into Gikere's house. A week later they registered their marriage at the D.C.'s office. That was how they became man and wife.

When Gikere's mother heard that her son had taken a wife and had married her without her approval, and when she realized who the woman was, she locked herself up in her house and wept for days. Finally she decided to leave the village and visit her son in the city and see the bride.

When she got to her son's house, she called him aside.

"Why did you choose her, my son?" she asked.

"I love her, mother."

"But do you know her well, do you know her people?"

"I know she loves me. That is all that matters."

"You must know her background. You must know her people. She is not a simple woman. You do not know her. She associates only with rich men. Do you know why she had decided to get married to a poor man like you?"

"She married me because she loves me."

"She does not love you. She does not know what love is. Leave her before you involve yourself too much into her kind of life."

"I cannot leave her. She is carrying my child."

"That is not a problem. We can take away the child if it is ever born."

"But I cannot abandon her."

"Think again, my son. A woman like Selina is not good for you. There are many women in the village, women who understand how to live with a man. Selina will never be one of us. Leave her alone."

"I cannot do that. I need her. She has a lot of money. I need her money. I can use it. We will do many things together. A village woman cannot understand my work. Selina is a nurse and I am a hospital assistant. We will build a clinic in the village together. That is my greatest dream. I must establish a clinic before my days are over! That is very important to me."

"But do you know where she comes from, my son?"

"She comes from Itukarua."

"Is that all you know?"

"Isn't that enough?"

"You must know more than that. A woman with money is not good for you. She will ruin your life."

"I love her and I cannot desert her now."

"Why not, my son?"

"I'm committed to her, mother."

"Then you will suffer all your life. And you will make us all suffer. Your children will be punished for the sins they never committed. Do you want this to happen, my son?"

"This will never happen."

"My son. Selina's past is important. Her people are important to your marriage. Do you know that her own mother had fits? Do you know that the woman you say you love used to suffer from fits during her childhood and was once raped as she lay unconscious by the roadside? And do you know that she was a woman of loose morals? Do you know all these things, my son? Do you know why no man has ever suggested marriage to her?"

"She has turned away a great number of men who have wanted to marry her!"

"That is not true. She is not a fool. She doesn't want anyone to know that she is not wanted. So, when she discovers that her lover is just about to abandon her, she jilts him before he does. That is how she keeps men cheated!"

"I do not believe all this. I know people are jealous of her. That is why they tell tales about her. I don't care whether she suffered from fits in her childhood. She is my wife and that is all I'm interested in now."

"I can see that you are lost, my son. I have lost you, lost everything. When your father deserted us, I hoped that you would be my support during my old age. I hoped you and I would find joy in each other. You were so close to me once but now I can see you moving away. I can see you have found another mother and you want to desert me. Gaciru is the only person I'm left with. But she too will go away. I know that. I know there is no happiness for an old woman like me. I'm alone in the village. My piece of land is full of weeds. My hands shake when I take a knife to turn the soil. What will happen to the land I have worked on so long? I thought that one day you would come back to live with me, and my grandchildren would help me to overcome the loneliness of old age. . . . But now you have chosen a woman of the city and I have lost you. You have chosen a conceited woman and I know she will bring you nothing but misery."

Adaora Lily Ulasi

?1932–

B orn in Aba, Eastern Nigeria, daughter of an Igbo chief, she was locally schooled then studied in Los Angeles, at Pepperdine University and at the University of Southern California, earning a BA in journalism in 1954. In the 1960s she was women's page editor of the Daily Times and Sunday Times of Nigeria, before marrying and moving to England, where her three children were born. After her divorce in 1972 she went to Nigeria as editor of Woman's World magazine, returning to England in 1976. Her first novel, Many Thing You No Understand (1970), controversially (for the time) used pidgin English to dramatize the interaction between colonial officers and local people in the pre-independence era, as did her subsequent works, Many Thing Begin for Change (1971), Who is Jonah? (1978) and The Man from Sagamu (1978). By contrast, The Night Harry Died (1974) is set in southern USA.

From

Many Thing Begin for Change

CHAPTER III

OBIEZE, having finished his breakfast, and, with nothing urgently requiring his attention, decided to call in and see one of his wives who had been shunning his advances lately.

Of all his eight wives, this one presented him with the greatest trouble. Either she must submit, or leave his compound. After all, he wasn't her brother, but her husband.

This problem so dominated his mind as he circled his vast compound on his way to this particular wife's house, that he started when out of nowhere, and so unexpectedly, a panting runner stood before him.

"Eh?" the Chief demanded.

"Chief, they close native court," the man said breathlessly.

The harsh words Obieze was about to pour on the man for having interrupted his journey and intruded on his thoughts, died instantly in his throat. "Who close court?"

The informer took a deep breath to steady himself before he replied. "I no know – nobody know. Interpreter tell all the people way get business for court, make them go home."

Obieze paused to digest this information fully. "You mean we no get court here anymore?" he asked in surprise, his thoughts scattered.

The informer had now gained proper control of himself, so he replied in a normal voice, "Me no know that. All I hear I tell you. I hear say they want for paint the place."

"Paint!" shouted Obieze in disbelief. "But the place no dirty!" Then the thought came to him that with MacIntosh gone, and Mason, unknown to his colleagues, out of the way, the region's headquarters would use painting the building as an excuse until a new man was appointed to replace MacIntosh and Mason. The anxiety Obieze felt at the outset left him. He was completely relaxed now. He afforded himself the luxury of a smile at a job well executed as far as his helping to get rid of MacIntosh, doing away with Mason, and putting the headquarters in complete disarray was concerned.

The informer, obeying the unwritten law that no one must interrupt a chief or speak without first being spoken to by His Highness, stood waiting Obieze's pleasure. But when something that seemed to him like eternity had passed, and since the next bit of information he was itching to give Obieze was very vital, he coughed discreetly to make the ruler aware that he was still standing there, and also to save himself from breaking the law. This diplomacy brought instant result. For Obieze murmured, "They lie, Foreigner lie too much!"

After this the informer felt he could now impart to the Chief the vital information he could no longer contain, and which was about to strangle him.

"Chief Obieze, I think I also for tell you say, another white man come for court this morning-time, and I think he still be there."

"Eh?" responded Obieze with shock.

Encouraged by this reaction, the informer went on. "He be still there when I lef for come here."

"What the man look like?" Obieze asked, his shock deepening.

The informer scratched his head in an attempt to recall any outstanding feature of the visiting expatriate. Finally he voiced what he could recall. "All white man look like the same to me," he began, "but this one long, and he get black-hair."

Obieze frowned and looked as if he was trying to put a name to the expatriate's face, or to remember whether he'd come across Jenkins before. When neither prospect proved successful he said, "I no think say I see this new man before. You think he be new A.D.O.?"

To this his informer replied, "Ah, that I no fit say. I no wait for hear."

"What be him name?"

"That too I no wait for hear."

"I want make you go back find out for me."

"Yes, Chief."

As his informer began to retreat, Obieze charged him with further responsibility. "Wait!" he ordered. "Make you tell Anako, but make you no tell him in front of new white man, you hear?" he warned, and the informer nodded. "I want make you tell Anako say I want him for come to see me for afternoon time today."

The informer left for the native court.

"You understand my instructions?" Jenkins once more asked the court interpreter.

"Yes, sir."

"Good. You're not to tell anyone anything about the missing keys until we know ourselves at headquarters." When Anako said he understood, Jenkins continued. "By the way, Mr MacIntosh is on leave. . ."

Anako cut it with, "Leave? But Mr MacIntosh just come. He no be for here long to go leave!"

Jenkins was momentarily silenced, and then tried to explain as best he could, averting his eyes from those of the court interpreter. "I know, Mr Anako, but these things happen."

"He go come back, from the leave I mean?"

"Eh . . . I don't really know. We'll have to wait and see."

Anako was no fool. He'd heard the hesitancy in Jenkins' voice, and caught the point from his fifteen years of experience of sensing A.D.O.s come and go.

"Maybe we go get another A.D.O.?" he pursued sadly.

Jenkins thought, "What the hell!" Why not tell the poor man the truth. After all, he's worked for the regional government for long enough. "Yes, I think so, Mr Anako," he replied.

This statement from Jenkins saddened Anako deeply. "Ah, Mr MacIntosh, he be good man," he said regretfully.

"Undoubtedly."

"What say?"

"Yes, Mr Anako, Mr MacIntosh is a very nice man indeed."

"Maybe you go come here yourself for replacement?" Anako asked Jenkins, looking up hopefully at him to confirm it.

"I doubt it. My line's entirely different. Look, I must get back to Utuka. The headquarters will be in touch with you."

"How for do about Mr MacIntosh him office?"

"Oh, yes. Let me have a look at it."

"But it lock," Anako reminded him.

"Yes, I'm aware of that. I just want to have a look at it from the outside."

As he and the interpreter walked, Jenkins turned to him and asked, "By the way, is the window through which you got in still open?"

Anako confirmed this. "Fanlight open too," he told Jenkins. When they reached the open window Anako climbed in after Jenkins. They looked round and found everything in order.

"Look, we'll have to close the fanlight and just leave the window half open so you can get in should you receive a call from headquarters."

"All right, sir."

Jenkins gathered what confidential papers he could find and prepared to leave. He had his feet on the window ledge ready to jump down when Onyeso mysteriously appeared. They stared at each other. Onyeso burst out laughing. "A government employee burgling government premises! I wish I'd a photographer with me to put it on celluloid!"

Jenkins looked embarrassed. "Look, Godfrey..." he began, but didn't know how to continue.

"Isn't it odd," Onyeso went on, pressing his advantage, "that a law court still in session, at least it was sitting up to last Friday, should be locked suddenly in order to have it painted?"

"Odd indeed, but odder things have happened. Godfrey, these things do happen," replied Jenkins when he had recovered himself and jumped down from the window ledge.

"What things?" Onyeso persisted.

"My friend, you ask too many questions!" Anako piped up from behind Jenkins.

"It's quite all right, Mr Anako. I'll take care of this," Jenkins told him. As he straightened up he continued, "It so happens that most of these cases here should really now go to the court of appeal at Utuka. All that's left here at the moment are merely petty thefts and things like that."

"But you have no keys?" Onyeso asked with feigned innocence. "You've just jumped out through an office window," he pointed out to Jenkins as if to refresh the latter's memory.

"You're absolutely right," Jenkins replied with equilibrium and went on. "And that's my privilege. But if you must know, I forgot the keys at Utuka in my hurry. It's just one of those things."

"But surely the residential official..." Onyeso started, and Jenkins finished it for him. "He's on leave," replied Jenkins. "He left the keys quite rightly with headquarters before he departed."

"But the relief and the official stationed here are always together for a short period for the handing over," Onyeso stubbornly pressed on.

Jenkins wiped perspiration from his eyes as he answered. "Yes. Mr MacIntosh however had to take his leave quickly, while there's a lull." He suddenly became angry. "Look here, Godfrey. I've told you the truth and all I know. You can either take it or leave it."

"Well, I'll leave you to it," replied the reporter, and walked off.

"Foolish man!" said Anako.

"Let's leave the matter here, Mr Anako," said Jenkins as he saw the anger in the interpreter's face. "Oh, he'll make trouble for us. Well," continued Jenkins, looking about him, "I leave the premises in your hands. We'll be in touch with you from headquarters as soon as possible."

"All right, sir."

Onyeso, having left Jenkins and Anako, ambled his way around the court grounds. His sharpened mind did not for one minute believe what Jenkins had told him. The more he thought about it, the more fishy it became, so he determined to find out the truth.

"You're the night-watchman?" Onyeso asked, as he came upon old Eze. "Yes, and janitor. What you want?" Eze wanted to know.

"I want you to do me a favour."

"Who me?" asked Eze, aghast.

"Yes, you," Onyeso told him, slightly amused at the startled look on the old man's face.

"Well, what dash [bribe] you want?" Eze asked, frowning, and Oyeso realized that the man had misunderstood his words. He burst out laughing as the full meaning of the situation hit him.

"I didn't mean that I wanted you to give me a dash. I'm the one who'll give you the dash if you do me a ..." he stopped as he searched for a simpler world which the night-watchman would understand. "A small favour," he finished patiently.

The alarmed expression on Eze's face at the thought of giving anyone dash out of his seven and sixpence monthly wage, relaxed, and he replied in a more friendly voice, "Ah, now I follow you!"

"Good." Onyeso then went on to enlighten him, "I want you to tell me the real reason behind the court being painted."

"Ah, Mr ..."

"Onyeso."

"Mr Onyeso, I no fit tell you," said Eze without thinking.

Onyeso's mouth twitched. His eyes danced viciously as he cornered Eze further. "Why can't you tell me?"

"The white man way jus' lef say make we no say anything to anybody if anybody ask," Eze continued stupidly.

"So there's another reason then?"

"Yes, I mean No!" Eze shouted on realizing his indiscretion, and threw away his tooth pick. But Onyeso, having trapped his man, pressed on, this time with the added temptation of a cash reward thrown in. "I'll give you one pound a month as a retainer fee if you tell me."

Eze swivelled his eyes to look Onyeso fully in the face. Was the man mad, he thought, or was he deceiving him? When he saw neither on Onyeso's face, and also took in the immaculate, and for him, expensive robe and trousers the reporter was wearing, he asked thickly, "One pound every month?" He'd never seen or handled such a lump sum at one go in his life. When Onyeso nodded with seriousness at the query, Eze looked at him, open mouthed. One pound just for simple information, with more to come each month! He looked mesmerized. "Jesu cry!" he shouted at last, and rubbed his nose.

"Well?" Onyeso asked after minutes, when it seemed that Eze had completely disappeared into a dream world and had forgotten his presence.

"Mr Onyeso," Eze began sorrowfully, "I no fit," he added with a shake of his head, having searched his soul.

"Why not?" Onyeso asked.

"Because Mr Jenkin way jus' lef go sack me if he find out say I tell you," he explained with an effort. The anguish of letting a pound enter and slip out of his hands was too great.

"Look, if you tell me I won't let anyone else know that it was you who gave me the information," persuaded Onyeso.

Eze looked up and searched the reporter's face. He began to think again. This new proposition certainly appealed to him. He cast his eyes on the ground to consider it further. He jerked his head up suddenly to express another vital point. "But you go put it for paper," he reminded Onyeso, his eyes narrowing at the corners.

"True, but I won't reveal my source of information. I won't betray you now, or in the future, ever," he told Eze softly.

Eze inclined his head as this sank in. He straightened up and thought of the things he could do with twenty shillings a month. The more he thought, the more the temptation to accept proved too great to resist. He could quit the job here as night-watchman cum janitor for the mere pittance of seven and six a month, and his stomach swollen night after night from the cold wind. But he threw that idea right out of his mind. If he did that the man standing before him would no longer be interested in him, and would withdraw his proposition. There would be no access for him to obtain the necessary information that he was willing to pay so handsomely for.

Another line of thought came to him as he stood, deciding. He suddenly remembered that the season for planting crops was upon them and that the additional money would go a long way to help him out. He looked about him to see if Anako or the driver were watching. When he saw neither he edged closer to this new benefactor and cleared his throat. "I go take the one pound. What you want for know?"

Onyeso, who had watched the struggle taking place in the night-watchman, and also witnessed the devil successfully gaining the upper hand, now murmured, "I've told you before. I want to know the truth about what's happening here."

"Give me the money first," Eze said, with a snap of his fingers.

Onyeso hedged. "Don't you trust me?"

Eze rubbed his eyes. "I do, Mr Onyeso, I do. But that no be for here or for there. I want make we finish the money palaver side first."

A crisp pound note changed hands. Eze glanced about him furtively as he folded the note and tucked it into his lappa. He smirked his lips with satisfaction when the task was completed. His breathing became normal again. "Mr MacIntosh go for leave, Mr Mason they no fit find. Somebody thief key."

"What d'you mean about the D.O.?" Onyeso asked his man. The news about Mason was unexpected, and of more interest.

"They say they no see him for headquarter," Eze said impatiently, anxious to get away in case someone saw him talking to the newspaper man.

"Oh? When was he missed?"

"That I no know. I think they 'fraid he loss, or they no go worry so." And with that Eze walked off to sweep up the leaves from under the trees.

Arthur Johnson, the government surveyor, knocked and entered the expansive office of the District Commissioner. Hughes watched his approach from behind his huge desk flanked on either side with leather chairs. He was a man of medium height when he stood up, but gave the impression of being tall as he sat behind his desk.

"You asked to see me?" said Johnson.

"Yes," Hughes replied abstractedly, and added, "Please sit down."

"Thank you."

The District Commissioner looked at some folders on his desk. He folded them and sat back in his seat. "It's been suggested that the soil here might be good for rubber planting. What d'you think?"

Johnson looked at him sharply. "You mean the soil here at Utuka?"

"No, generally."

Johnson considered for a moment. "I can't really say until I've tested the soil in other parts, but this area is definitely out of the question. The soil is barren. One has only to look at the harvest each year to see that."

"Hmm," mumbled Hughes, but Johnson added hastily. "Idom may be different. The yams grow to nearly three feet tall there. The circumference varies of course. Still, it's a rich harvest. I've seen them at the market."

"Is that so? I wonder why nothing grows very much here despite all the hard work the local people put in, and the heavy rainfall?" Hughes wondered.

"It's just barren, I suppose."

"Cultivation won't help?"

"We've tried that," Johnson told him. "We got the yams to grow just eight inches but no more. Two inches better than is normally produced by the locals."

"Pity," Hughes replied, looking again at the folders on his desk. "Going back to rubber," he went on, closing the folders once more. "How soon can you leave to sample the soil at the place you mentioned?"

"Idom? Now if you like."

"That's a bit quick." Hughes told him slightly amused as he wondered whether it was he who was driving the other man away, or if it was just enthusiasm for his job.

Johnson replied with equilibrium. "You sounded urgent when you mentioned the project."

"Yes, I know. I get all sorts of orders and requests from the Governor. I'm sure he thinks I've nothing else to do but sit here and wait for his commands!"

Johnson forced down the laugh that came to his voice and said, "I could leave for Idom this morning to start the necessary tests if you want me to."

"You know the place well, of course. D'you have any particular ground that you consider suitable? That is if the decision to experiment in rubber became definite."

"There's a stretch of land a mile long of very good earth between Idom and Uru. In fact one can't go wrong in that area as far as other produce is concerned. Rubber is something different."

"I see," said Hughes. "Well, I've leave it in your hands."

"Will that be all?" Johnson asked, preparing to get up.

Hughes looked up from the folder. "For the time being, yes."

Johnson stood up to leave. He added as an afterthought, "I think, George, I may as well survey the land I mentioned while I'm about it."

"How long will that take you?"

"Oh, allowing for delays and various other things, I should say a fortnight."

"But you've only just returned from trek last week. Why not have a week's break before you set out again."

Johnson inwardly moaned at the idea of Hughes showing some concern on his behalf. Aloud he said, "It doesn't matter," and added; "By the way, why I called earlier was to tell you that I'd some unfinished business in Ichara and wished to go back. However, it'll keep in view of the rubber venture."

Hughes' hazel eyes looked at him uncomprehendingly for a minute. "Oh, yes, I remember now, I did tell Mark to ask if you'd be kind enough to call back."

That's not the way it was related to me, thought Johnson, but what does it matter? He left the Commissioner's office for his own home to prepare for the trip.

He went through the lounge and up a flight of stairs to the main bedroom. As usual, Evelyn Johnson was sunbathing on the small balcony off their bedroom, with only a towel resting carelessly between her thighs, and the magazine, *Home from Home*, lying beside her. Johnson sighed and eyed her. What if their cook or steward wandered in, as servants often did unexpectedly, and saw her in that pose? he asked himself. A thought occurred to him which sent sparks of shock right through him as he stood gazing at the exquisite figure of his wife. He shook his head, as if by doing so he would shake the unpalatable thought off. No! he nearly screamed out, Evelyn couldn't descend that low – or could she? He'd heard of some wives buttonholing their servants while their husbands' backs were turned; the myth, or the reality being that men in this hemisphere went much longer than their counterparts in the west.

Mrs Johnson almost leapt as she heard her husband's voice say in controlled rage, "I'm off to survey a field at Idom for rubber planting and you're coming with me! I want no further gossip or near scandal behind my back. Take everything you'll require. We'll be away for two weeks or more, depending." And I'll also be out of the D.C.'s reach, he added to himself.

"That awful place?" Mrs Johnson asked after she heard her husband out. "There'll hardly be a soul in that rest house but us, or me, for most of the time!"

Johnson looked as if he couldn't care less if she stayed alone in the rest house until doomsday. "That awful place, as you put it my darling, also pays for our bread and butter!" he snapped.

"I know, you've told me before," Evelyn Johnson replied, getting up.

"Good. I'm glad it's sunk in," said Johnson sarcastically. He was determined to hurt her, and hurt her deeply.

"I'll pack a case," she replied, trailing the towel behind her from the balcony into their bedroom.

Johnson, having finished packing his own case, went downstairs to tell their cook to be ready in ten minutes with some utensils, and whatever food they had in the larder, to accompany them on trek. To their steward he said to come up in about five minutes to pick up the cases. He went back to their bedroom to find his wife in only her panties and brassière brushing her shoulder-length hair before the dressing-table mirror.

"I wish you'd hurry," he told her. "I want to reach Idom before it gets too hot."

"All in good time," she replied lazily, laying the brush aside and picking up her lipstick.

Johnson looked at her as if he wanted to strangle her. Instead he said, "I told Louis to come up in five minutes to pick up our cases."

"Well, I'm ready," said Mrs Johnson, as she rose from the dressing-table. Her husband watched as she buttoned her slim figure into a canary-yellow cotton frock. In another minute Louis knocked and went in and out again with the cases.

Walking behind her to their car Johnson remarked, "I wish you'd stop using that awful hair dye or whatever it is you use on your hair. I know you were once a redhead, but your hair's now the colour of a watered-down carrot."

Evelyn Johnson walked straight ahead without turning her head. "Watered-down carrot indeed! Planting vegetables has ruined your eyesight, Arthur. I'm only twenty-six and neither use, nor do I need, a hair dye," she hissed back at him.

Mrs Johnson was years younger than her husband, a fact that had pleased him at first, but which he now resented, as every male eye in the residential area and in the catering rest houses elsewhere always rested on her with undisguised lust. Husband and wife got in their car and drove all the way to Idom in complete silence.

Hughes picked up his receiver. "Extension two, please."

Jack Bailey came on the line. "Yes, sir?"

"Is Mark back yet?"

"No, sir."

"Have him call me when he gets back."

"Yes, sir."

As Bailey was about to ring off, Hughes added, "By the way, phone Ukana again, will you, and tell whoever's there to inform the Chief about the temporary closure of the court. If Mark's still there when you get through, ask him to do it – if not, anyone will do, "said Hughes and rang off.

Bailey looked at his watch. It said twelve fifteen. Another hour and forty-five minutes and I'll be off for the day, and away from Hughes, he thought to himself, and placed the call to Ukana. He looked around for something to do to make him look busy while the call went through. As he did so, two of the drivers sent out on routes that Mason could have taken to any one of the five sub-stations, excluding Ukana, returned, but with no heartening news. He decided against intruding on Hughes yet, until all the drivers were back.

Miriam Tlali

1933–

Born in Doornfontein, South Africa, she attended Witwatersrand University until it was closed to Blacks, then studied at the National University of Roma, Lesotho. Leaving there through lack of funds, she went to secretarial school and became an office clerk, on which experience she drew for her first novel Muriel at Metropolitan, which was written in 1968 but not published until 1975. A contributor to South African publications including the Rand Daily Mail and Staffrider, for which she wrote a popular series of interviews called "Soweto Speaking". Her second book, Amandla (1980) – which deals with the lives of the people of Soweto where she and her family live – was, like her first, banned in South Africa, Mihloti ("Tears"), which incorporates stories, journalism and interviews, appeared in 1984 and her collection of stories Mehlala Khatamping (Footprints in the Quag) was published in Britain as Soweto Stories (1989).

"Go in Peace, Tobias Son of Opperman"

JESSIE sat on the chair in the small kitchen. She was thinking. About five minutes had gone since Tobias, her husband, had disappeared into their bedroom. Would he be washing, she wondered? To her sluggish mind, it seemed like hours since he had shambled in that direction. "Alone again," she thought, "I'm alone." She dreaded the thought of being alone with only Tikie the cat and the old Big Ben clock on the old kitchen dresser over there, ticking away the seconds and the minutes, and the hours; endless hours of waiting. Waiting for someone to knock at the door.

She called out, her voice weak and shaky, "Tobie, where are you?"

"In here," her husband answered.

"What are you doing there for such a long time?"

Tobias did not answer. He was looking at his reflection on the piece of broken mirror on the rickety chest of drawers in the dimly lit bedroom, his shaky hands flapping the broad end of his neck-tie into the loop and pulling it down, adjusting it to hang over his sternum.

On such days there was only one thing to do. . . . Go . . . go anywhere; talk to people and not reflect on what might have been or might not have been, if, if, if. What had happened in their lives had happened. It was part of the past which no one could bring back or alter. It was one of those days again. Jessie was again in those moods of hers. If only she could accept her lot, her long protracted illness, and leave everything into the hands of the Creator. . . . He swallowed, he almost wished he could "swallow" the thought. If *he*, Tobias, ever tried to quote one verse from the Bible to Jessie – just one verse – he would regret it for the whole day. The dear woman seemed to have sunk deeper and deeper (in the twelve long years of her infirmity) into a world of despair and emptiness. Emptiness, nothingness. Even the prayers Matlome and Mma-Matlome their close friends came to comfort them with every week seemed of late to have no meaning to her. She no longer derived any strength from them. Matlome's words seemed to leave his lips, hit Jessie's hard stolid face and then bounce back to him without even reaching her ears. On such occasions, she just stared into the air and she would not utter a word of appreciation. At least whenever Matlome quoted verses from the scriptures, Jessie's stern face did not seem to recoil into a hard knot. She would not even stammer bitterly: "Don't come to me again with those 'holy' words, Tobias son of Opperman, please. I know you too well to take you seriously . . . words, words, words. You always say words you yourself do not mean, Tobiase."

It was still early but Tobias felt tired already. He cast a final look into the mirror before him, drawing back slowly and murmuring to himself, "Old age. You wake up tired as if you never slept at all!"

He had woken up early to make fire in their "Welcome Dover" coal stove. He had also prepared their breakfast, thin mealie-meal porridge as usual. As he moved towards the kitchen, he felt happy about his accomplishments. . . . The kitchen was warm and cosy. The pot of porridge was simmering slowly. He was thinking and his lips were moving, whispering the thoughts as they occurred to him. "I'll have to mix the powdered milk and make tea for both of us. . . . I must not forget to give Jessie the tablets for her arthritis," he mumbled almost loudly and slouched back into their bedroom. At that moment, he wished that Nakedi, his brother's twelve-year-old great-grand-daughter, was there to go on errands. He was wondering when the schools would reopen. The school holidays seem to be so much longer nowadays, he thought regretfully. It was so thoughtful of their great-grand-nephew and niece to have "offered" little Nakedi to stay with them to send around the house and to the shops. Now he would have to do everything himself until she returned from visiting her parents.

Tobias lumbered slowly back to the kitchen with the vial containing the pills for his wife. He looked at her, putting them on the table next to her, and advised, "Don't forget to take your tablets, Jessie, I'll. . . ."

"What's the use of taking them; they never work anyway," Jessie cut in sharply. She turned her head and looked at Tobias and asked, "How shall I forget them? You'll be here to. . . . You are not going away and leaving me alone again are you?" She nodded slowly, knowingly, added, "Oh, yes. Clean shirt, a suit, necktie and everything. You are ready to go again. You're so keen, you never even looked to see if your shirt is not inside-out!"

Tobias's hand moved immediately and unsteadily towards his neck. He had not yet buttoned his shirt and he had not noticed the mistake. "Oh, I didn't notice."

He shook his head. "Old age," he thought, "you never seem to do things right. And all the time you try so hard." He looked at Jessie again and added, "Shall I give you your porridge now? I have to go. Will you manage? I'll put everything next to you on the table – the bowl of porridge, the spoon, the soup and the sliced bread. Also sugar and the salt from the clinic. We don't have any more jam. Are you listening, Jessie?"

Jessie did not reply. She was thinking how she hated the very mention of *that* "clinic" salt. It tasted more like Epsom salt than salt! She looked ahead of her at nothing in particular. The aches in her legs were just beginning to intensify. She sat still, feeling the painful twinge come and go, come and go. The pains were spreading through her joints and piercing mercilessly all over her body like spikes of fire. That look of utter helplessness had come over her face again. She shut her eyes and said nothing.

A few minutes later, Tobias walked into the bedroom and picked up his hat and his umbrella. "I'll be back, Jessie," he mumbled as he went past her. He shut the door quietly behind him and walked slowly towards the gate.

With her eyes still closed, Jessie "spoke" to Tobias who she knew was not in the house and would not hear her.

"*Ikele ka kagiso, Tobiase Mor'waga Opperman. Balimo ba me ba tla sala le nna'* [Go well Tobias son of Opperman. My ancestors will remain with me]. The white man's language you speak, their ways which you learnt since you were born and their name that you carry with you, I thought that you would make me happy because you are not what they call 'die kraal-kaffer'. Like them (whites), you have no feelings for fellow human beings. You just have no "marrow". You're lost."

In the street, Tobias was thinking. Although he did not realize it, he was speaking loudly as if Jessie was still sitting next to him. He did not look back.

He just kept walking and walking and soliloquizing. . . . He knew deep down, however, that he would never say what was in his mind to his wife. . . . "I know what will happen if I stay next to you when you are like that, Jessie. You will be blaming me for everything that went wrong in our life; everything that was not gratifying and pleasant. You'll be blaming me for everything as if *I* make all the laws between human beings. Between men and women; the rich and the poor; white people and black people. What am I anyway? Just a struggling old man. . . . If during my youth I made mistakes, can they be worse than anybody else's? Like everybody else, I was only trying hard to eke out a living in a difficult world."

Tobias knew that he would never say all those things to his ailing wife. As you grow older, you learn the wisdom in the words "ho boloka khotso" in a marriage. You begin to appreciate how important it is. You come to realize that there are younger people around you who have to be assisted along the hazardous path of life shared, of marriage. Just like his father used to say to him and his sisters and brothers – all dead and buried now. "Trou is nie perde-koop nie," he would repeat again and again. The truth in those words sank deeper and deeper as he grew older and you have to pass on words of advice to your descendants and the sons and daughters of those you live with. He remembered the tumultuous early years of their marriage when they were still living in a one-room tin shack in S'deke-deke near Westbury Station long long ago. "*Jarelanang mef-okolo bana ba ka.*" An old Mosotho neighbour, old-man Nong, would pound on their door and enter without being asked to do so in an attempt to prevent what he thought would be a bloody duel of young people who had not learnt how to "carry the cross". "*Bolokang khotso bana ba ka! Jarelanang mefokolo,*" the old man would say, stepping in between him and Jessie. [Do preserve peace, my children. Bear with each other's weaknesses.] He could not remember how many times old-man Nong had stepped in, raising his hands high, reciting the words until they sounded like a commandment. He would then put his hands on Tobias's shoulder, pleading with him to sit down and "cool off". "Sit down, my child; do not raise your voice. A woman is a woman; you cannot compete with her tongue. Keep quiet or leave her and go elsewhere; when you return, she will have forgotten."

It was a long time ago and they had come to know one another through the years. Their quarrels had gradually ceased to be noisy and stormy because they had learnt – painfully – "*ho boloka khotso*". Or was it because he *had* finally come to know that there was no point in trying to compete with a woman's tongue?

Tobias had automatically walked in the direction of his old friend Matlome's house like his feet were drawn to it by an invisible magnet. He stopped opposite the house and hesitated for a while. He decided not to go in. It was still too early to pay anyone a visit and besides he was still too irritated and upset to speak to anyone. And Mma-Matlome was a very observant old woman who seemed always to see through people. She always seemed to be examining people's faces for any hidden traces of uneasiness. She was like a specialist who was an expert in diagnosing "maladies" associated with discontent, remorse or indignation.

Tobias hurried away from the spot before anyone noticed his procrastination.

Nobody seemed to care. Everyone went past him, obviously hurrying to wherever they were going. Who cares about an old man when there are more urgent matters to see to anyway, he thought, thankful that no one who knew him was near enough to notice his sadness and perhaps ask questions. Only the kids who were kicking the ball in the street saw him. They too were more concerned with the ball than with him. They were dodging the familiar figure of old Oupa. Tobias carrying the umbrella and the walking stick, always mumbling to himself. To them, it was fun to watch him as they kicked the ball around him; to look into his "unseeing" eyes without paying attention to his muttering.

In the open space between Zone 9 and Zone 10 Meadowlands, he was still thinking loudly, "speaking" to Jessie and listening to his own voice without making any effort to lower it. There was nobody in sight and he was grateful. . . .

"Even if I had tried to explain to you, you would have gone on and on accusing me of not caring. You would have told me again that all I cared about was *other* people – outside our house. What do you think would happen to us if I did not go round giving comfort to other old people and doing my part as a member of the Old Age Relief Committee in the church? The church gives us the milk powder, the soup powder, the beans, the mealie meal, the jam and the sugar. . . . Where would we get all that from if I did not help? Our pension money only manages to pay the rent; to buy coal, wood, the medicines, that's all. We can only buy meat two times a month, you know that. Unless some kind neighbour or relative brings us a packet now and again.

"It's your fault, Jessie; it's all your fault. I used to tell you to stop doing the washing for the whites and you never listened to me. All those bundles and bundles you carried on your head to and from the white suburbs day after day, week after week, month after month. And now all the joints in your body have given in. Now you are crippled; an invalid. *Twelve years* and you are still helpless. . . . You are no longer the sprightly beautiful Jessie I married."

Tobias shook his head at the thought and hot tears filled his eyes and he could not see the road ahead clearly. His boots kicked against the stones in the gravel path and he stumbled, holding tightly on to the stick in his hand. His limbs were tired and unsteady. He had been walking and walking without knowing where exactly he was going to. . . . Anywhere, anywhere away from the dark clouds which seemed forever to be engulfing his house. He thought of Nakedi. He continued to speak loudly, "If only little Nakedi was there then there would be someone to speak to. To relate the stories of old Madlera and Thulandivile, S'deke-deke and so on. To talk about the animals in the zoos and tell all sorts of tales about them. . . . The children, our children; why did they all go before us? When you give birth to children, you expect them to be there to close your eyes when you go. You do not expect them to leave you behind. . . . All three of them . . . all gone before us. Polio, meningitis, TB. . . . Why? If they were here, I would not have to bear the pain of watching Jessie alone . . . Jessie crawling like an insect before me; wasting away right there before my eyes. First a stroke, then arthritis and God-knows-what. . . . The children would help me carry Jessie from the chair to the toilet bowl; from the bed to the kitchen. . . . I have to 'carry the cross' alone. My shoulders, my arms, my legs – they're aching, tired. . . . Jessie, Jessie, daughter of Magolebane, I am tired."

In their little semi-detached house in Meadowlands, Jessie had long finished eating her breakfast. It was now long after lunchtime and she had not reached for her bread and cold soup. She did not feel hungry at all. She sat thinking and talking to herself, addressing Tobias who was not there to listen. It did not matter to her that he was not there to hear her. All she wanted to do was to speak out her mind. She went on and on: "Church work, church work . . . I know all about that, Tobias. You forget that I know you. I did not stay with you all my life for nothing. You are just a tramp – a born tramp, Tobias. 'I'm on the Committee; I must have a suit.' First it was the Boxing Board Committee, then it was the Football League Committee. Then followed the race-course and the 'boys'. You just had to go somewhere. . . . Durban, Cape Town, Port Elizabeth, Messina, Walvis Bay, everywhere. . . . Suits, suits, suits. A brown suit, a grey suit, a navy blue suit, a black suit. . . . What about the children, Tobias? The school fees, the school uniforms, the food, the children's shoes, coats for winter - what about *them?*" I would ask. The committees, the committees. They all came to nothing, nothing. Then you would come home with bloodshot eyes – drunk, after losing all your money at the race track.

"And now it's the Old Age Relief Committee. . . . Church work, church work. . . . Your field is becoming smaller and smaller just like mine. Ever since the 'street-corner' kids stole your bicycle, your field is becoming smaller and smaller and you still cannot see that. Mine is even smaller because I can no longer walk outside and greet people as they pass. I am now confined to the little square where I am sitting. I have to crawl on my knees to go into the toilet and just that takes a whole hour. Exercises, the clinic nurse says; 'Try to use your limbs, Ouma Jessie,' she says, piercing my tired flabby muscles with the long needle like she were poking a harmless stick into a dead piece of leather. . . . And now I have to go again to the toilet and I don't know how I'll manage. The cat. Tikie, you can't help me either. If only I could send you to bring the bowl to me. . . I have to crawl to that bowl over there. . . . What a cursed 'blessing' these Meadowlands toilets are inside the house! The smell – so near the pots and the pans – kitchen smells, bedroom smells, lavatory smells all mingling together on my nostrils. It's just like Vundla (P.Q.) used to say at our weekly meetings in Thulandivile's Communal Hall: 'The Boers want to take us to a *Me-e-e-do* [meadow]. They want us to go to a place where *Nxa ufun'uk'ye-bosh'* [(when you want to go and shit] and you are sitting outside, you go *into* the house to do that!' And we used to think he was mad, and the idea would be repulsive and nauseating, and we would spit. Everything put next to each other like that. . . . Fit only for derelicts like ourselves. People who have been used and discarded; forgotten by the glittering world of gold sixteen miles away. . . . We have helped to build their skyscrapers and now we are only fit for the rubbish heap. They can now sit in their posh buildings and forget about us, Tobias. . . . Now you have to hire a wheelbarrow and get a pair of strong youths to push it and take me to the superintendent's office every two months for us to collect our pension money because they will never give you *my* pension unless they *see* me. . . . That's what it has come to now, Tobias. . . . And now you too have cast me away to face the end alone."

The kitchen had gradually become darker and darker. Jessie wondered why Tobias had stayed away so late. It had started to rain and the dark clouds had made it look like it was late in the evening.

"Ouma! Ouma Jessie!" a child's voice called from outside the door. It sounded like it was coming nearer her. It was not easy to turn her head and see behind her. The muscles in her neck were stiff and it had been years since she could easily twist her neck-bones. It was typical of her type of illness, the doctor and the clinic nurses had said.

The child stopped as soon as he entered the little kitchen. He was surprised. Jessie was sitting on the floor, the cat cuddling on her dress between her knees. He stammered, "Ouma, I've brought Oupa Tobias. . . . But, but why is Ouma sitting on the floor?"

He moved to face Jessie squarely, puzzled. The child's face was familiar but Jessie could not say exactly whose child he was. Just one of the kids in the neighbourhood. He was holding on to Tobias with his one hand and clasping the umbrella and the walking-stick in the other. He did not wait for Ouma Jessie to reply, but explained because he could see that she was herself taken aback by what she was seeing. She tried to explain, her attention directed at Tobias. She drawled uncertainly, her tongue feeling heavy like it had suddenly become too big in her mouth, making it difficult for her to speak clearly.

"M-my s-stick, Tobias. . . . I tried to reach for it and it slipped and rolled away. I . . . I'm too tired. I could not reach it. It was only the cat Tikie and I. It was from the toilet over there. I could not get on to the chair without the stick. The . . . the cat could not give it to me. . . . I sat waiting for you to come and help me, Tobias. You've been gone for *so* long."

Tobias did not speak. His eyes seemed to be staring at something ahead of him. His knees began to sag and he dropped down with a thud on the floor next to Jessie.

"Oupa!" the child screamed. He jumped and tried to pick up the old man who was now sprawling, spreading his arms outward with his face towards the corrugated-iron roof and the rafters above.

"No, leave Oupa alone, my child! Go out and call somebody! A neighbour – anybody; go!"

Jessie could not mistake that look on Tobias's face. His head was just near her knees. She wished she could pick him up and put him on her lap. His eyes were still staring. She talked to the still form before her: "You are surprised, Tobias. So am I. You have cheated me once more. You were always so strong and now you have gone before me. Why are you so cruel, Tobias? How I wish I were you, Tobias. You will no longer have to reach for the umbrella and the walking-stick and trample the streets. . . . You have cheated me again. I always worked so hard for you and the children and all you can do is leave me alone. *Ikele ka kagiso Tobiase mor'wa Opperman . . . Jy het my vermors.* [You have wasted me]."

Jessie looked at the surprised expression on the face of her dead husband for a while, her mind failing to grasp clearly what was happening to her. Slowly her shaking hand moved towards his fixed eyelids and closed them.

Marion Patrick Jones
1934–

B orn in Trinidad, she is a graduate of St Joseph's Convent, Port
of Spain, won the Girls' Open Island Scholarship of 1950 and
was one of the first two female students admitted to the Imperial
College of Tropical Agriculture. She went to the USA in the mid 1950s and
lived in Brooklyn for a year, working in a ceramics factory. Returning
to Trinidad to work at Carnegie Free Library, she gained a diploma in
library science and in 1959 took graduate studies in social anthropology
at London University (1962). While in London she was a founder of the
Campaign Against Racial Discrimination. In 1973 she went to work with
Unesco in Paris and she has written non-fiction about Southern Africa
under her married name of O'Callaghan. She concerns herself with the
lives and changing aspirations of Trinidadians in her novels, Pan Beat
(1973) and J'Ouvert Morning (1976), from which this extract comes.

From

J'Ouvert Morning

ELIZABETH

F OR Elizabeth Grant one thing made this day different: she had met her
nephew, Junior, and he had spoken to her. She had been standing near
to Rosie's tray on Frederick Street ole talkin' about the price of khus khus
grass and wooden hangers when Junior hopped out of a pick up taxi, held
her by the elbow and said, "Aunt Liz, how you doing?" Until Junior had
come she had been dividing her time between Rosie and commenting on
the big shots who had passed her by. She knew them all, she assured Rosie,
personally. It was early in the day and she was not yet drunk. She had already
done her morning's quota of duties. She had been to mass, paid her periodic
visit to some "boys" who were starting a tailoring co-operative, cussed out a
policeman who had moved her on the day before, collected a loaf of hops
bread and cheese from a parlour in Duncan Street. The last stop before she
wandered to a rum shop was always Rosie's tray. She and Rosie had become
friendly over Ray Burnett and over politics. Rosie had spent most of her life –

since she was fifteen – selling cigarettes, matches, sweets, khus khus grass, and of late coconut-shell shac shacs especially put on for American tourists. She sat, legs apart, straw hat on, before a store front on Frederick Street. From there she viewed the scene around , registering each minute change in this person or that. Snippets of passing conversation were saved, sorted out, added to. The size of each person's shopping paper bag was noticed as well as which store had issued it. From all of this Rosie worked out the news of the day. Rosie had known them all when they were what Elizabeth called "snotty-nosed kids", but which Rosie primly called "runny-nosed children"! She had watched their parents shopping down town, or lingering at the street corners. There were some people in whom Rosie was particularly interested; those who had made it. They fascinated her. She had, she swore, picked them out when they were still young, noted their return to Frederick Street after being abroad, or the way they walked after having made a good marriage. Rosie's other preoccupation was with "independence". She counted the number of girls who had been discharged from the big bright stores, or the salesmen who were in a job today and out tomorrow and came to the conclusion that the only safety was in "independence". She was independent behind her tray sitting on the turned-over empty box which served her as a stool. She was not, she stressed, dependent on Ray Burnett for a job, or Bullseye Charlie for police protection, nor on any madam for a week's pay. She could, she added, dispose of her sugar cakes as she damn well felt like. She always kept one for Elizabeth. She had been doing that ever since Elizabeth was a girl at Convent school breaking Sister Marie's instructions never to eat in the street. Rosie always discussed the news with Elizabeth. They had a high regard for each other's intelligence. It was Rosie who had first warned Elizabeth that Ray Burnett was a son-of-a-bitch. She knew it from the precise skimping way he walked and she had heard he and Bullseye Charlie threatening to clean up the town and drive her off the street. Elizabeth had bust the warning when the boys were marching in 1970 and Rosie had had time to hide her tray, wrap a red cloth around her head and join their parade. She hadn't lost a thing and now Rosie's sugar cakes were bought by all the Black Power people. Rosie's tray was Elizabeth's main vantage point for Frederick Street, and it was through Rosie that Elizabeth had made friends in the barrack yards Behind the Bridge. Everyone was related to Rosie. Rosie had just whispered that John's wife Elaine was looking more and more like a soucouyant, up bright and early "foreday mornin" haunting down town, and that Ray Burnett and Bullseye Charlie looked as if the devil was catching up with them they were suddenly so mild, when Junior caught Elizabeth by the elbow. Rosie was particularly fond of Junior, she liked the way he wore his collar braked back like a man and he was always asking for his Aunt Elizabeth. The people Rosie liked were never those she prophesied would go far. It was a point on which she and Elizabeth disagreed. Junior had stood around for a while, shutting Rosie up with his presence and forcing her to push two shac shacs before a goggled, camera swinging, shirt-outside tourist. "Aunt Liz," he told Elizabeth, "where you been hidin', man, I haven't seen you for weeks."

"I have," Elizabeth assured him, pulling herself up, straightening an old fur around her shoulders, and pulling down her dress skirt, "been busy. Getting the country along proper lines is a hell of a job. You aren't finished with one thing when another starts up."

Junior agreed with her. Only the night before he and the boys had said the same thing. They had begun by wondering what they would do for Christmas. They would lime parangs at Arima now that the old custom had been revived. They had moved in imagination from one parang to the other, from one house to the other, dancing and singing and feteing. After that they had discussed a J'Ouvert morning band. They would play all the crazy people on the island. The little problem was who was crazy. They argued and argued over that. Each mad person had a backer among the boys who would produce cogent reasons for the person being perfectly sane. Everyone agreed that Elizabeth Grant was not mad at all, she had simply done what they all wished they could do. She had ditched the lot, "told them", Junior had said, "where to go and what to do when they got there", and she served as a reminder of the hypocrisy of their parents. She had been their friend, one of them – until she began shaking up the place. At first Junior had been ashamed of Aunt Elizabeth. Whenever she came to their house in Ellerslie Park a scandal would break out bringing the street to their verandas. He had feared meeting her, dirty half drunk on the corner of some street. He had had to live down the taunt of having an aunt who was known as "Stinking Fur Liz". As time went on shame turned to pride. He had moved into a group of boys who called themselves "The Gettysburg Patriots". Gettysburg had been chosen because someone had read Abraham Lincoln's address the day before they had to choose a name. Their main job was to bring Trinidad Culture to the schoolroom. They had emerged after the cultural anguish which followed the attempted revolution of 1970. They wrote poetry, painted, beat pan, went in force to parangs and calypso tents – and idolized Elizabeth. Last night he had been delegated to draw Elizabeth in as an honorary member of their group. They wanted her experience for the planning of their carnival J'Ouvert band.

The band this J'Ouvert was to be the culmination of their defiance, the manifesto of a new generation for a new society. The idea had arisen that night when his mother had stood on the veranda, her ragged hysterical voice one with her nervous face. There was something bordering on insanity in the way that she had come out, yelled, retreated, slamming doors and windows as if to escape something which was more than the harmless music that they were beating. Her housecoat was tied tightly around her waist, a pair of long hanging earrings jumped backwards and forwards. She seemed a wild haunted apparition which, in some inverted way, made what they were doing a revolution. After she had left they had named each other: Fidelista, Che Chica, Karlie Marx, Mao Meow, Malcolm, etcetera, and they had hit on the idea of a J'Ouvert band as their advertisement that the end had come. Elizabeth would lead it, carrying high the banner of the destruction from which would spring some unplanned future. The Pure One, they called her. Elizabeth the pure. For wasn't she untouched by the corruption, the disease that hollowed out his mother's eyes into dark mascara and ringed pencil? He had come upon Elizabeth once, carefully chalking a poem on a pavement to be erased by the passing feet hours later. He had seen her with a bundle of stolen faded flowers aimlessly talking to them and to herself. It was this Elizabeth to which he returned.

This evening Elizabeth was less drunk than she had been for months. The houses seemed starker, the streets straight, people distinguishable. She began her thinking where the calendar had interrupted her. It was impossible to analyse the "whys" in silence. Each attempt brought with it a desire to take another drink from the nip bottle she carried along with her. "I cannot let Junior meet me looking like an old hag," she told herself, "I used to be beautiful. When I walked into a room the whole room stopped, man. I'm not going to drink tonight. I'm going to talk over the past with Junior and plan for the future. Know your own past and the future will fend for itself. So we begin with the past." She kicked a tin can across the pavement. "Sounds like church bells, it's time for the 'Angelus'. Proof and the stars come out, one by one, one bright in the blue sky and then it's dark and on they come. Where shall I start? The wise men wandered over the desert until they came to a child in a manger. They followed stars. Wild dreams in the sky and proof one comes up, look yonder, Junior, proof one then two then a dozen and the Milky Way. Dreams that's where you begin and then madness. I'm not mad. But if I'm not, then what am I?" She stopped to consider it. "Dusk they call it. Twilight. Lasts a second and down the darkness and on the stars, flip on switch and on the stars. Can't count them. Shining above us. So on they walked across the desert to a hope that is a star. High in the sky, snap my fingers at them. Snap, snap thumb and finger. Last night I counted five hundred sitting on the pavement in one small space. Now if I had walked I could have found five hundred more, collected into an apron, gathered into a skirt, stars and they'd jump around sparkle around, spill over a Christmas tree. Eyes up, head up totter totter, I can almost walk straight heel first, toe next and in a line. Who says I'm drunk? The rum shops close at night for then they're the stars to give hope. But in the day oh they're cosy and we drink and klup klurp drink and kloop swallow and arrgh belcch, all drinking, waiting, equal. Looking alike and smelling alike and descending into hell. Finished. No, not that. Alike and ended and drunk and oh there's dreams in each eye. You can dream awake when you're drunk. The world merges into a cloud and there's nothing left that isn't fancy. All furry and slouched praying and all full of hope, drunk. Straight from the bottle, that's courage for you. Straight in a line toe after heel and a little bit, sway, like dem first-class women shaking their hips. Sway, Liz. Whew I used to be one of those and sometimes when I'm not drunk I remember and I feel myself pulled back in and going mad. When I'm not drunk something says: 'Liz, that's the way it is and it's no use fighting it.' It has always been like that, anything else is an illusion. But when I'm drunk then I see the truth that lives, faces, counters, buildings all are only part of a masquerade unreal world of pretence or hope. It's a choice. Sober and pretend, drunk or hope. Can't have both. Told that to Rosie this morning and she didn't believe me. I could see her thinking there goes crazy stinking Liz. But tell me who's sane if they don't go mad? Rosie is mad, give me a sugar cake that she could have sold to a bigtime tourist trying to escape into a holiday. Afraid, alone. I am so afraid of going back and afraid of staying out. There's a contradiction and I'm alone both ways. I can feel the pull back, back before the stars and back into it all and the past forgiven. What was the past? Let's see! It drops like darkness, swish down and I can't remember. If I drink I'll remember a little bit. But what? I feel as if, as if, Junior, I can't tell.

It makes me laugh the encounter with the future that is Junior or the future that hangs around waiting, waiting to be conceived. Carnival and we re-create the past in the present, I can tell him that. I'm afraid of that past and the future will exclude those like me, as if we weren't of one robe seamless and woven together without a stitch. Yourself is the best person to talk to. Once upon a time, so fairy stories begin because the past is only a tale, I used to address the people. Now I address myself and talk to myself a world within ours and body and head and feet and I can feel the aloneness as when, as now I hold out my finger-tips to trip them along the bars of a fence. Fast and it pains and you know that you exist and that hurt exists outside of you. Like people. So I talk to myself. I can mutter like water dripping down a wet hillside plip plop and a wet frond of a fern trembles. Plip and it glistens. Thoughts remain unstolen, and mad they are unsold unused, drunk they can be rustled apart to be stuck back into a puzzle. Carnival is the re-creation of the past. I said that before, didn't I?"

"Confessions. I have wanted to be great. Forgiveness for presumption. Forgive me father for I have sinned, I have wanted to be a saint. I confess that I hate it all and fear it all and love it all and that I would go back if the road was not blocked by the past and pot-holed by the future. Confession. I drink. Not too much, that's the problem, only enough to unload guilt on to a bottle. Junior is wrong. My mother suffered and my father suffered sacrificing today for what? For nothing any of us can repay them with. We sell them if we succeed and we sell them if we fail. Confession. I am the other side of Ray Burnett and of Elaine Grant. I hate them and I hate myself. HATE that's the way you spell hate. Creep up like a ghost and shoosh onto them out of the dark. Mother of the opt outs and the cop outs and those who refuse to build a future at all have mercy on us. We live roofless not even 'Zandolie find your hole' applies to us. Escaping torment in the illusion of drink and sanity in the illusion of madness. It's a fraud, it's not Stinking Fur Liz. I want to cry. To cry for myself. I used to be beautiful, do you know that? And clean, do you know that? I used to be and I want to be and I dare not be."

"Lord and our Lady, mercy. Power to the powerless, mercy. And we are the most powerless of all, threatening like my vomit yesterday – no, I wasn't drunk – to be spewed up, hiccuped up. Power, darlings, power. That's Junior, a power band, I'll lead it as I did that day when we sang to the end of the war and the beginning of peace. And I'll shoot my fist into the air, high out of despair. It will be enough to keep me sober for two damn days, drunkenness in itself."

"And middle class. From Woodbrook. A squared sterile place that used to be a plantation and that bred us in O'Connor Street, Gallus Street, Luis Street, Carlos Street, Alfredo Street, Cornelio Street. And I love it beyond talking or drinking or vomiting. It holds on to my heart and squeeze, squeeze and I hate myself, HATE, *Hate*. And hate it. HATE, *Hate*. It was pregnant with Ray Burnett, and Elaine Grant and with me too. Only a Behind the Bridge whored with St Clair. Aunt Dora and Douglah Mouse. That is history fer yer. Come on, fur, you're mink. God will awaken Woodbrook and Belmont and Cascade and Maraval and the statue will see. You're a fool, Stinking Fur Liz. You love it because it sleeps. Don't touch Woodbrook, leave it as it is. *Leave it*. A monument to dreams turned into nightmares. The skimping and the saving a blasted penny a day. Junior comes,

Aunt Liz, and I wish to return to Woodbrook out of the gutter. That's what they say. I'm in the gutter. But I made my vows. Mother Bridget was innocent. And the vows are poverty, chastity and obedience. To be innocent of money, love of power. That's Our Lady fer yer. Confession. We wanted all three. God, for a drink. Junior, I'll move a toast.

> Here's to Ash Wednesday morning.
> Hail Holy Queen, Mother of Mercy.
> Hail our life, our sweetness and our hope . . .

I haven't forgotten it, we used to say it after the rosary at lunchtime. St Joseph's Convent. Poor banished children of Eve. Ashes on your forehead in a cross. St Patrick's stands grey, sombre, shrugging aside its garden, unimpressed by the ghosts which walk and St Theresa's opens down its steps and on to the street. Pray for us Holy Mother of God. 'Hallelujah. Hallelujah,' said the Baptist woman, heads tied, hands clapping, shoulders swaying. 'Hallelujah,' she said with eyes closed and the Spirit descended groaning, shivering. 'Sing it out, sing it out. Eh, but leave something for we, na. Is every t'ing so dem spirits must t'ief?' Ray Burnett's mother, high priestess of the Children of Christ reformed, forehead knotted in purple cotton, a yellow embroidered black satin stole around her neck grabbed my elbow after Junior had left. 'Prayer, penance and mourning,' she continued whispering to me, 'for Ethopia shall arise saith the Lord. And then there shall be time for Hallelujahs and rejoicing. Scruntin' done.'"

Audre Lorde
1934–

B orn of Grenadian parentage in Harlem, New York, she describes
herself as "a black lesbian feminist warrior poet", writing importantly about the connection between sexism and racism. She
has a BA in literature and philosophy from Hunter College, MA from
Columbia University School of Library Science and also spent a year
at the University of Mexico. She was head librarian at City College,
New York, until 1968, after which she taught creative writing and was
poet-in-residence at Tougaloo College. She has lectured and read her
work internationally, addressing matters both personal and political.
She is the author of several books, of poems – The First Cities (1968),
Cables to Rage (1970), From a Land Where Other People Live (1973),
The New York Headshop and Museum (1975), Coal (1976), Between
Ourselves (1976), The Black Unicorn (1978), Chosen Poems – Old and
New (1982), Our Dead Behind Us (1987) – non-fiction, autobiography
and what she calls "biomythography" (fiction combining elements of
biography and history of myth), including The Cancer Journals (1980)
and Zami: A New Spelling of My Name (1982).

What My Child Learns of the Sea

What my child learns of the sea
Of the summer thunder
Of the bewildering riddle that hides at the vortex of spring
She will learn in my twilight
And childlike
Revise every autumn.

What my child learns
As her winters fall out of time
Ripened in my own body
To enter her eyes with first light.

That is why
More than blood
Or the milk I have given
One day a strange girl will step
To the back of a mirror
Cutting my ropes
Of sea and thunder and sun.
Of the way she will taste her autumns
Toast-brittle, or warmer than sleep
And the words she will use for winter
I stand already condemned.

Generation

How the young attempt and are broken
differs from age to age.
We were brown free girls
love singing beneath our skins
sun in our hair in our eyes
sun our fortune
and the wind had made us golden
made us gay.

In a season of limited power
we wept out our promises
and these are the children we try now
for temptations that wear our face.
But who comes back from our latched cities of falsehood
to warn them the road to nowhere
is slippery with our blood
to warn them
they need not drink the rivers to get home
for we have purchased bridges
with our mothers' bloody gold
and now we are more than kin
who have come to share
not only blood
but the bloodiness of failure.

How the young are tempted
and betrayed into slaughter
or conformity
is a turn of the mirror
Times question only.

Sonia Sanchez

1934–

B orn in Birmingham, Alabama, she was taken at the age of nine
to New York, grew up in Harlem, attended New York University
and has a BA in political science from Hunter College (1955).
Becoming involved in 1966 with the Black Studies movement at San
Francisco State College, she has taught Black literature and creative
writing at several institutions, including the University of Pittsburgh,
San Francisco State College, Rutgers University, Manhattan Community
College, Amherst College and Temple University. Mother of twin sons,
she has said: "My writing is a mixture of all that I do which includes
motherhood; thus, I am a writer because of my children – not in spite of
them." She has also said: "I am the continuation of Black women who have
gone before me and who will come after me. . . . I have tried to continue
the Black woman tradition of excellence." Her many books include
Homecoming (1969), We a BaddDDD People (1970), Love Poems (1973),
A Blues Book for Blue Black Magical Women (1974), I've Been a Woman:
New and Selected Poems (1978), Homegirls and Handgrenades: Poetry and
Prose (1984), Generations (1986) and Under a Soprano Sky (1987).

She edited the anthologies Three Hundred and Sixty Degrees of Blackness Comin' at You *(1971) and* We Be Word Sorcerers *(1973).*

Just Don't Never Give Up On Love

FEELING tired that day, I came to the park with the children. I saw her as I rounded the corner, sitting old as stale beer on the bench, ruminating on some uneventful past. And I thought, "Hell. No rap from the roots today. I need the present. On this day. This Monday. This July day buckling me under her summer wings, I need more than old words for my body to squeeze into."

I sat down at the far end of the bench, draping my legs over the edge, baring my back to time and time unwell spent. I screamed to the children to watch those curves threatening their youth as they rode their ten-speed bikes against midwestern rhythms.

I opened my book and began to write. They were coming again, those words insistent as his hands had been pounding inside me, demanding their time and place. I relaxed as my hands moved across the paper like one possessed.

I wasn't sure just what it was I heard. At first I thought it was one of the boys calling me so I kept on writing. They knew the routine by now. Emergencies demanded a presence. A facial confrontation. No long-distance screams across trees and space and other children's screams. But the sound pierced the pages and I looked around, and there she was inching her bamboo-creased body toward my back, coughing a beaded sentence off her tongue.

"Guess you think I ain't never loved, huh, girl? Hee. Hee. Guess that what you be thinking, huh?"

I turned. Startled by her closeness and impropriety, I stuttered, "I, I, I... Whhhaat dooooo you mean?"

"Hee. Hee. Guess you think I been old like this fo'ever, huh?" She leaned toward me, "Huh? I was so pretty that mens brought me breakfast in bed. Wouldn't let me hardly do no hard work at all."

"That's nice, ma'am. I'm glad to hear that." I returned to my book. I didn't want to hear about some ancient love that she carried inside her. I had to finish a review for the journal. I was already late. I hoped she would get the hint and just sit still. I looked at her out of the corner of my eyes.

"He could barely keep hisself in changing clothes. But he was pretty. My first husband looked like the sun. I used to say his name over and over again till it hung from my ears like diamonds. Has you ever loved a pretty man, girl?"

I raised my eyes, determined to keep a distance from this woman disturbing my day.

"No, ma'am. But I've seen many a pretty man. I don't like them though cuz they keep their love up high in a linen closet and I'm too short to reach it."

Her skin shook with laughter.

"Girl, you gots some spunk about you after all. C'mon over here next to me. I wants to see yo' eyes up close. You looks so uneven sittin over there."

Did she say uneven? Did this old buddah splintering death say uneven?

Couldn't she see that I had one eye shorter than the other; that my breath was painted on porcelain; that one breast crocheted keloids under this white blouse?

I moved toward her though. I scooped up the years that had stripped me to the waist and moved toward her. And she called to me to come out, come out wherever you are young woman, playing hide and go seek with scarecrow men. I gathered myself up at the gateway of her confessionals.

"Do you know what it mean to love a pretty man, girl?" She crooned in my ear. "You always running behind a man like that, girl, while he cradles his privates. Ain't no joy in a pretty yellow man, cuz he always out pleasurin' and givin' pleasure."

I nodded my head as her words sailed in my ears. Here was the pulse of a woman whose black ass shook the world once.

She continued. "A woman crying all the time is pitiful. Pitiful, I says. I wuz pitiful sitting by the window every night like a cow in the fields chewin' on cud. I wanted to cry out, but not even God hisself could hear me. I tried to cry out till my mouth wuz split open at the throat. I 'spoze there is a time all womens has to visit the slaughter house. My visit lasted five years."

Touching her hands, I felt the summer splintering in prayer; touching her hands, I felt my bones migrating in red noise. I asked, "When did you see the butterflies again?"

Her eyes wandered like quicksand over my face. Then she smiled, "Girl, don't you know yet that you don't never give up on love? Don't you know you has in you the pulse of winds? The noise of dragon flies?" Her eyes squinted close and she said, "One of them mornings he woke up callin' me and I wuz gone. I wuz gone running with the moon over my shoulders. I looked no which way at all. I had inside me 'nough knives and spoons to cut/scoop out the night. I wuz a tremblin' as I met the mornin'."

She stirred in her 84-year-old memory. She stirred up her body as she talked. "They's men and mens. Some good. Some bad. Some breathing death. Some breathing life. William wuz my beginnin'. I come to that man spittin' metal and he just pick me up and fold me inside him. I wuz christen' with his love."

She began to hum. I didn't recognize the song; it was a prayer. I leaned back and listened to her voice rustling like silk. I heard cathedrals and sonnets; I heard tents and revivals and a black woman spilling black juice among her ruins.

"We all gotta salute death one time or 'nother, girl. Death be waitin' outdoors trying to get inside. William died at his job. Death just turned 'round and snatched him right off the street."

Her humming became the only sound in the park. Her voice moved across the bench like a mutilated child. And I cried. For myself. For this woman talkin' about love. For all the women who have ever stretched their bodies out anticipating civilization and finding ruins.

The crashing of the bikes was anticlimactic. I jumped up, rushed toward the accident. Man. Little man. Where you bicycling to so very fast? Man. Second little man. Take it slow. It all passes so fast any how.

As I walked the boys and their bikes toward the bench, I smiled at this old woman waiting for our return.

"I want you to meet a great lady, boys."

"Is she a writer, too, ma?"

"No, honey. She's a lady who has lived life instead of writing about it."

"After we say hello, can we ride a little while longer? Please!"

"OK. But watch your manners now and your bones afterwards."

"These are my sons, ma'am."

"How you do, sons? I'm Mrs Rosalie Johnson. Glad to meet you."

The boys shook her hand and listened for a minute to her words. Then they rode off, spinning their wheels on a city neutral with pain.

As I stood watching them race the morning, Mrs Johnson got up.

"Don't go," I cried. "You didn't finish your story."

"We'll talk by-and-by. I comes out here almost everyday. I sits here on the same bench everyday. I'll probably die sittin' here one day. As good a place as any I 'magine."

"May I hug you, ma'am? You've helped me so much today. You've given me strength to keep on looking."

"No. Don't never go looking for love, girl. Just wait. It'll come. Like the rain fallin' from the heaven, it'll come. Just don't never give up on love."

We hugged; then she walked her 84-year-old walk down the street. A black woman. Echoing gold. Carrying couplets from the sky to crease the ground.

Zulu [Nwazulu] Sofola

1931–

Long Nigeria's only woman playwright, she was born of Igbo parentage in Bendel State, though she spent her adolescence and early womanhood in the USA, attending Southern Baptist Seminary, Nashville, and earning a BA in English at Virginia Union University and an MA in drama (1965) from the Catholic University of

*America, Washington, DC. Returning to Nigeria in 1966, she lectured in
the Department of Theatre Arts, University of Ibadan (where she obtained
a PhD in Drama) and currently is head of the Department of Performing
Arts at the University of Ilorin. She has written and directed many plays
for stage and television, including her own work, such as* King Emene.
*Among her other dramatic works, which range from historical tragedy
to domestic comedy and use both traditional and modern African settings, are* Wedlock of the Gods *(1970),* The Disturbed Peace of Christmas
(1971), The Wizard of Law *(1976) and* Old Wines Are Tasty *(1981). The
following extract is from her 1977 play,* The Sweet Trap, *a satire set
on a Nigerian university campus, dealing with the revolt of Mrs Clara
Sotubo, a well-educated young woman, against her husband's decree
that her annual birthday party may not be organized that year.*

From

The Sweet Trap

ACT I

SCENE ONE

*At Sotubo's house. It is supper time and Clara is busily preparing supper
while John sets the table. A loud riotous noise of festival music is heard
in the background rising to a crescendo, then suddenly coming to a stop.
Clara is attracted by the unusual noise and its sudden stop; she asks almost
absent-mindedly:*

CLARA: What was that?

JOHN [*in pidgin English*]: I tink say na Okebadan people, ma.

CLARA: That was an unusual noise for their activities. What [*not really addressing
John*] could be happening there?

JOHN: Na so dem want do-am dis year, madam.

CLARA: Where are the hot-pads for the table?

JOHN: Dem de inside, madam.

CLARA: Get them.

JOHN: Yes, madam. [*Goes for them; a knock at the door with the door opening
almost immediately.*]

MRS AJALA: Good evening, my dear [*talking while she enters.*]

CLARA [*moving towards her with pleasure*]: Good evening, Mrs Ajala. Is something wrong?

MRS AJALA: Those beasts out there are going beyond all limits of decency!

CLARA: The noise of a minute ago?

MRS AJALA: They are getting worse and worse every year.

CLARA: It's amazing how the government is doing absolutely nothing about this primitive festival.

MRS AJALA: How could it? The government is run exclusively by the male species, you know. The Okebadan festival is a ridicule of the female organs and nothing could be more exciting to the men than a legalized opportunity to take a swipe at us women.

CLARA [becoming engrossed in Mrs Ajala's exposition]: But wasn't Okebadan a festival of fertility?

MRS AJALA: In a male-dominated society, fertility means femininity.

CLARA: So it is our sex that this festival ridicules?

MRS AJALA: Obviously. Have you ever seen the participants ridiculing male sex organs? Mark you, the attack on the sexes in this rowdy festival was not originally restricted to the female sex only. It was only in recent years when our women began to resist male domination and brutality that this festival degenerated into a rowdy display where men could take revenge for their bruised egos.

CLARA [returns to preparing the table for supper]: That is just too bad. They will certainly have to do more than just ridicule our sexual sanctity.

MRS AJALA: Sometimes, of course, I feel sorry for them especially as it is crystal clear that their all-out war against our sex is bound to be wasted effort. But power is power; power intoxicates, it blinds. Men have enjoyed untold powers in this society for centuries and would resist any threat.

CLARA: But the movement is on.

MRS AJALA: Yes, and nothing can stop it.

CLARA [pause]: I didn't ask what you would like to drink.

MRS AJALA: Nothing, my dear.

CLARA: Not even some mild wine?

MRS AJALA: No, thank you. Those lunatics out there have got me out of tune. I was forced to take to my heels when it seemed they meant business.

CLARA: The women of this city should protest to the government.

MRS AJALA: We are getting ready for that. The Committee is presenting a paper on it at the next meeting.

CLARA: I hope they use language these men understand.

MRS AJALA: I am sure we will. [Pause.] Actually I came to see how plans are coming along for the birthday anniversary.

CLARA: I am still seriously at it.

MRS AJALA: Is he still opposed to it?

CLARA: Very much so, but his antagonistic disposition makes very little difference. My birthday anniversary will be celebrated willy-nilly.

MRS AJALA: You should maintain your stand, my dear. Don't yield an inch.

CLARA: Don't worry. I know what I want and I will get it, come what may.
[*The door opens to admit Dr Sotubo.*
Mrs Ajala rises automatically as she greets him.]

MRS AJALA: Good evening, Dr Sotubo. [*Realizes that she is standing and tries to underplay the fact that she had risen for him.*]

DR SOTUBO [*greets her with controlled warmth*]: Good evening, Mrs Ajala. How is the family?

MRS AJALA: We are well, thank you.

DR SOTUBO: How are things these days of traditional festivals?

MRS AJALA: There couldn't be a better time for fun, especially for you men who seize this opportunity to rail on us women folk.

DR SOTUBO [*laughs*]: It is interesting, isn't it, that our forefathers understood the value of psychological and emotional release of tensions. Okebadan is the epitome of their understanding of the human psyche.

MRS AJALA: Especially when this psyche has to do with boosting of the male ego, eh?

DR SOTUBO [*gets the idea*]: I believe that the battle of the sexes never existed in their times. The roles were so clearly defined and each person so meticulously upheld the *status quo* that nothing like the confusion of roles was ever dreamt of. Everyone knew his place and stayed there.

MRS AJALA: Is that so?

DR SOTUBO: Certainly.

MRS AJALA: How do you explain the one-sided attack on the female sex in Okebadan festival then?

DR SOTUBO: The female organs are more interesting, and may I add, infinitely more exciting. [*A glance at Clara with a grin.*]

MRS AJALA: I see. So rather than worship and adore it as the people of the civilized world do, our men decided to attack it.

DR SOTUBO: Well, that was how our forebears felt and so it was.

MRS AJALA: And that's that?

DR SOTUBO: What else? Our mothers never complained and I see no reason why anyone should now raise an eyebrow.

CLARA: No one is raising an eyebrow. Mrs Ajala was only making an interesting observation.

MRS AJALA: Well, I hope I have not hurt feelings. It was only an observation. I should be going now.

CLARA: I would have invited you to supper.

MRS AJALA: No thank you. I have to go now.

DR SOTUBO: You will please excuse me. I have to wash up for supper.

MRS AJALA: It's all right. [*To Clara*:] I shall see you later my dear.
   [*Exit Dr Sotubo.*]

CLARA: I am sorry for all this.

MRS AJALA: It's nothing at all. I am used to getting such from our uncouth men.
   [*At the door*:] Good evening, my dear.

CLARA: Bye-bye. [*Shuts the door, ponders a bit and goes to the table to
   finish setting it up for supper. Sotubo enters.*]

DR SOTUBO: Is she gone?

CLARA [*obviously annoyed with him*]: Is who gone?

DR SOTUBO: Your guest.

CLARA: Didn't you intend to drive her away?

DR SOTUBO: Me, drive Mrs Ajala away?

CLARA: It wouldn't be the first time. It has now become your favourite sport
   to drive my friends away.

DR SOTUBO [*sees where things are leading and ignores her remark*]: Is supper
   ready? [*Clara ignores him and steps into the kitchen. He looks around a bit
   and goes for the newspaper. John enters bringing food to the table.*]

CLARA [*announces disinterestedly*]: Supper is ready. [*Dr Sotubo lingers a second
   then goes to the table and takes his seat. His wife sits a few seconds after. A
   pause, then Dr Sotubo reaches for the rice dish; serves himself and puts the
   dish anywhere on the table. He serves himself with the stew and the vegetable.
   All the while Clara looks on with disgust; he pays her no attention. After
   serving himself he starts eating.*] Femi, you have done it again.

DR SOTUBO [*busy eating*]: I have done what again?

CLARA: Can't you see?

DR SOTUBO: See what?

CLARA: Don't tell me you don't know that the rice dish is not on the hot-pad.

DR SOTUBO: Hot-pad. Oh, well . . . [*He sets the rice dish on the hot-pad and
   continues to eat as if nothing had happened.*]

CLARA: It seems I have to remind you each time that civilized people know
   what to do at the table.

DR SOTUBO [*trying to control himself*]: Eat your supper.

CLARA: Why should I eat my supper?

DR SOTUBO: Let me eat mine if you don't want yours. I am very hungry.

CLARA: Every time I must remind you that this table-cloth cost me fifty naira. . .

DR SOTUBO [*anticipates the next phrase and starts it with her*]: "... and ten naira to ship it from England." I know but let me eat in peace for once. I am very hungry.

CLARA: That's all we know how to do in this house, food!

DR SOTUBO [*ignores her*]: John!

JOHN [*entering*]: Sir.

DR SOTUBO: Bring more chicken.

CLARA: There is no more chicken.

JOHN: Yes, sah. [*He is caught in between.*]
    CLARA: Where is the drinking water?

JOHN: Sorry, ma; I don forget 'am, I beg ...

CLARA: Idiot, fool, jackass! [*He runs off and returns promptly with a bottle of water.*] Fill our glasses!

JOHN: Yes, ma ...

CLARA: Look at him. Don't pour water on my table-cloth.

DR SOTUBO: Give him a chance.

CLARA: Let me handle this.
    [*Pause.*]

DR SOTUBO [*to John*]: Pass me the chicken.

JOHN [*he is somewhat nervous and fumbles*]: Yes, sah.

DR SOTUBO [*takes a chicken leg*]: Put the plate back.

JOHN: Yes, sah.

CLARA: Get out of here!

JOHN: Yes, madam. [*Exit.*]

CLARA [*helps herself to some chicken; her husband is chewing hard on his piece of chicken*]: Must you chew your chicken that hard? [*He ignores her and chews even harder.*] Femi, the noise from your chicken is blasting my eardrums.

DR SOTUBO: Clara, if I could blast those cursed ears of yours with my chicken bone, I would congratulate myself.

CLARA: Femi, withdraw that abuse.

DR SOTUBO: I said that if Femi Sotubo could burst those cursed elephant ears of yours with the noise of my chewing I would congratulate myself for my success!

CLARA: Olufemi Sotubo, I said to ...

DR SOTUBO: This is my castle, my kingdom, and I am the the king here...

CLARA [*interrupts him with unexpected hearty laugh. John re-enters; she unwittingly addresses John*]: Did you hear what he said? [*John is baffled.*] Femi

Sotubo is the king of this kingdom. Femi, you are very funny. [*John returns to the kitchen with chicken dish.*]

DR SOTUBO [*trying to check her*]: You must never forget that I am the man here. . .

CLARA: Dr Olufemi Sotubo, a man who flies after every skirt on the street has no kingdom. If this house is anybody's kingdom at all, it is mine. And I do whatever I deem fit in this castle. [*A knock at the door which calls them to a halt; a pause.*]

DR SOTUBO: John.

JOHN [*re-enters*]: Sah.

DR SOTUBO: Answer the door.
[*Clara steps into the bedroom.*]

JOHN [*opens the door to Mrs Oyegunle's steward*]: Na Amos, sah.

AMOS: Good evening, sah.

DR SOTUBO: What have you come for?

AMOS: Na my madam send me, sah.

DR SOTUBO: A message for me?

AMOS: No sah, na for madam, sah.
[*Enter Clara.*]

CLARA: Oh, Amos. A message from madam?

AMOS: Yes, madam. She say make I tell you say she go come for dee party.

DR SOTUBO: What party?

AMOS: Na dee party wey . . .

CLARA [*interrupting him*]: Tell her I will be expecting her.

AMOS: Yes, madam. Good night, sah, good night, madam.

CLARA: Good night, Amos.
[*Amos leaves; Clara heads for the bedroom; Sotubo stops her.*]

DR SOTUBO: What party was that?

CLARA: What party do you think it is?

DR SOTUBO: You don't mean you are still contemplating having that birthday anniversary.

CLARA: Yes, I am going ahead with it.

DR SOTUBO: After I have objected to it in clear terms?

CLARA: Yes, I am proceeding with the party in spite of your objections.

DR SOTUBO: And my decisions as to what should happen in my own house carry no weight?

CLARA: If the order is arrived at through a consensus of opinion by all parties concerned. . .

DR SOTUBO: Wonderful! Has it come to the point where every order I give in this house, every position I take in this place, every instruction I give here must be contemptuously thrown through the window?

CLARA: Did you think I would blindly accept orders from you without scrutinizing them first?

DR SOTUBO [*as if to the audience*]: Femi Sotubo cannot give an instruction in his own house and be assured that when he returns his orders will still be standing?

CLARA: You will find your instructions still standing if they can withstand the test of critical analysis, rational diagnosis, and intelligent scrutiny.

DR SOTUBO: Wonderful!

CLARA: You should have known that with my degree, I cannot be pushed around by the inflated ego of an undisciplined male partner. I stand on equal grounds with you and cannot be forced into any action that is against good reasoning.

DR SOTUBO [*suddenly grips her by the arms*]: To hell with you!

CLARA: Eh, Femi.

[*He pushes her into a chair still in his strong grip.*]

JOHN: Softly. sah.

DR SOTUBO: Get it into your head once and for all that your university education does not raise you above the illiterate fish seller in the market. Your degree does not make the slightest difference. You are a woman and must be treated as a subordinate. Your wishes, your desires and your choices are subject to my pleasure and mood. Anything I say is law and unalterable. When I say something, it stays; whether you like it our not, clear?

CLARA [*shocked and dumbfounded*]: You are breaking my arm.

DR SOTUBO: I won't mind breaking you into pieces if that will put some sense into you. [*Still holding her down into the seat.*] Now, that damned party of yours must be cancelled forthwith. You will not have it now, and you will not have it hereafter until I instruct you to the contrary. Your mention of anything about a birthday anniversary depends on whether or not I wake up one morning feeling like saying anything about your birthday, clear? [*Pushes her hard into the seat.*] Now, no more nonsense. [*Leaves her gradually with a steady stare into her face. She stares back at him, saying absolutely nothing.*] John, give me my coat.

JOHN: Yes, sah. [*Leaves and re-enters promptly with his suit coat; Sotubo takes the coat, puts it on; gives Clara one very hard look; takes his car key and heads outside. Car is heard driving off wildly.*]

CLARA [*rises slowly from the chair*]: He has gone too far this time. He'll see how I repay him. [*To John:*] John, fetch me my handbag.

JOHN: Yes, /madam. [*Leaves and re-enters with the handbag.*]

CLARA [*straightens up; snatches the handbag from John*]: He will smell pepper from me. [*Takes her car key from her handbag and heads outside.*] He will see hell from me. [*Leaves and slams the door behind her; car is heard driving off wildly.*]

JOHN [*looks on a second*]: I no sabi dis kind wahala-o.

SCENE TWO

[*At Dr Oyegunle's house. Both Fatima and Mrs Ajala are entering from the bedroom with some newly bought materials in hand. Mrs Ajala walks in front of Fatima and admires some of the materials as she talks.*]

FATIMA: And we will win.
　　[*A knock at the door.*]

CLARA: Mrs Oyegunle, I want to see Mrs Ajala.

MRS AJALA: Open the door quickly. It seems urgent.

FATIMA [*to Clara*]: I am coming. [*Opens the door and finds a very disturbed Clara.*] Mrs Sotubo, what is the matter?

MRS AJALA: My dear, what did your husband do to you?

CLARA [*trying to hold back tears*]: That beast!

MRS OKON: He laid his dirty hands on you?

MRS AJALA [*to Fatima*]: Fetch a glass of water. [*Fatima leaves for the water.*] Sit down and try to calm down. [*Fatima re-enters with a glass of water; Mrs Ajala takes it and tries to get Clara to drink some.*] Here is a glass of cold water. Take some and settle down a bit.

CLARA [*takes a sip*]: That beast has done the unbelievable! [*Tries again to hold back tears.*]

FATIMA: Please, don't be upset.

MRS AJALA: Did that brute lay his ugly hands on you?

CLARA: He broke a bottle of beer on my head and dared me to make a whimper. [*Breaks down in tears.*]

MRS AJALA: Impossible!

MRS OKON: And what did you do to him?

FATIMA [*trying to show off some learned phrase*]: Oh God, save us from the barbarity of the human beast.

CLARA: I was too dumbfounded . . . [*still crying*].

MRS AJALA: That animal of a husband beat this woman up because I dared to challenge him on the humiliation to which Okebadan celebrants subject the female citizens of this city. I tore asunder his pampered ego, so he chose this cheap way to retaliate.

CLARA: Me, daughter of lines of Balogun warriors, to be so terribly humiliated.

MRS AJALA: Never mind. We are fully armed for them. You have made the right decision. We shall all pull our forces together. Let us finish with your birthday anniversary first.

CLARA [*bursts into tears*]: There is not going to be a birthday anniversary.

MRS AJALA: No party?

CLARA: No party.

MRS OKON: For you?

CLARA: For me.

MRS AJALA [*to Fatima*]: Did you hear that?

FATIMA: I heard it.

MRS AJALA: Mrs Clara Kikelomo Oluremilekun Sotubo. You are going to have your birthday anniversary, dead or alive. That house is not the only home in town, is it?

FATIMA: Of course not.

MRS AJALA: We are going to have this party in this house. [*To Fatima:*] It will be a fight to finish.

FATIMA: We shall fight!

MRS AJALA [*to Fatima*]: Now, start things moving. This is already Thursday and we haven't got much time. Clara, contact all your invitees and give them notice of change of venue. I shall pour petrol where necessary.

MRS OKON: I still have some party decorations from last month.

CLARA [*to Fatima*]: Is the plan agreeable with you?

FATIMA: Fine by me.

MRS OKON: Like I always say, most men are beasts and the best among them are infants.

MRS AJALA [*to the audience*]: One has to show these men fire before they take one seriously. My husband was the worst of the pack until I showed him pepper. He decided to take to his heels, thinking that I would go looking for him. He learnt differently and has since been too ashamed to show his face.

FATIMA: Shame.

MRS AJALA: Look at Mrs Clara Sotubo, a degree holder from one of our best universities; an academician who has undergone the most scholarly discipline in the world; an intellectual who has attained the zenith of academic distinction, to be so meanly treated by a mere man.

FATIMA: We must fight!

MRS AJALA [*to Clara*]: Your fight is our fight. We must triumph!

FATIMA: We must win!

CLARA [*reassured of support*]: Sisters, I came here a few minutes earlier feeling terribly bruised; but your comforting words and support have renewed my courage and refuelled my energy. Femi will have to take it or leave it.

FATIMA: Right!

MRS AJALA: Sisters, the fight is on! Good evening and God bless you! [*Leaves*]

FATIMA: Amen!

MRS OKON: My dear Clara, don't give up. We are all with you.

CLARA: Thank you very much.

MRS OKON. I shall see you later. [*Exit.*]

CLARA [*to Fatima*]: I shall return early in the morning with all the things for the party. We don't have much time.

FATIMA: I shall start with what I have.

CLARA: Thank you very much.

FATIMA: Do gently-o.

CLARA: Good night.

FATIMA: Good night. [*Clara leaves; she pulls out from a cupboard some left-over party items, tries to sort out good ones; steps outside for something when Dr Oyegunle and Dr Sotubo enter from outside obviously enjoying a joke. Dr Oyegunle is surprised to find party items and newly bought clothes.*]

DR OYEGUNLE: What are all these?

DR SOTUBO: Your wife must be preparing for something.

DR OYEGUNLE: Couldn't be. We are not anticipating any function.

DR SOTUBO: You know how women suddenly have a brain wave. Nothing pleases them as much as a money-burning function.

DR OYEGUNLE: There is no such function. [*Still pondering.*]

DR SOTUBO: There is always a big function ticking at the back of their minds. My wife was seriously entertaining an idea for a big birthday party until I put a stop to it.

DR OYEGUNLE: Please have a seat while I prepare some drinks.

DR SOTUBO: Thank you. [*Sits.*] I had to get that nonsense off her head immediately.

*   *   *

DR JINADU: It was your auntie that persuaded me to come, so you owe her some thanks.

CLARA [*to Mrs Jinadu*]: Thank you very much, auntie.

MRS JINADU: Don't mention. You know how men can be stubborn when they think they are in the right.

CLARA: Thank you very much, Auntie. I know that you are angry with me, Uncle, but you will see that I have friends who know how much these things mean to us ladies.

DR JANADU: I can see that already. The party is bigger than I had expected.

CLARA: It is only that my husband complains about the wrong things, uncle. Most people think the way I think.

MRS JINADU: Let us join the others at the table.

DR JINADU: Where is your husband?

CLARA: He is busy inside with the drinks.

DR JINADU: That is good. He has obviously changed his mind.

CLARA: He had to, uncle.

MRS JINADU: Don't say that, my dear. Men don't like to feel they have been pressurized into doing anything.

DR OYEGUNLE [*joining them*]: Good evening, sir.

DR JINADU: Good evening, my dear chap.

DR OYEGUNLE: Good evening, madam. We are glad you could come.

MRS JINADU: Thank you.

DR OYEGUNLE: Please, come and serve yourselves.

DR JINADU: Thank you.

> [*As they serve themselves Dr Sotubo enters and goes to greet them. Everybody is busy serving themselves, eating and drinking. The jollof rice has entirely too much pepper. Prof. Davis and his wife are coughing with pepper. Some of the other guests are showing signs of it on their faces. Clara notices what's happening and is getting worried. Some other guests are pretending all is well. Mrs Ajala has gone for water for Prof. Davis. Fatima is wondering what's happening.*]

CLARA [*to Fatima*]: You must have poured all the pepper in the world into the rice.

FATIMA: It was only *ata rodo*. I put just small. I did not put any *ata wewe*.

CLARA: You put just small and everybody is coughing because of your poor cooking?

FATIMA: Ah . . . I did not know . . .

CLARA: I should have known better.

MRS JINADU [*interrupting*]: There is no need to panic. Everything will be all right.

CLARA: Auntie, her cooking is spoiling my party.

FATIMA: I put only *ata rodo*. It was only *ata rodo*. I did not put the small pepper. It was only *ata rodo*.

MRS JINADU: Big men don't eat as much pepper as our local people do.

CLARA: Auntie, she is too local to know that.

FATIMA: I am local, eh . . .

MRS JINADU: No, no. This is not the place for a fight. Let us get things under control. [*Mrs Ajala, Dr Sotubo and Dr Oyegunle have finally got things under some control. Most plates have been returned to the table with food untouched. Bola, Yetunde and Ngozi help clear the table of food. Salami puts on a good dancing record of either high-life, juju or rumba. People start dancing in an attempt to compensate for the inability to eat the hot-peppered rice.*]

DR SOTUBO [*to Mrs Ajala*]: Shall we have this dance?

MRS AJALA: Why not" [*They dance.*]
[*Clara goes back to her seat quite upset. Dr Azuka asks her for a dance.*]

DR AZUKA: Shall we honour your birthday anniversary with a dance?

CLARA: Well, why not? [*They dance.*]

MRS AJALA [*to Dr Sotubo*]: I hope you are having a good time this fine evening.

DR SOTUBO: Certainly. Who wouldn't with such a fabulous gathering?

MRS AJALA: Friends are good to have, aren't they?

DR SOTUBO: Surely. My wife has many good friends.

MRS AJALA: Reliable and trustworthy friends, I should say.

DR SOTUBO: Of course.

MRS AJALA: It has been my life philosophy always to flow in the goodly company of friends.

DR SOTUBO: Good friends are the *sine qua non* of life.

MRS AJALA: Indeed. [*They dance in silence for a second.*] I know that were it not for friends, Mrs Sotubo would have found this vital birthday celebration absolutely impossible.

DR SOTUBO: Perhaps so.

MRS AJALA: I know so. Certain unnecessary obstacles were being thrust in her way from some quarters. But thank heavens, those obstacles were conquered. We can now boast of another birthday anniversary added to the successes of the past. [*Music fades out.*]

DR SOTUBO: Congratulations!

FATIMA [*tries to get the people's attention. She carries a birthday cake held high; one candle on it*]: Ladies and gentlemen, we are ready for a very important part of tonight's party. [*People admire the cake and settle down.*] The cake is here, honourable Invitees! I have nothing much to say but Mrs Cecilia Ajala has a few words to say before our guest of honour and important celebrant cuts this lovely cake. [*Guests clap.*] Let me now call our dear friend and supporter to the front. Mrs Cecilia Ajala, our big sister!

MRS AJALA [*walks deliberately to the centre near Fatima in a matronly manner with airs of authority and justification*]: Ladies and gentlemen, I welcome each and every one of you here with heart-felt warmth. I would be deceiving myself if I told you that I expected to see anyone here this evening. [*Some whispers from the guests.*] The number of people here this evening shows that Mrs Clara Sotubo has friends of worth and value. I know, as a very close friend, what Mrs Sotubo had to overcome before this party could get on its feet. A leaf in an individual's chronological advance comes only once in a life-time, and when it passes it is gone for ever. It is for this reason that people with foresight, a good sense of value and an appreciation for the preciousness of life make it a point to mark the onset of a new leaf in the book of life. Our friend, Mrs Sotubo, has done it again this year, and I thank you for coming out in full force to help make this day a memorable one. I also express our appreciation to Mrs Oyegunle who made this occasion possible. Many things have proved this evening that a friend in need is a friend indeed. [*The guests clap.*] Mrs Sotubo has a few words to say.

CLARA [*trying hard to suppress her anger, she rises slowly and clears her throat*]: Ladies and gentlemen, I am most grateful to you for this honour done to me. My heart is touched with a new life and a renewed faith in the magnanimity of mankind. A few days ago my heart was heavy for fear that this day might never arrive. But thank God for good friends like you, especially Mrs Ajala who did not sleep until this day's celebration became a reality. I am indeed overwhelmed with joy. Thank you very much. [*Guests clap; Dr Oyegunle picks up a glass of wine and toasts to Mrs Sotubo's happiness. Clara, Mrs Ajala and Fatima are somewhat surprised.*]

DR OYEGUNLE: Shall we toast to the happiness and health of our great celebrant. [*Guests raise their glasses high and say almost in unison, "To the happiness and health of our great celebrant." They all drink. Dr Oyegunle starts the song "For she's a jolly good fellow", the guests join in; then voices outside join in the singing; the guests gradually stop but the intruders outside continue and become more boisterous; they sound drunk. The guests are stunned; Clara and Mrs Ajala are terribly disturbed, they frantically look to Dr Sotubo and Dr Oyegunle to do something; they are equally surprised and show great concern.*]

DR OYEGUNLE: John, go and drive those people away. Amos, join him.

JOHN & AMOS: Yes, sir. [*Not in unison; they go outside; there is a scuffle.*]

AMOS: Waitin you Ibadan people want here?

JOHN: Go away! Dis not dee place for Okebadan.

FIRST INTRUDER: Dis na Ibadan, abi? Make you comout, jare.

AMOS: Make unua no make wahala for my master-o.

DR OYEGUNLE [*to guests*]: Please, ladies and gentlemen, be calm. Things will get under control shortly.

SECOND INTRUDER: We no go make wahala for you master-o. He like fine sisi like me, abi?

FATIMA [*to Mrs Ajala*]: What are we going to do?
[*Clara is stunned.*]

DR OYEGUNLE [*to Fatima*]: Don't worry. I shall drive them away.

MRS AJALA: Ladies and gentlemen, please continue with the party. Everything will soon be brought under control.

DR SOTUBO [*to Dr Oyegunle*]: Shouldn't we call the police?

DR OYEGUNLE: Please do.
[*Dr Sotubo goes to telephone and begins dialling.*]

JOHN [*a struggle at the door*]: Ejo, make unua go away-o. Dee party no be for unua-o. [*First Intruder subdues John and bursts in. A pause.*]

FIRST INTRUDER: Good evening, ladies and gentlemen! [*He hiccups; looks behind for Second Intruder.*] Wey my darling now?

SECOND INTRUDER: I deh come jare. [*He enters; he is dressed in women's clothes and a mini; wears high heels, high wig, large earrings and is very heavily made-up. He tries hard to be feminine but his hard masculine features are very conspicuous; First Intruder is dressed like a cowboy and is heavily drunk while his partner is mildly drunk.*]

DR OYEGUNLE: Get out of here!

FIRST INTRUDER: Ah . . . na waitin? Abi we no fine? [*Hiccups again and makes a vomiting attempt at Dr Oyegunle who in turn is taken back.*]

SECOND INTRUDER [*to First Intruder*]: E rora-o.

FIRST INTRUDER: O jare.
[*Sotubo is still trying to get the police whose line is engaged. First Intruder flirts with Mrs Okon; Dr Okon protects her; they move away.*]

CLARA [*to her uncle and in tears*]: Uncle, they have ruined me.

DR OKON [*to his wife*]: Shall we go, darling?

DR JINADU: Don't worry. We shall soon get things under control.

CLARA [*nearly in tears*]: They have ruined me.

MRS JINADU: Come on. [*Takes her away into a room.*] Be calm.

SECOND INTRUDER [*struts like a woman of class*]: Ladies and gentlemen, I salute unua. [*Dr Oyegunle and Fatima panic.*]

FIRST INTRUDER [*flirtatiously slaps Second Intruder on the buttocks*]: Hello, my fine sisi.

SECOND INTRUDER: E rora-o. [*Giggles in a flirtatiously tantalizing manner.*]

FIRST INTRUDER [*to the audience*]: Na fine lady, abi? [*He pecks Second Intruder on the cheek, then struts away to the food table.*]

SECOND INTRUDER: I likam. He be lion.

[*Guests are starting to leave. Dr Oyegunle and Dr Sotubo appear helpless though still trying hard to restore order.*]

FIRST INTRUDER [*coming back munching piece of cake to Mrs Ajala*]: Hel. . .l. . .o, Mrs Beelzebub! [*She backs up with fury; guests have almost gone.*]

DR OYEGUNLE [*roughly handles First Intruder*]: Get your bloody self out of here.

FIRST INTRUDER: Ah . . . na waitin, oga?

SECOND INTRUDER: Dem no want fine people like we. Make we go, jare. [*Seeing that they have accomplished their mission.*]

FIRST INTRUDER: Make we go, jare. I no want man wey don drink belleful come spoil my body.

DR JINADU: You people must leave immediately.

FIRST INTRUDER: Ah . . . ah. Baba, se we don say we want go.

DR OYEGUNLE: Then get going.

[*First and Second Intruder leave of their own accord.*]

SECOND INTRUDER: Good night, ladies and gentlemen. [*Giggles flirtatiously, then they depart.*]

MRS AJALA: I can't believe this. Somebody must have sent them.

MRS JINADU [*as she re-enters from the bedroom*]: I'm sure nobody sent them. I have told my husband too often about the way ruffians are penetrating this reservation.

FATIMA [*in tears*]: I am sorry.

MRS JINADU: It was not your fault, my dear.

DR SOTUBO [*re-enters from the bedroom with Clara very depressed and in tears*]: This is unbelievable!

DR OYEGUNLE: I am terribly sorry. Please, help me apologize to madam.

FATIMA: I am sorry [*to Clara; still in tears, Clara is saying nothing*].

DR JINADU: Fellows, please pour oil on this troubled water. We must search out the root cause of this sabotage.

DR SOTUBO [*takes his wife's handbag, takes Clara by the waist and heads outside*]: Goodnight, everyone. [*They leave.*]

DR JINADU [*to Dr Oyegunle*]: I am sorry for this.

DR OYEGUNLE: Thank you, sir. [*Dr and Mrs Jinadu leave. Fatima is crying.*] Please, take it calmly.

FATIMA: The first time I am doing a big party. Those people came and spoilt it.

DR OYEGUNLE: We shall deal with them severely. [*He leads her to the bedroom consoling her as lights fade to blackout.*]

Lucille Clifton
1936–

orn in Depew, New York, she won a scholarship to Howard University at sixteen but left after two years, then attended Fredonia State Teachers' College. She has been Poet-in-Residence at Coppin State College, Baltimore, Visiting Writer at Columbia University School of Arts and a professor at other US universities. Among her works of poetry, which have won awards and earned her Pulitzer Prize nominations, are Good Times (1970), Good News About the Earth (1972), An Ordinary Woman (1974) and Two-Headed Woman (1980). In addition she has written books for children and a family history, Generations (1976).

Miss Rosie

When I watch you
wrapped up like garbage
sitting, surrounded by the smell
of too old potato peels
or
when I watch you
in your old man's shoes
with the little toe cut out
sitting, waiting for your mind
like next week's grocery
I say
when I watch you
you wet brown bag of a woman
who used to be the best looking gal in Georgia
used to be called the Georgia Rose
I stand up
through your destruction
I stand up

Jayne Cortez
1936–

*B*orn *in Arizona, she grew up in Watts, California, and now
lives in New York City. She performs her celebrated jazz poetry
throughout the USA, Africa, Europe, Latin America and the Caribbean, either alone or with musicians (in 1980 she formed a band named
the Firespitters, including her drummer son Denardo Coleman). The
inspiration and influence of music is strong in her work, which ranges
in mood from topical political militancy to soulful lyricism, and among
recordings she has produced are* Celebrations and Solitudes *(1975),*
Unsubmissive Blues *(1980),* There It Is *(1982),* Maintain Control *(1987)
and* Everywhere Drums *(1990). Her books include* Pisstained Stairs and
the Monkey Man's Wares *(1969),* Festivals and Funerals *(1971),* Scarifications *(1973),* Mouth on Paper *(1977),* Firespitter *(1982),* Coagulations:
New and Selected Poems *(1984) and* Poetic Magnetic *(1991). Her poems
have been widely anthologized and translated and she has received
awards from the National Endowment for the Arts, an American Book
Award and a New York Artists Foundation Award for poetry.*

Consultation

I have lived in circles of solitude
in support of my involved laughter
emerging from words
from an atmosphere of folded hands
and the half lip stroke of burnt respect
becoming noble while pounding an old love bone
in withered consultation
and without warning
i wiggle through dead hairs of dead gods
no change in volume
i too can be pain in the face of your body
speak to me about this confinement
this deep revelation
between pauses
and the earth fonk of discharge
pearl tongue submissions of enslaved tears

manhood   womanhood   childhood
the zigzag message from my teeth
heard by my lips
bold against painted spirits
of hunchback fear
   (as if i couldn't fly away from this road show of
   passing syringes)
No
it is the convulsion of limbs lying
in pose of a person
empty of all confidence
that will make the ritual invasion of death
spread like grease
through scalps of decorative hairdos

Push Back the Catastrophes

I don't want a drought to feed on itself
through the tattooed holes in my belly
I don't want a spectacular desert of
charred stems & rabbit hairs
in my throat of accumulated matter
I don't want to burn and cut through the forest
like a greedy mercenary drilling into
sugar cane of the bones

Push back the advancing sands
the polluted sewage
the dust demons   the dying timber
the upper atmosphere of nitrogen
push back the catastrophes
Enough of the missiles
the submarines
the aircraft carriers
the biological weapons
No more sickness   sadness   poverty
exploitation   destabilization
illiteracy and bombing
Let's move toward peace
toward equality and justice
that's what I want

To breathe clean air
to drink pure water to plant new crops
to soak up the rain to wash off the stink

to hold this body and soul together in peace
that's it
Push back the catastrophes

Jazz Fan Looks Back

I crisscrossed with Monk
Wailed with Bud
Counted every star with Stitt
Sang "Don't Blame Me" with Sarah
Wore a flower like Billie
Screamed in the range of Dinah
& scatted "How High The Moon" with Ella Fitzgerald
as she blew roof off the Shrine Auditorium
                    Jazz at the Philharmonic

I cut my hair into a permanent tam
Made my feet rebellious metronomes
Embedded record needles in paint on paper
Talked bopology talk
Laughed in high pitched saxophone phrases
Became keeper of every Bird riff
every Lester lick
as Hawk melodicized my ear of infatuated tongues
& Blakey drummed militant messages in
soul of my applauding teeth
& Ray hit bass notes to the last love seat in my bones
I moved in triple time with Max
Grooved high with Diz
Perdidoed with Pettiford
Flew home with Hamp
Shuffled in Dexter's Deck
Squatty rooed with Peterson
Dreamed a "52nd Street Theme" with Fats
& scatted "Lady Be Good" with Ella Fitzgerald
as she blew roof off the Shrine Auditorium
Jazz at the Philharmonic

Georgina Herrera

1936–

orn in Jovellanos, Matanzas province, in Cuba, she began writing as a very young woman. Her first collection of poems, Gentes y cosas (People and Things), was published in 1974; a second collection, Granos de sol y luna (Seeds of Sun and Moon), appeared in 1978. She works as a scriptwriter for the Cuban Institute for Radio and Television. She is the divorced mother of two children; her deep maternal attachment is one of the profoundest inspirations for her poetry. The following poems are translated from the Spanish by Kathleen Weaver.

Child Asleep

This girl
so peacefully asleep
has no more shelter than
my custom of
never being at rest but
always on sharp watch
for the future. . . .
To this child will come her hour.
The most ambitious pain will bend her low.
A thorn with its flower
will circle round her. Yet
if she is wise
she will be lucky.
For now, she sleeps in peace. Let
her dream be long,
the longest possible.

Cradle

Here beyond a cherishing wall
is the foremost lady of my stories
laid low
by the peaceable force of her dreams

Sweet-
ly guarded by my passion's soldiers
Remain so,
new queen, until
the king-father-sun
stretches and speaks the first word

That Way of Dying

They call it love –
those who lie in its giant shadow.
I would call it:
marine stone
lashing my heart with fish,
land
rock-hard
refusing moisture to my roots,
sky which bid my star farewell
and made it wandering.

June Jordan
1936–

Born in Harlem, New York, and raised in Brooklyn, where she
began writing poetry at the age of seven, she studied at Barnard
College (1953–5). Poet, journalist, essayist and Third World activist, she has also worked in city planning alongside Buckminster Fuller,
has taught African-American and women's studies at various institutions
and travels internationally to read her work and speak on literature and
politics. Her novel His Own Where (1971) was a finalist for the National

Book Award and won the Prix de Rome in Environmental Design, and among many other awards she has received are a Rockefeller Grant in Creative Writing, a National Endowment for the Arts fellowship and a Massachusetts Council for the Arts award for her essay "On the Difficult Miracle of Black Poetry in America, or Something Like a Sonnet for Phillis Wheatley". Her 1981 book of political essays Civil Wars *was the first such work published by a Black woman in the USA; her other prose collections are* On Call *(1985) and* Moving Towards Home *(1989) – in which her 1976 essay below is included. Her poetry books include* New Days: Poems of Exile and Return *(1973),* Things That I Do in the Dark: New and Selected Poems *(1977),* Passion: New Poems 1977–1980 *(1980) and* Lyrical Campaigns: Selected Poems *(1989). She has said: "My life seems to be an increasing revelation of the intimate face of universal struggle. You begin with your family and the kids on the block, and next you open your eyes to what you call your people and that leads you into land reform into Black English into Angola leads you back to your own bed where you lie by yourself, wondering if you deserve to be peaceful, or trusted or desired or left to the freedom of your own unfaltering heart. And the scale shrinks to the size of a skull: your own interior cage." Her writing makes a direct connection between the personal and the universal.*

Declaration of an Independence I Would Just as Soon Not Have

I F it is not apparent from the text, then let me make it clear that I wrote this from the inside. As a Black woman, and as a human being within the First World Movement, and as a woman who loves women as well as she loves men. *Ms.* magazine published this essay under their title, "Second Thoughts of a Black Feminist". My question at the end of this piece was answered by Black women who wrote to me, care of *Ms.*, from all over the country. Yes, they said, you are not alone!

*   *   *

I know I am not alone. There must be hundreds of other women, maybe thousands, who feel as I do. There may be hundreds of men who want the same drastic things to happen. But how do you hook up with them? How can you interlink your own struggle and goals with these myriad, hypothetical people who are hidden entirely or else concealed by stereotype and/or generalities of "platform" such as any movement seems to spawn? I don't know. And I don't like it, this being alone when it is clear that there will have to be multitudes working together, around the world, if radical and positive change can be forced upon the heinous status quo I despise in all its overwhelming power.

For example, suppose the hunger and the famine afflicting some 800 million lives on earth is a fact that leaves you nauseous, jumpy, and chronically enraged. No matter how intense your wrath may be, no matter how personally knowledgeable you may be about the cause and the conceivable remedies for this monstrous and unnecessary curse upon innocent human beings, you, by yourself, can do damned little, if anything, to destroy these facts of abject experience. But what can you join? Where can you sign up, sign in?

Or suppose you consider children, as I do, the only blameless people alive. And suppose you possess all the eyeball evidence, all the statistics, that indicate a majority of Black youngsters doomed to semi-illiteracy and/or obsolete vocational training for jobs, livelihoods, that disappeared from the real life marketplace at least five years ago. Or suppose you love children and you cannot forget that there are entire countries, even in this same hemisphere, where four- and five-year-olds, where nine- and ten-year-olds, have been abandoned, kicked out of their homes, or worse, where so-called packs of these little people must scavenge the garbage cans and the very streets for something to eat before they finally lie down to sleep in gutters and doorways, under the soiled newspapers that consistently fail to report the degrading fact that the children will probably not survive. What do you do? Where are the hands you can clasp in dedication against such enormous reasons for shame?

Or what about the poor, the dispossessed, families of America? Once you realize that Welfare supports have steadily declined, for instance, in the face of unprecedented, inflationary increases in the cost of living, once you understand what this particular disequilibrium implies for a family of five children and their mother who must, nevertheless, manage to secure food, heat, warm enough clothing, carfare, moneys for medical care, and the rent, where can you turn, effectively, to end this death-dealing disgrace? If you happen to be a Black woman, as I am, and a so-called female head of household, then, in an unlimited number of ways, you undoubtedly recognize that you are simply another unacknowledged single mother represented solely by official figures that bespeak a relentlessly rising percentage of Black people, per se: you are damned as Black, damned as a woman, and damned as a quote female head of household unquote. Can you point me toward the movement directly addressing the special, inexorable hardships borne by me and my sisters in like, involuntary circumstances?

Well, for a long time I thought it was perfectly fine to be alone, as far as political cause was concerned. You wrote poems, freelance exposé articles, essays proposing remedies, even novels demonstrating the feasibility of solutions that you ardently trusted as possibilities for activist commitment. Or you hitched onto ad hoc committees against this or that nightmare and, when and if you had the bucks, you made tax-deductible donations of endorsement for whatever public fight seemed to you among the most urgent to be won. What did this yield? I felt pretty good, yes, and comfortable with my conscience. But nothing changed, nothing ever really changed as the result of such loner activity.

So now I am no longer as silly, as vaingloriously innocent, as I was. It is plainly the truth that, whatever its vast and various dimensions, human misery is the predicted, aforethought consequence of deliberate, deliberated arrangements of power that would distort the whole planet into miserly, personal rights of property belonging to extremely few men and their egotistical and/or avaricious interests. Ad hoc, loner protests will not make the difference, will not impose the revolutionary changes such undue suffering demands. I think it is necessary to form or join a well-defined organization that can and will work to destroy the status quo as ruthlessly, as zealously, as nonstop in its momentum, as are the enemy forces surely arrayed against our goals. Accordingly, since the bloody close of the Civil Rights era I have sought, repeatedly, just such a body of intelligently inclusive feelings and aims. I have found that there are three movements that compel my willing respect and hopes. But I have also learned that there exists, in each of these movements, a ranking of priorities, a peculiarity of perspective, that conflicts with the other two, in an apparently irreconcilable manner. Furthermore, since every one of these movements calls for liberation of some kind, it has become necessary to try and define what liberation apparently signifies to the Black Movement, the Third World Movement, and the Women's Movement, respectively. In this effort, I have encountered a woeful magnitude of internecine, unfortunate, and basically untenable conflicts of analysis. Let me break down what I mean, exactly:

1.   The Black Movement: This is the battle I have attempted to help define, and forward, as though my own life depended on its success. In truth, my life does depend on the outcome of our Black struggles for freedom to be ourselves, in self-respecting self-sufficiency. But where can you find serious Black spokesmen, or women, for the impoverished, hungry, state-dependent Black peoples among us who still amount to more than a third of our total population? And why does it continue to be the case that, when our ostensible leadership talks about the "liberation of the Black man" that is precisely, and only, what they mean? How is it even imaginable that Black men would presume to formulate the Black Movement and the Women's movement as either/or, antithetical alternatives of focus? As a Black woman, I view such a formulation with a mixture of incredulity and grief: The irreducible majority of Black people continues to be composed of Black women. And, whereas many Black sons and daughters have never known our Black fathers, or a nurturing, supportive Black man in our daily lives, all Black people have most certainly been raised, and cared for, by Black women: mothers, grandmothers, aunts. In addition, and despite the prevalent bullshit to the contrary, Black women continue to occupy the absolutely lowest rungs of the labor force in the United States, we continue to receive the lowest pay of any group of workers, and we endure the highest rate of unemployment. If that status does not cry out for liberation, specifically as Black women, then I am hopelessly out of touch with my own pre-ordained reality.

On another front, I have difficulty comprehending our alleged Black leaders who postulate an antithetical relationship between the destinies of Afro-Americans and the fate of the First World – which is too commonly, and mistakenly, termed the "Third World". I cannot understand how we, Afro-Americans, have contended with racism, with life-denying exploitation, with brute-powerful despising of our culture, our languages, our gods, our children – how we have grappled with such a bedeviled history for more than four centuries and yet, today, cannot grasp the identical stakes, the identical sources of evil and oppression, that obtain in the lives of our First World brothers and sisters. Moreover, I cannot understand how any of us can fail to perceive the necessarily international nature of our oppression and, hence, our need for international unity and planned rebellion.

2.   The First World Movements: The multimillion-fold majority of the peoples on earth are neither white, nor powerful, nor exempt from terrifying syndromes of disease, hunger, poverty that defies description, and prospects for worse privation or demeaning subsistence. With all my heart and mind I would strive in any way I could to eradicate the origins of such colossal exploitation and abuse. But, except for the inspired exceptions of China, Cuba, and Tanzania, it appears that class divisions still suffocate the clearly legitimate aspirations of most First World Peoples, and that the status enjoined upon women is that of a serf, at best. Consequently, one can contribute to African liberation campaigns or to anti-famine collections, yes, but one must also wrestle with sober misgivings. Will these funds reach the afflicted peoples of your concern, or will the dollar bills merely fill the pockets of neo-colonial bourgeoisie who travel through the countryside in Mercedes-Benz limousines, air-conditioned and bullet-proofed against the men and women they have been empowered to serve? And how will the eventual victory be celebrated? Will the women cook the feast and then fear to share it with their menfolk at the same table, at the same time, on a basis of mutual regard and cherishing? What will victory mean for the traditional outcasts, the traditional lowest of the low: the poor, and women, generally? Will the changing of the color of the guards bring about a verifiable change of policy and objectives? Do we have to expect that formerly colonized, newly independent, nation states will mistakenly pursue paths that verily imitate the powers that enslaved them? Will none of the newly emerging leaders reject, for example, industrialization and their ongoing dependence upon outside, hostile corporations and military allies, and concentrate, instead, upon land reform and intensive agrarian development that will determine the actuality of their independence?

3.   The Women's Movement: I remain determined to fight for equal rights of fulfillment and exploration, as a person who is female. And for a while, and with exhilaration, I immersed myself in primer readings about the nature of women's subjugation, and about the legislative and social and economic proposals for corrective action. But then I began to falter in my excitement, in my sense of overdue confirmation, and sisterhood. The Women's Movement did not seem as large, in its avowed concerns, or as complicated, as I believe the world is large and complicated. Exceedingly little attention was granted to the problems of working-class or poor people, to the victimization of Black women who head families, by themselves. Nowhere did I see an espousal of the struggles to end the predicament of children everywhere – a cause that seemed natural to me, as a woman. Nor did I detect a feeling awareness that you cannot aid half a people; you have to seek to assist the men as well as the women of any oppressed group. Nor have I discovered a political breadth of response that

would certainly include, for example, the CIA murder of Patrice Lumumba, Martin Luther King, Jr, and President Allende of Chile, in a disastrous triumph of imperialistic will.

Finally, there is the question of the liberation of women. Will we liberate ourselves so that the caring for children, the teaching, the loving, healing, person-oriented values that have always distinguished us will be revered and honored at least commensurate to the honors accorded bank managers, lieutenant colonels, and the executive corporate elite? Or will we liberate ourselves so that we can militantly abandon those attributes and functions, so that we can despise our own warmth and generosity even as men have done, for ages?

And if women loving other women and/or women in love with women will be part and parcel of the manifest revolution we want to win, does that mean that we should condone lecherous, exploitative, shallow, acting out, and pathological behavior by women who term themselves lesbians – in much the same way that we, Black people, once voluntarily called ourselves *niggas* out of a convoluted mood of defiance, a mood that proved to be heavily penetrated by unconscious, continuing self-hatred? That is behavior, after all, that is the use of, that is submission to, an enemy concept such as we would never condone, or welcome, in interracial or heterosexual relationships of any sort.

I would hope that the sum total of the liberation struggles I have attempted to sketch, and briefly criticize would mean this: That I will be free to be who I am, Black and female, without fear, without pain, without humiliation. That I will be free to become whatever my life requires of me, without posturing, without compromise, without terror. That I will soon be able, realistically, to assume the dignified fulfillment of the dreams and needs and potentialities of most of the men, women, and children alive, today. That I can count upon a sisterhood and a brotherhood that will let me give my life to its consecration, without equivocating, without sorrow. That my son, who is a Black man, and that I, a Black woman, may keep faith with each other, and with those others whom we may have the privilege to serve, and to join.

Toward these ends, I have written this account of one woman's declaration of an independence I would just as soon not have. I believe I am not alone. Please verify:

Awa Thiam
1936–

B orn in Bamako, Mali, she is a politician. Her first book La Parole aux négresses *(1978), translated by Dorothy S. Blair as* Black Sisters, Speak Out: Feminism and Oppression in Black Africa *(1986), dealt with some of the practices – such as polygamy, clitoridectomy and infibulation – by which millions of women are controlled.*

From

Black Sisters, Speak Out

T HE problems that beset Black women are manifold. Whether she is from the West Indies, America or Africa, the plight of the Black woman is very different from that of her White or Yellow sisters, although in the long run the problems faced by all women tend to overlap. Their common condition is one of exploitation and oppression by the same phallocratic system, whether it be Black, White or Yellow. In Africa as in Europe, it is not unusual to find battered wives; in Europe as in Africa there are polygamous husbands. Whether polygamy is institutionalized or illegal, it is imposed on women by external forces. Women are still, in our own day, considered as objects, as sub-human. Everyone behaves as if women had no human sensitivities. The most convincing example of this is when little girls are married or betrothed as soon as they are born. In a country like Mali, and particularly in the Segu region, families can be found in which all the daughters are betrothed very young, some having been promised in marriage at birth. The reason given – true or false – is the wide-spread practice of polygamy, which would soon make for a shortage of wives. But this is only a hypothesis. If this partially explains the custom of child brides, it by no means justifies it. Among certain ethnic groups, the Tukolor and Fulani for instance, it is frequently accepted as a tradition.

Sometimes, these marriages may be contracted for reasons of social prestige. When a man marries a girl of "good family", he acquires greater social consideration, more respect. So, as soon as a son is born, some men hasten to ask for the hand of a girl for their son, sometimes before she is even conceived.

Polygamy seems to be rampant in every country in Black Africa. In the Republic of Guinea, which claims to be progressive, and whose first president, Ahmed Sékou Touré, opted for a socialist state, women are faced by the same problem as their Senegalese, Malian, Ghanaian or Nigerian sisters.

Polygamy continues to exist there, in spite of measures taken, not to forbid it, but to limit the number of people who practise it. So we read the words of the then President of Guinea, Sékou Touré, in Pierre Hanry's *Erotisme Africain* (p. 74):

> Guinean women must not be instruments of production in the economic life of the nation, nor domestic instruments in the life of the family. They must be workers, aware of the economic improvement of the nation and equal partners in the home.
>
> Young people of Guinea, polygamy is in your hands: you can maintain it or see that it disappears, according to the quality of your education and your strength of will in building a new Africa which will be permanently rid of the inferiority and oppression of women.

Hanry then goes on to say,

> Unfortunately as in all areas where it was exercised in 1965, the revolutionary action of the Secretary-General of the PDG (Parti Démocratique Guinéen) seems in this matter to have scarcely gone beyond the stage of words. (p. 75, *op. cit.*).

Polygamy certainly still exists in Guinea at the present time, but Pierre Hanry's point of view in this matter is not necessarily the correct one. To present the problem in this way is to blind ourselves, consciously or not, to the real issues. Arbitrary measures that the masses, especially women – the principal people concerned – cannot understand, will not help us arrive at equality of rights and duties, which still have to be defined. It is only by unremitting struggle that women will succeed in forcing action to be taken whereby they can obtain little scraps of equality, and in the end an equality that is imposed on everyone and observed by everyone.

The countries of Black Africa must certainly overhaul their economies, but social reform is also necessary. A close look must be taken at customs since, if women are to be liberated, the prerequisite must be a change in people's mental attitudes. In fact, there would have to be a total upheaval in the colonial and neo-colonial structures that still exist in Black Africa, and by this we mean a radical revolution. To conceive of the liberation of Black African women on any other footing is to delude ourselves. We deliberately speak of "liberation" of women, in preference to the term "emancipation", as the latter word suggests *a priori* the idea of a typical infantile character of women. It reduces a woman to the status of a minor, a child whom it would be necessary to emancipate. Is this not in fact what a large number of people think? And perhaps this is how we must understand the subjection of women.

We had to wait until the sixteenth century before women were acknowledged to have souls. How much longer must we wait before it is conceded that Black folk, and more especially Black women, also possess this attribute?

On the practical level, irrespective of all religious considerations, what is the situation respecting polygamy nowadays? In any European country, when a husband goes in for that form of semi-condoned polygamy that consists of taking a mistress – or several – the wife can have recourse to the law by instituting action for divorce, or at least obtain support for better treatment from him. Such a course of action is not possible for a Muslim woman, who grows up in a system of institutionalized polygamy, where this is not permitted. What is more, such action would appear aberrant in a Black African context, in which marriage is generally religious, not civil. This difference between the situation of Black and White women is found at practically all levels. And this is the main basis for our claim that the Black woman's struggle is of a different nature from that of her White sister. The majority of European women do not lack essentials, whereas Black women are fighting for survival as much in the field of institutions as in the manner of her daily existence. In other words, European women can gain much more advantage from their struggles – even if these don't lead to a radical revolution and a total upheaval of social structures. Where Black women have to combat colonialism and neo-colonialism, capitalism and the patriarchal system, European women only have to fight against capitalism and patriarchy.

Maryse Condé

1937–

Born in Pointe-à-Pitre, Guadeloupe, after local schooling she took university degrees in Paris and London, gaining a doctorate in Comparative Literature from the Sorbonne. For years she taught West Indian literature at the Sorbonne. Her career has embraced journalism, radio and television, teaching in Europe and Africa, and she is a reviewer and critic. She edited a collection of francophone literature (Ghana, 1966) and her published fiction includes the novels, Heremakhonon (1976), A Season in Rihata (Une Saison à Ribata, 1981) – extracted here – and Segu (1987). She lives in Guadeloupe with her husband Richard Philcox (who has translated her work into English), having spent much of her life in Africa, and lectures widely in the USA.

From

A Season in Rihata

CHAPTER I

T HE house stood somewhat askew in the middle of an immense, unkempt garden that had more guinea grass than actual lawn. A path led from the hedge of bougainvillaea up to the twin flight of front steps which enlaced a torch cactus and a dwarf frangipani between the shaky handrails. It still had a certain touch of grandeur. Twenty years earlier, before independence, it had been built by the local magistrate and his wife, both from Bordeaux and both fond of entertaining. Anything was a good excuse for celebrating: a new official arriving, an old one returning home, going on leave, repatriation for health reasons. When the French left, the house had remained shut for years and had slowly fallen into disrepair. Its architecture was too reminiscent of colonial times for the tastes of the new leaders of the one party's regional secretariat. They preferred to have moorish-style villas built on the plots down by the river outside the small town.

When Zek had arrived in Rihata with his wife Marie-Hélène, his growing family of children and his mother, the house had been hastily reopened, the walls whitewashed, the floors and windows done up and the garden weeded. Later, Zek had been offered more modern, less damp and less uncomfortable quarters. He had always refused them. Like his children, like Marie-Hélène perhaps, he had grown fond of this house which was unique of its kind, like his family.

Christophe was the only one who would have liked to live elsewhere – in a mud hut in the middle of a cluttered compound like some of his school friends; or in a cramped little villa in the civil servants' quarter; or even in the new residential district that the inhabitants of Rihata, who were never hard up for names, had nicknamed the "Garden of Allah". He regarded this unusual house as a symbol, a symbol that they were partly foreigners, poorly integrated into a community that put its own people first. Yet Zek had been born here, a son of one of the most illustrious Ngurka families, and his father, Malan, had founded the first union of planters and had become a dignitary in colonial times. The *griots* who gathered in the garden on feast days even traced his ancestors back to Bouraina, the mythical Ngurka hero and a household legend. It was Marie-Hélène who created this uneasiness and even Christophe, who adored her, sometimes felt like hating her for it.

Not that Marie-Hélène was the only one to have been born far from Rihata. The excesses of certain political regimes were driving an increasing number of men and women from their country to Rihata which had become a meeting place for many nationalities.

But she was the only one the market women, the traders in the rue Patrice-Lumumba, and the little date and peanut sellers, called "*Semela*", Ngurka for "the woman from over there". The "over there" was not just written in the colour of her skin or her hair. The inhabitants of Rihata were used to cross-breeding. The French, Lebanese and Greeks had left their quota of light-skinned, curly-haired little half-castes and nobody ostracized them. But there was a whole manner of being that was written into her gestures, attitudes and reactions which disconcerted, intimidated or attracted, depending on the case, and made her stand out as boldly as a birthmark in the middle of the forehead, a club foot or a crippled leg. Christophe was frightened of becoming like her. Every morning he anxiously examined his young mulatto face in the mirror. He too came from "over there". From Guadeloupe, through his mother Delphine, Marie-Hélène's sister. From Haiti, through his father, whom he had never known. He would have given anything not to be Zek's nephew, taken in out of kindness after his mother died; anything to be Zek's son, fruit of his loins and his desire and one of the children of this land.

He got up to put a record on the player he had received as a present the night before. It was Christmas which for a number of reasons Christophe hated, as it accentuated his feeling of loneliness. Not only did his school friends, who were mainly Moslem, pay little attention to Christmas, but at home he was the only one Marie-Hélène insisted should go to mass. Although Zek objected very little to anything, and respected his wife's and nephew's beliefs, he forbade his daughters to set foot inside the church. Christophe therefore had to accompany Marie-Hélène to Jacques Abouchar's, the Lebanese trader who was a Roman Catholic like them and at this time of year sold artificial Christmas trees, multicoloured candles, tinsel and sequins. Marie-Hélène made her choice under the fat man's lecherous gaze. Then Christophe escorted her to midnight mass in the little wooden church where there were fewer than fifty people, and came home to a Christmas Eve dinner that Bolanlé, the boy cook, had left heated up, and which always made him feel sick.

This year things had gone better since Marie-Hélène was almost at the end of her pregnancy and was too tired to bother about a Christmas tree, midnight mass or dinner. She had gone to bed soon after dinner and it was Zek who had brought Christophe his record player, which must have cost a fortune as such things were only available on the black market. Christophe wanted to tell him that at the age of seventeen he was no longer a child and that, knowing the family's finances, he did not want such a present. He hadn't dared and had stammered out his thanks, but Zek could see through him; he knew Christophe well enough to guess what he was thinking. Christophe put on his record and was about to go back to bed when Sia came in. Sia, the eldest daughter of Zek and Marie-Hélène, was his cousin and two years his junior. She was a solemn, detached teenager who seemed particularly gloomy that morning. She sat down at the foot of the bed biting the nails of her left hand in silence. "Uncle Madou is coming the day after tomorrow," she said after a while.

"Is he coming to see us?" Christophe asked in surprise.

She shrugged her shoulders. "No, of course not. He's coming to commemorate the anniversary of the *coup d'état*."

Zek had a brother, almost ten years his junior, who the previous year had been appointed Minister for Rural Development. The two brothers had not been on speaking terms for some years. Christophe knew that in actual fact their quarrel went back a long way. They were the only sons of Malan who had had four wives and fifteen daughters. Madou was the son of the first wife who had given birth to five daughters in a row, whereas the third wife, Sokambi, unloved by Malan and given him by a family of former servants as a mark of esteem, already had a son by the name of Zek. Zek and Madou had therefore been brought up as rivals, each vying for the attention and affection of their father. Without any apparent effort Madou had won. Other factors, of which Christophe knew nothing, had been grafted on to this initial discord. It had all started years earlier when they were living in N'Daru, the capital, before Zek had asked for his transfer to Rihata, this small town where nothing ever happened.

Christophe looked up at Sia who went on biting her nails. "Do you think he'll stay with us?"

She raised her eyes. "Not after what happened between him and Papa!"

In actual fact she did not know any more than Christophe, but she always spoke with a great deal of assurance, implying she knew more than she really did.

He followed her out on to the veranda. All the bedrooms were on the second floor and you could see the pilot rice schemes reaching down to the river where, at this time of year, the waters were still high. You could even make out some small, ragged members of the Sawale tribe poling their reed boats and, on the other bank, the minaret of the Mecoura mosque. Rihata was situated on a promontory of a lazy bend in the river. For this reason, even in the dry season, the vegetation was never parched and dusty as in other parts of the country. The rainy season seemed to linger on in the rich grass, in the leaves of the mango trees and in the blossom of the flame trees which were late producing pods.

Sia hated Rihata and everything about it. She could not understand how her mother, seemingly destined by birth and her intellectual and physical gifts to a brilliant life, could have married her father and followed him to this country where only the eccentricities of its dictator signalled its presence to the outside world. So she took refuge in this house, sometimes turning it into a fairy-tale castle, sometimes into a big West Indian great house complete with old nannies rocking babies in cradles. On this Christmas morning she would have liked to have found a pile of presents at the foot of her bed, and to have her fingers tangled in ribbons, as she pricked herself on the golden pins, her delighted parents looking on. Instead of which there was dead silence. The family was still asleep, except for Sara and Kadi, the fourth and fifth daughters respectively, who were playing at the foot of the front steps. There was Sokambi of course, the grandmother, up at dawn, who was busy with her *pagnes* and dye basins at the bottom of the garden. Zek and Marie-Hélène were locked away in the master bedroom, its ceiling pitted with mould. It was obvious that they no longer loved each other. Come to that, had they ever loved each other? Why then did they live together? Why did they have so many children? There were six already and a seventh was well on the way.

"Shall we go down to the river?"

She did not exactly jump at Christophe's suggestion, but there were hours to wait until lunch. A kind of bar cum restaurant stood on the river bank, where you could get fruit juice, Coca Cola and beer and nibble on fresh fried fish. For some time it had been a favourite meeting place for Rihata's bourgeoisie who used to listen to *kora* and *balafon* music far into the night. Then the fashion passed and the owner almost went bankrupt. Nothing ever lasted in Rihata. In this small town enthusiasm was short-lived.

She shrugged her shoulders, indifferently. "If you like."

The veranda went round the house like a flimsy footbridge and was shaky in places. She decided to change her *pagne* and while he waited for her Christophe stared at the flat grey river which well before noon would be sparkling in the sun. The river had always fascinated him. He imagined the silent journey of the waters to the delta, to the sea and to America on the other side. Perhaps one day he would have to go away and leave Rihata far behind him.

Bessie Head
1937–86

B orn in Pietermaritzburg, South Africa, to a white mother who was the daughter of a wealthy Natal racing family and a Black father who was a stablehand (after this alliance her mother was certified insane), she was brought up in a foster home until the age of thirteen, then was sent to a mission school before training as a teacher. After four years' teaching, she became a journalist, working for The Golden City Post and for Drum magazine. After a brief unhappy marriage, her involvement in the trial of a friend led her to apply for a teaching post in Botswana. She migrated there in her early twenties and in 1964 settled with her son in Serowe, her work as teacher and market gardener providing the economic base for her writing life. She had the precarious status of refugee for fifteen years before gaining citizenship in 1979. She drew heavily on the experiences of her traumatic life for her novels, which include When Rain Clouds Gather (1969), Maru (1971) and A Question of Power (1974). She also wrote numerous short stories and vignettes of life around her, published in The Collector of Treasures and Other

Botswana Village Tales *(1977, in which "The Special One" appeared) and* Tales of Tenderness and Power *(1990, where "The Woman from America" and "The Old Woman" are collected). On her untimely death at the age of forty-nine she was buried in Serowe.*

The Woman from America

T HIS woman from America married a man of our village and left her country to come and live with him here. She descended on us like an avalanche. People are divided into two camps. Those who feel a fascinated love and those who fear a new thing. The terrible thing is that those who fear are always in the majority. This woman and her husband and children have to be sufficient to themselves because everything they do is not the way people here do it. Most terrible of all is the fact that they really love each other and the husband effortlessly and naturally keeps his eyes on his wife alone. In this achievement he is seventy years ahead of all the men here.

We are such a lot of queer people in the southern part of Africa. We have felt all forms of suppression and are subdued. We lack the vitality, the push, the devil-may-care temperament of the people of the north of Africa. They do things first, then we. We are always going to be confederators and not initiators. We are very materialistically minded and I think this adds to our fear. People who hoard little bits of things cannot throw out and expand, and, in doing so, keep in circulation a flowing current of wealth. Basically we are mean, selfish. We eat each other all the time and God help poor Botswana at the bottom.

Then, into this narrow, constricted world came the woman from America. Some people keep hoping she will go away one day, but already her big strong stride has worn the pathways of the village flat. She is everywhere about because she is a woman, resolved and unshakeable in herself. To make matters more disturbing, she comes from the West of America, somewhere near California. I gather from her conversation that people from the West are stranger than most people. They must be the most oddly beautiful people in the world; at least this woman from the West is the most oddly beautiful person I have ever seen. Every cross-current of the earth seems to have stopped in her and blended into an amazing harmony. She has a big dash of Africa, a dash of Germany, some Cherokee and heaven knows what else. Her feet are big and her body is as tall and straight and strong as a mountain tree. Her neck curves up high and her thick black hair cascades down her back like a wild and tormented stream. I cannot understand her eyes, though, except that they are big, black and startled like those of a wild free buck racing against the wind. Often they cloud over with a deep, brooding look.

It took a great deal of courage to become friends with a woman like that. Like everyone here I am timid and subdued. Authority, everything can subdue me. Not because I like it that way but because authority carries the weight of an age pressing down on life. It is terrible then to associate with a person who can shout authority down. Her shouting-matches with authority are the terror and sensation of the village. It has come down to this. Either the woman is unreasonable or authority is unreasonable, and everyone in his heart would like to admit that authority is unreasonable. In reality, the rule is: if authority does not like you then you are the outcast and humanity associates with you at its peril. So try always to be on the right side of authority, for the sake of peace.

It was inevitable though that this woman and I should be friends. I have an overwhelming curiosity that I cannot keep within bounds. I passed by the house for almost a month, but one cannot crash in on people. Then one day a dog they have had puppies and my small son chased one of the puppies into the yard and I chased after him. Then one of the puppies became his and there had to be discussions about the puppy, the desert heat and the state of the world, and as a result of curiosity an avalanche of wealth has descended on my life. My small hut-house is full of short notes written in a wide sprawling hand. I have kept them all because they are a statement of human generosity and the wide carefree laugh of a woman who is as busy as women the world over about things women always entangle themselves in – a man, children, a home. Like this:

Have you an onion to spare? It's very quiet here this morning and I'm all fagged out from sweeping and cleaning the yard, shaking blankets, cooking, fetching water, bathing children, and there's still the floor inside to sweep, and dishes to wash and myself to bathe – it's endless!

Or again:

Have you an extra onion to give me until tomorrow? If so, I'd appreciate it. I'm trying to do something with these awful beans and I've run out of all my seasonings and spices. A neighbour brought us some spinach last night so we're in the green. I've got dirty clothes galore to wash and iron today.

Or:

I'm sending the kids over to get 10 minutes' peace in which to restore my equilibrium. It looks as if rain is threatening. Please send them back immediately so they won't get caught out in it. Any fiction at your house? I could use some light diversion.

And, very typical . . .

This has been a very hectic morning! First I was rushing to finish a few letters to send to you to post for me. Then it began to sprinkle slightly and I remembered you have no raincoat, so I decided to dash over there myself with the letters and the post key. At the very moment I was stepping out of the door, in stepped someone and that solved the letter posting problem, but I still don't know whether there is any mail for me. I've lost my p.o. box key! Did the children perhaps drop it out of that purse when they were playing with it at your house yesterday?

Or my son keeps getting every kind of chest ailment and I prefer to decide it's the worst:

What's this about whooping cough! Who diagnosed it? Didn't you say he had all his shots and vaccinations? The D.P.T. doesn't require a booster until after he's five years old. Diphtheria-Pertussis (Whooping cough) – Tetanus is one of the most reliable vaccinations I know; all three of mine and I have had hoarse, dry coughs but certainly it wasn't whooping cough. Here's Dr Spock to reassure you!

Sometimes, too, conversations get all tangled up and the African night creeps all about and the candles are not lit and the conversation gets more entangled, intense; and the children fall asleep on the floor dazed by it all. The next day I get a book flung at me with vigorous exasperation! "Here's C.P. Snow. Read him, dammit! And dispel a bit of that fog in thy cranium."

I am dazed, too, by Mr C. P. Snow. Where do I begin to understand the industrial use of electronics, atomic energy, automation in a world of mud-huts? What is a machine tool? he asks. What are the Two Cultures and the Scientific Revolution? The argument could be quaint to one who hasn't even one leg of culture to stand on. But it isn't really, because even a bush village in Africa begins to feel the tug and pull of the spider-web of life. Would Mr Snow or someone please write me an explanation of what a machine tool is? I'd like to know. My address is: Serowe, Bechuanaland, Africa.

The trouble with the woman from America is that people would rather hold off, sensing her world to be shockingly apart from theirs. But she is a new kind of American or even maybe will be a new kind of African. There isn't anyone here who does not admire her – to come from a world of chicken, hamburgers, TV, escalators and what not to a village mud-hut and a life so tough, where the most you can afford to eat is ground millet and boiled meat. Sometimes you cannot afford to eat at all. Always you have to trudge miles for a bucket of water and carry it home on your head. And to do all this with loud, ringing, sprawling laughter!

Black people in America care much about Africa and she has come here on her own as an expression of that love and concern. Through her, too, one is filled with wonder for a country that breeds individuals about whom, without and within, rushes the wind of freedom. I have to make myself clear, though. She is a different person who has taken by force what America will not give black people. We had some here a while ago, sent out by the State Department. They were very jolly and sociable, but for the most innocent questions they kept saying: "We can't talk about the government. That's politics. We can't talk politics." Why did they come here if they were so afraid of what the American government thinks about what they might think or say in Africa? Why were they so afraid? Africa is not alive for them. It seems a waste of the State Department's money. It seems so strange a thing to send people on goodwill projects if they are so afraid that they jump at the slightest shadow. Why are they so afraid of the government of America which is a government of freedom and democracy? Here we are all afraid of authority and we never pretend anything else. Black people who are sent here by the State Department are tied up in some deep and shameful hypocrisy. It is a terrible pity because such things are destructive to them and hurtful to us.

The woman from America loves both Africa and America, independently. She can take what she wants from us both and say: "Dammit!" It is a difficult thing to do.

The Old Woman

SHE was so frail that her whole body swayed this way and that like a thin stalk of corn in the wind. Her arms wee as flat as boards. The flesh hung loosely, and her hands which clutched the walking-stick were turned outwards and knobbled with age. Under her long dress also swayed the tattered edges of several petticoats. The ends of two bony stick-legs peeped out. She had on a pair of sand-shoes. The toes were all sticking out, so that the feet flapped about in them. She wore each shoe on the wrong foot, so that it made the heart turn over with amusement.

Yet she seemed so strong that it was a shock when she suddenly bent double, retched and coughed emptily, and crumbled to the ground like a quiet sigh.

"What is it, Mmm? What is the matter?" I asked.

"Water, water," she said faintly.

"Wait a minute. I shall ask at this hut here if there is any water."

"What is the matter?" they asked.

"The old lady is ill," I said.

"No," she said curtly. "I am not ill. I am hungry."

The crowd laughed in embarrassment that she should display her need so nakedly. They turned away; but old ladies have no more shame left. They are like children. They give way to weakness and cry openly when they are hungry.

"Never mind," I said. "Hunger is a terrible thing. My hut is not far away. This small child will take you. Wait till I come back, then I shall prepare food for you."

Then, it was late afternoon. The old lady had long passed from my mind when a strange young woman, unknown to me, walked into the yard with a pail of water on her head. She set it down outside the door and squatted low.

"Good-day. How are you?" I said.

She returned the greeting, keeping her face empty and carefully averted. It is impossible to say: what do you want? Whom are you looking for? It is impossible to say this to a carefully averted face and a body that squats quietly, patiently. I looked at the sky, helplessly. I looked at the trees. I looked at the ground, but the young woman said nothing. I did not know her, inside or out. Many people I do not know who know me, inside and out, and always it is this way, this silence.

A curious neighbour looked over the hedge.

"What's the matter?" she asked.

I turned my eyes to the sky again, shrugging helplessly.

"Please ask the young woman what she wants, whom she is looking for."

The young woman turned her face to the neighbour, still keeping it averted, and said quietly:

"No, tell her she helped our relative who collapsed this morning. Tell her the relatives discussed the matter. Tell her we had nothing to give in return, only that one relative said she passes by every day on her way to the water tap. Then we decided to give a pail of water. It is all we have."

Tell them too. Tell them how natural, sensible, normal is human kindness. Tell them, those who judge my country, Africa, by gain and greed, that the gods walk about her barefoot with no ermine and gold-studded cloaks.

The Special One

I WAS a newcomer to the village at that time and teaching at one of the primary schools. Mrs Maleboge was one of my colleagues, a short, stout woman, with a very sad face, who always wore a shawl and a white cotton kerchief wound rather unbecomingly around her head; the kerchief obscured a quarter part of her face so that her sad black eyes stared out from under it. She moved very slowly like the olden-day sailing ships blown by a steady breeze and her speech was as slow and steady as her walk. As soon as one became acquainted with her, she'd start to talk about the great tragedy in her life. Apparently, her husband had left her a small inheritance of cattle at his death, enough to have made her life comfortable in old age. The inheritance had been stolen from her by his brothers and so she was forced to seek employment in her old age when she should have been resting (she was sixty years old). She could stand for about an hour and outline details of the court case she had had with her brothers-in-law, and then stare quietly into the distance and comment: "I lost it because women are just dogs in this society." She did it to me twice, pinned me down and made me listen to the story, so that I developed an anxiety to avoid her. It was impossible to say: "Excuse me, I have to hurry somewhere" – she was too regal and commanded attention once she had started talking.

One day, without any change of expression, she said to me: "You must come to the baptismal party for my grandchild. It's on Sunday." Perhaps she didn't mean it, she was just self-absorbed, but her expression implied that the baptismal party was sad too like everything else. She also gave me directions to her home: "I live near the church. Just get near the church, then ask anyone in the surroundings where I live. They will show you my yard . . ."

So that was what I did, used the church as a guide-mark and then stood looking around, confused. Thousands of little footpaths spread out all round it towards thousands of yards, all with the same look. Where did I go from here? Suddenly along the footpath on which I was standing, a woman came walking towards me. She was walking rather rapidly and in a peculiar way with the wide, swaying footsteps of a drunk. She only cared about herself because she was looking at nothing and she would have walked right past me had I not said, with some desperation: "Please, do you know the yard of Mrs Maleboge?"

She stopped abruptly in the midst of her wide, swaying walk, turned around and looked directly at me.

"Why do you want to know where Mrs Maleboge lives?" she asked.

"She invited me to the baptismal party of her grandchild," I replied, uneasily. There was something wrong with the woman and she frightened me a little. To my surprise, she gasped and broke into a very friendly smile.

"How can Mrs Maleboge do this!" she exclaimed. "I am her best friend and she never told me that she was having a party! I am going to the party too! Come, I'll take you to her home. It's just around the corner."

That settled me a little and I was enchanted by the way she had had her mind entirely set on going somewhere else, and now had her mind entirely set on going to Mrs Maleboge's party. She had a light chiffon scarf wound around her head and she suddenly wrenched it off and began swinging it to and fro with the rhythm of her walk, like a young girl. I thought she might be in her late thirties and her mat of closely-cropped brown hair clung neatly to her head. She told me later that her name was Gaenametse, which literally translated means there-is-no-water but translated in a figurative way meant that at the time she was born, the marriage between her parents had been very unsatisfactory.

When we entered the yard of Mrs Maleboge, there were quite a number of guests assembled already. The old woman walked straight towards us, looking brighter and brisker than usual and taking me by the arm she said: "Special guests must enter the hut and be served separately. That is our custom."

Gaenametse and I entered the hut and as soon as the door was closed, my companion flung herself at Mrs Maleboge and began teasing and joking about the fact that her best friend had not invited her to the party but she was here all the same. They were really old friends, with a dialogue, and as soon as we were seated, Gaenametse picked up the dialogue at the exact point at which it had been left off when they last met.

"He's gone to her again!" she burst out. "I am at my wit's end, Mma-Maleboge. My love for my husband has reached the over-limit stage. I cannot part from him."

So acute was her misery that her whole body was shaken by sobs. And I thought: "That clears up the mystery of her frightening way of walking. She's at the point of breakdown."

I gathered from what they did next that they had been through this ritual a number of times. Mrs Maleboge sank to her knees, closed her eyes and began earnestly to implore Jesus to come to the aid of her friend. They formed a touching and complete circle of concentration. Gaenametse did not close her eyes. She stared intently at Mrs Maleboge's face as though expecting her at any moment to make contact with Jesus, and she did not want to miss that moment when it arrived. This effort of concentration so sharpened and heightened every feature in her face that I remember wondering why the unknown husband did not love such a beautiful woman. I had the impression of someone glowing with life, charm, and vitality.

Mrs Maleboge's prayer went on for well over fifteen minutes. Then she stood up and calmly carried on with her duties as hostess of a baptismal party. Neither woman was put out that a stranger had been witness to their private affairs. Gaenametse sat back, relaxed and calm, prepared to enjoy the party. She made some friendly conversation asking who I was and where I had come from. We were both handed plates of rice and chicken and salad by Mrs Maleboge. She had gone up in my estimation. I was deeply moved by the kindness she displayed towards her distressed friend and the touching and almost futile way in which the two women tried to cope with this eternal problem. Towards evening, Mrs Maleboge walked me a little way home and her final comment on the event was:

"Gaenametse has a very bad husband. He is off from woman to woman, but we are praying about the matter," and she stared quietly and sadly into the distance. She did not have to add that women are just dogs in this society. I believed her by then.

Six months later Gaenametse walked slowly down the road past my home; at least I saw someone I vaguely recognized. She had exchanged the lovely light chiffon scarf for the white cotton kerchief worn by Mrs Maleboge and wound it unbecomingly around her head so that only her eyes peeped out beneath it. A shawl was about her shoulders and her dress reached to the ankles. She had a piece of white crochet work in her hand and worked the crochet needle up and down as she walked. She looked very old and she recognized me more readily than I recognized her. She turned around with that sudden, impulsive movement and friendly smile.

"Oh," she said. "So this is where you live," and she turned in her path and walked straight up to my door.

I made tea, puzzled all the while. I just could not see the wild and beautiful woman of that Sunday. She soon informed me about this chameleon-like change of personality.

"I am divorced from my husband," she said, with a complacent smile.

"I'm sorry to hear that," I said, thinking that that was expected of me. I could see that she did not care a damn.

"Oh, everything is going to be all right," she said airily. "I have need of nothing. My father left me a lot of cattle when he died."

She put her head to one side, still with that complacent smile, and stroked the dead body of her marriage: "No one could have loved my husband as much as I did. I loved him too much."

"It's very sad when such things happen," I said.

"Oh, life isn't so bad," she said. "I can tell you a secret. Even old women like Mrs Maleboge are quite happy. They still make love."

I was so startled by this that I burst out: "You don't say!"

She put on the sweet and secret smile of a woman who knows much about this side of life.

"When you are old," she said, "that's the time you make love, more than when you are young. You make love because you are no longer afraid of making babies. You make love with young boys. They all do it but it is done very secretly. No one suspects, that is why they look so respectable in the day time."

It was just a bit beyond my imagination – Mrs Maleboge and a young boy! I shrugged my shoulders, lost. It never occurred to me either that this might also be Gaenametse's preoccupation. After we had drunk tea I walked her a little way down the road, and as I was returning to my own home I was accosted by a woman neighbour.

"What are you doing with *that one?*" she demanded.

I looked back at her, discomforted. It was the height of insult to refer to someone as *that one* but I was a bit appalled by that story of old women and young boys getting together.

"Don't you ever know what's going on in this village?" the gossipy neighbour persisted. "No one will talk to *her*. She's a wash-out! Everyone knows about her private life. She had a terrible divorce case. She was driving the husband mad. She pestered him day and night for the blankets, and even wanted him to do it during the time she was having her monthly bleeding. Many women have killed men by sleeping with them during that time. It's a dangerous thing and against our custom. The woman will remain alive and the man will die. She was trying to kill the husband, so the court ruled that he'd better be parted from such a terrible woman."

I stared back at her in petrified horror. She must have thought I understood and approved of some of the insane beliefs of a primitive society, and the society was primitive in certain respects – all primitive societies have their holy fear of a woman's menstrual cycle: during that time she is dirty, and a source of death and danger to the surroundings in general. No, what horrified me was the memory of that Sunday; the wide, drunken swaying walk of extreme emotional distress; the tender appeal two women had made to Jesus for help and a sudden insight into the depth of wickedness of the unknown man. He must have anticipated this social reaction to his wife and deliberately invoked the old tribal taboo to boost his image. How she must have cringed and squirmed, and after the divorce tried to build up an image of respect by dressing up like old Mrs Maleboge! It was impossible to convey all this to the snickering village gossip, so I simply told her quite seriously, without knowing anything definite about it, that where I came from the men usually slept with the women when they were menstruating so it was all right for me to talk to Gaenametse.

Shortly afterwards, I saw Gaenametse in the central shopping area of the village. She was dressed like Mrs Maleboge but she was off her beam again. Her walk was her own, wide, drunken, and swaying. Soon I noticed that she was following a young man and a young girl who were strolling casually down the dusty dirt road, hand in hand. She caught up with the couple and with a swift movement planted herself firmly in their path. She looked at the young man with a terribly ugly expression. Since I could read it, he must have read it too. It said plainly: "So, I am only good enough to visit at night. I'd like to stroll casually through the village with you, hand in hand." But no word was exchanged. She turned abruptly and swayed her way off into the distance. She was like that, a wild and wayward learner. She must have decided there and then that Mrs Maleboge's tricks were beyond her. She could not keep her emotions within bounds.

Her last image was the final one I saw. A business matter forced me to take a walk to a remote and far-flung part of the village. While on my way back a voice called out gaily: "Hey, what are you doing here?" I turned around and there was Gaenametse briskly sweeping a yard with a broom. She was still dressed like Mrs Maleboge but she looked happy in an complacent kind of way, like the day she had walked down the road with her crochet work.

"Won't you come in for tea?" she asked. "I watched you walking right to the end of the village and you must be thirsty."

As we walked towards the single mud hut in the yard, she lowered her voice to a whisper: "I have a husband. We are not quite married yet, but he is the priest of our church. He started the church himself because he can heal people. I went to him when my heart was troubled and so we found love. He is a very good man. He's inside the house now studying the Bible."

The man was seated on a low wooden stool. He was quite elderly, with greying hair. He stood up as we entered and politely clasped his hands together, exchanged greetings, and quietly went back to his Bible study. We drank tea, talked, and then she walked with me a little of the way home.

"You seem happy now," I said. "I cannot forget how unhappy you were that day at Mrs Maleboge's party."

She smiled, that sweetly secret smile of a woman who knows how to sort out her love life.

"I have all I need now," she said. "I have a good man. I am his mosadi-rra."

"What does that mean?" I asked.

"It means I am the special one," she said.

And as I walked on alone I thought that the old days of polygamy are gone and done with, but the men haven't yet accepted that the women want them to be monogamists.

Velma Pollard

1937–

*B*orn *in rural Jamaica to a school teacher and a farmer, she (and her younger sister, Erna Brodber) grew up in Woodside, St Mary. She has a PhD in Language Education, has taught in*

*Montreal, New York, Guyana and Trinidad and is a lecturer in the
Faculty of Education at the University of the West Indies, Jamaica. Her
special academic interests are teaching English in a creole-speaking
environment, language in Caribbean literature and language of the
Rastafari. Her critical articles, poems and short stories have appeared
in various periodicals, and she is the author of* Crown Point and Other
Poems *(1988),* Shame Trees Don't Grow Here *(poetry, 1991) and the
fiction collection* Considering Woman *(1989). Novelist Joan Riley has
said: "Pollard takes us on a journey through her world of women, Black
women whose warmth and humanity enfolds us through her pen."*

Bitterland

Listening your tale
tells me how woman I have felt for girls
fighting with wigs and powder caught strap-
hanging in the galleys of the USA

you tell me your New York
your Brooklyn and the Bronx
your island childhood cut in half
too soon a man
and all that little-understood
no longer folks
but black folks
hacks up there
where eyes forget to smile
and learn to bare unwilling
teeth in greeting (?)

the scars like keloids
mark the back of your remembering
like pictures shot too sharp
grow large in retrospect

A thousand spades
a thousand journeys
each generation's new roots
grown in air
or barely touching ground
twisted and gnarled. . .

Unless like yours
their luck
was in.

From

Considering Woman

CAGE I

I N the brown sofa, a geometrical figure, head lowered, trunk resting on a triangle of thighs and legs, Hugh sits. Joan passes the cup and seats herself in the couch opposite. The fragrance of Blue Mountain coffee clouds them slow, invisibly. Hugh, with great deliberateness, raises his head, waits, lowers it, and takes a quick, hot sip. Joan suddenly finds herself staring, contemplating a huge, brooding, over-sized bird; caught in a cage.

In the zoo, animals have enough space for the occasional short exploratory sally. A bird of Hugh's size would have a very large cage with enough space for a good whirl now and then. And even so they show claustrophobic tendencies.

"I want to talk to you."

"About what?"

"The marriage and everything."

"What about them?"

"How we and you not communicating at all."

"What you mean not communicating? I find we communicating quite well."

"I don't mean like that. I mean we not feeling comfortable and happy in the relationship with each other and I don't even feel sure you want me around."

This wasn't going very well. It sounded surprisingly like several earlier attempts on the same subject. The tone of response was the same too, gruff and impatient. This pause was too long; sort of ominous.

"What you want me to do now, tell you a love you and things like that?"

"I don't want you to lie to me and tell me things you don't mean."

"Is what you want then, woman? Listen, all I want now is to read this book and to be able to read it by myself. That is why I came out here in the first place. You ever hear about people needing to be alone? Well, that is what I need right now. A person can't even sit down a little by themselves without you coming with you stupid paranoia. You half-crazy, noh, but you not going send me off my head too."

Put like that, it all sounded very reasonable. Joan started to wonder whether she did, as Hugh frequently suggested, make her own problems then start to worry about them. Maybe she was complicating this marriage by her anxiety; she so desperately wanted it to go well. But could it really be so unfair to expect Hugh even just to talk to her sometimes? – in more than monosyllables, that is.

Joan lay in bed and moved out of the flat in a reverie that threatened to become obsessive. She must run away; leave Hugh and give him a chance; give herself a chance. They were destroying each other. He said he was okay but he probably just didn't want to think about it. She certainly wasn't. There had to be more than that to life. These days she found herself talking to herself after the older children had left for school. Nowhere had she read about or imagined such loneliness.

Married loneliness . . . call it what you will. You communicate all day with small children; you find yourself living for the evening and adult companionship and when it comes . . . it wants to be alone.

Hugh said she was like an octopus trying to hold him in a sort of multiple embrace. That sounded truly original and perhaps it was . . . great minds? Anyway she had noted the same image in a psychology book for laymen. Perhaps he even read psychology books on the sly all the while swearing they were confusing her brain:

"Listen, no two people alike; no two couples alike. How anybody can tell you how to fix yourself just because they fix some other people completely different from you . . . only a clown like you could swallow so much stupid-ness." She didn't want to own Hugh, or anything like that. She just wanted him to recognize the hand behind the coffee cup – sometimes. The thing with marriage is that it takes you out of your own little circle of girls and fellows then offers you nothing in exchange. And the man who spent so much time trying to be with you suddenly finds every ruse to be without you or starts looking very pained if he has to be with you.

But she had tried to make it bearable. Take the time Shadwell used to come by Sunday nights and bring his records so they could listen he to hers she to his such a fine selection between them . . . Hugh never liked her kind of music. Too melodramatic he used to say; those fantastic horns! So he would drift away to the bedroom. You can't expect to share all the same interests yourself and your husband so a guileless, young, sensible chap like Shads where is the harm in that? But one Sunday night he was a little late and Hugh said in his deadpan voice:

"What happen, you boyfriend not coming tonight?"

And you know that throw such a damper on the whole thing that she start to show the young man bad face. . . Amen to that. You either make a big fuss and a big point over a small thing like that; or forget it.

Or take the time she asked him whether she could invite Peter, the nice new fellow on the staff, over to the house so he could meet him:

"As long as when I bring any girls in here you don't mind." She hadn't meant it that way and Hugh knew that. So she never invited Peter though he collected blown glass pieces too and wanted to see her collection. Of course when he decided that girls was the thing, he went for them with a zest she hadn't seen him display about anything since he stopped stoning mangoes.

"You not sleeping?"

"Mmmmmm."

"What you setting up for without even a book in you hand?"

"I was just thinking. . ."

"I don't want to hear what you thinking. Every day for the past six years you been thinking the same thing. I want to sleep. You better try a little of that too."

In no time she was listening to him snore . . . curled up; his back a smooth curve, his knees forming an angle with his nose; accommodating his body, even in that peculiar shape, to the narrowness of the bed. Gathering the blanket about her, Joan settled into her small cage and concentrated on the shaft of light coming in through a peephole from the street outside. She knew she had found no answers.

Simone Schwarz-Bart

1938–

A fter spending her formative years in her native land, Guadeloupe, attending school there in Pointe-à-Pitre, she continued her education in Paris and in Dakar, Senegal. She now lives in Switzerland with her husband, writer André Schwarz-Bart, whom she met in 1959 and with whom she collaborated on the novel Une plat de porc aux bananes vertes *(1967). This extract comes from her prizewinning novel* Pluie et vent sur Télumée-Miracle *(1972), translated as* The Bridge of Beyond *(1974), an evocative tribute to the women of Guadeloupe whose indomitable spirit surmounts the deprivation in which they live as the descendants of ancestors enslaved by the French. Among her other works of fiction are* Ti Jean L'horizon *(1979) and a play,* Ton Beau Capitaine *(1987).*

From

The Bridge of Beyond

CHAPTER I

A MAN'S country may be cramped or vast according to the size of his heart. I've never found my country too small, though that isn't to say my heart is great. And if I could choose it's here in Guadeloupe that I'd be born again, suffer and die. Yet not long back my ancestors were slaves on this volcanic, hurricane-swept, mosquito-ridden, nasty-minded island. But I didn't come into the world to weigh the world's woe. I prefer to dream, on and on, standing in my garden, just like any other old woman of my age, till death comes and takes me as I dream, me and all my joy.

When I was a child my mother, Victory, often talked to me about my grandmother Toussine. She spoke of her with fervor and veneration: Toussine, she'd say, was a woman who helped you hold your head up, and people with this gift are rare. My mother's reverence for Toussine was such I came to regard her as some mythical being not of this world, so that for me she was legendary even while still alive.

I got into the habit of calling her, as men called her, Queen Without a Name. But her maiden name had been Toussine Lougandor.

Her mother was Minerva, a fortunate woman freed by the abolition of slavery from a master notorious for cruelty and caprice. After the abolition Minerva wandered in search of a refuge far from the plantation and its vagaries, and she came to rest at L'Abandonnée. Some runaway slaves came there afterwards, and a village grew up. The wanderers seeking refuge were countless, and many would not settle anywhere permanently for fear the old days might return. One Negro from Dominica vanished as soon as he learned he had sired a child, and those in L'Abandonnée whom Minerva had scorned now laughed at her swollen belly. But when dark-skinned Xango took on the shame of my great-grandmother Minerva, the laughter stopped dead, and those who had been amusing themselves at other's misfortunes choked on their own bile. Little Toussine came into the world, and Xango loved her as if she were his own. As the child grew, shooting up as gracefully as a sugar cane, she became the light of his eyes, the blood in his veins, the air in his lungs. Thus through the love and respect lavished on her by Xango, Minerva, now long dead, could walk without shame along the main street of the hamlet, head high, back arched, arms akimbo, and foul breath turned from her to blow over better pastures. And so life began for young Toussine, as delicately as dawn on a clear day.

They lived in a hamlet swept alternately by winds from the land and winds from the sea. A steep road ran along by cliffs and wastelands, leading, it seemed, to nothing human. And that was why it was called the deserted village, L'Abandonnée. At certain times everyone there would be filled with dread, like travellers lost in a strange land. Still young and strong, always dressed in a worker's overall, Minerva had a glossy, light mahogany skin and black eyes brimming over with kindness. She had an unshakeable faith in life. When things went wrong she would say that nothing, no one, would ever wear out the soul God had chosen out for her and put in her body. All the year round she fertilized vanilla, picked coffee, hoed the banana groves, and weeded the rows of sweet potatoes. And her daughter Toussine was no more given to dreaming than she. Almost as soon as she woke the child would make herself useful sweeping, gathering fruit, peeling vegetables. In the afternoon she would go to the forest to collect leaves for the rabbits, and sometimes the whim would take her to kneel in the shade of the mahoganies and look for the flat brightly coloured seeds that are made into necklaces. When she came back with a huge pile of greenstuff on her head, Xango delighted to see her with leaves hanging down over her face, and would fling both arms in the air and shout: "Hate me, so long as you love Toussine. Pinch me till you draw blood, but don't touch so much as the hem of her robe." And he would laugh and cry just to look at the radiant, frank-faced child whose features were said to be like those of the Negro from Dominica, whom he would have liked to meet once, just to see. But as yet she was not in full bloom. It was when she was fifteen that she stood out from all the other girls with the unexpected grace of a red canna growing on a mountain, so that the old folk said she in herself was the youth of L'Abandonnée.

There was also in L'Abandonnée at that time a young fisherman called Jeremiah who filled one's soul with the same radiance. But he paid no attention to girls, to whom his friends used to say, laughing, "When Jeremiah falls in love it will be with a mermaid." But this didn't make him any less handsome, and the girls' hearts shrivelled up with vexation. He was nineteen and already the best fisherman in Caret cove. Where on earth did he get those hauls of vivaneaux, tazars, and blue balarous? Nowhere but from beneath his boat, the *Headwind*, in which he used to go off forever, from morn till night and night till morn; all he lived for was hearing the sound of the waves in his ears and feeling the tradewinds caressing his face. Such was Jeremiah when Toussine was for everyone a red canna growing on a high mountain.

On windless days when the sea was dead calm Jeremiah would go into the forest to cut the lianas he made into lobster pots. One afternoon when he left the beach for this purpose, Toussine appeared in his path, right in the middle of a wood. She was wearing one of her mother's old dresses that came down to her ankles, and with her heap of greenstuff coming down over her eyes and hiding her face, she looked as if she didn't know where she was going. The young man asked her, "Is this L'Abandonnée's latest fashion in donkeys?" She threw down her burden, looked at him, and said in surprise, almost in tears: "A girl just goes to collect greenstuff from the forest, and here I am, insulted." With that, she burst out laughing and scampered off into the shadow. It was then Jeremiah was caught in the finest lobster pot he ever saw. When he got back from his excursion his friends noticed he looked absentminded, but they did not ask any questions. Real fishermen, those who have taken the sea for their native country, often have that lost look. So his friends just thought dry land didn't agree with Jeremiah, and that his natural element was the water. But they sang a different tune in the days that followed, when they saw Jeremiah neglecting the *Headwind*, deserting her and leaving her high and dry on the beach. Consulting among themselves, they came to the conclusion he must be under the spell of the Guiablesse, the most wicked of spirits, the woman with the cloven hoof who feeds exclusively on your desire to live, and whose charms drive you sooner or later to suicide. They asked him if he hadn't met someone that ill-fated day when he went up into the forest. Eventually Jeremiah confessed: "The only Guiablesse I met that day," he said, "is called Toussine – Xango's Toussine." . . .

On the day of the wedding all the village paths were swept and decorated as for the local feast day. Xango and Minerva's cottage was surrounded by huts of woven coconut palm. The one reserved for the bridal couple was a great bouquet of hibiscus, mignonette, and orange blossom – the scent was intoxicating. Rows of tables stretched as far as the eye could see, and you were offered whatever drink you were thirsty for, whatever meat would tickle your palate. There was meat of pig, sheep, and cattle, and even poultry served in the liquor it was cooked in. Blood pudding rose up in shining coils; tiered cakes were weighed down with lacy frosting; every kind of water ice melted before your eyes – custard-apple, water-lemon, coconut. But for the Negroes of L'Abandonnée all this was nothing without some music, and when they saw the three bands, one for quadrilles and mazurkas, one for the fashionable beguine, and the traditional combination of drum, wind instruments, and horn, then they knew they'd really have something worth talking about at least once in their lives. And this assuaged the hearts swollen with jealousy. For three days everyone left behind hills and plateaus, troubles and indignities of every kind, to relax, dance, and salute the bridal couple, going to and fro before them in the flower-decked tent, congratulating Toussine on her luck and Jeremiah on his best of luck. It was impossible to count how many mouths uttered the word luck, for that was the theme they decided to adopt for telling their descendants, in later years, of the wedding of Toussine and Jeremiah.

The years flowed over it all, and Toussine was still the same dragonfly with shimmering blue wings, Jeremiah still the same glossy-coated sea dog. He continued to go out alone, never bringing back an empty boat, however niggardly the sea. Scandalmongers said he used witchcraft and had a spirit go out fishing in his stead when no one else was about. But in fact his only secret was his enormous patience. When the fish would not bite at all, he dived for lambis. If there were no lambis, he put out long rods with hooks or live crabs to tempt the octopi. He knew the sea as the hunter knows the forest. When the wind had gone and the boat was hauled up on the shore, he would make for his little cottage, pour the money he'd earned into his wife's lap, and have a snack as he waited for the sun to abate. Then the two of them would go to tend their garden. While he dug, she would mark out the rows; while he burned weeds, she would sow. And the sudden dusk of the islands would come down over them, and Jeremiah would take advantage of the deepening dark to have a little hors d'oeuvre of his wife's body, there on the ground, murmuring all sorts of foolishness to her, as on the very first day. "I still don't know what it is I like best about you – one day it's your eyes, the next your woodland laugh, another your hair, and the day after the lightness of your step; another, the beauty spot on your temple, and then the day after that the grains of rice I glimpse when you smile at me." And to this air on the mandolin, Toussine, trembling with delight, would reply with a cool, rough little air on the flute: "My dear, anyone just seeing you in the street would give you the host without asking you to go to confession, but you're a dangerous man, and you'd have buried me long ago if people ever died of happiness." Then they would go indoors and Jeremiah would address the evening, casting a last look over the fields: "How can one help loving a garden?"
     Their prosperity began with a grass path shaded by coconut palms and kept up as beautifully as if it led to a castle. In fact it led to a little wooden house with two rooms, a thatched roof, and a floor supported on four large cornerstones. There was a hut for cooking in, three blackened stones for a hearth, and a covered tank so that Toussine could do her washing without having to go and gossip with the neighbours by the river. As the women did their washing they would pick quarrels to give zest to the work, comparing their respective fates and filling their hearts with bitterness and rancour. Meanwhile Toussine's linen would be boiling away in a pan in the back yard, and she took advantage of every minute to make her house more attractive. Right in front of the door she'd planted a huge bed of Indian poppies, which flowered all year round. To the right there was an orange tree with hummingbirds and to the left clumps of Congo cane from which she

used to cut pieces to give to her daughters, Eloisine and Meranee, for their tea. She would go to and fro amid all this in a sort of permanent joy and richness, as if Indian poppies, Congo canes, hummingbirds, and orange trees were enough to fill a woman's heart with complete satisfaction. And because of the richness of joy she felt in return for so little, people envied and hated her. She could withdraw at will into the recesses of her own soul, but she was reserved, not disillusioned. And because she bloomed like that, in solitude, she was also accused of being an aristocrat stuck-up. Late every Sunday evening she would walk through the village on Jeremiah's arm to look at the place and the people and the animals just before they disappeared in the darkness. She was happy, herself part of all that spectacle, that close and familiar universe. She came to be the thorn in some people's flesh, the delight of others, and because she had a distant manner they thought she put on aristocratic airs.

After the grass path came a veranda, which surrounded the little house, giving constant cool and shade if you moved the bench according to the time of day. Then there were the two windows back and front, real windows with slatted shutters, so that you could close the door and shut yourself safely away from spirits and still breathe in the scents of evening. But the true sign of their prosperity was the bed they inherited from Minerva and Xango. It was a vast thing of locust wood with tall head posts and three mattresses, which took up the entire bedroom. Toussine used to put vetiver roots under the mattresses, and citronella leaves, so that whenever anyone lay down there were all sorts of delicious scents: the children said it was a magic bed. It was a great object of curiosity in that poor village, where everyone else still slept on old clothes laid down on the floor at night, carefully folded up in the morning, and spread in the sun to get rid of the fleas. People would come and weigh up the grass path, the real windows with slatted shutters, the bed with its oval-panelled headboard lording it beyond the open door, and the red-bordered counterpane, which seemed an additional insult. And some of the women would say with a touch of bitterness, "Who do they take themselves for, these wealthy Negroes? Toussine and Jeremiah, with their two-roomed house, their wooden veranda, their slatted shutters, and their bed with three mattresses and red borders – do they think all these things make them white?"

Later on Toussine also had a satin scarf, a broad necklace of gold and silver alloy, garnet earrings, and high-vamped slippers she wore twice a year, on Ash Wednesday and Christmas Day. And as the wave showed no sign of flagging, the time came when the other Negroes were no longer surprised, and talked about other things, other people, other pains and other wonders. They had gotten used to the prosperity as they had gotten used to their own poverty. The subject of Toussine and wealthy Negroes was a thing of the past; it had all become quite ordinary.

Woe to him who laughs once and gets into the habit, for the wickedness of life is limitless: if it gives you your heart's desire with one hand, it is only to trample on you with both feet and let loose on you that madwoman bad luck, who seizes and rends you and scatters your flesh to the crows.

Eloisine and Meranee, twins, were ten years old when luck forsook their mother Toussine. A school had just opened in the village, and a teacher came twice a week to teach the children their letters in exchange for a few pennyworth of foodstuff. One evening as they were learning their alphabet, Meranee said her sister had all the light and told her to move the lamp to the middle of the table. And so just one little word gave bad luck an opening. "Have it all, then!" said Eloisine, giving the light an angry shove. It was over in an instant: the china lamp was in pieces and the burning oil was spreading all over Meranee's legs and shoulders and hair. A living torch flew out into the darkness, and the evening breeze howled around it, fanning the flames. Toussine caught up a blanket and ran after the child, shouting to her to stand still, but she rushed madly hither and thither, leaving a luminous track behind her like a falling star. In the end she collapsed, and Toussine wrapped her in the blanket, picked her up, and went back toward the house, which was still burning. Jeremiah comforted Eloisine, and they all sat in the middle of their beautiful path, on the damp grass of evening, watching their sweat, their life, their joy, go up in flames. A big crowd had gathered: the Negroes stood there fascinated, dazzled by the magnitude of the disaster. They stared at the flames lighting up the sky, shifting from foot to foot, in two minds – they felt an impulse to pity, and yet saw the catastrophe as poetic justice. It made them forget their own fate and compare the cruelty of this misfortune with the ordinariness of their own. At any rate, it's one thing that won't happen to us, they said.

Meranee's suffering was terrible. Her body was one great wound attracting more and more flies as it decayed. Toussine, her eyes empty of all expression, fanned them away, put on soothing oil, and grew hoarse calling on death, which, being no doubt occupied elsewhere, refused to come. If anyone offered to replace Toussine at the bedside for a while, she would say, smiling gently: "Don't worry about me. However heavy a woman's breasts, her chest is always strong enough to carry them." She spent seventeen days and seventeen nights cajoling death, and then, ill luck having gone elsewhere, Meranee expired. Life went on as before, but without one vestige of heart left, like a flea feasting on your last drop of blood, delighting in leaving you senseless and sore, cursing heaven and earth and the womb that conceived you.

Against sorrow and the vanity of things, there is and will always be human fantasy. It was thanks to the fantasy of a white man that Toussine and Jeremiah found a roof. He was a Creole called Colbert Lanony, who in the old days just after the abolition of slavery had fallen in love with a strange and fascinating young Negress. Cast out by his own people, he had sought refuge in a desolate and inaccessible wasteland far from the eyes that looked askance at his love. Nothing remained of all that now but some fine blocks of stone mouldering away in the wilderness, colonnades, worm-eaten ceilings, and tiles bearing witness still to the past and to an outlawed white man's fancy for a Negress. To those who were surprised to find a house like that in such a place, the local people got into the habit of saying, "It's L'Abandonnée," and the name later came to be used for the hamlet itself. Only one room on the first floor was habitable, a sort of closet, where the window openings were covered with sheets of cardboard. When it rained the water trickled through a hole in the roof into a bucket, and at night the ground floor was the resort of toads, frogs, and bats. But none of this seemed to bother Toussine, who had gone to live there like a body without a soul, indifferent to such details. As was the custom, she was visited there the first nine evenings by all the people of the village, who came to pay their respects to the dead and to keep the living company. Toussine did not weep or complain, but sat upright on a bench in a corner as if every breath of air were poison. People did not want to desert a ship like Toussine, but the sight of her was so unbearable they cut the ceremony short, just coming in, greeting her, and leaving, full of pitying kindness, thinking she was lost for ever.

The leaf that falls into the pond does not rot the same day, and Toussine's sorrow only grew worse with time, fulfilling all the gloomy predictions. At first Jeremiah still went to sea three times a week, but then only twice, then once, then not at all. The house looked as deserted as ever, as if there were no one living there. Toussine never left the room with the cardboard windows, and Jeremiah collected their food from the woods around – purslane, scurvy grass, pink makanga bananas. Before, the women going to market used to take a path that led by the ruined house; it was a shortcut to the main road and Basse-Terre, where they sold their wares. But now they were afraid, and they made a big detour through the forest rather than go near the pig-headed Toussine, who didn't speak, wouldn't even answer, but just sat staring into space, a bag of bones as good as dead. Every so often, when the conversation came around to her and Jeremiah and little Eloisine, a man would shin up a tree, peer toward the house, and report that it was still the same; nothing had changed, nothing had moved.

Three years went by before people began to talk about them again. As usual, a man climbed a tree and looked toward the ruins; but this time he didn't say anything, and showed no sign of coming down. When questioned he only signed for someone else to come up and look. It was the second man who announced that Toussine, the little stranded boat, the woman thought to be lost for ever, had come out of her cardboard tower and was taking a little walk outside in the sun.

Glad as they were at this news, the Negroes still waited, hesitating to rejoice outright until the kid was safely caught and tethered and they were sure they hadn't sharpened their knives for nothing. And as they looked, this is what they saw: Toussine was cutting down the weeds around the ruined house. She shivered a moment, went in, then came out again almost at once and began to cut down brushwood and scrub with the furious energy of a woman with something urgent to do and not a minute to lose.

From that day on the place began to be a little less desolate and the market women went back to using the shortcut to Basse-Terre. Toussine had taken her family into prison with her, and now she brought them back to life again. First Eloisine was seen in the village again, as slight and brittle as a straw. Next poor Jeremiah came down to the beach, filled his eyes with the sea and stood staring, fascinated, then went back smiling up the hill as in the days when the song of the waves sounded in his head. It could be seen plainly written across his brow that he would go back to sea again. Toussine put curtains up at the windows, and planted Indian poppies around the ruin, Angola peas, root vegetables, and clumps of Congo cane for Eloisine. And then one day she planted the pip of a hummingbird orange. But the Negroes did not rejoice yet. They still watched and waited, from a distance. They thought of the old Toussine, in rags, and compared her with the Toussine of today – not a woman, for what is a woman? Nothing at all, they said, whereas Toussine was a bit of the world, a whole country, a plume of a Negress, the ship, sail, and wind, for she had not made a habit of sorrow. Then Toussine's belly swelled and burst and the child was called Victory. And then the Negroes did rejoice. On the day of the christening they came to Toussine and said:

"In the days of your silks and jewels we called you Queen Toussine. We were not far wrong, for you are truly a queen. But now, with your Victory, you may boast that you have put us in a quandary. We have tried and tried to think of a name for you, but in vain, for there isn't one that will do. And so from now on we shall call you 'Queen Without a Name'!"

And they ate, drank, and were merry, and from that day forth my grandmother was called the Queen Without a Name.

Erna Brodber

1940–

*L*ike her writer sister Velma Pollard, she was born in the village *of Woodside, Jamaica, and before starting secondary school had three stories published in* The Weekly Times. *Graduating from high school, she worked in the civil service, then taught in Montego Bay. She earned a BA Honours degree in history from the University of the West Indies (UWI) and after a year in Trinidad as head of history at St Augustine High School for Girls she returned to Jamaica and was children's officer with the Ministry of Youth and Community Development.*

She won a Ford Foundation pre-doctoral scholarship and went to the University of Washington in 1967. She later received an MSc from UWI's Department of Sociology and became a lecturer there, joining the staff of the Institute of Social and Economic Research. Her first published books were sociological, and she has been involved with radio and drama, but it was with the appearance of Jane and Louisa Will Soon Come Home *(1980) – extracted here – in which she tellingly experiments with folk forms, that her unique contribution to the development of Caribbean fiction became evident. Jamaican literary critic Carolyn Cooper writes: "Brodber's narrative method exemplifies an interpretation of scribal and oral literary forms: a modernist, stream-of-consciousness narrative voice holds easy dialogue with the traditional teller of tales, the transmitter of anansi story, proverb, folk song and dance." Her second novel,* Myal *(1988), won the 1989 Commonwealth Writers' Prize.*

From

Jane and Louisa Will Soon Come Home

G RANNY Tucker prayed on Sunday mornings. In truth she always prays. Kneading her bread, she prays for health and strength to continue making bread to supply to the shops, to bring in money to pay Brother Jack to run the sugar mill to make sugar to feed the district. Granny Tucker prays for those who cannot afford to buy bread, for those who sing rag songs, and stray from the good book, waste their money on cock fights and cannot buy their bread. She prays for rain to moist the cabbage suckers. She prays that rain will stay away from the ripening tomato field. She prays for Parson Blair and the whole church militant. She prays constantly against Ole Joe, the devil who can tempt you, who can hide one foot of shoes and have you hunting for the other, who can cause your dough to fall.

Granny Tucker prays for the whole community. Give us faith O lord. Faith in our curing and sustaining power. Faith Dear God, not to fight evil with evil, to stand proud but not so proud that we insult you. Help us to beat down the disruptive force of the Tempter. Nowhere as in us dear God does evil have more sway. And you know why O lord (and she shakes her head). She prays for Tanny Stewart. Beating graves to get one square of land, to take that foolish woman from his brother, setting springe for that insipid khaki woman. Foolishness. What does it profit you to gain the world and lose your soul! And now facing the pearly gates, confessing to have known the devil. Stupid Fool. Lord take his tongue.

She prayed constantly. For evil is strong and only with God can it be fought.

But on Sunday mornings Granny Tucker prays especially for her children dispersed to the ends of the world... three, eight, forty miles and even overseas doing what she does not know but God knows best. On Sunday mornings, Granny Tucker rouses at Sheila's bark, rubs her eyes, says "Praise God for another day", breathes in heavily and says "Praise God" again, and like an alto sax tuning up or an organ finding the prelude to an anthem, she hums . . . just notes in different keys and octaves, sometimes in her chest, sometimes in her throat, sometimes with lips apart, eventually into song with words:

> Jesus still lead on
> Til our rest be won
> And although the way be cheerless
> We will follow calm and fearless.

Yes Lord, feed her spirit.

On Sunday mornings Granny Tucker prays on her knees, hands clasped and resting on her bed, knees joined to that vast expanse of dark, shine, broad, breadfruit wood, she prays for the six children "you put in this house". She prays for them by order of birth.

Granny prays for Eliza married before her time, married yes Lord but to a sinner. Touch his heart Lord if only for my chile's sake. Take away the rum and the dice. Hold his hand and steady him Lord. Keep your hand on him and mek we hold up our head.

She prays for Rita. In Colon. But you know best Lord. Keep her close to your feet and show her the way. I don't hear nothing Lord but keep her straight. Keep her from the pomp and vanity of this wicked world. Keep her from lip rouge and straighten hair. Take her hand Lord and keep her on the straight and narrow.

An Naomi. Only you dear Lord know why you take her in the prime of her life and leave these two little ones motherless and fatherless. Dear Jesus, show me how to keep them in the fold for I don't young again and you know it.

She prays for the boys. Don't strike me Lord, if I pray a little harder for my boy children, Lord. Is them must keep the name. Is them belong at your right hand. Bring them back Lord. Bring them back. I not kneeling down here for nothing. I don't go to church every Sunday for nothing. Bring them back Lord. You know I need them. Me one can't carry on. Brother Jack help. I thank you Lord. But blood thicker than water. What them doing in that wicked city. Can't even hear from them. Who to knock a nail if you want it knock. My hand weak now. Show them the joy of looking up into their mother eye. I stay with my father and get the blessing. Tell them what it is like.

You didn't bring Albert from the dead to work in no cock-fighting pit? You same one did give me a hard time with Obediah, Lord and it have to have some meaning. I not questioning you Lord, but what is this putting out, putting out to sea that he always writing to tell me 'bout? That just don't sound right Lord. Not even one of them you don't give a nose for your ministry, Lord!

Carlton is here Lord. Is it he? But he say he is going Lord and I can't stop in his way. Then who going to carry your cross?

It is Sarah's time.

– I have a wash belly Dear Saviour. You know it. You gave her to me. Didn't even get to see the father. Sarah is the name. I pick out teacher for her but you didn't want that for her. You turn her woman. You give her Alexander Richmond and two acres of land and six mouths to feed . . . Leaford Alfred, Gladys Maud, Joseph Obediah, William Alexander, Nellie, Rupie and the one she say coming. Pardon me Lord, those sneaking khaki people wouldn't let my chile rest. Every year so! I am only woman Lord and I beg you guide me for I can't question you. I can only say "Take the case Lord. Take the case for is your case." So take the case, Lord –

Granny Tucker sighs and makes to rise, half mumbling:

– You give me good man but you take him soon. Keep me Corpie good –

Eyes glazed and far away, Granny Tucker takes her hands from her nightdress and lets it fall to her hips; takes her stays from her bed head and hunches her shoulders, now one now the other as she pushes her arms through the openings. Lifts one, now the other breast, as she fits them into their sockets. From under her pillow, she takes her small clothes, a baggy affair, steps in and with her hand under her nightdress, pulls the string hard around her waist. She lets the dress slip to her feet and steps out of it; pulls her flannel merino over her head, ties her petticoat around her waist and hooks the bodice over this, smoothing out the bulges, the while. Then she takes her day frock from the rack, pulls it over her head, hooks the press-stud at the side and reaches for her tie-head all the while singing and humming "Guide me, O thou great Jehovah" as if in her toilet too she needs His guiding hand.

– Ham laughed at his father and was banished. You have to grow the children in the sight of the Lord – Granny mutters.

– Janey and Lou. Come over. It is time to pray –

– The children must be brought up in the sight of the Lord – Granny mutters. Granny Tucker get to her knees again with her granddaughters on either side:

– Lord defend this thy child and this thy child – she pats them on the head.

– Gentle Jesus meek and mild . . . go on Janey go on . . . Louise who you going to pray for? –

– You Granny –

– Not me one Lou. Pray for your aunts and your uncles. Pray for Aunt Sarah and her house. Call everybody by name. Say it now. God bless Aunt Sarah, bless Leaford Alfred, bless Gladys, Maud, bless Joseph Obediah, bless William Alexander, bless your play mate Nellie and little Rupie. You too Jane. Pray for each other. Pray to God to make you good girls –

– Mustn't pray for Uncle Alexander too –

– You know that Louise, you know that. Who else you going to pray for? –

– Everybody Granny –

– Not yet. Anybody else special? –

– Don't know Granny –

– Who you know that dying chile? –

– Mass Tanny Granny –

– Yes Mass Tanny. Pray that he reach the mercy seat. Pray that your grandfather and your mother and father stay there. They were good people. You come from good stock. Don't mind the evil 'round you. You must be proud and thankful for that –

The cool Christmas breeze is blowing.

– Put on your sweater. Wash your face and rinse your mouth and look after the chuunies –

The teasing Christmas breeze is blowing. It is early December and they too are eight.

Ann Moody
?1941–

Her *autobiography* Coming of Age in Mississippi *was published in 1968, a candid and powerful account of growing up Black in the southern USA, surviving bigotry, poverty and brutality to find self-awareness and later involvement with the civil rights movement. Christened Essie Mae, she used a different forename as a result of an error on her birth certificate. In this passage, it is 1955 and as a fourteen-year-old she is becoming increasingly aware of what it means to be Black in the US south, learning of the murder of teenage Emmett Till and of the existence of the National Association for the Advancement of Colored People.*

From

Coming of Age in Mississippi

CHAPTER X

Nот only did I enter high school with a new name, but also with a completely new insight into the life of Negroes in Mississippi. I was now working for one of the meanest white women in town, and a week before school started Emmett Till was killed.

Up until his death, I had heard of Negroes found floating in a river or dead somewhere with their bodies riddled with bullets. But I didn't know the mystery behind these killings then. I remember once when I was only seven I heard Mama and one of my aunts talking about some Negro who had been beaten to death. "Just like them low-down skunks killed him they will do the same to us," Mama had said. When I asked her who killed the man and why, she said, "An Evil Spirit killed him. You gotta to be a good girl or it will kill you too." So since I was seven, I had lived in fear for that "Evil Spirit". It took me eight years to learn what that spirit was.

I was coming from school the evening I heard about Emmett Till's death. There was a whole group of us, girls and boys, walking down the road headed home. A group of about six high school boys were walking a few paces ahead of me and several other girls. We were laughing and talking about something that had happened in school that day. However, the six boys in front of us weren't talking very loud. Usually they kept up so much noise. But today they were just walking and talking among themselves. All of a sudden they began to shout at each other.

"Man, what in the hell do you mean?"

"What I mean is these goddamned white folks is gonna start some shit here, you just watch!"

"That boy wasn't but fourteen years old and they killed him. Now what kin a fourteen-year-old boy do with a white woman? What if he did whistle at her, he might have thought the whore was pretty."

"Look at all these white men here that's fucking over our women. Everybody knows it too and what's done about that? Look how many white babies we got walking around in our neighborhoods. Their mamas ain't white either. That boy was from Chicago, shit, everybody fuck everybody up there. He probably didn't even think of the bitch as white."

What they were saying shocked me. I knew all of those boys and I had never heard them talk like that. We walked on behind them for a while listening. Questions about who was killed, where, and why started running through my mind. I walked up to one of the boys.

"Eddie, what boy was killed?"

"Moody, where've you been?" he asked me. "Everybody talking about that fourteen-year-old boy who was killed in Greenwood by some white men. You don't know nothing that's going on besides what's in them books of yours, huh?"

Standing there before the rest of the girls, I felt so stupid. It was then that I realized I really didn't know what was going on all around me. It wasn't that I was dumb. It was just that ever since I was nine, I'd had to work after school and do my lessons on lunch hour. I never had time to learn anything, to hang around with people my own age. And you never were told anything by adults.

That evening when I stopped off at the house on my way to Mrs Burke's, Mama was singing. Any other day she would have been yelling at Adline and Junior them to take off their school clothes. I wondered if she knew about Emmett Till. The way she was singing she had something on her mind and it wasn't pleasant either.

> I got a shoe, you got a shoe,
> All of God's chillun got shoes;
> When I get to hebben, I'm gonna put on my shoes,
> And gonna tromp all over God's hebben.
> When I get to hebben I'm gonna put on my shoes,
> And gonna walk all over God's hebben.

Mama was dishing up beans like she didn't know anyone was home. Adline, Junior, and James had just thrown their books down and sat themselves at the table. I didn't usually eat before I went to work. But I wanted to ask Mama about Emmett Till. So I ate and thought of some way of asking her.

"These beans are some good, Mama," I said, trying to sense her mood.

"Why is you eating anyway? You gonna be late for work. You know how Miss Burke is," she said to me.

"I don't have much to do this evening. I kin get it done before I leave work," I said.

The conversation stopped after that. Then Mama started humming that song again.

> When I get to hebben, I'm gonna put on my shoes,
> And gonna tromp all over God's hebben.

She put a plate on the floor for Jennie Ann and Jerry.

"Jennie Ann! You and Jerry sit down here and eat and don't put beans all over the floor."

Ralph, the baby, started crying, and she went in the bedroom to give him his bottle. I got up and followed her.

"Mama, did you hear about that fourteen-year-old Negro boy who was killed a little over a week ago by some white men?" I asked her.

"Where did you hear that?" she said angrily.

"Boy, everybody really thinks I am dumb or deaf or something. I heard Eddie them talking about it this evening coming from school."

"Eddie them better watch how they go around here talking. These white folks git a hold of it they gonna be in trouble," she said.

"What are they gonna be in trouble about, Mama? People got a right to talk, ain't they?"

"You go on to work before you is late. And don't you let on like you know nothing about that boy being killed before Miss Burke them. Just do your work like you don't know nothing," she said. "That boy's a lot better off in heaven than he is here," she continued and then started singing again.

On my way to Mrs Burke's that evening, Mama's words kept running through my mind. "Just do your work like you don't know nothing." "Why is Mama acting so scared?" I thought. "And what if Mrs Burke knew we knew? Why must I pretend I don't know? Why are these people killing Negroes? What did Emmett Till do besides whistle at that woman?"

By the time I got to work, I had worked my nerves up some. I was shaking as I walked up on the porch. "Do your work like you don't know nothing." But once I got inside, I couldn't have acted normal if Mrs Burke were paying me to be myself.

I was so nervous, I spent most of the evening avoiding them, going about the house dusting and sweeping. Everything went along fairly well until dinner was served.

"Don, Wayne, and Mama, y'all come on to dinner. Essie, you can wash up the pots and dishes in the sink now. Then after dinner you won't have as many," Mrs Burke called to me.

If I had the power to mysteriously disappear at that moment, I would have. They used the breakfast table in the kitchen for most of their meals. The dining room was only used for Sunday dinner or when they had company. I wished they had company tonight so they could eat in the dining room while I was at the kitchen sink.

"I forgot the bread," Mrs Burke said when they were all seated. "Essie, will you cut it and put it on the table for me?"

I took the cornbread, cut it in squares, and put it on a small round dish. Just as I was about to set it on the table, Wayne yelled at the cat. I dropped the plate and the bread went all over the floor.

"Never mind, Essie," Mrs Burke said angrily as she got up and got some white bread from the breadbox.

I didn't say anything. I picked up the cornbread from around the table and went back to the dishes. As soon as I got to the sink, I dropped a saucer on the floor and broke it. Didn't anyone say a word until I had picked up the pieces.

"Essie, I bought some new cleanser today. It's setting on the bathroom shelf. See if it will remove the stains in the tub," Mrs Burke said.

I went to the bathroom to clean the tub. By the time I got through with it, it was snow white. I spent a whole hour scrubbing it. I had removed the stains in no time but I kept scrubbing until they finished dinner.

When they had finished and gone into the living room as usual to watch TV, Mrs Burke called me to eat. I took a clean plate out of the cabinet and sat down. Just as I was putting the first forkful of food in my mouth, Mrs Burke entered the kitchen.

"Essie, did you hear about that fourteen-year-old boy who was killed in Greenwood?" she asked me, sitting down in one of the chairs opposite me.

"No, I didn't hear that," I answered, almost choking on the food.

"Do you know why he was killed?" she asked and I didn't answer.

"He was killed because he got out of his place with a white woman. A boy from Mississippi would have known better than that. This boy was from Chicago. Negroes up North have no respect for people. They think they can get away with anything. He just came to Mississippi and put a whole lot of notions in the boys' heads here and stirred up a lot of trouble," she said passionately.

"How old are you, Essie?" she asked me after a pause.

"Fourteen. I will soon be fifteen though," I said.

"See, that boy was just fourteen too. It's a shame he had to die so soon." She was so red in the face, she looked as if she was on fire.

When she left the kitchen I sat there with my mouth open and my food untouched. I couldn't have eaten now if I were starving. "Just do your work like you don't know nothing" ran through my mind again and I began washing the dishes.

I went home shaking like a leaf on a tree. For the first time out of all her trying, Mrs Burke had made me feel like rotten garbage. Many times she had tried to instill fear within me and subdue me and had given up. But when she talked about Emmett Till there was something in her voice that sent chills and fear all over me.

Before Emmett Till's murder, I had known the fear of hunger, hell, and the Devil. But now there was a new fear known to me – the fear of being killed just because I was black. This was the worst of my fears. I knew once I got food, the fear of starving to death would leave. I also was told that if I were a good girl, I wouldn't have to fear the Devil or hell. But I didn't know what one had to do or not do as a Negro not to be killed. Probably just being a Negro period was enough, I thought.

A few days later, I went to work and Mrs Burke had about eight women over for tea. They were all sitting around in the living room when I got there. She told me she was having a "guild meeting", and asked me to help her serve the cookies and tea.

After helping her, I started cleaning the house. I always swept the hallway and porch first. As I was sweeping the hall, I could hear them talking. When I heard the word "nigger", I stopped and listened. Mrs Burke must have sensed this, because she suddenly came to the door.

"Essie, finish the hall and clean the bathroom," she said hesitantly. "Then you can go for today. I am not making dinner tonight." Then she went back in the living room with the rest of the ladies.

Before she interrupted my listening, I had picked up the words "NAACP" and "that organization". Because they were talking about niggers, I knew NAACP had something to do with Negroes. All that night I kept wondering what could that NAACP mean?

Later when I was sitting in the kitchen at home doing my lessons, I decided to ask Mama. It was about twelve-thirty. Everyone was in bed but me. When Mama came in to put some milk in Ralph's bottle, I said, "Mama, what do NAACP mean?"

"Where did you git that from?" she asked me, spilling milk all over the floor.

"Mrs Burke had a meeting tonight –"

"What kind of meeting?" she asked, cutting me off.

"I don't know. She had some women over – she said it was a guild meeting," I said.

"A guild meeting," she repeated.

"Yes, they were talking about Negroes and I heard some woman say 'that NAACP' and another 'that organization,' meaning the same thing."

"What else did they say?" she asked me.

"That's all I heard. Mrs Burke must have thought I was listening, so she told me to clean the bathroom and leave."

"Don't you ever mention that word around Mrs Burke or no other white person, you heah! Finish your lesson and cut that light out and go to bed," Mama said angrily and left the kitchen.

"With a Mama like that you'll never learn anything," I thought as I got into bed. All night long I thought about Emmett Till and the NAACP. I even got up to look up NAACP in my little concise dictionary. But I didn't find it.

The next day at school, I decided to ask my homeroom teacher Mrs Rice the meaning of NAACP. When the bell sounded for lunch, I remained in my seat as the other students left the room.

"Are you going to spend your lunch hour studying again today, Moody?" Mrs Rice asked me.

"Can I ask you a question, Mrs Rice?" I asked her.

"You *may* ask me a question, yes, but I don't know if you *can* or not," she said.

"What does the word NAACP mean?" I asked.

"Why do you want to know?"

"The lady I worked for had a meeting and I overheard the word mentioned."

"What else did you hear?"

"Nothing. I didn't know what NAACP meant, that's all." I felt like I was on the witness stand or something.

"Well, next time your boss has another meeting you listen more carefully. NAACP is a Negro organization that was established a long time ago to help Negroes gain a few basic rights," she said.

"What's it gotta do with the Emmett Till murder?" I asked.

"They are trying to get a conviction in Emmett Till's case. You see the NAACP is trying to do a lot for the Negroes and get the right to vote for Negroes in the South. I shouldn't be telling you all this. And don't you dare breathe a word of what I said. It could cost me my job if word got out I was teaching my students such. I gotta go to lunch and you should go outside too because it's nice and sunny out today," she said leaving the room. "We'll talk more when I have time."

About a week later, Mrs Rice had me over for Sunday dinner, and I spent about five hours with her. Within that time, I digested a good meal and accumulated a whole new pool of knowledge about Negroes being butchered and slaughtered by whites in the South. After Mrs Rice had told me all this, I felt like the lowest animal on earth. At least when other animals (hogs, cows, etc.) were killed by man, they were used as food. But when man was butchered or killed by man, in the case of Negroes by whites, they were left lying on a road or found floating in a river or something.

Mrs Rice got to be something like a mother to me. She told me anything I wanted to know. And made me promise that I would keep all this information she was passing on to me to myself. She said she couldn't, rather didn't want to, talk about these things to other teachers, that they would tell Mr Willis and she would be fired. At the end of that year she was fired. I never found out why. I haven't seen her since then.

Nafissatou Diallo
1941–82

Born in Senegal, she was active in social services as a midwife and director of a maternal and child health care centre on the outskirts of Dakar, and in her writing described both tradition-al and modern aspects of Senegalese society. Her first work was an autobiographical novel, De Tilène au Plateau: Une enfance dakaroise (1976; translated by Dorothy Blair as A Dakar Childhood, 1982), which won an award from the International Association of French Language Speakers. Her other works of fiction are Le Fort Maudit (1980), Awa, la petite marchande (for children; 1982) and the novel extracted here, La Princesse de Tiali (1986; translated by Ann Woollcombe as Fary, Princess of Tiali, 1987) – a West African Cinderella story about the marriage of Fary, a beautiful village girl from the class of griots, to Prince Bocar, a royal prince. Fary's mother, Lala, is one of the four wives of her father Mayacine.

From

Fary, Princess of Tiali

LALA was small and unobtrusive. She accomplished her daily chores with submissiveness, serenity, and perseverance. Her skeletal body was surely the result of physical exhaustion, but more probably was due to her moral suffering which gnawed at her like a malignancy, whose name was Astou. Astou was her niece. She had been entrusted to her when her mother died in childbirth. Fary did not like Astou at all. More than once had she surprised her in conversation with Anta, discrediting Lala. Poor Anta! She did not in the least suspect what this snake in the grass had in store for her. The perverse girl had eyes on Anta's hus-band. Her respectful manners and her humble and innocent ways did not fool Fary. When Astou was alone with her father, she brushed against him with her firm young breasts, wiggled her behind, and looked at him longingly. Mayacine ignored her or pretended to ignore her, but the impertinent girl kept it up.

On that particular day Astou had kept to her bed. Mayacine, who had to go to old Bacar's funeral, did not go to the fields. Lala in her haste had forgotten part of the seeds. Halfway to the fields she remembered. Fary turned around and went home. Surprise! Her father was in her mother's bed holding Astou's breast as she gazed at him. Mayacine looked up and saw his daughter. Not at all embarrassed, Astou gave her a smile. Fary's heart jumped in her breast. She was torn by disgust and a terrible jealousy. The disdain and the determination in her face kept her father from slapping her. She took the seeds and left. She cried for a long time, but kept her secret.

A few days after this incident, the fourth wife was renounced. Her mush was too salty. Astou took her place. She made life miserable for Lala, whose shame was slowly killing her. In connivance with her brothers and sisters, Fary revenged her mother in her own way. Astou's poultry was mistreated, her *pagnes* cut up, her meals oversalted. Her father did his utmost to replace the wardrobe after each incident and to ignore the bad meals, but he had not counted on the children's determination. He never managed to catch them in the act.

On that particular day their father's deep voice pulled the children suddenly out of their sleep. Sensing some misfortune, for this was the first time in her life that her mother's soft voice had not awakened her, Fary ran towards the screen and lifted it. Her mother cowered in bed, trembling like a leaf, her body covered with perspiration. A cough rose from her throat like a complaint. Her father left the room to go over to Astou. Fary woke up her grandmother to tell her about her daughter's sudden illness.

Then Fary went into the forest to gather herbs which she put on her mother's body to make the fever go down. Her brothers and sisters were crying, "she is going to die, she is going to die," their eyes haggard. Fary reassured them the best she could, and with great courage took over the family. She gave orders and shared the work with an energy born of despair. Surprised by her authority, her brothers and sisters obediently did the tasks she assigned to them. After a few days of acute illness, Lala began to convalesce.

One morning when Fary straightened her bedcloths, her mother took her hand and whispered, "Daughter, come to see me when you have finished your work. Try to see to it that we are not disturbed. I want to talk to you."

Her father had suddenly become invisible, and appeared at the doorstep for a few seconds to inquire about the sick woman only if he happened to remember. Astou was expecting a child. Her nausea, her vomiting and her dizzy spells manifested themselves with violence even though her belly was still as flat as a board. Mayacine surrounded her with charms and all sorts of attentions to see to the end of this pregnancy which ill-intentioned rivals wanted to destroy at all costs. Fary was ashamed. Her father, even though he had enough children to form a regiment, acted as if he were expecting his first child.

"Here I am, Mother. We are alone. The family is in the fields. The 'snake' has gone out, probably to buy another talisman."

"Fary, if you want to please me, leave her alone. The blood of the chicken only soils the fingers of the one who kills it. I was wrong to have nourished an adder at my bosom. Who will live shall see. God is just. Forget Astou for now and listen to me carefully. Do you know the principality of Tiali?"

Fary opened her eyes wide. She had not expected such a question.

"No, Mother. I have only heard speak of it. It seems it is a wonderful place. But I don't like the prince who, just as he likes, can take away our best rams."

"That is his right, my daughter. We are his subjects and we in Mboupbène more so than others for we are also his *griots*. Tiali is governed by prince Bocar Djiwan Malik who is one of Ndiamal Djiwan's grandsons. Ndiamal had twelve sons. He set them up in twelve regions to which he gave their names and first names. His son Bocar received the county of Tiali. This is how Tiali Malick Bocar was founded. It is a day and a half's ride on horseback from Mboupbène. We depend on Bocar. If he has the goodness not to claim big yearly contributions, he can take a few animals from time to time for the needs of the court.

"When Bour Sine married his daughter, the prince was invited to the ceremony. He came back with one of the most humiliating and abject innovations for us as Muslims and as human beings. These terrible pagans bury their *griots* in tree trunks to ward off catastrophes. Putting them in one ground, they say, invites disasters such as lightning, drought, and earthquakes.

"Bocar Djiwan Malick has assigned the cursed baobabs east of Mboupbène to the members of our caste. From now on, these trees will be our cemetery. The prince has posted his policemen here to ensure that this new law is applied. Some people who thought they were more clever than others tried to bury their dead quickly in the fields or behind their fences during the night. They were found out and severely punished.

"You must wonder why I tell you all this. It is because I am afraid. Yes, I am afraid. I dreamed I saw myself thrown into this tree trunk. I can't sleep anymore when I think that my body will never know our traditional resting place, but in its place this pagan rite which is against our religion. It weighed like a stone on my head. Now I feel relieved since I have spoken to you."

Fary was speechless. The stone had moved from her mother's heart on to the daughter's. She left her mother and went to find Coura, her cousin on her father's side, her friend and only confidante. She told her about the talk she had had with her mother. Coura could scarcely believe it. Neither of them knew about the cemetery. Children, especially girls, never followed a funeral procession. Full of curiosity, they decided to hide in an adjoining field to see a funeral which was to take place that day.

They were barely hidden behind the trees when they heard the incantations with the words "*Allah! Allah!*" repeated incessantly. Some men carried the body of the deceased on their shoulders. They put it at the foot of the baobab and stood facing it. They prayed standing up without prostrating themselves, and repeated in chorus, "*Allakhou akbar!*" as if they were celebrating some strange rite. After a resounding "*Assala Malekoum,*" they took the body, wrapped it in a white shroud, and murmured while they put it in the hole, "You can see us, our Lord. We respect you and adore you. We believe in your messenger, the Prophet Mohammed. May peace be with him. This act is an order from down here below. It does not change our faith. May your clemency and your pity accompany him." Fary was speechless. The stone had moved from her mother's heart on to the daughter's. She left her mother and went to find Coura, her cousin on her father's side, her friend and only confidante. She told her about the talk she had had with her mother. Coura could scarcely believe it. Neither of them knew about the cemetery. Children, especially girls, never followed a funeral procession. Full of curiosity, they decided to hide in an adjoining field to see a funeral which was to take place that day.

They were barely hidden behind the trees when they heard the incantations with the words "*Allah! Allah!*" repeated incessantly. Some men carried the body of the deceased on their shoulders. They put it at the foot of the baobab and stood facing it. They prayed standing up without prostrating themselves, and repeated in chorus, "*Allakhou akbar!*" as if they were celebrating some strange rite. After a resounding "*Assala Malekoum*," they took the body, wrapped it in a white shroud, and murmured while they put it in the hole, "You can see us, our Lord. We respect you and adore you. We believe in your messenger, the Prophet Mohammed. May peace be with him. This act is an order from down here below. It does not change our faith. May your clemency and your pity accompany him."

Coura shivered; she was crying. Tears streamed down her smooth cheeks and fell in the cleavage of her young breasts shaped like papayas. From time to time her shoulders raised in a sob. She fought to suppress her emotion which made her eyes squint and pulled her lips into an ugly grimace. Fary moved close to her trying to comfort her, but she could hardly manage it. She was so moved that she was speechless. Her eyes were full of love and compassion when she looked at Coura. Better than her voice and lips could have done, her eyes expressed a consoling sympathy. She finally broke the silence.

"Coura, I should like to ask you a question which no one has been able to answer for me. I have heard explanations here and there. I have overheard conversations that were more or less evasive; I have listened at doors. I have discussed it with my mother and the elders, but I still don't know. You, whose father is a very wise man, can you tell me why we are different from other people? How have we come by this inheritance? How did we become *griots* and people of caste?"

"Fary, to be honest, I can only repeat my father's words. He often speaks of the right of man, of the equality of human beings as described in the Koran. This equality exists in the holy places of people from the worlds over, no matter what country they come from, what their color or race, regardless of their birth or attributes, they all wear the same white garment as a symbol of equality, of anonymity on this earth."

"Coura, this white garb, this Muslim rite is not known to the pagans that rule us."

"Fary, stop being difficult just for once. You asked me for an explanation and I am telling you exactly what my father said. You can believe it or not, just as you like. Either you are going to listen to me or I keep silent. What we have just seem has upset me. I am in no mood to argue."

"Go ahead. I'm listening."

"A long time ago, a very long time ago, my father says, people lived in wide open spaces, settled around a chief in order better to protect themselves against dangers. They domesticated animals, grew plants, and divided the work. For the sake of harmony in their lives, they divided into several groups. Some specialized in fishing or hunting. Others became weavers. This division of labor later turned into a social hierarchy, which, with the *ouoloffs*, was the origin of these classifications."

"The nobles were the *guerrs*, the jewelers the *teugnes*, the woodworkers were called *laobes*, the shoemakers became the *oudes*, the weavers the *rabes* and the slaves took the name of *diam*. We the *griots* are what we are, *Ngueol*.

"Except for the privileged class of the *guerr*, we travel in the same ship as our brothers. We are once again people of caste. To aspire to an alliance, be it male or female, with one of these beings of so-called superior origin, would be folly."

Once again Fary was speechless. Emotions of pain and helplessness choked her. She felt as if she would burst. Her heart expanded and contracted in her chest like a spring. This injustice had pitilessly destroyed her. With a great concentration of will, she ceased her laments. Terror was reflected on her face, followed by an expression of indescribable hatred. She was deadly angry at her ancestors who had fatalistically accepted the condition of slavery instead of refusing this inferior condition imposed on them by a domineering society. It was a real affront to human dignity. She, Fary, was a woman of caste, a *griotte*. Her world was for ever limited to the tiny circle of her race.

She became ill. The fever brought her down. One nightmare followed another in her burning head. Tree branches picked her up like the arms of an octopus and threw her into an immense black hole. She cried; she was choking. She fought against the invisible powers; she turned over and over, caught in a trembling that became a delirium.

Fary's illness became her mother's best remedy. She forgot her own sorrow to watch over Fary. The *marabouts* outdid each other finding remedies for her. She had seen what she must not see. She was possessed. One had to wash her face and close her eyes so that henceforth she could not see beyond the border of the mortals. Some thought it was the *djins*, the spirit, the *couyoum djin*, the male, the master of the *djins*, which lived in her small body. They had to be exorcised through incantations, concoctions, and incense. After two full weeks she was once again able to do her chores.

Sokhna was Coura's aunt. Her house, incontestably the most beautiful in Mboupbène, had brought her the nickname, "money-bags". Divorced a long time, she led a gay life. She was thought to have had a few adventures and her reputation was not spotless. Unbeknownst to her parents, Fary often went to see Sokhna because she had cowrie shells which never lied and also because of the few pennies Sokhna would give Fary on these occasions.

Her big house, hung with *pagnes*, always smelled of incense. Pretty mats covered the floor. A big bed covered with a colorful spread filled half the room. Sokhna was tall and strong. Her walk was graceful and her voice as soft and modulated as a lullaby. She had a whole string of admirers, of whom Mayoro was first in the running.

Fary and Coura came to consult her because their future worried them. Up to now there had not been one suitor on the horizon, even though marriage age rapidly approached. They had been careful not to reveal the real reasons for the consultation, leaving it to the ingenious Sokhna to ask her cowries.

A little maliciously she asked the girls, "What brings you here?"

"We want to consult your cowries for the usual sacrifices at the harvest dance."

Sokhna's eyes sparkled. She was not fooled. "Sacrifice, yes. But for what?

For the harvest or for the men?

"Whose turn first?"

"Fary's," answered Coura.

Fary stepped forward, trembling, her heart beating fast as it always did when she was going to learn about her destiny. She made her wishes, blew on the cowries, and threw them into the tray.

"You will give soured milk to the children on Thursday. Two cola nuts, one white, one red, to an old woman."

Fary hoped that the alms she must give would stop right there for her meager purse could not provide any more. And no more chances to get money from Bara!

"A young man of fair complexion, handsome, a scar on the right ear, here, right in front of you," Sokhna said, pushing a cowrie towards Fary. Her forehead wrinkled, her face serious, she continued, "A little man, fat, black, ugly but rich, even extremely rich, a prince, at any rate. A big name, right in front of you. Enormous wealth here, all around you.

"Ah," she said after a short silence, "This little cowrie is between you and all those riches and that man in front of you. But all this eliminated," she said, sweeping up the cowrie of bad omen, "fortune will smile on you." She looked at Fary as if seeing her for the first time, threw her cowries and looked at her again.

"Yes, Fary, three times thrown. Three times the cowries showed the same thing. You will be a princess. I swear by my ancestors that people will prostrate themselves before you. That is, if you manage to clear away this obstacle on your way," she said, angrily pushing away the small cowries.

"Could you tell me the nature of this obstacle?" Fary asked in a trembling voice.

"There might be several things. Offerings to be made, animals to be immolated, alms to be given. Let me look once more."

She threw the cowries and said, "It is neither a sacrifice nor alms to be given. It is a human being, more precisely a woman who stands in your way. She is the concrete to be poured, the tree to be felled, the obstacle to overcome to get at this fortune and this man."

"Will I get at it?" Fary asked, overexcited.

Again Sokhna gathered her cowries, consulted them, murmuring incantations.

"Probably yes, certainly yes, but not without great difficulties."

For a moment Fary abandoned herself to the predictions. Her eyes closed, she saw herself a princess. It lasted only a few seconds, then she was frightened.

"Coura, does this happy prediction not hide some misfortune? Did she not see my death? Old Fatim always predicts my early demise. And this woman in my path, wouldn't she be a *djin*?"

"No, Fary, she saw you as a princess, so don't worry. I don't know how it's going to happen, but happen it will. Her conclusion is the only thing that counts. That's what's essential. I believe in her. Her knowledge of the cowries is inherited. Her ancestor, who was known to all the princes, bequeathed her his knowledge. He chose her over the males in the family for the spirits saw in her the real repository of the spiritual powers. Make your sacrifices. We will see what happens."

"I can't believe it, Coura."

"Why shouldn't you be a princess, Fary? Kings have married *griottes* before. Why not you? Don't underestimate your beauty. It is exceptional."

"I must keep my feet on the ground. This sort of thing does not happen to a girl of my race. With the little bait I have, how could I land such a fish? Can you see me as a princess, me, Fary Mboup, *griotte*, untouchable, a woman of caste for generations, whose only wealth is this so-called beauty and a moth-eaten *pagne* around her hips! She is really good, but I'm afraid that today the spirits are not with her or are hiding something from her."

"If I didn't know you better, Fary, I would think you were cynical. I assure you that you will be a princess. Who wouldn't like that, my friend? It's the dream of every young girl, the realization of all dreams, wealth, jewels, clothes and honor."

"To become rich, me who never knew anything but poverty. What luck!" The words danced in her head. "Imagine, Coura, hundreds of slaves kissing the feet of Fary Mayacine Mboup? No, it's just a dream, but what munificence for my family and all the relatives!" Then she fell silent.

"What's the matter?" Coura asked, her eyes still bright with joy and excitement.

"Remember Sokhna's words? 'A small man, fat, black, ugly?' I hate ugliness."

"Don't jump to conclusions. Let's wait and when the time comes, we shall see. Besides, what does physical beauty matter in a man? In my opinion, it's the heart which is more important."

Mayacine often went to Tiali to give an account to the prince of all that went on in Mboupbène. These absences did not at all please Astou, who at the moment was more of a princess than Fary.

"Mayacine," she told her husband when he came home, "this is the fourth time you have skipped my turn. Why should your other wives enjoy your company twice a week? What have they got that I haven't got? The prince of Tiali always chooses *my* turn to call you to his side. You would think he does it on purpose. You are hardly better than his slaves. Do you have to hold the candle when he fulfills his obligations to his wives? Does he need your help so much? Answer me. You also have obligations to your wives, especially to me who is only sixteen years old. If you can't fulfill these obligations, I am going back to my parents."

Worn out by his long trip, surprised by this most insulting and amazingly humiliating reception, Mayacine raised the whip he still held and was going to hit Astou. Seeing his children there, their eyes lowered, he stopped short. His voice permitted no reply.

"Woman, in all my life I have not met anyone so rude, so perverse, and so abject and ill brought-up as you. You dare to blaspheme and berate my prince. You dare to insult me, your husband, your master. Pack your bags. From this moment on you mean nothing to me. Leave this house before I can no longer answer for myself, before I am obliged to kill you."

Astou, taken aback by her husband's words, nevertheless stood her ground, pointing to her swollen belly, and cried and carried on with all her might. Her frightened eyes went from child to child. Mayacine lifted his hand and a mighty slap resounded on the young woman's cheek. She started to laugh, looked at the children again, started to whine, and then to sob. Then, her hands on her waist, she twisted in pain. The generous Lala, forgetting the fate of her ancestor Yam Mademba Khary Mboup, interceded with her husband.

"Uncle, I beg you on my knees to keep her until she has the baby. Her grandparents live far away. She will be delivered prematurely."

"So be it," Mayacine answered. "She is acting. She is bluffing as usual. She won't spend the night here. Whoever gives her the slightest help will leave the house with her."

He threw her clothes and pots and pans into the courtyard. Her head bent, Astou went away. Fary was proud of her father who, as the master, had finally made a decision long overdue.

On the occasion of the new moon a week of festivities, matches, dances, and chants had been organized in Mboupbène. On that occasion Fary met the man on whom all her thoughts would now center. She noticed him in a group of spectators who were intently watching the fighters. She could not stop looking at his handsome face. There was a scar on the right ear. Sokhna's prediction was coming true. Their eyes sought each other and held each other in the light of the huge bonfire. Fary's heart was beating so fast it frightened her. She went away, ashamed of her strong emotions, and went to look for Coura.

"Are you ill? Have you seen a ghost?"

"No, nothing like that," she answered in a choking voice. "Follow me!" She pulled her friend behind a tree from where she could observe the object of her emotion.

"Ah, I see. Don't worry, you are not the only one. He breaks hearts wherever he goes. The young girls are smitten and the women sin. It's hard to resist his look. It's Gana Mboup, the son of Baye Daour the deaf man. Didn't you hear about the big fight the girls had over him last Thursday down by the river? It was a bloody battle where they tore each other's *pagnes*, hair and ears and threw rocks and shouted insanities. And yet, at night he is not so handsome. You must look at him tomorrow, in daylight. Try not to faint."

"What a surprise, Coura! Baye Daour's son? Such a beauty. How did that old deaf man produce such a marvel?"

"Be a little more charitable. Daour is old, but you can still see the traces of how handsome he was, even though he has lost all of his teeth. We'll see what happens to the son when he is his father's age. May God grant us a long life."

Fary was beautiful. She had that beauty which is authentically black, wild, pure, and enchanting. A black complexion, not a muddy black but a healthy clarity, shiny, and flawless, brightened by teeth that a kind nature had lined up in absolute perfection. Her eyes were lively, clear, a bit cunning and charming, her nose pert. Her eyes were full of fun and belied her submissive bearing. Her lips were sensual and would have moved a heart of stone. Gana, like many others, was receptive to so much charm. Fary was in love and was loved in return and lived only for the moments when they could meet in secret. For the moment, Gana was her prince.

Zee Edgell
1941–

*S*he grew up in Belize, a British colony until 1981. Her first job in the 1960s was as a reporter on the Daily Gleaner *in Jamaica. She subsequently taught at St Catherine Academy in Belize (1966–8) and edited a small newspaper in Belize City. After living in Jamaica, Britain, Nigeria, Afghanistan, Bangladesh and the USA with her husband and children, she returned to Belize to teach at St Catherine Academy and was appointed Director of the Women's Bureau in Belize. In 1982 she went to Somalia. The central character of her novel* Beka Lamb *(1982) is a fourteen-year-old Belizean schoolgirl, whose victory over a habit of lying is told in flashback, her reminiscences beginning when she wins an essay prize at her convent school. The book paints a vivid picture of ordinary life in a small community in the 1950s.*

From

Beka Lamb

CHAPTER IV

W HAT Beka recognized in herself as "change" began, as far as she could remember, the day she decided to stop lying. Things were getting almost beyond her control. She sat on the top step of the back porch that April Friday, seven months earlier, eating crayfish foot left over from tea and contemplating her latest, worst lie. The sun was going down, and a cool breeze from the Caribbean, several streets away, blew now and then reminding her that it was "Caye Time" once again.

Popping the last scrap of fish into her mouth, she tossed the shells between the railings and watched as they fell amongst the red bells and green crotons, dappled yellow, growing in the dry earth alongside the bottom of the stairs. Her parents had sat at the table finishing tea when Beka told them she had been promoted to second form. Without looking up from the report card he held between thumb and forefinger, Bill Lamb said, "It says here that anyone failing more than three subjects at the end of the school year must repeat the class. You failed four subjects, Beka."

The brown mulatto crust on her mother's cheek bones became extremely dark against the paleness of her skin. She said to Beka, perched on a chair opposite,

"Answer your father, girl."

"I pass in truth, Daddy!" Beka almost shouted. "Sister Virgil read my name off a list."

"Well, all I can say is that Sister Virgil must be helping you out, which for her is unusual. You are a lucky girl. Excuse me."

The chair scraped against the wooden floor as he pushed himself away from the mahogany table. Stalking into the living-room, he sat down in his easy chair, and snapped on the radio that stood on a high cabinet alongside one wall, and the radio announcer said,

"This is the British Honduras Broadcasting Service."

Lilla put her cup slowly down on the wet saucer, and with the forefinger of her right hand drew beads of sweat off her forehead. Beka opened her mouth, but before she could speak, her mother said quietly,

"Clear the table and wash the dishes now if you are finished, Beka. Your Gran and the boys ate before you came home from school. Change your uniform first."

Lying was one of the things about Beka that her parents detested most. When they discovered the truth about this latest one, her Dad was going to shout and holler, and definitely beat her till she couldn't stand up. She looked up at the blue sky and rosy clouds. Maybe there'll be a hurricane this year, she thought hopefully. If one came, the school records would all "wash way" and then her parents would never know she'd failed.

"Let's see," she murmured. "How does that rhyme go again? June, too soon; July, stand by; August, come it must; September, remember; October, all over." A hurricane couldn't come in time to rescue her then. School reopened in June. In any case, Sister Virgil, the American principal, would remember every girl that failed.

Beka shuddered at the thought of the leather belt her Dad wore. Sometimes Bill Lamb would come home from work, the tensions of the work day raging within him, and Lilla, filled with the frustrations of her own day, would sit down to tell him of Beka's insolence, her laziness, and her ingratitude. The story invariably concluded with Lilla saying,

"And the worst thing of all, Bill, is that she lied to me. I could see she hadn't swept the attic properly. Why did she lie to me?"

Because he was in a hurry at those times to have his tea before going for an hour's relaxation at the club, Bill Lamb would say impatiently,

"I don't want to hear a word from you, Beka. Go upstairs. I am going to put an end to this once and for all."

His felt hat askew on his head, Bill Lamb would follow Beka upstairs stamping his feet with emphasis. On the landing, Beka would begin to scream at the top of her voice before the belt touched her skin,

"No, Daddy! No, Daddy!"

Between lashes, Bill Lamb paused to ask,

"Do you know why I am beating you?"

"No, Daddy," Beka would reply.

"Not because of the thing you did, but because you lied!"

On one such occasion, the buckle end of the belt escaped accidentally from Bill Lamb's clenched fist and cut Beka on the left corner of her mouth. The next day at school, Beka told anyone who asked that she'd fallen down the back steps and cut her face on the concrete slab at the foot of the wooden stairs.

When her Dad returned from the club that night, he came up to Beka's bedside in the attic where Lilla was rubbing Beka's head and saying,

"It was all my fault, Bill. I can't understand why I complain so much to you about Beka. She had such a pretty smile, Bill, such a pretty smile. That was the nicest thing about her face."

Looking down at Beka's lip, Bill Lamb said,

"She still has a pretty smile. Smile, Beka! Show your mother what a pretty smile you still have."

Beka smiled as naturally as she could manage, because her parents always seemed to suffer for such a long time after Beka herself had forgotten the beating, and it was a rare child in the community that didn't get a whipping now, then, or more often.

Turning to go downstairs again, Bill Lamb said,

"Don't worry, pet. Your Gran will rub it with cocoa fat when it heals and then it won't scar." But although Granny Ivy rubbed it every night for a long time with cocoa fat, the scar browned over but remained visible, and Beka eventually gave up all hope that it would completely disappear.

After that, Lilla tried to keep her annoyance at Beka's shortcomings mostly to herself. She didn't talk much about them to Granny Ivy either, for Granny Ivy nearly always "took up" for Beka. Beka wondered if her Dad would be able to help himself from beating her when he found out about this latest, most provoking lie.

At those times when Beka's behaviour forced Lilla to complain, Beka's Dad resorted to calling her names. He couldn't understand how a girl with enough food to eat, decent clothes to wear, and a roof over her head could be such a trial. Beka didn't know which she disliked most, the beatings or the name calling. The worst and most hurtful name of all was when her Dad called her "phoney". Liar and thief were bad, but those words didn't really worry her. She knew she would never reach His Majesty's Prison where Uncle Curo, Granny Ivy's second son, worked as a warder. In any case, she had long ago stopped taking money from her Dad's pants pocket to buy panades and "cut-o-brute" from the vendors who set up shop outside the school playground at recess. And she was definitely through with lying as from today. But the word "phoney" peppered her insides good and hot.

On the outside, she probably looked phoney in truth. Twice a month she sat in Miss Doodie's kitchen, which smelled of stale fried beans and burnt rice, to have her hair hot-combed. Her Dad had been against straightening her hair from the start.

"I don't want Beka using hot irons on her hair, Lilla," Bill Lamb said. "None of the women on my side of the family hot-comb their hair. What's wrong with it anyway?"

"Clearing the tangles out of Beka's hair takes nearly an hour every morning, Bill. That's one of the reasons she's so often late for school. This way Beka can take care of it herself. Anyway it's only the style."

"Style! If you're not careful, she's going to grow up ashamed of herself and her people."

"Bill, if Beka grows up ashamed of herself, or her people, the hair straightening won't be the main cause of it."

"Go ahead, do what you want. I have no say in this family. I only provide the money!"

Lilla looked at her husband, and Bill Lamb rattled his paper and began reading aloud to them as they started stacking dishes, about the decision of the Workers' Union to support the People's Independence Party with funds.

But the lying was the thing that made her seem the most fake to her Dad. That, and perhaps the way she gave herself airs.

"I don't know who you are imitating," Bill Lamb would sometimes say on a Sunday evening. "We are a humble family. Wash that lipstick off before you leave this house! Your mouth looks like a red bell."

Beka didn't feel in the least bit humble. She felt all right most of the time, and her family wasn't all that humble compared to other families on Cashew Street. She looked at the house, set about three feet from the street side the way most Belizeans' houses were built. The house was a decent size, painted white with green blinds, shut now against the mosquitoes and sand-flies that often came out for a while in the evenings. In fact, the Lambs and the Hartleys were two of the few black families on Cashew Street that had much of anything at all. Most of the other prosperous families on Cashew Street were mestizos who owned shops or other businesses. But Beka knew that her Dad didn't mean a Good House and enough food to eat. He meant humble in the sense that the Lamb family was in a different class from the Blancos and the Hartleys. Bill Lamb was struggling to progress in the business world of the town, but he was quite satisfied to remain in the class where he was comfortable. He had no use for what he called artificiality and sham.

The green shutters of the back window jerked open and Chuku said,

"Beka! Mama wants to know when you are going to wash the tea things."

"Inmediatamente, nino," Beka answered, not moving.

"Show off!" Chuku snapped the shutters and returned noisily to the front veranda where Lilla sat with three-year-old Zandy and Granny Ivy watching the passersby.

Beka pulled dark brown knees up under her chin. The setting sun was throwing a tinselly gold light on the neighbourhood houses and yards all around, making everything seem much softer and prettier than it looked at midday, although it couldn't do anything extra for the lush redness of her bougainvillaea vine that arched over the back fence to waterfall into Miss Bouysie's yard. Miss Boysie didn't like that one bit. She said all that bloody bougainvillaea was taking up space in her yard, harboured flies, and was breaking down the fence besides.

The cooling wind, and the fright of what lay before her, made Beka shiver in her thin cotton blouse. She looked down at herself. One of her breasts was

growing but the other one remained flat. Dr Clark, a West Indian doctor resident
in the town, had said that the right one would soon catch up with the left. Beka
really hoped he was right.

Suppose when her Dad found out, he said she couldn't go back to school.
It would be the washing bowl underneath the house bottom for her then and
no mistake. How could she be a politician if she had to stand around a bowl
and barrel all day long? Last summer holidays, her mother had been sick, and
the family had not gone out to St George's Caye. Granny Ivy quarrelled with the
maid Daddy Bill hired the very first day. Beka did the washing. She remembered
the mosquitoes in the swampy yard buzzing around her face and arms, biting
her ankles even with long pants and rubber boots on, as she tried to hang out
the clothes. Then there had been the white clothes to boil in the big lard pan.
She struggled to light the fire with pine wood brought from Abrero's across the
street, but the stink from the outside latrine was so unbearable, she kept having
to run to the open space between the house, and the vat to take fresh breaths.

"Aie, ya yie!" Beka groaned.

Chilly, she sprang up and went into the darkening kitchen. Switching on
the light, she began scraping the shells from the plates piled on the counter
through the back window and into the yard below. From the window, she
could see the street through the branches of Mr Ulric's custard-apple tree.
A woman struggled by holding an aluminium bucket filled with water on her
head. She carried another full one in her free hand. Beka turned on the tap
and let just enough water run into the basin. She didn't want the vat to dry
up before the rainy season came for sure, otherwise, she would have to carry
buckets of water every day from the public pipe round the corner. The voices
of her brothers sounded subdued from the front veranda where they sat with
Granny Ivy. The latch on the bathroom door snapped back loudly making Beka
jump. Her mother came into the kitchen with an empty kettle in her hand.

Banging it down on the stove she said,

"Beka, how many times I tell you not to throw scraps into the yard? It's a
low down thing to do. That's why I put Sodie's expensive garbage pail on that
back porch!"

Beka began to cry. She couldn't help it, although crying was something
Lilla detested and rarely did herself that anybody could see. She used to tell
Beka when she was little and had hurt her knees in the yard,

"Stop that crying, Beka. Get tough. Be strong like London with all those
bombs falling. Our boys aren't crying over there, they're fighting so we can be
free."

"Who help them when they are hurt?" Beka would ask, brushing the
sand off her knees, and Lilla would say:

"Don't you remember Miss Nadine and Miss Dotsy went too? They are
doing the nursing." And with the wet sheet her mother was hanging on the
line flapping a pleasant coolness against her face, Beka listened again to the
story of Miss Darweather's boy whose plane got shot down over the sea, far
away in a place called Europe.

But this time, although Beka's tears were coming out in ugly gulps, Lilla
held her against soft breasts that seemed too big for her small frame and said,

"You failed, no true, Beka?"

"Yes, Mama, I fail, I fail."

"I know you failed, Beka. I could tell from your face. Your Dad knows too."

"Do you think Daddy will send me back, Mama?"

"It's too soon to think about that now, Beka. You'd better go and tell him first. I wish I could find a way to help you stop lying, my daughter."

Aminata Sow-Fall

1941–

B orn in Saint-Louis, Senegal, she was educated in Dakar and has a French literature degree from the Sorbonne, Paris (1967). She is considered the first published woman novelist from francophone Black Africa, publishing Le Revenant in 1976, followed in 1979 by La Grève des Bàttu ou les déchets humains (translated by Dorothy Blair as The Beggars' Strike, or the Dregs of Society, 1981), L'Appel des arènes (1982) and L'Ex-Père de la nation (1987).

From

The Beggars' Strike

CHAPTER II

A LL the beggars in the City have gathered in Salla Niang's courtyard for the daily draw on their subscription scheme: everyone puts down a premium of one hundred francs and the total sum thus collected – five thousand francs – is paid out to one or other of the subscribers; they are allowed to double or triple their stake and so increase their chances of "winning" by as many times. Salla Niang collects the subscriptions, acting as banker and making no compromises or concessions. She's a woman with plenty of guts and knows how to call to order any recalcitrants who claim their takings from the day's begging are less than the one hundred francs needed to put down.

"It hurts you to have to fork out the dough, eh! And when you get the chance of pocketing it, *Bissimilai!* Then you're happy enough. You just listen: don't try your tricks on me, you hear! Out with the dough! Nobody's allowed tick. You can't tell me! Even on the worst days anyone can collect more than a hundred francs."

"Not at every corner!" someone in the crowd ventures.

"You'd better learn to speak the truth! Name me any part of the City where it isn't everyone's first action, first thing in the morning, to give something to the beggars. Even in the white areas; the black *Toubabs* and the white *Toubabs* all respect this ritual. And if you're talking about the poor districts, then you've come to the wrong shop with that story; everyone knows the poor give more readily than the rich. So hand over the lolly, you bunch of skinflints!"

There is universal laughter as Salla Niang, from her chair in the doorway of her room, harangues the impressive crowd of beggars who fill the courtyard, carrying their *bàttu* – the calabash which serves as a begging bowl. Salla Niang holds a winnowing-basket on her lap and as she speaks she counts the money in the basket. The crowd comprises men and women of all ages and sizes, some crippled, some hale and hearty, all depending on their outstretched hands for their daily pittance.

Among them is blind Nguirane Sarr, always correctly dressed with his tie, soiled starched collar, dark, gold-rimmed spectacles, invariable navy-blue suit and white stick. Nguirane Sarr has a somewhat distinguished air, perhaps because he always holds his head high and bent slightly to the left. His vantage point is the roundabout near the Presidential Palace where he regularly receives a coin, to which is associated a wish, from everyone who is about to obtain an audience with the President of the Republic. Charity opens doors, so here goes a final coin to open the door of the President's heart.

And among the faces like masks with darkly protruding eyes, among the hoary heads and ulcerated limbs, covered with the pustules of scabies or eaten away with leprosy, among the rags which leave half-naked bodies which have long been innocent of any contact with water, among the beggars' crutches, sticks and *bàttu*, there are some adorable little tots who smile happily at life, twittering in rhythm with the clatter of pewter jugs.

Here, among the teeming crowd, is Papa Gorgui Diop – the old man who has the knack of winkling an extra mite out of the donors, thanks to his extraordinary comic talent; he's a perfect scream, the way he acts an old man in love with a young girl; he portrays one by one each of the old man's three wives who make bawdy fun of their husband's fads, then the old man himself, trying to make himself out a youngster, and finally the mischievous young girl who first bleeds her elderly lover white and then gives him a kick in the backside. Gorgui Diop is well-known all over the City and people come a great distance to see him do his act in his accustomed pitch, in front of "his" bank, from the twenty-fifth of the month to the tenth of the following month, and then at "his" market from the eleventh onwards.

When the draw is over the beggars proceed to the sale of produce: rice, sugar, millet, biscuits, candles, sometimes a few chickens. The sole purchaser is Salla Niang who pays thirty per cent less than the normal price for these goods, which serve to stock up the shop next to the house, which is managed by her husband. She's a real business woman is this Salla Niang. She had been in service as a maid-of-all-work, but had taken up begging as a career the day she gave birth to twins. One of her employers helped her to obtain a small plot of land, already cleared, on which she was able to build a house thanks to the proceeds from her begging. The twins are quite big now, so she can spend her days simply sitting in front of "her" hospital, not too much in evidence, and send the children chasing after patients and visitors, while she keeps a strict watch out in case any competitors try to take advantage of their superior age and shamelessly do the children out of their takings.

It is newcomers who most often indulge in this unfair play, for the regulars respect the law of the underworld, and even if competition is hard with hands jostling each other under the noses of the donors who then throw a few coins at random, just to get rid of the beggars, even then they only take what actually falls into their own outstretched palms.

On the day we are talking about, there is only one absentee from Salla Niang's courtyard: that is Madiabel, the lame beggar. He had been a tinker in his native village, mending pots and pans. But fewer and fewer people brought cooking-pots with holes needing to be patched up or old saucepans needing new handles to be fixed. He couldn't sell any more cookers, for the agent who collected them and took them to the City to dispose of them had disappeared one fine day without paying him for the results of a whole year's work. Madiabel had two wives and eight children to feed and clothe, so one day he upped and left for the City and became a "*bàttu*-bearer" – without a *bàttu* – simply holding out his hand for alms. Business was much better and he was able regularly to send his family clothes and money for food.

On this particular day. Salla Niang pointed out his absence as soon as the meeting started.

"Something's happened. Do you know what's the matter?"

"What's happened?"

"What's the matter?"

"It's not anything serious, is it?"

"Madiabel's had an accident," Salla replied.

"*Ashunalla! Chei waai!* Oh, dear! Oh, dear! How dreadful!"

"How did it happen?"

"Where was the accident?"

"Is he dead?"

"Oh, dear! Oh, dear!"

"I don't know if he's dead or not," said Salla. "It seems the manager of 'his' hotel complained to the police. They're bastards, those hotel people are. The police proceeded to organize a round-up. As he was trying to get away he ran out into the road without looking where he was going, just as a car came past at full speed."

"Oh! those round-ups! They make our life a misery. Poor Madiabel! He shouldn't have run, with his lame leg. It must be fate."

"Who wouldn't run, if he'd ever felt the sting of those whips? I take to my heels, I do, as soon as I catch sight of the fuzz. They lay about them like madmen; when they get worked up like that, they seem to forget that we're human beings."

"Some of them are quite decent sorts," Salla Niang intervenes. "They've never picked me up in their round-ups; they've never laid a hand on me. As soon as I see them coming, I arrange my scarf neatly on my head, I settle myself comfortably on my bench and I tell the children not to be afraid and not to run."

"The thing is, they don't take you for a beggar. In your smart *boubous* that are always freshly laundered and ironed, and with your children dressed as if they were going to a party, how could anyone imagine that you beg for a living?"

Everyone bursts out laughing. Poor Madiabel is forgotten. Narou, Salla's husband, happens to be passing at this moment with his kettle to go to his ablutions. He is delighted to hear the compliments addressed to his wife. Salla's *boubous* are very fine and she knows how to wear them. What is more, under her *boubou* she wears a *pagne*, and under this pagne she wears an immaculate little loincloth, and under this she has strings of white beads round her hips. Women nowadays disdain this custom, not realizing how much of their sexual attraction they lose thereby. The tinkle of these beads in the silence of the night in the Savanna, combined with the intoxicating smoke of *cuuraye* incense and the captivating perfume of *gongo* – what words can express the exhilarating effect this has on Narou!

"The old gossips in the district," he says to himself, "will never understand that."

"Narou is a weakling," they say.

"Salla wears the trousers."

"He's not really a man."

"They can go on slandering me; not one of them will ever know what ties me to Salla."

CHAPTER IV

"THEY'RE beginning to make our lives intolerable. Just because we're beggars, they think we're not quite human!"

It is Nguirane Sarr who is speaking. He's fed up with all the persecution. He's got the impression that "these madmen" have got it in for him especially. And yet he had thought he had won their respect and even their friendship. What had they got against him, when he always stayed quietly at "his" traffic-lights, never going up to accost people in their cars, knowing that he was dealing with his "regular patrons" who don't like being disturbed and who give to charity in any case, for their own benefit? And now "these madmen" don't stop to think any more. They don't make any distinction between people.

"They laid into me today. They tore my clothes, confiscated my stick and broke my glasses. It's too much, it's too much. Is that a way to treat a human being?"

Nguirane is at the end of his tether. Blood is oozing from a cut over his right eye that stretches down to his ear.

"They're quite vicious! When they start laying about them in a fury they're worse than mad dogs."

All the beggars are afraid now. They are being ceaselessly hunted down without respite. They are afraid and they suffer physically, but that does not stop them from returning to their strategic points every morning; they are drawn back as if by a magnet, armed only with the hope of being able to rely on the speed of their legs to escape from the stinging blows of the policemen's batons, or of hiding in some nearby house when the round-up parties come by.

"But what's got into them all of a sudden? Why this sudden zeal?"

"It's pure bloody-mindedness, that's all."

They don't understand – and, what is more, who is there to tell them – that they constitute a canker that must be hidden from sight. They have always considered themselves good citizens, practising a trade like everyone else, and because of this they have never tried to define what links them specifically to society. According to them, the contract that links every individual to society can be summed up in the words: giving and receiving. Well then, don't they, the poor, give their blessings, their prayers and their good wishes?

"It's too much, too much," Nguirane Sarr goes on. "Since they want war, let it be war."

"No, Nguirane," Gorgui Diop replies. "Don't talk like that. When you beg you have to learn to be patient, to put up with a lot of things. If you need something from someone, you have to satisfy his whims, besides Nguirane, those who give to us aren't the ones who knock us about."

Many voices are raised above the general murmurs.

"That's true, that's true. Gorgui Diop's quite right. You have to learn in life not to let a situation get out of hand."

"Gorgui Diop spoke the truth."

"Gorgui Diop's words are dictated by reason and wisdom."

"If we listened to the young we'd be in a nice mess!"

"At any rate, we wouldn't be in our graves," retorted Nguirane Sarr. "The young will never lead the way to the cemetery for you. Who was responsible for poor Madiabel's death? Wasn't it those madmen? If they hadn't hunted him down mercilessly, what happened would never have happened."

Madiabel had died of his injuries. He had lain at the hospital for five days without treatment, because he hadn't a penny on him, and to prove he was a pauper he had to have a certificate from the local authority; and as he was too badly injured to go and get this certificate of indigence which would exempt him from having to pay for treatment, he had lain in a corner, behind a general ward, whose inmates expressed sympathy for his suffering by endless exclamations of "*Ndeisan!* Shame! Shame!" whenever he groaned and writhed with the pain that racked him.

The day of his funeral, the whole brotherhood had accompanied him to his last resting-place and afterwards had collected a quite substantial sum of money to send to his family by way of assistance.

"We're not dogs!" Nguirane Sarr continues. "Are we dogs, now?"

His voice is shrill with anger and distress and it pierces the thin mist that lightly veils the last glimmer of twilight in the damp air that smells of burning wood. Tiny drops of water form like beads on the copper-coloured faces, expressive of distress and resignation.

"We're not dogs! You know perfectly well we're not dogs. And they've got to be convinced of this too. So we must get organized."

"How can we get organized? Beggars, get organized! You must be dreaming, Nguirane! You're young! Just leave them to the good Lord."

"Listen, we can perfectly well get organized. Even these madmen, these heartless brutes who descend on us and beat us up, even they give to charity. They need to give alms because they need our prayers – wishes for long life, for prosperity, for pilgrimages; they like to hear them every morning to drive away their bad dreams of the night before, and to maintain their hopes that things will be better tomorrow. You think that people give out of the goodness of their hearts? Not at all. They give out of an instinct for self-preservation."

The atmosphere had suddenly grown silent. Ears are pricked up; eyelids flicker, but remain closed. Little by little the mantle of twilight settles on the dark silhouettes which fill Salla Niang's courtyard. She herself stands in the doorway of her room, close to Nguirane. Seeing him so dishevelled, so cast down, at the sight of his face that had been pushed into the dust, and the large gash on his head that gives him the appearance of a martyr, she is filled with compassion. She is indignant. She shares the suffering of this man who she thinks of as her own brother, and who today presents such a downcast appearance. "Look what poverty." At the sight of his shirt which has been torn to ribbons, at the sight of a pair of underpants of doubtful whiteness that are visible through the wide rents in what was left of a pair of trousers – now nothing but a collection of rags floating round a semblance of a belt – at the sight of Nguirane's misfortunes Salla Niang has come to the conclusion that there are some forms of suffering that no one has the right to inflict on a human being.

"*Jog jot na! Jog jot na kal!* It's time we did something! It's really time we did something!"

As she speaks she points her right forefinger at the audience. When nobody reacts to this serious warning she goes on, "It's time we woke up, lads. Nguirane's right. People don't give out of love for us. That's quite correct. So, let's get organized! For a start, don't let's accept any more of those worthless coins they throw us, that won't even buy a lollipop. Eh, my little *talibés*, d'you hear! Spit on their one francs and their two francs; spit on their three lumps of sugar; spit on their handful of rice! D'you hear? Show them we're men as much as they are! And no more prayers for their welfare till we've received a good fat donation! Are you agreed, lads?"

"Ah, *loolu de yomb na*. That's quite easy."

"Yes, indeed. If one looks into it, what you've just said makes good sense."

"*Sa degg degg lef li mot naa seetaat*. Yes indeed, we must look into it. Let us do as Salla suggests."

"Agreed, agreed. We're all agreed."

They have confidence in Salla. They know she is a woman of experience. She has had plenty of opportunities of getting to know the world. Being orphaned quite young, she had to learn to make her own way in life very early. Her former job as a maid-of-all-work gave her the chance to get to know people, to learn their most intimate secrets and to judge the idiosyncracies of the rich as well as the poor; for she had swept sumptuous villas with their soft mattresses as well as sordid hovels in which at nightfall there were quarrels over a torn pallet whose straw swarmed with bed-bugs. The school of life is probably the best school! You see everything, you get hardened to everything. Nothing surprises you any more, not even a man's most contradictory behaviour.

Salla is now sitting just in front of her door. She rests her elbow on her right knee that is bent up before her; she leans her cheek on her hand.

"They always pretend to look down on the people they need. The last boss I worked for, the one who helped me get this plot of land, spent his time cursing all marabouts. I used to see him on television, I used to hear him on the radio, I recognized his picture in the newspaper when I took it to light the stove. His children explained to me that he wanted to wipe out the curse of the marabouts. He even received some decoration, I think, for his fine speeches. Yes . . . when he got his decoration, he organized a grand reception. And yet this man, a real black Frenchman, who drank beer when he was thirsty and whisky when he needed perking up, who only spoke French to his wife and children, well, he never left home in the morning without daubing himself with a mixture of powders and fermented roots that he kept in seven different pots. And those pots gave off such a sickening smell that it made me feel quite ill when I cleaned the bathroom, but it never upset Monsieur. And when he'd finished his speeches, what did he say to the marabouts he put up in his own house? . . . Yes, the house was always filled with marabouts; as soon as one left, more arrived with their dirty washing. Oh! their dirty washing! . . . Oh! Oh! what a peculiar man that boss was. . ."

She had noticed that Monsieur couldn't keep his eyes off her firm breasts. As soon as he got the chance, he'd try a little teasing and then make more definite advances. What a bastard! She had always held out. When Madame was present he didn't even look at her, or else rebuked her harshly on account of a speck of dust on the television or the collar of a shirt that had been badly ironed. Madame intervened and sometimes the matter degenerated into a quarrel.

"Leave the girl alone. She works here, but she's not our slave!"

"Oh! so you dare to question my authority, just over a servant! One of these fine days I'll give her the sack. And you'll follow her!"

"And then, one day, Madame discovered his little game! The villa was double-storeyed. The bedrooms were upstairs; the lounge, the dining-room and the kitchen were on the ground floor. Monsieur had a weakness for tea; he drank it after lunch and again about six o'clock after work, and again after dinner. Every working day he used to say, 'Salla, keep the last pot of tea for me.' And after his siesta, just before he went back to work, he used to come down to the kitchen while Madame was still resting. He took the opportunity to tease me, to pinch my bottom and fondle my tits. One day – I don't know if she suspected something – Madam suddenly burst into the kitchen while Monsieur was groping and I was trying to escape. We hadn't even heard her approach. When Monsieur caught sight of her standing near the kitchen door, not moving or saying anything, he looked like a man who's had a bucket of ice-cold water thrown over him in mid-winter. He looked shame-faced at Madame who just stood watching him, then he walked over to the table where the teapot was and began to pour the tea into the cups. Madame just stood there for a few minutes, then turned on her heels and left. I never knew if they had it out or not; though I listened with all my ears, I never heard any signs of a quarrel between them and soon afterwards I left the house as I was going to get married."

Ama Ata Aidoo

1942–

Born in Ghana's Central Region, she has a BA in English from the University of Ghana (1964) and began to write professionally as an undergraduate, after winning a prize in a short-story competition organized by the Mbari Club in Ibadan, Nigeria. In the 1980s she was appointed Secretary for Education in the Ghana government and she has lectured and consulted for universities and academic and research institutions in Ghana, other parts of Africa and the USA. She is based in Harare, Zimbabwe, with her daughter. Her writing – which includes literature for young people, poetry (Someone Talking to Sometime, 1985), plays (Dilemma of a Ghost and Anowa, 1970), short stories (collected in No Sweetness Here, 1970) and the novels Our Sister Killjoy: or Reflections from a Black-eyed Squint (1977) and Changes (1991) – is rooted in the oral tradition and has a directness born of African storytelling techniques combined with a talent for cross-cultural communication. She says she writes from the premise that "only an African knows what it is to be an African and only a woman knows what it is to be a woman and can give expression to the essence of being a woman".

Two Sisters

As she shakes out the typewriter cloak and covers the machine with it, the thought of the bus she has to hurry to catch goes through her like a pain. It is her luck, she thinks. Everything is just her luck. Why, if she had one of those graduates for a boy-friend, wouldn't he come and take her home every evening?

And she knows that a girl does not herself have to be a graduate to get one of those boys. Certainly, Joe is dying to do exactly that – with his taxi. And he is as handsome as anything, and a good man, but you know. . .Besides there are cars and there are cars. As for the possibility of the other actually coming to fetch her – oh well. She has to admit it will take some time before she can bring herself to make demands of that sort on *him*. She has also to admit that the temptation is extremely strong. Would it really be so dangerously indiscreet? Doesn't one government car look like another? The hugeness of it? Its shaded glass? The uniformed chauffeur? She can already see herself stepping out to greet the dead-with-envy glances of the other girls. To begin with, she will insist on a little discretion. The driver can drop her under the neem trees in the morning and pick her up from there in the evening. . .anyway, she will have to wait a little while for that and it is all her luck.

There are other ways, surely. One of these, for some reason, she has sworn to have nothing of. Her boss has a car and does not look bad. In fact the man is all right. But she keeps telling herself that she does not fancy having some old and dried-out housewife walking into the office one afternoon to tear her hair out and make a row. . . . Mm, so for the meantime, it is going to continue to be the municipal bus with its grimy seats, its common passengers and impudent conductors. . . . Jesus! She doesn't wish herself dead or anything as stupidly final as that. Oh no. She just wishes she could sleep deep and only wake up on the morning of her glory.

The new pair of black shoes are more realistic than their owner, though. As she walks down the corridor, they sing:

> *Count, Mercy, count your blessings*
> *Count, Mercy, count your blessings*
> *Count, count, count your blessings.*

They sing along the corridor, into the avenue, across the road and into the bus. And they resume their song along the gravel path, as she opens the front gate and crosses the cemented courtyard to the door.

"Sissie!" she called.

"*Hei* Mercy," and the door opened to show the face of Connie, big sister, six years or more older and now heavy with her second child. Mercy collapsed into the nearest chair.

"Welcome home. How was the office today?"

"Sister, don't ask. Look at my hands. My fingers are dead with typing. Oh, God, I don't know what to do."

"Why, what is wrong?"

"You tell me what is right. Why should I be a typist?"

"What else would you be?"

"What a strange question. Is typing the only thing one can do in this world? You are a teacher, are you not?"

"But. . .but. . ."

"But what? Or you want me to know that if I had done better in the exams, I could have trained to be a teacher too, eh, sister? Or even a proper secretary?"

"Mercy, what is the matter? What have I done? What have I done? Why have you come home so angry?"

Mercy broke into tears.

"Oh, I am sorry. I am sorry, Sissie. It's just that I am sick of everything. The office, living with you and your husband. I want a husband of my own, children. I want. . .I want. . ."

"But you are so beautiful."

"Thank you. But so are you."

"You are young and beautiful. As for marriage, it's you who are postponing it. Look at all these people who are running after you."

"Sissie, I don't like what you are doing. So stop it."

"Okay, okay, okay."

And there was a silence.

"Which of them could I marry? Joe is – mm, fine – but, but I just don't like him."

"You mean. . ."

"Oh, Sissie!"

"Little sister, you and I can be truthful with one another."

"Oh, yes."

"What I would like to say is that I am not that old or wise. But still I could advise you a little. Joe drives someone's car now. Well, you never know. Lots of taxi drivers come to own their taxis, sometimes fleets of cars."

"Of course. But it's a pity you are married already. Or I could be a go-between for you and Joe!"

And the two of them burst out laughing. It was when she rose to go to the bedroom that Connie noticed the new shoes.

"*Ei*, those are beautiful shoes. Are they new?"

From the other room, Mercy's voice came interrupted by the motions of her body as she undressed and then dressed again. However, the uncertainty in it was due to something entirely different.

"Oh, I forgot to tell you about them. In fact, I was going to show them to you. I think it was on Tuesday I bought them. Or was it Wednesday? When I came home from the office, you and James had taken Akosua out. And later, I forgot all about them."

"I see. But they are very pretty. Were they expensive?"

"No, not really." This reply was too hurriedly said.

And she said only last week that she didn't have a penny on her. And I believed her because I know what they pay her is just not enough to last anyone through any month, even minus rent. . . . I have been thinking she manages very well. But these shoes. And she is not the type who would borrow money just to buy a pair of shoes, when she could have gone on wearing her old pairs until things get better. Oh, I wish I knew what to do. I mean I am not her mother. And I wonder how James will see these problems.

"Sissie, you look worried."

"Hmm, when don't I? With the baby due in a couple of months and the government's new ruling on salaries and all. On top of everything I have reliable information that James is running after a new girl."

Mercy laughed.

"Oh, Sissie. You always get reliable information on these things."

"But, yes. And I don't know why."

"Sissie, men are like that."

"They are selfish."

"No, it's just that women allow them to behave the way they do instead of seizing some freedom themselves."

"But I am sure that even if we were free to carry on in the same way, I wouldn't make use of it."

"But why not?"

"Because I love James. I love James and I am not interested in any other man." Her voice was full of tears. But Mercy was amused.

"O God. Now listen to that. It's women like you who keep all of us down."

"Well, I am sorry but it's how the good God created me."

"Mm. I am sure that I can love several men at the same time."

"Mercy!"

They burst out laughing again. And yet they are sad. But laughter is always best.

Mercy complained of hunger and so they went to the kitchen to heat up some food and eat. The two sisters alone. It is no use waiting for James. And this evening, a friend of Connie's has come to take out the baby girl, Akosua, and had threatened to keep her until her bedtime.

"Sissie, I am going to see a film." This from Mercy.

"Where?"

"The Globe."

"Are you going with Joe?"

"No."

"Are you going alone?"

"No."

Careful, Connie.

"Whom are you going with?"

Careful, Connie, please. Little sister's nostrils are widening dangerously. Look at the sudden creasing-up of her mouth and between her brows. Connie, a sister is a good thing. Even a young sister. Especially when you have no mother or father.

"Mercy, whom are you going out with?"

"Well, I had food in my mouth! And I had to swallow it down before I could answer you, no?"

"I am sorry." How softly said.

"And anyway, do I have to tell you everything?"

"Oh, no. It's just that I didn't think it was a question I should not have asked."

There was more silence. Then Mercy sucked her teeth with irritation and Connie cleared her throat with fear.

"I am going out with Mensar-Arthur."

As Connie asked the next question, she wondered if the words were leaving her lips.

"Mensar-Arthur?"

"Yes."

"Which one?"

"How many do you know?"

Her fingers were too numb to pick up the food. She put the plate down. Something jumped in her chest and she wondered what it was. Perhaps it was the baby.

"Do you mean that member of Parliament?"

"Yes."

"But, Mercy. . ."

Little sister only sits and chews her food.

"But, Mercy. . ."

Chew, chew, chew.

"But, Mercy. . ."

"What?"

She startled Connie.

"He is so old."

Chew, chew, chew.

"Perhaps, I mean, perhaps that really doesn't matter, does it? Not very much anyway. But they say he has so many wives and girl-friends."

Please, little sister. I am not trying to interfere in your private life. You said yourself a little while ago that you wanted a man of your own. That man belongs to so many women already. . . .

That silence again. Then there was only Mercy's footsteps as she went to put her plate in the kitchen sink, running water as she washed her plate and her hands. She drank some water and coughed. Then as tears streamed down her sister's averted face, there was the sound of her footsteps as she left the kitchen. At the end of it all, she banged a door. Connie only said something like, "O Lord, O Lord," and continued sitting in the kitchen. She had hardly eaten anything at all. Very soon Mercy went to have a bath. Then Connie heard her getting ready to leave the house. The shoes. Then she was gone. She needn't have carried on like that, eh? Because Connie had not meant to probe or bring on a quarrel. What use is there in this old world for a sister, if you can't have a chat with her? What's more, things like this never happen to people like Mercy. Their parents were good Presbyterians. They feared God. Mama had not managed to give them all the rules of life before she died. But Connie knows that running around with an old and depraved public man would have been considered an abomination by the parents.

A big car with a super-smooth engine purred into the drive. It actually purrs: this huge machine from the white man's land. Indeed, its well-mannered protest as the tyres slid on to the gravel seemed like a lullaby compared to the loud thumping of the girl's stiletto shoes. When Mensar-Arthur saw Mercy, he stretched his arm and opened the door to the passenger seat. She sat down and the door closed with a civilized thud. The engine hummed into motion and the car sailed away.

After a distance of a mile or so from the house, the man started conversation.

"And how is my darling today?"

"I am well," and only the words did not imply tragedy.

"You look solemn today, why?"

She remained silent and still.

"My dear, what is the matter?"

"Nothing."

"Oh. . ." he cleared his throat again. "Eh, and how were the shoes?"

"Very nice. In fact, I am wearing them now. They pinch a little but then all new shoes are like that."

"And the handbag?"

"I like it very much too. . . .My sister noticed them. I mean the shoes." The tragedy was announced.

"Did she ask you where you got them from?"

"No."

He cleared his throat again.

"Where did we agree to go tonight?"

"The Globe, but I don't want to see a film."

"Is that so? Mm, I am glad because people always notice things."

"But they won't be too surprised."

"What are you saying, my dear?"

"Nothing."

"Okay, so what shall we do?"

"I don't know."

"Shall I drive to the Seaway?"

"Oh, yes."

He drove to the Seaway. To a section of the beach they knew very well. She loves it here. This wide expanse of sand and the old sea. She has often wished she could do what she fancied: one thing she fancies. Which is to drive very near to the end of the sands until the tyres of the car touched the water. Of course it is a very foolish idea as he pointed out sharply to her the first time she thought aloud about it. It was in his occasional I-am-more-than-old-enough-to-be-your-father tone. There are always disadvantages. Things could be different. Like if one had a younger lover. Handsome, maybe not rich like this man here, but well-off, sufficiently well-off to be able to afford a sports car. A little something very much like those in the films driven by the white racing drivers. With tyres that can do everything. . .and they would drive exactly where the sea and the sand meet.

"We are here."

"Don't let's get out. Let's just sit inside and talk."

"Talk?"

"Yes."

"Okay. But what is it, my darling?"

"I have told my sister about you."

"Good God. Why?"

"But I had to. I couldn't keep it to myself any longer."

"Childish. It was not necessary at all. She is not your mother."

"No. But she is all I have. And she has been very good to me."

"Well, it was her duty."

"Then it is my duty to tell her about something like this. I may get into trouble."

"Don't be silly," he said. "I normally take good care of my girl-friends."

"I see," she said and for the first time in the one month since she agreed to be this man's lover, the tears which suddenly rose into her eyes were not forced.

"And you promised you wouldn't tell her." It was father's voice now.

"Don't be angry. After all, people talk so much, as you said a little while ago. She was bound to hear it one day."

"My darling, you are too wise. What did she say?"

"She was pained."

"Don't worry. Find out something she wants very much but cannot get in this country because of the import restrictions." ·

"I know for sure she wants an electric motor for her sewing machine."

"Is that all?"

"That's what I know of."

"Mm. I am going to London next week on some delegation, so if you bring me the details on the make of the machine, I shall get her the motor."

"Thank you."

"What else is worrying my Black Beauty?"

"Nothing."

"And by the way, let me know as soon as you want to leave your sister's place. I have got you one of the government estate houses."

"Oh ... oh," she said, pleased, contented for the first time since this typically ghastly day had begun, at half-past six in the morning.

Dear little child came back from the playground with her toe bruised. Shall we just blow cold air from our mouth on it or put on a salve? Nothing matters really. Just see that she does not feel unattended. And the old sea roars on. This is a calm sea, generally. Too calm in fact, this Gulf of Guinea. The natives sacrifice to him on Tuesdays and once a year celebrate him. They might save their chickens, their eggs and their yams. And as for the feast once a year, he doesn't pay much attention to it either. They are always celebrating one thing or another and they surely don't need him for an excuse to celebrate one day more. He has seen things happen along these beaches. Different things. Contradictory things. Or just repetitions of old patterns. He never interferes in their affairs. Why should he? Except in places like Keta where he eats houses away because they leave him no choice. Otherwise he never allows them to see his passions. People are worms, and even the God who created them is immensely bored with their antics. Here is a fifty-year-old "big man" who thinks he is somebody. And a twenty-three-year-old child who chooses a silly way to conquer unconquerable problems. Well, what did one expect of human beings? And so as those two settled on the back seat of the car to play with each other's bodies, he, the Gulf of Guinea, shut his eyes with boredom. It is right. He could sleep, no? He spread himself and moved further ashore. But the car was parked at a very safe distance and the rising tides could not wet its tyres.

James has come home late. But then he has been coming back late for the past few weeks. Connie is crying and he knows it as soon as he enters the bedroom. He hates tears, for like so many men, he knows it is one of the most potent weapons in women's bitchy and inexhaustible arsenal. She speaks first.

"James."

"Oh, are you still awake?" He always tries to deal with these nightly funeral parlour doings by pretending not to know what they are about.

"I couldn't sleep."

"What is wrong?"

"Nothing."

So he moves quickly and sits beside her.

"Connie, what is the matter? You have been crying again."

"You are very late again."

"Is that why you are crying? Or is there something else?"

"Yes."

"Yes to what?"

"James, where were you?"

"Connie, I have warned you about what I shall do if you don't stop examining me, as though I were your prisoner, every time I am a little late."

She sat up.

"A little late! It is nearly two o'clock."

"Anyway, you won't believe me if I told you the truth, so why do you want me to waste my breath?"

"Oh, well." She lies down again and turns her face to the wall. He stands up but does not walk away. He looks down at her. So she remembers every night: they have agreed, after many arguments, that she should sleep like this. During her first pregnancy, he kept saying after the third month or so that the sight of her tummy the last thing before he slept always gave him nightmares. Now he regrets all this. The bed creaks as he throws himself down by her.

"James."

"Yes."

"There is something much more serious."

"You have heard about my newest affair?"

"Yes, but that is not what I am referring to."

"Jesus, is it possible that there is anything more important than that?"

And as they laugh they know that something has happened. One of those things which, with luck, will keep them together for some time to come.

"He teases me on top of everything."

"What else can one do to you but tease when you are in this state?"

"James! How profane!"

"It is your dirty mind which gave my statement its shocking meaning."

"Okay! But what shall I do?"

"About what?"

"Mercy. Listen, she is having an affair with Mensar-Arthur."

"Wonderful."

She sits up and he sits up.

"James, we must do something about it. It is very serious."

"Is that why you were crying?"

"Of course."

"Why shouldn't she?"

"But it is wrong. And she is ruining herself."

"Since every other girl she knows has ruined herself prosperously, why shouldn't she? Just forget for once that you are a teacher. Or at least, remember she is not your pupil."

"I don't like your answers."

"What would you like me to say? Every morning her friends who don't earn any more than she does wear new dresses, shoes, wigs and what-have-you to work. What would you have her do?"

"The fact that other girls do it does not mean that Mercy should do it too."

"You are being very silly. If I were Mercy, I am sure that's exactly what I would do. And you know I mean it too."

James is cruel. He is terrible and mean. Connie breaks into fresh tears and James comforts her. There is one point he must drive home though.

"In fact, encourage her. He may be able to intercede with the Ministry for you so that after the baby is born they will not transfer you from here for some time."

"James, you want me to use my sister!"

"She is using herself, remember."

"James, you are wicked."

"And maybe he would even agree to get us a new car from abroad. I shall pay for everything. That would be better than paying a fortune for that old thing I was thinking of buying. Think of that."

"You will ride in it alone."

"Well. . ."

That was a few months before the *coup*. Mensar-Arthur did go to London for a conference and bought something for all his wives and girl-friends, including Mercy. He even remembered the motor for Connie's machine. When Mercy took it to her she was quite confused. She had wanted this thing for a long time, and it would make everything so much easier, like the clothes for the new baby. And yet one side of her said that accepting it was a betrayal. Of what, she wasn't even sure. She and Mercy could never bring the whole business into the open and discuss it. And there was always James supporting Mercy, to Connie's bewilderment. She took the motor with thanks and sold even her right to dissent. In a short while, Mercy left the house to go and live in the estate house Mensar-Arthur had procured for her. Then, a couple of weeks later, the *coup*. Mercy left her new place before anyone could evict her. James never got his car. Connie's new baby was born. Of the three, the one who greeted the new order with undisguised relief was Connie. She is not really a demonstrative person but it was obvious from her eyes that she was happy. As far as she was concerned, the old order as symbolized by Mensar-Arthur was a threat to her sister and therefore to her own peace of mind. With it gone, things could return to normal. Mercy would move back to the house, perhaps start to date someone more – ordinary, let's say. Eventually, she would get married and then the nightmare of those past weeks would be forgotten. God being so good, he brought the *coup* early before the news of the affair could spread and brand her sister. . . .

The arrival of the new baby has magically waved away the difficulties between James and Connie. He is that kind of man, and she that kind of woman. Mercy has not been seen for many days. Connie is beginning to get worried. . . .

James heard the baby yelling – a familiar noise, by now – the moment he opened the front gate. He ran in, clutching to his chest the few things he had bought on his way home.

"We are in here."

"I certainly could hear you. If there is anything people of this country have, it is a big mouth."

"Don't I agree? But on the whole, we are well. He is eating normally and everything. You?"

"Nothing new. Same routine. More stories about the overthrown politicians."

"What do you mean, nothing new? Look at the excellent job the soldiers have done, cleaning up the country of all that dirt. I feel free already and I am dying to get out and enjoy it."

James laughed mirthlessly.

"All I know is that Mensar-Arthur is in jail. No use. And I am not getting my car. Rough deal."

"I never took you seriously on that car business."

"Honestly, if this were in the ancient days, I could brand you a witch. You don't want me, your husband, to prosper?"

"Not out of my sister's ruin."

"Ruin, ruin, ruin! Christ! See, Connie, the funny thing is that I am sure you are the only person who thought it was a disaster to have a sister who was the girl-friend of a big man."

"Okay; now all is over, and don't let's quarrel."

"I bet the *coup* could have succeeded on your prayers alone."

And Connie wondered why he said that with so much bitterness. She wondered if. . .

"Has Mercy been here?"

"Not yet, later, maybe. Mm. I had hoped she would move back here and start all over again."

"I am not surprised she hasn't. In fact, if I were her, I wouldn't come back here either. Not to your nagging, no thank you, big sister."

And as the argument progressed, as always, each was forced into a more aggressive defensive stand.

"Well, just say what pleases you. I am very glad about the soldiers. Mercy is my only sister, brother; everything. I can't sit and see her life going wrong without feeling it. I am grateful to whatever forces there are which put a stop to that. What pains me now is that she should be so vague about where she is living at the moment. She makes mention of a girl-friend but I am not sure that I know her."

"If I were you, I would stop worrying because it seems Mercy can look after herself quite well."

"Hmm," was all she tried to say.

Who heard something like the sound of a car pulling into the drive? Ah, but the footsteps were unmistakably Mercy's. Are those shoes the old pair which were new a couple of months ago? Or are they the newest pair? And here she is herself, the pretty one. A gay Mercy.

"Hello, hello, my clan!" and she makes a lot of her nephew.

"Dow-dah-dee-day! And how is my dear young man today? My lord, grow up fast and come to take care of Auntie Mercy."

Both Connie and James cannot take their eyes off her. Connie says, "He says to Auntie Mercy he is fine."

Still they watch her, horrified, fascinated and wondering what it's all about. Because they both know it is about something.

"Listen, people. I brought a friend to meet you. A man."

"Where is he?" from James.

"Bring him in," from Connie.

"You know, Sissie, you are a new mother. I thought I'd come and ask you if it's all right."

"Of course," say James and Connie, and for some reason they are both very nervous.

"He is Captain Ashley."

"Which one?"

"How many do you know?"

James still thinks it is impossible. "Eh...do you mean the officer who has been appointed the...the..."

"Yes."

"Wasn't there a picture in *The Crystal* over the week-end about his daughter's wedding? And another one of him with his wife and children and grandchildren?"

"Yes."

"And he is heading a commission to investigate something or other?"

"Yes."

Connie just sits there with her mouth open that wide...

Pamela Mordecai

1943–

J amaican-born, she was educated at the University of the West Indies (UWI) and in the USA. She taught English in schools and at Mico Teachers' College, has been a journalist and radio and television broadcaster, is currently Publications Officer at the UWI School of Education and edits the Caribbean Journal of Education. She has written on Caribbean literature and developed curriculum materials in language arts. Her poems have appeared in many journals and anthologies and in her book Journey Poem, she was also co-editor, with Mervyn Morris, of the anthology Jamaica Woman (1980).

Tell Me

So tell me what you have
to give: I have strong limbs
to make a lap of love
a brow to gaze at in
the quiet times half light and
lips for kissing: I'm well
fixed for all love's traffic

And further, I've an ear
open around the clock
you know, like those phone
numbers that you call at
anytime. And such soft eyes
that smile and ferret out
the truth. Extraordinary

eyes, and gentle – you can see
yourself. It's strong and warm
and dark, this womb I've got
and fertile: you can be
a child and play in
there: and if you fall and
hurt yourself, it's easy

to be mended: I know
it sounds a little much
but that's the way it seems
to me. So tell me, brother

what have you to give?

For Eyes to Bless You

Those times I have you when my flesh
wants nothing near it, you don't know
and even now you can't find out
that masquerade, that play.
It's old as woman, old as birth
that's joy and riddance both at once.
You will not know how much how
frequently, in that same way, I want
my body back. So do not ask

that what I said a week, a month
ago should be what I say now:
the only protest you may make
is that my eyes no longer bless
you – for the rest, the fires
that you lie so quietly against
are me: mercurial as hell
and heaven fixed in one
perpetual counterpoise:
there your intrusion may not reach,
That is a field where powers do
battle, principalities war on.
And what I say about it all
is little gauge. For eyes to bless
you then must be enough. . .

Carolyn M. Rodgers

1942–

B orn in Chicago, she attended the University of Illinois and holds
a BA from Roosevelt University. She worked with young people on
the South Side of Chicago, and has been a lecturer and writer-
in-residence at Columbia College, University of Washington, Malcolm
X Community College, Albany State College, Indiana University and
Chicago State University. Her awards include the first Conrad Kent Rivers
Writing Award in 1969, a National Endowment for the Arts Award in
1970, and PEN Awards. Her poetry can be forthright and militant, sensitive and complex, and deals with subjects ranging from revolution to
love, religion to the realities of Black womanhood. It has been published
in volumes including Paper Soul (1969), Songs of a Blackbird (1969),
How I Got Ovah (1976) and The Heart as Ever Green (1978). In the
1960s she was instrumental in defining a higher profile for poetry as a

Black art form, and she was an active member of the Organization of Black American Culture from 1967 to 1971.

Poem for Some Black Women

i am lonely,
all the people i know
i know too well

there was comfort in that
at first but now
we know each others miseries
   too well.

we are
   lonely women, who spend time waiting for
   occasional flings
we live with fear.
we are lonely.
we are talented, dedicated, well read
   BLACK, COMMITTED,

we are lonely,
we understand the world problems
Black women's problems with Black men
   but all
we really understand is
   lonely.

when we laugh,
we are so happy to laugh
we cry when we laugh
   we are lonely.
we are busy people
always doing things
fearing getting trapped in rooms
loud with empty. . .
                    yet
knowing the music of silence/hating it/hoarding it
loving it/treasuring it,
   it often birthing our creativity
              we are lonely

being soft and being hard
supporting our selves, earning our own bread

soft/hard/hard/soft/
knowing that need must not show
                    will frighten away
knowing that we must
walk back-wards nonchalantly on our tip-toeness
    into
happiness,
    if only for stingy moments

we know too much
we learn to understand everything,
to make too much sense out
of the world,
of pain
                    of lonely. . .

we buy clothes, we take trips,
we wish, we pray, we meditate, we curse, we crave, we coo,
we caw,

                    we need ourselves sick, we need, we need
we lonely we grow tired of tears we grow tired of fear
we grow tired but must al-ways be soft and not too serious. . .
                    not too smart not too bitchy not too sapphire
                    not too dumb not too not too not too
a little less a little more
                              add here detract there
                                   .lonely.

Pilar López Gonzales

1942–

One of the interviewees whose autobiographies are included in
Oscar Lewis's Four Women: Living the Revolution – An Oral
History of Contemporary Cuba (1977), she was born in her

grandparents' house in El Cerro. She describes her parents' quarrels, the hardship of home life in the barrio of Jesús María, the shame she felt at having to take a job as a housemaid, her marriage at fifteen to a man thirteen years her senior and the birth of her first daughter in 1958, after which she was advised to try working in a brothel by a girlfriend who told her, "It's all over in a minute. You get paid and that's that." Eventually she left prostitution to enter a rehabilitation school and make a fresh start, three years after the 1959 revolution.

It Was All Mamá's Fault

*P*APÁ's family was so different from *mamá*'s. There were only his parents, my *papá*, and his sister Gertrudis. Grandfather Raimundo and Grandmother Nicolasa were teachers and held sixth-grade classes in their home. She taught Spanish and he mathematics, until he got a job as a night watchman for Public Works.

I don't know whether my father finished high school, but he was pretty well educated and had good manners, and he became a photographer. Aunt Gertrudis was a schoolteacher even before the Revolution, so she must have passed the eighth grade. In those times it was really hard to find a teaching job, but since she was able to speak English, a friend of hers, an army captain, got her a job in the ten-cent store. The salary was good and Aunt Gertrudis always lived better than my mother's sisters, dressed better, and had more social poise, more polished manners. She used to go to the beach and other places to amuse herself. My mother's sisters never went anywhere.

The only nice one in *papá*'s family was Grandfather Raimundo. Nicolasa and Gertrudis were mean, hard women. Nicolasa had always opposed *papá*'s marriage, claiming that he had lowered himself by marrying a *mulata*. My grandmother helped us out a bit by sending food and things, but she was a selfish snob who hated my mother and never stopped reproaching *papá* for marrying her. So whenever *papá* visited his mother, there'd be a fight at home.

Nicolasa and Gertrudis favored Francisca, my eldest sister, who spent as much time at their house as I spent at *mima* Bella's, and even when we were both there I noticed that if visitors came, Grandmother would introduce Francisca but not me. I never complained, but it gave me intolerable pain. My sister had a higher position than the rest of us in all sorts of ways – she always, always, had plenty to eat, and she even had a Banker's Club credit card that Grandmother had bought her so she could go to the beach. My grandmother came right out and said that she took Francisca with her because my sister could pass for white and colored people weren't allowed in the places she went. My brother Aurelio was also on the light side, but Susana, Xiomara, and I were dark-skinned and she was embarrassed to be seen in public with us. Little Susana was even darker than I, and Grandmother used to call her "the monkey of the family".

So there was always some tension between the rest of us and the "white" girl of the family. If Nicolasa gave Francisca oranges she'd say, "Don't go giving your sisters any. They eat enough and you don't." Francisca had more clothes than we did because Aunt Gertrudis kept buying them for her, but Francisca would never lend them to the rest of us. She was very selfish about everything. Naturally we were a bit jealous.

Francisca had the kind of style that wins people over. I didn't – I was too dry and serious. She was proud and vain and I was quarrelsome and dominating, so we often fought, though when we were little we played together a lot, too. I'd get pretty mad at Francisca when they took her to parties or the beach, but I think I may also have been scared of her because she used to threaten me with her fingernails. We'd start fighting and then *mamá* would spank us both.

My paternal grandparents lived in the barrio Los Pinos in an apartment that Aunt Gertrudis got through a friend of hers. They had a corner apartment with two bedrooms, a living room, dining room, kitchen, bathroom, and terrace. After the Revolution Aunt Gertrudis found a better place and left that one to *mamá*.

Often on Saturdays Gertrudis would send for me to spend the day. That meant they were going to clean the house. I was the one who had experience, my aunt said, and Francisca didn't – meaning Francisca wouldn't lift a finger. Oh, my aunt was willing to use me when she needed me, but she never showed me any affection, nor did I ever get anything from her but cast-off clothes.

Grandfather Raimundo was different. He was very sweet to me and didn't pay much attention to Francisca, because, as he used to say, "She gets more than enough affection." He'd often argue with Grandmother about us, poor man! He'd say, "They're all your grandchildren. You should love every one of them. You shouldn't play favorites!" And it wasn't just words on his part. That's why he took me with him to buy the groceries. He used to buy me bananas because my sister was always getting special treats at mealtimes.

Papá never, never caught on to the situation. Oh, he knew his family liked Francisca best but he thought it was because she was the eldest and had spent the most time with them. Grandmother never said anything about skin color in front of him.

Papá adored his mother, and she respected him, even if she was always criticizing him and trying to run his life. She'd tell him he should come over more often because she was worried about his getting enough to eat, and she was always after him not to have any more children. He had to work hard enough as it was, and even so he couldn't support us all. How could he think of having more?

Papá didn't listen. He'd tell her, "I'm going to have at least a dozen and you needn't worry about what doesn't concern you." They were always arguing about that, but on the whole they were very loving with one another. My Aunt Gertrudis was forever complaining that Grandmother favored *papá*. "I'm the one who does everything for you. *I* make the sacrifices, and you thank me by paying more attention to Aurelio." Grandmother Nicolasa wasn't any model mother; she was self-centered and cared only about her own comfort, but at least there wasn't any violence in her home and nobody used foul language.

My grandmother made a slave of her husband. The problem was, he lost his job, and since he was home most of the time he did the woman's work – the cooking, the cleaning, the shopping. A cousin of Grandmother's lived with them too, an invalid in a wheelchair, and it was Grandfather who had to carry her and bathe her, even clean her and change the bed because she couldn't go to the toilet. Poor henpecked guy! And though he tried hard, Grandfather didn't really know how to give the house a good cleaning.

My aunt treated her father as if he were her servant, or even a woman. They all slept in the same room, my grandparents in one bed and my aunt in the other, and in the morning Gertrudis would get up in nothing but a transparent nightgown and go into the bathroom. She never took a bath, she just washed and used a lot of cream to keep herself from looking old. She always had a peculiar smell about her...I mean, it was horrible. Then she'd come out of the bathroom stark naked and say, "Hand me a bar of soap," or "*Papá*, get me my panties." I thought it was revolting.

I'd never seen my father or my brother naked. My sisters slept in the same things they wore during the day and changed in the bathroom, *papá* slept in his underwear but always covered himself, and *mamá* slept in a dress. My brother Aurelio never saw *mamá* without her clothes on. But Aunt Gertrudis wasn't ashamed for her *papá* to see her like that.

The first time Gertrudis got married, the groom brought her back home the day after the wedding. My aunt claimed it was because he wasn't a real man, but I heard a neighbor say, "What a brazen lie! Everybody knows why he brought her back – she's not a virgin." I also heard someone say that the only way she got her job at the ten-cent store was by giving herself to that captain. I don't know if it's true, but I don't suppose Grandmother cared what her daughter did as long as she herself was comfortable.

Aunt Gertrudis believes children should sacrifice themselves for their parents and that's what she's done all her life. Grandmother died a short time ago and now Raimundo lives with Gertrudis – he's ninety-two years old and a real nuisance. I don't mean he's bad, he's just troublesome because he's so old. Still, if my aunt really loved him she'd have taken his side when her mother was treating him so badly. As it was, he didn't dare open his mouth because every time he did, *boom!* they'd both jump all over him.

What with one thing and another, I never saw a happy marriage in my family. Not one! When it comes to that, I never saw one outside my family either.

Hattie Gossett
1942–

Born in central New Jersey, she now lives in Harlem and works as a writer. Her work has appeared in many publications, including Conditions, Essence, Jazz Spotlite News, Pleasure and Danger: Exploring Female Sexuality and Southern Africa. Her poetry collection, Sister No Blues, was published in 1988.

world view

theres more poor than nonpoor
theres more colored than noncolored
theres more women than men

> all over the world the poor woman of color is the mainstay of
> the little daddy centred family which is the bottom-line of big
> daddys industrial civilization

> when she gets off her knees and stands up straight the whole thing
> can/will collapse

> have you noticed that even now she is flexing her shoulder muscles
> and strengthening her thigh and leg muscles?

> and her spine is learning to stretch out long her brain and heart
> are pumping new energy already you can see the load cracking at
> the center as she pushes it off her

she is holding up the whole world
what you gonna do?
you cant stop her
you gonna just stand there and watch her with your mouth open?
or are you gonna try to get down?
you cant stop her
she is holding up the whole world

Micere Githae Mugo
1942–

orn in Kirinyaga on the slopes of Mount Kenya, she is one of
ten children whose parents were respected teachers and politically
active in Kenya's fight for Independence. She has a BA Honours
degree in literature and philosophy from Makerere University (1966), a
postgraduate diploma in Education from the University of Nairobi and,
after serving as headmistress of a girls' school, took her Master's and PhD
in literature at the University of New Brunswick, Canada. Previously senior lecturer in the Department of English at the University of Nairobi and
since 1982 Professor of Literature at the University of Zimbabwe, she has
published works of criticism (including Visions of Africa: The Fiction of
Chinua Achebe, Margaret Laurence, Elspeth Huxley, Ngugi wa Thiong'o;
1978), poetry (Daughter of My People, Sing!; 1976) and plays (The Long
Illness of Ex-Chief Kiti, 1976; and with Ngugi wa Thiong'o The Trial of
Dedan Kimathi, 1976).

Where Are Those Songs?

Where are those songs
my mother and yours
always sang
fitting rhythms
to the whole
vast span of life?

What was it again
they sang
          harvesting maize, threshing millet, storing the grain. . .

What did they sing
bathing us, rocking us to sleep. . .
and the one they sang
stirring the pot
(swallowed in parts by choking smoke)?

What was it
the woods echoed
as in long file

my mother and yours and all the women on our ridge
beat out the rhythms
trudging gaily
as they carried
piles of wood
through those forests
miles from home
What song was it?

And the row of bending women
hoeing our fields
to what beat
did they
break the stubborn ground
as they weeded
our *shambas*?

What did they sing
at the ceremonies
       child-birth
       child-naming
       second birth
       initiation. . .?
how did they trill the *ngemi*
What was
the warriors' song?
how did the wedding song go?
sing me
the funeral song.
What do you remember?

Sing
       I have forgotten
       my mother's song
       my children
       will never know.
This I remember:
Mother always said
       sing child sing
       make a song
       and sing
       beat out your own rhythms
       and rhythms of your life
       but make the song soulful
       and make life
       sing

Sing daughter sing
around you are
unaccountable tunes
some sung
others unsung
sing them
to your rhythms
observe
listen
absorb
soak yourself
bathe
in the stream of life
    and then sing
    sing
    simple songs
    for the people
    for all to hear
    and learn
    and sing
    with you

Eulalia Bernard

1940s–

Born in Limón, Costa Rica, of Jamaican forebears who had been brought there to work the banana plantations. A teacher and one-time cultural attaché in Jamaica following Independence in 1962, she founded the first Department of Afro-American Studies at the University of Central America, San José. She has also worked in education at the United Nations and as director of television programmes for

the Ministry of Public Education. Her publications include Ritmohéroe
*(1982), in which the following poems appeared; they were reproduced
in English in* Lovers and Comrades: Women's Resistance Poetry from
Central America, *edited and translated by Amanda Hopkinson (1989).*

We are the Nation of Threes

We are the nation of threes:
three great mountain ranges;
three colours to our flag;
three races intertwined;
speaking three languages;
governed by three powers;
three women to each man;
three children to a typical home.
We have three gods with three voices;
three national dishes, even
three national lifestyles.

We are the nation of threes
and of the third world.

Metamorphosis of your Memory

I remember you
then, dynamic
then, handsome
then, whole
then, abundant.

I regard you
now, weak
now, distorted
now, diminished
now, gone.

Christine Craig
1943–

B orn in Kingston, Jamaica, she studied at the University of the
West Indies. She lived for ten years in Britain, where she was a
founding member of the Caribbean Artists Movement in London
in the 1960s. Returning to Jamaica, she worked with the Women's Bureau
in the Office of the Prime Minister. She has published stories and poems in
journals such as Savacou and Arts Review and many anthologies, and
her writing includes scripts for radio, television and film. The following
poem is from her first collection, Quadrille for Tigers (1984).

The Chain

I no longer care, keeping close my silence
has been a weight,
a lever pressing out my mind.
I want it told and said and printed down
the dry gullies,
circled through the muddy pools
outside my door.
I want it sung out high by thin-voiced elders
front-rowing murky churches.
I want it known by grey faces queuing under
greyer skies in countries waking
and sleeping with sleet and fog.
I want it known by hot faces pressed against
dust-streaked windows of country buses.

And you must know this now.
I, me, I am a free black woman.
My grandmothers and their mothers
knew this and kept their silence
to compost up their strength,
kept it hidden
and played the game of deference
and agreement and pliant will.

It must be known now how that silent legacy
nourished and infused such a line,

such a close linked chain
to hold us until we could speak
until we could speak out
loud enough to hear ourselves
loud enough to hear ourselves
and believe our own words.

Joyce Sikakane

1943–

S *he was born in South Africa and brought up in the Orlando
district of Soweto. After completing her secondary education, she
worked as a reporter for* The World, *a newspaper run by Whites for
the Black community. She then became the first Black woman employed
by the* Rand Daily Mail. *She fell in love with a Scottish doctor, Kenneth
Rankin, a liaison then illegal since they were of different races. They were
engaged at the time he left the country and she planned to join him; but
she was arrested on charges of political subversion and was detained for
seventeen months, trial following trial until she was finally acquitted. In
1973 she left for Zambia, where she was reunited with her fiancé, whom
she had not seen for four years. They married and subsequently lived
in Scotland. An active anti-apartheid campaigner, she is a member of
the African National Congress and is currently based in Zimbabwe.
Her autobiographical book* A Window on Soweto (1977), *extracted
here, is a personal account of living in South Africa's largest township,
documenting the historical and social background to her experience. She
has also written poetry and fiction.*

From

A Window on Soweto

DETENTION

I WAS detained on May 12, 1969 at about 2 a.m. We heard knocking and woke to the flashing of torches outside and shouts of "Police! Police! Open the door!" We all got up – my mother, myself and my two brothers – and the police came in. There were three white policemen, one white policewoman and an African policeman, all in plain clothes.

They demanded Joyce Sikakane and I said it was myself and they produced a warrant of arrest under Section 6 of the Terrorism Act. They said they wanted to search the house. They were all brandishing their guns about and so they searched the house and took away whatever documents and personal papers – all my letters for example – they wished. The policewoman was guarding me the whole time.

After about two hours they told me to get dressed, as I was still in my nightie; I did so and was escorted to the car. I was afraid to wake Nkosinathi who was still sleeping, so I left him without saying goodbye.

On the way out of Soweto the car dropped off the African policeman in Meadowlands. I remember him saying, "Thank you, my baas, you caught the terrorist. I hope you get the information you want out of her."

We drove off to John Vorster Square (Security Police HQ), where another policeman got out, and then on again. When I asked where we were going, the only reply was that I was being detained under the Terrorism Act. I was terrified: I didn't see myself as a terrorist and didn't know why I should be detained under the Terrorism Act.

I was taken to Pretoria Central Prison. They knocked on the big door, the guard looked out and then opened the gate and I was led in. First we went to the office; they spoke to the matron and papers were signed. My engagement ring was taken from me – I was upset about that. Then we crossed the prison yard to another part of the prison. In the yard were about a hundred African women, some with babies on their backs, some sitting on the ground, some with vegetable baskets full of onions, pumpkins and so on, whom I could see were vendors who had been arrested for illegally selling vegetables in the street. As I came into the yard, the policeman shouted to the women to shut their eyes. This was because I was a Terrorism Act detainee, to be held incommunicado, which meant no one should know who or where I was. I was taken past and up some stairs, where the two policemen escorting me greeted another man as Colonel Aucamp.

He told the matron to take me to a cell. And I heard her ask, "Is she a condemned woman?" as I was shown into a cell with a bright blinding light that made me see sparks.

Aucamp immediately said, "No, no, not that one, I made a mistake." So I was taken out and led along to the common shower room, where there were lots of women prisoners, some naked under the showers, some undressing, some waiting their turn. The matron told me to undress, which I did, and got under the cold shower. I could tell the other women knew there was something special about me, being under escort and alone and jumping the queue like that.

After the cold shower I picked up my paper bag of clothes – the matron told me not to dress – and I was led to a cell. It was narrow and high, situated in what I later discovered was the isolation wing. The outer steel door was opened and then the inner barred door; I went in and the matron locked first one and then the other.

So there I was, in this tall narrow empty cell, gazing around. There was a small high hole covered with mesh, for ventilation. And it was very cold: May is the beginning of winter in South Africa and we had already had some frost. Suddenly I heard women's voices coming from outside in the yard, talking. I was horrified to hear them talking about their love affairs inside prison – the experienced women telling the freshers what to expect, how some were chosen as husbands and some as wives, and generally describing the whole scene to them. It gave me a real fright, standing there naked. I at once got my paper bag and put my panties on!

When I looked around at the contents of the cell all I saw was a damp sisal mat, rolled up, and three grey blankets, also damp and smelling of urine. That was all. I just sat down on the mat and waited.

It wasn't until 7 o'clock that evening that the cell door opened. There was a white wardress and an African woman prisoner in prison uniform, who shoved a plate of food through the door, along the floor, together with a galvanized bucket. All the time the wardress stood between me and the prisoner, so I should not be seen. Then they left, locking the doors behind them. But I heard them open the next cell and then I knew I wasn't alone: if the next cell was occupied I wasn't the only woman detainee.

From then on the pattern of prison life was always the same. In the morning at about 7 a.m. the cell door was opened, the shit bucket and empty plate taken out and a plate of porridge and cup of coffee put in. There was a bucket of sometimes warm water too, to wash oneself and one's underclothes. Lunch was usually about noon, though it could be earlier – on Sundays it was about 10.30 – and consisted of izinkobe or dry mealies – corn kernels – which had been boiled but were still dry and hard. There was a beverage too, some sort of drink, which the prisoners used to call puza'mandla – drink power! Then at about 2 p.m. came supper, which was soft maize porridge with one or two pieces of meat, possibly pork, in it. That was all until the next day.

For the first few days I didn't eat anything. I was frightened, angry, depressed, wondering why I had been detained, scared of what might happen, and crying most of the time. By the third day, I had cried all my tears out. At least, I think it was the third day. Two huge policemen, with layers and layers of chin, came for me. I asked where they were taking me and they said, to give an account of yours sins.

I was driven in a big Cadillac, with a policeman on either side of me and two more in front. We went to the Compol building (police HQ) in Pretoria. Knock, knock again, the police escort identify themselves and we drive in.

Down some corridors to an office. It looks like any other office except it has these wooden partitions. Right facing me is a stone sink and then there's a desk and a few chairs. I can see it's a work room. All along the walls is this wooden partitioning, covering the windows but capable of being drawn back. It kind of encloses the room, insulates it from outside. And just off this room is a sort of gym closet with punch bags – and a huge African policeman with fierce red eyes standing there. While I was being interrogated policemen kept trooping in to practice boxing on the punch bags.

INTERROGATION

THERE was a constant stream of policemen, about fifteen or twenty, coming into the room, as if they were going on stage. They were brandishing guns, holding documents, smoking cigarettes, greeting me, some scowling at me. They all looked different, some like bulldogs, some like Alsatians, some like timid cats. Some of them behaved with great politeness, like perfect gentlemen. I think this performance was just put on to confuse me, for the next thing was Major Swanepoel coming in. He is the most sadistic and most feared of all the police interrogators; several people have died as a result of his "questioning".

"Have you heard of Major Swanepoel?" he said. "I am Major Swanepoel." All the other policemen gave way to him, treating him very deferentially. Then interrogation began.

They fired questions and statements at me; all of a sudden they were all talking about me and my personal life – all my experiences, which they seemed to know better than I did! As they did so they incidentally revealed the extent of their informer network: I found they knew about all sorts of incidents in my career – the story about the Malawian air hostesses being allowed to stay in an all-white hotel, for instance, that I had been working on when I was detained. I also discovered, from things they said, who else had been questioned: Winnie Mandela, wife of ANC leader Nelson Mandela, and Rita Ndzanga, for instance. They had interrogated many other people I knew, and from what they knew I could see they had been tortured to extract the information.

From me they wanted confirmation: that certain things had been done, that I had knowingly participated, and whatever else I could add. From what they know one has to judge what to admit and what to hide and what one might not manage to hide – because it flashes into your mind what risk to others is involved, and also the possibility of being tortured yourself and whether the type of information you have is worth dying for. I knew that in our case what we had been doing was something that would not, in any other country, be considered "terroristic": we were involved with the welfare of political prisoners, helping to make arrangements for families of prisoners to visit their husbands or parents. And so why not admit it? Yes, I did that – so what? We hadn't been involved in anything connected with violence or arms – that would have called for other methods of interrogation. As far as I was concerned they were more interested in getting information about the underground communication network.

The interrogation lasted right through until the following day. They took turns, and took breaks. I was just standing there. I would be tired, I would squat down, I would jump about a bit. I was shown the bricks – the torture bricks on which the men detainees are made to stand. The questioning went on, without food, without anything, till the following morning. Then I was taken back to my cell.

It was about ten days before I was taken again for interrogation. This time it lasted for three whole days because this time they were concerned with taking a statement. Under the Terrorism Act a detainee may be held until a statement to the satisfaction of the Commissioner of Police has been given, and the purpose of the interrogation is to obtain such a statement which can then be used against you or someone else. They still ask questions: anything you admit goes down on the statement.

This time my interrogation took place on the third floor of Compol building, and the interrogators were Major Botha and Major Coetzee. They were trained and experienced political officers. Oh, they were courteous gentlemen, but I could sense hatred – they hated every bit of me. But they had to get what they wanted from me.

They put the proposal that I should be a state witness, giving evidence for the state against the others. I asked why should I do that? and they said, well, you're young, you're an intelligent girl, you have a fiancé outside the country. If you are afraid to give evidence because of what your organization will do to you, we can always give you another name and find a job in one of our embassies abroad – say in Malawi or London, where you can join your fiancé!

All the time, because of what they wanted out of me, they were at pains to explain that they were not against Africans or black people in general. They were only against communists. They argued that people like myself, young, intelligent, pretty, etc., were being misled by communists. They, on the other hand, were offering me a chance. I found this insulting. How could they sit there, admit that apartheid was a repressive system, which they did while maintaining that racism occurred all over the world. What hypocrites, I said inside me, to say communists had misled me into wanting to change the system. I didn't need any communists to tell me apartheid is evil. I know. Nor would I join the enemy camp for the sake of self-preservation.

So I told Major Botha and Major Coetzee I was not interested in their offer. They said in that case you are going to be here a long time. Others had given evidence, they said. If you refuse we have lots of other evidence we can use, the others are willing. . . .

. . . That same afternoon the cells were opened, first mine, and then four others, and we were taken out. I'll never forget the feelings of that moment, a kind of muted consternation, when we five women all saw each other. There was Winnie Mandela, Rita Ndzanga, Martha Dhlamini, Thokozile Mngoma – and of course we each half expected, as our interrogators had said, that the others had agreed to give evidence. But they hadn't. I remember we hugged each other hard: it was too good to be true. We felt this was a moment of victory and we were together. . . .

ON TRIAL

WE were charged on 21 main charges, most of them concerned with membership of the African National Congress, which had been officially banned in 1961. Some of the charges alleged plotting to obtain explosives and commit sabotage and other serious things, but mostly they alleged various activities on behalf of the ANC. We were all charged together, all incriminated with each other.

The first day was taken up with arranging about the defence lawyers, and with our parents and of course with finding out what had happened to each other, when and why each of us was interrogated and so on. Interrogation had taught us the enemy's workings and intentions – they wanted us to quarrel amongst ourselves, to be divided and, above all, to be bitter against each other. So we decided that this was something we just had to face; whatever information they had extracted from us was too bad and whatever they didn't manage to get from us – well and good. Some of the men had been tortured with electric shocks, and amongst the women Rita Ndzanga had been assaulted.

Rita had been a trade unionist, and of course trade union organizers are hated by the police. Toko Mngoma had been in the executive of the ANC Women's League and Martha Dhlamini was also an old ANC campaigner. Winnie Mandela was Nelson's wife and involved in past protest campaigns. In fact all the women had a history of political activity except me, so the police were only too happy to settle accounts and prosecute them. And amongst the younger people on trial including myself, our attempts to do something about apartheid repression were considered great audacity. As far as the state was concerned we too had a lot to answer for. There were several older men amongst us, such as one about 70 years old, who had been an active ANC member in Alexandra Township in the old days and who was tortured during interrogation. Lawrence Ndzanga was a trade unionist, and Elliot Shabangu had been an ANC organizer, so the police had something to settle with them as well.

Then the trial began, as usual with political trials in South Africa, with witnesses whose testimony can be shown to incriminate some or all of the accused. Often this testimony is very wide and is the sort of thing that wouldn't be considered incriminating anywhere else, only in South Africa.

At the time, the government was preparing for elections and wanted to use our trial for advertising purposes, to show that it was still very powerful and in control, that it had caught these communists and put them on trial. That was the political purpose behind our trial.

The first witnesses were some white people who had been in some kind of contact with the accused, and who gave evidence for the state and exposed the involuntary nature of it. Some had been tortured, some threatened and anyway, being detained under the Terrorism Act, how can they be said to have made a statement of their own volition, knowing that they would not be released until they did so? Other witnesses appeared, who said the same thing – their evidence was worthless. And even if it had been made voluntarily, it was nothing that proved any kind of terrorist conspiracy. There was nothing really there against us.

Shanthie Naidoo and Nomwe Mamkhala were brought into the witness box and refused to give evidence. This was after we had been told in court that Shanthie wanted to give evidence, and the prosecutor asked us if we were going to forgive her! Shanthie herself was brought from jail without being told where she was being taken. Suddenly she found herself in the witness box. She said she had been interrogated continuously for five days, during which she had not been allowed to sleep, rest or sit down. She had been threatened that her whole family would be arrested if she refused to speak. In court she said she would not give evidence against us because two of us were her friends – myself and Winnie Mandela. When asked by the judge for her reasons for refusing to give evidence, Shanthie answered, "I will not be able to live with my conscience if I do." For refusing, she and Nomwe were sentenced to two months imprisonment. They were not released from detention however. They went back to jail and were given prison clothes but none of the other prisoners' rights such as visits or letters etc. The security police can thus override the law and keep convicted prisoners incommunicado. At the end of the two months, the prison clothes were removed and ordinary clothes – the same ones they had brought with them when first detained – were returned. After that Shanthie spent four more months in solitary as a detainee under the Terrorism Act. We did not hear about Nomwe Mamkhala's fate.

As it turned out, the trial rebounded on the government, because instead of the evidence being to the liking of the state, it exposed the state's methods of getting evidence and demonstrated the bravery and resistance of the men and women on trial. There was good coverage in the white press and also internationally, and there was an observer from the International Commission of Jurists. The quality of the evidence made fools of the Special Branch and their accusations, it made fools of the whole Terrorism Act and all the conspiracy laws of South Africa because, as our lawyer pointed out, some of the acts alleged had taken place when one of the accused was still a toddler, so how could he be held responsible by association?

And because the evidence was so ridiculous and the publicity so bad, the state decided to abandon the case, to withdraw the charges. This was 16 February 1970. We could not believe it when we heard the judge say, "You are acquitted!" We began to leave the court in single file, between two rows of police, to go and meet our relatives, who were already singing and celebrating. The police refused to let us out and instead took us to a room, where Captain Dekker announced that he was detaining us again. There was a great protest: I remember shouting and I threw a fist at him, but I'm not sure if it landed. The police confiscated everything we had, including all our legal documents, and we were whisked off under guard, back to Pretoria Central.

It all happened so quickly that we hadn't time to get used to the idea of being free. Nor had we really believed in the acquittal – it just couldn't be true. In any case we had been told so many times during interrogation that we were going to spend 15 years in jail if we were lucky, more if we were not, and we had come to accept imprisonment. So we weren't so surprised to be taken back to detention.

But it was just as bad. I went back to the same cell, and there I stayed for the next four months.

This time there was no exercise, or only very occasionally. There were constant battles between us and the matron and the other officers because we kept demanding to be released, as the court had released us. A magistrate came fortnightly to hear our complaints, as a matter of routine, and we demanded to know why we were detained since we had already been tried and acquitted. We complained about conditions in the cells and demanded to be allowed various things. It all fell on deaf ears; the magistrate thought it was all our fault: "Why did you bring yourself here?" he would ask.

Nothing was improved: they didn't clean our cells, or give us cloths and polish so we could clean them ourselves. The food was just the same, and we could spend a week inside without any exercise, just the door opening three times a day to bring in the food and take out the shit bucket. We used to call these buckets SB's – the same name as we gave the Special Branch.

All the loneliness, emptiness and isolation came back, and so did the need to play games. But this time there were no ants to count.

Sometimes at night we would hear screams and the clatter of SB's on the concrete floors – the noise of prisoners fighting in their cells. Then there would be silence, followed by dogs barking, then men's voices and running footsteps towards where the screams had come from. And the next thing we would hear was the sound of real screams, screams of terror, screams of women being sjambokked. Then the screams would die out and we would hear the dogs being taken back and the men's voices, before everything died down to silence again.

Because we had no contact with the other prisoners we never got to know what the fights were about. But more painful than the screams was listening to the cries of the babies, all day and all night. Many women committed to Pretoria Central had small babies, or were pregnant, so throughout the jail there was this terrible forlorn crying, babies crying for their mothers or because they were hungry. It appeared that the women were taken off to work and the babies were just left in the cells, but we couldn't enquire about anything, so we didn't know why things were happening.

Except when condemned prisoners were going to be hanged, then we could hear singing coming from the men's section in the early hours of the morning, long, never-ending hymns. This meant the men knew a hanging was about to take place.

RE-TRIAL

EVENTUALLY after four months I was taken out to the charge office and the following day 18 June 1970 we were back in court. Two of the prisoners who had previously been charged were missing, and we were given to understand that they had agreed to give evidence against us. And as we were sitting there in the dock, wondering why there was a delay, we saw coming up from the cells a man chained between two policemen. As he was being unchained, he raised his head, threw his clenched fist in the air – "Amandla!" Then the older people in the dock recognized him as Benjamin Ramotse. He was a trained freedom fighter and had been captured in Botswana and so tortured he didn't know how he survived.

This was the reason for the new trial. We would be linked with him, according to the state, in an international ANC conspiracy, or whatever. We were thus charged with the offences he was alleged to have committed as well as the original charges, and the indictment had been changed from the Suppression of Communism Act to the Terrorism Act. Our lawyers objected to this.

They insisted on applying for a separation of trials, on the grounds that none of us had been connected with Ramotse. Our position was that if the state wanted to link us with him that was okay by us, we were prepared to stand trial with him. The lawyers insisted on trying the technical application. Ramotse himself felt we were mad – if there was a chance we should take it. If he stood trial he would continue the struggle.

In the end the application was successful: the trials were separated. We found it painful to be separated from Ramotse, for we had felt it an honour to be with him. The next step was to apply for a discharge, on the grounds that we couldn't be tried twice on the same charges. This application also succeeded, and once more we heard the judge say we were free. None of us stood up, we just sat, until we had to be evicted from court. We didn't believe we were really free.

We were released on 14 September.

Olive Senior

1943–

Born in a poor Jamaican village and brought up by urban relatives, she was educated in Jamaica and in Canada, she has worked as journalist, researcher, in publishing and public relations. She was Publications Officer at the University of the West Indies Institute of Social and Economic Research, editor of Social and Economic Studies and is managing director of the Institute of Jamaica Publishing Company and editor of Jamaica Journal. In 1987 she won the first Commonwealth Writers Award for Summer Lightning and Other Stores (1986), which *was followed by* Arrival of the Snake Woman and Other Stories *(1989). In addition to fictin she has written drama, non-fiction, and is the author of a book of poems,* Talking of Trees *(1985).*

Love Orange

Work out your own salvation with fear and trembling.

Philippians

SOMEWHERE between the repetition of Sunday School lessons and the broken doll which the lady sent me one Christmas I lost what it was to be happy. But I didn't know it then even though in dreams I would lie with my face broken like the doll's in the pink tissue of a shoebox coffin. For I was at the age where no one asked me for commitment and I had a phrase which I used like a talisman. When strangers came or lightning flashed, I would lie in the dust under my grandfather's vast bed and hug the dog, whispering "our worlds wait outside" and be happy.

Once I set out to find the worlds outside, the horizon was wide and the rim of the far mountains beckoned. I was happy when they found me in time for bed and a warm supper, for the skies, I discovered, were the same shade of China blue as the one intact eye of the doll. "Experience can wait," I whispered to the dog, "death too."

I knew all about death then because in dreams I had been there. I also knew a great deal about love. Love, I thought, was like an orange, a fixed and sharply defined amount, limited, finite. Each person had this amount of love to distribute as he may. If one had many people to love then the segments for each person would be smaller and eventually love, like patience, would be exhausted. That is why I preferred to live with my grandparents then since they had fewer people to love than my parents and so my portion of their love-orange would be larger.

My own love-orange I jealously guarded. Whenever I thought of love I could feel it in my hand, large and round and brightly coloured, intact and spotless. I had moments of indecision when I wanted to distribute the orange but each time I would grow afraid of the audacity of such commitment. Sometimes, in a moment of rare passion, I would extend the orange to the dog or my grandmother but would quickly withdraw my hand each time. For without looking I would feel in its place the doll crawling into my hand and nestling there and I would run into the garden and be sick. I would see its face as it lay in the pink tissue of a shoebox tied with ribbons beside the stocking hanging on the bedpost and I would clutch my orange tighter, thinking that I had better save it for the day when occasions like this would arise again and I would need the entire orange to overcome the feelings which arose each time I thought of the doll.

I could not let my grandmother know about my being sick because she never understood about the doll. For years I had dreamed of exchanging homemade dolls with button eyes and ink faces for a plaster doll with blue eyes and limbs that moved. All that December I haunted my grandmother's clothes closet until beneath the dresses I discovered the box smelling faintly of camphor and without looking I knew that it came from Miss Evangeline's toy shop and that it would therefore be a marvel. But the doll beside the Christmas stocking, huge in a billowing dress and petticoats, had half a face and a finger missing. "It can be mended," my grandmother said, "I can make it as good as new. 'Why throw away a good thing?' Miss Evangeline said as she gave it to me."

But I could no longer hear I could no longer see for the one China blue eye and the missing finger that obscured my vision. And after that I never opened a box again and I never waited up for Christmas. And although I buried the box beneath the allamanda tree the doll rose up again and again, in my throat, like a sickness to be got rid of from the body, and I felt as if I too were half a person who could lay down in the shoebox and sleep forever. But on awakening from these moments, I could find safely clutched in my hands the orange, conjured up from some deep part of myself, and I would hug the dog saying "our worlds wait outside."

That summer I saw more clearly the worlds that awaited. It was filled with many deaths that seemed to tie all the strands of my life together and which bore some oblique relationship to both the orange and the doll.

The first to die was a friend of my grandparents who lived nearby. I sometimes played with her grandchildren at her house when I was allowed to, but each time she had appeared only as a phantom, come on the scene silently, her feet shod in cotton stockings rolled down to her ankles, thrust into a pair of her son's broken down slippers. In all the years I had known her I had never heard her say anything but whisper softly; her whole presence was a whisper. She seemed to appear from the cracks of the house, the ceiling, anywhere, she made so little noise in her coming, this tiny, delicate, slightly absurd old woman who lived for us only in the secret and mysterious prison of the aged.

When she died it meant nothing to me, I could think then only of my death which I saw nightly in dreams but I could not conceive of her in the flesh, to miss her or to weep tears.

The funeral that afternoon was 5.00 p.m. on a hot summer's day. My grand-mother dressed me all in white and I trailed down the road behind her, my corseted and whaleboned grandmother lumbering from side to side in a black romaine dress now shiny in the sunlight, bobbing over her head a huge black umbrella. My grandfather stepped high in shiny black shoes and a shiny black suit ahead of her. Bringing up the rear, I skipped lightly on the gravel, clutching in my hand a new, shiny, bright and bouncy red rubber ball. For me, the funeral, any occasion to get out of the house was a holiday, like breaking suddenly from a dark tunnel into the sunlight where gardens of butterflies waited.

They had dug a grave in the red clay by the side of the road. The house was filled with people. I followed my grandparents and the dead woman's children into the room where they had laid her out, unsmiling, her nostrils stuffed with cotton. I stood in the shadows where no one saw me, filled with the smell of something I had never felt before, like a smell rising from the earth itself which no sunlight, no butterflies, no sweetness could combat. "Miss Aggie, Miss Aggie," I said silently to the dead old woman and suddenly I knew that if I gave her my orange to take into the unknown with her it would be safe, a secret between me and one who could return no more. I gripped the red ball tightly in my hands and it became transformed into the rough texture of an orange; I tasted it on my tongue, smelled the fragrance. As my grandmother knelt to pray I crept forward and gently placed between Miss Aggie's closed hands the love-orange, smiled because we knew each other and nothing would be able to touch either of us. But as I crept away my grandmother lifted her head from her hands and gasped when she saw the ball. She swiftly retrieved it while the others still prayed and hid it in her voluminous skirt. But when she sent me home, in anger, on the way the love-orange appeared comforting in my hand, and I went into the empty house and crept under my grandfather's bed and dreamt of worlds outside.

The next time I saw with greater clarity the vastness of this world outside. I was asked to visit some new neighbours and read to their son. He was very old, I thought, and he sat in the sunshine all day, his head covered with a calico skull cap. He couldn't see very clearly and my grandmother said he had a brain tumour and would perhaps die. Nevertheless I read to him and worried about all the knowledge that would be lost if he did not live. For every morning he would take down from a shelf a huge Atlas and together we would travel the cities of the world to which he had been. I was very happy and the names of these cities secretly rolled off my tongue all day. I wanted very much to give him my orange but held back. I was not yet sure if he were a whole person, if he would not recover and need me less and so the whole orange would be wasted. So I did not tell him about it. And then he went off with his parents to England, for an operation, my grandmother said, and he came back only as ashes held on the plane by his mother. When I went to the church this time there was no coffin, only his mother holding this tiny box which was so like the shoe box of the doll that I was sure there was some connection which I could not grasp but I thought, if they bury this box then the broken doll cannot rise again.

But the doll rose up one more time because soon my grandmother lay dying. My mother had taken me away when she fell too ill and brought me back to my grandmother's house, even darker and more silent now, this one last time. I went into the room where she lay and she held out a weak hand to me, she couldn't speak so she followed me with her eyes and I couldn't bear it. "Grandma," I said quickly, searching for something to say, something that would save her, "Grandma, you can have my whole orange," and I placed it in the bed beside her hand. But she kept on dying and I knew then that the orange had no potency, that love could not create miracles. "Orange," my grandmother spoke for the last time trying to make connections that she did not see, "orange.......?" and my mother took me out of the room as my grandmother died. "At least," my mother said, "at least you could have told her that you loved her, she waited for it."

"But..." I started to say and bit my tongue, for nobody, not then or ever could understand about the orange. And in leaving my grandmother's house, the dark tunnel of my childhood, I slammed the car door hard on my fingers and as my hand closed over the breaking bones, felt nothing.

Nikki Giovanni

1943–

Born in Tennessee, she and her family moved to Cincinnati when she was two months old. She majored in history and earned a BA from Fisk University, did graduate work at the University of Pennsylvania, then studied at Columbia School of Fine Arts. She also has a LHD from Wilberforce University. She made her name as a poet in the late 1960s and early 1970s, performing and publishing her work widely. She was editor of Black Dialogue and publisher of Black Dialogue Publications, and has held academic appointments at Queens College, City University of New York, and Livingston College, Rutgers University. She has honorary doctorates from several institutions including the University of Maryland, Ripon College and Smith College. She is Professor of English at Virginia Polytechnic Institute and State University in Blacksburg. Her poetry has been much anthologized and her books include Gemini: An Extended Autobiographical Statement: My First Twenty-Five Years of Being a Black Poet (1971) and several poetry collections, among them Black Feeling, Black Talk/Black Judgement (1970) and The Women and the Men (1975).

On Hearing "The Girl with the Flaxen Hair"

He has a girl who has flaxen hair
My woman has hair of gray
I have a woman who wakes up at dawn
His girl can sleep through the day

His girl has hands soothed with perfumes sweet
She has lips soft and pink
My woman's lips burn in midday sun
My woman's hands – black like ink

He can make music to please his girl
Night comes I'm tired and beat
He can make notes, make her heart beat fast
Night comes I want off my feet

Maybe if I don't pick cotton so fast
Maybe I'd sing pretty too
Sing to my woman with hair of gray
Croon softly, Baby it's you

Nikki-Rosa

childhood remembrances are always a drag
if you're Black
you always remember things like living in Woodlawn
with no inside toilet
and if you become famous or something
they never talk about how happy you were to have your mother
all to yourself and
how good the water felt when you got your bath from one of those
big tubs that folk in chicago barbecue in
and somehow when you talk about home
it never gets across how much you
understood their feelings
as the whole family attended meetings about Hollydale
and even though you remember
your biographers never understand
your father's pain as he sells his stock
and another dream goes
and though you're poor it isn't poverty that
concerns you
and though they fought a lot
it isn't your father's drinking that makes any difference
but only that everybody is together and you
and your sister have happy birthdays and very good Christmasses
and I really hope no white person ever has cause to write about me
because they never understand Black love is Black wealth and they'll
probably talk about my hard childhood and never understand that
all the while I was quite happy

Angela Yvonne Davis

1944–

B orn and raised in Birmingham, Alabama, she attended Brandeis
University, the University of California at San Diego and Goethe
University, Frankfurt. She joined the US Communist Party in 1968
and was a leading figure of the Black Power movement in the 1960s
and 1970s, active on issues of unemployment, judicial reform, police
repression and student rights, becoming involved with the Black Panthers. She taught philosophy at the University of California at Los Angeles
but was subsequently dropped from the staff. In 1970 the FBI accused
her of implication in an alleged kidnap attempt of three San Quentin
prisoners from Marin County Civic Center and she was put on their Ten
Most Wanted list. Hunted down, charged with murder, kidnapping and
conspiracy, she spent sixteen months in jail, but in 1972, following one
of the most famous trials in US history, she was acquitted after massive
national and international protests. Her prison writings were collected
in If They Come in the Morning (1971) and on her release she continued to write and teach. She was awarded the Lenin Peace Prize in
1979, and in 1980 and 1984 was nominated as the Communist Party's
vice-presidential candidate in the US elections. Her autobiography was
published in 1974, and the views that have informed her life are given
expression in her collections of essays, Women, Race and Class (1981)
and Women, Culture and Politics (1984), in which latter volume appears
the following piece – an address given at the National Women's Studies
Association annual conference, Spellman Colege, 25 June 1987.

Let Us All Rise Together: Radical Perspectives on Empowerment for Afro-American Women

T HE concept of empowerment is hardly new to Afro-American women.
For almost a century, we have been organized in bodies that have sought
collectively to develop strategies illuminating the way to economic and political power for ourselves and our communities. During the last decade of the
nineteenth century, after having been repeatedly shunned by the radically
homogeneous women's rights movement, Black women organized their own
Club Movement. In 1895 – five years after the founding of the General Federation

of Women's Clubs, which consolidated a club movement reflecting concerns of middle-class White women – one hundred Black women from ten states met in the city of Boston, under the leadership of Josephine St Pierre Ruffin, to discuss the creation of a national organization of Black women's clubs. As compared to their White counterparts, the Afro-American women issuing the call for this national club movement articulated principles that were more openly political in nature. They defined the primary function of their clubs as an ideological as well as an activist defense of Black women – and men – from the ravages of racism. When the meeting was convened, its participants emphatically declared that, unlike their White sisters, whose organizational policies were seriously tainted by racism, they envisioned their movement as one open to all women:

> Our woman's movement is woman's movement in that it is led and directed by women for the good of women and men, for the benefit of *all* humanity, which is more than any one branch or section of it. We want, we ask the active interest of our men, and, too, we are not drawing the color line; we are women, American women, as intensely interested in all that pertains to us as such as all other American women; we are not alienating or withdrawing, we are only coming to the front, willing to join any others in the same work and cordially inviting and welcoming any others to join us.[1]

The following year, the formation of the National Association of Colored Women's Clubs was announced. The motto chosen by the Association was "Lifting As We Climb".[2]

The nineteenth-century women's movement was also plagued by classism. Susan B. Anthony wondered why her outreach to working-class women on the issue of the ballot was so frequently met with indifference. She wondered why these women seemed to be much more concerned with improving their economic situation than with achieving the right to vote.[3] As essential as political equality may have been to the larger campaign for women's rights, in the eyes of Afro-American and White working-class women it was not synonymous with emancipation. That the conceptualization of strategies for struggle was based on the peculiar condition of White women of the privileged classes rendered those strategies discordant with working-class women's perceptions of empowerment. It is not surprising that many of them told Ms Anthony, "Women want bread, not the ballot."[4] Eventually, of course, working-class White women, and

[1] Gerda Lerner, *Black Women in White America* (New York: Pantheon Books, 1972), p. 443.
[2] These clubs proliferated the progressive political scene during this era. By 1916 – twenty years later – 50,000 women in 28 federations and over 1,000 clubs were members of the National Association of Colored Women's Clubs. See Paula Giddings's discussion of the origins and evolution of the Black Women's Club Movement in *When and Where I Enter* (New York: William Morrow, 1984), Chapters IV-VI.
[3] Miriam Schneir, ed., *Feminism: The Essential Historical Writings* (New York: Vintage, 1972), pp. 138–142.
[4] Ibid.

Afro-American women as well, reconceptualized this struggle, defining the vote not as an end in itself – not as the panacea that would cure all the ills related to gender-based discrimination – but rather as an important weapon in the continuing fight for higher wages, better working conditions, and an end to the omnipresent menace of the lynch mob.

Today, as we reflect on the process of empowering Afro-American women, our most efficacious strategies remain those that are guided by the principle used by Black women in the club movement. We must strive to "lift as we climb". In other words, we must climb in such a way as to guarantee that all of our sisters, regardless of social class, and indeed all of our brothers, climb with us. This must be the essential dynamic of our quest for power – a principle that must not only determine our struggles as Afro-American women, but also govern all authentic struggles of dispossessed people. Indeed, the overall battle for equality can be profoundly enhanced by embracing this principle.

Afro-American women bring to the women's movement a strong tradition of struggle around issues that politically link women to the most crucial progressive causes. This is the meaning of the motto, "Lifting As We Climb". This approach reflects the often unarticulated interests and aspirations of masses of women of all racial backgrounds. Millions of women today are concerned about jobs, working conditions, higher wages, and racist violence. They are concerned about plant closures, homelessness, and repressive immigration legislation. Women are concerned about homophobia, ageism, and discrimination against the physically challenged. We are concerned about Nicaragua and South Africa. And we share our children's dream that tomorrow's world will be delivered from the threat of nuclear omnicide. These are some of the issues that should be integrated into the overall struggle for women's rights if there is to be a serious commitment to the empowerment of women who have been rendered historically invisible. These are some of the issues we should consider if we wish to lift as we climb.

During this decade we have witnesses an exciting resurgence of the women's movement. If the first wave of the women's movement began in the 1840s, and the second wave in the 1960s, then we are approaching the crest of a third wave in the final days of the 1980s. When the feminist historians of the twenty-first century attempt to recapitulate the third wave, will they ignore the momentous contributions of Afro-American women, who have been leaders and activists in movements often confined to women of color, but whose accomplishments have invariably advanced the cause of white women as well? Will the exclusionary policies of the mainstream women's movement – from its inception to the present – which have often compelled Afro-American women to conduct their struggle for equality outside the ranks of that movement, continue to result in the systematic omission of our names from the roster of prominent leaders and activists of the women's movement? Will there continue to be two distinct continuums of the women's movement, one visible and another invisible, one publicly acknowledged and another ignored except by the conscious progeny of the working-class women – Black, Latina, Native American, Asian, and white – who forged that hidden continuum? If this question is answered in the affirmative, it will mean that women's quest for equality will continue to be gravely deficient. The revolutionary potential of the women's movement still will not have been realized. The racist-inspired flaws of the first and second waves of the women's movement will have become the inherited flaws of the third wave.

How can we guarantee that this historical pattern is broken? As advocates and activists of women's rights in our time, we must begin to merge that double legacy in order to create a single continuum, one that solidly represents the aspirations of all women in our society. We must begin to create a revolutionary, multiracial women's movement that seriously addresses the main issues affecting poor and working-class women. In order to tap the potential for such a movement, we must further develop those sectors of the movement that are addressing seriously issues affecting poor and working-class women, such as jobs, pay equity, paid maternity leave, federally subsidized child care, protection from sterilization abuse, and subsidized abortions. Women of all racial and class backgrounds will greatly benefit from such an approach.

For decades, white women activists have repeated the complaint that women of color frequently fail to respond to their appeals. "We invited them to our meetings, but they didn't come." "We asked them to participate in our demonstration, but they didn't show." "They just don't seem to be interested in women's studies."

This process cannot be initiated merely by intensified efforts to attract Latina women or Afro-American women or Asian or Native American women into the existing organizational forms dominated by white women of the more privileged economic strata. The particular concerns of women of color must be included in the agenda.

An issue of special concern to Afro-American women is unemployment. Indeed, the most fundamental prerequisite for empowerment is the ability to earn an adequate living. At the height of its audacity, the Reagan government boasted that unemployment had leveled off, leaving only (!) 7.5 million people unemployed. These claims came during a period in which Black people in general were twice as likely to be unemployed as white people, and Black teenagers almost three times as likely to be unemployed as white teenagers.[5] We must remember that these figures do not include the millions who hold part-time jobs, although they want and need full-time employment. A disproportionate number of these underemployed individuals are women. Neither do the figures reflect those who, out of utter frustration, have ceased to search for employment, nor those whose unemployment insurance has run out, nor those who have never had a job. Women on welfare are also among those who are not counted as unemployed.

At the same time that the Reagan administration attempted to convey the impression that it had successfully slowed the rise of unemployment, the AFL-CIO estimated that 18 million people of working age were without jobs. These still-critical levels of unemployment, distorted and misrepresented by the Reagan administration, are fundamentally responsible for the impoverished status of Afro-American women, the most glaring evidence of which resides in

[5] Children's Defense Fund, *Black and White Children in America: Key Facts* (Washington, D.C.: Author, 1985), pp. 21–22.

the fact that women, together with their dependent children, constitute the fastest-growing sector of the 4 million homeless people in the United States. There can be no serious discussion of empowerment today if we do not embrace the plight of the homeless with an enthusiasm as passionate as that with which we embrace issues more immediately related to our own lives.

The United Nations declared 1987 to be the Year of Shelter for the Homeless. Although only the developing countries were the initial focus of this resolution, eventually it became clear that the United States is an "undeveloping country". Two-thirds of the 4 million homeless in this country are families, and 40 percent of them are Afro-American.[6] In some urban areas, as many as 70 percent of the homeless are Black. In New York City, for example, 60 percent of the homeless population are Black, 20 percent Latino, and 20 percent white.[7] Presently, under New York's Work Incentive Program, homeless women and men are employed to clean toilets, wash graffiti from subway trains, and clean parks at wages of sixty-two cents an hour, a mere fraction of the minimum wage.[8] In other words, the homeless are being compelled to provide slave labor for the government if they wish to receive assistance.

Black women scholars and professionals cannot afford to ignore the straits of our sisters who are acquainted with the immediacy of oppression in a way many of us are not. The process of empowerment cannot be simplistically defined in accordance with our own particular class interests. We must learn to lift as we climb.

If we are to elevate the status of our entire community as we scale the heights of empowerment, we must be willing to offer organized resistance to the proliferating manifestations of racist violence across the country. A virtual "race riot" took place on the campus of one of the most liberal educational institutions in this country not long ago. In the aftermath of the World Series, white students at the University of Massachusetts, Amherst, who were purportedly fans of the Boston Red Sox, vented their wrath on Black students, whom they perceived as a surrogate for the winning team, the New York Mets, because of the pre-dominance of Black players on the Mets. When individuals in the crowd yelled "Black bitch" at a Black woman student, a Black man who hastened to defend her was seriously wounded and rushed unconscious to the hospital. Another one of the many dramatic instances of racist harassment to occur on college campuses during this period was the burning of a cross in front of the Black Students' Cultural Center at Purdue University.[9] In December 1986, Michael Griffith, a young Black man, lost his life in what amounted to a virtual lynching by a mob of White youths in the New York suburb of Howard Beach. Not far from Atlanta, civil rights marchers were attacked on Dr Martin Luther King's birthday by a mob led by the Ku Klux Klan. An especially outrageous instance in which racist violence was officially condoned was the acquittal of Bernhard Goetz, who, on his own admission, attempted to kill four Black youths because he *felt* threatened by them on a New York subway.

[6] *WREE-VIEW*, Vol. 12, nos. 1 & 2, January–April, 1987.
[7] Ibid.
[8] Ibid.

Black women have organized before to oppose racist violence. In the nine-teenth century the Black Women's Club Movement was born largely in response to the epidemic of lynching during that era. Leaders like Ida B. Wells and Mary Church Terrell recognized that Black women could not move toward empowerment if they did not radically challenge the reign of lynch law in the land. Today, Afro-American women must actively take the lead in the movement against racist violence, as did our sister-ancestors almost a century ago. We must lift as we climb. As our ancestors organized for the passage of a federal antilynch law – and indeed involved themselves in the woman suffrage movement for the purpose of securing that legislation – we must today become activists in the effort to secure legislation declaring racism and anti-Semitism as crimes. Extensively as some instances of racist violence may be publicized at this time, many more racist-inspired crimes go unnoticed as a consequence of the failure of law enforcement to specifically classify them as such. A person scrawling swastikas or "KKK" on an apartment building may simply be charged – if criminal charges are brought at all – with defacing property or malicious mischief. Recently, a Ku Klux Klanner who burned a cross in front of a Black family's home was charged with "burning without a permit". We need federal and local laws against acts of racist and anti-Semitic violence. We must organize, lobby, march, and demonstrate in order to guarantee their passage.

As we organize, lobby, march, and demonstrate against racist violence, we who are women of color must be willing to appeal for multiracial unity in the spirit of our sister-ancestors. Like them, we must proclaim: We do not draw the color line. The only line we draw is one based on our political principles. We know that empowerment for the masses of women in our country will never be achieved as long as we do not succeed in pushing back the tide of racism. It is not a coincidence that sexist-inspired violence – in particular, terrorist attacks on abortion clinics – has reached a peak during the same period in which racist violence has proliferated dramatically. Violent attacks on women's reproductive rights are nourished by these explosions of racism. The vicious anti-lesbian and anti-gay attacks are a part of the same menacing process. The roots of sexism and homophobia are found in the same economic and political institutions that serve as the foundation of racism in this country and, more often than not, the same extremist circles that inflict violence on people of color are responsible for the eruptions of violence inspired by sexist and homophobic biases. Our political activism must clearly manifest our understanding of these connections.

We must always attempt to lift as we climb. Another urgent point on our political agenda – for Afro-American and for all progressive women – must be the repeal of the Simpson-Rodino Law. The Simpson-Rodino Law is a racist law that spells repression for vast numbers of women and men who are undocumented immigrants in this country. Camouflaged as an amnesty program, its eligibility restrictions are so numerous that hundreds of thousands of people stand to be prosecuted and deported under its provisions. Amnesty is provided in a restricted way only for those who came to this country before 1982. Thus, the vast numbers of Mexicans who have recently crossed the border in an attempt to flee intensified impoverishment bred by the unrestricted immigration of US corporations into their countries are not eligible. Salvadorans and other Central

Americans who have escaped political persecution in their respective countries over the last few years will not be offered amnesty. We must organize, lobby, march, and demonstrate for a repeal of the Simpson-Rodino Law.[10] We must lift as we climb.

When we as Afro-American women, when we as women of color, proceed to ascend toward empowerment, we lift up with us our brothers of color, our white sisters and brothers in the working class, and, indeed, all women who experience the effects of sexist oppression. Our activist agenda must encompass a wide range of demands. We must call for jobs and for the unionization of unorganized women workers, and, indeed, unions must be compelled to take on such issues as affirmative action, pay equity, sexual harassment of the job, and paid maternity leave for women. Because Black and Latina women are AIDS victims in disproportionately large numbers, we have a special interest in demanding emergency funding for AIDS research. We must oppose all instances of repressive mandatory AIDS testing and quarantining, as well as homophobic manipulations of the AIDS crisis. Effective strategies for the reduction of teenage pregnancy are needed, but we must beware of succumbing to propagandistic attempts to relegate to young single mothers the responsibility for our community's impoverishment.

In the aftermath of the Reagan era, it should be clear that there are forces in our society that reap enormous benefits from the persistent, deepening oppression of women. Members of the Reagan administration include advocates for the most racist, anti-working-class, and sexist circles of contemporary monopoly capitalism. These corporations continue to prop up apartheid in South Africa and to profit from the spiraling arms race while they propose the most vulgar and irrational forms of anti-Sovietism – invoking, for example, the "evil empire" image popularized by Ronald Reagan – as justifications for their omnicidal ventures. If we are not afraid to adopt a revolutionary stance – if, indeed, we wish to be radical in our quest for change – then we must get to the root of our oppression. After all, *radical* simply means "grasping things at the root". Our agenda for women's empowerment must thus be unequivocal in our challenge to monopoly capitalism as a major obstacle to the achievement of equality.

I want to suggest, as I conclude, that we link our grassroots organizing, our essential involvement in electoral politics and our involvement as activists in mass struggles to the long-range goal of fundamentally transforming the socioeconomic conditions that generate and persistently nourish the various forms of oppression we suffer. Let us learn from the strategies of our sisters in South Africa and Nicaragua. As Afro-American women, as women of color in general, as progressive women of all racial backgrounds, let us join our sisters – and brothers – across the globe who are attempting to forge a new socialist order – an order which will reestablish socioeconomic priorities so that the quest for monetary profit will never be permitted to take precedence over the real interests of human beings. This is not to say that our problems will magically

[10] Unfortunately, the Simpson-Rodino bill was signed into law on November 6, 1987, with employer sanctions taking effect on June 1, 1988.

dissipate with the advent of socialism. Rather, such a social order should provide us with the real opportunity to further extend our struggles, with the assurance that one day we will be able to redefine the basic elements of our oppression as useless refuse of the past.

Thadious M. Davis
1944–

er poetry has been published in various journals and anthologies in the USA, including Obsidian, Pushcart Prize IV: Best of the Small Presses *(ed. Bill Henderson, 1979) and* Black Sister: Poetry by Black American Women, 1746–1980 *(ed. Erlene Stetson, 1981) and is collected in* Emergence. *In the 1980s she co-edited (with Trudier Harris) several volumes of the* Dictionary of Literary Biography *dealing with African-American writers.*

Asante Sana,[1] Te Te

Laughing eyes followed
the gold everywhere in our circle
gold rings reflecting red
afternoon sun

Precious links in a chain
surviving the crossing
Laughing eyes followed
the gold in my ears

---

[1] "Many thanks" in Swahili.

I do not know how to say in Fulani
My great-grandmother preserved the ritual
My great-grandmother Te Te
Three weeks after my birth
Great-grandmother Te Te
pierced my ears
and named me Marée Nage

Gloria T. Hull

1944–

B orn in Shreveport, Louisiana, she studied at Southern University, Baton Rouge (1962–6), earned a PhD in English from Purdue University (1972), and became Professor of English at the University of Delaware. From 1984 to 1986 she was Fulbright Senior Lecturer in the Department of English, University of the West Indies, Jamaica. Her critical work has appeared in many publications and she edited Give Us Each Day: The Diary of Alice Dunbar-Nelson (1982) and But Some of Us Are Brave: Black Women's Studies (with Patricia Bell Scott, Barbara Smith; 1982). She is also the author of Color, Sex and Poetry: Three Women Writers of the Harlem Renaissance (on Angelina Weld Grimké, Alice Dunbar-Nelson and Georgia Douglas Johnson; 1987). Of her first poetry book, Healing Heart, Poems 1973–1988 (1989), Gwendolyn Brooks said: "Gloria Hull is a Contemporary. She examines life without fright, observing alike garbage and roses – and reporting faithfully."

At My Age

At my age
now
I can see beauty
in the deep black shadows
of these green hills

Can appreciate the stealthy mold
fuzzing up the shoes in my closet
after fourteen days of rain

Dusk now is just as lovely as the sunset
Broad daylight as enchanting as the moon

Baby lizards play like children
        about my feet
and the drab little hummingbird in this red ixora
        surprises secret joy

At my age
now
I have taken up dancing
        and lip gloss
gone in for fashion
        and frivolity
vamp my hair into flying sexiness

I will speak my mind to whoever dares to listen:
        teach my son about heaven and the spirits
        warn daughters about the sweet and sour
                heaviness of men
        crack jokes with the corner idlers when I pass
        tell brown and black people about Blackness
                babies about their brothers in South Africa
        hold hands and run, shout clearly with my sisters
        preach sun and flow to every frozen soul
            who chills my path

I will leap up! speak up!
without fear of ridicule or broken bones

Crazy, you see, is the freest country
        in the world

Don't tell me – in other words –
about your fears of growth and change

Don't tell me what I should have done at fifteen
what was made to look good on flighty twenty-two-year-olds
how big, respectable women are supposed to act
what I should say, what I should do
then, what will people think? think, what will people say?

Look
I can't be bothered with such foolishness
now
at my age

Somebody, Some Body

I need somebody
to touch me
in a healing way

Somebody

Somebody

to touch me –
with love

somebody
who can hold
this depth of pain

hold me
crying tears
for every woman
whose
being a woman
has ever
made her cry

Unshed grief
running out slowly
in a river
of cleansing salt

Eintou Pearl Springer
1940s–

Born in Santa Cruz, Trinidad, she is a librarian and has been involved in dramatic arts since school, with the Caribbean Theatre Guild since 1970. A poet and playwright, she has also staged dramatized readings of her own poetry and prose. Her book of poems, Out of the Shadows, was published in 1986.

Women Over 30

Ripe –
in season
full blown
excellence.
No more half ripe
force ripe
fruit changed from green-ness
achieving fullness
of taste
of smell.

Ripe
in season
full ripened
excellence,
not just for any harvest
but for
cherished handling
mature sav'ring
of taste
of smell.

Ripe
knowing worth
enough
to refuse
to choose
who picks the fruit
who is allowed the fruit
at point of greatest
succulence.

Merle Hodge
1944–

B orn in Curepe, Trinidad, she received her early education in
the island before a scholarship in 1962 enabled her to study
French at London University, where she obtained a BA Honours
and an MPhil. After travelling widely in Europe and living for a time in
Africa, she returned to Trinidad and Tobago in the early 1970s, taught
French, English and West Indian literature there and later lectured in
French Caribbean and French African literature at the University of the
West Indies, Mona. In 1979 she went to Grenada to work with prime
minister Maurice Bishop, but left after his assassination in 1983 and
the subsequent US invasion of the island. Her novel Crick Crack, Monkey
(1970), from which this is an extract, is the story of a sensitive girl trying
to find her identity within the contradictory social context of Trinidad.

From

Crick Crack, Monkey

HER TRUE-TRUE NAME

T HE very next day we were being hustled off to Ma, away away up in
Pointe d'Espoir, with Toddan falling asleep on Mikey's lap as usual and
Mikey having to climb the track with him over one shoulder and the suitcase in
the other hand. When we came back it would be time for me to go to school, and
Toddan they could simply lose among Neighb' Ramlaal–Wife's own when there
was no one at home.

The August holidays had already begun, so that all the multitude was there.
Our grandmother was a strong, bony woman who did not smile unnecessarily,
her lower jaw set forward at an angle that did not brook opposition or argument.
She did not use up too many words at a time either, except when she sat on
the step with us teeming around her, when there was a moon, and told us
'nancy-stories. If the night was too dark or if it was raining there was no
story-telling – it was inconceivable to her that one should sit inside a house
and tell 'nancy-stories. At full moon there was a bonus and then we would
light a black-sage fire for the mosquitoes and sand-flies and the smoke smelt
like contented drowsiness. And when at the end of the story she said "Crick

crack?" our voices clambered over one another in the gleeful haste to chorus back in what ended on an untidy shrieking crescendo:

Monkey break 'e back
On a rotten pommerac!

And there was no murmur of protest when she ordered with finality: "That is enough. Find allyu bed."

On most afternoons we descended to the beach in a great band. Ma saluting houses on the way:

"Oo-oo Ma-Henrietta!"

"Oo-oo!" a voice would answer from the depths of the house or from somewhere in the backyard.

"Is me an' mih gran's passin'."

"Right, Ma-Josephine!"

Ma brought with her a wooden box and a stick. While we splashed about in the water she sat immobile and straight-backed on her box, her hands resting together on the stick which she held upright in front of her. When someone started to venture too far out she rapped sharply on the box with the stick. And when it was time to go she rapped again: "Awright. Come-out that water now!"

Then we walked along the sand, straggled and zig-zagged and played along the sand, to where they drew the nets in, and we "helped" in this latter operation, fastening ourselves like a swarm of bees to the end of the rope and adding as much to the total effort as would a swarm of bees bunched at the end of the thick hauling-rope. Afterwards we swooped down and collected the tiny fishes that they left on the beach, and Ma let us roast these in the fire at home.

Ma's land was to us an enchanted country, dipping into valley after valley, hills thickly covered with every conceivable kind of foliage, cool green darkness, sudden little streams that must surely have been squabbling past in the days when Brar Anancy and Brar Leopard and all the others roamed the earth outsmarting each other. And every now and then we would lose sight of the sea and then it would come into sight again down between trees when you least expected to see it, and always, it seemed, in a different direction; that was frightening too. We went out with Ma to pick fruit, she armed with a cutlass with which she hacked away thick vines and annihilated whole bushes in one swing. We returned with our baskets full of oranges, mangoes, chennettes, Ma bent under a bunch of plantains that was more than half her size.

Ma had a spot in the market on Sunday mornings, and she spent a great part of the week stewing cashews, pommes-cythères, cerises, making guava-cheese and guava jelly, sugar-cake, nut-cake, bennay-balls, toolum, shaddock-peel candy, chilibibi. . . . On these days we hung slyly about the kitchen, if only to feed on the smells; we were never afforded the opportunity of gorging ourselves – we partook of these delicacies when Ma saw fit, and not when we desired. She was full of maxims for our edification, of which the most baffling and maddening was:

Who ask
don't get
Who don't ask
don't want
Who don't want
don't get
Who don't get
don't care

For her one of the cardinal sins of childhood was gluttony: "Stuff yu guts today an' eat the stones of the wilderness tomorrow." (Ma's sayings often began on a note of familiarity only to rise into an impressive incomprehensibility, or vice versa, as in "Them that walketh in the paths of corruption will live to ketch dey arse.")

She was equal to all the vagaries of childhood. Nothing took her by surprise – she never rampaged, her initial reaction was always a knowing "Hm". Not that one permitted oneself the maximum of vagaries in Ma's house – her eye was too sharp and her hand too quick. But there were the odd times that somebody thought she wasn't looking. Sometimes there would be a chase, exciting but brief, when the culprit was hauled back panting to face the music in front of us all. Sometimes he was merely set free again, since he was already frightened to death and would certainly never try that one again.

Just as there were enough of us to play Hoop and Rescue and every conceivable game, so there were enough of us for the occasional outbreak of miniature gang-warfare. We sat for hours under the house in two camps proffering hearty insults. The division usually fell between those who were kept by Ma and those of us who didn't really live there. Ma's children were the "bush-monkeys" and "country-bookies" and they in turn made it known to us how deep was their longing for the day when we would all depart so they could have their house and their yard and their land to themselves again. This stung deep for though we knew beyond doubt that it was equally our house and yard and land yet it was those fiends who lived in the house all year round and played in the yard and went on expeditions into the land with Ma when we were not there. If hostilities lasted till a mealtime, then we placed ourselves on opposite sides of the table and eyed each other with contempt. And if they lasted until night-time, then going to bed was an uncomfortable affair, for it took rather longer to fall asleep when every muscle of your body and every inch of your concentration was taut with the effort of not touching your neighbour. But we the vacation batch always had our revenge when it was time to go home and our big-people had come to fetch us and we were all dressed up for the trip home and being fussed over – Ma's children looked a little envious then.

Ma awoke every morning with a groan quickly routed by a brief loud cheups. She rose at a nameless hour and in my half-sleep I saw a mountain shaking off mist in one mighty shudder and the mist falling away in little drops of cloud. The cheups with which Ma greeted the day expressed her essential attitude before the whole of existence – what yu mus' beat-up yuself for? In the face of the distasteful and unavoidable, the unexpected and irreversible, all that Ma could not crush or confound with a barked word or surmount with her lioness strength, she reacted to with a cheups, more or less loud, more or less long. Thus she sucked her teeth loudly and without further comment when the iron pot full of rice spitefully tipped itself over into the fire; when the sun took to playing monkey-wedding with the rain the moment she had put the final clothes-peg to her miles of washing strung from the breadfruit tree to the zaboca tree, from the zaboca tree to the house-post and from the house-post to the chicken-run post, Ma sucked her teeth and turned her back.

And there were the days of real rain. We could see it coming, down across the water, a dark ceiling letting down slow grey streamers into the horizon (that was God pee-peeing into his posie) and then it would be pounding the earth like a thousand horses coming at us through the trees. It was frightening and exciting. A sudden greyness had descended upon everything and we had seconds in which to race about the yard like mad-ants helping Ma to place her assortment of barrels and buckets in places where they would catch the water. And all the time the rain pounding nearer, racing to catch us. When the first messenger spray hit us there was pandemonium – we stampeded into the house, some squealing with a contagious excitement. We ran round shutting the windows, pulling out buckets and basins to place under the leaks, still squealing and colliding with each other. As the windows were closed one by one a cosy darkness crept in, and we felt as if our numbers were growing. We all collected into one room. Sometimes we piled onto the big-bed and made a tent of the coverlets, tying them to the four posts of the bed. Under the tent the commotion was sustained, rising to squealing pitch at every flash of lightning and crack of thunder, or every time the tent collapsed about us, or when a lath fell so that a part of the bed caved in under some of us; or when someone chose this situation of inescapable intimacy to emit an anonymous but very self-assertive poops. It was impossible to detect the owner, and chaos ensued while every man accused his immediate neighbour. In the end we had to count the culprit out by means of Ink-Pink-Mamma-Stink, and the man thus denounced was emitted bodily amidst a new burst of commotion.

Meanwhile Ma bustled about the house – we knew that she was just as excited as we were, barricaded into the darkened house with the rain drumming on the galvanize and surrounding us with heavy purring like a huge mother-cat. Ma seemed to be finding things to do so as not to yield to the temptation to come and crawl under the sheets and play tent with us. Then she came in with a big plate of sugar-cake and guava-cheese, and pretended to be scandalized at the way we were treating the bedclothes.

And when the rain had stopped we dressed up in Grampa's old jackets and went out with Ma to look at the river. This was like a ritual following upon the rain – she had to go and see the river. We walked behind her squelching joyously in the new puddles and mud. The air smelt brown and green, like when the earth was being made. From a long way off the river was calling to us through the trees, in one continuous groan, so that when we finally came to it, wet and splashed from the puddles and from the bushes we had brushed against, it was as though we had been straining along in it the whole time. Ma stopped abruptly and spread out both her arms to stop us, as though it were likely that we would keep on walking right into the fast ochre water. We counted how many trees it had risen past on the bank. If the river came down every week Ma's rapture would be quite as new.

"Eh!" she exclaimed, and then fell back into her trance. Then a little later on "Eh!" shaking her head from side to side, "Well, yes, well, yes!" We stood around her in an unlikely silence like spattered acolytes in our jumble-sale clothes, in the bright air hanging out crisp and taut to dry, and the river ploughing off with the dirt and everything drenched and bowing and satisfied and resting before the world started up again from the beginning.

We roamed the yard and swarmed down to the water and played hoop around the breadfruit tree as if we would always be wiry-limbed children whose darting about the sun would capture like amber and fix into eternity. Although Ma exclaimed upon our arrival each year at how big we'd got, yet all the holidays at Pointe d'Espoir were one August month, especially in the middle part of the day when everything seemed to set in the still, hanging brightness – our games and squabbling; the hens with their heads down scratching about the yard; the agreeableness of sitting clamped between Ma's knees having one's hair plaited. The cream air in the middle part of the day was like Time staring at itself in a mirror, the two faces locked dreamily in an eternal gaze.

I was Ma's own-own bold-face Tee, harden' as the Devil's shit but that is yu great great grandmother, that is she, t'ank Gord. Sometimes when the others were not about she would accost me suddenly: "An who is Ma sugar-cake?"

"Tee!"

"An who is Ma dumplin'?"

"Tee!"

And all at once she put on an expression of mock-displeasure and snapped at me gruffly: "Who tell yu that?"

"Ma tell mih!"

"Well, Ma is a liard ol'-fool," and she thrust a hunk of guava-cheese at me.

Ma said that I was her grandmother come back again. She said her grandmother was a tall straight proud woman who lived to an old old age and her eyes were still bright like water and her back straight like bamboo, for all the heavy-load she had carried on her head all her life. The People gave her the name Euphemia or Euph-something, but when they called her that she used to toss her head like a horse and refuse to answer so they'd had to give up in the end and call her by her true-true name.

Then Ma creased her forehead and closed her eyes and rubbed her temples and if anyone spoke she waved her hand with irritation. She sat like this for a long time. Then she would shake her head sorrowfully. She couldn't remember her grandmother's true-true name. But Tee was growing into her grandmother again, her spirit was in me. They'd never bent down her spirit and she would come back and come back and come back; if only she could live to see Tee grow into her tall proud straight grandmother.

Amryl Johnson
1940s–

Born in Tunapuna, Trinidad, she was brought up by her grand-mother until the age of eleven, when she joined her parents in England. She went to school in London and took a degree in African and Caribbean Studies at the University of Kent. She returned to the island of her birth in 1982, for four weeks, and finding herself almost "foreign" to her own culture, she determined to go back to the Caribbean at the earliest opportunity, which she did the next year for six months, staying in Trinidad, Tobago, Grenada, Barbados, St Lucia, Dominica and Guadeloupe. Out of this visit came a book on her experiences, Sequins for a Ragged Hem. She explains: "The 'ragged hem' of the book's title refers to the rape of slavery and all this had done to my people. 'Sequins' are the colour and sparkle they have woven into the state of being in exile." A contributor to anthologies such as News for Babylon (ed. James Berry, 1983), Watchers and Seekers (eds Cobham and Collins, 1987), Let It Be Told (ed. Ngcobo, 1987) and Caribbean New Wave (ed. Stewart Brown, 1990), in which "Yardstick" appeared, she is the author of the poetry collection Long Road to Nowhere (1985).

Yardstick

Is like the man don't sleep at all, at all. Don't matter how early I open the door, he there on he veranda, looking out.

"Morning, Mr Braffitt. How you?"

A toothless grin exposed the pink wealth of his gums.

"I dare, yes, Zelda girl. And yourself?"

His reply, the response was not always said. Sometimes, it was merely implied.

Today just like any other blasted Thursday. I have to wash the clothes, cook the food, get the first two ready for school in time, get myself ready for work then take the baby to the nursery. Her head was hot, she had to remember and –

Zelda went back to forcing clothes against the scrubbing board. She caught a glimpse of the old man in her line of vision just before she slapped the wet cloth against the board. He was still smiling.

Remember and – Then she had to –

"Yes, Mr Braffitt. Is true. Is true."

And when she finish doing that, she go have to –

"Is true. Is true what you saying, Mr Braffitt. I agree. I agree."

Zelda was only half listening. Her answers came almost mechanically. This was habit. Part of an early-morning ritual which had started from the very first morning, the very first morning she had moved into the yard.

"The old man always want to get you in some 'tory. Is like he always, always have something to say."

Old talk. Five in the morning, every morning. The old man would be there on his veranda, waiting to tell her something. I hear he have false teeth. I only hear. I ain't yet see he with he teeth in. All I ever see he doing, is skinning up he gum. Zelda could not always understand what he was saying. At times, she found herself blatantly guessing.

"Pa Braffitt does want talk politics. He ain't happy at all, at all with the way they running things in the country."

Mother Gloria who also lived in the yard, had laughed when she said it.

"He say he does remember when – . And the man travel all about, oui. He did work Panama Canal. The man go America, he go Canada, he go England. He –."

"And he come back here?!!"

Zelda's interruption had been high-pitched with incredulity. Mother Gloria had looked at her as if she was being disrespectful.

"Trinidad is he home, child. When he done he travelling, where else he go go?"

Zelda thought Mr Braffitt a fool.

Here? Me? Even if I did have a house here waiting. Empty.

Every now and then, her thoughts would drift back to that particular conversation with Mother Gloria. If she was at home, she would look around her and schueps. She would look at her poverty and deprivation and suck air through her teeth. She would do so loud with contempt. Sometimes, she would say it aloud.

"When I get out, you think I ever coming back here? Here? Christ, I tell you when I gone, I gone."

It was as if all her life had been spent in those two rooms he had taken her to when she was carrying their first child. Only for a while. Just a short while, he had said. Short while. Things were going to get better. Much better. And she had waited. More to the point, she had believed him. She had believed him. Ten years had gone by. Ten years of her sweet sweet life. Gone.

And Lord. And Lord, what? What, what, what? What did happen? What did go wrong, Lord? He in the same job he did have when I first meet he. And when last they give he a raise? I did think he have ambition. What ambition?

After a while, you done hoping. You done waiting for the rainbow. Every morning when you open your eye, you should feel good about life. Every day when I look up into the sky, was like every ray of sun less bright than the day before. And when you do hear the shout, you start to feel a tightening in your stomach even before you begin to open your eye. Was how it was for a while. And sudden sudden one day, I leave that behind. My inside start to get hollow hollow. Was like I empty. Was like I real real empty. Everything I feel getting less and less. Then like nothing inside me. Nothing. Nothing. Then like was I can't feel nothing at all, at all, something else start welling up inside me 'til the thing get full full. And it hurting. The thing hurting. I start to wonder if the pain ever going to go. I ever going to be free of this hurt? But it do. It leave me numb. I never going to feel nothing again. Everything I do from then on, I do it from duty. After that, every child I bring into this world, I shit out of me like vomit.

Zelda had not needed to go looking. She had found any, all yardsticks right there on her doorstep. Of late, she had taken to spending more and more time talking to herself.

"You see me, I not like Rosalie, eh. I still alive. I ain't dead."

Rosalie make ten. She, the man, and the children that ain't leave yet still in the board house where she make the first. Now she breast so dry up and shrivel, they hanging to she waist. She ain't never have no pleasure. She ain't never tasted no joy. She spend she whole life making baby. Making baby have she chain to the house. I never see she dress up. I never see she going no place. I just have to look in Rosalie eye to remind myself how I don't want to be. Of late, is like the two of we always catching one another glance. She don't talk much. Rosalie don't say much but she don't have to. Is there. Is right there in she face. Everything. Rosalie not old. Rosalie not an old woman but every line on she face does tell the story. Rosalie don't wear no expression. She don't look happy. She don't look sad. She don't look nothing. If wasn't for all the lines, I would think is mask the girl wearing. Is not a real face at all, at all. I feel every line on Rosalie face is she state of mind. She hiding behind mask to try and shield sheself. I feel so. But is when I look in Rosalie eye that I want to bawl. I want bawl for she. I want bawl for all of we. Anger does take me down below. I look in Rosalie eye and she telling me she life done. She trap. She in prison. I look in she eye and I want to scream for she. One time, I look at Rosalie and I make my decision. After that, my crying done. All my regret over. Long time now I make a vow and I have Rosalie to thank for that. I done make my decision. I getting out. By hook or crook, I getting out.

"Is true, Mr Braffitt. Is true. What you say is true."

The emphasis had now long since shifted. So much of what Zelda was doing was now done out of a sense of habit. No longer even duty.

"No, Mr Braffitt, I ain't think so. I sure the rainy season done."

Every morning the same chupid conversation. And sometimes when I come to think on it, I sure the reply I giving he ain't a fart anything to do with what he telling me. But what I go do? What? What?

It had slowly dawned on her. The truth and this decision had become more certain. More fixed. She had acquired a new found resilience. Zelda now had the stamina, the strength to go through the daily rigmarole, step by step. It was this determination which had recently found her sneaking days off work to spend hours in crowded waiting rooms, waiting. Just waiting. Waiting. Waiting her turn.

"You think it easy?!! It ain't easy, you hear! It ain't easy. You only *think* it easy."

It was his stock reply. Joseph had not shouted. He had only raised his voice. He had never been violent. He had never lifted a hand to Zelda or the children. While most women would have been grateful, it was this peaceful, to her mind docile, nature which had been the bone of contention in their marriage.

Too damn quiet for he own good. Too quiet and softy softy. People don't appreciate you for it. They does want take advantage. I ain't know how it is he ain't learn by now. They does take he for a fool again and again but the man never wise up. I did like he at first because he was gentle. He was gentle and nice. I did think sooner or later he go see you don't get nothing for nothing in this world. Yes, is true, when I first meet he, I did like he 'cause he quiet and gentle. But, Lord, when you see opportunity after opportunity slip through he finger 'cause he too softy softy to go out and fight and claw and devour, something does stick in your throat. And what the arse he know 'bout it? The man always giving me the same blasted reply. It ain't easy. It ain't easy. No, of course, it ain't easy. It have anything in life that easy? Tell me. Nothing in Trinidad going to come to we black people. We at the bottom of the ladder. Is not like the Indian and them. They helping one another. I tired telling he the stupidy little job he in since I know he, ain't worth nothing. When last he pay go up? Eh? Eh? When last? He working night watchman. Since I know he, he working night watchman for little little money. If wasn't for the job I holding down, I don't know how we would have manage. And the children does grow out of they clothes so fast. What sort of family we is, anyway? He working nights. I working in the day. On he days off, all he want do is sleep or he out with he boys and them. When the children and me does get to see he? Family? What family? We make three children together and is like he feel he work done. From the start, is like I alone doing the bringing up. I alone. I bathing them, I caring for them. I is the one does have to do the beating. Is me alone having to do everything. Everything. Father? What father? He is any father? I more father to them than he.

I twenty-six years of age and is still a fire in me, I still hungry and I want get out of this place before it dead. Look at me, juk, juk jukking. Jukking clothes against the blasted scrubbing board but why I have to – ?

Zelda's thoughts suddenly accelerated in time. She stood looking down at the clothes, her eyes almost glazed and her mouth now hung open with inspiration.

Girl, you stupid. You real real stupid, yes. You done. You fix-up, fix-up already. Don't wait 'til the end of the week. Why wait until the end of the week?

Zelda made an instant decision. The excitement she began feeling was reflected in her voice.

"Today a real special day, Mr Braffitt. You know that?"

He looked at her blankly for a few seconds as if trying to make sense of what she was saying.

"Is true, Zelda girl?"

Zelda always found it consoling when she and the old man were on the same wavelength.

"Yes, Mr Braffitt, today a real special day and tomorrow morning you go see why."

Zelda offered a broad smile. It tempted his own. At the best of times, his smile was never far from the surface.

Yes, Mr Braffitt, let we smile. Let we smile, you blasted old fool. What you think it is at all? You travel quite England. You travel quite America. You travel quite Canada. And when you done, you come back here? To this? Man, you real mad, oui. Old man, you real real chupid. You a vrai chupidy, yes. And I not too far short. Wait? No, man, my waiting done. I done run out of time. My time done. I pay my due. I serve my sentence. Yes, Mr Braffitt, let we smile together 'cause if wasn't for you, Mother Gloria and Rosalie, I would never've taken this thing so far. Every time I see the three of all you is like the devil and he fork chuking me, chuking me. He chuk, chuk, chuking me. He telling me, he reminding me that if I ain't take stock I going to end up like all of all you.

"Yes, Mr Braffitt, today is a real special day."

Zelda and the old man continued to smile at each other for a while longer. He seemed oblivious to the contempt which twisted her smile into a grimace.

Zelda cocked her head, listening to the seconds of a clock as it made its loud progress towards the bewitching hour. Midnight. Zelda sat waiting. A packed suitcase by her side. The room was in darkness. The moon's light through the open curtains seemed to highlight just one feature. A vase of plastic flowers on the small table by the window showed almost daylight colours. The glow also fell on the slip of white paper on the table next to the vase. The note read, simply.

> BOY, I GONE
> I NOT COMING BACK
> THEY IS YOUR CHILDREN TOO

Zelda went over recent events as she waited.

I have my papers. I done fix-up, fix-up. I get my passport. I get my visa from the American Embassy. I ready. I didn't plan to go 'til Saturday night. Straight from here to the airport. But something in me did snap when I pick up that piece of clothes. I know I didn't want spend no three more mornings slapping no one set of clothes against no jukking board and having to scrub it. I going now, tonight self. I go spend the rest of my time 'til the flight by Kevin and them. That is the last place he go think to look for me. And who say he go look?

Zelda heard the car as it screeched to a halt. Picking up the suitcase, she walked out of the door and, without a backward glance, closed it firmly behind her.

Granny in de Market Place

Yuh fish fresh?

Woman, why yuh holdin' meh fish up tuh yuh nose?
De fish fresh. Ah say it fresh. Ah ehn go say it any mo'

Hmmm, well if dis fish fresh den is I who dead an' gone
De ting smell like it take a bath in a lavatory in town
it here so long it happy. Look how de mout' laughin' at we
De eye turn up to heaven like it want tuh know 'e fate
Dey say it does take a good week before dey reach dat state

Yuh mango ripe?

Gran'ma, stop feelin' and squeezin' up meh fruit!
Yuh ehn playin' in no ban'. Meh mango eh no concertina

Ah tell yuh dis mango hard just like yuh face
One bite an' ah sure tuh break both ah meh plate
If yuh cahn tell de difference between green an' rosy red
dohn clim' jus' wait until dey fall down from de tree
Yuh go know dey ripe when de lizard an dem start tuh feed
but dohn bring yuh force-ripe fruit tuh try an' sell in here
it ehn burglars is crooks like all yuh poor people have to fear

De yam good?

Old lady, get yuh nails outta meh yam!
Ah mad tuh make yuh buy it now yuh damage it so bad

Dis yam look like de one dat did come off ah de ark
She brother in de Botanical Gardens up dey by Queens Park
Tourists with dey camera comin' from all over de worl'
takin' pictures dey never hear any yam could be dat ole
Ah have a crutch an' a rocking-chair someone give meh fuh free
If ah did know ah would ah bring dem an' leave dem here fuh she

De bush clean?

Well, I never hear more! Old woman, is watch yuh watching meh
young young dasheen leaf wit' de dew still shinin' on dem!

It seem tuh me like dey does like tuh lie out in de sun
jus' tuh make sure dat dey get dey edges nice an' brown
an' maybe is weight dey liftin' tuh make dem look so tough
Dey wan' build up dey strength fuh when tings start gettin' rough
Is callaloo ah makin' but ah 'fraid tings go get too hot
Yuh bush go want tuh fight an' meh crab go jump outta de pot

How much a poun' yuh fig?

Ah have a big big sign tellin' yuh how much it cos'
Yuh either blin' yuh dotish or yuh jus' cahn read at all

Well, ah wearing meh glasses so ah readin' yuh big big sign
but tuh tell yuh de trut' ah jus' cahn believe meh eye
Ah lookin' ah seein' but no man could be so blasted bol'
Yuh mus' tink dis is Fort Knox yuh sellin' fig as if is gol'
Dey should put all ah all yuh somewhere nice an' safe
If dey ehn close Sing-Sing prison dat go be the bestest place

De orange sweet?

Ma, it eh hah orange in dis market as sweet as ah does sell
It like de sun, it taste like sugar an' it juicy as well

Yuh know, boy, what yuh sayin' have a sorta ring
De las' time ah buy yuh tell meh exactly de same ting
When ah suck ah fin' all ah dem sour as hell
De dentures drop out an' meh two gum start tuh swell
Meh mout' so sore ah cahn even eat ah meal
Yuh sure it ehn lime all yuh wrappin' in orange peel?

De coconut hah water?

Red Jordan Arobateau
?1944

B orn to a Honduran father who came to Chicago and married a
light-skinned Black woman, she lives in San Francisco, describing
herself as "a lesbian, born-again christian, mongrel [the Mongrels are
a group of women born of mixed heritage], & witness on the sea of life". Her
works include The Bars Across Heaven (1975), Ho Stroll: A Novel in 5 Pars
(1975) and Stories from the Dance of Life #3 (1979).

Nobody's People

Mirror, mirror on the wall,
whose the fairest of them all?

T HAT'S an interesting accent you have, are you from the South?" Asked
the man.
She looked into space, tan face cold; profile of keen features. Her first

impulse was to slap him, but stayed cool.

"Where do you come from?" The man persisted. He was white.

"My Mommas wound." She replied with vennom.

"Where was that?"

"I can't remember, when she dropped me I wasn't thinking about what *state* it was, I was too busy looking around me wondering 'what's it gonna be like?'"

"What race are you?" If you don't mind me asking."

This question has persued me since before I learned how to talk – in infrences, facial expressions of curious people who saw me.

I am one drop black.

Raised black. This is the killer – your culture. What is *home* to a person.

By physical appearance one could easily say I'm white mixed with Native American. Nose & high cheek bones like an Indian. But I have nothing in common with that culture – envision them sitting around talking about things I don't know – Teepees, and the wilderness. Deer hunting.

& I'm a nigger to my heart.

This is what it bes like.

On my birth cirtificut are two words; NEGRO and SPANISH under Race for my mother & father, respectivily. My mother was yellow, & dad a latin from South America. I resemble a black maybe to an anthropoligist – faint traces in my face that must be studied to be seen, or recognized on instinct in an instent.

Thru grammar school & high school, misunderstanding blacks taunted me; made fun of me being so light. "Oh her nose is so big." "Oh, she's got a *pale* face. OOOWEE! I wouldn't want to be that *pale!*" Whites avoided me – once they heard the rummor; "she's part black." Or, "she associates with the Coloreds." & not really one of them.

Age 9, 10, I wondered why white girls shunned me. When I got older branching out from my Afro-American neighborhood and went into the larger world, when mixing with whites – inadvertently "passing", finally the question would spill out of their lips – "what nationality are you?" They wanted to justify the strange cast to my skin – not quite white; other impercievable characteristics. I told them I had Negro blood. They didn't like me too well after that.

I think back to age 13, the time my father took me aside & told me: "You can be anything you want to be!" But I didn't *want* to be anything! I wanted to be like mother & her family – Colored.

When he first told me this, it put words to my fears – "you can be anything." Freedom frightened me. "I'd rather be *something!*" A label has confort.

So what am I? White? Black? Latin? Mixed?

There's always been people like me. – Quadroons. All down thru herstory since my forebarers from Africa mated with those, Caucasian.

Not black, but black. This is why I can't be among my people in the same way as others. This is how I was raised – Colored; it is my home, and when too long gone, am hongry for my roots!

It is a passionate and angry thing, generating fierce emotions. Making me want to kick ass, but I won't.

A round table in a tavern; black women seated. A dark skinned woman walks in, boougiouse; dressed to her teeth; she greets those at the table giving all the soul-hand shake, except for the pale skin person. With her, the black woman switches up and shakes hands like white folks do. This point was not missed on the sister.

Later, I've forgotten the incident, am talking to an Asian woman when Miss Thang comes back over & speeks – aloof, her voice from a cool height like an inquisitor. "I been wanting to ask you something . . I *heard* you were black! This woman was talking about you. She said 'she's black,' and I was surprised."

"People are talking about me? Who? What's her name!"

"That's not important!" She drew back a little, a nasty smile played in her expression: "I *mean*, you don't *look* black, and you don't *act* black. To me, black is somebody who *looks* and *acts* black!"

The woman was silent, she'd been thru it before.

What an effort to put on the trappings of being black – if you don't possess them already – to curl her naturaly straight hair into an 'fro; to perfect black english when she was raised in a home of "proper speeking".

The cold voice continued, "You know I see your lips, your nose . . your *hair!*" Words dripping like acid. "How much black *are* you? One sixteenth? One 32nd?"

"One half."

The Asian sister intrupted. "Why are you comming on to her so angry?"

The black woman yelled, "I just want to know! Somebody say's the lady's black! I want to know is she? I couldn't tell!" She cried, defensivly. "She doesn't act black! She doesn't look black! She doesn't talk black!"

Insult after insult rolled out of her mouth; the black woman was angry, trembling with rage. The light complected woman only sat back, allowing the woman to convict herself. – She was tired of explaining. She'd been thru this scene a million times before. And made enough explinations to last her a lifetime. People wanting to mess with her just to get rid of their own frustrations.

"She hates white people." Said the Asian lady afterwords.

"She does that to everybody. I think it's for her ego. She *has* to."

"She acts like Miss *It*."

"Just ignore her. I know her. I'm gonna make her appologize."

"She want to act shitty, I can too."

"Ignore her, she's drunk."

"Bitch is drunk. I don't get drunk. And I don't trust *nobody*."

"I'll *make* her appologize." The Asian woman stated in a firm voice, eyes squinted in anger.

Around them, the sea of gay life was in full swing.

Many bars are a mixture of women & men, gay & straight, & all races. In them are danger trips with hostile men. And physical violence.

This particular bar, WOMANTIME was exclusively women – Middle class/ bougiouse. But women wounded each other just as deeply in the privacy of that smokey club with their words – glares of their eyes, knife edge like the karatee back hand chop – without knives. Hurt, not by lunging across the room fists flying, but the more advanced physological warfare, of the emotions. Acid on an intellectual level.

And subtely they turned a persons color against them and used it for hate.

She thought: "I have been confronted hundreds of times; and this is how it's always been – hostile."

She was not in grammer school anymore; "I stop worrying about them so much and worry about me."

In adult life, I spend 90% of my social life after dark, in clubs or partys. Lighting does strange things to skin complexion. It can make Latino's & fair blacks looks like whitefolks.

A yellow nigger like an Aryan with a tan.

"Those black women in the bars," she thought; "they hate my guts because they don't know what I am. Some have heard lies about me, some know the truth, but they don't know who I *am*."

Scenes such as these bring a lot of paranoia.

Here I am calling people "Sister & Brother," and not even looking like a sister or brother myself.

A mass of straight hair down to my sholders.

What race am I?

If I stay in the sun all summer and under a sunlamp by winter my skin is a shade darker. I could perminate my hair into an Afro to look black, and fit in; but to mee that's a lie. In the past it's been a hardship; – that's what people are made of, hardship.

I've started believeing in myself, so I can be free.

Got to be what I feel.

New York city

A white woman asks me; "What Nationality are you? Basque?"

"Basque?"

"It's in the Southern part of France."

"No,"

"Italian?"

"No, *guess again*."

"You must have an Indian grandparent."

Then she told her.

"OH!" Drawing back. "Well! You don't *look* like it!" Her white face flushes red. Suddenly the relationship between them has changed. The power balance must be readjusted. "OH. That must have been difficult for you, growing up!" (A few say. "Oh, you've had it easy!")

Or, "Excuse me!" And they walk away and avoid me like death.

In this world which literally bows down and worships anything but God, praises people for their whiteness – or their blackness, they can't have an attitude about me! They don't know what I am. They don't know much about my subject.

So politely, people don't mention me. Pretend I don't exist. My prescence makes them unconfortable. I'm too allusive – they can't pin me down.

Techinically I'm a freek – so people avoid me, or, race talk when I come around.

I am the leper Jesus talked about.

I am the one who the world casts out.

The one they said to Jesus – "why are you associating with her?"

Whites ask another white – "Why do you talk to her? she's not white!"

Blacks hiss at blacks, "leave that honkey alone!"

I am that one.

The one in question.

When we are different to the mainstream, the majority points the finger of scorn – and informs us we are lepers. We have the disease called, "you-don't-belong-to-my-people".

They put lepers in a prison, because we are the wrong color.

So lepers band together and be strong.

I am a leper with no one to join with.

An outcast from the outcasts. Outcast and outcast again.

There are no lepers in Jesus Christ.

Case in point:

Afro American's – the lepers of AmeriKKKa. Black people who are decendent from Africa, mixed with white, Indian, Asian & other.

Visable Characteristics:

Dark complexion

Kinky hair

Thick lips & nose

Invisable Characteristics

Soul

Black Power & Black Pride

This has been a tremendous up lift to Afro Americans; comming together as a race beging to love itself. And to feed itself inspiration. To be proud of it's characteristics both visable & invisable, and to build an economic support system for it's own.

Black Power & Black Pride.

It took the despised word – "black" the word our parents & grandparents only wispered – the word that meant stigma; misfortune, and raised the word up in an uplifted fist. Took the word "black" and made it a Crown. Black is beautiful! Glory filtering down the ladder from slavery in pride of our roots, into the future of black children.

Black is Beautiful made people come together and take care of business.

Afro Americans working in cooperation.

It was a breakthru. But, as any illusion, including white supremacy, it had it's flaws. Some became obbsessed to the point that Black is Beautiful became synonmous with Hate Whites. With Hate anything not Black.

My skin is not black.

These genes I carry in my body, that can show up in African-Trait offspring; one drop of black blood and a history of growing-up-Colored, is not enough. It is a tenuous hold on *blackness*.

So, she dropped out of her Momma's wound, grew like Topsey and went out into the highways & byways of the world, a lost lamb.

In pain she turned from God. We who are wanderers, people who have no places, in our troubles we search . . . taking whatever amount of time we need to be healed.

She was not even sure what love was like – the voluntary kiss of one mouth to another; a pelvic thrust accompanied by affection. Had seldom known it. That long deep reaching tongue between 2 people. The calling by a pet name. The days spent together in familiarity of a married couple. The voluntary cumming together in oral love of each others sex, without a bribe; of alcohol, or cash. Not a one night stand. Mostly she had known pickups, 2 week long "affairs," then, dialing a phonenumber, no answer. A handfull of dates with flowers then, "I'm sorry, but. . ." or, "I've got something to tell you. . ." The empty bed at night.

She didn't know how to be with people.

Didn't know how to belong in the human race in general. – Was selfconscious, shy, paranoid. . I mean, wouldn't you be? Being a labeless entity? A misunderstood stranger? A mixed so & so, that nobody knows your name? She had a lot of frustration which came out in rage. Cussing, putting her fist thru doors. Wouldn't believe after raising so much hell what she really wanted was peace.

She was proud. Was arrogant. She wore mens suits.

She had knocked but hadn't found a door.

The world; they lost a lot by not knowing her.

Los Angeles California:

My lover, a white woman says: "You're a black woman."

Chicago Illinois:

My psychiatrist informs me; "You are white." (He also tells me it's wrong to be a lesbian. He is white. And not homosexual. This is brainwashing.)

San Francisco California

Leaving a bar one night talking two 3 black sisters just met them: "Pardon me, can I ask you a question? – Don't take offence, but what race are you?"

"Part black," she says; & thinking, "here goes the whole thing again."

"No, I don't believe it." Says the woman sitting next to her.

"Part black." She states again in a low voice.

"Nobody is part black."

"Look at her hair." someone says. "Look." Reaching out, fingering her straight fine hair with nare' a curl. But she grabs the finger and points it back at the woman – who is a yellow bitch with soft, semi-curly hair. "LOOK AT YO' HAIR!" She sez back-at-her. "Well. . ." Sez the yellow gal, making a face.

"No such thing as half black. If you're part black you all black." The first sister declares.

"Multi-race."

"Well. . ." The sister says, begrudgingly; resigning herself to the facts; "one drop of black, you're black." Hating to acknowledge that this white-appearing stranger is of the same race as she.

As if this "white person" could be one of them.

This hated white looking type is actually one of their own.

This person can be white and can be black simotaneously.

That this person can claim the privledge of being black while still looking white.

Star filled night.

All it does is serve to remind me again that I am not black, but something different. I am part of the Afro American family – if they choose to take me in by the old laws of slavery, where one drop of African blood constitutes a Negro, – and also by my experience – in my formative years, and by relitives, Colored & black. But more often I am tollerated. Seen as different.

We who are, must forge a new identity for ourselves.

Meet a white sister in South Carolina.

Go home, take her to bed.

Wake up, daylight. My yellow belly on her lilly white one.

We talk. I mention, "I'm part black." Hesitent. Without blinking her big blue eyes she says;

"I knew you were."

"Oh."

"I was raised in the South, remember?"

The South – land of slavery, the cradle of misogany.

"You white."

Black woman informs me – she herself is fair, curly not Afro hair, but obviously black. Technically ¾ths white. Mother Caucasian, father half Caucasian, half black.

"You white!" She yells. Hate sputters out of her. – Or is it hurt?

In the dim lights of the çar she rants: "THERE'RE 5 RACES. BLACK, WHITE, BROWN, YELLOW & RED!" She lists them on her fair fingers; "YOU AIN'T *BLACK*, YOU AIN'T YELLOW, YOU AIN'T RED, YOU *WHITE!*" Accusing.

"BITCH IS GONNA LOOK AT ME AND TELL ME, SHE AIN'T WHITE! ALLRIGHT! YOU *BLACK* THEN!" she yells, taking a wild guess.

"*No*. I'm not black! This skin is not black!" Says the woman firmly, holding up her fair fair arm.

"I never seen no nigger with hair like *that!*" she says. "Yo' hair and a white girls hair are the same! You *White!*" She screems, showing her teeth like a cornored dog. "I don't care about your grandmammy, yo' racial heritage! It's what yo' is *now!* You is W.H.I.T.E!" She screems so loud her eyelids turn into slits as a jackolantern.

And I feel in my guts that terrible frustration when a free spirit and an imovable solid exchange blows. & tightening in my chest, walling up in cement in the region of the heart. A living entity – a heart, tissue that palpitates, can't live in cement it cracks. It needs to bust loose!

Rejected by both white & black; she was rejected by everyone, so found God.

Whites found she wasn't one of them.

Blacks didn't know her.

So, in the final anaylisis, it comes back to the Spirit. Maybe all this hell on earth has been to show us the way to God – the only escape route. I mean, I'm rejected everywhere I go in concrete, material, *facts*. Not black enough, not truely white, I don't hablé español.

I love it – just get so totally rejected, so, become totally free!

Jesus wants an army of people who have alligence to no other thing but love. – God is love.

To no other doctrin – because they all proove false.

For us to share space with no emotions of fear, hate; just love. We stand together in the world as at a party & rub elbows – so accept eachother.

"The stone that has rejected has become the cornorstone." – I can't get that phrase out of my mind.

In the Last Days they were sitting in the bar kissing & hugging like there was no tomorrow.

The pagen dance. So many humanbeings are living a life totally constituted by it.

They bow down to warped powers and let other people walk on their backs while they make fanfare, waving plumes as servants before the eunuchs; as eunuchs for the master. Applauding each other in the wrong they do.

I am Red.

A child of God.

Woman come up to her; jet black, fat & short & say's "I'm talking to you because I like white women."

"She thinks I'm white!"

An acquaintence: "You're black, don't be ashamed of it!"

"I'm not. Just sick of having to explain myself all the time."

By 35 she ran out of steam. "Don't care who knows what I am. Just gonna live on this good earth."

Today, my woman is yellow as I am, but looks black – except under bar lights when she can pass off as a white sister. Her hair is naturally blond.

"Kids in school use to give me hell about that. 'Who do you think you are? Why do you dye your hair? Isn't your natural hair color good enough for you? Why do you have to be different, you a nigger like we is!'

"I got sick of telling them my hair was naturally blond. (Her eye-brows are too) Finally I just stopped. Let them think what they want."

She sat at the kitchen table. A bowl of Gumbo on the stove.

Suddenly, she could no longer stand it! Remembered being knocked down by hostile blacks. The taunts from yesteryear – the jeers in black taverns. She recalled a man jumping at her, knocking her down to her knees; she remembered the rage at the sight of her own blood – the feeling of futility ... remembered nearly being killed by niggers. Asswhippings, mouth whippings. Niggers wild-angry because they fucked up theyselves.

She ran out of the house & thru the ghetto.

Back thru the neighborhood, the byways of my people – the members of this dis-placed African race, in AmeriKKKa. The world has ripped love from us, clamped red hearts in iron jaws of a garbage disposal of racial laws & color barriers & discrimination. "I'M ANGRY! SO ANGRY! BECAUSE I AM A MINORITY!

"TOO LONG BEEN TREATED LIKE A NOBODY! GODDAMN IT!"

She raced up to the first black she saw – by a barbeque shop.

"I'M NOT BLACK!" She yelled. Thrusting a pale arm out in front of the mans face she hollered; "MY SKIN IS NOT BLACK! NOT BROWN! MY FEATURES AIN'T NEGROID. I'M NOT BLACK, SO WHAT *AM* I? *TELL ME WHAT I AM*!!!!!"

The man stood, looking down at her. His face was ebony – color of the Queen of Spades.

The woman yelled; "I'M A VICTIM OF RACISM MORE THAN *ANYBODY!* AT LEAST YOU'RE *BLACK!* I'M NEITHER ONE!" She confronted the tall man.

"NIGGERS IS FOREVER TALKING ABOUT 'OUR PEOPLE THIS,' 'OUR PEO-PLE THAT,' 'OUR PEOPLE HAVE A LONG WAY TO GO!'" She mimicked in a mock tone; "I *HAVE* NO PEOPLE." She said. She was ready to die. "FOR THE LONGEST TIME, I'VE HAD NO POSITIVE IDENTITY!" A crowd of people in the barbeque house looked at her. Startled, black, imovable. "BEFORE BLACK WAS BEAUTIFUL, BLACKS HAD A UNITY – EVEN THO IT WAS NEGITIVE – NIGGERS! 'HEY NIGGER!' 'SAY NIGGER, WHAT'S HAPPENING!' YOU HEAR IT EVERY DAY! NOBODY CALLS ME NIGGER!" Said she, "UNLESS THEY KNOW MY MAMMY AND MY GRANDMAMMY!

"I'D RATHER BE *SOMETHING!* A LABLE! IT'S *CONFORTABLE!*"

She stood there and sinned in the sight of heaven. Got angry at those people staring at her in the barbeque house – did a stupid thing; and here she was baptized in water & in the Holy Ghost and at the very gates of heaven, she said:

"OHHHWEEEE I WANT *VENGENCE!!* BACK AT 'EM! IT'S UGLY! IT'S WRONG! WHAT THEY'VE SAID ABOUT ME! WHAT THEY'VE TRIED TO DO TO ME! I WANT TO DESTROY ALL OF THEM!

"THEY LOOK AT ME AND HATE, BECAUSE OF MY WHITE FACE!"

Shaking her fist at the crowd she yelled; "LOOK! BLACK SISTER AND BROTHER, OTHER BLACKS LOOK AT YOU, YOU ARE A 'SIS, OR 'BRO! – BUT THEY LOOK AT ME, AND THEY HATE. THIS IS NOT TRUE SISTERHOOD! THIS IS NOT UNITY!"

She assailed them all: "OOHHWEEEEE GOD I WANT *VENGENCE!* JESUS! DESTROY IT BECAUSE IT'S EVIL! RACE IS CORRUPT! THE POWER PEOPLE GIVE TO RACE DIFFERENCE!"

She whirled back to face the stoney face blackman who glared down at her.

"I'M GOD'S PEOPLE! THAT'S THE BLOOD I CLAIM! I DISOWN EVERYBODY ELSE!" And she spat on the sidewalk by his feet; her face in disgust; a grimace, making a downward motion, shoving her hands palm down as if pushing something ugly.

The tall black man opened his mouth; "I am the black sheep of America." He moaned.

"I am not responsible." He shrugged.

"I'm harmless." He shifted his giant weight from one foot to the other.

"My father was white, my mother is Marylin Monroe." He said, holding his hands, black side down, palms up as if to catch the rain and walked away.

Next week in the bar, the bogiouse sister came up to her appologized.

"We each have our own cross to bear." The woman thought. . "she's appologized, but I still have to live with it." The woman left, but the burdon was still on her.

But as I said before, the fight is not between black and white, woman against man, but between some people against some people.

I'm not going to break my heart in a cold white world, or loose my mind in a black stupid one.

Racism – I live it, believe me. I live it more honey, then you can believe; not belonging to anybody's race. *Nobody's.*

My experiences are different then most of yours.

No black complexioned person has ever gone thru the unique hell I go thru.

No white can understand the depth of it.

Only a person who claims the blood of a race they don't look like.

We are something different.

New realization of myself & what I am – an exact defination;

Nobody's people!

But my own self!

It is predicted that eventually race polirazition will cease. As slowly the planet becomes a huge metropolis, intermixing, in supersonic travel & economic exchange; in 10 generations there will be no more black, white, yellow, or red; just a range of brown to tan – a lot with slant eyes.

The bible declares we are all part of each other & all of us are part of God.

Personally I must say, I'm sick of black people. Not black rights, or black struggle which I support; but blackness. And also tired of whiteness and everybody's lousey little supremacy.

So will do the best I can, will sing my guts out on this page!

I take out my pen as a weapon to slay evil social practices which are killing us.

Currently, this is the winter of the soul. Everybody is out for themselves – a human race, humans racing to distruction – not a human family.

Those words which have been said to me were a shellshock, it's strong to think about. The shit I been thru – it's on a daily basis every day, drip drop drip droping acid. Because we live in races and walk in classes and unite in tribes & take up guns against the rest. I can never be free of it in the outside world, but must be free on my inside!

And *these* words in this story, this is my slap back. This is the ass-kick. The payback – translated into finer energy!

My enemys & their insults; I turn them into books. – I also make my enemys look like fools whenever possible.

I could choose the easy way; I too could sit back confortable, adapting the style of the master race; or tan my skin one shade darker and perminite the strands of my hair into curls so I would belong; one in a family of oppressed people and point the finger of scorn. But for all who hate me,

the pen is mightier then the sword.

The stone that was rejected has become the cornorstone.

Joan Cambridge
?1940s–

Brought up in Guyana, where she still lives in the interior, she has worked as a journalist and public relations officer. She has travelled extensively and lived in the USA, Germany and Britain. Clarise Cumberbatch Want to Go Home (1988) is her first novel.

From

Clarise Cumberbatch Want to Go Home

CHAPTER II

S TEEWPPS! Clarise let out a long suckteeth in Kennedy Airport.

Steewpps! Clarise suck her teeth again and start mumbling to herself now.

Eh-eh! Watch me in America? Is me Clarise in America ... But this was not how it was suppose to be. This wasn't how me and Harold did plan it. I shoulda been here with my husband waiting at de airport cause he send for me and later we going send for de children. I wasn't suppose to come here pon my *hardness* so! But I wonder if he still going say to me is lies, is all lies. And he didn't do it cause Leonie is his woman. He do it all for me, for we. And if I did stay home and wait he woulda write me soon and he woulda send for me and de children? I wonder if he would insult me so?

I have to find that man. All these years he gone and I *still* can't rest till we meet eyeball-to-eyeball. I ain't come here to row. I don't want to lick-down and fight-up with Leonie. This time I will make sure that Leonie and me don't butt-up. But I have to find him. He have to look me dead in my eye and tell me he was only fooling me. That he finish with the life we had together. This is justso he going forget he have two lil children that worship the dirt he walk pon. Eh-eh! That could never be. No! After all, is not me only make them. And he was a good father. Is what happen so? Pressure?

Yes, pressure. Pressure coming down pon everybody in Guyana these days. But when you call y'self a man and you swear that man is de greatest creature God ever make, you can't just blame everything pon de government and run away and gone justso without a word. If I use to complain to him bout pressure coming down pon me in that house trying to make de two cents he give me stretch to feed all o' we, plus buy school uniform for five hundred dollars and lil peas to nourish them children brain for eight dollars a pint with the pint-measure stuff up with newspaper underneath?

Steewpps! Clarise suck her teeth again. If I use to tell Harold all that? Is what he woulda done, eh? He woulda got away earlier. Cause if he can't stand his own pressure is what if he had to hear bout mine?

Clarise remembering now that all Harold use to do when she tell him the price of things is throw back his head and laugh like if he going mad and then start to sing: "Ban-um, Mr Burnham, ban-um."

But what I was to do? Run away? Justso? Abandon my home and gone away? Leave my children? My country? My husband? Cause pressure too much? Without evenself a explanation self? To he or anybody?

No! No! Is not so. That man in trouble, I telling you. He have to be in some sort of trouble or else he couldn't acting so. I know he in trouble. Is almost three years since he gone, and he ain't write one letter yet. Not *one single* letter, one *word* self. . .

"No!" Clarise say loud loud in the people airport. But she thought she say it in her mind; she didn't know she say it out loud till a woman with a wheelbarrow full of grips look round and say, "Yes?"

"No, not you, miz-lady. I not talking to you." And the woman look at her like she think Clarise crazy.

Then Clarise collect her grip from the merry-go-round. She poke in the clothes that spilling out the sides and she tie back the rope. Now all she have in her mind is passing through customs quick so she could go out in America and meet Mavis. Mavis mustbe waiting already. Thank God for Mavis Drakes. Mavis is Clarise friend. She understand what Clarise going through. She never did like Harold.

When Clarise write and tell Mavis she coming to America to search for Harold and she want somewhere to stay? Mavis write back and say that Clarise welcome to stay with her, but she not going to help her to find Harold cause she not encouraging her to find him.

In another letter Clarise tell Mavis that she trying hard to forget Harold but she still love him. Mavis write back:

"Clarise, you should thank your lucky stars that you got rid of that good-for-nothing Harold Cumberbatch. But if you say you still love him, that is the cross you will have to bear alone."

And is so Clarise picking up her canvasbag from the ground and her bust-up grip from the merry-go-round and putting them pon the wheelbarrow and rolling them off to the customsman at the counter with her mind telling her over and over and over again,

Clarise chile? You tired. Y'tired, tired, tired. The *Lawd knows* how you tired, Clarise.

"Anything to declare?"

"To declare? Lemme see. . . Nothing, sir. Nothing. Only that it cold. It cold bad, sir. I hope my friend Mavis bring de coat like she promise, cause I ain't accustom to no coldness. I come from Guyana, y'know?"

"What's that, ma'am?"

"I say in Guyana we don't have no coldness and it cold here. That is all I have to declare, sir. Is that it cold here."

And a dirtyskin Portuguese boy bust-out a big-laugh and say, "Hey! That's *dynamite*, man!"

But the customsman he not laughing at all. All Clarise seeing is rain setting-up in his face.

He saying, "I mean, do you have any gifts? Any plants? Alcohol? Fruits? Gold? Currency?"

"Ohhh! Oh-ho!" Clarise say. "I see . . . ha-ha ha-ha! Y'know what I did think? I did think you asking me what I have to declare bout de place? If I have anything to say bout America? And I say to m'self, Well, is how he expect me to say anything bout de place, eh? Is what I could know? I only just come. All I know is that it cold. It cold baaad!"

"Ma'am? Sorry, I didn't understand what you just said."

"Oh, no! You don't be sorry bout that, mister. I did know that would happen *before* I come here, cause I never learn to talk American. And I can't *understand* it, either. I have to strain my ears to hear what you saying. It ain't easy, but I know I have to try. Before I come a friend tell me that what I have to do is stand in front de mirror and practice to talk American, and she show me, like: *Haw aaarrre yah?* And talking in my nose like a cat. But I didn't have time for all that nonsense, so I never learn to do it right. And anyway, when I hear m'self sounding so stupid? I just —"

"You're holding up the line, ma'am."

"Don't mind me," the dirtyskin Portuguese boy say. "I have all the time in the world, and I'm *enjoying* this."

The customsman cutting-up his eye pon the dirtyskin Portuguese boy.

"Ohhh! Sorry! Sorry, sorry," Clarise saying, looking round at the rest of the people waiting. "Sorry, son," she say to the boy waiting in the line behind her. From behind the boy where two women just roll up she hear one long suckteeth and somebody saying:

"*Steeewwppps!* People like them do *really* embarrass me."

"Yes, country-come-to-town."

When you see so? Them-two mustbe just come back from showing off pon people or robbing them in Guyana, Clarise say to herself. She feel like turning back and saying to them, *Hey, allyuh-two ass-holes! This here not no ordinary town, this country come to, this here is America. This na Stabroek Market Square in Georgetown that me see with these two eyes how it could confuse buckman just come out de bush. This here is Kennedy Airport in New York and I never see nothing so yet in my livelong life and when allyuh did come first? Mustbe so y'all did feel, too. Cause a just-come is a just-come whenever you done.*

But Clarise say to herself that she is a woman know time and place, so she ain't say a word to them. She just tell the boy sorry and turn back to the customsman.

"Yes, mister, lemme see what I have..." And if you did see what Clarise start taking out Miz Goring canvasbag...

Is six green mangoes: "These is for my neighbor Miz Goring daughter. She getting baby and she write home to tell her mother how her mind steady calling for green mango with salt-and-pepper and she want to make achar, too."

In some corn-hassar wrap up in newspaper: "This is a sweet fish. It nice in curry or y'could cook it in dryfood, y'know? With ground-provisions ... metagee."

Is a plastic bottle with peppersauce.

Is another plastic bottle with the mouth seal-up with tape: "Casareep for de pepperpot. It does preserve de meat, make it last longer. All y'have to do is warm it up."

Is a bottle of XM Rum, Gold Medal: "To burn Mavis throat in all this cold weather. I hear you can't get good rum like this over here."

Is bush-pon-top-of-bush. Bush for tea, bush for medicine, purge, bush for seasoning. Is teesam, daisy, marrio-man-poke and sweetbroom. Is lemmon-grass and pear-leaf.

"Is that all?" the customsman say after he listen to Clarise telling him bout the things she spreading out pon the counter.

This time? The two women who talk bout how Clarise embarrass them? Not only embarrass now, they frighten somebody might think they like her cause they have Guyana passport like her. They give up they space in the line. They gone along to another line.

"That is all, sir," Clarise say.

The customsman breathe hard. "We'll have to take the fruit ..." and he start to pick up the green mangoes and put them aside.

Eh-eh! Well, what is this at all? Clarise voice ringing like a bell:

"No, mister! No! Ow, sir! Is how you could do such a thing? What I going to tell Miz Goring? Look! She was so nice to lend me her nice canvasbag to put everything in. That poor girl! Her mind is *calling!* Mister, you is a man, *you* don't know, you could *never* know what it is to get belly and your mind steady calling, calling for something you want to eat that you can't get. But *let me tell you*, sir, my mind use to call for black-pudding steady steady when I was getting Clarence. And one day? One day I walk three miles! *Five months pregnant,* just to – "

"Lady!" the customsman say sharp sharp, cutting Clarise.

But Clarise say quick quick before the man could talk, "Scuse me lil, sir, not to say I cutting you, but all I trying to say is that that poor girl baby is going to mark! Her baby is going to *mark*, mister, if she don't get these mangoes! She *expecting* them!"

"Lady, you can't bring fresh fruit or plants into the country. That's the law."

"Ohhh! Is de law? I didn't know was de law, sir. I didn't know was gainst de law."

The customsman say nothing. He take-out what he want and push aside the rest of Clarise things and then he turn his attention to the dirtyskin Portuguese boy haversack and start ransacking it like if he know what he looking for, and he sure he going find it.

"Clarise! Clarise!"

"Clarise Cumberbatch! Look me here! This side!"

Is so Clarise hearing her name calling in a daze, in a haze, cause she staring just staring with her mouth open and she thinking:

Is where they does put all these people when they go out de airport? America mustbe have plenty space. And watch how everything rush rush! How everybody hurry hurry!

Eh-eh!

Is why everybody here so hurry so? Is where they going so fast? Is everybody catching plane and all them late for it? Lawd! Mustbe *fire*? Mustbe fire make them hurry so? And watch this thing! Eh-eh! And that is not a *whiteman*? Is a whiteman, yes! And *that* is the work he doing? I never see whitepeople working laboring work before. And watch one there mopping-up de floor. Eh-eh! But what is this at all? And is where is de fire? That is what I want to know, is where de fire is.

Clarise shiver, then she remember that Mavis say she mustn't come out the airport till she bring her a coat.

"Clarise! Is me calling you. What happen to you? Like you gone deaf or something? Is me, Mavis!"

Is Mavis?

Eh-eh! Mavis dress-up high in high-heel shoe that come back in style. Mavis have on nice nice wig and wintercoat with fur collar like what you see people wearing in the photographs in the magazines and in the pictures pon the matinee screen. Mavis have on hat with feather!

Eh-eh! Mavis look nice!

Mavis always use to look nice, but now she look like a *real* American. Mavis take off that one gold chain she use to wear round her neck day-in-day-out till she send it to talk putagee in the pawnshop. That Portuguese man Mr Fernandes get rich off the interest Mavis pay on that chain. Cause regular regular you could mark it absent from her neck when things bad with her. Them was the hand-to-mouth days before she leave Guyana. Now watch Mavis! Just look at her!

Mavis have on a nice necklace to match her earrings. Mavis look *prosperous!*

And is so Clarise stand-up watching Mavis surprise! Eh-eh! Mavis look like a *real* American!

"Take care your eye don't drop out, hear?" Mavis say to Clarise and throw the coat round her shoulder and hug Clarise tight, laughing and saying, "Clarise! Clarise chile, y'come! Clarise in New York at last!"

"Eh-eh! Mavis? Mavis is really you?"

"Yeah, Clarise, is me. But what you watching me so for? I thief your mother white fowl?"

And Clarise laugh and hug-up Mavis. And Mavis laugh and hug-up Clarise. And then they start to talk. . . .

J. California Cooper

?1940s-

*A*merican-born, she has written seventeen plays, many of which have been produced on stage, public television, radio and college campuses (in 1978 she was named Black Playwright of the Year for her play Strangers) and is the author of three collections of fiction, A Piece of Mine *(1984),* Homemade Love *(1987) and* Some Soul to Keep

(1988). Alice Walker (whose Wild Trees Press published her first book) says: "In its strong folk flavor, Cooper's work reminds us of Langston Hughes and Zora Neale Hurston. Like theirs, her style is deceptively simple and direct, and the vale of tears in which some of her characters reside is never so deep that a rich chuckle at a foolish person's foolishness cannot be heard. It is a delight to read her stories, to come upon a saying like 'There ain't no sense beatin round the bush with the fellow who planted it,' and to know it will be with you perhaps for ever." She lives in Oakland.

Swingers and Squares

A IN'T life funny? This life thing will drive you crazy, if you let it! Me? I'm a hundred-degree woman and I ain't goin to let it! But life is funny, and some people don't know how to live it! They fools! They just come here and breathe and go thru the motions, as they say, then get on way from here! Ain't done nothing! Ain't lived! They just squares! I know, cause I got a window to one right here, next door, my neighbor. Not like me! I meant to do my livin and I have!

Now, like love. Oh, how sweet love is! I love love . . . all kinds of love! Any love, anytime, anyplace, chile! See? You got to taste of life! That what the books say. That's what I done and I ain't sorry one bit!

Take my friend next door. She been married to the same man twenty or twenty-five years! I don't know exactly cause I been busy living and ain't had time to know *all* her business. But I do know I ain't never ever seen her in a bar or no places to meet nobody else! Sho ain't gon' meet nobody else in church with that man sitting up side of her!

I remember when we was all younger and just getting married and all. Her husband was nice-looking. They made a nice-looking couple . . . got to give em that! But, honey, me and my husband, we was good-looking! My husband was fine, fine, fine. Didn't turn out to be worth nothing, but he sure was fine! Tall, big shoulders, football player-looking shoulders! Head full of hair and a smile to break your heart for days! He wore a big rhinestone ring trying to be a diamond, and cufflinks to match. Tried to smoke cigars. Wore them pointy-toe shoes. Oh, he was sharp! A heartbreaker! And that's what he did . . . broke my heart! Ten months we was together. That's all! Them women wouldn't leave him alone! I tried to keep up with him, going to all them parties and nightclubs and hanging round the pool hall, but I couldn't! I had one baby and one on the way when he left! Ohhh, I missed him! He had a way of slapping your hips when he made love. Hurt . . . but I loved it! Been looking for it, just never found it again. Yeah, I tried to keep him, but he didn't have good sense enough to try to keep a good woman like me, giving him a family! He never did nothing for me or his kids after that, cept once in a *big* while! He still round here! I know where he is. Right up there on that hill, done married a widow woman had a house! He got a real diamond now!

When I got home with my second baby from the county hospital, Lana, that's my neighbor, was just getting home with her first. He must didn't never make love to her if it took two years to have one child! I remember he carried her up the steps. Ain't that silly?! Her mama was carrying the baby and he was carrying her! Ain't that cute? Shit! Two years later they had another baby. And so did I! Me, three. Them, two. She said they planned theirs. Mine was a accident. Right in the middle of my good times! Chile, I was having a ball!

I had a little ole tiny job at the Hoot Owl niteclub and the lady next door watched my kids til they went to sleep. When I would get in in the morning I'd be so tired, but I'd fix them some toast and fall in bed and sleep while they play. See, the important thing is somebody in the house with em. That ole grown-ass daughter of mine messed it up once by burning herself half up when I was sleep! I'd been drinking and it was hard to wake me up. Well, I hafta drink doing the kind of job I do, keeping customers happy! Anyway, she made me so mad! Then she had to go running over to Lana's, and Lana put the fire out and even took her to the doctor's when she couldn't wake me up! Wasn't even my doctor! Cost me $30! I still owe it! I tole her to stay out of my business! Then I gave my daughter a good whipping for playing with fire and ruining my sleep! Hell! I had to go back to work, didn't I? I was sure glad when they got big enough to take care of themselves and the new baby!

Lana was always so silly! Didn't have a big thought in her head! Now, she sent her children to dancing school and them poor kids had to go take piano music lessons three times a week. And do you think she even let them be free after that? No, chile! Even in the summertime they had to come in the house by 6:30, light outside or not! My daughter told me! See, you got to have some sense and trust your kids. I trust my kids. They could stay out and play till 10:00 or 11:00, cause I remember how much fun I use to have playing! I didn't mess up my kids' fun! You got to remember when you was a child, when you get to be a parent! Sides, I had to work! I had to trust em!

Then when all the kids got measles and whooping cough and all them things? Lana practicly kept a doctor at her house. All that money! Me, I rubbed baking soda and water on my kids and taught them how to do each other. They came out all right ... just a few marks on they faces and backs and arms. But look at the money I saved! Didn't have it anyway! You got to dress when you work at a niteclub! Besides, I had a problem cause my son had started taken my clothes to sell to get sweets and things to eat! He wasn't never no good! Just like his daddy! Waiting till I leave, then be taken my clothes! Well, you do the best you can as a mother, but it don't do you no good! They don't preciate it!

Well, the years passed and that Lana hadn't progressed or changed one bit. Still doing the same ole things! Only difference was she was staying home now, not working. Just staying home fixing lunch for them kids and making them come home from school, walk three blocks, to eat lunch! Said they needed something hot when I told her she could be restin. Told you she was dumb! Kids can take a lot, and don't need a lot! Some folks just ain't got no sense!

I could tell what time it was, if I was home, by the time they turned their lights off! At 10:00 at night all the lights go out except the bathroom light they always leave on. She didn't never go nowhere! I know cause one of my daughters practicly lived there. She wouldn't let her daughter spend the night over here tho! That ole bitch! Just cause I had a man over here for the night sometime! Scared her chile gon learn somethin new! Ain't I human? She probably needed to learn somethin new sides all that boring stuff she had over there at home. Jive-time stuff!

Do you know, when them kids got to be teenagers, her kids was still wearing all them starched, stiff dresses? All that work? I'm telling you that woman Lana was a fool! Now, I got good sense as anybody and I know kids don't pay no mind to what they wearing! I let mine go down there to the secondhand store and pick out what they wanted. That's what being a kid is all about! Learning to choose stuff, do something different! Doing things for themselves! I couldn't work that hard round the house no more. I had had bout fifteen miscarriage, well, that's what I called em! And since I still had to work at the bar, I needed my strength for better, more important things than standing up over no ironing board doing dresses and things. Let em learn how to do their own, anyway! That's how they get to know bout life!

My son started staying out nights bout then. Well, boys will be boys! I don't want no sissy! He sposed to be a man someday! One day when I was laying out in the backyard sunning and having a cold beer with a friend and was talking bout having the landlord clean up this yard cause it was a mess, Lana called to me over the fence. I was so comfortable, but I got up and went to see what she wanted. She told me her husband saw my son hanging over there by the pool hall everyday when he should be in school, and sometimes very late at night when he should be in bed! Now, her husband works for the gas company and gets around quite a bit. I told her to mind her own business and tell her husband to mind his too! I'll run my family! Just run her own! Made me mad! In front of my company! My son wasn't gon be nothing but like his daddy, noway! I knew he was gonna have womens taken care of him someday. Wasn't he already using me? I tole him . . . "make em pay!" I don't want him laying on me all his life! He sure was good-lookin enough. Lana was just jealous cause she didn't have no son! Uh-huh! I had somethin she didn't have.

Bout that time Lana's husband got down real sick . . . some accident on the job, I think. He had to stay home in the bed. That Lana went on out and got a job! A job! I said to myself, "Good! Let's see how you make it out here stead of hiding in them four walls, you so smart! Thought you'd buy a house, huh? Now, let's see you pay them notes!"

Well, she worked while he just layed around the house! I said to myself again, "I bet them kids don't come home for lunch no more!" But they did! And I thought them starched white blouses and things would go too, but they didn't! The oldest girl and her daddy did it! Slaves! She was raisen a slave! And makin a woman outa her man! Ain't life funny?

Time passed and everything got back to normal, I guess.

Then the school cital or recital, whatever it was, it came up. My daughter, who hangs over to Lana's house all the time, worried me to death to go. Finally my boyfriend, at that time, told me to go, so I did. Honey, you could have blown me away when I looked up on that stage and saw my daughter singing! Alone! She wasn't singing nothing I liked or even knew, but she was singing pretty! "Look what I have done," I thought. I was so proud! One of Lana's daughter played the piano and the other played the violin with her singing. They played through the whole show, with her and everybody else! I got tired of them. They was alright but nothing special. Lana and her husband were there, of course, just grinning at the stage like fools! When the show was over and them kids ran to them, they grabbed them and said, "These are my daughters!" and the daughters said, "This is my mama! This is my daddy!" My daughter ran to them too, til I waved at her, then she came over to where I was. She didn't holler out that I was her mama, but she ask me to meet her teachers. I looked around me and pulled on out of there. I told her, "Honey, I done told them teachers so many lies, I don't want them to see me!" I laughed and thought she would, but she didn't! Too much hanging round Lana's house! She was losing her sense of humor! I told everybody at the bar about her later, but they didn't believe me!

High School graduation time came and, of course, my daughter needed a dress ... a white one! She liked to drove me crazy! See, my nerves is bad! I mean it! I told her I had a red dress she could wear, pretty dress, off the shoulders and all! She didn't want that. She cried and flung herself all over the house! I had to leave there to get some peace sometime! Just go on and go to work early, that's what I'd do. I knew my other, younger daughter was stealing, and I was wishing she would steal one for her sister to wear to graduation. But that fool never caught on and a person can't *tell* her daughter to steal! Hell, least not me, I ain't that kind of mama!

Lana, finally, said she would make one for her to graduate in if *we* bought the material! Ain't that something! If you gon do something, do it all! Do it right! Have some class bout yourself! Ain't life funny? Some people just don't know from nothing, and she was always acting like she knew everything! Anyway, we got the material some kind of way, and Lana made the dress. I didn't get to go to the graduation tho, I had a awful hangover and couldn't move my head. See, I'm not well. I been through a lot ... all by myself? Lana done had help – a husband. My daughter was beautiful tho, they told me bout it!

Problems never end, honey! My daughter wanted to go to college! Seems Lana's daughter was going. I told my child she better wake up and see what's happnin! College ain't nothing! I could help her get a job at the club where I work, but I never could be able to send her to no college! It wasn't gon help her no way! She had already done more than anybody in our family had ever done when she graduated from high school! Hell!

She settled down and pouted around the house for a month or so. Wouldn't take that job at the club! It all ended up with her marrying up with a soldier and she lived in Germany. I heard from her sometime. She divorced, but still lived and worked over there. Won't come home! She didn't get no babies. She smart, that one! My other daughter had three! Dropped out of school, married some jive-time boy, just like her daddy! Ain't life funny? No matter what I do I can't get they daddy out of them! That's what cause all their troubles! My son went to prison.

Well, time goes on by.

My oldest daughter never has come back home and she comes over here to New York sometimes. She's married again, some half-rich educated man she met in Italy. I think that's where she lives now. She got two children now I've never seen! They don't know they grandmama! A child should know the grandmama! My daughter don't send me no money either! Never! And I'm her mama ... raised her! And she know I need it! I wrote her and told her bout my troubles. Back gone out ... knees all swollen from arthritis and all! All these things I got working to support my kids! Being a mother! That Lana turned my baby against me, that's what! I shoulda kept her away from over there!

My other daughter got five kids now and she always trying to leave em here with me! I say, "Uh-uh, uh-uh! No, you don't! I raised mine, now you raise yours!" She be drunk and she try to fight me sometimes! She living with her fifth man! I tell her, "Fight him!" I have to call the police sometime! No matter how you raise them, they ain't gon come out right if it ain't in em! My son was out for a while from that prison, but he back in again now. When he was out, he got drunk and came over here and tried to get in bed with me! Said everyone else had! The liar! If my boyfriend, at that time, hadn't come in, I'd a had to fight my own son! As it was, he left, telling my friend not to "fall in, cause you'll never find your way out like I did!" Ain't that terrible? Do everything you can and still ... Ain't life funny?

I know you want to know, so I'll tell you! Lana's daughters. One lives in New York. Done married up with somebody big and travels a lot. She in concerts and things. The other one teaches in some college, married to some professor! Ain't done nothing but marry and settle down to slavery just like their mama! That's what you go to college for? To get married?! That's phoney! Me, I ain't no phoney! I'm for real!

Lana? I still think she stupid sometime. Her husband went back to work and worked til he retired. Ain't never done nothing big! Them two people still over there, next door, after all these years! I don't care if they did fix it up and added rooms to it and all. They put up a big fence between us on accounta my landlord never did clean up that yard! It's a mess! They take trips and all that square stuff and keep their grandchildren. Four, I believe. They repeating all the things they already done. Starched dresses and shirts and hot lunches! And smiling about it! Ain't life funny?

It's some people in this world never do learn! I rather be a swinger any day than be one of them squares! They fools and don't know it! Ain't life funny?

I got to rest now ... I hurt!

Jane Tapsubei Creider

?1940s–

S *he grew up near Lake Nyanza (formerly Lake Victoria), Kenya,
and, after working in Kisumu and Nairobi, went to live in Canada.
She and her American husband have two children. She works as an
artist in clay sculpture in London, Ontario, and has written articles on
the language and culture of her people, the Nandi. Her autobiography*
Two Lives: My Spirit and I *– extracted here – was published in 1986.*

From

Two Lives: My Spirit and I

I N my spirit life I was tall, beautiful, slender, long-limbed and brown-skinned,
with a well-shaped head, fine features, an attractive smile, kinky black hair,
and a stubborn character indeed.

About eighty years ago, Nandi customs were still followed rigidly and were
not scattered from sunrise to sunset the way they are now. It didn't matter how
powerful you were or how stubborn you were, you had to follow the traditional
rules. So I tried to be a good wife to my husband. We lived well, ate well, and
we agreed on almost everything. After a while I learned not to be bothered by
his age. My husband learned to look after cattle and to live like a Nandi. He was
even better than a Nandi because he used to help me with all kinds of work.
Perhaps men and women helped each other in this way in the country he had
come from.

Eventually we had a son, Marat Chok. The wealth of my family continued to
expand. Father had given me three goats when I got married and now there
were six. It was the same with the sheep and the cattle. By that time, however,
my father had passed away, and my brother made it very clear that it was his
wealth and that I could not just do what I wanted with it. For example, I couldn't
slaughter a goat or a cow for visiting friends without asking him. Sometimes I
would get no for an answer, which had never happened when my father was
alive.

I began to realize that I had started out with nothing and was going to end
up with nothing. It made me even sadder to think that my son might have the
same problems. I decided I would have to do something about it. One evening
I asked my husband, "What should we do? You know we have a son now, and
he must have things to begin his life with."

My husband told me that his people lived from day to day by hunting. They didn't plan for tomorrow or next week. Our son would be taught to live in the same way – I was not very happy to hear that.

In those days a woman lived only in the company of other women. You couldn't go and ask a man to help you raid cattle. Raiding was a dangerous business, many men lost their lives and no man would take a woman along. But raiding was the only thing I could do to have something of my own and to give my son a better future.

I had an idea of which people to raid from. Our custom didn't allow us to steal from our own and closely related tribes. One day I reached the decision to go raiding, by myself.

I headed into the trackless wilderness. There was no map, and I was guided only by the sun. I knew I was to go west. I would follow the sunset until I reached a place called Chemng'orng'or, the border between Nandi and another group of tribes called the Luyia. I didn't take anything with me except for some small gourds in which I carried a little milk. But it didn't matter really, for I had good looks, good manners and good health. I must have been very young, maybe about twenty, and attractive, because everywhere I went, people tried to make me stay with them. I would stay a couple of days, or until I found out how to get further towards my destination, and then I would disappear.

I travelled like that across the wilderness until I reached a place called Kapkeben. The people there spoke like the Nandi, but with a very strong accent so that sometimes a Nandi had trouble understanding them. I found a man gardening, and asked him if he knew of a place called Chemng'orng'or.

"Yes, I do," he said, and I asked him how far it was. He told me that it was about a mile and a half, and he asked me if I knew anyone there.

"No," I said. "I just want to see it. I've heard that there are some big caves there."

He knew that I didn't belong to his tribe, the Terik, so he asked me if I had some relatives to stay with. I said that I didn't but that I was sure I would find some place to stay for a few days until I had seen the caves, and then I would go back. He asked me to stay with him.

The country was very dry and full of rocks. It was so poor that people always wanted to leave to go to Mosop which is where I came from. This made me feel that the family I was staying with were not enemies so I asked them if they knew where someone could go to raid. They said yes, so I made a deal with Terigin, one of the sons of the family. I told him that if he helped me to go raiding and if we succeeded, I would take him back with me to Mosop so that he could start a new life in that rich land. He agreed right away.

We started immediately to plan our route and our course of action. I was given a sword and spear, a warrior's traditional equipment, and we set off. We travelled until we reached Chemng'orng'or, and the first thing we saw was a lot of sheep. The shepherd taking care of them was sleeping. I called Terigin and told him, "This is it. We won't go any further, we'll just take these animals."

"Oh, no," he said. "We haven't reached the place we are going to yet. These sheep belong to Terik. They are people just like me, and I speak the same language they do."

"You're not doing this for yourself," I said. "You're doing it for me. You take care of the sheep, and I'll look after the shepherd."

He didn't disagree any more, but pulled out his sword, and started taking the sheep. The shepherd was still asleep when we left. When we had gone about two miles we heard the sound of someone running after us. I told my friend to go ahead with the sheep and that I would deal with the shepherd. I pulled aside and waited behind a bush. When he came alongside me I grabbed him around his shoulders. He looked at me and started laughing, out of fear.

"Don't be afraid," I told him. "Tell me what you are running for."

"I'm running after my sheep," he said. "Did you see them?"

"Yes," I said, "I met a lot of men carrying weapons and taking sheep, and I'm sure some of them are still around. If I were you I wouldn't move from here."

I left the shepherd staring after me, open mouthed. Then I went after the sheep. When Terigin saw me he asked, "How did you get away from him?" He thought I must have killed the shepherd because I had a sword.

"I didn't kill him," I told my friend, "if that's what you're thinking."

"What happened?" he asked. "Did he get away from you?"

"No," I said. "I left him with the understanding that he wasn't to follow us."

My friend was afraid that the shepherd would get more men to come after us. I decided to go on in a different direction, hoping that he would be less afraid, but it didn't seem to help. Terigin wanted us to go in the direction of Mosop. But I wanted to plunge to the south-east into a great unknown forest called Kaimosi. I knew the forest was very dangerous, and we would be less likely to be followed there. People used to believe the forest was inhabited by animals called *kerinik* ("Nandi bears") that could grab people and eat their brains out, and by monsters called *chemosinik* who were people by day and animals by night that could swallow a person whole. I just planned to pray to my ancestors telling them, "*Omuta mutyo leye koinya ondowa.*" "Take me slowly, people of my family. Go ahead of me and scare away everything that wants to hurt me."

But Terigin didn't want to trust to luck any more, and he became really angry at me.

"I have no feeling of gratitude from you at all," he said. "I think you are stubborn and I have decided that you have the wrong personality for me. I had better let you go your way, and I go mine."

Between you and me I think he was afraid of the monsters in the forest. I told him that was all right with me, and I gave him directions to my home. There were no roads in those days and one gave directions by telling the person what country he would pass through on his way to where he was going.

I parted with him in mid-afternoon at a place called Siginwai. He went back to his home, and I headed towards the forest. I had decided to sleep at a place called Chebaraa and to go through the forest in the morning. I was hoping that the monster-animals would have gone to sleep for the day.

Meanwhile, people at home were asking everybody they met if they had seen me. Some people would say, "We saw her heading that way." My relatives went on asking until they worked out that I had gone to Chemng'orng'or and eventually they reached Terigin's home.

He told them I had been there but that I had left after I'd got what I came for.

Now no one from home knew what I had come for and they learned from my friend that I had gone raiding. They were very surprised because they thought I had run away for some unknown reason or for one of the usual reasons like a drunken or nagging husband.

Terigin told them everything. Since he knew where I was heading, he asked my people if he could go with them to show them the road. They agreed, and they all set off after me.

Meanwhile, I marched through the forest with my sheep safely. My dream was starting to come true. At that point I was no longer afraid of the enemy coming after me or of animals eating me up. I was in Nandi land, and all I had to do was walk slowly and let the sheep graze. My relatives were behind me following the spoor of the sheep through the forest and when they realized that I had got through safely they were very relieved. They decided to hurry home to tell people not to worry, that Tapsubei was coming. The trip to Mosop from there would take a person travelling alone only about an hour, but sheep are impossible to hurry. They never walk straight but go in a group sticking their heads together and meandering all over the place. So the trip of one hour took me an entire afternoon, and I got home in the evening.

When I got there everybody was waiting to cheer for me. My son, husband, brother, his wife, other relatives, and Terigin were all waiting for me to celebrate. When the celebration was finished, life went back to normal. I went back to being a housewife and my husband went on looking after cattle and sheep. Terigin decided to seek a new life in Nandi country because that was what he had always wanted. Land in Nandi country was not owned privately in those days. People used just to move around wherever they wanted. For a non-native, however, it was not so simple. He could be killed by Nandi people thinking he was an enemy trying to raid cattle. Therefore we had to adopt Terigin. That was the only thing we could do so that he could live freely like anyone else, move around, raid with other men, marry a Nandi girl, and have a home.

Barbara Makhalisa

?1940s–

Born in Zimbabwe, she studied at Gweru Teachers' College, majoring in English. Since 1969 she has had four books published in Ndebele and one, The Underdog and Other Stories (1984), in English.

Different Values

HELLO! – Ah, Clara, your voice sounded different, I thought it was your madam. Well, I'm so bored. Yes, well a few minutes back I was huffing and puffing away playing a game with Popi. Let me get a chair, hold on please! Hello! Oh, as usual! As it is, Popi is standing by the door, tongue out, drooling, waiting for me to come and resume the game. – Mh! – But I have to! – Yes, daily! – Of course! Anyone passes by and sees me racing Popi up and down the lawn, rolling with her and doing all sorts of silly little pranks would think I was a fifteen-year-old who was having a whirl of a time and had a lot of extra energy to burn away. Of course not! – I'm thirty-two, silly! – But it's a job, and I must do it! – Mh! – Yes, everyday, heh-heh! Can't you see that I have shelled off some of the extra fat? That is the only benefit I get for my efforts, though I am not particularly grateful, because I just hate it all. You know I've always hated dogs, – Yes, the worst of it is that Popi has no dog house outside so she sleeps in the kitchen. Her toilet is in the kitchen. – You just have never seen the likes of the mess which I have to clean up daily from the kitchen. And to think I cook their food in the same room! – No, no, no you are better because you have to contend with human mess. You have been a mother yourself, and there is nothing unnatural about that. At my home Popi would live outdoors and take care of his own mess. But here... – Yes, well, you've seen the likes of Popi all over. They're so precious, our *baases* would rather share the inside of a car with them than with their gardeners. What? – Poison Popi? – Don't be ridiculous! – I have two children to think about at home, cared for by my poor mother, to whom I must send money and food every month. Do you think I play with Popi for fun? – Call me what you will but I am paid for it just as you are paid to wash little Lolly's soiled nappies and the rest of it. One can't complain in the circumstances. Yes, and you know some of our friends do not even get the minimum wage still. Oh that... No! Do you think he'll ever change? Some of us who have not a bean to our names are better off than that woman, I tell you. Indeed yes! Tina was telling me only the other day that her Aunt came to visit them last Friday and did not stay the weekend through. Why? – How could she? – Although she lives in the communal area she is well off by communal people's standards. Tina says she complained that she could not live on vegetables from the garden when they had more than five hundred fowls cackling in the big fowl run. I'm not joking! – No, it was her very first visit to them, and the poor woman dared not slaughter one of the fowls to provide relish for her Aunt without his permission. He's a proper miser, that man is! Oh yes, she still goes to work. My dear – don't you be deceived by all this outward gloss and high and mighty airs about education from abroad. Some of these educated husbands like "Miser" treat their wives in the most atrocious fashion. Tina actually told me that the poor woman does not even touch her salary. It all goes into his fat bank book and she only gets a little pocket money at a time, which hardly sees her through the month. – Housekeeping? – Of course he buys the groceries, only a little of everything every week and is forever snapping at her for over using mealie-meal and all. Ha-ha! I laugh but it's not funny! – Yes – that's why those children are only ribs sticking out of their chests. Yes, probably that good furniture and other property in there are all for outward show and prestige, you know. – Shocking! – Of course she is highly educated. – Yes, she works in one of the big offices in town. – Well, I don't know whether it's love or fear of him. Goodness knows what she ever saw in a miser like him. – Yes. – Probably. – Well, if I were that educated, I don't see what I should be begging for in a man like that miser! – Oh yes, I've heard it too. It's true. I've heard from very reliable sources that she is not permitted to call him by his first name, yet all the office girls use his first name. – Imagine! I wonder what she used to call him when he was courting her. Oh yes, I've heard that one too, and have never seen her wearing lipstick yet she used to before she got married. But the girls he goes out with do. – It beats me! I wonder what he feels when other men are in the company of their dear wives at the parties he goes to. – Men! – Hey – hang on let me check. . . sounds like my madam's car! Hello! – No, it wasn't. Get off Popi! Come on, get off! Out, you beast! Out! I am coming in a minute! – Well, yes. He was tugging at my clothes as if he might tear them to pieces. – Mh, he still wants to play. – Aha! – Actually, is your madam in this morning? I know she is not finicky but we've been on the phone for ages. – Not again! – To the doctor's? That bad! – Honestly he'll kill her one of these days. – Buy why? – Yes, indeed, it's a mystery because I have seen them quite a few times together, and he behaves just like a proper gentleman. – Yes. That's why sometimes I tell myself that I should stay put and never worry about marriage. – What's the point? – Well, in a way. I agree it is every girl's wish to get the best deal in marriage. – Yes, a few people are lucky and experience bliss in marriage, but the bulk of unhappy marriages I notice is most discouraging. – Mh? – You think it's *muti*? – Might be! I for one cannot understand the *muti* science, but I believe people can do a lot of evil with it. You think it's the girls who are trying to displace her? – Yes. Possible. – What's that? – Alcoholic? – I don't understand. You mean, a little sip just makes his sense snap? – Really? – Well, well, I do not believe that. How many drunks do we see about who are hardly ever violent to their wives? – Hmm? – Her relatives have advised her to go to a *n'anga* to dispel the spell? – I don't know whether that is the best thing to do because most of these *n'angas* just cheat people out of their money. – Mh? – Set a thief to catch a thief? – Maybe, but I've seen many homes break and friends becoming enemies because of *n'angas*. – Poor woman – I feel so sorry for her because she's so sweet, she does not deserve such beastly treatment. – Yes, you were lucky unlike some of us here. – Hm? – What's that? No, thank you, my friend. Not at that hour! – Why not? I don't want to be caught in the snares of this notorious crackdown on suspected prostitutes. – Well, it's no longer a free for all world you know. We live in a men's world, and have to toe the line. – Yes, but do women commit the so-called crime on their own? – My *baas* and madam were discussing the issue yesterday, and I heard them say many advanced countries have tried to stamp out prostitution and have not really achieved abounding success. It is an age-old social cancer, they said. – Yes, well, I agree, but then the way it was done leaves one with a sour taste in the mouth. Imagine yourself window-shopping at about 7.00 in the evening, or going to catch a bus to visit your Auntie and you suddenly find yourself surrounded and turned from your way into a dreary truck, and the following day you are in Mushumbi Pools.

No, no, no, they were randomly picking up every woman they came across, guilty or innocent – and were not listening to explanations. Yes, I feel so sorry for some decent mums. It is agony for both their children at home and them. – Yes. – Well, I'm not taking any chances. If I am arrested, goodness knows how long I'd be kept before I was freed. I'd probably find my job gone, given to another. Oh, oh, madam's car! Bye!

"Good afternoon, madam?" very respectfully.

"Afternoon! Has Popi had enough exercise, Liza?"

"Yes, madam."

"I don't think so. He looks very restless."

"But, madam, I played with him for over an hour and have since sprained my ankle. I've been rubbing and rubbing it. I can no longer run, and I have to start on the ironing now."

"Where's Tommy?"

"He's watering the new flowers, madam."

"Tommy! Tommy!"

"Madam!"

Tommy runs in and stands before our mistress.

"Tommy when you finish with the new flowers, please race Popi for about 30 minutes. He's still restless and Liza has sprained her ankle."

Tommy glares at me, and I turn away without batting an eyelid and limp painfully towards the laundry room.

"Liza!"

"Madam!"

"You've been on my phone again!"

"No, madam!"

"Look at that!"

"But, madam, should I let the phone ring and ring and ring?"

"Who was calling?"

"It was a wrong number, madam."

"Wrong number! There are too many wrong numbers coming through. I think I'll get a lock now."

"As you please, madam. But in case of emergency, theft for instance, would it not waste a lot of time to run next door? You remember what happened at *Baas* Freddy's?"

"Yes, well, tell your friends to stop ringing wrong numbers. And don't threaten me with theft because I will get the police on your back before they search anywhere else."

I walk to the laundry-room smiling to myself. As I turn into the door, I see Tommy watching me intently, and his redshot eye reminds me that I am supposed to have a limp.

Myriam Warner-Vieyra
?1940s–

Born in Guadeloupe, in the French West Indies, she has for twenty years lived in Senegal, where she is a librarian and researcher at the University of Dakar. This extract is from her first novel, Le Quimboiseur l'avait dit... (published in 1980, and translated two years later by Dorothy S. Blair under the title As the Sorcerer Said). Her second novel, Juletane, appeared in 1984.

From

As the Sorcerer Said

THE day after Mr Felix's intervention, I went back to school as usual. Mrs Paule ignored me. That didn't worry me in the slightest; all I wanted was to pass my exam at the end of the year....

On Saturday afternoons Mrs Paule let us out half an hour early. Zelia and I rushed home and set off immediately to go for a swim in the river Corossol. A merry party of children were splashing about in the pool.

I washed my hair and then rinsed it with the prickly-pear infusion, and Zelia tied it in curling rags so that I would have curls for Mass the following day. Then we walked upstream with two schoolfriends, Laurence and Marie, to fill our water-bottles with drinking water, a long way up from the pool and the places where we usually did our washing.

The Corossol was not much more than six feet wide where we stopped. The water was unbelievably cold and clear; on the banks "pink apples" and wild peas grew in abundance. We sat down for a while to eat some on the spot. Then we ran back to the beach again. A few fishing-boats were coming in. The last rays of the setting sun were reflected in thousands of tiny copper-coloured flakes, turning the horizon red.

Father and Louis came back a little later than usual, their wide-brimmed hats pushed to the backs of their heads, their faces drawn. The catch had not been good, the sea was rough. A few small fish squirmed in the bottom of the boat. But we were in seventh heaven as Louis had caught a *chatou*, a shell-fish like a large lobster. We would have it for Sunday lunch cooked with rice and it would be a change from our daily diet of sweet potatoes with cod, or fish soup.

The next morning we were up early, as on every Sunday, so as to clean up the house a bit and prepare lunch before leaving for church. It was an absolute duty to go to Mass every Sunday. Father John was always saying it was a mortal sin to miss Mass unless one were seriously ill. So the whole village and the surrounding hamlets flocked to fill Cocotier's little Saint Sophie's Church, the only brick building in the village. It also served as a shelter in the event of a cyclone or a tidal wave. The men in their heavily starched white duck trousers arrived in a chorus of "plop! plop". The women, for the most part, wore long dresses of flowered cotton and funny straw hats with bunches of fruit, flowers and all sorts of ribbons, or else cotton headscarves.

Father John wouldn't let any women or girls into church without some sort of head covering. The Mass was always too long. Father John would go on and on, exhorting us to chastity, goodness, charity and many other virtues. He could see sin everywhere. Knowing, as all the inhabitants of Cocotier did, that I spent most of my leisure hours almost exclusively with Charles, he once asked me during confession, "Has Charles ever touched you, my child?" When I looked uncomprehending, he said, "Never let him see what you've got between your thighs, and much less touch you there; it would be a mortal sin." I felt terribly ashamed. He must have asked Charles the same question, but I never heard anything more about it. . . .

It was beautiful weather that Sunday, contrary to the forecast. The sky was quite clear. When we came out of the dim, cool church at eleven o'clock, the sun was quite dazzling. For once the idea of the succulent dish of rice and *chatou* sent us straight home, instead of dawdling for long outside the church. It's true that we never had anything to eat before Mass as we had to take communion on an empty stomach. . . .

In Cocotier nobody ever locked their doors, even if they had a lock on them. No one would ever think of entering a house when the occupants were out. One would just wait on the veranda till they came back. When we went out we used to put a big stone up against the front door; that was the way everyone shut up their houses.

When we got as far as the Felixes' we were astonished to see the stone moved and the door open. Someone was in our house. Not one of the inhabitants of the village, nor any of the surrounding hamlets; but perhaps it was an animal. . .and suppose it had eaten our *chatou.* . . . Without a word we started to walk faster and Louis and Jose broke into a run. When they reached the front door they stopped as if turned to stone, hesitated a moment, then went in. Zelia and I followed behind Father and Grandma, as we weren't very brave in circumstances like this.

As I reached the veranda I heard a woman's voice. A voice that I had not completely forgotten.

"Oh! How you've grown, Jose!"

My heart started to dance a frenzied *gros ka.* I recognized her immediately. . . .

She was even more beautiful than I had remembered. She looked like one of the ladies in fashion magazines. Her eyebrows were replaced by a pencil line, her lips and cheeks were made up. Her hair was drawn back to form an imposing chignon in the nape of her neck. She smiled. A cigarette was burning out in a plate that she had taken to use as an ashtray. Her white dress with little blue polka-dots was made out of a silky material with hundreds of tiny pleats in the skirt. She was wearing white shoes with heels so sharp that I wondered how anyone could really stand perched on them. The whole room was pervaded by a discreet but clinging perfume that was nothing like the cheap toilet waters we used on Sundays. It was as though a dazzling sunbeam were sitting there on the only decent chair that we still possessed, making everything look wretched and poverty-stricken in a way I had never noticed till then.

"Why now, my little Zetou, don't you recognize me? I'm your mother!"

I went up to her to kiss her. In spite of the smile on her face, her expression was quite different from the rest of her appearance; it was cold and almost contemptuous.

She had come back just as she had left six years ago, without any warning, once more upsetting the peaceful, regular rhythm of our simple life as a fisherman's children. Father, after a brief greeting, as if to someone he had left five minutes earlier, went off to the bar, probably to drown in rum the memory of his flouted love.

Jose, Louis, Zelia and I were too intimidated by this beautiful lady to say a word. Grandma was in ecstasies of joy at her daughter's return and asked her a thousand and one questions.

"What do you intend to do now?" she asked.

"I'm thinking of staying in town for two or three months to see about my divorce."

"Divorce!" cried Grandma.

"Yes, I want to be free, you understand?"

"Oh, well. . . I thought you were going to stay with us now. . . . Well, I'll go and see about lunch."

Grandma was clearly very disappointed. She must have thought that like the "prodigal son" in one of Father John's sermons, her child had returned, repentant.

When Grandma went out Mother turned to me.

"How are you getting on at school, Zetou?"

"Er...all right."

"What class are you in?"

"Standard six."

"Is that all! You're very behindhand. In France children of fifteen have already passed their School Certificate. And you haven't even got your primary certificate, have you?... It's true your father doesn't think education is of much use. I suppose he hasn't done anything to encourage you to study."

"I've never been kept down a year," I said.

She had forgotten that she had sent me to school very late, at eight and a half instead of at six, and that it had taken me a year to learn French. Like all the village children I had spoken Creole until I started school.

"And you, Jose, you're getting on all right?"

"Me! Oh, I'm all right!"

Jose, obviously too embarrassed to admit that he didn't go to school any more, after Mother's outcry on the subject, dashed out of the house. Zelia, who was not very talkative by nature, slipped away discreetly, to avoid any awkward questions.

Louis was fairly shy; nevertheless, he had no complexes; in fact he was rather proud of his job as a fisherman. Anticipating Mother's question, he said, "I've left school. I help Father with the fishing."

"You're going to become a fisherman, then!" she said, in a voice that clearly indicated that she meant "What a disgrace!"

"Mother, I want to go on studying after my primary certificate. Take me back to Paris with you."

I blurted this out rapidly, without thinking.

"We'll see....You're already old enough for secondary school....Look," she went on, pointing to a box on the table. "Open it. I've brought some little presents for you."

Then she took out her packet of cigarettes. They were Players. The only brand of cigarettes you could buy in Cocotier were called "Jobs". But most men smoked a pipe or rolled their own cigarettes with the thin papers that they bought from Mrs Felix. Normally I didn't like the smell of tobacco, but the smoke from the Players was like a real perfume, and I enjoyed sniffing it.

Louis got to the box first and opened it. There were clothes for all of us, including a shirt for Father. The dress intended for me was far too big. The fact is that at fifteen and a half I was small for my age. I was slender rather than thin, and quite strong.

The people in the village used to say that I took after my mother and that I was pretty like her. I didn't think I was beautiful, not even pretty, or even at all nice-looking. It's true I had my mother's big eyes, but my lips were thicker, my mouth bigger, my nose too large for my face and my front teeth decayed. I had never been to a dentist; whenever I'd had toothache it had been treated with cloves put into the cavity, which gave my breath a spicy smell.

Mother had healthy, even, white teeth. Her smile could have been used as an advertisement for some brand of toothpaste. . . .

Grandma had surpassed herself. The rice with *chatou* was delicious and Mother did our cooking the honour of taking a second helping. Grandma even found a few pence to buy us some iced lemonade from Mrs Felix.

At about three o'clock a black Peugeot 203 stopped in front of our house. It was Mr Milan. Mother left, promising to come and see us again while she was still in town. Father came in after supper. He had reverted to silence and did not answer when I asked him what he had been doing all day.

The next morning we all resumed our normal activities. School with Mrs Paule didn't bring me much satisfaction. I couldn't see how my school year was going to end. She was quite capable of refusing to enter me for the exam. She had taken me back, contrary to her custom, to do Mr Felix a favour. She never addressed a word to me, never asked me any questions in class. However, she did correct my exercises.

Mother did not come back to see us as she had promised. But she saw Grandma every Saturday at the market in town. Six weeks after she had turned up in Cocotier, she got her divorce without any difficulty, and under all the conditions that she had asked for. They had been married under community of property, but she let Father keep everything, not out of generosity, but simply because she had no use for a fishing-boat and a wooden hut – Father's sole possessions. She obtained custody of Zelia and myself, although she had no wish to take us away with her. We were to remain with Grandma. Mother's lawyer was a white man from town, a friend of Mr Milan. Father didn't engage a lawyer. He went off twice in Mr Felix's bus at six in the morning to attend the court hearings in town.

Having always associated his domestic troubles with too much schooling, Father decided to keep Zelia and me at home now, for fear of losing us too. He went to let Mrs Paule know and she was quite pleased since, as far as she was concerned, fisherfolk's children didn't need to know anything except the three Rs. Then he announced after supper that the next day Zelia and I were to go off to help Grandma in the fields.

"What!" I shouted. "I want to go on with my education!"

My left cheek smarted from the resounding slap I received. It was the very first time Father had ever struck me. I fled, more surprised than angry. . . .

The beach was deserted, the sand still warm, the sky sprinkled with twinkling stars. I sat down for a moment to try to see clearly into my own mind. I understood my poor father's reaction, nevertheless I was determined not to give in. Later on he would be only too pleased to have an educated daughter when he was too old to spend all day out at sea, waiting for the fish to bite, or pulling on a net that comes up empty more often than not. I couldn't understand how Zelia could accept Father's decision without a word. I couldn't understand how she could put up with everything with the same equanimity. . . .

A shooting star! I just had time to make a wish before it disappeared. . . .

Suddenly I remembered that Mother had not said no when I asked her to take me to Paris. I went home and wrote her a letter, asking her to help me; she was my only hope now. The next morning I went to Mr Felix's as he was leaving at six o'clock and gave my letter to Charles who knew where Mother was staying, telling him of this new nasty blow. I asked him to insist on Mother giving him an answer immediately, and in any case before she left town, which couldn't be very long now.

Mother took three days to think about it. I learnt some time later that it was Mr Milan who advised her to take me, saying that after all it was her duty as she had obtained custody of her daughters. So, three days after I had written my letter, I received a reply that surpassed all my hopes, as I had never imagined that Mother would decide to take me back with her straightaway. There was a five-franc note in the envelope and a few lines telling me to send three photos and my birth certificate so that she could get me a passport. . . .

Grandma was delighted that I was going with her daughter. I left her the responsibility of telling Father, whom I didn't dare confront since he had slapped my face.

Zelia was completely opposed to my leaving. She thought it was quite unwise for me to set off on this unknown venture. "You know what you're leaving behind, you don't know what you'll find over there." She wouldn't leave her village for anything in the world. Her ambitions went no further than the village of Cocotier, even the nearby town didn't attract her, as it was too noisy. I thought that Zelia was a little fool. What danger could I run? None at all. In Paris my future was assured; all I had to do was to settle down seriously to my school work; my future depended on myself, and so it was quite assured.

Two days after receiving Mother's letter I went off to town in Mr Felix's bus. Jose took me to a photographer who specialized in passport photos. Then I went to the hotel where Mother was staying. It was in the square from which the buses left for the different villages and regions of the island. I didn't know what name Mother was going under, so I asked for Mr Milan. Without taking his nose out of his newspaper, the grey-haired old white man, who must have been the proprietor of the hotel, replied that he was out.

"And the lady with him?"

"She's out."

"Can I wait for them?" I asked, more and more intimidated by this man who looked just like the polar bear in my reading book, with his hairy arms and mop of white hair.

"Please yourself."

Finally I decided to go and wait for them outside. I didn't feel at ease sitting opposite this man who seemed so starved for news that he was devouring his paper rather than reading it.

After a good half hour, during which I could have gone for a tour round the island in one of the multicoloured buses that were arriving and departing from the square, I caught sight of Mother coming back alone.

She was wearing trousers and low-heeled shoes. She didn't look like the lady I'd seen six weeks before at Cocotier; her hair was short, whereas I'd seen her at our house with a large bun, which gave the impression that she had long hair. Naturally I knew nothing at that time about how one could change one's appearance with wigs and false pieces. As for the trousers, it was the first time I'd seen a woman dressed like that.

She greeted me quite pleasantly, but without warmth.

"Well! How are you, Zetou? Have you got the papers and the passport photos?"

"Yes, Mother."

"Right then, give them to me. Roger" (she meant Mr Milan) "will see about your passport. He's got friends at the prefecture; it won't take long. . . . You'll have to have a smallpox vaccination . . . and . . . only take what you'll need on the boat. I'll buy you some decent clothes in Paris. We'll be leaving early next Tuesday, that's in one week's time exactly. You can sleep here on Monday night. Well, I must leave you, I've got a lot to do before lunch."

She left me standing there on the pavement and disappeared into the hotel. I couldn't go back to Cocotier before evening and anyway Mr Felix's bus was no longer in the square. I didn't dare wander off by myself as I didn't know my way about in town. Besides, I didn't know where to go for this vaccination. After several minutes' hesitation I plucked up all my courage and went back into the hotel.

"I'd like to see Mr Milan's lady."

"Number 6, first floor."

The old polar bear was still buried in his newspaper. I went along a rather dark corridor and found a staircase right at the end. On the first floor I knocked at the door which bore the number indicated. As soon as Mother opened it I blurted out very quickly, for fear she could intimidate me, "Excuse me, I don't know where to go for the vaccination and Mr Felix's bus isn't there any more. . . ."

"All right, come in. Roger won't be long. He'll show you where to go."

The room, which was really quite simple, seemed luxurious to me as I'd never seen anything like it. It was large and harmoniously furnished with curtains and a bedcover of flowered cretonne, a table and two bamboo armchairs.

As far as the "lot to do before lunch" was concerned, Mother was doing her long and carefully manicured nails. I felt ashamed as I watched her and crossed my arms, clenching my fists to hide my nails which were cut extremely short. We didn't exchange another word for the rest of the time until Roger arrived, which seemed an age to me. Finally he appeared, smiling and much more pleased to see me than my mother had been. He was sunburnt, with prominent cheekbones, grey-green eyes, golden-brown hair, an Adam's apple that bobbed up and down, and a genuinely warm smile.

"Hello! It's our little Zetou. Now, isn't she a little beauty! Of course we know who she takes after. . . ."

He took both my hands and planted a kiss on my forehead.

Mother smiled and a gleam of happiness appeared in her eyes; it must have been pleasure at Roger's return!

"Are you coming? I'm starving," he said.

Then, taking each of us by the hand, he led Mother and me into the hotel restaurant where five or six tables, covered with red-checked tablecloths, were set out in the courtyard under a pergola of apple-creepers. I greedily gobbled up the mixed hors d'oeuvres, not realizing that there would be two more courses to follow, taking no notice of Mother or Roger.

When I had wiped my plate clean I looked up, my hunger satisfied. Then I met my mother's cold angry gaze, while she said in a very sweet voice, "You eat too fast, Zetou!"

Whether it was the effect of the look she gave me, or the excessive sweetness of her voice, or a combination of the two, I can't say, but I felt as though a huge lump were blocking my throat and I could swallow nothing more for the rest of the meal.

That evening, on the way back to Cocotier, Charles and I had a long discussion. He was very pleased with the way things had turned out.

"You're very lucky, and then when I get to Paris, after I've got my matric, I shan't be lost as you can show me around."

"Of course," I said, "on one condition."

"What's that?"

"That you write to me every day for the next four years, giving me all the news of the village, even the most harmless gossip."

"Is that all! I don't make any promises; that's really asking a bit too much. One letter a week will be quite enough."

"All right! Then you can look for another guide when you get to Paris."

We burst out laughing noisily, waking a dried-up, bent old man who was a stranger to me, who had been dozing.

"That's right, young people can laugh at anything."

"You're not going to get much sleep today, Gaffer Tison, with those two," Mr Felix said to the old man.

"Mmm!" was his reply.

"That's Destinville's kid, the fisherman. She's going off to Paris next week with her mother. That's what they're all excited about."

"Hm! That's nothing to rejoice about. Those towns aren't the place for us. I was there in 1918 for their war with the Germans. In a whole week I never saw the sun once and it was so cold that one day when I had to sweep the yard with a Senegalese, we started to cry like two little kids, our fingers were so stiff and sore with the cold; we couldn't hold the broom. Fortunately it was nearly the end of the war; we were sent to the south where it wasn't so cold. All those who went out at the beginning of the war died; not a single one came back to the island. Those that weren't killed by the Germans, the cold must have done for."

Nobody believed a word of old Tison's rambling talk. Nevertheless we all listened in complete silence until he got out at Bananier, the little village before ours.

Father took things very well, at least outwardly. After his brief outburst, when he had hit me, he reverted to his taciturn habits. The news of my departure had spread rapidly through the village and the neighbouring hamlets. Many people came to see me; some of them brought me some little souvenir or other, according to their means. Unfortunately I had to leave the majority of their gifts behind: bags, shell-necklaces, fruit, among other things. Mother had insisted that I mustn't take anything useless. As far as she was concerned, nothing from Cocotier had any value. To avoid any temptation on my part, she had bought me the smallest possible suitcase.

Mrs Paule took the trouble to come and say goodbye to me the day before my departure. Now that I was going to live in Paris and go to school there, I was no longer simply a fisherman's daughter, good for nothing except sewing patches on the men's trousers. She gave me the address of her brother in Paris. I made a note of it, quite determined never to meet this brother.

When the last visitors had gone, it was half past ten. My brothers were chatting on the veranda with other boys and girls of their own age. Grandma then announced that we must set out for Corossol where we were to pay a visit to the sorcerer who would see if my journey was to take place under lucky omens.

Grandma took a chicken, a large yam, a candle and a little money to pay for the consultation.

It was a bright moonlit night. The cocks of the neighbourhood were paying their tribute to the silver moon in a noisy concert, to which the night birds added their cries and the rustle of their wings. We were lit on our way by a cheerful escort of fireflies. The ground was warm beneath our bare feet. A pleasant smell of freshly crushed grass mingled with the faint scent of the ylang-ylang. Oh! how pleasant my last night in Cocotier was. . . !

The sorcerer lived on the outskirts of Corossol. A tiny footpath behind the hamlet led to a hut that came into sight some little way from the steep climb. A dog greeted us in quite a friendly fashion. He seemed to know us, preceded us to the hut and growled slightly as if to say, "Here they are. . . ."

The man was smoking a long, crudely carved pipe. He was much younger than I had imagined a sorcerer to be. His sole garment was a piece of red material tied at his waist and he wore a necklace made of shells and the teeth of animals that I had never seen before.

"Ah! *Moune en moin! Moune en moin!* My people, my people!" the sorcerer said slowly. "Is this the child who is going on a journey?"

"Yes, Papa Logbo," Grandma replied.

Papa Logbo got up. Grandma took my hand and we followed him. The room we went into was smaller than the first one. Above the door was a wooden cross and opposite it was another cross drawn in white chalk in the middle of which was fixed a pair of scissors. Wooden statuettes stood on a table with rickety legs, projecting their shadows up to the roof of corrugated iron, from which hung a tangle of strings. At the end of each piece of string hung a bunch of leaves. The inside walls were covered with inscriptions and geometric drawings. An oil lamp made out of half a coconut shell cast a feeble light on a statue of Christ which stood on a shelf covered with a white cloth.

Papa Logbo sat down on the edge of a narrow bed covered with a jute cloth. He traced a cabalistic figure on the ground, composed of a double triangle that looked like a star. He wrote some letters and figures in it, then drew up a block of wood that served as a seat and made me sit on it. He lit the candle that Grandma had brought and gave it to me to hold. Still smoking his pipe he tapped the ground with his left foot. After a moment he gave a start, then began to snigger while he rocked backwards and forwards.

"Mamma Gastonia! Hee! hee! hee. . .! You ought to have come to see me sooner so that I could do something for the child. . . ."

"Yes?" said Grandma, very worried.

"*Enhan! Enhan!* I see good and bad. Our gods of Africa are not favourable for the immediate future. *Enhan! Enhan! Enhan!* I'll do what I can tonight. . . ."

Thereupon Papa Logbo left us and went out. After ten to fifteen minutes he came back carrying a large tub filled with a mixture of greenish water and leaves. He told me to undress and get into the tub. The water was warm and gave off an indefinable but pleasant smell. The sorcerer took the leaves and rubbed my body, while repeating incantations in a strange language – that of the gods of Africa, no doubt. Papa Logbo was really quite a nice person who knew where we came from and how to talk to the gods of Africa. I was so full of wonder that, forgetting my shyness, I asked him, "Have you been to Africa, Papa Logbo?"

"Yes, my child. I go back there every day, several times a day, to consult our gods."

After the bath, the sorcerer lit a charcoal fire in a clay pot. He poured a few drops of a liquid and various powders on to the fire, then made me step over this fire seven times.

"The river does not wash away what is meant for you."

Amelia Blossom House
?1940s–

Born in Wynberg, Cape Town, South Africa, she received a BA from the University of Cape Town (1961). After teaching in South Africa for seven years (using the name "Blossom" for her underground work), she went to London and studied drama at Guildhall School of Music & Drama, later acting on stage, television, radio and film. Since

1972 she has lived in Louisville, Kentucky. She received an MA from the University of Louisville in 1977 and at present teaches in the Fort Knox Community Schools System and part-time at the University of Louisville. She has had short stories, poems and critical essays published in many journals, including Staffrider, Présence Africaine, Callaloo, The Gar *and* Essence, *and has read her poetry (and performed it with percussion) in the USA, Canada, Norway and England. She compiled a* Checklist of Black South African Women Writers in English *(1980) and is the author of the poetry collections* Deliverance *(1986) and* Our Sun Will Rise: Poems for South Africa *(1989).*

Sacrifice

At your birth, my daughter
I heard you cry
a lamb unblemished
my new offering
to the world.

At your birth, my daughter
I heard your cry
for my pain
And your births
to come.

We Still Dance

today
yesterday
tomorrow
through and beyond time
we still dance
red dust
black mud
ochre sand
we still dance
birth
marriage
victory
we still dance
ankle rings
bracelets

feet drumming
soil
we still dance
yesterdays celebrations
for the soul
of the soil
todays celebrations
for the fight
of the soil
tomorrows
soul victory
we still dance.

Ifi Amadiume

1940s–

Born in Nigeria, she was educated there and in Britain, obtaining a first degree in Sociology and then a PhD in Anthropology from London University's School of Oriental and African Studies (SOAS). She was a research fellow for a year at the University of Nigeria, Enugu, has taught at SOAS and lectured in Canada, the USA and Senegal. She was founding editor of Pan-African Liberation Platform (1989–90) and now teaches and works as a community education officer in London. She is the author of Male Daughters, Female Husbands: Gender and Sex in an African Society (1987, Choice Book Award) and Afrikan Matriarchal Foundations: The Igbo Case (1987), from which this is an extract. As a poet she participated in 1977 in FESTAC, the second world festival of Black and African arts and culture, and her 1985 collection, Passion Waves, was nominated for the Commonwealth Poetry Prize.

From

Afrikan Matriarchal Foundations

"IKPU OKWA" FESTIVAL AND PATRIARCHAL IDEOLOGY

THE last time this festival was performed was in 1948. Most elderly Nnobi people therefore had a clear recollection of the activities and beliefs associated with the festival. Indeed, one of those interviewed, one of the oldest men in Nnobi called Ezudona, had himself gone through some of the rituals required for the taking of the *ozo Aho* title associated with this festival. Ezudona has also never been a Christian and still worships the goddess Idemili. Two other men whose vivid accounts are reported here, were Nnajide and Eze Enyinwa, neither of whom has ever stepped into a church or been a Christian. They also worship the goddess. I shall first describe the festival and then show its relationship to the goddess Idemili and the ideology of male dominance.

The central figures in this festival were the men with the title *ozo Aho*, associated with the spirit of Aho. Like the *Ekwe* title, it was involuntary, that is, taken as a result of spirit possession. But unlike the *Ekwe* title, which may be taken by any Nnobi woman possessed by the spirit of the goddess, only men from certain patrilineages in Umuona took the *ozo Aho* title. A possible candidate would consult the priest of Aho as soon as he experienced signs of possession, which may begin even in childhood. Through divination, the man would be told that Aho wished him to take his title. Only those who had taken the title and those in the process of taking the title carried the *okwa* masks during the festival. There were many taboos surrounding one who had taken the title. For example, when he was eating, he was not allowed to mention the names of certain birds, like *egbe, utugbe ugene oma*.[1] One was forbidden to mention the word *Nnokwa*[2] or to talk about the *ushie* dance.[3] In this, he was no different from the titled elites of the time and the protocol surrounding them.

The *ikpu okwa* festival took place in the tenth month of the traditional calendar and lasted for one month. It began with the roasting of yam, a very male thing. As with most Nnobi religious activities, ritual homage was paid. In this

---

[1] *Egbe*, hawk, which was the sign on the *okwa* mask, belongs to the kite family, and so possibly do the others.

[2] The Nnokwa taboo is associated with the story of how the neighbouring town Nnokwa "opened up rain" on *okwa* masqueraders returning from Agu Ukwu Nri when they were passing through Nnokwa. "Opened up rain" means using rain-makers to induce rainfall. As the story goes, only a certain old man called Eze Odije survived. This old man, when he noticed that it was raining, had taken off his mask from his head and put it on his shoulder. The water trickling down from the mask did not therefore enter his mouth and therefore he did not die. All the other men died as *ukpe*, which was really poison but used for painting the mask, got wet and entered their mouths. After that incident, *okwa* was always carried on the shoulder.

[3] *Ushie* or *ufie* was an exclusive dance performed only by *ozo* titled men.

case, the head of yam was circulated. Each male head of a household would send yam to his immediate social superior. Next was the looting ritual, when Umuona would invite all Nnobi major lineages in turn to eat roasted cocoyam. While a lineage group would be in Umuona eating cocoyam, the whole of Umuona, including women and children, would take to their heels and go rampaging in the compounds and gardens of their guests. This was called the gladness or joy of *okwa, onu okwa*. What Umuona aimed at getting were the things needed for the festival such as young yellow palm leaves, *omu*, from which the layers of raffia-like skirts which the masqueraders wore were brushed out. They also looted other petty foodstuffs such as coconuts, garden eggs and vegetables. They may drink any palm-wine left on the trees but may not loot any major economic item such as yam, cocoyam or livestock. The guests at Umuona in turn may do a bit of looting on their way home. This would go on until Umuona would have exchanged looting with all the other major patrilineages in Nnobi.

Next was the wrestling ceremony, whereby Umuona invited the different major patrilineages in turn for a wrestling bout[4] and which was performed before the *okwa* masks would be carried on the head.[5] The decoration of the masks was done in secret. This was the responsibility of a particular patrilineage in Umuona where the title *nwunye nonu*, wife *nonu*, was taken. Even though this title was held by a man, he was referred to as wife here in the sense of being in a domestic or service relationship to those holding the *ozo Aho* title. He and his patrilineage were responsible for preparing the *ukpe* dye which was rubbed on the masks. He was also responsible for decorating the body of the priest of Aho who carried the main mask with camwood dye, *ushie*. Several days before the emergence of the masqueraders, those who would perform the masquerade would spend each night performing a ritual called *iti nkpu Aho*, the night call to Aho to emerge from the wild.

Fully decorated in dyes and young yellow palm fronds, the masquerade, led by the priest of Aho, retraced the primordial route of Aho. They would emerge from a piece of forest in Umuona called *Agbo Aho*, go to the shrine of the Earth Spirit of Nnobi again in Umuona, and then proceed along the route to the shrine of Udide. From there, they would visit patrilineage shrines in the ancestral *obi* of each minor patrilineage in Nnobi to perform the ritual called *igwo ngwolo*, the sitting position of the lame. At each shrine, the priest of Aho would sit in this position while yam, cocoyam and money amd kola-nuts were filed out for him in eights. He would then invoke blessing on that shrine, purifying it and warding off evil spirits. He would continue thus till he had visited all the lineage shrines in the whole of Nnobi. He would then proceed to Aho's open space and the shrine, where the wrestling competition involving the whole town would be performed.

For this town competition, the titled men and women of all the different villages and patrilineages would gather in Aho square. These titled people would

---

[4] This wrestling competition was done by young men who were selected by each major patrilineage to represent them. Those who were victorious simply jubilated.
[5] It appears that the masks were carried on the head locally and on the shoulder for external visits.

take their individual chairs with them, with the *ozo* titled men wearing their eagle plumes. They usually sat in a circle, apart from other common spectators. The main masquerader, the priest of Aho known as *isi Aho*, and other masqueraders known as the children of Aho, *umu Aho*, would place themselves in the centre of the circle formed by the titled. The priest of Aho would again take the sitting position of the lame in the centre of the circle, hitting his hands and feet on the ground and boasting of his powers. As he would be doing this, people would strain forward to see what he was doing, while they would be shipped indiscriminately by the children of Aho. Then a ritual involving the cutting of ritual marks on the chest, *igbuchi obi*, would be performed by fearless young men. They would go in front of the priest of Aho and lie down. The priest would then cut them twice on their chests with a knife and rub medicine on the cuts. This indicated that from henceforth, Aho would protect them.

Then the priest of Aho, carrying the main *okwa* mask, would engage in ritual embrace with his wife in a dance exclusive to *ozo* titled men, *ushie*, for the whole *okwa* performance was exclusively male. For this reason, the priest's wife would have gone through a ritual which would give her male status so that she could participate in this dance with her husband. She would therefore wear a string anklet, like *ozo* titled men. After the priest had embraced his wife four times, he would stand in the middle of the open space with his legs astride. All pregnant women present would then crawl on hands and knees in between his legs to pick yellow palm leaf, *ikpa omu*. Each woman would hold one strand from behind and one from the front and break out tiny pieces. The women would then take them home to cook in sauce and eat. They were not expected to touch any other medicine till their babies were born.

Just like the deity Aho who punished by whipping, *okwa* masqueraders carried whips with which they whipped spectators indiscriminately but gently. After the performance at the open space in front of the Aho shrine, the whole masquerade would then pass through Nnokwa to Agu Ukwu Nri and retrace their steps back to Nnobi and go to the Afo central market-place, where the masqueraders continued their indiscriminate whipping. During this occasion, old women would go to be whipped, in the belief that by so doing, Aho took away any illness in their bodies. Finally, the priest would go back to the shrine of Aho. He would shake his body vigorously and shed the beautiful palm fronds on his body onto the ground. This was described as a very beautiful and amazing sight. He would then disappear into the virgin forest of Aho into the wild.

The *okwa* masquerade was extremely male, both in its composition, outlook and rituals. It is because of the very maleness of this ritual symbolism that the titled man who had to perform typical female domestic duty of preparing dyes and colourful decorations had to be called a wife. The mask itself was carved from strong heavy wood in the shape of a mortar for pounding, hence its name *okwa*. The assertion of patriarchy and male dominance are symbolized in three rituals, in particular, the visiting of village and patrilineage shrines to sanctify them, the crawling of pregnant women between the legs of the priest of Aho to pick young palm leaves, and the final ritual of undressing the goddess.

I was given two explanations as to why pregnant women had to crawl on hands and knees under the towering body of the masquerader of Aho to pick pieces of palm-leaf which they were supposed to cook and eat. According to one explanation, this was done to avoid having a baby who would sway its head from left to right or rock its head like the *okwa* mask carriers.[6] The very heavy weight of the mask made those carrying it sway their heads from side to side. Ezudona, who had spent most of his life and wealth taking the *ozo Aho* title, was more secretive and evasive about the reason why women picked and ate the palm-leaves. According to him, no one knew the reason, it was the custom, but, perhaps, it was done to avoid difficulty in childbirth. Apart from the assertion of male dominance, Aho might also be claiming the power of procreation. He publicly embraces his wife four times – a gesture never done in public under normal circumstances – and pregnant women crawl in between his legs. These all have sexual connotations.

PATRIARCHY VERSUS MATRIARCHY

A T the beginning of the season of ritual festivals, *omu*, young yellow palm leaves were decorated round the shrine of the goddess Idemili. This was done by the priest of Idemili shrine in conjunction with Umuona. At the end of the festival for Aho, which took place at the end of the period of religious activities, the priest of Aho would go to Idemili shrine to untie the palm leaves with which her shrine had been decorated. As Aho priest arrived for this ritual, spectators would laugh and tease the goddess, singing that her husband had arrived. This ritual was called *ito omu*, untying young yellow palm leaves, or *ito ogodo*, to untie a woman's wrapper or undress her.

There were two reasons given by Umuona people for the performance of this ritual. One was that Umuona was the head of Nnobi, the ancestral home of all Nnobi, and therefore had ritual prerogative. The second reason was that Aho was Idemili's husband and, as such, first protected his wife from public view at the beginning of the season of festivities by covering her, and at the end, I suppose as a husband would say in English, "the party is over, time to undress," he equally "undressed" her.

At the beginning of the *okwa* festival, before the commencement of the yam roasting ritual, the priest of Aho would take yam to Idemili as night food, *itu nni anyasi*. A husband customarily gave his wife yam as his contribution to the daily food in the household. Some saw this as a bribe or payment for a wife's sexual service and associated the expressed "night food" with the fact that sexual intercourse usually took place at night. The Nnobi saying which claims that a wife answers her husband's call reluctantly or sharply when she knows there is no yam left in the yam stack, may support this claim.

However, it is also possible to see the giving of yam to Idemili in the context of the paying of ritual homage which was done in Umuona at the beginning of the *okwa* festival. In this case, Umuona would not only be acknowledging the

---

[6] Nnobi people believed that objects or people's physical characteristics had strong influences on babies in the womb. Consequently, pregnant women avoided looking at "ugly" or deformed people for fear that their babies would resemble them.

ritual seniority of the goddess, but also the antiquity of the goddess with its embodied matriarchy. Umuona would also be acknowledging the male status of the goddess since, like a fully fledged independent male, she had an *obi* and an *ikenga*, as was mentioned by her priest, Eze Agba. The whole Aho cult therefore symbolizes the incursion of a patriarchal people on an indigenous matriarchal society. The fact that figurines of all the other deities in Nnobi which have their shrines elsewhere, including Aho himself, are represented in the main Idemili shrine supports this claim.

It is interesting that, even though Aho is seen as the husband of Idemili, and their relationship conceived of in terms of that of husband and wife in the household, Aho is not seen as a superior or more a power deity than Idemili, not even by Umuona people who, alone, worship him. Instead, Aho is seen as a man struggling to maintain a male authority over a very wealthy, independent and extremely popular woman. This idea is expressed in another myth which claimed that Aho was the husband of Idemili. Idemili, being very industrious, soon became a great woman; rich, powerful and much more popular than her husband, Aho. There is the belief that the way to humble an arrogant woman is to marry a second wife. So, Aho married Afo. Idemili, in her anger, closed all the other rivers, including that of Aho and Afo, and said that only her own river would continue to run. Aho, in male indignation, ruled that thenceforth, all important activities in Nnobi would be performed at Afo's place. *Afo* is one of the days of the week, the main market day and the name of the central market-place. Indeed, most festivals and activities take place there.

When I put it to the present priest of Idemili that it is said that Aho is Idemili's husband, he got angry and indignant. This is what he had to say:

No, he is not! Who was there when he went and took her for wife? You should ask them to say who witnessed the day that Aho took palm-wine to go and get Idemili. Who was there when *alusi nmuo*[7] originated? All I know is that my own fathers did not tell me this. Umuona is just boasting. It is only people who claim that Aho is Idemili's husband. These are things which people came to the world and began to say. Have you ever seen where people accompanied deities to go and get other deities for marriage?

It is when talking about customs that people tell these stories.

In reply to the denial of marriage by the priest of Idemili, Umuona people maintained that Aho gives yam to Idemili and that, in the household, yam is given to a wife by a husband!

---

7   Deities.

Grace Akello
?1940s–

orn in Eastern Uganda, she attended Makerere University and worked in Kenya and Tanzania before going to England in 1981. She is the author of Iteso Thought Patterns in Tales and her knowledge of Iteso traditions is also reflected in her poems, which have a strong traditional setting. Her poetry collection My Barren Song was published in 1980.

Encounter

Teach me to laugh once more
let me laugh with Africa my mother
I want to dance to her drum-beats
I am tired of her cries
Scream with laughter
roar with laughter
Oh, how I hate this groaning

Africa groans
under the load of her kwashiorkored children
she weeps
what woman would laugh
over her children's graves

I want to laugh once again
let me laugh with you
yes, even you my brother who blames me for breeding. . .
I laugh with you
even you who sell me guns
preserving world peace
while my blood, Africa's blood stains Earth
let laughter be my gift to you
my generous heart overflows with laughter
money and vanity harden yours
clogged in your veins, the blood no longer warms your heart
I will teach you yet

I am not bush, lion, savagery
mine are the sinews which built your cities
my sons fighting your wars
gave you victory, prestige
wherein lies the savagery in Africa. . .
Your sons in Africa looted our family chests
raping the very bowels of our earth
our gold lines the streets of your cities. . .
where are pavements in Africa

Laugh with me
Do not laugh at me
my smile forgives all
but greed fetters your heart
the nightmare of our encounter is not over
your overgrown offspring
swear by the western god of money and free enterprise
that they are doing their best for Africa
indeed, Africa the dumping ground
Africa the vast experimental ground
the army bases in the developing parts
enhanced military aid in the loyal parts
family planning programmes in the advanced parts

My son built your cities
What did your son do for me. . .

Lina Magaia

?1940s–

She was born in Maputo, capital of the former Portuguese colony of Mozambique, though her parents were originally from the south, and in order for her to attend secondary school her father had to become an assimilado, *renouncing African culture completely (by 1975 there were only 2,050 secondary school graduates in the whole country). While still at school she joined the Mozambican Liberation Front (FRELIMO) and was jailed for three months for political activities. She obtained a BSc in Economics on scholarship from the University of Lisbon, and then went to Tanzania for military training, becoming a member of the liberation army in 1975. She works in agricultural administration for the Mozambique government and is the author of two books. The following extract, translated from Portuguese by Michael Wolfers, is taken from* Dumba Nengue: Run For Your Life – Peasant Tales of Tragedy in Mozambique *(1989). "Dunba nengue" is a southern Mozambican proverb whose point is that "you have to trust your feet" and is also the name given to an area infested with the South African-backed armed terrorists known as the Mozambican National Resistance (or RENAMO), who in 1987, massacred 380 people in that region of the country.*

The Pregnant Well

B EFORE the bandit attacks began the settlement at Kamaxekana was rich. In the past, before independence, its leader was Matxene, respected and feared as headman since he was a landowner and had the confidence of the senior chief. He was also loved within his jurisdiction because he insisted that people to whom he allocated land for a house should plant cashew and other fruit trees (as he didn't want stealing from his) and because he had the Maxekane well built.

All the people of the settlement were members of a consumer cooperative, meaning they no longer had to make long treks into town for supplies. There was also a collective farm on which everyone in the area worked three days a week. This was the fruit of efforts by Celestino, a member of the cooperative management committee.

Many had built cement houses and also had made wells of cement with pullies used to draw water from the depths of the earth. Some even used the water to irrigate vegetables. Maxekane is seven kilometres from town, at most ten, depending on the route.

Old Madeu had benefited from the progress. He had built a house of blocks and cement, with four rooms, similar to the old reed and corrugated-roof house he had had as a clerk in Lourenço Marques.

Madeu did not live to see what the bandits did to the village because he died a few months before the start of this story. He left behind a widow, many cashew trees, mangoes and mafurras, and the family plot where he was buried.

The armed bandits came from around Nyambi, Xinyanguanine, Bunye, Mtlolonyana and other places where they were driving out the inhabitants and turning everything into thick bush. They reached Kamaxekana and drove out its inhabitants, including Madeu's widow. She took refuge, along with most of her neighbors, next to the railway line close to the town.

She was homesick, homesick for everything she had left behind – the trees, the house, the burial plot, the cashews in the flowering season, the hope she had had of buying new *capulanas*.[1] She was homesick and she wanted to go back to Kamaxekana, which is an area of Dumba Nengue.

She saw her house, with its doors broken open, she saw the cashews and the mangoes in flower, the mafurras in flower. She saw tracks. She saw the well – where she lives now, getting water is an act of heroism – and went to look inside it.

She says that she did not cry out because what she saw gripped her throat and struck her dumb. She says she did not believe she would get back to where she had come from.

She was running and it seemed an iron fist was holding her. She was afraid of her own footsteps even though they could not be heard on the sandy soil. In a frantic search for relief and safety, she sent the earth flying in all directions.

She said she did not believe that such cruelty was possible, that such horrors could have happened in her own well.

When she had looked into the well she had seen the heads of dead people staring at her as if pleading for help.

And the well had seemed pregnant to her.

Alice Walker

1944–

Born in Eatonton, Georgia, she attended Spelman College on scholarship (1961–3), during which time she wrote her first published story, and graduated from Sarah Lawrence College in 1965. *She was given a Merrill Fellowship for writing, was a Breadloaf Writers' Conference Scholar, a fellow at the McDowell Colony and Radcliffe Insti-*

---

[1] *Capulana* is the Mozambican word for the one and one-half metres of cloth peasant women wrap around their waists or use to tie their children on their backs.

tute, won the American Scholar *essay competition in 1967, received an NEA grant for her novel* The Third Life of Grange Copeland *(1970) and a Guggenheim Fellowship. Always politically active, she was involved in the civil rights movement as a student. Since 1968 she has taught Black studies and writing and lectured at many institutions, including Yale University, the University of California at Berkeley and Brandeis University. In 1974 she and her partner Robert Allen started Wild Trees Press in Navarro, California, their motto being: "We publish only what we love." In 1983 she won a Pulitzer Prize for her novel* The Color Purple *(1982), which was later made into a film by Stephen Spielberg. Her other novels are* Meridian *(1976),* The Temple of My Familiar *(1989), and* Possessing the Secret of Joy *(1992), and she is the author of works for children, the poetry volumes* Once *((1968),* Revolutionary Petunias *(1971),* Goodnight Willie Lee, I'll See You in the Morning *(1975),* Horses Make a Landscape Look More Beautiful *(1986) and* Her Blue Body Everything We Know *(1991), short stories –* In Love and Trouble: Stories of Black Women *(1967) and* You Can't Keep a Good Woman Down *(1981), in which the following story appears – and essays collected in* In Search of Our Mothers' Gardens: Womanist Prose *(1983) and* Living by the Word: Collected Writings 1973–1987 *(1988). Calling herself a womanist, she explains: "Womanist is to feminist as purple to lavender."*

Nineteen Fifty-Five

1955

THE car is a brandnew red Thunderbird convertible, and it's passed the house more than once. It slows down real slow now, and stops at the curb. An older gentleman dressed like a Baptist deacon gets out on the side near the house, and a young fellow who looks about sixteen gets out on the driver's side. They are white, and I wonder what in the world they doing in this neighborhood.

Well, I say to J. T., put your shirt on, anyway, and let me clean these glasses offa the table.

We had been watching the ballgame on TV. I wasn't actually watching, I was sort of daydreaming, with my foots up in J. T.'s lap.

I seen 'em coming on up the walk, brisk, like they coming to sell something, and then they rung the bell, and J. T. declined to put on a shirt but instead disappeared into the bedroom where the other television is. I turned down the one in the living room; I figured I'd be rid of these two double quick and J. T. could come back out again.

Are you Gracie Mae Still? asked the old guy, when I opened the door and put my hand on the lock inside the screen.

And I don't need to buy a thing, said I.

What makes you think we're sellin'? he asks, in that hearty Southern way that makes my eyeballs ache.

Well, one way or another and they're inside the house and the first thing the young fellow does is raise the TV a couple of decibels. He's about five feet nine, sort of womanish looking, with real dark white skin and a red pouting mouth. His hair is black and curly and he looks like a Loosianna creole.

About one of your songs, says the deacon. He is maybe sixty, with white hair and beard, white silk shirt, black linen suit, black tie and black shoes. His cold gray eyes look like they're sweating.

One of my songs?

Traynor here just *loves* your songs. Don't you, Traynor? He nudges Traynor with his elbow. Traynor blinks, says something I can't catch in a pitch I don't register.

The boy learned to sing and dance livin' round you people out in the country. Practically cut his teeth on you.

Traynor looks up at me and bites his thumbnail.

I laugh.

Well, one way or another they leave with my agreement that they can record one of my songs. The deacon writes me a check for five hundred dollars, the boy grunts his awareness of the transaction, and I am laughing all over myself by the time I rejoin J. T.

Just as I am snuggling down beside him though I hear the front door bell going off again.

Forgit his hat? asks J. T.

I hope not, I say.

The deacon stands there leaning on the door frame and once again I'm thinking of those sweaty-looking eyeballs of his. I wonder if sweat makes your eyeballs pink because his are sure pink. Pink and gray and it strikes me that nobody I'd care to know is behind them.

I forgot one little thing, he says pleasantly. I forgot to tell you Traynor and I would like to buy up all of those records you made of the song. I tell you we sure do love it.

Well, love it or not, I'm not so stupid as to let them do that without making 'em pay. So I says, Well, that's gonna cost you. Because, really, that song never did sell all that good, so I was glad they was going to buy it up. But on the other hand, them two listening to my song by themselves, and nobody else getting to hear me sing it, give me a pause.

Well, one way or another the deacon showed me where I would come out ahead on any deal he had proposed so far. Didn't I give you five hundred dollars? he asked. What white man – and don't even need to mention colored – would give you more? We buy up all your records of that particular song: first, you git royalties. Let me ask you, how much you sell that song for in the first place? Fifty dollars? A hundred, I say. And no royalties from it yet, right? Right. Well, when we buy up all of them records you gonna git royalties. And that's gonna make all them race record shops sit up and take notice of Gracie Mae Still. And they gonna push all them other records of yourn they got. And you no doubt will become one of the big name colored recording artists. And then we can offer you another five hundred dollars for letting us do all this for you. And by God you'll be sittin' pretty! You can go out and buy you the kind of outfit a star should have. Plenty sequins and yards of red satin.

I had done unlocked the screen when I saw I could get some more money out of him. Now I held it wide open while he squeezed through the opening between me and the door. He whipped out another piece of paper and I signed it.

He sort of trotted out to the car and slid in beside Traynor, whose head was back against the seat. They swung around in a u-turn in front of the house and then they was gone.

J. T. was putting his shirt on when I got back to the bedroom. Yankees beat the Orioles 10–6, he said. I believe I'll drive out to Paschal's pond and go fishing. Wanta go?

While I was putting on my pants J. T. was holding the two checks.

I'm real proud of a woman that can make cash money without leavin' home, he said. And I said *Umph*. Because we met on the road with me singing in first one little low-life jook after another, making ten dollars a night for myself if I was lucky, and sometimes bringin' home nothing but my life. And J. T. just loved them times. The way I was fast and flashy and always on the go from one town to another. He loved the way my singin' made the dirt farmers cry like babies and the womens shout Honey, hush! But that's mens. They loves any style to which you can get 'em accustomed.

1956

MY little grandbaby called me one night on the phone: Little Mama, Little Mama, there's a white man on the television singing one of your songs! Turn on channel 5.

Lord, if it wasn't Traynor. Still looking half asleep from the neck up, but kind of awake in a nasty way from the waist down. He wasn't doing too bad with my song either, but it wasn't just the song the people in the audience was screeching and screaming over, it was that nasty little jerk he was doing from the waist down.

Well, Lord have mercy, I said, listening to him. If I'da closed my eyes, it could have been me. He had followed every turning of my voice, side streets, avenues, red lights, train crossings and all. It give me a chill.

Everywhere I went I heard Traynor singing my song, and all the little white girls just eating it up. I never had so many ponytails switched across my line of vision in my life. They was so *proud*. He was a *genius*.

Well, all that year I was trying to lose weight anyway and that and high blood pressure and sugar kept me pretty well occupied. Traynor had made a smash from a song of mine, I still had seven hundred dollars of the original one thousand dollars in the bank, and I felt if I could just bring my weight down, life would be sweet.

1957

I LOST ten pounds in 1956. That's what I give myself for Christmas. And J. T. and me and the children and their friends and grandkids of all description had just finished dinner – over which I had put on nine and a half of my lost ten – when who should appear at the front door but Traynor. Little Mama, Little Mama! It's that white man who sings — — —. The children didn't call it my song anymore. Nobody did. It was funny how that happened. Traynor and the deacon had bought up all my records, true, but on his record he had put "written by Gracie Mae Still." But that was just another name on the label, like "produced by Apex Records."

On the TV he was inclined to dress like the deacon told him. But now he looked presentable.

Merry Christmas, said he.

And same to you, Son.

I don't know why I called him Son. Well, one way or another they're all our sons. The only requirement is that they be younger than us. But then again, Traynor seemed to be aging by the minute.

You looks tired, I said. Come on in and have a glass of Christmas cheer.

J. T. ain't never in his life been able to act decent to a white man he wasn't working for, but he poured Traynor a glass of bourbon and water, then he took all the children and grandkids and friends and whatnot out to the den. After while I heard Traynor's voice singing the song, coming from the stereo console. It was just the kind of Christmas present my kids would consider cute.

I looked at Traynor, complicit. But he looked like it was the last thing in the world he wanted to hear. His head was pitched forward over his lap, his hands holding his glass and his elbows on his knees.

I done sung that song seem like a million times this year, he said. I sung it on the Grand Ole Opry, I sung it on the Ed Sullivan show. I sung it on Mike Douglas, I sung it at the Cotton Bowl, the Orange Bowl. I sung it at Festivals. I sung it at Fairs. I sung it overseas in Rome, Italy, and once in a submarine *underseas*. I've sung it and sung it, and I'm making forty thousand dollars a day offa it, and you know what, I don't have the faintest notion what that song means.

Whatchumean, what do it mean? It mean what it says. All I could think was: These suckers is making forty thousand a *day* offa my song and now they gonna come back and try to swindle me out of the original thousand.

It's just a song, I said. Cagey. When you fool around with a lot of no count mens you sing a bunch of 'em. I shrugged.

Oh, he said. Well. He started brightening up. I just come by to tell you I think you are a great singer.

He didn't blush, saying that. Just said it straight out.

And I brought you a little Christmas present too. Now you take this little box and you hold it until I drive off. Then you take it outside under that first streetlight back up the street aways in front of that green house. Then you open the box and see. . . Well, just *see*.

What had come over this boy, I wondered, holding the box. I looked out the window in time to see another white man come up and get in the car with him and then two more cars full of white mens start out behind him. They was all in long black cars that looked like a funeral procession.

Little Mama, Little Mama, what it is? One of my grandkids come running up and started pulling at the box. It was wrapped in gay Christmas paper – the thick, rich kind that it's hard to picture folks making just to throw away.

J. T. and the rest of the crowd followed me out the house, up the street to the streetlight and in front of the green house. Nothing was there but somebody's gold-grilled white Cadillac. Brandnew and most distracting. We got to looking at it so till I almost forgot the little box in my hand. While the others were busy making 'miration I carefully took off the paper and ribbon and folded them up and put them in my pants pocket. What should I see but a pair of genuine solid gold caddy keys.

Dangling the keys in front of everybody's nose, I unlocked the caddy, motioned for J. T. to git in on the other side, and us didn't come back home for two days.

1960

WELL, the boy was sure nuff famous by now. He was still a mite shy of twenty but already they was calling him the Emperor of Rock and Roll. Then what should happen but the draft.

Well, says J. T. There goes all this Emperor of Rock and Roll business.

But even in the army the womens was on him like white on rice. We watched it on the News.

Dear Gracie Mae [he wrote from Germany],

How you? Fine I hope as this leaves me doing real well. Before I come in the army I was gaining a lot of weight and gitting jittery from making all them dumb movies. But now I exercise and eat right and get plenty of rest. I'm more awake than I been in ten years.

I wonder if you are writing any more songs?

Sincerely,
Traynor

I wrote him back:

Dear Son,

We is all fine in the Lord's good grace and hope this finds you the same. J. T. and me be out all times of the day and night in that car you give me – which you know you didn't have to do. Oh, and I do appreciate the mink and the new self-cleaning oven. But if you send anymore stuff to eat from Germany I'm going to have to open up a store in the neighborhood just to get rid of it. Really, we have more than enough of everything. The Lord is good to us and we don't know Want.

Glad to here you is well and gitting your right rest. There ain't nothing like exercising to help that along. J. T. and me work some part of every day that we don't go fishing in the garden.

Well, so long Soldier.

Sincerely,
Gracie Mae

He wrote:

Dear Gracie Mae,

I hope you and J. T. like that automatic power tiller I had one of the stores back home send you. I went through a mountain of catalogs looking for it — I wanted something that even a woman could use.

I've been thinking about writing some songs of my own but every time I finish one it don't seem to be about nothing I've actually lived myself. My agent keeps sending me other people's songs but they just sound mooney. I can hardly git through 'em without gagging.

Everybody still loves that song of yours. They ask me all the time what do I think it means, really. I mean, they want to know just what I want to know. Where out of your life did it come from?

Sincerely,
Traynor

1968

I DIDN'T see the boy for seven years. No. Eight. Because just about everybody was dead when I saw him again. Malcolm X, King, the president and his brother, and even J. T. J. T. died of a head cold. It just settled in his head like a block of ice, he said, and nothing we did moved it until one day he just leaned out the bed and died.

His good friend Horace helped me put him away, and then about a year later Horace and me starting going together. We was sitting out on the front porch swing one swummer night, dusk-dark, and I saw this great procession of lights winding to a stop.

Holy Toledo! said Horace. (He's got a real sexy voice like Ray Charles.) Look *at* it. He meant the long line of flashy cars and the white men in white summer suits jumping out on the drivers' sides and standing at attention. With wings they could pass for angels, with hoods they could be the Klan.

Traynor comes waddling up the walk.

And suddenly I know what it is he could pass for. An Arab like the ones you see in storybooks. Plump and soft and with never a care about weight. Because with so much money, who cares? Traynor is almost dressed like someone from a storybook too. He has on, I swear, about ten necklaces. Two sets of bracelets on his arms, at least one ring on every finger, and some kind of shining buckles on his shoes, so that when he walks you get quite a few twinkling lights.

Gracie Mae, he says, coming up to give me a hug. J. T.

I explain that J. T. passed. That this is Horace.

Horace, he says, puzzled but polite, sort of rocking back on his heels, Horace. That's it for Horace. He goes in the house and don't come back.

Looks like you and me is gained a few, I say.

He laughs. The first time I ever heard him laugh. It don't sound much like a laugh and I can't swear that it's better than no laugh a'tall.

He's gitting fat for sure, but he's still slim compared to me. I'll never see three hundred pounds again and I've just about said (excuse me) fuck it. I got to thinking about it one day an' thought: aside from the fact that they say it's unhealthy, my fat ain't never been no trouble. Mens always have loved me. My kids ain't never complained. Plus they's fat. And fat like I is I looks distinguished. You see me coming and know somebody's *there*.

Gracie Mae, he says, I've come with a personal invitation to you to my house tomorrow for dinner. He laughed. What did it sound like? I couldn't place it. See them men out there? he asked me. I'm sick and tired of eating with them. They don't never have nothing to talk about. That's why I eat so much. But if you come to dinner tomorrow we can talk about the old days. You can tell me about that farm I bought you.

I sold it, I said.

You did?

Yeah, I said, I did. Just cause I said I liked to exercise by working in a garden didn't mean I wanted five hundred acres! Anyhow, I'm a city girl now. Raised in the country it's true. Dirt poor – the whole bit – but that's all behind me now.

Oh well, he said, I didn't mean to offend you.

We sat a few minutes listening to the crickets.

Then he said: You wrote that song while you was still on the farm, didn't you, or was it right after you left?

You had somebody spying on me? I asked.

You and Bessie Smith got into a fight over it once, he said.

You *is* been spying on me!

But I don't know what the fight was about, he said. Just like I don't know what happened to your second husband. Your first one died in the Texas electric chair. Did you know that? Your third one beat you up, stole your touring costumes and your car and retired with a chorine to Tuskegee. He laughed. He's still there.

I had been mad, but suddenly I calmed down. Traynor was talking very dreamily. It was dark but seems like I could tell his eyes weren't right. It was like some*thing* was sitting there talking to me but not necessarily with a person behind it.

You gave up on marrying and seem happier for it. He laughed again. I married but it never went like it was supposed to. I never could squeeze any of my own life either into it or out of it. It was like singing somebody else's record. I copied the way it was sposed to be *exactly* but I never had a clue what marriage meant.

I bought her a diamond ring big as your fist. I bought her clothes. I built her a mansion. But right away she didn't want the boys to stay there. Said they smoked up the bottom floor. Hell, there were *five* floors.

No need to grieve, I said. No need to. Plenty more where she come from.

He perked up. That's part of what that song means, ain't it? No need to grieve. Whatever it is, there's plenty more down the line.

I never really believed that way back when I wrote that song, I said. It was all bluffing then. The trick is to live long enough to put your young bluffs to use. Now if I was to sing that song today I'd tear it up. 'Cause I done lived long enough to know it's *true*. Them words could hold me up.

I ain't lived that long, he said.

Look like you on your way, I said. I don't know why, but the boy seemed to need some encouraging. And I don't know, seem like one way or another you talk to rich white folks and you end up reassuring *them*. But what the hell, by now I feel something for the boy. I wouldn't be in his bed all alone in the middle of the night for nothing. Couldn't be nothing worse than being famous the world over for something you don't even understand. That's what I tried to tell Bessie. She wanted that same song. Overheard me practicing it one day, said, with her hands on her hips: Gracie Mae, I'ma sing your song tonight. I *likes* it.

Your lips be too swole to sing, I said. She was mean and she was strong, but I trounced her.

Ain't you famous enough with your own stuff? I said. Leave mine alone. Later on, she thanked me. By then she was Miss Bessie Smith to the World, and I was still Miss Gracie Mae Nobody from Notasulga.

The next day all these limousines arrived to pick me up. Five cars and twelve bodyguards. Horace picked that morning to start painting the kitchen.

Don't paint the kitchen, fool, I said. The only reason that dumb boy of ours is going to show me his mansion is because he intends to present us with a new house.

What you gonna do with it? he asked me, standing there in his shirtsleeves stirring the paint.

Sell it. Give it to the children. Live in it on weekends. It don't matter what I do. He sure don't care.

Horace just stood there shaking his head. Mama you sure looks *good*, he says. Wake me up when you git back.

Fool, I say, and pat my wig in front of the mirror.

The boy's house is something else. First you come to this mountain, and then you commence to drive and drive up this road that's lined with magnolias. Do magnolias grow on mountains? I was wondering. And you come to lakes and you come to ponds and you come to deer and you come up on some sheep. And I figure these two is sposed to represent England and Wales. Or something out of Europe. And you just keep on coming to stuff. And it's all pretty. Only the man driving my car don't look at nothing but the road. Fool. And then *finally*, after all this time, you begin to go up the driveway. And there's more magnolias – only they're not in such good shape. It's sort of cool up this high and I don't think they're gonna make it. And then I see this building that looks like if it had a name it would be The Tara Hotel. Columns and steps and outdoor chandeliers and rocking chairs. Rocking chairs? Well, and there's the boy on the steps dressed in a dark green satin jacket like you see folks wearing on TV late at night, and he looks sort of like a fat dracula with all that house rising behind him, and standing beside him there's this little white vision of loveliness that he introduces as his wife.

He's nervous when he introduces us and he says to her: This is Gracie Mae Still, I want you to know me. I mean. . .and she gives him a look that would fry meat.

Won't you come in, Gracie Mae, she says, and that's the last I see of her.

He fishes around for something to say or do and decides to escort me to the kitchen. We go through the entry and the parlor and the breakfast room and the dining room and the servants' passage and finally get there. The first thing I notice is that, altogether, there are five stoves. He looks about to introduce me to one.

Wait a minute, I say. Kitchens don't do nothing for me. Let's go sit on the front porch.

Well, we hike back and we sit in the rocking chairs rocking until dinner.

Gracie Mae, he says down the table, taking a piece of fried chicken from the woman standing over him, I got a little surprise for you.

It's a house, ain't it? I ask, spearing a chitlin.

You're getting *spoiled*, he says. And the way he says *spoiled* sounds funny. He slurs it. It sounds like his tongue is too thick for his mouth. Just that quick he's finished the chicken and is now eating chitlins *and* a pork chop. *Me* spoiled, I'm thinking.

I already got a house. Horace is right this minute painting the kitchen. I bought that house. My kids feel comfortable in that house.

But this one I bought you is just like mine. Only a little smaller.

I still don't need no house. And anyway who would clean it?

He looks surprised.

Really, I think, some peoples advance *so* slowly.

I hadn't thought of that. But what the hell, I'll get you somebody to live in.

I don't want other folks living 'round me. Makes me nervous.

You *don't*? It *do*?

What I want to wake up and see folks I don't even know for?

He just sits there downtable staring at me. Some of that feeling is in the song, ain't it? Not the words, the *feeling*. What I want to wake up and see folks I don't even know for? But I see twenty folks a day I don't even know, including my wife.

This food wouldn't be bad to wake up to though, I said. The boy had found the genius of corn bread.

He looked at me real hard. He laughed. Short. They want what you got but they don't want you. They want what I got only it ain't mine. That's what makes 'em so hungry for me when I sing. They getting the flavor of something but they ain't getting the thing itself. They like a pack of hound dogs trying to gobble up a scent.

You talking 'bout your fans?

Right. Right. He says.

Don't worry 'bout your fans, I say. They don't know their asses from a hole in the ground. I doubt there's a honest one in the bunch.

That's the point. Dammit, that's the point! He hits the table with his fist. It's so solid it don't even quiver. You need a honest audience! You can't have folks that's just gonna lie right back to you.

Yeah, I say, it was small compared to yours, but I had one. It would have been worth my life to try to sing 'em somebody else's stuff that I didn't know nothing about.

He must have pressed a buzzer under the table. One of his flunkies zombies up.

Git Johnny Carson, he says.

On the phone? asks the zombie.

On the phone, says Traynor, what you think I mean, git him offa the front porch? Move your ass.

So two weeks later we's on the Johnny Carson show.

Traynor is all corseted down nice and looks a little bit fat but mostly good. And all the women that grew up on him and my song squeal and squeal. Traynor says: The lady who wrote my first hit record is here with us tonight, and she's agreed to sing it for all of us, just like she sung it forty-five years ago. Ladies and Gentlemen, the great Gracie Mae Still!

Well, I had tried to lose a couple of pounds my own self, but failing that I had me a very big dress made. So I sort of rolls over next to Traynor, who is dwarfted by me, so that when he puts his arm around back of me to try to hug me it looks funny to the audience and they laugh.

I can see this pisses him off. But I smile out there at 'em. Imagine squealing for twenty years and not knowing why you're squealing? No more sense of endings and beginnings than hogs.

It don't matter, Son, I say. Don't fret none over me.

I commence to sing. And I sound – wonderful. Being able to sing good ain't all about having a good singing voice a'tall. A good singing voice helps. But when you come up in the Hard Shell Baptist church like I did you understand early that the fellow that sings is the singer. Them that waits for programs and arrangements and letters from home is just good voices occupying body space.

So there I am singing my own song, my own way. And I give it all I got and enjoy every minute of it. When I finish Traynor is standing up clapping and clapping and beaming at first me and then the audience like I'm his mama for true. The audience claps politely for about two seconds.

Traynor looks disgusted.

He comes over and tries to hug me again. The audience laughs.

Johnny Carson looks at us like we both weird.

Traynor is mad as hell. He's supposed to sing something called a love ballad. But instead he takes the mike, turns to me and says: Now see if my imitation still holds up. He goes into the same song, *our* song, I think, looking out at his flaky audience. And he sings it just the way he always did. My voice, my tone, my inflection, everything. But he forgets a couple of lines. Even before he's finished the matronly squeals begin.

He sits down next to me looking whipped.

It don't matter, Son, I say, patting his hand. You don't even know those people. Try to make the people you know happy.

Is that in the song? he asks.

Maybe. I say.

1977

FOR a few years I hear from him, then nothing. But trying to lose weight takes all the attention I got to spare. I finally faced up to the fact that my fat is the hurt I don't admit, not even to myself, and that I been trying to bury it from the day I was born. But also when you git real old, to tell the truth, it ain't as pleasant. It gits lumpy and slack. Yuck. So one day I said to Horace, I'ma git this shit offa me.

And he fell in with the program like he always try to do and Lord such a procession of salads and cottage cheese and fruit juice!

One night I dreamed Traynor had split up with his fifteenth wife. He said: *You meet 'em for no reason. You date 'em for no reason. You marry 'em for no reason. I do it all but I swear it's just like somebody else doing it. I feel like I can't remember Life.*

The boy's in trouble, I said to Horace.

You've always said that, he said.

I have?

Yeah. You always said he looked asleep. You can't sleep through life if you wants to live it.

You not such a fool after all, I said, pushing myself up with my cane and hobbling over to where he was. Let me sit down on your lap, I said, while this salad I ate takes effect.

In the morning we heard Traynor was dead. Some said fat, some said heart, some said alcohol, some said drugs. One of the children called from Detroit. Them dumb fans of his is on a crying rampage, she said. You just ought to turn on the TV.

But I didn't want to see 'em. They was crying and crying and didn't even know what they was crying for. One day this is going to be a pitiful country, I thought.

Nancy Morejón

1944–

I nternationally respected as a poet, she was born in Havana, Cuba, and studied French Language and Literature at Havana University. She is the author of several poetry collections, including the bilingual edition Where the Island Sleeps Like a Wing (1985, English translations by Kathleen Weaver), and her work has been translated into many languages and appears in a number of anthologies. She has written critical texts, in particular on the writings of Nicolás Guillén, and she works as director of Centro de Estudios del Caribe de las Americas/Casa de las Americas in Havana.

Looking Within

From the sixteenth century dates my suffering
though I barely felt it
for that nightingale
always sings in my suffering.

Coffee

Mama brings coffee
from over far-flung seas
as if her life's story
encircled each phrase of smoke
that swirled between us.
Surprised by dawn, she smiles
and over her sugary hair
gold bracelets leap.
The somber thread of her childhood
endures between us.

We would like a towering tree,
a mountain flamboyán,
in whose noble shade
the troubadour might sleep.

Mother

My mother had no patio garden
but rocky islands
floating in delicate corals
under the sun.
Her eyes mirrored no clear-edged branch
but countless garrottes.
What days, those days when she ran barefoot
over the whitewash of orphanages,
and didn't laugh
or even see the horizon.
She had no ivory-inlaid bedroom,
no drawing-room with wicker chairs,
and none of that hushed tropical stained-glass.
My mother had the handkerchief and the song
to cradle my body's deepest faith,
and hold her head high,
banished queen –
She gave us her hands, like precious stones,
before the cold remains of the enemy.

[Translated by Kathleen Weaver]

Black Woman

I can still smell the spray of the sea they made me cross.
The night, I can't remember.
Not even the ocean itself could remember.
But I can't forget the first alcatraz I saw.
High up, the clouds, like innocent witnessing presences.
By chance, I have forgotten neither my lost coast, nor my ancestral tongue.
They brought me here and here I have lived.
And because I worked like a beast
here I was born again.
How many a Mandinga legend have I resorted to.

        I rebelled.

His Honour bought me in a public square.
I made His Honour's shirt and a son.
My son was without a name.
And His Honour died by the hand of an impeccable English Lord.

        I wandered.

This is the land where I suffered the whip and degradation.
I trod the length of all her rivers.

Under her sun I planted and gathered harvests I did not eat.
My home was a barracoon.
I myself carried the stones to build it,
yet I sang to the natural rhythms of native birds.

I rose up.

In this same land I touched the damp blood
and the rotting bones of many others,
some brought to this place like me, others not.
And I never again thought of the road to Guinea.
Was it to Guinea? Or Benin? Was it to Madagascar? Or Cape Verde?

I worked harder.

I enhanced my hope and age-old song.
Here I built my world.

I went to the hills.

My real independence brought me to the fort
and I rode with Maceo's[1] troops.

Only a century later
with my descendants
of the blue mountain

would I come down from the Sierra[2]

to put an end to capital and moneylenders,
to generals and the bourgeoisie
Now I am: only today do we have and create.
Nothing is taken from us.
Ours is the land.
Ours the sea and the sky.
Ours the magic and the vision.
My peers, here I see you dance
around the tree we plant for communism.
Her prodigious wood already resounds.

[Translated by Julio Finn]

---

[1] Antonio Maceo (1845–96), a Black general, was one of the greatest leaders of
the Cuban Independence War of 1868. Later, with José Martí he led the war of 1895
against Spain, in which he died on the battlefield.
[2] Sierra Maestra, in Oriente, the rugged chain of mountains where the guerrilla
war began in 1956.

Buchi Emecheta
1944–

B orn of Ibuza parentage in Lagos, Nigeria, where she spent her
childhood and early married life, she came to London in 1962
with her student husband. She began writing while struggling to
adapt to life in Britain and support her husband and five young children,
at the same time studying for a BSc in sociology at London University.
She worked in the British Library and was a youth worker with the Inner
London Education Authority. She returned to Nigeria briefly to take up
a teaching post at the University of Calabar. With her sons, she founded
in the 1980s a small publishing company in London, Ogwugwu Afor,
producing some of her own work. A prolific novelist who draws for
subject matter on her own experiences as well as the lives of African
women in both traditional and foreign settings, she numbers among
her many books In the Ditch *(1972)*, Second-Class Citizen *(1974)*, The
Bride Price *(1976)*, The Slave Girl *(1977)*, The Joys of Motherhood *(1979;
extracted here) and* Gwendolyn *(1989); published in USA as* The Family*).*
She has also written plays and books for children.

From

The Joys of Motherhood

CHAPTER X

A MAN NEEDS MANY WIVES

H UMANS, being what we are, tend to forget the most unsavoury experiences
of life, and Nnu Ego and her sons forgot all the suffering they had gone
through when Nnaife was away.

The first important thing to attend to was the celebration at which they
would give their new child a name. All the Ibuza people living in Yaba, Ebute
Metta and in Lagos island itself were called to the feast. Palm wine flowed like
the spring water from Ibuza streams. People sang and danced until they were
tired of doing both. To cap it all, Nnaife brought plentiful supplies of the locally
made alcohol called *ogogoro* which he discreetly poured into bottles labelled
"Scotch Whisky". He assured Nnu Ego that he had seen the white men for whom
he worked on the ship drinking this whisky. Nnu Ego had asked wide-eyed,

"Why do they call our *ogogoro* illicit? Many of my father's friends were jailed just because they drank it."

Nnaife laughed, the bitter laugh of a man who had become very cynical, who now realized that in this world there is no pure person. A man who in those last months had discovered that he had been revering a false image and that under white skins, just as under black ones, all humans are the same. "If they allowed us to develop the production of our own gin, who would buy theirs?" he explained.

However Nnu Ego's long stay in Lagos and her weekly worship at St Jude's Ibo church had taken their toll. She asked suspiciously, "But our own gin, is it pure like theirs?"

"Ours is even stronger and purer – more of the thing. I saw them drink it on the ships at Fernando Po."

So on the day his baby boy was named, Nnaife served his guests with lots and lots of *ogogoro* and his guests marvelled at the amount of money he was spending, for they thought they were drinking spirits which came all the way from Scotland. They did not think of doubting him, since most ship crew members brought all sorts of things home with them. Their masters, not able to buy these workers outright, made them work like slaves anyway, and allowed them to take all the useless goods which were no longer of any value to them. They were paid – paid slaves – but the amount was so ridiculously small that many a white Christian with a little conscience would wonder whether it was worth anybody's while to leave a wife and family and stay almost a year on a voyage. Yet Nnaife was delighted. He was even hopeful of another such voyage. But on the day of his child's naming ceremony he spent a great portion of the money he brought home. He and his family had been without for so long that the thought of saving a little was pushed into the background.

Nnu Ego, that thrifty woman, threw caution to the winds and really enjoyed herself this time. She bought four different kinds of outfit, all cotton from the U.A.C. store. One outfit was for the morning, another for the afternoon, when the child was given the name Adim, Adimabua meaning "now I am two": Nnaife was telling the world that now he had two sons, so he was two persons in one, a very important man. She had another outfit for the late afternoon, and a costly velveteen one for the evening. This was so beautiful that even those women who had been her helpers in time of want looked on enviously. But she did not care; she was enjoying herself. Not to be outdone, Oshia and his father changed their clothes as many times as Nnu Ego. It was one of the happiest days of her life.

A month after that, Oshia started to attend the local mission school, Yaba Methodist. This made him very proud, and he didn't tire of displaying his Khaki uniform trimmed with pink braid. Nnu Ego sold off the spoils from her husband's ship over the next few months, and with this they were able to live comfortably.

Nnaife was developing a kind of dependence on his battered guitar. He would sing and twang on the old box, visiting one friend after another, and not thinking at all of looking for another job. "They promised to send for me," he said. "They said as soon as they were ready to sail again they would send for me."

Nnu Ego was beginning to realize something else. Since he had come back, Nnaife had suddenly assumed the role of the lord and master. He had now such confidence in himself that many a time he would not even bother to answer her questions. Going to Fernando Po had made him grow away from her. She did not know whether to approve of this change or to hate it. True, he had given her enough housekeeping money, and enough capital in the form of the things he brought from Fernando Po, but still she did not like men who stayed at home all day.

"Why don't you go to Ikoyi and ask those Europeans if they have other domestic work for you, so that when they are ready to sail you will go with them?"

"Look, woman, I have been working night and day non-stop for eleven months. Don't you think I deserve a little rest?"

"A little rest? Surely three months is a long time to rest? You can look for something while you are waiting for them."

If Nnu Ego went further than that he would either go out for the rest of the day or resort to his new-found hobby, the twanging of Dr Meers's old guitar. She decided to let him be for a while. After all, they still had enough money to pay for the rest. She also made sure of another term's fees for Oshia. She was now able to have a modest permanent stall of her own, at the railway yard, instead of spreading her wares on the pavement outside the yard. Oshia was helping, too. After school, he would sit by his mother's stand in front of the house, selling cigarettes, paraffin, chopped wood, and clothes blue. His mother would let him off to go and play with his friends as soon as she had finished washing and clearing the day's cooking things from the kitchen.

On one such evening, she sat with her neighbours in front of the house by the electric pole which provided light for yards around the house. Adim, Oshia's little brother, was now four months old, and he was propped up with sand around him to support his back, so he would learn how to sit up straight. He kept flopping on the sand like a bundle of loosely tied rags, much to the amusement of all. Nnu Ego had her stand by her, with her wares displayed, and Iyawo Itsekiri had started selling pork meat in a glass showcase. Another woman from the next yard had a large tray full of bread, so in the evenings the front of the house at Adam Street looked like a little market.

The women were thus happily occupied when they heard the guitar-playing Nnaife coming home. This was a surprise because when he went out these days he would not return until very late, sometimes in the early hours of the morning.

"Look," Iyawo Itsekiri pointed out to Nnu Ego, who was trying to make sure she was not seeing things. "Look, your husband is early today. Is something wrong?"

"Maybe he has decided to make use of his home this evening, for a change. And look at the group of friends he has with him. Are they going to have a party or something? Even our old friend Ubani is with them. I haven't seen him for a long time." With this statement, Nnu Ego forgot her husband's inadequacies and rushed enthusiastically to welcome their friends. They were equally glad to see her. Nnaife didn't stop twanging his guitar throughout the happy exchanges. Nnu Ego showed off her children and Ubani remarked how tall Oshia was growing and told Nnu Ego that his wife Cordelia would be pleased to know that he had seen them all looking so well.

"Oh, so you didn't tell her you were coming here tonight?"

"Few men tell their women where they are going," Nnaife put in, trying to be funny.

"I did not tell Cordelia that I would be seeing you all because I met your husband by accident in Akinwunmi Street, having a nice evening with some of his friends, so we all decided to come here and see you."

There was a kind of constraint on the faces of their visitors, she thought, though Nnaife did not seem to notice anything, but she was becoming uneasy. None the less, she said airily, "Please come in, come inside. Oshia, you mind the stand. I shall not be long."

Nnu Ego noticed that only Ubani was making an effort to talk. The others, Nwakusor, Adigwe and Ijeh, all men from Ibuza living around Yaba, looked solemn. Well, there was little she could do to alleviate their glumness, though she was going to try. She gave them some kolanut and brought out cigarettes and matches. Nnaife added his ever-present *ogogoro*, and soon the gathering resembled a party. After the prayers, Nwakusor gave a small tot of *ogogoro* to Nnaife, and another to his wife. When he urged them to drink it, Nnu Ego sensed that something was very wrong. These men were there to break bad news. All the same, like a good woman, she must do what she was told, she must not question her husband in front of his friends. Her thoughts went to her father, who was now ageing fast, and her heart pounded in fear. She started to shiver, but drank the home-made alcohol with a big gulp. She coughed a little, and this brought a smile to the faces of the men watching her. Nnu Ego was a good wife, happy with her lot.

Nwakusor cleared his throat, forcing furrows on to his otherwise smooth brow. He addressed Nnaife in the full manner, using his father's name Owulum. He reminded him that the day a man is born into a family, the responsibilities in that family are his. Some men were lucky in that they had an elder brother on whose shoulders the greater part of the responsibility lay. His listeners confirmed this by nodding in mute assent. It was an accepted fact.

"Now, you, Nnaife, until last week were one of those lucky men. But now, that big brother of yours is no more..."

Nnaife who all this time had kept his old guitar on his knee, waiting for Nwakusor to finish his speech so that he could start one of the songs he had learned during his short stay at Fernando Po, threw the instrument on the cemented floor. The pathetic clang it made died with such an echo of emptiness that all eyes hypnotically followed its fall, and then returned to Nnaife, who let out one loud wail. Thus there was silence. He stared at his friends with unseeing eyes. As Nnu Ego recovered from the shock of the loud guitar the news began to register. So that was it. Nnaife was now the head of his family.

"Oh, Nnaife, how are you going to cope? All those children, and all those wives." Here she stopped, as the truth hit her like a heavy blow. She almost staggered as it sank in. Nnaife's brother, the very man who had negotiated for her, had three wives even when she was still at home in Ibuza. Surely, surely people would not expect Nnaife to inherit them? She looked round her wildly, and was able to read from the masked faces of the men sitting around that they had thought of that and were here to help their friend and relative solve this knotty problem. For a time, Nnu Ego forgot the kind man who had just died; all she was able to think about was her son who had just started school. Where would Nnaife get the money from? Oh, God. . . She ran out, leaving her baby on the bed.

She ran into Mama Abby who with many others was wondering what the noise and crying was about. Nnu Ego blurted out the first thing that came into her head: "Nnaife may soon be having five more wives."

Seeing that her friends were in suspense, Nnu Ego went on to explain: "His brother has died and left behind several wives and God knows how many children."

"Oh, dear, are you bound to accept them all?" asked Mama Abby, who knew little of Ibo custom. "You have your own children to think of – surely people know that Nnaife is not in a steady job?"

"Maybe he'll be asked to come home and mind the farm," said one of the curious women.

They all started talking at the same time, this one telling Nnu Ego what to do, that one telling her what not to do. The voices jangled together, but Nnu Ego thanked the women and went back inside to her menfolk. Her husband was being consoled by his friends, who had poured him another glass of *ogogoro*. Nnu Ego was asked to bring more cigarettes from her display stand, with a vague promise of repayment by someone. Many neighbours and friends came in, and they held a small wake for Nnaife's brother.

Ubani was the first to take his leave. But before he did so, he called Nnu Ego and Nnaife out into the yard, as their room was filled with people who had come to commiserate with the bereaved family and stayed for a glass of gin or whisky and a puff of tobacco. The air outside was fresh, and the sky was velvety black. Stars twinkled haphazardly against this inky background, and the moon was partly hidden. Ubani told them that he could fix Nnaife up at the railways as a labourer cutting the grass that kept sprouting along the railway lines. Unless he wanted to go back to Ibuza, Ubani suggested he come the very next day.

Nnaife thanked him sincerely. No, he said, he would not go to Ibuza. He had been out of farming practice for so long that he would rather risk it here in Lagos. At home there would be no end to the demands his family would make on him. He had more chance of living longer if he didn't go into what looked like a family turmoil. Of course he would be sending money to the Owulum wives, and would see that their sons kept small farmings going. But he would help them more by being here in Lagos. He would definitely go with Ubani the next day to take up the job if they would accept him.

Ubani assured him that they would; he himself now cooked for the head manager of the whole Nigerian Railway Department and his work was permanent. He was employed by the Railway Department and not the manager himself, so that whenever he decided to leave he would simply be transferred to a new master. Ubani laughed bitterly. "I talk like an old slave these days, grateful to be given a living at all."

"Are we not all slaves to the white men, in a way?" asked Nnu Ego in a strained voice. "If they permit us to eat, then we will eat. If they say we will not, then where will we get the food? Ubani, you are a lucky man and I am glad for you. The money may be small, and the work slave labour, but at least your wife's mind is at rest knowing that at the end of the month she gets some money to feed her children and you. What more does a woman want?"

"I shall see you tomorrow, my friend. Mind how you go with these Hausa soldiers parading the streets."

Nnaife was given a job as a grass-cutter at the railway compound. They gave him a good cutlass, and he would wear tattered clothes while he cut grass all day, come sunshine or rain. The work was tiring, and he did not much like it, especially when he saw many of his own people making their various ways into the workshop every morning. However, like Ubani, he was working for the Department and not for a particular white man, and he intended using that as his basis for getting into the workshop.

One thing was sure: he gained the respect and even the fear of his wife Nnu Ego. He could even now afford to beat her up, if she went beyond the limits he could stand. He gave her a little housekeeping money which bought a bag of garri for the month and some yams; she would have to make up the rest from her trading profits. On top of that, he paid the school fees for Oshia, who was growing fast and was his mother's pride and joy. Adaku, the new wife of his dead brother, would be coming to join them in Lagos, and after some time the oldest wife Adankwo, who was still nursing a four-month-old baby, might come too. Ego-Obi, the middle wife, went back to her people after the death of Nnaife's brother Owulum. The Owulum family said that she was an arrogant person, and she for her part claimed that she was so badly treated by them when her husband died that she decided she would rather stay with her own people. In any case, she was not missed; first, she had no child, and secondly she was very abusive. Adaku, on the other hand, had a daughter, she was better-looking than Ego-Obi, and she was very ambitious, as Nnu Ego was soon to discover. She made sure she was inherited by Nnaife.

Nnu Ego could not believe her eyes when she came home from market one afternoon to see this young woman sitting by their doorstep, with a four-year-old girl sleeping on her knees. To Nnu Ego's eyes, she was enviably attractive, young-looking, and comfortably plump with the kind of roundness that really suited a woman. This woman radiated peace and satisfaction, a satisfaction that was obviously having a healthy influence on her equally well-rounded child. She was dark, this woman, shiny black, and not too tall. Her hair was plaited in the latest fashion, and when she smiled and introduced herself as "your new wife" the humility seemed a bit inconsistent. Nnu Ego felt that she should be bowing to this perfect creature – she who had once been acclaimed the most beautiful woman ever seen. What had happened to her? Why had she become so haggard, so rough, so worn, when this one looked like a pool that had still to be disturbed? Jealousy, fear and anger seized Nnu Ego in turns. She hated this type of woman, who would flatter a man, depend on him, need him. Yes, Nnaife would like that. He had instinctively disliked her own independence, though he had gradually been forced to accept her. But now there was this new threat.

"Don't worry, senior wife, I will take the market things in for you. You go and sit and look after the babies. Just show me where the cooking place is, and I will get your food ready for you."

Nnu Ego stared at her. She had so lost contact with her people that the voice of this person addressing her as "senior wife" made her feel not only old but completely out of touch, as if she was an outcast. She resented it. It was one thing to be thus addressed in Ibuza, where people gained a great deal by seniority; here, in Lagos, though the same belief still held, it was to a different degree. She was used to being the sole woman of this house, used to having Nnaife all to herself, planning with him what to do with the little money he earned, even though he had become slightly evasive since he went to Fernando Po – a result of long isolation, she had thought. But now, this new menace. . .

What was she to do? It had been all right when this was just a prospect. Not hearing anything definite from home, she had begun to tell herself that maybe the senior Owulum's wives had decided against coming. For she had sent messages to Ibuza to let Nnaife's people know that things were difficult in Lagos, that Lagos was a place where you could get nothing free, that Nnaife's job was not very secure, that she had to subsidize their living with her meagre profits. She could imagine this creature hearing all about it and laughing to herself, saying, "If it is so bad, why is she there? Does she not want me to come?" Yes, it was true, Nnu Ego had not wanted her to come. What else did Nnaife want? She had borne him two sons, and after she had nursed Adim there would be nothing to hold her back from having as many children as they wanted. She knew this kind of woman: an ambitious woman who was already thinking that now she was in Lagos she would eat fried food.

Nnu Ego knew that her father could not help her. He would say to her, "Listen, daughter, I have seven wives of my own. I married three of them, four I inherited on the deaths of relatives. Your mother was only a mistress who refused to marry me. So why do you want to stand in your husband's way? Please don't disgrace the name of the family again. What greater honour is there for a woman than to be a mother, and now you are a mother – not of daughters who will marry and go, but of good-looking healthy sons, and they are the first sons of your husband and you are his first and senior wife. Why do you wish to behave like a woman brought up in a poor household?" And all this for a husband she had not wanted in the beginning! A husband to whom she had closed her eyes when he came to her that first night, a husband who until recently had little confidence in himself, who a few months ago was heavy and round-bellied from inactivity. Now he was losing weight because of working hard in the open like other men did in Ibuza, Nnaife looked younger than his age, while she Nnu Ego was looking and feeling very old after the birth of only three children. The whole arrangement was so unjust.

She tried desperately to control her feelings, to put on a pleasant face, to be the sophisticated Ibuza wife and welcome another woman into her home; but she could not. She hated this thing called the European way; these people called Christians taught that a man must marry only one wife. Now here was Nnaife with not just two but planning to have maybe three or four in the not so distant future. Yet she knew the reply he would give her to justify his departure from monogamy. He would say: "I don't work for Dr Meers any more. I work as a grass-cutter for the Nigerian Railway Department, and they employ many Moslems and even pagans." He had only been a good Christian so long as his livelihood with Dr Meers depended on it. It was precisely that work, when they had seen each other every day and all day, that had made her so dependent on Nnaife. She had been in Lagos now for more than seven years, and one could not change the habits of so many years in two minutes, humiliating as it was to know that this woman fresh from Ibuza was watching her closely, reading all the struggles and deliberations going on in her mind. Adaku, however, was able to disguise any disgust she felt by wearing a faint smile which neither developed into a full smile nor degenerated into a frown.

Like someone suddenly awakened from a deep sleep, Nnu Ego rushed past her and, standing by their door with the key poised, said hoarsely, "Come on in, and bring your child with you."

Adaku, tired from her long journey, bit on her lower lip so hard that it almost bled. Without saying a word, she carried the sleeping child into the dark room, then went back to the veranda to bring in her things and, as expected of her, Nnu Ego's groceries. She had prepared herself for a reluctant welcome something like this; and what alternative did she have? After mourning nine whole months for their husband, she had had enough of Ibuza, at least for a while. People had warned her that Nnu Ego would be a difficult person to live with; yet either she accepted Nnaife or spent the rest of her life struggling to make ends meet. People at home had seen her off to Lagos with all their blessing, but this daughter of Agbadi so resented her. Nnu Ego was lucky there was no Ibuza man or woman to witness this kind of un-Ibo-like conduct; many people would not have believed it. Adaku did not care, though; all she wanted was a home for her daughter and her future children. She did not want more than one home, as some women did who married outside the families of their dead husbands. No, it was worth some humiliation to have and keep one's children together in the same family. For her own children's sake she was going to ignore this jealous cat. Who knows, she told herself, Nnaife might even like her. She only had to wait and see.

Nnaife was delighted at his good fortune. Beaming like a child presented with a new toy, he showed Adaku, as his new wife, round the yard. He pointed out this and that to her, and he bought some palm wine to toast her safe arrival. He took her daughter as his, and vowed to his dead brother that he would look after his family as his own. He called Oshia and introduced the little girl Dumbi to him as his sister. Oshia, who suspected that his mother did not like this new sister and her mother, asked:

"When will they go back to where they came from, Father?"

Nnaife reprimanded him, calling him a selfish boy and saying that if he was not careful he would grow into a selfish man who no one would help when he was in difficulty. Nnaife put the fear of the Devil into Oshia by telling him a story which he said happened on the ship, of a white man who died alone, because he was minding his own business.

Nnu Ego, who was busy dishing out the soup while this tirade was going on, knew that half the story was not true. She felt that Nnaife was being ridiculous and, rather like a little boy himself, was trying to show off his worldly knowledge to his new wife. Nnu Ego was the more annoyed because the latter was making such encouraging sounds, as if Nnaife were recounting a successful trip to the moon.

"For God's sake, Nnaife, was there anything that did not happen on that ship you sailed in so long ago?" She expected the others to laugh, but her son Oshia was so taken in by his father's stories that he strongly disapproved of his mother's interruption and protested indignantly:

"But it is true, Mother!"

"Some strange things do happen on those ships that sail on the big seas, and the men do see peculiar sights. This is well known even in Ibuza," Adaku put in, uninvited.

Nnu Ego stopped in her movements. She knew that if she did not take care she would place herself in a challenging position, in which she and Adaku would be fighting for Nnaife's favour. Strange how in less than five hours Nnaife had become a rare commodity. She ignored Adaku's remark as unanswerable but snapped at her son:

"What type of a son are you, replying to your own mother like that? A good son should respect his mother always; in a place like this, sons belong to both parents, not just the father!"

Nnaife simply laughed and told Oshia not to talk like that to his mother again, adding with a touch of irony, "Sons are very often mother's sons."

Again in came that cool, low voice, which Nnu Ego had been trying all day to accept as part of their life, at the same time as telling herself that the owner of the voice did not belong, or that, if she did, her belonging was only going to be a temporary affair – but Adaku, the owner of that disturbing voice, seemed determined to belong, right from the first:

"In Ibuza sons help their father more than they even help their mother. A mother's joy is only in the name. She worries over them, looks after them when they are small; but in the actual help on the farm, the upholding of the family name, all belong to the father. . ."

Adaku's explanation was cut short by Nnu Ego who brought in the steaming soup she had been dishing out behind the curtain. She sniffed with derision and said as she placed a bowl on Nnaife's table: "Why don't you tell your brother's wife that we are in Lagos, not in Ibuza, and that you have no farm for Oshia in the railway compound where you cut grass?"

They ate their food in silence, Nnu Ego, Adaku and the two children Oshia and Dumbi eating from the same bowl of pounded yam and soup. Nnu Ego's mind was not on the food and she was acting mechanically. She was afraid that her hold on Nnaife's household was in question. She took every opportunity to remind herself that she was the mother of the sons of the family. Even when it came to sharing the piece of meat for the two children, one of the duties of the woman of the house, she pointed out to Dumbi that she must respect Oshia, as he was the heir and the future owner of the family. Their few possessions – the four-poster iron bed which Nnaife had bought from his journey to Fernando Po and the large wall mirrors – were things of immense value to Nnu Ego, and if her son never grew up to be a farmer, she wanted to make sure that whatever there was should be his. She knew again that she was being ridiculous because no one challenged her; it was a known fact. However, she felt compelled to state the obvious as a way of relieving her inner turmoil.

After eating, Nnaife looked at her reflectively and said: "The food is very nice; thank you, my senior wife and mother of my sons."

It was Nnu Ego's turn to be surprised. Her husband had never thanked her for her cooking before, to say nothing of reminding her of being the mother of his two boys. What was happening to them all?

Nnaife was still studying her from his chair; the other members of the family were eating sitting on the floor.

"You see, my brother's death must bring changes to us all. I am now the head, and you are the head's wife. And as with all head wives in Ibuza, there are things it would be derogatory for you to talk about or even notice, otherwise you will encourage people to snigger and cause rumours to fly about you. No one wanted my brother's death. And do you think, knowing him as you did, that he was the sort of man to let you and Oshia beg if anything had happened to me?"

Nnu Ego could think of nothing apposite to say. She was a trifle disconcerted. To try and be philosophical like Nnaife might tempt her to ascribe profundity to the ordinary. None the less, she was intrinsically grateful to him for making what must have been a tremendous effort.

She was determined to attack with patience what she knew was going to be a great test to her. She was not only the mother of her boys, but the spiritual and the natural mother of this household, so she must start acting like one. It took her a while to realize that she was stacking the plates used for their evening meal and taking them out in the kitchen to wash.

"I should be doing that," Adaku cooed behind her.

Nnu Ego controlled her breath and held tight her shaking hands. Then she spoke in a voice that even surprised her: "But, daughter, you need to know your husband. You go to him, I'm sure he has many tales to tell you."

Adaku laughed, the first real laughter she had let herself indulge in since arriving that morning. It was a very eloquent sound, telling Nnu Ego that they were going to be sisters in this business of sharing a husband. She went into the kitchen still laughing as Mama Abby came in.

"Your new wife is a nice woman. Laughing with so much confidence and happiness on the day of her arrival."

"A happy senior wife makes a happy household," Nnu Ego snapped. She suspected that her unhappiness at Adaku's presence was by now common knowledge and she was not going to encourage it further. After all, Mama Abby had never had to live as a senior wife before, to say nothing of welcoming a younger wife into her family. To prevent her saying anything further, Nnu Ego added: "I must go and see to our guests."

She hurried in and, to take her mind off herself, busied herself entertaining people who came throughout the evening to see the new wife. Nnu Ego fought back tears as she prepared her own bed for Nnaife and Adaku. It was a good thing she was determined to play the role of the mature senior wife; she was not going to give herself any heartache when the time came for Adaku to sleep on that bed. She must stuff her ears with cloth and make sure she also stuffed her nipple into the mouth of her young son Adim, when they all lay down to sleep.

Far before the last guest left, Nnaife was already telling Oshia to go to bed because it was getting late.

"But we usually stay up longer than this, Father."

"Don't argue with your father. Go and spread your mat and sleep; you too, our new daughter Dumbi."

The neighbours who had come to welcome the new wife took the hint and left. Did Nnaife have to make himself so obvious? Nnu Ego asked herself. One would have thought Adaku would be going away after tonight.

"Try to sleep, too, senior wife," he said to her, and now Nnu Ego was sure he was laughing at her. He could hardly wait for her to settle down before he pulled Adaku into their only bed.

It was a good thing she had prepared herself, because Adaku turned out to be one of those shameless modern women whom Nnu Ego did not like. What did she think she was doing? Did she think Nnaife was her lover and not her husband, to show her enjoyment so? She tried to block her ears, yet could still hear Adaku's exaggerated carrying on. Nnu Ego tossed in agony and anger all night, going through in her imagination what was taking place behind the curtained bed. Not that she had to do much imagining, because even when she tried to ignore what was going on, Adaku would not let her. She giggled, she squeaked, she cried and she laughed in turn, until Nnu Ego was quite convinced that it was all for her benefit. At one point Nnu Ego sat bolt upright looking at the shadows of Nnaife and Adaku. No, she did not have to imagine what was going on; Adaku made sure she knew.

When Nnu Ego could stand it no longer, she shouted at Oshia who surprisingly was sleeping through it all: "Oshia, stop snoring!"

There was silence from the bed, and then a burst of laughter. Nnu Ego could have bitten her tongue off; what hurt her most was hearing Nnaife remark:

"My senior wife cannot go to sleep. You must learn to accept your pleasures quietly, my new wife Adaku. Your senior wife is like a white lady: she does not want noise."

Nnu Ego bit her teeth into her baby's night clothes to prevent herself from screaming.

J. J. Phillips
1944–

A poet and writer, she lives on the west coast of the USA. During
the Civil Rights Movement she was arrested in North Carolina
in 1962. Her novel Mojo Hand: An Orphic Tale, about a young
woman's involvement with a blues musician, was first published in 1966,
and was reissued in 1987.

From

Mojo Hand: An Orphic Tale

CHAPTER IX

SHE, the interloper, came to stay with him and learn his harsh ways.
Some days when she was home, she, X. L., and Blacksnake would go fishing,
relaxing down by the banks of the Little River. Time and thought crisscrossed
each other internally, silently, and the air was swollen with things unsaid, things
hoped to be said, or things expected to be said. Only the flies buzzed over their
heads waiting to settle on the catch of fish.

There was no real thought, only the vague aura of waiting lazily for something
agreeable to be said or listened to or not listened to but merely heard, for talk
was essential to the waiting which was the essence of this life. Sleep was superfluous because it cut short the wait with undeniable finality. However, though no
one said much it was not a sharp ennui; it was pleasant and quite in keeping with
the land, where everything only wanted to wait – for what, no one knew, or really
cared. The day was at hand and it was to be taken with a soft hand, dismembered
and sucked slowly, happily until another day revealed itself.

Sometimes though, there was in them the inability to take things in the way
they should; they had vague hintings at their abulia and it was often Blacksnake
who found himself dry. He would say to X. L., "Man, I just don't see why the
blues come in my house every morning 'fore day."

X. L. would shake his head in sympathy. "Yeah, man, I knows. Onliest
thing you can do is turn on your radio and let them waste away."

Blacksnake would carefully examine his shoes to see that every bit of the
surface was shined to a hard gloss. "Man, but I wakes up in a sweat with tears
all in my eyes and I just can't see why."

Eunice sat silently by, because she, too, was coming to know the ossification of judgment.

Blacksnake would grab a bottle of whiskey and violently rip off the cap, drinking with a vengeance. He'd look at X. L. "Yes, you take a man have the blues, he can't last very long."

X. L. smiled. "Can't say nothing to deny that, man."

"Yes, he wake up early in the morning all in a worry and he don't know what is going on."

"Shit, Snake, you *knows* you ain't got to tell me. Man, where them dice at?"

And so they would gamble to release the pitiful curiosity. The charts of disgust were of no use; moments were to be used, not listened to in their swiftly aging agony, and they had only themselves to answer to for the crimes of forgetfulness, and not the world. It was painful but easy to learn these ways to dispose the heart to the memory of things never to be experienced. Sitting, eating, drinking, loving – all were careless expressions of something gone long before, casual in their very intensity, outwardly justifying only themselves but binding the people involved to the true yet stale verbiage of mothers' warnings. Long afterward Eunice could distinctly retaste the unique flavor of a cigarette inhaled early in the morning when she and Blacksnake lay silently in each other's arms, unconsciously hoping for the ascendancy of some sort of permanence, yet merely toying with how they would deliver this new day to themselves, scrape some sort of definite pronunciation from it. For already a portion of it had been lost to them by sleep.

That remembered taste served to refire the flavor of being one's own hostage. Everyone else was concerned with the plight of thunder, while they lay responsible not even to each other. Yet, he still heralded the sun. Not that it was a task of so great importance, but it was a signal of hated finality that he had been chosen to amend into life. It was a disgusting but necessary avulsion for Eunice from easily being concerned about things of no real consequence to her, for now there were too many things to say, and not enough words to express. A song and a touch were the only means to combat the harrowing lack of communication that became a faked and enforced privacy, making one scream: *Have you ever looked over a mountain, a mountain you have never seen; have you ever lay down in your bed and had one of those lonesome dreams?* And slowly she came to taste more of the marrow of what made blues than she had ever imagined to be contained in such a thin, rigid fiber of expression.

Often Blacksnake would lie down for a short nap in the afternoon and when Eunice was home she too would rest. She would stretch out, her head slightly below his, low enough to look up at him as he slept. Always she would see first the wrinkles at the base of his neck behind each ear that reminded her of accordion-folded paper fans. But these were soft and small, and converged in a rumple at the back of his earlobe. Her eyes would then wander across his ear, usually with her hands following, tracing and quietly hoping to remember the sensation of his face. She would trace the razor pocks on his cheek. At the jaw they were long and thin, like lizard tracks in the sand, but as they went up his cheek they became small pinpoints and finally disappeared with confusion under his eyes. Her hands would jump over to his temple, her fingers feeling its throb. His eyebrows were those of a small child, very fine and extremely delineated, and on his forehead she could barely discern the grooves that made the diastrophic contortions rendering his face unrecognizable when he was cursing or singing.

His skin was a liquid chocolate, but under his eyes it deepened and dulled to a black velvet. Many times she would find his hands folded on his chest, take them in her own, and examine their weatherbeaten contour. The broken, distorted knuckles were the same black velvet and the veins knotted in and out, twining their way to invisibility at his wrists. His fingers were long, the tips calloused beyond feeling from pounding on the strings, and his nails ribbed and stained.

He would snore and sputter, sometimes chewing violently as if some tough hog hock was filling his mouth. Each time he would do this Eunice broke into laughter that woke him. His hand would fly up to check that his head rag was in place and his eyes would open. "Hey, woman," he would say, "what you laughing at?"

She would turn and try to stifle the laughter that rose in her every time she remembered the slow crackling of his teeth. "You were chewing in your sleep."

"I was having me a dream that my old lady was cooking me some food. She and you is the onliest peoples I lets fix my food, you knows. Somebody else might poison the Blacksnake. Shit, *you* just might."

"No, you know I would never do that."

"Yeah, I knows that, but, baby, I can't never be too sure." He would reach for a cigarette, so would Eunice. His hand would grab her arm and force it down. "Stop that. You going to kill youself smoking so much." Then she would put down the cigarette, get him some beer, and he would tell her stories as they drank.

"Yes, you knows, speaking 'bout killing peoples, one time I was living out to the country picking 'bacco. My wife was out there and she was Clarissa Mae then. She pick more 'bacco then them mens. I was a bad man then, and I used to take her money and go down to the town and gamble.

"In the camp I didn't pick no 'bacco. I let old Clarissa do that. I just used to play my guitar on Saturday nights and dance for them peoples. I was too slick for them when they would get to shooting the craps. I sure could roll them mollytrotters. I would get out there, set my point, and win all them store papers from them workers.

"It was them times when nobody couldn't get no liquor, so I'd go down and get me some malt syrup and sugar and some water and put it all in a crock churn during the week. Come Saturday night I play my box and sell the best-tasting beer you ever seen 'round Wake County, for thirty cent a bottle, and didn't no police ever get me for that."

He held up the beer to the light. "Shit, girl, it wasn't nothing like this. Then one time my brother came down from High Points to gamble. We all got to gambling and drinking my beer and he got to winning all the money. One of them mens got mad and left the game and my brother commenced to winning more money. Directly all the beer ran out and everybody got tired and wanted to go. My brother put all his little money away and just as soon as my brother gets out the screen door, this black fool what'd left earlier jumps out and stab him in his chest. My brother run down the street and he fell stone dead on the road. The other motherfucker hightailed his ass out of the country. I got so mad seeing my brother get kill for that little money, I got my gun. I used to had a fine old Colt pistol, shiny with a silver-and-mother-of-pearl handle. I got my gun and set out after that fool. I went and axed everybody if they'd seen him and I told them what he look like, 'cause he was a ugly fool. There was something wrong with his lip. He didn't have none, it just kept on running on up to his nose like somebody done hacked a passway right up his face. I was getting ready to hack one clear up from his black ass to his nappy head when somebody come and tell me where he be.

"As soon as I seed him I knowed who he was, and I just commenced to shooting. I *had* to kill his ass. His mama and papa come running and call the police on me. They carried me off to the penitench for five year. When I got out I went looking for the rest of his peoples, but they had gone to Chicago or someplace like that. I's sorry, sorry to my grave that I went to kill that fool. I don't want to be killing nobody. Now, I might just kill somebody accidental with my knife if I gets to fighting, but I don't be meaning to, and if I did they be sending me back to the penitench again."

He looked at his hands. "If I'm got to go back now, I knows, I *knows* I wouldn't never see the outside no more. I's too old for that shit." He looked at Eunice. "Yeah, woman, the prison blues is the baddest blues ever to fall down on this old daddy."

They would lie there in the receding light finishing the beer, telling lies and laughing, then listening quietly to their stomachs growl.

"Yeah, they sure do go on rumbling," Blacksnake would say.

Eunice would take a drink of beer, lie back, and laugh. "Well, it's not so much mine as yours."

He would pull the bottle of beer from her, take her hand, and flash his diamond in her face. "You kind of likes old Blacksnake. He mean though, going 'round killing peoples."

"Well, now," she would say, still laughing, "yes."

"Why, baby?"

"I suppose it's because your stomach growls so loud."

"Shit, woman. That all? You trying to tell poor me it just my stomach that make you love me? You a jiving mollytrotter if I ever seen one." Then he would take her and pluck from her his special blues. And she would curse the joy of the song as she sang it with him in the dying afternoon.

Sherley Anne Williams
1944–

B orn in Bakersfield, California, she attended school in Fresno, studied at California State University at Fresno (BA, 1966), Howard
University (1966–7) and Brown University (MA, 1972). She has
taught English at Federal City College in Washington, DC, California
State University and from 1975 at the University of California, San
Diego. As a literary critic, she has written widely on Black poetry and
music and in 1972 published Give Birth to Brightness: A Thematic Study
of Neo-Black Literature. She is also author of The Peacock Poems (1975),
Someone Sweet Angel Chile (1982) and the 1987 novel from which this
passage is taken, Dessa Rose (about a pregnant slave who is due to be
hanged for leading an insurrection – inspired by historical incidents that
took place in 1829–30 in Kentucky and North Carolina). She has said:
"I am the women I speak of in my stories, my poems. The fact that I am
a single mother sometimes makes it hard to bring this forth to embody it
in the world, but it is precisely because I am the single mother of an only
son that I try so hard to do this. Women must leave a record for their men;
otherwise how will they know us?"

From

Dessa Rose

THE WENCH

T HE days drifted by. Dessa slept, waking to the colored woman's gruff
urgings to "eat. Eat," the taste of some strongly flavored broth, the mealy
texture of cereal, thinned she thought with milk, the changing of the bloody
cloth. Acutely embarrassed and weak as a kitten, she bore the woman's gentle
touch. Often she woke to find the baby asleep in the curve of her arm and, hand
heavy, powerless to caress him, she pursed her lips and breathed him love. . .Or
opened her eyes to some smiling face – dark, peach-colored, hair like night or
the sun – whose name she ought to know. She would grin feebly; they would
pat her arm. Nathan, she would think. Cully. But already they were gone.

The colored woman chatted in a companionable way as she tended Dessa.
Not enough to require an answer or force Dessa to questions, but she did listen,

her mind holding enough to know the baby was doing well; the white woman meant no harm; she could sleep. She did not dream but she became cautious in her waking. The white woman seemed often in the room and Dessa woke, now and then, to find her settled in the rocker, hands quiet in her lap, dreamy-eyed, looking toward Dessa but apparently talking to herself. "...bonnet..." Dessa heard several times. Half-listening, fascinated, she watched the red mouth move. She knew she could understand what the white woman said if she would let herself. But if she understood the white woman, she would have to...have to, have to do – Something And – "...picnic," the white woman said. Dessa wanted to laugh. Where did you go to pick nits? Or was that something else only white folks did? She peered at the white woman; her dress looked neat enough. So they had bugs, just like some trashy buckra or freshwater negro who didn't know enough to keep clean. "Mammy..." That made no sense. Mammy's name came up often. What could this white woman know of mammy; or mammy of "dropped waists" and "Dutch sleeves" – unless these were cows?

Once she woke in arms, her face tangled in a skein of fine webbing that seemed alive, it clung and itched her skin so bad. She almost suffocated in her terror for she knew the white woman held her and they were together in the big feather bed. And, really, it was the white woman's breathing that saved her, brought her to her senses; its calm regularity imposing order on her own wildly beating heart. That breathing, punctuated by a drawn-out sigh of utter satisfaction and the small fragile bundle that nestled at her spine. Turning cautiously, moving with infinite patience, she inched herself and the baby toward the edge of the bed. Squirming carefully into the soft mattress she managed to nudge out a slight rise between herself and the other woman who, still breathing regularly, had likewise turned away. What kind of place had she come to? she thought as her heart thudded against her ribs. Her fingers touched briefly the satiny hair, the thin velvet of her baby's skin. It was a long time before she slept again.

The colored woman's name was Ada, Dessa realized one morning. The long windows had begun to gray with dawn light. No conch or bell sounded here; people must get up with the rooster's crow. This was the Sutton place except Master Sutton wasn't here. Ada called the white woman "Miz Ruint". There was something funny about the way Ada said the name, as though – Was the white woman crazy? Dessa sweated; the thin stuff of her shift clung to her. *Shift.* Dessa clutched at the garment. She had never in her life owned cloth as fine as the material her hand rubbed against her side. She moved uneasily between the unbelievable smoothness of the sheets. The white woman's breathing was barely audible in the stillness. Maybe she was crazy, Dessa thought, but not a killer. No, not a killer. Nathan and Cully would not have brought her here. Not a killer; but touched, maybe; strange in the head. What else could explain her own presence in this bed?

Touched; and Ada said, Miz Ruint said the master was coming home this harvest for sure. The other woman had laughed quietly. Ada said the white woman had said the same thing about the master's return last year and he hadn't come. Dessa remembered that; Ada had rolled her eyes as if to say – Dessa couldn't quite put her finger on it. Crazy – maybe, she assured herself now, but not no killer. Ada spoke also of "Dorcas". In her mind's eye, Dessa saw a thin, loam-colored face, surmounted by a tangle of even darker hair. No. That was Annabelle, Ada's daughter, seldom seen and then only briefly, a slender figure who hummed quietly and showed no interest in Dessa. Dorcas was someone Ada quoted, someone Dessa didn't think she had yet seen. Never mind, she told herself. Her hand moved to soothe the baby. There had to be someplace else to sleep. She would ask Ada.

Neither Ada nor her daughter belonged to the white woman; none of them did. Ada's words plucked at Dessa's attention. Ada's face beneath her bandanna was placid and Dessa wondered if she had heard right. Free? Dessa wondered silently, as she watched Ada stir the bowl she held. Dessa tried to gesture but her hand fell limply to her side. She swallowed. "Yo'all – " she croaked.

Ada paused with the spoon halfway to Dessa's mouth. "Free?" she said smiling, brown eyes looking closely at Dessa as she replaced the spoon in the bowl untouched. "Cat let loose your tongue, huh? Come on, it just a bit more." She stirred the remaining grits and lifted another spoonful toward Dessa. "Come on; eat up."

Dessa opened her mouth obediently. The grits had been thinned with milk and seasoned with butter and Dessa held the spoonful in her mouth savoring the richness.

"I wouldn't zactly call it free," Ada said, doubtfully. "We runned away," she added brightly, as though this explained it all. "She let us stay here; she need the he'p. Man gone; slaves runned off." Ada shrugged and smiled. "White folks think we hers but didn't none of us never belong to this place." She spooned the last of the cereal into Dessa's mouth and rose.

"Ada." Dessa managed to grasp a fold of the woman's skirt. "Ada, sleep with you?" She struggled to one elbow, then fell back weakly, her eyes seeking to hold the other woman's. "Me and the baby?" She couldn't spend another night in the white woman's bed.

"Honey." Ada bent over her, eyes warm with concern. "Honey, me and Annabelle sleeps in that little lean-to they calls a kitchen; it just barely big enough for us and it ain't no wise fitting. You ain't even out of childbed – "

"Quarters, we could – "

"Worse than a chicken run." Ada sat on the bed, stroking Dessa's hand. "Tell you, honey, these some *poor* white peoples. Oh, this room and the parlor fine enough, but you know what's outside that door? A great big stairway lead straight up to nothing cause they never did finish the second floor." She laughed. "The 'Quarters' is a cabin, one side for the womens, one side for the mens. 'Sides," she added when Dessa would have protested further, "she the only nursing woman on the place. Even if you go, you ought to leave the baby here."

Dessa had suspected from the way the baby turned from her, fretting and in tears, that she had no milk to speak of. Her baby, nursing – Her breathing quickened and her heart seemed to pound in her ears. There was more, but Dessa turned away.

Ada talked as much to herself as she did to Dessa, almost in the same way that the white woman did, never really expecting an answer. Already she seemed to have forgotten that Dessa had spoken. Dessa surrendered to the familiar lassitude. Runaways. Ada, Harker, how many others? And the white woman let them stay, nursed – Dessa knew the white woman nursed her baby; she had seen her do it. It went against everything she had been taught to think about white women but to inspect that fact too closely was almost to deny her own existence. That the white woman had let them stay – Even that was almost too big to think about. Sometimes it seemed to Dessa that she was drowning in milky skin, ensnared by red hair. There was a small mole on the white woman's forehead just above one sandy eyebrow. She smelled faintly of some scent that Dessa couldn't place. Why had they all run here? Because she let them stay. Why had she let them stay?

"...behind. She was that put out about it, too." The white woman was sewing this time, setting big, careless stitches in a white cloth draped over her knees. Against her will Dessa listened. "... night of the Saint Cecilia dinner and of course Mammy had to dress mother for that."

No white woman like this had ever figured in mammy's conversations, Dessa thought drowsily. And this would have been something to talk about: dinner and gowns – not just plain dresses.

"...all by myself. And scared, too – the Winstons was related to royalty or maybe it was only just a knight." The white woman paused a moment. "Now, often as Daphne told it, you'd think I'd know it by heart." She shook her head and laughed softly. "Mammy would know it."

Maybe, Dessa thought, with a sudden pang, Mammy hadn't "known" about Kaine, about Master selling Jeeter...

"...Mammy doubted that, when it all happened so long ago wasn't no one alive now who witnessed it."

I seen it, Dessa started to say. Master sold Jeeter to the trader same as Mistress sold me. But the white woman continued without pause.

"...the pretty clothes. Well, I know Mammy didn't know a thing about history, but I knew she was right about the clothes. She used to dress me so pretty. Even the Reynolds girls – and their daddy owned the bank; everyone said they wore drawers made out of French silk. They used to admire my clothes."

Dessa stared at the white woman. She was crazy, making up this whole thing, like, like –

"...pretend their clothes came from a fashionable *modiste*, but I always said, 'Oh, this is a little something Mammy ran up for me.' So when I walked into the great hall at Winston, I had on a dress that Mammy made and it was Mammy's –"

"Wasn't no 'mammy' to it." The words burst from Dessa. She knew even as she said it what the white woman meant. "Mammy" was a servant, a slave (Dorcas?) who had nursed the white woman as Carrie had nursed Young Mistress's baby before it died. But, goaded by the white woman's open-mouthed stare, she continued, "Mammy ain't made you nothing!"

"Why, she – " The white woman stopped, confused. Hurt seemed to spread like a red stain across her face.

Seeing it, Dessa lashed out again. "You don't even know mammy."

"I do so," the white woman said indignantly, "Pappa give her – "

"Mammy live on the Vaugham plantation near Simeon on the Beauford River, McAllen County." This was what they were taught to say if some white person asked them; their name and what place they belonged to. The white woman gaped, like a fish, Dessa thought contemptuously, just like a fish out of water. Anybody could make this white woman's wits go gathering.

"My, my – *My* Mammy – " the white woman sputtered.

The words exploded inside Dessa. "*Your* 'mammy' – " Never, never had that white baby taken Jessup's place with Carrie. "Your 'mammy'!" No *white* girl could ever have taken *her* place in mammy's bosom; no one. "You ain't got no 'mammy'," she snapped.

"I do – I did so." The white woman was shouting now, the white cloth crushed in her trembling hands.

"All you know about is this kinda sleeve and that kinda bonnet; some party here – Didn't you have no peoples where you lived? 'Mammy' ain't nobody name, not they real one."

"Mam – "

The white woman's baby started to cry and the white woman made as if to rise and go to it. Dessa's voice overrode the tearful wail, seeming to pin the white woman in the chair. "See! See! You don't even not know 'mammy's' name. Mammy have a name, have children."

"She didn't." The white woman, finger stabbing toward her own heart, finally rose. "She just had me! I was like her child."

"What was her name then?" Dessa taunted. "Child don't even know its own mammy's name. What was mammy's name? What – "

"Mammy," the white woman yelled. "That was her name."

"Her name was Rose," Dessa shouted back, struggling to sit up. "That's a flower so red it look black. When mammy was a girl they named her that count of her skin – smooth black, and they teased her bout her breath cause she worked around the dairy; said it smelled like cow milk and her mouth was slick as butter, her kiss tangy as clabber."

"You are lying," the white woman said coldly; she was shaking with fury. "Liar!" she hissed.

Dessa heaved herself to her knees, flinging her words in the white woman's face. "Mammy gave birth to ten chi'ren that come in the world living." She counted them off on her fingers. "The first one Rose after herself; the second one died before the white folks named it. Mammy called her Minta after a cousin she met once. Seth was the first child lived to go into the fields. Little Rose died while mammy was carrying Amos – carried off by the diphtheria. Thank God, He spared Seth." Remembering the names now the way mammy used to tell them, lest they forget, she would say; lest her poor, lost children die to living memory as they had in her world.

"Amos lived for a week one Easter. Seem like he blighted the womb; not another one lived till she had Bess." Mammy telling the names until speech became too painful.

"Them was the two she left, Seth and Bess; Seth was sold away when she come with Old Mistress to the Reeves place. Sold away like Jeeter, whose real name was Samuel after our daddy – only Carrie kept saying Jeeter when she meant Junior and that was the name he kept. Bess, born two years before Old Mistress married Old Master Reeves; left cause she was sickly; died before Rose reached her new home."

Even buried under years of silence, Dessa could not forget. She had started on the names of the dead before she realized that the white woman had gone. Both children were crying now but Dessa's voice continued through their noise:

"Jeffrey died the first year she come to the Reeves plantation; Caesar, two years older than Carrie: head kicked in by a horse he was holding for some guest. Carrie was the first child born at the new place to live. Dessa, Dessa Rose, the baby girl."

Anger spent now, she wept. "Oh, I pray God mammy still got Carrie Mae left."

Barbara Burford

1945–

B ritish-born poet, writer and editor, she is the author of a book of short stories, The Threshing Floor, *published in 1986, and her writing has appeared in many publications, including* A Dangerous Knowing: Four Black Women Poets *(1984), and* Everyday Matters: 2 *(1984), in which the story "Miss Jessie" appeared.*

Miss Jessie

B RA-AA-ANG!
     Miss Jessie's almost tuftless broom hit the discarded beer can with just the right applied force to spin it the length of the corridor, and bring it to a halt by the open carriage door. Two late commuters looked at each other with raised brows and slightly pursed lips. Miss Jessie, catching that well-known look,

stirred up the dust between their seats with her dirty broom till their still-shiny black toe-capped shoes became a more interesting mottled grey.

One of the men, moved to protest, looked at the figure behind the broom for the first time, encountering the fierce black eyes that mirrored generations of resentment and hatred. He was stunned, momentarily losing the initiative. Miss Jessie, expert in these encounters as a toreador, spun away, herding debris in front of her broom, down the corridor and off the train into her special upright dustpan.

Two other cleaners were exchanging raucous banter with a porter, in a patois unintelligible to the predominantly white travellers around them. Miss Jessie ignored them all; stomping off up the platform to empty her dustpan.

Miss Jessie – somehow no one ever called her just plain Jessie, or Miss Brown or Miss Smith. In fact, the only people who knew her last name were the ones in the finance and personnel offices. Miss Jessie was a short, black, Jamaican woman with an upright bearing. She wore a faded railway-issue overcoat tied round the waist with string; old, turning out at the ankles short winter boots; and on her head, almost as if moulded there, was an ancient, once blue beret; from under the rim of which peered the ends of her tightly braided short, pepper and salt hair.

Like most individuals who perform a menial task for the public, Miss Jessie was invisible to the great mass of people who surged through the station in tidal flows, to be drained down into the underground system or ferried away by bus or taxi. To most of her co-workers she was an object of mild fun, but paradoxically not really noticed, if they could help it, by most of the unnoticed themselves. She was often on the fringe of their conversations, but rarely took part in them. When she did, her acid tongue and sharpness of her unexpectedly penetrating black eyes usually ended the idle chatter of the moment.

Miss Jessie snorted now as she emptied her dustpan, standing on tiptoe to reach the rim of the huge cylindrical main bin.

"You hear dem talk," she muttered, "dem was all eider african prince or jamaican school teacher before them come here." She almost merged with a grimy wrought-iron pillar, as she stood with her dustpan and broom in her hands, waiting for the next dirty train.

She knew who she was, and although she was exiled in this babylon, that was a family matter and did not take away her position in life. One day the message *would* come, and she would be able to go home. Until then, she kept her memories, her real life, polished. Miss Jessie knew that she must not allow herself to forget a single thing; for to do so would be to drown in the hopeless degrading tide of second-class life in Britain.

Her boot-button eyes hooded themselves, and the lines etched on her face seemed to deepen, black on black, as the words dripped like acid inside her head.

By the waters of Babylon
We sat down and wept

When we remember thee,
Oh, Zion.

Once again, there was the hot high buzzing of the wasps above her as
she peered out of her hiding place under dense blue-flowered thicket.

With a conscious wrench that grew harder as she got older, Miss Jessie came
back to the hollow booming station. To another train insinuating itself between
the platforms, prematurely spilling people as it slowed.

Miss Jessie returned to the station that night, invisible, one of many in her
nylon fur coat, and an elaborately styled black wig. If anything, the station was
colder, although the wind had dropped. It was as if the friction of the thousands
of jostling bodies had generated a faint warmth earlier, which had died with the
outward ebb of the tidal flow.

There were no seats on the rubbish-strewn concourse. The pigeons, the
meths drinkers and the constant surveillance of the Transport Police would
have made them an unattractive prospect for the few late travellers. But the
youths scattered around the periphery, sitting on the cold asphalt, would have
welcomed the spurious comfort of wooden slats.

She stood quite still, only her sharp black eyes moved; the whites glistening in the harsh blue-white fluorescent glare. The young men wore a sort of
uniform: faded jeans, anoraks and old ski-hats. Only their footwear seemed to
differ, ranging from hiking boots to clogs worn over thick socks.

But as always, there was an obvious choice. He too was utterly still, his eyes
checking out those people standing about or passing through the concourse –
Miss Jessie unnoticed, outside his calculations.

"You look like you could do with a hot drink and a bath."

He was rising, responding to the message in the voice, before he registered
Miss Jessie in front of him. By the time he had straightened his wiry frame, his
eyes reflected only a cynical resignation.

She turned away, hiding her complacency. He would follow – they always
followed. Clumsily at first, but soon synchronizing his longer stride to her jerky
stump, he followed her along the cold, brightly lit streets near the station. Then
under the flyover, into the slightly seedy area on the edge of the ghetto in which
black people had been walled up by flyover, railway tracks, and prejudice.

When she stopped at a door, sandwiched between dusty boarded-up shops,
he almost cannoned into her. Miss Jessie snorted maliciously as she imagined
him losing all hope that she was the emissary, perhaps the servant, of someone
richer, or younger. She was sure that he was by now resolved to fall *very* deeply
asleep, as soon as he had eaten as much as he could. She opened the door and
walked straight into the unlit passageway.

He stood for a moment, a clumsy black silhouette, outlined by the faint frost
glitter of the deserted roadway behind him. Then the still, frozen air suddenly
eddied in the narrow hallway as he took a step into the darkness.

"Jack Frost nipping you heels!" Miss Jessie chortled, closing the door and
switching on the light.

They always followed.

She led the way up the stairs. On the first-floor landing Miss Jessie unlocked the stout Chubb lock on her second front door, and let the lights, the warmth, and the smell of chicken stew draw him into her home.

"Put you tings down." She looked up at him. "Put you tings down dere," she repeated gently, "and come in de kitchen. Ah give you something to eat." She opened one of the doors that led off the clean, noisily painted hallway, revealing an equally bright kitchen. Entering to check various saucepans on the cooker before returning past him to shed her coat and boots. Without shoes her feet suddenly seemed to find articulation, and she walked with an upright grace back to the kitchen, in her chainstore knitted dress, the elaborate wig incongruous on her head.

When he appeared in the doorway, his head slightly bent in the habitual stoop of the very tall going through doors and his eyes narrowed against the glare of the fluorescent tube light, Miss Jessie was already dishing up a huge platter of white, steaming rice, and saffron coloured chicken stew.

"I am dirty." He spoke for the first time, his voice faintly accented.

"Wash you hands in the sink dere." She jerked her head in the sink's direction, the wig wobbling slightly. "You can have a long hot bath after you eat." She clacked his plate down and moved to give him a small hand towel.

When he had satisfied his first, almost desperate, attack on his plate, he looked up to where she sat on the other side of the blue formica table.

"You do not eat? It is very good."

A smile touched her lips.

"Where you from?"

"I am from Norway."

"You don't have yellow hair." She got up to give him a second helping, scraping the clean-picked bones neatly into the pedal-bin.

"We are not all vikings with cows' horns on our heads," he said with lazy amusement.

Her eyes snapped, and he thought her annoyed, until she laughed. A surprising deep round laugh.

"Ah go upstairs and start you bath for you," was all she said. She left the kitchen and went noiselessly up the stairs.

In the blue and white bathroom, the light bouncing off the shiny surfaces, Miss Jessie started the bath, listening for the faint Whump! from the kitchen below as the gas water heater ignited.

After a moment she crossed the upper landing to her bedroom. She laughed softly, and did a few sideways shuffling dancesteps.

> *Life could be a dream*
> *If you would let me take you*
> *Up to paradise above.*

She sang softly to herself. When she emerged from her room she wore a starched white linen dress with inserts of crocheted lace. Her starched petticoats rustled over bare feet. The wig was gone from her head, replaced by a bright Madras cotton wrap with a flirtatious tail above one gold-hooped ear.

He looked up warily when she rustled into the kitchen, his eyes widening as he stood up instinctively.

"You see why Ah keep the place so bright and warm!" There was a dignity in her smiling face, laughter lines raying out from her eyes. "Is little Jamaica in my home."

He stood silent swaying slightly. Warm, replete.

"You go an have you bath." She rustled past him and started to clear the table. "You can put you tings in the room with de *single* bed." She laughed again, that same deep, round, happy laugh.

He lingered in the doorway.

"I have not thanked you. . . ."

"Go an have you bath," she insisted over her shoulder. "I will bring you a big cup of coffee."

He mumbled something, she was not sure what, perhaps in his own language. A moment later he was hefting his rucksack up the stairs, his boots clattering against the risers at the back of the narrower steps.

By the time Miss Jessie heard the rush of the cold water tap, and the Ascot went out she had washed up and the kitchen was again returned to its painfully bright cleanness.

When she entered the bathroom without even a knock, he was unsurprised, merely rolling his head sideways on the ledge of the satisfyingly big old bathtub. She placed the mug of coffee on the stool by the bath, then moved towards the taps.

"Ah fix dat clothesline. Is always hanging in de bath."

He vaguely noticed the end of a white plastic clothesline trailing into the water by his feet.

When a loop of the line was slipped over one ankle, he hardly felt it. It was only as his head was suddenly jerked under the water to emerge streaming and grasping that there was any inkling of danger. Even as he writhed suspended by one leg over the bath, and got out his first hoarse shout; there was a starched rustle, the bright wink of steel, then a loving smooth stroke against his throat, his hair gripped in iron fingers.

At the centre of her being Jacinta squeezed under the keening wasps' nests, and peered through the thicket at her father. Lije Punta; descendant of African Priest Kings, his sole remaining prerogative that of community butcher, was performing his ancient hereditary task on a young bullock.

"Speak dem fair. An wear clean clothes, no blood, an dem follow you. Dem always follow *us*, dey can't help it!" He had always boasted, laughing uproariously.

So why was it? when her cousin Tobias followed her to the place: And she did it sweetly, neatly, leaving him hanging there from the giant Akee tree in the centre of the clearing. Why was it they got so excited? Sending her away to this Babylon of exile? With no word since.

Valerie Belgrave
1940s–

*S*he grew up in Trinidad and studied at Sir George Williams
*(Concordia) University in Canada, obtaining a BA in Painting and
Literature. She still lives in Trinidad, where she is a working artist
and fabric designer specializing in batik. Her historical novel* Ti
Marie *(1988), from which this extract comes, has been described as "a
Caribbean* Gone with the Wind.*".*

From

Ti Marie

II

A BOUT a year after she had first come to the rescue of the sick baby and
had embarked on the role of foster mother to both of Diego's children, Yei
– who although known to occasionally absent herself had never been known to
so much as give a second glance to a man – became most obviously pregnant.
No one could persuade her to identify the father.

Once the babies were born and it became clear that their father was
either wholly or part white, suspicion naturally fell on Don Diego. It was
certainly remarkable that he never dismissed Yei. However, these two little
matched dolls, who looked like black and white versions of each other, were
the instant delight of Diego's children and indeed of everyone on the plantation.

Yei, in her natural wisdom, included both José and Juanita in care of the
babies. She captured for ever José's interest and affection by granting him the
privilege of naming them. He called the lighter one Carmen, and the darker,
Maria Eléna.

In no time it became clear that the twins were not identical, and indeed,
although undoubtedly similar, they matured differently.

Yei and her daughters demanded very little, and in any case Diego knew that in
the secluded estate of Santa Clara, nestled in the extensive and relatively remote
Maracas Valley some ten miles east of Port of Spain, he could have found nobody
else to befriend his otherwise solitary little daughter. Mixed households were
not unusual, anyway. In that depressed land, coloured mistresses and coloured
offspring were part of pragmatic compromise and made for survival.

M. Louis simply included them in his classes. In fact he became very fond
of the twins, particularly of the little brown-skinned girl. In her early displays
of intelligence and sensitivity, he saw a kindred spirit. Unlike the rest of the

household who had chosen to call her Eléna, he took to calling her *ma petite Marie Hélène*, which was shortened to *petite Marie* and eventually to *'ti Marie*.

One day, when the twins were only two years old, he was out of doors with his charges. He noticed Eléna reaching down. Looking shyly at M. Louis, the little toddler pointed her chubby finger at the weeds at her feet.

She was indicating the sensitive mimosa plant, which, like the folding of butterfly wings, closes its miniature fern-like leaves, magically, at the slightest touch. Louis remembered part of a verse which he had once heard somewhere, and he bent down to her, singing as he touched the plant, "Look, *ma petite*, 'ti Marie, 'ti Marie, close your door, policemen're coming to find you."

The little girl was delighted with the game and her face lit up with a glow that warmed Louis's heart. Completely overcome by her innocent charms, he hugged her to him and said, "*You* are my 'ti Marie, my little sensitive plant. See, you are as delightful as the tiny 'ti Marie flower. How the name suits you! Little wild flower, 'ti Marie."

III

DURING these years, when the twins were growing out of babyhood, the French, mostly from Grenada, were mivrating to Trinidad in modest numbers with their slaves. The island was beginning slowly to come to life, but this in no way affected the children.

Within the household, Carmen grew to look quite as Caucasian as Juanita. She was even held to bear her a certain resemblance, both having auburn hair and sparkling hazel eyes, Carmen's intense, sensitive personality proving perfectly harmonious with Juanita's sweet, lively character. Eléna, on the other hand, was not considered a beauty, but her reserved yet caring personality and her quick intelligence were endearing qualities. Without ingratiating herself, she would foster harmony around her. She showed a precocious maturity, being the least playful and the most academically inclined of the children. Were it not for her almost wayward sense of humour, her tutor would have worried at her serious-mindedness.

When the twins were five years old the ailing Tia Roma died, and Yei completely took over the reins of the household.

In the sixth year of the twins, when Eléna's intelligence and ingenuous personality were already evident, and Carman's undoubtedly gifted singing voice was the joy of those who cared to listen, Spain again made an effort to attract settlers to the island. Charles III passed a royal *Cedula* on colonization, a decree of wider scope than the previous one of 1776. This *Cedula* was aimed mostly at French colonizers of the other islands of the Caribbean.

That year Trinidad's meagre population rose to over six thousand souls. The French came, fleeing from their failed crops, from British persecution, from poor, depleted soils, or from their debts and mortgages.

Some of the immigrants were white families, but by far the greater number consisted of free blacks and mulattos, attracted by the promise of the *Cedula* to grant them land. Non-whites would get only half the white grant, but that was a generous offer to those generally oppressed peoples. Here, at least, their entitlement was assured and could even be considerable, depending of course on the quantity of their labourers; for with all these immigrants came thousands of African slaves, the number determining the size of land grants allowed their masters.

Apart from Louis's incomprehensible, forbidding declaration that development sometimes extracted a heavy price, these happenings had little, if any, effect on the lives of the happy family de Las Flores at Santa Clara.

Then one day Diego returned home, exclaiming to Louis, "*Gracias a Dios*, Louis, I met the new Governor today. Don José Maria de Chacon, a knight of Calatrava! No longer one of the scum of Spanish politics, but a real man, a man of vision!"

This Spanish nobleman, José Maria de Chacon, a linguist and a liberal, became well known and well liked by all but his fellow Spaniards. For naturally, in an island where they were fast being outnumbered, they did not like his equitable land distribution policy.

Many of these Spaniards left the island in pique, and those few who stayed were for the most part out of sympathy with the Governor. Finding himself isolated from his own countrymen, he welcomed friendship with Diego, occasionally making token protest over the indolent Diego's refusal to join the ruling *cabildo*.

Some evenings, escaping from the pressures of office, Chacon would visit Santa Clara. Since the house was not large, Eléna heard many of the gentlemen's conversations, learning of the wonderful improvements Don Chacon had instituted. They talked of the reorganization of the country into districts administered by overseers or commandants of quarters, possessing civil and judicial authority. They talked of the establishment of a medical board and a port health doctor. They talked of marvellous improvements to the town of Port of Spain, of the relocation, at Chacon's expense, of the Rio Santa Anna into the Dry River (a man-made bed at the foot of the low Laventille Hills that skirted the town).

They talked too of the construction of new government buildings, of a fort and mole on the Port of Spain waterfront, the improvements to public works and roadways and the construction of a proper carriage road linking St Joseph to Port of Spain.

The discussions that attracted Eléna's most serious interest, though, were those that dealt with Chacon's humanitarian projects: the establishment of new missions for the welfare of the Indians and the drafting of a new, liberal slave code. This code would protect slaves from harsh masters and neglect in their old age, allowing them to be instructed in the Roman Catholic religion and guaranteeing their right to live in families. There were to be regulations governing the quality of their food, hours of work, living quarters and punishment. Eléna began to understand a great deal, by inference, about all these matters. This "Code Noir" was of particular interest to her, for already she had begun to pay special attention to Diego's slave population.

One day, however, she found herself the subject under discussion, as Don

Chacon exclaimed to Diego, "What a beautiful black child!"

"Who? Eléna? Why, she is no match for her sister Carmen!"

"Oh, no, no! The other is fair, and has the obvious beauty of a mulatto, but this one is like a dark Spanish Moor, like a girl I once knew in Madrid. Her charm is still a sleeping bud, yet to open, but she will be a great beauty one day."

Eléna could not believe her ears. She did not then know that Chacon himself had a mulatto family, nor that she possessed exceptional good looks. For her, it was the first time that anyone but Yei had called her beautiful, so she remembered Don Chacon and his kind, complimentary words long after he had left the island of Trinidad.

Michelle Cliff

1946–

B orn in Kingston, Jamaica, spending her childhood there and in New York, she graduated from college with a BA in European history and then attended the Warburg Institute, London University, earning an MPhil degree in comparative historical studies of the Renaissance. She began to write after becoming involved in the 1970s feminist movement and is internationally known through her essays, articles, lectures and workshops on racism and feminism. She was co-editor (with Adrienne Rich) of the journal Sinister Wisdom (1981–3). Her first novel, Abeng (1984), is the story of Clare Savage, a light-skinned Jamaican, and her growing awareness of the relationship between colour and status; No Telephone to Heaven (1987), extracted here, follows Clare's development and involvement with revolutionary politics. Cliff has in addition published autobiographical works, poetry and prose poems, including Claiming an Identity They Taught Me to Despise (1980) and The Land of Look Behind (1985), and a collection of short stories, Bodies of Water (1990).

From

No Telephone to Heaven

AFTER her mother left her, in the days before she started school, Clare remained in the apartment until her father reappeared, abiding by his rule that she was to leave the house on no condition. So she stayed in, keeping house and watching television, moving within the space of her loss. But not allowed to be lost because her father said the family would be reattached. Soon.

She was taken by the magic of the television, and of her ability to conjure images by a switch, to change the images as she wished. Jamaica had not this sort of magic, this curious and wondrous choice; all man-made images were channeled into the cinemas, whose programs changed once a week, and over these selections there was no control. The island took what it was sent, not so different from the little black box catching waves in the Brooklyn apartment.

Jamaicans came in droves to see the pictures, to glimpse the world beyond the island, lose themselves, whether in theaters or in country gathering places – the picturegoers carried the images away with them, transforming them, eager always for more. In the streets and in the yards, Brer Anansi, about whom their grandparents taught them, Rhyging, about whom their mothers warned them, Sasabonsam, whose familiar image terrorized them, mixed in their games with Wyatt Earp, Legs Diamond, Tarzan the Apeman, and King Kong.

Playing in the dusk with Alexander, the boy of fourteen who kept the outside clean, while Clare waited for Dorothy to fix her supper, evenings when her parents were away, each child became a movie character. Alexander being Paul Newman being Billy the Kid, asking Clare to be the girl he rescued. These were forbidden games. And when her parents returned early one evening and caught the two circling a wagon train, Alexander was fired and Clare was condemned by her father for being "as thick as two thieves with a gardenboy".

In the dark of the basement apartment, trying to dismiss her mother, she watched pictures. Pictures she had not seen before. A white-haired butler teaching a little white girl to dance down stairs. When her father came home, Clare mentioned the movie to him and he told her about Bill Robinson and how he had tap-danced up Broadway once. His mother had written him about it from America when he was a boy and she worked the stage. Boy explained to his daughter what Broadway was and the difficulty of Robinson's task. Tapping up the sinking-rising cobblestones downtown, up the pitted avenue into Harlem. He talked on and on, telling his daughter how brave Robinson was, not just in dancing up Broadway but in making his way through America.

When she asked about the little girl in the picture, her father said that she was Shirley Temple, America's favorite child – no more, no less. Nothing was said about the little girl being as thick as two thieves with a butler. This was another country. This was make-believe.

"But, Clare, you mustn't spend all your time in front of that thing, you know; for it is a true time-waster. Read a book. You need to prepare yourself for school."

But Clare did not stop.

A large Black woman cooking and singing and laughing for Claudette Colbert and Monty Woolley in *Since You Went Away*. Clare recognized the woman (the large Black woman wearing a tiny little white cap) from *Gone With the Wind* (white cap replaced there by a plaid tiehead), which the third form of St Catherine's had seen at the Carib – during one of the annual showings of the film on the island. They were escorted by a teacher, a red-haired sunburned American woman who seemed confused. Who was led from King's Parade one Saturday morning for picking up a pair of pink pussboots in Bata's and neglecting to pay for them. Poor woman. Her color rose high. Downtown Kingston is a very small place, where nervous red-haired white women stand out, and her story made the front page of the Sunday *Gleaner*. It was too good to miss. She assured the police that one of the other patrons had asked her to hold the shoes for a minute, and when the police didn't believe her, she told them she had fully intended to pay for them but had taken the shoes outside to see how they looked in the sun. She was, after all, a member of the faculty of St Catherine's School for Girls, so she could be no thief. "Anyone can teef, missis," the constable told her.

"Nigger," she muttered – no one caught it.

Fired from school for causing embarrassment. Also for teaching the girls American history – she had told the headmistress she was a Canadian and would instruct the girls on the Commonwealth. A white woman washed up in Jamaica. What had possessed her to take on the American Civil War? Desperate. To lead, literally by the hand, a line of girls in burgundy tunics and sea island cotton blouses into the darkness of the Carib one afternoon when they should have been playing rounders, to see a "documentary", as she put it, of this "tragic phase", as she put it, of American history? Poor Miss America (which the girls called her behind her back; her name was Miss Peterkin), pacing the rows in the quiet cinema, telling girls impatient for the picture to begin, girls rustling their sweetie wrappers and surreptitiously slipping mangoes from their bookbags – exhorting them, in fact – telling them they needed to learn the lesson of the film, as the situation depicted therein was so similar to the situation on their island. Poor woman – where was her judgment? "Order is meant to be maintained," she stated vaguely to the fidgeting girls, whose color ranged from dark to light and back again. "A conflagration could take your nation down." Pause. "Do you want to forage for carrots and wear a dress made of draperies?" The girls kept silence, fighting the laughter in them. Her voice, already nasal in pitch, ran up the scale, out of control as her passion increased.

The picture began. Watching the burning of Atlanta, the teacher screeched suddenly, like a chicken disturbed at her roost, then bowed her head in tears. The girls assumed she was a fool.

She was the first American Clare ever met.

Sitting in the damp of the basement during a weekday afternoon, recognizing Hattie McDaniel, Clare remembered that other afternoon. She remembered the teacher. This led her to the other girls, her classmates, to whom she was not allowed to say goodbye because Boy owed the school money and was afraid of the complications should they find out Clare was leaving. So she didn't say goodbye. She merely disappeared from their lives. And they from hers.

Just like Miss America.

*   *   *

Magnanimous Warrior! She in whom the spirits come quick and hard. Hunting mother. She who forages. Who knows the ground. Where the hills of fufu are concealed. Mother who brews the most beautiful tea from the ugliest bush. Warrior who sheds her skin like a snake and travels into the darkness a fireball. Mother who catches the eidon and sees them to their rest. Warrior who labors in the spirit. She who plants gunga on the graves of the restless. Mother who carves the power-stone, center of the world. Warrior who places the blood-cloth on the back of the whipped slave. She who turns her attention to the evildoer. Mother who binds the female drumhead with parchment from a goat. Warrior who gathers grave-dirt in her pocket. Pieces of chalk. Packs of cards. Bits of looking-glass. Beaks. Feet. Bones of patoo. Teeth of dogs and alligators. Glass eyes. Sulfur. Camphor. Myrrh. Asafoetida. Frankincense. Curious shells. China dolls. Wooden images. She writes in her own blood across the drumhead. Obeah-woman. Myal-woman. She can cure. She can kill. She can give jobs. She is foy-eyed. The bearer of second sight. Mother who goes forth emitting flames from her eyes. Nose. Mouth. Ears. Vulva. Anus. She bites the evildoers that they become full of sores. She treats cholera with bitterbush. She burns the canefields. She is River Mother. Sky Mother. Old Hige. The Moon. Old Suck.

Rambling mother. Mother who trumps and wheels counterclockwise around the power-stone, the center of the world. Into whose cauldron the Red Coats vanished.

What has become of this warrior? Now that we need her more than ever. She has been burned up in an almshouse fire in Kingston. She has starved to death. She wanders the roads of the country with swollen feet. She has cancer. Her children have left her. Her powers are known no longer. They are called by other names. She is not respected. She lies on an iron bedstead in a shack in Trench Town. She begs outside a rumshop in Spanish Town. She cleans the yard of a woman younger than she. She lies in a bed in a public hospital with sores across her buttocks. No one swabs her wounds. Flies gather. No one turns her in the bed. The pain makes her light-headed. They tell her she is senile. They have taken away her bag of magic. Her teeth. Her goat's horn. We have forgotten her. Now that we need her more than ever. The nurses ignore her. The doctors make game of her. The priest tries to take her soul.

Can you remember how to love her?

Marsha Hunt
1946–

A merican-born singer, actress and writer who grew up in
        Philadelphia, she studied at the University of California, Berkeley,
        during the student riots of the 1960s but shortly afterwards went to
Europe. She has written of her varied experiences in Real Life: The
Story of a Survivor *(1985). In London she made her name in the hit*
musical Hair. *Her celebrated career that followed includes fifteen*
years in rock music, work in radio, on stage and screen. She has been a
member of the Royal National Theatre (1983–6) and the Royal Shakespeare
Company (1989). *Joy (1990), from which this passage is taken, was her*
first novel.

From

Joy

J oy was smart and knew she was smarter than me from when she was little,
    which is how come I think she was slow to listen to me. From when I first met
her, Joy could read and count faster, talk on the phone better and make sense of
all sorts quicker than I could. Like I couldn't never make head nor tail of them
cookbook recipes till she come along and give me a hand.

So when Joy got fourteen, which is how old she was when I caught her
hanging over at the playground, I reckon she still figured she was the smartest
out of both of us. And though I ain't claiming that she was completely wrong,
she didn't want to believe that I knew what I was talking about 'cause sometimes
age teaches things that all the brains and book learning in the world can't.

From that time at the playground, when I caught Joy flaunting herself in front
of them big ol' boys, I could see that without Tammy to stop her, Joy was fixing
to land herself in heap big trouble. I never forgave myself for tattling though,
'cause of the mean, hateful way I heard Tammy come down on the child. But
the very next day Joy said she forgave me. She was always real quick to forgive
me if I did something.

Thinking back on it, maybe I shouldn't of been so worried about Joy at the
time. Seeing how fast these young girls are today, maybe I was just making a
mountain out of a molehill.

What'd happened was that there was a whole bunch of teenaged boys in
the neighborhood that run around together though they wasn't trying to be
no gang. They was just boys being boys and played basketball a lot of time

at the local school ground. I was mortified to hear off of old Mrs Nathan, one of my church Sisters, that from her bedroom window, a few times she'd spied Joy lolling 'round the school yard fence like a cat in heat while them boys was playing basketball. Fourteen seemed way too early for a nice girl to have a hankering for them big ol' rough boys, but I couldn't tell Joy that I knew what she was really up to when the story she'd tell me was that she was staying late after school to set in the public library.

It was just lucky that Mrs Nathan's back bedroom had a good view of the school ground.

So to be exact, it was one Saturday afternoon in June just before summer vacation when Joy went out the house with Anndora after she slipped a note under my door, like she had to do if she was going out to say they was headed for the library. With a book each in their hands, I held my tongue when I saw from my bathroom window that the black shorts that Joy had on was too tight to be out in the streets in, even though I thought wasn't nobody in the library with their head stuck in a book gonna take no notice of a child no way. But I did know for sure that Joy and Brenda wasn't allowed to wear black since Tammy thought it looked hussyish on young girls and rightly believed that what her girls wore was a reflection on their upbringing and her. To tell the truth though, I thought sometimes she was too particular about what them girls of her'n put on to step out the front door, not that I dared to say it.

Anyway, Joy walked out in a pair of black short shorts that she'd cut from a Simplicity pattern she'd bought and stitched up on my sewing machine. There wasn't enough material in 'em to call them pants. So skimpy they was that they cut right into the crack of her behind. It sure didn't look ladylike. Though by then "ladylike" is something she said she couldn't see the point of.

But what worried me at the time when she walked out with Anndora in tow was that Joy had her head full of a chunky white boy named Max McDonald who hadn't long been moved into our street with his widowed mama and took him a job at Mr Houseman's son-in-law's drugstore unpacking boxes. Joy said Max was cute, but I couldn't see nothing cute about all them freckles and that curly red hair of his'n. Joy said he was seventeen, and wanted to become a pharmacist which is why he wanted that job in the drugstore.

Mrs McDonald, his mother, took a counter job over in the cleaner's which is how I got to know her. Freddie B guessed she didn't have no money which is the onliest reason he could see that she settled for living in a colored neighborhood. Poor white trash is how she looked to me but her talk was full of high faluting ideas about Max becoming a brain surgeon. She had her heart set on him going to Stanford to study on a scholarship, and I always got a earful from her about it when I'd take Freddie B's Sunday suit to the cleaner's every fourth Thursday of the month. I only listened to her going on about that boy of her'n 'cause I could tell from the number of times Joy'd mentioned him and found phony reasons to go to the drugstore that Joy had an eye for Max, and I wanted the low-down on him.

Aside from the fact that it wasn't the done thing for a white boy to be going with a colored girl, and aside from the fact that Joy was too young for him being practically at college, I didn't expect he'd of been eyeing Joy no way.

She had grown out of her looks around that time and there wasn't much pretty left to her throughout her teen years but her long hair which was thick and wavy and didn't need straightening. She kept it in a ponytail and had her some bangs to cover up all the pimples she had on her forehead. She hated 'em.

Anyway, 'bout half hour after her and Anndora'd walked out the house saying they was off to change their books at the library, Mrs Nathan rang me like I'd asked her to if she ever spotted Joy again hanging 'round that school yard fence while them boys was playing.

It was sure lucky to have had Mrs Nathan on the lookout, 'cause if it had of been any of them other women from my church that had seen Joy, I wouldn't of never heard the end of it. Whereas I trusted that Mrs Nathan, being eighty, was a good meaning soul and not one for gossiping and spreading tales.

I was in the middle of pressing my hair for church that day when she gave me the call. So, I quick put in some wire rollers at the back and tied a bandanna 'round my head, so that I could rush out to the A&P supermarket which was catty cornered to the school yard and I knew would give me a good excuse to be out in that direction. Usually I didn't never go to the A&P though, 'cause it was way too expensive, but I knew it would still give me a perfect reason for being across from the playground that was five blocks from Grange. I even took Anndora's old red wagon to make it look for real that I was out to shop for groceries. Although Anndora didn't use it no more, the wagon stayed in the little shed by our parking lot. Rusted though it was getting, she was still pernickety about it, and I always had to ask her if I could borrow it, anytime I wanted to use it for my shopping.

By the time I'd crossed the street in front of the A&P I could see Joy standing right by the fence near the basketball court and just like I thought, amongst all them six colored boys was Max McDonald, racing around bouncing the ball and pushing and shoving and shouting like the rest of 'em, supposed to be what ch'you call playing. You couldn't miss him. The onliest white one and with a carrot-top head. Joy didn't see me and neither did Anndora, and whereas I'd seen from my bathroom window that Joy'd gone out in them shorts, at least her hair had been drawn back neat in its usual ponytail. But there she was with it hanging loose down her back and her pink blouse made to look like a half blouse, 'cause it was unbuttoned halfway down so that she had the tail of it tied in a knot up under her bust. What bust she had. She had her collar pulled up and I was shocked to see that her whole belly was out. If she'd had any cleavage it would of being showing, but thank goodness, she wasn't buxom like Brenda. In fact, at fourteen Joy didn't have nothing to flaunt but her long legs, and I could tell she was trying to do her best with what little she had standing there.

I meant to look nonchalant like I just happened to be passing so I got to humming "Joshua Fit the Battle of Jericho" to calm myself, 'cause on top of everything else, I could feel my blood pressure up soon as I saw Joy. I was wearing a cotton dress that afternoon and some old sneakers that Brenda'd throwed out 'cause they had holes in the baby toes. The school yard fence was above ground level and you had to walk up some concrete steps to get to it.

Joy had her profile to me and I couldn't believe that it looked like her lips was painted red while she was lolling at the fence posing to be seen but acting casual, like she just happened to be standing half naked there. Miss Anndora had her face pressed against the wire mesh fence and she didn't look up once as I stood at the bottom of the steps and called Joy's name out, wanting to give her a chance to know I was there and planning to make my way up them steps. I knew that she was bound to be ashamed of herself caught red handed about fibbing to me about going to the library.

"Joy. Yoo hoo, there, Joy," I called out. But I reckon she had her eyes glued on Max and couldn't hear me above them boys running back and forth on the court and shouting and swearing at each other.

"Yoo hoo," I yelled out again, waving my arms. A colored boy noticed me and came over to the fence above where I was. "Could you tell that child in them shorts I want her."

Soon as he did, she turned around. I saw that she was wearing heavy lipstick and what must have been Maybelline or eyeliner or something like it on her eyes which really took me off guard. I'd seen her playing in makeup when she was little, but the way it was applied that day at the playground looked too for real, and if I hadn't known her, I'd have guessed her to be about sixteen, maybe older, even though she didn't have much bust.

"Joy! What's that on your face, girl?" I wasn't laughing at all 'cause the Joy Bang staring back at me with cold eyes was a stranger that I didn't know nothing about. She had a frisky streak in her, but if somebody'd told me she was sneaking around the boys claiming to be at the library and wearing lipstick I'd of called 'em a liar.

"Girl, you better get ch'you home 'fore I tan your hide." That was all I could think to say. I waited there for her to turn and come down the steps, but she just stood there looking through me as much to say "no". I thought I better go up them steps and grab her, but I didn't know what to do about Anndora's heavy red wagon that I didn't want to have to haul up the steps with me.

When Joy didn't answer I was glad I was wearing that old pair of white sneakers that Brenda'd thrown out, 'cause those sneaks carried me quick as a runner up them steps and I grabbed a handful of Joy's hair so that her head was pulled back before she knowed what was on her.

"Child, have you lost your mind," I said. "You better get your little hiney on home so that we can wash that mess off your face." I didn't want to shame her, but I was loud enough to let her know that I meant business. She didn't just have lipstick on. She had on rouge and with the eyeliner and that Maybelline gook too, she looked a madam.

"Let go!" she had the nerve to say, trying to wrestle away from me, but I'd got one strong grip and wasn't 'bout to let her shake loose without her leaving me with a hand full of her loose hanging hair.

"Leave you alone! Nigger, I'm here to rescue you from yourself!"

"I'm not doing anything wrong," Joy said. "Baby, let go...Baby Palatine! You're hurting me." I hadn't never laid hands on her in all the time I knew her but it was real lucky for Joy that I didn't yank her brains out her head. I ain't never even struck my sister Helen when she provokes, so it was a sure thing that

I wasn't gonna hit on Joy. Especially with Anndora and them boys watching me. Joy was a head shorter than me for a start and I knew if I held on to that hair of her'n long enough that she'd go home with me willing and not let me make no scene in front of Max. I didn't never have no temper where Joy was concerned but I couldn't believe how she was turned out and I wasn't going to stand for her twisting me 'round her finger like I was usually willing to let her do.

"You better get to stepping 'fore I shame you into it." I noticed out the corner of my eye that the boys had stopped bouncing that ball and they was just watching us. "Don't shame me and yourself, child. Now I ain't about to leave here without you and Anndora, so please come home willing." I could feel it when she'd stopped resisting, but I gripped her tighter in case it was just her tricking me. But when she rubbed at her temples where the hair was probably yanked from the root, I wanted to cry I was so sorry that I hurt her.

"You've practically pulled all my hair out," she whimpered, exaggerating to make me feel worse.

"I meant to," I said but I decided not to say no more as her, me and Anndora walked down them steps.

Of course, when I got to the bottom that red wagon was gone I knew the next mess was gonna be explaining to Anndora how her wagon got stole, but I was that mad that I didn't even bother to look up and down the street for it. I just walked on home with Joy following five paces behind. I couldn't care less whether she walked with me or not as long as she was walking. I didn't have nothing to say to her no way.

I couldn't even look at Anndora who I noticed had a bit of red smudged in the corners of her lips too, but not enough to say it was her wearing lipstick. It looked like she'd had it on and scraped it off, and I was willing to wager that she'd done that while I was fussing with Joy over at the playground, though I didn't have no way to prove it.

We headed up Archibald Street with the hot midday sun beating so hard on my head that the sweet smelling bergamot pomade on my hair kinda trickled down my scalp and made it itch. Of course nobody in their right mind was out walking which meant that nobody but Mrs Nathan must of seen the hullabaloo at the playground or us trailing up the street with Joy looking like a floozie and me too confounded to speak if spoken to.

When we rounded our corner I was feeling a bit calmer. "You better come on into my place," I said, "so we can clean that mess off your face." She just followed silent through the front door, but I could feel that she was mad, and Anndora said that she was going home to watch cartoons. I made straight for the bathroom and though I didn't have no cold cream left I knew that Vaseline Petroleum Jelly would do as good to get that makeup off Joy.

"Set yourself down there on the stool," I said sharpish, "and let me clean your face."

"I can do it," she sulked.

"Well, I'll watch." I was going to make sure that the job got done a hundred percent. My motive was selfish, 'cause I felt that I was in as much trouble with her mother as Joy was, if Joy got caught. Tammy was like them inspectors that come along to check up on things when you got an adopted child. They can walk in and lord over the place whenever they like.

I stood there while Joy smeared her face with Vaseline. Then I went into the kitchen to boil up some water, 'cause the hot tap in the bathroom had been broke for a week and Freddie B didn't have the right tool to fix it. Anyway it was that hot outdoors there wasn't no hurry to get it fixed. I wondered how long Joy had been sneaking out looking like that but I knew the question wouldn't bring no answer I would believe, so I didn't even bother to ask. Mainly what was going on in my head was how you can think you really know a child till you find out you don't.

While Joy was taking off that makeup, I remembered I had a icebox cake in my frigerator and took it out and cut off a couple pieces. Joy's silence was about to kill me, and I would have given a gold tooth to know what she was thinking setting there in the bathroom but I just served up the cake. I'd already done enough and was feeling bad, though what happened wasn't my fault. That came to be the way with us. Joy would do the doing, and I'd end up feeling bad.

I knew that Max McDonald was probably behind the makeup. I can't say that he forced her to wear the lipstick and them shorts cutting up her backside, but I'm sure that it was for him that she'd rigged herself up. He was always down the basketball court I figured, and that's why she'd traipsed down there.

"Max McDonald is too old and too white for you," I told her while she was pushing a cake crumb around her saucer. "Find somebody to have a crush on that's your own age and colored. There's nice enough boys at junior high school."

"They're silly."

"You're the one's silly," I told her but I realized looking at the one tear that come rolling down her cheek that I'd said enough. That was one thing I thought was always in my favor. I knew exactly when I'd said enough and she wasn't listening no more.

She was hard work during them teen years and used to have me worried that she was gonna end up as hard to handle as Anndora. But I prayed and prayed that Joy would pull her socks up and go back to being the sweet-natured easy child she'd always been. And by high school seemed like she was happy and sunny again. Maybe them pimples disappearing is what did it.

Joy kept getting As on her report cards but still had time for them extras at school. I was real proud when she went straight from being a cheerleader for the junior varsity track team over to being a pompom girl for the varsity football team. She was so excited the day she got chosen for that, and came running home and asked me if I'd help her take care of her pompom outfit that the school had give her. It was a pink and white gingham dress with so many white crinolines under it, that that dress could stand out about a mile when I got it starched and pressed.

Tammy wouldn't of bothered herself with nothing like ironing that pompom outfit. I kind of understood that she was tired from going to work everyday. But anyway, Joy got on that pompom squad, and she was really happy following the games around and whatnot, but I think she had something going with the blond halfback on the football team though.

She wouldn't let on to me 'cause he was another white one. Derek, I think was his name. He'd pick her up and drop her off, and pick up and drop off and never once did she get him to come in. I used to say to her, "Joy, you got to start as you mean to continue. Don't let that boy treat you like no trash now. Bring him in. Let me and your mama see him."

She'd say, "Oh, Baby Palatine, he doesn't want to come in. He's just giving me a lift." All them rides he give her, he didn't once take her out on no proper date but she wouldn't go out with nobody else neither and would set with me and Freddie B on a Saturday night watching the TV when them other girls was out.

In the back of my mind, I thought that's the price you pay if you don't stay with your own kind.

Sandi Russell
1946–

*S*he grew up in Harlem and is now living in Britain. As a professional jazz singer she has performed throughout the United States and Britain. She has written a book of literary criticism, Render Me My Song: African-American Women Writers from Slavery to the Present *(1990) and is co-editor of the* Virago Book of Love Poetry. *The short story reprinted here appeared in the anthology* Iron Women: New Stories By Women, *edited by Kitty Fitzgerald (1990).*

Sister

I T glistened in the sun and shards of sharp light hurt my eyes. I winced, and then decided it was time to cross the road and see cousin Sister.

The heat hunkered down and slumped my shoulders. The air was full of dust, and grit was on my tongue. Even the crepe myrtle bushes were fading, their pink and lavender softness reduced to a brown tinge.

I slid my sandals along the sandy dirt road and listened to my heart beat. It danced ahead of my own footsteps, keeping its own hurried pace. My hands were sweating. It had been ten years since I'd come to visit and everybody in the family was talking about how Sister wasn't right any more.

"I always thought she was a little touched, ever since she was a child."

"They shoulda put her away. Remember how Sister used to just stay all up under her momma's skirt when she was little? And talk to herself? She was real smart, but too sensitive, if you ask me."

"Well, girl, that's why she done got all crushed up over this thing. I tell you, it's a cryin' shame – she done grown to be a woman in her body, but since all this mess done happened to her, well. . . . She ain't gon' ever come out of it, if you want my opinion."

"Yeah, Sister done gone over the edge. And it seems like her momma done got real mean-spirited and gone over the edge with her. Sittin' up in that house all the time. They ain't even got a TV."

As I walked, Aunt Sippy and cousin Wilhemenia's voices soothed and shook me:

"We go back a long way round here, and we ain't never had nothin' like this happen to our people. We could always hold up against anything; you know, we'd get through it somehow. Seem like these youngins done got soft or somethin', done lost some part of themselves. I don't know, look like they lookin' for somethin' that ain't there, ain't never gonna be there. Got their heads up in some misty place. Floatin', seem like."

"Well, we all keep marryin' one 'nother down here anyway, bound to be some problems. . . ."

At first, it looked like some contemporary artist's idea of a sculpture. It was a mound of glittering substances: some wood intermingled with red-rust things, black shiny pieces and slabs of silver. Spread out on the ground, it rose in height to about six feet, at which it peaked, like a tent. I crept over to it, going around the back of the house, so as not to arouse Sister in the process. I accidentally stepped on some typewriter keys and looked up: tables, chairs, silverware, china, bits of a car, a bed-post, tires, a sofa hatefully punctured and an old mattress, sagging in the middle, with both sides flopped over trying to hide all that lay beneath it.

I stepped back, tripping a bit, swallowed hard, then turned around and walked to the front of the house.

A dog let out a wail and I heard slow-sliding footsteps coming toward me. "Shut-up, you ol' fool." Her voice was loud but it had no insistence in it. She was much bigger than the last time I saw her, her glowing mahogany-red skin pulled tight around the extra weight. Her black satiny hair had been clipped with spitefulness and hung in angry peaks. The faded, flower-print dress was spotted with circles of grey. She was shoeless, and as I looked at her toes, dusted with the dirt of the road, I remembered our long, languorous walks to Bubba Lane's store for a bottle of Crown Cola and a five-cent bag of peanuts. We'd open the peanuts and then watch them slither into the soda, making a plopping, fizzy sound. There was no explanation for this. It just meant we were different, special somehow.

As she pulled open the screen door, it resisted and made a throaty sound. Her mouth tried to turn upwards in a smile, but gravity's tug was stronger. "Missy," she said, "come on in." The words had no weight and floated away in the sweltering breeze.

How I hated being called "Missy", but Aunt Sadie gave me that name because she said I acted so dicty, like them Northern white women. When I was a little girl, we used to fight about the pronunciation of words:

"Missy, go on and pick them taters and maters."

"They're not taters and maters, Aunt Sadie, they're called potatoes and tomatoes."

"Listen, girl, I don't give a damn what you call 'em, but you better go out there and pick 'em *now*, if you knows what's good for you!"

I started up the steps but quickly moved to one side. Uncle Fletcher always sat on the second one from the bottom, in his faded overalls with his tobacco can just to the right of his leg. He seemed to live there, all closed up in himself. He shifted his head when I tried to pass and said, "How you doin', Missy?" Then he raised up somewhat, turned and spit tobacco juice through the two teeth he had in the front of his mouth. Gazing beyond me to the parched, grassy land, he smiled. His eyes gathered me in and mocked me at the same time. But Uncle Fletcher was dead, so I went on in, without swerving.

As I entered the kitchen, Sister was saying something, but I wasn't listening because the sights and the smells of the house came up on me so hard. Where simmering collards, hamhocks, baked bread and biscuits used to push you to the big, black wood-burning stove, now the air hung with the lives of uncared for cats and smothered sunlight. Pots with the grease of forgotten meals scattered the kitchen table. Clothes and bits of paper formed the pattern of a half-attempted patchwork quilt. One old red slipper, bent down at the heel, pointed the way toward the sitting room.

A far-away voice slipped through my senses and made me come alert.

"Well, well, look who's here. Let me look at you, child. Turn around. My, my, got them rich people's clothes on. You sure is lookin' good."

The sounds came from a shadowed presence in the far corner of the room. Behind the rocking-chair, where she moved back and forth, heavy closed curtains contained us. Aunt Sadie's bulk softly spilled over the contours of her chair. I couldn't see her cream-colored face, for shadows were laced across it, making a veil.

She turned her head away from me and started to hum: "Precious Lord, take my hand." Cousin Sister shifted her feet a few times, wiped her hands on her dress, then said, "Sit down, Missy." I sat down in the nearest chair. It was wooden, with a straight back made of cane rushing. As I eased into the seat, the legs protested. Moving forward, I sat stiffly on the edge.

Cousin Sister crossed the room and settled into another rocking-chair. There, in the dim light, they rocked in rhythm. I glanced around and noticed the dust.

Pictures crowded the mantelpiece and any other surface that would hold them. Generations peered out and boldly assessed. I was staring at a handsome face that I'd never seen before when Aunt Sadie said, "I don't know why she keep that picture. Ought to be put out front with the rest of their junk. He wasn't worth half that mess you got piled up outside. And she still grievin', like he were dead or somethin'. Sure should be."

"Who is he?" I whispered, and Sister replied:

"That's my husband, Jeffrey. I know he still love me, even though he ran off with that woman from DC. He comin' back though. I know it."

Her words came rushed and breathless now:

"All that money she got and them fine clothes ain't enough he from *here* and I understands him he gonna need that soon that's why I'm savin' all our stuff we gon' start all over again."

Aunt Sadie said, "Humpf," and started rocking real hard. The loudness of her voice made me jump: "Ain't you gon' offer Missy some water? Where's your manners?"

While Sister went for water, Aunt Sadie and I were sucked up in silence. My mind went back to all that junk outside. Why was Sister saving it? If she wanted to keep all her possessions, why not bring them in the house? Maybe all that stuff heaped up like that was her way of telling the world it really didn't matter; things, that is. But if she felt like that, why not throw them all away?

Aunt Sadie was staring at me. My chair moaned with each movement and my tongue felt thick. The air seemed to be getting tighter.

Sister placed the wet glass on the table next to me and started mumbling as she approached her chair. Suddenly, the words were distinct and resonated throughout the room:

> Come on, baby, come on back home.
> Better come on, baby, come on back home.
> I got the best lovin' round here, ain't no need to roam.

She kept repeating the words, but never put a tune to them. It was an incantation rising to a scream. She finally stopped in the middle of a verse and looked around. She seemed to fold into herself and sat down. Rocking again, speaking to no one in particular, she said: "I likes them old-timey songs. Most people round here don't though. They listens to Country and Western now."

Aunt Sadie reared forward. "Country and Western. You all done gone crazy. All you young folks."

"I ain't crazy . . . crazy like a fox!"

"Crazy, I tell you. Goin' to white churches and intergratin'. Where the preacher s'posed to be healin' your bodies. Can't nobody do that but the Lord and maybe the doctor. Born again. Born into what? Ya'll done left these black churches round here and hardly nobody in 'em any more. They used to really heal in the old days. Yes, Reverend Brown sure could preach."

Aunt Sadie's eyes held joy. I felt lifted and asked her if she still went to the church down the road.

"Ha, ha. Daddy died. Momma didn't go to the funeral. Said she was sick. Ha, ha."

Sister kept laughing, twisting from side to side in her own private dance, while Aunt Sadie kept rocking. The coolness of her voice shocked Sister into silence:

"Ain't no use goin'. Ain't nobody there. Peoples round here don't go nowhere no more. Don't seem to want to. And then again, other than the church, ain't nowhere else to go. Everybody either ridin' up and down in they car or sittin' up lookin' at all them television stations they got with that big silver dish outside they house. Ain't no visitin', neither. Folks just stays at home."

I thought for a moment and could find no response. Their rocking back and forth was beginning to make me anxious.

"Well, I better get back to the house. Momma will be waiting supper for me."

"I'm goin' on a trip to DC soon. Gonna drive up there. Wanna come, Missy?"

"Shut-up fool," Aunt Sadie said as she turned her face toward the back window. "You done been in five car crashes. You know you ain't got no more licence."

My mind went back to the heap of junk outside ... and there was Sister, standing on a dirt road, blood staining her best dress. Staring at the crushed car, her left eye twitched. She thought about how it would look with the other things. Nice touch of blue. Aunt Sadie started humming "Precious Lord" again, and as I rose to go, she murmured, never turning her face from the window, "Bye, child. You sure is lookin' good."

Cousin Sister walked me outside. We stood for a few moments without speaking. The air was stagnant and held no promise of clear and breezy days to come. Sister dug and prodded the earth with her feet. I wanted to hug her, to bring back that sweet summer closeness we used to have on our walks to Bubba Lane's. I started to raise my arms, but Sister had already left me.

I bowed my head and kicked the sand as I crossed the road. Shivering in the heat, I could hear Aunt Sippy's excited chatter bouncing brightly against a still sky:

"Maybe we should try and get all the folks together round here and have us a big picnic. Yes, we'll have it in the church yard. You know, everybody makin' somethin' and bringin' it. 'Member when we used to do that? We had us some good times then. Yeah, that's what we'll do. We'll have a real big bash, honey. It'll be somethin'. Just like the ol' times. I bet people be jumpin' to get this thing started. What you think?"

Marlene Nourbese Philip
1947–

Raised in Trinidad and Tobago, she lived in Jamaica and attended the University of the West Indies, then in 1968 moved to Canada, studied law in Ontario and was admitted to the Bar in 1975. After practising as a barrister and solicitor for seven years, until 1982, she turned to writing full-time, having first tried her hand at it in 1968. She has received Canada Council awards, has participated in poetry readings, including dramatic performances of her work, and has read for the BBC. Publications in which her work has appeared include Black Scholar and Présence Africaine and she has published poetry collections, Thorns (1983), Salmon Courage (1983) and She Tries Her Tongue, Her Silence Softly Breaks (1989), which in manuscript won the Casa de las Américas literary award. Her novel, Harriet's Daughter, was published in 1988.

Burn Sugar

IT don't come, never arrive, had not – for the first time since she leave, had left home; is the first, for the first time in forty years the Mother not standing, had not stood over the aluminum bucket with her heavy belly whipping up the yellow eggs them and the green green lime-skin. "People does buy cake in New York," she say, the Mother had said, "not make them."

Every year it arrived, use to in time for Christmas or sometimes – a few time well – not till January; once it even come as late as in March. Wherever she is, happen to be, it come wrap up and tie up in two or three layers of brown wrapping paper, and tape up in a Peak Freans tin – from last Christmas – over-blacked black black from the oven. And it address on both sides – "just to make sure it get there," she could hear the Mother saying – in the Mother funny printing (she could never write cursive she used to say). Air mail or sea mail, she could figure out the Mother's finances – whether she have money or not. When she cut the string she use to, would tear off the Scotch tape – impatient she would rip, rip off, rip the brown paper, prise off the lid, pause . . . sit back on she haunches and laugh – laugh she head off – the lid never match, never matched the tin, but it there all the same – black and moist. The cake.

The weeks them use to, would pass, passed – she eating the cake, would eat it – sometimes alone by sheself; sometimes she sharing, does share a slice with a friend. And then again – sometimes when she alone, is alone, she would, does cry as she eating – each black mouthful bringing up all kind of memory – then she would, does choke – the lump of food and memory blocking up, stick up in she throat – big and hard like a rock stone.

She don't know – when she begin to notice it she doesn't know, but once she has it always, was always there when she open the tin – faint – but it there, undeniable – musty and old it rise up, an odour of mouldiness and something else from the open tin making she nose, her nostrils twitch. Is like it cast a pall over she pleasure, shadowing her delight; it spoil, clouded the rich fruity black-cake smell, and every time she take a bit it there – in she mouth – hanging about it hung about her every mouthful. The Mother's advice was to pour some more make-sure-is-good-Trinidad rum on it. Nothing help, it didn't – the smell just there lingering.

And then she know, she knew that something on its annual journey to wherever she happened to be, something inside the cake does change, changed within the cake, and whether is the change that cause the funny smell, or the journey, the travel that cause the change that cause the funny smell . . . she don't know. . .

It never use to, it didn't taste like this back home is what the first bite tell she – back back home where she hanging round, anxiously hanging about the kitchen getting in the Mother's way – underfoot – waiting for the baking to start –

"Wash the butter!" The Mother want to get her out of the way, and is like she feeling the feel of the earthenware bowl – cool, round, beige – the Mother push at her. Wash the butter, wash the butter, sit and wash the butter at the kitchen table, cover with a new piece of oilcloth for Christmas; wash the butter, and the sun coming through the breeze blocks, jumping all over the place dappling spots on she hand – it and the butter running competition for yellow. Wash the butter! Round and round . . . she pushing the lumps of butter round with a wooden spoon.

Every year she ask the same question – "Is why you have to do this?" and every year the Mother tell she is to get the salt out of the butter, and every year she washing the butter. The water don't look any different, it don't taste any different – if she could only see the salt leaving the butter. The Mother does catch she like this every year, and every year she washing the butter for hours, hours on end until is time to make the burn sugar.

Now! She stop. The Mother don't tell she this but she know, and the Mother know – it was understood between them. The coal-pot waiting with it red coals – the Mother never let she light it – and the iron pot waiting on the coal-pot, and the Mother waiting for the right time. She push her hand in the sugar bag – suddenly – one handful, two handful – and the white sugar rise up gentle gentle in the middle of the pot, two handfuls of white sugar rise gently . . . she had never, the Mother had never let she do it sheself, but to the last grain of sugar, the very last grain, she know how much does go into the pot.

She standing close close to the Mother, watching the white sugar; she know exactly when it going change – after she count to a hundred, she decide one year; another year she know for sure it wasn't going change while she holding her breath; and last year she close she eyes and know that when she open them, the sugar going change. It never once work. Every time she lose, was disappointed – the sugar never change when she expect it to, not once in all the years she watching, observing the Mother's rituals. Too quick, too slow, too late – it always catch she – by surprise – first the sugar turn sticky and brown at the edges, then a darker brown – by surprise – smoke stinging, stings her eyes, tears run running down she face, the smell sharp and strong of burning sugar – by surprise – she don't budge, she stand still watching, watches what happening in the pot – by surprise – the white sugar completely gone leaving behind a thick, black, sticky mass like molasses – by surprise. If the pot stay on long enough, she wonder, would the sugar change back, right back to cane juice, runny and white . . . catching she – by surprise.

The Mother grab up a kitchen towel, grabs the pot and put it in the sink – all one gesture clean and complete – and it sitting there hissing and sizzling in the sink. The Mother open the tap and steam for so rise up and *brip brap* – just so it all over – smoke gone, steam gone, smoke and steam gone leaving behind this thick thick, black liquid.

She look down at the liquid – she use to call it she magic liquid; is like it have a life of it own – its own life – and the cake need it to make it taste different. She glance over at the Mother – maybe like she need the Mother to taste different. She wonder if the Mother need her like she need the Mother – which of them was essential to the other – which of them was the burn sugar?

She stick a finger in the pot and touch the burn sugar; turning she finger this way and that, she looking at it in the sunlight turning this way and that, making sure, she make sure you don't drop any of the burn sugar on the floor; closing she eyes she closes them, and touching she touch she tongue with her finger . . . gently, and she taste the taste of the burn sugar strong and black in its bitterness – it bitter – and she skin-up she face then smile – it taste like it should – strong, black and bitter it going make the cake taste like no other cake.

She hanging round again, watching and waiting and watching the Mother crack the eggs into the bucket – the aluminum bucket – and she dying to crack some in sheself – if she begged she got to crack a few but most of the time she just hanging, hung around watching and waiting and watching the Mother beat the eggs. Is like the Mother thick brown arm grow an appendage – the silver egg whisk – and she hypnotizing sheself watching the big arm go up and down scraping the sides of the bucket – a blur of brown and silver lifting up, lifts the deep yellow eggs – their pale yellow frothy Sunday-best tulle skirts – higher and higher in the bucket. The Mother stop and sigh, wipe she brow – a pause a sigh, she wipes her brow – and she throw in a piece of curly, green lime-skin, add a dash of rum – "to cut the freshness" – a curl of green lime-skin and a dash of rum. She don't know if the Mother know she was going to ask why, to ask her why the lime-skin – anticipating her question – or if she was just answering she own question, she don't know, but the arm continued, keep on beating as if it have a life of it own with a life of its own, grounded by the Mother's bulk which harness the sound of she own beat – the scrape, swish and thump of her own beat.

She watching the Mother, watches her beat those eggs – how they rise up in the bucket, their heavy, yellow beauty driven by the beating arm; she remember the burn sugar and she wonder, wonders if change ever come gently . . . so much force or heat driving change before it. Her own change had come upon her gently ... by surprise ... in the night of blood ... by surprise ... over the months them as she watch her changes steal up on her ... by surprise ... the days of bloodcloth, the months that swell up her chest ... by surprise ... as she watched watching the swelling, budding breasts, fearful and frighten of what they mean, and don't mean. There wasn't no force there, or was there? too old and ancient and gradual for she or her to notice as she watch the Mother and wait, waiting to grow up and change into, but not like – not like she, not like her, not like ... she watching ... the Mother face shiny with sweat shines, she lips tie up tight tight with the effort of the beating arm, lips held in tight and she wondering, wonders whether she, the Mother, have any answers ... or questions. Did she have any – what were they?

Nobody tell she but she hand over the bowl, the bowl of washed butter she pass to the Mother who pour off the water and put in the white sugar – granulated and white she add it to the lumpy yellow mass, and without a word the Mother pass it back to her. She hand too little to do it for long – cream the butter and sugar – her arm always grows too tired too soon, and then she does have to pass it back to the Mother. But once more, one more time – just before the Mother add the eggs, she does pass it back to her again for she to witness the change – surprise sudden and sharp all the way from she fingers right up she arm along she shoulder to she eyes that open wide wide, and she suck in her breath – indrawn – how smooth the texture – all the roughness smooth right out and cream up into a pale, yellow swirl. When she taste it not a single grain of sugar leave behind, is left to mar the smooth sweetness.

She want it to be all over now – quick quick, all this mixing and beating and mixing, but she notice the sound change now that the eggs meet the butter – it heavier and thicker, reminding her it reminds her of the Mother – she and the Mother together sharing in the Mother's sound.

She leans leaning over the bucket watching how the eggs and butter never want to mix, each resisting the other and bucking up against the Mother force. Little specks and flecks of butter, pale yellow in defiance, stand up to fight the darker yellow of the eggs them, and little by little they disappear until the butter give up and give in, yields – or maybe is the other way around – the eggs them give in to the butter. Is the Mother hand that win, the Mother's arm the victor in this battle of the two yellows.

The Mother add the dry fruit that soaking in rum and cherry brandy for months now, then the white flour; the batter getting thick thickens, stiffens its resistance to the Mother's hand, the beating arm, and all the time the Mother's voice encouraging and urging – "Have/to keep/beating/all the/time" – the words them heavy and rhythmical, keeping time with the strokes. The batter heavy and lumpy now, and it letting itself be pushed round and round the bucket – the Mother can only stir and turn now in spite of she own encouragement – but she refuse to let it alone, not giving it a minute's rest.

The Mother nod she head, and at last she know that *now* is the time – time for the burn sugar. She pick up the jar, holding it very carefully, and when the Mother nod again she begin to pour – she pouring the Mother stirring. The batter remain true to itself in how it willing to change – at first it turn from grey to brown – just like me she think, then it turn a dark brown like she sister, then an even darker brown – almost black – the colour of her brother, and all the time the Mother stirring. She empty the jar of burn sugar – her magic liquid – and the batter colour up now like she old grandmother – a seasoned black that still betray sometimes by whitish flecks of butter, egg and sugar, and the Mother arm don't stop beating and the batter turning in and on and over itself.

"How you know when it ready?"

"When the spoon can stand in it," and to show what she mean, the Mother stick the spoon the batter and it stand up stiff stiff.

Her spoon like the Mother's now stood at attention – stiff and alone in its turgid sea of black. It announced the cake's readiness for the final change of the oven. Was she ready? and was it the Mother's cake she now made? Or her own? Just an old family recipe – the cake had no other meaning – its preparation year after year only a part of painting the house, oiling the furniture, and making new curtains on the Singer machine that all together went to make up Christmas. She had never spoken to the Mother about it – about what, if anything, the cake and the burn sugar might mean...

It was its failure to arrive – the absence of the cake – even with its "funny" smell that drove her to this understanding, this moment of epiphany as she now stood over her cheap, plastic bowl and watched the spoon. She looked down at her belly, flat and trim where the Mother's easily helped balance the aluminum bucket – not like, not like, not like her – she hadn't wanted to be like her, but she *was* trying to make the Mother's black cake, and all those buckets of batter she had witnessed being driven through their changes were now here before her – challenging her. And she *was* different – from the Mother – as different perhaps as the burn sugar was from the granulated sugar, but of the same source. Here, over this bucket – it was a plastic bowl – she met – they met and came together – to share in this old old ritual of transformation and metamorphosis.

The Mother would surely laugh at all this – all this fancy talk with words like "transformation and metamorphosis" – she who had warned of change, yet was both change and constancy. "Is only black cake, child, is what you carrying on so for?" she could hear the voice. They didn't speak the same language – except in the cake, but now the Mother was sitting looking at her make the cake.

"Look, Mammy – look, see how you do it – first, the most important thing is the burn sugar – the sweetness of the cake need that bitterness – you can't have black cake without it." Mammy was smiling now,

"You was always a strange one."

"Shut up, Mammy, and listen," (gently of course) "just listen – the burn sugar is something like we past, we history, and you know that smell I always tell you about?" Mammy nod her head, "I now know what it is – is the smell of loneliness and separation – exile from family and home and tribe – even from the land, and you know what else, Mammy – is the same smell of – "

"Is only a cake, child – "

"The first ones – the first ones who come here rancid and rank with the smell of fear and death. And you know what else, Mammy? is just like that funny smell of the cake when I get it – the smell never leave – it always there with us – "

"Is what foolishness you talking, child – fear and death? Just make the cake and eat it."

"But, Mammy, that is why I remember you making the cake – that is what the memory mean – it have to mean something – everything have to have a meaning – "

"Let me tell you something, girl," Mammy voice was rough, her face tight tight – "some things don't have no meaning – no meaning at all, and if you don't know that you in for a lot of trouble. Is what you trying to tell me, child – that it have a meaning for we to be here – in this part of the world – the way we was brought here? That have a meaning? No, child" – the voice was gentler now – "no, child, you wrong and don't go looking for no meaning – it just going break you – "

"Mammy – "

But Mammy wasn't there, at least not to talk to. She looked down at the batter. The burn sugar she used was some she the Mother had made earlier that year, accompanied by the high-pitched whine of the smoke alarm. She had made the batter by hand, as much of it as she could, even adding the green green corkscrew of lime-skin, although according to Mammy "these modern eggs never smell fresh like they suppose to – like those back home."

When they were done she almost threw the cakes out. She had left them too long in the oven and a thick crust had formed around them; the insides were moist and tasted like they should – the bitter, sweet taste perfectly balanced by the deep, rich, black colour. But the crust had ruined them. Obviously she wasn't ready, and only the expense of the ingredients had prevented her from throwing them out immediately.

It was the Mother's advice that saved them. Following her instructions by phone she cut all the crusts off the cakes, then poured rum over them to keep them moist. She had smaller cakes now – not particularly attractive ones either, but they tasted like black cake should, and without that funny smell.

Was that hard crust a sign of something more significant than her newness at making the cake? Was there indeed no meaning to the memory, or the cake, or the funny smell? She wanted to ask the Mother – she almost did – but she knew the Mother would only laugh and tell her – "Cake is for eating not thinking about – eat it and enjoy it – stop looking for meaning in everything."

She thanked the Mother, lowered the receiver slowly and said to herself – "You wrong, Mammy, you wrong – there have to – there have to be a meaning."

Octavia E. Butler

1947–

Born in Pasadena, California, she attended Pasadena City College and State University, Los Angeles. One of the few Black writers to excel in the genre of science fiction, she is a Hugo and Nebula award-winner. Her books include Patternmaster (1976), Mind of My Mind (1977), Survivor (1978), Wild Seed (1980), Bloodchild (1985), Dawn, Xenogenesis: I (1987), Adulthood Rites, Xenogenesis: II (1988) and Imago, Xenogenesis: III (1989). This extract is from her 1979 novel, Kindred, in which Dana, a Black woman from contemporary Los Angeles, rescues a young boy, Rufus, from drowning and thereafter repeatedly finds herself snatched back 160 years to the Deep South in the threatening era of slavery.

From

Kindred

THE FIRE

1

I TRIED.

I showered, washed away the mud and the brackish water, put on clean clothes, combed my hair. . .

"That's a lot better," said Kevin when he saw me.

But it wasn't.

Rufus and his parents had still not quite settled back and become the "dream" Kevin wanted them to be. They stayed with me, shadowy and threatening. They made their own limbo and held me in it. I had been afraid that the dizziness might come back while I was in the shower, afraid that I would fall and crack my skull against the tile or that I would go back to that river, wherever it was, and find myself standing naked among strangers. Or would I appear somewhere else naked and totally vulnerable?

I washed very quickly.

Then I went back to the books in the living room, but Kevin had almost finished shelving them.

"Forget about any more unpacking today," he told me. "Let's go get something to eat."

"Go?"

"Yes, where would you like to eat? Someplace nice for your birthday."

"Here."

"But. . ."

"Here, really. I don't want to go anywhere."

"Why not?"

I took a deep breath. "Tomorrow," I said. "Let's go tomorrow." Somehow, tomorrow would be better. I would have a night's sleep between me and whatever had happened. And if nothing else happened, I would be able to relax a little.

"It would be good for you to get out of here for a while," he said.

"No."

"Listen. . ."

"No!" Nothing was going to get me out of the house that night if I could help it.

Kevin looked at me for a moment – I probably looked as scared as I was – then he went to the phone and called out for chicken and shrimp.

But staying home did no good. When the food had arrived, when we were eating and I was calmer, the kitchen began to blur around me.

Again the light seemed to dim and I felt the sick dizziness. I pushed back from the table, but didn't try to get up. I couldn't have gotten up.

"Dana?"

I didn't answer.

"Is it happening again?"

"I think so." I sat very still, trying not to fall off my chair. The floor seemed farther away than it should have. I reached out for the table to steady myself, but before I could touch it, it was gone. And the distant floor seemed to darken and change. The linoleum tile became wood, partially carpeted. And the chair beneath me vanished.

2

WHEN my dizziness cleared away, I found myself sitting on a small bed sheltered by a kind of abbreviated dark green canopy. Beside me was a little wooden stand containing a battered old pocket knife, several marbles, and a lighted candle in a metal holder. Before me was a red-haired boy. Rufus?

The boy had his back to me and hadn't noticed me yet. He held a stick of wood in one hand and the end of the stick was charred and smoking. Its fire had apparently been transferred to the draperies at the window. Now the boy stood watching as the flames ate their way up the heavy cloth.

For a moment, I watched too. Then I woke up, pushed the boy aside, caught the unburned upper part of the draperies and pulled them down. As they fell, they smothered some of the flames within themselves, and they exposed a half-open window. I picked them up quickly and threw them out the window.

The boy looked at me, then ran to the window and looked out. I looked out too, hoping I hadn't thrown the burning cloth onto a porch roof or too near a wall. There was a fireplace in the room; I saw it now, too late. I could have safely thrown the draperies into it and let them burn.

It was dark outside. The sun had not set at home when I was snatched away, but here it was dark. I could see the draperies a story below, burning, lighting the night only enough for us to see that they were on the ground and some distance from the nearest wall. My hasty act had done no harm. I could go home knowing that I had averted trouble for the second time.

I waited to go home.

My first trip had ended as soon as the boy was safe – had ended just in time to keep me safe. Now, though, as I waited, I realized that I wasn't going to be that lucky again.

I didn't feel dizzy. The room remained unblurred, undeniably real. I looked around, not knowing what to do. The fear that had followed me from home flared now. What would happen to me if I didn't go back automatically this time? What if I was stranded here – wherever here was? I had no money, no idea how to get home.

I stared out into the darkness fighting to calm myself. It was not calming, though, that there were no city lights out there. No lights at all. But still, I was in no immediate danger. And wherever I was, there was a child with me – and a child might answer my questions more readily than an adult.

I looked at him. He looked back, curious and unafraid. He was not Rufus. I could see that now. He had the same red hair and slight build, but he was taller, clearly three or four years older. Old enough, I thought, to know better than to play with fire. If he hadn't set fire to his draperies, I might still be at home.

I stepped over to him, took the stick from his hand, and threw it into the fireplace. "Someone should use one like that on you," I said, "before you burn the house down."

I regretted the words the moment they were out. I needed this boy's help. But still, who knew what trouble he had gotten me into!

The boy stumbled back from me, alarmed. "You lay a hand on me, and I'll tell my daddy!" His accent was unmistakably southern, and before I could shut out the thought, I began wondering whether I might be somewhere in the South. Somewhere two or three thousand miles from home.

If I was in the South, the two- or three-hour time difference would explain the darkness outside. But wherever I was, the last thing I wanted to do was meet this boy's father. The man could have me jailed for breaking into his house – or he could shoot me for breaking in. There was something specific for me to worry about. No doubt the boy could tell me about other things.

And he would. If I was going to be stranded here, I had to find out all I could while I could. As dangerous as it could be for me to stay where I was, in the house of a man who might shoot me, it seemed even more dangerous for me to go wandering into the night totally ignorant. The boy and I would keep our voices down, and we would talk.

"Don't you worry about your father," I told him softly. "You'll have plenty to say to him when he sees those burned draperies."

The boy seemed to deflate. His shoulders sagged and he turned to stare into the fireplace. "Who are you anyway?" he asked. "What are you doing here?"

So he didn't know either – not that I had really expected him to. But he did seem surprisingly at ease with me – much calmer than I would have been at his age about the sudden appearance of a stranger in my bedroom. I wouldn't even have still been in the bedroom. If he had been as timid a child as I was, he would probably have gotten me killed.

"What's your name?" I asked him.

"Rufus."

For a moment, I just stared at him. "Rufus?"

"Yeah. What's the matter?"

I wished I knew what was the matter – what was going on! "I'm all right," I said. "Look. . .Rufus, look at me. Have you ever seen me before?"

"No."

That was the right answer, the reasonable answer. I tried to make myself accept it in spite of his name, his too-familiar face. But the child I had pulled from the river could so easily have grown into this child – in three or four years.

"Can you remember a time when you nearly drowned?" I asked, feeling foolish.

He frowned, looked at me more carefully.

"You were younger," I said. "About five years old, maybe. Do you remember?"

"The river?" The words came out low and tentative as though he didn't quite believe them himself.

"You do remember then. It was you."

"Drowning. . .I remember that. And you. . .?"

"I'm not sure you ever got a look at me. And I guess it must have been a long time ago. . .for you."

"No, I remember you now. I saw you."

I said nothing. I didn't quite believe him. I wondered whether he was just telling me what he thought I wanted to hear – though there was no reason for him to lie. He was clearly not afraid of me.

"That's why it seemed like I knew you," he said. "I couldn't remember – maybe because of the way I saw you. I told Mama, and she said I couldn't have really seen you that way."

"What way?"

"Well. . .with my eyes closed."

"With your – " I stopped. The boy wasn't lying; he was dreaming.

"It's true!" he insisted loudly. Then he caught himself, whispered, "That's the way I saw you just as I stepped in the hole."

"Hole?"

"In the river. I was walking in the water and there was a hole. I fell, and then I couldn't find the bottom any more. I saw you inside a room. I could see part of the room, and there were books all around – more than in Daddy's library. You were wearing pants like a man – the way you are now. I thought you were a man."

"Thanks a lot."

"But this time you just look like a woman wearing pants."

I sighed. "All right, never mind that. As long as you recognize me as the one who pulled you out of the river. . ."

"Did you? I thought you must have been the one."

I stopped, confused. "I thought you remembered."

"I remember seeing you. It was like I stopped drowning for a while and saw you, and then started to drown again. After that Mama was there, and Daddy."

"And Daddy's gun," I said bitterly. "Your father almost shot me."

"He thought you were a man too – and that you were trying to hurt Mama and me. Mama says she was telling him not to shoot you, and then you were gone."

"Yes." I had probably vanished before the woman's eyes. What had she thought of that?

"I asked her where you went," said Rufus, "and she got mad and said she didn't know. I asked her again later, and she hit me. And she never hits me."

I waited, expecting him to ask me the same question, but he said no more. Only his eyes questioned. I hunted through my own thoughts for a way to answer him.

"Where do you think I went, Rufe?"

He sighed, said disappointedly, "You're not going to tell me either."

"Yes, I am – as best I can. But answer me first. Tell me where you think I went."

He seemed to have to decide whether to do that or not. "Back to the room," he said finally. "The room with the books."

"Is that a guess, or did you see me again?"

"I didn't see you. Am I right? Did you go back there?"

"Yes. Back home to scare my husband almost as much as I must have scared your parents."

"But how did you get there? How did you get here?"

"Like that." I snapped my fingers.

"That's no answer."

"It's the only answer I've got. I was at home; then suddenly, I was here helping you. I don't know how it happens – how I move that way – or when it's going to happen. I can't control it."

"Who can?"

"I don't know. No one." I didn't want him to get the idea that he could control it. Especially if it turned out that he really could.

"But. . . .what's it like? What did Mama see that she won't tell me about?"

"Probably the same thing my husband saw. He said when I came to you, I vanished. Just disappeared. And then reappeared later."

He thought about that. "Disappeared? You mean like smoke?" Fear crept into his expression. "Like a ghost?"

"Like smoke, maybe. But don't go getting the idea that I'm a ghost. There are no ghosts."

"That's what Daddy says."

"He's right."

"But Mama says she saw one once."

I managed to hold back my opinion of that. His mother, after all. . . Besides, I was probably her ghost. She had had to find some explanation for my vanishing. I wondered how her more realistic husband had explained it. But that wasn't important. What I cared about now was keeping the boy calm.

"You needed help," I told him. "I came to help you. Twice. Does that make me someone to be afraid of?"

"I guess not." He gave me a long look, then came over to me, reached out hesitantly, and touched me with a sooty hand.

"You see," I said, "I'm as real as you are."

He nodded. "I thought you were. All the things you did. . .you had to be. And Mama said she touched you too."

"She sure did." I rubbed my shoulder where the woman had bruised it with her desperate blows. For a moment, the soreness confused me, forced me to recall that for me, the woman's attack had come only hours ago. Yet the boy was years older. Fact then: Somehow, my travels crossed time as well as distance. Another fact: The boy was the focus of my travels – perhaps the cause of them. He had seen me in my living room before I was drawn to him; he couldn't have made that up. But I had seen nothing at all, felt nothing but sickness and disorientation.

"Mama said what you did after you got me out of the water was like the Second Book of Kings," said the boy.

"The what?"

"What Elisha breathed into the dead boy's mouth, and the boy came back to life. Mama said she tried to stop you when she saw you doing that to me because you were just some nigger she had never seen before. Then she remembered Second Kings."

I sat down on the bed and looked over at him, but I could read nothing other than interest and remembered excitement in his eyes. "She said I was what?" I asked.

"Just a strange nigger. She and Daddy both knew they hadn't seen you before."

"That was a hell of a thing for her to say right after she saw me save her son's life."

Rufus frowned. "Why?"

I stared at him.

"What's wrong?" he asked. "Why are you mad?"

"Your mother always call black people niggers, Rufe?"

"Sure, except when she has company. Why not?"

His air of innocent questioning confused me. Either he really didn't know what he was saying, or he had a career waiting in Hollywood. Whichever it was, he wasn't going to go on saying it to me.

"I'm a black woman, Rufe. If you have to call me something other than my name, that's it."

"But. . ."

"Look, I helped you. I put the fire out, didn't I?"

"Yeah."

"All right then, you do me the courtesy of calling me what I want to be called."

He just stared at me.

"Now," I spoke more gently, "tell me, did you see me again when the draperies started to burn? I mean, did you see me the way you did when you were drowning?"

It took him a moment to shift gears. Then he said, "I didn't see anything but fire." He sat down in the old ladder-back chair near the fireplace and looked at me. "I didn't see you until you got here. But I was so scared. . .it was kind of like when I was drowning. . .but not like anything else I can remember. I thought the house would burn down and it would be my fault. I thought I would die."

I nodded. "You probably wouldn't have died because you would have been able to get out in time. But if your parents are asleep here, the fire might have reached them before they woke up."

The boy stared into the fireplace. "I burned the stable once," he said. "I wanted Daddy to give me Nero – a horse I liked. But he sold him to Reverend Wyndham just because Reverend Wyndham offered a lot of money. Daddy already has a lot of money. Anyway, I got mad and burned down the stable."

I shook my head wonderingly. The boy already knew more about revenge than I did. What kind of man was he going to grow up into? "Why did you set this fire?" I asked. "To get even with your father for something else?"

"For hitting me. See?" He turned and pulled up his shirt so that I could see the crisscross of long red welts. And I could see old marks, ugly scars of at least one much worse beating.

"For Godsake. . .!"

"He said I took money from his desk, and I said I didn't." Rufus shrugged. "He said I was calling him a liar, and he hit me."

"Several times."

"All I took was a dollar." He put his shirt down and faced me.

I didn't know what to say to that. The boy would be lucky to stay out of prison when he grew up – if he grew up. He went on,

"I started thinking that if I burned the house, he would lose all his money. He ought to lose it. It's all he ever thinks about." Rufus shuddered. "But then I remembered the stable, and the whip he hit me with after I set that fire. Mama said if she hadn't stopped him, he would have killed me. I was afraid this time he would kill me, so I wanted to put the fire out. But I couldn't. I didn't know what to do."

So he had called me. I was certain now. The boy drew me to him somehow when he got himself into more trouble than he could handle. How he did it, I didn't know. He apparently didn't even know he was doing it. If he had, and if he had been able to call me voluntarily, I might have found myself standing between father and son during one of Rufus's beatings. What would have happened then, I couldn't imagine. One meeting with Rufus's father had been enough for me. Not that the boy sounded like that much of a bargain either. But, "Did you say he used a whip on you, Rufe?"

"Yeah. The kind he whips niggers and horses with."

That stopped me for a moment. "The kind he whips. . .who?"

He looked at me warily. "I wasn't talking about you."

I brushed that aside. "Say blacks anyway. But. . .your father whips black people?"

"When they need it. But mama said it was cruel and disgraceful for him to hit me like that no matter what I did. She took me to Baltimore City to Aunt May's house after that, but he came and got me and brought me home. After a while, she came home too."

For a moment, I forgot about the whip and the "niggers". Baltimore City. Baltimore, Maryland? "Are we far from Baltimore now, Rufe?"

"Across the bay."

"But...we're still in Maryland, aren't we?" I had relatives in Maryland – people who would help me if I needed them, and if I could reach them. I was beginning to wonder, though, whether I would be able to reach anyone I knew. I had a new, slowly growing fear.

"Sure we're in Maryland," said Rufus. "How could you not know that."

"What's the date?"

"I don't know."

"The year! Just tell me the year!"

He glanced across the room toward the door, then quickly back at me. I realized I was making him nervous with my ignorance and my sudden intensity. I forced myself to speak calmly. "Come on, Rufe, you know what year it is, don't you?"

"It's...eighteen fifteen."

"When?"

"Eighteen fifteen."

I sat still, breathed deeply, calming myself, believing him. I did believe him. I wasn't even as surprised as I should have been. I had already accepted the fact that I had moved through time. Now I knew I was farther from home than I had thought. And now I knew why Rufus's father used his whip on "niggers" as well as horses.

I looked up and saw that the boy had left his chair and come closer to me.

"What's the matter with you?" he demanded. "You keep acting sick."

"It's nothing, Rufe. I'm all right." No, I was sick. What was I going to do? Why hadn't I gone home? This could turn out to be such a deadly place for me if I had to stay in it much longer. "Is this a plantation?" I asked.

"The Weylin plantation. My daddy's Tom Weylin."

"Weylin..." The name triggered a memory, something I hadn't thought of for years. "Rufus, do you spell your last name, W-e-y-l-i-n?"

"Yeah, I think that's right."

I frowned at him impatiently. A boy his age should certainly be sure of the spelling of his own name – even a name like this with an unusual spelling.

"It's right," he said quickly.

"And...is there a black girl, maybe a slave girl, name Alice living around here somewhere?" I wasn't sure of the girl's last name. The memory was coming back to me in fragments.

"Sure. Alice is my friend."

"Is she?" I was staring at my hands, trying to think. Every time I got used to one impossibility, I ran into another.

"She's no slave, either," said Rufus. "She's free, born free like her mother."

"Oh? Then maybe somehow..." I let my voice trail away as my thoughts raced ahead of it fitting things together. The state was right, and the time, the unusual name, the girl, Alice...

"Maybe what?" prompted Rufus.

Yes, maybe what? Well, maybe, if I wasn't completely out of my mind, if I wasn't in the middle of the most perfect hallucination I'd ever heard of, if the child before me was real and was telling the truth, maybe he was one of my ancestors.

Maybe he was my several times great grandfather, but still vaguely alive in the memory of my family because his daughter had bought a large Bible in an ornately carved, wooden chest and had begun keeping family records in it. My uncle still had it.

Grandmother Hagar. Hagar Weylin, born in 1831. Hers was the first name listed. And she had given her parents' names as Rufus Weylin and Alice Green-something Weylin.

"Rufus, what's Alice's last name?"

"Greenwood. What were you talking about? Maybe what?"

"Nothing. I. . .just thought I might know someone in her family."

"Do you?"

"I don't know. It's been a long time since I've seen the person I'm thinking of." Weak lies. But they were better than the truth. As young as the boy was, I thought he would question my sanity if I told the truth.

Alice Greenwood. How would she marry this boy? Or would it be marriage? And why hadn't someone in my family mentioned that Rufus Weylin was white? If they knew. Probably, they didn't. Hagar Weylin Blake had died in 1880, long before the time of any member of my family that I had known. No doubt most information about her life had died with her. At least it had died before it filtered down to me. There was only the Bible left.

Hagar had filled pages of it with her careful script. There was a record of her marriage to Oliver Blake, and a list of her seven children, their marriages, some grandchildren. . .Then someone else had taken up the listing. So many relatives that I had never known, would never know.

Or would I?

I looked over at the boy who would be Hagar's father. There was nothing in him that reminded me of any of my relatives. Looking at him confused me. But he had to be the one. There had to be some kind of reason for the link he and I seemed to have. Not that I really thought a blood relation could explain the way I had twice been drawn to him. It wouldn't. But then, neither would anything else. What we had was something new, something that didn't even have a name. Some matching strangeness in us that may or may not have come from our being related. Still, now I had a special reason for being glad I had been able to save him. After all. . .after all, what would have happened to me, to my mother's family, if I hadn't saved him?

Was that why I was here? Not only to insure the survival of one accident-prone small boy, but to insure my family's survival, my own birth.

Vivian Glover
1947–

B orn in Orangeburg, North Carolina, she attended high school
in Camden, New Jersey, took a degree at Temple University,
Pennsylvania, and did graduate studies in political science at
Universidad de las Americas, Puebla, Mexico. She worked in radio for
many years and more recently in publishing. She has lived for some years
in Wiltshire, England, with her child. The First Fig Tree (1987) is her first
novel.

From

The First Fig Tree

"How did Adam and Eve put on fig leaves?"
The old woman heard the voice but didn't know where it had come from.
She blinked, trying to focus her eyes on the figure in front of her.

"Adam and Eve? How did they dress in fig leaves?" The little girl stood
before her clutching an armful of fig leaves.

"I want to make me a dress," the little girl continued. She dropped the
leaves on the ground where there was already a pile. "They sure needed a
lot."

The old woman stared at the leaves. Slowly she reached down and picked
up one as if to confirm that it was real, then put it back down again. "Whatever
done come over you?" she asked in wonderment. The old woman looked over
towards the orchard to see if any leaves were left on the tree. It didn't seem
possible that there were. "You tear off all them leaves?"

"I told you. So I can make a dress. How come they used fig leaves?"

"You sure gone and done it now. Didn't I tell you to leave those figs alone?"

"I did leave the figs alone. I just got some of the leaves." The little girl
stooped down and began to spread them about on the ground. "I'm going
to make a dress," she confirmed again.

The old woman sat back in her chair. "Well, if this don't take the rag
off the bush!"

"Adam and Eve did it," the little girl told her as she continued to spread
the leaves around.

"Well, I know one thing, Adam and Eve didn't get they leaves off your
grandaddy tree and if they had to, they'd be walking round buck-naked till this
day."

"But God didn't mind. Did He?"

"If this don't take the rag off the bush then I don't know what!"

"How did they get them to stay together?"

"I'm sure I don't know."

"Didn't you read it in the Bible?"

"Read what?"

"How they got all the leaves to stay together."

"I don't know," the old woman replied.

"Cause you didn't read it?"

"Cause it don't say."

"Did they have needles?" Undeterred, the little girl continued to arrange the fig leaves. She crawled around on her knees under the disapproving gaze of the old woman. "I could probably make two dresses," she said, after looking at the mound of leaves that remained. "And, I might give one to somebody."

"Sure enough?" the old woman snorted.

"This is going to be my dress," the little girl pointed, then leaned back to study her arrangement. "All I need to do is sew it up. That part's the front and that's the back." She looked around at all the leaves surrounding her and then sat back dissatisfied. "How come they used fig leaves?"

"I don't know." The old woman refused to be drawn into a conversation.

"They're not very big. How old was Adam and Eve? Maybe they were just standing by a fig tree. They might a been hiding in it."

The old woman didn't say anything.

"What does the Bible say?"

"That they dressed in fig leaves," the old woman admitted, thinking it might be unChristian to withhold knowledge from the Bible.

"Collard greens are bigger than fig leaves," the little girl observed. "They should a dressed up in collard green leaves." She looked over in the direction of the vegetable garden. The old woman followed her gaze.

"Well, you better be glad that they didn't cause if you had gone and pulled up your grandaddy greens, they wouldn't be nothing for you to do but leave town as fast as your feet could move."

The little girl gave a big, frustrated sigh. "But I want to know. How did they sew them? So they stayed together?"

"I told you I don't know. Maybe they got hold of some pine needles."

"Pine needles? Can they sew like real needles? I'm gonna go find some so you can show me." The little girl started to get up.

"Now you just hold on a minute." The old woman pointed her finger warningly at her. "If you think you gon get me twined up with these here fig leaves, then you got another think coming, cause that is your doing. You done it by yourself," the old woman paused for effect, "and you taking the blame by yourself." She nodded with finality. "So that's that."

The little girl sat back down and, chewing on her lower lip, stared at the leaves scattered around her. Slowly she brushed a few grains of sand off them.

The old woman had something else to say. "Plenty of time you could a just come on down out the tree. But, no, you had to stay up there climbing round till something take a hold of you and tell you to tear off all those leaves. Now that wouldna happen if you'd listen."

"I like being up in a tree," the little girl said quietly.

"Well, going up there got you into trouble. Didn't it?"

The little girl shrugged.

"Didn't it? It sure did," the old woman answered herself. "Those your grandaddy's trees out there" – the old woman pointed towards the orchard and then towards the house – "and this here his land and his house. Everything you see round here belong to him. You can't just go and do what you want with it. You just asking for trouble. What you think he go do if you start acting like that?"

"Send me away." The little girl didn't know where to look.

The old woman sank back in her chair. She had made her point sooner than she had expected and it had caused more dismay than she had intended. They sat in a heavy silence that couldn't be relieved, not even by the melodious chirping of a little bird perched on a branch of the pecan tree. The old woman raised her head to avoid seeing the drooping little figure sitting on the ground. "Nobody said nothing bout sending you away and it ain't nothing for you to be worrying about." She lowered her gaze and studied the little girl who was fingering the sand, then looked past her, catching sight of a bunch of flowers growing along the fence in front of the vegetable garden. Her daughter used these flowers to make bouquets for the living and dining rooms. The old woman had often wished that she had a few flowers in her own room, but did not feel comfortable about picking them and couldn't bring herself to ask her daughter. "You just have to learn about how other people like to have their things and how they do things and what not. That's having respect and you have to learn it while you growing up. That's what it is. Wasn't nobody talking about sending you away for nothing like no fig leaves."

The little girl's sigh ended with a quiver and she continued to play absently in the sand. After a while she said, "But God sent Adam and Eve away and my momma and daddy wanted to send me away."

"They want to send you away?"

The little girl nodded.

"Now what make you think they was go send you away?"

"They didn't want me cause I'm too bad."

"Well, I don't know what make you think your momma and daddy don't want you cause they do. Course they want you."

"No, they don't." The little girl shook her head.

"Course they do want you," the old woman repeated.

"Nope. Daddy said I'm too bad to be with."

"Well, they just say that so you'll try and be a good girl. That don't mean they don't want you. That's a bunch of stuff."

The little girl shook her head again. "Nope, cause my daddy told me he didn't want me till I was good."

"You know he didn't mean that. That's just something he said. All children get told that."

"And that's why he sent me away and then he went away."

"Now you don't believe that. You know you come up here to go to school and cause your daddy's gone off to the war and your mamma's gone back to school herself. You can't never get too much learning, specially these days. And when she come back, she'll be able to get a good job and be able to do more for you. If your daddy didn't go and fight in that war, then all those Germans a soon be over here bombing us all up. They didn't send you away. That's just how things happen. They're missing you a whole lot. They sure are. Course they didn't send you away. Don't you think they missing you?"

The little girl shrugged and then set her face so she wouldn't look bothered any more. She began to push sand away from her. "I don't care because I'm not missing them anyway. They don't care either and that's why my daddy didn't want to kiss me goodbye cause he said I was no good. And Grampy told me to get in the back of the car so he could take me away."

The old woman could think of no words which might remove the scowl from the tight little face. Finally, she was forced to look away, but she continued, through a wave of disconsolation, to hear the soft swishing sound of the sand as it was pushed away. It had brought back the memory of the heavy crocus sack, which as a child she had dragged up and down endless rows of cotton. It had got heavier and heavier. Her back and arms had ached, then grown numb, but still she was forced to carry on till all that she was aware of was the swish, swish sound of the cotton sack as she pulled it over the ground.

The old woman looked back down at the little girl. Some things do change, she told herself, while some things don't.

"You know what I was thinking bout just now?" she asked the little girl, then went on to answer the question. "Bout just how bad your daddy was when he was a little boy. I use to know your daddy before he grow up. I bet you didn't know that."

The little girl shook her head.

"Yeah, I used to know him. Your grandaddy had a farm down near Eautawville that wasn't too far from me and your daddy stayed down there till he was up a size. And talking about somebody full of devilment. Always wanting to play tricks on somebody. Bet he never told you about that."

The little girl looked up from the sand and shook her head. "No."

The old woman chuckled softly and picked up her fan. "Oh, yes. He used to get into a lot of devilment, specially after they got that house in Bowman. I can remember this one time, just after they moved there, when he caused a bit of fracas. See, the reason your grandaddy bought this house was because your grandmomma wanted somewhere nice for her daughters to take company. They were old enough to start courting and this house had a nice-size parlour.

"When your grandaddy bought it he decided to have electricity put in. Everybody used to talk about it because in those days hardly anybody had electricity. They all thought he must be rich so quite a few young men was asking to call on your aunts. Of course this got to be expensive and your grandaddy started to complain about all the bills. He said they were using too much electricity and finally he went round the house and took out all the light bulbs except one. He said they'd just have to make do because he was tired of paying out so much money on the house. So your grandmomma used to put this one light bulb in the front parlour when the girls had company.

"Now this particular Sunday evening your Aunt Ethel was seeing her beau. It happen to be your Uncle Bill cause later on they got married. But at this time they had just started to courting. Anyway, the light bulb was in the parlour and they were in there sitting together. Everything was going along fine till your daddy, he must a been about ten or eleven at the time, decided to go in there and sit between them. He would stay there long enough to get your Aunt Ethel mad and then run off laughing. Finally Aunt Ethel got fed up and told your grandmomma. And for a while they had some peace and quiet cause your grandmomma told your daddy he better not set foot in there again. But the next thing you know, he was standing there in the doorway making funny faces every time one of them would look his way. Your Uncle Bill couldn't help laughing and your Aunt Ethel got mad at him so he said he thought he better be going. Well, your aunt got worried because she figured he might not come back and she jumped up and slammed the parlour door in your daddy's face.

"Course it's not proper for a young lady to be in a room alone with a young man when the door's closed because she had to keep her reputation if she wanted to be respected and get married. Anyway closing the door didn't stop your daddy. He just started peeping through the keyhole and every time your uncle say something nice to your aunt, your daddy would start to say the same thing, just to mock them. There wasn't nothing they could do so they act like he wasn't there and sure enough that seem to do the trick and he went away. Your aunt was just beginning to relax and enjoy your uncle's attention when *BAM*! The parlour door flew open. Both of them jump. Your daddy come in and said, 'Mamma sent me to get the light bulb.' And he walk right up to the light in the middle of the room and take it out. They were left sitting there in the pitch-black and *BAM*! The parlour door shut.

"Your aunt didn't know what to do. It had happen so fast. She just sat there wondering what to do. Meanwhile, your daddy went to the kitchen where your grandmomma had the kerosene lamp and he told her that the light bulb had gone out in the front parlour and please could they have the kerosene lamp. Then he picked that up and was gone. So the whole house was in pitch-black and everybody sitting there thinking the other person had the light.

"After a while your aunt got so worried and she shout out from the front parlour: "Mamma, we sitting here in the dark." And she started crying cause she figured her reputation was ruined. Then when your grandmomma heard her she couldn't figure out how they come to be sitting in the dark. They kept on hollering back and forth to each other till they figured out what your daddy had done. Your grandmomma nearly had a fit and was insisting that your uncle leave the house and he was falling all over the furniture and messing up the parlour trying to find his way out the door. In the end, I believe that's why they rush your uncle through the courting and marry him into the family cause they didn't want too many people to hear about what had happened."

The old woman laughed for a good while. "Yes siree. He sure caused a fracas that time. Little imp!" She continued to smile and rocked thoughtfully while the little girl sat and watched with fascination. Then she stopped rocking and said, "You think he cut out all that foolishness when he and your momma got married?" She shook her head. "I believe it got worse."

"What did he do?" the little girl asked.

"He did plenty a things, but I remember this one in particular. It was just after your Uncle James and your daddy start farming together. Your uncle build himself a house just down the road and they would do a lot of the work from your daddy's house where the barn was. That's where they'd store everything. Now this particular year they made a whole lot of cider and they decide to put most of it in the shed next to your daddy's house.

"One evening after it had got dark, your Uncle James decided he would like a drink of cider so he sent the three children over to the house to fetch it. These were your cousins and they were just little children at the time. Naturally they were scared about walking down the road in the dark. But your uncle told them there was nothing to be scared of and gave them the kerosene lamp so they could see where they were going.

"When they got to the house, your daddy was already in the bed like he'd been sleeping and your momma, who was playing along with him, told the children that your daddy was asleep, so to be quiet, and she went out to the shed and got the cider. So there they were tiptoeing around trying to be quiet and your daddy done take the sheet off the bed and run out the house to hide in the field by the road.

"The children had been hoping that your daddy would a walked back down the road with them. It was bad enough having to come by themselves in the dark night, but to go back seem even worse. Your momma said she was sorry but they couldn't wake him up and so they left holding on to each other, the kerosene lamp and the cider jug.

"Well, by the time they got halfway down the road, they thought they heard this noise. Ooooh, it went. They told each it was just an ole owl. Ooooh, it went again and this time it sound even closer and even less like a owl. They started to walk a little faster. Ooooooh. Ooooooh. They were so scared they could hardly walk straight. Then they heard footsteps behind them and when they turn around to look there was this white thing weaving and waving about and running towards them.

"They didn't even stop when they got to your uncle's house. They just kept on running and hollering and your uncle had to go after them to make them stop. Course there wasn't nothing to see when they turn round to point to the ghost.

"They'd done dropped the jug of cider and the lamp in the middle of the road and when they got back to it the cider had just about leaked out. Your uncle was real cross because he knew it was his brother and not any ghost. He took the children back to your daddy's house so he could prove that it was him and also to get some more cider.

"Well, your daddy was lying up there in the bed snoring his head off. The children nearly bout died of fright. He never did admit it was him under that sheet, but your momma took pity on the children and said that it was your daddy. Even after those children had grown up they'd still asked your momma if that was really your daddy they saw that night."

The old woman leaned back in her chair. "Your daddy was something. And I expect wherever he is overseas, he got somebody wondering whether they coming or going. Both your momma and your daddy used to get the devil in them every so often so I guess you come by it honest."

"What does that mean?" the little girl asked.

"Means that you take after them cause you they child."

"Did my daddy do that for real?"

"Sure as I'm sitting here."

"And he was bad when he was little?"

"Bad? Times he would shame the devil himself!"

"Then how come he doesn't want me to be bad?"

"Cause that's how folks get when they grown and got children. They forget all the things they used to do. The ones that been bad children, they the worse, wanting their children to behave like angels. They don't remember how they used to behave when they say all kinda things to their children trying to get them to be a certain kind a way."

The little girl sat quietly for a moment. She looked down at the ground and began to doodle in the sand. "But they said they don't want any bad children. They only want good ones."

The old woman leaned forward in her chair, suddenly impatient with the woes that burdened the little girl. "There's no such a thing as a bad child. Sometimes they do bad things just like grown people, but that don't make them bad."

The little girl looked up puzzled. "Did God send Adam and Eve away cause he didn't want them?"

The old woman had to think for a while. "God love Adam and Eve. He was just angry about what they had done. He didn't never stop loving them. He was their father and fathers and mothers love their children. Sometimes they have to punish them when they do something wrong, but they don't never stop loving them."

The little girl sighed deeply, still bothered by unresolved questions. "But if children think their momma and daddy don't love them, then it's the same as when they really don't love them. Isn't it?"

The old woman nodded. "Yeah. Sometimes it seem like that's what it is. Sometimes grown people say the exact same thing about God. They say it seem like God don't love them cause they feel like He done left them and they all alone. But God hasn't left them. He just know that there come a time when a person got to find they own way. It seem like He left them, but He hasn't and it seem like He don't love them, but He do. And grown people have to have faith so they can believe in something when they can't see how it could be so."

The little girl began to push the sand again. "Well, I don't believe that my momma and daddy love me."

"They'd be mighty sad if they know that's what you was thinking."

"I'm not going to tell them anyway. When they get back, I'm not going to say nothing."

"Is that so?"

The little girl nodded without looking up.

"Well, I don't know," the old woman said. "Maybe I'm not going to say nothing neither. I don't know. Maybe," she said, and paused till she had the little girl's attention, "just maybe if you go and take those leaves and put them back there on that big pile of weeds they'll be all right. Ain't no use trying to dress up in fig leaves. The first ones couldn't a been too good else they'd still be wearing em. No, I don't think the Lord made the first fig tree for Adam and Eve to make dresses from."

The little girl began to gather up some of the leaves. "Then why did God make fig trees?"

"I can't say why the Lord decided to create a fig tree, but I got a pretty good idea why your grandaddy got that one growing in the garden."

"Why?"

"Well," the old woman replied, "if you take after your daddy side of the family, then one day you'll know." The old woman chuckled to herself. "Never mind," she said to the little girl who was frowning with puzzlement. "Just go on and do like I say."

The little girl, with an armload of leaves, ran towards the compost heap.

The old woman chuckled again. "I don't know," she said to herself, "maybe that is why he made the fig tree."

Lorna Goodison

1947–

Born in Kingston, Jamaica, she studied at the Jamaica School of Art and at the Art Student League of New York, and has worked as an art teacher, advertising copywriter and scriptwriter. An artist as well as writer, she has exhibited paintings in Jamaica and Guyana, has illustrated books (including her own work) and has read her poetry internationally. She has been much anthologized and her poetry publications include Tamarind Season (1980), the prizewinning I Am Becoming My Mother (1986) and Heartease (1988). Her first collection of short stories, Baby Mother and the King of Swords, appeared in 1990.

I Am Becoming My Mother

Yellow/brown woman
fingers smelling always of onions

My mother raises rare blooms
and waters them with tea
her birth waters sang like rivers
my mother is now me

My mother had a linen dress
the colour of the sky
and stored lace and damask
tablecloths
to pull shame out of her eye.

I am becoming my mother
brown/yellow woman
fingers smelling always of onions.

Guinea Woman

Great grandmother
was a guinea woman
wide eyes turning
the corners of her face
could see behind her
her cheeks dusted with
a fine rash of jet-bead warts
that itched when the rain set up.

Great grandmother's waistline
the span of a headman's hand
slender and tall like a cane stalk
with a guinea woman's antelope-quick walk
and when she paused
her gaze would look to sea
her profile fine like some obverse impression
on a guinea coin from royal memory.

It seems her fate was anchored
in the unfathomable sea
for great grandmother caught the eye of a sailor
whose ship sailed without him from Lucea harbour.
Great grandmother's royal scent of
cinnamon and escallions

drew the sailor up the straits of Africa,
the evidence my blue-eyed grandmother
the first Mulatta
taken into backra's household
and covered with his name.
They forebade great grandmother's
guinea woman presence
they washed away her scent of
cinnamon and escallions
controlled the child's antelope walk
and called her uprisings rebellions.

But, great grandmother
I see your features blood dark
appearing
in the children of each new
breeding
the high yellow brown
is darkening down.
Listen, children
it's great grandmother's turn.

Nanny

My womb was sealed
with molten wax
of killer bees
for nothing should enter
nothing should leave
the state of perpetual siege
the condition of the warrior.

From then my whole body would quicken
at the birth of everyone of my people's children.
I was schooled in the green-giving ways
of the roots and vines
made accomplice to the healing acts
of Chainey root, fever grass & vervain.

My breasts flattened
settled unmoving against my chest
my movements ran equal
to the rhythms of the forest.

I could sense and sift
the footfall of men
from the animals

and smell danger
death's odour
in the wind's shift.

When my eyes rendered
light from the dark
my battle song opened
into a solitaire's moan
I became most knowing
and forever sure.

And when my training was over
they circled my waist with pumpkin seeds
and dried okra, a traveller's jigida
and sold me to the traders
all my weapons within me.
I was sent, tell that to history.

When your sorrow obscures the skies
other women like me will rise.

Astrid Roemer
1947–

orn in Parimaribo, Surinam, she trained as a teacher but has
worked mainly as a journalist. From 1966 to 1975 she travelled
between Surinam and the Netherlands. Involved with working
against racism, she has said: "Through literature I'm trying little by little
to reach the continent of my ancestors. . . The themes I use in my work are
actually very universal. I write about love, death, sexuality and about the
struggle of individuals, very often black people, to be happy. I also use the

mother/daughter (son) relationship in my work, because I see that as the
most important relationship in my life. . . I place my writing in the service
of the struggle and my life. If novels do more good I'll write novels, and
if television writing is more effective then I'll do that." She has published
fiction and non-fiction in both Dutch and Sranen. The following extract
is from her novel Een naam voor de liefde (A Name for Love; *1987),*
translated by Rita Gircour.

From

A Name for Love

WHY shouldn't she look up to the triumphant cross when she walked back to her seat. All her suffering brought her closer to God. That the pew might one day be filled with children-in-law and grandchildren was the prayer she said as she carefully lit a candle at the Lady chapel – after Sunday mass.

Fortunately there was also a time when they still walked outside arm in arm – she and her mother, the youngest brother as a piece of blessing behind them. They stopped – arm in arm like that – to greet customers who had become friends and fellow believers who turned out to be customers. They let each other go and smile when gentlemen paid them compliments. And they walked hand in hand with the child along the waterfront. Without saying a word. Perhaps they thought, when they were looking at the river, that nothing lasts – only their services to God. Perhaps that idea gave them a feeling of peace-with-everything. Perhaps this internal search for quiet is the aim of their silence.

There was a time when I nearly forced her to read me fairy tales only to hear her voice. Long. For me. I stood listening at her door when she held business conversations. I loved her orders that cracked against the dance floor.

Don't get me wrong. I did not flee from her depressions. Because when she lay there bubbling like a volcano landscape I was lying next to her for hours, not realizing how I was healed by the thermal stream of her pain sources. I knew nothing about inside matters except for the contents of our refrigerator. I poured syrup for her, put ice cubes in it, held the glass to her lips. But then I was still small enough to be tender. Perhaps I did leave her in a dark hole when I was older. Don't think I am talking about guilt feelings. Let me point out where the grounds of complicity lie. Instead of bringing her closer to her mother I became their distance.

On the morning of my fourth birthday I was not put in the shower by my mother or by our housekeeper but by a curious incident. As I let myself be soaped my fingers are said to have slid across my grandmother's face in an attempt to find out what was underneath. I must have thought that my birthday had pulled a veil of decay over our house and felt lost in the hands of a woman who was so terribly like my mother, without being it up close. This is family history, because

I do not remember a thing about it. My grandmother says: You were looking for your mother in my eyes and you touched my skin – when I called your name you started trembling – you were crying when I told you I was the mother of your mother, especially when I poured milk over you, took it in my mouth and squirted it at your face. I am said to have cried out loud and kept my hands before my face until my mother picked me up. She remained fearful of close contact after that and looked for something we had in common to seal our relationship. It took her another four years to understand that my father had given himself to her daughter for ever. She did keep one comfort: like her mother and her grandmother and her great-grandmother and her great-great-grandmother their daughters and granddaughters remained earthed and fixed. This sort of shared trait does have its drawbacks of course. For example: my "first holy communion" party was threatened by my grandmother's demand to report my disrespectful behaviour to the priest; my mother refused but came with another demand: my teeth were never to touch the host again. And I had to stay in my room until I had promised that. I stood before the mirror like a bride who is to be given in marriage according to tradition and who rejects the bridegroom. For the first time I dearly loved myself. There was a little crown on my head with pink and white roses in a circle of leaves. Pure silk. Purely handmade. My dress had layers of satin and tulle and almost touched the ground. A hairdresser had made curls in my hair with a warm curling-iron. My mother had touched up the colour of my lips, cheeks and eyelids with small pots of cream. I stared at my mirror image for a long time in order to never lose it again.

"The guests are waiting, child."
    "I'm not promising anything."

Her voice had sounded peremptory after the umpteenth time. As if I were one of her pupils who did not stand in the correct position. My refusal was total. I could not confess to her that I did not want ever to become like her and her mother. She could see for herself how different I looked, couldn't she! That there wasn't anybody in the family who looked the least like me! Moreover I always got sick of the incense during mass. And, I did not believe a word they said about the creator of the universe.

"The guests are waiting, child."
    "I'm not promising anything."

It had not escaped me what my mother had to endure from her mother: that I am spoiled; too much alone to show consideration for others; that boarding school would do me a world of good; that my way of treating the housekeeper strikes her as arrogant; that the neighbourhood kids treat me as someone special; that I use the colour of my skin. My grandmother put the silver rosary she had brought as a present on my pillow. With an expression on her face of: I've done my duty. And left the room. That woman should never have done that. And her grandchild should not have walked up to her daughter and lied to her for the very first time: I will never chew on a host again!

In school I had already noticed that everyone paid me more attention than I actually liked. Because everyone saw my name in town constantly, I thought. Or because they admired my mother. Slowly, however, I realized that there were classmates who never heard a nice word from anyone. Then there were grease stains on their notebooks. Or they had to hand in their books because their tuition had not been paid. Usually they were not asked to run errands. They were always allowed to sit at the back of the class.

When I went downstairs with my mother that morning to present myself to the guests a blush of shame seems to have crept to my cheeks when the eyes of my friends lit up. I understood immediately what my grandmother had meant. The differences in skin colour in our living room were overwhelming. They were obtrusive and striking. One glance was enough to be ahead of time, because: there could be a moment in which the difference would put me in my place. Then without knowing where I was I could lose everything I had become attached to. Even though I was only seven and did not have the words to capture the newly gained insight: my guests sat there waiting for my arrival in clearly distinguishable groups. My mother felt how clammy my hands were, because she gave me her handkerchief. Everyone got up except for my grandmother. And they sang a song so-beautiful so-beautiful for me. I really don't know why I went through such a thing with my eyes cast down. Or why my mother took back the handkerchief. On the slides of Uncle Dispenser this sort of detail gives me a kind of hot flush – more violent than the memory of the ceremony.

I don't think that there has ever been a day since that has faded so delightfully. I loved the thoughts in my head so much. As if a gentle fire was burning inside my chest, as comforting as the sunlight. As if dying was closer than the music that engulfed our house. That was happiness. With the presents. At the party. With all the neighbourhood kids. Especially with the desire to grow before the eyes of my mother and her mother into a woman who makes her own decisions. There has not been a night since that has come over me so sensually.

Let me hold a three-minute silence.

I do not want to relate that my grandfather suddenly was no longer there. I do not want to talk about the sadness that blows constantly like the trade wind across our zone of silence. I do not want to long for another hug by him. I do not want to look for the night to call my name across the town. I do not want the day to bring me to his ovens.

What I want is a big raisin bun every day and to smell it, caress it, pick it crumb by crumb, swallow it bit by bit: *my doll's sweet little doll my darling's sweet little darling my girl's sweet little girl my baby's sweet little baby name of my name.*

I do not want to relate that my grandfather suddenly was no longer there. I do not want to talk about the sadness that blows constantly like the trade wind. . . .

That is how I grew up: the desire forced me to look at the world long enough to see only my self. So it was not the stories that my mother exhibited like archaeological findings in a showcase: Well, child, look, my grandfather held all the gold of this country in his hands, and, my daughter, keep in mind that there are even full-blooded Chinese who are your cousins and God knows why one cannot trust a single friend.

At that time I often dreamt I was floating over the town, and because dreams were traditionally told during breakfast our housekeeper remarked airily that I must have an air-spirit who loved me and also protected me – my mother should regularly give me ritual baths, she thought. But the meaningfulness of such a woman ended as soon as my mother looked in the mirror and rubbed lipstick on her mouth with a muscled fist to seal her tongue. With a mouth full of bread I sat down at the piano and I hammered the Arabischer Tanz through the room until she had finished her lemon juice and was no longer always dropping her earrings. I know that she was stuck in the thought about the jeweller who had become filthy rich since her grandfather had sailed to Hong Kong because his father was dangerously ill – the tradesman disappeared without a trace on this trip. But I did not feel like losing her in the early hours of the day to musings that rose early in the morning like mists of melancholy in order to leave deep in the night as resentment in yet another dream. I was sitting there after all when she recounted, still out of breath, how she had struggled to escape death from suffocation by waking up just in time. Sometimes it was water. Sometimes air. Usually it was bales of material that unrolled and trapped her. After all I heard with my own ears that the housekeeper ordered her to see a clairvoyant who could help her fight the sleeping dogs she did not let lie. Because even if it was a comfort that the Chinese eat dogs, the cadaverous smell that escapes when someone seeks blood revenge cannot be dispelled. But: the meaningfulness of such a woman ended as soon as my mother looked in the mirror and rubbed lipstick on her mouth with a muscled fist. And Tchaikovsky wailed through the room that it was primarily an Arab who had given her the right to exist.

So I had her, school and my crying fits – three fillies that really sucked me dry. I became visibly lighter and paler. It is remarkable that my grandmother and my mother also deteriorated outwardly. My mother's cheeks became hollow and her cheekbones gave her face a threatening quality. As if crows from everywhere had touched down briefly and violently on her sur-face, my grandmother became like an etching covered with chaotic grooves. And the vitamin preparation of Uncle Dispenser became the cores around which the housekeeper's vegetable dishes and fruit salads pivoted: we did not collapse – on the contrary! Plagued by sheets of rainwater we drove almost spluttering out of our yard, slowly along with the other vehicles on the tarmac roads over which the water gushed as if there was a flood somewhere close. God-oh-God, how I loved my country on those mornings – so full of children who broke from the heart of the city in all shades of colours with the fire of fabulous celestial bodies in their eyes. As if the rain was there to make them happy. As if the splashes could decorate them like body pearls. On one such Monday morning my mother caught me in one of the crying fits.

"Are you ill?"

"No."

"Are you unhappy?"
"No."
"Do you have a secret, dear?"
"No."

It was the first and in retrospect also the last time that my mother missed work to be with me. But neither she nor her mother, who also returned, hugged me. They stared at me and stayed with me and I dried up. They even made me crack under the abundance of their glow. That they wondered in the meantime what could be done to keep the rainy season out of the house was about as meaningful as my stubborn silence. My thoughts came together as lines, so that I saw squares everywhere in which the faces of children appeared like billions of light points, so illuminated by the sun that my tears stiffened to crystals on their skins. Another crying fit. Another flood of tears.

"Why do you cry?"
"Ask the rain."
"What should we do for you."
"Wait – wait till it's over – over."

Of course they saw another storm coming when the housekeeper held me against her skin and hummed the melodies of the popular songs she had sung in my preschool years: *Perun Perun mi patron san' wani kon' mak' a kon' Ingrisisma sa t jar' na planga go na Jobopan ala den grikibi den no sabi na fin' fin' wroka Kodjo Kodjo fa ju mofo langa so pur wan'* –
Even if this was the first time I could not laugh – I put my arms around her and I pressed my face deeper in her neck and I allowed the sound of my pain to come out with her so that I knew once and for all that, even after years of distance, nothing had come between us except the sort of knowledge that makes a difference.

The other two women, however, did not really stop to think about the full implications of the occasion. Not even interrupted by my sniffing – perhaps accompanied by the humming – they emptied the housekeeper's shopping bags. As in a rhythmic shift of image my grandmother bends to the floor and with her arm stretched she hands her daughter something ripe, something green, something wrapped. I get the urge to be even louder, not even to get their attention but to demand their skin. I get the idea of dying on the spot, not to receive their mourning but to demand their care. I would lie in state and they would kiss me repeatedly from head to toe – their fingertips would caress my skin in its most naked folds – they would cleanse my organs in palm-wine spiced with myrrh and cinnamon – they would wash my cavities with cedar oil – they would wrap me in hot Zanderij sand to dehydrate me – they would soak metres of linen in resin – they would cut the purple wood from the purpleheart tree for my coffin – they would pierce the soil of Albina to paint my face with minerals. Preserved by their care I would live on with artificial eyes that could resist especially the desire to die in my mother's arms. God, I should not have given in to this wishdream which was so charged that the housekeeper's body started to tremble – more and more strongly, as if the rhythm of my heart was imposing itself on her to turn her briefly into a messenger.

Actually my grandmother was an excellent wine-brewer. Fruits, grains, roots – they were made to ferment, and what first looks like gruel ripens into nectar of the gods. The most peaceful memories of her are the ones of her in her chalk-white chemist's coat airing her wine. Beside the poignant fragrance of bruised fruit there were the gulping sounds, caused by the transfer of the drink into a clean cask. She also did the bottling herself and with as much ritual as laying out the wine on the darkened racks. Nobody was allowed into her brewery without her. And apart from her daughter and me no other woman had seen the inside of the shed. Twice a year, as a sort of seasonal drink, her wines were sold on a small scale but labelled over the counter in the drugstore.
     Certainly not the fleshpots of Egypt this trade of my grandmother's, who never let her circle of clients influence her: the same families took the same wines in the same quantities year after year. As a matter of fact it was a shared interest of her and Uncle Dispenser, because he would drive all over on Sundays to buy the natural ingredients and he provided the necessary chemicals. For a woman who did not end a single day without a lengthy prayer the making of alcohol was at least improper. Like her husband who could only discuss his extramarital relationship personally with God she felt that Jehovah's own accomplices had handed her the secrets of the trade. Moreover, what water is to the soul, wine is to the heart – so water cleanses the spirit and wine cleans the blood. I was taught from early on that bathing in running water and drinking choice wines are as natural as going to bed and waking up. So what was so anti-Christian for God's sake about our housekeeper who, like a Venus of Willendorf turned to flesh, imposed the commandments as forcefully as a bull and in the name of a primeval god on three women from one belly to go out and bathe in the breakers of the Marowijne delta by moonlight – to cleanse the guilt – and have an open wine party afterwards with enough Chinese fireworks?
     The fortune our forefather had made by reporting French déportés, selling machetes, back-swords and daggers to the inlanders, enslaving men on his pontoons and misleading European gold expeditions, did eventually cost him his life, but his children were forced to live on – like vermin in a convent wall. His offspring has done enough penance – why didn't his friend who had guardianship over his money and whose sons now own a chain of businesses hang himself?! Arguments coming especially from my mother who had absolutely no intention of listening to the gibberish of her housekeeper.
     My grandmother opened the house Bible and read texts from it to expel the spirit – from the woman and our house. When that did not help she took rainwater out of the barrel next to the house and poured it gently around the tense woman's body while exclaiming sounds which together formed an intense prayer – a veiled accord to have at least a family meeting. Like she came the angel left us – in a close embrace with me.
     . . .

It was the year for changes; for example, the theme of the general election took the lid off a cesspool, the power struggle erected walls of dirt: Creoles are lazyish – Hindustani are slyish – Javanese are slowish; so the rest of the nation that had thought this up was naturally fit to lead the country intelligently, dependably and efficiently to their own top. Our housekeeper was remarkably active. Dressed in a grass-green robe of refined cotton she whizzed through the house, humming – she had become a propagandist for the alliance that should keep the country out of the hands of the light-skinned. My grandmother hardly got a chance to preach her own politics: Listen, God has only one chosen people. Sometimes my mother dealt a blow below the belt: You won't gain a thing from the election results – no matter what! Uncle Dispenser teased her that she was selling out by siding with Blacks. But even before her face could turn bright red and she could point out how acutely pigmented her own sons and daughters were, he showed his sympathy for her party by unbuttoning his coat and showing his propaganda shirt.

In general my mother was hardly involved in the things her brothers so staunchly defended. She fetched ashtrays, put cork mats under the glasses and took a sip herself once in a while. It showed in her eyes that she was occupied by matters that drowned out all the noise. She was thinking about me. Vague incidents had made her realize that I had not only grown beyond her skin but also beyond her will. Of course she was always very considerate of me so conflicts rarely occurred and because opinions occupy our house primarily as holes of emptiness there were no misunderstandings. But then, suddenly, like the smashing of precious china – my refusal to appear in line at any function. Don't get me wrong: the presence of my three uncles, their only sister and two wives on Sundays and holidays seemed like a dream come true. I think I loved each of them; moreover I saw how much good it did my grandmother; under apparent protest she let herself be worshipped by the offspring. Even if it was because only her wine was opened and only her cooking was praised and her beauty imposed itself on the looks of her children, it was also the patience with which they listened to her prayers of thanks. I have always looked at those faces which, closed like clockworks, reflected nothing but the moment, and thought: their mother is their love, their sorrow – their horizon. Because even the looks of their wives were a panorama of their mother's.

Suddenly a detail comes to mind. Suddenly a child has matured to understanding. Then a song no longer holds a melody but a complaint. Then the Mona Lisa is not a woman's portrait but a deception. For years and years my mother merely named the Country's Most Beautiful Virgin: with a voice so firm in its sound and with a courtliness that emphasized not so much her profession as her inflexibility. And it was not even what it seemed to be. All this time she carried a secret that crept to her shoulders and threatened to expose itself rather vulgarly right there at the fair pavilion: May I invite the public relations man from the Alcoa Bauxite Company! And he did nothing extraordinary when he gallantly kissed her. Perhaps it was the way in which her sisters-in-law bent their heads towards each other and furtively smiled just then. And from that moment on I understood the glow near her cheekbones and I knew how soft, how mercifully soft her lips were then. And instead of following her with the eyes of a jackal, as her mother did, I left this fairground for ever.

I still remember how I stood in front of the mirrors in the house that evening to see how true it was: my mother may have left me the space for much longer than nine months, the desire to make love did rush to her jaws from time to time. The fingers with which she could gesture so magnificently: Look, a spider for you! The hands that could reach so far: Wait, I'll pick a star, my child! The hips that only swung artificially! The legs that only spread for the *pas de chat*! In arabesque she had always stood before me, always-always ready, and suddenly I could only unbalance her.

Elean Thomas

1947–

B orn in St Catherine, Jamaica, she studied political science and history at the University of the West Indies and did postgraduate work in communications at Goldsmiths College, London. Rooted for many years in the women's struggle in the Caribbean, she has been active in the movement for Jamaican national independence and progress and involved in international diplomatic work and journalism. She was a founder of the Workers Party of Jamaica, and its International Secretary. She has given readings and conducted workshops in the Caribbean, Latin America, Eastern and Western Europe and Africa. Her writing encompasses articles, fiction and poetry. Her first two books were collections of poetry with some prose stories – Word Rhythms from the Life of a Woman (1986) and Before they Can Speak of Flowers: Word Rhythms (1988). (She says: "I call my pieces Word-Rhythms, I honestly believe it is pretentious to call them poems. They are merely word-sketches, word-photographs, word-drawings, word-paintings, word-beats.") She has also written a novel, The Last Room (1991).

Josina

I MET Josina when I was nine years old. To this day, I never knew how old she was. The day Josina came, I was washing dishes in the two pudding pans – one with water to wash, the other with water to rinse – in the kitchen. We, my mother, step-father and I, occupied the main front room of a three-room house. In the room at the back lived a Sugar Factory worker and his woman who took in washing. In the other room – the one opening to the side of the front verandah – lived the landlord (white Jamaican whose branch of the family had fallen from grace with their peers some time between slavery and colonialism and by now mainly drank rum and collected rent. He was also into the business of molesting little girls).

On our side of the road, there was the barber (called *Barber*) and his always-sick wife Miss Maude (people said that a girlfriend of his had obeahed her but I later came to understand that she suffered from the common female problem of fibroids); the respectable dressmaker, Miss Pat, married to the Prison Warder – and further down the road, the Browns – people who had lived on that same street, in that same house, in that same town for three generations and who were beginning to be doctors and civil servants before my people were even off the plantation.

My mother worked at the Textile Factory and my step-father at the Sugar Factory. The abysmal illusions of workers who are close to the petit-bourgeoisie! The working class on the road aspired to be like the dressmaker, Miss Pat, and her husband, the Prison Warder. Miss Pat and her husband, the Prison Warder, aspired to be like the Browns. And the Browns? They aspired to be what they were three generations ago before there was all this *indiscipline* with Rastas and Trade Unions and Political Parties and so on.

So that on my side of the road, its residents preferred to pretend that the other side of the road was not there. For on the other side of the road, was the Hangman's Cemetery, abandoned some years before but with the gravestones standing out among the tall stunted grass; perhaps to remind especially those on my side of the road where you would end up if you were not decent and mixed with only decent people.

If you walk alongside the cemetery, on the main road, just as you pass the train gate there is a wide track. On the left of this track, is a clearing, through which you can walk to get on to the trainline, or crossing the trainline, into the belly of the cemetery. On the other side is a gully which borders the clearing. Turning neither right nor left, after you have come off the main road into the clearing, but going straight, you come into Tawes Pen – a dirt-poor community of minute farmers, self-employed artisans, manual workers and perpetually unemployed. Children on our side of the road were reared from birth to view anything or anyone on the other side of the road as a specie of human being not quite human and certainly not decent. But it was from Tawes Pen that the Jonkonoo Band came every Christmas so even the most *well-behaved* children from my side of the road had, at one time or the other, ignored our parent's instructions not to mix with the Tawes Pen people.

I was telling you however about the day I met Josina for the first time. I was washing the dishes at about eleven in the morning during the holiday times when I heard a lot of excitement coming from over the other side of the road. I ran over there and saw that the activity was in the clearing. I saw some Rastas – about ten men, one woman and two children, setting up a settlement in the clearing on the cemetery land.

It was one year after the *general election* which brought the *Self-Government Party* to power. More importantly, it was four years after the Marxist-Socialists had been expelled from that Party and many of the leaders hounded off the island. It was also after all our prominent statesmen and politicians had agreed with the British that the best thing for the island was to model our self-government system on that of our colonial benefactors who had taught us so much for nearly 400 years. Of course, many of the workers either did not know of this consensus or were too ignorant to grasp its meaning. Because they continued to strike for better pay and conditions of work. Many of the unemployed continued to demand jobs. Many ruined farmers continued to migrate to the city and demand places to live. Some of all these joined Rastafari and increased their chants against *Babylon System*. The response of the authorities was terrible bulldozing of communities, mass arrests and evictions.

These people in the clearing had been evicted and like others of them, where there were no relatives to *kotch* with, no way else out, they *captured* land. These had *captured* a part of the Hangman's Cemetery.

They soon had up two shelters – a large one for the men, a smaller one for the woman and children. I stood along with other curious men, women and children as the newcomers set up residence and was there again in the evening when they started to drum and chant.

I used to steal away over there in the days, when mainly the woman, her children and the unemployed men were there. The men who had jobs worked on construction sites but most of them were either unemployed *hustlers* or sellers of some small thing – broom or bottles (in those days, sweeties and cigarettes were not such popular items of higglery as they are now). I used to steal away there in the nights also, when my parents were on night shift at the factory.

I had naturally noticed Josina on that first day but I came to know her and her children – one baby on breast, one toddler – better later on.

Josina had thick, black, coarse plaits, usually four or five sticking from her head, dark eyes, high forehead topping an oval face which was flat in front with African nose and black lips. Medium breasts (already *dropped* from being the only steady source of nutrient for the children), rounded belly, a high behind and strong legs come down to small ankles and feet. Just above the left ankle was the lasting deep scar of an ulcer which had taken gallons of hot water and Dettol, tons of Blue Stone and two years out of school before anyone could be sure she wouldn't lose the leg.

Josina didn't talk very much. She was one of those women – seen so often among our working people – who long ago decided that it took too much out of you to both talk and fight life, so just decided to fight life – quietly. With no one to leave the children with, looking for a job did not make much sense, even if there was any to find – for her. She stayed in the settlement, sewed, made things with her hands like crude wooden and stuffed toys for the children, tidied the place, cooked sometimes, washed and lived from day to day.

We would sit in the clearing on many a day, Josina and I. She doing something and watching the children, me trying to find out about their lives – how did they come there, where would they go from there. She never spoke about the children's father – who he was, what had happened to him, why was he not there with her and the children. The extent of her life that she was willing to bare was: she was a woman with two children who had nowhere to live and lived in that place at that moment. In terms of the men among whom she lived, she was everybody's woman – yet she was nobody's woman.

One evening when I went over there, they were quarrelling. One of their number had tried to crash Josina's hut in the night and force her submission to him. She had fought him off successfully and had raised it in the Council (the evening drumming and chanting). He sought to defend his action by saying it was a matter between Josina and himself. Class struggle raged between those who supported him in this and those who held onto *"this woman among us for us to protect her and her children; why should we seek to defile her just because she need our protection"*. These won out – one main reason being that the leader of the community, the highly respected Elder, carried this position firmly and would not back down.

I was at home alone again the day they came to root out Josina, her children and her brethren. They came in one jeep and one Black Maria – blue seams and red seams (the khaki must have stayed in the office).

Josina was there along with the children. They came like a hurricane – blue bag, blue stripe, red stripe hurricane. Quick as a flash, Josina grabbed up the children – one into her arms, the toddler in her skirts between her legs.

They started in with batons, with sledgehammers, with tearing hands, with stomping feet. They tore down the little shelter over the fireside, made up of sticks, crocus bags and old zinc. When that was down, they hammered the aluminum pot. They kicked the Dutch pot into the gully. They wouldn't even let the firestones remain but threw them into the gully too.

They tore down the two sleeping huts; they kicked the few meagre items of clothing into the dirt and the rubble.

And Josina just stood there, among the curious onlookers, watching the hurricane.

By this time some of the resident men had begun to drift to the scene one by one, word must have gotten to them. They helped to swell the crowd of onlookers, mainly from Tawes Pen. No one dared pierce the eye of the blue seam and red seam hurricane.

I had never before in my nine years seen such a scene of total violence.

When the police had beaten, thrashed and torn down everything. When the cardboard, the cellotex, the bits of board, the zinc, which had made up the huts, lay flat and scattered in the dust. When every last *grip*, suitcase, carton box containing their life's collections, had been mashed and crushed and flushed out in the dirt and into the gully, like hungry beasts unsated they kicked the dirt and looked around for more things to destroy. And prayed that one or more of the people forming a half-ring on the sidelines would intervene, so they could mash and crush some people too.

And then they saw Josina's pail. In those days every woman had a pail. My mother had a pail. I would soon have a pail. You soaked and washed your *small clothes* in the pail until they were so white and glistening on the clothes line, it hurt your eyes to look directly at them hanging in the sun.

Josina's pail was some way away from the settlement, behind a big cotton tree. The pail was neatly covered with a clean piece of cardboard weighted down by a stone.

At the same time they saw the pail, Josina remembered the pail. Putting the baby on the dirt, disentangling the toddler from between her legs, she started forward to rescue the pail. They reached it before she did. And one of the policemen kicked the pail high in the clearing. Bloody water and small clothes flew all around the clearing, the small clothes seeming to fly up and up and up – and then to come down and down and down – for an eternity – before settling plop, plop, plop, in the dirt.

For one moment, Josina and every man, woman and child, including some of the policemen themselves, stood together on the edge of the world. There was a thunderous silence, then an extended collective gasp – in the midst of which Josina walked to the middle of the clearing and began, as in a trance, to gather the small clothes from the dirt.

My nine-year-old belly began to tremble and thunder and roll and scream with razor-sharp pains from left to right (I learnt later that women feel things in our bellies). A rolling and groaning began in my belly and moved upwards and downwards, filling my legs, my stomach, my chest, till it filled my ears and head and it was all around me. And then I realized that the murmuring and rumbling were also coming from the hundred or so men, women and children gathered there. It started as a low murmur and then it rose like the mighty wave of a sea in the throes of a tidal wave beginning. Like a hurricane coming out of the gulf of Mexico and gathering force and fury.

And the Elder (the one who had defended Josina) brought out from the depths of his guts a terrible roar: *Babylon. . .Fall*!! The crowd picked up the ominous chant: *Babylon you must, you must fall down, Babylon you must fall down. . .* The chant followed me all the way over to my side of the street as I ran home. I never saw Josina again but for years her face was to remain with me as she stood in the clearing, the small clothes covered with dirt in her hands.

Black Woman's Love Song

I sang you love songs
as they dumped us
    together
amongst the cockroaches and rats
in the hole of the slave ship

I sang you love songs
when in that stinking hole
I helped you keep alive
for the new world fight to come

I sang you love songs
when they had us
    on the auction block
and took you east
dragging me north

I sang you love songs
through my cries
    of pain
begging you
please don't ever forget
    me

I sang you love songs
when they took me
for their concubine
and took you
for their stud

I sang you love songs
even when I ceased
to be their concubine
but you couldn't stop
being their stud

I sang you love songs
when the backra-massa
threw us off our land
paid for
by our sweat and blood
    together

I sang you love songs
when you said
"if we can't beat them
    join them"
and took up with the backra-missis

I sang you love songs
when we got our heads
   busted
   together
demonstrating for the right
to speak to strike
to politicize
to organize

I sang you love songs
when you cried upon my breast
and I rubbed healing herbs
into your wounds
   us both
   forgetting
that my own insides were torn
and shredded with wounds

I sang you love songs
when we took up arms
against the enemy
to reclaim our dignity

I sang you love songs
even as you disclaimed
our child
conceived from your hasty seed
shot into my womb
on a one-day furlough

I sang you love songs
after the war
when we worked together
to rebuild a whole people
and a free country

I sang you love songs
when you said
I was no longer bright enough
or good enough
to attend the State dinners
you were now being invited to

I keep singing
   you
   love songs
even as hate-songs
threaten to smother
   my very soul

I sing you love songs
   Black-man
so you can understand
that I want you
   strong
beside me
Singing me love songs too.

Pauline Melville

1940s–

S*he works as an actress and writer. Her poetry has been published in anthologies, including* Rented Rooms *(edited by David Dabydeen, 1989), in which her poem "Mixed" first appeared. In 1990 her first collection of stories,* Shape-Shifter, *was published, winning the* Guardian Fiction Prize, *the Macmillan Silver Pen Award and the Commonwealth Writers' Prize.*

Beyond the Pale

THERE is a Yoruba folktale of a trickster god who loves to cause strife. He walks down the main street of a village wearing a hat that is red on one side and blue on the other. When he has passed, the people on one side of the street say: "Did you see that god with the blue hat go by?" The people on the other side reply: "That hat was red. We saw it with our own eyes." And they fall to fighting and fisticuffs and interminable arguments while the god continues on his way, laughing.

I also cause confusion. I look completely English. My mother is English, second of ten children from a London family, a tribe of Anglo-Saxons if ever there was one, blonde and blue-eyed. The photographs show St Augustine's angels in hand-me-down clothes. My father was born in Guyana (or British Guiana as it was then), also the second of ten children. The photographs show a genetic bouquet of African, Amerindian and European features, a family gazing out from dark, watchful eyes – all except one, who turned out with the looks of a Dutchman. But then, Berbice, their birthplace, was a Dutch colony in the eighteenth century. I am the whitey in the woodpile. The trickster god now appears in another guise. He has donned the scientific mantle of genetics. I look English. At home, in a drawer, lies my great-great grandmother's baptism certificate. Dated 13 June 1832, it states: *Abode – Town of New Amsterdam. Occupation – Slave of D. Melville.*

White present, black past, a good position for breaking down preconceptions, stirring up doubt, rattling judgements, shifting boundaries and unfixing fixities. I am also well-placed to survey the ludicrous.

England. Over-eager hostess at dinner:
"Did you know Pauline was black?"
Bewildered silence. Forks poised halfway to mouths. People politely swallowing the evidence of their own eyes. Explanations. Sometimes they don't believe me. What am I supposed to do – wear the baptism certificate pinned to my lapel?

Guyana. On an occasion when I'd referred to myself as white:
"You're not white. I know your family. How can you call yourself white?"

England. "You're not black. That's crazy. You're as white as I am."

The confusion arises because there are overlapping definitions of race: race is what you look like; race is your genetic heritage, whatever you may look like; race is a cultural concept that might or might not coincide with what you look like. According to the first, I am white. According to the second, I am black. According to the third, I am mixed.

"Race is what you look like" fails as a useful criterion for grouping people. We all know of black Americans and black British who have returned to Africa and yet felt alien because their experience and culture bore little relation to that of the people they were with.

"Race is your genetic heritage, whatever you may look like" is a philosophy generally associated with the most pernicious of racists, imperialists and nose-measurers, whose power rested on such graded distinctions. A few years ago in Louisiana, a woman applied to have herself re-classified as Caucasian. As far as I remember, she claimed to be one-sixty-fourth part black and otherwise white. Her application was turned down. Imagine the aforementioned dinner party with a visibly black woman replacing myself: "Did you know that Charlene was white?"

"Race is a cultural concept" turns to look at an individual's interior landscape, the experience of region, class, gender and family history, all the multiple influences that go to build up an identity. Appearance matters less, unless the society has made it a factor of importance. We are more empowered to define ourselves. The transsexual man – a man who feels himself to be a woman – describes himself in accordance with this internal image. Unfortunately, we bump up against a real world outside where bureaucrats, civil-servants and form-fillers might choose to define us differently.

The telephone rings: "Would you be interested in contributing to an anthology of black women's literature?"

I hesitate. "Do you think I'm black?"

"That's for you to say."

Well, it's an odd thing to have a choice about. Perhaps I am the joker in the pack, able to turn up as any card. But I accept, through an unwillingness to disinherit myself or disclaim a past history, mainly through fear of betraying my father.

I cast my mind back to look for occasions when my identity was an issue. Vaguely I remember, in Guyana, being called "ice-cream face". Once, as a child, after coming to live in London (I think I was about eight or nine) I went with a friend to the hairdresser. My friend was going to have a shampoo and wash. I had never been inside a hairdresser's and wanted to tag along. Whether or not I was exercising some choice about being a West Indian, a Red Indian or an Asian Indian I do not know, but I insisted on accompanying her dressed as some sort of Indian. What the hairdresser made of this scrawny child, enveloped in a sheet, who remained totally mute during the whole of the visit (with the occasional mimed gesture), I have no idea. She was quite friendly and seemed to play along with it. It could have been just a kid's game. It might also have been, on my part, a small attempt to make visible what was invisible.

Years ago I watched an old British film called *Sapphire*, which was about the murder of a girl who looked white. Her fiancé's sister had bumped her off to stop her brother marrying a girl who was merely "passing" for white. I remember being disturbed and excited by the film. I tried to telephone one or two friends to tell them to watch the film because it was "about me".

Then again, recently I visited Liverpool for carnival. There the black community is one of the oldest and longest-standing in Britain, stretching back over some three hundred years. Many of the people were very light-skinned and I have to admit feeling in some way "authenticated" when I was among them. This leads to another story. During the Liverpool 8 riots of the 1980s, there were reports that white youths had joined the rioting. "But," said someone from Liverpool, "they weren't white. They were black. The police mistook them for white, but they were black." Here again, the cultural definition held sway. Here again, the same situation would not have arisen in reverse.

In Guyana I remember being at a dance when an Indo-Guyanese boy asked me to dance. Immediately, the Afro-Guyanese group I was with claimed me for theirs and cussed off the "coolie". Yet another division.

Parts of my life have been spent in the Caribbean, most of it in England. Because, in England, my appearance coincides with that of the majority, the dominant culture, I have not suffered discrimination in housing or work. I have not been picked on by the police. I have, so to speak, got away lightly. Some Afro-Caribbeans resent my being included among them when I have not undergone those bitter experiences. But let them not think that because I see with blue eyes I do not see what goes on. Why then do I feel faintly uncomfortable when people insist that I'm white? (Ironically, an elderly aunt of mine exploded into insanity at the fear of being called black – but attitudes shift in different places at different times.) There are several reasons: fear of being rejected by the black community; fear of being identified with an oppressor; and simply, for me, it does not feel like the whole truth.

But generally, the experiences I've mentioned have not been the most significant in my identity's shaping. When questioned about my identity, I would wish to echo Clark Gable in *Gone With the Wind*: "Frankly, my dear, I don't give a damn." In my interior landscape, the South American jaguar and the English chaffinch live easily together.

The quest for identity in roots is historically quite recent, a modern phenomenon just as psychology is a modern science. In the age of the individual, there needed to arise a science that could explain him/her. But it is an extraordinary notion to think of people roaming the world looking for their identity. As Louise Bennett put it:

> Wat a debil of a bump-and-bore
> Rig-jig and palam-pam
> Ef de whole worl start fi go back
> Whe dem great grampa come from!

Or, as Salman Rushdie said in *Shame*: "Sometimes, I think roots are a conservative myth designed to keep us in our place." Looking back, whether it be to Africa, the Amazonian rain forest or the primeval forests of Britain, can be an impulse driven by a pre-enlightenment engine where the golden age was in the past. The Age of Enlightenment shunted the golden age forwards. The engine that drives the desire for social justice is a post-enlightenment engine that puts the golden age in the future. Sometimes I think the race relations industry is a car with one of these engines at either end. There is a film with Steve Martin called *The Jerk*. In it he plays a white boy raised by a black family. One day he sets off to discover his white roots. Bob Marley chose to identify with his black roots. Had he pursued his father's Anglo-Scottish ancestry, he might have ended up in a kilt in the Highlands singing "Will ye no' come back again?" Culturally, he was pure Jamaican and, luckily for us, his voice came soaring out of the slums of the diaspora to personify the resistance of the Third World to oppression.

But how far back are roots supposed to go? I think of my Amerindian forebears. The Amerindians are thought to have come over originally from Mongolia. Do I have a Mongolian herdsman galloping along the spidery pathways of my DNA?

According to Darwin, I was a fish once.

Pinning down my identity is not what interests me most about life. I enjoy Carnival because anybody can take on any form: an Egyptian goddess; a Mabaruma warrior; a sultan; a demon; a frog. Race, gender, class, species and divinity are all in the melting-pot, and I am a champion of mixtures and hybrids. Carnival plays with identity. It is a masquerade where disguise is the only truth. A year ago at the Notting Hill Carnival I saw riot police cutting a swathe through the revellers. In a sense, they had joined the masquerade. They were the other side of the equation. The police were encased in Darth Vader black helmets with visors. They carried truncheons and dark plastic shields. The forces of death had come to confront the forces of life. Death comes in the guise of uniformity, mono-cultural purity, the externals of the state as opposed to the riot of the imagination.

And here we reach the crux of the matter. In most examinations of cultural identity, people are seen as mere repositories of experience. Excluded as a factor is the imagination. And this is where boundaries are crossed and hybrids fertilized. This is where everything is possible as there is a shuttle service between the imagination and the real world, they influence each other, and this is where things can begin to change. Through books, movies and TV we are able to enter other lives. We can identify with the plight of a Chinese fisherman, a Brooklyn housewife, a homosexual from Delhi, a musician from Zaïre, or even a hunted seal in Canada or a cartoon rabbit. The imagination is effortlessly trans-national, trans-racial, trans-gender, trans-species. It could be argued that some people are entirely practical, empiricists who deal in a world of pragmatism, without vision. It is nonsense, of course. There is no such person. Everybody is driven by dreams.

What good are dreams to a black youth who is being hit on the head by a white policeman? Or to a black nation sucked dry by a white one? Imagination leads to many things, and one of them is action for political justice. A youth without dreams is a youth who has already perished.

Meanwhile, I shall take as my tutelary spirits Legba, Exu and Hermes, the gods of boundaries, borders and crossroads.

Postscript: Two months after completing this piece I was diagnosed as having sickle-cell trait, a medical condition that affects only black people.

Mixed

Sometimes, I think
My mother with her blue eyes
And flowered apron
Was exasperated
At having such a sallow child,
And my mulatto daddee
Silenced
By having such an English-looking one.

And so my mother
Rubbed a little rouge on my cheeks
For school,
Lest people should think
She was not doing her job properly.

And my father chose to stay home
On sports days.

Becky Birtha
1948–

B orn in Virginia and now living in Philadelphia, she is, in her
own words, "a lesbian feminist poet who also writes fiction and
reviews." In 1985 she received an Individual Fellowship in Literature from the Pennsylvania Council on the Arts. Her work has appeared
in a number of literary and feminist journals and she has published a
poetry book, The Forbidden Poems (1991), and two collections of short
stories: For Nights Like This One: Stories of Loving Women (1983) and
Lovers' Choice (1987). This story appears in the latter.

Johnnieruth

S UMMERTIME. Nighttime. Talk about steam heat. This whole city get like
the bathroom when somebody in there taking a shower with the door shut.
Nights like that, can't nobody sleep. Everybody be outside, sitting on they steps
or else dragging half they furniture out on the sidewalk – kitchen chairs, card
tables – even bringing TVs outside.

Womenfolks, mostly. All the grown women around my way look just the
same. They all big – stout. They got big bosoms and big hips and fat legs,
and they always wearing runover house-shoes, and them shapeless, flowered
numbers with the buttons down the front. Cept on Sunday. Sunday morning
they all turn into glamour girls, in them big hats and long gloves, with they skinny
high heels and they skinny selves in them tight girdles – wouldn't nobody ever
know what they look like the rest of the time.

When I was a little kid I didn't wanna grow up, cause I never wanted to look
like them ladies. I heard Miz Jenkins down the street one time say she don't mind
being fat cause that way her husband don't get so jealous. She say it's more than
one way to keep a man. Me, I don't have me no intentions of keeping no man. I
never understood why they was in so much demand anyway, when it seem like
all a woman can depend on em for is making sure she keep on having babies.

We got enough children in my neighborhood. In the summertime, even the
little kids allowed to stay up till eleven or twelve o'clock at night – playing in
the street and hollering and carrying on – don't never seem to get tired. Don't
nobody care, long as they don't fight.

Me – I don't hang around no front steps no more. Hot nights like that,
I get out my ten-speed and I be gone.

That's what I like to do more than anything else in the whole world. Feel
that wind in my face keeping me cool as a air conditioner, shooting along like
a snowball. My bike light as a kite. I can really get up some speed.

All the guys around my way got ten-speed bikes. Some of the girls got em too, but they don't ride em at night. They pedal around during the day, but at nighttime they just hang around out front, watching babies and running they mouth. I didn't get my Peugeot to be no conversation piece.

My mama don't like me to ride at night. I tried to point out to her that she ain't never said nothing to my brothers, and Vincent a year younger than me. (And Langston two years older, in case "old" is the problem.) She say, "That's different, Johnnieruth. You're a girl." Now I wanna know how is anybody gonna know that. I'm skinny as a knifeblade turned sideways, and all I ever wear is blue jeans and a Wrangler jacket. But if I bring that up, she liable to get started in on how come I can't be more of a young lady, and fourteen is old enough to start taking more pride in my appearance, and she gonna be ashamed to admit I'm her daughter.

I just tell her that my bike be moving so fast can't nobody hardly see me, and couldn't catch me if they did. Mama complain to her friends how I'm wild and she can't do nothing with me. She know I'm gonna do what I want no matter what she say. But she know I ain't getting in no trouble, neither.

Like some of the boys I know stole they bikes, but I didn't do nothing like that. I'd been saving my money ever since I can remember, everytime I could get a nickel or a dime outta anybody.

When I was a little kid, it was hard to get money. Seem like the only time they ever give you any was on Sunday morning, and then you had to put it in the offering. I used to hate to do that. In fact, I used to hate everything about Sunday morning. I had to wear all them ruffly dresses – that shiny slippery stuff in the wintertime that got to make a noise every time you move your ass a inch on them hard old benches. And that scratchy starchy stuff in the summertime with all them scratchy crinolines. Had to carry a pocket-book and wear them shiny shoes. And the church we went to was all the way over on Summit Avenue, so the whole damn neighborhood could get a good look. At least all the other kids'd be dressed the same way. The boys think they slick cause they get to wear pants, but they still got to wear a white shirt and a tie; and them dumb hats they wear can't hide them baldheaded haircuts, cause they got to take the hats off in church.

There was one Sunday when I musta been around eight. I remember it was before my sister Corletta was born, cause right around then was when I put my foot down about that whole sanctimonious routine. Anyway, I was dragging my feet along Twenty-fifth Street in back of Mama and Vincent and them, when I spied this lady. I only seen her that one time, but I still remember just how she look. She don't look like nobody I ever seen before. I *know* she don't live around here. She real skinny. But she ain't no real young woman, neither. She could be old as my mama. She ain't nobody's mama – I'm sure. And she ain't wearing Sunday clothes. She got on blue jeans and a man's blue working shirt, with the tail hanging out. She got patches on her blue jeans, and she still got her chin stuck out like she some kinda African Royalty. She ain't carrying no shiny pocketbook. It don't look like she care if she got any money or not, or who know it, if she don't. She ain't wearing no house-shoes, or stockings or high heels neither.

Mama always speak to everybody, but when she pass by this lady she make like she ain't even seen her. She got a funny look on her face, almost like she think she know me from some place. After she pass on by, I had to turn around to get another look, even though Mama say that ain't polite. And you know what? She was turning around, too, looking back at me. And she give me a great big smile.

I didn't know too much in them days, but that's when I first got to thinking about how it's got to be different ways to be, from the way people be around my way. It's got to be places where it don't matter to nobody if you all dressed up on Sunday morning or you ain't. That's how come I started saving money. So, when I got enough, I could go away to some place like that.

Afterwhile I begun to see there wasn't no point in waiting around for handouts, and I started thinking of ways to earn my own money. I used to be running errands all the time – mailing letters for old Grandma Whittaker and picking up cigarettes and newspapers up the corner for everybody. After I got bigger, I started washing cars in the summer, and shoveling people sidewalk in the wintertime. Now I got me a newspaper route. Ain't never been no girl around here with no paper route, but I guess everybody got it figured out by now that I ain't gonna be like nobody else.

The reason I got me my Peugeot was so I could start to explore. I figured I better start looking around right now, so when I'm grown, I'll know exactly where I wanna go. So I ride around every chance I get.

Last summer, I used to ride with the boys a lot. Sometimes eight or ten of us'd just go cruising around the streets together. All of a sudden my mama decide she don't want me to do that no more. She say I'm too old to be spending so much time with boys. (That's what they tell you half the time, and the other half the time they worried cause you ain't interested in spending more time with boys. Don't make much sense.) She want me to have some girl friends, but I never seem to fit in with none of the things the girls doing. I used to think I fit in more with the boys.

But I seen how Mama might be right, for once. I didn't like the way the boys was starting to talk about girls sometimes. Talking about what some girl be like from the neck on down, and talking all up underneath somebody clothes and all. Even though I wasn't really friends with none of the girls, I still didn't like it. So now I mostly just ride around by myself. And Mama don't like that neither – you just can't please her.

This boy that live around the corner in North Street, Kenny Henderson, started asking me one time if I don't ever be lonely, cause he always see me by myself. He say don't I ever think I'd like to have me somebody special to go places with and stuff. Like I'd pick him if I did! Made me wanna laugh in his face. I do be lonely, a lotta times, but I don't tell nobody. And I ain't met nobody yet that I'd really rather be with than be by myself. But I will someday. When I find that special place where everybody different, I'm gonna find somebody there I can be friends with. And it ain't gonna be no dumb boy.

I found me one place already, that I like to go to a whole lot. It ain't even really that far away – by bike – but it's on the other side of the Avenue. So I don't tell Mama and them I go there, cause they like to think I'm right around the neighborhood someplace. But this neighborhood too dull for me. All the houses look just the same – no porches, no yards, no trees – not even no parks around here. Every block look so much like every other block it hurt your eyes to look at, afterwhile. So I ride across Summit Avenue and go down that big steep hill there, and then make a sharp right at the bottom and cross the bridge over the train tracks. Then I head on out the boulevard – that's the nicest part, with all them big trees making a tunnel over the top, and lightning bugs shining in the bushes. At the end of the boulevard you get to this place call the Plaza.

It's something like a little park – the sidewalks is all bricks and they got flowers planted all over the place. The same kind my mama grow in that painted-up tire she got out front masquerading like a garden decoration – only seem like they smell sweeter here. It's a big high fountain right in the middle, and all the streetlights is the real old-fashion kind. That Plaza is about the prettiest place I ever been.

Sometimes something going on there. Like a orchestra playing music or some man or lady singing. One time they had a show with some girls doing some kinda foreign dances. They look like they were around my age. They all had on these fancy costumes, with different color ribbons all down they back. I wouldn't wear nothing like that, but it looked real pretty when they was dancing.

I got me a special bench in one corner where I like to sit, cause I can see just about everything, but wouldn't nobody know I was there. I like to sit still and think, and I like to watch people. A lotta people be coming there at night – to look at the shows and stuff, or just to hang out and cool off. All different kinda people.

This one night when I was sitting over in that corner where I always be at, there was this lady standing right near my bench. She mostly had her back turned to me and she didn't know I was there, but I could see her real good. She had on this shiny purple shirt and about a million silver bracelets. I kinda liked the way she look. Sorta exotic, like she maybe come from California or one of the islands. I mean she had class – standing there posing with her arms folded. She walk away a little bit. Then turn around and walk back again. Like she waiting for somebody.

Then I spotted this dude coming over. I spied him all the way cross the Plaza. Looking real fine. Got on a three-piece suit. One of them little caps sitting on a angle. Look like leather. He coming straight over to this lady I'm watching and then she seen him too and she start to smile, but she don't move till he get right up next to her. And then I'm gonna look away, cause I can't stand to watch nobody hugging and kissing on each other, but all of a sudden I see it ain't no dude at all. It's another lady.

Now I can't stop looking. They smiling at each other like they ain't seen one another in ten years. Then the one in the purple shirt look around real quick – but she don't look just behind her – and sorta pull the other one right back into the corner where I'm sitting at, and then they put they arms around each other and kiss – for a whole long time. Now I really know I oughtta turn away, but I can't. And I know they gonna see me when they finally open they eyes. And they do.

They both kinda gasp and back up, like I'm the monster that just rose up outta the deep. And then I guess they can see I'm only a girl, and they look at one another – and start to laugh! Then they just turn around and start to walk away like it wasn't nothing at all. But right before they gone, they both look around again, and see I still ain't got my eye muscles and jaw muscles working right again yet. And the one lady wink at me. And the other one say, "Catch you later."

I can't stop staring at they backs, all the way across the Plaza. And then, all of a sudden, I feel like I got to be doing something, got to be moving.

I wheel on outta the Plaza and I'm just concentrating on getting up my speed. Cause I can't figure out what to think. Them two women kissing and then, when they get caught, just laughing about it. And here I'm laughing too, for no reason at all. I'm sailing down the boulevard laughing like a lunatic, and then I'm singing at the top of my lungs. And climbing that big old hill up to Summit Avenue is just as easy as being on a escalator.

Ntozake Shange

1948–

Born Paulette Williams in Trenton, New Jersey (as an act of protest against her Western roots, in 1971 she adopted Zulu names meaning "she who comes with her own things" and "she who walks like a lion"), she began writing when she was a child. She received a BA from Barnard College in 1970 and an MA from the University of California at Los Angeles and, becoming involved with the Black and women's movements, developed a writing style eminently suited for public readings. Her "choreopoem" For colored girls who have considered suicide/when the rainbow is enuf (1975) was produced on Broadway with dancer Paulette Moss, winning an Obie award. Among her many other works are A Photograph: A Study of Lovers in Motion (drama, 1977), Natural Disasters and Other Festive Occasions (poetry and prose, 1977), Nappy Edges (poetry, 1978), Boogie Woogie Landscapes (drama, 1978), Spell #7 (drama, 1979), See No Evil: Prefaces, Essays and Accounts 1976–83 (1984), Ridin' the Moon in Texas: Word Paintings (poetry and prose, 1987) and the novels Sassafrass, Cypress &

Indigo *(1982) and* Betsey Brown *(1985). About her characteristic use of lower-case letters, slashes and idiosyncratic spelling and syntax, she has said: "I like the idea that letters dance, not just that the words dance... I need some visual stimulation, so that reading becomes not just a passive act and more than an intellectual activity, but demands rigorous participation.... The spellings result from the way I talk or the way the character talks, or the way I heard something.... We do not have to refer continually to European art as the standard."*

aw, babee, you so pretty

not only waz she without a tan, but she held her purse close to her hip like a new yorker or someone who rode the paris métro. she waz not from here, but from there.

there some coloureds, negroes, blacks, cd make a living big enough to leave there to come here: but no one went there much any more for all sorts of reasons. the big reason being immigration restrictions & unemployment. nowadays, immigration restrictions of every kind apply to any non-european persons who want to go there from here. just like unemployment applies to most non-european persons without titles of nobility or north american university training. some who want to go there from here risk fetching trouble with the customs authority there. or later with the police, who can tell who's not from there cuz the shoes are pointed & laced strange/the pants be for august & yet it's january/the accent is patterned for port-au-prince, but working in crown heights. what makes a person comfortably ordinary here cd make him dangerously conspicuous there.

so some go to london or amsterdam or paris, where they are so many no one tries to tell who is from where. still the far right wing of every there prints lil pamphlets that say everyone from here shd leave there & go back where they came from.

anyway the yng woman i waz discussing waz from there & she was alone. that waz good. cuz if a man had no big brother in groningen. no aunt in rouen. no sponsor in chicago. this brown woman from there might be a good idea. everybody knows that rich white girls are hard to find. some of them joined the weather underground, some the baader-meinhof gang. a whole bunch of them gave up men entirely. so the exotic-lover-in-the-sun routine becomes more difficult to swing/if she wants to talk abt plastic explosives & the resistance of the black masses to socialism insteada giving head as the tide slips in or lending money just for the next few days. is hard to find a rich white girl who is so dumb, too.

anyway, the whole world knows, european & non-european alike, the whole world knows that nobody loves the blackwoman like they love farrah fawcett majors. the whole world dont turn out for a dead black woman like they did for marilyn monroe. (actually, the demise of josephine baker waz an international event, but she waz also a war hero) the worldwide un-beloved black woman is a good idea, if she is from there & one is a yng man with gd looks, piercing eyes, knowing of several romantic languages, the best dancing spots, the hill where one can see the entire bay at twilight, the beach where the seals & pelicans run free, the hidden "local" restaurants; or in paris, a métro map, in mexico city the young man might know where salsa is played, not that the jalisco folklorico is not beautiful. but if she is from there & black she might want to dance a dance more familiar. such a yng man with such information exists in great numbers everywhere. he stops a yng woman with her bag on her hip, demanding she come to his house for dinner that night. (they are very hospitable) when the black woman from there says she must go to antwerp at 6:00/ he says, then, when she comes back. his friends agree. (they are persistent) he asks, as he forces his number into her palm, are you alone. this is important. for the yng man from here with designs on a yng woman from there respects the territorial rights of another man, if he's in the country.

that is how the approach to the black woman works in the street. "aw babee/ you so pretty" begins often in the lobby of hotels where the bright handsome yng men wd be loiterers were they not needed to tend the needs of the black women from there. tourists are usually white people or asians who didn't come all this way to meet a black woman who isnt even foreign. so the hotel managers wink an eye at the yng men in the lobby or by the bar who wd be loitering, but they are going to help her have a gd time, maybe help themselves, too.

everybody in the world, everybody knows the black woman from there is not treated as a princess, as a jewel, a cherished lover. that's not how sapphire got her reputation, nor how mrs jefferson perceives the world. "you know/ babee/ you dont act like them. aw babee/ you so pretty."

the yng man in the hotel watches the yng black woman sit & sit & sit, while the european tourists dance with one another & the dapper local fellas mambo frenetically with secretaries from arizona. in search of the missing rich white girl. so our girl sits & sits & sits & sits. maybe she is courageous & taps her foot. maybe she is bold & enjoys the music, smiling, shaking shoulders. let her sit & know she is unwanted. she is not white and she is not from here. let her know she is not pretty enough to dance the next merengue. then appear, mysteriously, in the corner of the bar. stare at her. just stare. when stevie wonder's song "isn't she lovely" blares thru the red-tinted light, ask her to dance & hold her as tyrone power wda. hold her & stare. dance yr ass off. she has been discovered by the non-european fred astaire. let her know she is a surprise. . .an event. by the look on yr face you've never seen anyone like this. black woman from there. you say, "aw/ you not from here?" totally astonished. she murmurs that she is from there. as if to apologize for her unfortunate place of birth, you say, "aw babee/ you so pretty." & it's all over.

a night in a pension near the sorbonne. pick her up from the mattress. throw her gainst the wall in a show of exotic temper & passion: *"maintenant, tu es ma femme. nous nous sommes mariés."* unions of this sort are common wherever the yng black women travel alone. a woman travelling alone is an affront to the non-european man, who is known the world over, to european & non-european alike, for his way with women, his sense of romance, how he can say "aw babee/ you so pretty" & even a beautiful woman will believe no one else ever recognized her loveliness, till he came along.

he comes to a café in willemstad in the height of the sunset, an able-bodied, sinewy yng man who wants to buy one beer for the yng woman. after the first round, he discovers he has run out of money. so she must buy the next round, when he discovers what beautiful legs she has, how her mouth is like the breath of tiger lilies. the taxi driver doesnt speak english, but he knows to drop his countryman off before he takes the yng woman to her hotel. the tab is hers.

but hers are, also, the cheeks that grandma pinches, if the yng man has honorable intentions. all the family will meet the yng black woman from there. the family has been worried abt this yng man for a while. non-european families dont encourage bachelors. bachelorhood is a career we associate with the white people: dandies on the order of errol flynn, robert de niro. the non-european men have women, some women they marry & stay with forever. get chicken on sunday (chicken fricassee, arroz con pollo, poulet grillee, smothered chicken, depending on what kinda black woman she is & whether she is from here or there). then some women they just are with for years or a day. but our families do expect a yng man to waltz in with somebody at sometime. & if she's from there, the family's very excited. they tell the yng woman about where they are from & how she cd almost be from the same place, except she is from there. but more rousing than coincidental genealogical traits is the torrid declaration: "we shall make love in the. . .how you call it/ yes in the earth, in the dirt. i will have you. . ./aw/ yes. i will have you in the soil." probably under the stars & smelling of wine an unforgettable international affair can be consummated.

at 11.30 one evening i waz at the port authority, new york, united states, myself. now i was there & i spoke english & i waz holding approximately $7 american currency, when a yng man from there came up to me from the front of the line of people waiting for the princeton new jersey united states local bus. i mean to say, he gave up his chance for a good seat to come say to me: "i never saw a black woman reading nietzsche." i waz demure enough, i said i had to for a philosophy class. but as the night went on i noticed this yng man waz so much like the yng men from here who use their bodies as bait & their smiles as passport alternatives. anyway the night did go on. we were snuggled together in the rear of the bus going down the jersey turnpike. he told me in english/ which he had spoken all his life in st louis/ where he waz raised/ that he had wanted all his life to meet someone like me/ he wanted me to meet his family, who hadnt seen him in a long time, since he left missouri looking for opportunity/ opportunity to sculpt. he had been everyplace, he said, & i waznt like any black woman he had ever met anywhere. there or here. he had come back to new york cuz of immigration restrictions & high unemployment among black american sculptors abroad.

just as we got to princeton, he picked my face up from his shoulder where i had been fantasizing like mad & said: "aw babee/ you so pretty." i believe that night i must have looked beautiful for a black woman from there. though a black woman from anywhere cd be asked at any moment to tour the universe. to climb a six-story walk-up with a brilliant & starving painter. to share kadushi.

to meet mama. to getta kiss each time the swing falls toward the willow branch. to imagine where he say he from. & more/ she cd/ she cd have all of it/ she cd not be taken/ long as she dont let a stranger be the first to say: "aw babee/ you so pretty." after all, immigration restrictions & unemployment cd drive a man to drink or to lie. so if you know yr beautiful & bright & cherishable awready. when he say, in whatever language, "aw babee/ you so pretty." you cd say, "i know, thank you." & then when he asks yr name again cuz yr answer was inaudible. you cd say: "difficult." then he'll smile. & you'll smile. he'll say: "what nice legs you have." you can say: "yes, they run in the family."

"aw babee/ i've never met any one like you."

"that's strange. there are millions of us."

Zoë Wicomb
1948–

*S*he was born in Cape Province, South Africa, and after completing *an Arts degree at the University for Cape Coloureds, Western Cape, she went to England in 1970 and studied English Literature at Reading University. She now lives in Nottingham, where she teaches English and lectures on Black literature and in women's studies. An active member of the Anti-Apartheid Movement, she has written articles for journals such as* The Southern African Review of Books. *Her collection of short stories,* You Can't Get Lost in Cape Town, *was published in 1987.*

You Can't Get Lost in Cape Town

I N my right hand resting on the base of my handbag I clutch a brown leather purse. My knuckles ride to and fro, rubbing against the lining. . .surely cardboard. . .and I am surprised that the material has not revealed itself to me before. I have worn this bag for months. I would have said with a dismissive wave of the hand, "Felt, that is what the base of this bag is lined with."

Then, Michael had said, "It looks cheap, unsightly," and lowering his voice to my look of surprise, "Can't you tell?" But he was speaking of the exterior, the way it looks.

The purse fits neatly into the palm of my hand. A man's purse. The handbag gapes. With my elbow I press it against my hip but that will not avert suspicion. The bus is moving fast, too fast, surely exceeding the speed limit, so that I bob on my seat and my grip on the purse tightens as the springs suck at my womb, slurping it down through the plush of the red upholstery. I press my buttocks into the seat to ease the discomfort.

I should count out the fare for the conductor. Perhaps not; he is still at the front of the bus. We are now travelling through Rondebosch so that he will be fully occupied with white passengers at the front. Women with blue-rinsed heads tilted will go on telling their stories while fishing leisurely for their coins and just lengthen a vowel to tide over the moment of paying their fares.

"Don't be so anxious," Michael said. "It will be all right." I withdrew the hand he tried to pat.

I have always been anxious and things are not all right; things may never be all right again. I must not cry. My eyes travel to and fro along the grooves of the floor. I do not look at the faces that surround me but I believe that they are lifted speculatively at me. Is someone constructing a history for this hand resting foolishly in a gaping handbag? Do these faces expect me to whip out an amputated stump dripping with blood? Do they wince at the thought of a hand, cold and waxen, left on the pavement where it was severed? I draw my hand out of the bag and shake my fingers ostentatiously. No point in inviting conjecture, in attracting attention. The bus brakes loudly to conceal the sound of breath drawn in sharply at the exhibited hand.

Two women pant like dogs as they swing themselves on to the bus. The conductor has already pressed the bell and they propel their bodies expertly along the swaying aisle. They fall into seats opposite me – one fat, the other thin – and simultaneously pull off the starched servants' caps which they scrunch into their laps. They light cigarettes and I bite my lip. Would I have to vomit into this bag with its cardboard lining? I wish I had brought a plastic bag; this bag is empty save for the purse. I breathe deeply to stem the nausea that rises to meet the curling bands of smoke and fix on the bulging bags they grip between their feet. They make no attempt to get their fares ready; they surely misjudge the intentions of the conductor. He knows that they will get off at Mowbray to catch the Golden Arrow buses to the townships. He will not allow them to avoid paying; not he who presses the button with such promptness.

I watch him at the front of the bus. His right thumb strums an impatient jingle on the silver levers, the leather bag is cradled in the hand into which the coins tumble. He chants a barely audible accompaniment to the clatter of coins, a recitation of the newly decimalized currency. Like times tables at school and I see the fingers grow soft, bending boyish as they strum an ink-stained abacus; the boy learning to count, leaning earnestly with propped elbows over a desk. And I find the image unaccountably sad and tears are about to well up when

I hear an impatient empty clatter of thumb-play on the coin dispenser as he demands, "All fares, please" from a sleepy white youth. My hand flies into my handbag once again and I take out the purse. A man's leather purse.

Michael too is boyish. His hair falls in a straight blond fringe into his eyes. When he considers a reply he wipes it away impatiently, as if the hair impedes thought. I cannot imagine this purse ever having belonged to him. It is small, U-shaped and devoid of ornament, therefore a man's purse. It has an extending tongue that could be tucked into the mouth or be threaded through the narrow band across the base of the U. I take out the smallest note stuffed into this plump purse, a five-rand note. Why had I not thought about the busfare? The conductor will be angry if my note should exhaust his supply of coins although the leather bag would have a concealed pouch for notes. But this thought does not comfort me. I feel angry with Michael. He has probably never travelled by bus. How would he know of the fear of missing the unfamiliar stop, the fear of keeping an impatient conductor waiting, the fear of saying fluently, "Seventeen cents please," when you are not sure of the fare and produce a five-rand note? But this is my journey and I must not expect Michael to take responsibility for everything. Or rather, I cannot expect Michael to take responsibility for more than half the things. Michael is scrupulous about this division; I am not always sure of how to arrive at half. I was never good at arithmetic, especially this instant mental arithmetic that is sprung on me.

How foolish I must look sitting here clutching my five-rand note. I slip it back into the purse and turn to the solidity of the smoking women. They have still made no attempt to find their fares. The bus is going fast and I am surprised that we have not yet reached Mowbray. Perhaps I am mistaken, perhaps we have already passed Mowbray and the women are going to Sea Point to serve a nightshift at the Pavilion.

Marge, Aunt Trudie's eldest daughter, works as a waitress at the Pavilion but she is rarely mentioned in our family. "A disgrace," they say. "She should know better than to go with white men."

"Poor whites," Aunt Trudie hisses. "She can't even find a nice rich man to go steady with. Such a pretty girl too. I won't have her back in this house. There's no place in this house for a girl who's been used by white trash."

Her eyes flash as she spits out a cherished vision of a blond young man sitting on her new vinyl sofa to whom she serves gingerbeer and koeksisters, because it is not against the law to have a respectable drink in a Coloured home. "Mrs Holman," he would say, "Mrs Holman, this is the best gingerbeer I've had for years."

The family do not know of Michael even though he is a steady young man who would sit out such a Sunday afternoon with infinite grace. I wince at the thought of Father creaking in a suit and the unconcealed pleasure in Michael's successful academic career.

Perhaps this is Mowbray after all. The building that zooms past on the right seems familiar. I ought to know it but I am lost, hopelessly lost, and as my mind gropes for recognition I feel a feathery flutter in my womb, so slight I cannot be sure, and again, so soft, the brush of a butterfly, and under cover of my handbag I spread my left hand to hold my belly. The shaft of light falling across my shoulder, travelling this route with me, is the eye of God. God will never forgive me.

I must anchor my mind to the words of the women on the long seat opposite me. But they fall silent as if to protect their secrets from me. One of them bends down heavily, holding on to the jaws of her shopping bag as if to relieve pressure on her spine, and I submit to the ache of my own by swaying gently while I protect my belly with both hands. But she having eyed the contents of her full bag carefully, her hand becomes the beak of a bird dipping purposefully into the left-hand corner and rises triumphantly with a brown paper bag on which grease has oozed light-sucking patterns. She opens the bag and her friend looks on in silence. Three chunks of cooked chicken lie on a piece of greaseproof paper. She deftly halves a piece and passes it to her thin friend. The women munch in silence, their mouths glossy with pleasure.

"These are for the children," she says, her mouth still full as she wraps the rest up and places it carelessly at the top of the bag.

"It's the spiced chicken recipe you told me about." She nudges her friend. "Lekker hey!"

The friend frowns and says, "I like to taste a bit more cardamom. It's nice to find a whole cardamom in the food and crush it between your teeth. A cardamom seed will never give up all its flavour to the pot. You'll still find it there in the chewing."

I note the gaps in her teeth and fear for the slipping through of cardamom seeds. The girls at school who had their two top incisors extracted in a fashion that raged through Cape Town said that it was better for kissing. Then I, fat and innocent, nodded. How would I have known the demands of kissing?

The large woman refuses to be thwarted by criticism of her cooking. The chicken stimulates a story so that she twitches with an irrepressible desire to tell.

"To think," she finally bursts out, "that I cook them this nice surprise and say what you like, spiced chicken can make any mouth water. Just think, it was yesterday when I say to that one as she stands with her hands on her hips against the stove saying, 'I don't know what to give them today, I've just got too much organizing to do to bother with food.' And I say, feeling sorry for her, I say, 'Don't you worry about a thing, Marram, just leave it all in cook's hands (wouldn't it be nice to work for really grand people where you cook and do nothing else, no bladdy scrubbing and shopping and all that). . .in cook's hands,' I said," and she crows merrily before reciting: "And I'll dish up a surprise / For Master Georgie's blue eyes.

"That's Miss Lucy's young man. He was coming last night. Engaged, you know. Well, there I was on my feet all day starching linen, making roeties and spiced lentils and sweet potato and all the lekker things you must mos have with cardamom chicken. And what do you think she says?"

She pauses and lifts her face as if expecting a reply, but the other stares grimly ahead. Undefeated she continues, "She says to me, 'Tiena,' because she can't keep out of my pots, you know, always opening my lids and sniffing like a brakhond, she says, 'Tiena,' and waits for me to say, 'Yes, Marram,' so I know she has a wicked plan up her sleeve and I look her straight in the eye. She smile that one, always smile to put me off the track, and she say looking into the fridge, 'You can have this nice bean soup for your dinner so I can have the remains of the chicken tomorrow when you're off.' So I say to her, 'That's what I had for lunch today,' and she say to me, 'Yes, I know, but me and Miss Lucy will be on our own for dinner tomorrow,' and she pull a face, 'ugh, how I hate reheated food.' Then she draws up her shoulders as if to say, That's that.

"Cheek, hey! And it was a great big fowl." She nudges her friend. "You know for yourself how much better food tastes the next day when the spices are drawn right into the meat and anyway you just switch on the electric and there's no chopping and crying over onions, you just wait for the pot to dance on the stove. Of course she wouldn't know about that. Anyway, a cheek, that's what I call it, so before I even dished up the chicken for the table, I took this," and she points triumphantly to her bag, "and to hell with them."

The thin one opens her mouth, once, twice, winding herself up to speak.

"They never notice anyway. There's so much food in their pantries, in the fridge and on the tables; they don't know what's there and what isn't." The other looks pityingly at her.

"Don't you believe that. My marram was as cross as a bear by the time I brought in the pudding, a very nice apricot ice it was, but she didn't even look at it. She know it was a healthy grown fowl and she count one leg, and she know what's going on. She know right away. Didn't even say, 'Thank you, Tiena.' She won't speak to me for days but what can she do?" Her voice softens into genuine sympathy for her madam's dilemma.

"She'll just have to speak to me." And she mimics, putting on a stern horse face. "We'll want dinner by seven tonight,' then, 'Tiena, the curtains need washing,' then, 'Please, Tiena, will you fix this zip for me, I've got absolutely nothing else to wear today.' And so on the third day she'll smile and think she's smiling forgiveness at me."

She straightens her face. "No," she sighs, "the more you have, the more you have to keep your head and count and check up because you know you won't notice or remember. No, if you got a lot you must keep snaps in your mind of the insides of all the cupboards. And every day, click, click, new snaps of the larder. That's why that one is so tired, always thinking, always reciting to herself the lists of what's in the cupboards. I never know what's in my cupboard at home but I know my Sammie's a thieving bastard, can't keep his hands in his pockets."

The thin woman stared out of the window as if she had heard it all before. She has finished her chicken while the other, with all the talking, still holds a half-eaten drumstick daintily in her right hand. Her eyes rove over the shopping bag and she licks her fingers abstractedly as she stares out of the window.

"Lekker, hey!" the large one repeats, "the children will have such a party."

"Did Master George enjoy it?" the other asks.

"Oh, he's a gentleman all right. Shouted after me, 'Well done, Tiena. When we're married we'll have to steal you from madam.' Dressed to kill he was, such a smart young man, you know. Mind you, so's Miss Lucy. Not a prettier girl in our avenue and the best-dressed too. But then she has mos to be smart to keep her man. Been on the pill for nearly a year now; I shouldn't wonder if he don't feel funny about the white wedding. Ooh, you must see her blush over the pictures of the wedding gowns, so pure and innocent she think I can't read the packet. 'Get me my headache pills out of that drawer, Tiena,' she say sometimes when I take her cup of cocoa at night. But she play her cards right with Master George; she have to 'cause who'd have what another man has pushed to the side of his plate? A bayleaf and a bone!" and moved by the alliteration the image material- izes in her hand. "Like this bone," and she waves it under the nose of the other who starts. I wonder whether with guilt, fear or a debilitating desire for more chicken.

"This bone," she repeats grimly, "picked bare and only wanted by a dog."

Her friend recovers and deliberately misunderstands, "Or like yesterday's bean soup, but we women mos know that food put aside and left to stand till tomorrow always has a better flavour. Men don't know that hey. They should get down to some cooking and find out a thing or two."

But the other is not deterred. "A bone," she insists, waving her visual aid, "a bone."

It is true that her bone is a matt grey that betrays no trace of the meat or fat that only a minute ago adhered to it. Master George's bone would certainly look nothing like that when he pushes it aside. With his fork he would coax off the fibres ready to fall from the bone. Then he would turn over the whole, deftly, using a knife, and frown at the sinewy meat clinging to the joint before pushing it aside towards the discarded bits of skin.

This bone, it is true, will not tempt anyone. A dog might want to bury it only for a silly game of hide and seek.

The large woman waves the bone as if it would burst into prophecy. My eyes follow the movement until the bone blurs and emerges as the Cross where the head of Jesus lolls sadly, his lovely feet anointed by sad hands, folded together under the driven nail. Look, Mamma says, look at those eyes molten with love and pain, the body curved with suffering for our sins, and together we weep for the beauty and sadness of Jesus in his white loincloth. The Roman soldiers stand grimly erect in their tunics, their spears gleam in the light, their dark beards are clipped and their lips curl. At midday Judas turns his face to the fading sun and bays, howls like a dog for its return as the darkness grows around him and swallows him whole with the money still jingling in the folds of his saffron robes. In a concealed leather purse, a pouch devoid of ornament.

The buildings on this side of the road grow taller but oh, I do not know where I am and I think of asking the woman, the thin one, but when I look up the stern one's eyes already rest on me while the bone in her hand points idly at the advertisement just above my head. My hands, still cradling my belly, slide guiltily down my thighs and fall on my knees. But the foetus betrays me with another flutter, a sigh. I have heard of books flying off the laps of gentle mothers-to-be as their foetuses lash out. I will not be bullied. I jump up and press the bell.

There are voices behind me. The large woman's "Oi, I say" thunders over the conductor's cross "Tickets please." I will not speak to anyone. Shall I throw myself on the grooved floor of this bus and with knees drawn up, hands over my head, wait for my demise? I do not in any case expect to be alive tomorrow. But I must resist; I must harden my heart against the sad, complaining eyes of Jesus.

"I say, Miss," she shouts and her tone sounds familiar. Her voice compels like the insistence of Father's guttural commands. But the conductor's hand falls on my shoulder, the barrel of his ticket dispenser digs into my ribs, the buttons of his uniform gleam as I dip into my bag for my purse. Then the large woman spills out of her seat as she leans forward. Her friend, reconciled, holds the bar of an arm across her as she leans forward shouting, "Here, I say, your purse." I try to look grateful. Her eyes blaze with scorn as she proclaims to the bus, "Stupid these young people. Dressed to kill maybe, but still so stupid."

She is right. Not about my clothes, of course, and I check to see what I am wearing. I have not been alerted to my own stupidity before. No doubt I will sail through my final examinations at the end of this year and still not know how I dared to pluck a fluttering foetus out of my womb. That is if I survive tonight.

I sit on the steps of this large building and squint up at the marble façade. My elbows rest on my knees flung comfortably apart. I ought to know where I am; it is clearly a public building of some importance. For the first time I long for the veld of my childhood. There the red sand rolls for miles, and if you stand on the koppie behind the house the landmarks blaze their permanence: the river points downward, runs its dry course from north to south; the geelbos crowds its banks in near straight lines. On either side of the path winding westward plump little buttocks of cacti squat as if lifting their skirts to pee, and the swollen fingers of vygies burst in clusters out of the stone, pointing the way. In the veld you can always find your way home.

I am anxious about meeting Michael. We have planned this so carefully for the rush hour when people storming home crossly will not notice us together in the crush.

"It's simple," Michael said. "The bus carries along the main roads through the suburbs to the City, and as you reach the Post Office you get off and I'll be there to meet you. At five."

A look at my anxious face compelled him to say, "You can't get lost in Cape Town. There," and he pointed over his shoulder, "is Table Mountain and there is Devil's Peak and there Lion's Head, so how in heaven's name could you get lost?" The words shot out unexpectedly, like the fine arc of brown spittle from between the teeth of an old man who no longer savours the tobacco he has been chewing all day. There are, I suppose, things that even a loved one cannot overlook.

Am I a loved one?

I ought to rise from these steps and walk towards the City. Fortunately I always take the precaution of setting out early, so that I should still be in time to meet Michael who will drive me along de Waal Drive into the slopes of Table Mountain where Mrs Coetzee waits with her tongs.

Am I a loved one? No. I am dull, ugly and bad-tempered. My hair has grown greasy, I am forgetful and I have no sense of direction. Michael, he has long since stopped loving me. He watched me hugging the lavatory bowl, retching, and recoiled at my first display of bad temper. There is a faraway look in his eyes as he plans his retreat. But he is well brought up, honourable. When the first doubts gripped the corners of his mouth, he grinned madly and said, "We must marry," showing a row of perfect teeth.

"There are laws against that," I said unnecessarily.

But gripped by the idyll of an English landscape of painted greens, he saw my head once more held high, my lettuce-luscious skirts crisp on a camomile lawn and the willow drooping over the red mouth of a suckling infant.

"Come on," he urged. "Don't do it. We'll get to England and marry. It will work out all right," and betraying the source of his vision, "and we'll be happy for ever, thousands of miles from all this mess."

I would have explained if I could. But I could not account for this vision: the slow shower of ashes over yards of diaphanous tulle, the moth wings tucked back with delight as their tongues whisked the froth of white lace. For two years I have loved Michael, have wanted to marry him. Duped by a dream I merely shook my head.

"But you love babies, you want babies some time or other, so why not accept God's holy plan? Anyway, you're a Christian and you believe it's a sin, don't you?"

God is not a good listener. Like Father, he expects obedience and withdraws peevishly if his demands are not met. Explanations of my point of view infuriate him so that he quivers with silent rage. For once I do not plead and capitulate; I find it quite easy to ignore these men.

"You're not even listening," Michael accused. "I don't know how you can do it." There is revulsion in his voice.

For two short years I have adored Michael.

Once, perched perilously on the rocks, we laughed fondly at the thought of a child. At Cape Point where the oceans meet and part. The Indian and the Atlantic, fighting for their separate identities, roared and thrashed fiercely so that we huddled together, his hand on my belly. It is said that if you shut one eye and focus the other carefully, the line separating the two oceans may rear drunkenly but remains ever clear and hair-fine. But I did not look. In the mischievous wind I struggled with the flapping ends of a scarf I tried to wrap around my hair. Later that day on the silver sands of a deserted beach he wrote solemnly: Will you marry me? and my trembling fingers traced a huge heart around the words. Ahead the sun danced on the waves, flecking them with gold.

I wrote a poem about that day and showed Michael. "Surely that was not what Logiesbaai was about," he frowned, and read aloud the lines about warriors charging out of the sea, assegais gleaming in the sun, the beat of tom-toms riding the waters, the throb in the carious cavities of rocks.

"It's good," he said, nodding thoughtfully, "I like the title, 'Love at Logiesbaai (Whites Only)', though I expect much of the subtlety escapes me. Sounds good," he encouraged, "you should write more often."

I flushed. I wrote poems all the time. And he was wrong; it was not a good poem. It was puzzling and I wondered why I had shown him this poem that did not even make sense to me. I tore it into little bits.

Love, love, love, I sigh as I shake each ankle in turn and examine the swelling.

Michael's hair falls boyishly over his eyes. His eyes narrow merrily when he smiles and the left corner of his mouth shoots up so that the row of teeth form a queer diagonal line above his chin. He flicks his head so that the fringe of hair lifts from his eyes for a second, then falls, so fast, like the tongue of a lizard retracted at the very moment of exposure.

"We'll find somewhere," he would say, "a place where we'd be quite alone." This country is vast and he has an instinctive sense of direction. He discovers the armpits of valleys that invite us into their shadows. Dangerous climbs led by the roar of the sea take us to blue bays into which we drop from impossible cliffs. The sun lowers herself on to us. We do not fear the police with their torches. They come only by night in search of offenders. We have the immunity of love. They cannot find us because they do not know we exist. One day they will find out about lovers who steal whole days, round as globes.

There has always been a terrible thrill in that thought.

I ease my feet back into my shoes and the tears splash on to my dress with such wanton abandon that I cannot believe they are mine. From the punctured globes of stolen days these fragments sag and squint. I hold, hold these pictures I have summoned. I will not recognize them for much longer.

With tilted head I watch the shoes and sawn-off legs ascend and descend the marble steps, altering course to avoid me. Perhaps someone will ask the police to remove me.

Love, love, love, I sigh. Another flutter in my womb. I think of moth wings struggling against a window pane and I rise.

The smell of sea unfurls towards me as I approach Adderley Street. There is no wind but the brine hangs in an atomized mist, silver over a thwarted sun. In answer to my hunger, Wellingtons looms on my left. The dried-fruit palace which I cannot resist. The artificial light dries my tears, makes me blink, and the trays of fruit, of Cape sunlight twice trapped, shimmer and threaten to burst out of their forms. Rows of pineapple are the infinite divisions of the sun, the cores lost in the amber discs of mebos arranged in arcs. Prunes are the wrinkled backs of aged goggas beside the bloodshot eyes of cherries. Dark green figs sit pertly on their bottoms peeping over trays. And I too am not myself, hoping for refuge in a metaphor that will contain it all. I buy the figs and mebos. Desire is a Tsafendas tapeworm in my belly that cannot be satisfied and as I pop the first fig into my mouth I feel the danger fountain with the jets of saliva. Will I stop at one death?

I have walked too far along this road and must turn back to the Post Office. I break into a trot as I see Michael in the distance, drumming with his nails on the side of the car. His sunburnt elbow juts out of the window. He taps with anxiety or impatience and I grow cold with fear as I jump into the passenger seat and say merrily, "Let's go," as if we are setting off for a picnic.

Michael will wait in the car on the next street. She had said that it would take only ten minutes. He takes my hand and so prevents me from getting out. Perhaps he thinks that I will bolt, run off into the mountain, revert to savagery. His hand is heavy on my forearm and his eyes are those of a wounded dog, pale with pain.

"It will be all right." I try to comfort and wonder whether he hears his own voice in mine. My voice is thin, a tinsel thread that springs out of my mouth and flutters straight out of the window.

"I must go." I lift the heavy hand off my forearm and it falls inertly across the gearstick.

The room is dark. The curtains are drawn and a lace-shaded electric light casts shadows in the corners of the rectangle. The doorway in which I stand divides the room into sleeping and eating quarters. On the left there is a table against which a servant girl leans, her eyes fixed on the blank wall ahead. On the right a middle-aged white woman rises with a hostess smile from a divan which serves as sofa, and pats the single pink-flowered cushion to assert homeliness. There is a narrow dark wardrobe in the corner.

I say haltingly, "You are expecting me. I spoke to you on the telephone yesterday. Sally Smit." I can see no telephone in the room. She frowns.

"You're not Coloured, are you?" It is an absurd question. I look at my brown arms that I have kept folded across my chest, and watch the gooseflesh sprout. Her eyes are fixed on me. Is she blind? How will she perform the operation with such defective sight? Then I realize: the educated voice, the accent has blinded her. I have drunk deeply of Michael, swallowed his voice as I drank from his tongue. Has he swallowed mine? I do not think so.

I say "No," and wait for all the cockerels in Cape Town to crow simultaneously. Instead the servant starts from her trance and stares at me with undisguised admiration.

"Good," the woman smiles, showing yellow teeth. "One must check nowadays. These Coloured girls, you know, are very forward, terrible types. What do they think of me, as if I would do every Tom, Dick and Harry. Not me, you know; this is a respectable concern and I try to help decent women, educated, you know. No, you can trust me. No Coloured girl's ever been on this sofa."

The girl coughs, winks at me and turns to stir a pot simmering on a primus stove on the table. The smell of offal escapes from the pot and nausea rises in my throat, feeding the fear. I would like to run but my feet are lashed with fear to the linoleum. Only my eyes move, across the room where she pulls a newspaper from a wad wedged between the wall and the wardrobe. She spreads the paper on the divan and smooths with her hand while the girl shuts the door and turns the key. A cat crawls lazily from under the table and stares at me until the green jewels of its eyes shrink to crystal points.

She points me to the sofa. From behind the wardrobe she pulls her instrument and holds it against the baby-pink Crimplene of her skirt.

"Down, shut your eyes now," she says as I raise my head to look. Their movements are carefully orchestrated, the manoeuvres practised. Their eyes signal and they move. The girl stations herself by my head and her mistress moves to my feet. She pushes my knees apart and whips out her instrument from a pocket. A piece of plastic tubing dangles for a second. My knees jerk and my mouth opens wide but they are in control. A brown hand falls on my mouth and smothers the cry; the white hands wrench the knees apart and she hisses, "Don't you dare. Do you want the bladdy police here? I'll kill you if you scream."

The brown hand over my mouth relaxes. She looks into my face and says, "She won't." I am a child who needs reassurance. I am surprised by the softness of her voice. The brown hand moves along the side of my face and pushes back my hair. I long to hold the other hand; I do not care what happens below. A black line of terror separates it from my torso. Blood spurts from between my legs and for a second the two halves of my body make contact through the pain.

So it is done. Deflowered by yellow hands wielding a catheter. Fear and hypocrisy, mine, my deserts spread in a dark stain on the newspaper.

"OK," she says, "get yourself decent." I dress and wait for her to explain. "You go home now and wait for the birth. Do you have a pad?"

I shake my head uncomprehendingly. Her face tightens for a moment but then she smiles and pulls a sanitary towel out of the wardrobe.

"Won't cost you anything, lovey." She does not try to conceal the glow of her generosity. She holds out her hand and I place the purse in her palm. She counts, satisfied, but I wave away the purse which she reluctantly puts on the table.

"You're a good girl," she says and puts both hands on my shoulders. I hold my breath; I will not inhale the foetid air from the mouth of this my grotesque bridegroom with yellow teeth. She plants the kiss of complicity on my cheek and I turn to go, repelled by her touch. But have I the right to be fastidious? I cannot deny feeling grateful, so that I turn back to claim the purse after all. The girl winks at me. The purse fits snugly in my hand; there would be no point in giving it back to Michael.

Michael's face is drawn with fear. He is as ignorant of the process as I am. I am brisk, efficient and rattle off the plan. "It'll happen tonight so I'll go home and wait and call you in the morning. By then it will be all over." He looks relieved.

He drives me right to the door and my landlady waves merrily from the stoep where she sits with her embroidery among the potted ferns.

"Don't look," she says anxiously. "It's a present for you, for your trousseau," and smiling slyly, "I can tell when a couple just can't wait any longer. There's no catching me out, you know."

Tonight in her room next to mine she will turn in her chaste bed, tracing the tendrils from pink and orange flowers, searching for the needle lost in endless folds of white linen.

Semi-detached houses with red-polished stoeps line the west side of Trevelyan Road. On the east is the Cape Flats line where electric trains rattle reliably according to timetable. Trevelyan Road runs into the elbow of a severely curved Main Road which nevertheless has all the amenities one would expect: butcher, baker, hairdresser, chemist, library, liquor store. There is a fish and chips shop on that corner, on the funnybone of that elbow, and by the side, strictly speaking in Trevelyan Road, a dustbin leans against the trunk of a young palm tree. A newspaper parcel dropped into this dustbin would absorb the vinegary smell of discarded fish and chips wrappings in no time.

The wrapped parcel settles in the bin. I do not know what has happened to God. He is fastidious. He fled at the moment that I smoothed the wet black hair before wrapping it up. I do not think he will come back. It is 6 a.m. Light pricks at the shroud of Table Mountain. The streets are deserted and, relieved, I remember that the next train will pass at precisely 6.22.

Jewelle L. Gomez
1948–

Born in Boston, she describes herself as a "lesbian activist and cultural worker". She has lived in New York since 1971 and is currently Director of Literature at New York State Council on the Arts, a state funding agency. She writes literary and social criticism, which has been published in The Nation, New York Times, Village Voice and Belles Lettres, and her fiction and poetry has appeared in publications such as Essence, Conditions, Azalea, Black Scholar and in anthologies, including Serious Pleasure (Sheba) and Home Girls (edited by Barbara Smith). She is the author of a book of poetry, Flamingoes and Bears (1987), and her first novel is The Gilda Stories (1991).

A Swimming Lesson

AT nine years old I didn't realize my grandmother, Lydia, and I were doing an extraordinary thing by packing a picnic lunch and riding the elevated train from Roxbury to Revere Beach. It seemed part of the natural rhythm of summer to me. I didn't notice how the subway cars slowly emptied of most of their Black passengers as the train left Boston's urban center and made its way into the Italian and Irish suburban neighborhoods to the north. It didn't seem odd that all of the Black families stayed in one section of the beach and never ventured onto the boardwalk to the concession stands or the rides except in groups.

I do remember Black women perched cautiously on their blankets, tugging desperately at bathing suits rising too high in the rear and complaining about their hair "going back". Not my grandmother, though. She glowed with unashamed athleticism as she waded out, just inside the reach of the waves, and moved along the riptide parallel to the shore. Once submerged, she would load me onto her back and begin her long, tireless strokes. With the waves partially covering us, I followed her rhythm with my short, chubby arms, taking my cues from the powerful movement of her back muscles. We did this again and again until I'd fall off, and she'd catch me and set me upright in the strong New England surf. I was thrilled by the wildness of the ocean and my grandmother's fearless relationship to it. I loved the way she never consulted her mirror after her swim, but always looked as if she had been born to the sea, a kind of aquatic heiress.

None of the social issues of 1957 had a chance of catching my attention that year. All that existed for me was my grandmother, rising from the surf like a Dahomean queen, shaking her head free of her torturous rubber cap, beaming down at me when I finally took the first strokes on my own. She towered above me in the sun with a benevolence that made simply dwelling in her presence a reward in itself. Under her gaze I felt part of a long line of royalty. I was certain that everyone around us – Black and white – saw and respected her magnificence.

Although I sensed her power, I didn't know the real significance of our summers together as Black females in a white part of town. Unlike winter, when we were protected by the cover of coats, boots and hats, summer left us vulnerable and at odds with the expectations for women's bodies – the narrow hips, straight hair, flat stomachs, small feet – handed down from the mainstream culture and media. But Lydia never noticed. Her long chorus-girl legs ended in size-nine shoes, and she dared to make herself even bigger as she stretched her broad back and became a woman with a purpose: teaching her granddaughter to swim.

My swimming may have seemed a superfluous skill to those who watched our lessons. After all, it was obvious that I wouldn't be doing the backstroke on the Riviera or in the pool of a penthouse spa. Certainly nothing in the popular media at that time made the "great outdoors" seem a hospitable place for Black people. It was a place in which we were meant to feel comfortable at best and hunted at worst. But my prospects for utilizing my skill were irrelevant to me, and when I finally got it right I felt as if I had learned some invaluable life secret.

When I reached college and learned the specifics of slavery and the Middle Passage, the magnitude of that "peculiar institution" was almost beyond my comprehension; it was like nothing I'd learned before about the history of my people. It was difficult making a connection with those Africans who had been set adrift from their own land. My initial reaction was "Why didn't the slaves simply jump from the ships while they were still close to shore, and swim home?" The child in me who had learned to survive in water was crushed to find that my ancestors had not necessarily shared this skill. Years later when I visited West Africa and learned of the poisonous, spiny fish that inhabit most of the coastal waters, I understood why swimming was not the local sport there that it was in New England. And now when I take to the surf, I think of those ancestors and of Lydia.

The sea has been a fearful place for us. It swallowed us whole when there was no escape from the holds of slave ships. For me, to whom the dark fathoms of a tenement hallway were the most unknowable thing so far encountered in my nine years, the ocean was a mystery of terrifying proportions. In teaching me to swim, my grandmother took away my fear. I began to understand something outside myself – the sea – and consequently something about myself as well. I was no longer simply a fat little girl: My body had become a sea vessel – sturdy, enduring, graceful. I had the means to be safe.

Before she died last summer I learned that Lydia herself couldn't really swim that well. As I was splashing, desperately trying to learn the right rhythm – face down, eyes closed, air out, reach, face up, eyes open, air in, reach – Lydia was brushing the ocean's floor with her feet, keeping us both afloat. When she told me, I was stunned. I reached into my memory trying to combine this new information with the Olympic vision I'd always kept of her. At first I'd felt disappointed, tricked, the way I used to feel when I'd learn that a favorite movie star was only five feet tall. But then I quickly realized what an incredible act of bravery it was for her to pass on to me a skill she herself had not quite mastered – a skill that she knew would always bring me a sense of accomplishment. And it was more than just the swimming. It was the ability to stand on any beach anywhere and be proud of my large body, my African hair. It was *not* fearing the strong muscles in my own back; it was gaining control over my own life.

Now when the weather turns cold and I don the layers of wool and down that protect me from the eastern winters, from those who think a Black woman can't do her job, from those who think I'm simply sexual prey, I remember the power of my grandmother's broad back and I imagine I'm wearing my swimsuit. Face up, eyes open, air in, reach.

'Molara Ogundipe-Leslie
1949–

Born in Lagos, Nigeria, of Yoruba parentage, she was educated at Queen's School, Ede, and University College, Ibadan, earning a first-class BA Honours degree in English (1977). She has taught English and African Literature in universities in Nigeria and the USA, including Columbia, Berkeley, Harvard and Northwestern. An outspoken Marxist and feminist literary critic, she was Professor and Head of the Department of English in Ogun State University, Ago-Iwoye, and Senior Lecturer in the English Department at the University of Ibadan. She has written for numerous academic and general publications and for the Nigerian Guardian, of which she is an Editorial Board member. She was appointed a member of the Nigerian Federal directorate for Social Mobilization and Chair of its Ogun State branch. Her poetry, which ranges from the lyrical to the satirical, is collected in Sew the Old Days and Other Poems (1986).

tendril love of africa

I see again and again in my eyes
the smile flit over your cheekbones
Reach like a tendril to caress your face
in those lean days that startled
do you joy
that life does not slaughter our dreams
our secret thoughts on its butcher bench of time
that we gather to ourselves
the scraps and bones of our dismembered being
hoard to nurse them
that death may not out-stare us?

Bird-song

Every day we die more.
I wake to hunger brushed a-face my soul
Brushed like harmattan dust
Dream-startle to your cry that says:
"Nothing is joined, my friend, today,
Any everything is joined."

Yoruba Love

When they smile and they smile
and then begin to say
with pain on their brows
and songs in their voice:
"the nose is a cruel organ
and the heart without bone
for were the nose not cruel,
it would smell my love for you
and the heart if not boneless,
would feel my pain for you
and the throat, O, has no roots
or it would root to flower my love";
run for shelter, friend,
run for shelter.

Aline França

?1949–

B orn in Brazil into a family of five, she comes from the small
town of Teodoro Sampaio in Bahia (near where in the past slaves
plunged into a river, thinking that they would surface in Africa).
*She began writing at the age of fifteen and began to gain recognition
with the publication of her first novel,* Negao Dony (A Big Black Man)
*in 1978. She has since received national attention and honours and her
work has been staged in Rio as a musical,* Goodbye Aleduma. *This extract
(translated from the Portuguese by Penda de Longeville and Julio Finn) is
from her 1981 novel* A Mulher de Aleduma (*The Woman from Aleduma*),
*which uses language and imagery in which the Yoruba retentions are
markedly clear.*

From

The Woman from Aleduma

O N a certain continent on Earth, many thousands of years ago, there arrived
from Outer Space a Black of divine appearance: his mission was to found a
race destined to be of primordial importance on this continent. It was Aleduma,
a Black God of superior intelligence, come from the planet IGNUM, ruled by
the Goddess Salópia. His upright figure, his shining, slightly wavy hair, his feet
turned front-to-back, his braided beard (which touched the ground) gave him
a singular appearance. He came looking for a site where the Black race could
flourish. In IGNUM it was a holiday in honour of the Goddess Salópia. The
women wore pretty hairdos and stalwartly held their wooden lances. They were
ready to mount IZIBUM, a ferocious animal who snorted and faced them with
his great horns. The winner of the contest would win a trip to the planet Earth:
along with a companion (the winner of a former competition) she would make
the trip in order to populate a region chosen by Aleduma the Ancient One.

From IGNUM, Aleduma followed the events by means of telepathy; he
arranged to meet the couple, who were already on their way to Earth.

Aleduma the Ancient One found himself in an immense forest, full of
resplendent trees and wild animals who, curiously, became tame and friendly
towards the unknown being. It was as if the atmosphere had undergone a change
in order to celebrate the event that was about to happen amidst the trees. The

Black God extended his hands and, with a mystical gesture, said: "This is your new home; Take these fruits, they belong to you, alone."

The couple, amazed, took in every aspect of the scene. They were nude and examined their genitals which, strangely enough, were very different in form. The penis had, the whole of its length, a skin which began in the region of the anus. The vagina had a system of adaptation on one of its two lips which clasped on to the skin of the penis: they made veritable coinciding tools during the sexual act. Their progeniture grew each day and the population of this region of the Earth augmented day after day, in accord with the will of IGNUM.

Some genetic modifications took place among their offspring, perhaps because of the influence of the place where the couple procreated. It could already be seen that the feet no longer completely turned back-to-front, as in the case of their parents, but a lateral position, which provoked in these individuals a slight forward lean.

The Blacks of IGNUM did not possess typical nervous cells but had a pouch situated in the brain, full of electrical charges, which regulated the sensations in the body, and which gave them a very high potential of intelligence.

The population born on Earth had normal neurons and a high intelligence, though less than that of their progenitors.

Aleduma the Ancient One looked upon the accomplishment of his mission with satisfaction. The Black race had taken root in the chosen region. Thousands of years passed in this way and the Black God observed the genetic changes that took place in his descendants.

He alone remained genetically unchanged.

IGNUM, the planet of the sea, the most beautiful and majestic, exercised total sway over the seas of the Earth. The movement of the tides on Earth is controlled by the movement of the Sea of IGNUM, the great sea, the queen of seas, the alpha and omega of all the seas in the Universe. When it is low tide on Earth, it is because the Sea of IGNUM is calm, like the whiteness of a dove gliding, serenely, across the skies.

Aleduma the Ancient One sensed a call from Salópia and prepared to leave. He spoke to his people in a soft voice and said: "I must go, but be without fear, you will overcome your future sufferings . . ."

In festive mood, IGNUM welcomed Aleduma the Ancient One who, smiling and reverent, approached the Goddess Salópia who, extending her hand, touched his head, saying: "Your return gives us great energy, we are full of beneficial fluids . . ."

The storm lashes on the Blacks on Earth, that suffering foreseen by Aleduma the Ancient One had come to pass, slavery overtakes this people, the joyful song of creation is silent, and the continent quivers.

Now, emptiness beats down on their dwellings, and their children are scattered to the four corners of the world, devastated by white selfishness, wrecked by the white feudal desire of ruling, in conformity with the predictions of Aleduma. The Old Black, the tribal chief, invoked the help of IGNUM: "Oh! Ancient Aleduma, return and save us."

Coinjá, island of marvels, with its becalming landscape, its beaches of immaculate sand and moon of pale beauty, was the place chosen as a refuge for the

Blacks who managed to escape the horrors of slavery. Perhaps it will prove a propritious place for regenerating the population.

The Old Black, a man recognized for his chiefly bearing, was there and in his mind's eye saw the tribe he had commanded in times gone by.

A glimpse of home flashed in his eyes and he invoked Aleduma in these words: "Thanks, Black God – this place will be called by all the Isle of Aleduma and this little isle of blue waters will be your refuge."

Time passed and the Isle of Aleduma grew. Walking, one could already see houses, a place was reserved for workers. It was enjoyable to sit in the shade of the foliage and sleep the sleep of liberty.

Gayl Jones
1949–

Born in Lexington, Kentucky, she is the third generation of women writers in her family. She attended schools in Lexington, received a scholarship to Connecticut College, graduating with a BA in 1971, and in 1973 she completed a master's degree in creative writing at Brown University, followed by a doctorate in 1975. She later was a professor of English at the University of Michigan. Her writing deals with the harsh realitites of Black American life, particularly for women, exposing the rawness of intimate relationships in a way that has disturbed some critics; it often has a historical aspect, reflecting her study of the African presence in Brazil and Mexico in past centuries. Her books include novels – Corregidora (1975) and Eva's Man (1976) – the collection of stories White Rat (1977), Song of Anninho (1981), an extended ballad about an eighteenth-century slave revolt in Brazil, and Xarque and Other Poems (1985). She has said: "The question of significant events/actions/relationships in fiction and how one's sex, history, culture and geography influence them has been something that has interested me – not only in terms of writing, but in terms of how it affects one's critical response to a work."

Ensinança

I

HE was a man who did not like to be much in evidence. He would disappear if given half the opportunity. But he had a malady that kept him visible – conspicuous hairy nevus. The top of him was all black, the bottom was all white. His navel divided him into night and day.

The women he knew were either too surprised or too afraid. He learned that surprise and fear were the same.

His mother, an innkeeper in Olinda, said he had had the "thing" happen to him because he had betrayed his destiny, his gift from heaven.

"You were born to be a healer, a *curandero*."

But he was a man of modern times and modern possibilities, an engineering student in Rio.

"Men make their destiny," he said.

"I'll call you Heaven's Punishment then, Ensinadelo, not Ensinança, because He gave you the special gift of making men and women whole again, and you've traded it for pottage."

"I want to build bridges and skyscrapers," he said.

"In the old days it was what *He wants*."

The woman rubbed her eyes with her brown knuckles.

"You can't work against heaven. No. And look what heaven's given you. Its own evidences, that you can't lift one finger against. Go design your bridges, half-one-half-other. Only heaven can make you whole again."

"Perhaps heaven has made me whole already," he said.

"You were meant to be a *curandero*. To poke a shoulder and make it well. To turn a head and make it better. To make a dumb man talk. To draw the pain from knuckles. To make them whole. To stop a cough. To mend a knee. To see where the devil's hiding and draw him out. Eh, you've betrayed your destiny."

There is no convincing her. They seem opposing spirits. But doesn't he carry two worlds? He hides one part of himself in denim, the other in white cotton shirts.

II

ENSINANÇA met a woman staying at his mother's boarding house. They were not strangers long.

The sky opened. The world changed from trouble to kisses. She was not afraid or surprised when she discovered him.

"You are the first woman," he said. "Why don't you fear me? Why do you look at me as if you've always seen me, as if I've always been? Why do you look at me as if I'm possible?"

She didn't answer. They sat in cane chairs. They kissed each other. They kissed the sun. They ate oranges and coconuts. They touched fingertips. They played games. They lifted each other up. They named and renamed each other.

"Why don't you think I'm a monster?" he persisted.

"If you are a monster, you are the loveliest monster," she said.

She welcomed him into her arms again. She kissed his forehead. She kissed his moustache. She kissed his stomach where his landscape changed.

"Are you happy?"

"Yes."

"You were not surprised or afraid?"

"No."

III

"TELL me what you believe," he asks.

She only kisses him.

"Can I survive with kisses?" he asks. "Tell me what you believe."

She plays with his armpits. She kisses his elbows. She won't answer.

"Are you superstitious? Do you believe in destiny?" he asks.

The woman laughs at him and chews an olive.

"Shall I tell you my destiny?" he asks.

She smiles.

"If it's a gift from heaven," she says, "you should take it."

"Who have you been talking to?" His look is intense and fierce.

She lights a cigarette. She sits in a turquoise chair.

He calls her a dishonest woman, the worst kind.

"I am a little," she says.

She kisses the nape of his neck.

"What are you here for?" he asks.

She opens her mouth, and there's oil on her tongue. He flies to the center of her.

IV

IN the daytime, he designs with steel and stone. At night, he rebuilds flesh and spirit.

Sometimes he dreams of a peregrine woman neither afraid nor surprised at his differentness, the landscapes above and below his navel, who herself could draw light from darkness, darkness from light.

"I came to ask you, where's the devil hiding?" a client asks.

He drives the devil out in a hurry. He makes them wonder what manner of man he is.

Jamaica Kincaid
1949–

orn in St John's, Antigua, to a Carib-Indian mother from Dominica, she went in 1966 to the USA to pursue her education, and
still lives in New York with her husband and daughter. She began
writing for magazines such as Ms and The New Yorker, on which she
has been a staff writer since 1976, and her work has also appeared in
Rolling Stone and Paris Review. In 1984 she won the Morton Dauwen
Zabel Award of the American Academy and Institute of Arts and Letters
for her first book At the Bottom of the River (1983), a collection of her
stories. Her second book was Annie John (1985), from which this is an
extract; a semi-autobiographical novel which also explores Caribbean
identity in a wider sense, it is about a young girl's gradual realization
that she must leave the enchanted landscape of the island of her birth,
the dreams and magic of childhood, as surely as she must reach womanhood. A Small Place (1988) was a critique in extended essay-form of
Antigua's colonial past and present tourist development, and her most
recent novel is Lucy (1991).

From

Annie John

CHAPTER VIII

A WALK TO THE JETTY

"My name is Annie John." These were the first words that came into my
mind as I woke up on the morning of the last day I spent in Antigua,
and they stayed there, lined up one behind the other, marching up and down,
for I don't know how long. At noon on that day, a ship on which I was to be a
passenger would sail to Barbados, and there I would board another ship, which
would sail to England, where I would study to become a nurse. My name was
the last thing I saw the night before, just as I was falling asleep; it was written
in big, black letters all over my trunk, sometimes followed by my address in
Antigua, sometimes followed by my address as it would be in England. I did
not want to go to England, I did not want to be a nurse, but I would have
chosen going off to live in a cavern and keeping house for seven unruly men

rather than go on with my life as it stood. I never wanted to lie in this bed again, my legs hanging out way past the foot of it, tossing and turning on my mattress, with its cotton stuffing all lumped just where it wasn't a good place to be lumped. I never wanted to lie in my bed again and hear Mr Ephraim driving his sheep to pasture – a signal to my mother that she should get up to prepare my father's and my bath and breakfast. I never wanted to lie in my bed and hear her get dressed, washing her face, brushing her teeth, and gargling. I especially never wanted to lie in my bed and hear my mother gargling again.

Lying there in the half-dark of my room, I could see my shelf, with my books – some of them prizes I had won in school, some of them gifts from my mother – and with photographs of people I was supposed to love forever no matter what, and with my old thermos, which was given to me for my eighth birthday, and some shells I had gathered at different times I spent at the sea. In one corner stood my washstand and its beautiful basin of white enamel with blooming red hibiscus painted at the bottom and an urn that matched. In another corner were my old school shoes and my Sunday shoes. In still another corner, a bureau held my old clothes. I knew everything in this room, inside out and outside in. I had lived in this room for thirteen of my seventeen years. I could see in my mind's eye even the day my father was adding it onto the rest of the house. Everywhere I looked stood something that had meant a lot to me, that had given me pleasure at some point, or could remind me of a time that was a happy time. But as I was lying there my heart could have burst open with joy at the thought of never having to see any of it again.

If someone had asked me for a little summing up of my life at that moment as I lay in bed, I would have said, "My name is Annie John. I was born on the fifteenth of September, seventeen years ago, at Holberton Hospital, at five o'clock in the morning. At the time I was born, the moon was going down at one end of the sky and the sun was coming up at the other. My mother's name is Annie also. My Father's name is Alexander, and he is thirty-five years older than my mother. Two of his children are four and six years older than she is. Looking at how sickly he has become and looking at the way my mother now has to run up and down for him, gathering the herbs and barks that he boils in water, which he drinks instead of the medicine the doctor has ordered for him, I plan not only never to marry an old man but certainly never to marry at all. The house we live in my father built with his own hands. The bed I am lying in my father built with his own hands. If I get up and sit on a chair, it is a chair my father built with his own hands. When my mother uses a large wooden spoon to stir the porridge we sometimes eat as part of our breakfast, it will be a spoon that my father has carved with his own hands. The sheets on my bed my mother made with her own hands. The curtains hanging at my window my mother made with her own hands. The nightie I am wearing, with scalloped neck and hem and sleeves, my mother made with her own hands. When I look at things in a certain way, I suppose I should say that the two of them made me with their own hands. For most of my life, when the three of us went anywhere together I stood between the two of them or sat between the two of them. But then I got too big, and there I was, shoulder to shoulder with them more or less, and it became not very comfortable to walk down the street together. And so now

there they are together and here I am apart. I don't see them now the way I used
to, and I don't love them now the way I used to. The bitter thing about it is that
they are just the same and it is I who have changed, so all the things I used to
be and all the things I used to feel are as false as the teeth in my father's head.
Why, I wonder, didn't I see the hypocrite in my mother when, over the years,
she said that she loved me and could hardly live without me, while at the same
time proposing and arranging separation after separation, including this one,
which, unbeknownst to her, *I* have arranged to be permanent? So now I, too,
have hypocrisy, and breasts (small ones), and hair growing in the appropriate
places, and sharp eyes, and I have made a vow never to be fooled again."

Lying in my bed for the last time, I thought, This is what I add up to. At that,
I felt as if someone had placed me in a hole and was forcing me first down and
then up against the pressure of gravity. I shook myself and prepared to get up.
I said to myself, "I am getting up out of this bed for the last time." Everything I
would do that morning until I got on the ship that would take me to England I
would be doing for the last time, for I had made up my mind that, come what
may, the road for me now went only in one direction: away from my home, away
from my mother, away from my father, away from the everlasting blue sky, away
from the everlasting hot sun, away from people who said to me, "This happened
during the time your mother was carrying you." If I had been asked to put into
words why I felt this way, if I had been given years to reflect and come up with
the words of why I felt this way, I would not have been able to come up with so
much as the letter "A". I only knew that I felt the way I did, and that this feeling
was the strongest thing in my life.

Kebbedesh

?1950–

Women in Ethiopia's impoverished northern province of Tigray
have contributed much to the liberation struggle waged since
1975 against repression by the Addis Ababa central govern-

ment. The feudal system that obtained meant that the poor subsistence peasant farmers who were in the majority had most of their produce taken from them; needless to say, peasant women were at the bottom of the hierarchy, with absolutely no rights. During the next fifteen years the Tigrayan people worked toward a democratic society through a gradual process of revolution, led by the Tigrayan People's Liberation Front (TPLF), operating on principles of equality and participation by women, who are fundamental to the changes that have taken place. Kebbedesh is one of the thousands of former prostitutes who returned to Tigray from surrounding countries to support the struggle. She was interviewed in 1989 for the book Sweeter Than Honey: Testimonies of Tigrayan Women *(1989) by Jenny Hammond of Third World First. Though her specific experience, recounted below, represents an exceptional model of strength, in her determination to transform her life she is typical of many women.*

From

"No one knew more about women's oppression than I did. . ."

M Y family were peasants. I never knew my father – he was murdered by outlaws when my mother was pregnant with me. My mother faced many problems after his death. She was shocked and her health was not good. Because of her troubles she called me Kebbedesh, "a heavy burden".

After a while my mother remarried. She left for another village but I went to live with my aunts. When I was seven, my aunts arranged for me to be married to a wealthy neighbour. He was rich, chauvinistic and rather foolish. He was huge, with a beard, and he seemed like a giant to me. My uncles told him not to have sex with me. They made him promise in front of a priest that he would wait until I was mature, but this did not work.

I went to his house, which was strange to me. I saw him for the first time inside the house. He was like a giant, like something that makes you afraid. At that time I didn't know what marriage, or being husband and wife, meant. After three terrible nights I escaped back to my aunt's house. My family insulted me, shouted at me, "Why did you come back, you stupid girl?" They forced me to return.

After some weeks I escaped again, this time to the forest. I passed several very difficult days there. I was hungry and thirsty and I just wanted to die. I fainted and a peasant found me and took me back to his house. He knew me and knew my family were angry so he kept me in his house. He gave me milk because I couldn't eat *injera* [fermented grain pancake, the basic food of the region]. After a few days he took me back to my home. My family took me in but then they tried to persuade me to return to my husband. They said he was rich and owned many cattle. They wanted me to go and live with him again.

They took me to him for the third time. I lived there for some months, maybe a year, but then I escaped again. I felt it was too difficult to live in the world. I took a rope and went to the forest to hang myself. A neighbouring peasant who was tending his cattle in the forest found me standing under a tree. He was surprised and asked me what I was doing there with a rope. I told him I was collecting wood. He didn't believe me and tried to take me back to my husband. I refused to go – I said I was looking for wood.

After two days in the forest, I became so hungry that I returned to a neighbour's house. They tried to reconcile me to my family. When I was eight, one year after I was married, they made me return to my so-called husband. My husband forced me to have sex when I was eight years old. I was sick for many days after that. I just didn't know what to do or how to help myself. All paths seemed closed to me. All the people in the area were against me. They said I should stay with my husband because he was rich. They couldn't see it from my point of view – they thought it was natural.

I continued like this until I was eleven, escaping and being returned by my family. At last my mother learned what was happening to me. She came back to the village, divorced me from that man and took me away with her to her village.

But once I was there I faced another problem. The people there insulted me. Because I didn't know my father, they said I was undisciplined. They said I was rubbish because I had been brought up by a woman, without a father. They said a woman could not bring up a child properly, that I was undisciplined to divorce my husband and so they teased and insulted me. Things weren't easy for my mother either. She also felt insulted because I had left my husband. So I decided to go to Asmara. A friend had come to visit us from Asmara, so I went to her and begged her to take me away with her. I was fifteen at that time.

But when I reached Asmara I didn't like it. There was nothing for me there. After a miserable time there I went to T'senay near the Sudan border and got a job in a bar. In the bar I was badly treated – men came and kicked me, spat in my face. They could do whatever they wanted. The owner of the bar also was cruel. If I broke a glass she would not pay me. I worked there for two years but was not even able to buy any clothes. The male customers cheated me. They said they would give me money to pass the night with me, but after they slept they would leave without paying.

At last some women came to the bar from Sudan. They had jewellery and good clothes so I asked them about their life in the Sudan. They encouraged me to go there with them, saying I could have a good life. So I went to Sudan after two years in T'senay. I lived in the Sudan for ten years. I rented a room and worked as a prostitute for ten miserable years. The life of prostitution is clear to you, so I don't need to explain it.

In 1977, TPLF members were trying to agitate the people in Sudan and to establish underground movements wherever there were Tigrayans. I became interested in this news. TPLF didn't need to politicize me – I had led a terrible life. No one knew more about women's oppression than I did. I became an active participant in TPLF activities and worked for two years with them. I learned sewing and then, in 1980, I decided to come to the Field as a fighter. After I finished training, I was assigned to the workshop as a tailor. Then, three years ago, I was assigned here to Marta School.[1] I am a student and I teach sewing. I am also a fighter.

I feel proud and happy to be here. We are many women with different miserable experiences. We discuss our past lives all the time. This gives me a very special feeling. Before I came here I was fighting without a full consciousness. I understood more than anyone that women are oppressed by men and by class oppression, but still I was not fighting consciously. I had not examined the "woman question" scientifically. Since coming here I have studied the "woman question" and have come to realize that the solution is to struggle and to bring about a new society.

It makes me happy that I came both to learn and to teach. I feel so happy to be teaching my sisters, to be producing skilled sisters. I feel joy and happiness when I see the results of my teaching.

Saida Hagi-Dirie Herzi
?1950s–

Born in Mogadishu, Somalia, she has a BA in English Literature from King Abdulaziz University in Jedda, Saudi Arabia (where she currently teaches English) and a Master's degree from American University in Cairo, Egypt. She is married, with two sons and two daughters. "Against the Pleasure Principle, her first published story, appeared in Index on Censorship in 1990.

Against the Pleasure Principle

RAHMA was all excitement. Her husband had been awarded a scholarship to one of the Ivy-League universities in the United States, and she was going

---

[1] Named after two women called Marta: one a member of the Tigrayan resistance who was executed with other university students after a failed attempt to hijack a plane; the other, the first woman fighter to join the TPLF.

with him. This meant that she was going to have her baby – the first – in the US. She would have the best medical care in the world.

But there was the problem of her mother. Her mother did not want her to go to the US. Rahma was not sure just what it was that her mother objected to but partly, no doubt, she was afraid she'd lose Rahma if she let her go. She had seen it happen with other girls who went abroad: most of them did not come back at all and those who did came only to visit, not to stay. And they let it be known that they had thrown overboard the ways of their people and adopted the ways of the outside world – they painted their lips and their faces; they wore western dress; they went about the city laughing and singing outlandish songs; they spoke in foreign languages or threw in foreign words when they spoke the local language; and they generally acted as though they were superior to all those who stayed behind.

Her mother also seemed worried about Rahma having her baby in the US. Rahma had tried and tried again to reassure her that there was nothing to worry about: she would have the best medical attention. Problems, if any, would be more likely to arise at home than there. But it had made no difference. Her mother kept bombarding her with horror stories she had heard from Somali women coming back from the US – the dreadful things that happened to them when they went to US hospitals, above all when they had their babies there.

Like all women in her native setting, Rahma was circumcised, and, according to her mother, that would mean trouble for her when she was going to have a baby unless there was a midwife from her country to help her. Her mother was convinced that US doctors, who had no experience with circumcised women, would not know what to do.

Rahma had never given much thought to the fact that she had been only four years old when it happened, and nineteen years had passed since then. But she did remember.

It had not been her own feast of circumcision but that of her sister, who was nine then. She remembered the feeling of excitement that enveloped the whole house that morning. Lots of women were there; relatives were bringing gifts – sweets, cakes, various kinds of delicious drinks, trinkets. And her sister was the centre of attention. Rahma remembered feeling jealous, left out. Whatever it was they were going to do to her sister, she wanted to have it done too. She cried to have it done, cried and cried till the women around her mother relented and agreed to do it to her too. There was no room for fear in her mind: all she could think of was that she wanted to have done to her what they were going to do to her sister so that she too would get gifts, she too would be fussed over.

She remembered the preliminaries, being in the midst of a cluster of women, all relatives of hers. They laid her on her back on a small table. Two of the women, one to the left of her and the other to the right, gently but firmly held her down with one hand and with the other took hold of her legs and spread them wide. A third standing behind her held down her shoulders. Another washed her genitals with a mixture of *melmel* and *hildeed*, a traditional medicine. It felt pleasantly cool. Off to one side several women were playing tin drums. Rahma did not know that the intent of the drums was to drown the screams that would be coming from her throat in a moment.

The last thing she remembered was one of the women, a little knife in one hand, bending over her. The next instant there was an explosion of pain in her crotch, hot searing pain that made her scream like the rabbit when the steel trap snapped its legs. But the din of the drums, rising to a deafening crescendo, drowned her screams, and the women who held her expertly subdued her young strength coiling into a spring to get away. Then she must have passed out, for she remembered nothing further of the operation in which all the outer parts of her small genitals were cut off, lips, clitoris and all, and the mutilated opening stitched up with a thorn, leaving a passage the size of a grain of sorghum.

When she regained consciousness, she was lying on her mat in her sleeping corner, hot pain between her legs. The slightest movement so aggravated the pain that tears would well up in her eyes. She remembered trying to lie perfectly still so as not to make the pain worse.

For some time after the operation she walked like a cripple: her thighs had been tied together so that she could move her legs only from the knees down, which meant taking only the tiniest of steps. People could tell what had happened to her by the way she walked.

And she remembered how she dreaded passing water. She had to do it sitting because she could not squat, and she had to do it with her thighs closed tightly because of the bindings. To ease the pain of urine pushing through the raw wound of the narrow opening, warm water was poured over it while she urinated. Even so, it brought tears to her eyes. In time the pain abated, but urinating had been associated with discomfort for her ever since.

She remembered being told that she had needed only three thorn stitches. Had she been older, it would have taken four, perhaps five, stitches to sew her up properly. There are accepted standards for the size of a girl's opening: an opening the size of a grain of rice is considered ideal; one as big as a grain of sorghum is acceptable. However, should it turn out as big as a grain of maize, the poor girl would have to go through the ordeal a second time. That's what had happened to her sister; she herself had been luckier. When the women who inspected her opening broke out into the high-pitched *mash-harad* with which women in her society signalled joy, or approval, Rahma knew that it had turned out all right the first time.

Rahma's culture justified circumcision as a measure of hygiene, but the real purpose of it, Rahma was sure, was to safeguard the woman's virginity. Why else the insistence on an opening no larger than a grain of sorghum, one barely big enough to permit the passing of urine and of the menstrual blood? An opening as small as that was, if anything, anti-hygienic. No, if the kind of circumcision that was practised in her area had any purpose, it was to ensure that the hymen remained intact. Her society made so much of virginity that no girl who lost it could hope to achieve a decent marriage. There was no greater blow to a man's ego than to find out that the girl he married was not a virgin.

Rahma knew that, except for the first time, it was customary for women to deliver by themselves, standing up and holding on to a hanging rope. But the first time they needed assistance – someone to cut a passage large enough for the baby's passage. That was what so worried Rahma's mother. She did not think a US doctor could be trusted to make the right cut. Not having had any experience with circumcised women he would not know that the only way to cut was upward from the small opening left after circumcision. He might, especially if the baby's head was unusually big, cut upward *and* downward. How was he to know that a cut towards the rectum could, and probably would, mean trouble for all future deliveries? Nor would he know that it was best for the woman to be stitched up again right after the baby was born. It was, Rahma's mother insisted, dangerous for a circumcision passage to be left open.

When it became obvious that her words of warning did not have the desired effect on Rahma, her mother decided to play her last trump card – the *Kur*, a ritual feast put on, usually in the ninth month of a pregnancy, to ask God's blessing for the mother and the baby about to be born. Friends and relatives came to the feast to offer their good-luck wishes. It was her mother's intention to invite to the *Kur* two women who had had bad experiences with doctors in the US. They would talk about their experiences in the hope that Rahma would be swayed by them and not go away.

The *Kur* feast was held at her mother's place. When the ritual part of it was over and the well-wishers had offered their congratulations, some of the older women, who had obviously been put up to it by her mother, descended on Rahma trying to accomplish what her mother had failed to do – persuade her to put off going away at least until after the baby's birth.

It did not work. From the expression on Rahma's face that was only too obvious. So her mother signalled for the two special guests to do their part. The first, whose name was Hawa, had spent two years in the US as a student. She talked about the problems of a circumcised woman in a society that did not circumcise its women. "When people found out where I was from," she told her audience in a whisper, "they pestered me with questions about female circumcision. To avoid their questions, I told them that I had not been circumcised myself and therefore could not tell them anything about it. But that did not stop them from bugging me with more questions." The topic of circumcision, she told them, continued to be a source of embarrassment for as long as she was there.

Hawa then talked about her experience at the gynaecologist's office. She had put off seeing a gynaecologist as long as possible, but when she could not put it off any longer, she looked for, and found, a woman doctor, thinking that she would feel more comfortable with a woman. When the doctor started to examine her, Hawa had heard a gasp. The gasp was followed by a few stammering sounds that turned into a question. The doctor wanted to know whether she had got burned or scalded. When Hawa signalled by a shake of her head that she had done neither, the doctor asked her whether she had had an operation for cancer or something, in which the outer parts of her genital had been amputated. Again Hawa denied anything, and to avoid further questions quickly added that the disfigurement which the doctor found so puzzling was the result of circumcision.

At that, Hawa's doctor went on with the examination without further questions. When she was finished, she turned to Hawa once more. "You had me confused there," she muttered, more to herself than to Hawa. "Don't hold my ignorance against me. I have heard and read about circumcision, but you are the first circumcised woman I have seen in my career. I neither knew that it was still practised nor did I have any idea it went so far.

"You know," she continued after a moment's pause, "I cannot for the world of me understand why your people have to do this to their women. Intercourse cannot be much fun for someone mutilated like that. Perhaps that's why they do it, to make sure the women won't get any pleasure out of sex. And what misery it must be for a woman sewn up like that to have a baby."

Hawa said she went away from the doctor's office thinking how right the doctor was about sex not being fun for circumcised women. She remembered the first time her husband made love to her, how horribly painful it had been. And it had continued to be painful for her even after she got used to it. She knew that for most of the women in her society sex was something to be endured not enjoyed. With all the sensitive parts of womanhood cut away, it was all but impossible for them to be sexually aroused and quite impossible for them to experience any of the pleasurable sensations that would redeem the act.

Hawa said she walked home feeling like a freak: what was left of her genitals must look pretty grim if the sight of it could make a doctor gasp. Why did her people do this to their women? Hundreds of millions of women the world over went through life the way God had created them, whole and unmutilated. Why could her people not leave well enough alone? It seemed to her, at least in this case, that man's attempts to improve on nature were a disaster.

The second woman, Dahabo, seemed to believe in circumcision as such. However, when a circumcised woman moved to a part of the world that did not practise circumcision problems were bound to arise. She too had lived in the US. She too had had her encounters with US doctors. She talked at length about her first such encounter. Like Hawa's doctor, hers was a woman; unlike Hawa's hers was familiar with the idea of female circumcision. Nevertheless, Dahabo was her first case of a circumcised woman. Dahabo told her audience about the questioning she was subjected to by her doctor after the examination:

Doctor: Did you have any sort of anaesthesia when they circumcized you?

Dahabo: No, I did not, but I did not really fell any pain because I fainted and remained unconscious during the whole operation.

Doctor: Is circumcision still practised in your culture?

Dahabo: Yes, it is. I had it done to my five-year-old daughter before coming here.

Doctor: Any difference between your way and your daughter's way?

Dahabo: None whatsoever: the same women who circumcised me circumcised her.

At that point, Dahabo told her listeners, something happened that puzzled her: her doctor, eyes full of tears, broke into loud sobs, and she continued to sob while she opened the door to usher her patient out into the corridor. Dahabo said she had never understood what had made her doctor cry.

Rahma had no trouble understanding what it was that had moved the doctor to tears. She was close to tears herself as she left her mother's house to walk home. How much longer, she wondered, would the women of her culture have to endure this senseless mutilation? She knew that, though her people made believe circumcision was a religious obligation, it was really just an ugly custom that had been borrowed from the ancient Egyptians and had nothing to do with Islam. Islam recommends circumcision only for men.

The *Kur* did not achieve what her mother had hoped. Rahma was more determined than ever to accompany her husband to the US. True, there was still the problem of her mother; no doubt her mother meant well, no doubt she wanted the best for her, but Rahma had different ideas about that. She was, for instance, convinced that having her baby in the US was in the best interest of her and of the baby. She would like to have her mother's blessing for the move, but if that was not possible she would go without it. She had always hated circumcision. Now she hated it more than ever. No daughter of hers would ever be subjected to it.

Zaynab Alkali

1950–

Her Islamic family came from a village in Borno State, Nigeria, but moved to a Christian village in Gongola State, where she was brought up. She graduated from Bayero University, Kano, with a BA in 1973, obtaining an MA in African Literature in English in 1979. The first woman novelist from Northern Nigeria, she is Senior Lecturer in English at the University of Maiduguri, Borno State. She has written two novels, The Stillborn (1984), from which this passage is taken – a lively story of family life, centring on the adolescent Li and her hopes of independence, while illustrating how the dreams of women are often stillborn in a society ordered by men – and the The Virtuous Woman (1987).

From

The Stillborn

CHAPTER II

"OH! How I wish I could try the dance steps," Li piped, wriggling beside Awa on the bench.

"Uhmm, you will do no such thing. You really are forgetting yourself. Besides, people will laugh at your awkwardness," Awa said.

"Well, at least I'll be noticed. Someone will probably sing in praise of me in the dancing arena."

"Ridicule you, you mean. And what happens if Baba learns of it?"

"Baba! Big sister," Li exclaimed. "Can't you forget Father for a while?"

"We have to be careful, Li," Awa cautioned.

"He won't learn of this. If he does we'll have to pay."

"You'll have to pay, you mean."

"Both of us. We are here together, remember?" she said mischievously.

"Nobody will see me dancing. I could deny it, you know," Awa said.

"That would be difficult, big sister. You still would have to say where you were when I was dancing."

"All right, wise one. You aren't going to dance and Baba will never learn of this either," Awa said lightly.

Suddenly there was applause from the bystanders. Li's attention was drawn to the centre of the arena. A richly dressed young man was pasting a ten-shilling note on a woman's forehead. Li cheered and clapped with the rest.

"That's Alhaji Bature," she said, pointing to the man.

"And who is the woman?" Awa asked.

"I don't know," Li said absent-mindedly. "That is the part I like best," still referring to the man's action. "Someone is sure to paste a shilling on my forehead," she exclaimed.

"You are worth more than a shilling," a deep slow voice boomed, startling them both. Li turned her head and looked straight into a pair of bold eyes.

"Besides," the man continued, "you really don't have to be in the centre to be admired."

He was so confident and sure of himself that Li was spellbound. Awa hardly looked at him but Li was already summing him up. "He must be new around here," she thought. "The dialect is strangely different, something about the accent."

She observed also that he was good looking, but poorly dressed. As he drew closer, Li noticed his muscular thighs under a pair of brown shorts, which looked like part of a school uniform. Hanging loosely, and barely covering his hairy chest, was a threadbare shirt which had seen a lot of soap and water. Li looked down at his feet and saw a pair of white canvas shoes with one or two toes peeping from a gap.

She looked up and met the owner's proud eyes evenly. Her heart missed a beat. "By God, the man is attractive," she thought. He was tall, several inches taller than Li, and a shade darker. He was healthy-looking, almost robust. "He must spend all he has on food and forget about clothes," she thought again with amazement.

Now he was smiling at Li. He had an odd habit of casting side-glances. Li felt nervous. She wondered why he didn't seem to notice Awa at all. She smiled back, convinced she could handle him, given the chance. She was becoming aware of her power over men. Not that she had any experience of them yet – perhaps it was the way they fixed their gaze on her body but avoided her eyes. A neighbour once said that only a lover could look into those large eyes. But she knew the man was different, bold and aggressive. She was the first to avert her eyes.

"You are a stranger here?" Li ventured and almost jumped with pain from a sharp jab on her thigh. It was a warning from her cautious sister to take her time. Li turned to look at her with a puzzled expression and repeated her question.

"Be silent, Li, and stop bothering the man," Awa said angrily.

"No bother," the young man smiled broadly, looking at Awa for the first time. His eyes rested on her arms and he observed that she too was beautiful, a beautiful shining ebony black. He studied her face carefully and concluded that she must be the older of the two. Her face carried a weight of responsibility that was absent in the younger girl. The man observed also that, although she was much smaller, her body was fully rounded and matured. Nevertheless, she was completely overshadowed by the other's liveliness. "Yes," he thought, "this part of the village has its share of beautiful girls." Aloud he said, "May I sit down?"

"Is this not a public place?" Awa countered with dignity. Li gave her a funny look. She sensed that Awa disliked the man and wondered why. After all, they'd only just met. He sat next to Li, leaving a decent gap between them.

"Why aren't you two dancing?" he asked with a puzzled expression.

"The same reason you are not," Awa answered his question coldly.

She was playing to the tune of a traditional courtship. A woman was not supposed to show interest in a man on their first meeting. His seriousness would only be determined by how well he took a rebuff and how persistently he pursued his woman. The man turned to Li and found her smiling. Ignoring Awa completely, he kept his head inclined towards Li, waiting for her answer.

"The truth is that we don't know how," Li replied.

The man was not convinced by her reply. "You don't know how? It can't be true! Every small child in these parts knows the new steps. Are you strangers here?"

"No," Li replied.

"Well, where have you been hiding?"

"Under Baba's. . ."

Awa's terrible look interrupted her. "Enough of that, Li. You've poured enough into the ears of a stranger."

"All right, big sister," Li said sullenly and they fell silent. Each was lost in thought. Li was the first to break the silence which was becoming embarrassing.

"You haven't told us where you come from."

The man looked at her mysteriously and maintained silence, then added, "Or who I am."

"Or who you are," Li replied with amusement.

"I am a young man," he replied with a ghost of a smile.

"Obviously," Awa said, surveying him from head to toe. "We can see that much." She sounded humorous but for the look on her face. Li and the man burst into laughter. Awa could not contain herself and joined in. The laughter helped to establish a more cordial atmosphere and Awa relaxed a little.

"What are your traditional names?" he asked and Li looked at him with a triumphant smile.

"You tell us your name first."

"No, yours first," he insisted.

"Uhmm, he is playing hard to get," Li commented.

"Who wants to get him anyway?" Awa replied, eyeing his clothes once more. The girls giggled. Awa could be funny without meaning to. Awa stood up and took hold of Li's arm. They'd stayed far too long and their parents would soon miss them, but Li protested. They'd only just come, she argued and, besides, the dance was just beginning to warm up.

"Obey your sister, Li," the stranger put in. "She knows best."

Li got to her feet grudgingly. She was a bit disappointed in the man. She had felt he was on her side. Other girls were much more lucky, she thought, and wished she was in one of those so-called heathen homes.

"May the day break well then, son-of-the-chief," Li said mockingly.

"May we live to see tomorrow, girls. Greet your people for me," he added.

"Uhmmm," Awa grunted, "see who is sending his greetings to my people." It was a calculated insult which the man ignored completely.

"And who might we say sent his greetings?" Li asked with a suggestive glint in her eyes.

The man, who was also standing by this time, moved closer to Li and inclined his head towards her. But he addressed himself to Awa. "I am the son-of-the-chief of London Traku, the famous Habu Adams."

"And pompous too, you might add," Li said mischievously.

The piece of information had a comic effect on Awa. She stared at Habu Adams for a minute and roared with laughter. She slapped her thighs and hissed, "By God, I should have guessed you are from London Traku. Only your type comes from there, a typical villager."

Habu Adams' face clouded for a second, but only for a second. Li looked open-mouthed at her sister who she thought had been behaving out of character ever since the man walked up to them. Calm and collected, she never behaved like this even in private. She must dislike Habu Adams very much. It was Li's turn to urge them to leave.

"Let us go, big sister," she said.

And as Awa bent to retrieve her shoes from under the log, the two exchanged a meaningful look over her head. They both knew then that they would meet again that night.

The next morning Baba called all the children, except the small ones. He stood, feet apart and arms akimbo, scowling at a large opening in the fence behind Mama's hut. When he saw that they had all assembled, he turned to face them.

"Who went out last night?" he asked, looking at them one by one in his usual direct way. Nobody answered him and he repeated the question twice, his face darkening with anger. Awa gave Li a warning glance.

"I am talking to all of you. Have you lost your tongues?"

Still no one said anything. They looked at each other furtively. Above their heads a long oiled whip hung loosely from the end of a bamboo pole. The silence was becoming intolerable. Suddenly, Li opened her mouth to speak but was forestalled by Awa.

"Nobody went out as far as I know," she said uncertainly.

"Then can you explain the gaping hole, Awa?"

"No, Father."

"A dog could have done that," Li blundered and regretted it immediately. Her father might be a shortsighted bigot, but he was no fool.

"Uhmm, a dog. You really want me to believe a dog made this neat opening, do you?" he reached for the oiled whip as he spoke. Sule gave Li a look that seemed to say, "Keep quiet, let me handle this."

Sule had known Li went out the previous night. Frustrated at the thought that all his friends were at the dance, he himself had been unable to sleep. He had tossed on his bed for hours, his heart throbbing in rhythm to the drumbeat. He knew the dance steps and ached to try them in the dancing arena. He had thought of stealing out over the fence, but dispelled such thoughts immediately. The dance wasn't worth the disgrace.

At midnight he had gone behind his mother's hut to smoke a little to ease the tension. He could not smoke inside his hut because Baba had a disturbing habit of barging in on him – a sort of check on his daily habits. He had thought of school and wished the holidays were over. School was much better. He lit a cigarette and immediately nipped at it, burning his finger in the process. A sudden rustling sound had scared him. He quickly dropped the cigarette and stepped on it. He braced himself for a confrontation with his father, but instead came face to face with Li.

"God in heaven, small one, you scared my insides," he exclaimed, bending low and searching for the cigarette in the clear moonlight. "See what you have cost me," he raised his hand to her nose. "A costly stick and a burnt finger."

"Ssh, son-of-my-mother, Father might hear us," Li whispered, coming closer to him. "I've been to the dance," she said excitedly. "I will tell you all about it in the morning."

"Uhmm," Sule granted. "To the dance, Li?"

"Say nothing to anybody or. . ." she paused a while, "I might just be tempted to mention this." She touched the cigarette.

"You know I won't," Sule said soberly, "but I am afraid for you though. You shouldn't have broken the fence." He moved close and examined the fence. "You are really empty-headed. You should have climbed over the fence."

"Allah! That's an idea," she explained. "I'll remember that another time."

"If you survive this time," Sule said. "Now wait," he took hold of her arm as she made to leave. "What are you going to do about the fence?"

"Mend it, of course," she said easily.

"Before morning?"

She thought for a minute and said, "I don't know. I guess it'll have to wait until morning."

"Until he sees it, you mean?"

"I will have to get up at cockcrow."

"Wake me up and I will help you."

"Thank you, son-of-my-mother."

"Don't worry, little sister. Aren't we friends?"

"Plotters," Li said and they laughed quietly. They both heard a slight cough from the direction of Baba's room and stole away quietly. In the morning Baba had forestalled them, much to their horror. They had overslept.

Awa looked at the oiled whip and shot a glance at Li. She too knew who had gone out last night, although she hadn't known how until now. At midnight, she had got up to look for her blanket and had found Li's bed empty. "Useless child," Awa had thought. "She must have gone after that worthless beggar."

Now, standing in front of Baba who was angry beyond description, Awa wondered what Li saw in that stranger to risk their father's anger. Good-looking, yes, but what woman needed a man for his face? For that was all he had, a face. In those clothes he looked like a market beggar. Why, the shorts hardly covered his buttocks. And he called himself "the son-of-the-chief'. Awa stifled a giggle at the train of her thoughts. "No," she said to herself. "The man isn't worth the trouble. Li would be in serious trouble if Baba found out. God knows, the girl has the brain of a chicken. She could have climbed over the fence". For some strange reason she was glad this had happened. If Li was punished, she thought, she might forget about the stranger. But why did she dislike Habu so much? She tried asking herself that question. Surely it wasn't because he looked poor? What had poverty to do with it? After all, no one in her family could present a better picture.

"Awa," Baba cut into her thoughts.

"Yes, Father."

"Are you sure you know nothing about the hole?"

"No, Father." She was glad he hadn't asked if she had gone to the dance. She wouldn't have known how to answer that.

"I know Sani slept in his mother's hut, because he was ill," he began. "Mari is only six and still afraid of the dark. The twins are only four years old, not to talk of Bata who is still a baby," he pushed on, looking at them one by one. His eyes landed momentarily on Sani's immediate senior. "Where were you last night, Becki Hirwa?"

"I was in bed, Baba. You can ask Mama," she said and their father nodded, convinced. Li knew what was coming. Baba wasn't getting any answers, so he had started a calculated process of elimination, bent on finding the truant. Well, she would have to own up, she thought. It was the price she had to pay for the clandestine meeting. She braced herself for the ordeal by taking a deep breath. Her eyes dilated – half with fear half with expectation – as Baba's eyes settled on her finally.

"What about you, Li? Were you at the dance?"

"I was, Father." Again Li was forestalled – this time by Sule's deep voice which jolted everybody. Li looked up in surprise. Sule was shielding her. Awa looked from Li to Sule and back, obviously confused.

"I had to go," Sule was still speaking. "All my friends were there. I could not sleep."

There was a charged silence. No one moved or spoke. Finally Baba moved in Sule's direction. He stood and faced his son and they stared at each other. Baba had been taken unawares. He knew that Sule was capable of this sort of thing but, somehow, he had suspected Li this time. He could not say exactly why. Was it the mad glint in her eyes when she had said it could be a dog, or was it the furtive glances? Maybe she was trying to protect Sule, or was it the other way round? Whichever way it was, Baba knew someone was lying somewhere along the line. What worried him now was, what was he to do with this man-child? He was a man now and it wasn't just his age, but what he stood for. He could beat Awa easily if she erred, no matter how old she was, but not Sule, his firstborn malechild. And to beat a man for going out to dance at night was outrageous. He decided to give him a chance to apologize. That way both could salvage their pride.

"I am ashamed of you breaking a fence like that," he said and waited. Silence. He fixed Sule with a hard stare and with his eyes begged him to apologize, but Sule stared back, a new kind of look creeping into his eyes. It was a defiant look as if he was challenging his father to a duel. Baba was suddenly infuriated and said to himself, "What has come over the children of today? They are not only rebellious but completely immodest. Now what am I to do with Sule?" The others sensed Baba's dilemma and moved closer.

Li no longer looked fidgety. Her eyes grew bold. She was beginning to enjoy the drama. Sule had covered for her, but Li knew very well that Sule's heroism was on his own account. There was no way he could have escaped their father's wrath this day, because Li wasn't one to take any beating alone and Sule was well aware of that.

"I went out, and so did big sister Awa," she would have blurted out. "As for big brother Sule, he smoked something awful."

Nevertheless, Li had her good points. Now that Sule had covered for her first, she was going to do the same. If Baba insisted on beating Sule, she was going to confuse the whole issue by confessing. That way Baba would never know who actually went out, and he wasn't one to punish anyone if in doubt. Li smiled wickedly. It seemed to her that that was one of Baba's few virtues.

Awa was in a different frame of mind. She wasn't concerned about Sule's plight. It served him right, she thought. The wayward children must have gone out together – Sule wasn't the type to stand up for anybody, not even Li. Now he was in real trouble and Awa couldn't help wanting to see his ego deflated. She moved closer and waited for what seemed like an eternity for the drama which never came.

Her father stood with one hand holding the whip loosely, and the other resting on his hip. His shoulders drooped and his eyes looked tired. Presently, Baba dropped the whip and turned to go into his hut. "What an impotent gesture," Awa thought.

Li and Sule smiled mischievously at each other. Awa felt like a traitor. "What an affinity between two people," she said to herself. "Why, they should have come as a husband and wife, not as a brother and sister."

She turned to leave and was arrested by a loud guffaw from behind. Grandma was laughing wildly. She had been watching the scene from the security of her courtyard. "Foolish man," she murmured toothlessly. "He is never tired of playing god with his children." Her mouth twisted into a funny smile. "Crack, crack, crack, crack." The shells of the groundnuts were gradually piling high between her legs.

Kaka walked in slowly, muttering to himself. He stopped abruptly and surveyed the courtyard. The atmosphere was tense. The air, polluted with hostility, assailed him. He watched his son disappear into his hut and observed Mama's grim expression as she walked past him. Kaka knew then that there had been another explosion in his absence. He always knew when there was one – people behaved strangely. With a tottering step, he crossed over to his yard.

The twisted smile on Grandma's face confirmed his worst suspicion. "The witch," he thought. "She is never happy until there is trouble in the family. Wicked, barren woman." In Kaka's opinion, the woman had been the root of all his troubles and of his son's too.

But deep down in his heart, he knew Grandma wasn't the only reason for his son's abnormal behaviour. Other things helped to confuse his sense of moral values. Mainly the quest for modern living coupled with a foreign culture, a thing that was sweeping the whole community like wildfire.

Kaka covered his mouth with the back of his hand and let out a loud yawn. Many things his son did went against his own sense of judgement, but who was he to talk? He was only an old man and nobody listens to old men these days.

In fact his stay in the compound was on condition that he refrained from questioning or interfering with the family's lifestyle. He stayed but lived a different life, unknown to most members of the family. When he felt sick, he visited Heman, the herbalist, in secret. Of the hospital he had this to say, "How can a stranger know the diseases of the people? What does he know about the wrath of the gods of my ancestors? Let those that are beginning to go funny in the head swallow white clay for medicine and have their stomachs slit open for a cure." In the privacy of his room he worshipped his gods. Behind the Hill Station, among the hills, he sacrificed to the gods of his ancestors. Whenever there was a Christian or Muslim festival in the village, he attended both diligently. "At least there's a man alive who is trying to keep the village clean," he would say to his friends.

Kaka could have lived peacefully this way, deriving comfort from his private activities, but for what he termed his son's mad obsession with discipline. He could not close his eyes to the constant beatings that took place at the slightest pretext in the name of discipline. He decided to speak to his son in spite of the warning to keep quiet. Children shouldn't be caged, he reasoned, for if the cage got broken by accident or design, they would find the world too big to live in.

Already the cage was too small for most of them. A week ago, Kaka had gone to ask the price of a goat from a neighbour who brewed home-made beer, burukutu. He had found Sule there among friends having a good time. For both their sakes, Kaka had made a big show of not seeing him there.

Yesterday, too, he had passed by the dancing arena on his way to visit a sick friend. He had seen his two granddaughters talking with a tall, young man. Kaka had wondered if that was the first time they had met. The man had seemed sure of himself, inclining his head towards Li as he spoke.

"Men are utterly shameless and callous these days," he had thought disapprovingly. "He speaks to a woman even before he's met her parents. He could be speaking to the daughter of a leper or a lunatic, or, worse still, the daughter of the accursed."

He chuckled to himself now. "This is what they call modern living."

His mind came back to the present crisis in the compound. He wouldn't be surprised if it had something to do with the girls' presence at the dance yesterday. His son never went out due to his fragile constitution, but he had a strong nose and he could smell a rat a mile away.

He sighed and drew up his rickety chair close to Grandma. "What happened?" he asked in a conspiratorial whisper as he made to sit down.

"Where?" she asked contemptuously without looking up.

He stared at her bent head for a second and flopped into the chair. "In this compound, of course, where else do you think?" His tone was now one of suppressed anger.

"Nothing happened," she replied nonchalantly.

"Don't nothing me, woman. You don't wear that face in this house for nothing," he shouted at her.

"Which face?" she asked stubbornly.

"Your silly twisted face," he answered angrily.

"My face," she said "has always been silly in this house. As for being twisted, your abusive tongue is enough to twist a virgin's face. Listen, friend, why do you bother to look for answers to your daily problems on my silly twisted face? You had better ask your precious son if you want to know what's happening in your family." She continued to shell the groundnuts as she spoke.

Kaka was silent for a long time. He cleared his throat and finally said, "Thank you for your advice, and now listen to mine, woman. Next time anything happens in my absence, you scrub that dirty face well before I come in, or else I will scrub it for you." He fell silent and she raised her head for the first time to see if he had finished with her. He seemed to have.

"Ei ei ei," she cackled. "I shouldn't be surprised, friend. It sounds all too familiar. It must be in the blood."

Kaka got up angrily, knocking his chair over. Her mirthless laughter followed him to his hut.

Merle Collins
1950–

*S*he was born in Aruba and brought up in Grenada, where she was
a teacher and researcher. *She was a public worker in the Ministry
of Foreign Affairs during the Grenada Revolution and a member
of Grenada's National Women's Organization until 1983. Now settled
in London, she is a popular reader of her own work and a member of
African Dawn, an orature collective that performs dramatized poetry
fused with African music. She has published* Because the Dawn Breaks!
Poems Dedicated to the Grenadian People *(1986), a novel* Angel *(1987),
and the short-story collection in which "The Walk" appears,* Rain Darling
(1990). She also co-edited, with Rhonda Cobham, Watchers and Seekers:
Creative Writing by Black Women in Britain *(1987).*

The Walk

F AITH reached up and unbuttoned the apron at the back. Let it drop to
the front. Reached back and loosened the knot at her waist. Pulled off
the apron and dropped it on to the barrel behind the door. She slumped on
to the bench just inside the kitchen door. She looked across at the fireside, at
the scattered bits of wood, at the ashes cold and grey around the wood. Her eyes
moved automatically towards the coalpot, where the yellow butter-pan rested on
partly burnt-out coals. She wondered whether Queen had prepared anything. To
tell the truth, she was too tired to really care. She turned and looked at the bucket
of water on the dresser, at the two pancups hanging from a nail above it. She took
a deep breath, released it and let her head fall forward on to the rough board of
the kitchen table.

"Oh, God, ah tired!" For a few moments, Faith remained like that, letting
her body savour what it was like to be sitting down, letting it relax. And then
her bottom registered that there was something hard on the bench. Faith's hand
found the pebble, removed it. She sat up with a sigh and threw the pebble
through the window over the shelf. Faith looked down at the floor. Yes. Queen
had scrubbed it. A good child, when she put her mind to it.

Faith leaned back against the brown board of the partition and closed her eyes.

"Queen! Queenie oh! Bring some water give me!"

Queen came running. "Mammie, I didn't hear you come, non! And I look out
the back window and I see light in the Great House still, and I see a lot of cars
go up, so I say they having party, and. . ."

"All right. All right!"

Faith held the pancup with both hands, drinking the water in great gulps.

"Ah! Dat good! You boil de cocoa tea?"

"Yes, Mammie."

"The lady pay me dis evening. I want you to go up for me tomorrow mornin."

Queen sucked her teeth. "Mammie, I. . ."

"You what?" Faith sat up, her eyes demanding the response they defied her daughter to make. "Look, child! If you know what good for you, move out of me eyesight, eh! You have to go up for me tomorrow and pay de society, an Cousin Kamay have the little pig mindin so I could turn me hand to something. I want you to pass and see if it drop already. You remember de house where I did show you Cousin Sésé daughter livin?"

"De house wid de green gate and the yellow curtain in the window?"

"So if they change de curtain you won't know de house?"

"Ay! Yes, Mammie, it bave a big mammie apple tree in the yard."

"Right. Pass there and tell Cousin Sésé daughter, Miss Ivy, I ask if de message ready already."

"Yes, Mammie."

Faith looked at her daughter standing beside the bucket of water, at her bony, long-legged frame in the baggy dress. She sighed. It would be a long walk, but Queen was used to it. She wished she didn't have to take the child away from school to make these errands, but what with living so far away and not being able to get a job nearer to the family! And she *must* pay the society. If she dropped down tomorrow morning, what would happen to Queen? A person must make sure to put by a little. You never know when you time would come without warning! And if the pig drop now, she could sell one and have enough to at least buy a little bed. And perhaps she might even be able to take out a better susu hand. Anyway, don't count you chickens! Just hope for the best. Just hope!

"Don't drink too much water, Queen. Next thing you know, you playin baby give me an wetting you bed. Is time for you to go an sleep. You have to get up early. You drink the coraile bush for the cold?"

"Yes, Mammie, an I make some bakes and put in de safe."

"Good. That good. You a real help to me, yes. I don't know what I would do without you, child! Take de small lamp an go inside and sleep. Leave de masanto here for me. What light you sit down inside there with? You have a candle?"

"No, Mammie, I was just sitting down looking out of the back window at the Great House lights."

"Sitting down in the dark, Queen? Why you didn't take the small lamp all the time?"

"Was only for a little while, yes, Mammie, after I finish clean up the kitchen."

"All right, go on! Go on and get ready for bed!"

Queen took the lamp and walked out of the kitchen door. For just a moment she glanced to the left, at the quiet, dark outline of coconut trees. But she didn't like the way the coconut trees rustled, and besides you could never trust a sudden breeze not to put the lamplight out.

Queen climbed the two wooden steps into the house, placed the lamp on the shelf and prepared for bed. She was thinking of the following morning's walk as she pulled the pile of bedding from under the sofa in the corner and spread it out. Queen did not like having to walk all the way to River Sallee. The road was long. She was always afraid to walk that long road. Queen stood for a long while staring at the lamp. She looked at the partition above the lamp, at the picture which had written on it, *God Save Our Gracious King*. Thrown over the top of this picture was her mother's chaplet, the cross resting on the king's forehead. Queen wasn't really *seeing* the picture. She was thinking. Wondering who and who was going to make that walk to River Sallee with her tomorrow morning. Who else was going up? In her hand was the old, torn dress that her mother no longer wore and which she was about to spread out on the floor over the other things already there. Queen walked to the door, her dress band trailing. She had already undone the fastener at the back, and the dress was drooping, baring one bony shoulder.

"Mammie! Cousin Liza goin up tomorrow too?"

"Yes. She goin to call for you early in the morning. You say you prayers yet?"

"No, Mammie. I goin an say it now."

Queen changed quickly, knelt down, bent her forehead to touch the sofa, and prayed aloud: "Gentle Jesus, meek and mild, look upon a little child!"

She lifted her head and looked at the crucifix over the bed. "Papa God, help me to grow up into a big strong girl for me please. God, don't let me die tonight or any other night please. Bless Mammie and Cousin Dinah and Maisie and Mark. Make the walk tomorrow not hard please and don't let me and Cousin Liza meet anything in the road. Bless Cousin Liza too and let me have a lot a lot of money when I get big, please, God. Amen."

Still on her knees, Queen lifted her head.

"Good-night, Mammie."

"Good-night, chile. Turn down de lamp low."

"You not goin an sleep now, Mammie?"

"Yes. I just takin a little rest fus."

"Well, come and rest inside here, non, Mammie."

"Queenie, hush you mouth an sleep now. You pray already. Stop talkin like dat after you pray."

About an hour later, Faith, having eaten some of the bake from the safe and allowed the day's weariness to seep from her body through the boards to the still, hot air outside, walked heavily up the two board steps and into the house. There was some noise as she passed briefly through the watching darkness; a cat scuttling, perhaps, a dog scratching, a frog hopping by. Faith didn't look around. She hardly heard them. The sounds of darkness were always with her. Nothing strange.

Her young Queen was fast asleep, mouth slightly open, left hand thrown wide and resting on the floor outside the bedding, the cover partly twisted around her waist. The mother stood staring for a moment, then stooped to straighten the piece of bedding which served as a cover and pulled it up over her daughter's body. She turned to the sofa, then sank to her knees and bowed her head. Faith spoke no words aloud. She talked silently to the Lord. Her last waking thoughts were, Today is the madam party. I wonder if Mr Mark suit. . .

When Cousin Liza pounded at the door on that February morning in 1931, it was still the time of day when everyone whispered. Dark and cold in the kind of way it never was when the sun came up. It was still the time that the trees claimed as their own as they whispered secrets against the sky. They whispered something when Cousin Liza knocked, and she looked around nervously, but they became silent then.

The walk from St David's to River Sallee was a long and arduous one. It was best started early. Queen was still half-asleep when they left. But the way Cousin Liza walked, sleep didn't stay around for long. It departed with a frown and an irritated yawn. Wide awake after the first few minutes, Queen pushed the straw hat more firmly on to her hand, held the cloth bag securely on her shoulder, and kept running to keep up.

Cousin Liza had planned to start at five a.m. She must have made a mistake, though. Day was a long time coming, and the trees and the shadows and the frogs shouting in the drains kept insisting that it was still their time. They had been walking for more than two hours when the first glimmers of dawn appeared. At one time they had passed a house in which a light burned brightly. The man inside may have seen them, for the door was open. Into the darkness he shouted, "Wey dis two woman goin at this hour?" and his feet pounded on the floor as though he were coming out to get them. If she had known who he was, Cousin Liza wouldn't be afraid, but you never knew with people who were up that late. They could be doing all sorts of things with the supernatural. So Cousin Liza pulled Queen and they pelted off down the road, feet flying on the broken pavement. After this, Queen was afraid, for she realized that Cousin Liza, too, walked with fear.

At one point, when they got to a place where the road forked in three directions, Queen did not find it strange to see a cock standing in the middle of the crossroads. She was accustomed to fowls. It was only when she felt Cousin Liza jerk her towards the drain that she froze. They passed in the drain at the side of the road and walked without looking back. Cousin Liza did not have to tell Queen it would be dangerous to look back. She *knew*! Queen's whole body was heart. It pounded with a painful thump that resounded in her steps. Her bare feet felt neither the stones in the road nor the effect of the miles. Suspended in a twilight between conscious thought and puppetry, she knew neither where she was nor where she was going to. And worse was yet to come.

They were making their way through a track in Hope, St Andrew's, which could cut down on the distance to Grenville town, when Queen pulled convulsively on Cousin Liza's hand. Liza's twenty-eight years on what she knew of earth had not given her the fearlessness that Queen expected her to possess. Queen stood, one hand now on top of the straw hat the brim of which framed her round face, the thick black plaits sticking out on both sides, the other hand lifted towards the distance. Liza froze. With a taut, tense movement she boxed down the child's shaking finger.

"Don't point," she whispered hoarsely. "Bite you finger," she remembered to add.

On the hill next to the gravestone, something moved. No house was in sight. Above the watching women, the branches of the trees leaned across and linked leaves, touching each other caressingly in the stillness of the morning. The thing moved again. A pale light from a wandering, waning moon flashed across it and the thing bent towards them, beckoning, encouraging them forward. Queen's arms were thrown around Liza and she clung tightly, mouth open, the breath pushed from her throat to her lips in audible sobs, eyes wide with terror. Liza, body and hands hard with fear, held on to the child. She uttered no prayer with her lips, none in her heart. Her whole body was a throbbing prayer. Papa God! Papa God!

Whatever it was was quiet now. Still, no longer beckoning. The leaves above, too, had stopped their furtive caressing. Liza's feet moved. One quiet dragging step. Two, the left foot following because it couldn't go off on its own in a different direction. T-h-r-ee. Queen's body, with no will or separate identity of its own, did whatever Liza's did. The thing bent towards them. Queen screamed. With sudden decision, Liza dragged Queen along the edge of the track. And as this living fear drew level with the taunting thing above, it stopped in unbelief.

"Jesus!" said Cousin Liza. "Jesus!"

The plantain leaf bowed again.

Queen, sobbing now with the release of terror, clung to Cousin Liza's hand and was dragged along the track. Her destination was daylight. It was only when the sky lightened and she could hear cocks crowing and see people moving about in the yards that she became once more a conscious being. She started to feel tired and told Cousin Liza that she wanted to rest.

They had been walking for seven hours and were in Paradise with the sun blazing down upon their heads when the bus from St David's passed them on its way to Sauteurs. Queen ate her coconut-drops and stretched out her tongue at the people looking back from the back seat of the bus. Years later, an older Queen learnt that the threepence she and Cousin Liza had spent to buy things to eat along the way could have paid a bus fare. Even though she had known then, the knowledge would have been of little use. Faith would have called her damn lazy if she had suggested going by bus.

"Liza, girl, you must be tired. How you do? Come, come, come girl. Come an sit down. Queenie, child, me mind did tell you me mother would send you up today."

Cousin Kamay accepted their arrival as a matter of course.

"Constance, put some food in the bowl for Cousin Liza. Go in the kitchen an see what you get to eat, Queen. It have food dey. Help yourself to what you want. How you mother?"

"She well, tanks."

"'Well, tanks' *who*?"

"She well tanks, Cousin Kamay."

Cousin Kamay watched her. "Hm! You gettin big! These children nowadays you have to keep a eye on them yes. Go an see what you get to eat!"

The journey was over. In two days' time, after being about her mother's business, eleven-year-old Queen would leave again with Cousin Liza or whoever else happened to be making the trip to St David's. The one thing that remained to haunt her was the knowledge that the return trip would have to be made in darkness, when the sun was down, and when those who had to walk always made their journeys.

Grace Nichols

1950–

B orn in Georgetown, Guyana, she took a Diploma in Communications from the University of Guyana, taught (1967–70), was a
reporter and journalist and worked in government information
services before migrating to Britain in 1977. She now lives in Lewes, East
Sussex, with poet John Agard and her daughters. She has given readings
of her poetry widely and published in numerous publications, including
Artrage, City Limits, Third Eye, Frontline, Ambit, Kunapipi and Poetry
Review. Her cycle of poems about Caribbean womanhood, i is a long
memoried woman (1983) won the Commonwealth Poetry Prize, since
when she has published other collections including The Fat Black Woman's Poems (1984) and Lazy Thoughts of a Lazy Woman (1989). She has
also written books for children, and a novel, Whole of a Morning Sky
(1986), which draws on her childhood memories to recreate vividly a
Georgetown to which political turmoil comes, with strikes, riots and
racial clashes intensifying the pattern of daily family life.

Praise Song for My Mother

You were
water to me
deep and bold and fathoming

You were
moon's eye to me
sunrise to me
rise and warm and streaming

You were
the fishes red gill to me
the flame tree's spread to me
the crab's leg/the fried plantain smell
                              replenishing replenishing

Go to your wide futures, you said

Skin-Teeth

Not every skin-teeth
is a smile "Massa"

if you see me smiling
when you pass

if you see me bending
when you ask

Know that I smile
know that I bend
only the better
to rise and strike
again.

Grease

Grease steals in like a lover
over the body of my oven.
Grease kisses the knobs
of my stove.
Grease plays with the small
hands of my spoons.
Grease caresses the skin
of my table-cloth,
Getting into my every crease.
Grease reassures me that life
is naturally sticky.

Grease is obviously having an affair with me.

From

Whole of A Morning Sky

L URLEENA, the new girl who come to live in the house at the side of the
passageway opposite Mr Castello. Lurleena, tall, thin, dark with short neat
plaits around her head. Lurleena with her wide smile and slightly crooked teeth.
Lurleena with her bad temper. The two of you become inseparable. You live at
her house. She at yours. "The two of you like batty and poe," her grandmother
would say. "The two of you too bewitched," your mother would say. You like the
same kinds of books; schoolgirl and superman comics, Enid Blyton, Nancy Drew
mysteries. You play concerts on her bed, using the bedstead as stage, dancing on
the springs, driving her grandmother wild. Then the two of you would get to the
window, throwing tiny bricks on Mr Castello rooftop, ducking and giggling when
he come out and start to curse. Sometimes you play old higue. You like being
the ole higue, glad for the chance to come hobbling along in an old sheet, then
quietly pulling back the covers off Lurleena and nibbling at her neck. She would
start shrieking and laughing the moment you reach the bed.

Sometimes you play husband and wife, spreading ricebags under the steps,
shutting off the sides with pieces of boards and boxes so no one could see.
Lying quietly together in a tangle of legs.

CHAPTER XI

I VY Payne groaned, turned, lifted herself up, he elbows supporting her body on the
hard fibre mattress that lay on a bed of wooden planks. She stayed that way for a
few nodding moments, then gently hoisted herself over the sleeping limbs of her
children and stumbled, not quite fully awake, into the dark passageway that led to
the kitchen. On her way she passed a small bedroom in which her eldest son and his
wife and children were sleeping. Her second son, Vibert, had again slept out for she
couldn't see his long, awkward frame curled up on the bedding on the
drawing-room floor.

Ivy didn't feel like going down to the yard bathroom and contented herself
with splashing cold water on her face at the back window, scrubbing her teeth
with some kitchen salt and rinsing the night away.

Today was Friday and she must hurry down to the abattoir before all the
good runners and blood for her black pudding were sold out. She had taken
up with the business ever since her trawler fishing husband had died four years
ago, leaving her with the six children. After his death she was forced to sell their
Broad Street cakeshop and take up residence in one of the Ramsammys' run-
down little houses in the Charlestown yard. She supported herself and children
with the black pudding money and from what she made at her weekly Saturday
night dances. She couldn't depend on her eldest son for anything, now that he
had his own family. But she did get some extra help from her manfriend, Cyril.

Cyril, a plumpish middle-aged man, came about twice a week. On these occasions Ivy made up a bed for the other children on the floor outside with Vibert so they would have some privacy. Cyril always came very late at nights, picking his way around the sleeping bodies, and left in the morning before they woke up. He himself worked on the waterfront as a stevedore and his contributions to Ivy's family came in useful.

Vibert hated the best bone in Cyril for reasons peculiar to himself. At nineteen he was sullen and brooding and at nights would lie staring at the quiet face of his father's photograph which his mother had carefully hung on the drawing-room wall. He could hear the shaking of the bed in his brother's room. He could endure that. What he couldn't stand was the sight of his mother's locked door and the knowledge that Cyril was inside there with her.

The thought of Cyril's smooth body and slick hair next to his mother's healthy darkness aroused such a fury in him. He felt she had no shame. He remembered the way she had carried on at his father's funeral, throwing herself across the coffin, but that was like a woman all over, he thought, quick to forget. Now he had to restrain himself from kicking the shaky door in and dragging the man out of the house, down the steps and right through the passageway. Also the way his mother had of putting aside Cyril's food first in the glass bowl made him sour inside.

Ever since the night that Vibert had ripped away her nightdress Ivy felt that some indefinable thread in the relationship between mother and son had been severed. That was the last time she had tried beating him.

Vibert would always remember the look of outraged astonishment on her face, her tears afterwards. He didn't know what had possessed him that night. It had nothing to do with her shouting that he had no ambition or the blows she rained about his head and neck. In the act of deliberately ripping her nightdress he thought he was showing her the complete disrespect which he felt he now had for her.

Ivy lit the kerosene stove in the kitchen, then hurried back to the bedroom to dress. When she came out she added three heaping potspoons of sugar to the water on the stove, unplugged two tiny balls of paper from a tin of evaporated milk and poured a little in. She didn't trust her biggest girl, June, with the milk. She lifted down a basket of bread which she had baked the day before and placed a tin of margarine beside it. June would give the others their bread and tea later. Ivy helped herself only to a cup of the hot thin tea as she didn't want to get wind in her stomach, then she tied her head with a blue headtie, picked up her red shopping bag and hurried out of the house.

She picked her way along the passageway, stepping on the odd pieces of board precariously laid down. Apart from the clanking of pans which came from Mrs Lall's hut and which only reinforced Ivy's belief that she was haunted, the yard was still asleep. Ivy passed the remaining range rooms, patches of black crouching in the softening dawn, and stepped out into the cool streets.

She walked like a woman filled with sweet life, the red shopping bag with two large brown bottles fitted snugly into the crook of her arm, her cotton shift of red and yellow flowers blowing gently at the knees of her sturdy polished legs. A pale half moon still hovered in the skies and the streets had hardly begun to stir. Passing a rumshop, Ivy spat at the scent of urine that would dissipate itself in the sunshine later in the day.

She liked to start a day like this, untouched by the hungry, peevish faces of her children or the bawling of her son's baby. On days like this she felt strong, basking in her ability to cut and contrive and to make a living for her children. It wasn't good to depend on any man and, even though she appreciated Cyril's help, she intended to make life her own way.

Ivy's thoughts continued to flow in serene contentment until she neared the Stabroek Market with all the buses lined up from the night before. Then it all came back. The news about the general strike last night.

Ivy stopped in her tracks, the red bag slipped down her arm to her fingers. "Oh, Christ! I forget everything bout dis kiss-me-ass strike," the words broke involuntarily from her lips in a strangled kind of way. "Shit," she went on, sucking her teeth, "don't tell me dis going mean I kyant get no runners and blood to buy." Ivy looked around in agitation as if seeking someone to tell her just what the strike would mean.

When she had heard the news from her eldest son, Marcus, last night, the thought that it would affect her black pudding had never entered her head for some reason. Now realization was beginning to dawn.

Ivy stood there in a fit of indecision for a full five minutes. Across by the market she could see a few vendors standing uncertainly around their boxes of produce. Then she decided that she wouldn't turn back. She would go down to the abattoir and beg someone there to help her. There must be someone there, one of the men she joked with week after week. She didn't mind waiting the entire morning just as long as she got some blood and runners. She had come to depend too much on it, not only the money which made things stretch far into the week, but on the activity itself, the stuffing and the boiling and the cutting in a kitchen full of the scents of thyme and peppers, while every few minutes someone came around to the back door for a "fifty cents black pudding" or "a dollar black pudding".

Ivy was just in time to see the night watchman rolling his bicycle away from the faded government abattoir building as she swung the corner into the street. He was moving away from her and she raised her arms and began to clap frantically, calling, "Hee-ooo, hee-ooo."

He heard her and turned his bicycle around. "Is what you doing here, girl? You en hear bout de strike?" he asked as he came near her.

"Jesus Christ," said Ivy.

"Is where you living, girl?" he chided her.

"But I must get mih blood and runners," said Ivy. "You kyant help me?"

"Me!" he exclaimed, "Sista, I would advise you to go home. You wasting yuh time waiting here. Nobody coming to work here dis morning. You see me. Is home I going home. No more nightshift till I hear dis strike call off. I would advise you to go home. When dem abattoir people come down here they en coming to work. They coming fuh demonstrate like de union say. I been at the meeting yesterday an I know what I talking bout."

Ivy was only half listening to him. Already she could visualize how hard the coming week would be if she failed. But when the watchman suggested slyly that she meet him later that afternoon, her eyes returned swiftly to the present, and with a "haul yuh ole tail," she sent him riding slowly away.

Ivy could feel the fingers of the sun eating into the hollow of her back, could feel the cool little trickles of perspiration running down her neck. She had been waiting for hours outside the abattoir along with four other women, all regular black puddings makers, all sticking around to see if they would have any luck. So far no luck.

The workers inside the compound who kept arriving in ones and twos were there to picket, not work. Some squatted in front of the main doorway in the shade while the bolder ones walked slowly up and down to display the placards pinned on their chests. Fresh from yesterday's bidding by the union, they were determined to play their part.

Ivy went up to one of the women carrying placards to find out exactly what was going on. The woman whose sign read, "Workers Will Die For Their Rights", simply said, "Is up to youall if you want to wait but I don't think the abattoir opening up today."

The other black pudding women didn't seem as put out as Ivy. In fact they seemed to be enjoying the novelty of seeing women like themselves strolling up and down with placards.

"Come, Ivy girl, what you going do?" they advised her with good-humoured resignation. "Don't let lil black pudding money kill yuh."

"We have to do something to bring down this bold face cammanist," Mavis, a hardened woman, philosophized.

Ivy sucked her teeth. "What de hell you know bout cammanist?" she said contemptuously.

"But how yuh mean, mih dear darling," retorted Mavis, "dem cammanists does take away everything. Down to yuh own quarter pound here," she said, putting her hand protectively between her legs, "yuh can't call yuh own."

A burst of belly laughter followed.

"Mind yuh jokes, Mavis, yuh know I have a weak bladder," another woman admonished.

After a while Ivy detached herself from the women and went up to the man leaning against the door. She had seen him several times before giving orders inside the abattoir.

"God, this woman ent mean to give up," said the man. "Look, lady, you don't understand a strike on? The store close. Nobody working today, an I can't help you. You going just have to do without de lil black-pudding money this week."

Midday, and the sun glinting harshly on galvanized zinc roofs; glistening on the heavy brown of the Demerara River; wilting the heads of hibiscus flowers; beating down on the mass demonstration at the parade ground, and on the different pickets being staged in front of government buildings around Georgetown.

The police, responding to the government's ban on all public meetings, were on their way, not so much out of concern or sympathy with the government, but just complying with orders from their chief. Truckloads of them with batons and shields and teargas began to arrive at the various scenes.

Outside the Ministry of Labour, a crowd had already entrenched itself. Women were sitting flat out in front of the building, thighs spread out before them like giant hams. As the black-clad figures hopped out of the police truck, the women broke into the workers' song: "We shall not, no, we shall not be moved. We shall not, no, we shall not be moved. Just like the trees standing by the water, we shall not be moved."

The women indeed looked as if they couldn't be moved, massive flesh sunk below, making themselves as heavy as possible. The police regarded them hesitantly. Each face wore the same taunting provocative expression, daring to be moved.

But the police had to do something. Two young policemen each placed a hand under the sweating armpits of a woman and heaved. A tall woman got up and deliberately threw herself against one of the policemen, twisting the angle of his hat, and turning to the crowd: "Yuh see. Yuh see. Yuh see how he push me?"

"Yes, we see. We see. We see how he push yuh," the crowd chanted back.

At the electricity company the mood was ugly as crowds sent bricks and bottles flying into the building in protest at the work still taking place inside by some staff members.

"All you scabs, bring yuh tail out here," was the cry. As the bricks and bottles increased the police moved in. People rushed madly to escape the sudden fumes of teargas, stumbling into nearby yards for water to wet their faces. A woman cried out, "O God, de gas choking me baby."

Even though the baby recovered, rumour spread that police teargas had just killed a baby. Two babies.

And that was all it took to set gangs of youths who had attached themselves to the pickets and demonstrations kicking over street bins and smashing store windows.

Ivy and Mavis were still on the streets when news reached them that looting had started and the white superintendent of police had just been shot in another part of the city.

"Something been telling me all marning dat dis woulda happen," said Mavis, panting to keep up with Ivy.

From the smaller side streets they could see people swarming out to join the crowds. Ivy even recognized some of the prostitutes who strolled around the Tiger Bay area.

"Wha happen? Wha happen?" she said, running forward a little to stop the man panting heavily towards them on his bicycle. But the man, his dark face oozing perspiration, didn't stop. "Is madness break loose," he said, continuing on his way.

Another man flew by, doubled over his bicycle handles, laden down with all sorts of bags, three shoe boxes clipped on to the carrier at the back of his bike, two new umbrellas still in their plastic cases dangling from the back of his collar.

"Christ!" said Ivy, standing still for a moment and watching the thickening movement of people ahead of her.

As she and Mavis got closer to the crowds and stores, they could see that the looting was in full swing. Men, women and youngsters, looking as if they'd just been through a bad scuffle, emerged from stores with bolts of cloth, shoes, arms full of clothing, anything they could manage to carry. Seeing one rumpled woman stagger past her with arms full of bath towels and nylon panties, Ivy was suddenly filled with the same madness. Good underwear is a luxury.

With Mavis' bony fingers clutching her arm, she half ran to the other side of the road and pressed herself against the mob of people now trying to get into another store, Singh & Sons Ltd. Pushed from behind, her own body was squashed up against the hardness of a man's wet back, the scent of his sweat filling her nostrils.

The next moment she was swept into the store, minus Mavis on her arm. The only thought in Ivy's head was to grab as much as possible. Things like this didn't happen every day. With a fearful exhilaration she was thrust again, this time with more than a dozen other people, into an aisle packed with brand new clothing and a counter with bolt upon bolt of cloth.

Ivy decided to forget the bolts of cloth. They would only hinder her, she needed her hands. But she must hurry, more and more people coming in, snatching left right and centre.

A man chucked her out of the way; "When you getting freeness, lady, you can't pick and choose."

Possessed, Ivy began to grab. About a dozen negligees from an open box on the top shelf; another open box of men's shirts; a handful of half-slips from below; some brassières. Shirts under her arm and other things stuffed into her red bag, Ivy looked further down the line to a bottom shelf of lacy panties disappearing with lightning swiftness, some into a man's shirt front, some into a woman's bosom. By the time Ivy got to the shelf only crumpled plastic wrapping remained.

The store was hot and crowded now with people snatching just about anything, even two left-side shoes. At the back a raging tug-o-war was going on for bolts of cloth.

Ivy, who was almost being suffocated, pushed her way through on to the pavement, her neatly brushed, back-pressed hair standing in tufts all over her head.

You wonder about her, Miss Sheila. Did she really throw that acid on Mr Percy face? Because she look so quiet. If she did, did he really forgive her or only pretending? Why she didn't go out like the other women to the shops and stores and market? Why only looking through her window, dressed up, with that smile on her face? One day she ask you to buy a pack of biscuits from the shop for her. You run up her clean wooden steps quickly, but you can't really see inside her house properly. She hand you the money at the door and when you come back let you keep the three cents change.

But one day you discover you can see into her house, at least into her drawing-room, from a small round hole in your toilet. Sometimes you peep at her and she don't even know. Sometimes she'd walk around in a pink half-slip alone and you see her nice big heavy breasts, just a shade lighter than the rest of her skin. You stare, wondering about she and Mr Percy, touching your own tiny breasts, only a little bigger than the halves of a twin guenip.

CHAPTER XII

IT was Gem who heard the urgency in the voice of the old Indian woman next door.

"Nabe, nabe!"

Perhaps it was the urgency in the voice that made her drop her book so quickly and rush to the back window.

"You want something, Mrs Lall?" Gem inquired breathlessly, sensing instinctively that something was wrong.

"Tell yuh mudda to look quick," Mrs Lall managed, leaning heavily against the wooden paling, a strange ashy look about her face.

"Mummy, Mrs Lall say to look quick," Gem called out, startled by the fright she saw in the old woman's face.

Clara came in swiftly, wiping her soapy hands on the end of her dress, her brow knitting into its familiar pucker whenever she suspected something was wrong.

"Mrs Lall," she pushed her head out of the window in a half-confiding, half-alarmed manner.

"Nabe, nabe, the town pan fire," the words came out in a plaintive cry.

Clara's face paled. "Fire, which fire?" she asked in bewilderment.

"Owh, nabe, dem ah burn down de whole town. Dem thiefing up everything in de stores and market dem. Ah prapa run, nabe. Look to de front window, de fire all bout de sky."

At this point Gem listened no further. She ran to the front window and was confronted by the unmistakable smoke and flames blotting the northern skies. Her cry sent her father, who was resting inside, leaping up, and Dinah and Anthony too. Behind them Clara was witnessing the scene, three distinctive fires, in quiet amazement.

"God, to think all this going on and we don't know a word," her voice held a note of accusation. Archie had turned the radio off earlier in the day, a natural act of conservation on his part.

The news of the fire and looting seemed to have reached the rest of the Charlestown yard at the same time, for moments later, snatches of excited conversation could be heard all around the yard.

Dinah and Clara went back to the kitchen window to listen to the rest of Mrs Lall's distraught outpourings. The Ramsammys closed up their rumshop quickly and Mrs Ramsammy hurried down from the big house to join Mrs Lall at the paling, walking in quick, agitated steps.

The two children, Gem and Anthony, bounded around the house. The sight of the flames seemed to have released a mad surge within them as they grappled with the two emotions, excitement and fear.

"Control yourselves," snapped Archie as they collided with him in the passageway. But a grimness had settled over his own countenance. When he switched back on the radio only a solemn interlude of music was coming through.

Ivy Payne's children were all out at the front of the road; only Jeanette came across crying for her Mammy, and Clara placed an arm around her waist and told her that her Mammy was sure to come back just now.

For the rest of the afternoon the Walcotts remained at their front window. The rest of the yard population kept drifting in and out, standing around with the growing number of people gathered on the grassy sides of the road to watch the looters going by, or simply to stare at the unruly billowings of smoke and flames licking the skies.

"Guianese people really stupid," observed Dinah contemptuously, her hair in brown paper screws. "Look how they burning down their own country, and look at this fool..." she continued, referring to Crazy-Mannie, the black man who spent most of his time sitting on a box outside the rumshop, plucking out his eyebrows.

Crazy-Mannie kept coming and going, giving everyone a running commentary on what was happening downtown.

"Santos gone," he announced in a loud dramatic voice, throwing up his hands in the air.

Fifteen minutes later he returned. "Kirpilany gonnnne...Singh and Brothers gonnnnne...Bookers gonnnne" – gonnnne, meaning under fire, and at the pronouncement of each "gonnnne" a wave of mounting murmurings came from the watching people.

The people cheered as a short wiry man, his dark face swimming in sweat, came by, pushing a medium-sized refrigerator laid across the handle bar of his bicycle.

"Today is black people birthday," he called out, the muscles in his arms steeling against any shift in his luxurious burden. Others followed with bolts of cloth on their heads, chairs, tables, stereo sets.

Dinah wanted to go out to see some of the action in the streets but Clara was adamant. She could have insisted, but seeing the anxiety on her mother's face she gave a resigned but not unhappy suck-teeth and retired to bed with a book, getting up every once in a while to see the progress of the flames, sparing a thought for Hartley and what he might be doing.

In spite of the upheaval, there was a quality of unreality about the hot, almost oppressively bright afternoon, like something out of a Western film, the way the sky was calmly receiving the growing procession of flames.

"Aiee," said Archie, as he watched more and more people deserting the sides of the road to join the crowds sweeping downtown for a share in the goodies. "Well, I choose a bad time to move to this place," he admitted to Clara, rubbing his forehead, "I tell you, when the British pull out of here, it's going to be hell to pay."

"The British, the British," muttered Dinah inside, "he's a real colonialist."

There is something holy about Georgetown at dusk. The Atlantic curling the shoreline, brown and laced with foam; further out, rough and glowing faintly in the last rays of the afternoon sunlight. The Atlantic, vast and overwhelming, but so native, as if it belongs to Guiana alone. The Atlantic, kept out by the solid grey sea wall where the Georgetown people love to meet. The shadow of the ocean and the shield of the wall make a perfect foil for lovers locked below. At the edge of the jetty a man throwing his castnet to the deceptively calm water below is framed against the horizon and a little further inland, the white cathedral and the wooden houses cast peaceful shadows on to the avenues and streets, the trade winds gentle at this hour.

Dusk tonight over the city of wood is all dancing, orange-black flames, billowing like a biblical catastrophe.

Some of the Charlestown people were already fetching their belongings out on to the street in a bid to save something in case the fires reached them.

Archie, who regarded most of them as foolish people out to dramatize every situation, paid no attention to his children's pleas to let them start fetching out their own furniture.

"The big heavy piano alone gun take an age to lift out," said Gem in despair. "Is what we waiting for?" The earlier excitement had long receded, leaving an icy coldness in her hands. She and Anthony kept up their vigil at the window, counting all the fires they could see, making guesses as to how close they were, how long before reaching their house. "That one look like it by the jail now," said little Anthony, "three more corners and then is our house."

They had to keep calm, Archie thought, as he switched back on the radio. A reporter was describing the worst of all the fires which began at a Drug Company on Lombard Street and was sweeping everything in its wake. The work stoppage at the electricity company meant that the mains were without water and the fire brigades were grappling with water pumps in the nearby canals.

Archie listened to the crackling explosions in the background as the reporter described the exquisite colours of the flames caused by the chemicals, the blues, the greens, the pinks.

Then he heard a sound coming from under the house and rushed to the back window. Two figures were fetching some heavy equipment through his backgate. It was Marcus and Vibert, taking a short cut with the afternoon's spoils. Ivy had already come back and Clara had sent Jeanette over.

"Well, that is what I call presumption to its height, man," he said to Clara, "coming through my yard with stolen goods. I don't know how people could be so barefaced."

"Archie, I have more to think about than people fetching things through yard," cried Clara vexedly.

Then Mohabir came on the air. He said he had asked the Governor to send for British troops but that Governor Rothschild had only sent a cable, telling them to be on standby.

Clara, who no longer worried to hide her fear from the children, said, "But is what the hell he waiting for, for the whole blasted place to burn down? And we can't even see Conrad," she added, thinking how much they could all do with his dangerous, reassuring presence.

They had forgotten all about Mrs Lall. The children giggled nervously as her short, stout frame came swiftly and silently into the yard, carrying a brown bag stuffed with clothes. Her voice floated up before her thinly as she reached the steps, "Nabe nabe."

Mrs Lall was shaking her head from side to side when they opened the door for her.

She looked shorter and older under the bright fluorescent light. Her thin mouth which gave her a sneering appearance merely looked pathetic now and she seemed like a woman about to make some desperate move. "Teacha Teacha," she said to Archie, holding on to the back of a chair to support herself.

Archie, who responded to names of that nature, softened a bit, but his voice when it came was still matter-of-fact, "So you're here," he said, eyeing her brown bag suspiciously. "Well, we have to wait and see what happens. This is what Guiana has come to."

"I love black people," wailed Mrs Lall, clutching at Clara's hand distractedly, "I really love dose people."

"Don't distress yourself too much, Mrs Lall," said Clara, "All we can do is leave everything in God's hands."

As soon as Archie went inside Mrs Lall began to plead, "Owh nabe, I-yuh must tek me with I-yuh when you going, me na go give no trouble."

"We don't know what we doing yet, nabe," said Clara.

But around eight o'clock it was decided that Dinah and the children should spend the night at their Cousin Wilma in Agricola, a small village on the East Bank, just outside Georgetown. Dinah could be depended on to get them there safely.

You, Dinah and Anthony walk quickly, taking short cuts through some of the quieter back streets. Groups of people still standing about the roads gazing up at the skies. As you walk you keep looking back at the skies too, counting all the orange blazes like billowing bottle lamps in the sky. You feel like a girl in one of those schoolgirl comics. A heroine looking back at her city in ruins.

As you walk, with a bag of clothes hanging from your shoulder, nothing tell you that you'd ever see your home again. The rocking-chair, the settee, the big piano, the small coconut palm at the front of the yard and that purple plant, the gooseberry tree. All would be gone, maybe the entire Charlestown yard, nothing remaining in the morning but the blackened earth. But you feel calm. Full of a calm, frightened excitement.

"If the worst comes to the worst," Dinah say, "Mummy and Daddy will follow, bringing Mrs Lall, I suppose."

CHAPTER XIII

ALTHOUGH she had received no word about their coming, Cousin Wilma, who was a distant cousin, welcomed them as if she's been expecting them all afternoon. She lived at the end of a long dark yard in a small house, almost hidden by a tremendous guenip tree which seemed to be guarding the house in its immense shadow.

Cousin Wilma, who was in her mid-forties and due to be married soon, was a seamstress, a plump, light brown woman with wavy hair and eyes that spoke of many calamities. Within the last week a zinc sheet had come off her kitchen roof, she had twisted her ankle and her bicycle was stolen. "I don't know, it just seem to be my luck," she would say.

Her house, which gave off an earthy, musty scent was strewn with ends of cloth, strips of blue, patches of green and flowered triangles. Her bed was covered with half-finished dresses, fashion books and new, folded materials as yet untouched by her femininely fashioning hands. She could never complete anything in time though, so the people who gave her work usually lied that they needed the particular dress or skirt a day or two before they actually did. In any case, they still had to undergo hours of sulky waiting while she stitched, pinned and hemmed, and related the incident that had prevented her from completing it.

Tonight she was thirsty for news of the fire which she couldn't see because of the big factory buildings at the head of the main road. Dinah told her all about it and she responded, "But is whuh we coming to nuh," in her soft, rounded voice which flowed between English and Creole, as the mood swayed her.

She cleared the bed by gathering everything up and dropping it loosely into a sheet on the floor. Dinah and Gem could sleep with her on the bed and Anthony on the carpet in the corner. She wasn't making her own bridal dress, she said, because it was unlucky for a bride to do that. It was a good thing she had some bakes left back. She made them some Ovaltine to go with the bakes and they devoured them hungrily.

Then she went on talking. She needed reassurance about marrying James. She didn't know whether she was doing the right thing at her age. She had met him one afternoon as she was crossing a street in Georgetown. He was driving his car and had pulled up to let her pass, then he had turned around and offered her a lift. Dinah had met him only once and thought he was horrible, a big vulgar-looking man of about sixty with flat, squashy lips in a sour, pompous face. But she didn't say any of these things. Instead she just listened and smiled as if this marriage was going to be the most natural and beautiful thing. Cousin Wilma's house seemed miles away from the frantic burning world she had left an hour ago.

Archie, Clara and Mrs Lall kept their vigil. The fires did seem to be looking more under control and at about five o'clock the next morning the British troops arrived. The Governor had sent another cable ordering them in.

As the skies gave way to greyish dawn, Mrs Lall slowly made her way back to her own home. She didn't look relieved but merely like one whose fate had been suspended. Although they hadn't slept a wink, on the morning after the fires both Clara and Archie felt in lighter spirits. Perhaps it was the knowledge of the sober-looking British soldiers in the country.

With a calm air of propriety the troops were now guarding the charred, smoking ruins around the city which they had already cordoned off – what was left of big department stores and shops and buildings. It would take at least a week before anyone could venture to search among the twisted black wreckage of mattress springs and bicycle frames, chromium tables and steel chests and other red hot junk – iron and black metal skeletons, the only survivors of a death by fire.

Throughout the week people left their homes specifically to see the sight, standing around in chastened little crowds, staring in awe at the disfigurements. Staring too at the green-clad soldiers whose presence, more than anything, said that what had happened was a really big thing.

The police began their laborious and almost fruitless task of searching for stolen goods, prising up the floor boards of the homes of people whom they suspected. But everything, it seemed, was too well buried or hidden. A curfew too came into being every night from ten.

But in spite of everything, things began to resume a more normal rhythm. Many modifications were made in the budget. The strike was called off. People were going to work again, except for those who had lost their jobs with the fires. Buses were running. Factories were humming.

On Dinah's first morning back after the fires, Hartley came in late and threw down his haversack.

"We never learn. We never learn," he said in despair at her table. "This is just what the Americans want. We've played right into their bloody hands. Now we have the British troops to take care of the natives who can't take care of themselves."

And as the laws of nature would have it, every action has a reaction: so too the coming of the soldiers on the female section of the population. Within a few weeks of their coming soldiers and young women were being married, no less than three or four couples every week in the city's various churches.

The Sunday papers gave their full blessings to these weddings which were een as a tribute to the beauty of Guianese womanhood. Week after week they carried the smiling photographs of each couple and the accompanying tender story of soldier and local girl who had fallen in love at first sight.

One man boasted how he was able to marry off all his daughters in the space of a few months and more and more people flocked the churches to witness the sight of meek, blond- and dark-haired bridegrooms being whisked away by smiling local girls. A hardy British soldier even managed to drag one of the well-known Georgetown prostitutes to the altar and some of the "unluckier" women gnashed their teeth, marriage to a white foreigner being synonymous with a life of luxury and ease.

Then there was Cousin Wilma's wedding. It was decided that, since her yard was so long and treacherous and the church in which she was being married was so close to the Walcotts', she should dress from their home.

And though it was the smallest of weddings it seemed that the traditional confusion would still reign. It was a seven o'clock wedding but up to six-thirty the bridal dress hadn't arrived as yet. Clara combed out her hair hurriedly, and started out for the seamstress who lived a ten-minute walk away, leaving Wilma in her underwear on the verge of tears.

She met the seamstress about halfway down the street, a short, dark, god-fearing woman who broke out in cold sweat at the sight of Mrs Walcott. There had been some mishap, she explained in an agonized fashion. She had finished Wilma's dress at twelve o'clock the night before and had it all wrapped up to deliver early this morning. But her eldest daughter, without looking inside the parcel, had handed it to the young boy who had come early this morning to collect his sister's dress. The sister was also going to a wedding. She was on her way to remedy the mishap, she explained, breathing hard, her eyes pleading for understanding. "For God sake, hurry then," said Clara, and at these words the seamstress broke into a run.

Back at the Walcotts' house, a group of women were standing at the gate even though nobody knew how they had heard of the wedding. At a quarter to seven a grey car containing Wilma's elderly cousin drove up to the gate and honked twice. He was a small-chested man, dressed in an impressive grey suit with a neatly folded white handkerchief at his breastpocket. Today he was the father giver, and his face reflected the task.

Some of the women who were standing at the head of the bridge went to stare at him through the car window and he regarded them coldly and told the chauffeur to blow his horn again. Gem came running out to tell him that Wilma wasn't ready and that he must come back in about ten minutes. The car drove off with the elderly cousin sitting straight-faced.

At the promptings of the women, Gem explained to them about the dress.

"I don't like the sound of that attall," a plump woman broke out even before Gem had finished speaking, and they turned to give each other knowing looks.

"Something fishy guying on," said another woman eagerly and they began to talk among themselves, putting forward their own reasons as to the delay of the dress. All felt that obeah was involved. All sided with the bride.

Meanwhile, Wilma, who had taken Clara's advice on everything, insisted on wearing foundation make-up and rouge and outlining her nicely shaped brows in heavy black pencil, drawing them down in two arcs which immediately gave her a hooded look. But she felt that she needed a new face to cope with the new identity she was going to assume.

Like many Guianese brides, she looked completely different from her usual self. The smooth texture of her still firm cheeks had taken on a putty-like appearance. Her hair, which had been pressed too straight the day before, fell lank and flat around her skull. Her face looked strained from the constriction of the white corset she had struggled into.

At exactly five minutes to seven the grey car with Aunt Wilma's cousin drove up again and honked. The elderly cousin waited for about a minute then hopped out in vexation and said in a trembling voice, "Doesn't Wilma know the time? It's now," he said, pausing for effect, "two minutes to the hour."

"But is wha is he case?" asked a gruff-voiced woman loudly. "He en know de woman ent get she frack as yet."

"Youall don't have anything better to do," said the cousin, getting back into the car and slamming the door.

"But look de dry up old shrimp," laughed another woman.

Five minutes later the sweat-covered seamstress came hurrying in. As she passed the bridge one of the women said loudly so that she could hear, "They trying to stop de woman from getting she man." The seamstress who felt on the verge of tears herself, silently helped Wilma, who had resigned herself to fate at this stage, into the dress. It was a little tight in the bosom but Clara pressed a prayer book with two long white streamers into Wilma's hand and led her out of the door.

All around Georgetown at this time, there's a rustling among the poorer segments of the population, a burgeoning of new clothes, new shoes, new dresses, new shirts and trousers, nighties and hats: a resurrection of the smaller items looted in the recent fires. People who had been nowhere near the scene of the looting come into little bonanzas through friends of friends, relatives of relatives, and other far-reaching connections.

Deprived little girls are beginning to play around in spanking new dresses; deprived shirt-tail boys in crisp trousers; men and women stepping out in high-priced leather shoes. The clothes are being worn with discretion, as totally new outfits from top to bottom would only arouse suspicion.

Though the bigger luxury goods like fridges and stereos still remain hidden, the smaller items begin to circulate generously, unexpected gifts coming to even those who had condemned the looting.

On Easter Sunday morning blind Mrs Castello, leaning on Mr Castello's arm, stepped out in a pair of bright blue leather wedge-heels which fitted her like a soft glove. Holding on to the pew in church, she sang *Up From the Grave He Arose* in her most soulful of voices. On bended knee she prayed generously, praying not only for her devoted Mr Castello, who had left her by the church door and would later come to collect her, but praying also for the contentious neighbours in the yard, praying for the country ("Lord, stop the strife and troubles and guide us through to peace and harmony"), praying for the gift of her new shoes ("Lord, you don't come but you does send"), Mr Castello himself being blessed with two expensive leather shoes, a left-sided pair, which he mashed down at the heels to accommodate his feet.

These "godsends" or windfalls extended even to the Walcott household. Clara got some cotton print from one of her cousins, Cousin Lucille, and made from it a puff-sleeved dress for Gem, a shirt for Anthony and housecoat for Dinah. Archie got a box of handkerchiefs, and he considered it best not to question the source as he mopped his brow.

The children were all unbelievably proud of these clothes, even Dinah, old as she was. Lying around in her red-flowered housecoat, she felt as though she was wearing a piece of her country.

Gloria Naylor

1950–

B*orn in New York to working-class parents who were migrants from the south, she worked as a telephone operator (1968–75) and subsequently earned a BA in English from Brooklyn College*

(1981) and an MA in Afro-American Studies from Yale University (1983).
She has lectured and held writer-in-residence posts and in 1985 received
a National Endowment for the Arts grant. She is the author of three books
of fiction that locate and explore the experience of Black women in
varied types of communities: The Women of Brewster Place: A Novel in
Seven Stories *(1982, the interwoven stories of seven Black women in a*
Black ghetto) – from which "The Two" is taken – Linden Hills *(1985) and*
Mama Day *(1988).*

From

The Women of Brewster Place

THE TWO

A T first they seemed like such nice girls. No one could remember exactly
when they had moved into Brewster. It was earlier in the year before Ben
was killed – of course, it had to be before Ben's death. But no one remembered
if it was in the winter or spring of that year that the two had come. People often
came and went on Brewster Place like a restless night's dream, moving in and
out in the dark to avoid eviction notices or neighborhood bulletins about the
dilapidated condition of their furnishings. So it wasn't until the two were clocked
leaving in the mornings and returning in the evenings at regular intervals that
it was quietly absorbed that they now claimed Brewster as home. And Brewster
waited, cautiously prepared to claim them, because you never knew about young
women, and obviously single at that. But when no wild music or drunken friends
careened out of the corner building on weekends, and especially, when no
slightly eager husbands were encouraged to linger around that first-floor apartment and run errands for them, a suspended sigh of relief floated around the
two when they dumped their garbage, did their shopping, and headed for the
morning bus.

The women of Brewster had readily accepted the lighter, skinny one. There
wasn't much threat in her timid mincing walk and the slightly protruding teeth
she seemed so eager to show everyone in her bell-like good mornings and
evenings. Breaths were held a little longer in the direction of the short dark
one – too pretty, and too much behind. And she insisted on wearing those thin
Qiana dresses that the summer breeze molded against the maddening rhythm
of the twenty pounds of rounded flesh that she swung steadily down the street.
Through slitted eyes, the women watched their men watching her pass, knowing
the bastards were praying for a wind. But since she seemed oblivious to whether
these supplications went answered, their sighs settled around her shoulders too.
Nice girls.

And so no one even cared to remember exactly when they had moved
into Brewster Place, until the rumor started. It had first spread through the
block like a sour odor that's only faintly perceptible and easily ignored until it

starts growing in strength from the dozen mouths it had been lying in, among clammy gums and scum-coated teeth. And then it was everywhere – lining the mouths and whitening the slips of everyone as they wrinkled up their noses at its pervading smell, unable to pinpoint the source or time of its initial arrival. Sophie could – she had been there.

It wasn't that the rumor had actually begun with Sophie. A rumor needs no true parent. It only needs a willing carrier, and it found one in Sophie. She had been there – on one of those August evenings when the sun's absence is a mockery because the heat leaves the air so heavy it presses the naked skin down on your body, to the point that a sheet becomes unbearable and sleep impossible. So most of Brewster was outside that night when the two had come in together, probably from one of those air-conditioned movies downtown, and had greeted the ones who were loitering around their building. And they had started up the steps when the skinny one tripped over a child's ball and the darker one had grabbed her by the arm and around the waist to break her fall. "Careful, don't wanna lose you now." And the two of them had laughed into each other's eyes and went into the building.

The smell had begun there. It outlined the image of the stumbling woman and the one who had broken her fall. Sophie and a few other women sniffed at the spot and then, perplexed, silently looked at each other. Where had they seen that before? They had often laughed and touched each other – held each other in joy or its dark twin – but where had they seen *that* before? It came to them as the scent drifted down the steps and entered their nostrils on the way to their inner mouths. They had seen that – done that – with their men. That shared moment of invisible communication reserved for two and hidden from the rest of the world behind laughter or tears or a touch. In the days before babies, miscarriages, and other broken dreams, after stolen caresses in barn stalls and cotton houses, after intimate walks from church and secret kisses with boys who were now long forgotten or permanently fixed in their lives – that was where. They could almost feel the odor moving about in their mouths, and they slowly knitted themselves together and let it out into the air like a yellow mist that began to cling to the bricks on Brewster.

So it got around that the two in 312 were *that* way. And they had seemed like such nice girls. Their regular exits and entrances to the block were viewed with a jaundiced eye. The quiet that rested around their door on the weekends hinted of all sorts of secret rituals, and their friendly indifference to the men on the street was an insult to the women as a brazen flaunting of unnatural ways.

Since Sophie's apartment windows faced theirs from across the air shaft, she became the official watchman for the block, and her opinions were deferred to whenever the two came up in conversation. Sophie took her position seriously and was constantly alert for any telltale signs that might creep out around their drawn shades, across from which she kept a religious vigil. An entire week of drawn shades was evidence enough to send her flying around with reports that as soon as it got dark they pulled their shades down and put on the lights. Heads nodded in knowing unison – a definite sign. If doubt was voiced with a "But I pull my shades down at night too," a whispered "Yeah, but you're not *that* way" was argument enough to win them over.

Sophie watched the lighter one dumping their garbage, and she went out-side and opened the lid. Her eyes darted over the crushed tin cans, vegetable peelings, and empty chocolate chip cookie boxes. What do they do with all them chocolate chip cookies? It was surely a sign, but it would take some time to figure that one out. She saw Ben go into their apartment, and she waited and blocked his path as he came out, carrying his toolbox.

"What ya see?" She grabbed his arm and whispered wetly in his face.

Ben stared at her squinted eyes and drooping lips and shook his head slowly. "Uh, uh, uh, it was terrible."

"Yeah?" She moved in a little closer.

"Worst busted faucet I seen in my whole life." He shook her hand off his arm and left her standing in the middle of the block.

"You old sop bucket," she muttered, as she went back up on her stoop. A broken faucet, huh? Why did they need to use so much water?

Sophie had plenty to report that day. Ben had said it was terrible in there. No, she didn't know exactly what he had seen, but you can imagine – and they did. Confronted with the difference that had been thrust into their predictable world, they reached into their imaginations and, using an ancient pattern, weaved them-selves a reason for its existence, because even though it was deceptive enough to try and look as they looked, talk as they talked, and do as they did, it had to have some hidden stain to invalidate it – it was impossible for them both to be right. So they leaned back, supported by the sheer weight of their numbers and comforted by the woven barrier that kept them protected from the yellow mist that enshrouded the two as they came and went on Brewster Place.

Lorraine was the first to notice the change in the people on Brewster Place. She was a shy but naturally friendly woman who got up early, and had read the morning paper and done fifty sit-ups before it was time to leave for work. She came out of her apartment eager to start her day by greeting any of her neighbors who were outside. But she noticed that some of the people who had spoken to her before made a point of having something else to do with their eyes when she passed, although she could almost feel them staring at her back as she moved on. The ones who still spoke only did so after an uncomfortable pause, in which they seemed to be peering through her before they begrudged her a good morning or evening. She wondered if it was all in her mind and she thought about mentioning it to Theresa, but she didn't want to be accused of being too sensitive again. And how would Tee even notice anything like that anyway? She had a lousy attitude and hardly ever spoke to people. She stayed in that bed until the last moment and rushed out of the house fogged-up and grumpy, and she was used to being stared at – by men at least – because of her body.

Lorraine thought about these things as she came up the block from work, carrying a large paper bag. The group of women on her stoop parted silently and let her pass.

"Good evening," she said, as she climbed the steps.

Sophie was standing on the top step and tried to peek into the bag. "You been shopping, huh? What ya buy?" It was almost an accusation.

"Groceries." Lorraine shielded the top of the bag from view and squeezed past her with a confused frown. She saw Sophie throw a knowing glance to the others at the bottom of the stoop. What was wrong with this old woman? Was she crazy or something?

Lorraine went into her apartment. Theresa was sitting by the window, reading a copy of *Mademoiselle*. She glanced up from her magazine. "Did you get my chocolate chip cookies?"

"Why, good evening to you, too, Tee. And how was my day? Just wonderful." She sat the bag down on the couch. "The little Baxter boy brought in a puppy for show-and-tell, and the damn thing pissed all over the floor and then proceeded to chew the heel off my shoe, but, yes, I managed to hobble to the store and bring you your chocolate chip cookies."

Oh, Jesus, Theresa thought, she's got a bug up her ass tonight.

"Well, you should speak to Mrs Baxter. She ought to train her kid better than that." She didn't wait for Lorraine to stop laughing before she tried to stretch her good mood. "Here, I'll put those things away. Want me to make dinner so you can rest? I only worked half a day, and the most tragic thing that went down was a broken fingernail and that got caught in my typewriter."

Lorraine followed Theresa into the kitchen. "No, I'm not really tired, and fair's fair, you cooked last night. I didn't mean to tick off like that; it's just that. . .well, Tee, have you noticed that people aren't as nice as they used to be?"

Theresa stiffened. Oh, God, here she goes again. "What people, Lorraine? Nice in what way?"

"Well, the people in this building and on the street. No one hardly speaks anymore. I mean, I'll come in and say good evening – and just silence. It wasn't like that when we first moved in. I don't know, it just makes you wonder; that's all. What are they thinking?"

"I personally don't give a shit what they're thinking. And their good evenings don't put any bread on my table."

"Yeah, but you didn't see the way that woman looked at me out there. They must feel something or know something. They probably – "

"They, they, they!" Theresa exploded. "You know, I'm not starting up with this again, Lorraine. Who in the hell are they? And where in the hell are we? Living in some dump of a building in this God-forsaken part of town around a bunch of ignorant niggers with the cotton still under their fingernails because of you and your theys. They knew something in Linden Hills, so I gave up an apartment for you that I'd been in for the last four years. And then they knew in Park Heights, and you made me so miserable there we have to leave. Now these mysterious theys are on Brewster Place. Well, look out that window, kid. There's a big wall down that block, and this is the end of the line for me. I'm not moving anymore, so if that's what you're working yourself up to – save it!"

When Theresa became angry she was like a lump of smoldering coal, and her fierce bursts of temper always unsettled Lorraine.

"You see, that's why I didn't want to mention it." Lorraine began to pull at her fingers nervously. "You're always flying up and jumping to conclusions – no one said anything about moving. And I didn't know your life has been so miserable since you met me. I'm sorry about that," she finished tearfully.

Theresa looked at Lorraine, standing in the kitchen door like a wilted leaf, and she wanted to throw something at her. Why didn't she ever fight back? The very softness that had first attracted her to Lorraine was now a frequent cause for irritation. Smoked honey. That's what Lorraine had reminded her of, sitting in her office clutching that application. Dry autumn days in Georgia woods, thick bloated smoke under a beehive, and the first glimpse of amber honey just faintly darkened about the edges by the burning twigs. She had flowed just that heavily into Theresa's mind and had stuck there with a persistent sweetness.

But Theresa hadn't known then that this softness filled Lorraine up to the very middle and that she would bend at the slightest pressure, would be constantly seeking to surround herself with the comfort of everyone's goodwill, and would shrivel up at the least touch of disapproval. It was becoming a drain to be continually called upon for this nurturing and support that she just didn't understand. She had supplied it at first out of love for Lorraine, hoping that she would harden eventually, even as honey does when exposed to the cold. Theresa was growing tired of being clung to – of being the one who was leaned on. She didn't want a child – she wanted someone who could stand toe to toe with her and be willing to slug it out at times. If they practiced that way with each other, then they could turn back to back and beat the hell out of the world for trying to invade their territory. But she had found no such sparring partner in Lorraine, and the strain of fighting alone was beginning to show on her.

"Well, if it was that miserable, I would have been gone a long time ago," she said, watching her words refresh Lorraine like a gentle shower.

"I guess you think I'm some sort of a sick paranoid, but I can't afford to have people calling my job or writing letters to my principal. You know I've already lost a position like that in Detroit. And teaching is my whole life, Tee."

"I know," she sighed, not really knowing at all. There was no danger of that ever happening on Brewster Place. Lorraine taught too far from this neighborhood for anyone here to recognize her in that school. No, it wasn't her job she feared losing this time, but their approval. She wanted to stand out there and chat and trade makeup secrets and cake recipes. She wanted to be secretary of their block association and be asked to mind their kids while they ran to the store. And none of that was going to happen if they couldn't even bring themselves to accept her good evenings.

Theresa silently finished unpacking the groceries. "Why did you buy cottage cheese? Who eats that stuff?"

"Well, I thought we should go on a diet."

"If *we* go on a diet, then you'll disappear. You've got nothing to lose but your hair."

"Oh, I don't know. I thought that we might want to try and reduce our hips or something." Lorraine shrugged playfully.

"No, thank you. We are very happy with our hips the way they are," Theresa said, as she shoved the cottage cheese to the back of the refrigerator. "And even when I lose weight, it never comes off there. My chest and arms just get smaller, and I start looking like a bottle of salad dressing."

The two women laughed, and Theresa sat down to watch Lorraine fix dinner. "You know, this behind has always been my downfall. When I was coming up in Georgia with my grandmother, the boys used to promise me penny candy if I would let them pat my behind. And I used to love those jawbreakers – you know, the kind that lasted all day and kept changing colors in your mouth. So I was glad to oblige them, because in one afternoon I could collect a whole week's worth of jawbreakers."

"Really. That's funny to you? Having some boy feeling all over you."

Theresa sucked her teeth. "We were only kids, Lorraine. You know, you remind me of my grandmother. That was one straight-laced old lady. She had a fit when my brother told her what I was doing. She called me into the smokehouse and told me in this real scary whisper that I could get pregnant from letting little boys pat my butt and that I'd end up like my cousin Willa. But Willa and I had been thick as fleas, and she had already given me a step-by-step summary of how she'd gotten into her predicament. But I sneaked around to her house that night just to double-check her story, since that old lady had seemed so earnest. 'Willa, are you sure?' I whispered through her bedroom window. 'I'm tellin' ya, Tee,' she said. 'Just keep both feet on the ground and you home free.' Much later I learned that advice wasn't too biologically sound, but it worked in Georgia because those country boys didn't have much imagination.

Theresa's laughter bounced off of Lorraine's silent, rigid back and died in her throat. She angrily tore open a pack of the chocolate chip cookies. "Yeah," she said, staring at Lorraine's back and biting down hard into the cookie, "it wasn't until I came up north to college that I found out there's a whole lot of things that a dude with a little imagination can do to you even with both feet on the ground. You see, Willa forgot to tell me not to bend over or squat or – "

"Must you!" Lorraine turned around from the stove with her teeth clenched tightly together.

"Must I what, Lorraine? Must I talk about things that are as much a part of life as eating or breathing or growing old? Why are you always so uptight about sex or men?"

"I'm not uptight about anything. I just think it's disgusting when you go on and on about – "

"There's nothing disgusting about it, Lorraine. You've never been with a man, but I've been with quite a few – some better than others. There were a couple who I still hope to this day will die a slow, painful death, but then there were some who were good to me – in and out of bed."

"If they were so great, then why are you with me?" Lorraine's lips were trembling.

"Because – " Theresa looked steadily into her eyes and then down at the cookie she was twirling on the table. "Because," she continued slowly, "you can take a chocolate chip cookie and put holes in it and attach it to your ears and call it an earring, or hang it around your neck on a silver chain and pretend it's a necklace – but it's still a cookie. See – you can toss it in the air and call it a Frisbee or even a flying saucer, if the mood hits you, and it's still just a cookie. Send it spinning on a table – like this – until it's a wonderful blur of amber and brown light that you can imagine to be a topaz or rusted gold or old crystal, but the law of gravity has got to come into play, sometime, and it's got to come to rest – sometime. Then all the spinning and pretending and hoopla is over with. And you know what you got?"

"A chocolate chip cookie," Lorraine said.

"Uh-uh." Theresa put the cookie in her mouth and winked. "A lesbian." She got up from the table. "Call me when dinner's ready, I'm going back to read." She stopped at the kitchen door. "Now, why are you putting gravy on that chicken, Lorraine? You know it's fattening."

Marita Golden

?1950–

From the USA, she has a BA (from American University) and and MA (from Columbia University). She has received grants from DC Commission on Arts and Humanities to support her writing Mother of a son, she teaches at George Mason University, Virginia. She says: "There is a recurring theme in all of my books. It's not conscious, but I find that the women in my work find themselves negotiating the tension between personal and political choices and are compelled to leave home to further their self-definition." Her autobiographical fiction includes Migrations of the Heart: A Personal Odyssey (1983), A Woman's Place (1986, extracted here) and Long Distance Life (1989).

From

A Woman's Place

CRYSTAL

WHEN I told Aisha about Neil she merely asked, "Is he a good man?" The charity of her response caught me unawares and I roughly replied, "How do I know? He cares for me, has a sensitivity I think is special, but how do I know what that means ultimately?"

"I remember when I met Rasheed," she mused gently. "I had to figure out what I saw when I looked at him. Mama had told my sister Beth about him and she asked me why I wanted a man as old as Rasheed. I knew he was old enough to be my father. Knew there'd be some things he'd give me and some things he'd deny, because of that. But when I looked at him I didn't see an old man. I just saw an answer to a prayer I hadn't heard myself whisper."

"But Rasheed isn't white."

"Don't get in your own way, Crystal. Don't try so hard to understand what's happening to you. I think you're afraid to fall in love."

"Why should I be?"

"You can't dissect it, analyze it, put it on a piece of paper and then type it up."

I looked at Aisha, embarrassed and flattered that she had accumulated such a precise knowledge of me. And then I remembered that friendship is nothing more, really, than that.

"Love makes you wonder rather than know," she said. "You have to face up to being its prisoner as long as it will let you. And there aren't always words to say what it means. There don't always have to be."

"Is that how you feel about Rasheed?"

"For a long time I only knew I had to be with him. It's only just now, in the past year, that I could say I loved him."

"So now are you happy?"

"I don't believe anymore that's what being with someone is about. I don't know if I'm happy. I just know we've made something together that, so far, we can survive and that serves us."

"You make it sound so simple, so easy."

"Then you haven't heard a word I said. Giving myself over to Rasheed has been the hardest thing I've ever done. But I wanted him and I didn't have any choice. And I don't think I could've done much better even if I had."

"Neil asked me one day if I would ever forgive or forget. I told him I could do neither."

"Do you think you're strong enough to go the distance with him?"

"I don't know what the distance is. I don't know if he would lead, aid or abandon me – if we tried to go so far."

"What do you think? Don't give me a lecture, give me an answer," Aisha said.

"I think, if I wanted him, if he proved necessary, I could go farther than the distance. But I don't know what I'd have to do in order to reach it."

The letter from Serena lay on the desk in the room Neil helped me turn into a study. It has been months since I last heard from her. So I removed my shoes, settled comfortably on the sofa and slit the seal.

Dear Crystal,

Kano is hot, dry and ancient, completely different from the southern part of Nigeria. Despite the fact that the northern section of the country is more populous, because of the rambling, unending openness of the desertlike land you don't feel crowded. After the madness of Lago, Kano is a joy. The major influence here of course is Islam and I've enclosed several pictures of the mosques. Forward them on to Aisha. The call to worship resounds throughout the city several times a day like some primeval chant, and men gather at the nearest mosque, women reverently kneel on mats spread on the floors of kitchens or bedrooms. Most of the women are in purdah and they only come out at night, walking through the streets cloaked in long veils that in the darkness make them seem like a flock of surreal invading birds. Several weeks ago I attended the opening ceremonies for a new university with the black American couple I am staying with. The university is partially endowed by Alhaji Ibrahim, a leader in the early post-independence period and a wealthy agri-businessman. After the dedication, there was a reception, and since Denise and Walker knew the Alhaji, they introduced us. Two days later he showed up at their house and invited me to dinner. The next day in the afternoon, he drove me on a tour of the city, to the places only someone who was born here would recognize as special. He has four wives and his children are almost my age.

One night I asked him to tell me what it was like in the early days of independence. He gave me a veritable history of the country up to the present. When he finished his account, which was as dramatic as anything I'd ever heard, he said, "Nigerians are a people who love the process of making laws and the challenge of breaking them."

And do you know, he likes my body, my big breasts, even my ass which refuses to go away. All 165 pounds of me!!!! When I told him I preferred to undress in the dark, he insisted on removing my clothes himself, with all the lights on. I was embarrassed, and speechless the first time he did it, yet relieved by the appreciation I saw in his eyes as he looked at me sitting on the edge of the bed, my hands trying idiotically to hide everything he saw. He took off his robes and then turned off the lights and in the dark said, "You are a woman, and as you should, you have a woman's body."

A week later I traveled with him to the Ivory Coast to attend an economic development conference. The men who represented twelve West African countries wore three-piece suits, spit-shined shoes, carried briefcases, were dressed in tribal robes. They were well fed and prosperous. France, Britain, and America was stamped all over them. I tried to think of them as servants of the people they represented but couldn't. They looked like politicians caucusing to determine their individual fates.

The women in Abidjan were supremely feminine, their hair neatly braided, their long dresses snug on their bodies. The young ones walked along the streets that are designed like boulevards, past mock-French cafés, looking like dark-skinned gazelles, their heads high and proud. The French women, wives of two- and three-year contract technicians, doctors, engineers, who hold 60% of the jobs requiring a college degree, walked the same streets in sheer see-through dresses.

The Alhaji wants me to remain in Kano. I will for a while longer. But he is used to buying and owning at will, on impulse, because he has the power. I don't want to become just another thing he owns. I don't know when I'll be back stateside. Every morning I wake up like this is where I belong. In your letter you asked me to be your judge. I'm your friend and will offer you no more than that.

You're a black woman beginning to love a white man. You decide if what's happening to you is what you need. I don't envy you. But you are the echo of my own heart and I wish you well.

Love,
Serena.

That night I tried to explain to Neil how much Serena means to me, how much she is missed. When I asked him if he had a best friend, he said, "My mother and now you." I knew that would be his answer. The fleeting, sporadic nature of men's bonds to one another always amazes me. Their ties appear to be purely expedient. I recall my father's reliance on my mother and now Neil's assumption of my loyalty as well as my love. How do women survive being considered superfluous yet claimed as indispensable? The fear that I could not survive being either was why I kept my apartment even after moving in with Neil.

"So you don't trust me," he had accused when I told him I wanted to keep my own place for a while.

"Sometimes you'll have to leave me alone. I can't explain it any other way."

"And what am I supposed to say to that?"

"I don't know. Maybe there's nothing you can say. I hope you can care enough to understand it. And if you feel it's necessary, to forgive me."

I didn't know how to tell my father about Neil, and so for a long time I did not. Mother knew from the beginning. Knew that Neil was white, and told me that was the least interesting thing I'd told her about him. I'd told her that I would tell Father myself, wondering even as I made this extraordinary promise, how I would find the words to do it. So, finally, I went home last weekend. It wasn't until my last day that I told my father. I had driven with him to an open, grassy field near our house where he likes to go to practice his golf swing. It had been a good visit. Since I now have my master's degree and have begun teaching, my father no longer looks upon me as some crazy artistic kook. And the irony is that my father wanted, once, to write. That's what he told me, anyway.

"I wanted to be a writer once," he said, "but I decided to just go on and be a teacher when I realized I didn't really enjoy being alone. Writing makes you publicly accountable for every sin, every act of courage. If you think it's just about putting some words together so they sound pretty, you're wrong. And that's why I don't support so much your urge to write. I want you to be free." It was important, I know, for my father as a product of his times not to be vulnerable, so he chose and I can't say that I blame him, to live his life rather than create it.

He is aging with sublime dignity, and whatever physical strength he loses is supplemented, it seems, by an increase in mental vigor. Sometimes I look at him and am convinced he will never die.

I stood beside him in the field, watching him take the clubs out of the trunk. After he'd slammed it closed, I heard myself blurting out, "I've got a new boyfriend. We're living together."

"Well, don't tell me all the details. I don't approve of those kinds of arrangements and your coming to tell me in person won't lessen my disappointment one bit." He'd hoisted the clubs onto his shoulder and was striding onto the field. I walked faster to keep pace with him. Matching him step for step, I said, "He's white."

He didn't say anything, just continued to walk and then stopped abruptly, pulled out the club he wanted, meticulously placed the ball onto the tee, placed himself before it and then swung with a vigor that I had not expected. The ball landed about sixty feet away. He looked at the spot where the ball stood, searching that distant spot for nearly a minute, then he turned to me.

"I didn't raise you for something like that."

"He loves me."

"Hell, white men been loving black women since they first brought us over here. That ain't nothing new."

"I love him."

"That's nothing new either," he said in disgust, placing the iron back in the holder and spitting on the grass, hard and loud as if spitting out an unpleasant taste.

"Just tell me why you chose their side."

"It's not about sides. It's not about choosing." I heard my voice weak and unconvincing.

"You'd better believe it's about choosing. You better believe it's about sides. About choosing sides and being on the right one. Everything is. If we don't choose, we look back and discover a string of accidents, one mistake after another. I wanted you to go through all those doors they finally opened up. I wanted you to understand 'the man' for your own self-defense. I never intended for you to become them."

"Well, I'm through fighting for you, for everybody," I shouted. "I want to belong to me, not you, not us, not them."

"I didn't raise you to be your own woman," he shouted. My father gazed at me as though his words had unlocked some dreaded family secret my actions had forced him to reveal. "Your life don't belong to just you. It belongs to me, your mother, your people. And now you'll turn into somebody no one will recognize or accept."

He stalked angrily back to the car, leaving me standing in the middle of the field. His words shattered the chirping of the birds and the frivolous shouts of children jumping rope across the street. I could never have released all the tears that I felt then, because it would have required the rest of my life. We drove home in silence. At the house I went upstairs to pack my bags and then sat with my mother trying to tell her what my father had said. But I could not tell her because I refused to give a second life to what felt more and more like an evil spell he had cast upon me.

Christine (Douts) Qunta

1952–

Born in Kimberley, South Africa, she was on the regional executive of the South African Students Organization and the Black People's Convention in the Western Cape in the 1970s, among the hundreds of students who gave up their studies during the 1973 walk-out to work more closely with their community. While doing active political work she was detained and forced to flee the country in order to avoid being forced to testify against her colleagues or face trial with them in 1975. She was granted political asylum in Botswana and later completed a Law degree in Sydney, Australia. She subsequently worked in Botswana and now practises as a solicitor in Zimbabwe, where she lives with her husband and two daughters. Her poetry has been published in Africa, New Zealand, the USA and Britain and in a collection, Hoyi Na! Azania – Poems of an African Struggle (1979). She was also the editor of Women in Southern Africa (1987).

The know

the know
is in the brown-red broken nipples
of my pregnant breasts
from which the warm milk
will spurt in gleeful dance
the know is written
on the innocent swelling of my hips
the know is in the
majestic black glint in my eye
it is in the pulsating
sometimes lilting tunes
flowing from the sadness in my voice
spilling from oceans of angry waves
the know
lives in sweet-sad gaiety
exuberant utterances of self-pride
viciousness
bitterness
love
enlightenment
the know is in knowing him
better than him knowing me
it is tasting and spitting him out.

The procession

If tenderness could
envelope us in completeness
hate would stampede out
and that procession of mourning
children led by coffins
filled with dynamite and victory
scribbled even in the
smallest corner. it will dance
to the graves with
plastic grass and flowers
growing vigorously taunting
the unspoken beauty of the
immediate universe which
gasps at the sombre message
of the plaintive songs
and drums trailing in the night
of the day of that procession.

Rita Dove

1952–

B orn in Akron, Ohio, she was educated at Miami University (Oxford, Ohio), Universität Tübingen (Germany) and the University of
Iowa. A recipient of a Fulbright/Hays scholarship and of National
Endowment for the Arts and Guggenheim fellowships for her poetry,
as well as a Portia Pitt Fellowship as writer-in-residence at Tuskegee
Institute, she spent several years in Europe before becoming Professor
of Literature, teaching creative writing, at Arizona State University. In
1986 she was the second African-American (after Gwendolyn Brooks in
1950) to win a Pulitzer Price for poetry, for Thomas and Beulah (1986).
Her other books of poems are The Yellow House on the Corner (1980),
Museum (1983) and Grace Notes (1989). Her short-story collection, Fifth
Sunday, was published in 1985.

The Zulus

L IKE their name, they soared on the dark edges of adventure and superstition
– young men on heavy Japanese machines, custom-made leather jackets
rippling over their chests and across the backs, at the shoulders the biker's
name and their trademark, a flaming spear and a skull, stitched in silver and
crimson. They poured through the streets of a dying city, honking and shouting
to the uninitiated behind curtains. *Where were you when the lights went out?* they
sang, *in Buffalo, Pittsburgh, Cleveland, Chi-town, Motown, Gary Indiana . . .* for
they had been to all these places which belched along the glittery soiled neckline
of North America.

They were high-school age, though some had dropped out. Parents warned
their daughters away: *if nothing else, think of your family.* The members of the
High School Honor Society officially shunned them. Girls tittered nervously
whenever one of them sauntered down the corridor.

Which was why, when I heard that Swoop had asked Caroline Mosley to
the Prom, I laughed. Actually, I snorted. It was absurd. His real name was
Leander Swope, but everybody called him Swoop because that's the sound
the basketball net made whenever he was there for the handoff. Like a kiss,
his shots were perfect. Swoop! The crown went wild.

Leander Swope may have been a thing of beauty on the court, but in classes he
was just another beetle-browed athlete, dim-witted and sullen. Rumor had it that
the two diagonal gouges on his left cheek were dug there by a girl's fingernails as

she tried to defend herself. But I knew those scars were the marks of dishonor – the brand for those brave enough to undergo the initiation into the Zulus.

And Caroline? Caroline was beyond reproach. When everyone in fourth grade had to give a demonstration speech, Caroline brought in a mop and dustcloths and explained how one cleaned a house. As the youngest daughter of a broken home, I guess she had had lots of practice. She was dimpled and was fun to be around; although she had lots of boyfriends they all spoke well of her. The girls liked her, too.

"The men in this town are spoiled," she would say. "Somehow they got it into their heads that they're a blessing to us all, and they run around with their noses in the stratosphere. Have you ever heard of a guy expecting the girl to call him up before? They'll stand there bold as day and scribble their phone number on a greasy slip of paper. And when another girl tries to steal him, he expects you to fight for him! Look at them – a bunch of the sorriest mangy dogs around. When are these gals going to do something for themselves? Look at the women in this town – aren't they some of the prettiest women you've ever seen?" We looked around. It was true.

And when her father discovered Black Power and moved into an apartment where he could put up his H. Rap Brown posters and entertain turbanned sisters under black lights, Caroline went on as if nothing had happened. And we followed her lead. After all, we knew nothing about divorces and too many children. We were friends, but we never spoke much about personal matters.

So when I heard about Swoop and Caroline, I didn't ask her if it was true. I waited. . .and when Prom night came, watched with the others in amazement as the band opened with a fanfare of saxes and Swoop and Caroline appeared in matching baby blue, looking like the plastic dolls on a wedding cake.

It is not to be comprehended, but we didn't have time to ponder. We had to pack for college. We were already in the world of Shetland sweaters and meal tickets.

The summer after our first year at college, we saw Caroline again. She was working at Pittsburgh Plate Glass; Swoop had lost his job at the potato chip factory. She hadn't changed at all – she laughed at our descriptions of the "educated turkeys" we'd dated and gave us an update on the exploits of our former Homecoming queen. She giggled as she told us how her mother nearly caught her and Lee buck naked on the leather E-Z chair in the basement. We had all lost our virginity that year, so we tried not to make a big deal of it, but inside we were shocked. It was something you didn't talk about.

In August the announcement came: a garden wedding. DeeDee, Caroline's older sister, met three of us in a movie and offered the services of her boyfriend – a tall dark-skinned dude with a diamond stud in one ear – for driving us to the wedding, since it was on the north side of town. DeeDee was what we called "fast". She had very fine features and slightly slanted black eyes set in a heart-shaped face the color of pale coffee, and it seems everything she wore was calculated to hide her beauty – she tacked on false eyelashes and fake clover-leafed "beauty marks", she dyed her hair a different shade every month (this time it was the color of sherry) and poked heavy gold hoops through her ears.

On the day of the wedding a blossom-white convertible spun into the driveway and out he unfolded, long limbs resplendent in royal blue with a lavender silk shirt. He arranged us with all due courtesy in the leather upholstery and spun off again. After a year with no opportunity to dress up, we had outdone ourselves – there were even white gloves tucked in the side pockets of our purses. But our hair! DeeDee's friend's convertible had no mercy. In collective dismay we felt our upsweep tugged loose, the curls swept from a pageboy, a silk gardenia flapping indignantly on the last bobby pin.

The garden was nothing more than a hastily mown lawn. Folding chairs had been set up in the back yard and the side lot, surrounded by a latticed fence, bordered on a dead-end street. The path between the folding chairs led up to a wicker arbor laced with vines and studded with blue carnations.

We took our places on the side designated for "friends of the bride" and waited for the music. A quarter of an hour passed. People began to whisper: Lee was mad because he couldn't invite his motorcycle buddies; someone had forgotten the marriage license; Lee was inside watching baseball on T.V. and wouldn't come out until the game was over. From the window behind us could be heard muted voices, interrupted by sporadic cheering. Poor Caroline! What an ending for the most admired girl in the city, one who owed it to herself to do better. And for what – Love? Here, in a backyard where roses dropped, babies squawled, bees attacked and here and there a dandelion showed its impertinent proletarian head? No, it wasn't possible.

The voices stopped and the mothers – Lee's in pale blue and Caroline's in yellow – marched down the aisle and seated themselves in the front row. The bridegroom and the minister appeared at the arbor; Leander looked surprisingly handsome in a light blue tuxedo with a cream-colored ruffled shirt. The beautiful, whorish DeeDee skimmed by, followed by an entourage of blue silks and unfamiliar faces, concluding with the intolerably cute ring bearer with his plump pillow.

A white cloth was rolled out, and in its wake came Caroline – the old Caroline, with a spray of blue and white flowers and the dimples held in check. Her father, aware of his uselessness, tried to look inconspicuous. When the Lohengrin – which had been assaulting us from a stereo at the back of the house – stopped, the babies started up again. In a short while it was over, and without having heard a word we made our way to the adjoining yard where the tables were stacked with plates of ham and chicken.

There was nothing left to say. It was done. Caroline presented a dimpled cheek and looked genuinely happy. We looked for a hostess but none was introduced.

Some guests had already lined up for a second piece of cake when a low-pitched noise grew above the general hum of voices. It was a fuzzy rumble that sharpened as it drew nearer, stopping all conversation, inspiring even the babies to silence. When it seemed the sound could come no nearer, the first of them appeared, helmets flashing the gilt insignia of the Zulus, a spear and a skull. They drove up the dead-end street and parked their bikes along the fence, clustering in a dark glittering knot. Swoop greeted them with a shout, and they clapped him on the back. They wouldn't come in but they would have some cake – which Swoop passed over the fence in crumbling chunks while Caroline, a rose among thorns, stood by smiling.

Terry McMillan
1951–

B orn in Port Huron, Michigan, she studied at the University of California, Berkeley, and Columbia University. She teaches creative writing at the University of Arizona in Tucson, where she lives with her son. Her first novel Mama, from which this is an extract, was published in 1987 and her second, Disappearing Acts, in 1989.

From

Mama

S INCE Mildred and Crook had broken up, she hadn't exactly resigned herself to being a widow, so to speak, but the men in Point Haven not only bored her to death but barely had a pot of their own to piss in, and if they did, helping out a woman with five kids was not their idea of having a good time, no matter how good she could make them feel in bed.

Mildred had stopped wearing that awful platinum wig, even though she knew she looked damn good in it. Now she wore her own hair, rusty red to suit her reddish skin tone. She let Curly trim it for her every now and then because it grew so fast and got too bushy and thick. A lot of colored women envied her shoulder-length hair. They thought if your hair was long and thick and halfway straight and didn't roll up into tight black pearls at the nape of your neck, you were full of white blood, which made you lucky. In 1966 most colored women in Point Haven wanted desperately to have long straight hair instead of their own knotty mounds. To get it like that, they wore wigs or rubbed Dixie Peach or Royal

Crown hair grease into their scalps and laid the straightening comb over the gas burner and whipped it through their hair until it sizzled. Sometimes Mildred didn't feel like being bothered, sitting in that chair for almost an hour just for the straightening part, and maybe another hour to get it bumper-curled. Most of the time she would roll it up with brush rollers and let it go at that. Mildred usually didn't care what people thought.

Whenever she went to the bar, somebody's husband usually offered to buy her a drink. They always had that I've-been-waiting-for-you-to-get-rid-of-that-sorry-niggah look in their eyes. But Mildred would just accept their drink offer, make small talk – usually about the condition of their wives – then turn her back to them and continue running her mouth with her female friends.

Mildred didn't believe in messing around with anybody's husband, no matter what kind of financial proposition they made. The way she figured it, when and if she ever did get herself another husband, she damn sure didn't want a soul messing with hers. She truly believed in the motto that what goes around comes around. She'd seen it come true too many times. Janey Pearl got caught in the Starlight Motel under the Bluewater Bridge, laying up with Sissie Moncrief's old man, and Sissie tried to strangle Janey Pearl with her own garter belt and stockings. Shirley Walker's husband caught her in bed with his brother. Put both of them in the hospital with a .38.

This town was entirely too small to be sneaky and slick. Be different if this was a city like Detroit. Messing around was the surest way to get yourself killed by some jealous church-going woman, especially if she was a Baptist. Them Baptists could get the spirit all right, Mildred thought, right on your ass, and the very words they chastised their children for using would sizzle off their tongues like water hitting a hot skillet.

Mildred didn't have any trouble getting the attention of most men because she was still young – a few months shy of thirty – and well equipped. Her hips didn't exactly curve out now, but when she turned to the side her behind looked like someone had drawn it on, made it a little too perfect, and it was this luscious behind that drew many a man's eye. Even though she still stuffed her bra with a pair of the girls' anklets to give her breasts more cleavage, Mildred wasn't what you'd call promiscuous. She liked to look her best and had gotten tired of sitting around the house all those months getting sucked in by soap operas. It wasn't even so much romance she was looking for as it was to have some fun, maybe roll over and feel a man's body in her bed again. These days no one was there except maybe one or two of the kids, trying to keep warm.

One night a tall, caramel-skinned man strolled through the doors of the Red Shingle. He walked right past Mildred. She could hardly swallow her drink; couldn't believe something this handsome would set foot inside the Shingle without advance notice. In all the years she'd been in here and even when she worked here, she'd never seen anybody that caused her to do a double take.

This man had deep-set eyes and thick bushy eyebrows and a smile like you saw in toothpaste commercials. His hair was charcoal mixed with gray and he was as tall as a basketball player. He had a body like a boxer and instead of walking, he strutted like his ego was sitting on his shoulders. Mildred liked his style immediately. This man had class. She could barely speak when he walked up to her and introduced himself. His name was Sonny Tyler. She told him her name, then tucked in her lip and broke out her long-forgotten-that-she-still-had "Yes, I'm alone" smile. He sat down next to her at the bar and offered to buy her a drink but all she asked for was ginger ale.

Sonny told her he was stationed at Selfridge Air Force Base in St Clemens, which was thirty-odd miles from Point Haven. One of his old running buddies was playing at the Shingle tonight and he had come to hear him since he hadn't seen him in almost a year. "Is that so," was all Mildred could say. She was trying to sound intelligent and figuring out the best way to carry on a conversation with this man, who was causing her panties to get wet.

They talked through two shows.

"I'm divorced and got five kids. The oldest is thirteen and the baby is seven," she told him.

"You sure know how to keep yourself up," he said, smiling. Mildred was shocked that he didn't go flying to the other end of the bar where there were quite a few women with less responsibility but also less sex appeal. They were all tapping their stirrers on the rim of their glasses to the beat of the music, and watching Mildred like hawks.

Sonny asked Mildred for her phone number, which made her feel seventeen again. She loved it. A few nights later he called her. He wanted to come over to her house; wanted to meet her kids. "Not yet," she said, but she met him at a motel in Canada. She told him she didn't let just any man in her bed, didn't care how good he looked or how good he smelled. "What's that you wearing anyway, Sonny? Lord, it smells good."

"Old Spice," he'd said, caressing her in all the right places. She knew it smelled familiar because Crook had always worn it, and so did Percy. It smelled different on Sonny. Tantalizing.

After a few weeks of making excuses to the kids as to why she'd been staying out so late or not coming home until daylight, Mildred decided to tell them. Hell, she was a grown woman with needs just like any other female. What was wrong with her feeling a little pleasure?

She made Sonny whisper when she let him in. "This is a nice house," he said softly.

"Shhh," she said, and guided him to her bedroom, where she hung his clothes over the door and left it cracked. She didn't want the kids to barge in unannounced and find her in bed with a man who wasn't their father. Sonny was a much better lover than either Crook or Percy had been. He was so warm and big that Mildred woke up whistling the next morning, anxious to fix him a hot breakfast. She wanted to make him as comfortable as possible because she wanted him to come back. And keep coming back. It had been so long since she'd been kissed, especially the way Sonny did. She'd almost forgotten what else lips were good for. And what he had rekindled between her legs was another story altogether.

Sonny put on everything except his shirt and walked out into the living room when he heard the kids laughing at cartoons. When Freda first saw his hairy chest, her eyes widened like she'd seen a ghost.

"Who are you?" she asked, turning up her nose at him.

"I'm Sonny," he said smiling, all friendly-like. "I'm a friend of your mother's."

"Since when? And how come you don't have all your clothes on? You coming or going? Did you spend the night over here? With my mama, in *her* bed?"

"Yes, your mother is a very nice lady, and I like her a lot. I hope to get to know you and the other kids better, too."

"Hmph. I hope you ain't staying long," she said, and huffed away.

Mildred walked back into the living room, not having heard this, and slid her arms around his waist like a high schooler satisfying a crush. She called the kids to introduce him. Each of them sat down on the couch, lined up like dominoes, and when Freda crossed her arms and grunted, the rest of them imitated her. They watched her for the next move, hardly even noticing Sonny.

"Sonny is a friend of your mama's, and he's nice. I like him, and I want y'all to treat him nice. He's in the air force and he's going to be visiting us quite regularly, so y'all might as well get used to him."

"Why we gotta get used to him? He ain't coming to see us," Freda said.

"You got a quarter?" asked Money, holding out his hand.

"Boy, stop begging, what I tell you about that. And Freda, you better watch the tone of your voice, you ain't grown. I'm still the mama in this house."

"How'd you get a name like Money?" Sonny asked.

Money hunched his shoulders. He didn't know.

It was Freda who had started calling him that. It seemed that Money always begged, and nobody knew where he got the habit from. He was barely old enough to tell you his address, but he'd beg coins from anyone who came to the house or wherever Freda had dragged him. "You got a dime?" he'd ask, and if they said no, he'd say, "You got a nickel?" And if they still said no, he'd press the point. "Well, you got *any* money?" Freda would smack his hand and tell him he shouldn't be begging and if Mildred ever found out he was doing it, she would beat the stew out of him. He ignored her threats. "Money! Money! Money! Those the only words you know, ain't it?" Freda would say. After that, to embarrass him she started calling him Money all the time. So did everybody else.

It was commonplace in black neighborhoods to have a nickname. By the time a child was sucking his bottle or thumb, people were already staring at him like a specimen, asking, "What you gon' call him?" Then they would give the child a name that showed no consideration for his own. Baby boys got names like Lucky, BooBoo, Sugar Pie, PeeWee, and Homeless. "Don't he look just like a little fat pumpkin?" And that's what he'd be called thereafter. Little girls' names were at least softer to the ear: Peaches, Babysister, Candy, Bo-Peep, and Cookie. There was a set of twins called Heckle and Jeckle.

Money kept his hand out when he saw Mildred take the plates back in the kitchen.

"Here, I've got a quarter, for all of you," Sonny said, reaching into his pockets. Their attitudes seemed to change then, but when Freda refused hers, the girls pulled their hands back too. Not Money. He slid his quarter into his pocket and told Sonny he could give all of the coins to him and he'd see to it that his sisters got theirs later on when he knew they'd change their minds. The girls looked at him like he was a traitor, but it didn't bother Money.

Sonny kept coming for a few months and Mildred was glowing, always humming some song. Then he found out he was getting sent to Okinawa. He told Mildred it was a strong possibility that he might not see her for at least a year. And if he was ordered to fight in Vietnam, he might not ever see her again. Before he'd met her, he'd asked to be transferred to Texas, which is where he'd be stationed if he made it back to the States. Mildred didn't whine or cry. She just thanked Sonny for the best four months she'd had since her divorce, especially since he'd gotten her juices back in circulation. It wasn't like she was madly in love with him. Hell, Mildred said to herself, wasn't no use crying over spilt milk.

Percy hadn't exactly given up on her, even though he'd married a shy woman who knew a good thing when she saw one. Percy was the kind of man who would try to enter a jalopy in a stock car race and wouldn't be able to figure out why he didn't qualify, and if by chance they did let him in, he'd be at a total loss as to why he didn't win. The only thing he was good at figuring out was his long-overdue and stored-up passion for Mildred. Dreaming about her was enough for Percy. His wife suspected it, though she never said anything to him so long as he paid the bills.

Percy had told Mildred time and time again that if she ever needed anything, anything at all, to drop her pride and call him first. She decided to keep him on the back burner in case of a real emergency. After all, he *was* married, and she didn't want his wife knocking on her door in the middle of the night ready to blow her brains out. So Mildred left Percy just where he was: on simmer. Besides, he was too nice, she thought, and not once had Mildred ever seen him lose his temper. She wondered if he had one.

Mildred applied for another job. This time at Prest-o-Lite, though they weren't hiring. Those welfare checks were barely making the house note, let alone everything else. She wanted to work, not sit around the house all day trying to drum up things to keep her busy. She was getting fidgety and the least little thing that didn't go right got on her nerves. She was sick of standing and waiting in line for the flour and cheese and margarine and Spam they gave her at the welfare office.

She sat at the kitchen table and started going through a stack of envelopes that she had already shuffled and reshuffled in order of importance over the past few weeks. It didn't make a difference. Most of them were going to have to go unpaid. Bills. The coal bill. The gas bill. The light bill. The water bill. The garbage man. The insurance man. The washer and dryer bill. The house note. Groceries. Lunch money. Special field trip money. Gym suit money. School books. Notebook paper. Tennis shoes. Sunday shoes. The dentist. Popsicles.

Everything was piling up and it was as if Mildred were caught in a snow storm and was constantly shoveling the sidewalk. It kept snowing over where she had just shoveled. In spite of the welfare checks and the occasional day work she managed to get on the side, Mildred was getting deeper and deeper into debt. Everything kept getting more expensive and her kids were growing entirely too fast.

It cost so much to keep up a three-bedroom house like this, and trying to raise five kids, she thought. Hell, twenty years is a long-ass time to be paying for anything. What will I do with all this room when the kids is grown? Which won't be long. Sit in here by myself and run from room to room? Maybe I'll have some grandbabies. But the thought of being a grandmother was unfathomable to her. She decided not to think so far ahead. Shit. Right now what she needed was some money. A decent job. Maybe even a sugar daddy, which Mildred was seriously considering about now.

"Mama, can I make some cocoa?" asked Bootsey, walking into the kitchen. She was starting to look like a miniature Mildred. Everybody had been telling Bootsey this, but Bootsey didn't see it.

"I don't care what you make, girl," Mildred said.

"Here's the mail," Bootsey said, handing it to her.

Interruptions. Always interruptions. Mama this. Mama that. Mama Mama Mama Mama. Can I have this? Can I have that? Yes. No. Maybe. I need this. I need that. Not now. Mama, please? Why not? Because. Because why? Because I said so. Because because. Her kids were everywhere she turned and everywhere she looked. A hand. A mouth open. Asking asking asking. Do something. Anything. Gimme gimme gimme. And always the very things she didn't have, except her love, which they never once asked her for.

Mildred went through the envelopes quickly, tossing aside the ones she didn't want to look at, and then she came across a letter from her oldest brother, Leon. He lived in Phoenix. What would he be writing me for? she wondered.

She opened the letter and read it. She was surprised to discover that he was well informed about her financial situation and she wondered who had filled him in. It had to be one of her sisters, most likely old fat-ass Georgia or motor-mouth Lula. Mildred let the thought pass when she got to the part where he suggested she consider selling the house and moving out to Phoenix. He said there were better job opportunities out there for colored people, the weather was hot and dry all year long, which meant hardly any mosquitoes, the kids might meet some civilized children instead of those hoodlums running loose in Point Haven, and, above all else, Mildred might meet a stable and loveable serviceman with a pension and she might even consider getting her high school diploma.

She folded the letter and put it back in the evelope, letting her fingers crease it over and over again. She could hear the furnace clicking on. Heat, Mildred thought. Wouldn't need no furnace in Arizona. She walked over and flicked off the switch. She had never really thought of leaving Point Haven before. All her people were here. But she wasn't afraid of taking chances. Always knew something had to happen to make things better. Was this it? She looked down at her puffy hands and saw how years of bleach and ammonia and detergent had made her skin like spiderwebs.

Ain't nothing gon' ever change unless I make it change, she thought. And I need a change, that's for damn sure. Shit, I'm tired of playing catch-up. Working and scrimping and scraping, to get where? Nowhere. Not even past the starting line. She went to the sink and turned on the faucet though there were no dirty dishes in the basin. She poured almost two cups of Tide in the water and let the suds ooze through her fingers. She stood in front of the window and let her hands soak until they felt like liquid silk. Then she pushed the starched curtains aside to unblock the view. Her view. Of Herman and Beulah Dell's ugly brown house. The grass in the side yard was growing too fast. And before spring this house would have to be painted again. The Mercury was starting to fall apart too. Mildred dried her hands on the curtains and picked up the letter again. Then she found Leon's phone number in the junk drawer and picked up the telephone.

Mary Monroe

?1950s-

Born on a cotton plantation in Choctaw County, Alabama, she left the South at twenty-one and later settled in Oakland, California, with her two daughters. Her first novel, The Upper Room, (1985), set in a migrant labour camp amid the Forida Everglades, is a magical story about young Maureen, torn between the world of her larger-than-life mother Mama Ruby and the harsh reality of outside society.

From

The Upper Room

CHAPTER XXVII

"**B**LESS this girl, Lord. For she know not her sins! Shake that devil out of poor Ruby Jean's life for once and for all. She done kilt her husband. She is guilty of just about some of everything. Runnin with a Cajun wild woman. Takin up with a carnival. Not communicatin with her family in a coon's age. And" – Ruby's father began his sermon with vigor – "what all else, daughter?" he asked. Ruby sat on a footstool in front of the whole congregation of the Reed Street Church of God in Christ, surrounded by flowers and crucifixes. "What else that devil had you doin, girl?"

Ruby shrugged before speaking.

"Gluttony. . .bad credit. . .tellin lies." She paused to think, rolling her eyes off to the side, as the silent audience waited in a fever of anticipation to hear her story. "Let me see now. . .name-callin and associatin with foreigners, all the usual backslidin activities."

Her father turned to face her with his hands on his hips. He was a big man, even more rotund than Ruby. He wore a long black robe that was noticeably shorter in the back than it was in the front and in his hand he clutched a thick white cloth he used to wipe his brow during his foot-stomping sermons.

"I ax yall," he continued, turning back to the audience. "I ax yall if you ever knowed of a sister with so much of the devil in her as Ruby Jean? My child done spent the last half of her life ridin Satan's coattails!"

"AMEN!" the congregation shouted.

"She been lost!" the preacher yelled.

"LOST!" the congregation agreed.

"But now she done found her way back home!" the preacher grinned. "Now, brethren. . .we got to get her boy Virgil back home. Lord, the boy done slid from the embrace of his mama's bosom into a heathen country. A country that don't even recognize the Holy Ghost! A country where the folks don't even believe in eatin meat! Can yall imagine not bein allowed to eat *ribs*?"

"NO!" the congregation hollered.

"A country where they worship *cows* when Jesus done told em he was the *only* way! A *cow*, yall!"

"COWS!" came the response.

Some of the younger members of the congregation looked at one another with puzzled expressions on their faces.

"Hey – he don't know what he talkin about! That's India where they worship and don't eat cows, not V-Eight Nam!" a young boy said, snickering. He received sharp looks from his elders.

"What's the difference?!" a woman asked the boy. The boy quickly returned his attention to the preacher.

"And the girl's been misled and raped and – and robbed and beat up and, and – what else, Ruby Jean?" the preacher asked, turning to Ruby again.

She looked out into the audience at Maureen sitting in the front row of benches, an incredulous look on her face.

". . .Um. . .my husband got involved with another woman," she said.

The preacher turned to his congregation with his mouth open and his hands held up high in the air.

"As if the girl ain't got troubles enough, the devil walked into her house and carried her man off, before she kilt him. Came in the guise of a hussy!"

"A *white* woman at that!" Ruby added.

The congregation went wild.

"THE WHITE MAN IS THE DEVIL!" they shrieked.

Maureen's heart was beating fast. She was terribly frightened. The reverend started to dance about the stage and speak in tongues and Ida began to hit random keys on the red piano sitting in a corner near the stage. Women, men, and children joined in the confusion, dancing. Some started to sing, no two people singing the same song, and they all shouted and spoke in tongues. Some fell to the floor writhing. A woman sitting next to Maureen lost her wig and some young boys grabbed it up from the floor and started tossing it back and forth across the room.

Maureen rose from her seat, eased out of the church, and ran down the street back to her grandparents' house two blocks away.

When Ruby and the others returned home Maureen was sitting on the bed in Ruby's old room staring off into space. Ruby stood in the doorway for a moment looking at Maureen lovingly before making her presence known.

"What's the matter, Mo'reen?" Ruby gently closed the door. She moved to the bed and sat next to Maureen.

Ruby's former room looked a lot like it had during the days she occupied it. Neat and homey, with bright-colored curtains, bedspread, and throw rugs. A large cloth illustration of the Last Supper almost covered half of one wall.

"I want to go home," Maureen answered.

"Don't you like it here?"

"Naw. Do you?"

"Of course I like it here! This is where I come from," Ruby said. She made a sweeping gesture with her hand and glanced around the room.

"Then how come you left and stayed away so long, Mama Ruby? How can you leave somethin you like. . .I'd never do that."

Ruby looked at Maureen's lips as she spoke, then looked up alongside her head.

"Do you like me, Mo'reen?"

"Ma'am?"

"I ax you if you like me?"

"Yes, ma'am."

"Then you'll never leave me?"

"I don't know."

"You just said you'd never leave nothin you like."

"I wouldn't. . .I guess. . .I ain't never leavin you then," Maureen smiled. "Unless. . ." her voice trailed off.

"Unless what?" Ruby asked with alarm.

"Unless I. . .unless I get carried off by the devil, like you say my daddy was."

Ruby turned away and considered Maureen's words.

"I won't let the devil get near you. I'm tough," Ruby whispered, looking toward the door.

"Then how come he carried off my daddy? You couldn't stop the devil from carryin off my daddy, how you goin to stop him from carryin me off?"

"Remember that day me and you was sittin on the porch and you axed me if I was the devil?"

"Yeah. You said. . . ."

Ruby looked toward the door again, then leaned closer to Maureen, glancing about the room nervously. "I ain't goin to mention it, but I am. Don't you never tell nobody I told you this. Don't tell Cousin Hattie. Don't tell nobody back in Florida. They wouldn't be able to handle havin the devil so close to em. How you think Roscoe would feel knowin he was engaged to marry the devil? What you think Irene and Bishop would say if they knowed they best friend was the devil? And what would my daddy say?"

"If you is the devil, how can you be a Christian too?" Maureen asked, cocking her head to the side and looking at Ruby out of the corner of her eye.

"The devil is the master of disguises! He the only one, cept the Lord, what can be more than one thing at the same time. Though I am filled with the Holy Ghost, I also am the doorway to darkness."

Maureen covered her mouth with her hand to suppress a giggle. "Mama Ruby, you so funny. You ain't the devil. The devil was a man."

Ruby sighed and moved to the window. She started talking with her back to Maureen.

"Virgil's dead. I just know it. He done died in that foreign country. He took secrets with him," Ruby said. "Secrets I will carry with me to my grave."

"About what?"

"You for one. Me. Him. Things I can never tell nobody. Not even you." Ruby turned slightly to see Maureen's reaction.

"Bad things?"

Ruby looked at Maureen thoughtfully and nodded.

"Don't never tell me what they is," Maureen said softly.

"I hadn't planned to," Ruby said firmly.

Maureen leaped up from the bed, ran to Ruby, and grabbed her hand.

"Mama Ruby, let's stop talkin sad talk. Tell me again about that ole white lady we goin to visit this week."

Ruby lifted Maureen up, returned to the bed with her, and sat down, putting Maureen on her lap.

"Her name is Miss Mo'reen."

"That's my name!"

"It was Miss Mo'reen's name first. She the one I named you after. She live in New Orleans and got two plum trees in her front yard."

"She got any kids I can play with?" Maureen asked, her eyes wide and her heart thumping madly.

"She got kids but they all growed up and livin in a foreign country called Ireland. That's where Miss Mo'reen come from."

"You said foreigners was the devil's relations."

"Not all foreigners. See, Miss Mo'reen been in America most of her life. She don't even talk like no foreigner. She talk regular English like me and you. None of them crazy accents or nothin."

"She a nice lady?"

"If God made anything better than Miss Mo'reen, he kept it for hisself. She made me what I am today," Ruby said proudly. "Girl, I am some successful!"

Maureen looked at Ruby carefully, from her feet up to her face.

"What she make you into, Mama Ruby?"

Ruby looked at Maureen with surprise on her face.

"What Miss Mo'reen make you into?"

"A Christian. In spite of Satan's toe hold," Ruby answered. She lightly touched her bosom, confirming the presence of her cross and her switchblade.

Michele Wallace
1952–

B orn and brought up in Sugar Hill, Harlem, and privately schooled,
she gained much attention for her discussion of the relationship
between Black men and women, based on the masculinist bias of
the Black Power culture of the 1960s. When Black Macho and the Myth
of the Superwoman *was first published in 1978, with its controversial
interpretation of the way Black women were being metaphorically dis-
enfranchised by both the Women's Movement and the Black Movement,
it aroused fierce protest; however in her introduction to the revised 1990
edition she makes it clear how she has modified some of the views for
which she was criticized, having returned to graduate school at Yale in
1980 to focus on Afro-American Studies and then American Studies. She
subsequently completed a master's degree in Afro-American Literature
and Literary Criticism at the City College of New York, where she now
teaches English and Women's Studies. Her latest book,* Invisibility Blues:
From Pop to Theory *(1990), is a work of cultural criticism that considers
the work of her mother, artist Faith Ringgold, her own development as
a writer and the historical and conceptual questions that an emergent
Black feminist theory must address.*

From

Black Macho and the Myth of the Superwoman

. . . THROUGHOUT the entire span of her existence on American soil,
the Negro woman has been alone and unprotected, not only socially
but psychologically as well. She has *had* to fend for herself as if she were a
man; being black, even more so. I am not implying that the Negro woman has
become frigid or "masculine." In fact, she is potentially, if not already, the most
sexual animal on this planet. It is not frigidity that I am describing. It is *rigidity*.
And it has been this quality of austerity in the Negro woman which has enabled
her to survive what few other women have ever lived through. . . (Hernton, *Sex
and Racism in America.*)

*Sapphire. Mammy. Tragic mulatto wench. Workhorse, can swing an ax, lift a
load, pick cotton with any man. A wonderful housekeeper. Excellent with chil-*

dren. Very clean. Very religious. A terrific mother. A great little singer and dancer and a devoted teacher and social worker. She's always had more opportunities than the black man because she was no threat to the white man so he made it easy for her. But curiously enough, she frequently ends up on welfare. Nevertheless, she is more educated and makes more money than the black man. She is more likely to be employed and more likely to be a professional than the black man. And subsequently she provides the main support for the family. Not beautiful, rather hard looking unless she has white blood, but then very beautiful. The black ones are exotic though, great in bed, tigers. And very fertile. If she is middle class she tends to be uptight about sex, prudish. She is hard on and unsupportive of black men, domineering, castrating. She tends to wear the pants around her house. Very strong. Sorrow rolls right off her brow like so much rain. Tough, unfeminine. Opposed to women's rights movements, considers herself already liberated. Nevertheless, unworldly. Definitely not a dreamer, rigid, inflexible, uncompassionate, lacking in goals any more imaginative than a basket of fried chicken and a good fuck.

From the intricate web of mythology which surrounds the black woman, a fundamental image emerges. It is of a woman of inordinate strength, with an ability for tolerating an unusual amount of misery and heavy, distasteful work. This woman does not have the same fears, weaknesses, and insecurities as other women, but believes herself to be and is, in fact, stronger emotionally than most men. Less of a woman in that she is less "feminine" and helpless, she is really *more* of a woman in that she is the embodiment of Mother Earth, the quintessential mother with infinite sexual, life-giving, and nurturing reserves. In other words, she is a superwoman.

Through the years this image has remained basically intact, unquestioned even by the occasional black woman writer or politician. In fact, if anything, time has served to reinforce it. Even now I can hear my reader thinking, *Of course she is stronger. Look what she's been through. She would have to be. Of course she's not like other women.* Even for me, it continues to be difficult to let the myth go. Naturally black women want very much to believe it; in a way, it is all we have.

But just image, for a moment, that you had a little girl and circumstances dictated that she be released in a jungle for a period of time to get along the best way she could. Would you want her to think she was invulnerable to the sting of the snake, the claws of the panther? Would you like her to believe that she could go without sleep and food indefinitely and that she needed no shelter? Or would you want her to know something of her actual capabilities and human weaknesses, not enough to make her give up before she had begun, but just enough to make her want to protect herself? How long do you think she'd survive if you deceived her? And, more importantly, in what state would she survive? Imagine further that she believed her wounds were just another proof of her strength and invulnerability.

Now I want you to picture a little black girl in a jungle that has no tigers and lions, but poverty, ignorance, welfare centers, tenements, rats, roaches, inadequate schools, malevolent teachers, pimps, Forty-second Streets, Eighth Avenues, heroin, hypodermic needles and methadone, opportunistic preachers and community leaders, a narrow range of career possibilities, always impending pregnancies, sterilization, poor medical services, corrupt lawyers, an insensitive and illogical court system, and two races of men who prey upon her as a sexual chattel and a beast of burden. And suppose that behind this black girl, there was a whole string of little black girls who had faced this same jungle with their imaginary advantages and been defeated. Would it not be an act of unkindness, of extreme injustice really, to tell her that she was a woman of special strengths, of exceptional opportunities?

I remember once I was watching a news show with a black male friend of mine who had a Ph.D. in psychology and was the director of an out-patient clinic. We were looking at some footage of a black woman who seemed barely able to speak English, though at least six generations of her family before her had certainly claimed it as their first language. She was in bed wrapped in blankets, her numerous small, poorly clothed children huddled around her. Her apartment looked rat-infested, cramped, and dirty. She had not, she said, had heat and hot water for days. My friend, a solid member of the middle class now but surely no stranger to poverty in his childhood, felt obliged to comment – in order to assuage his guilt, I can think of no other reason – "That's a *strong* sister," as he bowed his head in reverence.

bell hooks (Gloria Watkins)
1952–

Born in Kentucky and advocate of anti-racist, anti-sexist, anti-capitalist politics, she is one of the few Black women whose writing explicitly identifies itself as feminist. As she says: "By and large, Black women are still reluctant to call themselves feminists. One reason is deep resentment of white women. By rejecting feminism at the historical moment that white women embraced it, we took the opportunity to reject them." She has taught at Yale University and Oberlin College, Ohio, and is the author of four books on the politics of race and gender and cultural criticism: Ain't I a Woman: Black Women and Feminism (1981), Feminist Theory: From Margin to Center (1984), Talking Back: Thinking Feminist – Thinking Black (1989) – in the passage below she describes her decision *to speak out, despite the constraints of a southern Black upbringing, and to use a pseudonym – and* Yearning: Race, Gender, and Cultural Politics *(1991).*

From

Talking Back: Thinking Feminist – Thinking Black

TALKING BACK

I N the world of the southern black community I grew up in, "back talk" and "talking back" meant speaking as an equal to an authority figure. It meant daring to disagree and sometimes it just meant having an opinion. In the "old school", children were meant to be seen and not heard. My great-grandparents, grandparents, and parents were all from the old school. To make yourself heard if you were a child was to invite punishment, the back-hand lick, the slap across the face that would catch you unaware, or the feel of switches stinging your arms and legs.

To speak then when one was not spoken to was a courageous act – an act of risk and daring. And yet it was hard not to speak in warm rooms where heated discussions began at the crack of dawn, women's voices filling the air, giving orders, making threats, fussing. Black men may have excelled in the art of poetic preaching in the male-dominated church, but in the church of the home, where the everyday rules of how to live and how to act were established, it was black women who preached. There, black women spoke in a language so rich, so poetic, that it felt to me like being shut off from life, smothered to death if one were not allowed to participate.

It was in that world of woman talk (the men were often silent, often absent) that was born in me the craving to speak, to have a voice, and not just any voice but one that could be identified as belonging to me. To make my voice, I had to speak, to hear myself talk – and talk I did – darting in and out of grown folks' conversations and dialogues, answering questions that were not directed at me, endlessly asking questions, making speeches. Needless to say, the punishments for these acts of speech seemed endless. They were intended to silence me – the child – and more particularly the girl child. Had I been a boy, they might have encouraged me to speak believing that I might someday be called to preach. There was no "calling" for talking girls, no legitimized rewarded speech. The punishments I received for "talking back" were intended to suppress all possibility that I would create my own speech. That speech was to be suppressed so that the "right speech of womanhood" would emerge.

Within feminist circles, silence is often seen as the sexist "right speech of womanhood" – the sign of woman's submission to patriarchal authority. This emphasis on woman's silence may be an accurate remembering of what has taken place in the households of women from WASP backgrounds in the United States, but in black communities (and diverse ethnic communities), women have not been silent. Their voices can be heard. Certainly for black women, our struggle has not been to emerge from silence into speech but to change the nature and direction of our speech, to make a speech that compels listeners, one that is heard.

Our speech, "the right speech of womanhood", was often the soliloquy, the talking into thin air, the talking to ears that do not hear you – the talk that is simply not listened to. Unlike the black male preacher whose speech was to be heard, who was to be listened to, whose words were to be remembered, the voices of black women – giving orders, making threats, fussing – could be tuned out, could become a kind of background music, audible but not acknowledged as significant speech. Dialogue – the sharing of speech and recognition – took place not between mother and child or mother and male authority figure but among black women. I can remember watching fascinated as our mother talked with her mother, sisters, and women friends. The intimacy and intensity of their speech – the satisfaction they received from talking to one another, the pleasure, the joy. It was in this world of woman speech, loud talk, angry words, women with tongues quick and sharp, tender sweet tongues, touching our world with their words, that I made speech my birthright – and the right to voice, to authorship, a privilege I could not be denied. It was in that world and because of it that I came to dream of writing, to write.

Writing was a way to capture speech, to hold onto it, keep it close. And so I wrote down bits and pieces of conversations, confessing in cheap diaries that soon fell apart from too much handling, expressing the intensity of my sorrow, the anguish of speech – for I was always saying the wrong thing, asking the wrong questions. I could not confine my speech to the necessary corners and concerns of life. I hid these writings under my bed, in pillow stuffings, among faded underwear. When my sisters found and read them, they ridiculed and mocked me – poking fun. I felt violated, ashamed, as if the secret parts of my self had been exposed. brought into the open, and hung like newly clean laundry, out in the air for everyone to see. The fear of exposure, the fear that one's deepest emotions and innermost thoughts will be dismissed as mere nonsense, felt by so many young girls keeping diaries, holding and hiding speech, seems to me now one of the barriers that women have always needed and still need to destroy so that we are no longer pushed into secrecy or silence.

Despite my feelings of violation, of exposure, I continued to speak and write, choosing my hiding places well, learning to destroy work when no safe place could be found. I was never taught absolute silence, I was taught that it was important to speak but to talk a talk that was in itself a silence. Taught to speak and yet beware of the betrayal of too much heard speech, I experienced intense confusion and deep anxiety in my efforts to speak and write. Reciting poems at Sunday afternoon church service might be rewarded. Writing a poem (when one's time could be "better" spent sweeping, ironing, learning to cook) was luxurious activity, indulged in at the expense of others. Questioning authority, raising issues that were not deemed appropriate subjects brought pain, punishments – like telling mama I wanted to die before her because I could not live without her – that was crazy talk, crazy speech, the kind that would lead you to end up in a mental institution. "Little girl," I would be told, "if you don't stop all this crazy talk and crazy acting you are going to end up right out there at Western State."

Madness, not just physical abuse, was the punishment for too much talk if you were female. Yet even as this fear of madness haunted me, hanging over my writing like a monstrous shadow, I could not stop the words, making thought, writing speech. For this terrible madness which I feared, which I was sure was the destiny of daring women born to intense speech (after all, the authorities emphasized this point daily), was not as threatening as imposed silence, as suppressed speech.

Safety and sanity were to be sacrificed if I was to experience defiant speech. Though I risked them both, deep-seated fears and anxieties characterized my childhood days. I would speak but I would not ride a bike, play hardball, or hold the gray kitten. Writing about the ways we are traumatized in our growing-up years, psychoanalyst Alice Miller makes the point in *For Your Own Good* that it is not clear why childhood wounds become for some folk an opportunity to grow, to move forward rather than backward in the process of self-realization. Certainly, when I reflect on the trials of my growing-up years, the many punishments, I can see now that in resistance I learned to be vigilant in the nourishment of my spirit, to be tough, to courageously protect that spirit from forces that would break it.

While punishing me, my parents often spoke about the necessity of breaking my spirit. Now when I ponder the silences, the voices that are not heard, the voices of those wounded and/or oppressed individuals who do not speak or write, I contemplate the acts of persecution, torture – the terrorism that breaks spirits, that makes creativity impossible. I write these words to bear witness to the primacy of resistance struggle in any situation of domination (even within family life); to the strength and power that emerges from sustained resistance and the profound conviction that these forces can be healing, can protect us from dehumanization and despair.

These early trials, wherein I learned to stand my ground, to keep my spirit intact, came vividly to mind after I published *Ain't I A Woman* and the book was sharply and harshly criticized. While I had expected a climate of critical dialogue, I was not expecting a critical avalanche that had the power in its intensity to crush the spirit, to push one into silence. Since that time, I have heard stories about black women, about women of color, who write and publish (even when the work is quite successful) having nervous breakdowns, being made mad because they cannot bear the harsh responses of family, friends, and unknown critics, or becoming silent, unproductive. Surely, the absence of a humane critical response has tremendous impact on the writer from any oppressed, colonized group who endeavors to speak. For us, true speaking is not solely an expression of creative power; it is an act of resistance, a political gesture that challenges politics of domination that would render us nameless and voiceless. As such, it is a courageous act – as such, it represents a threat. To those who wield oppressive power, that which is threatening must necessarily be wiped out, annihilated, silenced.

Recently, efforts by black women writers to call attention to our work serve to highlight both our presence and absence. Whenever I peruse women's bookstores, I am struck not by the rapidly growing body of feminist writing by black women, but by the paucity of available published material. Those of us who write and are published remain few in number. The context of silence is varied and multi-dimensional. Most obvious are the ways racism, sexism, and class exploitation act to suppress and silence. Less obvious are the inner struggles, the efforts made to gain the necessary confidence to write, to re-write, to fully develop craft and skill – and the extent to which such efforts fail.

Although I have wanted writing to be my life-work since childhood, it has been difficult for me to claim "writer" as part of that which identifies and shapes my everyday reality. Even after publishing books, I would often speak of wanting to be a writer as though these works did not exist. And though I would be told, "you are a writer", I was not yet ready to fully affirm this truth. Part of myself was still held captive by domineering forces of history, of familial life that had charted a map of silence, of right speech. I had not completely let go of the fear of saying the wrong thing, of being punished. Somewhere in the deep recesses of my mind, I believed I could avoid both responsibility and punishment if I did not declare myself a writer.

One of the many reasons I chose to write using the pseudonym bell hooks, a family name (mother to Sarah Oldham, grandmother to Rosa Bell Oldham, great-grandmother to me), was to construct a writer-identity that would challenge and subdue all impulses leading me away from speech into silence. I was a young girl buying bubble gum at the corner store when I first really heard the full name bell hooks. I had just "talked back" to a grown person. Even now I can recall the surprised look, the mocking tones that informed me I must be kin to bell hooks – a sharp-tongued woman, a woman who spoke her mind, a woman who was not afraid to talk back. I claimed this legacy of defiance, of will, of courage, affirming my link to female ancestors who were bold and daring in their speech. Unlike my bold and daring mother and grandmother, who were not supportive of talking back, even though they were assertive and powerful in their speech, bell hooks as I discovered, claimed, and invented her was my ally, my support.

That initial act of talking back outside the home was empowering. It was the first of many acts of defiant speech that would make it possible for me to emerge as an independent thinker and writer. In retrospect, "talking back" became for me a rite of initiation, testing my courage, strengthening my commitment, preparing me for the days ahead – the days when writing, rejection notices, periods of silence, publication, ongoing development seem impossible but necessary.

Moving from silence into speech is for the oppressed, the colonized, the exploited, and those who stand and struggle side by side a gesture of defiance that heals, that makes new life and new growth possible. It is that act of speech, of "talking back", that is no mere gesture of empty words, that is the expression of our movement from object to subject – the liberated voice.

Marsha Prescod

1950s–

S *he went to England from Trinidad as a child with her parents in
the 1950s' wave of immigration from the Caribbean. Encouraged
by the Black Writers' Workshop in Brixton, she has written poetry
since 1980. Brent Black Music Workshop helped her develop her style and
confidence as a performance poet. Her book of poems* Land of Rope and
Tory *was published in 1985. She also writes short stories and is developing
a genre of "African-Caribbean science fiction".*

Auntie Vida's Hair Salon

I F you wanted to play sociology professor, and do an analysis of Caribbean
women's humour, it could be divided into categories like Sayings, Irony,
Socio-political comment, Mother-wit and Survival techniques. For example, take
my Auntie Vida's unique way of giving advice. If you came to her, crying about
unhappiness over job/man/friends, she would say "Child, what you want to carry
round this big load of problems for? You ever see problems in a coffin? You a
go dead and bury and leave these self-same problems here."

I remember my grandmother cracking them up in the DHSS.[1] She'd gone
into the office in Harlesden 'cos her giro hadn't arrived. They told her that her
name was on their computer, but not on the main computer up in Newcastle
due to some error, hence the delay. Quick as a flash she'd retorted, "Eh-eh!
So just because your computer vex with the computer up in Newcastle, and
they ain't talking, you mean I can't get me money? You better tell the one in
Newcastle that if it don't start behaving, I going to get 'my' computer to cuss its
arse!" Needless to say, she got her money.

I also remember my own mother cracking me up with her sharp comments
in times of crisis. Like the day she came into my room and said, "Marsha, I
think you better enter that red skirt you like to wear in the Olympics." When
I asked her why, she retorted, "Because within ten seconds of you putting it
in the machine with the other clothes, it run all over your father's best dress
shirt." Or the example she gave when commenting on a friend of hers who
would take no nonsense from anybody, and in giving a list of the actions carried
out in retaliation against her ex-husband, each harder than the last, concluded
triumphantly: ". . .so he give her six children. . .and she give them right back!"

---

[1] Department of Health and Social Security.

Thinking of some of these incidents, and others, when asked to write something on the topic of our humour, I thought that the best place to go and sample some of the vintage stuff was Auntie Vida's hair salon.

Now, my Auntie Vida has what she calls, "Qualifications in Life". As a result, her wisdom is legendary throughout the South (Croydon, Brixton, Peckham, Camberwell), and her salon is known for attracting customers with a deadly line of repartee.

I decided to venture there one Saturday morning when I knew it would be full of her cronies. When they heard what I'd come to research, there was a burst of raucous laughter.

Wiping her eyes after a good giggle, Mrs Euphacine Williams commented: "Of course Black women are good at comedy. We have a fantastic sense of humour. Look at me, I left a happy little life in Grenada to come here and work in a shitty little factory for chickenfoot wages and break me neck to buy a house the size of a dog kennel. Ain't that a big joke?"

"No", Aunt Vida snapped, quick as a whip. "But that hairdo you get from Maxiecurls is!"

"Nah," put in Wrencilla, Auntie Vida's trusty lieutenant. "The biggest joke is the fact that she pay them money for it." That was the cue for a second burst of raucous laughter, while I asked Mrs Williams what she meant by the phrase "chickenfoot wages".

"Well," she said, "those is wages that is so small, that when you get them the only thing you can afford to buy to cook is chickenfoot."

"You see, child," said another lady I only knew as Miss CC, "we does have to put up with so much to survive in this country that you gots to have a sense of humour to deal with it."

"*Um-hm!*" echoed a big, cocoa-coloured woman by the name of Mrs Lucille Leslyn Lewis. "Imagine, I go into the bank yesterday to get a loan to buy a car, and though I have me house fully paid for and no debts, the little hard-faced clerk still keep telling me 'Oh, Mrs Loo-seel, what *hexactly* are your assets?' In the end I had to get *stink*. I tell him, 'Assets? What you mean – a little ass? Because that must be what you think I am, cross-questioning me for half an hour for this small bit of money. I start dealing with money over thirty years ago, when you was so small your pee couldn't even make froth and your mother was still cleaning the doo-doo from your baggie. So don't tell me nothing about assets, to raas.'"

That was the cue for the third burst of raucous laughter. By now, I could hardly keep a straight face. I told the gathering that I'd noticed in the past that politics seemed to provide a continuous source of inspiration to women of my mother's generation.

"Of course," said Madame Wavis Wills, a regular at the salon, who liked to describe herself as being "strained in economics" (i.e. hard up). "That's a tradition in the West Indies, in the popular songs there. And over here, well, you gots to laugh at a government that running the economy using a Christopher Columbus strategy." We all looked puzzled at this description, so this was how she explained it:

"Well, they like to say that Christopher Columbus is a big hero, how he discover this place and that place, is just so this government is boasey. They like to boast about all the economic miracles they invent. But when you really check out the story of Christopher Columbus, what you find, eh? Christopher Columbus was a real arsehole. He leave for a long journey and he didn't know where the hell he was going. When he get there, he didn't know *where* he was.

"He met a set of people living there and he didn't know who the hell they where. When he leave, he couldn't have said where he was leaving from. And up to the day he died, he didn't know where he'd been. When they tell me about him in school, when I was about ten, I said to myself, what an idiot. And when a few months later I get on the bus to go to school and I find out the driver's name was Christopher Columbus, I get frighten; and climb right back off, 'cos I did figure that instead of going to St James, I woulda end up in Japan." Cue for the fourth burst of raucous laughter.

There was more, much more, that morning at Auntie Vida's hair salon, and I'm sorry to say that as the women got warmed up, I was laughing so hard my hand was too shaky to write down what I'd heard. But the amount of what our African-American sisters could call Attitude, Bodaciousness and Sass that flew around was such, that when I left there, I was high, ready to take on the world. They'd shown me how our community's daughters, mothers, aunties, grandmothers had survived the trials and tribulations of migration to a country that is often hostile and indifferent, using humour as a deadly weapon.

Let's celebrate!

Exiles

Forty years in the factory,
Thirty years on the bus,
Twenty years with machinery,
They don't make them any more like us.

Happy to know which place to go,
Canada, US and Britain,
Whether is canal to build,
War to fight,
Land to till,
We eager to make we heaven.

Small fish in an ocean
Of greed, and gold,
All we dreaming is how to get rank.
So, is families wasted,
An health all gone,
Whilst we putting we lives in the bank.

An when you hear the shout –
We can't get out,
Our pride and spirit get break.
At home prices too high,
An no jobs left to try,
Here,
We is crippled by the Welfare State.

Is a little beer here,
Little dominoes there,
And a lot of funeral to follow,
Having ketch as ketch arse,
Just a pensioner's pass,
An a old folks home come tomorrow.

Forty years in the factory,
Thirty years on the bus,
Twenty years with machinery,
Yes. . .
They don't make them anymore like us.

Dionne Brand

1953–

Born in Guayaguayare in Trinidad, she was educated locally until high school, then in 1970 moved to Canada, graduating from the University of Toronto in 1975 with a degree in English and philosophy. She worked for a year as an information/communications coordinator in Grenada until the American invasion of the island in October 1983, when she returned to Canada, where she has been active in Black community work in Toronto. Her books of poems include 'Fore Day Morning (1979), Primitive Offensive (1982) and Chronicles of the Hostile Sun (1984). She has also published a collection of short stories, Sans Souci and Other Tales (1988).

From

Primitive Offensive

CANTO XIII

I hated evenings like this
when I fall asleep
in the afternoon
and wake up when it has
already turned evening,
a smell of muddy oil
in the air
a scent of dirty water
trapped under the earth,
it would be damp
a breeze every now and again
got through
the grey watery sky,
and they would hang,
the clouds I mean,
there is no one else
in the world
on those evenings
those absolutely quiet evenings
waking up, looking across to the window,
hearing shoes on the pavement outside
hollow
heeled, spiked, woman's
and those man's
flat, slap of leather,
slithering,
I know he has a smile
gold teeth in his mouth
perhaps,
rings on his index, middle
and little fingers,
I'm sure he's wearing tan
she, her face is tight
as the pavement and the
heel of her shoe
her mouth is full of sand
her legs are caught
in that hobbled skirt
and the leaves of the trees
above those sounds

of steps
made a deceitful silky sound
like that
not all the time,
there is no one else in the world
on those evenings,
that dog's voice
barking through,
that child screaming
surprised to be awakened,
astonished at the quiet,
so startling,
to wake up at the wrong time,
the man and the woman
are a dream
knocking at my sleep,
betrayal of an evening
let me sleep
I am afraid of them
I lie still
waiting for them to leave,
the man's smile, his gold
the woman's tight face
her armpits
tight with sand
they hollow and slither
in turn,
it is endless,
they cover me like gauze
like a master-weaver spider,
no matter where I am
these unforgiving evenings
fallen asleep and forgotten,
centuries in this huge and ruined
room.

Andrea Lee
?1953–

A native of Philadelphia, Pennsylvania, the youngest of a Baptist minister's three children, she has a BA and MA in English literature from Harvard University, where she met her husband, a PhD candidate in Russian history. Accompanying him to Moscow and Leningrad for ten months of study (1978–9), she recorded her observations in a diary, which formed the basis of her highly praised first book, Russian Journal (1981). She subsequently became a staff writer for the New Yorker magazine and in 1980 was given the Front Page Award for Distinguished Journalism by the Newswomen's Club of New York. This is a chapter from her first novel, Sarah Phillips (1984), a story of middle-class Black America and a young Black woman's journey of self-discovery in Europe and Philadelphia, which takes her back to memories of childhood.

From

Sarah Phillips

AN OLD WOMAN

EARLY one Saturday morning my mother and I had a long, monotonous argument about a nifty pair of French jeans that I wanted to buy at Saks. My mother said that the jeans were overpriced and indecently tight, and that she and my father didn't give me an allowance to have me waste it on any fad that came along; I contended that the jeans were a necessity, that I had fewer pairs than any other girl in the neighborhood, and that she just wanted to keep me badly dressed and looking like a child.

We were driving around doing errands. Mama sat up very straight behind the steering wheel, looking prim and slightly ruthless in a dark-green suit, and I slumped in the seat beside her, biting my nails and tapping the toes of my sneakers with boredom. After stopping in at Saks, we had bought some groceries, picked up some flats of marigolds at Korvettes, dropped in at my orthodontist's office to see about a possible crack in my retainer, and stopped at Mrs Rindell's house to deliver some tickets Mama was selling for a benefit given by her club, the Wives of Negro Professionals. It was a hot, hazy morning, one of a spell of unseasonably warm September days in Philadelphia. Along City Line Avenue the trees were slowly turning brown, and in the diffused light the big street with its crowded shopping centers and dense streams of traffic looked as if it had been lightly powdered by a fall of yellowish dust – it was the same yellow tint that comes over old Polaroid snapshots.

There was one more errand left to do: my mother indicated a brown bag that held a quarter of a poundcake wrapped in wax paper. "I want to take this over to poor old Mrs Jeller," she said. "Roosevelt Convalescent Home is only five minutes away, and we can just duck in and say hello, and then we can go home."

"Oh, God, Mom – do I have to go in?" I asked.

"You certainly do," said my mother emphatically. "Mrs Jeller was one of your father's most faithful parishioners a long time ago – possibly in early Christian days – and it would be a pleasure for her to see you. Sit up straight, and stop gnawing at your thumb."

The convalescent home wasn't five minutes away, it was twenty-five, the amount of time it took to go from the crowded thoroughfare of suburban shopping centers at the edge of town to a run-down, oddly deserted city street lined with boarded-up row houses and brick apartment buildings. The wheels of our car rattled on the cobblestones between the trolley tracks; at one end of the street I saw a group of little girls jumping double-dutch, their thin brown legs flying between the whirling ropes.

Old Mrs Jeller's room opened off a shiny red linoleum corridor on the eighth floor of a tall dismal building of pale, graffiti-covered brick. The room was a tiny cubicle half filled by a double bed covered with a yellow satin spread; a big television with the picture on but the sound off flickered in the corner. The air was smotheringly hot and smelled strongly of liniment. When I came with my mother through the doorway, I was embarrassed to see Mrs Jeller seated bare-legged on the bed, wearing a short, rather tight cotton shift that revealed the shape of her large, limp breasts. The old woman was brown-skinned, with a handsome square face; her loose gray hair bounced in a wild frizzy mass around her shoulders, and she kept tossing it back from her face with a petulant gesture that was like a macabre parody of the way a flirtatious teenager might behave. Her expression, which had been drawn and querulous, brightened somewhat when she saw us.

"Come on in, pastor's wife, and sit down!" she called out to my mother in a voice that seemed over-loud and silly to me. She gestured us toward two rangy oak side chairs that looked as if they had come out of a country parlor. "Me and Miz Bryant was just watching TV."

Mrs Bryant turned out to be the resident social worker, a white woman of about thirty, wearing an Indian-print dress and with a hairdo of untidy curls over a face with a receding chin and a mild, regretful expression, like that of a sheep. Mama handed her the package for Mrs Jeller, and then all of us sat down. For a minute or two the old woman stared at Mama and me with bright eyes and an unsmiling mouth, still tossing back her hair with that petulant gesture; then she gave a small chuckle. "I can tell you all is mother and daughter," she said. "They ain't no way you could deny that."

"Is that *your* mother over there in the picture, Mrs Jeller?" asked my mother, indicating an almost indecipherable yellow daguerreotype of a woman that stood on a table beside the bed.

"Yes, ma'am it is," said Mrs Jeller. "But she didn't raise me. I came up the hard way."

She moved laboriously backward on the bed and then stretched out her bare legs on the mattress until they lay stiffly in front of her like a doll's legs. On the other side of the bed, the social worker had turned her mournful sheep's face toward the silent television, where a game-show host, like a genie, conjured up prize after prize for a woman who seemed to be weeping with excitement.

"Oh, dear," began my mother. "What a shame. How – "

"The hard way," repeated Mrs Jeller, striking the mattress with a loud whack. She flung her bushy hair back impatiently and turned to address me as if we were alone in the room. "How old are you, missy? Fifteen?"

"Sixteen," I muttered, abashed. The sight of this wild old woman with the bare legs and shamelessly tossing breasts both disgusted and fascinated me; seeing her was shocking in a curiously intimate way, like learning a terrifying secret about myself.

Mrs Jeller sat up a little straighter and went on staring at me. Her gaze was severe, as if she were about to chastise me for something. "You're a pretty thing," she said in a reproving tone, and was silent for a minute, her eyes glittering like two black beads in her dry brown face.

"Do you know, girl," she continued abruptly, "that I had my first man – that a man first had his way with me – when I was twelve years old? *Twelve years old!*'

The old woman drew out these last three words into a plaintive wail that sounded like the voice of an abandoned child. As she spoke, she suddenly turned her head from me and began staring out of the window.

My mother gave a dry little cough and asked, "What town did you grow up in, Mrs Jeller? Was it Philadelphia?"

Mrs Jeller shook her head. "No, ma'am. It was out in the back of nowhere in Kentucky. Mama worked for the white folks, so I lived with Uncle Mills and Aunt Treece. They were country folks, and up until I was twelve, they kept me innocent. I was so innocent that when I first got Eve's curse, my monthly flow of blood, I thought I had cut myself in the privy. I came running back to the house, shouting to my uncle and aunt, 'I've hurt myself!'

"Aunt Treece took my upstairs and showed me the cloths I must use to catch the blood, and how I must boil and wash them. And Uncle Mills called me into the parlor and told me that now I was a woman, and from that night on, I must only take my pants down for two reasons – to wash, and to go to the privy.

"Both of them warned me never to allow any men or boys near me. But strict as they could be, a man did get to me. He was the brother of two girls who lived down the road. They were fast girls, bad girls, older than I was; they used to smoke little violet-colored cigarettes. They would always say 'Come on!' to me whenever they went places, and like a fool I'd go. And then their brother took to hanging around, and one night the girls left the two of us alone, and he did something to me. He hurt me, and I didn't even know what it was he was doing. I ran home and didn't stop to speak to my uncle and aunt – I just went right on up to bed and cried. Three weeks later my uncle looked at me and said, 'Honey, you been with a man. Who was it?'

"I started to cry and told him all about it. It turned out that I had gotten a baby from that man, from just that one time. A man's seed is a powerful thing. It wiggles and jumps until it gets where it's going, even inside a child who was a virgin.

"The next morning my uncle went out, and when he came back, he said to me, 'Hattie, we are going to have a wedding here, so go and invite whoever you want.'

"I invited my teacher from school, and a girl I played with from next door, and I stood in the parlor, and the preacher married me to that man – his name was John. And after that, John lived in our house, and slept in my room, though I hardly spoke to him. Oh, it was frightening, I tell you, to wake up with that strange head alongside of me on the pillow. One night he touched me, and I felt a leaping and a hopping inside of me, as if my baby was trying to come out. After that I wouldn't let him touch me. And in June, when my baby came, my uncle had the marriage annulled."

Mrs Jeller shivered suddenly and clasped her hands with a sudden movement that shook her limp breasts under the cotton shift. "I can't seem to get warm, even on hot days," she said. "I can't even sleep with regular sheets now," she continued, indicating the bed, which was made up with a pair of thin, stained cotton blankets. Through the window came the hazy September sunlight, and from the street below, faintly, drifted the shouts of children and the noise of passing cars.

My mother and I both had our eyes fixed on the old woman as if we were hypnotized. "What happened to your baby?" I asked, almost involuntarily.

Mrs Jeller looked off toward Mrs Bryant, the social worker, who was still watching the silent television. "For a year and a half, my baby lived," she said. "It was a baby girl. I left school and went out to work for white folks, and my lady, Miz Guthrie, was crazy about my baby. 'Little Daisy,' she named her, and kept her in a big basket in the dining room. She called me every hour to nurse the baby. That child saw more white society than I ever did. But she sickened and died; a lot of children died in those days. Two years later I was fourteen and free of husband and daughter. Free of both of them, and still a child myself."

The old woman suddenly turned her head back toward Mama and me, and gave us a toothless smile so wide and so swift that it seemed demonic. We both rose abruptly from our chairs as if we'd been struck from behind. Once on my feet, I really felt as if I might faint from the stifling heat of the room and the smell of liniment.

"It's been very nice to see you," said my mother, after making a bit of small talk.

"Nicer for me than for you," said Mrs Jeller, with a wink.

When we stood waiting for the elevator in the red linoleum hallway of the nursing home, I felt unwilling to look my mother in the face, and she seemed disinclined to look at me. We stood awkwardly, half facing away from each other, and I felt very aware of my body under my clothes. For the first time, I was sensing the complicated possibilities of my own flesh – possibilities of corruption, confused pleasure, even death. The tale we'd heard – that had burst so unexpectedly upon a dullish Saturday afternoon – had a disturbing archaic flavor; it seemed, even, in a vague way, obscene. In its light it was hard for us to face each other as mother and child. We had not yet arrived at an acquaintance with each other as two women, and so we had to remain silent.

"I never heard *that* story before," said Mama finally, taking a handkerchief from her purse and patting the sides of her neck. "Poor old thing, she's gotten very senile."

"It was awfully hot in there," I said, gathering up my hair in my hands and flapping it to make a breeze.

"Old people like hot rooms. Their limbs don't seem to hold any warmth."

We got in the car and began the long drive back to the suburbs, and after a minute or two it was possible to talk naturally. We never, however, resumed our formulaic argument over the French jeans: one visible effect of our visit to old Mrs Jeller was that ever afterward I was allowed to pick out my own clothes. My mother explained it by saying that she guessed I was old enough to make any mistake I chose.

Sekai Nzenza

?1950s–

B orn and trained as a nurse in Zimbabwe, she did additional nursing studies in England and subsequently went to live in Australia. Her autobiography, Zimbabwean Woman: My Own Story, was published in 1988.

From

Zimbabwean Woman: My Own Story

CHAPTER I

THE African sun was getting hot. It's supposed to be a winter's sun; but here in Africa, we do not have a real cold winter. We have never seen snow. May is a dull month and the days are shorter than the nights. The fields are dry and the season's harvest was done two months ago. There is not much to do in this season except to collect the cattle from the valleys. These cattle roam about and enjoy their freedom because nobody looks after them or whips them unnecessarily. The herdboys love this season because all they have to do is get the herds of cattle out of the kraal and direct them down to the valley or up in the mountains, then the boys go climbing trees, looking for the wild fruits when the sun gets hot at midday. They go down to the rivers to fish, to swim and to fight just for the sake of finding out who is more powerful. At sunset they go looking for the cattle and would often find them; but sometimes they don't and have to face a bit of boxing of the ears by a usually drunk father.

My mother is a middle-aged woman. It's ever so difficult to tell her age. She is medium built, quite brown in complexion which means that she must have been considered beautiful as a young girl. She is heavily pregnant with her sixth child. Her oldest child is ten, which means she has been pregnant every other year. She has done very well; and what's more, she has had two boys and three girls. This pregnancy is definitely going to be another boy. Her ten-year-old daughter has gone to collect some firewood nearby. The eight-year-old boy has gone to leave the cattle in the hills today. The six-year-old girl is washing the dishes from last night. The four-year-old boy is chasing flies and bees behind the hut. This hut is the kitchen, the bedroom, as well as the food store. The two-year-old girl has had a bad night and has to be carried on her mother's back, even though she is heavily pregnant.

The woman sits and watches her four-year-old son running around and she smiles, because he does not often run around like that. He often just sits and stares. He prefers to have on his khaki shirt which hardly covers his front, but covers his back and bottom very well. He never has his pants on. It's funny how these shirts are designed to cover the back part so well and leave the front exposed. Who cares anyway. The boy, Chorosi is his name, laughs as he grasps one fly. He crushes it in his hand, the legs, the head, the wings but no eyes. Flies do not have eyes, he concludes. No wonder they keep on falling into my bowl of milk and also sit on my waste matter soon after I have done it.

His mother looks at him and sighs. She looks down at her mother-in-law's hut. There is smoke coming out through the thatched roof. Maybe her mother-in-law is cooking. That will keep her in for some time and she will not start shouting and swearing at people at mid-day, anyway. This old woman is neurotic and is in fact in control of this village, because everybody is scared of her. She is a terror. Her husband left her to have three other women, but she still has her status; for did she not have five children: three boys, two girls, all strong and healthy? She was the first wife and therefore in charge and had authority over every woman married into the village. But today, she chooses to grind some corn and perhaps do some cooking.

The woman feels pain in her tummy. She feels some wetness and she knows that the baby is on the way. It's almost a week overdue. She takes the baby off her back to put her down, but the two-year-old screams in protest and clings on to her. The woman decides to take a walk in the bush nearby. The pain is getting worse. She pulls the leaves off bushes and branches to forget her pain – but it gets worse and she feels weak and heavy in the legs – she squats and grips her teeth. The child on her back cries because she does not feel comfortable when her bearer is squatting. The woman gets up; quickly walks home. She gets into the kitchen and calls her four-year-old boy Chorosi.

"Go and call your grandmother quick."

The boys stares at her confused. However, he gets the message and slowly walks to his grandmother's hut. On the way he stops and examines the insides of a fly. The fly has no tummy. So why does it drink my milk and follow me when I go to help myself? Flies are so naughty, but so clever. He wishes he was a fly and starts pretending to fly, forgetting that he has been sent to call his grandmother.

The woman writhes and sweats with labour pains.The two-year-old, Giji, looks at her and cries for attention. Pai, the ten-year-old, gets back from collecting fire-wood. She takes hold of the situation. For did not her mother feel like this two years ago?

"Go call the midwife and tell her the water is all out and the head is coming."

Pai goes to her grandmother first and finds her busy grinding corn. She stops grinding, looks up, frowns and says:

"What is it? I thought your mother cooked for you last night. I haven't got any food to give the whole village. I work so hard in my old age and nobody says thank you. Your mother basks in the sun all day nursing her pregnancy. She is not the first woman to get pregnant and being pregnant is not an illness. Did she not get enough teaching where she came from? Can you teach a woman to cook, sweep and look after her own house, can you?"

"Grandma, Mother is going in..." Pai said; and before she finished, her grandma cut in.

"Going where? Going across to the river to gossip. Eh? Gossip is all your mother can do. Why she ever gave birth to you as a first-born child is what I do not understand. You should have been a boy to take control of my son's house because your stupid mother is too lazy to care and all she thinks of is getting pregnant and giving birth to more girls. There are three of you now and I would not be surprised if the next one is a girl. Now go away and let me get on with my work." She said this as she blew her nose into the dying fire nearby, wipes gers on her clothes and started grinding.

"Mother is going into labour and she wants you," Pai shouted this time.

Grandmother looked up, a bit surprised. Got up. Blew her nose again and wiped it with the back of her hand, leaving marks of white mealie-meal on her face and nose.

Pai ran back to her mother and shouted that grandmother was coming. Then she rushed off to call the midwife, who lived two miles across the stream.

The woman was getting tired as the pain got worse and she could feel the head coming out. Grandmother got in and saw the head coming out.

"I did not believe you were in labour. Now take it easy and relax. Do not push hard. I'm not a good midwife but I can see you well all right," she said, holding her by the shoulders and rubbing her back. She put a blanket below for the water and blood to flow on.

Nobody noticed Chorosi sitting behind the door watching. He had given up chasing and crushing flies, fascinated by this extraordinary event.

Two women neighbours shouted a greeting from outside. When they got no reply, they decided to come in. The door was open, which meant there was somebody at home. They looked at the woman on the floor in pain and they sat down. One of them, Mai Keti, just pushed her hand inside to check the progress.

"You are all right, my friend. There is lots of space. This is your sixth baby, isn't it? Well, a sixth baby is as easy as eating sadza with okra soup. Take it easy, woman," she said, as she wiped the water off her hands and sat down to watch the progress.

Pai finally got there. The midwife was sitting beside her hut, smoking her black snuff.

"My mother is in labour, she says do come quickly."

Without a word the old woman got up, picked up a stone nearby and put it on her back, secured it with a piece of cloth and tied it round. The stone on her back is supposed to delay delivery and prevent complications before she, the expert midwife in the village, got there.

"It's coming and it hurts S-s-s-t!" the woman screamed in pain.

"You have to push now. Push, harder," the women urged her.

She pushed harder and harder and slowly but surely the baby was coming out. First the small head with loads of black silky, wet hair, then the shoulders, the back, the bottom and the legs. With a scream the baby finally got out.

"It's yet another girl," grandmother said.

"Cut off the cord with the razor," Mai Keti said, as she gave grandmother a razor which was rather blunt, but did its job. The other woman had got a piece of string from the fresh bark of a tree ready and tied the cord.

"She is black and ugly."

"Yes, she is black, but she going to be beautiful."

"A black baby can never be beautiful."

The midwife and Pai arrived soon afterwards but they were a little late. The stone did not work or maybe the baby just decided to come too early.

The women talked and laughed about their labour experiences. Even grandmother talked and laughed as well.

The baby was well wrapped in blankets and put to the breast. It started sucking immediately.

"What an appetite! She is going to be a ravenous monster, but she has given you the easiest labour you will ever have. It did not last long, did it?" Mai Keti said, as she rose up to go.

"I want to have a baby to play with," Chorosi said and everybody laughed.

The other children came to see the baby. Sidi, the eight-year-old boy refused to believe the baby had actually come out of his mother. There were no men in the village except old grandpa Sosia who came to see the baby.

"A real black one indeed. There is no doubt she is our blood for she has taken well after us and after the women in our generations. Thanks be to the spirits of the earth who guide us well and give us little ones to keep our name," he said, and took the baby into his hands and blessed it in the name of the spirits of the living, the spirits of the ancestors.

Dulcie September
1953–88

*S*he *was born in Western Cape, South Africa, received secondary schooling at Athlone High School and attended Battswood Teacher Training College, Wynberg, Cape Province. Forced to leave teaching because of her stand against educational policies and Bantu Education Act practices, she was arrested and convicted for political work in April 1974 and banned after her release – five years restriction. She left South Africa that year and was later posted to Paris as chief African National Congress representative in France. She was killed by a bomb placed in her office. This story was posthumously published in* One Never Knows: An Anthology of Black South African Women Writers *(ed. Mabuza, 1989).*

A Split Society – Fast Sounds on the Horizon

BELLA gave the impression that she was always ready to embrace everybody – she always had a friendly smile, a friendly word. Her home was a place where everybody felt free to call at any time. Sometimes she did not have much to offer them in the line of refreshments, but she would give them what she could even if it meant standing behind the kitchen door beating her head with her fists because she could not think of things that she could prepare.

When she eventually appeared in the lounge with a tray of nice things to eat, nobody could have guessed just how exhausted, both mentally and physically, she was.

"Come along, help yourself to some mince pie. I curried the meat. It is lovely and spicy, just the way you like it. And what about some toast and sardines? With tomato salad? We'll have these while the stamp *mielies* and beans are cooking.

"Who's for coffee? Or tea?

"Let's see now: one, two, three coffees; one, two, three teas. I'll bring the milk and sugar so that you can help yourself." Off she would dart to the kitchen to make the tea and coffee.

"I have some more pies in the oven. So don't be afraid to help yourself," Bella would shout from the kitchen.

At last, the coffee and tea would be ready. She could then go and sit down and have a lovely chit-chat with her friends. That was how she liked it. Shoulders down, handing around whatever was wanted, chin at the wag.

It was always very obvious that Bella's home was the focal point of life because it was there that she could cut herself off from all the ugliness of the society in which she lived. She was actually saying: Let it be just us and those who understand what I mean.

Eric, a tall, well-built character, who would sport a crew-cut hair-style today and a few months later would have his hair lying on his shoulders, would always tell Bella that he loved her just the way she was. But under his breath he would mumble so that only those near him would hear: "I must be hard-up for friends, to be saying this to her!" Those who overheard him would have a hearty laugh and good-natured Bella would know that something nasty had been said about her. But she would laugh along with the others at a remark about herself, that was not meant for her ears but which she vaguely heard.

Poppie was there in that happy atmosphere that Bella created, but was never part of it. She could not meet her friends or visit them. She was forced by an order which banned her and stopped her from being a social being. A knock at the door at any time of the day or night could mean that her jailers were coming to check whether she was breaking some clause in the order. This order which made her her own jailer.

Very often Poppie would say to herself: "But I am my own wardress. I am putting myself into jail every evening at six o'clock; only allowed to unlock that gate again at six o'clock in the next morning."

Yes, Bella's happy home was Poppie's jail where Poppie lived a twilight existence. Her whole lifestyle had suddenly changed. This order that banned her, suddenly changed everything. Suddenly there were no more weekend meetings, or midnight watermelon feasts on the open beaches.

"No, there is nothing like that now because this blasted order is making all my decisions for me. It decides that I have to deposit myself on my side of the garden gate every evening at six o'clock, with myself as company. I can't pick up the phone and ask my friends to call and spend the evening with me." All of a sudden Poppie was no longer supposed to be a social being.

Parked cars in the vicinity of Poppie's home always meant that there were some prying, watching eyes checking whether she would be on her side of the gate by the time the clock in the tower of the Nederduitse Gereformeerde Church struck six in hollow, off-tune beats.

When Poppie was still a child she used to wonder about this Nederduitse Gereformeerde Kerk, where only white people used to go on Sundays. She would sit on the pavement and wriggle her filthy toes while watching all these white people going to church.

"I wonder why they pull their lips so tightly together. They are so tight-lipped, no smile. It can't be very nice to be a white person going to church on Sundays to pray. Mama says they pray in there, pray to God. But I don't think I'll want to pray in there, even if I could, because I don't want to look sad. I saw Mama being sad when Papa died but now she is all right, I think. And they wear such strange clothes. They always mourn on Sundays. When my Papa died everybody, almost everybody wore black. Mama said they did so because they were mourning and were very sad. Those stiff-starched collars seem to be choking them. I suppose that is the reason why they pull their lips together in such tight lines."

Mama says that the women wear sensible clothes. I wonder what Mama means by that. I did not want to ask her. I wonder whether the clothes that I have on are sensible? Mama always says that I look a real disgrace in my tatters, in my filthy khaki shorts and shirts. But it is so puzzling to me that I can't keep them clean or without holes. They just get dirty and torn.

These women always wear hats when they go and pray in this Nederduitse Gereformeerde Church. I wonder why. I wonder whether the men also put their hats on again when they get inside the church because I notice that they take their hats off as they move up the pathway towards the church door. Rather funny, this is.

Today I stay here in the gutter and wait for them to come out of church because I must see whether they will be smiling then. At school the teacher told us that God was good. If he does good things to them then they must be happy. Look how happy I am when Mama brings me fruit and sweets. That is good and I laugh and thank Mama and Mama smiles. So, if God is good to them then they should be smiling. Oh, I don't understand all this. Maybe God is not good to them.

"Oh, here they come, first the Dominee. He is shaking hands with the people as they leave the church. I see no difference in the faces and expressions of these people. They seem to be just as tight-lipped and unhappy. I wonder whether God has scolded them. When Mama scolds me, I also look unhappy because I don't like Mama to scold me. That's it. They must have had a scolding from God."

Today Poppie knows all too well that these tight-lipped people are indoctrinated with false belief that they are here by virtue of the fact that they are white and therefore superior to people of colour. Those with darker skins are naturally inferior according to their doctrine, and not to be trusted.

"Oh! No! What's to-be-trusted? Let's arm ourselves, brother and sisters, old and young, against the dangers of people of colour." The minister ventriloquizes through his tight lips. So these people with their stiffly starched collars and tight lips are the upholders of Afrikanerdom and Christian Nationalism, the pure superior race – civilization. The women in their sensible clothes cover up, because it is degrading for a good woman to show her arms or chest: "Good women cover up! Don't expose your flesh, which is the curse of this world. Cover up good women or our Christian society will go to the dogs," preaches the Dominee. The silly little hats that these good women wear cannot hide the shallowness of their thoughts, their empty way of life, which revolves around floral decorations, the latest recipe and their ability to play some musical instrument. While they prattle away on empty topics, somewhere a mother is watching a young baby starve to death. There cannot be idle prattle about floral decorations, the latest recipes or musical instruments. The only music this mother knows is the death rattle of her starving, dying baby.

This death rattle that gnaws away at her brain until she thinks that she is going crazy. And when that death rattle stops besides her, that gnawing, gnawing goes on in her brain like a needle that has got itself stuck in the grooves of a record. When she again finds herself sitting in the same position, again listening to the death rattle of yet another baby, she knows that the sound of the death rattle in her brain has never stopped. But she firmly knows that it must stop some time.

Poppie says quietly to her: "I know of another kind of nationalism which just a few decades ago had the whole world bleeding. Is this not a very similar nationalism, under cover of Christianity which breeds, breeds, but which will eventually erupt and have the whole world bleeding again."

"These upholders of Afrikanerdom are the thieves in our country, the plunderers, the murderers. They stole everything that once belonged to us. Today they dump us in the worst areas that cannot bring forth anything but barrenness. The best land these thieves have stolen, and are now plundering everything – our land, our gold, our coal, our diamonds – everything. And while they steal and plunder they murder. Murder by starvation: murder by hanging: murder in the mines, on the streets, in jails.

"Murder to these Christian Nationalists is not crime. Stealing is not a crime because of the superior white position they hold. But the suffering millions have already decided that they will bring these criminals to justice."

In Poppie's frustration she calls out: "What crime have I committed to be sitting here in jail, Bella's happy home, my jail? That I am forced to create it for myself. No social life, home at six, no talking to a crowd of people, no meeting, nothing! House arrest because I dare oppose the wrong that we have to endure. No! We won't let them go unpunished!"

From time to time Poppie's mind dwells on Bella and she says to herself, "Bella's life is too insular. She means well but her whole life actually revolves around herself. . ."

Bella's home was comfortable. There was happiness. But just down the road there was a shanty town where the shacks in which the people lived were constructed of zinc, cardboard, rags and sticks – any material for that matter could help towards putting a roof over the heads of those who have nothing at all.

In a shanty town like this everybody is congested, with one shack built right on top of the other, as it were. There is no breathing space. And one very often gets the impression that the wind turns the other way and blows in the opposite direction when it gets anywhere near this shanty-town. Even the wind is shocked at these conditions.

Yes, here even God does not temper the wind to help the shorn lambs. There is no drainage and on a sweltering day, the flies seem to attack not only the filth but everything including the people, especially the bare-backed children. For some reason they seem to be looking for some opening so that they can get into that hollowness inside. The bare-backed children run the streets looking for more morsels to fill that hollowness inside. To these children the gutters and the garbage bins are like Bella's pleasant refreshment trays, laden with nice things to eat. A velvety green mouldy crust of bread, a gravel-encrusted toffee in a green-infested hand, rescued from a garbage bin, will keep those howling hollow pangs away long enough until the next meal of the same dreary fare.

There are some who are fortunate enough to have employment. They run like mad march hares to collect garbage from palatial homes with rows and rows of pretty flowers, sprawling lawns: for you it is the path which leads to the back of the house. For you the paths which lead to those lovely ornate doors are out of bounds. As Sam, the garbage collector, runs, he says to himself.

"Is that a green carpet lying over there? No, man, you old silly, it is only the green lawn you are squinting at as you run, run for the garbage." "Now, the garbage bin, then run, run after the blasted truck that never stops. Run, run or else you'll miss it and you won't be able to toss the garbage on the truck. If you could only run as fast as you do when you run from the police who are always around to arrest you for vagrancy – some type of violation of the vagrancy laws. Vagrant in my own country?"

Run, run, run, Sam!

"Vagrancy laws! Made it! I won't let this blasted truck with its white driver get me. I'll show them both that I can still run, run. But I am really sorry that I could not scrounge around in this bin for bits of waste which I know are there. If only I could have laid my hands on them then I could have stilled these hunger pains in my stomach. Had only a cup of weak, black sugarless tea this morning. It was all my Rachel had for me. But what are you doing, thinking about food in garbage bins that you could have had if it had not been for this blasted truck-collector of garbage – that never stops. Run, Sam, run, back to those palatial houses for their garbage. This is the house where I always get a little parcel of waste neatly wrapped in tin foil. Oh! This woman who works here always keeps some of the scraps for my children.

Sam grabs the bin and hoists it on his shoulder. He runs, runs, out by the gate and into the street. He thinks to himself: "I must run carefully because I know that the white truck driver that never stops that truck is watching in his rear-view mirror. Now let's run slowly towards the left of the truck while you push your hand under the lid. Now pull off the lid. The silver parcel, where is it? There! Grab it! Push it into the front of your shirt and at the same time empty the bin. Now back to the house with your empty bin."

As Sam leaves the next house he wonders what day of the week it is. Monday, is it? That means that this household has had fish for their Friday supper. They obviously have not heard the Pope say that they could eat other things besides fish on Fridays. Sam mumbles to himself: "Oh, this fish house again. I must run, run faster so that I can get the contents of this bin emptied as fast as possible. Look, even the cats turn and walk the other way."

What a stink!

Sam grabs the awfully smelling bin that has had fish entrails, fish heads and fried fish-bones in it since Friday night. And it has been boiling hot the whole weekend. I wonder what the neighbours say and think of this revolting stench here in civilization alleys. But then their noses are so far above this revolting fish stench that it does not bother them. And, they don't exactly live on top of one another. No, no there is no congestion here.

Sam runs and tosses the contents of the bin into the truck. Filth, dried, stinking fish entrails, heads and bones. The stench almost makes Sam throw up. But there is only emptiness, hollowness. Even the weak, black, sugarless tea is no longer there. It has mingled with the sweat and salt on the surface of his skin.

At last it is Friday night and Sam feels happier with his pay in his packet. It is nothing much, not enough to give his wife and family the bare necessities of life. This pay packet is actually worthless, but Sam must go to the shebeen to meet his friends and have a few glasses of Oom Tas, which is specially brewed for us to help us forget the ugliness of this society and that damned truck that never stops. On the one hand it helps us to forget our problems, but on the other hand it also subdues our tempers.

As Sam walks into the shebeen where he has decided to meet his friends and to have some Oom Tas that will drown his frustrations, it is:

"Hello, John, man. Hello, Jack, hello hello hello."

"Hello, man," my friends chorus, "you are a bit late, are you not?"

"Yes, fellows. These old legs are not what they used to be. They get tired much faster than they used to," laughs Sam.

"One Oom Tas, please, Queen Marie. How are you then, Queen Marie?"

Queen Marie smiles and says that she is fine. "She has been our shebeen queen for as long as we can remember. She is part of our little community. If she should leave us one day then part of us will be lost," thinks Sam fondly.

Queen Marie is big and does not fear any of her regular customers. Sometimes after a few bottles of Oom Tas many troublesome ones have had a foretaste and five fingers of Queen Marie's big brown fist that has had them fully tasting dust before they knew where they were. Nobody argues with Queen Marie. No, you pick yourself up, that is if you can, dust yourself back, with a sheepish look: Queen Marie is not a bad old soul at all. What would this community do without her?

Queen Marie, like so many in her "profession", is a victim of this rotten society. As a little girl Queen Marie had a vision of becoming a nurse. Oh! Those lovely starched uniforms, the hustle and bustle of a busy hospital. She wanted to be part of it. She pictures herself looking very tenderly after all the ill people in the overcrowded hospitals. She would have had to write so carefully that she did not make mistakes and administered the wrong medicines and pills. That could be dangerous and people could die. Well, she knows of people who have died because they were given the wrong medicines and pills. But the poor overworked nurses and doctors can't be blamed. How can they possibly do their work properly with patients lying all over the place – on the floor, under the beds, on benches, in the corridors. There are even two or three children to a cot. When Queen Marie was still a child she went to a hospital with her Mama where she saw the people in the hospital turn very ill patients away, or send very ill patients home because there was no place for them. Yes, conditions are still bad, very bad.

But Queen Marie never became a nurse because she had to leave school before completing high school to help her family. They did not have enough money to feed and clothe the family. So Queen Marie also went to work in the Vineyards where her mother, father and elder brother were working. Then she could not help her family much because the pay was so low and every night they were each given a bottle of cheap, patent wine as part of their wages. This only meant that her father had an extra bottle of wine to drink each night and was in a perpetual drunken stupor. The children had less and less to eat.

There was many a weekend when they each brought home only a bottle of wine because they owed so much at the farm shop that the debts took all their wages – every penny. It was on these occasions that they used to live for that bottle of wine with which to drown their problems. But you had to eat sometimes and what of the younger children? You went back to the farm shop and asked that bloodsucker behind the counter for more credit which tied you more and more tightly to this farm.

When Marie got married she came to live with her husband's family: the property belonged to the same person whose vineyards she had worked. He wanted to get rid of his liquor, so he brought it to her to sell. What else could she do but comply? She already had two children with a third on the way. Her Ernie was out of work, had been for more than a year and she was unemployed as well. If she had not agreed to sell that octopus liquor, she, her Ernie and family would have been out in the cold street. Yes, Queen Marie called him an octopus because he had his big, ugly tentacles everywhere.

But Friday nights at Queen Marie's shebeen must also come to an end and one has to pick up one's quivering bones, this time not from the tiredness of running after blasted garbage trucks, but a nice shivery Oom Tas feeling in one's bones.

"So come now, friend, John Jack, let's find our way home," says Sam. Slowly and laboriously they pick themselves up.

"Night, Queen Marie, sleep well," they chorus, and: "Night", calls Queen Marie. "Be careful," and then: "Oh, look at that moon and the majestic mountain! What about a song, pals?" asks Sam.

As they stumble their way home the stillness of the night is disturbed by "Mona Lisa! Now let's mind the pot holes, we don't want to break our legs because we'll have to run, run again early on Monday morning after garbage trucks that won't stop," says Sam.

"You so like the lady with thaat mystic smiileee. . ." their drunken voices rend the still air.

"Oops! Jack has lost his balance and is here somewhere in the gutter," says John.

"Now where is that blasted moon? I can't see!" shouts Sam.

"Here he is, let's help him up," hiccups John.

But this is not such an easy task because Jack seems to have acquired such a lot of weight – a dead weight. At last he is on his feet and stumble-stumble, "Mona-Lisa" – stumble-stumble, "mystic-smilee". They get to shanty-town.

It takes ages for old friends to say good night to each other. But at last after a lot of back-patting and stumbling they bid each other fond farewell and stumble along their respective paths, narrow, dirty and covered in pot-holes.

"Must be careful that I get to my shack and not to that of somebody else. These shacks are all so close to one another and look so alike especially in the darkness. I don't think that the moon shines on this place. And I wish that these scraggy dogs will stop barking. What is that that I hear in the distance? It is a blood-curdling scream. Some poor fellow on his way home is being attacked by knife-wielding thugs, I'm sure. Poor fellow! I hope Jack and John get home safely," thinks Sam.

Like Queen Marie in her shebeen, these knife-wielding thugs are also victims of this society. Unemployment, boredom, a feeling of rejection, make them what they are.

"Here is my door. Yes, number 56 in big white figures," murmurs Sam to himself. He pushes the rickety door open and stumbles over his sleeping children. In the far corner a lonely candle burns on the old rickety table that his long-suffering wife, Rachel, salvaged from her white employer, for whom she cleans and cooks. As Sam stumbles nearer, he can see Rachel's tired features. As she glares at him the tired lines in her face seem to get deeper and deeper.

"The same old thing," thinks Rachel. "The children had to go and sleep without anything decent to eat. The money that she got this evening for clean-ing, and cooking lovely suppers for these white people, had to be given to the landlord for having this – a shack of sticks, zinc, cardboard and rags – on his property. There was only enough money left for a loaf of bread and some tea. No milk. No sugar."

Suddenly something gives way inside Rachel. "What does this Sam of mine think he is doing, drinking the way he is, while there is nothing for the children to eat! There is little Grace, three months old, who has been coughing for a week and needs some cough mixture. The other children, five of them, need shoes, books, clothing," thinks Rachel, fuming with anger.

Not even thinking about what she is doing, Rachel punches Sam in the face. She had to vent her anger and frustration on somebody, and Sam's drunken face was just the place. Rachel is angry and fed-up with everything around her. This poverty, hunger, disease, filth. She knows very well that it is not Sam's fault that she and the children suffer in this way. She knows that Sam is very hard-working and needs to relax with his friends, but not when she needs the money so badly just to survive on.

The blow makes Sam stagger, almost fall, but he manages to keep on his feet. "What do you think you are doing, woman?" He yells at Rachel. He stumbles towards her, grabs her and the punching, screaming, tearing, pushing, shake the little shack.

The little children are all wide awake. They instinctively huddle wide-eyed and frightened in the remotest corner and wish that this fighting would stop. Elsie, the eldest, edges across to the crying baby and gathers her up. The other children know that this is a sign for them to escape into the dark night with the dogs howling and barking all around them.

With one of her hardest punches, Rachel gets Sam falling to the ground like a ton of bricks. This is her chance. She struggles towards the door over bags which do for bedding, boxes which are used for sitting on, to get away from Sam and to find her children so that they can somewhere find a sheltered nook where they can huddle close together to spend the rest of the night.

At least, tonight it is not raining.

Poppie sits back in the armchair at the window and closes her eyes. She can hear Bella in the kitchen where she is preparing nice things because she is going to entertain again this evening.

Bella, unfortunately, is one of those people who became part of the system in which she lived. She had a piece of land on which she used cheap labour that worked that land for her. These men, that she fetched from the Transkei to work her land for her, slaved long hours in the hot sun, and in wind and rain. They lived in shacks on her property, where they had no amenities. The pay was low, extremely low, and very often they were hungry. But there was no way they could get back to Transkei, and Bella's place was the only home they knew. They were actually chained to her and her piece of land.

Bella sold her vegetables on the local market where she had a stall. Over the years her profits grew and Bella was able to get a comfortable house built where she liked to entertain her friends and relatives. She saw no wrong in exploiting those men that she brought from the Transkei. This was what the system was all about and she was part of it.

But even now at night when Bella goes and sleeps, she can't help hearing the shouts of the Rachels being beaten up. She can't help hearing the blood-curdling screams of those that are being attacked by knife-wielding thugs. When Bella goes down the road, when she has to leave this cocoon that she has created for herself, she can't miss shanty-town and all its misery. She sees, hears and smells that misery. it scares her but she is not prepared to do anything to change what she sees. Bella usually falls asleep uneasily.

On this night, while Bella is entertaining, she suddenly feels a pain across her chest. The pain becomes worse although Bella tries to keep a brave face. But eventually Bella can no longer ignore the pain across her chest. She goes to the room and a doctor is sent for. On her arrival Bella is certified dead.

Death came to Bella the way she liked to live – with her friends, her relatives, the remains of a party, and Poppie.

Poppie likes being in her room at night with her thoughts, with her plans. She smiles to herself as she thinks of the plans. Everything is going well. The children are on strike up and down the country. Tomorrow the workers are coming out on strike as well to bring the economy of this country, that bleeds them, starves them, to a standstill. The oppressed of this country know too well how to use the strike weapon.

And in the distance we can hear sounds of steadily running feet, steadfast feet, steady feet. And we know that these sounds that we hear are the sounds of those who are going to eradicate all this ugliness. These sounds that we hear are drawing nearer and nearer. They are getting very close, drawing closer and closer. And the sun creeps over the horizon, adding long silhouettes to the sounds of the steady running feet.

Abena P. A. Busia
1953–

*B*orn *in Accra, Ghana, she spent the first years of her childhood at home as well as in Holland and Mexico, before her family settled in Oxford, England, where she had her secondary and university education; she read for a BA in English Language and Literature at St Anne's College (1976) and a DPhil in Social Anthropology at St Antony's College (1984). She has been an external tutor at Ruskin College, Oxford, a visiting lecturer in the Department of Afro-American Studies at Yale University and has held post-doctoral fellowships at Bryn Mawr College and the Center for Afro-American Studies, University of California at Los Angeles. She is now Associate Professor of English at Rutgers State University, where she has taught since 1981. Her articles have appeared in many journals and anthologies, and she is working on a critical book,* Song in a Strange Land: Narrative and Rituals of Remembrance in the Novels of Black Women of Africa and the African Diaspora. *Her poetry collection,* Testimonies of Exile, *was published in 1990.*

Exiles

Funerals are important.
Away from home we cannot lay
our dead to rest
for we alone have given them
        no fitting burial.

Self-conscious of our absence
brooding over distances in western lands
we must rehearse
the planned performance of our rites
                    till we return.

And meanwhile through the years
our unburied dead eat with us
follow behind through bedroom doors.

"Though I Have Sworn"

Though I have sworn
never to do the same,
today I saw myself patient
like my mother –
pregnant in a foreign land
waiting to bear the child

Liberation

We are all mothers,
and we have that fire within us,
of powerful women
whose spirits are so angry
we can laugh beauty into life
and still make you taste
the salt tears of our knowledge –
For we are not tortured
anymore;
we have seen beyond your lies and disguises,
and *we* have mastered the language of words,
we have mastered speech.
And know
we have also seen ourselves.
We have stripped ourselves raw
and naked piece by piece until our flesh lies flayed
with blood on our *own* hands.
What terrible thing can you do us
which we have not done to ourselves?
What can you tell us
which we didn't deceive ourselves with
a long time ago?

You cannot know how long we cried
until we laughed
over the broken pieces of our dreams.
Ignorance
shattered us into such fragments
we had to unearth ourselves piece by piece,
to recover with our own hands such unexpected relics
even we wondered
how we could hold such treasure.
Yes, we have conceived
to forge our mutilated hopes
into the substance of visions
beyond your imaginings
to declare the pain of our deliverance:
So do not even ask,
do not ask what it is we are labouring with *this* time;
Dreamers remember their dreams
when we are disturbed –
And you shall not escape
what we *will* make
of the broken pieces of our lives.

Angelika Einsenbrandt

?1953–

Related when she was aged thirty-three, her story of growing up in Germany in an atmosphere of alienation and her determination to overcome the resultant self-doubt is one of the poignant contributions to the anthology Farbe bekennen, *edited by Katharina Oguntoye, May Opitz and Dagmar Schultz (1986; translated by Anne V. Adams as* Showing Our True Colour: Afro-German Women on the Traces of Their History).

"Suddenly I knew what I wanted"

M Y family lives in E—, a small town near Kassel. I grew up there with my brother and sister with my grandparents. My brother and I did not know our father, who was an American soldier. My sister's father was white. All three of us are illegitimate. My brother had the easiest time as he was given the most support. I suffered most at the things adults said. For example, at my girlfriend's house they would always tell me, "You have to go now, Angelika – we're expecting company."

The fact that my brother and I looked different only became apparent when we started school. When we played with other kids in our large garden it wasn't noticeable. But whenever visitors came we were dressed up and our hair brushed. We were always supposed to look pretty and cute.

Sometimes my brother would put down my sister. He would say she was different from us and that anyway there were two of us. I didn't understand this and would cry. Later on I felt more and more that I looked different, and my grandmother seemed to dress me in particular clothes. I only wore light colours like white and yellow. She used to say, "Red doesn't suit you; it doesn't go with the colour of your skin." I didn't say anything but it would make me annoyed. Once I had some red checked trousers. I thought they were great and that they suited me. My grandma took them away. My mother didn't interfere with any of this. She was too exhausted from working all day. She cleaned in a bakery from 4 a.m., came home at 7 a.m. and from 8 a.m. she worked in a photographic laboratory.

Funny, though, when I became independent and while I was married I only bought red things. I never really gave it any thought. Up till now I still love the colour.

I could never understand why Granny said my brother and I shouldn't have vaccinations. She said our blood was different and that it could be dangerous for us. Only my sister was vaccinated. Later my brother was vaccinated for a boat trip and nothing happened. That surprised me.

I believe my Granny loved us but simply had difficulty with our being different. She was afraid that people would talk about us. When my daughter S— was born Granny was very disappointed and said, "She isn't all that dark." She could somehow accept the skin colour in an infant but she became uneasy about it as the child grew older.

During my school days I never went out to discos or things like that with the others. I was allowed to, but lacked the self-confidence to go out by myself. My sister took me along sometimes and I found it quite normal that she went out and coped. I liked it best when my brother took me along. I worshipped him at that time, thought he was the greatest because he always did so much and had such a large circle of friends. I only found him irritating within the family. He was admired and spoiled by everybody. What was so unfair was that if he wanted something different to eat rather than what was cooked for us, he got it and we didn't. . . .

I met my husband through my sister. He was a friend of her boyfriend. I liked him from the first moment that I spoke to him. Probably because he was six years older than me and was more experienced. Lots of people told him that he couldn't marry me as there would be too many problems, such as finding a home. He said, "That's not true at all." I was very impressed by that.

After a while I thought my husband had married me just so he could feel special. He wanted someone he could show off with. That's how I felt, above all when he would say things like, "Do your hair differently – you know, like the Africans who have it all curly." I myself found short straight hair great. He wanted me to look African, so that people could see that I was different.

I married to get away from my mother. As long as we had lived together we had serious disagreements. I had looked forward to living with her as I had almost always lived with my Granny. I thought that I could finally establish a relationship with my mother. To start with, when I was still going to school it worked quite well. We talked a lot and got to know each other well. Later on, when I wanted to speak of my problems at work or made more demands on her, things got more difficult. Even though I was working I had to ask her first if I wanted to buy anything. We lived together for six years. My sister stayed with us in the beginning and again much later. She never got on well with our mother but she was still allowed to do more that I was. She simply demanded more and achieved what she wanted, whereas I had to ask over and over again. Nowadays she has a better relationship with my mother than I do.

My mother is a woman who can't show her emotions. As long as I lived with my Granny I knew I was loved. My grandparents were kind and tender. When I had to deal with my mother directly I thought that she didn't love me. In spite of all that, I really liked my mother and loved her.

I came into contact with other women through my daughter S— and realized that there was a lot that I hadn't done and didn't understand. . . .

While I was at school and since S— went to kindergarten I've always had to work. I often argued with my husband about things we had to buy, but as I wasn't strong enough he got his way most times. Now I live alone with my daughter and feel great.

I still haven't managed to get rid of all the problems to do with my colour. I notice that I'm not always taken seriously when I say something, even when I mean it seriously.

I still discover that my appearance is unusual at my daughter's school. They are amazed and ask her, "That's your mum? You look quite different." I find it hard to go to the school and to cross the playground during the break. My daughter doesn't have these problems.

[Translated by George Busby]

Opal Palmer Adisa
1954–

Born in Kingston, Jamaica, she has a BA in Communications from Hunter College, New York, and an MA in Creative Writing from San Francisco State University. She has taught at City College of San Francisco, has written for children, written and directed plays for Black Repertory and other theatres in the Bay Area, and has written and produced material for television. She was a producer with the Educational Broadcasting Service of the Jamaican Ministry of Education. She is also the author of various poetry collections. The following story is one of four collected in Bake-Face and Other Guava Stories (1986), all about ordinary Jamaican women, particularly as they relate to their mothers and to each other.

Duppy Get Her

Duppy nuh wan yuh drop
  yuh picknie deh, guh home
Dappy nuh wan yuh drop
  yuh picknie deh, guh home
Duppy nuh wan yuh drop
  yuh picknie deh, guh home, gal
tie yuh belly, gal, guh home.

EVENING falls like dewdrops on oleander petals glistening under the sun. Oshun, goddess of love, is present, her orange-yellow skirt swaying coquettishly. Mosquitoes are like kiskode petals on skin, blown off by the lax odor whispering mischief in the air. Cane fields rustle in frolic; answered by the evening breeze, they dance the merenge, twirling to giddiness. What are the cane fields saying? What is uttered by the leaves? Listen! Listen – with wide eyes.

Suddenly the murmur of the cane fields – almost hypnotic – forces everyone to look in their direction. Swirling, they sing:

Steal away, steal away;
  duppy gwana get yuh, gal, steal away.
Steal away, steal away;
  duppy a come get yuh, gal, steal away.

The labyrishers – gossipers – do not hear; they don't hear, save one – Lilly.

Lilly cleans house, cooks food, washes clothes, irons and does other domestic chores for her living. She has been since she was sixteen; she is eighteen, now, and with child due any day. She sits with Beatrice, her cousin, also a domestic; with Richard, her baby's father and a pot-boiler at the sugar estate; and with Basil and Errol, two other factory hands. They are gathered together, feeling contented at being their own bosses for at least the next twelve hours.

The evening is rare in its simple grace. The sun, sinking beyond the cane fields, dominates the sky. All the land kneels in homage to this god of energy and sustainer of life – fully orange, gigantic and mystic, surrounded by black-purple haze. The clouds stand back, way off in respect. The sun, heedful of his power, gyrates and snarls. Lilly glances at him just as he flaps his ears, emitting fire from his nostrils; she checks her laughter. So awed is she by the sun's fire she scarcely breathes. After some moments, Lilly mumbles: "Lawd, de sun mitey tonite, sah. Look, im on im way home nuh." Suddenly, the turning of the child in her belly elicits a laugh that escapes deep from her womb.

Beatrice, seated by her, places her hand on Lilly's stomach, feeling the baby's position. "Dis a definite boy picknie yuh a guh ave. See how yuh belly pointed and de sonofabitch won gi yuh nuh peace."

"Im mus tek afta im fada."

Richard turns away in vexation; he chups, kissing his teeth: "Is me yuh ave mout fah, nuh? Ooman neba satisfy. Wen dem nuh ave nutten else fi seh, dem chat stupidness." He moves to leave, but changes his mind; he chups again: "Nuh boda me backside dis evenin yah, gal, nuh boda me backside."

The breeze whistles by. The dogs cover their ears in embarrassment, while the frogs exchange glances which ask, "What's troubling him this nice evening, eh? What's troubling him?" A green lizard, in response, croaks; its bulging eyes are lit by the sun. There is silence amidst the gathering of two women and three men – maids, pot-boiler and factory-hands.

Silence dominates but the undercurrent there is anger mingled with amusement and foreboding. Again, the swishing of the cane fields seems to grab everyone's attention. Lilly is rocking. Suddenly noticing a flock of birds in the sky, she points like an excited child. Again, silence. The sun is almost gone. Lilly sees a star, and thinking it must be the very first one in the sky this evening, she quickly makes a wish, anxious for its fulfillment. She resumes her rocking, forgetting what it was she wished for. A rooster cackles near the barbed wire fence separating them from the canal and the cane field beyond. Two dogs are stuck, one in the other.

Richard picks up a stone, throws it at them; he swears under his breath: "Damn dog – dem nuh ave nuh shame. Look how much bush bout de place, yet dem a fi come rite inna de open."

Beatrice snickers. Lilly retorts, "Nuh eberybode wait till nite fi cova dem act inna de darkness like yuh."

"Ooman, me nuh tell yuh nuh boda me soul-case. If yuh nuh ave nutten fi seh, shet yuh backside."

Beatrice comments, "Some people hot tonite, Lawd. Mus all dat boiling molasses. De sweetness keep de heat inna de body." Again silence. Beatrice fidgets in the chair, which is too small for her large behind. Suddenly, she starts singing, a mischievous smile on her face. Her voice is full and melodious, and her song is aimed at Richard, whom she always provokes to anger:

> *Gentle Jesas, meek an mile,*
> *look upon a trouble man.*
> *East im soul an let im rest,*
> *for im is a soul distress.*

Lilly bursts out in loud belly-laughter and Errol and Basil sputter. Richard's color is rising like the pink of a cat's tongue. Anger is clearly written on his face. A sudden wind blows dirt into Beatrice's eye, putting an end to her song.

Richard keenly observes the little gathering and feels excluded. He looks at the dark bodies, envying them. He is the "red nega" among them. All during his school days, the boys teased him, saying his mother had slept with a sailor. And even though he knew it wasn't true (although he was the fairest one in his family), he was still always hurt; he didn't care if his great-great-grandfather had married an Irish settler whom he resembled. He wanted to be purple-dark like the rest of them so his face wouldn't turn red like the color of sorrel fruit whenever he got angry. Staying out in the sun didn't help either; it only made his skin tomato. Lean and muscular, he stood out like a guinep among star-apples.

Lately, however (that is, ever since meeting Lilly not yet twelve months ago), Richard has been relaxed. Lilly, lusted after by all the men, the gentlemen of the community included, chose him. Although every once in a while she teases him about his complexion and stings his hand to see her fingerprints revealed, he knows she cares for him.

Richard doesn't feel like being anyone's beating stick tonight, however. He looks from Lilly, sitting with a smile crowning her face, to Errol and Basil, with mischief twinkling in their eyes, to Beatrice, playing her usual pious role. Richard wants to remind Beatrice of the nightly utterances of her mattress, and bedsprings, but he holds his tongue as he isn't sure whether it is Errol or Basil or both who pray to the Lord between her thighs at night. He chuckles, stomping the balls of his feet, and then chups, kissing his teeth, before turning to fidget with his bicycle. "One of dese days oonuh gwane wan fi serious and kyan," he warns.

Richard catches a glimpse of the sun just before it disappears, and it whispers to him: "Steal away, steal away – duppy gwane box yuh, duppy nuh like yuh, steal away. . ." He looks over his shoulder to see if anyone else heard. No one did; the group is already onto something else.

The cane fields whimper, swishing to and fro. The evening is alive. All the creatures stop to say their piece. Sparkling fireflies called penewales dart in and out of the darkness; crickets are in argument. Even the water in the canal tastes the omen. It rumbles like a vexed child who is sent to sweep up the dirt and gather leaves; the task adds to the child's vexation when the twirling leaves blind his eyes while playing rounders with the breeze. So is the evening sweet yet wicked – as even the nicest woman can be.

The rustling of the cane fields is louder. Beatrice shivers. Blossoms from the ackee tree fall and the wind takes them, blowing them everywhere. Lilly tries to catch the blossoms, but the movement in her belly stops her. She relaxes and pats her stomach.

Beatrice feels her head growing big; it is a ton of bricks on her body. She rubs her arms, feeling the cold-bumps. Something is going to happen. She looks around at Richard, who is still angry, and Basil and Errol, who are sharing some private joke. Beatrice reaches over and rubs Lilly's belly, feeling the child inside kicking. She is certain it's a boy. Again, the murmur of the cane fields. Beatrice quickly blows into her cupped palms and throws the air over her left shoulder. It is her way of telling the duppies to step back. She cannot see the ghosts, but she senses their presence near. Again she cups her palms, blows, and throws her cupped hands over her right shoulder, cursing a bad-word with the motion before mumbling, "De Lawd is me Shepherd, Ah fear nuh evil. . ." Still she senses an outside force. Lilly is smiling to herself and rocking, one hand patting her stomach.

Beatrice's head swells; she feels it much larger than her body, much larger than the veranda where they are sitting, much larger than the evening. She hugs her bosom and rocks, trying to put aside the fear that has crept upon her without invitation.

After her mother died when she was six and her father wandered to another town and another woman, Beatrice was taken in by Lilly's mother, who was her aunt. She was two years older than Lilly, so their lives followed similar paths until at fifteen Beatrice's was partially ruined by her Sunday school teacher. Fear made her keep her mouth shut; prayer made the child born dead. Soon thereafter she left, getting several jobs as domestic help before settling in this quiet community. Eight years ago, Beatrice and Lilly both attended their grandparents' funerals, three months apart. They were always close, so over the years, they kept in touch. When Lilly complained of being restless and wanting to leave the overprotective shield of her mother two years ago, Beatrice found her a job with her own employer Mrs Edwards. That was how they came to be together again.

Before Beatrice lost her child, she had promised the Lord that she would spread his name if he killed the life that was growing in her womb. When the child was born strangled, she kept her word, but it was already too late, because she had discovered the joy which lay buried between her legs. As she wasn't pretty, it was easy to have several men without ruining her reputation. No one wanted to boast of sleeping with the coarse, big busted, no ass, Jesus-crazy maid. This way she had it her way all the time, not really trusting any man in the first place.

Putting aside her reflections, Beatrice leans her head to hear what Basil is saying.

"Oonuh look like oonuh inna anoda world."

Richard is still fidgeting with his bicycle; Errol has gone to help him. Lilly, rocking on the seatless cane rocker, is hypnotized by the rustling cane field beyond. Beatrice and Basil notice her staring at what to them appears to be nothing. They feel her strangeness like silence between them. Pausing to take it in, they resume their conversation. An ackee blossom falls, disquieting Richard, and he curses: "See yah, Lawd, yuh nuh test me fait tuh dis yah nite."

A man and woman have crept out of the cane field. They stand right at the edge on the bank of the canal. To look at the woman is to see an older Lilly. The man is all grey. The woman wears a plaid dress gathered at the waist, and her feet are without shoes. Her husband wears rubber shoes and stained khaki pants turned up at the ankles. His faded shirt is partially unbuttoned, his arm is around his wife's waist. They exude a gentleness like the petals of roses. The woman uses her index finger to beckon to Lilly. Jumping as if pulled from her seat, Lilly bounds toward the man and woman by the cane field beyond the canal and beyond the barbed wire fence. She scrambles over Beatrice's feet.

Beatrice yells, "Lilly, Lilly, weh yuh a guh? Lilly! Is mad? Yuh mad? Min yuh fall down hurt yuhself. Lilly! Gal, weh yuh a guh?'

Richard runs after Lilly.

Beatrice repeats, "Lilly, gal, wha get inna yuh?"

Lilly: "Yuh rass-cloth, leabe me alone. Yuh nuh ear me granny a call me?" She points to what appears to be the canal.

They all stare, seeing no one, hearing nothing. Lilly is close to the fence, running, tearing off her clothes. Fearing that she is going to dive in, Richard reaches for her, but she clutches and attempts the barbed wire fence; Richard pulls at her. She boxes and derides him till he releases her. She tries scrambling through. Richard takes firm hold of her and pulls her safely from the fence. Beatrice is by their side; she helps with Lilly. Errol stands transfixed by the bicycle, while Basil cranes his neck from the veranda. Richard and Beatrice struggle with Lilly, pulling her away from the fence; they are breathless, but luckily, Lilly settles down for a moment.

The woman in the cane field beckons to Lilly, cajoling: "Lilly, me picknie, come kiss yuh granny and granpa; yuh nuh long fi see we?"

Lilly, strident, gesticulates wildly like a man cheated out of his paycheck. She calls, "Yes, Granny, me a come, me long fi see yuh."

Beatrice and Richard struggle with Lilly. Their fright and confusion are as loud as Lilly's screams, Richard tries to rough her up but she merely bucks him off. Beatrice's jaws work, sweat forms on her forehead, and her fleshy arms flail about, comical.

Again, she tries to reason with Lilly: "Lilly, gal, memba me and you did help dress Granny fah er funeral? Memba, memba, Lilly, how we did cry til we eye swell big? Granny dead. She nah call yuh."

"Granny nuh dead; see, she stan deh wid Granpa. Oonuh leh me guh." At this, Lilly spits at Beatrice and Richard and frees herself from their hold.

She rushes toward the cane field like a man afire in search of water. Richard seizes her, but she now has the strength of many persons; he hollers for Errol and Basil. Lilly rips off her blouse and brassière, and her ample breasts flap about. Richard remembers the taste of her milk, only last night. More hands take hold of her; she bites, scratches and kicks. Miss Maud from next door, hearing the commotion, runs to her fence to learn all about it.

"Leh me guh, leh me guh! Yuh nuh see me granny a call me? Leh me guh."

Richard: "Lilly, shet yuh mout. Min Miss Edward ear yuh an yuh loose yuh wuk. Nuhbody nah call yuh."

"Miss Edward bumbu-hole – Miss Edward rasscloth. Oonuh leave me alone mek me guh tuh me granny and granpa."

Beatrice scolds: "Lilly, gal, shet yuh mout. How yuh can speak suh bout Miss Edward? Gal, shet yuh mout for yuh loose yuh wuk."

"Oonuh rass-cloth, oonuh bumbu-hole, oonuh leabe me alone – mek me guh to me granny."

The four find it difficult to hold Lilly. She kicks, bucks and tears at her remaining cloths. The evening sings:

> Steal away, steal away, duppy get yuh.
> Steal away. . .duppy get yuh. . .

From across the fence, Miss Maud offers: "Lawd, God, duppy done mad me picknie, Lawd God. Jesas! Rub er up wid some frankincense and white rum; rub er up quick come." Before anyone can respond, she is climbing through the barbed wire fence which separates her yard from theirs, opening a bottle. In her haste, her dress catches on the fence, but she pulls it, ripping the hem. The pungent smell from the bottle vapors into the air.

Miss Maud rubs Lilly's hands, face and neck with the potion, then makes the sign of the cross in the air. Now she sprinkles some of the substance on the ground, muttering: "Steal away, duppy, steal away. De deed well done; steal away. . ." She looks around her, pats her head and turns to Beatrice. "Fin piece a red tag, tie er head. Duppy fraid red, fraid red. Our Fada who in heaven, duppy afraid red. Dy kingdom come, tie er head. Dy will be done, tie er head. Ave Mercy, Pupa Jesas."

Lilly breathes heavily; Richard, Errol and Basil hold her firmly.

Says Beatrice, "She kyan stay ere; dem nuh wan er stay ere."

Maud explains, "Dem jus wan er home. No arm will be done. Lawd ave mercy."

Richard stares at Lilly: "Who obeah me sweet Lilly? Who?"

Beatrice explodes: "Shet yuh mout, Richard, nuhbody nuh set nuh spell pan Lilly, nuhbody obeah er."

> Steal away, chile, steal away.
> Duppy nuh wan yuh ere, chile,
>   duppy nuh wan yuh ere.
> Dem nuh wan yuh ere.

It is generally agreed that Lilly must be returned to her place of birth – that for whatever reason, her dead grandparents don't want her where she is. Mrs Edwards is consulted and a car is summoned. Kicking and frothing at the mouth, Lilly is forced into the back of the car, Richard to her right and Basil to her left. Beatrice sits up front with the driver armed with Miss Maud's flask of potion. The car pulls off, leaving a trail of dust.

Mrs Edwards returns to her house; she fumbles inside her medicine cabinet and comes up with a brown vial, the contents of which she sprinkles at each doorway and window and in all four corners of every room. Then she goes back to her rocking chair, her hands folded in her lap, her eyes searching the grey sky.

Miss Maud, the community myalist – healer – returns to her backyard. Her lips are pouted and her eyes intent, as if seeking a shiny shilling in the road; she shakes her head from side to side.

Suddenly she is possessed; she twirls around her yard, her wide skirt billowing out, her hands lifted to the sky, her feet marching time to an invisible drum. Her voice, deep bass, echoes like a man's throughout the entire community:

> *Duppy nuh wan yuh drop*
> *yuh picknie deh, guh home*
> *Duppy nuh wan yuh drop*
> *yuh picknie deh, guh home*
> *Duppy nuh wan yuh drop*
> *yuh picknie deh, guh home, gal,*
> *Tie yuh belly, gal, guh home.*
> *Yuh muma seh she neba raise*
> *Nuh picknie fi guh lego*
> *Yuh muma seh she neba raise*
> *Nuh picknie fi guh lego*
> *Yuh muma seh she neba raise*
> *Nuh picknie fi guh lego*
> *Tie yuh belly, guh home.*
> *Duppy nuh wan yuh drop*
> *yuh picknie deh*
> *Tie yuh belly, guh home.*
> *Guh home.*

Mrs Edwards feels cold-bumps covering her arms as she watches Miss Maud twirling and singing in her yard. The swishing of the cane fields has stopped and suddenly, a sense of desolation – abandonment – takes over. The sky turns a deep mauve, a lone donkey somewhere in the distance brays, brays, brays and the night is on so fully all creep to the safety of their homes and pull the covers tightly over their heads. Only Mrs Edwards sits for a long time on her veranda in the dark, rocking and rocking away the fear and doubt.

Upon returning from taking Lilly home, Beatrice reports that Lilly calmed gradually as she approached her place of birth. In fact, by the time she got home, she was reasonable enough to request from her mother a cup of water sweetened with condensed milk. After drinking the milk, Lilly hugged her mother and they both cried; no one had to restrain her thereafter. Nothing needed to be explained to Lilly's mother, who had been expecting them all day. It appeared she had had a dream from her dead mother the night before.

Prior to this incident, Lilly always claimed that she saw duppies in Mrs Edwards's house and around the estate in general. Since no one else professed such powers, there was no way to verify her claim. Many came to her when they wanted to ask for protection from those in the other world. Often, when they were in Lilly's presence, they asserted that they felt their heads rise and swell to twice their size, but again, since this was only a feeling and nothing visible, nothing could be proven. There were others who wanted to be able to see duppies like Lilly and asked her how they could obtain such powers. Lilly's recommendations were the following: "Rub dog matta inna yuh eye or visit a graveyard wen de clock strike twelve midnight. Once dere, put yuh head between yuh legs, spit, then get up an walk, not lookin back. Afta dat, yuh will see duppy all de time."

It is not known if anyone ever followed Lilly's advice, although two women who went to see Lilly had taken to visiting the graveyard daily and were now in the habit of talking to themselves.

Lilly returns to Mrs Edwards's employment exactly ten weeks after the incident, healthy and as sane as before, with her bubbling, carefree manner. She gave birth to a seven-and-a-half pound boy, the spitting image of Richard, the day after her departure. The child was left behind with her mother, who christened him Sam, after his deceased grandfather.

Now when Lilly looks into the cane field, nothing bursts forth and no dead are brought back to life, but every time people see her looking, they remember that evening and somehow, the cane field starts rustling and a voice much like Lilly's rings throughout the entire community, stopping people at their chores:

> Let me guh, leh me guh, oonuh rass-cloth!
> Le me guh – me granny a call me, oonuh leh me guh.
> Mrs Edwards bumbu-hole; leh me guh.

No one referred to Mrs Edwards, a highly respected member of her community, in such a manner before, and no one has after Lilly. Lilly, of course, apologized to Mrs Edwards, who graciously forgave her as she was not in possession of herself at the time. And although Mrs Edwards was committed to taking Lilly back in her employment after she gave birth, whenever Mrs Edwards was around her, she was always full of trepidation.

Lilly goes off one other time since the cane field incident. Several years have passed; Lilly is getting married to Richard. This is the big day. She is dressed, waiting to be taken to the church. Her grandmother appears again, but this time alone. Lilly rips her bridal dress to shreds and runs naked to the river, cursing everyone she meets, while Richard waits by the altar. For nine days she has to be tied down with ropes. For nine days, the breeze sings:

> Steal away, steal away.
> Duppy seh nuh, duppy seh nuh.
> Steal away. . .

Lilly's face is a dimpled cake pan. Her body is pleasing like a mango tree laden with fruits. She has eight children, now, six for her husband and two for Richard, the first two. Richard stole away after duppy boxed him the second time. The last that was heard of him, it was reported that he was seen walking and talking to himself, his hair matty and his skin black with dirt. Lilly now has a maid to help her with her many chores; her husband owns a fleet of trucks.

Beatrice has opened up a storefront church in another community far from where the main part of this story took place. Her congregation is said to be ninety-two per cent sturdy black men. Basil is still working as a pot-boiler at the sugar factory. Errol went abroad to England, it could be Canada or America as well, where he is said to have married an East Indian girl, so now he eats with his fingers.

After Lilly left Mrs Edwards's employment, Mrs Edwards swore confidentially to Mrs Salmon, her best friend, that she would never again hire a maid from Agusta valley – that was the district from which Lilly came. Mrs Edwards, of course, did not admit to a belief in local superstitions.

At least once a year, Miss Maud can still be heard singing at the top of her voice:

> *Duppy nuh wan yuh drop*
> *yuh picknie deh, guh home*
> *Duppy nuh wan yuh drop*
> *yuh picknie deh, guh home*
> *Duppy nuh wan yuh drop*
> *yuh picknie deh, guh home, gal,*
> *Tie yuh belly, guh home.*

Ayse Bircan
1954–

*B*orn *in Istanbul, Turkey, she studied sociology at the University of Istanbul (1971) but could not finish her degree there because of the political situation in the country. She was the editor of the Turkish progressive newspaper* Young Socialist *in 1975, and as a result of her work with this publication was tried and sentenced to imprisonment. She went into hiding in 1979 after her trial and subsequently left the country. She was also an organizer of Ilerici Kadinlar Derneği, the Progressive Women's Organization of Turkey, and a founder member in 1977 of the Turkish Peace Association. Since 1983 she has been a*

political refugee in London, where she was instrumental in founding the
Turkish Community Centre. The following autobiographical essay dates
from May 1991.

Black and Turkish

I WAS born in Istanbul, my parents' third child. My mother worked for a while
as a house cleaner, then she stayed home; my father first worked in a factory
then was a fireman for a bus company. I have an older brother and three sisters,
one younger than me. I don't know a lot about my family's history; my mother's
parents were also Black but she didn't tell us much about their own background,
so I don't know that part of the history. But my father was always talking about his
history, especially when *Roots* came out on television; he tried to find out and
began to write our family's history, but I haven't seen it yet because I was here
when he died. When I go back I will see what he wrote. He was always thinking
of writing about our history.

My father's grandfather was sold in Mecca as a slave and freed by a rich
Turkish man who adopted him as a seven-year-old child. We don't know
my great-grandfather's original country; of course he was from Africa, but
we don't know which part. During that period there was slavery not only
to the West of the world but in that area too. I've tried to find out when
but I can't; it could be the middle of the 1880s or so. In the west of Turkey,
capitalist trade started earlier than the other part and there were more slaves.
In that area – Múgla – after slavery was banned some small villages were only
Black people; I recently found that out, from a few Turkish novels of about the
1920s. But I can't find out exactly where. My mother's village (Gökçekōy) and
my father's village (Seyītoba) neighbour each other in Mansia, a city near Izmir
– which is an ancient Greek area, full of famous places like Ephesus. There was
only one Black family in my father's village and one Black family in my mother's,
but they were always matching people so they kept their colour. An old women
who was a matchmaker in my mother's village told my mother about my father.
My mother escaped to his village without her parents' permission, and they got
married. My parents are both Black. It's not that there's a real problem about
intermarriage. In some parts of Turkey you can't easily marry with a white man
or woman, but in that part we are mixed. It depends on your wealth, not your
colour.

The man who took my great-grandfather was the richest man in Father's
village and had no children, so he bought himself a son in Mecca. Of course,
he was there to make the religious pilgrimage but at the same time to buy a
son. He chose to free and adopt a Black slave because it was more valuable
in terms of religion and going to Heaven. Later he had his own children and
when he died he divided all his lands equally. Now we call them "Uncle" and
so on; they are the same family, though they are white. We get on well but have
different surnames, because surnames were taken after the Independence War.
Before, we shared the same surname but when it was allowed to take another
surname my grandfather took a different one – Bircan, which means "Alone" –

"the only one", "the one Black", something like that. It's more meaningful in Turkish. He separated himself from the others, I think. He was sent to the town to be educated and when his father died he left and came back to the village.

My parents married when they were 18 and then my father went into the military for four years – it's usually two but during the Second World War it was four years. Then there was a famine and when he came back he had to move to Istanbul for work, so after 1945 our family lived there. He didn't go to school, he taught himself to write and read on cigarette boxes. And when he was 45 he got a primary school diploma – we already had ours! He gave us a lot of Black identity and consciousness, especially us three girls, because although there isn't much colour prejudice in Turkey still he felt we had to have an occupation, had to be well educated and have a good status. The three of us girls went to university. When I was seven we moved to an area. . .like a slum area, something like a ghetto. . .a shanty town. You built your own small shack. It was illegal – we were squatters on the land, didn't pay anything for it. In the 1960s there was an important change in Turkey in terms of industry, in terms of a new constitution, and everything was changing politically, economically. When industry started to increase, many peasants came to Istanbul and established this area. It was the best part of my childhood. . .my best memories. They were all workers, they had to work, men and women, and we kids were alone in the area; and if someone was sick, or in any case, all the elderly looked after the children. It was very different from anywhere else. You could be another family's daughter, they would feed you, wash you. The whole area was like an extended family. If someone wanted to go to their village for harvest they left their children with their neighbours. It was a nice thing. That's why I really know how to share everything and feel responsible for others.

I was bright. . .we all were, because my father encouraged us. For example, he never let us do housework. Instead, he would say: "Leave it." So I don't know how to do sewing, for example. If he saw me doing it he just put it in the dustbin and said, "Take a book and read it. This is what you need. Those are easy and silly things you can do whenever you want but they aren't important in terms of the outside world. You must learn other things first. You can't be dependent on your husband when you grow up, and if you don't want to be spoiled by him you must have your own occupation and economic freedom. Then you can sack him whenever you want." It was really unusual for Turkey. It's not an ordinary story about my father. He wasn't formally educated; he educated himself with our school books. Every day when we came home we would all sit together and discuss what we had learned, putting arguments for and against. It was fun.

We mostly read school books, because there weren't facilities like local libraries. But my sister who is six years older than me found whatever she could, and whatever she found I could also read, but she showed responsibility in what she chose and we didn't read any rubbish. She always chose good things for me. Because of her I read many translated world classics – Tolstoy, Dostoevsky, Balzac, Voltaire. But I was really more interested in the outside world in my area, not just what I learned out of a book, I think, because in that area there was always something happening and you had to help each other. So when I was twelve, before I got my period, I saw bleeding after birth, because people had come from their village and didn't have any relatives, so when a woman gave birth I stayed with her and looked after her. And sometimes a big storm broke down all the shanty houses and we helped them, we'd get them together. I think that was more important than the books. And of course you apply something from what you read to what you live.

In the 1960s when I was in primary school I was very lucky to have a woman teacher who taught me for five years who was a really good person. In my area there was no school; I had to walk miles to go to school. Istanbul is the biggest city in Turkey but because that area was so newly established there was no school, no bus, and the school we had to go to was in a posh area. My teacher talked about the Black civil rights fighters in America and showed me English magazines – I couldn't understand English but I saw Martin Luther King, etcetera – and she told me about racism in America.

Of course there is some racism in Turkey. For example, when you walk down the street, small kids call after you, "Negro, Negro!" In Turkish it's "*Arab*". Yes, Arab! It's funny. It's a kind of ignorance to call a Black person that; educated people don't do it. In religious terms it's a sin to exclude Blacks or any others. The most important thing is whether you're Muslim or not. It's different from in the West. Religion, not colour, divides. Older people especially respect that anyone can be a true Muslim. But kids, seeing someone different for the first time, may call after you, though your white friends will challenge them, "What are you saying?" So colour prejudice isn't that strong. I mean, if you go to any institution you don't feel threatened because you are Black. There are some limitations. You can't, for example, be a general in the army if you are Black. I don't know if it is written or not, but you definitely can't be. You can only go to a certain level. So there are some things, but not as hard as here. There aren't many Black people high in Turkish life. There is a Black woman singer who is like a mascot, you know – she was on television. People like her. For me, she's not that good, actually, but because she is Black she is given sympathy. I don't think there is that much pressure on Black people, especially in the big cities. When you go to the other part of Turkey which is less developed, or not developed, because they haven't seen Blacks in their lives they are shocked; then they realize and come up and say, "Sorry, if I've done something it's because I didn't know, that's why I was afraid of you, but now I'm not afraid." Things like that happen. The population of Turkey is very great – about 50 million or so, with maybe not even one per cent Blacks. Maybe in total we Blacks are less than three thousand.

My own situation was more important for me than my colour: being among other working-class families. I wasn't much aware of difference in terms of being Black. Maybe because we Blacks aren't a big population we don't threaten anyone's power. Whatever the cause, it doesn't make sense to say I really experienced racism. Yet my father was very careful; he was always telling us that we were Black and had to be aware of it. Once he was asked to be in a film with a famous blonde actress. He was pleased, but when he went to the set they told him, "You just hold her horse." He refused because he didn't think it was work for him; he could act other things as well. When I was fifteen I wanted to go into the theatre, to study acting; and he just said, "Yes, you can do whatever you want, I'm not saying you can't, but think about it – think about what kind of roles you can get." I realized there wasn't much opportunity as a Black, you couldn't be really famous even if you had ability.

In the newly developing working-class district of Istanbul where I grew up, girls usually were not sent to school. They either just about finished primary school or went straight to work in factories before even finishing primary education. I was the only girl of my age-group who was allowed to go on to secondary school, which thrust great responsibilities upon me. The whole neighbourhood knew when I was going to sit an exam. All the women waited for me on their doorsteps in the morning of any important exam and each one gave me something sweet to eat to – according to superstition – "make my brain work better"! They were all anxious for me to do well at school. It was a matter of pride for them that a child, a girl at that, should be successful among the rich children. Support and solidarity among the neighbours were tremendous. After the end of my secondary schooling when I was 16, I went to the main university in Istanbul and choose to study sociology. While I was attending university I became involved in politics and I left home to find a job. I didn't get any money from my family; we all had to earn our own money. And that way you aren't dependent on your family and can do whatever you want. My father was afraid for my future if I was involved in politics, because in Turkey being in politics means you may die.

I was involved in the socialist movement. I published a newspaper, *Socialist Youth*. I did all the technical things at first and someone else was the editor, but he had to leave Turkey because he was taken to court and faced many years' sentence – it's illegal to write about class struggle – so he had to leave Turkey. I took over the editorship as well as writing and doing the technical things. It was published openly but you had to take copies to the authorities. They check and if they find things that were illegal they take you to court, open a trial and you can easily get many years. It happened to me in 1975. I was taken to court. But the process can take a long time. When in 1979 my trial ended they gave me 6 years and 8 months, and two years' refuge in another city in Turkey; but after that, I faced many other trials which would have meant 40 years' imprisonment. One trial was over but my others were also coming to an end. Altogether my sentence would have been 40 years. When my first trial finished, I tried to appeal, but they refused my application. Then I went into hiding, living in an illegal flat.

In another capacity I was working in a mass women's organization, Ilerici Kadinlar Derneği, the Progressive Women's Organization of Turkey, which was founded in 1975. I was one of the organizers, responsible for one of seven parts of Turkey, a big area, including Istanbul. That organization was banned in 1979, at the same time as my trial, and that's why I had to go into hiding. Then in 1980 the military coup came. I couldn't really be free, but I did work sometimes. Many people also had to hide from the police, and while I was hiding I hid other people in my flat. I changed my name, I used a false identity card, I moved to another place – Istanbul is a big place, so you can hide. Even with so few Black people, I could still hide. But twice they asked me for my passport –

I changed my appearance, didn't wear what I usually wear; I looked really different then...more like a model – all my money went on clothing! Once I was going somewhere in a taxi and they stopped it and asked for my passport. I shouted, "I'm Turkish! How dare you?"

In 1983 it was really a narrow space to move in Istanbul because a lot of friends who were members of democratic organizations from Anatolia came into the city and the police knew that most of them were living there because it was so easy to hide. They became stricter, increased the pressure, and I realized I couldn't stay there any longer. I found a false passport but when I got to the border the man checking passports told me, "We can't let you out." My heart stopped, and I asked him why. He said, "Is this you? Are you Turkish?" He had never seen a Black person before, so he was confused and I took advantage of this, shouting: "How dare you? I am Turkish!" He forgot about anything else. Then other people in the queue shouted, "Ignorant man, how can you ask?" But my passport was false! I left with one of the friends I had been hiding in my flat for about a year; sometimes I would put him in a cupboard when guests came, because I was acting at being another woman. I came to England because I had friends here.

I could go back to Turkey from now on. Last week there was an important new Act passed: it is no longer the case that you can't write about class struggle – this was abolished. Still I don't think you can write freely; since there is another new Act which in another sense makes it illegal. You can write but you can't organize; so if you write or say something about organizing it is still illegal. It means you still can't do anything against the government, I think. But many people have been freed from prison; most of them are out since last week. It is good for the time being, but for the future it's not literally an amnesty, because there are conditions. For example, if you offend again you go to prison and have to serve out what was left of your previous sentence.

I left university in 1975 – when I was pregnant – because fascist students occupied our faculty. In the History and other departments there were many fascist students, and because I was Black and politically active they knew me; also my husband was the leader of an organization. I couldn't get into the university even for the exams. One of my friends who tried spent eight days in hospital. He was beaten almost to death. Eight days he stayed in hospital. So I just left. Once when my husband was in prison and my son was three and a half months I tried to go back to take my exams in order to get a better job...I worked in a really bad place. It was hard to tackle all those problems with the uneducated bosses. (You could work as well as study; it wasn't compulsory to go full-time to lectures, that's why I chose that university.) So I tried to complete my studies and get a good job; but I couldn't achieve that. I had to work so hard because my husband was in prison and I was paying for a private crèche for my son. . . . He's in Sweden now, with his father.

He chose to live there. At first I couldn't get him here. The government didn't give him a passport. His father went to Sweden, I came here. We both ran away but left our son in Turkey and for five years they wouldn't give him a passport. At that time there was a problem with Turkish people in Bulgaria. There was a girl who was split from her family and a big campaign was mounted to get her out of Bulgaria to Turkey to rejoin her family, and during that time there were magazine articles about my son as well, some publishers took up the case and said he should be given a passport. Then I got my son back, after five years. He lived with me in London for a year and a half, then he wanted to see Sweden and what life is like there, and he found it better than here. He's sixteen now. . . .

I was also a founder of the Peace Movement in Turkey, in 1977. It's banned and the executive committee were in prison for a long time, but they've now been released. When the Gulf war began in January [1991], I was so sad just because Turkey is a neighbour of Iraq and it will cost us more than other people living in America, for example, or in England. But fortunately the Turkish people were against war and that was very hard, because the government is a kind of dictatorship, despite there being elections. There isn't democracy like here, yet still people – as in Germany – marched against war. I'm really proud of them. The government wanted to be involved with their army, but just before the war the top general of the army resigned, it's said because of the dangers of involvement in the war, which was the first time in the history of Turkey it happened; so they were afraid of the army itself, couldn't find any support for becoming involved with their forces. Still I think Turkey lost many things but in terms of manpower they didn't.

The situation for Kurdish people is a long and sad story. There are 12 million Kurdish people living in Turkey and in Turkish history there are three big riots – Kurds against the Turkish government. Kurds and Turks fought together in the war of independence; and in the first parliament of 1920 there were Kurdish MPs representing not just Kurdish people but others as well. But it changed. Kurds began to rebel against the government. After the military coup in 1980, it wasn't law that you couldn't speak Kurdish – there was no mention in an Act – but that's what happened after 1980; there are many Kurdish prisoners in prison whose family know no other language but Kurdish and they couldn't speak to their relatives since it was banned. Some are in prison just for speaking Kurdish, others were involved with banned democratic organizations – youth organizations, trade unions – and were imprisoned for being representatives of those organizations, as my former husband was.

There is a big Kurdish-Turkish war in our history, and Kurdish people really have a lower status. Most want their own rights as Kurds, but some of them. . .there are still Kurdish MPs who are. . .you know how some Blacks are called "coconut", Black on the outside, white on the inside? It's kind of like that. That whole area – the Iran, Iraq and Turkish border – has Kurdish people. But the Kurdish refugee problem after the Gulf War happened while some Kurdish organizations were fighting with the Turkish army in the east of Turkey, so that's why the Turks didn't respect them when they came, kicked them, didn't really want to help them in humanitarian terms, since in the meantime they were fighting with another part of the Kurdish population in their own land. It's horrible. . . . For a long time there has been this massacre in all parts of that area. The Kurds have to have their own country to stop this sad story. It's horrible – you can't imagine. . . . There is racism against Kurds in Turkey. When I was a child in Istanbul, some people said Kurdish men had tails which they hid in their clothes. Like what people elsewhere used to say about

Blacks. Because Kurds have a sizeable population, they are noticeable – not just a few of them, like us. They are 12 million. And they had their own land which is occupied by the Turkish. So this is where there is racism. My ex-husband was Kurdish and I was asked, "Has he got a tail?" I was taught and brought up in different attitudes; because I was Black I was conscious about excluding people or feeling against them. My family don't have any attitudes towards different, other people. But some people. . . .

I think my son has an identity problem, being Black and Turkish. Yes, he has lots of problems. It's not easy for him to be like us, because he was weaker than us when he came – I came here when I was nearly 30; he came when he was 12. He became ashamed of himself. In his London school, for example, the Turkish kids weren't very dominant but the Black kids were. He identified with the Jamaican boys and I was afraid for him because he copied everything they did. Copying them wasn't the problem. The problem was his identification – I wanted to make him proud of himself but I couldn't achieve that. And he stopped studying hard. He was really good in Turkey, always got distinction for schoolwork. He stopped, because he was called chicken for studying, so he didn't want to do it any more. The same thing is continuing now in Sweden. There he's the only Black in his school and no one wants to go out with him. It's sad, it's sad for him. His father is white, so maybe he is mixed up. . . . This is the worst part of it – I think being mixed-race sometimes brings identity problems, thinking of yourself as neither Black nor White. He didn't have that problem in Turkey. Being an immigrant brought those kinds of problems, I think.

One of my sisters didn't finish university, got married, had daughters and now works as a secretary; the other finished university and is a high-school English teacher. My elder brother – he's twelve years older – was a driver but has stopped work now, he is pensioned.

In Turkey women share the same problems of oppression as women any-where, but their position is changing as a result of industrialization. Old attitudes have begun to change. Before the 1960s there were different attitudes towards women. In big cities women can go to school and do whatever they want, but it's not the same everywhere. Women can also vote in all parts of Turkey; they have the right to vote and to be elected, which is before in some European countries. Because in the war of independence women fought along with men, when the new country was established (it was the Ottoman Empire before) Atatürk gave women all these rights – yet there are many barriers. There are laws. For example, if a man doesn't sign that his wife can work, she can't work; it has to be written on paper. But the situation doesn't arise in the first place, since women, being oppressed, anyway ask their husbands. After the industrialization of the 1960s many women went into the workplace. Their labour was needed because it's cheap and a woman generally isn't a danger for a boss. In the textile industry especially, most of the workforce is female. In the women's organization I worked in an area that has the country's highest popu-lation of women workers. It was in Bursa, where there are many textile factories, 90 per cent staffed by women; only the managers were men. Our organization lasted four years before it was banned, but during those years it expanded very quickly.

When I came to Britain, because I was a political refugee I thought I should continue working with Turks till I went back, since I came as a guest, not to settle down and stay for ever. Most of the Turkish workers here didn't know any English or what their rights were and didn't have a good organization to help them, or any organized social life, so I and some of my friends decided to found an organization. I am also a founder of a Turkish community centre in Stoke Newington where I worked voluntarily for four or five years; all my effort and time went there. I didn't want to do anything for myself while I had left my son in Turkey; I felt guilty and – I can say it now, I couldn't then – I think I punished myself deeply, doing nothing for myself, even in terms of personal relations – I didn't settle down or choose a man to live with, didn't want to make myself happy because of my feelings of guilt. When I brought my son here I realized that I had to and wanted to do something for myself because I had paid enough. The year he came, I went to an English class and got a certificate, applied to London University and began studying sociology again at Goldsmith College in 1989. This is my second year. I don't know what I will do after I get my degree. I may work with women again, in London or in Turkey. It depends on the situation here and in Turkey.

I don't have much contact with other Black or British people here, having spent so many years in the Turkish community. Also after a certain age you can't easily get on together when attitudes, culture, everything is so different. For example, I met a man at a party, and in Turkey I could be his friend rather than girlfriend, and I told him we could see each other because we really had a good chat – about Black people here, about racism, about teenage problems, etcetera – it wasn't like something soft or to do with love and sex. He brought me home and I gave him my phone number but when he came to see me I understood that he took it in another way. That sort of thing wouldn't easily happen among Turkish people; they can infer what you really mean...it's not only about language, it's about custom: it's not strange for Turks of opposite sexes to be just friends. But here it seems in the first place it's either sexual relations or nothing.... But I have friends from the political movement, and I was involved also with two solidarity organizations we established – one was about solidarity with women in Turkey; the other about solidarity with peace fighters in Turkey, and many British MPs were also members of that organization – during that time I had English friends and still have some of them. But most of my friends are Turkish, though now in college I have good friends.

I have begun writing about my family, but because of studying I haven't been able to finish. I started with my grandfather's father, imagining what he might have thought, what he might have felt; I know the area, the village we came from, the people and their attitudes. I just have to build up the story of his family history, including my sisters', brother's and father's life. My mother's history is very sad and important for me. Her father was not poor; it was the fashion for rich white people to adopt Black children, so my grandfather – Mother's father – gave her up to a rich white family as an adopted child. But when the rich man who adopted my mother died, everything spoiled; she and her sister were alone. She often told us about what she lived through. When she was 16 she escaped and caused many problems for the family; she had no

money, knew nothing of how to go to her village and she could only imagine –
she didn't know how to return to her village – but eventually through the police
she was taken back to her own family. My mother and my aunt were together but
my aunt didn't go with my mother and her life is now worse than my mother's.
She's all right now, though her youth was spoiled as a cleaner in huge houses,
being sexually abused, and so on. It is important that I write my family's story. I
really want to write, but I have to be settled.

Womi Bright Neal

1954–

*B*orn *in Monrovia, Liberia, she was educated there, in England
and in Switzerland, before attending university in the USA. Until
recently she was principal of a small private school in Monrovia.
She has written and produced films and serials for Liberian television as
well as several stage plays. She currently lives in the USA.*

The Weeping Tree

I T was a warm night in January. Hours after the little town of Besowa
had succumbed to slumber, Jaa Musa, husband and hunter, found himself
running breathlessly toward the hut of Ma Jabohn, the midwife.

Collecting her lappa about her shoulders the old lady responded with haste
to the emergency, quickening her steps through the unkempt bush towards the
banana patch. The full moon glazed the field with its pale light, enabling her to
deftly select a young banana leaf before hurrying on through the town to the
weather-beaten shack where Zoe lay whimpering in pain. As they came within
sight of the hut, Jaa took seat on the reeds in the adjacent kitchen and waited,

deferring to the custom of Besowa which prohibited men from looking upon women as they underwent this trauma.

Zoe's time had come early. Barely seven months had passed since they were bound to each other as husband and wife. Jaa allowed his thoughts to drift to the day that they were married. He had admired Zoe from the moment he saw the young girl toting a pile of wood on her head, striding toward her mother's fire-hearth. Her back was erect and strong and her front showed all signs of bloom. He did not delay in obtaining her parent's consent to tie the knot about their daughter's wrist. They agreed and Jaa immediately set himself to work in order to pay the girl's dowry. A superb hunter, he supplied Zoe's family with an abundant variety of game from his daily hunting trips.

On the nuptial day, their families and friends had congregated beneath the thatch shade specifically constructed for the ceremony. Handsomely attired in a magnificent hand-woven gown, the groom showered his in-laws with an assortment of clothing to be distributed among members of their immediate family as a gesture of appreciation for providing him with his lovely bride. Amidst wild cheers, Jaa proudly laid on the table the bride-price of forty rollods. Silence fell upon the assembly as the rope around the girl's wrist, symbolic of their betrothal, was cut by the groom, and Zoe, thenceforth, belonged to him.

Jaa Musa loved Zoe. When they were apart the longing he felt for her was always so evident that his friends would tease him, calling him not "woman-lappa", a term of derision they reserved for men who spent their lives wrapped, like an item of clothing, around some woman or another, but rather "Zoe-lappa". And what could Jaa do but laugh since it was true. His friends were always amazed that he showed no hint of embarrassment at this and began to regard him with new respect. It was not that they believed Zoe to be anything out of the ordinary, but the effect she had on their friend was so startling that they all fell just a little in love with her. "Ah, Zoe-Lappa," the unmarried among them would say, "see that shine to his skin? I will never marry until I find me a 'Zoe'!"

That day, as he listened keenly for the high-pitched wail signalling the birth, he could only thank fate yet again as he thought of the woman who was now his wife, who was soon to alter once more the way the world saw him. Jaa Musa, Hunter, Husband and yes, soon, Father. Tightening his eyelids he prayed that his first-born would be a girl, "and she will carry the name Maissa, after the mother of my mother."

"To sire a girl child first," he told his friends one evening over a game of draughts, "means good luck for the man".

"If your child is a girl," young Momo Fan Sando announced, "I want her for my wife."

There was great laughter in the room as the men drank to Momo.

"It is good to propose while the child is yet in the womb. That way, you can be sure no other man will comebefore you." Jaa gulped the last dregs from the palm wine bottle and passed it on to Zoe who happily recharged it.

"Let's leave this baby talk, my friends, because you all have a long time to wait," she said, serving the men roasted deer and filling their bottles before going about her evening chores.

Hard to believe that that was barely a week ago and now here he was waiting for the child to be born. Occasionally he forced his ear against the cracks of the wooden window but the only sounds filtering through were low grunts and groans. Suddenly, the rooster crowed, startling him out of his reverie. Jaa could hardly contain himself. This baby was taking an exceptionally long time to be born. It must be a boy, he concluded, since a girl would have had the sense to be considerate of her mother.

He shrugged as he resigned himself to accepting a son and allowed his mind to wander. He envisioned the boy by his side hunting in the deep dark forest. He imagine the face of his son. Perhaps he would be blessed with the high forehead of his mother that betrayed her intelligence, and the dark twinkling eyes that would win many a maiden's heart. And maybe he would have the stubborn cleft chin that would tell all he met that he was the son of Jaa Musa. Yes, Jaa Musa thought, a son would be preferable. When the time came he would have him initiated into the Poro, the men's bush society where he would be schooled for manhood and in the great mysteries of life.

He dreamt of how a month after Zoe gave birth Besowa Town would come to life with jubilation and merriment. Their child would be delivered from hand to hand as each villager in turn welcomed the infant to Besowa and to the society of the living. He imagined the masked dancers whirling their straw-covered bodies, kicking up dust and finally moving into the surrounding forest while the beat of the congas became a loud tumultuous bass heralding the Besowa boys dance troupe. A wonder to behold, yes, but not such a wonder as the precious infant whose birth they would celebrate with such vigour. Grandma Maissa, his mother's mother would, in time-honoured tradition, take to the floor and dance non-stop for fifteen minutes and it would be well nigh dusk before the play would simmer down. In his mind Jaa saw himself standing in the midst of the spectators, raising his offspring towards the heavens.

The cock crowed once more as darkness lifted slowly from the face of Besowa and a cool breeze swept across the waking village. Just as Jaa yielded to an uncontrollable doze, he thought he heard a baby wail and imagined his son or daughter opening its doe-eyes to the world at the precise moment that its father stirred. At last the wait was over. He knew that minutes after the baby was born Ma Jabohn would shuffle toward him and quietly lodge a small parcel of banana leaf in his palm. The parcel would contain the infant's umbilical cord which he would press firmly against his forehead before burying it unseen beneath a young almond tree at the side of the house that he had picked out for this very purpose. All these thoughts were like quickfire in his mind, jostling with each other for space but disappearing almost instantaneously.

He glanced through the door, uncertain about what he should now do, nervous about disturbing his wife and very very happy that she had come through this ordeal and had brought forth life. He chuckled to himself about his behaviour and thought, finally I have joined the long tradition of men, fathers all, who have behaved as I for as long as women have conceived.

"Jaa Musa, Jaa Musa," he thought he heard Zoe whisper. But no, it was not her, he realized, it was Ma Jabohn. The old midwife's body was bent over the bed heaving, wracked with sobs, and he instantly understood that something too terrible to contemplate had happened.

It was not the child. Or rather, it was not *just* the child. He felt a sharp pain hit his gut and dropped to his knees, knocking the old lady over as he fell. He could not find the strength to stand and so crawled with his belly almost touching the floor, feeling like hot lead had been poured into it. As he came closer to the bed the distance seemed too interminable to conquer. Zoe's mouth was open and her neck bent back, grotesquely arched as though through some superhuman effort she was willing the pain to leave her body. He took all this in within seconds, and his body began to contort as though he was holding in his pain with the same ferocity that Zoe had tried to expel her own. After what seemed hours, he let out a scream, which assaulted the air and shocked the town people of Besowa out of their early morning dreams. When the men came to move Jaa Musa from the body it took five of them and they understood that they were witnessing something they were never likely to see again: an eternal mourner, succumbing to a veritable sea of grief.

That morning in a dry parched field on the edge of Besowa town, where children dare no longer pass, Jaa Musa hanged himself from a tree. After his death drops of moisture began to fall day and night from the leaves of this tree, nourishing a little patch of flowers and green grasses that sprang up in its shade. The only one who does not fear the weeping tree is the daughter Zoe gave to the world and whom Jaa Musa, drowning in his grief, simply failed to see. She was named Maissa, after the mother of his mother.

Véronique Tadjo
1955–

Born in *Côte d'Ivoire, she is the author of a volume of poetry,* Latérite; *two novels –* A Vol d'Oiseau *(1986) and* Le Royaume aveugle *(1991); a children's book,* Lord of the Dance *(1988); and a collection of short stories,* La Chanson de la vie *(1990). Married and a mother, she teaches in the English department of the University of Abidjan. All her poems are untitled and are usually capitalized throughout; the first three are from* Latérite *(here translated into English by the author) and the last two are previously unpublished.*

Five Poems

LIFE IS MADE
OF BLACKBERRY BUSHES
AND DARK THORNS
I WOULD HAVE LIKED IT
MORE MELLOW AND LESS BITTER
BUT YOU KNOW
THE LIMIT OF THINGS
SHRINKS AT EVERY MOMENT
OUR FACES CHANGE
AND OUR LOVES CRASH
AGAINST ONE ANOTHER
YOU KNOW IT WELL
THE NIGHT OF YOUR BIG FRIGHT
THERE'LL ONLY BE YOU

*　　　*　　　*

YOU MUST GIVE BIRTH
TO CHILDHOOD
SPIT OUT THE VENOM
WHICH BREAKS YOUR VIOLENCE
EMBRACE THE PRESENT
AND LEAVE FROM THE PLATFORM
THE WARMTH OF THE FOETUS
IS THE NIGHT OF ALL TIMES

*　　　*　　　*

HE IS MY SHADOW
MY STEP-BY-STEP
MY FURTIVE GLANCE
HE IS MY MAYBE
MY NEWBORN DESIRE
HE IS MY STRENGTH
AND MY WEAKNESS
THE WATER WHICH CARRIES ME
AND THE WATER WHICH DROWNS ME
HE IS WHERE I'D LIKE TO GO
TOMORROW AS WELL AS YESTERDAY

*　　　*　　　*

DID YOU SEE
HOW THE FATHER CRIED
WHEN HIS DAUGHTER LEFT?

WHEN SHE WALKED AWAY
HIS FACE A GRIMACE
HIS MOUTH A GAPING HOLE
AND HIS BROW LINED WITH CREASES
THEN HE LOWERED HIS HEAD

TO GO OVER THERE
FURTHER AWAY FROM EVERYTHING
THAT MADE YOU

BUT THERE IS THE TELEPHONE
WHICH ECHOES ONE MORNING
IN THE HALF SLEEP OF A DAY
ALREADY TURNING GREY
THE VOICE OF THE FATHER
OVER LAND
AND OVER WATER
TELLING EVERYDAY WORDS
WORDS CARVED BY YEARS
WORDS SO ORDINARY
THEY SOUND LIKE A REVELATION
AND IN THE MIDST OF
SUCH EMOTION
OF THIS OUTSTRETCHED HAND
THE CLICK OF THE TELEPHONE
SENDING SILENCE
WHICH BECOMES OBSESSION
UNENDING UPROAR
OF A TRUER REALITY
EMPTINESS & THE FORGETTING OF BODIES

*   *   *

Life is walking fast
It wasn't how I wanted it, but I had to take what I could.
I used to think time was on my side. That has changed now.
I can't risk it
I can't wait
I had to touch you
I don't know what tomorrow will bring.
I had to gamble.

Lucinda Roy
?1956–

Born in Britain to a Jamaican father (novelist/sculptor Namba Roy) and an English mother, she has lived in Africa and is currently Assistant Professor in English and Creative Writing at Virginia State Polytechnic and State University. Appearing in US journals, her poems have won many awards. Her collection Wailing the Dead to Sleep was published in 1988.

Points of View

Even now, women bend to rivers
Or to wells; they scoop up life and offer it
To men or to their children, to their elders,
To blistered cooking-pots. Heavy with light,
And the brief mosaics of the world,
Water is carried home. Even now,
Women bend to see themselves in rivers
Or catch unsteady faces in buckets drawn
From wells. And water sucks them in,
Catching the wild geometry of the soul
Tossing it onto a plane. The wells
Are brimming with women's fluid faces;
The rivers are alive with women's hands.
Reflections savoured for a while, then gone.

From up here, what can I know of water?
I catch it tamed from metal spouts encased
In quiet glass, contoured in porcelain.
I compartmentalize the beast in ice,
Then serve it, grinning, to distant friends.
What do I know of water? Tomorrow
I must go again to find it. I will swim
In rivers thick with time, permanent as eyes
Of sleepy crocodiles. I will watch women
In slow genuflections ease water
Into round bowls. The river-blinded boys
With jellied eyes transparent in the sun
Will look at me. Children will jump from element

To element making paths through air to water,
Shooting diamond-drops along trajectories
Too long for me to measure. "This is water,"
They will tell me. This intense immersion.
A new baptism free of metaphor
Will be mine. Water will be water,
And I, a newly-evolved fish, will hear
The aquabatic rippling of gills.

If You Know Black Hair

If you know, you really know black hair,
the way it feels like bunched-up cloud
or dense-packed candy floss,
if you know, you really know the smell
of milky coconut easing through
the careful braids or the relaxed curls
of women just as bold with chemicals
as all the white girls with their tightly perms,
if you know all this, then you know
that there is nothing softer sweeter tougher
than black hair. Look at how the rain
perches like snow on foamy curls.
Look at how the hair springs back
to its original position.
Look at how it struggles against the comb
reasserting itself like an old mother
who's seen more than she ever
wanted to.

So when my mother smiles at my son's
effervescent hair, and when I smile too
seeing bubbles brownly crown his head
we are rejoicing in the thing my father gave
my son, a kind of indomitability.
May it cling to his head like memory.
May hands that touch it feel the soft of strength.

Iiola Ashundie
1956–

B orn on the Caribbean island of St Kitts, she spent her early years
in the capital, Basseterre, joining her family in Britain in 1964, at
the age of seven. She has said: "As I grew with this country called
England, my heart longed to be in the place of my birth. . . . My writings
are based on my own life experience, recollecting those early childhood
memories that are still with me." A mother of three, she writes both prose
and poetry, which she performs, and has taught creative writing and
literacy for Black women. Her work appears in the anthology Sojourn
(edited by Zhana, 1988).

Mother of Mine

I REMEMBER you when you looked after me when I was ill. You nursed me
until I was well again, my dear mother. I ran and played under Grandmother's
house making my mud pies and I truly eat them. It tasted like it had been mixed
with salt from the sea, then I was ill again. This time I had worms. I screamed as
I sat upon the pot; they wiggled and jiggled, as you helped withdraw them from
my body. Yes, it was you, my mother.

I watched you when you baked the cassava bread and fried the fish upon
the open stove in the yard. You giggled and played with me and your other
children, yes, my two brothers and my sister. When it was time to sleep you
kneeled beside me making sure that I said my prayers. Yes, I remember, it
was "Gentle Jesus meek and mild", but my tongue told me it was "Seventy
Jesus make a mile". You slapped me for talking utter nonsense.

Then one day you told me I was going to England. Where it was I did not
know, I only knew that the big silver aeroplane took you there high in the sky. I
used to shout to it, yelling out to bring me lots of things, little that I knew that it
couldn't hear me. You came out into the hot sun, it's radiance brightened your
smile as you looked at me. Happy go lucky, I ran about the yard with my sisters
and brothers, chasing the fowls up and down, until I stepped on one of the
baby chicks, squeezing out its inside. It went all over my foot. I was frightened,
I ran under the house to hide myself from you. You were totally vexed. All the
shouting that you did couldn't get me out. There I stayed until evening, when you
called me for my food. Thinking that you had forgotten about the baby chick, yes,
Mother, I got a beating that very evening.

On Sundays when you plaited my hair, we popped the peas from their pods.
I listened to you and Grandmother laughing. There you sat and put your paper

curls in your shiny black hair. Yes, Mother, I was there. Again you told me I was going to England and that the snow was going to bite me. I cried because I didn't want the snow to bite me, believing that it was some sort of animal. You said that there was lots of fog too. I hid myself beneath Grandmother's bed, believing that a multitude of frogs was going to get me. I ran along the alley jumping fence, oh so high and mighty, for I was only as small as a flea. Again I had an injury. Yes, Mother, I jumped upon a nail so large and rusty. I hopped and cried while you put purple violet upon my feet. I thought I was going to die. For days I could not walk, as the pain went through my thigh.

The hot sun shone down as I ran down the bay. There I stayed catching crabs all day, until they bit my finger so. I hurried home dry as can be, where you told me that I looked like I have just come from salt-pan alley. "Go and get yourself clean up," you shouted. Indeed, I gleamed as a mirror for I had used all the Vaseline.

You told me to go down my Aunt Vicky. I hopscotched all the way. There I was bitten by her dog, Bully.

The star shone from above, yes, it was the middle of the night. I was sick again, this time I had diarrhoea. Someone had given me beer. I sat upon the pot, filling it completely, as I emptied the contents of my stomach in another before me. Yes, I remember, I was sick as can be. Then something flickered in the breadfruit tree. It crashed upon the tin roof. I ran as fast as could be and you comforted me. Yes, Mother, for I was frightened of Jumbie.

You dressed me in my pretty dress and we went to church. I began to climb the steps. The rude boys began to look up at me from beneath. Little did I realize that I had forgotten to put on my panties.

I looked at you while you scaled the fish. I ran and scaled the mango tree, even bruising my knee.

The yard was empty. You were not there. Only the fire flickered there, and little brother began to play there. He said he was making pull-pull-sweetie and how I loved pull-pull-sweetie. It looked so real. He flicked it at me, almost blinding me. My bottom was bare. He had got me there. The scar is still there.

Then again you told me I was going to England and that it was cold as ice. I didn't want to be frozen like ice, like the ice that came upon the donkey cart. Thinking I was smart, I used to pull the donkey's tail. The man said he was going to send me to jail for pulling the donkey's tail.

Something stunk in the air, as the flies were everywhere. I climbed the kitchen top. There I saw Mr Thomas giving the shark the chop.

Once again, Mother, you told me I was going to England. How I was going to Daddy. It's funny but I didn't remember him leaving. He weren't there in the evening.

The car drew up. I got inside. I saw the houses going by. You placed me with a guide, who always peeled my hide. You kissed me goodbye and told me not to cry, with my handbag by my side. Oh, Mother dear, you were not there as the ship drew in at the pier. I looked up to find my daddy. There were thousands of daddies everywhere. Yes, Mother, you were not there. Only sorrow there was to bear.

For many years I tried to get over there, to hear your laughter from your long gone daughter. I grew to be a teenager with children later. Again my thoughts wandered over many waters. The emptiness grew deeper as life grew dimmer, never hearing your laughter. My inner energies began to take hold of me to find you again, my dear mother, to catch that plane to that far-off land.

I walked down the stairs with my ticket in one hand. Someone looked at me. I didn't recognize him, my dear long lost brother.

It was dark as the stars lighted my heart. I stood upon the sidewalk. This old woman stood there. Then I was told it was you, my mother. I looked with wonder, seeing you for the first time. Should I cry, as I hugged you? Yes, Mother, I had returned. It seemed like a century to fill this heart that is empty. Yes, it's my mother and me, your long lost daughter.

Valerie Bloom

1956–

B orn in Clarendon, Jamaica, she attended schools and teacher training college in Kingston. She taught there, at Frankfield High School (1977–9), then came to England and taught music in Manchester. She obtained a first-class Honours degree in English with African and Caribbean Studies from the University of Kent. She has broadcast on television and radio in Britain and in Jamaica, performs her work extensively and conducts workshops all over England. She has also lectured on folk traditions in dance, song and poetry. She now lives in Manchester, where she is a Multicultural Arts Officer. She has said: "I work within the old oral tradition that goes back to Africa, rather than the newer one of reggae and dub poetry. The differences are partly of rhythm: I usually use normal speech rhythms rather than the musical rhythms of dub music." Her first volume of poetry, Touch Mi, Tell Mi!, was published in 1983 and her work has been much anthologized.

Carry-go-bring-come

Mi hear sey yuh a go foreign,
A true dat, sista Cole?
Yuh can trus me wid yuh bizniz
For me wouldn' tell a soul.

Den a true yuh an Charlie mash up?
Unoo no deh agen?
No bada fret yuh heart, mi chile,
For yuh can always go back to Ben.

An' smaddy tell mi sey yuh sista
Engage fi married soon.
A which one a dem, mi dear Miss Cole?
Mi mine tell mi sey a June.

No bada fraid fi tell me
For not a wud wi pass mi mout'
Mi a ooman kip to meself
Mi no carry news go bout.

For from mawnin' mi hear piece o' news
An mi no tell nobody yet
(At least mi ongle tell Sta Gwen
An Aunt Sue and Miss Ginnet).

No badda go back go sey mi sey
For a yuh one mi dis a tell
But mi hear sey Joshie Williams
A sen fi Lucy Bell.

Mark oh, a no mi sey so
A smaddy dis wispa it to mi.
But tell mi sumpn', if dat true
Wha a go appen to Miss Mary?

Den mi tell yuh bout de news
Whey Fanny tell mi bout Mass Jim?
Mi hear sey im plan fi run whey
For Miss Ivy won' tap nag im.

Doah no bada tell nobody
For mi promise no fi talk
An mi no wan mi name go call
Far no cyah how yuh secret dark

If yuh pinch tell mi yuh bizniz
Yuh won' ever haffe fret
For from mi bawn mi no hear nobody
Call mi 'mout-a-massy' yet.

Tell mi bout Mass Charle
An mi wi tell yuh about Aunt Sue
An if yuh tell mi who dah married
Mi wi tell yuh bout Miss Lou.

A gawn yuh gawn, yuh nah tell mi
Well, silent mean consent.
Dat mean whey mi sey mussa true,
Mek a run go tell Mass Clement.

Jean Binta Breeze

1956–

Acknowledged as the first female "dub" poet, she was born in the village of Pattyhill, Jamaica, in Hanover parish (her grandparents were peasant farmers, her father a sanitary inspector, her mother a nurse and a Community Development Officer), and has four sisters. In 1978, while studying acting, directing, stage management and community drama at the Jamaica School of Drama, she added the African name "Binta" (meaning "close to the heart") to her own. She subsequently became a teacher of English, Geography, Spanish and Drama, among other subjects, for five years and also worked for two years with the Jamaican Cultural Development Commission as a co-ordinator for their speech and literacy programme. Since January 1985, when she travelled to London, she has performed her poetry widely, and she has also made

recordings of her work and has written fiction and plays, including
Hallelujah Anyhow *which was televised in 1990. This is the title poem*
from her collection Riddym Ravings and Other Poems *(1988).*

Riddym Ravings
(The Mad Woman's Poem)

de fus time dem kar me go a Bellevue
was fi di dactar an de lanlord operate
an tek de radio outa mi head
troo dem seize de bed
weh did a gi mi cancer
an mek mi talk to nobady
ah di same night wen dem trow mi out fi no pay de rent
mi haffi sleep outa door wid de Channel One riddym box
and de DJ fly up eena mi head
mi hear im a play seh

Eh, Eh,
no feel no way
town is a place dat ah really kean stay
dem kudda – ribbit mi han
eh – ribbit mi toe
mi waan go a country go look mango

fah wen hungry mek King St pavement
bubble an dally in front a mi yeye
an mi foot start wanda falla fly
to de garbage pan eena de chinaman backlat
dem nearly chap aff mi han eena de butcha shap
fi de piece a ratten poke
ah de same time de mawga gal in front a mi
drap de laas piece a ripe banana
an mi – ben dung – pick i up – an nyam i
a dat time dem grab mi an kar mi back a Bellevue
dis time de dactar an de lanlord operate
an tek de radio plug outa mi head
dem sen mi out, seh mi alright
but – as ah ketch back outa street
ah push een back de plug
an ah hear mi DJ still play, seh

Eh, Eh,
no feel no way

town is a place dat ah really kean stay
dem kudda – ribbit mi han
eh – ribbit mi toe
mi waan go a country go look mango

Ha Haah. . .Haa

wen mi fus come a town
mi use to tell everybady 'mawnin'
but as de likkle rosiness gawn outa mi face
nobady nah ansa mi
silence tun rags roun mi bady
in de midst a all de dead people dem
a bawl bout de caast of livin
an a ongle one ting tap mi fram go stark raving mad
a wen mi siddung eena Parade
a tear up newspaper fi talk to
sometime dem roll up
an tun eena one a Uncle But sweet saaf
yellow heart breadfruit
wid piece of roas saalfish side a i
an if likkle rain jus fall
mi get cocanat rundung fi eat i wid
same place side a weh de country bus dem pull out
an sometime mi a try board de bus
an de canductar bwoy a halla out seh
'dutty gal, kum affa de bus'
ah troo im no hear de riddym eena mi head
same as de tape weh de bus driva a play, seh

Eh, Eh,
no feel no way
town is a place dat ah really kean stay
dem kudda – ribbit mi han
Eh – ribbit mi toe
mi waan go a country go look mango
so country bus, ah beg yuh
tek mi home
to de place, where I belang. . .

an di dutty bway jus ran mi aff

Well, dis mawnin, mi start out pon Spanish Town Road,
fah mi deh go walk go home a country
fah my granny use to tell mi how she walk from wes
come a town
come sell food

an mi waan ketch home befo dem put de price pon i'
but mi kean go home dutty?
fah mi parents dem did sen mi out clean
Ah!
see wan stanpipe deh!
so mi strip aff all de crocus bag dem
an scrub unda mi armpit
fah mi hear di two mawga gal dem laas nite
a laugh an seh
who kudda breed smaddy like me?
a troo dem no know seh a pure nice man
weh drive car an have gun
visit my piazza all dem four o'clock a mawnin
no de likkle dutty bway dem weh mi see dem a go home
wid
but as mi feel de clear water pon mi bady
no grab dem grab mi
an is back eena Bellevue dem kar mi
seh mi mad an a bade naked a street
well dis time de dactar an de lanlord operate
an dem tek de whole radio fram outa mi head
but wen dem tink seh mi unda chloroform
dem put i dung careless
an wen dem gawn
mi tek de radio
and mi push i up eena mi belly
fi keep de baby company
fah even if mi nuh mek i
me waan my baby know dis yah riddym yah
fram before she bawn
hear de DJ a play, seh

Eh, Eh
no feel no way
town is a place dat ah really kean stay
dem kudda – ribbit mi han
eh – ribbit mi toe
mi waan go a country go look mango

an same time
de dactar an de lanlord
trigger de electric shack
an mi hear de DJ vice bawl out, seh

Murther
Pull up Missa Operator!

Iyamidé Hazeley
1957–

Born of Sierra Leonean parentage in London, she spent her formative years in West Africa. She has a BA Honours degree in Social
Science (1979) and in 1986 received an MA from London University's Institute of Education. She has been a teacher, designer and painter
and has given lectures and workshops on creative writing to adults and
children, in addition to writing poetry, fiction and articles. She received
a Minority Rights Group/Minority Arts Advisory Service (MAAS) award for
poetry in 1983 and in 1986 was a joint winner of the Greater London
Council Black Experience filmscript competition. She was co-founder of
Zora Press, a Black women's publishing cooperative, whose first book was
her own collection of poems Ripples and Jagged Edges (1987).

Women of Courage

There will be a morning song
for those who clean the dust
from the children's bruises
the blood of the wounds from bullets
those who wipe the sleep
from the eyes of the weary
and whose labour shields
the frail bodies of the old
those whose pain is multiplied
by the pleas of their young
scarred by the precision
of their inquisitors
who refuse to retreat in battle
and who are dying with the sum of this knowledge
There will be a future.

When You Have Emptied Our Calabashes

When you have emptied our calabashes
Into your porcelain bowls overflowing
the surplus spilling and seeping
into foreign soil
when you have cleaved the heads of our young
and engraved upon the soft papyrus there
an erasure of our past
having built edifices to your lies
filled them with so many bad books and distorts
and sealed the cracks in the structure
with some synthetic daub,
when you stock and pile arms
and talk about the nuclear theatre
want to make the world your stage
limiting the chance of world survival
it confirms your calculations, your designs
your ambitions which we'll thwart
which we'll resist
which we'll fight in all manner of ways.

We will rebuild
we will choose our most knowing
most eloquent old women
to spit in the mouths
of the newborn babies
so that they will remember
and be eloquent also
and learn well
the lessons of the past
to tell their grandchildren
so that if you come again
in another time
with your trinkets and arms
with porcelain bowls
and scriptures
they will say
we know you.

Political Union

You call me "Sister", Brother,
yet it seems you speak with the empty kernel of the word,
and sometimes
when you talk to me

there lingers after
a void
far more empty than existed before.

When you hear my anguished silence and are reassured by it,
then I know that your strength depends
    on my becoming weak,
    that you have not questioned
    the bars, deeply entrenched,
    of the barbed cage externally defined
    that is the oppressor's role you so emulate.

When you look above the waist,
    see my face,
    touch my skin,
    nestle on my breast as though
    to reclaim the ease of infancy,
then I know
    that you have concretized my body
    in your mind
    into a temple for your fantasies.
When you fraternize with my sisters while demanding my fidelity
then I know
    that you yourself are unfulfilled.

Many times you have seen my nakedness
    but not noticed my eyes
    as you surrounded me in your taunting caress.
Can you, physically a part of this body,
try to see inside this body
    the joy and pain at once housed side by side?
Can you stop wearing me, playing me,
    stop strumming my emotions?

You call me "Sister", Brother,
yet I know
    that is simply a psychological lever
    to prise apart my legs.
"Sister, make coffee for the movement,
Sister, make babies for the struggle."
You raped my consciousness with your body,
    my body with reason,
    and assuage your unconscious guilt
    by oral politicking,
      make believing
"Sister, Sister".

When you yourself acknowledge the occidental fetters
    that truss you,
when you yourself see the hidden fenders
    that seal the seal
    over your mind's eye
    against me,
When you can see that my political significance is
    a vertical one,
that my contribution is
    a vanguard one,
    and you can see my total,
Then you can call me Sister
Then you will be my Comrade.

Joan Riley

1959–

B orn in St Mary, Jamaica, youngest of eight children, she studied at universities in Britain, obtaining a postgraduate degree in communications. She now lives with her young daughter and son in London and teaches culture and Black history in literacy programmes. Her novels – The Unbelonging (1985), Waiting in the Twilight (1987) and Romance (1988) – deal particularly with Caribbean women in Britain and their personal and family relationships. In The Unbelonging, from which this passage comes, eleven-year-old Hyacinth leaves her aunt's home in Kingston to join her father in England, and, plunged into a confusing and alienating environment both at school and at home, where she is confronted by the nightmare of incest, she finds escape in daydreams of a better life in Jamaica.

From

The Unbelonging

S HE was moving! Hyacinth heard the news with mingled joy and disbelief. She had wanted to move for such a long time. Already she had been at the centre for over a year. Other children had come and gone, but there was never anywhere suitable for her. She often wished she had the courage to ask to see one of the places they thought so unsuitable. Anything would have been better than staying where she was. If only they knew how much she had grown to hate the reception centre. Littlethorpe, the home she was moving to, sounded ideal, even though it was further out in the countryside than the reception centre. Any apprehension she might feel was buried deep. There was no one to talk to about it anyway. They could never understand how it felt to stand exposed and naked in her blackness, frightened by the hostile stares always turned on her.

The large rambling house her social worker took her to looked dusty and neglected, the red brick walls chipped and crumbling, the pale, watery afternoon sun exposing all the weaknesses and highlighting the dingy, run-down appearance. Hyacinth's heart had sunk as she watched the place approaching, knowing with certainty that that was where she was going. She wished with all her might that they would drive straight past. This place looked condemned and dilapidated. For a fleeting moment she wondered if it could possibly be better than the modern reception centre she had just left.

The interior lived up to the promise of the outside. It had an air of dirt about it, a dinginess that clung to the worn and faded carpet, the discoloured wallpaper and the musty-smelling, ageing furniture. Hyacinth stood in the middle of the large hallway, feeling strange and alone, wishing she had never agreed to come. She wished that she had the courage to tell her social worker just how she felt, but the thought of returning to the reception centre after leaving so triumphantly was more than she could bear. She felt misery weigh on her, longing for somewhere else to go, that she could somehow return to Jamaica. She was glad when her social worker went to search for the woman who ran the home.

The woman her social worker came back with was fat and greasy, eyes small blue chips in her long, heavy face.

"I'm Auntie Susan," she said coldly. "My husband, Uncle Alan, and myself are the house-parents here."

Hyacinth nodded, not quite sure how she should respond to that. She wondered if she was expected to call the woman "Auntie". She could sense the woman's dislike, and it made her feel alone and desperate. It would be like this everywhere, all of them being polite – hating you, but hiding it. A sudden longing to be with black people surged within her, mingled with her usual sense of shame and guilt about her colour.

Hyacinth hated being the new girl at the home. The other children did not like her and it was like the nightmare of coming to England all over again. She felt bitter at the way the staff ignored her suffering, trapped and desperate as she became the butt of jokes and cruelties, both within Littlethorpe and among the children from the surrounding homes. Going to school was liberation, but her feet dragged in the evenings in much the same way as they had done going home to the house of her father. She would have to steel herself for the taunts and jeers, the vicious pokes in her back, the slyly extended foot that tripped her when she was least aware. Most nights found her shaking and tearful as she crawled wretchedly into her bed. She often wished that she had nice hair, that her skin was lighter. She was sure they would not pick on her then. The more she suffered, the more she clung to thoughts of Jamaica, sinking further into her world of dreams, where she was never older than ten, never had to face the unpleasant reality that was England. It was only in the nightmares that her father came, the bulge exposed and menacing eyes spitting and burning with evil fire. But waking always brought reality, brought bitterness at the knowledge of her blackness, her ugliness a shameful weight that hung her head and bowed her shoulders. Try as she might she could not block out the other children's taunts, or even deny the truth of their words.

There was one girl in particular whom she watched with wary eyes. Sylvia Bell was a big, stocky girl, a few months younger than Hyacinth. She had often heard the other children whisper among themselves about the bad things she did with girls, and she kept out of her way as best she could. Sylvia reminded her of Margaret White and the humiliation she had heaped on her. She had no illusion that she could fight the bigger girl. Her fight with Margaret had been a fluke and the thought of getting into a fight with Sylvia left her shaking with fear.

One day, coming in from school, tired and buffeted by the wind, they met. Hyacinth stiffened when Sylvia appeared and moved to block her way up the stairs. The gleam of anticipation in the girl's eyes told Hyacinth that she had been waiting for her, and the familiar desperation seemed to swamp her. She was miserable and hungry, unable to cope with the other girl's taunts. She prayed that she would let her pass.

"You better say excuse me, liver lip, or you're not going anywhere," the white girl said aggressively, as Hyacinth stood uncertainly at the bottom of the stairs. She felt unhappy and embarrassed about the whole situation, wanting only to be left alone.

"Can you excuse me, please?" she asked humbly.

Sylvia threw her head back, roaring with laughter. "Can you excuse me, please?" she mimicked.

Hyacinth heard Auntie Susan's door open, close again with a definite click, and tears of self-pity rushed to her eyes. A sudden kick on her shin made her flinch, and she stepped hastily backwards, mind spiralling back to the nightmare days of her first school years in Britain. She could almost hear them shouting, "Kill the wog!" and her stomach churned sickeningly with fear of remembered pain. Panic welled up inside her. Sylvia's face looked evil and threatening, looming over her wickedly. She could not face another beating, could not go back to those days, not after so many years had passed. She had to do something, had to stop the panic spiralling up inside, and suddenly she dived at the other's leering face, wanting to tear it out of her way. She wanted, needed to escape to the safety of the waiting dormitory. Her fingers curled and sank into the pink cheek while her foot kicked viciously at the pale shin. She hated these white people, feared them, envied them, and the three emotions merged into a frustrated burst of feeling. At that moment she wanted to tear the girl apart, rob her of that skin that was so much a badge of acceptance.

Sylvia screamed, scrambling away from the sudden attack, sprawling down the stairs as her legs got tangled up and buckled under the unexpected attack.

Hyacinth wasted no time scrambling on top of her, pounding at her, banging her head, trying to destroy her and the torment that she caused.

"Let Sylvia go this minute!" The woman's voice was like cold water trickling down her spine, seeping into her mind with the knowledge of what she had been doing, sobering her. Hyacinth's fist unclenched reluctantly, fingers slowly loosening their hold on the other girl's dress. Fear and alarm were rapidly replacing the satisfaction of pounding out her frustration on the girl's defeated head. She knew the woman would blame her for the fight, heard it in the impatience of the voice, felt the long knowledge of her hate.

"I want to talk to you in my room," Auntie Susan said, as Sylvia struggled groggily to her feet. "No, not you, Sylvia. I want to talk to Hyacinth."

Hyacinth's heart sank; the woman blamed *her* for what had happened. Bitterness welled up inside her as she remembered the door opening, and the finality of rejection as it clicked shut, leaving her to her fate. It would have been different if Sylvia had beaten her up, she was convinced of this. They were all the same these white people, they would always stick together against black people.

"I will not allow you to come here and establish jungle law!"

Hyacinth stiffened, sick with shame, hating the way the woman always lumped her in with other blacks. She knew she was different from other black people, even if she did look like them. She was not violent. But how could she tell this hard-eyed woman? How could she explain her fear? It was not her fault Sylvia had caused her to lose her temper. She knew it was wrong, that nothing the girl did would excuse her in the woman's eyes. But what else could she have done? She would have liked to have interrupted Auntie Susan, told her how she felt. Instead she hung her head, shame welling inside her, feeling small and disgusting.

"Having you here is one thing," the woman was saying now, "I had no choice about that. But one more incident like this evening and you are out. Do you hear me? Out!"

Hyacinth flinched, bitterness turning to panic, her tenuous hold on security slipping from under her feet, the nightmare of homelessness rapidly turning into reality. What would she do if Auntie Susan turned her out? Memories of the night she had left her father's house swam into her mind. The cold, the loneliness; the fat man in the car. No, she could not let that happen, she just could not. At the same time the unfairness of the situation bore down on her. She wanted to scream the truth at the woman, fear and anger mingling, warring inside her. She had to struggle to keep her mouth shut.

"Go and apologize to Sylvia, and let's have no more of this kind of behaviour from you," Auntie Susan said finally, dismissively.

Hyacinth's head shot up, and she had to bite back the bitter words that threatened to spill over. The woman knew the fight had not been her fault, yet she was forcing her to apologize to the other girl. She felt tears clogging up her throat, anger making her head hurt. She wished she could refuse, could tell the woman she would not do it, but the memory of that terrible night was still with her, and she bowed her head in defeat.

"It's always the same," she thought bitterly, "just because I am black. I have to take the blame for everything. I'll never be treated same as them." It was humiliating to have to apologize to her tormentor, and she wondered what the other girl would do once she found out that she had been blamed. She could imagine how it would spread around the three cottages of the home. Everybody would pick on her now. They would know that she would be held responsible for anything that happened, and she knew she would be too afraid of being kicked out of the home to fight back.

As it happened, the fight with Sylvia stopped the teasing. Now the others watched her warily, avoiding her as much as they could. Hyacinth was glad of this. She knew they still talked about her behind her back, but that was something she could live with. Even the unbelonging, the unwanted feeling was bearable, for at least they allowed her peace. "One day I will have friends again," she vowed often to herself. "One day I will be back where I belong." Jamaica was all she ever wanted, and she still visited it in her dreams, still treasured her aunt and confided in her friends. If the dreams were not always free from fear, she censored them, dismissed the unpleasant parts to the nightmares from which they had escaped. Yet for all that, the dreams were comforting in their unchanging state: security in an uncertain world.

At the same time there was an emptiness about her life, in her half-real world. Often she would lie awake in the silence of the night, perfectly still, the combined breathing of the other five girls in the room underlining her isolation. She would lie there staring into the impenetrable darkness, silent tears trickling from the corners of her eyes. She would have given anything for someone to talk to, someone to confide in.

By the time she reached sixteen the feeling that something was missing from her life had become an obsession. She often heard the other girls whispering among themselves, giggling with excitement. Often she would pretend to read a book, sitting in her corner, quiet and withdrawn, while thrilling to stories of what they did with boys. Yet always for her the image of her father would intrude, loom big and threatening above her; sick reality in the lump, exposed and obscenely menacing. The memory made her feel dirty, and she often thought the other children guessed. And still the emptiness grew inside her, yawned wide and open in her life. Now her night dreams left her strangely dissatisfied, peopled as they were with shadowy figures and flickering lights like fires. Now she no longer clung to the dreams as day broke, instead pushing them furtively to the back of her mind like something to be ashamed of. Even at school she would often catch herself staring absently through the window, wishing something new and exciting would happen to her today.

In this mood she discovered romance, found it between the pages of a stack of old Mills and Boon books that Auntie Susan had been about to throw away. Hyacinth loved the stories from the start, reading them from cover to cover, finding it hard to put them down, to concentrate on anything else. Now her lonely nights were peopled with tall, dark, handsome strangers, Spanish caballeros with warm brown eyes, romantic and intense Frenchmen. Sometimes in her secret fantasies she would be swept off her feet by a rich, passionate stranger and taken to live in his wild, remote castle. Always her hair would be blonde and flowing, her skin pale and white. Even at school she would daydream, ignoring the way her classmates nudged each other, pointed and sniggered, deaf to their crude comments and knowing looks.

She knew that many of the girls at school and at the home had boyfriends, and sometimes she envied them, envied the casualness with which they went to discos and youth clubs. She would never dare to go to one of the discos around Littlethorpe, conscious as she was of her colour, her strangeness. She could imagine them laughing at her, poking fun at her awkwardness, making rude comments about her skinny body and large bottom. The more she saw other girls dressed up, the more she envied them and wished she had been anything but black. They could never understand what it was like, how much she hated her brittle hair, the thickness of her lips. How could they understand what it was to be born like her? she often thought with bitterness. It wasn't fair. She had never done anything to deserve it. But she knew that no amount of anger and bitterness would change things. She envied the casual way the white children would cut their hair, secure in the knowledge that it would quickly grow again. Try as she might, her hair refused to grow, remaining stubbornly short and ugly; and she struggled to comb through the brittle dryness, afraid to use hair oil in case they thought her primitive. She always felt they were judging her, finding her wanting. And every time she felt inadequate, she would bury herself in another involved romantic plot, finding temporary relief as she had done for many years in a make-believe world.

Zindzi [Zindziswa] Mandela

1959–

Born in South Africa, younger daughter of Nelson and Winnie Mandela, she wrote her collection of poems, black as i am (with photographs by Peter Mugubane, 1978), at the age of sixteen. Her work has appeared in the ANC journal Sechaba and in anthologies such as Somehow We Survive: An Anthology of South African Writing (ed. Plumpp, 1982).

I Waited for You Last Night

I waited for you last night
I lay there in my bed
like a plucked rose
its falling petals my tears

the sound that my room
   inhaled
   drew in softly
   swallowed
in my ears
was the tapping on the window

getting up
I opened it
and a moth flew in
powdering my neck
shrugging
I caught its tiny wings
and kissed it
I climbed back into bed
with it
and left it to flutter around my head

I waited for you last night

Gcina Mhlope
1959–

Born in Hammarsdale, near Durban, South Africa, the youngest of a large family (her name Gcina means "the last"), she began writing poems and stories in Xhosa while at high school in the

Transkei: "I started writing English much later, when I was already in Johannesburg, using a public toilet as my study room. Most of my published works were written in that toilet." Well known as an actress with the Market Theatre, Johannesburg, she has also acted at the Edinburgh Festival and toured in Europe and the USA. Among plays in which she has appeared are The Nurse *(1982),* Black Dog, Born in the RSA *(for which she received the Obie award) and her own play* Have You Seen Zandile? *(1987), and she played the lead in the film* A Place of Weeping. *Her work has appeared in* Sometimes When It Rains *(ed. Oosthuizen, 1987), in* Spare Rib *and in* A Land Apart *(eds Brink and Coetzee, 1987).*

Nokulunga's Wedding

M OUNT Frere was one of the worst places for a woman to live. A woman had to marry whoever had enough money for lobola[1] and that was that. Nokulunga was one of many such victims whose parents wholeheartedly agreed to their victimization. She became wife to Xolani Mayeza.

By the time Nokulunga was sixteen years old she was already looking her best. One day a number of young men came to the river where she and her friends used to fetch water. The men were strangers. As the girls came to the river, one of the men jumped very high and cried in a high-pitched voice.

"Hayi, hayi, hayi!
Bri – bri mntanam uyagula!"

He came walking in style towards the girls and asked for water. After drinking he thanked them, went back to his friends and they left. This was not a new thing to Nokulunga and her friends, but the different clothes and style of walking left them with mixed feelings. Some were very impressed by the strangers but Nokulunga was not. She suspected they were up to something but decided not worry about people she did not know. The girls lifted their water pots on to their heads and went home.

In late February the same strange men were seen at the river, but their number had doubled. The day was very hot but they were dressed in heavy overcoats. Nokulunga did not see them until she and her friends were near the river. The girls were happily arguing about something and did not recognize the men as the same ones they had seen before. Only when the same man who had asked for water came up to them again did they realize who the strangers were. Nokulunga began to feel uneasy.

He drank all his water slowly this time, then he asked Nokulunga if he could take her home with him for the night. She was annoyed, and filled her water pot, balanced it on her head and told the others she had to hurry home. One of her friends did the same and was ready to go with Nokulunga when the other men came and barred their way.

---

[1] *lobola* dowry

Things began to happen very fast. They took Nokulunga's water pot and broke it on a rock. Men wrapped Nokulunga in big overcoats before she could scream. They slung the bundle on to their shoulders.

The other girls helplessly looked on as the men set off. The men chanted a traditional wedding song as they quickly climbed the hillside, while many villagers watched.

Nokulunga twisted round, trying to breathe. She had witnessed girls being taken before. She thought of the many people in the neighbourhood who seemed to love her. They couldn't love her if they could let strangers go away with her without putting up a fight. She felt betrayed and lost. She thought of what she had heard about such marriages. She knew her mother would not mind, as long as the man had enough lobola.

The journey was long and she was very hot inside the big coats. Her body felt so heavy, but the rhythm of her carriers went on and on. . .her lover Vuyo was going back to Germiston to work. He had promised her that he would be away for seven months then he would be back to marry her. She had been so happy.

Her carriers were walking down a very steep and uneven path. Soon she heard people talking and dogs barking. She was put down and the bundle was unwrapped. A lot of people were looking to see what the newcomer looked like. She was clumsily helped to her feet and stood there stupidly for viewing. She wanted to pee. For a while no one said anything, they all stood there with different expressions on their faces. The children of the house came in to join the viewing one by one and the small hut was nearly full.

She was in Xolani, her "husband's", room. She was soon left alone with him for the night. She sat down calmly, giving no indication that she was going to sleep at all. Xolani tried to chat with her but she was silent, so he got undressed and into the big bed on the floor. He coughed a few times, then uneasily invited her to join him. She sat silent. He was quiet for a while, then asked if she was going to sleep that night. No. For a long time she sat staring at him. She was watchful.

But Nokulunga was tired. She thought he was sleeping. Xolani suddenly lunged and grabbed her arm. His eyes were strange, she could not make out what was in them, anger or hatred or something else.

She struggled to free her arm, he suddenly let go and she fell. She quickly stood up, still watching him. He smiled and moved close to her. She backed off. It looked like a game, he following her slowly, she backing round and round the room. Each round they moved faster. Xolani decided he had had enough and grabbed her again. She was about to scream when he covered her mouth. She realized it was foolish to scream, it would call helpers for him.

She still stood a chance of winning if they were alone. He was struggling to undress her when Nokulunga went for his arm. She dug her teeth deep and tore a piece of flesh out. She spat. His arm went limp, he groaned and sat, gritting his teeth and holding his arm.

Nokulunga sat too, breathing heavily. He stood up quickly, cursing under his breath and kicked her as hard as he could. She whined with pain but did not stand up to defend herself.

Blood was dripping from Xolani's arm and he softly ordered her to tear a piece of sheet to tie above the bite. She did it, then wiped blood from the floor. Xolani got under the bedcovers in silence. Nokulunga pulled her clothes together. She did not dare to fall asleep. Whether Xolani slept or not, only he knows. The pain of his arm did not make things easier for him.

Day came. Xolani left, and Nokulunga was given a plate of food and locked in the room. She had just started eating when she heard people talking outside. It sounded like a lot of men. They went into the hut next to the one she was in and came out talking even louder. They moved away and she gave up listening and ate her food, soft porridge.

The men sat next to the big cattle-kraal. Xolani was there, his father Malunga and his eldest brother Diniso. The rest were uncles and other family members. They were slowly drinking their beer. They were all very angry with Xolani. Malunga was too angry to think straight. He looked at his son with contempt, kept balling his hands into fists.

No one said anything. They stole quick glances at Malunga and their eyes went back to stare at the ground. Xolani shifted uneasily. He was holding his hurt arm carefully, his uncle had tended to it but the pain was still there. His father sucked at his pipe, knocked it out on the piece of wood next to him, then spat between his teeth. The saliva jumped a long way into the kraal and they all watched it.

"Xolani!" Malunga called to his son softly and angrily.

"Yes, Father," Xolani replied without looking up.

"What are you telling us, are you telling us that you spent all night with that girl and failed to sleep with her?"

"Father, I. . .I. . ."

"Yes, you failed to be a man with that girl in that hut. That is the kind of man you have grown into, unable to sleep with a woman the way a man should."

Silence followed. No one dared to look at Malunga. He busied himself refilling his pipe as if he was alone. After lighting it he looked at the other men.

"Diniso, are you listening with me to what your brother is telling us? Tell us more, Xolani, what else did she do to you, my little boy? Did she kick you on the chest too, tell me, father's little son?" He laughed harshly.

An old man interrupted. "Mocking and laughing at the fool will not solve our problem. So please, everyone think of the next step from here. The Mjakuja people are looking for their daughter. Something must be done fast." He was out of breath when he finished. The old man was Malunga's father from another house.

The problem was that no word had been sent to Nokulunga's family to tell them of her whereabouts. Thirteen cattle and a well-fed horse were ready to be taken to the family, along with a goat which was called *imvulamlomo*, mouth opener.

The sun was about to set. Nokulunga watched it for a long time. She was very quiet. She stared at the red orange shape as it went down into the unknown side of the mountain.

By the time the colours faded she was still looking at the same spot but her eyes were taking a look at her future. She had not escaped that day. She felt weak and miserable. A group of boys sat all day on the nearby hill watching her so that she did not try running away. She was there to stay.

She did not know how long she stood there behind the hut. She only came to when she heard a little girl laughing next to her. The girl told her that people had gone out to look for her because they all thought she had managed to get away while the boys were playing. She went back into the house. Her mother-in-law and the other women also laughed when the little girl said she'd found Nokulunga standing behind the hut. More boys were sent to tell the pursuers that Nokulunga was safe at home.

She hated the long dress and doek she had been given to wear, they were too big for her and the material still had the hard starch on it. The people who had gone out to look for her came back laughing and teasing each other about how stupid they had been to run so fast without even checking behind the house first.

Nokulunga was trembling as it grew dark. She knew things would not be as easy as they had been the night before. She knew the family would take further steps although she did not know exactly what would happen.

She was in her husband's room waiting for him to come in. The hut suddenly looked so small she felt it move to enclose her in a painful death. She held her arms across her chest, gripping her shoulders so tight they ached.

The door opened and a number of men about her husband's age came in quietly. They closed the door behind them. She watched Xolani undress as if he did not want to. His arm did not look better as he stood there in the light of the low-burning paraffin lamp. She started to cry.

She was held and undressed. Her face was wet with sweat and tears and she wanted to go and pee. The men laughed a little.

One of them smiled teasingly at her and ordered her to lie down on the bed. She cried uncontrollably when she saw the look on Xolani's face. He stood there with eyes wide open as if he was walking in dreamland, his face had the expression of a lost and helpless boy. Was that the man she was supposed to look upon as a husband? How was he ever to defend her against anything or anyone?

Hands pulled her up and her streaming eyes did not see the man who shouted to her that she should lie like a woman. She wiped her eyes and saw Xolani approaching her.

She jumped and pushed him away, grabbed at her clothes. The group of men was on her like a mob. They roughly pulled her back on to the bed and Xolani was placed on top of her. Her legs were each pulled by a man. Others held her arms.

Men were cheering and clapping hands while Xolani jumped high, now enjoying the rape. One man was saying that he had had enough of holding the leg and wanted a share for his work. Things were said too about her bloody thighs and she heard roars of laughter before she fainted.

"The bride is ours
The bride is ours
Mother will never go to sleep
without food
without food

"The bride is ours
The bride is ours
Father will never need for beer
will never want for beer. . ."

The young men were singing near the kraal. Girls giggled as they sang and did Xhosa dances. Soon they would be expected to dance at Xolani's wedding. They were trying new hairstyles so each would look her best. The young men too were worried about how they would look. Some of them were hoping for new relationships with the girls of Gudlintaba. That place was known for the good-looking girls with their beautiful voices. Others knew too that some relationships would break as a result of that wedding. Everyone knew the day was in their hands, whether fighting or laughter ended the day.

Women prepared beer and took turns going to the river for water, happy and light-footed in the way they walked. Time and again a woman would run from hut to hut calling at the top of her voice, ululating joyfully:

"Lilililili. . .lili. . .lili. . .liiiiii!

To give birth is to stretch your bones!

What do you say, woman who never gave birth?"

Nokulunga spent most of the time inside the house with one of her friends and her mother's sister tending to her face. They had a mixture of eggs and tree barks as part of the concoction. All day long her face was crusted with thick liquids supposed to be good for her wedding complexion. Time and again her mother's sister would sit down and tell her how to behave now that she was a woman. How she hated the subject. She wished days would simply go by without her noticing them.

"*Ingwe iyawavula amathambo 'mqolo.*

The leopard opens the back bones."

She heard the girls happily singing outside. She hated the bloody song. The only thing they all seemed to care about was the food they were going to have on that day she never wanted to come. Many times she would find herself sitting there with her masked face looking out of the tiny window. She hated Xolani and his name. She felt that he was given that name because he would always do things to hurt people, then he would keep on apologizing and explaining. Xolani means "please forgive".

The day came. Nokulunga walked slowly by Xolani's side with lots of singing and laughing and ululating and clapping of hands around her. She did not smile, when she tried only tears came rolling down to make her ashamed.

It was the day of his life for Xolani, such a beautiful wife and such a big wedding. He was smiling and squeezing her hand when Nokulunga saw

Vuyo. He was looking at Xolani with loathing, his fists very tight and his lips so hard. She pulled her hand from Xolani's and took a few steps. She began to cry. Xolani went to her and tried to comfort her. A lot of people saw this, they stood watching and sympathizing and wondering. . . .

Months passed. Nokulunga was sitting by the fire, in her arms a five-day-old baby boy was sleeping so peacefully she smiled. Her father-in-law had named it Vuyo. How thankful she had been to hear that, she would always remember the old Vuyo she had loved.

Nokulunga now accepted that Xolani was her lifetime partner and there was nothing she could do about it. Once she saw Vuyo in town and they had kissed. It had been clear to them that since she was already pregnant, she was Xolani's wife, and Vuyo knew he would have to pay a lot of cattle if he took Nokulunga with the unborn baby. There was nothing to be done.

Maud Sulter

1960–

B orn in Glasgow to a Scots mother and a Ghanaian father, she has given seminars and readings internationally. Her poem "As a Blackwoman" won the Vera Bell Prize in the Afro-Caribbean Education Resource's 1984 Black Penmanship Awards in London, and the following year her collection of the same title was first published. Her subsequent publications include Zabat: Poetics of a Family Tree *(1990) and a novel,* Necropolis *(1991). She is also an artist and photographer whose work has appeared in exhibitions, and she was awarded the MoMart Fellowship at the Tate Gallery, Liverpool, 1990–91.*

As a Blackwoman

As a blackwoman
the bearing of my child
is a political act.

I have
been mounted in rape
   bred from like cattle
   mined for my fecundity

I have
been denied abortion
   denied contraception
   denied my freedom to choose

I have
been subjected to abortion
   injected with contraception
   sterilized without my consent

I have
borne witness to the murders
of my children
by the Klan, the Front, the State

I have
borne sons hung for rape
for looking at a white girl

I have
borne daughters shot
for being liberationists

As a blackwoman
I have taken the power to choose
to bear a black child

– a political act?

As a blackwoman
every act is a personal act
every act is a political act

As a blackwoman
the personal is political
holds no empty rhetoric

Dinah Anuli Butler

1960–

Daughter of an English mother and an absent Nigerian father, she grew up in Barking, east London, taught in Kenya for two years after leaving school, then studied anthropology at Sussex University. Her writing has appeared in journals such as Spare Rib, Women's Review, West Africa and in several anthologies, including Black Women Talk Poetry (ed. Da Choong et al., 1987).

To My Father

you
black man
made me raw umber
abandoned my mother
dead you claim me
for your lineage and I
rage a friction
to stay warm in my mother's
cool cramped land where
care bent gentle toward me
and flesh was split
I owe you less than minus
stand fire eyed and innocent
no stepping slow reverent
around the stone thrones of
peerless ancestors
till my curiosity
trails your blackness
you head the column
my life
I hover a question
should I bring you fine children
and tears crusting salt tracks
or the anger of a stale betrayal to

keep you on the cold side of a shuttered moment
for I cannot hide
in luscious Nigeria imagined
tied to a wishworld by your bequest of confusion

Tsitsi Dangarembga
?1960–

F rom Harare, Zimbabwe, she began medical studies at university in
Cambridge then read psychology at university in Zimbabwe before
turning to writing, drama and film. Her novel, Nervous Conditions
(1988, winner of a Commonwealth Writers' Prize), is about growing up in
pre-independence Rhodesia, evoking the loss involved in the colonization
of one culture by another. In this extract, Tambu, a young girl from a poor
rural community, has gone to stay with her aunt, Maiguri, and wealthy
uncle, Babamukuru, who has agreed to sponsor her education. Tambu
begins to feel misgivings about the worldly ways of her cousin Nyasha, who
has been brought up in England.

From

Nervous Conditions

I WAS not half-way through the door before Nyasha was on me with a big
hug, which I understood, and a kiss on both cheeks, which I did not. She
was excited to see me, she was pleased she said. I was surprised to see her in
such high spirits, pleasantly surprised, since this was not the cousin I had been
steeling myself to meet. . . .

Nyasha was baking a cake, she said, for her brother. . . . Not wanting to impose
I busied myself with inspecting the kitchen. It looked very sophisticated to me at
the time. But looking back, I remember that the cooker had only three plates,
none of which was a ring; that the kettle was not electric; that the refrigerator
was a bulky paraffin-powered affair. . . .

Later, as experience sharpened my perception of such things, I saw too that the colours were not co-ordinated. The green and pink walls – it was the fashion to have one wall a different colour from the others – contrasted harshly with each other and with the lino. It pleased me, though, to see that the kitchen was clean. What dirt that could be removed from the lino was removed regularly by thorough scrubbing with a strong ammonia cleaner, which was efficient but chapped your hands much more roughly than ash dissolved in water from Nyamarira ever did. The enamel of the cooker and the plastic of the fridge, although not shining, were white, and the kitchen sink gleamed greyly. This lack of brilliance was due, I discovered years later when television came to the mission, to the use of scouring powders which, though they sterilized 99 per cent of a household, were harsh and scratched fine surfaces. When I found this out, I realized that Maiguru, who had watched television in England, must have known about the dulling effects of these scourers and about the brilliance that could be achieved by using the more gentle alternatives. By that time I knew something about budgets as well, notably their inelasticity. It dawned on me then that Maiguru's dull sink was not a consequence of slovenliness, as the advertisers would have had us believe, but a necessity.

Anna came back with the news that Maiguru was resting. She would be with me in the time that it took to get out of bed and dressed. She would show me to the living-room, where I was to wait for my aunt.

Hoping that it was not illness that had put my aunt in bed at that time of the day, I followed Anna to the living-room, where I made myself comfortable on a sofa. It was impossible not to notice that this sofa was twice as long and deep and soft as the one in the house at home. I took stock of my surroundings, noting the type, texture and shape of the furniture, its colours and its arrangement. My education had already begun, and it was with a pragmatic eye that I surveyed Maiguru's sitting-room: I would own a home like this one day; I would need to know how to furnish it.

Since I had entered my uncle's house through the back door, and so had moved up a gradient of glamour from the kitchen, through the dining-room to the living-room, I did not benefit from the full impact of the elegance of that living-room, with its fitted carpet of deep, green pile, tastefully mottled with brown and gold, and chosen to match the pale green walls (one slightly lighter than the other three according to the fashion). The heavy gold curtains flowing voluptuously to the floor, the four-piece lounge suite upholstered in glowing brown velvet, the lamps with their tasselled shades, the sleek bookcases full of leather-bound and hard-covered volumes of erudition, lost a little, but only a very little, of their effect.

Had I entered from the driveway, through the veranda and the front door, as visitors whom it was necessary to impress would enter, the taste and muted elegance of that room would have taken my breath away. As it was, having seen the kitchen, and the dining-room, which was much smarter than the kitchen, with shiny new linoleum covering every square inch of floor and so expertly laid that the seams between the strips were practically invisible, I was a little better prepared for what came next. This was not altogether a bad thing, because the full force of that opulent living-room would have been too much for me. I remember feeling slightly intimidated by the dining-room, with its large, oval table spacious enough to seat eight people taking up the centre of the room. That table, its shape and size, had a lot of say about the amount, the calorie content, the complement of vitamins and minerals, the relative proportions of fat, carbohydrate and protein of the food that would be consumed at it. No one who ate from such a table could fail to grow fat and healthy. Pushed up against a window, and there were several windows flanked by plain, sensible sun-filters and sombre, blue cotton curtains, was a display cabinet. Glossy and dark as the table, it displayed on greenish glass shelves the daintiest, most delicate china I had ever seen – fine, translucent cups and saucers, teapots and jugs and bowls, all covered in roses. Pink on white, gold on white, red on white. Roses. Old English, Tea, Old Country. Roses. These tea-sets looked so delicate it was obvious they would disintegrate the minute you so much as poured the tea into a cup or weighted a plate down with a bun. No wonder they had been shut away. I fervently hoped I would not be expected to eat or drink from them. I was relieved to find out in due course that everyone was a bit afraid of those charmingly expensive and fragile tea-sets, so they were only ever admired and shown off to guests.

If I was daunted by Maiguru's dainty porcelain cups, the living-room, as I have said, would have finished me off had I not been inoculated by the gradient I have talked of, although calling it a glamour gradient is not really the right way to describe it. This increase in comfort from kitchen to living-room was a common feature of all the teachers' houses at the mission. It had more to do with means and priorities than taste. Babamukuru's taste was excellent, so that where he could afford to indulge it, the results were striking. The opulence of his living-room was very strong stuff, overwhelming to someone who had first crawled and then toddled and finally walked over dung floors. Comfortable it was, but overwhelming nevertheless. Some strategy had to be devised to prevent all this splendour from distracting me in the way that my brother had been distracted. Usually in such dire straits I used my thinking strategy. I was very proud of my thinking strategy. It was meant to put me above the irrational levels of my character and enable me to proceed from pure, rational premises. Today, though, it did not work.

Every corner of Babamukuru's house – every shiny surface, every soft contour and fold – whispered its own insistent message of comfort and ease and rest so tantalizingly, so seductively, that to pay any attention to it, to think about it at all, would have been my downfall. The only alternative was to ignore it. I remained as aloof and unimpressed as possible.

This was not easy, because my aunt took a long time to come from her bedroom. I put this interval to good use in building up my defences. I had only to think of my mother, with Netsai and Rambanai superimposed in the background, to remember why and how I had come to be at the mission. And having seen how easily it could happen, I judged my brother less harshly. Instead, I became more aware of how necessary it was to remain steadfast. Then, to make sure that I was not being soft and sentimental in revising my opinion of Nhamo, I had to survey my surroundings again to see whether they really were potent enough to have had such a devastating effect on him, thus exposing myself again to all the possible consequences. I triumphed. I was not seduced.

You might think that there was no real danger. You might think that, after all, these were only rooms decorated with the sort of accessories that the local interpretations of British interior-decor magazines were describing as standard, and nothing threatening in that. But really the situation was not so simple. Although I was vague at the time and could not have described my circumstances so aptly, the real situation was this: Babamukuru was God, therefore I had arrived in Heaven. I was in danger of becoming an angel, or at the very least a saint, and forgetting how ordinary humans existed – from minute to minute and from hand to mouth. The absence of dirt was proof of the other-worldly nature of my new home. I knew, had known all my life, that living was dirty and I had been disappointed by the fact. I had often helped my mother to resurface the kitchen floor with dung. I knew, for instance, that rooms where people slept exuded peculiarly human smells just as the goat pen smelt goaty and the cattle kraal bovine. It was common knowledge among the younger girls at school that the older girls menstruated into sundry old rags which they washed and reused and washed again. I knew, too, that the fact of menstruation was a shamefully unclean secret that should not be allowed to contaminate immaculate male ears by indiscreet reference to this type of dirt in their presence. Yet at a glance it was difficult to perceive dirt in Maiguru's house. After a while, as the novelty wore off, you began to see that the antiseptic sterility that my aunt and uncle strove for could not be attained beyond an illusory level because the buses that passed through the mission, according to an almost regular schedule, rolled up a storm of fine red dust which perversely settled in corners and on surfaces of rooms and armchairs and bookshelves. When the dust was obvious it was removed, but enough of it always remained invisibly to creep up your nose and give you hay fever, thus restoring your sense of proportion by reminding you that this was not heaven. Sneezing and wiping my nose on the back of my hand, I became confident that I would not go the same way as my brother.

A shrill, shuddering wail pulled me abruptly out of my thoughts, made my armpits prickle and my mouth turn bitter. It wailed and trembled for ten long seconds, during which images of witches on hyenas' backs, both laughing hellishly, flitted through my mind. This was no time to be frightened, when I needed all my wits about me to take advantage of all the opportunities the mission could offer. So I became annoyed instead, with myself for being caught unaware by everyday mission sounds and with the mission for having such sounds. Deliberately, nonchalantly, clenching my moist palms and in spite of the fact that there was no one but myself to be impressed by this intrepid display of courage, I stood up to see through the window the results of that shuddering wail. Through the jacarandas in my uncle's yard and the blue gums at a distance, the pale-green school buildings flittered in the evening sun and boarding pupils strolled or walked or ran to the largest of these buildings, which I learnt later was the Beit Hall. The boys wore khaki shirts and shorts as usual, the girls were in dark-blue, belted gym-slips over pale-blue blouses.

"It's for them to go to assembly," chuckled Anna from the dining-room. "We'd had a rest from it during the holiday, but now it's begun again. It's frightening, isn't it? The day I first heard it, my whole body dried up. Dry and stiff. Like bark. That sireen! But you get used to it."

"You really are dying to get to school, aren't you?" joked Maiguru from the door opposite the window. "E-e-h! Sisi Tambu," she smiled, advancing to greet me with her right arm bent upwards from the elbow, with her palm facing me and swinging her hand down so that I was forced to slap palms with her by way of greeting, in the way that you do when you greet your age mates or friends. "So you have arrived, Sisi Tambu. That is good. I always think there is something wrong with my house when BabawaChido's relatives do not want to visit."

Maiguru was too modest. I did my best to reassure her. "Don't even think such things, Maiguru. Everybody loves to come here. They all say you treat them so kindly. If they could, they'd be here every day."

Maiguru smiled ruefully and then recovered her good spirits. "Then it is all right," she said. "But you never know with some people. You see them leave quietly and you think they are satisfied, but what they say afterwards, that is another story."

"Oh, no, Maiguru," I hastened, "I've not heard anyone say anything bad. They are proud of you. They say you work so hard for them." Then I greeted her. It was necessary to sit on the floor to do this. I sat, folding my legs up under my bottom. I clapped my hands. "*Nyamashewe*, Maiguru. How are you?"

"We are all fit and jolly," Maiguru answered. "But get up, child, and sit comfortably in the seat." Maiguru called Anna to ask her to prepare tea. While we waited she asked me about my mother, the tone of her voice saying much more about the concern she was feeling than her words. I answered as briefly as was polite, because it was not something I liked to talk about. I preferred to keep thoughts of my mother's condition to myself.

Anna returned carrying a tray with the tea things on it. There were pots and jugs and cups and saucers, all flowery and matching, with a teaspoon for the sugar and two more for Maiguru and me to stir our tea with. It was all very novel and refined. At home we boiled the milk up with the water, when we had milk, and then added the tea leaves. Lifting a round spoon-shaped object from the tray, Maiguru poured my tea.

"What has amused you, Sisi Tambu?" she asked, seeing a smile hover over my mouth.

"That little sieve, Maiguru. Is it really just for sifting tea?"

"The tea-strainer?" my aunt replied. "Haven't you seen one before? The tea wouldn't be drinkable without it. It would be all tea-leaves."

So this tea-strainer was another necessity I had managed without up until now. Maiguru seemed to think it was absolutely vital to have one. I would hardly have described it like that. Interesting, yes, but vital? And imagine spending money on a sieve so small it could only be used for sifting tea! When I went home I would see whether tea really was less pleasant to drink without the strainer.

There was food too, lots of it. Lots of biscuits and cakes and jam sandwiches. Maiguru was offering me the food, but it was difficult to decide what to take because everything looked so appetizing. We did not often have cake at home. In fact, I remembered having cake only at Christmas time or at Easter. At those times Babamukuru brought a great Zambezi slab home with him and cut it up in front of our eager eyes, all the children waiting for him to distribute it. This he did one piece each at a time so that for days on end, long after the confectionery had lost its freshness, we would be enraptured. We would spend many blissful moments picking off and nibbling, first the white coconut and then the pink icing and last the delicious golden cake itself, nibbling so slowly such little pieces at a time that we could hardly taste them, but could gloat when everyone else had finished that we still had some left. Biscuits were as much of a treat as cake, especially when they were dainty, dessert biscuits with cream in the middle or chocolate on top. Jam was another delicacy that appeared only on festive occasions.

Maiguru must have guessed my thoughts from the expression on my face and the way I hesitated to help myself. Cordially she invited me to eat as much as I liked of anything I liked, even if that meant everything. Not wanting my aunt to think me greedy, I had to be more restrained than usual after that, so I chose one small biscuit that did not even have cream in the middle and bit into it slowly so that I would not be obliged to take anything else. This made Maiguru anxious. My sweet little aunt, who liked to please, interpreted my diffidence as her own shortcoming.

"Did you want Mazoe, Sisi Tambu? Or Fanta? Ginger Ale maybe? It is all there. Just say what you want."

I hastened to reassure her by taking a great gulp of tea. Being used to enamel mugs which warned you when the tea was too hot by burning your lips before you let the liquid reach your mouth, the boiling tea scalded my tongue. I was in agony. My eyes watered and my nose too. Choking and spluttering, I deposited my cup shakily back in its saucer.

"What are you doing to her, Mum? She looks about to burst into tears," asked Nyasha, bouncing into the living-room, all flour and rich baking smells.

"Go and clean yourself up, Nyasha. Say hello to your cousin," instructed Maiguru.

"Hello," my cousin said cheerfully, half-way across the room.

"Nyasha!" Maiguru insisted.

"I have said hello, before you came out," Nyasha called, passing out of the living-room into the depths of the house. "Anyway," she added pointedly, "I'm going to clean myself up."

It really was very sad that Maiguru, who was the embodiment of courtesy and good breeding, should have such a rumbustious daughter. It was so embarrassing, the way Nyasha thought she could say anything to her mother. I did not know where to look.

"They are too Anglicized," explained Maiguru, with a little laugh so that it was difficult to tell whether she was censoring Nyasha for her Anglicized habits or me for my lack of them. "They picked up all these disrespectful ways in England," she continued conversationally, "and it's taking them time to learn how to behave at home again. It's difficult for them because things are so different. Especially this business of relatives. Take you, for example, Sisi Tambu, the way your brother was here and the way you have come yourself. They didn't see these things while they were growing up in England so now they are a bit confused. But it doesn't matter. You mustn't worry about Nyasha's little ways. We keep trying to teach her the right manners, always telling her: Nyasha, do this; Nyasha, why didn't you do that. But it's taking time. Her head is full of loose connections that are always sparking. Nyasha! Ha, Nyasha! That child of mine has her own thoughts about everything! Have you finished your tea, Sisi Tambu?" she asked, glancing into my empty cup. "Then come, I will show you where you will sleep."

I followed Maiguru into the hall, which was dark, there being no windows, but not too dark to hide a long row of pegs in the wall from which hung heavy overcoats and lightweight raincoats. These people, I saw, never got wet or cold.

Maiguru stopped in front of a closed door, knocked and entered. I followed into a room that comfortably contained two three-quarter beds, a wardrobe that must have been too big for one person's clothes and a dresser with a full-length mirror so bright and new that it reflected only the present. Nyasha lounged, propped up against the headboard of her bed, which was the one against the wall, her legs raised and crossed at the knee, apparently deeply engrossed in a novel, although her eyes strayed from time to time to observe herself in the mirror. Maiguru and I stood in the doorway for a long time. I think we were both wondering what was going to happen next.

"What are you reading, Nyasha-washa, my lovey-dove?" Maiguru eventually asked, advancing into the room. Nyasha raised her book so that her mother could see for herself.

Maiguru's lips pursed into a tight, disapproving knot. "Oh, dear," she breathed, "that's not very good. Nyasha, I don't want you to read books like that."

"There's nothing wrong with it, Mum," Nyasha reassured her.

"Don't tell me that, Nyasha," Maiguru warned in a tone that I approved of although I could not follow the language very well. I thought Nyasha ought to be more respectful. "I read those books at postgraduate level," Maiguru continued. "I know they are not suitable books for you to read."

"But it's meant to be good, Mum. You know D. H. Lawrence is meant to be good," objected Nyasha.

"You mustn't read books like that. They are no good for you," Maiguru insisted.

"But, Mum, I get so bored. I've read everything in the house that you say I can and there's not much of a library at school. What's all the fuss about anyway? It's only a *book* and I'm only *reading* it."

Maiguru's face tightened, I thought in annoyance, but she may have been wincing. Ignoring Nyasha (who also began to ignore her mother, diverting her attention sternly to her book so that the concentration furrowed her brow with delicate lines of mental activity) Maiguru turned to me. "Well, Sisi Tambu, this is where you will sleep," she smiled vivaciously, adding unnecessarily, "with Nyasha." She indicated the unoccupied bed.

If I had been apprehensive from the minute we entered my cousin's bedroom, I was thoroughly distressed now that my fate had been made clear. From what I had seen of my cousin, I was intrigued and fascinated with one part of my mind, the adventurous, explorative part. But this was a very small part. Most of me sought order. Most of me was concrete and categorical. These parts disapproved of Nyasha very strongly and were wary of her. Nyasha, I thought, would have too many surprises; she would distract me when all I wanted was to settle down to my studies. There was something about her that was too intangible for me to be comfortable with, so intangible that I could not decide whether it was intangibly good or intangibly bad. There was a certain glamour to the idea of sharing a room with my Anglicized cousin. Nyasha herself was glamorous in an irreverent way that made me feel, if not exactly inadequate, at least uneducated in some vital aspect of teenage womanliness. But for all the glamour, the thought persisted that Nyasha would not be good for me. Everything about her spoke of alternatives and possibilities that if considered too deeply would wreak havoc with the neat plan I had laid out for my life. The sense of being alien and inadequate that had departed while I drank tea under Maiguru's maternal surveillance reasserted itself. Needing a scapegoat I blamed Nyasha, who had not been cordial enough to say a single word to me in all the time that I had been standing in her room.

Maiguru was fussing, cooing and clucking and shaking her feathers. "These are your things, Sisi Tambu, your clothes and your washing things," she chirped brightly, pulling a suitcase from beneath the bed that was to be mine, and opening the suitcase to display my new wardrobe. There was the uniform, two dark-blue gym-slips with wide box pleats and four light-blue short-sleeved shirts to wear underneath the gym-slips. There were half a dozen pairs of white ankle-socks and a pair of black side-buckled shoes that turned out to be half a size too small, which was not too small to wear. My aunt showed me too the underwear, the smooth nylon slips and sensible panties. To my great joy there were two smart casual dresses in pastels – pale pink and pale yellow – both brand new with little puffed sleeves and full, gathered skirts set into chicly dropped waists. My heart brimmed over with gratitude and love for my aunt and uncle. All the excitement, uncertainty, anxiety and happiness mixed into such a steamy emotion that I was almost reduced to tears. I tried to say something to my aunt, some appropriate words of thanks, but Miguru was still chirruping away. "You see, Sisi Tambu, you see, don't you, what good care your uncle is taking of you? He has fixed everything. Here the toothbrush, here the Vaseline and the flannel and a comb. You see, everything! But if something has been forgotten, don't be shy. Tell us at once. Or tell Nyasha. She'll help you get settled. Nyasha, sugar pie!" I held my breath.

"Yes, Mum?" answered the daughter decorously. I breathed again.

"Help Tambudzai get settled, lovey."

"Yes, Mum," Nyasha murmured.

May Opitz
?1961–

S he co-edited, with Katharina Oguntoye and Dagmar Schulz, Farbe
*Bekennen (1986), an anthology of Afro-German women – trans-
lated into English by Anne V. Adams as* Showing Our True Colour:
Afro-German Women on the Traces of Their History *– and Afro-Germans
and their history was the topic of her Master's thesis. Both in her poems
and her prose she writes with remarkable candour about the potential
external and internal conflicts attendant on being a Black German
woman.*

Departure

O N the day I was born, stories about my life were born too. Each one
contains its own truth and wisdom. Those who experienced my childhood
may tell a different story of it than I would. I can only tell the story in the way
that it left impressions on me. I don't need to apologize if negative occurrences
are clearer in my memory than positive ones. That's the way it is. Here I shall
surrender some of myself, without accusing or forgiving, without any claim to
reality and in the experience of truth, and in the certainty that whoever reads
my story will understand it differently.

When I was born I was neither black nor white. The name I was called
most of all was "half-caste". It is hard to surround a child with love when the
grandparents say that the child does not fit in. It is hard when the child doesn't
fit in with the mother's plans and when money is short. It becomes even harder
when a white mother doesn't want her child kidnapped to a black world. And
German laws don't allow African fathers to take their German daughters to an
African mother.

It's not easy to put a child into an orphanage. The child stays there for
eighteen months.

I hear on the radio about couples with children like me: about children
who don't find parents because there are "GI children", because they are
handicapped or not blond enough or because they were born in prison. I
became the planned child of a white German family and forgot the months
in the orphanage. My foster parents' stories are all that remain from that time:
"You couldn't even stand. You had rickets as a result of the unbalanced diet.
Your body was fat and overfed and your little legs so crooked that the doctor
thought they'd never straighten out."

There are no "cute" baby photos from that period. I remember my foster parents' repeated warnings: "Be careful. A fat baby will be fat later on. Take care what and how much you eat." My fear of getting fat and old has stayed with me ever since, reinforced by the stereotype of the "black mamma" that was pointed out to me in the movies.

Childhood is a time when a child thinks about many things but the words a child uses are not understood. Childhood is when a child wets its bed and so gets a spanking. Childishness is when the child does everything wrong, is naughty, doesn't understand, is dull and makes the same mistakes again and again. Childhood is when a child repeatedly wets the bed and no one understands that the child isn't doing it to punish the parents. Childhood is living in fear of being beaten and not being able to come to terms with it. Childhood is getting bronchitis every year and being sent away to convalesce. Years later I was astonished that my chronic bronchitis disappeared when I was 15. A doctor told me, "Didn't you know that bedwetting is a psychosomatic problem?"

Fear blocking the respiratory tract? There was enough fear. Probably claustrophobia. Or fear of exploding. Fear of dissolving as a result of scoldings and beatings, and being unable to find my way back again. Don't protest – swallow it all – until it isn't possible any more and it escapes into the bed or as vicious coughing spasms. Spasms that would drive any normal person who heard it to insomnia and rage. That's the way it is with suppression. As soon as you begin to bottle it up you can be sure that a limit will be reached sometime. The bottom falls out or else it overflows. Then it's a self-protective mechanism that is either not understood at all or totally misunderstood. I can still hear my mother moan: "This permanent cough is enough to drive one mad!"

Childhood is laughter too. Playing in the sand or going rollerskating, playing on a scooter or learning to ride a bicycle. Laddering a thousand pairs of tights and accepting Mother's anger as the price of a wonderful day. And love.

Love is when Mother cooks something delicious or takes the child to town with her. When the kid gets a stick of rock at the funfair, when Christmas casts a spell over everything and the child can go to the pictures. Love is to get up early in the morning and set the breakfast table for Mum and Dad and think up pretty little presents. Love is when we all set off on holiday in good spirits.

Longing is the need to hear someone say, "Well, kid, are you OK? We love you. No matter if you're black or white, fat or thin, clever or stupid, I love you. Come to me!" Longing is to know what you want to hear yet to wait in vain for it to be said. Sadness is when a child finds out she is too black and ugly. Horror is when Mummy won't wash the child white. Why not? Everything would be much easier. The other children wouldn't shout "Nigger". The child wouldn't need to be ashamed any longer and wouldn't have to be extra well behaved. "Always behave decently. Whatever people think of you they'll think of all others with your colour."

Life is too hard for me.

1.   This damned fear of doing everything wrong. The nights spent crying whenever I lost something at school. "Please, God, don't let Mum and Dad

beat me when I tell them." Constant trembling from fear of doing something wrong, then dropping twice as much because of the tremble. "No wonder no one likes me."

2.   The damned primary school with the damned homework. Mum supervises everything, especially maths, with a wooden spoon. If the child doesn't do her sums fast enough she gets rapped on the head, and if homework isn't written neatly enough the page gets torn out. Apart from the breaks and sports, I don't really like school. Why can't I invite anyone round or visit anyone? "Dear God, let Mum and Dad die and let us have other parents who are nice all the time."

3.   My parents often said that I can't do anything, am nothing and do everything too slowly. I secretly take one of my father's razor blades and hide it under my pillow. The fear and the longing for suicide. "The child is playing with razor blades in bed! You must be abnormal. Don't you know how dangerous that is? This child will drive me crazy!" Once I decided to run away. I tell my baby brother and say goodbye to him. I was about nine and he was five years old. He recognized how serious things were and began to scream and he squealed to my parents. Everyone is a bit nicer to me. "Dear God, let me go to sleep and never wake up."

4.   Who destroyed my dream? My dream of "being white" is shattered on my parents' lack of will, the lack of charming power in the soap. My dream of "being black" is shattered by my father's physical appearance. But first, my secret. When I grow up I shall go to Africa. Everyone there looks like me. When Mum and Dad and my brothers and sisters come to visit me, people will point at them. I would comfort them and say, "Don't do that!" And my parents would understand how I felt in Germany.

Look! That's my Father! Completely black. "You are white by comparison" – "Are all people in Africa black?" – "Of course." You have destroyed my dream!

Once when my father came to visit, all the children run away – he had brought sweets for us all. Maybe we had played "Who's afraid of the Black man?" too often. "What happens if he comes?" "We'll run away." Perhaps the inoculation of fear, of the black lies, black sins and black bogeymen sat too deep. My brother and I would have liked to run away too but we knew we couldn't. Besides which he brought nice gifts.

My father was Uncle E. He was Uncle E because he was Uncle E for my white brother, and he was Uncle E for me even when I began to write to him using "Dear Father". My foster father wanted me to do it. He thought that Uncle E would be happy about this. As I knew that he was far away and that bar a visit every two or three years he would stay, I humoured him and wrote "Dear Father". I wrote about my last holiday, about my next holiday, about school results and endlessly about the weather. My foster father made sure that I did so for years.

I never asked myself if I should be proud of my father or if I should despise him. As far as I could gather from all reports, he seemed to be a positive, intellectual man who happened to have a child whom he could not raise. I once asked for a story about the woman who gave birth to me. "What woman? She was a slut!" I never asked again.

The feeling of being excluded caused my head to spin. Especially my foster parents' fear that I could drift from the straight and narrow held me in its clutches. The fear that I would come home pregnant was the reason for forbidding me to go out. Their worries and fears strangled me. Before I left home I spent a year of silence and this finalized the split that then came.

On reflection I know that my parents loved me. They took me in and cared for me in order to counteract the prejudice in society. To give me a chance in life that I would not have had in an orphanage. My strict upbringing, the beatings, and being imprisoned by my foster parents was done out of love, responsibility and ignorance. Knowing the prejudices that existed in German society, they unwittingly adapted my upbringing to these prejudices. I grew up with the same feelings that they had – the need to prove that a "half-caste", a "nigger", an "orphan child" could be a whole person. Alongside all that there was hardly time for me to discover my "me".

It took a long time for me to become aware that I had a value. As soon as I was able to say "Yes" to myself without secretly wanting to transform myself, it was possible for me to see the cracks in myself and my surroundings, to come to terms with them and learn from them. The fact that I couldn't duck away from things forced me actively to tackle them and I found that it was no longer a burden but rather a challenge to be honest.

The fact that I always had to explain my situation and words helped me towards the recognition that I owed no one an explanation. I hold no grudge against those to whose power and helplessness I was exposed, to whom I subjugated myself or by whom I was subjugated. I have often allowed myself to be made into something; and it's up to me to make something out of what they made out of me.

I'm on my way.

Afro-German

You're Afro-German?
...oh, *I* see: African *and* German.
An interesting mixture!
You know, there are people who still think
    mulattos won't get
    as far in life
    as whites

I don't believe that
I mean: given the same type of education....
    You're pretty lucky to have grown up *here*.
    With German parents, even. Think of that!

Do you want to go back some day?
What, you've never been to your Dad's country?
   That's so sad.... Listen, if you ask me:
A person's origin, see, leaves quite a mark.
Take me, I'm from Westfalia,
and I feel
that's where I belong....

Oh, boy! All the misery there is in the world!
  Be glad
    you don't still live in the bush.
    You wouldn't be where you are today!
I mean, you're really quite an intelligent girl, you know.
   If you work hard at your studies,
   you can help your people in Africa: That's
   what you're predestined to do;
     I'm sure they'd listen to you,
whereas people like us –
  there's such a difference in cultural levels...

What do you mean, do something here? What would you want to do here?
OK, OK, so it's not all sunshine. But I think
  everyone should put their own house in order first!

Afro-German II

...hm, I understand.
You can thank your lucky stars you're not Turkish, right?
I mean: it's awful the way they pick on foreigners,
  do you ever come up against that at all?

"..."

Well, sure but I have *those* problems, too.
I think a person can't blame everything on the colour of their skin,
and things are never easy for a woman.
Take this friend of mine:
  she's pretty heavy,
  and what problems she has!
Compared to her, now, you seem quite relaxed.
Anyway, I think
  that Blacks have kept a sort of natural
  outlook on life

While here: everything's pretty screwed up.
I think I'd be glad if I were you.
   German history isn't something one
   can really be proud of, is it?
And you're not that black anyway, you know.

[Translated by George Busby]

Jackie Kay
1961–

S*he was born in Edinburgh, Scotland, and brought up by white adoptive parents in Glasgow. She earned a BA Honours in Literature from Stirling University and now lives in London, with her young son, and works for the Arts Council of Great Britain. Since she was very young she has written poetry and short stories and has also written plays. She reads her work widely and her sequence of poems,* The Adoption Papers *(1991), was dramatized on BBC Radio 3 in 1990 and published in 1991. Her writing has appeared in collections including* A Dangerous Knowing: Four Black Women Poets *(1984),* Beautiful Barbarians *(ed. Mohin, 1986),* Black Women Talk Poetry *(eds Choong et al., 1987),* Dancing the Tightrope *(eds Burford et al., 1987) and she co-edited* Charting the Journey: Writings by Black and Third World Women *(1988).*

Diary of Days for Adjoa

I am carrying your grin
with me and all your many faces:
imagined face of your teens
loss across your cheek
bones after your abortion
hurt hanging from different angles
over the years I haven't known you;
and your face this morning

You make me travel
past my past
hands raking earth
trusting you enough to
dig for worms or treasures
old dry roots coming unstuck

this land I've found in you
is frightening too
how far might we go
how far could we go

longing does not listen to reason
but trust – need meeting past
and making friends – carries
me buoyant to our next time

I could write you a diary
of days since I last saw you:
how I sang to Ella Fitzgerald
in the car going north east from Brixton
how although love is old
Ella doesn't sing of two black women
watching *Falling in Love* eating
nan and mutter paneer drinking
gin and talk talk talking
till our eyes held onto our fire
till our bodies took over the telling of stories

I listened to all Ella's devils
watching for signs and glancing at the map
I never knew I had and
I'd left something behind in Brixton
I carried your grin and your smell
that whole journey wearing your soft yellow
these past days I've caught that smile
at odd hours – you surprising me
you around me, me sometimes wishing
I could let go for a while
stop your dancing in my head

And   I know no definites except
how much I love the caring you bring
the way your eyes travel places and
then suddenly stop and stare
amazed – a comment on our happening
I am missing you it seems so long since

your arms held my need
And still, I don't know
what it is you want
or what it is I want
but I know we will give
each other something
something
like a raging wind
a scorching sun
an echo from the wilderness.

Jacqueline Rudet
1962–

B orn in the East End of London, where her parents were trying
to make a new life in Britain, she went to Dominica at the age
of two to live for some years with her grandparents. Returning
to Britain for her secondary education, she took a drama course and
began her career in theatre as an actress (with Cast Theatre Company
and Belt and Braces), before forming the group Imani-Faith in 1983
to present theatre for and by Black women, in 1983. Her plays which
have been performed at London's Royal Court Theatre Upstairs include
Money to Live (1984) and God's Second in Command (1986; broadcast
on BBC Radio 4, 1990, directed by Frances Solomon). Basin (directed
at the Royal Court Theatre Upstairs by Paulette Randall, 1985), which
is extracted here, was her first attempt at writing and was previously
called With Friends Like You. After a visit to Dominica reminded her of
the local word "zammie", meaning a close female friend (though not
necessarily a lesbian), she reworked the play with the aim of showing
that Black women have much in common, and used for its new title a
symbol of cleanliness and wifely service that all women possess. Also a
director, she is based in London.

From

Basin

ACT ONE

SCENE ONE

MONA's *flat. She is clearing up after the previous night's party. She sings to herself.*

MONA: Honey, pepper, leaf green limes,
    Pagan fruit whose names are rhymes,
    Mangoes, breadfruit, ginger root,
    Grandilliars, bamboo shoots,
    Sugar cane, kola nuts,
    Citrons, hairy coconuts,
    Fish, tobacco, native hats,
    Gold bananas, woven mats,
    Plantains, wild thyme, pallid leaks,
    Pigeons with their scarlet beaks,
    Saffron, yams,
    Baskets, ruby guava jams,
    Frustles, goat skins, cinnamon, allspice,
    Oh, island in the sun
    Gave to me by my father's hand,
    La, la, la, la. . .

MONA *hears a knock at the door.*

MONA: Coming!

MONA *goes to open the door.* SUSAN *kisses her and comes in.*

SUSAN: Mona, I've been knocking and knocking. Were you asleep?

MONA: Sorry, I was miles away. Back home, in fact. Thinking about all the good times.
    So, you decided to come? Don't you think you're a little late?

SUSAN: Looks like you had a good time here!

MONA: Well, if you'd come, you'd've enjoyed yourself too.

SUSAN: What happened?

MONA: It was great! I mean! Pat and her new man business! The boy is so dry! He spent the whole night in that corner giving everybody cut eye! He's a joke. I don't know what she sees in him. I said, "Pat, what do you see in this boy? He must have one big wood!" You could see Pat was shame. First, she kept making excuses that he wasn't feeling well, then, she couldn't take it any more, just walked out and left him! It was really funny.

Everybody enjoyed themselves. And listen to this, nah! Herbert brought this box full of whisky. I don't know where he got it from because every minute him just a peep through the window to see if bull a come. So Michael plays this trick on him. He rushes in and says, "Bull outside! Someone thief a box of whisky from the off licence!" Girl, I never see Herbert move so fast! When Herbert found out, him so vexed him fit to burst!

SUSAN: I would've liked to see that. Good! I can't stand him. And how was your Michael?

MONA: The boy makes me sick. The guy love woman! I'm serving drinks and the guy's got some piss an' tail gal in the corner a wind-up in front of me in my own fucking house! I'm fed-up with the guy. All he wants me for is jook, jook, jook.

SUSAN: I thought all you wanted was jook, jook, jook!

MONA: Michael's just taking the piss.

SUSAN: I've told you that too many times.

MONA: Never mind about me. Look at you! You look well miserable!

SUSAN *tries to speak, but can't.*

MONA: Come on, start at the beginning. I'll listen, no matter how boring.

SUSAN: Thank you!

MONA: Only joking! (*Pause.*) Come on!

SUSAN: Well. . .you remember when I was at drama school?

MONA: Back that far!

SUSAN: Are you interested?

MONA: All ears! Come on!

SUSAN (*pause*): I was the only black student. I felt really proud of myself. I was the only one of my friends to get somewhere and achieve something. I was being kept back and not being given the chance to prove myself but, I knew I had the talent, so I just kept on going.

MONA: This isn't what's on your mind!

SUSAN: I'm getting to it. (*Pause.*) One month, I missed my period. . .

MONA: What's this got to do with drama school?

SUSAN: I'm jumping. Sorry. While I was at drama school, one month, I missed my period, took a test, found it was positive but, I felt so stupid, I couldn't bring myself to tell you. Anyway, I had an abortion, of course.

Pause.

MONA: Are we getting to it?

SUSAN: We're getting there.

MONA: This is all stuff to set the mood, is it?

SUSAN: I'm building up to it.

MONA: Is this why you didn't come to the party?

SUSAN: I would've liked to have come, but I had so much on my mind.
    MONA: I organized the party so everyone could cast aside the troubles in their life and have a good time. Everyone said, "Where's Susan?" I said, "She's probably down Handsworth earning some pocket money."

SUSAN: I was at home. I got to the top of your road and turned back.

MONA: There's this really cheap psychiatrist I can recommend.

SUSAN: I got to the top of your road and just turned back. I couldn't face it.

MONA: Face what?

SUSAN: Everyone.

MONA: Our friends?

SUSAN: The noise, the smoke, the chat-up lines, Michael. . .

MONA: You wouldn't have seen him anyway! He was tucked away in this corner getting all slippery with this little girl. I don't even know who invited her!

SUSAN: That's what I couldn't have stood! Michael: fucking around with another woman right under your nose!

MONA: What's new?

SUSAN: I would've said something.

MONA: We used to go out to parties. I'd go and get some drinks, or go to the toilet, and when I'd get back, where would he be? Pressing some girl up against a wall, supposedly dancing! Michael's a big slag, he always has been.

SUSAN: I've never understood this about you. You can't tell me you love him!

MONA: You've never been in love, have you? Michael was my first real man. He's been the only man in my life since I was nineteen. A man like that becomes part of your life. You don't "go out" with him, it's not a "love affair", he's just there. It's pathetic, I know, but I can't imagine life without him.

SUSAN: I can't bear the way he treats you.

MONA: And that's why you didn't come to the party?

SUSAN: You never rang me last night. You can't have been that bothered what had happened to me!

MONA: So, you need an invitation and then a call on the night to check you're coming? What's eating you, woman?

A knock on the door. MONA *opens the door.* MICHELE *walks in.*

MONA: Ah, now we come to the interesting part of the story!

MICHELE: What story? Hi, Sue, where were you?

MONA: Now we come to the *very* interesting part of the story!

MICHELE *helps* MONA *clean up.*

MICHELE: What story?

MONA: Michele finds herself in the unenviable position of being in the same room as four of her ex-boyfriends.

SUSAN: Michele, you're good!

MICHELE: Where were you?

SUSAN: I didn't feel like it.

MICHELE: You missed one party!

MONA: What does Michele do?

SUSAN: Dunno.

MONA: She ignores all her ex-boyfriends and takes up with someone man!

SUSAN: Michele, you're good!

MICHELE: They're ex-boyfriends. Ex. You know, in the past.

SUSAN: So, who's the new one?

MICHELE: A guy called Steven. I don't know where he came from. Heaven. I'm sure!

MONA: Of course, Michele's looking so good, all of her man dem a eye up her backside. So Michele's getting it on with number five while numbers one to four try their best, all night long, to get a dance.

SUSAN: Michele, you're a star!

MONA: Could it be charisma?

MICHELE: Leave it out!

MONA: Could it be the perfume she uses?

SUSAN: What perfume do you use?

MICHELE: Who'll make the tea?

MONA: She's just a regular girl really. See? She drinks tea like the rest of us.

SUSAN: Want a cup, Mona?

MONA: No thanks.

> SUSAN *goes into the kitchen.*

MICHELE: Mona?

MONA: Yes.

MICHELE: Have you still got that nice red dress?
>   MONA: You want to borrow it?

MICHELE: Could I?

MONA: Whatever you want.

MICHELE: And do you still have those nice red shoes?

MONA: Take them too.

MICHELE: Thanks, Mona. I'm going out tonight but all my stuff needs mending or dry cleaning.

MONA: Aren't you tired?

MICHELE: Yeah, but I feel like going out. (*Beat.*) Mona, you did see that Steven boy, didn't you? Don't you think he's nice?

MONA: He bores me.

MICHELE: I could really check f'him!

> SUSAN *enters and puts two cups of tea on the table.*

MONA: You're always talking about man and going out.

MICHELE: What should I talk about?

MONA: I tell you, you love man. Man fever, you have. It'll be a real problem in time to come.

MICHELE: How could it?

MONA: You rely too much on men. You think all a man thinks about is you? He's got lots of things on his mind, other women, for a start!

MICHELE: What can I do? I seem to get on better with guys. Girls really irritate me; they look at me and see where they can fault me.
    Have you ever been to a party where women are just looking you up and

down, checking you out to see which parts of them are more expensive than you. I've never been able to get into girls and what they talk about. All these girls at my school, all they ever talked about was marriage, kids and having big houses. I never wanted that. I always dreamt of having a little place of my own and doing what I wanted.

SUSAN: Your wish came true.

MICHELE: I'm working on it.

SUSAN: Sounds like you're overdoing it!

MICHELE: We all like being complimented, don't we? Where else am I going to get praise? If you stick with a guy too long, the compliments dry up, so do the presents, so does the passion. That's why I keep checking new men. When you first get a guy, he takes real good care of you; takes you out, buys you things, tells you how good you look, and the loving is sweet! I like that.

SUSAN: You can't live on that.

MICHELE: I live on it. Believe me. I live on it.

MONA: Like I said, you rely too much on men. You've never been alone for two minutes. You don't even know who you are and what you're capable of.

MICHELE: Don't give me a hard time. All I came here to do was borrow the dress and some shoes.

MONA: The way you bring my things back sometimes, I might as well throw them away!

MICHELE: That's not true. I'll have the dress back, washed and ironed, by tomorrow night.
Mona,. . .I'm going out with Marcus tonight. . .and I've got to have money. Could you lend us a fiver?

MONA: You think I print money?

MICHELE: As soon as I get my cheque. I'll pay you back.

MONA: By Friday. No later.

MICHELE: Mona. . .(*Long pause.*). . .you know that whisky?

MONA: Yes.

MICHELE: What did you do with it? Have you got any left?

MONA: Yes, lots, take a bottle.

MICHELE: You're an angel. (*To* SUSAN:) So, where were you? Having a little party of your own, were you?

SUSAN: I just didn't feel like it.

MICHELE (*to* MONA): If you can't find the red dress, I'll take the black one.

MONA (*wearily*): Take whatever you want, Michele.

MICHELE: Have you got Steve's number?

MONA (*looking in her bag for her address book*): What, are you going to go from Marcus to Steve tonight? Michele, your poom-poom must be well hot! (*She finds address book and shows* MICHELE *the number.*) You want Michael too? Michael's probably got some for you if you want it!

MICHELE (*copying the number on a piece of paper*): Thanks. No, I'm not going to Steve tonight. Tomorrow.

MONA: Go on, have another pickney! That's what you want, innit? You can't breed pickney like dog!

MICHELE: Everyone's allowed one mistake. I'm all equipped now, anyway, so it won't happen again. (*Beat.*) He's so nice though! How can I resist?

MONA: There are so many pretty boys, Michele.

MICHELE: I like pretty boys. Girl, I could eat him!

MONA (*to* MICHELE): Have you got any weed?

SUSAN (*to* MONA): You smoke too much weed.

MICHELE: No, she doesn't.

SUSAN: I wasn't talking to you!

MICHELE: There's nothing wrong with a smoke every now and then.

SUSAN: I don't like people who smoke a lot of weed. Everything's too cool with them. They haven't got a job, that's cool. They haven't paid the rent, that's cool. They just got pregnant, that's cool. Everyt'ing cool!

MONA: Have you?

MICHELE: Not with me.

MONA: I've got some, but just enough for one. I don't like not having any. Sometimes, you just fancy a spliff.

SUSAN *looks at her disapprovingly.* MONA *shrugs her shoulders.*

I don't know why you two bicker at each other.

SUSAN: We don't bicker.

MICHELE: No, you just dig at me.

SUSAN: I dig at you only when I have a reason. It just so happens that I find your manners a little lacking these days.

MICHELE: What have manners got to do with it?

MONA: Are you sure all this doesn't date back to Roland?

SUSAN: That was years back! I got over that years ago!

MONA: Are you sure?

SUSAN: Roland and I fell out, we split up, Michele was his next woman. I was glad to get rid of him.

MONA: That's not what you said at the time.

SUSAN: I was caught up in the heat of the moment.
MONA: You accused Michele of one set of crimes!

SUSAN: Mona, stop shit-stirring! I wasn't going to fall out with a friend over a man, a good friend at that.

MONA: So what is it between you two?

MICHELE: It's nothing.

SUSAN: It's not nothing, Michele. I don't like to see you abuse Mona.

MICHELE: Times are bad for me right now. I'm supporting myself. What I need to find is a rich man.

SUSAN: You won't find a rich man. You don't move in those circles.

MICHELE: I feel bad but I just haven't got any money. I'm feeding my baby rubbish. Things'll get better. I'll pay Mona back.

SUSAN: Things will get better?

MICHELE (*irritated; to* MONA): Can I just take those things and go?

MONA: Go look in the bedroom, you'll find them.

MICHELE: And where's the whisky?

MONA (*pointing*): Over there in the corner.

MICHELE: Mona. . .(*Long pause*). . .I know what Susan was just saying. . .but I haven't got any food in the flat. My dole comes on Friday. Is there anything left over from the party?

MONA: There's a tin of cheese biscuits on top of the fridge. I didn't even open them.

MICHELE: Are you sure that's all right?

MONA: You just sit there. I'll get it all together for you.

> MONA *goes into the kitchen, then the bedroom, collecting things for* MICHELE *in some plastic bags. Uncomfortable silence between* SUSAN *and* MICHELE.

SUSAN: It's getting a bit bad these days, isn't it?

MICHELE: What?

SUSAN: The way people treat each other.

MICHELE *shrugs her shoulders, not understanding.*

SUSAN: The world is run by those who get the breaks. Some people are born into the breaks, others just strike lucky. Those who get the breaks – there's not many of them – they rule our lives; we; the mass; the majority. There's no such thing as an oppressed minority, most of us are part of the oppressed majority. What do we do, we minions, what do we do? We squabble amongst ourselves. They find that very funny.

MICHELE: Who?

SUSAN: Those in power; those who get the breaks. They laugh at us. As long as we run around in circles, they'll be all right.

MICHELE, *not really understanding, looks blankly at* SUSAN, *not sure what to say.*

I'm talking about us, Michele. We help you. You're meant to help us at some stage of the day.

MICHELE: I'm having it bad right now.

SUSAN: You're always having it bad!

MICHELE: It's not my fault, is it?

SUSAN: Whose fault is it? It takes two to make a baby. What, are you going to blame him for the pregnancy? Who spends all the money that comes into your hands? Someone else? No, you. It's your fault. You let men into your life. Try and give your fanny a rest and you might be able to save some money for yourself, and spend some time with your child.

MICHELE: All right, I feel bad. Happy?

SUSAN *looks mildly remorseful.*

Happy?

SUSAN: I'm sorry. You seem to upset me whenever I see you. You keep saying, "Things will get better", but it's not "things" that need to get better. It's you!

MONA *comes back in with several plastic bags, which she gives to* MICHELE, *who gets up and makes for the door.*

MICHELE (*to* MONA): So, when am I going to see you again?

MONA: When you want something.

MICHELE: Don't say that!

MONA: Michele, it doesn't really matter.

MICHELE (*to* SUSAN): I'll see you, madam.

SUSAN: Girl, just don't work it too hard tonight!
MICHELE: You jealous?

MICHELE *opens the door.*

See you both.

MICHELE *exits.* MONA *pulls a tobacco tin out from underneath a cushion, throws it to* SUSAN, *who rolls a spliff for her.*

SUSAN: Just this once.

MONA: Share it with me. Stay over?

SUSAN: You want me to stay?

MONA: It'll be good for you to relax and have a laugh. (*Beat.*) It used to be different when we were young. We were all living with our parents, money was something they had. We had nothing to give, nothing that could be borrowed.

SUSAN: It's like a blind spot with Michele. You've lent her more fivers than you can remember. She's forgotten about them all, that's for sure.

MONA: Maybe it gets to the point – that point where you can't feed your shrieking infant – when you don't really care what you're doing, you don't really care what you've become.

SUSAN: You can't say "no", though. She needs all the support she can get.

MONA: You never did tell me what was bugging you.

SUSAN: It's not really distressing me. It's something that's rather pleasing me, actually. I'm not unhappy at all. I feel great.

MONA: Tell me about that.

SUSAN (*pause*): There's someone I like.

MONA: You must definitely tell me about that! Yes-I! News for me! Come on, tell me, who is it?

SUSAN: Well. . .

MONA: Having a quiet one on the sly, eh? Now tell your Auntie Mona.

SUSAN: What would you do if you liked someone but you weren't sure how they felt?

MONA: I'd tell them.

SUSAN: But what if it was someone you'd known a long time?

MONA: I'd tell them.

SUSAN: Mona, I'm really confused. I know little girls go through phases but I'm really not sure about some of the phases I'm going through!

MONA: There's nothing the matter with you. Everyone gets confused. That shows how normal you are. If you're caught up in some dilemma, you're at peak fitness. Whatever's going on in your head, it's not going to shock me, is it?

SUSAN *finishes rolling the spliff and lights it. She takes a few puffs and passes it on to* MONA.

MONA: Come on, girl. Before this makes us into a pair of idiots. What's your problem?

Pause.

SUSAN: I was walking down the road the other day, and I could see this young guy walking towards me. I could feel him looking at me and, as he got closer, I watched his eyes. He was obviously into tits 'cause he was staring at my chest. Then he moved down to my lower half; a few seconds on my crotch, a few seconds on my legs. Something seemed to please his eyes 'cause he then moved up to my face, seeing if I was good-looking. Not that that matters. Haven't you heard guys say that they don't need to look at the mantelpiece to stoke the fire?

Systematically, this guy checked me out. If he'd looked in my eyes, he wouldn't have seen something he liked, but my head didn't interest him. First he wanted to see if my implements for fucking were all in order. I really hate that, you know.

It's true, there are more female politicians, more businesswomen, more women in influential jobs, but that still hasn't improved men's outlook on women. I'm still, first and foremost, a fuck. I really can't stand that.

What I'm struggling to say is that I think I'm growing tired of that lovable, household pet known as the boyfriend.

SUSAN *kneels before* MONA, *opening her arms, asking to be held.* MONA *hugs her.* SUSAN *pulls back and tries to kiss* MONA. MONA *is shocked and stands up.*

MONA: Susan!

SUSAN (*embarrassed*): I'm sorry.

MONA: You're fed-up with boys and you want women instead?

SUSAN: Not really...I just...I just feel something for you. It's not really that I'm really turned off men, it's not really that I'm turned on by women, it's just...well...you're really special. You're so patient with Michele, you're so patient with me, you're so patient with Michael...

MONA: I don't know about that.

SUSAN: . . .and that's the reason I didn't come to the party; I couldn't bear to see you in public with Michael. I couldn't bear to see him treat you with such disdain in public. He's disgusting. I don't know why you care for him, I don't know how you ever did. You're too maternal; I can't bear to see Michele and Michael take and take and give nothing in return.
    You're really special. . .

MONA (*embarrassed*): Cut it out!

SUSAN: Mona, seriously, you're just the best friend I'll ever have. I think you're really great. . .and I just happen to fancy you as well.
    MONA *passes the spliff to* SUSAN.

MONA: This is getting well out of order. . .

SUSAN: . . .stop and think about it. . .

MONA: . . .this is the spliff talking. . .

SUSAN: . . .when was the last time you felt loved?

MONA: Maybe there is something wrong with you!

SUSAN: There's nothing wrong with me!

MONA: This is one of the phases that little girls go through. Come on, girl, pass it, nah!

    Playfully, SUSAN *moves away.*

SUSAN: Come and get it then.

MONA: Come on, pass it, before I give you two kick!

    SUSAN *moves behind a chair.*

SUSAN: If you want it, come and get it.

    MONA *comes towards* SUSAN *and tries to retrieve the spliff.* SUSAN *dodges out of her way.*

MONA: Look, I'm not joking, Susan, pass it!

    MONA *tries to make a grab at the spliff and burns her hand.*

    Ouch! Stupid!

SUSAN: Who tell you to put your hand on burning weed? (*Pause.*) Are you all right, Mona?

MONA: No, I'm not all right. Look what you've done! I'm scarred! Why can't you behave yourself? What's got into you today?

SUSAN *tries to look at* MONA's *hand but* MONA *moves away.*

Don't bother. I'm fed up with your foolishness.

MONA *exits.* SUSAN *raises her eyes to the ceiling, feeling regret, but picks up the tobacco tin and follows* MONA *out.*
                        Blackout.

SCENE TWO

MONA's *flat. The morning after. She walks from the kitchen, dressed in dressing-gown and slippers, carrying a bowl of cornflakes and a cup of tea. She sits down and starts eating.* SUSAN *wanders in wearing similar attire.*

SUSAN (*cheerily*): Good morning!
No reply from MONA. SUSAN *goes into the kitchen – to put the kettle on – then comes back out again.*

Tea?

MONA: I've got some, thank you.

SUSAN: Sleep well?

MONA: Yes, thank you.

SUSAN: Feeling talkative? Feeling revived and refreshed, are we?

MONA *gets up, gets out her carpet cleaner and starts, aimlessly, pushing it up and down the floor.*

SUSAN: What's wrong, Mona? Are we still friends? Don't you feel well? I feel wonderful. I feel really happy. Don't you feel any kind of happiness? I knew this is how it would be, you know? I feel really different, don't you? Mona, please say something! Please! What's wrong?

MONA *continues Hoovering.*

MONA: Look, it may be important to you but I don't intend to discuss last night.

SUSAN: But I really want to talk about it!

MONA: I know you do!

SUSAN: It's important to me, Mona, don't dismiss it.

MONA: I said I don't intend to discuss it!

SUSAN: Come on, Mona. . .

MONA: Don't "Come on, Mona" me! It's a bit of a shock to the system, you know. I've got a boyfriend, you know. It's a bit of a shock.

SUSAN: Can't we talk?

MONA: Stop it! In fact, I'm seeing Michael later on.

SUSAN: How can you!

MONA: He's my boyfriend and while I'm going out with him, you'd better relax.

SUSAN: Last night meant nothing to you, did it?

MONA: You're right, I'm too maternal, I'm too soft, I make sacrifices for everyone. You wanted me, I complied.

SUSAN: How can you say that!

MONA: People act funny when they're charged. I just let you do what you wanted.

SUSAN: That's really considerate of you. So, now you're off to Michael so he can do what he wants. You could run a little business, you know. Make people pay, Mona. Tell them they can do what they want, all they have to do is stick a coin in the slot!

MONA: Why don't you get hysterical! Why don't you insult me!

SUSAN: I just can't bear to see Michael use you. He doesn't need you, I do!

MONA: We go a long way back, you know. Michael and me talk. I like him – strange as it may seem – I like him. He was the first person that ever talked to me. He taught me a lot, he still does.

SUSAN: He just calls you when he want a jook!

MONA: Don't stop there, Susan, get really unpleasant!

SUSAN: Come on, Mona, admit it, you enjoyed last night. Don't let it bother you.

MONA: Get dressed and piss off, nah!

SUSAN: Don't be like that.

MONA: I don't want to talk!

Pause.

SUSAN: What are you doing tonight?

MONA: I'll probably end up staying at Michael's, won't I?

SUSAN: Okay. (*Pause.*) I'll see you tomorrow?

MONA: Don't start all that again. We made love. I don't know why. I don't know what's come over you. Maybe you were just upset.

SUSAN: Upset? I was happy! I'm really happy!
     When we were back home, didn't we sleep together? As kids, didn't we kiss? Didn't we touch? Have you erased it from your memory?

MONA: Susan, we were kids. We didn't know what we were doing.

SUSAN: Didn't we?

MONA: Did you?

SUSAN: I did. You didn't know what you were doing? You didn't love me?

MONA: Susan, we were kids. This is now.

SUSAN: But you love me, don't you?

MONA: Of course I do.

SUSAN: In love?

MONA: In love? (*Dawning on her:*) Well, yes, I suppose I am. (*Pause*) But we're talking being "lovers"!

SUSAN: Not that much difference.

MONA: Of course not.

SUSAN: I'll come back here around tea-time. I'm auditioning for this small, touring production today. This left-wing group are dragging some radical piece all over Britain. They obviously feel they should have a black person in the group, so I'm going along to keep the side up.

MONA: You don't look happy at the prospect of work.

SUSAN: It'll carry me miles away from you.

MONA: Don't worry about me. I'll be here when you get back.

Blackout.

Gabriela Pearse

1962–

Born in Bogata, Colombia, to a Trinidadian mother and English father, she grew up in Colombia-Chile-Switzerland-Grenada-Trinidad-England, studied at Warwick University and now lives in London, where she is a training consultant. A committed feminist, she has written stories and poems for years; with her mother she wrote a children's play performed by the Theatre of Black Women (1987). Her poetry has appeared in anthologies including A Dangerous Knowing: Four Black Women Poets (1985) and Black Women Talk Poetry (1987).

Today

A woman with a gash
so deep and wide in
her black soul
came and spilled her
self over me.

Asking to be held
like no-one held her

Asking to be fed
like no-one fed her.

She crawled beneath
my skirt trembling and
afraid and clasped
my lifeboat legs.

But I had meetings
to go to,
and a world to save.

Yelena Khanga

1962–

The daughter of a Russian-born Black woman whose father was American-born and of a Tanzanian, she lives in Moscow and since receiving her degree in journalism from Moscow State University in 1979 has been a reporter at Moscow News. She made her first visit to her grandfather's native land in November 1987, on a journalism exchange that enabled her to spend three months with the Christian Science Monitor in Boston. Her article "Black Russian" (translated by T. Butkova) first appeared in Essence magazine, August 1989.

Black Russian

A BLACK Russian is a strong but very nice cocktail I first tasted in the United States, where I spent three months in 1987–88. I don't know the recipe to this day, I confess, but the name awoke a chain of associations in my mind: I mean Black Russians, to whose number my ancestors belong.

My grandfather, Oliver Golden, was the son of a runaway Mississippi slave and a Tuskegee Institute undergraduate who met a white heiress in New York City. Oliver and Bertha married in 1929, when American society stringently ostracized mixed marriages. At that time, thousands of specialists from all countries went to work in the new Soviet Union, eager to build an unheard-of community based on social justice. There were lots of Americans among them, and Oliver Golden, an agricultural specialist, had the brilliant idea of a Black family colony in the Soviet Union. Sixteen families joined him, several top-class agricultural experts among them, and went to the country of their choice in 1931.

My grandparents had many friends and enjoyed their work. Several years after Lily, my mother, was born, they made up their minds to stay in the Soviet Union for good. Mother grew up like other Soviet young people. She went to high school and music school, and she excelled in tennis. She went to study at the history department of Moscow State University and got her doctorate ten years later. Lily met Abdulla Khanga, a Tanzanian who was a student at Oxford University at that time. He later moved to Moscow to be with Lily and attended the Patrice Lumumba People's Friendship University. The young couple fell in love and soon got married. I was born on May 1, 1962. After Daddy got his degree in Moscow, he went home to take a key government post. He died in 1968, a young man.

My mother published her book *Africans in Russia* in Britain and France in 1966. It tells the story of the first Ethiopian in Russia, Ibrahim Hannibal, godson and foster child of Russian emperor Peter the Great, brought to my country as a child late in the seventeenth century. Alexander Pushkin, his great-grandson, was the greatest-ever Russian poet. Mother tells of Ira Aldridge, the renowned African-American actor and an inimitable Othello, who was triumphantly touring the best Russian theaters for about ten years in the mid-nineteenth century.

Like parents the world over, Mother thought her daughter a child prodigy. I disappointed her in whatever she made me take up, whether ballet or figure skating. I took music lessons from three to ten years of age – it was torture for me and the instrument. So Mother switched her parental ambition to tennis. She saw me as another Althea Gibson, Black world champion, or playing mixed doubles with Arthur Ashe. At last I got some of her zeal, and tennis became my passion. I got the dream of playing with Arthur Ashe from Mother and cherished it for many years.

Recordings of Ray Charles, Louis Armstrong, Ella Fitzgerald and Stevie Wonder were played nonstop in our household – and were the only things to remind me of my Black roots. I grew up in Russian cultural surroundings, went to a Russian school and mixed with Russians from morning till night. Although I was the only Black girl in my school, I never felt I was any different and remembered my dark color only when I looked in the mirror. But my frizzy hair was a problem. There are no special combs and no conditioners for it in our country, and I saw new styles only in the rare issues of *Essence* that came my way by sheer chance. Hairstyles present a problem for many other Black girls in the Soviet Union, so an American stylist should start a Black beauty parlor in my country. It would be a great success, not only with us Black Russians but also with thousands of female African students and with the wives of African diplomats.

Dick Gregory's book *Nigger* once came my way. It was a revelation. For the first time, I felt one with my African-American brothers and sisters. Another time I squealed with delight when I got an invitation to take part in a crowd scene in the film *Black Like Me*, about racial prejudice in the United States. Next I played the daughter of the Congolese leader Patrice Lumumba in the film *Black Sun*.

After I entered the department of journalism at Moscow State University, in 1979, I seriously took up Black American history. I wrote my graduation thesis on the African-American press. My adviser, Professor Evgenia Privalova, supplied me with books on my topic. Her ideas were profound and extremely interesting.

I'm afraid I can't tell you the exact number of Black Soviet citizens, because my country doesn't keep racial statistics. I think there are about a hundred people like me in Moscow, most of them offspring of mixed marriages between Soviet young men and women and African students. Soviet towns have no Black neighborhoods, so we are dispersed.

I have many Black friends in Moscow. There's Lyuda, an actress and cabaret singer whose mother was Ukrainian and whose father is Cuban; Alena, a pop singer and daughter of a Ghanaian student and a Russian woman; and Misha, a young rebel who has just left high school and never thinks about a career. He and his crowd are a source of constant anxiety for the law and his mother.

Many Black Russian children are fatherless, or live with a stepfather. My mother, stepdad and I live in Moscow's center, in a fine four-room apartment. I owe my journalistic career to Ma's husband, the writer Boris Yakovlev. He is the strictest critic of everything I write.

I am a reporter at *Moscow News* and write, under my "Welcome" rubric, about problems of foreign businesspeople, correspondents and tourists in our country, about joint-venture companies, performers touring the Soviet Union and, most regrettably, about frequent conflicts, let's say, between Finnish tourists and our militia, or between American millionaires and Russian waiters. I have been working at *Moscow News* for five years since I got my university degree. I also interview foreign political leaders and notables of the arts and sports worlds who visit my country.

Until recently I was a Young Communist League activist in my weekly's office, responsible for athletic events. I arranged lots of them: table-tennis tournaments, chess contests, football matches and so on. I even organized marathons.

I am one of those lucky people who love their job above all. An interesting interview is a treat for me even on a weekend. My days are packed, but whenever I have an evening at my disposal, I spend it with my boyfriend at the movies or the theater. I sometimes wish a girlfriend could accompany me, but none can: all have little children and have become stay-at-homes.

The year before last, the Soviet Union and the United States had their first journalism exchange [cosponsored by the New England Association of Newspaper Editors and the Union of Soviet Journalists]. Two American reporters worked for three months on the *Moscow News* staff. They gave much first-rate information to the weekly, which is published in five languages, English included, and distributed in 140 countries. I was chosen to spend a three-month term at the *Christian Science Monitor* in Boston.

I had thousands of questions and was eager to find answers to them in America. Why did I meet so few Blacks among the many American tourists I met in Moscow? Did they feel no interest in a country almost wholly populated by whites? Or maybe they just couldn't afford expensive holidays overseas? I bombarded my American acquaintances with queries.

I came to Grandad's native land in November 1987. I was at a loss at first when Black people greeted me in the streets. I thought they were mistaking me for a movie star or something like that. Only later did I learn that many Blacks exchange greetings even if they don't know one another. I was moved to tears when strangers addressed me as "sister".

I made many friends from the start and grew especially fond of Lisa and Mary, Boston women my age from the *Christian Science Monitor* staff. I also liked Armin, a visitor from India, a kind and extremely intelligent young woman. We shared an apartment and grew to be fast friends. As we talked our problems over, I often forgot I was no longer in Moscow with girls I had known for years.

I'm especially grateful to Luix V. Overbea, staff correspondent for the *Christian Science Monitor*. He is like a father to all Black journalists and was an example to me of Black brotherhood – as I had imagined it back home when I dreamed of my ancestral land.

I owe my best and merriest hours in America to Karen Saunders, a Black ABC-TV producer from New York City. She showed me the city and introduced me to her friends. She became something of an elder sister, and time and again I caught myself seeing through her eyes.

A man I didn't know once called me from Los Angeles at the *Monitor* office. He introduced himself and showered me with questions about the Soviet Union. This businessman invited me to spend the weekend with him and his family, and the next day I received my plane ticket. It was a wonderful weekend. I gave a talk at the Sheraton. Close to 150 professional people came to listen. My host and his friends and family drove me around Los Angeles and Hollywood, and we visited Disneyland. I didn't feel in the least like a stranger.

But I don't have only sunny reminiscences of Black brotherhood. Once when I sat alone in my Boston apartment, the doorbell rang. Through the peephole I saw a nice-looking young Black man. He had brought me my salary from the office, he explained through the closed door. I knew he was lying, and when I refused to let him in, he flew into a rage and tried to break in. Luckily the landlord came to my rescue and the young man beat a hasty retreat. I realized then how wrong I was about African-American solidarity. I later found out that statistics, too, say that crime is at its highest in Black neighborhoods.

I thought I would find a monolithic Black community in America. The real situation was not so simple and radiant. It was a community like any other, ridden by class, social and other prejudice. Some of its members make their way to the top, but many people from poor families live a miserable existence to the end.

What I disliked most was racial prejudice in the Black community itself. After we saw the movie *School Daze* together, a friend of mine proudly said that he never made passes at dark women – not that they weren't his type, he just preferred lighter complexions. I was dumbfounded: I'd never heard a thing like that, even from prejudiced whites. That was when I realized that legal desegregation was much easier than rooting out prejudice itself.

Your great scholar Dr W. E. B. Du Bois predicted that race relations would present the biggest problem of the twentieth century. To all appearances, it will remain so in the century to come. I see America as a testing-ground of race relations, and I see its experience, positive and negative, as relevant to many countries. So I concentrated on the racial issue – not that three months was enough to make me an expert on it.

I pestered my friendly and cooperative American acquaintances with questions about their life. They paid in kind.

"Why are there no Blacks on the Soviet Olympic team?"

"I wish I knew just one Soviet Black athlete. Most Soviet Blacks take up scientific research, engineering, teaching, acting or medicine, not sports."

"What can Soviets take from Americans, and vice versa?"

"I'd love us Soviets to borrow the 'keep smiling' motto from you and be as careful about our health. I think you Americans would do well to be as interested as we are in the rest of the world, to be more politically minded."

"Are American boyfriends any different from Soviet ones?"

"I didn't have enough time for comparison. But I think men are alike all over."

Now that I am back home, the American situation is duplicated. For several months my friends have been showering me with questions about America, especially its Black community. I repeat, three months wasn't long, but I did my best to get as much information as possible. To get objective impressions, I met people from all walks of life. I interviewed Jesse Jackson and Arthur Ashe, my childhood idol. At Christmas I visited a shelter for the homeless. I met Michael Jackson and spoke by telephone to Stevie Wonder. I even visited a jail near Boston when a prisoner asked me to meet him. I met the Reverend Dr Samuel D. Proctor, then pastor of the Abyssinian Baptist Church in Harlem, the writer Dick Gregory and many others. The more I talked to my American blood brothers and sisters, the better I saw how little we know one another.

Today is the time to build economic and cultural bridges between the Soviet Union and the United States. Black Americans are welcome to join the effort. The soil is well prepared: Soviet jazz lovers admire Louis Armstrong, Duke Ellington, Ella Fitzgerald, Oscar Peterson and Count Basie. Their Soviet-made records appear everywhere. Michael Jackson's recordings are played nonstop in our discos. Stevie Wonder's "I Just Called to say I Love You" was top of the pops in the Soviet Union a couple of years ago. Then there are sports fans, for whom Carl Lewis and other Black athletes are household names.

No official delegation exchange, no movies or documentaries, no books or TV linkups replace direct communication at the public level. Let's meet one another. Let's join hands across the ocean.

Abena Adomako

?1963–

A contributor at the age of twenty-three to Farbe bekennen (eds Ogyntoye et al. 1986; translated by Anne V. Adams as Showing Our True Colour: Afro-German Womenon the Traces of Their History), she here describes her continuing search for selfhood in the face of unabashed prejudice and racism.

Mother: Afro-German, Father: Ghanaian

MY skin is black. As a result I am seen as a foreigner – African or American. I am always asked why my German is so good, where I come from, etc. These questions are irritating. Mostly I answer provocatively that I am German. Even then the questions don't stop – Why, how come, how so?

I am African but I am also German. My appearance makes me African, my thoughts and my behaviour are German, the way I move is European.

Africans are described as lovable, dumb, stupid and dirty. My mother and grandmother grew up as Afro-Germans in Germany. To avoid prejudice they brought me up to be particularly neat and clean and to perform well in school and in my profession. I had to be better than the others, or at least among the best.

Whenever I go to Ghana to see my relatives it's always a big adjustment for me at first. Then I just mix with all the Africans, even though my European manner makes me stand out. Ghana! I'm at home, but it's not my home. Yet I feel comfortable there.

I used to be jealous whenever I saw lighter coloured Afro-Germans. I thought their skin colour was more beautiful, like a suntan, and that they would have fewer problems and would be sooner accepted by society. I never recognized that they had problems simply because their colour was visible.

As a child I knew very few other Afro-German children. There was one boy in my class with whom I didn't really have much contact. I'd have been interested to find out what he thought and felt. There was another girl in our neighbourhood and I started to wonder about things when she was going with a friend of mine. Was I too dark to be someone's girlfriend? I can't blame everything on the colour of my skin. Maybe I just wasn't the right type. I still wonder about that today.

At that age I really didn't have any opportunities at all to go out with boys. Some of my girlfriends already had boyfriends and I felt excluded not being able to discuss boys with them. One even said that I was too dark to have a boyfriend. I kept hearing this until I actually had my first boyfriend. I still think that, while I was liked and accepted, the boys were afraid to show too much affection for me or to be too friendly towards me in case obligations and complications arose, such as my bringing a really Black girlfriend along.

I also suffered through not being able to take part in pranks since I would have been too easily recognized if a group of us played at ringing doorbells and running. I'd always been told to be careful, to behave. That's the way I was until I was 17.

All families aim at good behaviour in their children to give them a good upbringing. Our parents had the additional burden of prejudice. Don't draw attention to yourself in any negative way, no matter the cost. Always be polite and nice to everyone. That's what was expected from "decent" Africans. That's how one had to be and what was expected.

When contact games between boys and girls began at the onset of puberty, I felt excluded. I was usually made the custodian of coats and bags on those occasions. Up to today I react badly whenever anyone tries to give me chores like that.

I went to London as an *au pair* in 1980. My consciousness of my colour and origins was strengthened and developed. I felt good. I didn't stand out among the many different nationalities. The pressure and stress to appear superior and cool, and the feeling of being constantly watched and picked on disappeared. It was a liberating feeling to be able to move freely among people on the streets and on the subway. I learned to accept my skin colour completely there. I did not want to be paler any more. I am Black. Abena and everything to do with her is me.

As soon as I got back to Berlin all the stress and pressure, the staring, the feeling of inferiority began all over again. My environment once more demanded the well-brought-up obedient Abena it had known up till then. If I had been quiet and introverted before, now I was lively and self-assured and confident. I talked ceaselessly and swapped my conservative clothes for second-hand rags. My behaviour went against all the expectations of my family and friends.

On my return from England I started to look for a job. I had trained as a foreign-language secretary, and I began making applications in writing and by phone. They asked for information: age, nationality. My mind began to work. Could I go for a job with my Berlin accent and colour? Was I asked about my nationality because of my surname Adomako? I go for interviews. Amazing performances take place to conceal xenophobia and prejudice from me. So I write and phone endlessly in the search for a halfway neutral person who will employ me. Even once I'm employed, it all continues; I sense the prejudices of colleagues and superiors. "You wrote that wrong." Doubts about my ability. Africans just aren't supposed to be able to do this. But I trained for this job. Then I'm not so sure who is right. It's a spiral and I continue to fight my battle.

In recent years in Germany I've lost some of my strength and confidence. The desire and wish to leave for a place where people can move free of prejudice, where I can cross the street without being seen as a foreign object, begins to grow. People always say, "If you leave, you'll miss your homelend." That may be true, but rather a little homesickness than unhappiness "at home".

When it's time for discos, pubs and relationships – to dress up, to go out and go dancing – this means stress for me from start to finish.

(1) Getting ready. I must appear clean and well groomed. Why? There are prejudices against grubby, poor-looking African girls, or those just the opposite – too chic and she can almost certainly be bought. So what to wear? I choose something neutral if possible, so as not to appear sexy. . . .

(2) At the disco. The stares and whispers of men and women and the pressure of my escort at being observed too. Or maybe enjoying being the centre of attention.

(3) Dancing. Generally it is assumed that people of African descent can dance better. So I go on to the dancefloor with special attention being paid to "little old me". It doesn't matter whether I think I danced well or if I don't really feel up to it – I am always congratulated.

(4) Flirting. All women are flirted with. With me there's absolutely no restraint shown. I find the way it's done degrading and clumsy. "Everyone knows what a Black woman can offer a man." First, she is a sexually attractive woman, secondly, a woman with character. I like to be complimented on looking good, but the question is whether it's an insult. Wherever I go, I get a lot of reaction but I would prefer not to stand out all the time. I'm not the type who likes to put on a show in the way that is often expected of me. To protect myself from undesirable suitors it was necessary for me to erect a wall around myself. I have no desire to be chatted up by pimps and horny old goats. That's not how I want to live. Being full of mistrust and caution all the time, I appear to be hard, rejecting, quiet and try to hide any possible attraction. That's when I am left in peace.

This hardness carries over into my normal daily life. It's difficult for a really nice guy to get to me and I can hardly recognize his honesty. At this point I begin unconsciously to set tests. It's hard to explain why it's like this. Maybe it's because I want to know whether he's able to stick to me in spite of the prejudice and opposition from outside. But all this only makes me sad.

Even when it sounds as if some of my experiences have been harsh, I have learned to stand by myself and to find a way to be myself and to develop myself. I am finding more and more courage to stand out, and the courage to show my body without hiding in buttoned-up blouses and loose skirts and feeling ashamed. That's important for me.

I have to establish myself in a society which may appear to be neutral but which is not so in fact. I can appear self-assured, but I'm only strengthened by the thought: *You must or you'll go under*. Why can't I simply be the way I want to be, without taking up a fighting stance?

[Translated by George Busby]

Kristina Rungano

1963–

She was born into a Zimbabwean Roman Catholic family, and spent her childhood years between the Dominican-run Martindale Primary School, St John's High School and Kutama in Zvimba, where her father ran a small business. After high school she went to Britain, returning to Zimbabwe in 1982 after taking a diploma in computer science. The poems in her collection, A Storm is Brewing (1984), were largely written when she was an eighteen-year-old.

The Woman

A minute ago I came from the well
Where young women drew water like myself;
My body was weary and my heart tired.
For a moment I watched the stream that rushed before me
And thought how fresh the smell of flowers,
How young the grass around it.
And yet again I heard the sound of duty
Which ground on me – made me feel aged
As I bore the great big mud container on my head
Like a great big painful umbrella.
Then I got home and cooked your meal
For you had been out drinking the pleasures of the flesh
While I toiled in the fields
Under the angry vigilance of the sun,
A labour shared only by the bearings of my womb.
I washed the dishes – yours –
And swept the room we shared
Before I set forth to prepare your bedding
In the finest corner of the hut,
Which was bathed by the sweet smell of dung
I had this morning applied to the floors.
Then you came in,
In your drunken lust
And you made your demands.
When I explained how I was tired
And how I feared for the child – yours – I carried,

You beat me and had your way.
At that moment
You left me unhappy and bitter
And I hated you.
Yet tomorrow I shall again wake up to you,
Milk the cow, plough the land and cook your food;
You shall again be my lord,
For isn't it right that woman should obey,
Love, serve and honour her man?
For are you not the fruit of the land?

Jenneba Sie Jalloh
1964–

B orn in West London, to an Irish mother from Limerick and an African father from Freetown, Sierra Leone, she still lives in Ladbroke Grove where she grew up. She writes fiction and poetry, some of which appeared in the anthology Common Thread: Writings by Working-Class Women (eds Burnett et al; 1989). In one of her poems she has described herself as "a black woman, an African with an alternate Irish heartbeat". This autobiographical passage is taken from Across the Water: Irish Women's Lives in Britain (Virago, 1988).

Alternate Heartbeats

I T's only now as I get older that I feel Irish, I feel my Irish blood. When I was a child, like most children, I just took things for granted, but my mum was always at the forefront, and my Irish background was always there. She's always talked to me, and told me about her experiences and her childhood in Ireland. It all seeped through to me, it all went into my subconscious.

My mum was born in Limerick, in a really small village. When she was five years old she moved with all her family to Dublin, to Cabra. Some of my relations in Ireland are still living there now.

My father's from Freetown, Sierra Leone. My grandmother is Creole, and my grandfather was from the Fulla tribe. They're a market tribe, shop-keepers, things like that. When he was sixteen my father stowed away and came to Glasgow. He never went back after that, never visited Sierra Leone after that time. So he spent sixteen years in Freetown, and the rest of his life – he was fifty-two when he died – all around England, Scotland and Tiger Bay in Wales.

I was born in the centre of London, in Paddington Hospital. I'm an only child. My mum wanted a family for me, so I went every summer to Archway to stay with one of my aunts and cousins when they came over from Dublin. When I was seven I went to Brittas Bay in Wicklow for one summer. That was really good, we stayed in a caravan with my aunt and three cousins. The second time I went I was about fourteen, and I went on my own to stay with my aunt and cousins who used to come over here. But I always felt like an outsider. I think it wasn't only because I'm black, but also because I'm a Londoner, and they thought of me as English. I think I was kept away from the family in a lot of ways, obviously because my father's black and my mother's a bit of an outsider because of it. There was no contact between my dad and my mum's family.

As a child I really wanted my mother's family, because none of my father's family is here. Then at about the age of fourteen I decided I didn't want them any more, because I really felt that they didn't want me. Then last year I met all my cousins at a wedding. I went through traumas deciding whether or not to go. I thought to myself, after all these years do I really want to see them and relive the memories of childhood? I was scared of being with my mum where she would be part of the family, and maybe I wouldn't be. I was scared of losing her, just for that day. In fact, everybody was really nice to me. I'm glad I went though I was always aware of myself. One cousin actually asked me if I "knew my father" which showed that they knew nothing about me and resorted to stereotypes. At fourteen that would have affected me, but at twenty-two I was prepared.

They're two great influences, the African and the Irish, but they both came in different ways. My father talked to me about Africa. His stories were wonderful. He used to tell me about smoking weed in the jungle, about the beach, about bunking off and sitting on the dock watching the ships going to England, and saying he wanted to go. . .but they were just snippets of information. I remember having my ears pierced when I was six, because my grandmother was going to send me earrings and all African girls had their ears pierced. He always said to me, "You're African." He called me Jenneba, when everybody else called me Jenny. The one thing I regret is that because my dad died when I was fourteen, I never spoke to him as an adult. Now I can speak to my mother woman to woman, but I never spoke to my father in that way. I can romanticize about my dad – when the African influence came, it came hard and strong. But if I was to be honest, the influence of my mum and the Irish heritage is a lot more profound, because it was constant. I was surrounded by Irish, hearing colloquialisms and my mother's accent. I was hearing things as I grew up, and it had a great influence on me in many ways, a more subtle influence.

My mum is republican, so I've always been brought up really strongly for a united Ireland. I was taught rebel songs – I used to sing them to people when they came round, things like that. I remember my mum telling me that her grandmother saw people dying on the road with grass in their mouths during the Famine, but I wasn't taught Irish history at school. I was taught it first at college, doing A levels. They said, "We're now going to deal with 'the Irish Problem'." I said, "The Irish *problem?*" I questioned it, and that was the first time that I didn't like the way it was being put across. The second time, at the poly, we were doing literature and they said, "We're doing English literature here, the poets and playwrights, Shaw and Oscar Wilde and Sheridan." I said, "Excuse me, I really don't think they're English." We argued for about half an hour. The whole class was bored because I wouldn't let it drop. But I really felt indignant. It's a real English thing anyway, it's like what they do with black athletes. They claim who they want, when they want, when it serves their nationalism. But the thing is, those lecturers have been lecturing the same thing for years, they're not going to change it.

As a small child I had no conflict about my mum being white. She told me that when I was about four or five I said to her, "Mummy, am I black?" She was taken aback by this and she said, "Yes, yes, you are black." She told my dad and my dad thought it was really funny. Later on, in school, the biggest thing for me was that my father was African rather than West Indian. My school was 80 per cent black and mainly West Indian. I used to say he was American, because Africans were, you know, called monkeys and savages and cannibals and the rest of it. It's awful now, when I look back on it. It's all part of what the colonialists have left us.

My mum and dad never sat down and talked to me about racism and being mixed race. My dad would talk about Africa and say I was an African child. My mum would talk about Ireland and say that I'd get on because everyone would like me for what I am. With a lot of children of mixed race now, their parents consciously tell them. Looking back on it, I can remember feeling apart at primary school. There weren't very many black people, so my friends were white – funnily enough they were all Catholics, but they were white English. I can remember feeling a bit different. Maybe when I was younger I put it down to other things, but I know I felt a bit like an outsider. I was about eighteen years old when I actually sat down and confronted it, and cried about it, and felt I didn't belong. My identity crisis came at eighteen, which is quite late, you know.

At school we learnt about the slave trade, we learnt that it was really bad, that it was really wrong, but we never learnt about how great the civilizations were in Africa, before the people were taken as slaves. So, although we were given a sympathetic view, we were given a really negative view. It wasn't put into perspective – they left out a very fundamental part that could have given a lot of black children a lot of pride, because to be taught that your history started at the time of slavery is pretty tragic.

My mother didn't really let me explore my African heritage as I was growing up, she didn't go into it as much as she could have done. Some younger white women now, being married to black men, take time and trouble to spell out the history to their children. But my mother came from a different generation. I think in a way she was a bit scared that she'd be losing me to my father. Many times, especially in my teenage years, I must have caused her so much agony. If I didn't get what I wanted I'd say, "If I was white you'd have given it to me." It must have really pained her – I know now that it did. She didn't want to hear about racism, because it caused her too much pain. It's really silly, because she knew through her own experience of being Irish in the 1950s, you know, "No Blacks, No Irish, No Dogs". Whenever there was a bomb scare, she used to say that she'd ask for her fare in a really low voice 'cause she didn't want them to know that she was Irish – it used to pain me inside to think of it. So, from somebody who's had those same experiences I've always found it really odd that she didn't want to accept it for black people. The reason is that she didn't want to accept it for *me*. It's me who's made her aware – well she's been aware, but it's me who's actually made her come to terms and face it, that black people are discriminated against.

I think you can only condemn a person for thinking things that maybe racist or sexist if, after you've told them or you've made them aware, they still believe those things. I've argued with my mum about things, and then, with other people she'll make all the points that I've made in our arguments! I took her to the Irish Women's Centre when I was doing the poetry reading and some women said to me, "Why do you think of yourself as black and not Irish?" I was just about to reply, when my mum stood up in front of me and said, "Well, obviously...," and she took over. I didn't get a word in edgeways, and she was arguing with these women about why I see myself as black, you know. And it was a lovely thing to hear as well, I was really proud of her.

When I read my mum the poem I wrote to her, she just cried. Part of that poem said:

> To break the bond
>   And tell the person from whose womb you came,
> That your struggle is a different one
>   You fight a different fight
> Where you go, they can't follow,
>   They must remain outside
> And let you fight for what's rightfully yours
>   Away from their love and their guiding light.
>
> How different are we?
>   Are we as different as they say?
> I hear all round me that it is
>   The white man, the white oppressor,
> Who is keeping me down.
>
> But when I need that love,
>   That guiding light,
> That heart in tune with mine,

Who can I turn to but my Mother,
That person whose skin colour is different to mine.

She cried, and she said, "I shouldn't have had you." But I tried to explain that you can't say things like that. I'm trying to be a realist. I know there are things we can't relate on because she is white, but that could be the same for anybody whose mother or father is from a different culture. There's a bond between my mother and myself that could never be equalled and could never be surpassed.

I've had to deal with racism from my own flesh and blood. What really struck me once was my aunt actually sounding quite bitter about black people standing up and, you know, protesting. She said what I think maybe other Irish people living in London say, "We went through it, and we never made all that fuss and nonsense. We got on with it." What she hears is that black people have got equal this and equal that, and that you have to give certain jobs to black people, which of course, isn't true. So, she says, "We don't have any of that." And there's a kind of bitterness. It's a kind of jealousy in a way. It could be partly because Irish people are white people. It could be that when people are together under the same oppression, some want to stay apart and think they'll get on better if they don't meet other people who are oppressed. Some black people feel like that too. But I feel more hurt by Irish people being racist, because I am a part of them.

As a black person of mixed race, you are always fighting to say "I am black", and sometimes it can be a bit difficult to bring in another part of your background, especially if it is white. For me, I am part of my Irish heritage. I am stirred by Irish music, by the haunting pipes; I'm proud of the history of struggle and resistance to British imperialist forces; I want to see Ireland united as a socialist republic; I can visualize the wild countryside, and when I hear Irish people, or something about Ireland on telly, my ears do prick up straight away, same as if I hear black. If I hear anti-Irish jokes, I *always* say something – people moan about that. I was really proud and excited to read my poetry at the Irish Women's Centre. I've never, ever attempted to deny any part of my heritage, African or Irish. But there are people in the Irish community, and in the Black community, who would want to rob me of my identity. I've been told "you're black", "you're white", "half-caste", I'm this, that and the other. I'm not denying any part of my heritage by stating what I am. I'm not white, I'm black. I'm part Irish, part African. I call myself an African woman with an Irish mother, and a Londoner. I want to pass on whatever I've got to my children, so I've got to work it out for myself. So, for those people who want to deny me, well, I think it's them who've got the problem, not me.

Julia Berger

?1969–

L ike others in the anthology *Farbe bekennen* (eds Oguntoye et al., *1986; translated into English by Anne V. Adams under the title* Showing Our True Colour: Afro-German Women on the Traces *of Their History), she wrote optimistically and defiantly, as a seventeen-year-old, of how she has come to terms with everyday reactions to her dual heritage.*

"I do the same things others do"

M Y father was Italian and my mother Afro-German. I lived with my grand-parents in Italy during the three or four years my mother was training. I guess I was very spoiled and got everything I wanted.

It was clear that I looked different but all that anyone said was, "How sweet!" One day my mother simply collected me and took me to Berlin. I started school at the age of five but had already had a year of school in Italy. At first I still spoke Italian as well as German, but I can't so well any longer. Whenever my mother would tell me that I had an African grandfather I would say, "That's not true. I come from Italy." It was just that I didn't know my grandparents on my father's side.

I didn't have much contact with my father even though he lives here in Berlin. He owns restaurants here. I used to wish my parents could get on with one another and that we could build together. Now I can understand why my mother separated from my father. He had a new girlfriend and a baby. While I was in Italy they always tried to keep the fact that I had a half-sister a secret from me. She must be 10 by now. I'd really like to see her but I don't think she knows I exist. At the moment I see my father more frequently.

I feel less of an Italian now and more of a German. I do the same things others do and have lots of friends. No one says to me, "We don't want anything to do with you because you are brown." I never had problems in school, except once. A boy said, "What are you doing here? Go back where you came from." Another time in elementary school a girl said, "I'm not playing with you. You are a mulatto." So I said to her, "So what? Your father is an alcoholic." I don't know why she said that to me. Maybe she was unhappy and wanted to take it out on someone. She certainly picked the wrong person with me.

The teachers treated me like everyone else. Once when I came back from Africa I had to give a talk at school. They thought it was great and I got good marks for it. Whenever I go to a disco I meet lots of people who look like me. It's not a rare sight in Berlin. I don't know if their parents are American or African. I don't ask them about it. There's also a girl at school and I'd like to talk to her. I don't have any hang-ups in that respect. But when my friends say, "I saw your sister," I don't know how to react, so I say: "That's nice. Show her to me." I don't find it unpleasant. I've never known children to call out after me. Sometimes strangers ask me if I speak German. I was asked that yesterday as I was sitting in a café with my mother. Most people are surprised at my good German. If I'm out with white Germans that hardly ever happens.

More often than not, I'm taken for a half-American and people are amazed when I say that my grandparents were African. I don't want to be white. I am the way I am. I have to live with it and don't find it hard to live with.

My friends do ask where I come from. Then I have to tell my story again and again; but I'm not considered a foreigner either in school or anywhere else.

I once went to see a careers adviser and said I wanted to work in a travel agency. He asked me if I was aware that I'd have to send a photo with my application. "Of course," I answered. He then said that I might come up against people who wouldn't take me on because I was brown or because they didn't employ foreigners. So I said, "Look, I am not a foreigner."

I had thought it might be difficult because of my qualifications but I didn't think people would react that way. There are so many foreigners living in Germany, it's quite normal. We aren't living in the Stone Age any more. They can't refuse to give someone work.

It was tough for me in Africa. People were nice and I liked it there. But I don't think I could live there. I'm used to life here. I've never lived in a village before, either.

When I went there I thought the people would be darker. What I didn't expect was for them to call out "Whites" after us. They said "Toubab", which means "Stranger", but in a friendly manner, and the children waved and laughed. I had expected them to accept me as one of their own.

Here they shout "Black". There they shout "White". Where does one really belong?

[Translated by George Busby]

Serena Gordon

1972–

S *he was born in London, to a father born in Bermuda and a*
German-born mother, and was educated mainly at Copthall School
in Mill Hill, where she took her GCSE and A level exams. She lists as
her main interests "Ireland – politically and historically – competitive
riding, music, reading and writing" and is a member of Amnesty Inter-
national and Greenpeace.

Into the Light

I 'VE passed through the tunnel, into the light. I'm standing on a hill with
the world spread before me – fields, deserts, rivers and mountains and all
the cities of the world laid out at my feet. The choice is mine; I've fought and
struggled to reach the choice, and now it's arrived it daunts me.

As I look behind, I see the chains discarded on the ground, and an empty
black void. The demons have been rejected and can be seen no more. I've held
on to myself and my soul and have reached the light intact. Now I have to justify
that struggle and keep the demons away for ever.

I need to find the right way through the world, the way that is right for me,
the way that will keep the spark inside me glowing brightly. Nothing must ever
extinguish the spark, because then the true heart and soul dies. So far I've kept
alive and now I can walk slowly on into the light. . . .

Sources and Individual Works by Authors

Studies/biographies are in square brackets at the end of individual entries; for further reading see Select Bibliography

Adisa, Opal Palmer: *Bake-Face and Other Guava Stories* [short stories], Berkeley: Kelsey Street Press, 1986; London: Flamingo, 1989.
——*Jackfruit Survival*.
——*Market Woman*.
——*Pina, the Many-Eyed Fruit* [for children], San Francisco: Julian Richardson Associates, 1985.
——*Tamarind and Market Woman*.
——*Travelling Women* [with Devorah Major], Oakland, Ca: Jukebox Press, 1989.
Adomako, Abena: autobiography in Oguntoye *et al.* (eds) *Farbe bekennen*, Berlin: Orlanda, 1986; trans. Anne V. Adams as *Showing Our True Color*, Amherst: University of Massachusetts Press, 1992; London: Open Letters, 1992.
Aidoo, Ama Ata: *Changes* [novel], London: Women's Press, 1991.
——*The Dilemma of a Ghost/Anowa* [plays], Harlow, Essex: Longman, 1965, 1985; New York: Collier-Macmillan, 1971.
——*No Sweetness Here* [short stories], Harlow, Essex: Longman, 1970, 1988; Garden City, NY: Doubleday, 1971.
——*Our Sister Killjoy: or Reflections from a Black-eyed Squint* [novel], Harlow, Essex: Longman, 1977, 1981; New York: Nok, 1979.
——*Someone Talking to Sometime* [poems], Zimbabwe: College Press, 1985.
——*A Very Angry Letter in January* [poems], Australia/Denmark/Coventry, UK: Dangaroo Press, 1992.
——[Jane W. Grant, *Ama Ata Aidoo – The Dilemma of a Ghost*, London: Longman (Longman Guide to Literature), 1980.]
Akello, Grace: *My Barren Song* [poems], Arusha/Dar-es-Salaam: East Africa Publishing House, 1979.
——*Self Twice-Removed: Uganda Woman*, London: Change International Reports, 1982.
——*Iteso Thought Patterns in Tales* [non-fiction].
Alkali, Zaynab: *The Stillborn* [novel], Harlow: Longman, 1984, 1988.
——*The Virtuous Woman* [novel], Harlow: Longman, 1987; Nigeria; Gong, 1987.
Amadiume, Ifi: *Afrikan Matriarchal Foundations: The Igbo Case* [non-fiction], London: Karnak House, 1987.
——*Passion Waves* [poems], London: Karnak House, 1985.

Angelou, Maya: *All God's Children Need Travelling Shoes*, New York: Random House, 1987; London: Virago, 1987.

——*And Still I Rise* [poems], New York: Random House, 1978, Bantam, 1980; London: Virago, 1986.

——*Conversations with Maya Angelou* [non-fiction], ed. Jeffrey M. Elliot, London: Virago, 1989.

——*Gather Together in My Name* [autobiography], New York: Random House, 1974, Bantam, 1975; London; Virago, 1985.

——*The Heart of a Woman* [autobiography], New York: Random House, 1981, Bantam, 1982; London: Virago, 1986.

——*I Know Why the Caged Bird Sings* [autobiography], New York: Random House, 1970, Bantam, 1971; London: Virago, 1984.

——*I Shall Not Be Moved* [poems], New York: Random House, 1990, Bantam, 1991; London: Virago, 1990.

——*Just Give Me a Cool Drink of Water 'Fore I Diiie* [poems], New York: Random House, 1971, Bantam, 1973; London: Virago, 1988.

——*Maya Angelou Omnibus Volume I [I Know Why the Caged Bird Sings; Gather Together in My Name; Singin' and Swingin' and Gettin' Merry Like Christmas]*, New York: Random House, 1991; London: Virago, 1991.

——*Now Sheba Sings the Song* [poems], New York: Dutton, 1987; London: Virago, 1987.

——*Oh Pray My Wings Are Gonna Fit Me Well* [poems], New York: Random House, 1975, Bantam, 1977.

——*Poems*, New York: Bantam, 1986.

——*Shaker, Why Don't You Sing?* [poems], New York: Random House, 1983, Bantam, 1986.

——*Singin' and Swingin' and Gettin' Merry Like Christmas* [autobiography], New York: Random House, 1976, Bantam; London: Virago, 1985.

——[Dolly A. McPherson, *Order Out of Chaos: The Autobiographical Works of Maya Angelou*, New York: Peter Lang, 1990; London: Virago, 1991.]

Arobateau, Red Jordan: *The Bars Across Heaven* [novel], Berkeley: author, 1975, 1979.

——*Ho Stroll: A Novel in Five Parts*, author, 1975.

——*Stories from the Dance of Life*, 1979.

Ashundie, Iiola: in Zhana (ed.), *Sojourn*, London: Methuen, 1988.

Bâ, Mariama: *Le chant écarlate* [novel], Dakar: Nouvelles Éditions Africaines, 1981; trans. Dorothy S. Blair as *Scarlet Song*, Harlow, Essex: Longman, 1986.

——*Une Si Longue Lettre* [novel], Dakar: Nouvelles Éditions Africaines, 1979; trans. Modupé Bodé-Thomas as *So Long a Letter*, London: Heinemann Educational Books, 1981; Virago, 1982.

Baba: Mary F. Smith, *Baba of Karo: A Woman of the Muslim Hausa* [oral history], London: Faber, 1954; New York: Praeger, 1964; New Haven: Yale University Press, 1981.

Bambara, Toni Cade: *Gorilla, My Love* [short stories], New York: Random House, 1972, Vintage, 1981; London: Women's Press, 1984.

——*The Salt Eaters* [novel], New York: Random House, 1980; London: Women's Press, 1982.

——*The Sea Birds Are Still Alive: Collected Stories* [short stories], New York: Random House, 1977; London: Women's Press, 1984.

Belgrave, Valerie: *Ti Marie* [novel], London: Heinemann International, 1988.

Bennett, Gwendolyn: poems in James Weldon Johnson (ed.), *Book of American Poetry*, New York: Harcourt, Brace & World, 1971; Erlene Stetson (ed.), *Black Sister*, Bloomington: Indiana University Press, 1981.

Bennett, Louise: *Anancy and Miss Lou*, Kingston, Jamaica: Sangster's Book Stores, 1971.

——*Anancy Stories and Dialect Verse and Proverbs*, Kingston: Pioneer Press, 1945.

——*Anancy Stories and Dialect Verse by Louise Bennett and Others*, Kingston: Pioneer Press, 1957.

——*Dialect Verse by Louise Bennett*, comp. George K. Bowen, Kingston: Herald, 1942.

——*Jamaica Labrish: Jamaica Dialect Poems*, Kingston: Sangster, 1966.

——*Jamaica Maddah Goose* [for children], Kingston: Friends of the Jamaica School of Art, 1981, illus.

——*Jamaican Dialect Verse*, Kingston: Herald, 1942.

——*Jamaican Humour in Dialect*, Kingston: Jamaica Press Association, 1943.

——*Laugh with Louise: A Pot-Pourri of Jamaica Folklore*, Kingston: City Printery, 1961.

——*Lulu Sez: Dialect Verses with Glossary*, Kingston: Gleaner, 1952.

——*Miss Lulu Sez: A Collection of Dialect Poems*, Kingston: Gleaner, 1947.

——*Selected Poems*, ed. Mervyn Morris, Kingston: Sangster's Book Stores, 1982.

——*Verse in Jamaican Dialect*, Kingston: Herald, 1942.

——[Paula Grace Anderson, *Jamaica's Miss Lou: Louise Bennett*, Washington, DC; Three Continents Press, 1984.]

Berger, Julia: autobiography in Oguntoye *et al.* (eds), *Farbe bekennen*, Berlin: Orlanda, 1986; trans. Anne V. Adams as *Showing Our True Color*, Amherst: University of Massachusets Press, 1992; London: Open Letters, 1992.

Bernard, Eulalia: *Nuevo Ensayo sobre Existencia y la Libertad Política* [poems], San José, 1981.

——*Ritmohéroe* [poems], San José, 1982.

Birtha, Becky: *The Forbidden Poems*, Seattle: Seal Press 1991.

——*For Nights Like This One: Stories of Loving Women* [short stories], East Palo Alto, CA: Frog in the Well, 1983.

——*Lovers' Choice* [short stories], Seattle: Seal Press, 1987; London: Women's Press, 1988.

Bloom, Valerie: *Touch Mi! Tell Mi!* [poems], London: Bogle-L'Ouverture, 1983, 1990.

Bonner, Marita: *Frye Street and Environs: The Collected Works of Marita Bonner*. Eds Joyce Flynn and Joyce Occomy Stricklin, Boston: Beacon Press, 1987.

——*The Purple Flower* [play], in *Crisis*, January 1928; Hatch and Shine (eds), *Black Theatre USA*, 1974.

Brand, Dionne: *Chronicles of the Hostile Sun* [poems], Ontario: Williams-Wallace, 1984.

——*Earth Magic* [poems], Toronto: Kids Can Press, 1980.

——*'Fore Day Morning*, Toronto: Khoisan Artists, 1979.

——*No Language is Neutral* [poems], 1990.

——*Primitive Offensive* [poems], Ontario: Williams-Wallace, 1982.

——*Rivers Have Sources, Trees Have Roots: Speaking of Racism* [with Krisantha Sri Bhaggiyadatta; non-fiction], Toronto: Cross-Cultural Communication Centre, 1986.

——*Sans Souci and Other Tales* [short stories], Ontario: Williams-Wallace, 1988.

——*Winter Epigrams and Epigrams to Ernesto Cardenal in Defense of Claudia* [poems]. Ontario: Williams-Wallace, 1983.

Breeze, Jean Binta: *Answers* [poems], Jamaica: Masani, 1983.

——*Riddym Ravings and Other Poems*, ed. Mervyn Morris, London: Race Today, 1988.

——*Spring Cleaning* [poems], London: Virago, 1992.

Brindis de Salas, Virginia: *Cien Cárceles de Amor* [One Hundred Prisons of Love; poems], Montevideo, 1949.

——*Pregón de marimorena* [poems], intr. Julio Guadelupe; Montevideo: Sociedad Cultural Editora Indoamericana, 1946.

Brodber, Erna: *Abandonment of Children in Jamaica* [non-fiction], Mona, Jamaica: University of the West Indies, 1974.

——*Jane and Louisa Will Soon Come Home* [novel], London: New Beacon Books, 1980.

——*Myal* [novel], London: New Beacon, 1988.

——*Perceptions of Caribbean Women: Towards a Documentation of Stereotypes* [non-fiction], Cave Hill, Barbados: UWI, 1982.

——*Reggae and Cultural Identity in Jamaica* (with J. Edward Greene) [non-fiction], 1981.

——*A Study of Yards in the City of Kingston* [non-fiction], Mona: UWI, 1975.

Brooks, Gwendolyn: *Aloneness* [for children], Detroit: Broadside Press, 1971.

——*Annie Allen* [poems], New York: Harper & Brothers, 1949; in *Blacks*, 1987.

——*The Bean Eaters* [poems], New York: Harper & Brothers, 1960; in *Blacks*, 1987.

——*Beckonings* [poems], Detroit: Broadside Press, 1975.

——*Blacks* [omnibus volume], Chicago: David Co., 1987.

——*Bronzeville Boys and Girls* [for children], New York: Harper & Brothers, 1956.

——*A Capsule Course in Black Poetry Writing* (with Keorapaetse Kgositsile, Haki Madhubuti and Dudley Randall), Detroit: Broadside Press, 1973.

——*Family Pictures* [poems], Detroit: Broadside Press, 1970; in *Blacks*, 1987.

——*For Illinois 1968: A Sesquicentennial Poem*, 1968.

——*Gottschalk and the Grande Tarantelle* [poems], Chicago: David Co., 1988.

——*Maud Martha* [autobiographical novel], New York: Harper & Brothers, 1953; in *Blacks*, 1987.

——*Mayor Harold Washington and Chicago, the* I Will *City*, Chicago: David Co., 1983.

——*In the Mecca: Poems*, New York: Harper, 1953; in *Blacks*, 1987.

——*In the Time of Detachment, In the Time of Cold*, 1963.

——*The Near-Johannesburg Boy and Other Poems*, Chicago: David Co., 1986; in *Blacks*, 1987.

——*Primer for Blacks: Three Preachments* [poems/prose], Chicago: Brooks Press, 1980; in *Blacks*, 1987.

——*Report from Part One: The Autobiography of Gwendolyn Brooks*, Detroit: Broadside Press, 1972.

——*Riot* [poems], Detroit: Broadside Press, 1969; in *Blacks*, 1987.

——*Selected Poems*, New York: Harper & Row, 1963; in *Blacks*, 1987.

——*A Street in Bronzeville* [poems], New York: Harper & Brothers, 1945; in *Blacks*, 1987.

——*The Tiger Who Wore White Gloves, or What You Really Are, You Are* [for children; illus. Timothy Jones], Chicago: Third World Press, 1974.

——*To Disembark* [poems], Chicago: Third World Press, 1981.

——*Very Young Poets* [for children], Chicago: David Co., 1983.

——*The Wall*, Detroit: Broadside Press, 1967.

——*We Real Cool*, Detroit: Broadside Press, 1966.

——*Winnie* [poetry], Chicago: David Co., 1988; in *Gottschalk and the Grande Tarantelle*, 1988.

——*The World of Gwendolyn Brooks*, New York: Harper & Row, 1971.

——*Young Poet's Primer* [for children], Chicago: David Co., 1980.

——Paul M. Angle, *We Asked Gwendolyn Brooks*, Chicago: Illinois Bell Telephone Co., 1967.

——D. H. Melhem, *Gwendolyn Brooks: Poetry and the Heroic Voice*, Lexington: University Press of Kentucky, 1987.

——George E. Kent, *A Life of Gwendolyn Brooks*, Lexington: University Press of Kentucky, 1989.

——Haki Madhubuti (ed.), *Say That the River Runs: The Impact of Gwendolyn Brooks*, Chicago: Third World Press, 1987.

——Maria K. Mootry and Gary Smith, *A Life Distilled: Gwendolyn Brooks, Her Poetry and Fiction*, Urbana/Chicago: University of Illinois Press, 1987, 1989.

——Harry Shaw, *Gwendolyn Brooks*, Boston: Twayne, 1980.]

Burford, Barbara: 12 poems in *A Dangerous Knowing: Four Black Women Poets*, London: Sheba, 1984.

——*The Threshing Floor* [short stories], London: Sheba, 1986; Ithaca, NY: Firebrand Boks, 1987.

Burton, Annie Louise: *Memories of Childhood's Slavery Days* [autobiography], Boston: Ross Publishing Co., 1909; in *Six Women's Slave Narratives*, ed./intr. William L. Andrews, New York/Oxford: Oxford University Press, Schomburg Library of Nineteenth-Century Black Women Writers, 1988.

Busia, Abena P. A.: *Testimonies of Exile* [poems], Trenton, NJ: Africa World Press, 1990; Accra: Woeli Publications, 1990.

Butler, Dinah Anuli: poems in Ilona Linthwaite (ed.), *Ain't I a Woman!* London: Virago, 1987; Da Choong *et al.* (eds), *Black Women Talk Poetry*, London: Black Womantalk, 1987; Shabnam Grewal *et al.* (eds), *Charting the Journey*, London: Sheba, 1988.

Butler, Octavia E.: *Adulthood Rites: Xenogenesis II* [novel], New York: Warner, 1988; London: Gollancz, 1987.
——*Bloodchild* [novel], New York, 1985.
——*Clay's Ark* [novel], New York: St Martin's Press, 1984; London: Arrow, 1984, VGSF (Gollancz), 1991.
——*Dawn Xenogenesis I* [novel], New York: Warner, 1987; London: Gollancz, 1988.
——*Imago: Xenogenesis III* [novel], New York: Warner/Questar, 1989; London: Gollancz, 1989.
——*Kindred* [novel], Garden City, NY: Doubleday, 1979, Pocket Books, 1981; Boston: Beacon, 1988; London: Women's Press, 1988.
——*Mind of My Mind* [novel], Garden City, NY: Doubleday, Avon, 1977.
——*Patternmaster* [novel], New York, 1976.
——*Survivor* [novel], New York: 1978, New American Library, 1979.
——*Wild Seed* [novel], New York, 1980, Pocket Books, 1981; London: Gollancz, 1990.

Cambridge, Joan: *Clarise Cumberbatch Want to Go Home* [novel], New York: Ticknor & Fields, 1987; London: Women's Press, 1988.

Cartagena Portalatín, Aída: *El culto sincrético en villa mella, música, canto y danzas de los indios de española* [sociomusiclogy].
——*Del sueño al mundo* [poems], n.p., 1944.
——*En la casa del tiempo* [poems], Santo Domingo: Colección Montesinos 5, 1984.
——*Escalera para Electra* [novel], Santo Domingo: Ed. de la Universidad Autónoma de Santo Domingo, 1970, Editorial Taller, 1975.
——*José Vela Zanetti* [art criticism], Santo Domingo: La Isla Necesaria, 1954.
——*Llámale verde* [poems], Santo Domingo: Ed. La Poesia Sorprendido, 1945.
——*Una mujer está sola* [poems], Ciudad Trujillo: Sol. La Isla Necesaria, 1953, 1955.
——*Mi mundo el mar* [poems], Ciudad Trujillo: La Isla Necesaria, 1953; Santo Domingo: Libreria Dominicana, No. 10, 1955.
——*Tablero* [poems], Santo Domingo: Editorial Taller, 1978.
——*La tarde en que murió Estefania* [poems], Santo Domingo: Editorial Taller, 1983.
——*La tierra escrita* [poems], San Domingo: Brigadas Dominicanas, Baluarte 15, 1967.
——*Tierra Vania* [poems], 1981
——*Víspera del sueño al mundo* [poems], San Domingo: Ed. La Poesia Sorprendido; 1944.
——*La voz desatada* [poems], Santo Domingo: Bridadas Dominicanas, 1962.
——[Daisy Cocco de Filippis (ed.), *From Desolation to Compromise: The Poetry of Aída Cartagena Portalatín*, Santo Domingo: Alfa y Omega, 1988.]

Casely-Hayford, Adelaide: *Memoirs and Poems* [by Adelaide and Gladys Casely-Hayford], ed. Lucilda Hunter; Sierra Leone University Press, 1983.
——*Reminiscences* [autobiography], 1953.
——[Adelaide M. Cromwell, *An African Victorian Feminist: The Life and Times of Adelaide Smith Casely-Hayford 1868–1960*, London: Frank Cass, 1986.]

Casely-Hayford, Gladys May [Aquah Laluah]: *Memoirs and Poems* [by Adelaide and Gladys Casely-Hayford], ed. Lucilda Hunter; Sierra Leone University Press, 1983.

——*Take 'um So* [poems], Freetown: New Era Press, 1948.

Chauvet, Marie (Marie Vieux): *Amour, colère et folie* [Love, Anger and Madness; 3 novels], Paris: Gallimard, 1968.

——*La Danse sur le volcan* [novel], Paris: Plon, 1957; trans. Salvator Attanasio as *Dance on the Volcano*, New York: Willian Sloane Associates, 1959.

——*Fille d'Haiti* [Daughter of Haiti; novel], Paris: Editions Fasquelle, 1954.

——*Fonds-des-Nègres* [novel], Port-au-Prince, Haiti: Imprimerie Henri Deschamps, 1961.

——*La Légende des fleurs*, Port-au-Prince: Imprimerie Henri Deschamps, 1949.

——*Les Rapaces* [Birds of Prey; novel], Port-au-Prince: Editions Deschamps, 1986.

Childress, Alice: *Florence, A One-Act Drama* [play], in *Masses and Mainstream* 3 (October 1950), pp. 34–47.

——*A Hero Ain't Nothin' But a Sandwich* [novel], New York: Coward, McCann & Geoghegan, 1973.

——*Let's Hear It for the Queen* [children's play], New York: Coward, McCann & Geoghegan, 1976.

——*Like One of the Family: Conversations from a Domestic's Life* [short stories], Brooklyn, NY: Independence Publishers, 1956; intr. Trudier Harris, Boston: Beacon Press, 1986.

——*Rainbow Jordan* [novel], New York: Coward, McCann & Geoghegan, 1981, Avon/Flare, 1982.

——*A Short Walk* [novel], New York: Coward, McCann & Geoghegan, 1979.

——*String* [play], New York: Dramatists Play Service, 1969.

——*String and Mojo: Two Plays*, New York: Dramatists Play Service, 1971.

——*Trouble in Mind* [play], in Lindsay Patterson (ed.), *Black Theatre*, New York: Dodd, Mead, 1971.

——*Wedding Band: A Love/Hate Story in Black and White* [play], New York: Samuel French, 1973.

——*When the Rattlesnake Sounds* [play], New York: Coward, McCann & Geoghegan, 1975.

——*Wine in the Wilderness: A Comedy-Drama* [play], New York: Dramatists Play Service, 1969.

——*The World on a Hill* [play], in *Plays to Remember*, Literary Heritage Series, New York: Macmillan, 1968.

Cliff, Michelle: *Abeng* [novel], Trumansburg, NY: Crossing Press, 1984.

——*Bodies of Water* [short stories], London: Methuen, 1990, Minerva/Mandarin, 1991.

——*Claiming an Identity They Taught Me to Despise* [poems], Watertown: Persephone, 1980.

——*The Land of Look Behind: Prose and Poetry*, Ithaca, NY: Firebrand Books, 1985.

——*No Telephone to Heaven* [novel], New York: Dutton, 1987; London: Methuen, 1988, Minerva.

Clifton, Lucille: *All Us Come Cross the Water* [for children], 1973.

——*Amifika* [for children], New York, 1977.

——*The Black BC's* [for children], New York: Dutton, 1970.

——*The Boy Who Didn't Believe in Spring* [for children], New York: Dutton, 1973.

——*Don't You Remember?* [for children], New York, 1974.

——*Everett Anderson's Christmas Coming* [for children], New York: Holt, Rinehart & Winston, 1975.

——*Everett Anderson's Friend* [for children], New York: Holt, Rinehart & Winston, 1976.

——*Everett Anderson's Nine Month Long* [for children], New York: Holt, Rinehart & Winston, 1978.

——*Everett Anderson's 1-2-3* [for children], New York: Holt, Rinehart & Winston, 1977.

——*Everett Anderson's Year* [for children], New York: Holt, Rinehart & Winston, 1971.

——*Generations: a Memoir* [non-fiction], New York: Random House, 1976.

——*Good News about the Earth* [poems], New York: Random House, 1972.

——*Good, Says Jerome* [for children], New York: Dutton, 1973.

——*Good Times* [poems], New York: Random House/Vintage, 1970.

——*Good Woman: Poems and a Memoir 1969–1980*, Brockport, NY: Boa Editions 1987.

——*The Lucky Stone* [for children], New York, 1979.

——*My Brother Fine with Me* [for children], New York, 1975.

——*My Friend Jacob* [for children], New York: Harper & Row, 1980.

——*Nest: New Poems*, BOA Editions, 1987.

——*An Ordinary Woman* [poems], New York: Random House, 1974.

——*Some of the Days of Everett Anderson* [for children], New York: Holt, Rinehart & Winston, 1970.

——*Sonora Beautiful* [for children], New York, 1981.

——*The Times They Used to Be* [for children], New York, 1974.

——*Two-Headed Woman* [poems], Amherst, Mass.: University of Massachusetts Press, 1980.

Collins, Merle: *Angel* [novel], London: Women's Press, 1987.

——*Because the Dawn Breaks! Poems Dedicated to the Grenadian People*, London: Karia Press, 1985.

——*Rain Darling* [short stories], London: Women's Press, 1990.

Condé, Maryse: *Cahiers d'un retour au pays natal de Césaire*, Paris: Hatier, 1978.

——*La Civilisation du bossale: Réflexions sur la littérature orale de la Guadeloupe et de la Martinique*, Paris: L'Harmattan, 1978.

——*Dieu nous l'a donné* [play], Paris: Editions Pierre-Jean Oswald, 1972; trans. Washington, DC: Three Continents Press, 1984.

——*Hérémakhonon* [novel], Paris: Union Générale d'Editions, 1976; trans. Richard Philcox, Washington, DC: Three Continents Press, 1982.

——*Moi, Tituba, sorcière noire de Salem* [novel], Paris: Mercure de France, 1986.

——*The Morne of Massabielle* [play], trans. Richard Philcox; Washington, DC; Three Continents Press, 1990.

——*Mort d'Oluwemi d'Ajumako* [play], Paris: Pierre-Jean Oswald, 1973; trans. Washington, DC: Three Continents Press, 1984.

——*La Parole des femmes: essai sur des romancières des Antilles de langue française* [criticism], Paris: L'Harmattan, 1979.

——*Pays Mêlé suivi de Nanna-ya* [short stories], Paris: Hatier, 1985; Abidjan: CEDA, 1986.

——*Une Saison à Rihata*, [novel], Paris: Laffont, 1981; trans. Richard Philcox as *A Season in Rihata*, London: Heinemann Educational Books, 1988.

——*Ségou I: Les Murailles de terre* [novel], Paris: Laffont, 1984.

——*Ségou II: La Terre en miettes* [novel], Paris: Laffont, 1985; trans. Barbara Bray, *Segu*, New York: Viking Penguin, 1987; as *Children of Segu*, New York: Ballantine, 1989.

——*La Vie scélérate* [novel], Paris, 1987.

Cooper, Anna Julia: *L'Attitude de la France à l'égard de l'esclavage pendant la Révolution* [non-fiction], Paris: Maréthev, 1925.

——*The Life and Writings of the Grimké Family*, Washington, DC: author, 1951.

——*Le Pèlerinage de Charlemagne* [non-fiction], Paris: A. Lahure, 1925.

——*The Third Step*, 1925.

——*A Voice from the South: By a Black Woman of the South* [non-fiction], Xenia, Ohio: Aldine Publishing House, 1892; intr. Mary Helen Washington, New York/Oxford: Oxford University Press, Schomburg Library of Nineteenth-Century Black Women Writers, 1988.

——[Leona C. Gabel, *From Slavery to the Sorbonne and Beyond: The Life and Writings of Anna J. Cooper*, Northampton, Mass.: Smith College Publications, 1982.

——Louise Daniel Hutchinson, *Anna J. Cooper: A Voice from the South*, Washington, DC: Smithsonian Institution Press, 1981.]

Cooper, J. California: *Family* [novel], New York: Doubleday, 1991.

——*Homemade Love* [short stories], New York: St Martin's Press, 1986; London: Women's Press, 1987.

——*A Piece of Mine* [short stories], Navarro, Ca: Wild Trees Press, 1984; London: Women's Press, 1986.

——*Some Soul to Keep* [short stories], New York: St Martin's Press, 1987.

Cortez, Jayne: *Celebrations and Solitudes* [recording with music], New York: Strata East Records, 1975.

——*Coagulations: New and Selected Poems* [illus. Mel Edwards], New York: Thunder's Mouth, 1984; London: Pluto, 1985.

——*Everywhere Drums* [recording with music], New York, Bola Press, 1990.

——*Festivals and Funerals* [poems; illus. Mel Edwards], New York: Phrase Text, 1971.

——*Firespitter* [poems; illus. Mel Edwards], New York: Bola Press, 1982.

——*Maintain Control* [recording with music], New York: Bola Press, 1986.

——*Merveilleux Coup de Foudre: Poetry of Jayne Cortez and Ted Joans*, Paris: Handshake Editions, 1982.

——*Mouth on Paper* [poems; illus Mel Edwards], New York: Bola Press, 1977.

——*Pisstained Stairs and the Monkey Man's Wares* [poems; illus. Mel Edwards], New York: Phrase Text, 1969.

——*Poetic Magnetic* [poems from *Everywhere Drums* and *Maintain Control*; illus. Melvin Edwards], New York: Bola Press, 1991.

——*Scarifications* [poems; illus. Mel Edwards], New York: Bola Press, 1973.

——*There It Is* [recording with music], New York: Bola Press, 1982.

——*Unsubmissive Blues* [recording with music], New York: Bola Press, 1980.

——[*Jayne Cortez in Concert* (video), Workhorse Productions, 1983.

——*Life and Influences of Jayne Cortez* (video), Sâo Paulo: Museu da Literature, 1987.]

Craig, Christine: *Emmanuel and his Parrot* [for children], London: Oxford University Press, 1970.

——*Emmanuel Goes to Market* [for children], London: Oxford University Press, 1971.

——*I Can Be A* [career booklet], Kingston: Women's Bureau, 1974.

——*Quadrille for Tigers* [poems], Sebastopol, CA: Mina Press, 1984.

Creider, Jane Tapsubei: *Two Lives: My Spirit and I* [autobiography], London: Women's Press, 1986.

Dangarembga, Tsitsi: *Nervous Conditions* [novel], London: Women's Press, 1988.

Davis, Angela: *If They Come in the Morning*, New York, 1971; London: Orbach & Chambers/Angela Davis Defence Committee, 1971.

——*Lectures on Liberation* [essays], 1972.

——*Violence Against Women and the Ongoing Challenge to Racism* [pamphlet], New York: Kitchen Table: Women of Color Press, Freedom Organizing Series #5, 1985.

——*With My Mind on Freedom: An Autobiography*, New York: Random House, Bantam, 1974; London: Hutchinson, 1975; as *Angela Davis: An Autobiography*, London: Women's Press, 1990.

——*Women, Culture & Politics* [essays], New York: Random House, 1984; London: Women's Press, 1990.

——*Women, Race and Class* [essays], New York: Random House, 1981; London: Women's Press, 1982.

——[J. A. Parker, *Angela Davis: The Making of a Revolutionary*, New Rochelle, NY: Arlington House, 1973.

——"The Professor", *Angela: Portrait of a Revolutionary*, foreword Melvin M. Belli; London: Sphere Books, 1972.]

Davis, Thadious M.: poems in Erlene Stetson (ed.), *Black Sister*, Bloomington: Indiana University Press, 1981.

——*Emergence* [poems].

——*Faulkner's "Negro": Art and the Southern Context* [criticism], Baton Rouge: Louisiana State University Press, 1983.

Delaney, Lucy A.: *From the Darkness Cometh the Light: or, Struggles for Freedom*, St Louis: Publishing House of J. T. Smith, 1892; in *Six Women's Slave Narratives*, ed./intr. William L. Andrews, New York/Oxford: Oxford University Press, Schomburg Library of Nineteenth-Century Black Women Writers, 1988.

De Sousa, Noémia: poems in Dickinson (ed./trans.), *When Bullets Begin to Flower*, 1972.

Diallo, Nafissatou: *Awa la petite marchande*, Dakar: Edicef/Nouvelles Éditions Africaines, 1982.

——*De Tilène au Plateau: Une enfance dakaroise* [autobiography], Dakar: Nouvelles Éditions Africaines, 1975; trans. Dorothy Blair as *A Dakar Childhood*, Harlow, Essex: Longman, Drumbeat, 1982.

——*Le Fort maudit*, Abidjan: CEDA/Paris: Hatier, 1960.

——*La Princesse de Tiali* [novel], Dakar: Nouvelles Éditions Africaines, 1986; trans. Ann Woollcombe as *Fary, Princess of Tiali*, Washington: Three Continents Press, 1987.

Dove Danquah, Mabel: *The Torn Veil and Other Stories* [short stories], with Phebean Itayemi-Ogundipe; London: Evans Bros, 1976.

Dove, Rita: *Fifth Sunday* [short stories], Lexington: University of Kentucky, 1985.

——*Grace Notes* [poems], New York: Norton, 1989.

——*Museum* [poems], Pittsburgh: Carnegie-Mellon University Press, 1986.

——*Thomas and Beulah* [poems], Pittsburgh: Carnegie-Mellon, 1986.

——*The Yellow House on the Corner* [poems], Pittsburgh: Carnegie-Mellon, 1980.

Drumgoold, Kate: *A Slave Girl's Story: Being an Autobiography of Kate Drumgoold*, Brooklyn, NY, 1898; in *Six Women's Slave Narratives*, ed./intr. William L. Andrews, New York/Oxford: Oxford University Press, Schomburg Library of Nineteenth-Century Black Women Writers, 1988.

Dunbar-Nelson, Alice [Alice Ruth Moore]: *An Alice Dunbar-Nelson Reader*, ed. R. Ora Williams, Washington, DC: University Press of America, 1979.

——*Give Us Each Day: The Diary of Alice Dunbar-Nelson*, ed. Gloria T. Hull, New York/London: W. W. Norton, 1984.

——*The Goodness of St Rocque, and Other Stories* [short stories], New York: Dodd, Mead and Co., 1899.

——*Violets and Other Tales* [short stories and poems], Boston: Monthly Review Press, 1895; 1898.

——*The Works of Alice Dunbar-Nelson* [3 vols; poems, short stories, nonfiction], ed. Gloria T. Hull, New York/Oxford: Oxford University Press, Schomburg Library of Nineteenth-Century Black Women Writers, 1988.

——[Gloria T. Hull, *Color, Sex and Poetry: Three Women Writers of the Harlem Renaissance*, Bloomington: Indiana University Press, 1987.]

Edgell, Zee: *Beka Lamb* [novel], London: Heinemann Educational Books, 1982.

——*In Times Like These* [novel], London: Heinemann International, 1991.

Einsenbrandt, Angelika: autobiography in Oguntoye *et al.*, *Farbe bekennen*, Berlin: Orlanda, 1986; trans. Anne V. Adams as *Showing Our True Color*, Amherst: University of Massachusetts Press, 1992; London: Open Letters, 1992.

Elaw, Zilpha: *Memoirs of the Life, Religious Experience, Ministerial Travels and Labours of Mrs Zilpha Elaw, an American Female of Colour* [autobiography], London: author, 1846; in Andrews (ed.), *Sisters of the Spirit*, Bloomington: Indiana University Press, 1986.

Elizabeth: *Memoir of Old Elizabeth, a Coloured Woman* [autobiography], Philadelphia: Collins, printer, 1863; in *Six Women's Slave Narratives*, ed./intr. William L. Andrews, New York/Oxford: Oxford University Press, Schomburg Library of Nineteenth-Century Black Women Writers, 1988.

Emecheta, Buchi: *Adah's Story* [*In the Ditch/Second-Class Citizen*], London: Allison & Busby, 1983, Fontana, 1988.

——*The Bride Price* [novel], London: Allison & Busby, 1976, Fontana, 1978, Flamingo, 1989; New York: George Braziller, 1976.

——*Destination Biafra* [novel], London: Allison & Busby, 1982, Fontana, 1983.

——*Double Yoke* [novel], London: Ogwugwu Afor, 1984, Fontana, 1985, Flamingo, 1989; New York: Braziller, 1984.

——*Gwendolen* [novel], London: Collins, 1989, Fontana, 1990; as *The Family*, New York: Braziller, 1990.

——*Head Above Water* [autobiography], London: Ogwugwu Afor, 1986, Fontana/Flamingo, 1986.

——*In the Ditch* [novel], London: Barrie & Jenkins, 1972, Pan, 1973; revised, Allison & Busby, 1979, Flamingo, 1988.

——*The Joys of Motherhood* [novel], London: Allison & Busby, 1979, Heinemann Educational Books, African Writers Series, 1980; New York: Braziller, 1979.

——*The Moonlight Bride* [for young adults], London: Oxford University Press, 1977; New York: Braziller, 1983.

——*Naira Power* [novel], London: Macmillan Educational, Pacesetter, 1982.

——*Nowhere to Play* [for children; illus.], London: Allison & Busby, 1980.

——*The Rape of Shavi* [novel], London: Ogwugwu Afor, 1984, Fontana, 1985; New York: Braziller, 1984.

——*The Rebel* [novel], forthcoming, 1992.

——*Second-Class Citizen* [novel], London: Allison & Busby, 1974, Fontana/Flamingo, 1977, 1987; New York: Braziller, 1975.

——*The Slave Girl* [novel], London: Allison & Busby, 1977, Fontana, 1979, Flamingo, 1989; New York: Braziller, 1977.

——*Titch the Cat* [for children; illus.], London: Allison & Busby, 1979.

——*The Wrestling Match* [for young adults], London: Oxford University Press, 1980; New York: Braziller.

Espírito Santo, Alda do: *O Jorgal das Ilhas* [poems], Sâo Tomé: np, 1976.

——*O Nosso o Solo Sagrado de Terra* [poems], Lisbon: Ulmeiro, 1978.

Evans, Mari: *I Am a Black Woman* [poems], New York: William Morrow, 1970.

——*I Look at Me!* [for children; illus. Mike Davis], Chicago: Third World Press, 1974.

——*J. D.* [for children], New York: Avon, 1973.

——*Jim Flying High* [for children], 1979.

——*Nightstar 1973–1978* [poems], Los Angeles: UCLA Center for Afro-American Studies, 1981.

——*The Day They Made Biriyani* [for children], 1982.

——*Where Is All the Music?*, London: Paul Breman, 1968.

Fauset, Jessie Redmon: *The Chinaberry Tree: A Novel of American Life*, New York: Frederick A. Stokes, 1931; College Park, Md: McGrath, 1969.

——*Comedy American Style* [novel], New York: Frederick A. Stokes, 1933.

——*Plum Bun: A Novel Without a Moral*, New York: Frederick A. Stokes, 1928; London/Boston: Pandora, 1985.

——*There Is Confusion* [novel], New York: Boni & Liveright, 1924, AMS Press, 1974.

——[Carolyn Wedin Sylvander, *Jessie Redmon Fauset, Black American Writer*, Troy, NY: Whitson Publishing, 1981.]

Forten [Grimké], Charlotte: *The Journal of Charlotte L. Forten: A Free Negro in the Slave Era*, ed. Ray A. Billington, New York: Dryden Press, 1953, Collier Macmillan, 1961, Norton, 1981; *The Journals of Charlotte Forten Grimké*, ed. Brenda Stevenson, New York/Oxford: Oxford University Press, Schomburg Library of Nineteenth-Century Black Women Writers, 1988.

——[Anna J. Cooper, *The Life and Writings of the Grimké Family*, 2 vols, Washington, DC: author, 1951.]

Franca, Aline: *A Mulher de Aleduma* [The woman from Aleduma; novel], Brazil; Organizacao Clarindo Silva, 1981.

——*Negao Dony* [A big Black man; novel], Brazil, 1978.

Fullor, Henrietta: Letter to John McDonough, 24 Oct 1849 (John McDonogh Papers, Special Collections Division, Tulane University Library, New Orleans), in Robert Starobin (ed.), *Blacks in Bondage*, NY: New Viewpoints, 1974.

Garvey, Amy Jacques: *Garvey and Garveyism*, Kingston, Jamaica: author, 1963; New York: University Place, 1963, Collier Macmillan, 1970.

Gilroy, Beryl: *Black Teacher* [autobiography], London: Cassell, 1979.

——*Boy-Sandwich* [novel], London: Heinemann, 1989.

——*Business at Boom Farm* [for children], London: Macmillan Caribbean, 1977.

——*Echoes and Voices (Open-heart Poetry)*, New York: Vantage Press, 1991.

——*Frangipani House* [novel], London: Heinemann Educational Books, 1986.

——*Grandpa's Footstep* [for children], London: Macmillan Caribbean.

——*In Bed* [for children], London: Macmillan, 1975.

——*In for a Penny* [short stories for teenagers], London: Cassell Compass Books, 1980; Holt Saunders, 1982.

——*Inkle and Yarico* [novel], forthcoming.

——*The Little Green Donkey* [for children], London: Macmillan.

——*Stedman and Joanna: A Love in Bondate* [novel], New York: Vantage Press, 1991.

——*A Time Remembered: Long-Time Story*, 1991.

Giovanni, Nikki: *All I Gotta Do* [poems], Detroit: Broadside Press.

——*Black Feeling, Black Talk/Black Judgement* [poems], New York: William Morrow, 1970.

——*Black Judgement* [poems], Detroit: Broadside Press, 1969.

——*Cotton Candy on a Rainy Day* [poems], New York: William Morrow/Quill, 1978.

——*A Dialogue: James Baldwin and Nikki Giovanni* [non-fiction], 1972.

——*Ego Tripping and Other Poems for Young Readers*, Westport, Conn.: Lawrence Hill, 1973.

——*Gemini: An Extended Autobiographical Statement on My First Twenty-Five Years of Being a Black Poet* [autobiography], Indianapolis: Bobbs-Merrill, 1971; New York: Viking Compass, 1973, Penguin, 1976.

——*My House* [poems], New York: William Morrow, 1972.

——*Poem of Angela Yvonne Davis*, New York: NikTom, 1970.

——*A Poetic Equation: Conversations Between Nikki Giovanni and Margaret Walker* [non-fiction], Washington, DC: Howard University Press, 1974.

——*Re-Creation* [poems], Detroit: Broadside Press, 1970.

——*Spin a Soft Black Song: Poems for Children*, New York: Hill & Wang, 1971.

——*Those Who Ride the Nightwinds* [poems], New York: William Morrow, 1983.

——*Vacation Time: Poems for Children*, New York, 1980.

——*The Women and the Men: Poems*, New York: William Morrow, 1975.

Glover, Vivian: *The First Fig Tree*, [novel], London: Methuen, 1987; New York: St Martin's Press, 1988.

Golden, Marita: *Long Distance Life* [novel], New York, 1989; London: Judy Piatkus, 1990, Bantam, Bantam New Fiction, 1991.

——*Migrations of the Heart* [autobiography], New York, 1983.

——*A Woman's Place* [novel], New York: Doubleday, 1986; London: Methuen, 1988.

Gomez, Jewelle L.: *Flamingoes and Bears* [poems], New Brunswick, NJ: Grace Publications, 1986.

——*The Gilda Stories* [novel], New York: Firebrand, 1991.

Gonzales, Pilar López: autobiography in Lewis *et al.* (eds), *Four Women: Living the Revolution*, Urbana: University of Illinois Press, 1977.

Goodison, Lorna: *Baby Mother and the King of Swords: Short Stories*, Harlow, Essex: Longman, 1990.

——*Heartease* [poems], London: New Beacon Books, 1988.

——*I Am Becoming My Mother* [poems], London: New Beacon, 1986.

——*Lorna Goodison* [from *I am Becoming My Mother* and *Heartease*], New York: Research Institute for the Study of Man, 1989.

——*Tamarind Season* [poems], Kingston: Institute of Jamaica, 1980.

Gossett, Hattie: *Presenting . . . Sister No Blues* [poems], Ithaca, NY: Firebrand Books, 1988.

Grimké, Angelina Weld: *Rachel: A Play in Three Acts*, Boston: Cornhill, 1921; Washington, DC: McGrath Publishing Co., 1969; in Hatch and Shine (eds), *Black Theatre USA*, New York: Free Press, 1974.

——[Gloria T. Hull, *Color, Sex and Poetry: Three Women Writers of the Harlem Renaissance*, Bloomington: Indiana University Press, 1987.]

Guy, Rosa; *And I Heard a Bird Sing*, London: Victor Gollancz.

——*Bird at My Window* [novel], Philadelphia: Lippincott, 1966; London: Souvenir, 1966, Allison & Busby, 1985, Virago, 1989.

——*Children of Longing* [novel], New York: Holt, Rinehart & Winston, 1971; London: Gollancz, 1981.

——*The Disappearance* [novel], New York: Delacorte, 1979; London: Gollancz, 1980, Puffin, 1985.

——*Edith Jackson* [novel], New York: Viking, 1978; London: Gollancz, 1979, Puffin, 1985.

——*The Friends* [novel], New York: Holt, Rinehart & Winston, 1973; London: Gollancz, 1974, Puffin, 1977.

——*A Measure of Time* [novel], New York: Holt, Rinehart & Winston, 1983; London: Virago, 1984.

——*Mirror of Her Own*, New York: Delacorte, 1981.

——*Mother Crocodile "Maman Caiman": An Uncle Amadou Tale from Senegal* [folklore], New York: Delacorte, 1981.

——*My Love, My Love, or the Peasant Girl* [fiction], New York: Holt, Rinehart & Winston, 1985; London: Virago, 1987.

——*The New Guys Around the Block*, New York: Holt, Rinehart & Winston, 1983; London: Gollancz, 1983, Puffin.

——*Paris, Pee Wee and Big Dog* [for children], New York: Delacorte, 1984; London: Gollancz, 1984, Puffin.

——*Ruby* [novel], New York: Viking, 1976; London: Gollancz, 1981; Penguin, 1981.

——[Jerrie Norris, *Presenting Rosa Guy*, Boston: Twayne, 1988.]

Hansberry, Lorraine: *Les Blancs: The Collected Last Plays of Lorraine Hansberry*, New York: Random House, 1972, Vintage 1973.

——*The Movement: Documentary of a Struggle for Equality* [non-fiction], New York: Simon & Schuster, 1964; as *A Matter of Colour*, Harmondsworth: Penguin, 1964.

——*A Raisin in the Sun: a drama in three acts* [play], New York: Random House, 1959, Signet, 1961, 1988; London: Methuen, 1960.

——*The Sign in Sidney Brustein's Window* [play], New York: Random House, 1965; in *Three Negro Plays*, Harmondsworth: Penguin, 1969.

——*To Be Young, Gifted and Black: An Informal Autobiography* [adapted by Robert Nemiroff], Englewood Cliffs, NJ: Prentice-Hall, 1969; New York: New American Library, 1970.

——["Lorraine Hansberry: Art of Thunder, Vision of Light", *Freedomways*, special issue, 19:4, Fourth Quarter, December 1979.]

Harper, Frances Ellen Watkins ["Effie Afton"]: *Atlanta Offering. Poems*, Philadelphia: George S. Ferguson, 1895.

——*A Brighter Coming Day: A Frances Ellen Watkins Harper Reader*, ed. Frances Smith Foster, New York: Feminist Press, 1990.

——*The Complete Poems of Frances E. W. Harper*, ed. Maryemma Graham, New York/Oxford: Oxford University Press, Schomburg Library of Nineteenth-Century Black Women Writers, 1988.

——*Eventide. A series of tales and poems*, Boston: Ferridge & Co., 1854.

——*Forest Leaves [Autumn Leaves]* [poems], Baltimore: privately printed, 1851.

——*Idylls of the Bible* [poems], Philadelphia: author, 1893, George S. Ferguson, 1901.

——*Iola Leroy; or, Shadows Uplifted* [novel], Philadelphia; Garrigues Brothers, 2nd edn 1892, intr. William Still; Philadelphia: AMS Press, 1971; Boston: Beacon, 1987; intr. France Smith Foster, New York/Oxford: Oxford University Press, Schomburg Library of Nineteenth-Century Black Women Writers, 1988.

——*Light Beyond the Darkness* [poems], Chicago: Donohue & Henneberry, nd.

——*The Martyr of Alabama and Other Poems*, c. 1895.

——*Moses: A Story of the Nile* [poem and essay], Philadelphia: Merrihew & Son, 2nd edn 1869, 1889.

——*Poems*, Philadelphia: Merrihew & Son, 1871; Providence, RI: A. Crawford Greene & Sons, 1880; New York: AMS Press, 1975.

——*Poems*, Philadelphia: George S. Ferguson, 1896, 1900.

——*Poems on Miscellaneous Subjects*, Boston: Y. B. Yerrington & Son, 2nd edn 1854; Philadelphia: Merrihew & Thompson, 1857, Merrihew & Son, 1871.

——*Sketches of Southern Life* [poems], Philadelphia: Merrihew & Son, 1872; expanded, Ferguson Brothers, 1886.

——*The Sparrow's Fall and Other Poems*, np, c. 1894.

——[Montgomery, Janey Weinhold, *A Comparative Analysis of the Rhetoric of Two Negro Women Orators: Sojourner Truth and Frances E. Watkins Harper*, Fort Hays, Kans.: Fort Hays Kansas State College, 1968.]

Hatshepsut: in Miriam Lichtheim (ed.), *Ancient Egyptian Literature*, Vol. II, Berkeley: University of California Press, 1971.

——[Amr Hussein, *Hatshepsut*, trans. Samia M. Shereef; Egypt: Amr Hussein, 1989.]

Hazeley, Iyamidé: *Ripples and Jagged Edges* [poems], London: Zora Press, 1987.

Head, Bessie: *A Bewitched Crossroad: An African Saga*, 1984.

——*The Collector of Treasures, and Other Botswana Village Tales* [short stories], London: Heinemann Educational Books, 1977.

——*A Gesture of Belonging: Letters from Bessie Head*, ed. Randolph Vigne; London: SA Writers/Portsmouth, NH: Heinemann Educational Books, 1991.

——*Maru* [novel], London: Gollancz, 1971, Heinemann Educational Books, African Writers Series 101, 1972, 1987: New York: McCall, 1971, Humanities Press, 1977.

——*A Question of Power* [novel], London: Davis-Poynter 1974, Heinemann Educational Books, African Writers Series 149, 1974, 1987; New York: Humanities Press, Pantheon, 1977.

——*Serowe: Village of the Rain Winds* [non-fiction], London: Heinemann Educational Books, 1981.

——*Tales of Tenderness and Power*, London: Heinemann International, 1990.

——*When Rain Clouds Gather* [novel], London: Gollancz, 1969, Heinemann Educational Books, 1972; New York: Simon & Schuster, 1969.

——*A Woman Alone: Autobiographical Writings*, London: Heinemann International, 1990.

——[C. Abrahams (ed.), *The Tragic Life: Bessie Head and Literature in Southern Africa*, Trenton, NJ: Africa World Press, 1990.]

Herrera, Georgina: *Gentes u cosas* [People and Things; poems], 1974.

——*Granos de sol y luna* [Seeds of Sun and Moon; poems], 1978.

Herzi, Saida: short story in *Index on Censorship* (London), October 1990 Achebe and Innes (eds), *The Heinemann Book of Contemporary African Short Stories*, 1992.

Hodge, Merle: *Crick Crack, Monkey* [novel], London: André Deutsch, 1970; intr. Ray Narinesingh, Heinemann Educational, 1981.

Holiday, Billie: *The Best of Billie Holiday*, New York: Edward B. Marks Music Corp., 1962.

——*Billie Holiday, Anthology: Lady Sings the Blues*, California: Creative Concepts Publishing Corp., 1976.

——*Lady Sings the Blues* [with William Dufty; autobiography], Garden City, NY: Doubleday, 1956, Popular Library; London: Barrie, 1958, revised 1973, Ace Books, 1960, Abacus/Sphere, 1975; Penguin, 1984.

——[Jon Chilton, *Billie's Blues: The Billie Holiday Story, 1933–1959*, New York: Stein & Day, 1975.]

——Alexis DeVeaux, *Don't Explain: A Song of Billie Holiday*, New York: Harper & Row, 1980.]

——Bud Kliment, *Billie Holiday-Singer*, New York: Chelsea House, 1990, Los Angeles: Melrose Square, 1990.

Hooks, Bell (Gloria Watkins): *Ain't I a Woman: Black Women and Feminism* [non-fiction], Boston: South End Press, 1981; London, Pluto, 1982.

——*Feminist Theory: From Margin to Center* [non-fiction], Boston: South End Press, 1984.

——*Talking Back: Thinking Feminist – Thinking Black* [non-fiction], Boston: South End Press; London: Sheba, 1989.

——*Yearning: Race, Gender, and Cultural Politics* [non-fiction], Boston: South End Press; London: Turnaround, 1991.

Hopkins, Pauline (Sarah A. Allen): *Contending Forces: A Romance Illustrative of Negro Life North and South* [novel], Boston: Colored Cooperative Publishing, 1900; Miami: Mnemosyne, 1969; Carbondale: Southern Illinois University Press, 1978; intr. Richard Yarborough, New York/Oxford: Oxford University Press, Schomburg Library of Nineteenth-Century Black Women Writers, 1988.

——*Hagar's Daughters, a Story of Southern Caste Prejudice* [novel], in *Colored American* 2, March 1901–March 1902.

——*The Magazine Novels of Pauline Hopkins* (including *Hagar's Daughter*, *Winona*, *Of One Blood*, intr. Hazel V. Carby; New York/Oxford: Oxford University Press, Schomburg Library of Nineteenth-Century Black Women Writers, 1988.

——*Of One Blood: or, The Hidden Self* [novel], in *Colored American* 6, November 1902–November 1903).

——*Poems on Miscellaneous Subjects*, Boston: J. B. Yerrinton & Sons, 1854.

——"Topsy Templeton" [novella], in *New Era (Washington, DC), 1916.*

——*Winona: A Tale of Negro Life in the South and Southwest* [novel], in *Colored American* 4–5, May 1902–October 1902.

——*A Primer of Facts Pertaining to the Early Greatness of the African Race and the Possibility of Restoration by Its Descendants – with Epilogue* [non-fiction], Cambridge, Mass.: P. E. Hopkins & Co., Black Classics Series 1, 1905.

House, Amelia Blossom: *Black Women Writers from South Africa: A Preliminary Checklist*, Evanston: Northwestern University Program on Women, 1980.

——*Deliverance* [poems], 1986.

——*Our Sun Will Rise: Poems for South Africa*, Washington, DC: Three Continents Press, 1989.

Hull, Gloria T.: *Color, Sex and Poetry: Three Women Writers of the Harlem Renaissance*, Bloomington: Indiana University Press, 1987.

——*Healing Heart, Poems 1973–1988*, New York: Kitchen Table: Women of Color Press, 1989.

Hunt, Marsha: *Free* [novel], London: Hamish Hamilton, 1992.

——*Joy* [novel], London: Random Century, 1990, Arrow, 1991; New York: Dutton, 1991.

——*Real Life: The Story of a Survivor* [autobiography], London: Headline, 1985.

Hunter, Kristin: *Boss Cat* [for children], New York: Avon, 1981.

——*God Bless the Child* [novel], New York: Scribner, 1964; Washington, DC: Howard University Press, 1986.

——*Guests in the Promised Land* [novel], 1973.

——*The Lakestown Rebellion* [novel], New York: Scribner, 1978.

——*The Landlord* [novel], New York: Avon, 1969.

——*Lou in the Limelight*, [novel], New York: Scribner, 1981.

——*The Soul Brothers and Sister Lou* [novel], New York: Scribner, Avon, 1968; London: Women's Press, 1987.

——*The Survivors* [novel], 1975.

Hurston, Zora Neale: *Color Struck* [play], in *Fire*, November 1927.

——*Dust Tracks on a Road* [autobiography], Philadelphia: J. B. Lippincott, 1942; London: Hutchinson, 1944; New York: Arno, 1969; intr. Robert Hemenway, Chicago/Urbana: University of Illinois Press, 1984; London: Virago, 1986.

——*The First One* [play], in Charles S. Johnson (ed.), *Ebony and Topaz*, New York: Opportunity, 1927.

——*I Love Myself When I Am Laughing. . .And Then Again When Looking I'm Mean and Impressive: A Zora Neale Hurston Reader*, ed. Alice Walker, intr. Mary Helen Washington, New York: Feminist Press, 1979.

——*Jonah's Gourd Vine* [novel], intr. Fannie Hurston; Philadelphia: J. B. Lippincott, 1934; New York: Harper & Row, 1971, Viking Penguin; London: Duckworth, 1934, Virago, 1987.

——*Moses, Man of the Mountain* [novel], Philadelphia: J. B. Lippincott, 1939; London: J. M. Dent, 1941; as *Man of the Mountain*, intr. Blyden Jackson, Chicago: University of Illinois Press, 1984; foreword Deborah E. McDowell, New York: Harper Perennial, 1991.

——*Mule Bone: A Comedy of Negro Life* [with Langston Hughes; play], New York: Harper Perennial, 1991.

——*Mules and Men* [folklore], Philadelphia: J. B. Lippincott, 1935; London: Kegan Paul & Co., 1936; New York: Negro Universities Press, 1969; intr. Darwin Turner, Harper & Row, 1970; Chicago: University of Illinois Press, 1978; pref. Franz Boaz, Foreword Arnold Rampersad, Perennial Library, 1990.

——*The Sanctified Church: The Folklore Writings of Zora Neale Hurston* [nonfiction], foreword Toni Cade Bambara, Berkeley, CA: Turtle Island Press, 1981.

——*Seraph on the Suwanee* [novel], New York: Scribner, 1948, AMS Press, 1974; foreword Hazel V. Carby, New York: Harper Perennial, 1991.

——*Spunk: The Selected Short Stories of Zora Neale Hurston*, Berkeley: Turtle Island Foundation, 1985; London: Camden Press, 1987.

——*Tell My Horse: Voodoo and life in Haiti and Jamaica* [folklore], Philadelphia: J. B. Lippincott, 1938; London: J. M. Dent, 1938; intr. Ishmael Reed, New York: Harper & Row Perennial Library, 1990; as *Voodoo Gods: An Inquiry into Native Myths and Magic in Jamaica and Haiti*, intr. Bob Callahan, Berkeley, CA: Turtle Island Foundation, 1981.

——*Their Eyes Were Watching God* [novel], Philadelphia: J. B. Lippincott, 1937; London: J. M. Dent; Greenwich: Fawcett, 1965, 1971; New York: Negro Universities Press, 1969; foreword Sherley Anne Williams, Urbana: University of Illinois Press, 1978; London: Virago, 1986.

——[Michael Awkward (ed.), *New Essays on* Their Eyes Were Watching God, Cambridge University Press, 1990.

——Robert E. Hemenway, *Zora Neale Hurston: A Literary Biography*, Urbana: University of Illinois, 1977; London: Camden Press, 1986.

——Lillie P. Howard, *Zora Neale Hurston*, Boston: Twayne Publishers, 1980.

——Marian Murray, *Jump at the Sun: The Story of Zora Neale Hurston*, New York: Third Press/Odarkai, 1975.

——N. Y. Nathiri (ed.), *Zora! Zora Neale Hurston: A Woman and Her Community*, with essay by Alice Walker, Orlando, Fla.: Sentinel Communications Co., 1991.

——Adele S. Newson, *Zora Neale Hurston: A Reference Guide*, Boston: G. K. Hall, 1987.

——Ruthe T. Sheffey (ed.), *Rainbow Round Her Shoulder: The Zora Neale Hurston Symposium Papers*, Baltimore: Morgan State University Press, 1984.

——George C. Wolfe (adapt.) *Spunk: Three Tales By Zora Neale Hurston*, New York: Theater Communications Group, 1991.]

Jabavu, Noni: *Drawn in Colour: African Contrasts* [non-fiction], London: John Murray, 1960; New York: St Martin's Press, 1962.

——*The Ochre People: Scenes from South African Life* [non-fiction], London: Murray, 1963, New York: St Martin's, 1963; Johannesburg: Ravan Press, 1982.

Jackson, Mattie J.: *The Story of Mattie J. Jackson: A True Story. Written and arranged by Dr L. S. Thompson (formerly Mrs Schuyler) as given by Mattie*, Lawrence, 1866; in *Six Women's Slave Narratives*, ed./intr. William L. Andrews, New York/Oxford: Oxford University Press, Schomburg Library of Nineteenth-Century Black Women Writers, 1988.

Jacobs, Harriet [Linda Brent]: *Linda, or Incidents in the Life of a Slave Girl: An Authentic Historical Narrative Describing the Horrors of Slavery as Experienced by Black Women*, ed. L. Maria Child, Boston: author, 1861; London: W. Tweedie, 1862; New York/Oxford: Oxford University Press, Schomburg Library of Nineteenth-Century Women Writers, 1988.

Jesús, Carolina Maria de: *Casa de alvenaria: Diário de uma ex-favelada* [journal], Rio de Janeiro: Liv. Francisco Alves, 1961.

——*Quarto de despejo: Diário de uma favelada* [journal], Sao Paulo, Brazil: Liv. Francisco Alves, 1960; trans. David St Clair as *Child of the Dark: The Diary of Carolina Maria de Jesús*, New York: Dutton, 1962, New American Library, 1969; as *Beyond All Pity*, London: Souvenir Press, 1962, Panther, 1970, Earthscan, 1990.

Johnson, Alice Perry: *Africa Is a Woman* [poems and prose], Liberia, 1976.

——*One Step Ahead* [poems and prose], Monrovia: Liberian Publishing Co., 1972.

Johnson, Amryl: *Long Road to Nowhere* [poems], London: Sable Publications, 1982, Virago, 1985, Cofa Press, 1991.

——*Sequins for a Ragged Hem* [travel memoir], London: Virago, 1988.

Johnson, Georgia Douglas: *An Autumn Love Cycle* [poems], intr. Alain Locke, New York: Harold Vinal, 1928; New York: Neal, 1938; facsimile of 1928 edn, Freeport, NY: Books for Libraries Press, 1971.

——*Blue Blood* [play; 1926], in Frank Shay (ed.), *Fifty More Contemporary One-Act Plays*, New York: Appleton, 1928.

——*Bronze: A Book of Verse*, intr. W. E. B. Du Bois, Boston: B. J. Brimmer, 1922; New York: Books for Libraries Press, 1971.

——*Frederick Douglass* [play], in Richardson and Miller (eds), *Negro History in Thirteen Plays*, Washington, DC: Associated Publishers, 1935.

——*The Heart of a Woman and Other Poems*, intr. William Stanley Braithwaite, Boston: Churchill, 1918; New York: Books for Libraries Press, 1971.

——*Plumes* [play], in Locke and Gregory (eds), *Plays of Negro Life*, New York: Harper, 1927.

——*Share My World: A Book of Poems*, Washington, DC: Half-Way House, 1962.

——*A Sunday Morning in the South* [play], in Hatch and Shine (eds), *Black Theatre USA*, New York: Free Press, 1974.

——*William and Ellen Craft* [play], in Richardson and Miller (eds), *Negro History in Thirteen Plays*, Washington, DC: Associated Publishers, 1935.

——[*Catalog of Writings by Georgia Douglas Johnson*, Washington, DC: Half-Way House, n.d..

——Gloria T. Hull, *Color, Sex and Poetry: Three Women Writers of the Harlem Renaissance*, Bloomington: Indiana University Press, 1987.]

Jones, Claudia: *An End to the Neglect of the Problems of the Negro Woman*, New York: National Women's Commission, 1930.

——[Buzz Johnson, *"I Think of My Mother": Notes on the Life and Times of Claudia Jones*, London: Karia Press, 1985.]

Jones, Gayl: *Corregidora* [novel], New York: Random House, 1975; Boston: Beacon Press, 1986; London: Camden Press, 1989.

——*Eva's Man* [novel], New York: Random House, 1976; Boston: Beacon Press, Black Women Writers series, 1987.

——*The Hermit Woman* [poems], Detroit: Lotus Press, 1983.

——*Liberating Voices: Oral Tradition in African American Literature* [criticism], Cambridge, Mass./London: Harvard University Press, 1991.

——*Song for Anninho* [poems], Detroit: Lotus Press, 1981.

——*White Rat* [short stories], New York: Random House, 1977.

——*Xarque and Other Poems,* Detroit: Lotus Press, 1985.

Jordan, June (June Meyer): *Civil Wars* [essays], Boston: Beacon Press, 1981.

——*Dry Victories* [non-fiction], New York: Holt, 1972, Avon, 1975.

——*His Own Where* [novel], New York: Dell, 1971, 1972.

——*Living Room: New Poems*, Chicago: Thunder's Mouth Press, 1985.

——*Lyrical Campaigns: Selected Poems*, London: Virago, 1989.

——*Moving Towards Home: Political Essays*, London: Virago, 1989.

——*Naming Our Destiny: New and Selected Poems*, New York: Thunder's Mouth Press.

——*New Days: Poems of Exile and Return*, New York: Emerson Hall, 1973.

——*New Life, New Room* [poems], New York: Crowell, 1975.

——*Okay Now* [novel], New York: Simon & Schuster, 1975.

——*On Call: Political Essays*, Boston: South End Press, 1985; London, Pluto, 1986.

——*Passion: New Poems, 1977–1980*, Boston: Beacon Press, 1980.

——*Some Changes* [poems], New York: Dutton, 1971.

——*Soulscript: Afro-American Poetry*, New York: Doubleday, 1970.

——*Things That I Do in the Dark: New and Selected Poems*, New York: Random House, 1977; Boston: Beacon, 1981.

——*Who Look at Me* [poems for children], New York: Crowell, 1969.

Kay, Jackie: *The Adoption Papers* [poems], London: Bloodaxe, 1991.

——*Chiaroscuro*, London: Methuen, 1988.

——poems in *A Dangerous Knowing: Four Black Women Poets*, London: Sheba, 1984.

Kebbedesh: oral history in Hammond and Druce (eds), *Sweeter than Honey: Testimonies of Tigrayan Women*, Oxford: Third World First, 1989.

Khaketla, Caroline N. M.: *'Mantsopa* [poems], Cape Town: Oxford University Press, 1963.

——*Mosali eo u 'neileng eena* [The Woman You Gave Me; Sotho play], Morija: Morija Sesuto Book Depot, 1954.

——*Pelo ea Monna* [The Heart of a Man; Sotho play], Maseru: author, 1976.

Khanga, Yelena: "Black Russian" in *Essence* 20:4 (August 1989).

Kincaid, Jamaica: *Annie John* [novel], New York: Farrar, Straus & Giroux, 1985, Plume/New American Library, 1985; London: Picador, 1985.

——*At the Bottom of the River* [short stories], New York: Farrar, Straus & Giroux, 1983, Aventura/Vintage, 1985; London: Picador, 1984.

——*Lucy* [novel], New York: Farrar, Straus & Giroux, 1991; London: Cape, 1991.

——*A Small Place* [non-fiction], New York: Farrar, Straus & Giroux, 1988.

Kuzwayo, Ellen: *Call Me Woman* [autobiography], Cape Town: David Philip Publishers; London: Women's Press, 1985.

——*Sit Down and Listen: Stories from South Africa* [non-fiction], Cape Town: David Philip; London: Women's Press, 1990.

Lara, Alda: *Poemas*, Sá da Bandeira: Edicoes Imbondeiro, 1966.

——*Poesia*, Luanda: Caderinos Lavra & Oficina, 1979.

——*Tempo de chuva* [short stories], Lobito: Capricórnio, 1973.

Larsen, Nella: *Passing* [novel], New York/London: Knopf, 1929, Arno/New York Times, 1969, Collier-Macmillan, 1971.

——*Quicksand* [novel], New York/London: Knopf, 1928, Negro Universities Press, 1969, Collier-Macmillan, 1971.

——*Quicksand and Passing* [novels], Rutgers University Press, 1986; London: Serpent's Tail, 1989.

Lee, Andrea: *Russian Journal* [non-fiction], New York; Random House, 1979.

Sarah Phillips [novel], New York: Random House, 1984; London: Faber, 1985.

Lorde, Audre: *Between Ourselves* [poems], Point Reyes: Eidolon Editions, 1976.

——*The Black Unicorn* [poems], New York: W. W. Norton, 1978; London, 1981.

——*A Burst of Light* [essays], Ithaca, NY: Firebrand, 1988; London: Sheba, 1989.

——*Cables to Rage* [poems], London: Paul Breman, Heritage Series, 1970.

——*The Cancer Journals* [autobiography], Argyle, NY: Spinsters Ink, 1980; London: Sheba, 1985.

——*Chosen Poems: Old and New*, New York: Norton, 1982.

——*Coal*, [poems], New York: Norton, 1968, 1976.

——*The First Cities* [poems], New York: Poets Press, 1968.

———*From a Land Where Other People Live* [poems], Detroit: Broadside Press, 1973.

———*Need: A Chorale for Black Women Voices*, New York: Kitchen Table Freedom Organizing Series #6.

———*The New York Headshop and Museum* [poems], Detroit: Broadside Press, 1975.

———*Our Dead Behind Us: Poems*, New York: Norton, 1986; London: Sheba, 1987.

———*Sister Outsider: Essays and Speeches*, Freedom, CA: Crossing Press, Crossing Press Feminist Series, 1984.

———*Uses of the Erotic: The Erotic as Power* [non-fiction], New York: Out & Out Pamphlet, 1978.

———*Zami: A New Spelling of My Name* [autobiography], Watertown: Persephone, 1982; London: Sheba, 1984.

McDougald, Elise Johnson: "The Double Task: The Struggle of Negro Women for Sex and Race Emancipation", *Survey Graphic* 6:6 (March 1925); Baltimore: Black Classic Press, 1980.

McMillan, Terry, L.: *Disappearing Acts* [novel], London: Cape, 1989, Black Swan, 1991.

———*Mama* [novel], Boston: Houghton Mifflin, 1987, Washington Square Press/ Pocket Books, 1987; London: Cape, 1987, Pan/Pavanne, 1988, Black Swan, 1991.

Madgett, Naomi Long: *Exits and Entrances* [poems], Detroit: Lotus Press, 1978.

———*One and the Many* [poems], New York: Exposition Press, 1956.

———*Pink Ladies in the Afternoon* [poems], Detroit: Lotus Press, 1972, 1990.

———*Songs to a Phantom Nightingale* [poems], New York: Fortuny's Publishers, 1941.

———*Star by Star* [poems], Detroit: Harlo Press, 1965.

Magaia, Lina: *Dumba Nengue: Run for Your Life – Peasant Tales of Tragedy in Mozambique* [non-fiction], trans. Michael Wolfers, Trenton, NJ: Africa World Press, 1988; London: Karnak House, 1989.

Makhalisa, Barbara C.: *Impilo Yinkinga* [Ndebele, fiction], Zimbabwe: Longman, 1964.

———*Qilindini* [Ndebele, fiction], 1969.

———*Umendo* [Marriage; Ndebele, fiction], Gwelo, Zimbabwe: Mambo Press/ Rhodesia Literature Bureau, 1977.

———*Umhlaba Io!* [What a world!; Ndebele, fiction], Gwelo: Mambo/Rhodesia Literature Bureau, 1977.

———*The Underdog and Other Stories* [short stories], Gweru: Mambo, 1984.

Mandela, Zindziswa: *Black As I Am* [poems], Los Angeles: Guild of Tutors Press, 1978.

Marshall, Paule: *Brown Girl, Brownstones* [novel], New York: Random House, 1959, Avon, 1970; Chatham, NJ: Chatham Bookseller, 1972; Old Westbury, NY: Feminist Press, 1981; London: Virago, 1981.

———*The Chosen Place, the Timeless People* [novel], New York: Harcourt, Brace & World, 1969, Vintage, 1984.

———*Daughters* [novel], New York: Atheneum, 1991.

——*Praisesong for the Widow* [novel], New York: G. P. Putnam, 1983; London: Virago, 1983.

——*Reena and Other Stories* [short stories], Old Westbury, NY: Feminist Press, 1983; as *Merle and Other Stories*, London: Virago, 1985.

——*Soul Clap Hands and Sing* [short stories], New York: Atheneum, 1961; Chatham, NJ: Chatham Bookseller, 1971; London: W. H. Allen, 1962; Old Westbury, NY: Feminist Press, 1981.

Marson, Una: *Heights and Depths* [poems], Kingston: Gleaner Co., 1931.

——*The Moth and the Star* [poems], Kingston: Gleaner, 1937.

——*Towards the Stars* [poems], Bickley, Kent: University of London Press, 1945.

——*Tropic Reveries* [poems], Kingston: Gleaner, 1930.

M'Baye, Annette: *La Bague de cuivre et d'argent* [for children], Dakar: Nouvelles Éditions Africaines/AGECOOP, 1983.

——*Chansons pour Laity* [poems], Dakar/Abidjan: Nouvelles Éditions Africaines, 1976.

——*Kaddu* [poems], Dakar: Imprimerie A. Diop, 1967.

——*Le Noël du vieux chasseur* [for children], Dakar: NÉA/AGECOOP, 1983.

——*Poèmes africains*, Paris/Toulouse: Centre d'Art National Francais, 1965.

Melville, Pauline: *Shapeshifter* [short stories], London: Women's Press, 1990, Picador, 1991.

——poems in David Dabydeen (ed.), *Rented Rooms*, London, 1989; Ramabai Espinet (ed.), *Creation Fire*, 1990.

Meriwether, Louise: *Daddy Was a Number Runner* [novel], Englewood Cliffs, NJ: Prentice-Hall, 1970; New York: Feminist Press; London: Hodder & Stoughton, 1972.

——*Don't Take the Bus on Monday: The Rosa Parks Story*, Englewood Cliffs, NJ: Prentice-Hall, 1973.

——*The Freedom Ship of Robert Smalls*, Englewood Cliffs, NJ: Prentice-Hall, 1971.

——*The Heart Man: Dr Daniel Hale Williams*, Englewood Cliffs, NJ: Prentice-Hall, 1972.

Mhlope, Gcina: *Have You Seen Zandile?* [play; with Thembi Mtshali and Maralin Vanrenen], London: Methuen, 1991.

——in Oosthuizen (ed.), *Sometimes When It Rains*, London/New York: Pandora, 1987.

Monroe, Mary: *The Upper Room* [novel], New York: St Martin's Press, 1985, Ballantine; London: Allison & Busby, 1986.

Moody, Ann: *Coming of Age in Mississippi* [autobiography], New York: Dial, 1968, Dell, 1970, Camel, 1976.

Mordecai, Pamela: *Journey Poem*, Kingston: Sandberry Press, 1989.

——*Shooting the Waves* [poems].

Morejón, Nancy: *Amor, Ciudad Atribuida* [Love, Attributed City; poems], Havana: El Puente, 1964.

——*Cuaderno de Granada*, Havana: Casa de Las Américas, 1984; trans. Lisa E. Davis, *Grenada Notebook*, New York: Circulo de Cultura Cubana, 1984.

——*Elogio de la danza* [In Praise of Dance; poems], National Autonomous University of Mexico, 1982.

——*Lengua de pájaro* [Bird's Tongue; poems], with Carmen Gonce, Havana, 1971.

——*Mutismos* [Silences; poems], Havana, 1962.

——*Nación y Mestizaje en Nicolás Guillén* [non-fiction], Havana: Ediciones Unión, 1982.

——*Octubre imprescindible* [Essential October; poems], Havana: Ediciones Unión, 1983.

——*Ours the Earth* [poems] trans. J. R. Pereira, Mona, Jamaica: University of West Indies, Institute of Caribbean Studies, Caribbean Writers Series 2, 1990.

——*Parajes de una época* [Parameters of an Epoch; poems], Havana, 1979.

——*Poemas*, National Autonomous University of Mexico, 1980.

——*Recopilación de textos sobre Nicolás Guillén* [criticism], Havana, 1974.

——*Richard trajo su fluta y otras argumentos* [Richard Brought his Flute; poems]. Havana: Instituto del Libro, 1967.

——*Where the Island Sleeps Like a Wing: Selected Poetry*, bilingual, trans. Kathleen Weaver, San Francisco: Black Scholar Press, 1985.

Morrison, Toni: *Beloved* [novel], New York: Alfred A. Knopf; London: Chatto, 1987.

——*The Bluest Eye* [novel], New York: Holt, Rinehart & Winston, 1970, Pocket Books, 1972; London: Chatto, 1981, Triad Grafton, 1987.

——*Jazz* [novel], New York: Knopf, London: Chatto, 1992.

——*Song of Solomon* [novel], New York: Knopf, 1977, New American Library, 1977; London: Chatto, 1978, Triad Grafton, 1987.

——*Sula* [novel], New York: Knopf, 1974, NAL/Plume; London: Chatto, 1980, Triad Grafton, 1982.

——*Tar Baby* [novel], New York: Knopf, NAL; London: Chatto, 1981, Triad Grafton, 1983.

——[Nellie F. McKay (ed.), *Critical Essays on Toni Morrison*, Boston: G. K. Hall, 1988.]

Msham, Mwana Kupona: "Advice of Mwana Kupona Upon the Wifely Duty" (trans. Alice Werner; Azania Press, 1932) in Elspeth Huxley, *Nine Faces Of Kenya*, London: Collins Harvill, 1990.

Mūgo, Mīcere Gīthae: *Daughter of My People, Sing!* [poems], Nairobi: East African Literature Bureau, 1976.

——*The Long Illness of Ex-Chief Kiti* [play], Nairobi: East African Literature Bureau, 1976.

——*A New Approach to the Teaching of Literature in Schools in Kenya* [non-fiction], with L. Wasambo Were, Nairobi: East African Publishing House.

——*The Trial of Dedan Kimathi* [play], with Ngugi wa Thiong'o, Nairobi/London: Heinemann Educational Books, 1976.

——*Visions of Africa: The Fiction of Chinua Achebe, Margaret Laurence, Elspeth Huxley, Ngugi wa Thiong'o* [criticism], Nairobi: Kenya Literature Bureau, 1978.

Murray, Pauli: *"All For Mr Davis": The Story of Sharecropper Odell Waller* [non-fiction], New York: Workers Defense League, 1942.

——*The Autobiography of a Black Activist, Feminist, Lawyer, Priest, and Poet* [formerly *Song in a Weary Throat: An American Pilgrimage*, New York: Harper & Row, 1978, 1982; autobiography], Knoxville: University of Tennessee Press, 1989.

——*Dark Testament and Other Poems*, Norwalk, Conn.: Silvermine, 1970.

——*Proud Shoes: The Story of an American Family* [non-fiction], New York: Harper & Brothers, 1956, 1978, Perennial Library, 1987.

Naylor, Gloria: *Linden Hills* [novel], New York: Ticknor & Fields, 1985; London: Hodder & Stoughton, 1985, Methuen, 1986.

——*Mama Day* [novel], New York: Ticknor & Fields, 1988, Vintage Contemporaries, 1989; London: Hutchinson, 1988.

——*The Women of Brewster Place: A Novel in Seven Stories*, New York: Viking Penguin, 1982; London: Hodder & Stoughton, 1983, Methuen, 1987.

Ndaaya, Citèkù: in Cosman *et al.* (eds), *Penguin Book of Women Poets*, Harmondsworth: Penguin, 1978.

Ngcobo, Lauretta: *And They Didn't Die* [novel], London: Virago, 1990; New York: Braziller, 1991.

——*Cross of Gold* [novel], London: Longman, 1981.

Nichols, Grace: in *A Dangerous Knowing: Four Black Women Poets*, London: Sheba, 1985.

——*Baby Fish and Other Stories from Village to Rain Forest* [for children], London: Nanny Books, 1983.

——*Can I Buy a Slice of Sky?* [children's poems].

——*Come On Into My Tropical Garden: Poems for Children*, London: A. & C. Black, 1988.

——*The Fat Black Woman's Poems*, London: Virago, 1984.

——*i is a long-memoried woman* [poems], London: Karnak House, 1983.

——*Lazy Thoughts of a Lazy Woman* [poems], London: Virago, 1989.

——*Leslyn in London* [for children], London: Hodder & Stoughton, 1984.

——*Poetry Jump Up*, Harmondsworth: Penguin, 1989.

——*Trust You, Wriggly* [for children], London: Hodder & Stoughton, 1981.

——*Whole of a Morning Sky* [novel], London: Virago, 1986.

——*A Wilful Daughter* [for children], London: Hodder & Stoughton, 1983.

Nisa: Marjorie Shostak, *Nisa: The Life and Words of a !Kung Woman*, New Haven: Harvard University Press, 1981; London: Allen Lane, 1982, Earthscan, 1990.

Njau, Rebeka: *The Hypocrite* [short stories], Nairobi: Uzima Press, 1977, 1980.

——*Kenyan Women Heroes and Their Mystical Power*, Vol. 1 with Gideon Malaki, Nairobi: Risk Publications, 1984.

——*Ripples in the Pool* [novel], Nairobi: Transafrica Publishers, 1975; London: Heinemann Educational Books, African Writers Series 203, 1978.

——*The Scar: A Tragedy in One Act* [play], Moshi, Tanzania: Kibo Art Gallery, 1965.

Nwapa, Flora: The Adventures of Deke [for children], Enugu: Flora Nwapa Co., 1980.

——*Cassava Song and Rice Song* [poems], Enugu, Nigeria: Tana Press, 1986.

——*Efuru* [novel], London: Heinemann Educational Books, 1966.

——*Emeka, Driver's Guard* [for children], London: University of London, 1972.

——*Idu* [novel], London: Heinemann Educational Books, 1969.

——*Journey to Space* [for children], Enugu: Flora Nwapa Co., 1980.

——*Mammy Water* [for children], Enugu: Flora Nwapa Co., 1979.

——*The Miracle Kittens* [for children], Enugu: Flora Nwapa Co., 1980.

——*My Animal Colouring Book* [for children], Enugu: Flora Nwapa Co., 1979.

——*My Animal Numbering Book*, [for children], Enugu: Flora Nwapa Co., 1981.

——*My Tana Alphabet Book* [for children], Enugu: Flora Nwapa Co., 1981.

——*My Tana Colouring Book* [for children], Enugu: Flora Nwapa Co., 1979.

——*Never Again* [novel], Enugu: Tana Press, 1975, Nwamife Publishers, 1976.

——*One is Enough* [novel], Enugu: Flora Nwapa Co., 1981, Tana Press, 1984.

——*This is Lagos and Other Stories* [short stories], Enugu: Nwamife, 1971.

——*Wives at War and Other Stories* [short stories], Enugu: Nwamife, 1980, Flora Nwapa Co./Tana Press, 1984.

——*Women Are Different* [novel], Enugu: Tana Press, 1986.

——[Anna Githaiga, *Notes on Flora Nwapa's "Efuru"*, Nairobi: Heinemann Educational Books, 1979.]

Nzenza, Sekai: *Zimbabwean Woman: My Own Story* [autobiography], London: Karia Press, 1988.

Ogot, Grace: *The Graduate* [novel], Nairobi: Uzima Press, 1980.

——*The Island of Tears* [short stories], Nairobi: Uzima Press, 1980.

——*Land Without Thunder* [short stories], Nairobi: East African Publishing House, 1968.

——*The Other Woman and Other Stories* [short stories], Nairobi: Transafrica, 1976.

——*The Promised Land* [novel], Nairobi: East African Publishing House, 1966.

——*The Strange Bride* [folklore; originally published in Dholuo as *Miaha*, 1983], Nairobi: Heinemann Kenya, 1989.

Ogundipe-Leslie, 'Molara: *Sew the Old Days and Other Poems*, Ibadan, Nigeria: Evans Bros, 1986.

Opitz, May: autobiography in Oguntoye *et al.* (eds), *Farbe bekennen*, Berlin: Orlanda, 1986; trans. Anne V. Adams as *Showing Our True Color*, Amherst: University of Massachusetts Press, 1992; London: Open Letters, 1992.

Patrick Jones, Marion: *J'Ouvert Morning* [novel], Port of Spain: Columbus Publishers, 1976.

——*Pan-Beat* [novel], Port of Spain: Columbus Publishers, 1973.

Pearse, Gabriela: poems in Da Choong *et al.* (eds), *Black Women Talk Poetry*, London: Black Womantalk, 1987.

Petry, Ann: *Country Place* [novel], Boston: Houghton Mifflin, 1947; London: Michael Joseph, 1948; Chatham, NJ: Chatham Bookseller, 1971.

——*The Drugstore Cat* [for children; illus Susanne Suba], New York: Crowell, 1949; Boston: Beacon, 1988.

——*Harriet Tubman, Conductor on the Underground Railroad* [non-fiction], New York: Crowell, 1955; as *The Girl Called Moses: The Story of Harriet Tubman*, London: Methuen, 1960.

——*Legends of the Saints* [fiction; illus. Anne Rockwell], New York: Crowell, 1970.

——*Miss Muriel and Other Stories* [short stories], Boston: Houghton Mifflin, 1971.

——*The Narrows*, [novel], Boston: Houghton Mifflin, 1953; London: Gollancz, 1954, Ace, 1961; intr. Nellie Y. McKay, Boston: Beacon Press, 1988.

——*The Street* [novel], Boston: Houghton Mifflin, 1946; New York: Pyramid, 1961; Boston: Beacon Press, 1985; London: Michael Joseph, 1947; Ace Books, 1958; Virago, 1988.

——*Tituba of Salem Village* [non-fiction], New York: Crowell, 1964; Harper Trophy, 1991.

Philip, Marlene Nourbese: *Harriet's Daughter* [novel], London: Heinemann International, 1988; Toronto: Women's Press, 1989.

——*Salmon Courage* [poems], Toronto: Williams-Wallace, 1983.

——*She Tries Her Tongue, Her Silence Softly Breaks* [essay and poems], Charlottetown, Canada: Ragweed Press, 1989.

——*Thorns* [poems], Toronto: Williams-Wallace, 1980.

Phillips, J. J.: *Mojo Hand: An Orphic Tale* [novel], New York: Trident Press/Simon & Schuster, 1966; City Miner Books, 1985; London: Serpent's Tail, 1987.

Plato, Ann: *Essays: Including Biographies and Miscellaneous Pieces in Prose and Poetry*, Hartford: author, 1841; intr. Kenny J. Williams, New York/Oxford: Oxford University Press, Schomburg Library of NIneteenth-Century Black Women Writers, 1988.

——*Poems*, South Carolina, 1834.

Pollard, Velma: *Considering Woman* [short stories], London: Women's Press, 1989.

——*Crown Point and Other Poems*, Leeds: Peepal Tree Press, 1988.

——*Shame Trees Don't Grow Here* [poems]. Leeds: Peepal Tree Press, 1991.

Prescod, Marsha: *Land of Rope and Tory* [poems], London: Akira Press, 1985.

Prince, Mary: *The History of Mary Prince, a West Indian Slave, Related by Herself* [autobiography]. London: F. Westley & A. H. Davis/Edinburgh: Waugh & Innes, 1831; London: Pandora, 1987; in *Six Women's Slave Narratives*, ed./intr. William L. Andrews, New York/Oxford: Oxford University Press, Schomburg Library of Nineteenth-Century Black Women Writers, 1988.

Prince, Nancy: *A Narrative of the Life and Travels of Mrs Nancy Prince. Written by Herself* [autobiography], Boston: author, 1850; 1853; 1856; intr. William L. Andrews, in *Six Women's Slave Narratives*, New York/Oxford: Oxford University Press, Schomburg Library of Nineteenth-Century Black Women Writers, 1988; as *A Black Woman's Odyssey Through Russia and Jamaica*, intr. Ronald G. Walters, Markus Wiener, 1990.

——*The West Indies: Being a Description of the Islands, progress of Christianity, Educ. and Liberty among the Colored Population Generally* [non-fiction], Boston: Dow & Jackson Printers, 1841.

Queen of Sheba: "On the wisdom of Solomon", trans. Sir E. A. Wallis Budge in *The Queen of Sheba and her Only Son, Menyelek*, London/Liverpool/Boston: Medici Society, 1922.

Qunta, Christine Douts: *Heroes and Other Treasures* [poems], Johannesburg: Seriti Sa Sechaba, 1990.

——*Hoyi Na! Azania: Poems of an African Struggle*, New South Wales, Australia: Marimba Enterprises, 1979.

Riley, Joan: *A Kindness to the Children* [novel], forthcoming.

——*Romance* [novel], London: Women's Press, 1988.

——*The Unbelonging* [novel], London: Women's Press, 1985.

——*Waiting in the Twilight* [novel], London: Women's Press, 1987.

Rodgers, Carolyn: *For Flip Wilson* [poems], Detroit: Broadside Press, 1971.

——*For H. W. Fuller* [poems], 1970.

——*The Heart as Ever Green* [poems], Garden City, NY: Doubleday/Anchor, 1978.

——*How I Got Ovah* [poems], New York: Doubleday, 1971.

——*Long Rap/Commonly Known as a Poetic Essay*, Detroit: Broadside Press, 1971.

——*Now Ain't That Love*, Detroit: Broadside Press, 1970.

——*Paper Soul* [poems], Chicago: Third World Press, 1969.

——*Songs of a Black Bird* [poems], Chicago: Third World Press, 1969.

Roemer, Astrid: *Alarm Ach Alarm* [play], Haarlem: In der Knipscheer, 1984.

——*De Buiksluiter* [radio play], Haarlem: In de Knipscheer, 1981.

——*Eeen Nati Bot Uit!* [radio play], Haarlem: In der Knipscheer, 1982.

——*Levenslang gedicht* [Life-long poem; novel], Haarlem: In der Knipscheer, 1987; as *Een naam voor de liefde*, Amsterdam: Rainbow Pocketboek, 1990; trans. Rita Gircour as *A Name For Love*, MS.

——*Liederatuur* [poems], Haarlem: In der Knipscheer, 1985.

——*Lijf Eigenen* [play], Haarlem: In der Knipscheer, 1984.

——*Neem mij terug, Suriname* [Take me back, Surinam; novel], author, 1974.

——*Nergens, ergens* [Nowhere, somewhere; novel], Haarlem: In der Knipscheer, 1983; Amsterdam: Rainbow, 1987.

——*Over de gekte van een vrouw* [About a woman's madness; novel], Haarlem: In der Knipscheer, 1982; Amsterdam, Rainbow.

——*Paramaribo! Paramaribo!* [play], Haarlem: In der Knipscheer, 1982.

——*Sasa, Mijn actuele zijn* [poems], Paramaribo, Surinam: Eldorado, 1970.

——*Schoon en Schofterig* [novel], Haarlem: In der Knipscheer, 1985.

——*Waarom de Rivier Zo Nat Is* [play], Haarlem: In der Knipscheer, 1984.

——*Waaram zou je huilen, mijn lieve lieve* [Why should you cry, my darling darling], 1976.

——*De Wereld heeft gesicht verloren* [The world has lost face; novel], 1975.

——*De Zak van Santa Claus* [play], Haarlem: In der Knipscheer, 1983.

Rojas Rodriguez, Marta: *El Aula verde* [The Green Classroom; non-fiction], Havana, 1981.

——*El Columpio de Rey Spencer* [Rey Spencer's Swing; novel], MS, 1990.

——*La Cueva del Muerto* [Dead Man's Cave; novel], Havana: Ediciones Union, 1983, José Martí Publishers, 1989.

——*Escenas de Viet Nam* [Vietnam Scenes; non-fiction], Havana, 1969.

——*El Juicio del Moncada* [The Moncada Trial; non-fiction], Havana: Ediciones R, 1964, Scientias Sociales, 1988.

——*El Médico de la familia* [Family Doctor non-fiction], Havana, 1986.

——*El Que debe vivir* [Right to Live; non-fiction], Havana, Casa de las Américas, 1978.

——*Relatos de Viet Nam del Sur* [Reports from South Vietnam; non-fiction], Havana: Editorial Instituto del Libro, 1976.

——*Tania, la guerrillera inolvidable* [non-fiction], Havana, 1974; trans. *Tania, the Unforgettable Guerrilla*, New York: Random House, Ocean Press.

Roy, Lucinda: *Wailing the Dead to Sleep* [poems], London: Bogle-L'Ouverture, 1988.

Rudet, Jacqueline: *Basin*, in Yvonne Brewster (ed.), *Black Plays*, London: Methuen, 1987.

——*Money To Live*, in Mary Remnant (ed.), *Plays by Women: 5*, London: Methuen, 1987.

Rungano, Kristina: *A Storm is Brewing* [poems], Harare: Zimbabwe Publishing House, 1984.

Russell, Sandi: "Sister" in Kitty Fitzgerald (ed.), *Iron Women: New Stories by Women*, North Shields: Iron Press, 1990.

Sanchez, Sonia: *The Adventures of Small Head, Square Head and Fathead* [for children], New York: Third Press/Joseph Okpaku Publishing Co., 1973.

——*A Blues Book for Blue Black Magical Women* [poems], Detroit: Broadside Press, 1974.

——*The Bronx Is Next* [play], in *Tulane Drama Review* 12 (Summer 1968); in Davis and Redding (eds), *Cavalcade*, Boston: Houghton Mifflin, 1971.

——*Crisis in Culture: Two Speeches by Sonia Sanchez*, New York: Black Liberation Press, 1983.

——*Generations: Selected Poems*, London: Karnak House, 1986.

——*Homecoming* [poems], Detroit: Broadside Press, 1970.

——*Homegirls and Handgrenades: Poetry and Prose*, New York/Chicago: Thunder's Mouth Press, 1984.

——*It's a New Day: Poems for Young Brothas and Sisthus*, Detroit: Broadside Press, 1971.

——*I've Been a Woman: New and Selected Poems*, Sausalito, Ca: Black Scholar Press.

——*Love Poems*, New York: Third Press, 1973.

——*Sister Son/ji* [play], in Ed Bullins (ed.), *New Plays from the Black Theatre*, New York: Bantam, 1969.

——*A Sound Testament and Other Stories* [for children; illus. Larry Crowe], Chicago: Third World Press, 1980.

——*Uh, Uh, But How Do It Free Us?* [play], in *The New Lafayette Theatre Presents: Plays with Aesthetic Comments by 6 Black Playwrights*, New York: Doubleday/Anchor, 1974.

——*Under a Soprano Sky* [poems], Trenton, NJ: Africa World Press, 1987.

——*We a BaddDDD People* [poems], Detroit: Broadside Press, 1970.

Schwarz-Bart, Simone: *Between Two Worlds*, New York: Harper & Row, 1981.

——*Un Plat de porc aux bananes vertes* [with André Schwarz-Bart; novel], Paris: Seuil, 1967.

——*Pluie et vent sur Télumée-Miracle* [novel], Paris: Seuil, 1972; trans. Barbara Bray as *The Bridge of Beyond*, New York: Atheneum, 1974; London: Gollancz, 1975; intr. Bridget Jones, London: Heinemann Educational Books, Caribbean Writers Series, 1982.

——*Ti Jean L'horizon* (novel], Paris: Seuil, 1979 trans. Barbara Blay, *Between Two Worlds*, New York: Harper & Row, 1981; Oxford: Heinemann International 1992.

——*Ton Beau Capitaine* [play], Paris: Seuil, 1987.

——[Fanta Toureh, *L'Imaginaire dans l'oeuvre de Simone Schwarz-Bart: Approche d'une mythologie antillaise*, Paris: Harmattan, 1987.]

Seacole, Mary: *Wonderful Adventures of Mrs Seacole in Many Lands* [autobiography], ed. W. J. S., London: James Blackwood, 1857; ed. Ziggi Alexander and Audrey Dewjee, Bristol: Falling Wall Press, 1984; intr. William L. Andrews, New York/Oxford: Oxford University Press, Schomburg Library of Nineteenth-Century Black Women Writers, 1988; as *Jamaican Nightingale: The Wonderful Adventures of Mary Seacole in Many Lands*, ed. George Cadogan, Ontario: Williams-Wallace Publishers.

——[Ziggi Alexander and Audrey Dewjee, *Mary Seacole: Jamaican National Heroine and "Doctress" in the Crimean War*, London: Brent Library Service, 1982.]

Segun, Mabel: *Conflict and Other Poems*, Ibadan: New Horn Press, 1987.

——*Friends, Nigerians, Countrymen* [prose], Ibadan: Oxford University Press, 1977; as *Sorry, No Vacancy*, Ibadan: University Press, 1985.

——*My Father's Daughter* [for children], Lagos: African Universities Press, 1965.

——*Olu and the Broken Statue* [for children], Ibadan: New Horn, 1985.

——*Under the Mango Tree: Songs and Poems for Primary Schools, Books 1 & 2* [ed. with Neville Grant], Longman, 1980.

——*Youth Day Parade*, Ibadan: Daystar Press, 1984.

Senior, Olive: *Arrival of the Snake Woman and Other Stories*, Harlow, Essex: Longman, 1989.

——*A-Z of Jamaican Heritage*, Kingston: Heinemann/Gleaner, 1983.

——*Discerner of Hearts* [short stories], forthcoming.

——*Grandfather Never Danced the Tango* [novel], forthcoming.

——*The Message is Change*, Kingston: Kingston Publishers, 1972.

——*Summer Lightning and Other Stories* [short stories], Harlow, Essex: Longman, 1986.

——*Talking of Trees* [poems], Kingston: Calabash Press, 1985.

——*Working Miracles: Lives of Caribbean Women* [non-fiction], London: James Currey, 1991.

September, Dulcie: stories in Mabuza (ed.), *One Never Knows*, 1989.

Shange, Ntozake: *Betsey Brown: A Novel*, New York: St Martin's Press, 1985; London: Methuen, 1985.

——*Boogie Woogie Landscapes* [play], 1978.

——*A Daughter's Geography* [poems], New York: St Martin's Press, 1983: London: Methuen, 1985.

——*For colored girls who have considered suicide/ when the rainbow is enuf* [choreopoem] New York: Macmillan, 1977; London: Eyre Methuen, 1978; new edn, with *spell #7*, London: Methuen Drama, 1990.

——*From Okra to Greens/a Different Kinda Love Story* [play], New York: Samuel French, 1983.

——*The Love Space Demands (a continuing saga)* [poems], New York: St Martin's Press, 1991.

——*Nappy Edges* [poems], New York: St Martin's, 1978; London: Methuen, 1987.

——*Natural Disasters and Other Festive Occasions*, 1977.

——*A Photograph: A Study of Lovers in Motion*, New York: Samuel French, 1981.

——*Ridin' the Moon in Texas: Word Paintings* [prose/poems], New York: St Martin's Press, 1987.

——*Sassafrass* [novella], San Lorenzo, CA: Shameless Hussy Press, 1976.

——*Sassafrass, Cypress & Indigo* [novel], New York: St Martin's, 1982; London: Methuen, 1983.

——*See No Evil: Prefaces, Essays and Accounts 1976–1983*, San Francisco: Momo's Press, 1984.

——*Spell #7* [play], New York: St Martin's Press, 1981; London: Methuen, 1985; new edn, with *for colored girls. . . .*, London: Methuen Drama, 1990.

——*Three Pieces: Spell #7, A Photograph: Lovers in Motion, Boogie Woogie Landscapes*, New York: St Martin's Press, 1981.

Sie Jalloh, Jenneba: autobiography in Mary Lennon, Marie McAdam, Joanne O'Brien (eds), *Across the Water: Irish Women's Lives in Britain*, London: Virago, 1988.

Sikakane, Joyce: *A Window on Soweto* [autobiography], London: International Defence and Aid Fund for Southern Africa, 1977.

Sofola, Zulu: *The Deer Hunter and the Hunter's Pearl* [plays], London: Evans Bros, 1969.

——*The Disturbed Peace of Christmas* [play], Ibadan: Daystar, 1971.

——*King Emene: Tragedy of a Rebellion* [play], London: Heinemann Educational Books, 1974.

——*Old Wines Are Tasty* [play], Ibadan: Oxford University Press, 1981.

——*The Sweet Trap* [play], Ibadan: Oxford University Press (Nigeria), 1977.

——*Wedlock of the Gods* [play], Ibadan: Evans, 1972.

——*The Wizard of Law* [play], Ibadan: Evans, 1975.

Sow-Fall, Aminata: *L'Appel des arènes* [novel], Dakar: Nouvelles Éditions Africaines, 1982.

——*L'Ex-Père de la nation* [novel], Paris: Harmattan, 1987.

——*La Grève des Bàttu ou les déchets humains* [novel], Dakar; Nouvelles Éditions Africaines, 1979; trans. Dorothy Blair as *The Beggars' Strike, or the Dregs of Society*, London: Longman, 1981, 1986.

——*Le Revenant*, Dakar: Nouvelles Éditions Africaines, 1976.

Spencer, Anne: poems in Erlene Stetson (ed.), *Black Sister*, Bloomington: Indiana University Press, 1981.

Springer, Eintou Pearl: *Godchild* [poems for children], London: Karia Press, 1987.

——*Out of the Shadows* [poems], London: Karia Press, 1986.

Stewart, Maria W.: *Meditations from the Pen of Mrs Maria Stewart*, Washington, DC: Enterprise Publishing Co., 1879; Garrison & Knopp, 1932; in *Spiritual Narratives*, New York/Oxford: Oxford University Press, Schomburg Library of Nineteenth-Century Black Women Writers, 1988.

——*Maria W. Stewart: America's First Black Woman Political Writer – Essays and Speeches*, ed. Marilyn Richardson, Bloomington: Indiana University Press, 1987.

Sulter, Maude: *As A Blackwoman: Poems 1982–1985*, London: Akira Press, 1985; Hebden Bridge, Yorks: Urban Fox Press, 1990.

——*Calabash of Dreams* [for children], Hebden Bridge, Yorks: Urban Fox Press, 1991.

——*Necropolis* [novel], Hebden Bridge, Yorks: Urban Fox Press, 1991.

——*Zabat: Narratives*, Hebden Bridge, Yorks: Urban Fox Press, 1991.

——*Zabat: Poetics of a Family Tree. Poems 1986–1989*, Hebden Bridge, Yorks: Urban Fox Press, 1989.

Sutherland, Efua: *Anansegoro: Story-Telling Drama in Ghana*, Accra: Afram, 1975.

——*Edufa* [play], London: Longman, 1969; Washington, DC: Three Continents Press, 1979.

——*Foriwa: A Play in Three Acts*, Accra-Tema: Ghana Publishing Corp., 1967.

——*The Marriage of Anansewa* [play], London: Longman, 1977, 1980; Washington, DC: Three Continents Press, 1980.

——*The Marriage of Anansewa/Edufa* [plays; combined edn], Harlow: Longman.

——*Odasani* [play], Accra: Anowuo Educational Publications, 1967.

——*The Original Bob* [play], Accra: Anowuo Educational Publications, 1969.

——*Playtime in Africa* [for children], New York: Atheneum, 1962.

——*The Roadmakers* [for children], London: Newman Neame, 1963.

——*Vulture! Vulture! and Tahina: Two Rhythm Plays*, Tema: Ghana Publishing Corp., 1968.

Tadjo, Véronique: *La Chanson de la vie* [for children], Paris: Hatier, Monde Noir Poche Jeunesse, 1990.

——*Latérite* [poems], Paris: Hatier, Monde Noir Poche, 1984.

——*Lord of the Dance: An African Retelling* [for children], London A. & C. Black, 1988.

——*Le Royaume aveugle* [novel], Paris: L'Harmattan, 1991.

——*À Vol d'oiseau* [As the crow flies; poems], Paris: Fernand Nathan, 1986.

Taylor, Susie King: *Reminiscences of My Life in Camp with the 33rd United States Colored Troops Late 1st SC Volunteers* [autobiography], Boston: author, 1902; intr. Anthony G. Barthelemy in *Collected Black Women's Narratives*, New York/Oxford: Oxford University Press, Schomburg Library of Nineteenth-Century Black Women Writers, 1988; as *Reminiscences of My Life: A Black Woman's Civil War Memoirs*, eds Patricia W. Romero and Willie Lee Rose; New York: Markus Wiener Publishing Co., 1988.

Teodoro, Maria de Lourdes: *Agua-Marinha ou Tempo Sem Palavra* [poems], Brasilia, Brazil, 1978.

Terrell, Mary Church: *A Colored Woman in a White World* [autobiography], Washington, DC: Ransdell Publishing Co., 1940; New York: Arno Press, 1980.

Terry, Lucy: "Bars Fight, August 28, 1746", from *The American Museum or Repository of Ancient and Modern Fugitive Pieces, etc. Prose and Poetical*, vol. I, no. vi (June 1787); in Josiah Gilbert Holland, *History of Massachusetts*, 1855.

Thiam, Awa: *Continents noirs* [non-fiction], Paris: Editions Tiercé, 1987.

——*La Parole aux Négresses* [non-fiction], Paris: Denoël-Gonthier, 1978; as *Black Sisters, Speak Out*, London, Pluto, 1986.

Thomas, Elean: *Before They Can Speak of Flowers: Word Rhythms* [poems/short stories], London: Karia Press, 1988.

——*The Last Room* [novel], London: Virago, 1991.

——*Word Rhythms from the Life of a Woman*, London: Karia Press, 1986.

Tlali, Miriam: *Amandla* [novel], Johannesburg: Ravan Press, 1980; Soweto: author, 1986.

——*Footprints in the Quag* [*Mehlala Khatamping*: short stories], Soweto: author, 1986; Cape Town: David Philip, 1989; as *Soweto Stories*, London: Pandora, 1989.

——*Mihloti* [Tears; short stories], Johannesburg: Skotaville, 1984.

——*Muriel at Metropolitan* [novel], Johannesburg: Ravan, 1975; London: Longman, 1979; Washington, DC: Three Continents, 1979.

Truth, Sojourner: *The Narrative of Sojourner Truth, a Northern Slave, Emancipated from Bodily Servitude by the State of New York, in 1828* [autobiography, written down by Olive Gilbert], Boston: author, 1850, 1875.

——[Jacqueline Bernard, *Journey Toward Freedom: The Story of Sojourner Truth*, New York: Norton, 1967; intr. Nell Irvin Painter, New York: Norton, 1967, Feminist Press, 1990.

——Arthur Huff Fauset, *Sojourner, God's Faithful Pilgrim*, Chapel Hill: University of North Carolina Press, 1938.

——Peter Krass, *Sojourner Truth – Antislavery Activist*, New York: Chelsea House, 1988, Los Angeles: Melrose Square, 1990.

——Janey Weinhold Montgomery, *A Comparative Analysis of the Rhetoric of Two Negro Women Orators: Sojourner Truth and Frances E. Watkins Harper*, Fort Hays, Kans.: Fort Hays Kansas State College, 1968.

——Victoria Oritz, *Sojourner Truth: A Self-Made Woman*, New York: Lippincott, 1974.

——Hertha Pauli, *Her Name Was Sojourner Truth*, New York: Appleton-Century-Crofts, 1962.]

Tubman, Harriet: Sarah H. Bradford, *Harriet, the Moses of Her People*, New York: J. Little & Co., 1886, Corinth Books, 1961.

——Sarah Bradford, *Scenes In the Life of Harriet Tubman*, New York: n.p., 1869.

——Earl Conrad, *Harriet Tubman: Negro Soldier and Abolitionist*, New York: International Publisher, 1942.

——Ann Petry, *Harriet Tubman, Conductor on the Underground Railroad*, New York: Crowell, 1955; as *The Girl Called Moses: The Story of Harriet Tubman*, London: Methuen, 1960.

——Dorothy Sterling, *Freedom Train: The Story of Harriet Tubman*, Garden City, NY: Doubleday, 1954.

Ulasi, Adaora Lily: *The Man from Sagamu* [novel], London: Collins/Fontana, 1978; New York: Collier Macmillan, 1978.

——*Many Thing Begin for Change* [novel], London: Michael Joseph, 1971, Fontana, 1975.

——*Many Thing You No Understand* [novel], London: Michael Joseph, 1970, Fontana, 1973.

——*The Night Harry Died* [novel], Lagos: Research Institute Nigeria, 1974.

——*Who Is Jonah?* [novel], Ibadan: Onibonoje Press, 1978.

Veney, Bethany: *The Narrative of Bethany Veney, a Slave Woman.* [autobiography], Worcester, Mass., 1889; intr. Anthony G. Barthelemy, in

Collected Black Women's Narratives, New York/Oxford University Press, Schomburg Library of Nineteenth-Century Black Women Writers, 1988.

Waciuma, Charity: *Daughter of Mumbi* [autobiography], Nairobi: East African Publishing House, 1969.

——*The Golden Feather* [for children], Nairobi: East African Publishing House, 1966.

——*Merry-Making* [for children], Nairobi: East African Publishing House, 1972.

——*Mweru, the Ostrich Girl* [for children], Nairobi: East African Publishing House, 1966.

——*Who's Calling?* [for children], Nairobi: East African Publishing House, 1973.

Walker, Alice: *The Color Purple* [novel], New York: Harcourt Brace 1982; London: Women's Press, 1983.

——*Five Poems*, Detroit: Broadside Press, 1972.

——*Goodnight, Willie Lee, I'll See You in the Morning: New Poems*, New York: Dial/Harvest/Harcourt Brace, 1975, 1979, 1984; London: Women's Press, 1987.

——*Her Blue Body Everything We Know: Earthling Poems 1965-1990 Complete*, New York, 1991; London: Women's Press, 1991.

——*Horses Make a Landscape Look More Beautiful* [poems], New York: Harcourt Brace, 1984; London: Women's Press, 1985.

——*In Love and Trouble: Stories of Black Women* [short stories], New York: Harcourt Brace, 1967, 1973; London: Women's Press, 1984.

——*In Search of Our Mothers' Gardens: Womanist Prose* [essays], New York: Harcourt Brace, 1983; London: Women's Press, 1984.

——*Langston Hughes, American Poet* [for children], New York: Crowell, 1974.

——*Living by the Word: Collected Writings 1973–1987* [prose], London: Women's Press, 1988.

——*Meridian* [novel], New York: Harcourt Brace, 1976; London: Deutsch, 1976, Women's Press, 1982.

——*Once* [poems], New York: Harcourt Brace, 1968; London: Women's Press, 1986.

——*Possessing the Secret of Joy* [novel], New York: Harper & Row, 1992; London: Jonathan Cape, 1992.

——*Revolutionary Petunias and Other Poems*, New York: Harcourt Brace, 1971, 1973; London: Women's Press, 1988.

——*The Temple of My Familiar* [novel], New York: Harcourt Brace, 1989, Pocket Books, 1991; London: Women's Press, 1989, Penguin, 1990.

——*The Third Life of Grange Copeland* [novel], New York: Harcourt Brace, 1970, Avon, 1971; London: Women's Press, 1985.

——*To Hell With Dying* [for children], New York: Harcourt Brace, 1988.

——*You Can't Keep a Good Woman Down* [short stories], New York: Harcourt Brace, 1981; London: Women's Press, 1982.

——[Harold Bloom (ed.), *Alice Walker: Modern Critical Views*, New York/Philadelphia: Chelsea House Publishers, 1989.

——Louis H. Pratt and Darnell D. Pratt, *Alice Malsenior Walker: An Annotated Bibliography, 1968–1986*, Westport/London: Meckler, 1988.]

Walker, Margaret: *Come Down from Yonder Mountain* [novel], 1962.

——*The Daemonic Genius of Richard Wright* [biography], New York: Amistad, 1988.

——*For My People* [poems], New Haven: Yale University Press, 1942.

——*How I Wrote Jubilee* [essays], Detroit: Broadside Press, 1971.

——*How I Wrote Jubilee and Other Essays on Life and Literature*, ed. Maryemma Graham, New York: Feminist Press, 1990.

——*Jubilee* [novel], Boston: Houghton Mifflin, 1966, Bantam, 1967; London: Star Books, 1978.

——*October Journey* [poems], Detroit: Broadside Press, 1973.

——*A Poetic Equation: Conservations Between Nikki Giovanni and Margaret Walker* [non-fiction], Washington, DC: Howard University Press, 1974.

——*Prophets for a New Day* [poems], Detroit: Broadside Press, 1970.

——*This Is My Century: New and Collected Poems* [poems], Athens, GA/London: University of Georgia Press, 1989.

Wallace, Michele: *Black Macho & the Myth of the Superwoman* [non-fiction], New York: Warner, Dial, 1978; London: Calder, 1979, Verso, revised 1990.

——*Invisibility Blues: From Pop to Theory* [non-fiction], London/New York: Verso, 1990.

Warner-Vieyra, Myriam: *Femmes échouées* [novel], Paris: Présence Africaine, 1988.

——*Juletane* [novel], Paris: Présence Africaine, 1984; London: Heinemann Educational Books, 1987.

——*Le Quinboiseur l'avait dit...* [novel], Paris: Présence Africaine, 1980; trans. Dorothy S. Blair, *As the Sorcerer Said*, London: Longman, 1982.

Wells, Ida B.: *Crusade for Justice: The Autobiography of Ida B. Wells*, ed. Alfreda M. Duster, Chicago/London: University of Chicago Press, 1970, 1972.

——*Mob Rule in New Orleans: Robert Charles and His Fight to the Death* [non-fiction], Chicago: author, 1900.

——*On Lynchings: Southern Horrors; A Red Record; Mob Rule in New Orleans* [non-fiction], New York: Arno Press/New York Times, 1969.

——*The Reason Why: The Colored American is not in the World's Columbian Exposition* [non-fiction], Chicago: author, 1893.

——*A Red Record: Tabulated Statistics and Alleged Causes of Lynchings in the US, 1892–1893–1894* [non-fiction], Chicago: Donohue & Henneberry, 1895; New York: Arno Press, 1971.

——*Southern Horrors: Lynch Law in All Its Phases* [non-fiction], New York: New York Age Print, 1892.

West, Dorothy: *The Living Is Easy* [novel], Boston: Houghton Mifflin, 1948; New York: Arno Press/New York Times, 1969, Feminist Press, 1982; London: Virago, 1987.

Wheatley, Phillis: *A Beautiful Poem on Providence...*, Halifax, 1805.

——*The Collected Works of Phillis Wheatley*, ed. John C. Shields, New York/Oxford: Oxford University Press, Schomburg Library of Nineteenth-Century Black Women Writers, 1988.

——*An elegiac poem, on the death of...George Whitefield...By Phillis, a servant girl, of 17 years of age, belonging to Mr J. Wheatley, of Boston: she has been but 9 years in this country from Africa.*, Boston: Ezekial Russell and John Boyles, 1770.

——*An elegy, sacred to the memory of. . .Dr Samuel Cooper*, Boston: E. Russell, 1784.

——*Liberty and Peace: a poem*, Boston, 1784.

——*Memoir and Poems of Phillis (Wheatley), A Native African and a Slave*, Boston: Geo. W. Light, 1834, Isaac Knapp, 1938.

——*The Poems of Phillis Wheatley*, ed. Julian D. Mason Jr, Chapel Hill/London: University of North Carolina Press, 1966, 1989; *The Poems of Phillis Wheatley, as they were originally published in London, 1773*, Philadelphia: R. R. & C. C. Wright 1909, 1930.

——*Poems on comic, serious and moral subjects*, London, 1787.

——*Poems on Various Subjects, Religious & Moral.*, London, 1773; Philadelphia, 1786, 1787, 1789; Albany, NY, 1793; Walpole, NH, 1802; Hartford, 1804; Halifax, 1813, 1814, 1819; New England, 1816; Denver, 1887.

——[Charles F. Heartman, *Phillis Wheatley (Phillis Peters): A Critical Attempt and a Bibliography of Her Writings*, New York: author, 1915.

——G. Herbert Renfro, *Life and Works of Phillis Wheatley, containing her complete poetical works, numerous letters, and a complete biography of this famous poet of a century and a half ago*, 1916; 1968; Salem, NH: Ayer Co., 1988.

——Merle A. Richmond, *Bid the Vassal Soar: Interpretive Essays on the Life and Poetry of Phillis Wheatley and George Moses Horton*, Washington, DC: Howard University Press, 1974.

——B. B. Thatcher, *Memoir of Philis Wheatley, A Native African and a Slave*, Boston: Geo. W. Wright, 1834.

——William H. Robinson, *Phillis Wheatley in the Black American Beginnings*, Broadside Critics Series no. 5, Detroit: Broadside Press, 1975.

——William H. Robinson, *Phillis Wheatley: a Bio-Bibliography*, Boston: G. K. Hall, 1981.]

Wicomb, Zöe: *You Can't Get Lost in Cape Town* [short stories], London: Virago, 1987.

Williams, Sherley Anne: *Dessa Rose* [novel], New York: Morrow, 1986, Berkley Books, 1987; London: Macmillan, 1987, Futura, 1988.

——*Give Birth to Brightness: A Thematic Study of Neo-Black Literature* [non-fiction], New York: Dial, 1972.

——*The Peacock Poems*, Middletown, Conn.: Wesleyan University Press, 1975, 1977.

——*Someone Sweet Angel Chile* [poems], New York: William Morrow, 1982.

Wilson, Harriet E.: *Our Nig: or, Sketches from the Life of a Free Black, In a Two-Story White House, North. Showing That Slavery's Shadows Fall Even There* [novel], Boston: author, 1859; New York: Random House/Vintage, 1983; London: Allison & Busby, 1984.

Wynter, Sylvia: *The Hills of Hebron: A Jamaica novel*, London: Cape, 1962; Longman, 1984; New York: Simon & Schuster, 1962.

——*Jamaica Is the High of Bolivia*, New York: Vantage Press, 1979.

Bibliography of Further Reading

(including anthologies, with some women contributors named in square brackets)

Abrahams, Roger D., and John F. Szwed, *After Africa: Extracts from British travel accounts and journals of the 17th, 18th and 19th centuries concerning the slaves, their manners and customs in the British West Indies*. Cambridge/London: Harvard University Press, 1983.

Abrash, Barbara (ed.), *Black African Literature in English, Since 1952: Works and Criticism*, New York: Johnson Reprint Corp., 1967.

Abdul, Raoul (ed.), *The Magic of Black Poetry*, New York: Dodd, Mead, c. 1972. [Gwendolyn Brooks, Jackie Earley, Mari Evans, Saundra Sharp]

Achebe, Chinua, *The Insider: Stories of War and Peace from Nigeria*, Enugu: Nwamife Publishers, 1971. [Flora Nwapa]

Achebe, Chinua, and C. L. Innes (eds), *African Short Stories*, London: Heinemann Educational Books, 1985. [Ama Ata Aidoo, Bessie Head, Grace Ogot, Alifa Rifaat]

——, *The Heinemann Book of Contemporary African Short Stories*, London/Portsmouth, NH: Heinemann Educational Books, 1992. [Assia Djebar, Saida Herzi, Lindiwe Mabuza]

Adams, William (ed.), *Afro-American Authors*, Boston: Houghton-Mifflin, 1972. [Gwendolyn Brooks]

Addai-Sebo, Akyaaba, and Ansel Wong (eds), *Our History: A Handbook of African History and Contemporary Issues*, London: London Strategic Policy Unit, 1988.

Ademola, Frances (ed.), *Reflections: Nigerian Prose and Verse*, preface Ezekiel Mphahlele; Lagos: African Universities Press, 1962; intr. Nnamdi Azikiwe, 1965. [Mabel Segun]

Adoff, Arnold (ed.), *Black Out Loud: An Anthology of Modern Poems by Black Americans*, New York: Macmillan, 1969. [Gwendolyn Brooks, Kattie M. Cumbo, Mari E. Evans, Nikki Giovanni, Mae Jackson, Alicia Loy Johnson, Sonia Sanchez]

——(ed.), *Brothers and Sisters: Modern Stories by Black Americans*, New York: Macmillan, 1970. [Gwendolyn Brooks, Eugenia Collier, Pearl Crayton, Nikki Giovanni, Diane Oliver, Carolyn M. Rodgers]

——(ed.), *I Am the Darker Brother: An Anthology of Modern Poems by Negro Americans*, New York: Macmillan, 1968. [Mari Evans, Georgia Love, Margaret Walker]

——(ed.), *The Poetry of Black America: Anthology of the Twentieth Century*, intr. Gwendolyn Brooks; New York: Harper & Row, 1976. [Nanina Alba, Johari Amini, Gwendolyn B. Bennett, Gwendolyn Brooks, Carole Gregory Clemmons, Lucille Clifton, Jayne Cortez, Margaret Danner, Clarissa Scott Delany, Mari E. Evans, Sarah Webster Fabio, Jessie Redmon Fauset, Julia Fields, Carol Freeman, Nikki Giovanni, Angelina Weld Grimké, Mae Jackson, Georgia Douglas Johnson, Helene Johnson, June Jordan, Bette Dulcie Latimer, Elouise Loftin, Pearl Cleage Lomax, Audre Lorde, Naomi Long Madgett, Barbara Mahone, Pauli Murray, Effie Lee Newsome, Gloria Oden, Julianne Perry, Quandra Prettyman, Carolyn M. Rodgers, Sonia Sanchez, Anne Spencer, Alice Walker, Margaret Walker]

Agetua, John (ed.), *Interviews with Six Nigerian Writers*, Benin City: Bendel Newspapers Corporation, 1976. [Flora Nwakuche (Nwapa)]

Albrecht, Lisa, and Rose M. Brewer (eds), *Bridges of Power: Women's Multicultural Alliances*, Santa Cruz, CA: New Society, 1991, [Gloria Anzaldúa, Audre Lorde]

Alibar, France, and Pierrette Lembeye-Boy, *Le Couteau seul... (Sé Kouto sèl...): La condition féminine aux Antilles*, 2 vols, Paris: Editions Caribéennes, 1981.

Alkalimat, Abdul, and associates, *Introduction to Afro-American Studies: A People's College Primer*, Chicago: Twenty-first Century Books, 1973.

Allen, Samuel (ed.), *Poems from Africa*, New York: Thomas Y. Crowell, 1973. [Ama Ata Aidoo, Mabel Segun]

Amateshe, A. D. (ed.), *An Anthology of East African Poetry*, Harlow, Essex: Longman, 1988. [Philippa Namutebi Barlow, Lillian Ingonga, Micere Githae Mugo]

Ambrose, Amanda (ed.), *My Name Is Black: An Anthology of Black Poets*, New York: Scholastic Book Service, 1973. [Amanda Ambrose, Fanny Berry, Gwendolyn Brooks, Mari E. Evans, Nikki Giovanni, Angelina Weld Grimké, Helene Johnson, Audre Lorde, Susie Melton, Pauli Murray, Sharon Porter, Blossom Powe, Kathy Sterling, Kathy Weathers, Lula Lowe Weedon, Millie Williams]

Amos, Valerie, Gail Lewis, Amina Mama and Pratibha Parmar (eds), *Many Voices, One Chant: Black Feminist Perspectives, Feminist Review* 17 (Autumn 1984).

Amosu, Margaret (ed.), *Creative African Writing in the European Languages: A Preliminary Bibliography*, Ibadan: Institute of African Studies, University of Ibadan, African Notes Bulletin Special Supplement, 1964.

Andreski, Iris (comp.), *Old Wives Tales: Life Stories of African Women*, New York: Schocken, 1971.

Andrew, Natalie Charles, *Fanm Kouway: Profiles of Seven Rural Women in Dominica's Development*, Roseau: Small Projects Assistance Team, 1990.

Andrews, William L. (ed.), "Annotated Bibliography of Afro-American Biography, Beginnings to 1930", *Resources for American Literary Study* 12:2 (Autumn 1985), pp. 119–33.

——, *Sisters of the Spirit: Three Black Women's Autobiographies of the Nineteenth Century*, Bloomington: Indiana University Press, 1986. [Zilpha Elaw, Julia Foote, Jarena Lee]

——(ed.), *Six Women's Slave Narratives*, Oxford/New York: Oxford University Press, Schomburg Library of Nineteenth-Century Black Women Writers, 1988. [Mary Prince, Mattie J. Jackson, Old Elizabeth, Lucy A. Delaney, Kate Drumgoold, Annie L. Burton]

——, *To Tell a True Story: The First Century of Afro-American Autobiography, 1760–1865*, Urbana/Chicago: University of Illinois Press, 1988.

Andrzejewski, B. W., and I. M. Lewis, *Somali Poetry: An Introduction*, Oxford: Clarendon Press, 1965.

Andrzejewski, B. W., S. Pitaszewicz and W. Tyloch, *Literatures in African Languages:* Theoretical Issues and Sample Surveys, Cambridge University Press, 1985.

Angoff, Charles, and John Povey (eds), *African Writing Today*, New York: Manyland Books, 1969. [Ama Ata Aidoo]

Anstey, Roger T., *The Atlantic Slave Trade and British Abolition, 1760–1810*, London: Macmillan, 1975; Atlantic Heights, NJ: Humanities Press, 1975.

Anyidoho, Kofi, Peter Porter and Musaemura Zimunya (eds), *The Fate of Vultures: New Poetry from Africa, London: Heinemann International, 1989. [Ama Asantewa Ababio, Beverley Jensen, Valerie Nkomeshya, Felicity Atuki Okoth, Gloria Sandak-Lewin]*

Anzaldúa, Gloria (ed.), *Making Face, Making Soul: Hacienda Caras. Creative and Critical Perspectives by Women of Color*, San Francisco: Aunt Lute Foundation, 1990. [Opal Palmer Adisa, Norma Alarcón, Paula Gunn Allen, Siu Wai Anderson, Judith Francisca Baca, Beth Brant, Anne Mi Ok Bruining, Andrea R. Canaan, Lynn Weber Cannon, Lorna Dee Cervantes, Sucheng Chan, Barbara Christian, Chrystos, Sandra Cisneros, Michelle Cliff, Nora Cobb, Judith Ortiz Cofer, Elena Tajima Creef, Julia De Burgos, Bonnie Thornton Dill, Edna Escamill, Gisele Fong, Jewelle L. Gomez, Janice Gould, Joy Hrjo, Virginia R. Harris, Elizabeth Higginbotham, Bell Hooks, June Jordan, Rosemary Cho Leyson, Audre Lorde, María C. Lugones, Lynda Marín, Trinh T. Minh-Ha, Janice Mirikitani, Papusa Molina, Pat Mora, Cherrie Moraga, Carmen Morones, Laura Munter-Orabona, Ekua Omosupe, Trinity A. Ordoña, Pat Parker, Kit Yuen Quan, Tey Diana Rebolledo, Catalina Rios, Barbara Ruth, Elba Rosario Sánchez, Chela Sandoval, Barbara Smith, Aleticia Tijerina, Lynet Uttal, Helena María Viramontes, Alice Walker, Anne Waters, Shirley Hill Witt (Akwesasne Mohawk), Mitsuye Yamada, Gloria Jennifer Jackson Yamato, Canéla Jaramillo, Alice Walker, Anne Waters, Shirley Hill Witt (Akwesasne Mohawk), Mitsuye Yamada, Bernice Zamora, Maxine Baca Zinn, Kristal Brent Zook]

Anzaldúa, Gloria, and Cherrie Moraga (eds), *This Bridge Called My Back: Writings by Radical Women of Color*, foreword Toni Cade Bambara; Watertown, Mass.: Persephone, 1981; Latham, NY: Kitchen Table Press, 1983. [Norma Alarcón, Barbara M. Cameron, Andrea Canaan, Jo Carillo, Chrystos, Cheryl Clarke, Gabrielle Daniels, doris juanita davenport, hattie gossett, mary hope lee, Audre Lorde, Aurora Levina Morales, Rosario Morales, Naomi Littlebear Morena, Pat Parker, Mirtha Quintanales, Donna Kate Rushin, Barbara Smith, Beverly Smith, Luisah Teish]

Aptheker, Bettina (ed.), *Women's Legacy: Essays on Race, Sex, and Class in American History*, Amherst: University of Massachusetts Press, 1982.

Aptheker, Herbert (ed.), *A Documentary History of the Negro People in the United States. Vol. 1: From the Colonial Times through the Civil War. Vol. 2: From the Reconstruction to the Founding of the NAACP*, New York: Citadel Press/Carol Publishing Group, 1951. [Harriet Tubman, Ida B. Wells-Barnett]

Arkin, Marian, and Barbara Shollar (eds), *Longman Anthology of World Literature by Women, 1875–1975*, New York/London: Longman, 1989. [Ama Ata Aidoo, Nawal al-Saadawi, Louise Bennett, Gwendolyn Brooks, Lydia Cabrera, Andrée Chedid, Nafissatou Diallo, Assia Djebar, Patricia Grace, Bessie Head, Zora Neale Hurston, Gayle Jones, Nella Larsen, Carolina Maria de Jesus, Annette M'Baye d'Erneville, Nancy Morejón, Efua Sutherland, Alice Walker, Kath Walker, Sherley Anne Williams]

Ascher, Carol, Louise DeSalvo and Sara Ruddick (eds), *Between Women: Biographers, Novelists, Critics, Teachers and Artists Write About Their Work on Women*, Boston: Beacon Press, 1984. [Michelle Cliff, Gloria Hull, Erlene Stetson]

Ashcroft, B. Griffiths, and H. Tiffin, *The Empire Writes Back: Theory and practice in post-colonial literatures.*

Awkward, Michael, *Inspiriting Influences: Tradition, Revision, and Afro-American Women's Novels*, New York: Columbia University Press, 1989.

Awoonor, Kofi, and G. Adali-Mortty (eds), *Messages: Poems from Ghana*, London: Heinemann Educational Books, African Writers Series 42, 1971. [Efua Sutherland]

Baker, Houston A., Jr (ed.), *Black Literature in America*, New York: McGraw-Hill, 1971.

——, *Blues, Ideology, and Afro-American Literature*, Chicago: University of Chicago Press, 1984.

——(ed.), *Reading Black: Essays in the Criticism of African, Caribbean and Black American Literature*, Cornell University, 1976.

——, *Workings of the Spirit: The Poetics of Afro-American Women's Writing*, phototext by Elizabeth Alexander and Patricia Redmond, Chicago: University of Chicago Press, Black Literature and Culture Series, 1991.

Bankier, Joana, Carol Cosman, Doris Earnshaw, Jean Keefe, Deirdre Lashgari, Kathleen Weaver (eds), *The Other Voice: Twentieth-Century Women's Poetry in Translation*, foreword Adrienne Rich; New York: Norton, 1976. [Noémia de Sousa, Alda do Espírito Santo, Gertrudis Gomez de Avellaneda, Caroline Khaketla, Nancy Morejón, Mririda n'Ait Attik]

Bankier, Joana, and Deirdre Lashgari (eds), *Women Poets of the World*, New York: Macmillan, 1983. [Andrée Chédid, Leila Djabali, Alda do Espírito Santo, Hatshepsut, Minji Karibo, Lindiwe Mabuza, Maria Margarido, Stella Ngatho, Dorothy Obi]

Banks-Henries, A. Doris (ed.), *Poems of Liberia (1836–1961)*, London: Macmillan, 1963. [Rebecca J. N. Ware, Beverley Wilson]

Baraka, Amina, and Amiri Baraka (eds), *Confirmation: An Anthology of African-American Women*, New York: Morrow, 1983. [Janus Adams, Fatimah Afif, Fayola Kamaria Ama, Johari Amini, Maya Angelou, Toni Cade Bambara, Amina Baraka, Gwendolyn Connor Bey, Gwendolyn Brooks, Lucille Clifton, Jayne Cortez, Alexis De Veaux, Y. W. Easton, Mari Evans, Lois Elaine Griffith,

Nikki Grimes, Safiya Henderson, Akua Lezli Hope, Mariah Britton Howard, Lateifa-Ramona Lahleet Hyman, Adrienne Ingrum, Rashidah Ismaili, Mae Jackson, Gayl Jones, Anasa Jordan, June Jordan, Abbey Lincoln, Audre Lorde, Esther Louise, Paule Marshall, Malkia M'buzi, Rosemari Mealy, Louise Meriwether, Toni Morrison, Margaret Porter, Aishah Rahman, Faith Ringgold, Carolyn M. Rodgers, Sandra Rogers, Sonia Sanchez, Judy Dothard Simmons, Vértàmàè Smart-Grosvenor, Eleanor Traylor, Alice Walker, Margaret Walker, Michelle Wallace, Regina Williams, Sherley Anne Williams, Geraldine Wilson, Nzadi Zimele-Keita (Michelle McMichael)]

Baraka, Amiri [Leroi Jones], and Larry Neal (eds), *Black Fire: An Anthology of Afro-American Writing*, New York: Morrow, 1968. [Carole Freeman, Lethonia Gee, Sonia Sanchez, Barbara Simmons]

Baratte-Eno Belinga, Thérèse, Jacqueline Chaveau-Rabut and Makala Kadima-Nzuji (eds), *Bibliographie des auteurs africains de langue française*, Paris: Nathan, Classiques du Monde, 1979.

Bardolph, Richard, *The Negro Vanguard*, New York: Rinehart, 1959, Vintage, 1961.

Barksdale, Richard, and Kenneth Kinnamon (eds), *Black Writers of America: A Comprehensive Anthology*, New York: Macmillan, 1972. [Gwendolyn Brooks, Mari E. Evans, Nikki Giovanni, Angelina Weld Grimké, Frances E. W. Harper, Zora Neale Hurston, Elizabeth Keckley, Paule Marshall, Barbara Molette, Anne Petry, Anne Spencer, Margaret Walker, Phillis Wheatley]

Barlow, Judith E. (ed.), *Plays by American Women: 1900–1930*, New York: Applause Theatre Book Publishers. [Georgia Douglas Johnson]

Barrett, Jane, Aneene Dawber, Barbara Klugman, Ingrid Obery, Jennifer Shindler and Joanne Yawitch, *Vukani Makhosikazi: South African Women Speak*, London: Catholic Institute for International Relations, 1985.

Barthelemy, Anthony (ed.), *Collected Black Women's Narratives*, Oxford/New York: Oxford University Press, Schomburg Library of Nineteenth-Century Black Women Writers, 1988. [Nancy Prince, Susie King Taylor, Bethany Veney, Louisa Picquet]

Barton, Rebecca Chalmers, *Witnesses for Freedom: Negro Americans in Auto-biography*, New York: Harper & Co., 1948; Oakdale, NY: Dowling College Press, 1976.

Bassir, Olumbe (ed.), *An Anthology of West African Verse*, Ibadan: Ibadan University Press, 1967. [Efua Sutherland]

Bastide, Roger, *Les Amériques Noires: les civilisations africaines dans le nouveau monde*, Paris: Payot, 1967; trans. Peter Green as *African Civilisations in the New World*, London: Hurst, 1971; New York: Harper & Row, 1972.

——(ed.), *La Femme de couleur en Amérique Latine*, Paris: Editions Anthropos, 1974.

Baxter Miller, R. (ed.), *Black American Poets Between Worlds, 1940–1960*, Knoxville: University of Tennessee Press, Tennessee Studies in Literature, Vol. 30, 1988.

Beachy, R. W. A., *A Collection of Documents on the Slave Trade of Eastern Africa*, London: Rex Collings, 1976.

Bean, Richard, *The British Trans-Atlantic Slave Trade, 1650–1775*, New York: Arno Press, 1975.

Beasley, Delilah L., *The Negro Trail Blazers of California*, Los Angeles: Times Mirror Print & Bind House, 1919; San Francisco: R & E Research Associates, 1968.

Beauvue-Fougerollas, *Les Femmes antillaises*, Paris: L'Harmattan, 1976.

Beckles, Hilary McD., *Natural Rebels: A Social History of Enslaved Black Women in Barbados*, Rutgers/Zed, 1989.

Beier, Ulli (ed.), *African Poetry: An Anthology of Traditional African Poems*, London/New York: Cambridge University Press, 1966.

——(ed.), *Black Orpheus: An Anthology of New African and Afro-American Stories*, London: Longman, 1964; New York: McGraw-Hill, 1965.

——(ed.), *An Introduction to African Literature: An Anthology of Critical Writing*, London: Longman; Evanston, Ill.: Northwestern University Press, 1967; London/New York: Longman, revised 1979.

——(ed.), *Political Spider: Stories from Black Orpheus*, London: Heinemann Educational Books, African Writers Series 58, 1969; New York: Africana Publishing Corp., 1969. [Ama Ata Aidoo]

Bell, Bernard W. (ed.), *Modern and Contemporary Afro-American Poetry*, Boston: Allyn & Baker, 1972. [Gwendolyn Brooks, Lucille Clifton, Margaret Danner, Julia Fields, Nikki Giovanni, Frances E. W. Harper, Audre Lorde, Naomi Long Madgett, Gloria Oden, Sonia Sanchez, Margaret Walker]

Bell, Roseann P., Bettye J. Parker and Beverly Guy-Sheftall (eds), *Sturdy Black Bridges: Visions of Women in Literature*, Garden City, NY: Anchor/Doubleday, 1979. [Eintou Apandaye (Springer), Melba Joyce Boyd, Mary Williams Burgher, Iva Carruthers, Daryl C. Dance, Mari E. Evans, Gloria Gayles, Nikki Giovanni, Beverly Guy-Sheftall, Bessie Head, Gloria T. Hull, Jacquelyn Fergus Hunter, Mae Jackson, Gloria Joseph, Winifred Oyoko Loving, Paule Marshall, Toni Morrison, Judy Mutunhu, Bettye J. Parker, Carolyn M. Rodgers, Andrea Benton Rushing, Sonia Sanchez, Ellease Southerland, Hortense Spillers, Lynn Wheeldin Suruma, Marie Linton Umeh, Margaret Walker, Mary Helen Washington, Paulette Childress White, Lorna V. Williams]

Bell-Scott, Patricia, Beverly Guy-Sheftall, Jacqueline Jones Royster, Janet Sims-Wood, Miriam DeCosta-Willis and Lucie Fultz (eds), *Double Stitch: Black Women Write About Mothers and Daughters*, Boston: Beacon Press, 1991.

Bennett, Lerone, Jr, *Before the Mayflower: A History of Black America*, 5th edn, New York/Harmondsworth: Penguin, 1984.

Bernal, Martin, *Black Athena: The Afroasiatic Roots of Classical Civilisation. Vol. I: The Fabrication of Ancient Greece 1785–1985*, London: Free Association Books, 1987; *Vol. II: The Archaeological and Documentary Evidence*, New York: Rutgers University Press, 1991; London: Free Association Books, 1991.

Bernikow, Louise (ed.), *The World Split Open: Four Centuries of Women Poets in England and America*, New York: Vintage, 1974.

Bernstein, Hilda, *For Their Triumphs and for Their Tears: Conditions and Resistance of Women in Apartheid South Africa*, London: International Defence & Aid Fund, 1975.

Berrian, Brenda F., *Bibliography of African Women Writers and Journalists (Ancient Egypt–1984)*, Washington, DC: Three Continents Press, 1985.

——(ed.), *Critical Perspectives on Women Writers from Africa*, Washington, DC: Three Continents Press, 1990.

Berrian, Brenda F., and Aart Broek, *Bibliography of Women Writers from the Caribbean*, Washington DC: Three Continents Press, 1989.

Berry, James (ed.), *Bluefoot Traveller*, London: Harrap, 1981. [Sandra Agard, Pauline Brown, Joan Davidson, Rosemarie Chung, Lorraine Flynn]

——(ed.), *News for Babylon: The Chatto Book of Westindian-British Poetry*, London: Chatto & Windus/Hogarth Press, 1984. [Valerie Bloom, Accabre Huntley, Amryl Johnson, Grace Nichols]

Berry, John P. (ed.), *Africa Speaks: A Prose Anthology*, London: Evans Brothers, 1970. [Barbara Kimenye]

Berzson, Judith R., *Neither White nor Black: The Mulatto Character in American Fiction*, New York: New York University Press, 1978.

Bethel, Lorraine, and Barbara Smith (eds), *Conditions: Five – The Black Women's Issue*, Vol. II, No. 2, New York, Autumn 1979. [Donna Allegra, Lorraine Bethel, Becky Birtha, Cheryl Clarke, Michelle T. Clinton, Wilie M. Coleman, Toi Derricotte, Alexis De Veaux, Audrey Ewart, Ruth Farmer, Yvonne Flowers, Carole C. Gregory, Gloria T. Hull, Eleanor Johnson, Cheryl L. Jones, Muriel Jones, Patricia Jones, Hillary Kay, Audre Lorde, Deirdre McCalla, Chirlane McCray, Pat Parker, Michelle D. Parkerson, Linda C. Powell, Rashida, Donna Kate Rushin, Fahamisha Shariat, Ann Allen Shockley, Judy Simmons, Barbara Smith, Beverly Smith, Niobeh Tsaba, Mary Watkins, Rita Weems]

Black and Priceless: The Power of Black Ink, Manchester: Crocus/Commonword, 1988. [Cindy Artiste, Karryn Ewers, Jenny MacDonald, Donna Montague, Monika Montsho, Sally Neaser, Pauline Omoboye, Anne-Marie Thompson]

Black Anthology Group, *Not All Roses and Prose*, London: Centreprise Publishing Project, 1987. [Dee Barnett, Thandiwe Benjamin, Catherine Goodman Boyce, Deborah Boyce, Maxine Fields, Gwendolyn Goodman, Ethel Thomas, Veronica Venner, Pauline Wiltshire]

Blackburn, Dougal, Alfred Horsfall and Chris L. Wanjala (eds), *Attachments to the Sun*, London: Edward Arnold, 1978. [Stella Nagatho, Noemia De Sousa]

Blacksong Series I: Four Poetry Broadsides by Black Women, Detroit: Lotus Press, 1978.

Blain, Virginia, Patricia Clements and Isobel Grundy (eds), *The Feminist Companion to Literature in English*, London: Batsford, 1990.

Blair, Dorothy S., *African Literature in French: A History of Creative Writing in French from West and Equatorial Africa*, London/New York: Cambridge University Press, 1976.

Blakely, Allison, *Russia and the Negro: Blacks in Russian History and Thought*, Washington, DC: Howard University Press, 1986.

Blassingame, John W., *The Slave Community: Plantation Life in the Antebellum South*, New York: Oxford University Press, 1973.

Bone, Robert A., *Down Home: A History of Afro-American Short Fiction from Its Beginnings to the End of the Harlem Renaissance*, New York: G. Putnam's Sons, 1975.

——, *The Negro Novel in America*, New Haven: Yale University Press, 1958, revised 1965.

Bontemps, Arna W. (ed.), *American Negro Poetry*, New York: Hill & Wang, 1963; revised 1974. [Gwendolyn B. Bennett, Gwendolyn Brooks, Catherine Cater, Clarissa Scott Delany, Mari E. Evans, Julia Fields, Yvonne Gregory, Angelina Weld Grimké, Georgia Douglas Johnson, Helene Johnson, Pauli Murray, Effie Lee Newsome, Gloria Oden, Anne Spencer, Margaret Walker]

——(ed.), *Golden Slippers: An Anthology of Negro Poetry for Young Readers*, New York: Harper, c. 1941. [Gladys May Casely-Hayford, Josephine Copeland, Jessie Redmon Fauset, Ariel Williams Holloway, Dorothy Vena Johnson, Georgia Douglas Johnson, Helene Johnson, Clara Ball Moten, Beatrice M. Murphy, Effie Lee Newsome, Marva Tatum Smith]

——(ed.), *The Harlem Renaissance Remembered*, New York: Dodd, Mead, 1972. [Mae Gwendolyn Henderson]

Boserup, Ester, *Woman's Role in Economic Development*, London: George Allen & Unwin, 1970; intr. Swasti Mitter, London: Earthscan, 1989; New York: St Martin's Press, 1970.

Bousquet, Ben, and Colin Douglas, *West Indian Women at War: British Racism in World War II*, foreword Jocelyn Barrow, London: Lawrence & Wishart, 1991.

Bowles, Juliette (ed.), *In the Memory and Spirit of Frances, Zora and Lorraine: Essays and Interviews on Black Women and Writing*, Washington, DC: Howard University, Institute for Arts & Humanities, 1979.

Bowman, W. G. (intr.), *When I Awoke*, Nairobi: East African Publishing House, 1966. [Anges Kagondu, Esther Kisangi, R. Lucy Kuria, Beatrice Mwangi, Pauline Wanjiru, Doris May Waruhiu]

Bown, Lalage (ed.), *Two Centuries of African English: A survey and anthology of non-fictional English prose by African writers since 1769*, London: Heinemann Educational Books, 1973, African Writers Series 132.

Bracey, John H., *Black Matriarchy: Myth or Reality*, Belmont, CA: Wadsworth Publishing Co., 1971.

Brasch, Ila Wales, and Walter Milton Branch, *A Comprehensive Annotated Bibliography of American Black English*, Baton Rouge: Louisiana State University Press, 1974.

Brathwaite, Edward Kamau, *The Folk Culture of the Slaves in Jamaica*, London: New Beacon Books, 1981.

——, *History of the Voice: The Development of Nation Language in Anglophone Caribbean Literature*, London: New Beacon Books, 1984.

Brawley, Benjamin Griffith (ed.), *Early Negro American Writers*, New York: Denver Publications, 1970. [Frances E. W. Harper, Phillis Wheatley]

Braxton, Joanne M., *Black Women Writing Autobiography: A Tradition Within a Tradition*, Philadelphia: Temple University Press, 1989.

Braxton, Joanne M., and Andrée Nicola McLaughlin, *Wild Women in the Whirlwind: Afra-American Culture and the Contemporary Literary Renaissance*, New Brunswick, NJ: Rutgers University Press, 1990; London: Serpent's Tail, 1990. [Zala Chandler, Chinosole, Barbara Christian, Angela Davis, Joanne V. Gabbin, Daphne Duval Harrison, Gale P, Jackson, June Jordan, Gloria I.

Joseph, Régine Altagrace Latortue, Vashti Crutcher Lewis, Audre Lorde, Nellie Y. McKay, Andrée Nicola McLaughlin, Barbara Omolade, Barbara Smith, Billie Jean Young]

Breman, Paul (ed.), *Sixes and Sevens: An Anthology of New Negro Poetry*, London: Paul Breman, 1962. [Audre Lorde]

——(ed.), *You Better Believe It: Black Verse in English from Africa, the West Indies, and the United States*, Harmondsworth/New York/Baltimore: Penguin, 1973. [Christina Ama Ata Aidoo, Vera Bell, Musu Ber (Carol Luther), Gwendolyn Brooks, Margaret Danner, Julia Fields, Nikki Giovanni, Alice M. Jones, Audre Lorde, Barbara Malcom (Nayo), D. T. Ogilvie, Carolyn M. Rodgers, Sonia Sanchez, Margaret Walker]

Brewer, John Mason (ed.), *Heralding Dawn: An Anthology of Verse*, Dallas, TX: Superior Typesetting Co., c. 1936. [Gwendolyn Bennett, Lauretta Holman Gooden, Maurine L. Jeffrey, Lillian Tucker Lewis, Birdelle Wycoff Ransom, Bernice Love Wiggins]

Brewster, Yvonne (ed.), *Black Plays*, London: Methuen, 1987. [Jacqueline Rudet]

——(ed.), *Black Plays: Two*, London: Methuen, 1989. [Maria Oshodi, Winsome Pinnock]

Brignano, Russell, *Black Americans in Autobiography: An Annotated Bibliography of Autobiographies and Autobiographical Books Written Since the Civil War*, Durham: Duke University Press, 1984.

Brink, André, and J. M. Coetzee (eds), *A Land Apart: A South African Reader*, London: Faber, 1987. [Gcina Mhlope, Maria Tholo]

Brooks, Gwendolyn (ed.), *A Broadside Treasury*, Detroit: Broadside Press, 1971. [Gwendolyn Brooks, Margaret Danner, Ronda M. Davis, Sarah Webster Fabio, Nikki Giovanni, Joyce Whitsett Lawrence (Malaika Wangara), Naomi Long Madgett, S. Carolyn Reese, Carolyn M. Rodgers, Sonia Sanchez, Stephany, Margaret Walker]

——(ed.), *Jump Bad: A New Chicago Anthology*, Detroit: Broadside Press, 1971. [Johari Amini, Ronda Davis, Peggy Susberry Kenner, Linyatta, Carolyn M. Rodgers, Sharon Scott]

Brown, Hallie Quinn (ed.), *Homespun Heroines and Other Women of Distinction*, Xenia, Ohio: Aldine, 1926; intr. Randall K. Burkett, Oxford/New York: Oxford University Press, Schomburg Library of Nineteenth-Century Black Women Writers, 1988.

Brown, Lloyd W., *Women Writers in Black Africa*, Westport, Conn.: Greenwood Press, 1981.

Brown, Patricia L., Don L. Lee and Francis Ward (eds), *To Gwen with Love: An Anthology Dedicated to Gwendolyn Brooks*, Chicago: Johnson Publishing, 1971. [Johiri Amini, Carole Gregory Clemmons, Cynthia M. Conley, Margaret Danner, Maxine Hall Elliston, Sarah Webster Fabio, Nikki Giovanni, Alicia Johnson, Paulette Jones, Delores Kendrick, Helen H. King, Barbara A. Reynolds, Carolyn M. Rodgers, Sonia Sanchez, Sharon Scott, Maami Verano, Margaret Walker, Val Gray Ward]

Brown, Sterling A., *Negro Poetry and Drama*, Washington, DC: Associates in Negro Folk Education, 1937.

Brown, Sterling A., Arthur P. Davis and Ulysses Lee (eds), *The Negro Caravan: Writings by American Negroes*, New York: Dryden, 1941, Arno, 1970. Intr. Julius Lester, Salem, NH: Ayer, 1987. [Katherine Dunham, Jessie Redmon Fauset, Charlotte Forten, Angelina Weld Grimké, Frances E. W. Harper, Zora Neale Hurston, Georgia Douglas Johnson, Elizabeth Keckley, Eslanda Goode Robeson, Anne Spencer, Margaret Walker, Phillis Wheatley, Lucy Ariel Williams]

Brown, Stewart (ed.), *Caribbean Poetry Now*, London: Hodder & Stoughton Educational, 1984, 1986. [Louise Bennett, Valerie Bloom, Gloria Escoffery, Lorna Goodison, Pamela Mordecai, Grace Nichols, Opal Palmer, Helen Royes, Shana Yardan]

——, *Caribbean New Wave*, Oxford: Heinemann International, 1990. [Opal Palmer Adisa, Hazel D. Campbell, Zoila Ellis, Lorna Goodison, Amryl Johnson, Jamaica Kincaid, Velma Pollard, Olive Senior, Janice Shinebourne]

——, *Writers from Africa*, London: Book Trust, 1989.

Brown, Stewart, Mervyn Morris and Gordon Rohlehr (eds), *Voiceprint: An Anthology of Oral and Related Poetry from the Caribbean*, intr. Gordon Rohlehr; Harlow/Kingston/San Juan: Longman, 1989. [Louise Bennett, Valerie Bloom, Dionne Brand, Jean Binta Breeze, Christine Craig, Lorna Goodison, Amryl Johnson, Pamela Mordecai, Grace Nichols, Opal Palmer, Velma Pollard, Lucinda Roy, Olive Senior]

Brown, Susan, Isabel Hofmeyr and Susan Rosenberg (eds), *LIP from Southern African Women*, Johannesburg: Ravan Press, 1983. [Petunia Buthelezi, Bessie Head, Gcina Mhlope, Christine Rembawawasvika, Rose Zwi]

Brown, Wesley, and Amy Ling (eds), *Imagining America: Stories from the Promised Land*, New York: Persea Books, 1991. [Toni Cade Bambara, Marita Bonner, Paule Marshall, Alice Walker]

Brown, Wilmette, *Black Women and the Peace Movement*, Bristol: Falling Wall Press, 1983.

Brown-Guillory, Elizabeth, *Their Place on the Stage: Black Women Playwrights in America*, Westport, Conn.: Greenwood, 1988.

Bruner, Charlotte H. (ed.), *Unwinding Threads: Writing by Women in Africa*, London: Heinemann Educational Books, 1983. [Ama Ata Aidoo, Fadhma Amrouche, Marguerite Amrouche, Mariama Bâ, Adelaide Casely-Hayford, Andrée Chedid, Mabel Dove Danquah, Assia Djebar, Latifa el-Zayat, Buchi Emecheta, Bessie Head, Flora Kimenye, Helen Mugot, Martha Mvungi, Flora Nwapa, Grace Ogot, Alifa Rifaat, Efua Sutherland, Miriam Tlali, Charity Waciuma]

Bryan, Beverley, Stella Dadzie and Suzanne Scafe (eds), *The Heart of the Race: Black Women's Lives in Britain*, London: Virago, 1985.

Bulkin, Elly, Minnie Bruce Pratt and Barbara Smith, *Yours in Struggle: Three Feminist Perspectives on Anti-Semitism and Racism*, Long Haul Press, 1984; Ithaca, NY: Firebrand Books, 1988.

Burford, Barbara, Lindsay MacRae and Sylvia Paskin (eds), *Dancing the Tightrope: New Love Poems by Women*, London: Women's Press, 1987. [Barbara Burford, Iyamidé Hazeley, Jackie Kay, Maud Sulter]

Burness, Don (ed./trans.), *A Horse of White Cloud: Poems from Lusophone*

Africa, Foreword Chinua Achebe; Athens, OH: Ohio University Press, 1989. [Noémia de Sousa, Alda Lara]

Burnett, June, Julie Cotterill, Annette Kennerley, Phoebe Nathan and Jeanne Wilding (eds), *The Common Thread: Writings by Working-Class Women*, London: Mandarin, 1989. [Rozena Maart, Maria Noble, Jenneba Sie Jalloh, Maud Sulter, Lesley Summers, Tina Wildebeest]

Burnett, Paula (ed.), *The Penguin Book of Caribbean Verse in English*, Harmondsworth: Penguin, 1986. [Lillian Allen, Louise Bennett, Valerie Bloom, Dionne Brand, Gloria Escoffery, Barbara Ferland, Lorna Goodison, Claire Harris, Una Marson, Judy Miles, Pamela Mordecai, Grace Nichols, Marlene Nourbese Philip, Olive Senior]

Bush, Barbara, *Slave Women in Caribbean Society 1650–1838*, London: James Currey/Kingston: Heinemann (Caribbean)/Bloomington: Indiana University Press, Columbus Series of Caribbean Studies, 1990.

Butcher, Maggie (ed.), *Tibisiri: Caribbean Writers and Critics*, Sydney, Australia/Denmark: Dangaroo, 1989. [Diane Brown, Lorna Goodison, Elaine Savory, Olive Senior]

Butcher, Margaret Just, *The Negro in American Culture* [based on materials left by Alain Locke], New York: Knopf, 1956, Mentor/NAL, 1957.

Byerman, Keith, *Fingering the Jagged Grain: Tradition and Form in Recent Black Fiction*, Athens, Ga.: University of Georgia Press, 1985.

Cade [Bambara], Toni (ed.), *The Black Woman: An Anthology*, New York: Signet/NAL, 1970, [Frances Beale, Helen Cade Brehon, Grace Lee Boggs, Jean Carey Bond, Carole Brown, Joanna Clark, Ann Cook, Francee Covington, Nikki Giovanni, Joanne Grant, Joyce Green, Adele Jones, Maude White Katz, Abbey Lincoln, Kay Lindsey, Audre Lorde, Paule Marshall, Gwen Patton, Patricia Peery, Pat Robinson, Fran Saunders, Verta Mae Smart-Grosvenor, Gail Stokes, Alice Walker, Helen Williams, Shirley Williams]

——(ed.), *Tales and Stories of Black Folks*, New York, 1971. [Alice Walker]

Carby, Hazel, *Reconstructing Womanhood: The Emergence of the Afro-American Woman Novelist*, Oxford: Oxford University Press, 1987.

Carew, Jan, *Fulcrums of Change: African Presence in the Americas*, Trenton, NJ: Africa World Press, 1988.

Carruthers, Iva, "Africanity and the Black Woman", *Black Books Bulletin* Vol. 6, No. 4 (1980), pp. 14–20, 71.

Carson, Josephine, *Silent Voices: The Southern Negro Woman Today*, New York: Dell/Delacote Press, 1969.

Cashmore, Ernest, and Barry Troyna (eds), *Black Youth in Crisis*, London: Allen & Unwin, 1982.

Centre for Contemporary Cultural Studies, *The Empire Strikes Back: Race and Racism in 70s Britain*, London: Hutchinson/University of Birmingham, 1982. [Hazel V. Carby, Pratibha Parmar]

Chamberlain, Mary (ed.), *Writing Lives: Conservations Between Women Writers*, London: Virago, 1988. [Maya Angelou, Rosa Guy, Paule Marshall, Mary Helen Washington]

Chambers, Bradford, and Rebecca Moon (eds), *Right On! An Anthology of Black Literature*, New York/Toronto: NAL/Mentor, 1970. [Nikki Giovanni,

Naomi Long Madgett, Diane Oliver, Ann Petry, Malaika Wangara]

Chapman, Abraham, *The Negro in American Literature, and a Bibliography of Literature by and about Negro Americans*, Madison: Wisconsin State University, Wisconsin Council of Teachers of English, special publication no. 16, 1966.

——(ed.), *Black Voices: An Anthology of Afro-American Literature*, New York: New American Library, 1968. [Gwendolyn Brooks, Mari E. Evans, Audre Lorde, Naomi Long Madgett, Paule Marshall, Diane Oliver, Ann Petry, Margaret Walker]

——(ed.), *New Black Voices: An Anthology of Contemporary Afro-American Literature*, New York: NAL/Mentor, 1972. [Gwendolyn Brooks, Johnetta B. Cole, Jayne Cortez, Mari E. Evans, Naomi Faust, Val Ferdinand, Nikki Giovanni, Audre Lorde, Naomi Long Madgett, Nayo (Barbara Malcolm), Sonia Sanchez, Stephany, Jeanne A. Walker, Margaret Walker]

——, *Steal Away: Slaves Tell Their Own Stories*, London: Ernest Benn, 1973.

Chapman, Dorothy Hilton (comp.), *Index to Poetry by Black American Women*, Westport, Conn.: Greenwood Press, 1986.

Charles, Christophe (ed.), *La Poésie féminine haïtienne (histoire et anthologie)*, Port-au-Prince: Editions Choucoune, 1980. [Suzette Antoine, Jacqueline Beauge-Rosier, Aline Belance, Emmelyne Carrie Lemaire, Devige Clermont, Mme Frantz Colbert Saint-Cyr, Marie Thérèse Colimon, Muriel Darly, Celie Diaquoi Deslandes, Marie Laurette Destin, Ida Faubert, Marie Marcelle Ferjuste, Mona Rouzier Guerin, Marie Ange Jolicoeur, Michaelle Lafontant-Medard (Marguerite Deschamps), Soeurette Mathieu, Hélène Morpeau, Nyllde (Eddlyn Telhomme), Rose-Marie Perrier Casias, Virginie Sampeur, Jacqueline Tavernier Louis, Cleantes Desgraves Valcin (Mme Virgile Valcin), Jacqueline Wiener Silvera]

Chemain-Degrange, Arlette, *Emancipation féminine et roman africain*, Dakar: Nouvelles Editions Africaines, 1980.

Cherry, Gwendolyn, *et al.*, *Portraits in Color: The Lives of Colorful Negro Women*, Paterson, NJ: Pageant Books, 1962.

Chester, Laura (ed.), *Deep Down: New Sensual Writing by Women*, London: Faber, 1988, [Ai, Toni Cade Bambara, Wanda Coleman, Toi Derricotte, Audre Lorde, Toni Morrison, Ntozake Shange, Alice Walker]

Chester, Laura, and Sharon Barba (eds), *Rising Tides: Twentieth-Century American Women Poets*, intr. Anais Nin; Kangaroo/Pocket Books, 1973. [Lucille Clifton, Nikki Giovanni, June Jordan, Sonia Sanchez]

Chevrier, Jacques (ed.), *Anthologie africaine*, Paris: Hatier, 1981, Monde noir poche 9. [Mariama Bâ]

Child, Lydia Maria (ed.), *The Freedmen's Book*, Ticknor & Fields, 1865; New York: Arno Press/New York Times, 1968. [Charlotte Forten, Frances E. W. Harper, Harriet Jacobs, Phillis Wheatley]

Chinoy, Helen Krich, and Linda Walsh Jenkins, *Women in American Theatre*, New York: Crown Publishers, 1981, Theatre Communications Group, 1987.

Chinweizu (ed.), *Voices from Twentieth-Century Africa: Griots and Towncriers*, London: Faber, 1988.

Chisholm, Shirley, "Racism and Anti-Feminism", *Black Scholar* v:1 (3–4), January–February 1970, pp. 40–45.

Choong, Da, Olivette Cole-Wilson, Bernardine Evaristo and Gabriela Pearse (eds), *Black Women Talk Poetry*, London: Black Womantalk, 1987, [Adjoa Andoh, M. Ayoi, Dinah Anuli Butler, Zeina Carrington, Debjani Chatterjee, Bernardine Evaristo, Patricia Hilaire, Meiling Jin, Jackie Kay, Bekleen Leong, Sylvia Parker, Gabriela Pearse, Avril Rogers-Wright, B. B. Samuel, Shabnam, Dorothea Smartt, Roma Thomas, Carmen Tunde, Tina Wildebeest, Zhana]

Choong, Da, Olivette Cole Wilson, Sylvia Parker and Gabriela Pearse (eds), *Don't Ask Me Why: An Anthology of Short Stories by Black Women*, London: Black Womantalk, 1991. [Teresa Alexander, Monica Aguilhas, Sheila Auguste, Debjani Chatterjee, Joyoti Grech, Rahila Gupta, Meiling Jin, Margaret Mukama, Catherine Proctor, Joy Russell, a-dZiko Simba, Pauline Stewart, Shaziya Suleyman]

Christian, Angela, "The Place of Women in Ghana Society", *African Women*, III:3, 1959, pp. 57–9.

Christian, Barbara, *Black Women Novelists: The Development of a Tradition 1892–1976*, Westport/London: Greenwood, 1980.

——, *Black Feminist Criticism: Perspectives on Black Women Writers*, New York: Pergamon, 1985.

Clark, Bori S. (comp.), *Trinidad Women Speak*, Redlands, CA: Libros Latinos, 1981.

Clark, Edith, *My Mother Who Fathered Me*, London: George Allen & Unwin, 1957.

Clark, Leon E. (ed.), *Coming of Age in Africa: Continuity and Change*, New York: Praeger, 1969. [Anna Apoko]

Cobham, Rhonda, and Merle Collins (eds), *Watchers and Seekers: Creative Writing by Black Women in Britain*, London: Women's Press, 1987; New York: Peter Bedrick, 1988. [Valerie Bloom, Iyamidé Hazeley, Amryl Johnson, Grace Nichols, Maud Sulter]

Cock, Jacklyn, *Maids and Madams*, Johannesburg: Ravan Press, 1980.

Cole, Johnetta B., *All-American Women: Lines That Divide, Ties That Bind*, New York: Free Press, 1985.

——, "Black Women in America: An Annotated Bibliography", *Black Scholar* 3 (December 1971), pp. 42–54.

College of the Bahamas (ed.), *Bahamian Anthology*, London: Macmillan Caribbean, 1983. [Ava Adams, Cheryl Albury, Meta Davis Cumberbatch, Eunice Humblestone, Ileana McDermott, Melissa Maura, Antoinette Smith, Marcella Taylor, Mizpah Tertullien, Telcine Turner-Rolle, Susan Wallace]

Collier-Thomas, Bettye, *Black Women in America: Contributors to Our Heritage*, Washington, DC: Bethune Museum Archives, 1983.

——, *Black Women: Organizing for Social Change 1800–1920*, Washington, DC: Bethune Museum Archives, 1984.

——, *National Council of Negro Women, 1935–1980*, Washington, DC: Bethune Museum Archives, 1981.

Collins, Patricia Hill, *Black Feminist Thought: Knowledge, Consciousness, and the Politics of Empowerment*, Boston/London: Unwin Hyman, 1990, HarperCollins Academic, 1991.

Condé, Maryse (ed.), *Anthologie de la littérature africaine d'expression françaises*, Accra: Institute of Languages, 1966.

——, *La Paroles des femmes: essai sur des romancières des Antilles de langue française*, Paris: L'Harmattan, 1979.

——(ed.), *La Poésie antillaise*, Paris: Fernand Nathan, 1977. [Marie-Magdeleine Carbet, Florette Morand-Capasso]

——(ed.), *La Roman antillaise*, 2 vols, Paris: Fernand Nathan, 1977.

Conlon, Faith, Rachel de Silva and Barbara Wilson (eds), *The Things That Divide Us: Stories by Women*, Seattle: Seal, 1985; London: Sheba, 1986. [Cheryl Ann Alexander, Becky Birtha, Barbara Neely]

Contin y Aybar, Pedro René, *Poseía dominicana*, Santo Domingo: Julio D. Postigo, 1969.

Cook, David (ed.), *In Black and White: Writings from East Africa with broadcast discussions and commentary*, Nairobi: East African Literature Bureau, 1976. [Margaret Alifaijo, Sister Anselm, Charu Damani, Nazaru Jethu, Joy Lehai, Rose Mbowa, Grace Ogot, Proscovia Rwakyaya]

——(ed.), *Origin East Africa – a Makerere Anthology*, London: Heinemann Educational Books, African Writers Series 15, 1965.

Coombs, Orde (ed.), *We Speak as Liberators: Young Black Poets, An Anthology*, New York: Dodd, Mead, 1970. [Fareedah Allah, Nikki Giovanni, Carolyn M. Rodgers, Sonia Sanchez]

Condor, S. Henry (ed.), *New Voices from West Africa: The first major anthology of contemporary Liberian short stories*, Monrovia: Liberian Literary and Educational Publishing, 1979. [Patricia Jabbeeh, Elizabeth M. Mitchell, Maima Roberts, Elizabeth Tulay]

Cornwell, Anita R., *Black Lesbian in White America*, foreword Becky Birtha; Tallahassee: Naiad Press, 1983.

Cortez, Jayne (ed.), *Black Scholar* 19:4 & 5, special issue "Word within a word" (July/August–September/October 1988). [Susan Alexander, Amina Baraka, Melba Joyce Boyd, Gwendolyn Brooks, Xam Wilson Cartier, Cheryl Clarke, Michelle T. Clinton, Wanda Coleman, Jayne Cortez, Toi Derricotte, Alexis De Veaux, Rita Dove, J. E. Franklin, Jewelle L. Gomez, Safiya Henderson, Rashidah Ismaili, Angela Jackson, Amryl Johnson, June Jordan, Nubia Kai, Jackie Kay, Naomi Long Madgett, Louise Meriwether, Nancy Morejón, May Opitz, Sonia Sanchez, Ellease Southerland, Lourdes Teodoro, Margaret Walker (Alexander), Marilyn Nelson Waniek]

Cosman, Carol, Joan Keefe and Kathleen Weaver (eds), *The Penguin Book of Women Poets*, Allen Lane, 1978, New York: Viking/Penguin, 1979. [Christina Ama Ata Aidoo, Oumar Ba, Amina Baraka, Gwendolyn Brooks, Noémia De Sousa, Toi Derricotte, Rita Dove, Alda de Espírito Santo, Naomi Long Madgett, Annette M'baye, Louise Meriwether, Nancy Morejón, Mririda N'ait Attik, Citèkù Ndaaya, Glória de Sant'Ana, Margaret Walker]

Couzens, Tim, and Essop Patel (eds), *The Return of the Amasi Bird: Black South African Poetry, 1891–1981*, Johannesburg: Ravan, 1982. [Christine Douts (Qunta), Bessie Head, Mavis Kwankwa, Lindiwe Mabuza, Rebecca Matlou, Lindiwe Mvemve, Joyce Sikakane]

Crane, Louise, *Ms Africa: Profiles of Modern African Women*, New York: J. B. Lippincott, 1973.

Cromwell, Otelia, Lorenzo Dow Turner and Eva B. Dykes (eds), *Readings from Negro Authors for Schools and Colleges, with a Bibliography of Negro Literature*, New York: Harcourt, Brace, 1931. [Ethel Caution, Caroline Stewart Day, Clarissa Scott Delany, Blanche Dickinson, Alice Dunbar-Nelson, Eva B. Dykes, Jessie Redmon Fauset, Angelina Weld Grimké, Florence Harmon, Zora Neale Hurston, Georgia Douglas Johnson, Helene Johnson, Gertrude Parthenia McBrown, Esther Popel]

Crowley, Daniel J., *African Folklore in the New World*, Austin/London: University of Texas Press, 1977.

Cruikshank, Margaret (ed.), *New Lesbian Writing: An Anthology*, San Francisco: Grey Fox Press, 1985. [Paula Gunn Allen, SDiane Bogus, Beth Brant, Audrey Ewart, LindaJean Brown, doris davenport, Suniti Namjoshi]

Cudjoe, Selwyn R. (ed.), *Caribbean Women Writers: Essays from the First International Conference*, Wellesley, Mass: Calaloux Publications, 1990. [Opal Palmer Adisa, Valerie Belgrave, Erna Brodber, Afua Cooper, Leah Creque-Harris, Daryl Cumber Dance, Jean D'Costa, Clara Rosa De Lima, Beryl Gilroy, Lorna Goodison, Veronica Marie Gregg, Rosa Guy, Merle Hodge, Glasceta Honeyghan, Marion Patrick Jones, Lucille Mathurin Mair, Grace Nichols, Marlene Nourbese Philip, Sybil Seaforth, Olive Senior, Marie-Denise Shelton, Janice Shinebourne, Ena Thomas, Helen Pyne Timothy]

Cullen, Countee (ed.), *Caroling Dusk: An Anthology of Verse by Negro Poets*, New York, Harper & Bros, 1927; Harper & Row, 1974. [Gwendolyn B. Bennett, Gladys Casely-Hayford, Clarissa Scott Delany, Blanche Taylor Dickinson, Alice Dunbar-Nelson, Jessie Redmon Fauset, Angelina Weld Grimké, Georgia Douglas Johnson, Helene Johnson, Mary Effie Lee Newsome, Anne Spencer, Lula Lowe Weedon, Lucy Ariel Williams]

Cummings, Gwenna, "Black Women: Often Discussed by Never Understood", in *The Black Power Revolt*, ed. F. B. Barbour, Boston: Extending Horizons Books, 1968.

Cunard, Nancy (ed.), *Negro: An Anthology*, London, 1934; New York: Negro Universities Press (Greenwood Publishing), 1969; abridged, New York: Frederick Ungar, 1970. [Carrie Williams Clifford, Olga Comma, Maud Cuney Hare, Zora Neale Hurston, Georgia Douglas Johnson, Pauli Murray, Gladis Berry Robinson]

Curley, Richard T., *Elders, Shades and Women: Ceremonial Change in Lango, Uganda*, Berkeley: University of California Press, 1973.

Cutrufelli, Maria Rosa, *Women in Africa: Roots of Oppression*, London: Zed Press, 1983.

Dabydeen, David (ed.), *The Black Presence in English Literature*, Manchester: Manchester University Press, 1985.

Dabydeen, David, and Nana Wilson-Tagoe, *A Reader's Guide to West Indian and Black British Literature*, London: Hansib Publishing, 1988.

Dallas, R. C., *The History of the Maroons*, London: T. N. Longman and O. Rees, 1803.

Dalphinis, Morgan, *Caribbean and African Languages*, London: Karia Press, 1985.

Damas, Léon-Gontran, *Latitudes françaises: poètes d'expression françaises*, Paris: Seuil, 1947. [Gisele Armelin, Draste Houel, Lucie Thesee]

Dance, Daryl Cumber (ed.), *Fifty Caribbean Writers: A Bio-Bibliographical Critical Sourcebook*, Westport, Conn.: Greenwood, 1986. [Entries on Louise Bennett, Dionne Brand, Erna Brodber, Jean D'Costa, Merle Hodge, Marion Patrick Jones, Jamaica Kincaid, Sylvia Wynter]

Dandridge, Rita, "On Novels by Black American Women: A Bibliographic Essay", *Women's Studies Newsletter* 6 (Summer 1978), pp. 28–30.

Daniel, Sadie Iola, *Women Builders*, Washington, DC: Associated Publishers, 1931.

Dannett, Sylvia G. L., *Profiles of Negro Womanhood 1619–1900*, 2 vols; Yonkers, NY: Educational Heritage, 1964–66.

Dathorne, O. R. (ed.), *African Poetry for Schools and Colleges*, London: Macmillan, 1969.

——, *The Black Mind: A History of African Literature*, Minneapolis: University of Minnesota Press, 1974, 1975; abridged as *African Literature in the Twentieth Century*, London: Heinemann Educational Books, 1976.

——(ed.), *Caribbean Verse: An Anthology*, London: Heinemann Educational Books, 1967. [Vera Bell, Vera Margon, Stella Mead, Daisy Myrie]

Dathorne, O. R., and Willfried Feuser (eds), *Africa in Prose*, Harmondsworth: Penguin, 1969. [Adelaide Casely-Hayford]

David, Jay (ed.), *Black Joy*, Chicago: Cowles Book Co., 1971; Toronto: General Publishing Co., 1971. [Alice Childress, Mari E. Evans, Ruby Goodwin, Angelina Weld Grimlé, Zora Neale Hurston, Ethel Waters]

Davidson, Basil, *Black Mother: Africa and the Atlantic Slave Trade*, London, 1961; revised edn, Harmondsworth: Penguin, 1980.

——, *History of West Africa 1000–1800*, London: Longman, revised 1977.

Davidson, Elizabeth (comp.), *Some English Writings by Non-European South Africans, 1928–1971: A bibliography*, Johannesburg: University of the Witwatersrand, Dept of Bibliography, Librarianship and Typography, 1972.

Davies, Carole Boyce (ed.), *Black Women's Writing: Crossing the Boundaries*, Frankfurt: Verlag Holger Ehling, Matatu 6, 1989. [Catherine Obianuju Acholonu, Anne V. Adams, Irène Assiba d'Almeida, Abena P. A. Busia, Carole Boyce Davies, Arlene Elder, Yannick François, Jewelle L. Gomez, bell hooks, Fawzziya Abu Khalid, Omolara Ogundipe-Leslie, Velma Pollard, Sonia Sanchez, Joyce Hope Scott]

Davies, Carole Boyce, and Elaine Savory Fido (eds), *Out of the Kumbla: Caribbean Women and Literature*, Trenton, NJ: Africa World Press, 1990. [Abena P. A. Busia, Jenipher Carnegie, Vèvè Clark, Rhonda Cobham, Carolyn Cooper, Carole Boyce Davies, Elaine Savory Fido, Janice Lee Liddell, Pamela Claire Mordecai, Nancy Morejón, Evelyn O'Callaghan, Marlene Nourbese Philip, Joyce Stewart, Elizabeth Wilson, Sylvia Wynter]

Davies, Carole Boyce, and Anne Adams Graves (eds), *Ngambika: Studies of Women in African Literature*, Trenton, NJ: Africa World Press, 1986. [Irène Assiba d'Almeida, Naana Banyiwa-Horne, Brenda Berrian, Abena P.

A. Busia, Carole Boyce Davies, Elaine Savory Fido, Anne Adams Graves, Mildred Hill-Lubin, Beverly B. Mack, Rafika Merini, Esther Y. Smith, Karen Smyley-Wallace, Marie Linton Umeh]

Davis, Angela, "Reflections on the Black Woman's Role in the Community of Slaves", *Black Scholar* 3 (December 1971), pp. 2–15.

——, *Women, Culture and Politics*, New York: Random House, 1984; London: Women's Press, 1990.

——, *Women, Race and Class*, New York: Random House, 1981; London: Women's Press, 1982.

Davis, Arthur Paul (ed.), *From the Dark Tower: Afro-American Writers 1900– 1960*, Washington, DC: Howard University Press, 1974.

——, *The New Negro Renaissance*, New York: Holt, Rinehart & Winston, 1975. [Jessie Redmon Fauset, Angelina Weld Grimké, Georgia Douglas Johnson, Helene Johnson, Mae Smith Johnson, May Miller, Effie Lee Newsome, Andrea Razafkerlefo, Anne Spencer, Margaret Walker, Phillis Wheatley]

Davis, Arthur P., and Saunders Redding (eds), *Cavalcade: Negro American Writing from 1760 to the present*, Boston: Houghton Mifflin, 1971. [Gwendolyn Brooks, Margaret Danner, Charlotte Forten Grimké, Alicia Loy Johnson, Elizabeth Keckley, Naomi Long Madgett, Paule Marshall, Sonia Sanchez, Anne Spencer, Margaret Walker]

Davis, Charles T., and Daniel Walden (eds), *On Being Black: Writings by Afro-Americans from Frederick Douglas to the Present*, New York: Fawcett, 1970.

Davis, Elizabeth L., *Lifting as They Climb: The National Association of Colored Women*, Washington, DC: National Association of Colored Women, 1933.

Davis, Lenwood G., *Black Women in the Cities: 1872–1972: A Bibliography of Published Works on the Life and Achievements of Black Women in the United States*, Monticello, Ill.: Council of Planning Librarians, 1972.

——, *The Black Woman in American Society: A Selected Annotated Bibliography*, Boston, G. K. Hall, 1975.

——, *The Black Family: A Selected Bibliography of Annotated Books and Articles*, Westport, Conn.: Greenwood Press, 1978.

Davis, Marianna W. (ed.), *Contributions of Black Women to America. Vol. I: The Arts, Business and Commerce, Media, Law, Sports. Vol. II: Civil Rights, Politics and Government, Education, Medicine, Sciences*, Columbia, SC: Kenday Press, 1982.

Dawes, Neville, and Anthony McNeill (eds), *The Caribbean Poem*, Carifesta, 1976. [Jennifer Brown, Pamela Mordecai, Olive Senior]

Dearborn, Mary V., *Pocohontas's Daughters: Gender and Ethnicity in American Culture*, New York: Oxford University Press, 1986.

Debrunner, Hans Werner, *Presence and Prestige: Africans in Europe: A History of Africans in Europe before 1918*, Basel: Basler Afrika Bibliographien, 1979.

Dee, Ruby (ed.), *Glowchild, and Other Poems*, New York: Third Press, Joseph Okpaku Publishing Co., 1972. [Constance Berkley, Elaine Brown, Linda Brown, Pam Brown, Margaret Burroughs, LaVerne Davis, Nora Davis, Risa Gerson, Ruth Duckett Gibbs, Mrs J. W. Hammond, Beth Hollander, Lisa

McCann, Rhonda Metz, Dorothy Randall, Jo Nell Rise, Ridhiana, Linda Thomas, Susan Tobbins, Ann Wallace, Debbie Whitely, Gwendolyn Williams]

Degler, Carl N., *Neither Black nor White: Slavery and Race Relations in Brazil and the United States*, New York: Macmillan, 1971.

Dendridge, Rita, "Male Critics/Black Women's Novels", *CLA Journal*, 23:1 (September 1979).

———, "On Novels by Black American Women: A Bibliographical Essay", *Women's Studies Newsletter*, 6:3 (Summer 1978), pp. 28–30.

Dennis, Ferdinand, *Behind the Frontlines: Journey into Afro-Britain*, London: Victor Gollancz, 1988.

Denny, Neville (ed.), *Pan African Short Stories*, London: Nelson, 1965. [Ama Ata Aidoo, Barbara Kimenye, Grace Ogot, Efua Sutherland]

Deodene, Frank, and William P. French, *Black American Poetry since 1944: A Preliminary Checklist*, Chatham, NJ: Chatham Bookseller, 1971.

Desalmand, P., *L'Emancipation de la femme en Afrique et dans le monde*, Nouvelles Editions Africaines, 1977.

Dhondy, Farrukh (comp.), *Ranters, Ravers and Rhymers: Poems by Black and Asian Poets*, London: Collins, 1990. [Grace Nichols, Jean Binta Breeze, Lorna Goodison, Kristina Rungano]

Dickinson, Margaret (ed.), *When Bullets Begin to Flower*, Nairobi: East African Publishing House, 1972. [Noémia De Sousa]

Diggs, Irene, *Black Chronology: From 4000 BC to the Abolition of the Slave Trade*, Boston: G. K. Hall, 1983.

Dill, Bonnie, "The Dialectics of Black Womanhood", *Signs*, 4 (Spring 1979), pp. 543–55.

Dillard, J. L., *Black English: Its History and Usage in the United States*, New York: Random House, 1972, Vintage, 1973.

———, *Lexicon of Black English*, New York: Seabury Press, 1977.

Diop, Cheikh Anta, *The African Origin of Civilization: Myth or Reality* [compilation of selections from *Nations Nègres et Culture* and *Antériorité des Civilisations Nègres*], Paris: Présence Africaine (1955 and 1967), ed./trans. Mercer Cook; New York/Westport: Lawrence Hill & Co., 1974.

———, *The Cultural Unity of Black Africa: The Domains of Patriarchy and of Matriarchy in Classical Antiquity*, new intr. Ifi Amadiume; London: Karnak House, 1989.

———, *Precolonial Black Africa*, Westport: Lawrence Hill.

Dodgson, Elyse, *Motherland: West Indian Women to Britain in the 1960s*, London: Heinemann Educational Books, 1984.

Donnan, Elizabeth, *Documents Illustrative of the History of the Slave Trade to America*, 4 vols, Washington, DC: Carnegie Institute, 1930–35.

Doob, Leonard W. (ed.), *Ants Will Not Eat Your Fingers: A Selection of Traditional African Poems*, New York: Walker & Co./Toronto: George J. McLeod, 1966.

Drachler, Jacob (ed.), *African Heritage: Intimate Views of the Black Africans from Life, Lore, and Literature*, preface Melville J. Herskovits; New York: Crowell-Collier, 1963, Macmillan, 1964; London: Collier Macmillan, 1969.

Dreer, Herman (ed.), *American Literature by Negro Authors*, New York:

Macmillan, 1950. [Gwendolyn Brooks, Rosa Paul Brooks, Floretta Howard, Georgia Douglas Johnson, Naomi Long Madgett, Ophelia Robinson, Alice McGee Smart, Anne Spencer, Evelyn Watson, Phillis Wheatley]

Driberg, J. H., *Initiation: Translations from Poems of the Didinga and Lango Tribes*, London: Golden Cockerel Press, 1932.

——, *People of the Small Arrow*, New York: Payson & Clarke, 1930.

——(ed.), *Poems of the Didinga and Lango Tribes*, Golden Cockerel Press.

DuBois, Ellen Carol, and Vivki L. Ruiz (eds), *Unequal Sisters: A Multi-Cultural Reader in US Women's History*, New York/London: Routledge, 1990. [Elsa Barkley Brown, Hazel V. Carby, Darlene Clark Hine, Deborah Gray White]

Du Bois, W. E. B., *The Negro American Family*, Atlanta: Atlanta University Press, 1908.

——, *The Suppression of the African Slave-Trade to the United States of America, 1638–1870*, Cambridge, Mass.: Harvard University Press, 1896; New York: Russell & Russell, 1965.

Duerden, Dennis, and Cosmo Pieterse, *African Writers Talking*, London: Heinemann Educational Books, 1972. [Ama Ata Aidoo, Efua Sutherland]

Duignan, Peter, and Clarence Clendenen, *The United States and the African Slave Trade, 1619–1862*, Stanford: Hoover Institute, 1963.

Dunbar-Nelson, Alice (ed.), *The Dunbar Speaker and Entertainer, containing the best prose and poetic selections by and about the Negro race, with programs arranged for special entertainments*, Naperville, Ill.: Nichols Publishing Co., 1920. [Charlotte Forten Grimké]

——(ed.), *Masterpieces of Negro Eloquence: the best speeches delivered by the Negro from the days of slavery to the present time*, New York: Bookery, 1914; Chicago: Johnson Reprint Corp., 1970. [Fanny Jackson Coppin, Alice Dunbar-Nelson, Frances E. W. Harper, Josephine St Pierre Ruffin]

Dupland, E. (ed.), *Les Poètes de la Guadeloupe*, Paris: J. Grassin, 1978. [Viviane Berdier, Jacqueline Bloncourt-Herselin, Paule Dursus de Kermadec, Francine Firmo, Jeanne de Kermadec, Maryse Pakardine, Jacqueline Plenet, Agathe Reache, Francesca Velayduron]

Earthy, E. Dora, *Valenge Women: The Social and Economic Life of the Valenge Women of Portuguese East Africa*, London: Cass, 1968.

Edwards, Paul (ed.), *West African Narrative*, Edinburgh: Nelson, 1963. [Adelaide Casely-Hayford]

Edwards, Paul, and David Dabydeen (eds), *Black Writers in Britain 1760–1890*, Edinburgh: Edinburgh University Press, 1992. [Harriet Jacobs, Mary Prince]

Edwards, Paul, and James Walvin, *Black Personalities in the Era of the Slave Trade*, London: Macmillan, 1983.

Elliott, Lorris (ed.), *Bibliography of Literary Black Writings in Canada*, Stratford, Ontario: Williams-Wallace Publishers.

——(ed.), *Other Voices: Writings by Blacks in Canada*, Stratford, Ontario: Williams-Wallace Publishers.

Ellis, Pat (ed.), *Women of the Caribbean*, London: Zed/Kingston Publishers, 1986. [Jeanette Bell, Agnes Hammel-Smith]

Emanuel, James A., and Theodore L. Gross (eds), *Dark Symphony: Negro Literature in America*, New York: Free Press/London: Collier Macmillan,

1968. [Gwendolyn Brooks, Mari E. Evans, Paule Marshall, Margaret Walker]

Equiano, Olaudah, *Interesting Narrative of the Life of Olaudah Equiano, or Gustavus Vassa, the African, written by himself*, London, 1789; ed. Paul Edwards, Heinemann Educational Books, 1967.

Erro-Peralta, Nora, and Caridad Silva-Núñez, *Beyond the Border: A New Age in Latin American Women's Fiction*, Pittsburgh/San Francisco: Cleis Press, 1990. [Lydia Cabrera, Aída Cartagena Portalatín]

Espinet, Ramabai (ed.), *Creation Fire: A CAFRA Anthology of Caribbean Women's Poetry*, Toronto, Ontario: Sister Vision: Black Women and Women of Colour Press/Tunapuna, Trinidad & Tobago: CAFRA [Caribbean Association for Feminist Research and Action], 1990. [Opal Palmer Adisa, V. M. Albert, Lillian Allen, Karin Ammon, Lynette Atwell, Louise Bennett, Kamla Best, Sandra Bihari, Jean Binta Breeze, Priscilla Brown, Rosanne Brunton, A. M. Burgos, Anielli J. Camrhal, Peggy Carr, Christene Clarkson, Michelle Cliff, Merle Collins, Afua Cooper, Madeline Coopsammy, Christine Craig, Pauline Crawford, Pauline Crawford, Cheza Dailey, Nydia Bruce Daniel, Mahadai Das, Maria C. Diwan, Gladys Do Rego-Kuster, R. H. Douglas, Nydia Ecury, Ushanda Io Elima, Zoila M. Ellis, Aimée Eloidin, Ramabai Espinet, Evelyne, Lima Fabien, Honor Ford-Smith, Bernice Fraser, Dawn French, Joan French, Frome Cultural Club, Mary Garcia Castro, Lydia Geerman, Charmaine Gill, Margaret D. Gill, Lorna Goodison, Carolle Grant, Gladys August Hall, Claire Harris, Gina Henriquez, Jane King Hippolyte, Germaine Y. Horton, Audrey Ingram-Roberts, Celene Jack, Meryl James-Bryan, Meiling Jin, Amryl Johnson, Stacy Johnson, Lorraine F. Joseph, C. Carrilho-Fazal Ali Khan, Belen Kock-Marchena, Randi Gray Kristensen, Ruffina Lee Sheng Tin, Sharon Lee Wah, Audre Lorde, Joy Mahabir, Niala Maharaj, Ahdri Zhina Mandiela, Angelique Marsan, Marina Ama Omowale Maxwell, Pauline Melville, Nancy Morejón, Amy Nicholas, Grace Nichols, Norma Nichols, Nneka, Grace Nobbee-Eccles, Sita Parsan, Joyce Peters-McKenzie, Marlene Nourbese Philip, Velma Pollard, Asha Radjkoemar, Vanda Radzik, Jennifer Rahim, Triveni Rahim, Rajandaye Ramkissoon-Chen, Indrani Rampersad, Dawn Mahalia Riley, Nelcia Robinson, Tiffany Robinson, Leone Ross, Rumeena, Evelyn St Hill, Ruth Sawh, Seketi, Olive Senior, Kiren Shoman, Hazel Simmons-MacDonald, Dorothy Wong Loi Sing, Deborah Singh-Ramlochan, Shirley Small, Leleti Tamu, Yvonne Mechtelli Tijn-a-Sie, Martha Tjoe-Nij, Annette L. Trotman, Imelda Valerianus-Fermina, Gladys Waterberg, Margaret Watts, Marie-Ella Williams, Joy Wilson-Tucker, Marguerite Wyke]

Evans, Mari (ed.), *Black Women Writers (1950–1980): A Critical Evaluation*, Garden City, NY: Anchor/Doubleday, 1984: as *Black Women Writers: Arguments and Interviews*, London: Pluto, 1985. [Maya Angelou, Toni Cade Bambara, Gwendolyn Brooks, Alice Childress, Lucille Clifton, Mari E. Evans, Nikki Giovanni, Gayl Jones, Audre Lorde, Paule Marshall, Toni Morrison, Carolyn M. Rodgers, Sonia Sanchez, Alice Walker, Margaret Walker]

Exum, Pat Crutchfield (ed.), *Contemporary Black Women Writers*, Deland, Fla: Everett/Edwards, 1976.

——(ed.), *Keeping the Faith: Writings by Contemporary Black American Women*, Greenwich, Conn.: Fawcett Publications/Premier, 1974, 1981. [Barbara

A. Banks, Alice Childress, Gayl Jones, Audre Lorde, Paule Marshall, Toni Morrison, Alice Walker]

Fabre, Michel, *From Harlem to Paris: Black American Writers in France, 1840-1980*, Urbana/Chicago: University of Illinois Press, 1991.

Fage, John D., *A History of Africa*, London: Hutchinson, 1978.

Feinberg, Barry (ed.), *Poets to the People: South African Freedom Songs*, London: Allen & Unwin, 1974: Heinemann Educational Books, African Writers Series 230, 1980. [Lindiwe Mabuza, Ilva Mackay, Rebecca Matlou]

Fernandes, Florestan, *The Negro in Brazilian Society*, trans. Jacqueline D. Skiles, A. Brunel, Arthur Rothwell; New York: Atheneum, 1971.

Ferreira, Manuel, and Gerard Moser (comps), *Bibliography of Portuguese-African Literature*, Lisbon: Edicoes 70 and Instituto de Alta Cultura, 1981.

Fetterley, Judith (ed.), *Provisions: A Reader from Nineteenth-Century American Women*, Bloomington: Indiana University Press, 1985. [Charlotte Forten Grimké, Harriet Jacobs, Maria W. Stewart]

Figueroa, John (ed.), *Caribbean Voices*, Vol. 1: *Dreams and Visions*, London: Evans Brothers, 1966. [Gloria Escoffery, Barbara Ferland, Vivette Hendriks, Constance Hollar, Mary Lockett, Una Marson, Stella Mead, Daisy Myrie]

——(ed.), *Caribbean Voices*, Vol. 2: *The Blue Horizons*, London: Evans, 1970. [Louise Bennett, Gloria Escoffery, Barbará Ferland, Vivette Hendriks, Una Marson, Dorothy Phillips, Clovis Scott]

——(ed.), *Caribbean Voices* [above 2 vols combined], 1971; Washington. DC: Robert Luce, 1973.

——(ed.), *An Anthology of African and Caribbean Writing in English*, London: Heinemann Educational Books/Open University, 1982, 1987. [Louise Bennett, Christine Craig, Buchi Emecheta, Gloria Escoffery, Honor Ford-Smith, Sally Henzell, Heather Royes, Olive Senior]

File, Nigel, and Chris Power, *Black Settlers in Britain 1555–1958*, London: Heinemann Educational Books, 1981.

Finn, Julio, *Voices of Négritude*, London: Quartet, 1988. [Nancy Morejón]

Finnegan, Ruth, *Oral Literature in Africa*, Oxford: Clarendon Press, 1970.

Fisher, Dexter (ed.), *The Third Woman: Minority Women Writers of the United States*, Boston: Houghton Mifflin, 1980. [Colleen McElroy]

Fisk University Library, *Dictionary Catalog of the Negro Collection of the Fisk University Library*, 6 vols, Boston: G. K. Hall, 1974,

Fitzgerald, Kitty (ed.), *Iron Women: New Stories by Women*, North Shields, Tyne & Wear: Iron Press, 1990. [Devi Maharaj, Sandi Russell]

Foster, Frances S., "Changing Concepts of the Black Woman", *Journal of Black Studies* 3 (June 1973), pp. 433–54.

Fox-Genovese, Eugene, *Within the Plantation Household: Black and White Women of the Old South*, Chapel Hill: North Carolina University Press, 1988.

Franklin, John Hope, *From Slavery to Freedom: A History of American Negroes*, New York: Knopf, 1947, 4th edn 1974.

Frazier, E. Franklin, *The Negro Family in the United States*, Chicago: University of Chicago Press, 1939.

Frazier, E. F., *Black Bourgeoisie*, Glencoe, Ill.: Free Press, 1957.

——, *The Negro in the United States*, New York: Macmillan, 1949.

Freedman, Frances (ed.), *The Black Experience*, New York: Bantam, 1970. [Nikki Giovanni]

Frickey, Pierrette, and Elaine Campbell (eds). *Women Writers from the Caribbean*, Washington, DC: Three Continents Press, 1990.

Frucht, Richard (ed.), *Black Society in the New World*, New York: Random House, 1971.

Fryer, Peter, *Black People in the British Empire: An Introduction*, London: Pluto, 1988.

——, *Staying Power: The History of Black People in Britain*, London: Pluto, 1984.

Ganz, David L., and Donald E. Herdeck (comps), *A Critical Guide to Anthologies of African Literature*, Waltham, Mass.: Brandeis University, African Studies Association, Literature Committee, 1973.

Gaptooth Girlfriends (eds), *Gaptooth Girlfriends: An Anthology*, Brooklyn, NY: Gaptooth Girlfriends Publications, 1981.

——, *Gaptooth Girlfriends: The Third Act*, New York: Third Act Press, 1985.

Gates, Henry Louis, Jr (ed.), *Black Literature and Literary Theory*. New York: Methuen, 1984; New York/London: Routledge, 1990. [Barbara E. Bowen, Barbara Johnson, Mary Helen Washington, Susan Willis]

——(ed.), *Reading Black, Reading Feminist: A Critical Anthology*, New York: Meridian/NAL, 1990. [Hazel V. Carby, Barbara Christian, Rita Dove, Elizabeth Fox-Genovese, Jewelle L. Gomez, Mae Gwendolyn Henderson, Zora Neale Hurston, Barbara E. Johnson, Jamaica Kincaid, Deborah E. McDowell, Nellie Y. McKay, Valerie Smith, Hortense J. Spillers, Michele Wallace, Mary Helen Washington, Sherley Anne Williams]

Gayle, Addison, Jr (ed.), *The Black Aesthetic*, Garden City, NY: Anchor/Doubleday, 1972. [Sarah Webster Fabio, Carolyn F. Gerald, Toni Morrison]

——(ed.), *Black Expression: Essays by and about Black Americans in the creative arts*, New York: Weybright & Talley, 1969. [Toni Cade (Bambara), Barbara Christian, Sarah Webster Fabio, Jessie Redmon Fauset, Margaret Walker]

Genovese, Eugene D., *Roll, Jordan, Roll: The World the Slaves Made*, New York: Pantheon, 1972.

Giddings, Paula, *In Search of Sisterhood: Delta Sigma Theta and the Challenge of the Black Sorority Movement*, New York: Morrow, 1988.

——, *When and Where I Enter: The Impact of Black Women on Race and Sex in America*, New York: Morrow, 1984, Bantam, 1985.

Gilroy, Paul, *"There Ain't No Black in the Union Jack": The Cultural Politics of Race and Nation*, London: Hutchinson, 1987.

Giovanni, Nikki (ed.), *Night Comes Softly: An Anthology of Black Female Voices*, Newark, NJ: Medic Press, 1970. [Sonia Sanchez]

Glikin, Ronda, *Black American Women in Literature, a Bibligraphy, 1976 through 1987*, Jefferson, NC: McFarland, 1987.

Gloster, Hugh M., *Negro Voices in American Fiction*, Chapel Hill: University of North Carolina Press, 1948; New York: Russell & Russell, 1965.

Golden-Hanga, Lily, *Africans in Russia*, Moscow: Novosti Press, 1966.

Gomez, Alma, Cherrie Moraga and Mariana Romo-Carmona (eds), *Cuentos:*

Stories by Latinas, Latham, NY: Kitchen Table, 1987. [Cenen, Alma M. Gomez, Carolina Maria de Jesús, Aurora Levins Morales, Milagros Perez-Huth, Aleida Rodriguez, Sara Rosel, Luz Selenia Vazquez, Iris Zavala]

Gonzales, Lelia, and Carlos Hasenbalg, *Lugar de Negro*, Rio de Janeiro: Editora Marco Zero, 1982.

Goodwin, June, *Cry Amandla! South African Women and the Question of Power*, New York: Africana Publishing, 1984.

Gordon, Eugene, *The Position of Negro Women*, New York: Workers' Library, 1935.

Gordon, Suzanne, *A Talent for Tomorrow: Life Stories of South African Servants*, Johannesburg: Ravan Press, 1985.

Gordon, Vivian, *Black Women, Feminism, and Black Liberation: Which Way?*, Chicago: Third World Press, 1985.

Goss, Linda, and Marian E. Barnes (eds), *Talk That Talk: An Anthology of African-American Storytelling*, intr. Henry Louis Gates, Jr, New York: Touchstone/Simon & Schuster, 1989.

Goveia, Elsa, *The West Indian Slave Laws of the Eighteenth Century*, Caribbean Universities Press, 1970.

Grahn, Judy (ed.), *True to Life Adventure Stories*, Vol. 1, Diana Press, 1978; Trumansburg, NY: Crossing Press, 1983; [Red Jordan Arobateau, Pat Parker]

Granqvist, Raoul, and John Stotesbury (eds), *African Voices: Interviews with Thirteen African Writers*, Australia/Denmark/Coventry, UK: Dangaroo, 1990. [Ama Ata Aidoo, Buchi Emecheta, Lauretta Ngcobo, Miriam Tlali]

Grant, Douglas, *The Fortunate Slave: An Illustration of African Slavery in the Early Eighteenth Century*, London: Oxford University Press, 1968.

Gray, Stephen (ed.), *On the Edge of the World: Southern African Stories of the Seventies*, Johannesburg: Ad. Donker, 1974. [Sheila Fugard, Bessie Head] ——(ed.), *The Penguin Book of South African Stories*, Harmondsworth: Penguin. [Bessie Head]

Green, Veronica (comp.), *The Rhythm of Our Days,* Cambridge: Cambridge University Press, 1991. [Maya Angelou, Gwendolyn Brooks, Nikki Giovanni, Grace Nichols, Marsha Prescod, Alice Walker]

Grewal, Shabnam, Jackie Kay, Liliane Landor, Gail Lewis and Pratibha Parmar (eds), *Charting the Journey: Writings by Black and Third World Women*, London: Sheba, 1988. [Adjoa Andoh, Kum-Kum Bhavnani, Avtar Brah, Barbara Burford, Dinah Anuli Butler, Zeina Carrington, Olivette Cole-Wilson, Bernardine Evaristo, Stephanie George, Rahila Gupta, Shaheen Haque, Linda King, Gail Lewis, Liliane Landor, Audre Lorde, Isha McKenzie-Mavinga, Eveline Marius, Pauline Moure, Elaine Okoro, Sona Osman, Ingrid Pollard, Mo Ross, Agnes Sam, Joyce Spencer, Maud Sulter, Lola Thomas, Protasia Torkington, Carmen Tunde, Jacqueline Ward, Yvonne Weekes, Claudette Williams]

Gross, Seymour L., and John E. Hardy, "Bibliography: The Negro in American Literature, A Checklist of Criticism and Scholarship", *Images of the Negro in American Literature*, eds S. L. Gross and J. E. Hardy; Chicago: University of Illinois Press, 1966.

Guptara, Prabhu, *Black British Writing: An Annotated Bibliography*, London: Dangaroo, 1987.

Gutman, Herbert G., *The Black Family in Slavery and Freedom, 1750–1925*, New York: Pantheon, 1976; Random House, 1977.

Guy, Rosa (ed.), *Children of Longing*, New York: Bantam, 1970. [Nikki Giovanni]

Guyonneau, Christine H., "Francophone Women Writers from Sub-Saharan Africa", *Callaloo* 8:2 (Spring–Summer 1985), pp. 453–83.

Gwaltney, John Langston (ed.), *Drylongso: A Self-Portrait of Black America*, New York: Random House/Vintage, 1980. [Erica Allen, Avis Briar, Carolyn Chase, Velma Cunningham, Celia Delaney, Mabel Johns, Harriet Jones, Hattie Lanarck, Margaret Lawson, Mabel Lincoln, Angela McArthur, Janet McCrae, May Anna Madison, Gloria Melton, Hannah Nelson, Estelle O'Connor, Johnetta Ray, Alberta Roberts, Ellen Saunders, Janice Saunders, Ruth Shays, Ellen Turner Surry, Nancy White]

Gwin, Minrose C., *Black and White Women in the Old South: The Peculiar Sisterhood in American Literature*, Knoxville: University of Tennessee Press, 1985.

Habekast, Christian, *Dub Poetry: 19 Poets from England and Jamaica*, Neustadt, Germany: Michael Schwinn, 1986. [Jean Binta Breeze, Sista Nita, Anita Steward]

Hafkin, Nancy, and Edna G. Bay (eds), *Women in Africa: Studies in Social and Economic Change*, Stanford, CA: Stanford University Press, 1976.

Haley, Alex, *Roots*, New York: 1977; London: Hutchinson, 1977.

Halsey, Peggy L., Gail J. Morlan and Melba Smith (eds), *If You Want to Know Me: Reflections of Life in South Africa*, New York: Friendship Press, 1976. [Josina Machel, Zindzi Mandela, Gladys Thomas]

Hamilton, Kelly, *Goals and Plans of Black Women: A Sociological Study*, Hicksville, NY: Exposition Press, 1975.

Hamilton, Russell G., *Voices from an Empire: A History of Afro-Portuguese Literature*, Minneapolis: University of Minnesota Press, 1975.

Hammond, Jenny, and Nel Druce (eds), *Sweeter Than Honey: Testimonies of Tigrayan Women*, Oxford: Links/Third World First, 1989.

Hammonds, Evelyn, "Towards a Black Feminist Aesthetic", *Sojourner* (October 1980).

Haniff, Nesha, *Blaze a Fire: Significant Contributions of Caribbean Women*.

Hanry, Pierre, *Erotisme africain*, Paris: Payot, 1970.

Harding, Vincent, *There Is a River: The Black Struggle for Freedom in America*, New York: Harcourt Brace Jovanovich, 1981.

Harley, Sharon, and Rosalyn Terborg-Penn (eds), *The Afro-American Woman: Struggles and Images*, Port Washington: NY/London: National University Publications, Kennikat, 1978. [Sharon Harley, Cynthia Neverdon-Morton, Harriet Pipes McAdoo, Rosalyn Terborg-Penn]

Harper, M., and R. Stepto (eds), *Chant of Saints: A Gathering of Afro-American Literature, Art, and Scholarship*, Champaign/London: University of Illinois Press, 1979. [Gayl Jones, Alice Walker]

Harris, Joseph E. (ed.), *The African Presence in Asia*, Evanston: Northwestern University Press, 1971.

——, *Global Dimensions of the African Diaspora*, Washington, DC: Howard University Press, 1982.

Harris, Trudier, *Exorcising Blackness: Historical and Literary Lynching and Burning Rituals*, Bloomington: Indiana University Press, 1984.

——, *From Mammies to Militants: Domestics in Black American Literature*, Philadelphia: Temple University Press, 1982.

Harris, Trudier, and Thadious M. Davis (eds), *Dictionary of Literary Biography, 50: Afro-American Writers Before the Harlem Renaissance*, Detroit: Gale, 1986. [Entries on Charlotte Forten, Frances E. W. Harper, Pauline Hopkins, Alice Dunbar-Nelson, Henrietta Cordelia Ray, Phillis Wheatley]

——(eds), *Dictionary of Literary Biography, 51: Afro-American Writers from the Harlem Renaissance to 1940*, Detroit: Gale, 1987. [Entries on Gwendolyn B. Bennett, Marita Bonner, Jessie Redmon Fauset, Zora Neale Hurston, Georgia Douglas Johnson, Helene Johnson, Nella Larsen, Anne Spencer]

——(eds), *Dictionary of Literary Biography, 76: Afro-American Writers 1940–1955*, Detroit: Gale, 1988. [Entries on Shirley Graham, Naomi Long Madgett, Beatrice M. Murphy, Effie Lee Newsome, Ann Petry, Dorothy West]

——(eds), *Dictionary of Literary Biography, 38: Afro-American Writers after 1955, Dramatists and Prose Writers*, Detroit: Gale, 1985. [Entries on Maya Angelou, Toni Cade Bambara, Alice Childress, Alexis DeVeaux, Lorraine Hansberry, June Jordan, Adrienne Kennedy, Arthenia J. Bates Millican, Ntozake Shange]

Harrison, Paul (ed.), *Muntu: Plays of the African Continuum*, New York: Grove Press, 1974. [Adrienne Kennedy]

Hatch, James V., and Abdullah Omanii, *Black Playwrights, 1823–1977: An Annotated Bibliography of Plays*, New York: R. R. Bowker, 1977.

Hatch, James V., and Ted Shine (eds), *Black Theater, USA: Forty-five Plays by Black Americans 1847–1974*, New York: Free Press, 1974. [Marita Bonner, Mary Burrill, Martie Charles, Alice Childress, Alice Dunbar-Nelson, Ruth Gaines-Shelton, Angelina Weld Grimké, Georgia Douglas Johnson, Adrienne Kennedy, Myrtle Smith Livingston, May Mille, Eulalie Spence]

Hay, Margaret Jean, and Sharon Stichter (eds), *African Women South of the Sahara*, London/New York: Longman, 1984.

Hayden, Robert E. (ed.), *Kaleidoscope: Poems by American Negro Poets*, New York: Harcourt, Brace & World, 1967. [Gwendolyn Brooks, Margaret Danner, Mari E. Evans, Julia Fields, Frances E. W. Harper, Georgia Douglas Johnson, Naomi Long Madgett, Gloria Oden, Anne Spencer, Margaret Walker, Phillis Wheatley]

Henderson, Gwyneth (ed.), *African Theatre: Eight prize-winning plays for radio*, London: Heinemann Educational Books, African Writers Series 134, 1973. [Derlene Clems, Elvania Namukwaya Zirimu]

Henderson, Gwyneth, and Cosmo Pieterse (eds), *Nine African Plays for Radio*, London: Heinemann Educational Books, African Writers Series 127, 1973. [Patience Henaku Addo, Derlene Clems, Jeanne Ngo Libondo]

Henderson, Stephen (ed.), *Understanding the New Black Poetry: Black Speech and Black Music as Poetic References*, New York: Morrow, 1973. [Johari Amini, Lillie Kate Walker Benitez, Gwendolyn Brooks, Sharon Bourke, Margaret Danner, Mari E. Evans, Sarah Webster Fabio, Betty Gates, Nikki Giovanni, Pamela Woodruff Hill, Audre Lorde, Daphne Dianne Page, Gertrude "Ma" Rainey, Carolyn M. Rodgers, Sonia Sanchez, Judy Dothard Simmons, Margaret Walker]

Herdeck, Donald E. (ed.), *African Authors: A Companion to Black African Writing, Vol. I: 1300–1973*, Washington, DC: Black Orpheus Press/Inscape Corporation, 1974.

——(ed.), *Caribbean Writers: A Bio-Bibliographical-Critical Encyclopaedia*, Washington, DC: Three Continents Press, 1979.

Hernton, Calvin, *Sex and Racism in America*, New York: Doubleday, 1965, Grove, 1966.

——, *The Sexual Mountain and Black Women Writers: Adventures in Sex, Literature, and Real Life*, Garden City, NY: Anchor/Doubleday, 1987.

Herskovits, Melville J., *Dahomey*, New York: Augustin, 1938.

——, *The Myth of the Negro Past*, Boston: Beacon Press, 1941, 1958.

Higgins, Chester, *Black Woman*, New York: McCall, 1970.

Hill, Errol (ed.), *Black Heroes: Seven Plays*, New York: Applause Theatre Book Publishers, 1989. [May Miller]

Hill, Herbert (ed.), *Black Voices: New Writing by American Negroes*, New York: Knopf, 1963; London: Elek, 1964. [Gwendolyn Brooks, Katherine Dunham, Betty Gates, Pauli Murray, Ann Petry, Dorothy West]

——(ed.), *Soon, One Morning: New Writing by American Writers, 1940–1962*. New York: Knopf, 1963.

Hiro, Dilip, *Black British, White British: A History of Race Relations in Britain*, London: Eyre & Spottiswoode, 1971; revised, Pelican, 1973; Grafton, 1991.

Hoetink, H., *Slavery and Race Relations in the Americas*, New York, 1973.

Hogg, Peter C., *The African Slave Trade and its Suppression, A Classified and Annotated Bibliography of Books, Pamphlets and Periodical Articles*, London: Frank Cass, 1973.

Honey, Maureen (ed.), *Shadowed Dreams: Women's Poetry of the Harlem Renaissance*, Foreword Nellie Y. McKay; New Brunswick/London: Rutgers University Press, 1989. [Gwendolyn B. Bennett, Lillian Byrnes, Joyce Sims Carrington, Gladys Casely-Hayford, Ethel M. Caution, Anita Scott Coleman, Mae V. Cowdery, Clarissa Scott Delany, Blanche Taylor Dickinson, Ruth G. Dixon, Alice Dunbar-Nelson, Jessie Redmon Fauset, Angelina Weld Grimké, Virginia A. Houston, Mary Jenness, Georgia Douglas Johnson, Helene Johnson, Rosalie M. Jonas, Dorothy Kruger, Elma Ehrlich Levinger, Marjorie Marshall, Bessie Mayle, Dorothea Mathews, Isabel Neill, Effie Lee Newsome, Esther Popel, Anne Spencer, Margaret L. Thomas, Eloise Bibb Thompson, Eda Lou Walton, Lucy Ariel Williams, Octavia Beatrice Wynbush, Kathleen Tankersley Young]

Hood, Elizabeth, "Black Women, White Women, Different Paths to Liberation", *Black Scholar* 9 (April 1978), pp. 45–56.

Hooks, Bell, *Ain't I a Woman? Black Women and Feminism*, London: Pluto, 1982.

——, *Feminist Theory: From Margin to Center*, Boston: South End Press, 1984.

——, *Talking Back: Thinking Feminist – Thinking Black*, Boston: South End Press; London: Sheba, 1989.

——, *Yearning: Race, Gender, and Cultural Politics*, Boston: South End Press; London: Turnaround, 1990.

Hopkins, Lee Bennett (ed.), *On Our Way*, New York: Knopf, 1974. [Lucille

Clifton, Linda Curry, Mari E. Evans, Nikki Giovanni, Naomi Long Madgett, Linda Porter, Jo Nell Rice, Yolande Zealy]

Hopkinson, Amanda (ed.), *Lovers and Comrades: Women's resistance poetry from Central America*, trans. Amanda Hopkinson and members of El Salvador Solidarity Campaign Cultural Committee, London: Women's Press, 1989. [Eulalia Bernard, Nancy Morejón]

House, Amelia, *Black Women Writers from South Africa: A Preliminary Checklist*, Evanston: Northwestern University Program on Women, 1980.

Howard University Founders Library, *Moorland Foundation Dictionary Catalog of the Jesse E. Moorland Collection of Negro Life and History*, 9 vols, Boston: G. K. Hall, 1962.

Howard University Library, *Dictionary Catalog of the Arthur B. Spingarn Collection of Negro Authors*, 2 vols; Boston: G. K. Hall, 1970.

Howe, Florence, and Ellen Bass (eds), *No More Masks: An Anthology of Poems by Women*, Garden City, NY: Anchor/Doubleday, 1973. [Gwendolyn Brooks, Carole Gregory Clemmons, Lucille Clifton, Mari E. Evans, Carole Freeman, Nikki Giovanni, June Jordan, Audre Lorde, Pauli Murray, Carolyn M. Rodgers, Sonia Sanchez, Alice Walker, Margaret Walker]

Howes, Barbara (ed.), *From the Green Antilles*, New York: Macmillan, 1966; London: Souvenir Press, 1967, Panther, 1971. [Lydia Cabrera, Florette Morand]

Huggins, Nathan (ed.), *Voices from the Harlem Renaissance*, New York: Oxford University Press, 1975. [Gwendolyn B. Bennett, Jessie Redmon Fauset, Georgia Douglas Johnson, Helene Johnson]

Hughes, Carl Milton, *The Negro Novelist: A Discussion of the Writings of American Negro Novelists, 1949–1950*, New York: Citadel, 1953.

Hughes, Langston (ed.), *An African Treasury: articles, essays, stories, poems by black Africans*, New York: Crown, 1960, Pyramid; London: Gollancz, 1961. [Adelaide Casely-Hayford, Mabel Dove-Danquah, Marion Morel, Phyllis Ntantala, Efua Sutherland]

——(ed.), *Poems from Black Africa*, Bloomington: Indiana University Press, 1963. [Gladys Casely-Hayford, Marina Gashe (Rebeka Njau), Francesca Pereira-Emanuel]

——(ed.), *New Negro Poets USA*, intr. Gwendolyn Brooks, Bloomington: Indiana University Press, 1964. [Vivian Ayers, Helen Morgan Brooks, Isabella Maria Brown, Margaret Danner, Mari E. Evans, Julia Fields, Vilma Howard, Audre Lorde, Georgia Love, Naomi Long Madgett, Gloria Oden, Lucy Smith]

——(ed.), *The Best Short Stories by Negro Writers: An Anthology From 1899 to the Present*, Boston: Little, Brown & Co., 1967. [Helen Morgan Brooks, Alice Childress, Paule Marshall, Alice Walker]

Hughes, Langston, and Arna Bontemps (eds), *The Poetry of the Negro: 1746–1949*, Garden City, NY: Doubleday, 1949, 1953; revised as *The Poetry of the Negro: 1746–1970*, see below. [Gwendolyn B. Bennett, Gwendolyn Brooks, Helen Johnson Collins, Margaret Danner, Clarissa Scott Delany, Alice Dunbar-Nelson, Mari E. Evans, Jessie Redmon Fauset, Angelina Weld Grimké, Frances E. W. Harper, Constance Hollar, Ariel Williams Holloway, Dorothy Vena Johnson, Helene Johnson, Bette Darcie Latimer, Mary Lockett, Paule Marshall, Beatrice M. Murphy, Effie Lee Newsome, Stephanie Ormsby, Mary

Carter Smith, Anne Spencer, Lucy Terry, Margaret Walker, Phillis Wheatley]
——(eds), *The Poetry of the Negro, 1746–1970*, Garden City, NY: Doubleday, 1971. [Nanina Alba, Gwendolyn B. Bennett, Gwendolyn Brooks, Helen Morgan Brooks, Isabella Maria Brown, Helen Johnson Collins, Margaret Danner, Clarissa Scott Delany, Alice Dunbar-Nelson, Mari E. Evans, Sarah Webster Fabio, Jessie Redmon Fauset, Carol Freeman, Angelina Weld Grimké, Frances E. W. Harper, Constance Hollar, Ariel Williams Holloway, Dorothy Vena Johnson, Georgia Douglas Johnson, Helene Johnson, Naomi Long Madgett, Beatrice M. Murphy, Effie Lee Newsome, Gloria Oden, S. Carolyn Reese, Lucy Smith, Mary Carter Smith, Anne Spencer, Lucy Terry, Margaret Walker, Phillis Wheatley, Sarah E. Wright]

Hull, Gloria T., *Color, Sex and Poetry: Three Women Writers of the Harlem Renaissance* [on Alice Dunbar-Nelson, Angelina Weld Grimké, Georgia Douglas Johnson], Bloomington: Indiana University Press, 1987.

Hull, Gloria T., Patricia Bell Scott and Barbara Smith (eds), *All the Women Are White, All the Blacks Are Men, But Some of Us Are Brave: Black Women's Studies*, Old Westbury, NY: Feminist Press, 1982. [Lorraine Bethel, Martha Hursey Brown, Constance Carroll, Combahee River Collective, Tia Cross, Rita Dandridge, Jacquelyn Grant, Elizabeth Higginbotham, Gloria T. Hull, Freada Klein, Ramona Blair Mathewson, Jeanne-Marie Miller, Ellen Pence, Michele Russell, Patricia Bell Scott, Joan R. Sherman, Barbara Smith, Beverly Smith, Erlene Stetson, Alice Walker, Michele Wallace, Mary Helen Washington, R. Ora Williams, Dora Wilson, Jean Fagan Yellin]

Indiana University, *The Black Family and the Black Woman: A Bibliography*, Bloomington: Indiana University Library and Afro-American Studies Dept, 1972.

Inge, M. Thomas, Maurice Duke and Jackson R. Byer, *Black American Writers: Bibliographical Essays. Vol. 1: Beginnings Through the Harlem Renaissance and Langston Hughes*, New York: St Martin's Press; London: Macmillan, 1978.

International Defence and Aid Fund for Southern Africa, *To Honour Women's Day: Profiles of Leading Women in the South African and Namibian Liberation Struggles*, London: IDAF, 1981.

——, *Women Under Apartheid*, London: IDAF, 1981.

Irwin, Graham W., *Africans Abroad: A Documentary History of the Black Diaspora in Asia, Latin America and the Caribbean during the Age of Slavery*, New York: Columbia University Press, 1977.

Jackson, Jacquelyn J., "A Partial Bibliography on or Related to Black Women", *Journal of the Study of Behavioural Sciences* 21 (Winter 1975), pp. 90–135.

——, *Labor of Love, Labor of Sorrow: Black Women, Work, and the Family from Slavery to the Present*, New York: Basic Books, 1985.

Jackson, Richard L., *Afro-Spanish American Authors: An Annotated Bibliography of Criticism*, NY/London: Garland, 1980.

——, *The Black Image in Latin American Literature*, New York: John Wiley & Sons, 1973; New Mexico: New Mexico University Press, 1976.

——, *Black Writers in Latin America*, Albuquerque: University of New Mexico Press, 1979.

Jahadhmy, Ali A. (ed.), *Anthology of Swahili Poetry*, London: Heinemann

Educational Books, African Writers Series 192, 1977. [Mwana Kupona Msham]

Jahn, Jahnheinz, *A Bibliography of Neo-African Literature from Africa, America and the Caribbean*, New York: Praeger, 1965; London: André Deutsch, 1965.

Jahn, Jahnheinz, and C. P. Dressler (comps), *Bibliography of Creative African Writing*, Nendeln, Liechtenstein: Kraus-Thomson Organization, 1971.

Jahn, Jahnheinz, Ulla Schild and Almut Nordmann (eds), *Who's Who in African Literature: Biographies, Works and Commentaries*, Tübingen: Horst Erdmann Verlag, 1972.

James, Adeola (ed.), *In Their Own Voices: African Women Writers Talk*, London: James Currey/Nairobi: Heinemann Kenya/Portsmouth, NH: Heinemann Educational Books, 1990. [Ama Ata Aidoo, Zaynab Alkali, Buchi Emecheta, Pamela Kola, Ellen Kuzwayo, Muthoni Likimani, Micere Githae Mugo, Penina Muhando, Joyce Ochieng, Asenath Odaga, Ifeoma Okoye, 'Molara Ogundipe-Leslie, Rebeka Njau, Flora Nwapa, Zulu Sofola]

James, C. L. R., *The Black Jacobins: Toussaint L'Ouverture and the San Domingo Revolution*, London: Secker & Warburg, 1938; revised edn, Allison & Busby, 1980; New York: Vintage, 1963.

——, *A History of Negro Revolt*, London, *Fact* monograph no. 18, September 1938; New York: Haskell, 1967; revised as *A History of Pan-African Revolt*, intr. Marvin Holloway, Washington, DC: Drum and Spear Press, 1969; London: Race Today Publications, 1985.

James, Louis, *Writers from the Caribbean*, London: Book Trust, 1990.

Jenkins, Davis, *Black Zion: The Return of Afro-Americans and West Indians to Africa*, London: Wildwood House, 1975.

Johnson, Charles S. (ed.), *Ebony and Topaz: A Collectanea*, New York: Opportunity, National Urban League, 1927; Plainview, NY: Books for Libraries Press, 1971. [Gwendolyn B. Bennett, Marita Bonner (Joseph Maree Andrew), Lillian Brown, Mae V. Cowdery, Lois Augusta Cuglar, Blanche Taylor Dickinson, Alice Dunbar-Nelson, Angelina Weld Grimké, Maud Cuney Hare, Katherine Jackson Hunter, Zora Neale Hurston, Gladys M. Jameson, Georgia Douglas Johnson, Helene Johnson, Brenda Ray Moryck, Dorothy R. Peterson, Anne Spencer]

Johnson, James Weldon (ed.), *The Book of American Negro Poetry*, New York: Harcourt, Brace & World, 1922; revised 1931; 1950, 1958; Plainview, NY: Books for Libraries Press, 1971. [Gwendolyn B. Bennett, Alice Dunbar-Nelson, Jessie Redmon Fauset, Georgia Douglas Johnson, Anne Spencer, Phillis Wheatley, Lucy Ariel Williams]

Johnson, Willa D., and Thomas Green (eds), *Perspectives on Afro-American Women*, Washington, DC: ECCA Publications, 1975.

Jones, Eldred Durosimi, Eustace Palmer and Marjorie Jones (eds), *Women in African Literature Today*, London: James Currey/Trenton, NJ: Africa World Press, 1987.

Jones, Gayl, *Liberating Voices: Oral Tradition in African American Literature*, Cambridge, Mass./London: Harvard University Press, 1991.

Jones, Jacqueline, *Labor of Love, Labor of Sorrow: Black Women, Work and the Family, from Slavery to the Present*, New York: Vintage/Random House, 1986.

Jones, Patricia (ed.), *Ordinary Women: An Anthology of New York City*

Women, New York: Ordinary Women Books, 1978.

Jordan, June (ed.), *Soulscript: Afro-American Poetry*, Garden City, NY: Doubleday, 1970. [Julia Alvarez, Gwendolyn Brooks, Linda Curry, Jackie Earley, Nikki Giovanni, Gayl Jones, June Jordan, Audre Lorde, Naomi Long Madgett, Sonia Sanchez]

Jordan, Winthrop D., *White over Black: American Attitudes Towards the Negro, 1550–1812*, Chapel Hill: University of North Carolina Press, 1968.

Joseph, Gloria, and Jill Lewis, *Common Differences: Conflicts in Black and White Feminist Perspectives*, New York: Anchor/Doubleday, 1981.

Joyce, Donald Franklin, *Gatekeepers of Black Culture: Black-Owned Book Publishing in the United States, 1817–1981*, Westport, Conn.: Greenwood, 1983.

Kaberry, Phyllis M., *Women in Grassfields: A Study of the Economic Position of Women in Bermuda, British Cameroons*, 2nd edn, New York: Humanities Press, 1969.

Kaiser, Ernest (ed.), *A Freedomways Reader: Afro-America in the Seventies*, foreword James Baldwin; Berlin: Seven Seas, 1977. [Arlene P. Bennett, Jean Carey Bond, Dorothy Burnham, Eugenia Collier, Brenda L. Jones, Nancy L. Moore, Augusta Strong, Jacqueline Lee Young]

Kallenbach, Jessamine S. (comp.), *Index to Black American Literary Anthologies*, Boston: G.K. Hall, 1979.

Kanter, Hannah, Sarah Lefanu, Shaila Shah and Carole Spedding (eds), *Sweeping Statements: Writings from the Women's Liberation Movement 1981–83*, London: Women's Press, 1984. [Linda Bellos, Brixton Black Women's Group, Zee Clarke]

Katz, Naomi, and Nancy Milton (eds), *Fragment From a Lost Diary and Other Stories: Women of Asia, Africa, and Latin America*, New York: Random House, 1973; Boston: Beacon Press, 1975; Toronto: Sanders, 1975. [Ama Ata Aidoo, Marjorie Mbilinyi]

Katz, William Loren, *Eyewitness: The Negro in American History*, New York: Pitman, 1967.

Kayper-Mensah, A. W., and Horst Wolff (eds), *Ghanaian Writing: Ghana as Seen by Her Own Writers as well as by German Authors*, Tübingen: Horst Erdmann Verlag, 1972. [Joyce Addo, Ama Ata Aidoo, Efua Sutherland]

Kearns, Francis E. (ed.), *The Black Experience*, New York: Viking, 1970. [Gwendolyn Brooks, Margaret Walker]

Kellner, Bruce (ed.), *The Harlem Renaissance: A Historical Dictionary for the Era*, Westport/London: Greenwood Press, 1984.

Kendricks, Ralph (ed.), *Afro-American Voices: 1770s–1970s*, New York: Oxford Book Co., 1970. [Gwendolyn Brooks, Jymi Jones, Margaret Walker, Phillis Wheatley]

Kenyon, Olga, *Writing Women: Contemporary Women Novelists*, London: Pluto, 1991.

Kerlin, Robert T. (ed.), *Negro Poets and Their Poems*, New York: Associated Publishers, Inc., 1923; Washington, DC: Associated Publishers, 3rd edn 1935. [Gwendolyn Bennett, Gladys May Casely-Hayford, Clarissa Scott Delany, Alice

Dunbar-Nelson, Jessie Redmon Fauset, Sarah Lee Brown Fleming, Charlotte Forten, Angelina Weld Grimké, Mrs J. W. Hammon, Frances E. W. Harper, Eva A. Jessye, Georgia Douglas Johnson, Helene Johnson, Mae Smith Johnson, Corinne Lewis, H. Cordelia Ray, Anne Spencer, Phillis Wheatley]

Kgositsile, Keorapetse (ed.), *The Word Is Here: Poetry from Modern Africa*, New York: Double/Anchor, 1973. [Ama Ata Aidoo]

King, Woodie, Jr (ed.), *Black Short Story Anthology*, New York: NAL, 1972. [Alice Walker]

——(ed.), *Black Spirits: A Festival of New Black Poets in America*, New York: Random House/Vintage, 1972. [Johari Amini, Jackie Earley, Mari E. Evans, Nikki Giovanni, Kali Grosvenor, Mae Jackson, Carolyn M. Rodgers, Sonia Sanchez]

——(ed.), *The Forerunners: Black Poets in America*, Washington, DC: Howard University Press, 1975. [Gwendolyn Brooks, Margaret Goss Burroughs, Margaret Danner, Frances E. W. Harper, Naomi Long Madgett, Margaret Walker]

King, Woodie, Jr, and Ron Milner (eds), *Black Drama Anthology*, New York: NAL, 1971. [Martie Charles, Elaine Jackson]

Klotzman, Phyllis R., and Wilmer H. Baatz, *The Black Family and the Black Woman: A Bibliography*, New York: Arno Press, 1978.

Kochman, Thomas (ed.), *Rappin' and Stylin' Out: Communication in Urban Black America*, Urbana: University of Illinois Press, 1972.

Komey, Ellis A., and Ezekiel Mphahlele (eds), *Modern African Stories*, London: Faber, 1964. [Ama Ata Aidoo, Adelaide Casely-Hayford, Grace Ogot]

Konek, Carol, and Dorothy Walters (eds), *I Hear My Sisters Saying: Poems by Twentieth-Century Women*, New York: Thomas Y. Crowell, 1976. [Maya Angelou, Gwendolyn Brooks, Mari E. Evans, Nikki Giovanni, Naomi Long Madgett, Sonia Sanchez, Alice Walker, Kath Walker]

Kratochvil, Laura, and Shauna Shaw, *African Women: A Select Bibliography*, Cambridge: African Studies Centre, Cambridge University, 1974.

Kubitschek, Missy Kehn, *Claiming the Heritage: African American Women Novelists and History*, University Press of Mississippi.

Kwakwa, B. S. (ed.), *Ghanaian Writing Today: 1*, Accra: Ghana Publishing Corp., 1974. [Ama Ata Aidoo, Mabel Dove-Danquah, Efua Sutherland]

Ladner, Joyce, *Tomorrow's Tomorrow: The Black Woman*, Garden City, NY: Doubleday, 1971.

Lane, Pinkie Gordon (ed.), *Poems by Blacks*, 2 vols, Fort Smith, Ark.: South and West, 1973–5.

Lanker, Brian (photos/interviews), *I Dream a World: Portraits of Black Women Who Changed America*, ed. Barbara Summers, Foreword Maya Angelou, New York: Stewart, Tabori and Chang, 1989. [Margaret Walker Alexander, Ernestine Anderson, Marian Anderson, Maya Angelou, Daisy Bates, Mary Frances Berry, Unita Blackwell, Gwendolyn Brooks, Yvonne Brathwaite Burke, Harriet Elizabeth Byrd, Sherian Grace Cadoria, Alexa Canady, Elizabeth Catlett, Leah Chase, Shirley Chisholm, Septima Poinsetta Clark, Jewel Plummer Cobb, Johnetta B. Cole, Janet Collins, Elizabeth Cotten, Angela Davis, Ruby Dee, Ophelia De Vore-Mitchell, Katherine Dunham, Marian Wright Edelman, Myrlie Evers, Ruby Middleton Forsythe, Althea Gibson, Berthe Knox Gilkey,

Clara McBride Hale, Anna Arnold Hedgeman, Dorothy Irene Height, Lena Horne, Winson and Dovie Hudson, Charlayne Hunter-Gault, Jean Blackwell Huson, Eva Jessye, Cora Lee Johnson, Barbara Jordan, Leontine T. C. Kelly, Coretta Scott King, Autherine Lucy, Jewell Jackson McCabe, Josephine Tiley Matthews, Queen Mother Audley Moore, Toni Morrison, Constance Baker Motley, Eleanor Holmes Norton, Odetta, Rosa Parks, Carrie Saxon Perry, Georgia Montgomery Davis Powers, Leontine Price, Beah Richards, Rachel Robinson, Wilma Rudolph, Sonia Sanchez, Gloria Dean Randle Scott, Betty Shabazz, Althea T. L. Simmons, Norma Merick Sklarek, Willia Mae Ford Smith, Ellen Stewart, Niara Sudarkasa, Johnnie Tillmon, Jackie Torrence, Cicely Tyson, Wyomia Tyus, Sarah Vaughan, Alice Walker, Maxine Waters, Faye Wattleton, Priscilla L. Williams, Oprah Winfrey]

Lapchick, Richard E., and Stephanie Urdang, *Oppression and Resistance: The Struggle of Women in Southern Africa*, Westport, Conn.: Greenwood Press, 1982.

Larson, Charles R. (ed.), *African Short Stories: A collection of contemporary African writing*, New York: Macmillan, 1970; revised as *Modern African Stories*, London: Collins/Fontana, 1971. [Ama Ata Aidoo]

——(ed.), *Opaque Shadows and Other Stories from Africa*, London: Fontana/Collins, 1975; Washington, DC: Inscape, 1975. [Bessie Head, Peninah Ogada]

Laurence, Margaret, *Long Drums and Cannons: Nigerian Dramatists and Novelists*, London: Macmillan, 1968; New York: Praeger, 1969.

Lawson, Lesley, *Working Women in South Africa*, Johannesburg: Ravan Press/Sached Trust, 1985; London: Pluto, 1986. [Alice, Alfie, Anna Catherine, Dolly, Flora, Lydia Konie, Ma Dlomo Lugogo, Mabel, Liza Makalela, Emma Mashinini, Elsie Mbatha, Gugu Mhlongo, Mildred, Mjekula, Rose Modise, Thembi Nabe, Margaret Nhlapo, Nomvula, Rose, Kate Sibiya, Maureen Sithole, Agnes Thulare, Elizabeth Tshayinca, Louise Yekwa]

Leith-Ross, Sylvia, *African Women: A Study of the Ibo of Nigeria*, London: Routledge & Kegan Paul, 1965.

Lerner, Gerda (ed.), *Black Women in White America: A Documentary History*, New York: Random House/Pantheon, 1972, Vintage Press, 1973. [Dara Abubakari (Virginia Collins), Ella Baker, Maria L. Baldwin, Ida B. Wells Barnett, Charlotta Bass, Daisy Bates, Mary McLeod Bethune, Dorothy Bolden, Eva D. Bowles, Charlotte Hawkins Brown, Jean Collier Brown, Nannie Burroughs, Mary Shand Cary, Shirley Chisholm, Septima Poinsetta Clark, Anna J. Cooper, Luanna Cooper, Fannie Jackson Coppin, Ellen Craft, Sarah Mapps Douglass, Elizabeth Piper Ensley, Renee Ferguson, Estelle Flowars, Amy Jacques Garvey, Frances A. Joseph Gaudet, Charlotte Forten Grimké, Fannie Lou Hamer, Frances E. W. Harper, Martha Harrison, Elizabeth Ross Haynes, Anna Arnold Hedgeman, Helen Howard, Charlotte Anne Jackson, Mahalia Jackson, Amanda Smith Jemanda, Lucy Laney, Mollie V. Lewis, Elise Johnson McDougald, Sabina Martinez, Louise Meriwether, Anne Moody, Pauli Murray, Mrs Robert R. Patterson, Florence Rice, Patricia Robinson, Josephine St Pierre Ruffin, Emma L. Shields, Maranda Smith, Amy Spain, Maria Stewart, Ellen Tarry, Susie King Taylor, Mary Church Terrell, Sojourner Truth, Harriet Tubman, Sarah Tuck, Margaret Murray Washington, Mrs Henry Weddington,

Fannie Barrier Williams, Margaret Wright]

Levine, Lawrence, *Black Culture and Black Consciousness*, New York: Oxford University Press, 1977.

Lewis, David Levering, *When Harlem Was in Vogue*, New York: Knopf, 1981, Vintage, 1982.

Lewis, Gail, and Pratibha Parmar, "Black Women's Writing", *Race and Class* 25:2 (1983).

Lewis, Gordon K., *The Growth of the Modern West Indies*, New York: Monthly Review Press, 1968.

Lewis, Oscar, Ruth Lewis and Susan Rigoder, *Living the Revolution: An Oral History of Contemporary Cuba. Vol. 2: Four Women*, Chicago: University of Illinois Press, 1977.

Lichtheim, Miriam, *Ancient Egyptian Literature: A Book of Readings. Vol. II: The New Kingdom*, Berkeley: University of California Press, 1971.

Lindfors, Bernth (ed.), *Black African Literature in English: A Guide to Information Sources*, Detroit: Gale Research Co., 1979.

——(ed.), *Mazungumzo: Interviews with East African Writers, Publishers, Editors and Scholars*, Athens, OH/London: Ohio University Center for International Studies, Africa Programme, 1980. [Grace Ogot]

Linthwaite, Ilona (ed.), *Ain't I a Woman! Poems by Black and White Women*, London: Virago, 1987; as *Ain't I a Woman! A Book of Women's Poetry from around the World*, New York: Peter Bedrick Books, 1988. [Dazzly Anderson, Maya Angelou, Valerie Bloom, Gwendolyn Brooks, Jennifer Brown, Dinah Butler, Lourdes Casal, Cheryl Clarke, Michelle T. Clinton, Jayne Cortez, Christine Craig, Charmaine Crowell, Noémia De Sousa, Nilene O. A. Foxworth, Kath Fraser, Nikki Giovanni, Carole E. Gregory, Frances E. W. Harper, Audre Lorde, Sandy McIntosh, Zindziswa Mandela, Nancy Morejón, Mwana Kupona Msham, Grace Nichols, Taiwo Olalete-Oruene, Marsha Prescod, Margaret Reckord, Sojourner Truth, Alice Walker, Sherley Anne Williams]

Lipman, Beata, *We Make Freedom: Woman in South Africa*, London: Pandora Press, 1984.

Little, Kenneth L., *Negroes in Britain: A Study of Racial Relations in English Society*, London: Kegan Paul, Trench, Trubner & Co., 1947.

——, *The Sociology of Urban Women's Image in African Literature*, London: Macmillan, 1980.

Litto, Frederic (ed.), *Plays from Black Africa*, New York: Hill & Wang, 1968. [Efua Sutherland]

Locke, Alain (ed.), *The New Negro: An Interpretation*, New York: Albert & Charles Boni, 1925; New York: Atheneum, 1968. [Gwendolyn B. Bennett, Jessie Redmon Fauset, Angelina Weld Grimké, Georgia Douglas Johnson, Elise Johnson McDougald, Anne Spencer]

Locke, Alain, and Montgomery Gregory (eds), *Plays of Negro Life: a source book of native American drama*, New York: Harper, 1927. [Thelma Duncan, Angelina Weld Grimké, Georgia Douglas Johnson, Eulalie Spence, Lucy White]

Loewenberg, Bert James, and Ruth Bogin (eds), *Black Women in Nineteenth-Century American Life: Their Words, Their Thoughts, Their Feelings*, University Park, PA: Pennsylvania University Press, 1976. [Ida B. Wells Barnett, Anna J.

Cooper, Elizabeth, Frances E. W. Harper, Ann Plato, Nancy Prince, Amanda Smith, Susie King Taylor, Fannie Barrier Williams]

Lomax, Alan, and Raoul Abdul (eds), *Three Thousand Years of Black Poetry: An Anthology*, New York: Dodd, Mead, 1970. [Gwendolyn Brooks, Noémia De Sousa, Mari E. Evans, Carol Freeman, Nikki Giovanni, Frances E. W. Harper, Georgia Douglas Johnson, Gladys Casely-Hayford (Aquah Laluah), Agnes Maxwell-Hall, Phillis Wheatley]

Long, Richard A., and Eugenia W. Collier (eds), *Afro-American Writing: An Anthology of Prose and Poetry*, New York: New York University Press, 1972; 2 vols. [Gwendolyn Brooks, Mari E. Evans, Nikki Giovanni, Frances E. W. Harper, Georgia Douglas Johnson, Naomi Long Madgett, Carolyn M. Rodgers, Margaret Walker, Phillis Wheatley]

Lorde, Audre, "Feminism and Black Liberation: The Great American Disease", *Black Scholar* 10 (May/June 1979), pp. 17–20.

Lorimer, Douglas A., *Colour, Class and the Victorians: English attitudes to the Negro in the mid-nineteenth century*, New York/London: Holmes & Meier/Leicester University Press, 1978.

Mabuza, Lindiwe (ed.), *One Never Knows: An Anthology of Black South African Women Writers in Exile*, Braamfontein: Skotaville, 1989. [Baleka Kgositsile, Ponkie Khazamula, Susan Lamu, Lindiwe Mabuza, Rebecca Matlou, Mavis Nhlapho, Dulcie September]

McCluskey, Audrey T. (ed.), *Women of Color: Perspectives on Feminism and Identity*, Bloomington: Women's Studies Program, 1985.

McDougall, Harold, *Black Woman*, New York: Saturday Review Press, McCall Books, 1970.

McEwen, Christian (ed.), *Naming the Waves: Contemporary Lesbian Poetry*, London: Virago, 1988; Freedom, CA: Crossing Press, 1989. [Jackie Kay, Irma Kendall, Linda King, Audre Lorde, Sapphire]

McFarlane, John E. Clare (ed.), *A Treasury of Jamaican Poetry*, London: University of London Press, 1949. [V. M. Clark, Clara Maud Garrett, Faith Goodheart, Constance Hollar, Ruth Hornor, Albinia C. Hutton, Lena Kent, Mary Lockett, Una Marson, Agnes Maxwell-Hall, Arabel Moulton-Barrett, Eva R. Nicholas, Nellie Frances Ackerman Olson, Stephanie Ormsby, Tropica (Mary Adella Wolcott), Dorothy Whitfield]

——(ed.), *Voices from Summerland. An Anthology of Jamaican Poetry*, London: Fowler Wright, 1929. [Constance Hollar, Albinia Catherine Hutton, Nellie Frances Ackerman Olson, Barbara Stephanie Ormsby, N. Eileen Ormsby Cooper]

MacInnes, C. M., *England and Slavery*, Bristol: Arrowsmith, 1934.

McLean, Scilla (ed.), *Female Circumcision, Excision and Infibulation: The Facts and Proposals for Change*, London: Minority Rights Group, Report No. 47, 1980.

McMillan, Terry (ed.), *Breaking Ice*, New York: Penguin, 1990; London: Vintage, 1991. [Tina McElroy Ansa, Doris Jean Austin, Toni Cade Bambara, Barbara Neely, Becky Birtha, Octavia Butler, Xam Wilson Cartiér, Carolyn Cole, Wanda Coleman, J. California Cooper, Rita Dove, Grace Edwards-Yearwood, Sandra Hollin Flowers, Marita Golden, Safiya Henderson-Holmes, Kristin Hunter,

Angela Jackson, Gayl Jones, Colleen McElroy, Paule Marshall, Mary Monroe, Gloria Naylor, Fatima Shaik, Ntozake Shange, Ellease Southerland, Barbara Summers, Alice Walker]

McNeill, Pearlie, Marie McShea and Pratibha Parmar (eds), *Through the Break: Women in Personal Struggle*, London; Sheba, 1986. [Patricia Brunner, Lola Hatmil, Linda King, Isha McKenzie-Mavinga, Pratibha Parmar, Maud Sulter]

McPherson, James M., Laurence B. Holland, James M. Banner Jr, Nancy J. Weiss and Michael D. Bell, *Blacks in America: Bibliographical Essays*, Garden City, NY: Doubleday, 1971.

Madgett, Naomi Long (ed.), *Deep Rivers: a Portfolio: 20 Contemporary Black American Poets*, Detroit: Lotus Press, 1974.

Maitland, Sara (ed.), *Very Heaven: Looking Back at the 1960s*, London: Virago, 1988. [Lee Kane, Terri Quaye]

Maja-Pearce, Adewale, (ed.), *The Heinemann Book of African Poetry in English*, Oxford: Heinemann International, 1990. [Catherine Obianuju Acholonu, Marjorie Oludhe Macgoye, 'Molara Ogundipe-Leslie]

Major, Clarence (ed.), *The New Black Poetry*, New York: International Publishers, 1969. [Gloria Davis, Julia Fields, Nikki Giovanni, Carole Gregory (Clemmons), Alicia L. Johnson, Audre Lorde, June Meyer (Jordan), D. T. Ogilvie, Helen Quigless, Niema Rashidd, Ridhiana, Sonia Sanchez, Malaika Ayo Wangara (Joyce Whitsitt)]

Majors, Gerri, and Doris Saunders, *Black Society*, Chicago: Johnson Publishing Co., 1976.

Majors, Monroe Alphus, *Noted Negro Women: Their Triumphs and Activities*, Chicago: Donohue and Henneberry, Printers, 1893; Freeport, NY: Books for Libraries Press, 1971.

Makward, Edris, and Leslie Lacy (eds), *Contemporary African Literature*, New York: Random House, 1972. [Ama Ata Aidoo]

Malson, Micheline R., Elisabeth Mudimbe-Boyi, Jean F. O'Barr and Mary Wyer (eds), *Black Women in America*, Chicago/London: University of Chicago Press, 1990. [Elsa Barkley Brown, Rita Carroll-Seguin, Patricia Hill Collins, Bonnie Thorton Dill, Cheryl Townsend Gilkes, Sharon Harley, Martha S. Hill, Deborah K. King, Diane K. Lewis, Micheline Ridley Malson, Elizabeth Mudimbe-Boyi, Mary Wyer]

Malveaux, Julianne, "Political and Historical Aspects of Black Male/Female Relationships: the Sexual Politics of Black People: Angry Black Women, Angry Black Men", *Black Scholar* 10 (May/June 1979), pp. 32–5.

Mama, Amina, *The Silent Study: Responses to Violence Against Black Women*, London: Runnymede Trust.

Mamonsono, Léopold P., and Sylvain Bemba, *Bio-bibliographie des écrivains congolais: belles lettres, littérature*, Brazzaville: Editions Littéraires Congolaises, Ministère de la Culture et des Arts de la République Populaire du Congo, 1979.

Manley, Edna (ed.), *Focus: An Anthology of Contemporary Jamaican Writing*, Kingston: City Printery, 1943, 1948, 1956, 1960.

Mansour, Mónica, *La poesia negrista*, Mexico: Ediciones Era, 1973.

Mapanje, Jack, and Landeg White (comps), *Oral Poetry: An Anthology*, Harlow/New York: Longman, 1983.

Markham, E. A. (ed.), *Hinterland: The Bloodaxe Book of Caribbean Poets*, London: Bloodaxe, 1989. [Louise Bennett, Lorna Goodison, Grace Nichols, Olive Senior]

Martin, Tony, *The Pan-African Connection: From Slavery to Garvey and Beyond*, Cambridge, Mass.: Schenkman Publishing Co., 1983.

Mascarenhas, Ophelia, and Marjorie Mbilinyi, *Women in Tanzania: An Analytical Bibliography*, Uppsala: Scandinavian Institute of African Studies/Stockholm: Swedish International Development Authority, 1983.

Mathurin, Lucille, *The Rebel Woman in the West Indies During Slavery*, Kingston, Jamaica: African Caribbean Publications, 1975.

Mathurin-Mair, Lucille (ed.), *Savacou* 13, Caribbean Woman issue. Kingston, Jamaica: Gemini 1977. [Myrna Bain, Peta-Ann Baker, Carol-Maureen Thompson Brown]

Matthews, Geraldine O., *Black American Writers, 1773–1949: A Bibliography and Union List*, Boston: G. K. Hall, 1975.

Matthews, James (ed.), *Black Voices, Shout!*, Athlone, SA: BLAC Publishing House, 1974; Austin, TX: Troubador Press, 1975, Foreword Dennis Brutus. [Ilva McKay, Christine Qunta]

Mberi, S. K., and Cosmo Pieterse (eds), *Speak Easy Speak Free*, New York: International Press, 1975. [Lindiwe Mabuza]

Meer, Fatima, *Factory and Family: The Divided Lives of South African Women Workers*, Durban: Institute for Black Research, 1984.

Melhem, D. H., *Heroism in the New Black Poetry: Introduction and Interviews*, Lexington: University Press of Kentucky, 1990. [Gwendolyn Brooks, Jayne Cortez, Sonia Sanchez]

Mérand, Patrick, and Séwanou Dabla, *Guide de littérature africaine: de langue française*, Paris: L'Harmattan, 1979.

Merriam, Eve, *Growing Up Female in America: Ten Lives*, Garden City, NY: Doubleday, 1971; Boston: Beacon, 1987.

Metzger, Linda (ed.), *Black Writers: A Selection of Sketches from Contemporary Authors*.

Meyer, Doris, and Margarite Fernández Olmos, *Contemporary Women Authors of Latin America*, New York: Brooklyn Humanities Institute Series, 1983.

Mickelwait, Donald R., *et al.*, *Women in Rural Development: A Survey of the Roles of Women in Ghana, Lesotho, Kenya, Nigeria, Bolivia, Paraguay and Peru*, Boulder: Westview Press, 1976.

Miller, Adam David (ed.), *Dices or Black Bones: Black Voices of the Seventies*, New York: Houghton Mifflin, 1970. [Lucille Clifton, Sarah Webster Fabio, Patricia Parker]

Miller, Elizabeth W. (comp., for American Academy of Arts and Sciences), *The Negro in America: A Bibliography*, Foreword Thomas F. Pettigrew, Cambridge, Mass.: Howard University Press, 1966; revised 1970.

Miller, Ruth (ed.), *Blackamerican Literature: 1760–Present*, Beverly Hills: Glencoe Press, 1971; New York: Macmillan, 1971. [Mari Evans, Phillis Wheatley]

Milwaukee County Welfare Rights Organization, *Welfare Mothers Speak Out: We Ain't Gonna Shuffle Anymore*, New York: W. W. Norton, 1972.

Mirza, Sarah, and Margaret Strobel (eds), *Three Swahili Women: Life Histories from Mombasa, Kenya*, Bloomington: Indiana University Press, 1989. [Kaje wa Mwenye Mtano, Mishi wa Abdala, Shamsa Muhumad Muhashamy]

Mohin, Lilian (ed.), *Beautiful Barbarians: Lesbian Feminist Anthology*, London: Onlywomen Press, 1986. [Barbara Burford, Bernardine Evaristo, Jackie Kay, Tina Kendall, Suniti Namjoshi]

Molefe, Sono (ed.), *Malibongwe – ANC Women: Poetry is also their weapon*, African National Congress, nd. [Mpho Segomotso Dombo, Rebecca Matlou, Baleka Kgositsile, Sono Molefe, Lerato Kumalo, Jaimaimah Motangg, Susan Lamu, Gloria Mtungwa, Lindiwe Mabuza, Duduzile Ndelu, Ilva Mackay, Gloria Nkadimeng, Fezeka Makonese, Jeanette Solwande, Zinziswa Mandela, Alice Tsongo, Mpho Maruping, Fumzile Zulu]

Molette, Barbara, "They Speak: Who Listens? Black Women Playrights", *Black World* 25 (April 1976), pp. 28–34.

Moore, Gerald, and Ulli Beier (eds), *Modern Poetry from Africa*, Harmondsworth/ Baltimore: Penguin, 1963, revised 1968. [Alda do Espirito Santo, Noémia De Sousa]

Moraga, Cherrie, and Gloria Anzaldúa (eds), *This Bridge Called My Back: Writings by Radical Women of Color*, Foreword Toni Cade Bambara, Watertown, Mass.: Persephone Press, 1981; revised, New York: Kitchen Table: Women of Color Press. [Andrea R. Canaan, Chrystos, Cheryl Clarke, Gabrielle Daniels, Doris Juanita Davenport, Hattie Gossett, Mary Hope Lee, Audre Lorde, Pat Parker, Donna Kate Rushin, Barbara Smith, Beverly Smith, Luisah Teish]

Morales, Jorge Luis (ed.), *Poesía Afro-antillana y negrista*, Puerto Rico: Universidad de Rio Piedras, 1976.

Mordecai, Pamela (ed.), *From Our Yard: Jamaican Poetry Since Independence*, Kingston: Institute of Jamaica Publications, 1987. [Louise Bennett, Valerie Bloom, Beverley Brown, Christine Craig, Gloria Escoffery, Lorna Goodison, Jean Goulbourne, Judith Hamilton, Rachel Manley, Pamela Mordecai, Olive Senior]

Mordecai, Pamela, and Mervyn Morris (eds), *Jamaica Woman: An Anthology of Poems*, Kingston/London: Heinemann Educational Books, Caribbean Writers Series 29, 1980. [Christine Craig, Dorothea Edmonson, Lorna Goodison, Pamela Mordecai, Velma Pollard, Cyrene Tomlinson]

Mordecai, Pamela, and Betty Wilson (eds), *Her True-True Name: An Anthology of Women's Writing from the Caribbean*, London: Heinemann International, Caribbean Writers Series, 1989. [Omega Aguero, Dionne Brand, Erna Brodber, Marie Chauvet, Michelle Cliff, Merle Collins, Maryse Condé, Hilma Contreras, Christine Craig, Zee Edgell, Rosario Ferré, Carmen Lugo Filippi, Magalia Garcia Ramis, Beryl Gilroy, Rosa Guy, Merle Hodge, Jamaica Kincaid, Paule Marshall, Grace Nichols, Marion Patrick-Jones, Velma Pollard, Joan Riley, Simone Schwarz-Bart, Olive Senior, Janice Shinebourne, Ana Lydia Vega, Myriam Warner-Vieyra, Sylvia Wynter Carew, Mirta Yánez]

Morgan, Robin (ed.), *Sisterhood is Global: The International Women's Movement Anthology*, Garden City, NY: Anchor/Doubleday, 1984; Harmondsworth: Penguin, 1985. [Peggy Antrobus, Rose Adhiambo Argungu-Olende, Motlalepula Chabaku, Sonia M. Cuales, Nawal El Saadawi, Lorna Gordon, Gwendoline Konie, Olivia M. Muchena, 'Molara Ogundipe-Leslie, Marie-Angelique Savané]

——(ed.), *Sisterhood is Powerful: An Anthology of Writing from the Women's Liberation Movement*, New York: Random House/Vintage, 1970. [Frances M. Beal, Florynce Kennedy, Eleanor Holmes Norton]

Morris, Mervyn (ed.), *The Faber Book of Contemporary Caribbean Short Stories*, London/Boston, 1990. [Erna Brodber, Hazel D. Campbell, Merle Hodge, Jamaica Kincaid, Olive Senior]

Mortimer, Mildred, *Journeys in the French African Novel*, London: James Currey/ Portsmouth, NH: Heinemann Educational Books, Studies in African Literature, 1990.

Mossell, N. F. [Gertrude Bustill Mossell], *The Work of the Afro-American Woman*, Philadelphia: George S. Ferguson Co., 1894; 1908; Freeport, NY: Books for Libraries Press, 1971; intr. Joanne Braxton, NY/Oxford: Oxford University Press, Schomburg Library of Nineteenth-Century Black Women Writers, 1988.

Mphahlele, Ezekiel (ed.), *African Writing Today*, Harmondsworth: Penguin, 1967. [Christina Ama Ata Aidoo, Grace Ogot]

——(ed.), *Voices in the Whirlwind*, [Audre Lorde]

Mulford, Wendy (ed.), with Helen Kidd, Julia Mishkin, Sandi Russell, *The Virago Book of Love Poetry*, London, 1990. [Maya Angelou, Ruth Asher-Pettipher, Gwendolyn B. Bennett, Jean Binta Breeze, Gwendolyn Brooks, Lucille Clifton, Jayne Cortez, Ida Cox, Alexis De Veaux, Rita Dove, Alice Dunbar-Nelson, Carole C. Gregory, Angelina Weld Grimké, Frances E. W. Harper, Iyamidé Hazeley, Georgia Douglas Johnson, Helene Johnson, Audre Lorde, Naomi Long Madgett, Memphis Minnie, Grace Nichols, Marsha Prescod, Gertrude "Ma" Rainey, Jessie Redmon Fauset, Sonia Sanchez, Ntozake Shange, Bessie Smith, Anne Spencer, Rita Anyiam St John, Alice Walker, Margaret Walker]

Mullard, Chris, *Black Britain*, London: George Allen & Unwin, 1973.

Müller, W. M., *Die Liebespoesie der alten Ägypter*, Leipzig, 1899.

Murphy, Beatrice M. (ed.), *Negro Voices: An Anthology of Contemporary Verse*, New York: Harrison-Hilton Books, 1939; Ann Arbor, Mich.: University Microfilms, 1971. [Lycurgus J. Alee, Marie E. Alexandre, Josie Craig Berry, Katharine Beverly, Bernardine Blessitt, Jane W. Burton, Helen F. Chappell, Bessie A. Cobb, Anita Scott Coleman, Ethel Coleman, Portia Bird Daniel, Ionie Daniels, Juanita M. Dickerson, Ruby Berkeley Goodwin, Edythe Mae Gordon, Edna Gullins, Clara H. Haywood, Edna White Hill, Ethlynne E. Holmes, Virginia Houston, Royal Hughes, Eleanor C. Hunter, Dorothy Vena Johnson, Helen Aurelia Johnson, Helene Hubell Johnson, Leighla Lewis, Leona Lyons, Corinne Lytle, Eleanor McDuffie, Jeanette V. Miller, Isabelle H. Moneow, Myra Estelle Morris, Clara Ball Moten, Beatrice M. Murphy, Constance Nichols, Georgiana Oliver, Beatris Oversby, Valerie Parks, Lucia Mae Pitts, Myntora J. Roker, Dorothy Lee Louise Shaed, Edna Shaw, Laura E. Smith, Ruby Stevens, Claire Turner, Lucy May Turner, Coston Vale, Naomi Evans Vaughn, Eleanor Weaver]

—— (ed.), *Ebony Rhythm: An Anthology of Contemporary Negro Verse*, New York: Exposition Press, 1948, revised Freeport, NY: Books for Libraries Press, Granger Index reprint series, 1968. [Alice D. Anderson, Edna L. Anderson, Ruby Berkley, Katharine Beverly, Louise Blackman, Dorothy F. Blackwell, Iola M. Brister, Dolores A. Brown, Naomi E. Buford, Frederica Katheryne Bunton, Nell Chapman, Helen F. Clarke, Mary Wilkerson Cleaves, Dolores

Clinton, Anita Scott Coleman, Katherine L. Cuestas, Ylessa Dubonee, Catherine L. Findley, Lenora Gillison, Ruby Berkley Goodwin, Myrtle Campbell Gorham, Emily Jane Greene, Helen C. Harris, Edna L. Harrison, Ethlynne E. Holmes, Lois Royal Hughes, Dorothy Vena Johnson, Georgia Douglas Johnson, Leanna F. Johnson, Ruth Brownlee Johnson, Georgia Holloway Jones, Martha E. Lyons, Corinne Lytle, Gertrude Parthenia McBrown, Cora Ball Moten, Beatrice M. Murphy, Constance Nichols, Gladys Marie Parker, Lucia M. Pitts, Constantia E. Riley, Ruth E. J. Sarver, Isabelle McClennan Taylor, Tomi Carolyn Tinsley, Nanny M. Travis, Countess M. Twitty, Naomi Evans Vaughn, Hazel L. Washington, Deborah Fuller Weiss, Bessie Woodson Yancey]

——(ed.), *Today's Negro Voices: An Anthology by Young Negro Poets*, New York: Julian Messner, 1970. [Barbara Anne Baxter, Thelma Parker Cox, Nikki Giovanni, Bernette Golden, Roslyn Greer, Vera Guerard, Marsha Ann Jackson, Yvette Johnson, Barbara Marshall, Beatrice M. Murphy, Carolyn J. Ogletree, Henrietta C. Parks, Dorothy C. Parrish, Antoinette T. Payne, Helen G. Quigless, Valerie Traver]

Murray, Jocelyn, *A Preliminary Bibliography: Women in Africa*, Los Angeles: Graduate Women in History, UCLA, 1974.

Mutiso, G. C. M., "Women in African Literature", *East African Journal* v:8 (3), March 1971, pp. 4–13.

Mutloatse, Mothobi (ed.), *Forced Landing: Writings from the Staffrider Generation*, Johannesburg: Ravan, Staffrider Series 3, 1980; as *Africa South: Contemporary Writing*, London: Heinemann Educational Books, African Writers Series 243, 1981. [Bessie Head, Miriam Tlali]

Myers, Carol Fairbanks, *Women in Literature: Criticism of the Seventies*, Metuchen, NJ: Scarecrow Press, 1976.

Nketia, J. H. Kwabena, *Folk Songs of Ghana*, Legon: University of Ghana, 1963.

Mzamane, Mbulelo (ed.), *Hungry Flames and Other Black South African Short Stories*, Harlow, Essex: Longman, 1968. [Bessie Head, Gladys Thomas]

Nasta, Susheila (ed.), *Motherlands: Black Women's Writing from the Caribbean, Africa and South Asia*, London: Women's Press, 1991.

Nazareth, Peter (ed.), *African Writing Today*, special edn of *Pacific Moana Quarterly* 6:3–4, Hamilton: Outrigger Publications, 1981. [Grace Akello, Nadia Bishai, Amelia House]

——, *Literature and Society in Modern Africa: Essays on Literature*, Nairobi: East African Literature Bureau, 1972; Evanston: Northwestern University Press, 1974.

Nekola, Charlotte, and Paula Rabinowitz (eds), *Writing Red: An Anthology of American Women Writers, 1930–1940*, New York: Feminist Press at City University of New York, 1987. [Lucille Boehm, Marita Bonner, Gladys Casely-Hayford, Edith Manuel Durham, Thyra Edwards, Elaine Ellis, Mary LeDuc Gibbons, Mollie Lewis, Toni Morrison, Susan McMillan Shepherd, Elizabeth Thomas, Margaret Walker]

Ngcobo, Lauretta (ed.), *Let It Be Told: Essays by Black Women Writers in Britain*, London: Pluto, 1987; Virago, 1988. [Valerie Bloom, Beverley Bryan/Stella Dadzie/Suzanne Scafe, Amryl Johnson, Lauretta Ngcobo, Grace Nichols, Marsha Prescod, Agnes Sam, Maud Sulter]

Nichols, Lee (ed.), *Conversations with African Writers*, Washington, DC: Voice of America, 1981. [Bessie Head, Penina Mlama (Muhando), Grace Ogot, Zulu Sofola, Efua Sutherland]

Niven, Alastair (ed.), *The Commonwealth Writer Overseas: Themes of Exile and Expatriation*, Brussels: Didier, 1976.

Nketia, J. H. Kwabena, *Folk Songs of Ghana*, Legon: University of Ghana, 1963.

Nkosi, Lewis, *Tasks and Masks: Themes and Styles of African Literature*, Harlow, Essex: Longman, 1981.

Noble, Jeanne L., *Beautiful, Also, Are the Soul's of My Black Sisters: A History of the Black Woman in America*, Englewood Cliffs, NJ: Prentice-Hall, 1978.

Nolen, Barbara (ed.), *Africa is People: First-hand Accounts from Contemporary Africa*, New York: Dutton, 1967. [Noni Jabavu]

——(ed.), *Voices of Voices*, New York: Fontana/Collins, 1972. [Bessie Head]

Nommo 2: Remembering Ourselves Whole: An OBAC Anthology of Contemporary Black Writing, preface Toni McConnell: Chicago: OBAhouse, 1990. [Sherifah Akorede, Collette Armstead, S. Brandi Barnes, Marion L. Tumblewood Beach, Barbara Cochran, Y. A. Folayan (Kim Hoskins), Lisa Gillard, Lorraine Harrell, Angela Jackson, Sandra Jackson-Opoku, Harriet Jacobs, Jacqueline Johnson, Chiquita Mullins Lee, Toni McConnell, Michelle Dacus Mason, Judy B. Massey, Rose Marie Tompkins, Jeanne Towns, Sharon Warner, Damita Willis]

Nouvelle somme de poésie du monde noir [New sum of poetry from the Negro World], *Présence Africaine* (Paris) 57, 1966. [Alda do Espírito Santo, Maria Carvalho da Margarido, Annette M'baye, Nancy Morejón, Jacqueline Tavernier Louis]

Ntantala, Phyllis P., *An African Tragedy: The Black Woman Under Apartheid*, Chicago: Agascha Productions, 1975.

Nwoga, Donatus Ibe (ed.), *West African Verse: an annotated anthology*, London: Longman, 1965. [Gladys Casely-Hayford]

Obbo, Christine, *African Women: Their Struggle for Economic Independence*, London: Zed Press, 1981.

O'Brien, John (ed.), *Interviews with Black Writers*, New York: Liveright, 1973. [Toni Morrison, Alice Walker]

Ogunbiyi, Yemi (ed.), *Perspectives on Nigerian Literature 1700 to the Present* [A Critical Selection from the Guardian Literary Series], Foreword Stanley Macebuh; Lagos: Guardian Books (Nigeria), 1988, 2 vols. [Articles on Zaynab Alkali, Buchi Emecheta, Flora Nwapa, Ifeoma Okoye, Tess Onwueme, Mabel Segun, Zulu Sofola, Adaora Ulasi]

Oguntoye, Katharina, May Opitz and Dagmar Schultz (eds), *Farbe bekennen: Afro-deutsche Frauen auf den Spuren ihrer Geschichte*, Berlin: Orlanda Frauenverlag, 1986; trans. Anne V. Adams as *Showing Our True Color: Afro-German Women on the Traces of Their History*, Foreword Audre Lorde; Amherst: University of Massachusetts Press, 1992; London: Open Letters. [Angelika Adomako, Laura Baum, Julia Bergen, Astrid Berger, Katharina Birkenwald, Angelika Eisenbrandt, Helga Emde, Miriam Goldschmidt, Corinna N., Katharina Oguntoye, May Opitz, Gloria Wekker, Ellen Wiedenroth]

Ojo-Ade, Femi, *Analytic Index of Présence Africaine (1947–1972)*, Washington, DC: Three Continents Press, 1977.

Oliphant, Andries Walter, and Ivan Vladishlavić (eds), *Ten Years of Staffrider Magazine, 1978–1988*, Johannesburg: Ravan, 1988. [Gladys Thomas, Miriam Tlali]

Oliver, Clinton F., and Stephanie Stills (eds), *Contemporary Black Drama: From A Raisin in the Sun to No Place to Be Somebody*, New York: Scribner, 1971. [Adrienne Kennedy]

Olney, James (ed.), *Afro-American Writing Today: An Anniversary Issue of the Southern Review*, Baton Rouge/London: Louisiana State University Press, 1985. [Kathy Elaine Anderson, Josephine Baker, Rita Dove, Pinkie Gordon Lane, Brenda Marie Osbey, Charlotte Pierce-Baker, Valerie Smith, Margaret Walker, Marilyn Nelson Waniek]

Oosthuizen, Ann (ed.), *Stepping Out: Short Stories on Friendship Between Women*, London: Pandora, 1986. [Barbara Burford, Jackie Kay]

——(ed.), *Sometimes When It Rains: Writings by South African Women*, London/New York: Pandora (Routledge & Kegan Paul)/Methuen Inc., 1987. [Bessie Head, Ellen Kuzwayo, Liseka Mda, Fatima Meer, Gcina Mhlope, Bernadette Mosala, Maud Motanyane, Gladys Thomas, Miriam Tlali]

Oppong, Christine (ed.), *Female and Male in West Africa*, London: Allen & Unwin, 1983. [Katherine Abu, Eugenia Date-Bah, Eleanor R. Fapohunda, Wambui Wa Karanja, Christine Okali, Kamene Okonjo, Christine Oppong]

Ormerod, Beverley, *An Introduction to the French Caribbean Novel*, London: Heinemann Educational Books, 1985.

Osei, G. K. *Caribbean Women: Their History and Habits*, New York: University Place Bookstore, 1979.

Osler, Audrey, *Speaking Out: Black Girls in Britain*, London: Virago, Virago Upstarts, 1989.

O'Sullivan, Sue (ed.), *Turning the Tables: Recipes and Reflections from Women*, London: Sheba, 1987. [Akwe Amosu, Linda Bellos, Jewelle L. Gomez, Yvonne Spencer, Protasia Torkington, Claudette Williams, Melba Wilson]

——(ed.), *Women's Health: A Spare Rib Reader*, London: Pandora, 1987. [Tsehai Berhane Selassie, Stella Efua Graham, Audre Lorde, Dorothea Smartt, Protasia Torkington]

Otekunefor, Henrietta, and Obiageli Nwolo (eds), *Nigerian Female Writers: A Critical Perspective*, Lagos: Mathouse Press, 1989.

Owusu, Kwesi (ed.), *Storms of the Heart: An anthology of Black Arts and Culture*, London: Camden Press, 1988. [Merle Collins, Carolyn Cooper, Ruhi Hamid, Shaheen Haque, Jan McKenley, Pratibha Parmar, Suzanne Scafe, Adeola Solanke]

Pankhurst, Sylvia, *Ethiopia*, Essex: Lalibela House, 1959.

Páricsy, Pál (comp.), *A New Bibliography of African Literature*, Budapest: Center for Afro-Asian Research of the Hungarian Academy of Sciences, Studies on Developing Countries 24, 1969.

Park, Christine, and Caroline Heaton (eds), *Close Company: Stories of Mothers and Daughters*, London: Virago, 1987. [Ama Ata Aidoo, Jamaica Kincaid, Efua Sutherland, Alice Walker]

Parks, Carole A. (ed.), *Nommo: A Literary Legacy of Black Chicago (1967–1987): An OBAC Anthology*, Chicago: OBAhouse, 1987. [Johari M. Amini-Hudson, Debra Anderson, Collette Armstead, S. Brandi Barnes, Nora Brooks Blakely, Gwendolyn Brooks, Pamela Cash-Menzies, Eileen C. Cherry, Barbara Cochran, Pauline Cole-Onyango, Eugenia Collier, Alfreda Collins, Ronda Davis, Janice Dawson, Mari Evans, Eunice Favors, Angela Jackson, Maga Jackson, Sandra Jackson-Opoku, Jamila-Ra (Maxine Hall Ellison), Helen King, Denise Love, Antoinette McConnell, Barbara Mahone, Judy B. Massey, Maria K. Mootry, Carole A. Parks, Carolyn M. Rodgers, Sandra Royster, Adalisha Safi, Jeanne Towns, Patricia Washington, Birdie Williams]

Patai, Daphne, *Brazilian Women Speak : Contemporary Life Stories*, New Brunswick/London: Rutgers University Press, 1988.

Patel, Bhadra, and Jane Allen (eds), *A Visible Presence: Black People Living and Working in Britain Today* [annotated anti-racist booklist], London: National Book League, 1985.

Patten, Margaret D., *Ghanaian Imaginative Writing in English, 1950–1969: an annotated bibliography*, Legon: University of Ghana, Dept of Library Studies, Occasional Paper 4, 1971.

Patterson, Lindsay (ed.), *Black Theater: A Twentieth-Century Collection of the Work of its Best Playwrights*, New York: Dodd, Mead, 1971, Signet/NAL. [Alice Childress, Lorraine Hansberry]

——(ed.), *Introduction to Black Literature in America from 1746 to the Present*, New York: Publishers Corp. Inc., 1968. [Gwendolyn Bennett, Gwendolyn Brooks, Mari E. Evans, Julia Fields, Frances E. W. Harper, Georgia Douglas Johnson, Gloria Oden, Anne Spencer, Lucy Terry, Margaret Walker, Phillis Wheatley]

——(ed.), *A Rock Against the Wind: Black Love Poems*, New York: Dodd, Mead, 1973. [Dolores Abramson, Jeannette Adams, Fareedah Allah, Johari Amini, Gwendolyn Bennett, Gwendolyn Brooks, Helen Morgan Brooks, Jayne Cortez, Linda Cousins, Blanche Taylor Dickinson, Jackie Earley, Mari E. Evans, Jessie Redmon Fauset, Julia Fields, Lethonia Gee, Paula Giddings, Nikki Giovanni, Linda Goss, Angelina Weld Grimké, Femi Funmi Ifetayo (Regina Micou), Georgia Douglas Johnson, Helene Johnson, Alice Jones, June Jordan, Pearl Cleage Lomax, Dee Dee McNeil, Pauli Murray, E. Marie Newsome, Gloria Oden, S. Carolyn Reese, Carolyn M. Rodgers, Loretta Rodgers, Sandra Royster, Sonia Sanchez, Saundra Sharp, Aishah Sayyida Mali Toure, Alice Walker]

Paulme, Denise, *Women of Tropical Africa*, Berkeley/Los Angeles: University of California Press, 1963, 1971; London: Routledge & Kegan Paul, 1963 [trans. from *Femmes d'Afrique Noir*, Paris: Mouton, 1960].

Pellow, Deborah, *Women in Accra: Options for Autonomy*, Michigan: Reference Publications, 1977.

Peplow, Michael W., and Arthur P. Davis (eds), *The New Negro Renaissance: An Anthology*, New York: Holt, Rinehart & Winston, 1975. [Jessie Redmon Fauset, Angelina W. Grimké, Zora Neale Hurston, Georgia Douglas Johnson, Helene Johnson, Mae Smith Johnson, Nella Larsen, Effie Lee Newsome, Anne Spencer, Margaret Walker]

Peristiany, J. G., *The Social Institutions of the Kipsigis*, London: Routledge & Kegan Paul, 1939.

Perkins, Kathy A. (ed.), *Black Female Playwrights: An Anthology of Plays Before 1950*, Bloomington/Indianapolis: Indiana University Press, 1989. [Marita Bonner, Mary P. Burrill, Shirley Graham, Zora Neale Hurston, Georgia Douglas Johnson, May Miller, Eulalie Spence]

Perry, Margaret, *Silence of the Drums: A Survey of the Literature of the Harlem Renaissance*, Westport: Greenwood, 1976.

Peterson, Kirsten Holst, and Anna Rutherford (eds), *A Double Colonization: Colonial and Post-Colonial Women's Writing*, Aarhus, Denmark: Dangaroo, 1986. [Grace Akello, Bev Brown, Abena P. A. Busia, Elaine Campbell, Lauretta Ngcobo, Agnes Sam]

——, *Into the Nineties: Post-Colonial Women's Writing*, Australia/Denmark/ Coventry, UK: Dangaroo, 1991.

Pichanick, J., A. J. Chennells and L. B. Rix (comps), *Rhodesian Literature in English: a bibliography (1890–1974½)*, Gwelo, Zimbabwe: Mambo Press, Zambeziana 2, 1977.

Piercy, Marge (ed.), *Early Ripening: American Women's Poetry Now*, London/ New York: Pandora Press (Routledge & Kegan Paul), 1987. [Ai, Rita Dove, Beth Brant, June Jordan, Michelle Cliff, Audre Lorde, Jayne Cortez, Colleen J. McElroy, Thulani Davis, Brenda Marie Osbey, Toi Derricotte, Sonia Sanchez]

Pieterse, Cosmo (ed.), *Eleven Short African Plays*, London: Heinemann Educational Books, African Writers Series 78, 1971. [Rebeka Njau]

Pieterse, Cosmo, and Dennis Duerden (eds), *African Writers Talking*, New York: Africana Publishing Corp., 1972. [Ama Ata Aidoo, Efua Sutherland]

Plumpp, Sterling (ed.), *Somehow We Survive: An Anthology of South African Writing*, New York: Thunder's Mouth, 1982. [Christine Douts (Qunta), Bessie Head, Amelia House, Baleka Kgositsile, Ilva MacKay, Zindzi Mandela, Barbara Masakela]

Poems by Blacks, Fort Smith, Arkansas: South and West, Inc., nd, v. 2. [Constance E. Berkeley, Gwendolyn Brooks, Juanita Brown, Carolyn Coleman, Bobbretta M. Elliston, Naomi M. Faust, Patricia Ford, Beth Jackson, Barbara Jean Knight, Thelma Lamar, Pinkie Gordon Lane, Lois Miller, Mary Nell Nash, Stella Ngatho, Geraldine Peterson, Kathleen Reed, Lotus Schaefer]

Pollard, Velma (ed.), *Anansesem*, Kingston: Longman Jamaica, 1985. [Daphne G. Cuffie, Vilma Dube, Belinda Edmondson, Shauna Fern Godfrey, Sheryl Gordon, Constance Hollar, Phyllis Inniss, Una Marson, Daisy Myrie, Nellie Frances Ackerman Olson, Lisa Salmon]

Pool, Rosey E. (ed.), *Beyond the Blues: New Poems by American Negroes*, Lympne, Kent: Hand & Flower Press, 1962. [Gwendolyn Brooks, Linda Brown, Katherine L. Cuestas, Margaret Danner, Mari Evans, Julia Fields, Audre Lorde, Naomi Long Madgett, May Miller, Margaret Walker, Sarah E. Wright]

Porter, Dorothy B., "Early American Negro Writing: A Bibliographical Study", *Papers of the Bibliographical Society of America* 39 (1945), pp. 132–268.

——(ed.), *Early Negro Writing, 1769–1837*, Boston: Beacon, 1971.

——, *North American Negro Poets: A Bibliographical Checklist of Their Writings (1760–1944)*, Hattiesburg, Miss.: Book Farm, 1945; New York: Burt Franklin, 1963.

——, *A Catalogue of the African Collection in the Moorland Foundation*,

Howard University Library, Washington, DC: Howard University Press, 1958.
——, "A Bibliographical Checklist of American Negro Writers about Africa", *Africa Seen by American Negroes*, *Présence Africaine* (1958), pp. 379–99.
——, "African and Caribbean Creative Writings: A Bibliographic Survey", *African Forum* 1 (Spring 1966), pp. 107–11.
——, *A Working Bibliography on the Negro in the United States*, Ann Arbor, 1969; rpt (modified) as *The Negro in the United States: A Selected Bibliography*, Washington, DC: Library of Congress, 1970.
Povey, John, and Charles Angoff (eds), *African Writing Today*, New York: Manyland Books, 1969. [Ama Ata Aidoo]
Prescod-Roberts, Margaret, and Norma Steele, *Black Women: Bringing It All Back Home*, Bristol: Falling Wall Press, 1980; reissued 1986, afterword Wilmette Brown.
Price, Richard (ed.), *Maroon Societies: Rebel Slave Communities in the Americas*, Baltimore/New York: John Hopkins University, 1979.
Pryse, Marjorie, and Hortense Spillers (eds), *Conjuring: Black Women, Fiction and the Literary Tradition*, Bloomington: Indiana University Press, 1985. [Deborah E. McDowell, Madonne M. Miner, Thelma J. Shinn, Hortense Spillers, Claudia Tate]
Quarles, Benjamin, *The Negro in the Making of America*, New York: Collier Books/London: Collier Macmillan, 1964, 3rd expanded edn 1987.
Qunta, Christine (ed.), *Women in Southern Africa*, London: Allison & Busby/ Johannesburg: Skotaville, 1987. [Nomvo Booi, Nora Chase, Ruvimbo Chimedza, Zuky N. Mihyo, Sibongile Mkhabela, Lesego Molapo, Olivia N. Muchena, Margaret Nananyane Nasha, Teurai Ropa Nhonga, Dabi Nkululeko, Christine Qunta, Letticia Rutashobya, Ntomb'elanga Takawira]
Rainwater, Catherine, and William J. Scheick (eds), *Contemporary American Women Writers: Narrative Strategies*, Lexington: University of Kentucky, 1985. [Elizabeth Filer, Toni Morrison, Linda Wagner]
Ramchand, Kenneth, *The West Indian Novel and its Background*, 2nd edn, London/Kingston/Port of Spain: Heinemann Educational Books, 1983.
Ramchand, Kenneth, and C. Gray (eds), *West Indian Poetry: An Anthology for Schools*, London: Longman, 1971, new edn 1989. [Cheryl Albury, Vera Bell, Louise Bennett, Dionne Brand, Christine Craig, Gloria Escoffery, Barbara Ferland, Lorna Goodison, Judy Miles, Pamela Mordecai, Grace Nichols, Alma Norman, Heather Royes, Shana Yardan]
Ramdin, Ron, *The Making of the Black Working Class in Britain*, London: Gower, 1987.
Randall, Dudley (ed.), *The Black Poets: A New Anthology*, New York: Bantam, 1971. [Johari Amini, Gwendolyn Brooks, Lucille Clifton, Margaret Danner, Mari E. Evans, Nikki Giovanni, Frances E. W. Harper, June Jordan, Naomi Long Madgett, Carolyn M. Rodgers, Sonia Sanchez, Stephany, Lucy Terry, Margaret Walker, Phillis Wheatley]
——(ed.), *Black Poetry: A Supplement*, Detroit: Broadside Press, 1969. [Nikki Giovanni, Naomi Long Madgett, Sonia Sanchez, Margaret Walker]
Randall, Dudley, and Margaret Goss Burroughs (eds), *For Malcolm: Poems on the Life and Death of Malcolm X*, Detroit: Broadside Press, 1967. [Marcella

Caine, Mari E. Evans, Carmen Auld Goulbourne, Christine Claybourne Johnson, Patricia, Sonia Sanchez, Malaika Wangara]

Randall, Margaret (ed.), *Breaking the Silences: Twentieth-Century Poetry by Cuban Women*, Vancouver, BC: Pope Press, 1981.

Rattray, R. S., *Religion and Art in Ashanti*, Oxford: Clarendon, 1927.

Redding, Jay Saunders, *They Came in Chains: Americans from Africa*, Philadelphia: J. B. Lippincott, 1950.

Reed, Ishmael (ed.), *Calafia: The California Poetry*, Berkeley, CA: Y'bird Books, 1979. [Maya Angelou, Eva Carter Buckner, Sadie H. Calbert, Jayne Cortez, Ntozake Shange, Mrs Patricia Stewart]

Reed, John, and Clive Wake (eds), *A Book of African Verse*, London/Ibadan: Heinemann Educational Books, African Writers Series 8, 1964. [Minji Karibo]

Reese, Lyn, Jean Wilkinson and Phyllis Sheon Koppelman (eds), *I'm On My Way Running: Women Speak on Coming of Age*, New York: Avon/Discus Books, 1983. [Gwendolyn Brooks, Paule Marshall, Toni Morrison, Micere Mugo, Nisa, Miriam Khamadi Were]

Rehse, Hermann, *Kizibia: Land und Leute*, Stuttgart: Strecker & Schröder, 1910.

Reid, Inez, *"Together" Black Women*, New York: Emerson Hall, 1971; Third Press, 1975.

Reid, Willie Mae, *Black Women's Struggle for Equality*, New York: Pathfinder, 1976.

Reynolds, Edward, *Stand the Storm: A History of the Atlantic Slave Trade*, London/New York: Allison & Busby, 1985.

Rice, C. Duncan, *The Rise and Fall of Black Slavery*, London: Macmillan, 1975.

Richards, Audrey I., *Chisungu: A Girl's Initiation Ceremony Among the Bemba of Northern Rhodesia*, London: Faber, 1956.

Richardson, Marilyn, *Black Women and Religion* [bibliography], Boston: G. K. Hall, 1980.

Richardson, Willis, and May Miller (eds), *Plays and Pageants from the Life of the Negro*, Washington, DC: Associated Publishers, 1930. [Inez Burke, Thelma Duncan, Dorothy C. Guinn, Frances Gunner, Maud Cuney Hare, May Miller]

——(eds), *Negro History in Thirteen Plays*, Washington, DC: Associated Publishers, 1935. [Helen Webb Harris, Georgia Douglas Johnson, May Miller]

Rive, Richard (ed.), *Modern African Prose*, London: Heinemann Educational Books, African Writers Series 9, 1964. [Efua Sutherland]

Roberts, J. R. (comp.), *Black Lesbians: An Annotated Bibliography*, Tallahassee, Fla: Naiad Press, 1981.

Roberts, G. W., and S. Sanchez, *Women in Jamaica*, New York: KTO Press, 1978.

Robertson, Claire C., and Martin A. Klein, *Women and Slavery in Africa*, Madison: University of Wisconsin Press, 1983.

Robinson, William H. (ed.), *Early Black American Poets*, Dubuque, Iowa: William C. Brown Co., 1969. [Frances E. W. Harper, Josephine D. Heard, Ann Plato, Henrietta Cordelia Ray, Lucy Terry, Phillis Wheatley]

——(ed.), *Nommo: An Anthology of Modern Black African and Black American Literature*, New York: Collier-Macmillan, 1972. [Sonia Sanchez, Efua Sutherland]

Rodgers, Carolyn M. (ed.), *For Love of Our Brothers*, Chicago: Third World Press, 1970.

Rodgers-Rose, LaFrances (ed.), *The Black Woman*, Beverly Hills/London: Sage, 1980. [Delores P. Aldridge, Christina Brinkley-Carter, Christine H. Carrington, Bonnie Thornton Dill, Rhetaugh Graves Dumas, Eleanor Engram, Gloria Wade-Gayles, Cheryl Townsend Gilkes, Janice Hale, Willa Mae Hemmons, Cheryl Bernadette Leggon, Harriette Pipes McAdoo, Carrie Allen McCray, Lena Wright Myers, Jewel L. Prestage, LaFrances Rodgers-Rose, Essie Manuel Rutledge, Geraldine L. Wilson]

Rollins, Charlemae (ed.), *Christmas Gif'*, Chicago: Follett, 1963. [Gwendolyn Brooks, Eve Lynn (Evelyn C. Reynolds), Effie Lee Newsome]

Romero, Patricia W. (ed.), *Life Histories of African Women*, London/Atlantic Highlands, NJ: Ashfield Press, 1988.

Roses, Lorraine Elena, and Elizabeth Ruth Randolph, *Harlem Renaissance and Beyond: Literary Biographies of 100 Black Women Writers, 1900–1945*, Boston: G. K. Hall, 1990.

Ruck, S. (ed.), *The West Indian Comes to England*, London: Routledge & Kegan Paul, 1960.

Rugg, Akua, *Brickbats and Bouquets: Black Woman's Critique – Literature, Theatre, Film*, London: Race Today, 1984.

Ruiz del Vizo, Hortensia (ed.), *Black Poetry of the Americas (A Bilingual Anthology)*, Miami: Ediciones Universal, 1972. [Ana H. Gonzalez, Anisia Meruelo Gonzales, Ana Rosa Nunez]

Runnymede Trust and Radical Statistics Race Group, *Britain's Black Population*, London: Heinemann Educational Books, 1980.

Rush, Theressa Gunn, Carol Fairbanks Myers and Esther Spring Arata, *Black American Writers Past and Present: A Biographical and Bibliographical Dictionary*, 2 vols, Metuchen, NJ: Scarecrow Press, 1975.

Rushing, Andrea, "An Annotated Bibliography of Images of Black Women in Black Literature", *CLA Journal* 21 (March 1978), pp. 435–42.

Russell, Diana E. H., *Lives of Courage, Women for a New South Africa*, New York: Basic Books, 1989; London: Virago, 1990. [Rhoda Bertelsmann-Kadalie, Feziwe Bookholane, Florence De Villiers, Gertrude Fester, Leila Issel, Shahieda Issel, Lydia Kompe, Rozena Maart, Winnie Mandela, Mavivi Manzini, Emma Mashinini, Connie Mofokeng, Elaine Mohamed, Ruth Mompati, Seth-embile N., Ela Ramgobin, Nontsikelelo Albertina Sisulu]

Russell, Michele, "Black-eyed Blues Connection: Teaching Black Women", *Women's Studies Newsletter* 4 (Fall 1976), pp. 6–7; 5 (Winter/Spring 1977), pp. 24–8.

Russell, Sandi, *Render Me My Song: African-American Women Writers from Slavery to the Present*, London: Pandora, 1990, New York: St Martin's Press.

Rutherfoord, Peggy (ed.), *Darkness and Light: An anthology of African Writing*, Johannesburg: Drum Publications, 1958; as *African Voices: An anthology of native African writing*, New York: Vanguard Press, 1958, Grosset & Dunlap/Universal Library, 1970. [Gladys Casely-Hayford, "Gbemi"]

Saint-André Utudjian, Eliane (comp.), *A Bibliography of West African Life and Literature*, Waltham, Mass.: Crossroads Press, 1977.

Sainville, Léonard (ed.), *Anthologie de la littérature Négro-Africaine: Romanciers et conteurs*, 2 vols; Paris: Présence Africaine, 1963 and 1968.

[Mayotte Capecia, Madeleine Carbet, Carolina Maria de Jesus, Michèle Lacrosil]

Sanchez, Sonia (ed.), *Three Hundred and Sixty Degrees of Blackness Comin'
at You*, 5X Publishing Co., 1971; New York: Bantam, 1971. [Jeanette Adams,
Delores Abramson, Judith Bracey, Tyki Brown, Jacqueline Copps, Linda
Cousins, Frances Garcia, Mara Moja Tu Kali, Mitchelene Morgan, Nilata,
Nia n'Sabe, Dorothy Randall, Jo Nell Rice, Loretta Rodgers, Ava Sanders,
Bernadette Simmons, Maami Verano]

——(ed.), *We Be Word Sorcerers: 25 Stories by Black Americans*, New York:
Bantam, 1973. [Toni Cade Bambara, Alice Walker]

Scafe, Suzanne, *Teaching Black Literature*, London: Virago/University of London
Institute of Education, 1989.

Scanzoni, John H., *The Black Family in Modern Society*, Chicago: University
of Chicago Press, 1977.

Schapera, Isaac, *Married Life in an African Tribe*, Evanston: Northwestern
University Press, 1965; London: Faber.

——, *"Premarital Pregnancy and Native Opinion"*, *Africa*, v:6 (1933), pp. 59–89.

Scheffler, Judith A., *Wall Tappings: An Anthology of Writings by Women
Prisoners*, Boston: Northeastern University Press, 1986. [Ericka Huggins,
Joyce Sikakane]

Schipper, Mineke (ed.), *Source of All Evil: African Proverbs and Sayings
on Women*, London: Allison & Busby, 1991.

——(ed.), *Unheard Words: Women and Literature in Africa, the Arab World,
Asia, the Caribbean and Latin America*, London: Allison & Busby, 1985.

Schoener, Allon (ed.), *Harlem on My Mind*, New York: Random House, 1968.

Schomburg, Arthur, Alfonso (comp.), *A Bibliographical Checklist of American
Negro Poetry*, New York: Charles F. Heartman, 1916.

Schuster, Ilsa, *The New Women of Lusaka*, Palto Alto: Mayfield Publishing
Co., 1979.

Scobie, Edward, *Black Britannia: A History of Blacks in Britain*, Chicago:
Johnson Publishing Co., 1972.

Scott, Kesho Yvonne, *The Habit of Surviving: Black Women's Strategies for
Life*, New Brunswick, NJ: Rutgers University Press, 1991.

Sealy, Clifford (ed.), *Voices*, Independence Anniversary Issue, Port of Spain,
Trinidad: PEN Club of Trinidad & Tobago, 1964.

Senior, Olive, *Working Miracles: Women of the English-speaking Caribbean*,
London: James Currey/Institute of Social and Economic Research, University
of the West Indies, 1991.

Sergeant, Howard (ed.), *New Voices of the Commonwealth*, London: Evans, 1968.

——(ed.), *African Voices*, London: Evans; Westport, Conn.: Lawrence Hill, 1974.

Seymour, A. J. (ed.), *New Writing in the Caribbean: Carifesta '72*, Georgetown:
Guyanese Lithographic Co., 1972. [Carmen Alicia Cadilla, Elizabeth Clarke,
Thea Doelwijt, Marie-Ange Jolicoeur, Mitzie Townsend, Shana Yardan]

——(ed.), *A Treasury of Guyanese Poetry*, Georgetown: Guyana and Trinidad
Mutual Fire Insurance Co., 1984. [Jean Brutus, Mahadai Das, Laurie De Jonge,
Jacqueline De Weever, Mercedes Pierre-Dubois, Maureen Prince, Helen Taitt,
Annette Warren-Rollins, Shana Yardan]

Seymour, A. J., and Elma Seymour (eds), *My Lovely Native Land: an anthology of Guyana*, Port-of-Spain: Longman Caribbean, 1971. [Jacqueline De Weever, Celeste Dolphin, Rajkumari Singh]

Shapiro, Norman R. (ed./trans.), *Négritude: Black Poetry from Africa and the Caribbean*, intr. Wilfred Cartey, New York: October House, 1970. [Joselyn Étienne, Marie-Thérèse Rouil]

Sheba Collective (ed.), *Serious Pleasure: Lesbian Erotic Stories and Poetry*, London: Sheba, 1989. [Jewelle Gomez]

Shelton, Austin J. (ed.), *The African Assertion: A Critical Anthology of African Literature*, New York: Odyssey Press, 1968. [Adelaide Casely-Hayford, Mabel Dove-Danquah, Efua Sutherland]

Sheridan, R. B., *Sugar and Slavery: An Economic History of the British West Indies 1623–1775*, Baltimore: Johns Hopkins University Press, 1973.

Sherman, Joan R. (ed.), *Invisible Poets: Afro-Americans of the Nineteenth Century*, Urbana: University of Illinois Press, 1974. [Frances E. W. Harper, Charlotte Forten Grimké, Ann Plato, Henrietta Cordelia Ray, Eloise Bibb Thompson]

——(ed.), *Collected Black Women's Poetry*, 4 vols, Oxford/New York: Oxford University Press, Schomburg Library of Nineteenth-Century Black Women Writers, 1988.

Sherwood, Marika, *Many Struggles: West Indian Workers and Service Personnel in Britain 1939–1945*, London: Karia Press, 1985.

Shillington, Kevin, *History of Africa*, London: Macmillan, 1989.

Shinnie, Margaret, *Ancient African Kingdoms*, New York: New American Library, 1970.

Shockley, Ann Allen (ed.), *Afro-American Women Writers 1746–1933: An Anthology and Critical Guide*, Boston: G. K. Hall, NAL/Meridian, 1988. [Olivia Ward Bush Banks, Charlotte Hawkins Brown, Mary Louise Burgess, Anna Julia Cooper, Alice Dunbar Nelson, Zilpha Elaw, Jessie Redmon Fauset, Sarah Fleming, Charlotte Forten, Miss Garrison, Angelina Weld Grimké, Maud Cuney Hare, Frances Ellen Watkins Harper, Josephine Henderson Heard, Pauline Hopkins, Harriet Jacobs, Amelia Etta Hall Johnson, Georgia Douglas Johnson, Elizabeth Keckley, Emma Dunham Kelley-Hawkins, Jarena Lee, Victoria Earle Matthews, Ann Plato, Nancy Prince, Henrietta Cordelia Ray, Amanda Berry Smith, Mary Etta Spencer, Lucy Terry, Susie Baker King Taylor, Clara Ann Thompson, Clarissa Minn Thompson, Eloise Bibb Thompson, Priscilla Jane Thompson, Lillian E. Wood, Ida Wells-Barnett, Phillis Wheatley, Frances Ann Rollin Whipper, Harriet Wilson, Zara Wright]

Showalter, Elaine (ed.), *The New Feminist Criticism: Essays on Women, Literature, and Theory*, New York: Pantheon, 1985.

Shuman, R. Baird (ed.), *Nine Black Poets*, Durham, NC: Moore Publishing Co., 1968. [Carole Gregory Clemmons, Kattie M. Cumbo, Julia Fields, Alicia Loy Johnson]

——(ed.), *A Galaxy of Black Writing*, Durham, NC: Moore, 1970. [Mary Bohanon, Carole Gregory Clemmons, Kattie M. Cumbo, Katherine Dunham, Julia Fields, Linda B. Graham, Linda G. Hardnett, Claudia E. Jemmott, Alicia Loy Johnson, Mattie T. Lakin, Doris Ann Shaw, Sandra E. Stevens, Virginia Williams]

Shyllon, F. O., *Black People in Britain 1555–1833*, London: Oxford University

Press for Institute of Race Relations, 1977.

——, *Black Slaves in Britain*, London: Oxford University Press for Institute of Race Relations, 1974.

Simon, H. J., *African Women: Their Legal Status in South Africa*, Evanston: Northwestern University Press, 1968; London: Christopher Hurst, 1968.

Sims, Janet L., *The Progress of Afro-American Women: A Selected Bibliography and Resource Guide*, Westport, Conn.: Greenwood, 1980.

Singh, Amritjit, *The Novels of the Harlem Renaissance: Twelve Black Writers, 1923–1933*, University Park: Pennsylvania State University Library, 1976. [Jessie Fauset, Nella Larsen]

Sistren Theatre Collective and Honor Ford Smith, *Lionheart Gal: Life Stories of Jamaican Women*, London: Women's Press, 1986.

Sivanandan, A., *Coloured Immigrants in Britain: A Select Bibliography*, London: Institute of Race Relations, Special Series, 1969.

Smith, Barbara (ed.), *Home Girls: A Black Feminist Anthology*, Latham, NY: Kitchen Table: Women of Color Press, 1983. [Donna Allegra, Tania Abdulahad, Barbara A. Banks, Becky Birtha, Julie Carter, Cenen, Cheryl Clarke, Michelle Cliff, Michelle T. Clinton, Willie Coleman, Toi Derricotte, Alexis De Veaux, Jewelle L. Gomez, Gloria T. Hull, Eleanor Johnson, Patricia Jones, June Jordan, Audre Lorde, Raymina Y. Mays, Deirdre McCalla, Chirlane McCray, Pat Parker, Linda C. Powell, Bernice Johnson Reagon, Spring Redd, Gwendolyn Rogers, Donna Kate Rushin, Ann Allen Shockley, Barbara Smith, Beverly Smith, Shirley O. Steele, Luisah Teish, Jameelah Waheed, Alice Walker, Renita Weems]

——, *Toward a Black Feminist Criticism*, Trumansburg, NY: Crossing Press, 1982.

Smith, Valerie, *Self-Discovery and Authority in Afro-American Literature*, Cambridge: Harvard University Press, 1987.

Smitherman, Geneva, *Talkin' and Testifyin': The Language of Black America*, Boston: Houghton Mifflin, 1977.

Soyinka, Wole (ed.), *Poems of Black Africa*, London: Secker & Warburg, 1975; Heinemann Educational Books, African Writers Series 171, 1975; New York: Hill & Wang, 1975. [Noémia De Sousa, Susan Lwanga]

Spelman, Elizabeth V., "Theories of Race and Gender: The Erasure of Black Women", *Quest* 5 (1979), p. 42.

Stack, Carol, *All Our Kin: Strategies for Survival in a Black Community*, New York: Harper & Row, 1974.

Stadler, Quandra Prettyman (ed.), *Out of Our Lives: A Collection of Contemporary Black Fiction*, Washington, DC: Howard University Press, 1981. [Toni Cade Bambara, Pearl Crayton, Deloris Harrison, Louise Meriwether, Ann Petry, Ann Allen Shockley, Alice Walker]

Standford, Barbara (ed.), *I, Too, Sing America*, New York: Hayden Book Co., 1971. [Gwendolyn Brooks, Mari E. Evans, Nikki Giovanni, Phillis Wheatley]

Staples, Robert, *The Black Woman in America: Sex, Marriage, and the Family*, Chicago: Nelson-Hall Publishers, 1973; Chicago: Nelson-Hall, 1978.

Starling, Marion, *The Slave Narrative: Its Place in Literary History*, Boston: G. K. Hall, 1982.

Staunton, Irene (comp./ed.), *Mothers of the Revolution: The War Experience of Thirty Zimbabwean Women*, Harare: Baobab Books, US/Canada: Indiana University Press, London: James Currey, 1991.

Steady, Filomina Chioma (ed.), *The Black Woman Cross-Culturally*, Cambridge, Mass.: Schenkman, 1981. [Agnes Akosua Aidoo, Nancie L. Solien Gonzalez, Darlene Clarke Hine, Irene V. Jackson, Bennetta Jules-Rosette, Joyce Bennett Justus, Joyce A. Ladner, Regine LaTortue, Susan Makiesky-Barrow, Yolanda T. Moses, Maria Luisa Nunes, Achola Pala Okeyo, Kamene Okonjo, Linda M. Perkins, Elizabeth Thaele Rivkin, Andrea Benton Rushing, Ruth Simms (Hamilton), Carol B. Stack, Filomina Chioma Steady, Niara Sudarkasa (Gloria A. Marshall), Constance R. Sutton, Rosalyn Terborg-Penn]

Sterling, Dorothy, *Black Foremothers: Three Lives*, intr. Margaret Walker; Old Westbury, NY: Feminist Press, Women's Lives/Women's Work project, 1979. [Ellen Craft, Ida B. Wells, Mary Church Terrell]

——(ed.), *We Are Your Sisters: Black Women in the Nineteenth Century*, Bloomington: Indiana University Press, 1981; New York/London: Norton, 1984.

Stetson, Erlene (ed.), *Black Sister: Poetry by Black American Women, 1746–1980*, Bloomington: Indiana University Press, 1981. [Ada, Fareedah Allah (Ruby C. Saunders), Gwendolyn B. Bennett, Bessie Calhoun Bird, Gwendolyn Brooks, Margaret Goss Burroughs, Della Burt, Carrie Williams Clifford, Lucille Clifton, Alice S. Cobb, Jayne Cortez, Mae V. Cowdery, Kattie M. Cumbo, Margaret Danner, Thadious Davis, Alice Dunbar-Nelson, Mari Evans, Sarah Webster Fabio, Jessie Redmon Fauset, Charlotte Forten Grimké, Nikki Giovanni, Carole C. Gregory, Angelina Weld Grimké, Jo Ann Hall-Evans, Frances E. W. Harper, Georgia Douglas Johnson, Helene Johnson, Rosalie M. Jonas, Gayl Jones, Patricia Jones, June Jordan, Johari M. Kunjufu (Johari Amini), Pinkie Gordon Lane, Audre Lorde, Irma McClaurin, Colleen J. McElroy, Naomi Long Madgett, May Miller, Pauli Murray, Gloria C. Oden, Patricia Parker, Linda Piper, Ann Plato, Henrietta Cordelia Ray, Carolyn M. Rodgers, Sonia Sanchez, Ntozake Shange, Lucy Terry, Clara Ann Thompson, Sojourner Truth, Alice Walker, Margaret Walker, Phillis Wheatley, Lucy Ariel Williams, Sherley Anne Williams]

Strobel, Margaret, *Muslim Women in Mombasa*, New Haven: Yale University Press, 1979.

Sudarkasa, Niara, *Where Women Work: A Study of Yoruba Women in the Marketplace and in the Home*, Ann Arbor: University of Michigan Press, 1973.

Sulter, Maud (ed.), *Passion: Discourses on Blackwomen's Creativity*, Hebden Bridge, Yorks: Urban Fox Press, 1990. [Pat Agana, Asian Women Writers Collective, Frederica Brooks, Chila Kumari Burman, Nina Edge, Bernardine Evaristo, Lubaina Himid, Roshini Kempadoo, Yemi Morgan, Nailah, Olusola Oyeleye, Ingrid Pollard, Olive Pollard, Patricia St Hilaire, Dionne Sparks, Delta Streete, Veena Stephenson, Maud Sulter, Meera Syal]

——(ed.), *Zenobia*, Hebden Bridge, Yorks: Urban Fox Press, forthcoming.

Sweetman, David, *Women Leaders in African History*, London: Heinemann Educational Books, 1984.

Taiwo, Oladele, *Female Novelists of Modern Africa*, London: Macmillan, 1984.

Talkers Through Dream Doors: Poetry and Short Stories by Black Women,
intr. Vastiana Belfon; Manchester: Crocus Books, 1989. [Nayaba Aghedo,
Cindy Artiste, Jolina Black, Georgina Angela Blake, Lorna Euphemia Griffiths,
Lorraine Griffiths, Loretta Harris, Sua Huab, Gloria Knowles, Carlene Mon-
toute, Sally Neaser, Pauline Omoboye, Annette Reis, Kanta Walker]

Tarn, Nathaniel (ed./trans.), *Con Cuba: An Anthology of Cuban Poetry of the Last
Sixty Years*, London: Cape Goliard, 1969; New York: Grossman, 1969. [Lydia
Cabrera, Belkis Cuza Male, Gloria Escoffery, Lina de Feria, Barbara Ferland,
Fina Garcia Marruz, Vivette Hendricks, Constance Hollar, Una Marson, Agnes
Maxwell-Hall, Stella Mead, Florette Morand, Nancy Morejón, Arabel Moulton-
Barrett, Phyllis May Myers, Daisy Myrie, Stephanie Ormsby, Millicent Payne,
Isel Rivero, Monica Skeete, Flora Squires]

Tate, Claudia (ed.), *Black Women Writers at Work: Conversations*, New York:
Continuum, 1983; Harpenden, Herts: Oldcastle Books, 1985. [Maya Angelou,
Toni Cade Bambara, Gwendolyn Brooks, Alexis De Veaux, Nikki Giovanni,
Kristin Hunter, Gayl Jones, Audre Lorde, Toni Morrison, Sonia Sanchez,
Ntozake Shange, Alice Walker, Margaret Walker, Sherley Anne Williams]

Terborg-Penn, Rosalyn, Sharon Harley, Andrea Benton Rushing (eds), *Women
in Africa and the African Diaspora*, Washington, DC: Howard University
Press, 1987. [Andrea Benton Rushing, Lynn Bolles, Martha K. Cobb, Sha-
ron Harley, Sylvia Jacobs, Bennetta Jules-Rosette, Harryette Pipes McAdoo,
Bernice Johnson Reagon, Filomena Chioma Steady, Niara Sudarkasa, Rosalyn
Terborg-Penn, Karen Smyley Wallace, Miriam Khamadi Were]

Thornton, Louise, Jan Sturtevant and Amber Coverdale Sumrall, *Touching Fire:
Erotic Writings by Women*, London: Robert Hale, 1989. [Ai, Beth Brant, Lucille
Clifton, Zora Neale Hurston, Audre Lorde, Terry McMillan]

Tibble, Anne (ed.), *African English Literature*, London: Peter Owen, 1965,
New York: October House, 1965. [Noni Jabavu, Noémia De Sousa, Efua
Sutherland]

Times Like These, intr. Rhonda Cobham, Foreword Edward Kamau Brathwaite;
London: Obatala Press, 1988. [Sandra A. Agard, Monique Griffiths, Brenda
Hayde-Agard]

Toppin, Edgar A., *A Biographical History of Blacks in America since 1528*,
New York: McKay, 1969, 1971.

Trask, Willard (ed.), *The Unwritten Song*, New York: Macmillan Inc.

Trotman, Donald A. R. (ed.), *An Anthology: Voices of Guyana* [poetry], Georgetown, Guyana: Sheik Sadeek, 1968. [Evadne D'Oliviera, Syble Douglas, Sheila
King]

Troupe, Quincy, and Rainer Schulte (eds), *Giant Talk: An Anthology of Third
World Writing*, New York: Random House, 1975. [Ama Ata Aidoo, Toni Cade
Bambara, Lucille Clifton, Carole Clemmons Gregory, Lindiwe Mabuza, Toni
Morrison, Margaret Walker, Phillis Wheatley]

Tsikang, Seageng, and Dinah Lefakane, *Women in South Africa: From the Heart
– an anthology of stories written by a new generation of writers*, intr. Ellen
Kuzwayo; Johannesburg: Seriti sa Sechaba Publishers, 1988. [Emelda Damane,
Fatima Dike, Thandeka Nomkhita Kgantsi, Mercy Lebakeng, Dinah Lefakane,
Boitumelo Makhema, Nomavenda Mathiane, Dumisile Mavimbela, Julia Mjali

Mji, Faith Humang Mokoka, Kefiloe Tryphina Mvula, Mantu Ngakane, Rose
Lineo Nketu, Sobhna Poona, Fikiswa Pupuma, Mpine Qakisa, Ndlaleni Radebe,
Portia Rankoane, Ntsoaki Senokoanyane, Florence Shabalala, Stella Alexander
Stevens, Kenalemang M. Tau, Seageng Tsikang]

Turner, Darwin T. (ed.), *Black American Literature: Essays, Poetry, Fiction,
Drama*, Columbus, Ohio: Charles E. Merrill, 1970. [Gwendolyn Brooks,
Georgia Douglas Johnson, Naomi Long Madgett, Margaret Walker, Phillis
Wheatley]

——, *Afro-American Writers*, New York: Appleton-Century-Crofts, 1970.

——(ed.), *Voices from the Black Experience: African and Afro-American Literature*, Lexington, Mass.: Ginn, 1972.

Tuttle, Lisa, *Encyclopedia of Feminism*, Longman, 1986; Arrow Books, 1987.

Uma, Alladi, *Woman and her Family: India and Afro-America – A Literary
Perspective*, New Delhi: Sterling Publishers, 1989.

Urdang, Stephanie, *And Still They Dance: Women, War and the Struggle for
Change in Mozambique*, New York: Monthly Review Press; London: Earthscan,
1989.

——, *Two Colonialisms: Women in Guinea-Bissau*, New York: Monthly Review
Press, 1979.

Van Sertima, Ivan (ed.), *Black Women in Antiquity*, New Brunswick/London:
Transaction Books, 1988.

——(ed.), *Egypt Revisited*, New Brunswick/London: Transaction Publishers,
1989.

——, *They Came Before Columbus: The African Presence in Ancient America*,
New York: Random House, 1976.

Vinson, James (ed.), *Contemporary Dramatists*, preface Ruby Cohn, London:
St James Press, New York: St Martin's Press, 1977. [Ama Ata Aidoo, Efua
Sutherland]

——(ed.), *Contemporary Novelists*, New York: St Martin's Press, 1972. [Gwen-
dolyn Brooks, Bessie Head, Kristin Hunter, Ann Petry, Margaret Walker]

Voorhees, Lillian W., and Robert W. O'Brien (eds), *The Brown Thrush: An
Anthology of Verse by Negro Students at Talladega College*, Bryn Athyn,
Penn: Lawson-Roberts Publishings Co., c. 1932. [Arlene Howard Benton,
Elaine Behel, Lillian Brown, Thelma T. Clement, Margaret Danner, Gertrude
Davenport, Julia Gaillard, Ariel Williams Holloway, Katherine Jackson Hunter,
Olivia M. Hunter, Audrey Johnson, Katie Kelly, L. Doretta Lowery, Portia Lucas,
W. Blanche Nivens, Hilda Preer, Eleanor A. Thompson, Thersea Thorpe, Edna
Mae Weiss]

Wade-Gayles, Gloria, *No Crystal Stair: Visions of Race and Sex in Black
Women's Fiction*, New York: Pilgrim Press, 1984.

Wagner, Jean, *Les Poètes Nègres des Etats Unis*, Librarie Istra, 1963; trans.
Kenneth Douglas as *Black Poets of the United States: From Paul Laurence
Dunbar to Langston Hughes*, Urbana: University of Illinois Press, 1973.

Walker, Cheryl, *Women and Gender in Southern Africa to 1945*, Johannesburg:
David Philip; London: James Currey, 1991.

——, *Women and Resistance in South Africa*, London: Onyx, 1982.

Walker, Melissa, *Down from the Mountaintop: Black Women's Novels in the

Wake of the Civil Rights Movement, 1966–1989, London: Yale University Press, 1991.

Wall, Cheryl A. (ed.), *Changing Our Own Words: Essays on Criticism, Theory, and Writing by Black Women*, New Brunswick, NJ: Rutgers University Press, 1989; London: Routledge, 1990. [Abena P. A. Busia, Barbara Christian, Mae Gwendolyn Henderson, Gloria T. Hull, Deborah McDowell, Valerie Smith, Hortense Spillers, Claudia Tate, Cheryl Wall, Susan Willis]

Wallace, Ann (ed.), *Daughters of the Sun, Women of the Moon: Anthology of Canadian Black Women Poets*, Ontario: Williams-Wallace Publishers, 1991. [Dionne Brand, Afua Cooper, Claire Harris, Ahdri Zhina Cooper, Marlene Nourbese Philip]

Wallace, Michele, *Black Macho and the Myth of the Superwoman*, London/New York: Verso, 1990.

——, *Invisibility Blues: From Pop to Theory*, London/New York: Verso, 1990.

Wallis Budge, Sir E. A., *The Queen of Sheba and her only Son Menyelek*, London: Medici Society, 1922.

Walmsley, Anne, and Nick Caistor (eds), *Facing the Sea: a new anthology from the Caribbean region*, London/Kingston: Heinemann Educational Books, 1986. [Hazel D. Campbell, Christine Craig]

Walrond, Eric, and Rosey Pool (eds), *Black and Unknown Bards: A Collection of Negro Poetry*, Aldington, Kent: Hand & Flower Press, 1962. [Gwendolyn B. Bennett, Gwendolyn Brooks, Frances E. W. Harper, Margaret Walker]

Walsh, William, *Commonwealth Literature*, London: Oxford University Press, 1973.

Walvin, James, *The Black Presence: A Documentary History of the Negro in England, 1555–1860*, London: Orbach & Chambers, 1971.

Warner, Keith (ed.), *Critical Perspectives on Caribbean Literature in French*, Washington, DC: Three Continents Press, 1990?

Washington, Mary Helen (ed.), *Black-Eyed Susans/Midnight Birds: Stories by and about Black Women*, New York: Anchor/Doubleday, 1990. [Toni Cade Bambara, Gwendolyn Brooks, Alexis De Veaux, Frenchy Hodges, Gayl Jones, Paule Marshall, Louise Meriwether, Toni Morrison, Ntozake Shange, Jean Wheeler Smith, Alice Walker, Paulette Childress White, Sherley Anne Williams]

——(ed.), *Black-Eyed Susans: Classic Stories by and about Black Women*, Garden City, NY: Anchor/Doubleday, 1975; as *Any Woman's Blues*, London: Virago, 1981. [Toni Cade Bambara, Gwendolyn Brooks, Paule Marshall, Louise Meriwether, Toni Morrison, Jean Wheeler Smith, Alice Walker, Mary Helen Washington]

——(ed.), *Memory of Kin: Stories About Family by Black Writers*, New York: Anchor, 1991. [Toni Cade Bambara, Lucille Clifton, Toi Derricotte, Alexis De Veaux, Rita Dove, June Jordan, Jamaica Kincaid, Andrea Lee, Audre Lorde, Paule Marshall, Alice Walker, Marilyn Waniek, Paulette Childress White]

——(ed.), *Midnight Birds: Stories of Contemporary Black Women Writers*, Garden City, NY: Anchor/Doubleday, 1980. [Toni Cade Bambara, Alexis De Veaux, Frenchy Hodges, Gayl Jones, Toni Morrison, Ntozake Shange, Alice Walker, Mary Helen Washington, Paulette Childress White, Sherley Anne Williams]

——(ed.), *Invented Lives: Narratives of Black Women 1860–1960*, Garden City, NY: Anchor/Doubleday, 1987; London: Virago, 1989. [Marita Bonner, Gwendolyn Brooks, Frances E. W. Harper, Pauline E. Hopkins, Zora Neale Hurston, Harriet Jacobs, Nella Larsen, Ann Petry, Dorothy West, Fannie Barrier Williams]

Waters, Harold A., *Théâtre Noir: Encyclopédie des pièces écrites en français par des auteurs noirs*, Washington, DC: Three Continents Press, 1988?

Watkins, Mel, and Jay David (eds), *To Be a Black Woman: Portraits in Fact and Fiction*, New York: Morrow, 1970. [Mari Evans, Carlene Hatcher Polite]

Watkins, Sylvester C. (ed.), *Anthology of American Negro Literature*, New York: Random House, 1944.

Watts, Margaret (ed.), *Washerwoman Hangs Her Poems in the Sun: Poems by Women of Trinidad and Tobago*, Trinidad & Tobago, 1990. [Laura June Alleyne, Llima Cole, Clara Rosa De Lima, Maya Devi, Sharon Francis-Thomas, Joya Gomez, Melvina Hazard, Laurel Ince, Cynthia James, Candyce Kelshall, Naomi Laird, Diana Mahabir, Sybil Maundy, Marina Ama Omowale Maxwell, Dionyse McTair, Carol-Ann Mohammed, Esther H. Moore, Lorna Pilgrim, Jennifer Rahim, Rajandaye Ramkissoon-Chen, Dawn Mahalia Riley, Eintou Pearl Springer, Joy Valdez, Lisa Wells, Marguerite Wyke, Margaret Watts]

Watson, Carole McAlpin, *Prologue: The Novels of Black American Women, 1891–1965*, Westport/London: Greenwood, 1985.

Weaver, Robert, and Joseph Bruchac (eds), *Aftermath: An Anthology of Poems in English from Africa, Asia, and the Caribbean*, New York: Greenfield Review Press, 1977. [Ama Ata Aidoo, Louise Bennett, Suroj Dutta, Gloria Escoffery, Margaret Gill, Delphine King, Rose Mbowa, Stella Ngatho, Shana Yardan]

Welsch, Erwin K., *The Negro in the United States. A Research Guide*, Bloomington: Indiana University Press, 1965.

West, Richard, *Back to Africa: A History of Sierra Leone and Liberia*, London: Jonathan Cape, 1970.

White, Deborah Grey, *Ar'n't I a Woman? Female Slaves in the Plantation South*, New York/London: W. W. Norton, 1985.

White, Evelyn C. (ed.), *The Black Women's Health Book: Speaking for Ourselves*, Seattle: Seal, 1990. [Opal Palmer Adisa, Denise Alexander, Georgiana Arnold, Byllye Y. Avery, Sheila Battle, Melissa Blount, Lorraine Bonner, Julia A. Boyd, Forrestine A. Bragg, Andrea R. Canaan, Lucille Clifton, Angela Davis, Bridgett M. Davis, Marian Wright Edelman, Janis Coombs Epps, Vanessa Northington Gamble, Jewelle L. Gomez, Imani Harrington, Rev. Linda H. Hollies, Linda Janet Holmes, Zora Neale Hurston, Vida Labrie Jones, Cheryl M. Killon, Mary Lou Lee, Marsha R. Leslie, Andrea Lewis, Gloria Lockett, Audre Lorde, Lulu F., Pat Parker, Rachel V., Sean Reynolds, Beth Richie, Kate Rushin, Pamela Sherrod, Judy D. Simmons, Barbara Smith, Alice Walker, Faye Wattleton, Evelyn C. White, K. Malaika Williams]

White, Newman Ivey, and Walter Clinton Jackson (eds), *An Anthology of Verse by American Negroes*, Durham, NC: Trinity College Press, 1924; Durham, NC: Moore Publishing Co., 1968. [Jessie Redmon Fauset, Sarah Collins Fernandis, Frances E. W. Harper, Georgia Douglas Johnson, Ann Plato, H. Cordelia Ray,

Clara Ann Thompson, Priscilla Jane Thompson, Phillis Wheatley, Myra Viola Woods]

Whitehead, Winifred, *Different Faces: Growing Up with Books in a Multicultural Society*, London: Pluto, 1988.

Whiteley, W. H. (ed.), *A Selection of African Prose. Vol. 1: Traditional Oral Texts. Vol. 2: Written Prose*, Oxford: Clarendon Press, 1964. [Mabel Dove-Danquah]

Whiteman, Maxwell, *A Century of Fiction by American Negroes, 1853–1952: A Descriptive Bibliography*, Philadelphia: Albert Saifer, 1955.

Wilentz, Ted, and Tom Weatherley (eds), *Natural Process: An Anthology of New Black Poetry*, New York: Hill & Wang, 1970. [Nikki Giovanni, Audre Lorde, Carolyn M. Rodgers, Sonia Sanchez]

Wilkerson, Margaret B. (ed.), *Nine Plays by Black Women*, New York: NAL/Mentor, 1987. [Alice Childress, Kathleen Collins, Alexis DeVeaux, P. J. Gibson, Lorraine Hansberry, Elaine Jackson, Aishah Rahman, Beah Richards, Ntozake Shange]

Wilkinson, Jane (ed.), *Talking with African Writers: Interviews with African poets, playwrights and novelists*, London: James Currey, 1991. [Tsitsi Dangarembga, Micere Githae Mugo]

Wilkov, A. (comp.), *Some English Writings by Non-Europeans in South Africa, 1944–1960*, Johannesburg: Department of Librarianship, University of the Witwatersrand, 1962.

Williams, Chancellor, *The Destruction of Black Civilization: Great Issues of a Race from 4000 BC to 2000 AD*, Chicago: Third World Press, 1976.

Williams, Eric, *Capitalism and Slavery*, Chapel Hill: University of North Carolina Press, 1944.

——, *From Columbus to Castro: The History of the Caribbean 1492–1969*, London: André Deutsch, 1970.

Williams, Maxine, *et al.* (eds), *Black Women's Liberation*, New York: Pathfinder Press, 1971.

Williams, Ora, "A Bibliography of Works Written by American Black Women", *CLA Journal*, 15 (March 1972), pp. 354–77.

——, *American Black Women in the Arts and Sciences: A Bibliographic Survey*, Metuchen, NJ: Scarecrow Press, 1973.

Williams, Sherley Anne, *Give Birth to Brightness: A Thematic Study of Neo-Black Literature*, New York: Dial Press, 1972.

Willis, Susan, *Specifying: Black Women Writing: The American Experience*, Madison: University of Wisconsin Press, 1987.

Wilson, Amrit, *The Challenge Road: Women and the Eritrean Revolution*, London: Earthscan, 1991.

Wolfers, Michael (ed.), *Poems from Angola*, London: Heinemann Educational Books, African Writers Series 215, 1979. [Deolinda Rodrigues de Almeida]

Woodson, Carter G., *African Heroes and Heroines*, Washington, DC: 1969 (reissue).

Work, Monroe N., *A Bibliography of the Negro in Africa and America*, New York: Octagon, H. W. Wilson, 1928; 1965.

Yellin, Jean Fagan, *Women and Sisters: Antislavery Feminists in American Culture*, New Haven: Yale University Press, 1990.

Young, Ann Venture (ed./trans.), *The Image of Black Women in Twentieth-Century South American Poetry*, Washington, DC: Three Continents Press, 1987.

Zahava, Irene (ed.), *Love, Struggle and Change*, Freedom, CA: Crossing Press, 1988. [Toni Cade Bambara, Becky Birtha, Jewelle L. Gomez]

——(ed.), *My Father's Daughter: Stories by Women*, Freedom, CA: Crossing Press, 1990. [Gloria Anzaldúa, Jewelle L. Gomez, Audre Lorde, Alice Walker]

Zandy, Janet (ed.), *Calling Home: Working-Class Women's Writings – An Anthology*, New Brunswick/London: Rutgers University Press, 1990. [Toni Cade Bambara, Beth Brant, Sandra Cisneros, Sharon Doubiago, Rayna Green, Daphne Duval Harrison, Endesha Ida Mae Holland, Myung-Hee Kim, Audre Lorde, Cherrie Moraga, Barbara Smith, Helena Maria Viramontes, Nellie Wong, Judy Yung]

Zell, Hans M. (ed.), *African Books in Print/Livres Africains disponibles*, 2 vols, London: Mansell/Westview: Meckler Books/Paris: France Expansion, 1978.

Zell, Hans M., Carol Bundy and Virginia Coulon (eds), *A New Reader's Guide to African Literature*, London/Ibadan/Nairobi: Heinemann Educational Books, 1983.

Zettersten, Arne (ed.), *East African Literature: An Anthology*, London/New York: Longman, 1983. [Micere Mugo, Rebeka Njau, Grace Ogot]

Zhana (ed.), *Sojourn* [anthology of prose and poetry by Black women in Britain], London: Methuen, 1988. [Iiola Ashundie, Debjani Chatterjee, Najma Kazi, Lennie St Luce, Zindika S. Macheol, Isha McKenzie-Mavinga, Tod Perkins, Judith Kaurmekeli Greenidge]

Zimunya, Musaemura, *Birthright: A Selection of Poems from Southern Africa*, Harlow, Longman, 1989. [Noémia De Sousa]

Geographical Listing of Authors

(by region of birth and/or association or residence)

Africa

ANGOLA
Alda Lara

BOTSWANA
Bessie Head
Nisa

CÔTE D'IVOIRE
Véronique Tadjo

EAST AFRICA
Mwana Kupona Msham

EGYPT
Hapshepsut

ETHIOPIA
Kebbedesh
Makeda, Queen of Sheba

GHANA
Ama Ata Aidoo
Abena P. A. Busia
Gladys May Casely-Hayford
Mabel Dove-Danquah
Efua Sutherland

KENYA
Jane Tapsubei Creider
Micere Githae Mugo
Rebeka Njau

Grace Ogot
Charity Waciuma

LESOTHO
Caroline Ntseliseng Khaketla

LIBERIA
Henrietta Fullor
Alice Perry Johnson
Womi Bright Neal

MALI
Awa Thiam

MOZAMBIQUE
Noémia De Sousa
Lina Magaia

NIGERIA
Zaynab Alkali
Ifi Amadiume
Baba
Buchi Emecheta
Flora Nwapa
'Molara Ogundipe-Leslie
Mabel Segun
Zulu Sofola
Adaora Lily Ulasi

SÃO TOMÉ
Alda do Espírito Santo

SENEGAL
Mariama Bâ
Nafissatou Diallo
Annette M'Baye
Aminata Sow-Fall
Myriam Warner-Vieyra
Phillis Wheatley

SIERRA LEONE
Adelaide Casely-Hayford
Gladys May Casely-Hayford
Iyamidé Hazeley

SOMALIA
Saida Herzi

SOUTH AFRICA
Bessie Head
Amelia Blossom House
Noni Jabavu
Ellen Kuzwayo
Zindzi Mandela
Gcina Mhlope
Laurette Ngcobo
Christine Qunta
Dulcie September
Joyce Silakane
Miriam Tlali
Zoë Wicomb

TIGRAY
Kebbedesh

UGANDA
Grace Akello

WEST AFRICA
Lucy Terry

ZAÏRE
Citèkù Ndaaya

ZIMBABWE
Tsitsi Dangarembga
Barbara Makhalisa
Sekai Nzenza
Kristina Rungano

Caribbean, Latin America and South America

ANTIGUA
Jamaica Kincaid

ARUBA
Merle Collins

BARBADOS
Paule Marshall

BELIZE
Zee Edgell

BERMUDA
Mary Prince

BRAZIL
Aline França
Carolina Maria de Jesús
Lourdes Teodoro

COLOMBIA
Gabriela Pearse

COSTA RICA
Eulalia Bernard

CUBA
Pilar López Gonzales
Georgina Herrera
Nancy Morejón
Marta Rojas

DOMINICA
Jacqueline Rudet

DOMINICAN REPUBLIC
Aída Cartagena Portalatín

GRENADA
Merle Colins
Audre Lorde

GUADELOUPE
Maryse Condé
Simone Schwarz-Bart
Myriam Warner-Vieyra

GUYANA
Joan Cambridge
Beryl Gilroy
Pauline Melville
Grace Nichols

HAITI
Marie Chauvet

JAMAICA
Opal Palmer Adisa
Louise Bennett
Eulalia Bernard
Valerie Bloom
Jean Binta Breeze
Erna Brodber
Michelle Cliff
Christine Craig
Amy Jacques Garvey
Lorna Goodison
Una Marson
Pamela Mordecai
Velma Pollard
Joan Riley
Mary Seacole
Olive Senior
Elean Thomas
Sylvia Wynter

ST KITTS
Iiola Ashundie

SURINAM
Astrid Roemer

TRINIDAD AND TOBAGO
Valerie Belgrave
Dionne Brand
Rosa Guy
Merle Hodge
Amryl Johnson
Claudia Jones

Marion Patrick Jones
Marlene Nourbese Philip
Marsha Prescod
Eintou Pearl Springer

URUGUAY
Virginia Brindis de Salas

Europe

DENMARK
Nella Larsen

ENGLAND
Ifi Amadiume
Iiola Ashundie
Valerie Boom
Jean Binta Breeze
Barbara Burford
Dinah Anuli Butler
Merle Collins
Buchi Emecheta
Beryl Gilroy
Serena Gordon
Iyamide Hazeley
Marsha Hunt
Amryl Johnson
Claudia Jones
Jackie Kay
Pauline Melville
Lauretta Ngcobo
Grace Nichols
Gabriela Pearse
Marsha Prescod
Mary Prince
Joan Riley
Lucinda Roy
Jacqueline Rudet
Sandi Russell
Jenneba Sie Jalloh
Maud Sulter
Zoë Wicomb

FRANCE
Maryse Condé
Simone Schwarz-Bart

GERMANY
Abena Adomako
Julia Berger
Angelika Eisenbrandt
May Opitz

IRELAND
Jenneba Sie Jalloh

NETHERLANDS
Astrid Roemer

RUSSIA
Yelena Khanga

SCOTLAND
Jackie Kay
Maud Sulter

TURKEY
Ayse Bircan

North America

CANADA
Dionne Brand
Jane Tapsubei Creider
Marlene Nourbese Philip

USA
Maya Angelou
Red Jordan Arobateau
Toni Cade Bambara
Gwendolyn B. Bennett
Becky Birtha
Marita Bonner
Gwendolyn Brooks
Abena P. A. Busia
Octavia E. Butler
Annie L. Burton
Alice Childress
Lucille Clifton
Anna J. Cooper
Jayne Cortez
Angela Davis
Thadious Davis

Lucy Delaney
Rita Dove
Kate Drumgoold
Alice Dunbar-Nelson
Zilpha Elaw
Elizabeth ("Old Elizabeth")
Mari E. Evans
Jessie Redmon Fauset
Charlotte Forten (Grimké)
Henrietta Fullor
Nikki Giovanni
Vivian Glover
Marita Golden
Jewelle L. Gomez
Hattie Gossett
Angelina Weld Grimké
Rosa Guy
Lorraine Hansberry
Frances E. W. Harper
Billie Holiday
bell hooks
Pauline E. Hopkins
Gloria T. Hull
Marsha Hunt
Kristin Hunter
Zora Neale Hurston
Harriet Jacobs (Linda Brent)
Mattie Jackson
Alice Perry Johnson
Georgia Douglas Johnson
Claudia Jones
Gayl Jones
June Jordan
Jamaica Kincaid
Nella Larsen
Andrea Lee
Audre Lorde
Elise Johnson McDougald
Naomi Long Madgett
Terry McMillan
Paule Marshall
Louise Meriwether
Mary Monroe
Ann Moody
Toni Morrison
Pauli Murray
Gloria Naylor

Ann Petry
J. J. Phillips
Ann Plato
Mary Prince
Nancy Prince
Carolyn M. Rodgers
Sandi Russell
Sonia Sanchez
Ntozake Shange
Anne Spencer
Maria E. Stewart
Susie King Taylor
Mary Church Terrell
Lucy Terry
Sojourner Truth
Harriet Tubman
Bethany Veney
Alice Walker
Margaret Walker
Ida B. Wells (Barnett)
Dorothy West
Phillips Wheatley
Sherley Anne Williams
Harriet Wilson

Copyrights and Permissions

The editor and publishers would like to thank the following for permission to reproduce material in this anthology:

OPAL PALMER ADISA: "Duppy Get Her" from *Bake-Face and Other Guava Stories* by Opal Palmer Adisa reprinted by permission of Kelsey Street Press and HarperCollins Publishers Ltd., copyright © 1989 by Opal Palmer Adisa. ABENA ADOMAKO: "Mother: Afro-German; Father: Ghanaian" by Abena Adomako from *Farbe bekennen: Afro-deutsche Frauen auf den Spuren ihrer Geschichte*, eds. Oguntoye et al. (Orlanda Frauenverlag, 1986), this translation copyright © 1991 by George Busby. AMA ATA AIDOO: "Two Sisters" from *No Sweetness Here* by Ama Ata Aidoo (Longman, 1988) reprinted by kind permission of the author, copyright © 1988 by Ama Ata Aidoo. GRACE AKELLO: "Encounter" from *My Barren Song* by Grace Akello by kind permission of Dangaroo Press, copyright © 1979 by Grace Akello. ZAYNAB ALKALI: extract from *The Stillborn* by Zaynab Alkali reprinted by permission of Longman Group Limited, copyright © 1984 by Zaynab Alkali. IFI AMADIUME: extract from *Afrikan Matriarchal Foundations: The Igbo Case* by Ifi Amadiume reprinted by permission of Karnak House, copyright © 1987 by Ifi Amadiume. ANCIENT EGYPTIAN LOVE POEMS: "Verses 2, 2, 6, 8" from Papyrus Harris 500 IIb, the second collection, in *Ancient Egyptian Literature* by Miriam Lichtheim reprinted by permission of The University of California Press, copyright © 1973–80 by Regents. MAYA ANGELOU: "A Good Woman Feeling Bad" from *Shaker, Why Don't You Sing?* by Maya Angelou reproduced by permission of Random House, Inc., copyright © 1983 by Maya Angelou; "The Reunion" by Maya Angelou from *Confirmation*, eds. Baraka & Baraka (Morrow, 1983), reprinted by kind permission of the author, copyright © 1983 by Maya Angelou. RED JORDAN AROBATEAU: "Nobody's People" (*Sinister Wisdom* 21) from *Stories from the Dance of Life* by Red Jordan Arobateau reprinted by kind permission of the author, copyright © 1979 by Red Jordan Arobateau. IIOLA ASHUNDIE: "Mother of Mine" by Iiola Ashundie from *Sojourn*, ed. Zhana, reprinted by permission of Methuen London, copyright © 1988 by Iiola Ashundie. MARIAMA BÂ: extract from *So Long A Letter* by Mariama Bâ reprinted by kind permission of Heinemann Educational Books, this translation copyright © 1979 by Modupé Bodé-Thomas. BABA: extract from *Baba of Karo: A Woman of the Muslim Hausa* by Mary F. Smith reprinted by permission of Yale University Press, copyright © 1954 by Mary F. Smith. TONI CADE BAMBARA: "Maggie of the Green Bottles" from *Gorilla, My Love* by Toni Cade Bambara reprinted by permission of The Women's Press and Random House, Inc., copyright © 1960, 1963, 1964, 1965, 1968, 1970, 1971, 1972 by Toni Cade Bambara. VALERIE BELGRAVE: extract from *Ti Marie* by Valerie Belgrave reprinted by kind permission of Heinemann Educational

Books, copyright © 1988 by Valerie Belgrave. GWENDOLYN BENNETT: "To a Dark Girl" by Gwendolyn Bennett in *Opportunity* 5, 1927 and "Hatred", in *The Book of American Negro Poetry*, ed. James Weldon Johnson (Harcourt, Brace and World, 1931); "Advice" by Gwendolyn Bennett in *Caroling Dusk*, ed. Countee Cullen (Harper & Bros, 1927). LOUISE BENNETT: "Back to Africa" from *Jamaica Labrish* by Louise Bennett reprinted by kind permission of Sangster's Book Stores Ltd., copyright © 1966 by Louise Bennett. JULIA BERGER: "I do the same things others do" by Julia Berger from *Farbe bekennen*, eds. Oguntoye et al. (Orlanda Frauenverlag, 1986), this translation copyright © 1991 by George Busby. EULALIA BERNARD: "We Are the Nation of Threes" and "Metamorphosis of Your Memory" from *Ritmoberoe* (San José, 1982 by Eulalia Bernard, translated by Amanda Hopkinson in *Lovers and Comrades: Women's Resistance Poetry from Central America* (Women's Press, 1989). AYSE BIRCAN: "Black and Turkish" by Ayse Bircan reproduced by kind permission of Ayse Bircan, copyright © 1991 by Ayse Bircan. BECKY BIRTHA: "Johnnieruth" from *Lovers' Choice* by Becky Birtha reprinted by kind permission of Seal Press, copyright © 1987 by Becky Birtha. VALERIE BLOOM: "Carry-go-bring-come" from *Touch Mi, Tell Mi!* by Valerie Bloom reprinted by kind permission of Bogle-L'Ouverture Publications, copyright © 1983 by Valerie Bloom. MARITA BONNER: "On Being Young – a Woman – and Colored" by Marita Bonner from *Frye Street and Environs: The Collected Works of Marita Bonner*, eds. Joyce Flynn and Joyce Occomy Stricklin, reprinted by permission of Beacon Press, copyright © 1987 by Joyce Flynn and Joyce Occomy Stricklin. DIONNE BRAND: "Canto XIII" from *Primitive Offensive* by Dionne Brand reprinted by kind permission of Williams-Wallace Publishers, copyright © 1982 by Dionne Brand. JEAN BINTA BREEZE: "Riddym Ravings (the mad woman's poem)" from *Riddym Ravings and Other Poems* by Jean Binta Breeze reprinted by permission of Race Today Publications, copyright © 1988 by Jean Binta Breeze. VIRGINIA BRINDIS DE SALAS: "Song for a South American Black Boy" by Virginia Brindis de Salas from *Voices of Négritude* by Julio Finn, reprinted by kind permission of Quartet Books and Julio Finn, this translation copyright © 1988 by Julio Finn. ERNA BRODBER: extract from *Jane and Louisa Will Soon Come Home* by Erna Brodber reprinted by permission of New Beacon Books, copyright © 1980 by Erna Brodber. GWENDOLYN BROOKS: extract from *Maud Martha* and "To Black Women" from *To Disembark* (Third World Press, 1981) by Gwendolyn Brooks reprinted by kind permission of the author, copyright © 1987 Gwendolyn Brooks Blakely. BARBARA BURFORD: "Miss Jessie" by Barbara Burford from *Everyday Matters 2* reprinted by permission of Sheba Feminist Publishers, copyright © 1984 by Barbara Burford. ABENA P. A. BUSIA: "Though I Have Sworn" and "Exiles" from *Testimonies of Exile* by Abena P. A. Busia and "Liberation" reprinted by permission of the author and Africa World Press, copyright © Abena P. A. Busia. DINAH ANULI BUTLER: "To my Father" by Dinah Anuli Butler in *Charting the Journey* (Sheba, 1988) reprinted by permission of Sheba Feminist Publishers, copyright © by Dinah Anuli Butler. OCTAVIA E. BUTLER: extract from *Kindred* by Octavia E. Butler reprinted by permission of The Women's Press and Writers House Inc., copyright © 1979 by Octavia E. Butler. JOAN CAMBRIDGE: extract from *Clarise Cumberbatch Want to Go Home* by Joan Cambridge reprinted by permission of Houghton Mifflin and The Women's Press, copyright © 1988 by Joan Cambridge. AÍDA CARTAGENA PORTALATÍN: "Black Autumn" by Aída Cartagena Portalatín in *Antología Panorámica de la Poesía Dominicana*, ed. Rueda (Santiago: UCMM, 1972), translated by Daisy C. DeFilippis. ADELAIDE CASELY-HAYFORD: "Mista Courifer" by Adelaide Casely-Hayford reprinted by kind permission of Kobe Hunter, copyright © Kobe Hunter. GLADYS CASELY-HAYFORD: "The Serving Girl", "Junior Geography Lesson", "To My Mother", "The Ideal", "Distance", "The Might Have Been" by Gladys May Casely-Hayford used by kind permission of Kobe Hunter, copyright © Kobe Hunter. MARIE CHAUVET: "Love" from *Amour, colère et folie* by Marie Chauvet in *Her True-True Name*, eds. Mordecai and Wilson (Heinemann International), this translation copyright © 1989 by Betty Wilson. ALICE CHILDRESS: "Like One of the Family" and "The Pocketbook Game" from *Like One of the Family: Conversations from a Domestic's Life* by Alice Childress (Beacon Press, 1956) reprinted by permission of Flora Roberts Inc., copyright © 1986 by Alice Childress. MICHELLE CLIFF: extracts from *No Telephone to Heaven* by Michelle Cliff reprinted by permission of the author and Dutton, an imprint of New American Library, a division of Penguin Books USA Inc., copyright © 1987 by Michelle Cliff. LUCILLE CLIFTON: "Miss Rosie" from *Good Times* by Lucille Clifton reprinted by permission of Random House Inc., copyright © 1969 by Lucille Clifton. MERLE COLLINS: "The Walk" from *Rain Darling* by Merle Collins reprinted by kind permission of The Women's Press, copyright © 1990 by Merle Collins. MARYSE CONDÉ: extract from *A Season in Rihata* by Maryse Condé reprinted by kind permission of Heinemann Educational Books, copyright © 1988 by Maryse Condé. J. CALIFORNIA COOPER: "Swingers and Squares" from *Homemade Love* by J. California Cooper (St Martin's Press, 1986) copyright © 1986 by J. California Cooper. JAYNE CORTEZ: "Consultation", "Jazz Fan Looks Back" and "Push Back the Catastrophes" by Jayne Cortez reprinted by kind permission of the author, copyright © 1991 by Jayne Cortez. CHRISTINE CRAIG: "The Chain" from *Quadrille for Tigers* by Christine Craig (Mina Press, 1984) reprinted by kind permission of the author, copyright © 1984 by Christine Craig. JANE TAPSUBEI CREIDER: extract from *Two Lives: My Spirit and I* by Jane Tapsubei Creider reprinted by kind permission of The Women's Press, copyright © 1986 by Jane Tapsubei Creider. TSITSI DANGAREMGBA: extract from *Nervous Conditions* by Tsitsi Dangaremgba reprinted by kind permission of The Women's Press, copyright © 1988 by Tsitsi Dangaremgba. ANGELA DAVIS: "Let Us All Rise Together: Radical Perspectives on Empowerment for Afro-American Women" from *Women, Culture and Politics* by Angela Davis reprinted by permission of Random House, Inc., copyright © 1984, 1985, 1986, 1987, 1988, 1989 by Angela Davis. THADIOUS M. DAVIS: "Asante Sana, Te Te" by Thadious M. Davis in *Black Sister*, ed. Stetson, reprinted by permission of Indiana University Press, copyright © Thadious Davis. NOÉMIA DE SOUSA: "If You Want to Know Me" by Noémia De Sousa in *When Bullets Begin to Flower* (East African Publishing House), translated by Margaret Dickinson, copyright © by Noémia De Sousa. NAFISSATOU DIALLO: extract from *Fary, Princess of Tiali* by Nafissatou Diallo reprinted by permission of Three Continents Press of Washington, DC, this translation copyright © 1987 by Ann Woollcombe. RITA DOVE: "The Zulus" from *Fifth Sunday* by Rita Dove (University of Kentucky, 1985) reprinted by permission of the author, copyright

© 1985 by Rita Dove. MABEL DOVE-DANQUAH: "Anticipation" by Mabel Dove-Danquah reprinted by kind permission of the author, copyright © Mabel Dove-Danquah. ZEE EDGELL: extract from *Beka Lamb* by Zee Edgell reprinted by kind permission of Heinemann Publishers Ltd., copyright © 1982 by Zee Edgell. ANGELIKA EISENBRANDT: "Suddenly I knew what I wanted" by Angelika Eisenbrandt from *Farbe bekennen*, eds. Oguntoye et al. (Orlanda Frauenverlag, 1986), this translation copyright © 1991 by George Busby. BUCHI EMECHETA: "A Man Needs Many Wives" from *The Joys of Motherhood* by Buchi Emecheta reprinted by permission of HarperCollins Publishers Limited, copyright © 1979 by Buchi Emecheta. ALDA DO ESPÍRITO SANTO: "The Same Side of the Canoe" by Alda do Espírito Santo in *Penguin Book of Women Poets*, eds. Cosman, Keefe and Weaver (Allen Lane, 1987) reprinted by permission of Kathleen Weaver, this translation copyright © 1978 by Kathleen Weaver and Allan Francovich. MARI EVANS: "I Am a Black Woman" and "Where Have You Gone" from *I Am a Black Woman* by Mari Evans (Morrow, 1970) reprinted by kind permission of Mari Evans Phemster, copyright © 1970 by Mari Evans. JESSIE REDMON FAUSET: "Dead Fires" and "Oriflamme" by Jessie Redmon Fauset reprinted by permission of *Crisis* magazine. ALINE FRANÇA: extract from *The Woman of Aleduma* (*A Mulher de Aleduma*) by Aline França (Clarindo Silva, 1981), this translation copyright © 1991 by Julio Finn. BERYL GILROY: extract from *Franjipani House* by Beryl Gilroy reprinted by kind permission of Heinemann Publishers Ltd., copyright © 1986 by Beryl Gilroy. NIKKI GIOVANNI: "On Hearing 'The Girl with the Flaxen Hair'" and "Nikki-Rosa" from *Black Feeling Black Talk/Judgement* by Nikki Giovanni reprinted by permission of William Morrow and Co. Inc., copyright © 1970 by Nikki Giovanni. VIVIAN GLOVER: extract from *The First Fig Tree* by Vivian Glover reprinted by permission of Methuen, London and Faith Childs Literary Agency, copyright © 1987 by Vivian Glover. MARITA GOLDEN: "Crystal" from *A Woman's Place* by Marita Golden reprinted by permission of Methuen, London and Doubleday, a division of Bantam Doubleday Dell Publishing Group Inc., copyright © 1986 by Marita Golden. JEWELLE L. GOMEZ: "A Swimming Lesson" by Jewelle L. Gomez (*Essence*, August 1990) reprinted by kind permission of the author, copyright © 1990 by Jewelle L. Gomez. PILAR LÓPEZ GONZALES: "It Was All Mamá's Fault" by Pilar Lopez Gonzales from *Four women: Living the Revolution*, by Lewis, Lewis and Rigdon, reprinted by permission of University of Illinois Press, copyright © 1977 by Lewis et al. LORNA GOODISON: "I Am Becoming My Mother", "Guinea Woman" and "Nanny" from *I Am Becoming My Mother* by Lorna Goodison reprinted by permission of New Beacon Books, copyright © 1986 by Lorna Goodison. SERENA GORDON: "Into the light" by Serena Gordon reproduced by kind permission of the author, copyright © 1991 by Serena Gordon. HATTIE GOSSETT: "world view" from *Presenting ... Sister No Blues* by Hattie Gossett reprinted by permission of the author and Firebrand Books, Ithaca, New York, copyright © 1988 by Hattie Gossett. ANGELINA WELD GRIMKÉ: "The Black Finger" and "At April" by Angelina Weld Grimké from *Opportunity*, magazine of the National Urban League. ROSA GUY: extract from *A Measure of Time* by Rosa Guy reprinted by permission of Virago Press and Henry Holt and Company, Inc., copyright © 1983 by Rosa Guy. LORRAINE HANSBERRY: extract from *A Raisin in the Sun* by

Lorraine Hansberry reprinted by permission of Methuen Drama, copyright ©. HATSHEPSUT: "Speech of the Queen" in *Ancient Egyptian Literature*, Vol. II, by Miriam Lichtheim, reprinted by permission of the University of California Press, copyright © 1973–80 by the Regents. IYAMIDÉ HAZELEY: "When You Have Emptied Our Calabashes", "Women of Courage" and "Political Union" by Iyamidé Hazeley reprinted by kind permission of the author, copyright © 1987, 1991 by Iyamidé Hazeley. BESSIE HEAD: "The Special One" from *The Collector of Treasures* by Bessie Head reprinted by kind permission of Heinemann Publishers Ltd; "The Old Woman" (1967) and "The Woman from America" from *Tales of Tenderness and Power* by Bessie Head reprinted by kind permission of John Johnson Ltd., copyright © 1989 by the Estate of Bessie Head and Ad. Donker Pty Ltd. GEORGINA HERRERA: "Child Asleep", "Cradle" and "That Way of Dying" by Georgina Herrera, translated by Kathleen Weaver, reprinted by permission of the author and CENDA Cuban Center for Authors' Rights, these translations copyright © 1991 by Kathleen Weaver. SAIDA HERZI: "Against the pleasure principle" by Saida Herzi (*Index on Censorship*, October 1990) reprinted by kind permission of the author, copyright © 1990 by Saida Herzi. MERLE HODGE: extract from *Crick Crack, Monkey* by Merle Hodge reprinted by permission of André Deutsch Ltd., copyright © 1970 by Merle Hodge. BILLIE HOLIDAY: extract from *Lady Sings the Blues* by Billie Holliday (with William Dufty) reprinted by kind permission of Doubleday, a division of Bantam Doubleday Dell Publishing Inc., copyright © 1956 by Eleanor Fagan and William F. Dufty. BELL HOOKS: "Talking Back" from *Talking Back* by bell hooks reprinted by permission of South End Press, Boston, MA, copyright © 1988 by bell hooks. AMELIA BLOSSOM HOUSE: "Sacrifice" and "We Still Dance" from *Our Sun Will Rise* by Amelia Blossom House reprinted by permission of Three Continents Press Inc., copyright © 1989 by Amelia Blossom House. GLORIA T. HULL: "At My Age" and "Somebody, Some Body" from *Healing Heart, Poems 1973–1988* by Gloria T. Hull reprinted by permission of Kitchen Table: Women of Color Press, copyright © 1989 by Gloria T. Hull. MARSHA HUNT: extract from *Joy* by Marsha Hunt reprinted by permission of Random Century Group, copyright © 1990 by Marsha Hunt. KRISTIN HUNTER: extract from *God Bless the Child* by Kristin Hunter reprinted by permission of Howard University Press, copyright © 1964 by Kristin Hunter. ZORA NEALE HURSTON: extracts from *Mules and Men* by Zora Neale Hurston reprinted by permission of HarperCollins Publishers, copyright © 1935 by Zora Neale Hurston, renewed 1963 by John C. Hurston; extract from *Their Eyes Were Watching God* by Zora Neale Hurston reprinted by permission of HarperCollins Publishers, copyright © 1937 by J. B. Lippincott Company, renewed 1965 by John C. Hurston and Joel Hurston. NONI JABAVU: extract from *The Ochre People* by Noni Jabavu (John Murray, 1963) reprinted by permission, copyright © 1963 by Noni Jabavu. CAROLINA MARIA DE JESÚS: extract from *Beyond All Pity* by Carolina Maria de Jesús reprinted by permission of Souvenir Press Ltd., this translation copyright © by David St Clair. ALICE PERRY JOHNSON: "The Beginning of a Kpelle Woman" from *One Step Ahead* by Alice Perry Johnson (Liberian Publishing Co., 1972) reprinted by kind permission of the author, copyright © 1972 by Alice Perry Johnson. AMRYL

JOHNSON: "Yardstick" by Amryl Johnson from *Caribbean New Wave: Contemporary Short Stories*, eds. Brown (Heinemann International, 1990) and "Granny in de Market Place" from *Long Road to Nowhere* by Amryl Johnson (Virago, 1985) reprinted by permission of the author, copyright © 1990, 1985 by Amryl Johnson. GEORGIA DOUGLAS JOHNSON: "I Want to Die While You Love Me" in *Caroling Dusk*, ed. Countee Cullen (Harper and Bros, 1927). CLAUDIA JONES: from "An End to the Neglect of the Problems of Negro Women!" by Claudia Jones from *"I Think of My Mother": Notes on the Life and Times of Claudia Jones* by Buzz Johnson, reprinted by kind permission of Karia Press, copyright © 1985 by Buzz Johnson. GAYL JONES: "Ensinanca" by Gayl Jones in *Confirmation*, eds. Baraka and Baraka (Morrow, 1983), reprinted by permission, copyright © 1983 by Gayl Jones. JUNE JORDAN: "Declaration of an Independence I Would Just as Soon Not Have" (1976) from *Moving Towards Home* by June Jordan reprinted by permission of Virago Press, copyright © 1989 by June Jordan. JACKIE KAY: "Diary of Days for Adjoa" by Jackie Kay in *Dancing the Tightrope*, eds. Burford, MacRae, Paskin (Women's Press, 1987) reprinted by kind permission of the author, copyright © 1987 by Jackie Kay. KEBBEDESH: from *Sweeter than Honey: Testimonies of Tigrayan Women*, eds. Hammond and Druce (Third World First, 1989) reproduced by kind permission of Third World First, copyright © 1989 by Third World First. CAROLINE N. M. KHAKETLA: "The White and the Black" from *'Mantsopa* by Caroline Khaketla reproduced by permission of Oxford University Press South Africa, copyright © 1963 by Oxford University Press South Africa. YELENA KHANGA: "Black Russian" by Yelena Khanga (*Essence*, August 1989) reprinted by permission of the author, copyright © 1989 by Yelena Khanga. JAMAICA KINCAID: "A Walk to the Jetty" from *Annie John* by Jamaica Kincaid reprinted by permission of Farrar, Straus and Giroux, Inc., and Pan Books, copyright © 1983, 1984, 1985 by Jamaica Kincaid. ELLEN KUZWAYO: "The Reward of Waiting" from *Sit Down and Listen* by Ellen Kuzway reprinted by permission of The Women's Press, copyright © 1990 by Ellen Kuzwayo. ALDA LARA: "Testament" by Alda Lara in *A Horse of White Clouds: Poems from Lusophone Africa*, translated by Don Burgess, reprinted by permission of The Ohio University Monographs in International Studies, Athens, Ohio, copyright © 1989 by Don Burness. NELLA LARSEN: extracts from *Quicksand and Passing* by Nella Larsen, edited by Deborah E. McDowell, reprinted by permission of Rutgers University Press and Serpent's Tail, copyright © 1986 by Rutgers. ANDREA LEE: "An Old Woman" from *Sarah Phillips* by Andrea Lee reprinted by permission of ICM and Random House Inc., copyright © 1984 by Andrea Lee. AUDRE LORDE: "What My Child Learns of the Sea" and "Generation" from *Chosen Poems – Old and New* by Audre Lorde reprinted by permission of Charlotte Sheedy and W. W. Norton Inc., copyright © 1963, 1966 by Audre Lorde. TERRY MCMILLAN: extract from *Mama* by Terry McMillan first published in the UK by Jonathan Cape Publishers, 1987, reprinted by permission of the author and her agents, the Aaron Priest Literary Agency, copyright © by Terry McMillan. NAOMI LONG MADGETT: "New Day" from *Exits and Entrances* by Naomi Long Madgett (Lotus Press, 1978) and "Black Woman" from *Pink Ladies in the Afternoon* by Naomi Long Madgett (Lotus Press, 1972, 1990) reprinted by permission of the author, copyright © 1978, 1972, 1990 by

Naomi Long Madgett. LINA MAGAIA: "The Pregnant Well" from *Dumba Nengue: Run for Your Life* by Lina Magaia reprinted by kind permission of Karnak House, copyright © 1989 by Lina Magaia. BARBARA C. MAKHALISA: "Different Values" from *The Underdog and Other Stories* by Barbara Makhalisa reprinted by kind permission of the Mambo Press, copyright © 1984 by Barbara Makhalisa. ZINDZI MANDELA: "I waited for you last night" by Zindzi Mandela, in *Somehow We Survive*, ed. Plumpp, reprinted by permission of Thunder's Mouth, copyright © 1982 by Thunder's Mouth. PAULE MARSHALL: "To Da-Duh, In Memoriam" from *Reena and Other Stories* by Paule Marshall (Feminist Press, 1983) reprinted by permission of The Feminist Press and the author, copyright © 1983 by Paule Marshall. ANNETTE M'BAYE: "Silhouette" by Annette M'Baye (translated by Kathleen Weaver), in *Penguin Book of Women Poets*, eds. Cosman, Keefe, Weaver, reprinted by permission of Kathleen Weaver, this translation copyright © 1978 by Kathleen Weaver. PAULINE MELVILLE: "Beyond the Pale" and "Mixed" by Pauline Melville reproduced by permission of Curtis Brown Group on behalf of the author, copyright © 1991 by Pauline Melville. LOUISE MERIWETHER: "A Happening in Barbados" by Louise Meriwether in *Black-Eyed Susans*, ed. Washington, reprinted by permission of the author, copyright © 1968 by Louise Meriwether. GCINA MHLOPE: "Nokulunga's Wedding" by Gcina Mhlope reprinted by kind permission of Tony Peake Associates, copyright © 1983 by Gcina Mhlope. MARY MONROE: extract from *The Upper Room* by Mary Monroe (St Martin's, 1985) reprinted by permission, copyright © 1985 by Mary Monroe. ANN MOODY: extract from *Coming of Age in Mississippi* by Ann Moody reprinted by permission of Doubleday, a division of Bantam Doubleday Dell Publishing Group Inc., copyright © 1968 by Ann Moody. PAMELA MORDECAI: "Tell Me" and "For Eyes to Bless You" by Pamela Mordecai reprinted by permission of the author, copyright © 1978, 1979 by Pamela Mordecai. NANCY MOREJÓN: "Looking Within", "Coffee" and "Mother" from *Where the Island Sleeps Like a Wing: Selected Poetry* by Nancy Morejón, translated by Kathleen Weaver (Black Scholar Press, 1985), reprinted by kind permission of Kathleen Weaver, this translation copyright © 1985 by Kathleen Weaver; "Black Woman" by Nancy Morejón in *Voices of Négritude* by Julio Finn, reprinted by kind permission of Quartet Books, this translation copyright © 1988 by Julio Finn. TONI MORRISON: extract from *Beloved* by Toni Morrison reprinted by permission of the author and Chatto and Windus, part of the Random Century Group, copyright © 1987 by Toni Morrison. MWANA KUPONA MSHAM: from "Poem of Mwana Kupona" from *Advice of Mwana Kupona Msham Upon Wifely Duty* by Mwana Kupona Msham (translated by Alice Werner, Azania Press, 1932) in *Nine Faces of Kenya* by Elspeth Huxley (Collins Harvill, 1990). MĨCERE GĨTHAE MŨGO: "Where are those songs?" from *Daughter of My People, Sing* by Mĩcere Mũgo (East African Literature Bureau, 1976) reprinted by permission of the author, copyright © by Mĩcere Mũgo. PAULI MURRAY: "Ruth" from *Dark Testament and Other Poems* by Pauli Murray (Silvermine Publishers, 1970) reprinted by permission of Frances Collins Literary Agency, copyright © 1970 by Pauli Murray. GLORIA NAYLOR: "The Two" from *The Women of Brewster Place* by Gloria Naylor reprinted by permission of Viking Penguin, a division of Penguin Books USA Inc., copyright © 1980, 1982 by Gloria Naylor. CITÈKÙ NDAAYA: extract from "Ndaaya's Kàsàlà" by Citèkù Ndaaya in *Penguin Book of Women Poets*, eds. Cosman, Keefe and Weaver (Allen Lane, 1978), this translation copyright © 1978 by Judith Gleason. WOMI BRIGHT NEAL: "The Weeping Tree" by Womi Bright Neal reproduced by kind permission of the author, copyright © 1991 by Womi Bright Neal. LAURETTA NGCOBO: extract from *And They Didn't Die* by Lauretta Ngcobo (Virago, 1990; George Braziller, 1991) reprinted by permission of Shelley Power Literary Agency Ltd. and Virago Press, copyright © 1990 by Lauretta Ngcobo. GRACE NICHOLS: "Praise Song for My Mother" by Grace Nichols in *Watchers and Seekers*, eds. Cobham and Collins (Women's Press, 1987) reprinted by permission of Curtis Brown Group Ltd. on behalf of Grace Nichols; "Skin-Teeth" from *The Fat Black Woman's Poems* by Grace Nichols, "Grease" from *Lazy Thoughts of a Lazy Woman* by Grace Nichols, and extract from *Whole of a Morning Sky* by Grace Nichols reprinted by permission of Virago Press, copyright © 1981, 1989, 1986 by Grace Nichols. NISA: extract from *Nisa: The Life and Words of a !Kung Woman*, by Marjorie Shostak (Harvard University Press, 1981; Earthscan, 1989) reprinted by permission of Harvard University Press and Earthscan Publications, copyright © 1981 by Marjorie Shostak. REBEKA NJAU: extract from *Ripples in the Pool* by Rebeka Njau reprinted by kind permission of Heinemann Publishers Ltd., copyright © 1975 by Rebeka Njau. FLORA NWAPA: "This is Lagos" from *This is Lagos and Other Stories* by Flora Nwapa reprinted by kind permission of Nwamife Publishers Ltd., copyright © 1971 by Flora Nwapa. SEKAI NZENZA: extract from *Zimbabwean Woman: My Own Story* by Sekai Nzenza reprinted by kind permission of Karia Press, copyright © 1988 by Sekai Nzenza. GRACE OGOT: "The Rain Came" from *Land Without Thunder* by Grace Ogot (East African Publishing House, 1968) reprinted by permission, copyright © 1968 by Grace Ogot. 'MOLARA OGUNDIPE-LESLIE: "tendril love of africa", "Bird-song" and "Yoruba Love" from *Sew the Old Days and Other Poems*" by 'Molara Ogundipe-Leslie. MAY OPITZ: "Departure", "Afro-German" and "Afro-German II" by May Opitz in *Farbe bekennen*, eds. Oguntoye et al. (Orlanda Frauenverlag, 1986), this translation copyright © 1991 by George Busby. MARION PATRICK-JONES: extract from *J'ouvert morning* by Marion Patrick-Jones reprinted by kind permission of the author, copyright © 1976 by Marion Patrick-Jones. GABRIELA PEARSE: "Today" by Gabriela Pearse in *Black Women Talk Poetry* (Black Womantalk, 1987) reprinted by kind permission of the author, copyright © 1987 by Gabriela Pearse. ANN PETRY: extract from *The Street* by Ann Petry reprinted by permission of Houghton Mifflin Co. and Virago Press, copyright © 1946 by Anne Petry, renewed 1974 by Anne Petry. MARLENE NOURBESE PHILIP: "Burn Sugar" by Marlene Nourbese Philip (in *Panurge 7* and *Imagining Women*, ed. The Women's Press, Ontario) reprinted by permission of the author, copyright © 1988 by Marlene Nourbese Philip. J. J. PHILLIPS: extract from *Mojo Hand: An Orphic Tale* by J. J. Phillips reprinted by permission of Serpent's Tail and City Miner Books, Berkeley, copyright © 1966 by J. J. Phillips. VELMA POLLARD: "Bitterland" from *Crown Point and Other Poems* by Velma Pollard reprinted by permission of Peepal Tree Press, copyright © 1988 by Velma Pollard; "Cage I" from *Considering Woman* by Velma Pollard reprinted by kind permission of The Women's Press, copyright © 1989 by Velma Pollard.

MARSHA PRESCOD: "Exiles" and "Womanist Blues"; "Auntie Vida's Hair Salon" by Marsha Prescod (*Spare Rib*, October 1990) reprinted by kind permission of the author, copyright © 1990 by Marsha Prescod. QUEEN OF SHEBA: "On the Wisdom of Solomon", from *The Queen of Sheba and her Only Son, Menyelek* by E. A. Wallis Budge. CHRISTINE QUNTA: "The know" and "The procession" from *Hoyi Na! Azania: Poems of an African Struggle* by Christine Qunta (Sydney: Marimba Press, 1979) reprinted by kind permission of the author, copyright © 1979 by Christine Douts Qunta. JOAN RILEY: extract from *The Unbelonging* by Joan Riley reprinted by kind permission of The Women's Press, 1985, copyright © 1985 by Joan Riley. CAROLYN RODGERS: "Poem for Some Black Women" from *How I Got Ovah* by Carolyn Rodgers reprinted by permission of Doubleday, a division of Bantam Doubleday Dell Publishing Group Inc., copyright © 1971 by Carolyn Rodgers. ASTRID ROEMER: extract from *A Name For Love* (*Een naam voor de liefde*) by Astrid Roemer (In de Knipscheer, 1987), translated by Rita Gircoor, reproduced by kind permission of the author, copyright © 1990 by Astrid Roemer. MARTA ROJAS: extract from *Rey Spencer's Swing* (*El Columpio de Rey Spencer*) by Marta Rojas Rodriguez (MS), published by permission of the author, Jean Stubbs and CENDA Cuban Center for Authors' Rights, this translation copyright © 1991 by Pedro Sarduy and Jean Stubbs. LUCINDA ROY: "Points of View" and "If You Know Black Hair" from *Wailing the Dead to Sleep* by Lucinda Roy reprinted by kind permission of Bogle-L'Ouverture Publications, copyright © 1988 by Lucinda Roy. JACQUELINE RUDET: extract from *Basin* by Jacqueline Rudet, in *Black Plays*, ed. Brewster, reprinted by permission of Methuen Drama, copyright © 1987 by Jacqueline Rudet. KRISTINA RUNGANO: "The Woman" from *A Storm is Brewing* by Kristina Rungano reprinted by permission of Zimbabwe Publishing House, copyright © 1984 by Kristina Rungano. SANDI RUSSELL: "Sister" by Sandi Russell in *Iron Women: New Stories by Women*, ed. Fitzgerald (Iron Press, North Shields, 1990), reprinted by permission of the author, copyright © 1990 by Sandi Russell. SONIA SANCHEZ: "Just Don't Never Give Up On Love" from *Homegirls and Handgrenades* by Sonia Sanchez (Thunder's Mouth, 1984) reprinted by kind permission of the author, copyright © 1984 by Sonia Sanchez. SIMONE SCHWARZ-BART: extract from *The Bridge of Beyond* by Simone Schwarz-Bart reprinted by permission of Victor Gollancz and George Borchardt Inc., copyright © 1972 by Editions du Seuil, 1974 by Atheneum Publishers. MABEL SEGUN: "The Pigeon-Hole" by Mabel Segun in *Reflections: Nigerian Prose and Verse*, ed. Ademola, reprinted by permission of African Universities Press, copyright © 1962 by Mabel Segun; "Polygamy – Ancient and Modern" from *Sorry, No Vacancy* by Mabel Segun reprinted by permission of University Press Ibadan, copyright © 1977 by Mabel Segun. OLIVE SENIOR: "Love Orange" from *Summer Lightning* by Olive Senior reprinted by permission of Longman Group UK, copyright © 1986 by Olive Senior. DULCIE SEPTEMBER: "A Split Society – Fast Sounds on the Horizon" by Dulcie September in *One Never Knows*, ed. Mabuza, reprinted by permission of Skotaville Publishers, copyright © 1989 by Dulcie September. NTOZAKE SHANGE: "aw, babee, you so pretty" (*Essence*, April 1979) in *Midnight Birds*, ed. Washington (Anchor, 1980) reprinted by permission of A. M. Heath, copyright © 1980 by Ntozake

Shange. JENNEBA SIE JALLOH: "Alternate Heartbeats" by Jenneba Sie Jalloh, from *Across the Water: Irish Women's Lives in Britain*, eds. Lennon, McAdam, O'Brien, reprinted by permission of Virago Press and Marie McAdam, copyright © 1988 by Jenneba Sie Jalloh. JOYCE SIKAKANE: extract from *A Window on Soweto* by Joyce Sikakane reprinted by kind permission of the author and International Defence and Aid Fund for Southern Africa, copyright © 1977 by Joyce Sikakane. ZULU SOFOLA: extract from *The Sweet Trap* by Zulu Sofola reprinted by permission of University Press Ibadan, copyright © 1977 by Zulu Sofola. AMINATTA SOW-FALL: extract from *The Beggars' Strike* by Aminata Sow-Fall, translated by Dorothy S. Blair, reprinted by permission of Longman Group UK, copyright © 1981 by Aminata Sow-Fall. ANNE SPENCER: "Letter to My Sister" by Anne Spencer in *Caroling Dusk*, ed. Countee Cullen (Harper & Bros, 1927); "White Things" by Anne Spencer, in *Crisis*, 1923, reprinted by kind permission of *Crisis* magazine; "Lady, Lady" by Anne Spencer in *The New Negro*, ed. Locke (Macmillan, 1925). EINTOU PEARL SPRINGER: "Women Over 30" from *Out of the Shadows* by Eintou Pearl Springer reprinted by kind permission of Karia Press, copyright © 1986 by Eintou Pearl Springer. MAUD SULTER: "As a Blackwoman" from *As A Blackwoman* by Maud Sulter (Akira Press, 1985) reprinted by kind permission of the author, copyright © 1985 by Maud Sulter. EFUA SUTHERLAND: "New Life at Kyerefaso" by Efua Sutherland in *The African Assertion* by J. Shelton (Bobbs-Merrill) reprinted by permission of Ghana Broadcasting Association, copyright © 1958 by Efua Sutherland. VÉRONIQUE TADJO: "Five poems" from *Latérite* by Véronique Tadjo reprinted by permission of the author and Hatier, copyright © 1984 Véronique Tadjo. LOURDES TEODORO: "The Generation of Fear" from *Agua-Marinha ou Tempo sem Palavra* by Lourdes Teodoro (Brasilia, 1978), translated by Iain Bruce, reprinted by permission of the author, copyright © 1978 by Lourdes Teodoro. AWA THIAM: extract from *Black Sisters, Speak Out* by Awa Thiam reprinted by permission of Pluto Press Ltd., copyright © 1986 by Awa Thiam. ELEAN THOMAS: "Josina" from *Word Rhythms from the Life of a Woman* by Elean Thomas and "Black Woman's Love Song" from *Before They Can Speak of Flowers* reprinted by kind permission of the author and Karia Press, copyright © 1986, 1988 by Elean Thomas. MIRIAM TLALI: "Go in Peace, Tobias Son of Opperman" from *Soweto Stories* by Miriam Tlali (Pandora, 1989) reprinted by permission of HarperCollins Publishers, copyright © 1989 by Miriam Tlali. TRADITIONAL AFRICAN POEMS: "Initiation Song of Girls" translated from Bemba by Audrey Richard in *Chisunqu* (Faber, 1956) reprinted by permission of Faber and Faber Ltd; "Song for Dance of Young Girls" translated by J. H. Driberg in *People of the Small Arrow* (Payson and Clarke, 1930) reprinted by permission of Associated University Presses; "Girls' Secret Love Song" from *The Social Institutions of the Kipsigis* by J. G. Peristiany (Routledge and Kegan Paul, 1939) reprinted by permission of John Peristiany; "A Woman Sings of Her Love" from *Somali Poetry*, ed. Andrzejewski and Lewis (Clarendon, 1964) reprinted by permission of Ioan Lewis; "A Mother to Her First Born" from *Initiation* translated by J. H. Driberg (Golden Cockerel Press, 1932) reprinted by permission of Associated University Press; "A Mother Praises Her Baby", translated by Willard Trask, from *The Unwritten Song*, reprinted by permission of Macmillan Inc; "Chorus Sung by Co-wives to One Another", translated by Leonard Doob, from *Ants Will Not Eat Your Fingers*, reprinted with permission from Walker and Company, copyright © 1966 by Leonard Doob; "Love Song" from *The Folk Songs of Ghana* by J. H. Kwabena Nketia (University of Ghana) reprinted by permission of J. H. Kwabena Nketia, copyright © 1963 by J. H. Kwabena Nketia; "Pounding Songs" from *Oral Poetry from Africa: An Anthology*, eds. Mapanje and White (Macmillan, 1983); "I Am Your Betrothed" from *Married Life in an African Tribe* by I. Schapera reprinted by permission of Faber and Faber Ltd; "Grinding Song" from *Sweeter Than Honey: Testimonies of Tigrayan Women*, eds. Hammond and Druce, reprinted by kind permission of Third World First, copyright © 1989 by Third World First. ADAORA LILY ULASI: extract from *Many Thing Begin for Change* by Adaora Lily Ulasi (Michael Joseph, 1971) reprinted by permission of Adaora James, copyright © 1971 by Adaora Lily Ulasi. CHARITY WACIUMA: "Itega and Irua" from *Daughter of Mumbi* by Charity Waciuma (East African Publishing House, 1969) reprinted by permission of East African Publishing House, copyright © 1969 by Charity Waciuma. ALICE WALKER: "Nineteen Fifty-Five" from *You Can't Keep a Good Woman Down* by Alice Walker reprinted by permission of Harcourt Brace Jovanovich, Inc., copyright © 1981 by Alice Walker. MARGARET WALKER: "For My People" and "Lineage" from *For My People* by Margaret Walker (Yale University Press, 1942) reprinted by permission of Margaret Walker Alexander, copyright © 1942 by Margaret Walker. MICHELE WALLACE: extract from *Black Macho and the Myth of the Superwoman* by Michele Wallace (Verso, 1990) reprinted by permission of Verso, copyright © 1978, 1990 by Michele Wallace. MYRIAM WARNER-VIEYRA: extract from *As the Sorcerer Said* by Myriam Warner-Vieyra, translated by Dorothy S. Blair (Longman, 1982), copyright © 1982. DOROTHY WEST: extract from *The Living Is Easy* by Dorothy West, published 1982 by the Feminist Press at CUNY, used with permission, copyright © 1948, 1975 by Dorothy West. ZOË WICOMB: "You Can't Get Lost in Cape Town" from *You Can't Get Lost in Cape Town* by Zoë Wicomb reprinted by permission of Virago Press and Pantheon Books, a division of Random House Inc., copyright © 1987 by Zoë Wicomb. SHERLEY ANNE WILLIAMS: extract from *Dessa Rose* by Sherley Anne Williams reprinted by permission of William Morrow Inc., copyright © 1987 by Sherley Anne Williams. SYLVIA WYNTER: extract from *The Hills of Hebron: A Jamaican Novel* by Sylvia Wynter (Jonathan Cape) reprinted by permission of Random Century Group, copyright © 1962 by Sylvia Winter.

Every effort has been made to trace the copyright holders of the material reprinted in this anthology. The editor and publisher would be glad to hear from copyright holders they have not been able to contact and to print due acknowledgement in the next edition.

Index

(Bold type indicates main entries)